MW00834892

International Business Transactions

Documents

[...] = edits by editor

International Business Transactions

Documents

edited by

Professor Dr. Talia Einhorn
and
Professor Dr. Frank Emmert, LL.M.

COUNCIL on INTERNATIONAL LAW and POLITICS

2nd ed., rev. 2013

© 2013 by the Council on International Law and Politics

All rights reserved. No part of this publication may be reproduced, stored in a retrieval system, or transmitted, in any form or by any means, without the prior permission in writing of the Council on International Law and Politics.

Copyright Acknowledgments: Documents contained in this book are reproduced with permission from the following institutions:
American Arbitration Association,
American Law Institute,
European Union,
Hague Conference on Private International Law,
International Bar Association (IBA),
International Centre for Dispute Resolution (ICDR - AAA),
International Chamber of Commerce (ICC),
International Civil Aviation Organization (ICAO),
International Court of Arbitration (ICC),
International Institute for the Unification of Private Law (UNIDROIT),
International Underwriting Association (IUA),
Lloyd's Market Association,
National Conference of Commissioners on Uniform State Laws,
Organization of American States,
United Nations,
United Nations Commission on International Trade Law (UNCITRAL),
United Nations Conference on Trade and Development (UNCTAD)

In the text of the various materials, "[...]" indicates deletions by the editors; "[text in brackets]" indicates editorial additions or changes.

Although great care has been taken to include the precise language of the different documents and to have an accurate list of signatories at the end of the different conventions, the editors cannot accept any liability for mistakes in this volume. When in doubt, users are advised to double-check the wording of documents and to obtain the latest status list of signatory countries from the respective organizations that administer the documents.

Published by
Council on International Law and Politics
411 North LaSalle Street
Suite 200
Chicago, Illinois 60654
http://www.cilpnet.org

Publications Coordinator: Mark L. Shope

Cover design: Salma Taman
Cover art: Frank Emmert, for more information see http://www.TheIMAC.co

Font Myriad Pro

Printed by CreateSpace

17 16 15 14 13 12 1 2 3 4 5 6

ISBN: 978-0-9858156-2-2

TABLE OF CONTENTS

Part IV - Insurance

Part V - Enforcement of International Contracts and Agreements

Part I - Sales Contracts

1955 HAGUE CONVENTION ON THE LAW APPLICABLE TO INTERNATIONAL SALE OF GOODS[1]

Article 1

This Convention shall apply to international sales of goods.

It shall not apply to sales of securities, to sales of ships and of registered boats or aircraft, or to sales upon judicial order or by way of execution. It shall apply to sales based on documents.

For the purposes of this Convention, contracts to deliver goods to be manufactured or produced shall be placed on the same footing as sales provided the party who assumes delivery is to furnish the necessary raw materials for their manufacture or production.

The mere declaration of the parties, relative to the application of a law or the competence of a judge or arbitrator, shall not be sufficient to confer upon a sale the international character provided for in the first paragraph of this Article.

Article 2

A sale shall be governed by the domestic law of the country designated by the contracting parties.

Such designation must be contained in an express clause, or unambiguously result from the provisions of the contract.

Conditions affecting the consent of the parties to the law declared applicable shall be determined by such law.

Article 3

In default of a law declared applicable by the parties under the conditions provided in the preceding Article, a sale shall be governed by the domestic law of the country in which the vendor has his habitual residence at the time when he receives the order. If the order is received by an establishment of the vendor, the sale shall be governed by the domestic law of the country in which the establishment is situated.

Nevertheless, a sale shall be governed by the domestic law of the country in which the purchaser has his habitual residence, or in which he has the establishment that has given the order, if the order has been received in such country, whether by the vendor or by his representative, agent or commercial traveller.

In case of a sale at an exchange or at a public auction, the sale shall be governed by the domestic law of the country in which the exchange is situated or the auction takes place.

Article 4

In the absence of an express clause to the contrary, the domestic law of the country in which inspection of goods delivered pursuant to a sale is to take place shall apply in respect of the form in which and the periods within which the inspection must take place, the notifications concerning the inspection and the measures to be taken in case of refusal of the goods.

Article 5

This Convention shall not apply to:
1. The capacity of the parties;
2. The form of the contract;
3. The transfer of ownership, provided that the various obligations of the parties, and especially those relating to risks, shall be subject to the law applicable to the sale pursuant to this Convention;
4. The effects of the sale as regards all persons other than the parties.

---

1 © Hague Conference on Private International Law.

Article 6

In each of the Contracting States, the application of the law determined by this convention may be excluded on a ground of public policy.

Article 7

The contracting States have agreed to incorporate the provisions of Articles 1-6 of this Convention in the national law of their respective countries.

Articles 8 - 12 [Omitted]

Entry into Force: 1 September 1964
Ratifications: Denmark (1964), Finland (1964), France (1964), Italy (1964), Niger (1971), Norway (1964), Sweden (1964), Switzerland (1972)

1986 HAGUE CONVENTION ON THE LAW APPLICABLE TO CONTRACTS FOR THE INTERNATIONAL SALE OF GOODS[1]

The States Parties to the present Convention,
DESIRING to unify the choice of law rules relating to contracts for the international sale of goods,
BEARING IN MIND the *United Nations Convention on Contracts for the International Sale of Goods*, concluded at Vienna on 11 April 1980,
HAVE AGREED upon the following provisions:

Chapter I - Scope of the Convention
Article 1

This Convention determines the law applicable to contracts of sale of goods -
a)   between parties having their places of business in different States;
b)   in all other cases involving a choice between the laws of different States, unless such a choice arises solely from a stipulation by the parties as to the applicable law, even if accompanied by a choice of court or arbitration.

Article 2

The Convention does not apply to -
a)   sales by way of execution or otherwise by authority of law;
b)   sales of stocks, shares, investment securities, negotiable instruments or money; it does, however, apply to the sale of goods based on documents;
c)   sales of goods bought for personal, family or household use; it does, however, apply if the seller at the time of the conclusion of the contract neither knew nor ought to have known that the goods were bought for any such use.

Article 3

For the purposes of the Convention, "goods" includes -
a)   ships, vessels, boats, hovercraft and aircraft;
b)   electricity.

Article 4

(1)   Contracts for the supply of goods to be manufactured or produced are to be considered contracts of sale unless the party who orders the goods undertakes to supply a substantial part of the materials necessary for such manufacture or production.
(2)   Contracts in which the preponderant part of the obligations of the party who furnishes goods consists of the supply of labour or other services are not to be considered contracts of sale.

Article 5

The Convention does not determine the law applicable to -

---

1   © Hague Conference on Private International Law.

a)   the capacity of the parties or the consequences of nullity or invalidity of the contract resulting from the incapacity of a party;
b)   the question whether an agent is able to bind a principal, or an organ to bind a company or body corporate or unincorporate;
c)   the transfer of ownership; nevertheless, the issues specifically mentioned in Article 12 are governed by the law applicable to the contract under the Convention;
d)   the effect of the sale in respect of any person other than the parties;
e)   agreements on arbitration or on choice of court, even if such an agreement is embodied in the contract of sale.

Article 6
The law determined under the Convention applies whether or not it is the law of a Contracting State.

Chapter II - Applicable Law
Section 1 - Determination of the Applicable Law
Article 7
(1)   A contract of sale is governed by the law chosen by the parties. The parties' agreement on this choice must be express or be clearly demonstrated by the terms of the contract and the conduct of the parties, viewed in their entirety. Such a choice may be limited to a part of the contract.
(2)   The parties may at any time agree to subject the contract in whole or in part to a law other than that which previously governed it, whether or not the law previously governing the contract was chosen by the parties. Any change by the parties of the applicable law made after the conclusion of the contract does not prejudice its formal validity or the rights of third parties.

Article 8
(1)   To the extent that the law applicable to a contract of sale has not been chosen by the parties in accordance with Article 7, the contract is governed by the law of the State where the seller has his place of business at the time of conclusion of the contract.
(2)   However, the contract is governed by the law of the State where the buyer has his place of business at the time of conclusion of the contract, if -
a)   negotiations were conducted, and the contract concluded by and in the presence of the parties, in that State; or
b)   the contract provides expressly that the seller must perform his obligation to deliver the goods in that State; or
c)   the contract was concluded on terms determined mainly by the buyer and in response to an invitation directed by the buyer to persons invited to bid (a call for tenders).
(3)   By way of exception, where, in the light of the circumstances as a whole, for instance any business relations between the parties, the contract is manifestly more closely connected with a law which is not the law which would otherwise be applicable to the contract under paragraphs 1 or 2 of this Article, the contract is governed by that other law.
(4)   Paragraph 3 does not apply if, at the time of the conclusion of the contract, the seller and the buyer have their places of business in States having made the reservation under Article 21, paragraph 1, sub-paragraph b).
(5)   Paragraph 3 does not apply in respect of issues regulated in the United Nations Convention on Contracts for the International Sale of Goods (Vienna, 11 April 1980) where, at the time of the conclusion of the contract, the seller and the buyer have their places of business in different States both of which are Parties to that Convention.

Article 9
A sale by auction or on a commodity or other exchange is governed by the law chosen by the parties in accordance with Article 7 to the extent to which the law of the State where the auction takes place or the exchange is located does not prohibit such choice. Failing a choice by the parties, or to the extent that such choice is prohibited, the law of the State where the auction takes place or the exchange is located shall apply.

Article 10

(1) Issues concerning the existence and material validity of the consent of the parties as to the choice of the applicable law are determined, where the choice satisfies the requirements of Article 7, by the law chosen. If under that law the choice is invalid, the law governing the contract is determined under Article 8.

(2) The existence and material validity of a contract of sale, or of any term thereof, are determined by the law which under the Convention would govern the contract or term if it were valid.

(3) Nevertheless, to establish that he did not consent to the choice of law, to the contract itself, or to any term thereof, a party may rely on the law of the State where he has his place of business, if in the circumstances it is not reasonable to determine that issue under the law specified in the preceding paragraphs.

Article 11

(1) A contract of sale concluded between persons who are in the same State is formally valid if it satisfies the requirements either of the law which governs it under the Convention or of the law of the State where it is concluded.

(2) A contract of sale concluded between persons who are in different States is formally valid if it satisfies the requirements either of the law which governs it under the Convention or of the law of one of those States.

(3) Where the contract is concluded by an agent, the State in which the agent acts is the relevant State for the purposes of the preceding paragraphs.

(4) An act intended to have legal effect relating to an existing or contemplated contract of sale is formally valid if it satisfies the requirements either of the law which under the Convention governs or would govern the contract, or of the law of the State where the act was done.

(5) The Convention does not apply to the formal validity of a contract of sale where one of the parties to the contract has, at the time of its conclusion, his place of business in a State which has made the reservation provided for in Article 21, paragraph 1, sub-paragraph c).

Section 2 - Scope of the Applicable Law
Article 12

The law applicable to a contract of sale by virtue of Articles 7, 8 or 9 governs in particular -
a) interpretation of the contract;
b) the rights and obligations of the parties and performance of the contract;
c) the time at which the buyer becomes entitled to the products, fruits and income deriving from the goods;
d) the time from which the buyer bears the risk with respect to the goods;
e) the validity and effect as between the parties of clauses reserving title to the goods;
f) the consequences of non-performance of the contract, including the categories of loss for which compensation may be recovered, but without prejudice to the procedural law of the forum;
g) the various ways of extinguishing obligations, as well as prescription and limitation of actions;
h) the consequences of nullity or invalidity of the contract.

Article 13

In the absence of an express clause to the contrary, the law of the State where inspection of the goods takes place applies to the modalities and procedural requirements for such inspection.

Chapter III - General Provisions
Article 14

(1) If a party has more than one place of business, the relevant place of business is that which has the closest relationship to the contract and its performance, having regard to the circumstances known to or contemplated by the parties at any time before or at the conclusion of the contract.

(2)   If a party does not have a place of business, reference is to be made to his habitual residence.

Article 15
In the Convention "law" means the law in force in a State other than its choice of law rules.

Article 16
In the interpretation of the Convention, regard is to be had to its international character and to the need to promote uniformity in its application.

Article 17
The Convention does not prevent the application of those provisions of the law of the forum that must be applied irrespective of the law that otherwise governs the contract.

Article 18
The application of a law determined by the Convention may be refused only where such application would be manifestly incompatible with public policy (ordre public).

Article 19
For the purpose of identifying the law applicable under the Convention, where a State comprises several territorial units each of which has its own system of law or its own rules of law in respect of contracts for the sale of goods, any reference to the law of that State is to be construed as referring to the law in force in the territorial unit in question.

Article 20
A State within which different territorial units have their own systems of law or their own rules of law in respect of contracts of sale is not bound to apply the Convention to conflicts between the laws in force in such units.

Article 21
(1)   Any State may, at the time of signature, ratification, acceptance, approval or accession make any of the following reservations -
a)   that it will not apply the Convention in the cases covered by sub-paragraph b) of Article 1;
b)   that it will not apply paragraph 3 of Article 8, except where neither party to the contract has his place of business in a State which has made a reservation provided for under this sub-paragraph;
c)   that, for cases where its legislation requires contracts of sale to be concluded in or evidenced by writing, it will not apply the Convention to the formal validity of the contract, where any party has his place of business in its territory at the time of conclusion of the contract;
d)   that it will not apply sub-paragraph g) of Article 12 in so far as that sub-paragraph relates to prescription and limitation of actions.
(2)   No other reservation shall be permitted.
(3)   Any Contracting State may at any time withdraw a reservation which it has made; the reservation shall cease to have effect on the first day of the month following the expiration of three months after notification of the withdrawal.

Article 22
(1)   This Convention does not prevail over any convention or other international agreement which has been or may be entered into and which contains provisions determining the law applicable to contracts of sale, provided that such instrument applies only if the seller and buyer have their places of business in States Parties to that instrument.
(2)   This Convention does not prevail over any international convention to which a Contracting State is, or becomes, a Party, regulating the choice of law in regard to any particular category of contracts of sale within the scope of this Convention.

Article 23
This Convention does not prejudice the application -

a)   of the United Nations Convention on Contracts for the International Sale of Goods (Vienna, 11 April 1980);

b)   of the Convention on the Limitation Period in the International Sale of Goods (New York, 14 June 1974), or the Protocol amending that Convention (Vienna, 11 April 1980).

Article 24

The Convention applies in a Contracting State to contracts of sale concluded after its entry into force for that State.

Chapter IV - Final Clauses

Article 25

(1)   The Convention is open for signature by all States.

(2)   The Convention is subject to ratification, acceptance or approval by the signatory States.

(3)   The Convention is open for accession by all States which are not signatory States as from the date it is open for signature.

(4)   Instruments of ratification, acceptance, approval and accession shall be deposited with the Ministry of Foreign Affairs of the Kingdom of the Netherlands, depositary of the Convention. [...]

Article 27

(1)   The Convention shall enter into force on the first day of the month following the expiration of three months after the deposit of the fifth instrument of ratification, acceptance, approval or accession referred to in Article 25. [...]

Article 28

For each State Party to the Convention on the law applicable to international sales of goods, done at The Hague on 15 June 1955, which has consented to be bound by this Convention and for which this Convention is in force, this Convention shall replace the said Convention of 1955.

Article 29

Any State which becomes a Party to this Convention after the entry into force of an instrument revising it shall be considered to be a Party to the Convention as revised.

Article 30

(1)   A State Party to this Convention may denounce it by a notification in writing addressed to the depositary.

(2)   The denunciation takes effect on the first day of the month following the expiration of three months after the notification is received by the depositary. Where a longer period for the denunciation to take effect is specified in the notification, the denunciation takes effect upon the expiration of such longer period after the notification is received by the depositary.

Article 31

The depositary shall notify the States Members of the Hague Conference on Private International Law and the States which have signed, ratified, accepted, approved or acceded in accordance with Article 25, of the following -

a)   the signatures and ratifications, acceptances, approvals and accessions referred to in Article 25;

b)   the date on which the Convention enters into force in accordance with Article 27;

c)   the declarations referred to in Article 26;

d)   the reservations and the withdrawals of reservations referred to in Article 21;

e)   the denunciations referred to in Article 30.

In witness whereof the undersigned, being duly authorised thereto, have signed this Convention.

Done at The Hague, on the 22nd day of December, 1986, in the English and French languages, both texts being equally authentic, in a single copy which shall be deposited in the archives of the Government of the Kingdom of the Netherlands, and of which a certified copy shall be sent, through diplomatic channels, to each of the States Members of the Hague Conference on

Private International Law as of the date of its Extraordinary Session of October 1985, and to each State which participated in that Session.

Entry into force: requires at least 5 ratifications
Ratifications to date: Argentina (1991), Moldova (1997)

1978 HAGUE CONVENTION ON THE LAW APPLICABLE TO AGENCY[1]

THE STATES SIGNATORIES TO THE PRESENT CONVENTION,
DESIRING to establish common provisions concerning the law applicable to agency,
HAVE RESOLVED to conclude a Convention to this effect, and have agreed upon the following provisions -

Chapter I - Scope of the Convention
Article 1

The present Convention determines the law applicable to relationships of an international character arising where a person, the agent, has the authority to act, acts or purports to act on behalf of another person, the principal, in dealing with a third party.

It shall extend to cases where the function of the agent is to receive and communicate proposals or to conduct negotiations on behalf of other persons.

The Convention shall apply whether the agent acts in his own name or in that of the principal and whether he acts regularly or occasionally.

Article 2

This Convention shall not apply to -
a)   the capacity of the parties;
b)   requirements as to form;
c)   agency by operation of law in family law, in matrimonial property regimes, or in the law of succession;
d)   agency by virtue of a decision of a judicial or quasi-judicial authority or subject to the direct control of such an authority;
e)   representation in connection with proceedings of a judicial character;
f)   the agency of a shipmaster acting in the exercise of his functions as such.

Article 3

For the purposes of this Convention -
a)   an organ, officer or partner of a corporation, association, partnership or other entity, whether or not possessing legal personality, shall not be regarded as the agent of that entity in so far as, in the exercise of his functions as such, he acts by virtue of an authority conferred by law or by the constitutive documents of that entity;
b)   a trustee shall not be regarded as an agent of the trust, of the person who has created the trust, or of the beneficiaries.

Article 4

The law specified in this Convention shall apply whether or not it is the law of a Contracting State.

Chapter II - Relations Between Principal and Agent
Article 5

The internal law chosen by the principal and the agent shall govern the agency relationship between them.

---

1   © Hague Conference on Private International Law.

This choice must be express or must be such that it may be inferred with reasonable cer–tainty from the terms of the agreement between the parties and the circumstances of the case.

Article 6

In so far as it has not been chosen in accordance with Article 5, the applicable law shall be the internal law of the State where, at the time of formation of the agency relationship, the agent has his business establishment or, if he has none, his habitual residence.

However, the internal law of the State where the agent is primarily to act shall apply if the principal has his business establishment or, if he has none, his habitual residence in that State. Where the principal or the agent has more than one business establishment, this Article refers to the establishment with which the agency relationship is most closely connected.

Article 7

Where the creation of the agency relationship is not the sole purpose of the agreement, the law specified in Articles 5 and 6 shall apply only if -
a)   the creation of this relationship is the principal purpose of the agreement, or
b)   the agency relationship is severable.

Article 8

The law applicable under Articles 5 and 6 shall govern the formation and validity of the agency relationship, the obligations of the parties, the conditions of performance, the consequences of non-performance, and the extinction of those obligations.
This law shall apply in particular to -
a)   the existence and extent of the authority of the agent, its modification or termination, and the consequences of the fact that the agent has exceeded or misused his authority;
b)   the right of the agent to appoint a substitute agent, a sub-agent or an additional agent;
c)   the right of the agent to enter into a contract on behalf of the principal where there is a potential conflict of interest between himself and the principal;
d)   non-competition clauses and *del credere* clauses;
e)   clientele allowances (*l'indemnité de clientèle*);
f)   the categories of damage for which compensation may be recovered.

Article 9

Whatever law may be applicable to the agency relationship, in regard to the manner of perfor-mance the law of the place of performance shall be taken into consideration.

Article 10

This Chapter shall not apply where the agreement creating the agency relationship is a contract of employment.

Chapter III - Relations with the Third Party

Article 11

As between the principal and the third party, the existence and extent of the agent's authority and the effects of the agent's exercise or purported exercise of his authority shall be governed by the internal law of the State in which the agent had his business establishment at the time of his relevant acts.

However, the internal law of the State in which the agent has acted shall apply if -
a)   the principal has his business establishment or, if he has none, his habitual residence in that State, and the agent has acted in the name of the principal; or
b)   the third party has his business establishment or, if he has none, his habitual residence in that State; or
c)   the agent has acted at an exchange or auction; or
d)   the agent has no business establishment.
Where a party has more than one business establishment, this Article refers to the establish-ment with which the relevant acts of the agent are most closely connected.

Article 12

For the purposes of Article 11, first paragraph, where an agent acting under a contract of employment with his principal has no personal business establishment, he shall be deemed to have his establishment at the business establishment of the principal to which he is attached.

Article 13

For the purposes of Article 11, second paragraph, where an agent in one State has communicated with the third party in another, by message, telegram, telex, telephone, or other similar means, the agent shall be deemed to have acted in that respect at the place of his business establishment or, if he has none, of his habitual residence.

Article 14

Notwithstanding Article 11, where a written specification by the principal or by the third party of the law applicable to questions falling within Article 11 has been expressly accepted by the other party, the law so specified shall apply to such questions.

Article 15

The law applicable under this Chapter shall also govern the relationship between the agent and the third party arising from the fact that the agent has acted in the exercise of his authority, has exceeded his authority, or has acted without authority.

Chapter IV - General Provisions

Article 16

In the application of this Convention, effect may be given to the mandatory rules of any State with which the situation has a significant connection, if and in so far as, under the law of that State, those rules must be applied whatever the law specified by its choice of law rules.

Article 17

The application of a law specified by this Convention may be refused only where such application would be manifestly incompatible with public policy (ordre public).

Article 18 [Reservations]

Any Contracting State may, at the time of signature, ratification, acceptance, approval or accession, reserve the right not to apply this Convention to -
(1)   he agency of a bank or group of banks in the course of banking transactions;
(2)   agency in matters of insurance;
(3)   the acts of a public servant acting in the exercise of his functions as such on behalf of a private person.
      No other reservation shall be permitted.
Any Contracting State may also, when notifying an extension of the Convention in accordance with Article 25, make one or more of these reservations, with its effect limited to all or some of the territories mentioned in the extension.
      Any Contracting State may at any time withdraw a reservation which it has made; the reservation shall cease to have effect on the first day of the third calendar month after notification of the withdrawal.

Article 19

Where a State comprises several territorial units each of which has its own rules of law in respect of agency, each territorial unit shall be considered as a State for the purposes of identifying the law applicable under this Convention.

Article 20

A State within which different territorial units have their own rules of law in respect of agency shall not be bound to apply this Convention where a State with a unified system of law would not be bound to apply the law of another State by virtue of this Convention.

Article 21

If a Contracting State has two or more territorial units which have their own rules of law in respect of agency, it may, at the time of signature, ratification, acceptance, approval or accession, declare that this Convention shall extend to all its territorial units or to one or more of them, and may modify its declaration by submitting another declaration at any time.

These declarations shall be notified to the Ministry of Foreign Affairs of the Kingdom of the Netherlands, and shall state expressly the territorial units to which the Convention applies.

Article 22

The Convention shall not affect any other international instrument containing provisions on matters governed by this Convention to which a Contracting State is, or becomes, a Party.

Chapter V - Final Clauses [...]

In witness whereof the undersigned, being duly authorised thereto, have signed this Convention.

Done at The Hague, on the 14th day of March, 1978, in the English and French languages, both texts being equally authentic, in a single copy which shall be deposited in the archives of the Government of the Kingdom of the Netherlands and of which a certified copy shall be sent, through diplomatic channels, to each of the States Members of the Hague Conference on Private International Law at the date of its Thirteenth Session.

Entry into force: 1 May 1992
Ratifications and binding effect: Argentina (1992), France (1992), Netherlands (1992), Portugal (1992)

1994 INTER-AMERICAN CONVENTION
ON THE LAW APPLICABLE TO INTERNATIONAL CONTRACTS[1]
"Mexico Convention"

The States Parties to this Convention,
REAFFIRMING their desire to continue the progressive development and codification of private international law among member States of the Organization of American States;
REASSERTING the advisability of harmonizing solutions to international trade issues;
BEARING in mind that the economic interdependence of States has fostered regional integration and that in order to stimulate the process it is necessary to facilitate international contracts by removing differences in the legal framework for them,
HAVE AGREED to approve the following Convention:

Chapter I - Scope of Application
Article 1

This Convention shall determine the law applicable to international contracts.
It shall be understood that a contract is international if the parties thereto have their habitual residence or establishments in different States Parties or if the contract has objective ties with more than one State Party.

This Convention shall apply to contracts entered into or contracts to which States or State agencies or entities are party, unless the parties to the contract expressly exclude it. However, any State Party may, at the time it signs, ratifies or accedes to this Convention, declare that the latter shall not apply to all or certain categories of contracts to which the State or State agencies and entities are party.

---

1   © Organization of American States, Washington DC.

Any State Party may, at the time it ratifies or accedes to this Convention, declare the categories of contract to which this Convention will not apply.

Article 2
The law designated by the Convention shall be applied even if said law is that of a State that is not a party.

Article 3
The provisions of this Convention shall be applied, with necessary and possible adaptations, to the new modalities of contracts used as a consequence of the development of international trade.

Article 4
For purposes of interpretation and application of this Convention, its international nature and the need to promote uniformity in its application shall be taken into account.

Article 5
This Convention does not determine the law applicable to:
a) questions arising from the marital status of natural persons, the capacity of the parties, or the consequences of nullity or invalidity of the contract as a result of the lack of capacity of one of the parties;
b) contractual obligations intended for successional questions, testamentary questions, marital arrangements or those deriving from family relationships;
c) obligations deriving from securities;
d) obligations deriving from securities transactions;
e) the agreements of the parties concerning arbitration or selection of forum;
f) questions of company law, including the existence, capacity, function and dissolution of commercial companies and juridical persons in general.

Article 6
The provisions of this Convention shall not be applicable to contracts which have autonomous regulations in international conventional law in force among the States Parties to this Convention.

Chapter 2 - Determination of Applicable Law
Article 7
The contract shall be governed by the law chosen by the parties. The parties' agreement on this selection must be express or, in the event that there is no express agreement, must be evident from the parties' behavior and from the clauses of the contract, considered as a whole. Said selection may relate to the entire contract or to a part of same.

Selection of a certain forum by the parties does not necessarily entail selection of the applicable law.

Article 8
The parties may at any time agree that the contract shall, in whole or in part, be subject to a law other than that to which it was previously subject, whether or not that law was chosen by the parties. Nevertheless, that modification shall not affect the formal validity of the original contract nor the rights of third parties.

Article 9
If the parties have not selected the applicable law, or if their selection proves ineffective, the contract shall be governed by the law of the State with which it has the closest ties.

The Court will take into account all objective and subjective elements of the contract to determine the law of the State with which it has the closest ties. It shall also take into account the general principles of international commercial law recognized by international organizations.

Nevertheless, if a part of the contract were separable from the rest and if it had a closer tie with another State, the law of that State could, exceptionally, apply to that part of the contract.

Article 10

In addition to the provisions in the foregoing articles, the guidelines, customs, and principles of international commercial law as well as commercial usage and practices generally accepted shall apply in order to discharge the requirements of justice and equity in the particular case.

Article 11

Notwithstanding the provisions of the preceding articles, the provisions of the law of the forum shall necessarily be applied when they are mandatory requirements.

It shall be up to the forum to decide when it applies the mandatory provisions of the law of another State with which the contract has close ties.

Chapter 3 - Existence and Validity of the Contract
Article 12

The existence and the validity of the contract or of any of its provisions, and the substantive validity of the consent of the parties concerning the selection of the applicable law, shall be governed by the appropriate rules in accordance with Chapter 2 of this Convention.

Nevertheless, to establish that one of the parties has not duly consented, the judge shall determine the applicable law, taking into account the habitual residence or principal place of business.

Article 13

A contract between parties in the same State shall be valid as to form if it meets the requirements laid down in the law governing said contract pursuant to this Convention or with those of the law of the State in which the contract is valid or with the law of the place where the contract is performed.

If the persons concerned are in different States at the time of its conclusion, the contract shall be valid as to form if it meets the requirements of the law governing it as to substance, or those of the law of one of the States in which it is concluded or with the law of the place where the contract is performed.

Chapter 4 - Scope of the Applicable Law
Article 14

The law applicable to the contract in virtue of Chapter 2 of this Convention shall govern principally:
a)   its interpretation;
b)   the rights and obligations of the parties;
c)   the performance of the obligations established by the contract and the consequences of nonperformance of the contract, including assessment of injury to the extent that this may determine payment of compensation;
d)   the various ways in which the obligations can be performed, and prescription and lapsing of actions;
e)   the consequences of nullity or invalidity of the contract.

Article 15

The provisions of Article 10 shall be taken into account when deciding whether an agent can obligate its principal or an agency, a company or a juridical person.

Article 16

The law of the State where international contracts are to be registered or published shall govern all matters concerning publicity in respect of same.

Article 17

For the purposes of this Convention, "law" shall be understood to mean the law current in a State, excluding rules concerning conflict of laws.

Article 18

Application of the law designated by this Convention may only be excluded when it is manifestly contrary to the public order of the forum.

Chapter 5 - General Provisions
Article 19

In a State Party, the provisions of this Convention shall apply to contracts concluded subsequent to its entry into force in that State.

Article 20

This Convention shall not affect the application of other international conventions to which a State Party to this Convention is or becomes a party, insofar as they are pertinent, or those concluded within the context of integration movements.

Article 21

When signing, ratifying or acceding to this Convention, States may formulate reservations that apply to one or more specific provisions and which are not incompatible with the effect and purpose of this Convention.

A State Party may at any time withdraw a reservation it has formulated. The effect of such reservation shall cease on the first day of the third calendar month following the date of notification of withdrawal.

Article 22

In the case of a State which has two or more systems of law applicable in different territorial units with respect to matters covered by the Convention:
a)   any reference to the laws of the State shall be construed as a reference to the laws in the territorial unit in question;
b)   any reference to habitual residence or place of business in that State shall be construed as a reference to habitual residence or place of business in a territorial unit of that State.

Article 23

A State within which different territorial units have their own systems of law in regard to matters covered by this Convention shall not be obliged to apply this Convention to conflicts between the legal systems in force in such units.

Article 24

If a State has two or more territorial units in which different systems of law apply in relation to the matters dealt with in this Convention, it may, at the time of signature, ratification or accession, declare that this Convention shall extend to all its territorial units or to only one or more of them.

Such declaration may be modified by subsequent declarations, which shall expressly indicate the territorial unit or units to which the Convention applies. Such subsequent declarations shall be transmitted to the General Secretariat of the Organization of American States, and shall take effect ninety days after the date of their receipt.

Chapter 6 - Final Clauses
Article 25

This Convention shall be open to signature by the member States of the Organization of American States.

Article 26

This Convention shall be subject to ratification. The instruments of ratification shall be deposited with the General Secretariat of the Organization of American States.

Article 27

This Convention shall remain open for accession by any other State after it has entered into force. The instruments of accession shall be deposited with the General Secretariat of the Organization of American States.

Article 28

This Convention shall enter into force for the ratifying States on the thirtieth day following the date of deposit of the second instrument of ratification.

For each State ratifying or acceding to the Convention after the deposit of the second instrument of ratification, the Convention shall enter into force on the thirtieth day after deposit by such State of its instrument of ratification or accession.

Article 29

This Convention shall remain in force indefinitely, but any of the States Parties may denounce it. The instrument of denunciation shall be deposited with the General Secretariat of the Organization of American States. After one year from the date of deposit of the instrument of denunciation, the Convention shall no longer be in force for the denouncing State.

Article 30

The original instrument of this Convention, the English, French, Portuguese and Spanish texts of which are equally authentic, shall be deposited with the General Secretariat of the Organization of American States, which shall forward an authenticated copy of its text to the Secretariat of the United Nations for registration and publication in accordance with Article 102 of its Charter. The General Secretariat of the Organization of American States shall notify the Member States of the Organization and the States that have acceded to the Convention of the signatures, deposits of instruments of ratification, accession and denunciation, as well as of reservations, if any, and of their withdrawal.

IN WITNESS WHEREOF the undersigned Plenipotentiaries, being duly authorized thereto by their respective Governments, do hereby sign the present Convention.
DONE AT MEXICO, D.F., MEXICO, this seventeenth day of March, one thousand nine hundred and ninety-four.

Entry into force: 15 December 1996
Ratifications and binding effect: Venezuela (1996), Mexico (1996)

EU REGULATION 593/2008 OF 17 JUNE 2008 ON THE LAW APPLICABLE TO CONTRACTUAL OBLIGATIONS (ROME I)[1]

THE EUROPEAN PARLIAMENT AND THE COUNCIL OF THE EUROPEAN UNION,
HAVING REGARD to the Treaty establishing the European Community, and in particular Article 61(c) and the second indent of Article 67(5) thereof, [...]
ACTING IN ACCORDANCE with the procedure laid down in Article 251 of the Treaty,
Whereas:
(1)   The Community has set itself the objective of maintaining and developing an area of freedom, security and justice. For the progressive establishment of such an area, the Community is to adopt measures relating to judicial cooperation in civil matters with a cross-border impact to the extent necessary for the proper functioning of the internal market.
(2)   According to Article 65, point (b) of the Treaty, these measures are to include those promoting the compatibility of the rules applicable in the Member States concerning the conflict of laws and of jurisdiction.
(3)   The European Council meeting in Tampere on 15 and 16 October 1999 endorsed the principle of mutual recognition of judgments and other decisions of judicial authorities as the cor-

---

1   OJ 2008 L 177, p. 6. This Regulation, as well as many other EU documents, can also be found in Frank Emmert (ed.), Eúropean Union Law - Documents, The Hague 2011.

nerstone of judicial cooperation in civil matters and invited the Council and the Commission to adopt a programme of measures to implement that principle.

(4)   On 30 November 2000 the Council adopted a joint Commission and Council programme of measures for implementation of the principle of mutual recognition of decisions in civil and commercial matters. The programme identifies measures relating to the harmonisation of conflict-of-law rules as those facilitating the mutual recognition of judgments.

(5)   The Hague Programme, adopted by the European Council on 5 November 2004, called for work to be pursued actively on the conflict-of-law rules regarding contractual obligations (Rome I).

(6)   The proper functioning of the internal market creates a need, in order to improve the predictability of the outcome of litigation, certainty as to the law applicable and the free movement of judgments, for the conflict-of-law rules in the Member States to designate the same national law irrespective of the country of the court in which an action is brought.

(7)   The substantive scope and the provisions of this Regulation should be consistent with Council Regulation 44/2001 of 22 December 2000 on jurisdiction and the recognition and enforcement of judgments in civil and commercial matters (Brussels I) and Regulation 864/2007 of the European Parliament and of the Council of 11 July 2007 on the law applicable to non-contractual obligations (Rome II).

(8)   Family relationships should cover parentage, marriage, affinity and collateral relatives. The reference in Article 1(2) to relationships having comparable effects to marriage and other family relationships should be interpreted in accordance with the law of the Member State in which the court is seised.

(9)   Obligations under bills of exchange, cheques and promissory notes and other negotiable instruments should also cover bills of lading to the extent that the obligations under the bill of lading arise out of its negotiable character.

(10) Obligations arising out of dealings prior to the conclusion of the contract are covered by Article 12 of Regulation 864/2007. Such obligations should therefore be excluded from the scope of this Regulation.

(11) The parties' freedom to choose the applicable law should be one of the cornerstones of the system of conflict-of-law rules in matters of contractual obligations.

(12) An agreement between the parties to confer on one or more courts or tribunals of a Member State exclusive jurisdiction to determine disputes under the contract should be one of the factors to be taken into account in determining whether a choice of law has been clearly demonstrated.

(13) This Regulation does not preclude parties from incorporating by reference into their contract a non-State body of law or an international convention.

(14) Should the Community adopt, in an appropriate legal instrument, rules of substantive contract law, including standard terms and conditions, such instrument may provide that the parties may choose to apply those rules.

(15) Where a choice of law is made and all other elements relevant to the situation are located in a country other than the country whose law has been chosen, the choice of law should not prejudice the application of provisions of the law of that country which cannot be derogated from by agreement. This rule should apply whether or not the choice of law was accompanied by a choice of court or tribunal. Whereas no substantial change is intended as compared with Article 3(3) of the 1980 Convention on the Law Applicable to Contractual Obligations (the Rome Convention), the wording of this Regulation is aligned as far as possible with Article 14 of Regulation 864/2007.

(16) To contribute to the general objective of this Regulation, legal certainty in the European judicial area, the conflict-of-law rules should be highly foreseeable. The courts should, however, retain a degree of discretion to determine the law that is most closely connected to the situation.

(17) As far as the applicable law in the absence of choice is concerned, the concept of 'provision of services' and 'sale of goods' should be interpreted in the same way as when applying Article 5 of Regulation 44/2001 in so far as sale of goods and provision of services are covered by that

Regulation. Although franchise and distribution contracts are contracts for services, they are the subject of specific rules.

(18) As far as the applicable law in the absence of choice is concerned, multilateral systems should be those in which trading is conducted, such as regulated markets and multilateral trading facilities as referred to in Article 4 of Directive 2004/39 of the European Parliament and of the Council of 21 April 2004 on markets in financial instruments, regardless of whether or not they rely on a central counter-party.

(19) Where there has been no choice of law, the applicable law should be determined in accordance with the rule specified for the particular type of contract. Where the contract cannot be categorised as being one of the specified types or where its elements fall within more than one of the specified types, it should be governed by the law of the country where the party required to effect the characteristic performance of the contract has his habitual residence. In the case of a contract consisting of a bundle of rights and obligations capable of being categorised as falling within more than one of the specified types of contract, the characteristic performance of the contract should be determined having regard to its centre of gravity.

(20) Where the contract is manifestly more closely connected with a country other than that indicated in Article 4(1) or (2), an escape clause should provide that the law of that other country is to apply. In order to determine that country, account should be taken, *inter alia*, of whether the contract in question has a very close relationship with another contract or contracts.

(21) In the absence of choice, where the applicable law cannot be determined either on the basis of the fact that the contract can be categorised as one of the specified types or as being the law of the country of habitual residence of the party required to effect the characteristic performance of the contract, the contract should be governed by the law of the country with which it is most closely connected. In order to determine that country, account should be taken, *inter alia*, of whether the contract in question has a very close relationship with another contract or contracts.

(22) As regards the interpretation of contracts for the carriage of goods, no change in substance is intended with respect to Article 4(4), third sentence, of the Rome Convention. Consequently, single-voyage charter parties and other contracts the main purpose of which is the carriage of goods should be treated as contracts for the carriage of goods. For the purposes of this Regulation, the term 'consignor' should refer to any person who enters into a contract of carriage with the carrier and the term 'the carrier' should refer to the party to the contract who undertakes to carry the goods, whether or not he performs the carriage himself.

(23) As regards contracts concluded with parties regarded as being weaker, those parties should be protected by conflict-of-law rules that are more favourable to their interests than the general rules.

(24) With more specific reference to consumer contracts, the conflict-of-law rule should make it possible to cut the cost of settling disputes concerning what are commonly relatively small claims and to take account of the development of distance-selling techniques. Consistency with Regulation 44/2001 requires both that there be a reference to the concept of directed activity as a condition for applying the consumer protection rule and that the concept be interpreted harmoniously in Regulation 44/2001 and this Regulation, bearing in mind that a joint declaration by the Council and the Commission on Article 15 of Regulation 44/2001 states that 'for Article 15(1)(c) to be applicable it is not sufficient for an undertaking to target its activities at the Member State of the consumer's residence, or at a number of Member States including that Member State; a contract must also be concluded within the framework of its activities'. The declaration also states that 'the mere fact that an Internet site is accessible is not sufficient for Article 15 to be applicable, although a factor will be that this Internet site solicits the conclusion of distance contracts and that a contract has actually been concluded at a distance, by whatever means. In this respect, the language or currency which a website uses does not constitute a relevant factor.'.

(25) Consumers should be protected by such rules of the country of their habitual residence that cannot be derogated from by agreement, provided that the consumer contract has been concluded as a result of the professional pursuing his commercial or professional activities in that particular country. The same protection should be guaranteed if the professional, while not pursuing his commercial or professional activities in the country where the consumer has his habitual residence, directs his activities by any means to that country or to several countries, including that country, and the contract is concluded as a result of such activities.

(26) For the purposes of this Regulation, financial services such as investment services and activities and ancillary services provided by a professional to a consumer, as referred to in sections A and B of Annex I to Directive 2004/39, and contracts for the sale of units in collective investment undertakings, whether or not covered by Council Directive 85/611 of 20 December 1985 on the coordination of laws, regulations and administrative provisions relating to undertakings for collective investment in transferable securities (UCITS), should be subject to Article 6 of this Regulation. Consequently, when a reference is made to terms and conditions governing the issuance or offer to the public of transferable securities or to the subscription and redemption of units in collective investment undertakings, that reference should include all aspects binding the issuer or the offeror to the consumer, but should not include those aspects involving the provision of financial services.

(27) Various exceptions should be made to the general conflict-of-law rule for consumer contracts. Under one such exception the general rule should not apply to contracts relating to rights *in rem* in immovable property or tenancies of such property unless the contract relates to the right to use immovable property on a timeshare basis within the meaning of Directive 94/47 of the European Parliament and of the Council of 26 October 1994 on the protection of purchasers in respect of certain aspects of contracts relating to the purchase of the right to use immovable properties on a timeshare basis.

(28) It is important to ensure that rights and obligations which constitute a financial instrument are not covered by the general rule applicable to consumer contracts, as that could lead to different laws being applicable to each of the instruments issued, therefore changing their nature and preventing their fungible trading and offering. Likewise, whenever such instruments are issued or offered, the contractual relationship established between the issuer or the offeror and the consumer should not necessarily be subject to the mandatory application of the law of the country of habitual residence of the consumer, as there is a need to ensure uniformity in the terms and conditions of an issuance or an offer. The same rationale should apply with regard to the multilateral systems covered by Article 4(1)(h), in respect of which it should be ensured that the law of the country of habitual residence of the consumer will not interfere with the rules applicable to contracts concluded within those systems or with the operator of such systems.

(29) For the purposes of this Regulation, references to rights and obligations constituting the terms and conditions governing the issuance, offers to the public or public take-over bids of transferable securities and references to the subscription and redemption of units in collective investment undertakings should include the terms governing, *inter alia*, the allocation of securities or units, rights in the event of over-subscription, withdrawal rights and similar matters in the context of the offer as well as those matters referred to in Articles 10, 11, 12 and 13, thus ensuring that all relevant contractual aspects of an offer binding the issuer or the offeror to the consumer are governed by a single law.

(30) For the purposes of this Regulation, financial instruments and transferable securities are those instruments referred to in Article 4 of Directive 2004/39.

(31) Nothing in this Regulation should prejudice the operation of a formal arrangement designated as a system under Article 2(a) of Directive 98/26 of the European Parliament and of the Council of 19 May 1998 on settlement finality in payment and securities settlement systems.

(32) Owing to the particular nature of contracts of carriage and insurance contracts, specific provisions should ensure an adequate level of protection of passengers and policy holders. Therefore, Article 6 should not apply in the context of those particular contracts.

(33) Where an insurance contract not covering a large risk covers more than one risk, at least one of which is situated in a Member State and at least one of which is situated in a third country, the special rules on insurance contracts in this Regulation should apply only to the risk or risks situated in the relevant Member State or Member States.

(34) The rule on individual employment contracts should not prejudice the application of the overriding mandatory provisions of the country to which a worker is posted in accordance with Directive 96/71 of the European Parliament and of the Council of 16 December 1996 concerning the posting of workers in the framework of the provision of services.

(35) Employees should not be deprived of the protection afforded to them by provisions which cannot be derogated from by agreement or which can only be derogated from to their benefit.

(36) As regards individual employment contracts, work carried out in another country should be regarded as temporary if the employee is expected to resume working in the country of origin after carrying out his tasks abroad. The conclusion of a new contract of employment with the original employer or an employer belonging to the same group of companies as the original employer should not preclude the employee from being regarded as carrying out his work in another country temporarily.

(37) Considerations of public interest justify giving the courts of the Member States the possibility, in exceptional circumstances, of applying exceptions based on public policy and overriding mandatory provisions. The concept of 'overriding mandatory provisions' should be distinguished from the expression 'provisions which cannot be derogated from by agreement' and should be construed more restrictively.

(38) In the context of voluntary assignment, the term 'relationship' should make it clear that Article 14(1) also applies to the property aspects of an assignment, as between assignor and assignee, in legal orders where such aspects are treated separately from the aspects under the law of obligations. However, the term 'relationship' should not be understood as relating to any relationship that may exist between assignor and assignee. In particular, it should not cover preliminary questions as regards a voluntary assignment or a contractual subrogation. The term should be strictly limited to the aspects which are directly relevant to the voluntary assignment or contractual subrogation in question.

(39) For the sake of legal certainty there should be a clear definition of habitual residence, in particular for companies and other bodies, corporate or unincorporated. Unlike Article 60(1) of Regulation 44/2001, which establishes three criteria, the conflict-of-law rule should proceed on the basis of a single criterion; otherwise, the parties would be unable to foresee the law applicable to their situation.

(40) A situation where conflict-of-law rules are dispersed among several instruments and where there are differences between those rules should be avoided. This Regulation, however, should not exclude the possibility of inclusion of conflict-of-law rules relating to contractual obligations in provisions of Community law with regard to particular matters. This Regulation should not prejudice the application of other instruments laying down provisions designed to contribute to the proper functioning of the internal market in so far as they cannot be applied in conjunction with the law designated by the rules of this Regulation. The application of provisions of the applicable law designated by the rules of this Regulation should not restrict the free movement of goods and services as regulated by Community instruments, such as Directive 2000/31 of the European Parliament and of the Council of 8 June 2000 on certain legal aspects of information society services, in particular electronic commerce, in the Internal Market (Directive on electronic commerce).

(41) Respect for international commitments entered into by the Member States means that this Regulation should not affect international conventions to which one or more Member States are parties at the time when this Regulation is adopted. To make the rules more accessible, the Commission should publish the list of the relevant conventions in the *Official Journal of the European Union* on the basis of information supplied by the Member States.

(42) The Commission will make a proposal to the European Parliament and to the Council concerning the procedures and conditions according to which Member States would be entitled to negotiate and conclude, on their own behalf, agreements with third countries in individual and exceptional cases, concerning sectoral matters and containing provisions on the law applicable to contractual obligations.

(43) Since the objective of this Regulation cannot be sufficiently achieved by the Member States and can therefore, by reason of the scale and effects of this Regulation, be better achieved at Community level, the Community may adopt measures, in accordance with the principle of subsidiarity as set out in Article 5 of the Treaty. In accordance with the principle of proportionality, as set out in that Article, this Regulation does not go beyond what is necessary to attain its objective.

(44) In accordance with Article 3 of the Protocol on the position of the United Kingdom and Ireland, annexed to the Treaty on European Union and to the Treaty establishing the European Community, Ireland has notified its wish to take part in the adoption and application of the present Regulation.

(45) In accordance with Articles 1 and 2 of the Protocol on the position of the United Kingdom and Ireland, annexed to the Treaty on European Union and to the Treaty establishing the European Community, and without prejudice to Article 4 of the said Protocol, the United Kingdom is not taking part in the adoption of this Regulation and is not bound by it or subject to its application.

(46) In accordance with Articles 1 and 2 of the Protocol on the position of Denmark, annexed to the Treaty on European Union and to the Treaty establishing the European Community, Denmark is not taking part in the adoption of this Regulation and is not bound by it or subject to its application,

HAVE ADOPTED THIS REGULATION:

Chapter I Scope

Article 1 Material Scope

1.   This Regulation shall apply, in situations involving a conflict of laws, to contractual obligations in civil and commercial matters.

It shall not apply, in particular, to revenue, customs or administrative matters.

2.   The following shall be excluded from the scope of this Regulation:

(a)   questions involving the status or legal capacity of natural persons, without prejudice to Article 13;

(b)   obligations arising out of family relationships and relationships deemed by the law applicable to such relationships to have comparable effects, including maintenance obligations;

(c)   obligations arising out of matrimonial property regimes, property regimes of relationships deemed by the law applicable to such relationships to have comparable effects to marriage, and wills and succession;

(d)   obligations arising under bills of exchange, cheques and promissory notes and other negotiable instruments to the extent that the obligations under such other negotiable instruments arise out of their negotiable character;

(e)   arbitration agreements and agreements on the choice of court;

(f)   questions governed by the law of companies and other bodies, corporate or unincorporated, such as the creation, by registration or otherwise, legal capacity, internal organisation or winding-up of companies and other bodies, corporate or unincorporated, and the personal liability of officers and members as such for the obligations of the company or body;

(g)   the question whether an agent is able to bind a principal, or an organ to bind a company or other body corporate or unincorporated, in relation to a third party;

(h)   the constitution of trusts and the relationship between settlors, trustees and beneficiaries;

(i)   obligations arising out of dealings prior to the conclusion of a contract;

(j)   insurance contracts arising out of operations carried out by organisations other than undertakings referred to in Article 2 of Directive 2002/83 of the European Parliament and of the Council of 5 November 2002 concerning life assurance the object of which is to provide benefits for employed or self-employed persons belonging to an undertaking or group of undertakings, or to a trade or group of trades, in the event of death or survival or of discontinuance or curtailment of activity, or of sickness related to work or accidents at work.

3.   This Regulation shall not apply to evidence and procedure, without prejudice to Article 18.
4.   In this Regulation, the term 'Member State' shall mean Member States to which this Regulation applies. However, in Article 3(4) and Article 7 the term shall mean all the Member States.

Article 2 Universal Application

Any law specified by this Regulation shall be applied whether or not it is the law of a Member State.

Chapter II Uniform Rules

Article 3 Freedom of Choice

1.   A contract shall be governed by the law chosen by the parties. The choice shall be made expressly or clearly demonstrated by the terms of the contract or the circumstances of the case. By their choice the parties can select the law applicable to the whole or to part only of the contract.
2.   The parties may at any time agree to subject the contract to a law other than that which previously governed it, whether as a result of an earlier choice made under this Article or of other provisions of this Regulation. Any change in the law to be applied that is made after the conclusion of the contract shall not prejudice its formal validity under Article 11 or adversely affect the rights of third parties.
3.   Where all other elements relevant to the situation at the time of the choice are located in a country other than the country whose law has been chosen, the choice of the parties shall not prejudice the application of provisions of the law of that other country which cannot be derogated from by agreement.
4.   Where all other elements relevant to the situation at the time of the choice are located in one or more Member States, the parties' choice of applicable law other than that of a Member State shall not prejudice the application of provisions of Community law, where appropriate as implemented in the Member State of the forum, which cannot be derogated from by agreement.
5.   The existence and validity of the consent of the parties as to the choice of the applicable law shall be determined in accordance with the provisions of Articles 10, 11 and 13.

Article 4 Applicable Law in the Absence of Choice

1.   To the extent that the law applicable to the contract has not been chosen in accordance with Article 3 and without prejudice to Articles 5 to 8, the law governing the contract shall be determined as follows:
(a)   a contract for the sale of goods shall be governed by the law of the country where the seller has his habitual residence; (default)
(b)   a contract for the provision of services shall be governed by the law of the country where the service provider has his habitual residence;
(c)   a contract relating to a right *in rem* in immovable property or to a tenancy of immovable property shall be governed by the law of the country where the property is situated;
(d)   notwithstanding point (c), a tenancy of immovable property concluded for temporary private use for a period of no more than six consecutive months shall be governed by the law of the country where the landlord has his habitual residence, provided that the tenant is a natural person and has his habitual residence in the same country;
(e)   a franchise contract shall be governed by the law of the country where the franchisee has his habitual residence;
(f)   a distribution contract shall be governed by the law of the country where the distributor has his habitual residence;
(g)   a contract for the sale of goods by auction shall be governed by the law of the country where the auction takes place, if such a place can be determined;
(h)   a contract concluded within a multilateral system which brings together or facilitates the bringing together of multiple third-party buying and selling interests in financial instru-

ments, as defined by Article 4(1), point (17) of Directive 2004/39, in accordance with non-discretionary rules and governed by a single law, shall be governed by that law.

2.   Where the contract is not covered by paragraph 1 or where the elements of the contract would be covered by more than one of points (a) to (h) of paragraph 1, the contract shall be governed by the law of the country where the party required to effect the characteristic performance of the contract has his habitual residence. (OR)

3.   Where it is clear from all the circumstances of the case that the contract is manifestly more closely connected with a country other than that indicated in paragraphs 1 or 2, the law of that other country shall apply.

4.   Where the law applicable cannot be determined pursuant to paragraphs 1 or 2, the contract shall be governed by the law of the country with which it is most closely connected.

Article 5 Contracts of Carriage

1.   To the extent that the law applicable to a contract for the carriage of goods has not been chosen in accordance with Article 3, the law applicable shall be the law of the country of habitual residence of the carrier, provided that the place of receipt or the place of delivery or the habitual residence of the consignor is also situated in that country. If those requirements are not met, the law of the country where the place of delivery as agreed by the parties is situated shall apply.

2.   To the extent that the law applicable to a contract for the carriage of passengers has not been chosen by the parties in accordance with the second subparagraph, the law applicable shall be the law of the country where the passenger has his habitual residence, provided that either the place of departure or the place of destination is situated in that country. If these requirements are not met, the law of the country where the carrier has his habitual residence shall apply.

The parties may choose as the law applicable to a contract for the carriage of passengers in accordance with Article 3 only the law of the country where:
(a)   the passenger has his habitual residence; or
(b)   the carrier has his habitual residence; or
(c)   the carrier has his place of central administration; or
(d)   the place of departure is situated; or
(e)   the place of destination is situated.

3.   Where it is clear from all the circumstances of the case that the contract, in the absence of a choice of law, is manifestly more closely connected with a country other than that indicated in paragraphs 1 or 2, the law of that other country shall apply.

Article 6 Consumer Contracts

1.   Without prejudice to Articles 5 and 7, a contract concluded by a natural person for a purpose which can be regarded as being outside his trade or profession (the consumer) with another person acting in the exercise of his trade or profession (the professional) shall be governed by the law of the country where the consumer has his habitual residence, provided that the professional:
(a)   pursues his commercial or professional activities in the country where the consumer has his habitual residence, or
(b)   by any means, directs such activities to that country or to several countries including that country, and the contract falls within the scope of such activities.

2.   Notwithstanding paragraph 1, the parties may choose the law applicable to a contract which fulfils the requirements of paragraph 1, in accordance with Article 3. Such a choice may not, however, have the result of depriving the consumer of the protection afforded to him by provisions that cannot be derogated from by agreement by virtue of the law which, in the absence of choice, would have been applicable on the basis of paragraph 1.

3.   If the requirements in points (a) or (b) of paragraph 1 are not fulfilled, the law applicable to a contract between a consumer and a professional shall be determined pursuant to Articles 3 and 4.

4. Paragraphs 1 and 2 shall not apply to:
(a) a contract for the supply of services where the services are to be supplied to the consumer exclusively in a country other than that in which he has his habitual residence;
(b) a contract of carriage other than a contract relating to package travel within the meaning of Council Directive 90/314 of 13 June 1990 on package travel, package holidays and package tours;
(c) a contract relating to a right *in rem* in immovable property or a tenancy of immovable property other than a contract relating to the right to use immovable properties on a time-share basis within the meaning of Directive 94/47;
(d) rights and obligations which constitute a financial instrument and rights and obligations constituting the terms and conditions governing the issuance or offer to the public and public take-over bids of transferable securities, and the subscription and redemption of units in collective investment undertakings in so far as these activities do not constitute provision of a financial service;
(e) a contract concluded within the type of system falling within the scope of Article 4(1)(h).

Article 7 Insurance Contracts

1. This Article shall apply to contracts referred to in paragraph 2, whether or not the risk co-vered is situated in a Member State, and to all other insurance contracts covering risks situated inside the territory of the Member States. It shall not apply to reinsurance contracts.
2. An insurance contract covering a large risk as defined in Article 5(d) of the First Council Directive 73/239 of 24 July 1973 on the coordination of laws, regulations and administrative provisions relating to the taking-up and pursuit of the business of direct insurance other than life assurance shall be governed by the law chosen by the parties in accordance with Article 3 of this Regulation.

To the extent that the applicable law has not been chosen by the parties, the insurance contract shall be governed by the law of the country where the insurer has his habitual residen-ce. Where it is clear from all the circumstances of the case that the contract is manifestly more closely connected with another country, the law of that other country shall apply.
3. In the case of an insurance contract other than a contract falling within paragraph 2, only the following laws may be chosen by the parties in accordance with Article 3:
(a) the law of any Member State where the risk is situated at the time of conclusion of the contract;
(b) the law of the country where the policy holder has his habitual residence;
(c) in the case of life assurance, the law of the Member State of which the policy holder is a national;
(d) for insurance contracts covering risks limited to events occurring in one Member State other than the Member State where the risk is situated, the law of that Member State;
(e) where the policy holder of a contract falling under this paragraph pursues a commercial or industrial activity or a liberal profession and the insurance contract covers two or more risks which relate to those activities and are situated in different Member States, the law of any of the Member States concerned or the law of the country of habitual residence of the policy holder.

Where, in the cases set out in points (a), (b) or (e), the Member States referred to grant greater freedom of choice of the law applicable to the insurance contract, the parties may take advan-tage of that freedom.

To the extent that the law applicable has not been chosen by the parties in accordance with this paragraph, such a contract shall be governed by the law of the Member State in which the risk is situated at the time of conclusion of the contract.
4. The following additional rules shall apply to insurance contracts covering risks for which a Member State imposes an obligation to take out insurance:
(a) the insurance contract shall not satisfy the obligation to take out insurance unless it com-plies with the specific provisions relating to that insurance laid down by the Member State

that imposes the obligation. Where the law of the Member State in which the risk is situated and the law of the Member State imposing the obligation to take out insurance contradict each other, the latter shall prevail;

(b) by way of derogation from paragraphs 2 and 3, a Member State may lay down that the insurance contract shall be governed by the law of the Member State that imposes the obligation to take out insurance.

5.   For the purposes of paragraph 3, third subparagraph, and paragraph 4, where the contract covers risks situated in more than one Member State, the contract shall be considered as constituting several contracts each relating to only one Member State.

6.   For the purposes of this Article, the country in which the risk is situated shall be determined in accordance with Article 2(d) of the Second Council Directive 88/357 of 22 June 1988 on the coordination of laws, regulations and administrative provisions relating to direct insurance other than life assurance and laying down provisions to facilitate the effective exercise of freedom to provide services and, in the case of life assurance, the country in which the risk is situated shall be the country of the commitment within the meaning of Article 1(1) (g) of Directive 2002/83.

Article 8 Individual Employment Contracts

1.   An individual employment contract shall be governed by the law chosen by the parties in accordance with Article 3. Such a choice of law may not, however, have the result of depriving the employee of the protection afforded to him by provisions that cannot be derogated from by agreement under the law that, in the absence of choice, would have been applicable pursuant to paragraphs 2, 3 and 4 of this Article.

2.   To the extent that the law applicable to the individual employment contract has not been chosen by the parties, the contract shall be governed by the law of the country in which or, failing that, from which the employee habitually carries out his work in performance of the contract. The country where the work is habitually carried out shall not be deemed to have changed if he is temporarily employed in another country.

3.   Where the law applicable cannot be determined pursuant to paragraph 2, the contract shall be governed by the law of the country where the place of business through which the employee was engaged is situated.

4.   Where it appears from the circumstances as a whole that the contract is more closely connected with a country other than that indicated in paragraphs 2 or 3, the law of that other country shall apply.

Article 9 Overriding Mandatory Provisions

1.   Overriding mandatory provisions are provisions the respect for which is regarded as crucial by a country for safeguarding its public interests, such as its political, social or economic organisation, to such an extent that they are applicable to any situation falling within their scope, irrespective of the law otherwise applicable to the contract under this Regulation.

2.   Nothing in this Regulation shall restrict the application of the overriding mandatory provisions of the law of the forum.

3.   Effect may be given to the overriding mandatory provisions of the law of the country where the obligations arising out of the contract have to be or have been performed, in so far as those overriding mandatory provisions render the performance of the contract unlawful. In considering whether to give effect to those provisions, regard shall be had to their nature and purpose and to the consequences of their application or non-application.

Article 10 Consent and Material Validity

1.   The existence and validity of a contract, or of any term of a contract, shall be determined by the law which would govern it under this Regulation if the contract or term were valid.

2.   Nevertheless, a party, in order to establish that he did not consent, may rely upon the law of the country in which he has his habitual residence if it appears from the circumstances that it would not be reasonable to determine the effect of his conduct in accordance with the law specified in paragraph 1.

Article 11 Formal Validity

1.   A contract concluded between persons who, or whose agents, are in the same country at the time of its conclusion is formally valid if it satisfies the formal requirements of the law which governs it in substance under this Regulation or of the law of the country where it is concluded.

2.   A contract concluded between persons who, or whose agents, are in different countries at the time of its conclusion is formally valid if it satisfies the formal requirements of the law which governs it in substance under this Regulation, or of the law of either of the countries where either of the parties or their agent is present at the time of conclusion, or of the law of the country where either of the parties had his habitual residence at that time.

3.   A unilateral act intended to have legal effect relating to an existing or contemplated contract is formally valid if it satisfies the formal requirements of the law which governs or would govern the contract in substance under this Regulation, or of the law of the country where the act was done, or of the law of the country where the person by whom it was done had his habitual residence at that time.

4.   Paragraphs 1, 2 and 3 of this Article shall not apply to contracts that fall within the scope of Article 6. The form of such contracts shall be governed by the law of the country where the consumer has his habitual residence.

5.   Notwithstanding paragraphs 1 to 4, a contract the subject matter of which is a right *in rem* in immovable property or a tenancy of immovable property shall be subject to the requirements of form of the law of the country where the property is situated if by that law:

(a)   those requirements are imposed irrespective of the country where the contract is concluded and irrespective of the law governing the contract; and

(b)   those requirements cannot be derogated from by agreement.

Article 12 Scope of the Law Applicable

1.   The law applicable to a contract by virtue of this Regulation shall govern in particular:

(a)   interpretation;

(b)   performance;

(c)   within the limits of the powers conferred on the court by its procedural law, the consequences of a total or partial breach of obligations, including the assessment of damages in so far as it is governed by rules of law;

(d)   the various ways of extinguishing obligations, and prescription and limitation of actions;

(e)   the consequences of nullity of the contract.

2.   In relation to the manner of performance and the steps to be taken in the event of defective performance, regard shall be had to the law of the country in which performance takes place.

Article 13 Incapacity

In a contract concluded between persons who are in the same country, a natural person who would have capacity under the law of that country may invoke his incapacity resulting from the law of another country, only if the other party to the contract was aware of that incapacity at the time of the conclusion of the contract or was not aware thereof as a result of negligence.

Article 14 Voluntary Assignment and Contractual Subrogation

1.   The relationship between assignor and assignee under a voluntary assignment or contractual subrogation of a claim against another person (the debtor) shall be governed by the law that applies to the contract between the assignor and assignee under this Regulation.

2.   The law governing the assigned or subrogated claim shall determine its assignability, the relationship between the assignee and the debtor, the conditions under which the assignment or subrogation can be invoked against the debtor and whether the debtor's obligations have been discharged.

3.   The concept of assignment in this Article includes outright transfers of claims, transfers of claims by way of security and pledges or other security rights over claims.

Article 15 Legal Subrogation

Where a person (the creditor) has a contractual claim against another (the debtor) and a third person has a duty to satisfy the creditor, or has in fact satisfied the creditor in discharge of that duty, the law which governs the third person's duty to satisfy the creditor shall determine whether and to what extent the third person is entitled to exercise against the debtor the rights which the creditor had against the debtor under the law governing their relationship.

Article 16 Multiple Liability

If a creditor has a claim against several debtors who are liable for the same claim, and one of the debtors has already satisfied the claim in whole or in part, the law governing the debtor's obligation towards the creditor also governs the debtor's right to claim recourse from the other debtors. The other debtors may rely on the defences they had against the creditor to the extent allowed by the law governing their obligations towards the creditor.

Article 17 Set-off

Where the right to set-off is not agreed by the parties, set-off shall be governed by the law applicable to the claim against which the right to set-off is asserted.

Article 18 Burden of Proof

1.   The law governing a contractual obligation under this Regulation shall apply to the extent that, in matters of contractual obligations, it contains rules which raise presumptions of law or determine the burden of proof.

2.   A contract or an act intended to have legal effect may be proved by any mode of proof recognised by the law of the forum or by any of the laws referred to in Article 11 under which that contract or act is formally valid, provided that such mode of proof can be administered by the forum.

Chapter III Other Provisions

Article 19 Habitual Residence

1.   For the purposes of this Regulation, the habitual residence of companies and other bodies, corporate or unincorporated, shall be the place of central administration.

The habitual residence of a natural person acting in the course of his business activity shall be his principal place of business.

2.   Where the contract is concluded in the course of the operations of a branch, agency or any other establishment, or if, under the contract, performance is the responsibility of such a branch, agency or establishment, the place where the branch, agency or any other establishment is located shall be treated as the place of habitual residence.

3.   For the purposes of determining the habitual residence, the relevant point in time shall be the time of the conclusion of the contract.

Article 20 Exclusion of renvoi

The application of the law of any country specified by this Regulation means the application of the rules of law in force in that country other than its rules of private international law, unless provided otherwise in this Regulation.

Article 21 Public Policy of the Forum

The application of a provision of the law of any country specified by this Regulation may be refused only if such application is manifestly incompatible with the public policy (*ordre public*) of the forum.

Article 22 States with More Than One Legal System

1.   Where a State comprises several territorial units, each of which has its own rules of law in respect of contractual obligations, each territorial unit shall be considered as a country for the purposes of identifying the law applicable under this Regulation.

2.   A Member State where different territorial units have their own rules of law in respect of contractual obligations shall not be required to apply this Regulation to conflicts solely between the laws of such units.

Article 23 Relationship with Other Provisions of Community Law
With the exception of Article 7, this Regulation shall not prejudice the application of provisions of Community law which, in relation to particular matters, lay down conflict-of-law rules relating to contractual obligations.

Article 24 Relationship with the Rome Convention
1.   This Regulation shall replace the Rome Convention in the Member States, except as regards the territories of the Member States which fall within the territorial scope of that Convention and to which this Regulation does not apply pursuant to Article 299 of the Treaty.
2.   In so far as this Regulation replaces the provisions of the Rome Convention, any reference to that Convention shall be understood as a reference to this Regulation.

Article 25 Relationship with Existing International Conventions
1.   This Regulation shall not prejudice the application of international conventions to which one or more Member States are parties at the time when this Regulation is adopted and which lay down conflict-of-law rules relating to contractual obligations.
2.   However, this Regulation shall, as between Member States, take precedence over conventions concluded exclusively between two or more of them in so far as such conventions concern matters governed by this Regulation.

Article 26 List of Conventions
1.   By 17 June 2009, Member States shall notify the Commission of the conventions referred to in Article 25(1). After that date, Member States shall notify the Commission of all denunciations of such conventions.
2.   Within six months of receipt of the notifications referred to in paragraph 1, the Commission shall publish in the *Official Journal of the European Union*:
(a)   a list of the conventions referred to in paragraph 1;
(b)   the denunciations referred to in paragraph 1.

Article 27 Review Clause
1.   By 17 June 2013, the Commission shall submit to the European Parliament, the Council and the European Economic and Social Committee a report on the application of this Regulation. If appropriate, the report shall be accompanied by proposals to amend this Regulation. The report shall include:
(a)   a study on the law applicable to insurance contracts and an assessment of the impact of the provisions to be introduced, if any; and
(b)   an evaluation on the application of Article 6, in particular as regards the coherence of Community law in the field of consumer protection.
2.   By 17 June 2010, the Commission shall submit to the European Parliament, the Council and the European Economic and Social Committee a report on the question of the effectiveness of an assignment or subrogation of a claim against third parties and the priority of the assigned or subrogated claim over a right of another person. The report shall be accompanied, if appropriate, by a proposal to amend this Regulation and an assessment of the impact of the provisions to be introduced.

Article 28 Application in Time
This Regulation shall apply to contracts concluded after 17 December 2009.

Chapter IV Final Provisions
Article 29 Entry Into Force and Application
This Regulation shall enter into force on the 20th day following its publication in the *Official Journal of the European Union*.

It shall apply from 17 December 2009 except for Article 26 which shall apply from 17 June 2009.

This Regulation shall be binding in its entirety and directly applicable in the Member States in accordance with the Treaty establishing the European Community.
Done at Strasbourg, 17 June 2008.

1980 UNITED NATIONS CONVENTION ON CONTRACTS FOR THE INTERNATIONAL SALE OF GOODS[1]

THE STATES PARTIES TO THIS CONVENTION,
BEARING IN MIND the broad objectives in the resolutions adopted by the sixth special session of the General Assembly of the United Nations on the establishment of a New International Economic Order,
CONSIDERING that the development of international trade on the basis of equality and mutual benefit is an important element in promoting friendly relations among States,
BEING OF THE OPINION that the adoption of uniform rules which govern contracts for the international sale of goods and take into account the different social, economic and legal systems would contribute to the removal of legal barriers in international trade and promote the development of international trade,
HAVE DECREED as follows:

PART I – SPHERE OF APPLICATION AND GENERAL PROVISIONS
CHAPTER I - SPHERE OF APPLICATION
Article 1 [Scope of Application]

see Art.10

(1)   This Convention applies to contracts of sale of goods between parties whose places of business are in different States:

both

(a)   when the States are Contracting States; or
(b)   when the rules of private international law lead to the application of the law of a Contracting State. *(not both, but only one State has ratified)*

seller's law or closest conn. -ection. see Art.95

(2)   The fact that the parties have their places of business in different States is to be disregarded whenever this fact does not appear either from the contract or from any dealings between, or from information disclosed by, the parties at any time before or at the conclusion of the contract.
(3)   Neither the nationality of the parties nor the civil or commercial character of the parties or of the contract is to be taken into consideration in determining the application of this Convention.

Article 2 [Sales Contracts Not Covered]
This Convention does not apply to sales:
(a)   of goods bought for personal, family or household use, unless the seller, at any time before or at the conclusion of the contract, neither knew nor ought to have known that the goods were bought for any such use;
(b)   by auction;
(c)   on execution or otherwise by authority of law;
(d)   of stocks, shares, investment securities, negotiable instruments or money;
(e)   of ships, vessels, hovercraft or aircraft;
(f)   of electricity.

Article 3 [Contracts Involving Works or Services]
(1)   Contracts for the supply of goods to be manufactured or produced are to be considered sales unless the party who orders the goods undertakes to supply a substantial part of the materials necessary for such manufacture or production.

---

1   © United Nations, 1489 UNTS 3, all rights reserved.

1(1)(c) - if CISG was chosen as the applicable law

(2)   This Convention does not apply to contracts in which the preponderant part of the obligations of the party who furnishes the goods consists in the supply of labour or other services.

Article 4 [Scope in Substantive Contract Law]
This Convention governs only the formation of the contract of sale and the rights and obligations of the seller and the buyer arising from such a contract. In particular, except as otherwise
expressly provided in this Convention, it is not concerned with:
(a)   the validity of the contract or of any of its provisions or of any usage;
(b)   the effect which the contract may have on the property in the goods sold.

Article 5 [No Application in Tort Law]
This Convention does not apply to the liability of the seller for death or personal injury caused
by the goods to any person.

Article 6 [Priority of Contractual Clauses]
The parties may exclude the application of this Convention or, subject to Article 12, derogate
from or vary the effect of any of its provisions.

CHAPTER II - GENERAL PROVISIONS
Article 7 [Interpretation of the CISG]
(1)   In the interpretation of this Convention, regard is to be had to its international character
and to the need to promote uniformity in its application and the observance of good faith in international trade. (precedent is persuasive, regardless of Xi)
(2)   Questions concerning matters governed by this Convention which are not expressly settled in it are to be settled in conformity with the general principles on which it is based or, in the
absence of such principles, in conformity with the law applicable by virtue of the rules of private
international law.

Article 8 [Interpretation of Conduct and Statements]
(1)   For the purposes of this Convention statements made by and other conduct of a party are
to be interpreted according to his intent where the other party knew or could not have been
unaware what that intent was.
(2)   If the preceding paragraph is not applicable, statements made by and other conduct of a
party are to be interpreted according to the understanding that a reasonable person of the
same kind as the other party would have had in the same circumstances.
(3)   In determining the intent of a party or the understanding a reasonable person would have
had, due consideration is to be given to all relevant circumstances of the case including the negotiations, any practices which the parties have established between themselves, usages and
any subsequent conduct of the parties.

Article 9 [Usages of the Parties and the Industry]
(1)   The parties are bound by any usage to which they have agreed and by any practices which
they have established between themselves.
(2)   The parties are considered, unless otherwise agreed, to have impliedly made applicable to
their contract or its formation a usage of which the parties knew or ought to have known and
which in international trade is widely known to, and regularly observed by, parties to contracts
of the type involved in the particular trade concerned.

Article 10 [Definition of "Place of Business"]
For the purposes of this Convention:
(a)   if a party has more than one place of business, the place of business is that which has the
      closest relationship to the contract and its performance, having regard to the circumstan-
      ces known to or contemplated by the parties at any time before or at the conclusion of the
      contract;
(b)   if a party does not have a place of business, reference is to be made to his habitual resi-
      dence.

Article 11 [Freedom of Form]

A contract of sale need not be concluded in or evidenced by writing and is not subject to any other requirement as to form. It may be proved by any means, including witnesses.

Article 12 [Exceptions to the Freedom of Form]

Any provision of Article 11, Article 29 or Part II of this Convention that allows a contract of sale or its modification or termination by agreement or any offer, acceptance or other indication of intention to be made in any form other than in writing does not apply where any party has his place of business in a Contracting State which has made a declaration under Article 96 of this Convention. The parties may not derogate from or vary the effect or this article.

Article 13 [Definition of Written Form]

For the purposes of this Convention "writing" includes telegram and telex. fax, e-mail, etc.

PART II – FORMATION OF THE CONTRACT

Article 14 [Offer or Invitation]

(1)   A proposal for concluding a contract addressed to one or more specific persons constitutes an offer if it is sufficiently definite and indicates the intention of the offeror to be bound in case of acceptance. A proposal is sufficiently definite if it indicates the goods and expressly or implicitly fixes or makes provision for determining the quantity and the price.

(2)   A proposal other than one addressed to one or more specific persons is to be considered merely as an invitation to make offers, unless the contrary is clearly indicated by the person making the proposal.

Article 15 [Effective and Withdrawn Offers]

(1)   An offer becomes effective when it reaches the offeree.

(2)   An offer, even if it is irrevocable, may be withdrawn if the withdrawal reaches the offeree before or at the same time as the offer.

Article 16 [Revocable and Irrevocable Offers]

(1)   Until a contract is concluded an offer may be revoked if the revocation reaches the offeree before he has dispatched an acceptance.

(2)   However, an offer cannot be revoked:

(a)   if it indicates, whether by stating a fixed time for acceptance or otherwise, that it is irrevocable; or

(b)   if it was reasonable for the offeree to rely on the offer as being irrevocable and the offeree has acted in reliance on the offer.

Article 17 [Rejection of Offers]

An offer, even if it is irrevocable, is terminated when a rejection reaches the offeror.

Article 18 [Acceptance of Offers]

(1)   A statement made by or other conduct of the offeree indicating assent to an offer is an acceptance. Silence or inactivity does not in itself amount to acceptance.

(2)   An acceptance of an offer becomes effective at the moment the indication of assent reaches the offeror. An acceptance is not effective if the indication of assent does not reach the offeror within the time he has fixed or, if no time is fixed, within a reasonable time, due account being taken of the circumstances of the transaction, including the rapidity of the means of communication employed by the offeror. An oral offer must be accepted immediately unless the circumstances indicate otherwise.

(3)   However, if, by virtue of the offer or as a result of practices which the parties have established between themselves or of usage, the offeree may indicate assent by performing an act, such as one relating to the dispatch of the goods or payment of the price, without notice to the offeror, the acceptance is effective at the moment the act is performed, provided that the act is performed within the period of time laid down in the preceding paragraph.

Article 19 [Modified Acceptance or Counter-offer]

(1)   A reply to an offer which purports to be an acceptance but contains additions, limitations or other modifications is a rejection of the offer and constitutes a counter-offer.

(2)   However, a reply to an offer which purports to be an acceptance but contains additional or different terms which do not materially alter the terms of the offer constitutes an acceptance, unless the offeror, without undue delay, objects orally to the discrepancy or dispatches a notice to that effect. If he does not so object, the terms of the contract are the terms of the offer with the modifications contained in the acceptance.

(3)   Additional or different terms relating, among other things, to the price, payment, quality and quantity of the goods, place and time of delivery, extent of one party's liability to the other or the settlement of disputes are considered to alter the terms of the offer materially.

Article 20 [Time Limit for Acceptance]

(1)   A period of time for acceptance fixed by the offeror in a telegram or a letter begins to run from the moment the telegram is handed in for dispatch or from the date shown on the letter or, if no such date is shown, from the date shown on the envelope. A period of time for acceptance fixed by the offeror by telephone, telex or other means of instantaneous communication, begins to run from the moment that the offer reaches the offeree.

(2)   Official holidays or non-business days occurring during the period for acceptance are included in calculating the period. However, if a notice of acceptance cannot be delivered at the address of the offeror on the last day of the period because that day falls on an official holiday or a non-business day at the place of business of the offeror, the period is extended until the first business day which follows.

Article 21 [Late Acceptance]

(1)   A late acceptance is nevertheless effective as an acceptance if without delay the offeror orally so informs the offeree or dispatches a notice to that effect.

(2)   If a letter or other writing containing a late acceptance shows that it has been sent in such circumstances that if its transmission had been normal it would have reached the offeror in due time, the late acceptance is effective as an acceptance unless, without delay, the offeror orally informs the offeree that he considers his offer as having lapsed or dispatches a notice to that effect.

Article 22 [Withdrawal of Acceptance]

An acceptance may be withdrawn if the withdrawal reaches the offeror before or at the same time as the acceptance would have become effective.

Article 23 [Conclusion of Contract]

A contract is concluded at the moment when an acceptance of an offer becomes effective in accordance with the provisions of this Convention.

Article 24 [Definition of "Reaches"]

For the purposes of this Part of the Convention, an offer, declaration of acceptance or any other indication of intention "reaches" the addressee when it is made orally to him or delivered by any other means to him personally, to his place of business or mailing address or, if he does not have a place of business or mailing address, to his habitual residence.

PART III – SALE OF GOODS

CHAPTER I - GENERAL PROVISIONS

Article 25 [Definition of "Fundamental Breach"]

A breach of contract committed by one of the parties is fundamental if it results in such detriment to the other party as substantially to deprive him of what he is entitled to expect under the contract, unless the party in breach did not foresee and a reasonable person of the same kind in the same circumstances would not have foreseen such a result.

Article 26 [Declaration of Avoidance]

A declaration of avoidance of the contract is effective only if made by notice to the other party.

Article 27 [Delay or Error in Transmission of Communications]

Unless otherwise expressly provided in this Part of the Convention, if any notice, request or other communication is given or made by a party in accordance with this Part and by means appropriate in the circumstances, a delay or error in the transmission of the communication or its failure to arrive does not deprive that party of the right to rely on the communication.

Article 28 [Specific Performance]

If, in accordance with the provisions of this Convention, one party is entitled to require performance of any obligation by the other party, a court is not bound to enter a judgement for specific performance unless the court would do so under its own law in respect of similar contracts of sale not governed by this Convention.

Article 29 [Modification or Termination by Agreement]

(1)   A contract may be modified or terminated by the mere agreement of the parties.

(2)   A contract in writing which contains a provision requiring any modification or termination by agreement to be in writing may not be otherwise modified or terminated by agreement. However, a party may be precluded by his conduct from asserting such a provision to the extent that the other party has relied on that conduct.

CHAPTER II - OBLIGATIONS OF THE SELLER
Article 30 [Primary Obligations]

The seller must deliver the goods, hand over any documents relating to them and transfer the property in the goods, as required by the contract and this Convention.

Section I. Delivery of the Goods and Handing over of Documents
Article 31 [Place of Delivery]

If the seller is not bound to deliver the goods at any other particular place, his obligation to deliver consists:

(a)   if the contract of sale involves carriage of the goods - in handing the goods over to the first carrier for transmission to the buyer;

(b)   if, in cases not within the preceding subparagraph, the contract related to specific goods, or unidentified goods to be drawn from a specific stock or to be manufactured or produced, and at the time of the conclusion of the contract the parties knew that the goods were at, or were to be manufactured or produced at, a particular place - in placing the goods at the buyer's disposal at that place;

(c)   in other cases - in placing the goods at the buyer's disposal at the place where the seller had his place of business at the time of the conclusion of the contract.

Article 32 [Carriage and Insurance]

(1)   If the seller, in accordance with the contract or this Convention, hands the goods over to a carrier and if the goods are not clearly identified to the contract by markings on the goods, by shipping documents or otherwise, the seller must give the buyer notice of the consignment specifying the goods.

(2)   If the seller is bound to arrange for carriage of the goods, he must make such contracts as are necessary for carriage to the place fixed by means of transportation appropriate in the circumstances and according to the usual terms for such transportation.

(3)   If the seller is not bound to effect insurance in respect of the carriage of the goods, he must, at the buyer's request, provide him with all available information necessary to enable him to effect such insurance.

Article 33 [Time of Delivery]

The seller must deliver the goods:

(a)   if a date is fixed by or determinable from the contract, on that date;

(b)   if a period of time is fixed by or determinable from the contract, at any time within that period unless circumstances indicate that the buyer is to choose a date; or

"time is of the essence" = every delay is a fundamental breach

(c)   in any other case, within a reasonable time after the conclusion of the contract.

Article 34 [Delivery of Related Documents]

If the seller is bound to hand over documents relating to the goods, he must hand them over at the time and place and in the form required by the contract. If the seller has handed over documents before that time, he may, up to that time, cure any lack of conformity in the documents, if the exercise of this right does not cause the buyer unreasonable inconvenience or unreasonable expense. However, the buyer retains any right to claim damages as provided for in this Convention.

Section II. Conformity of the Goods and Third Party Claims

Article 35 [Conformity of Goods to Contract]

(1)   The seller must deliver goods which are of the quantity, quality and description required by the contract and which are contained or packaged in the manner required by the contract.

(2)   Except where the parties have agreed otherwise, the goods do not conform with the contract unless they:

(a)   are fit for the purposes for which goods of the same description would ordinarily be used;

(b)   are fit for any particular purpose expressly or impliedly made known to the seller at the time of the conclusion of the contract, except where the circumstances show that the buyer did not rely, or that it was unreasonable for him to rely, on the seller's skill and judgement;

(c)   possess the qualities of goods which the seller has held out to the buyer as a sample or model;

(d)   are contained or packaged in the manner usual for such goods or, where there is no such manner, in a manner adequate to preserve and protect the goods.

(3)   The seller is not liable under subparagraphs (a) to (d) of the preceding paragraph for any lack of conformity of the goods if at the time of the conclusion of the contract the buyer knew or could not have been unaware of such lack of conformity.

Article 36 [Time When Goods Must Be in Conformity]

(1)   The seller is liable in accordance with the contract and this Convention for any lack of conformity which exists at the time when the risk passes to the buyer, even though the lack of conformity becomes apparent only after that time.

(2)   The seller is also liable for any lack of conformity which occurs after the time indicated in the preceding paragraph and which is due to a breach of any of his obligations, including a breach of any guarantee that for a period of time the goods will remain fit for their ordinary purpose or for some particular purpose or will retain specified qualities or characteristics.

Article 37 [Seller's Right to Cure Defects Before Due Date for Delivery]

If the seller has delivered goods before the date for delivery, he may, up to that date, deliver any missing part or make up any deficiency in the quantity of the goods delivered, or deliver goods in replacement of any non-conforming goods delivered or remedy any lack of conformity in the goods delivered, provided that the exercise of this right does not cause the buyer unreasonable inconvenience or unreasonable expense. However, the buyer retains any right to claim damages as provided for in this Convention.

Article 38 [Buyer's Obligation to Examine Goods]

(1)   The buyer must examine the goods, or cause them to be examined, within as short a period as is practicable in the circumstances.

(2)   If the contract involves carriage of the goods, examination may be deferred until after the goods have arrived at their destination.

(3)   If the goods are redirected in transit or redispatched by the buyer without a reasonable opportunity for examination by him and at the time of the conclusion of the contract the seller knew or ought to have known of the possibility of such redirection or redispatch, examination may be deferred until after the goods have arrived at the new destination.

Article 39 [Buyer's Obligation to Notify Non-Conformity]

(1)   The buyer loses the right to rely on a lack of conformity of the goods if he does not give notice to the seller specifying the nature of the lack of conformity within a reasonable time after he has discovered it or ought to have discovered it.

(2)   In any event, the buyer loses the right to rely on a lack of conformity of the goods if he does not give the seller notice thereof at the latest within a period of two years from the date on which the goods were actually handed over to the buyer, unless this time-limit is inconsistent with a contractual period of guarantee.

Article 40 [Seller's Knowledge of Non-Conformity]

The seller is not entitled to rely on the provisions of Articles 38 and 39 if the lack of conformity relates to facts of which he knew or could not have been unaware and which he did not disclose to the buyer.

Article 41 [Delivery with Title and Free from Encumbrances]

The seller must deliver goods which are free from any right or claim of a third party, unless the buyer agreed to take the goods subject to that right or claim. However, if such right or claim is based on industrial property or other intellectual property, the seller's obligation is governed by Article 42.

Article 42 [Third Party Industrial or Intellectual Property Rights]

(1)   The seller must deliver goods which are free from any right or claim of a third party based on industrial property or other intellectual property, of which at the time of the conclusion of the contract the seller knew or could not have been unaware, provided that the right or claim is based on industrial property or other intellectual property:

(a)   under the law of the State where the goods will be resold or otherwise used, if it was con- templated by the parties at the time of the conclusion of the contract that the goods would be resold or otherwise used in that State; or

(b)   in any other case, under the law of the State where the buyer has his place of business.

(2)   The obligation of the seller under the preceding paragraph does not extend to cases where:

(a)   at the time of the conclusion of the contract the buyer knew or could not have been un- aware of the right or claim; or

(b)   the right or claim results from the seller's compliance with technical drawings, designs, for- mulae or other such specifications furnished by the buyer.

Article 43 [Buyer's Obligation to Notify Third Party Claims]

(1)   The buyer loses the right to rely on the provisions of Article 41 or Article 42 if he does not give notice to the seller specifying the nature of the right or claim of the third party within a rea- sonable time after he has become aware or ought to have become aware of the right or claim.

(2)   The seller is not entitled to rely on the provisions of the preceding paragraph if he knew of the right or claim of the third party and the nature of it.

Article 44 [Exception to Article 39(1) and 43]

Notwithstanding the provisions of paragraph (1) of Article 39 and paragraph (1) of Article 43, the buyer may reduce the price in accordance with Article 50 or claim damages, except for loss of profit, if he has a reasonable excuse for his failure to give the required notice.

Section III. Remedies for Breach of Contract by the Seller

Article 45 [Buyer's Remedies in the Event of Seller's Breach]

(1)   If the seller fails to perform any of his obligations under the contract or this Convention, the buyer may:

(a)   exercise the rights provided in Articles 46 to 52;

(b)   claim damages as provided in Articles 74 to 77.

(2)   The buyer is not deprived of any right he may have to claim damages by exercising his right to other remedies.

(3)   No period of grace may be granted to the seller by a court or arbitral tribunal when the buyer resorts to a remedy for breach of contract.

Article 46 [Priority of the Right to Require Performance]
(1)   The buyer may require performance by the seller of his obligations unless the buyer has resorted to a remedy which is inconsistent with this requirement.
(2)   If the goods do not conform with the contract, the buyer may require delivery of substitute goods only if the lack of conformity constitutes a fundamental breach of contract and a request for substitute goods is made either in conjunction with notice given under Article 39 or within a reasonable time thereafter.
(3)   If the goods do not conform with the contract, the buyer may require the seller to remedy the lack of conformity by repair, unless this is unreasonable having regard to all the circumstances. A request for repair must be made either in conjunction with notice given under Article 39 or within a reasonable time thereafter.

Article 47 [Additional Time Limit for Performance]
(1)   The buyer may fix an additional period of time of reasonable length for performance by the seller of his obligations.
(2)   Unless the buyer has received notice from the seller that he will not perform within the period so fixed, the buyer may not, during that period, resort to any remedy for breach of contract. However, the buyer is not deprived thereby of any right he may have to claim damages for delay in performance.

Article 48 [Seller's Right to Remedy Performance Even After Date for Delivery]
(1)   Subject to Article 49, the seller may, even after the date for delivery, remedy at his own expense any failure to perform his obligations, if he can do so without unreasonable delay and without causing the buyer unreasonable inconvenience or uncertainty of reimbursement by the seller of expenses advanced by the buyer. However, the buyer retains any right to claim damages as provided for in this Convention.
(2)   If the seller requests the buyer to make known whether he will accept performance and the buyer does not comply with the request within a reasonable time, the seller may perform within the time indicated in his request. The buyer may not, during that period of time, resort to any remedy which is inconsistent with performance by the seller.
(3)   A notice by the seller that he will perform within a specified period of time is assumed to include a request, under the preceding paragraph, that the buyer make known his decision.
(4)   A request or notice by the seller under paragraph (2) or (3) of this Article is not effective unless received by the buyer.

Article 49 [Buyer's Right to Avoid]   *see See. V (pg. 39)*
(1)   The buyer may declare the contract avoided:
(a)   if the failure by the seller to perform any of his obligations under the contract or this Convention amounts to a fundamental breach of contract; or *see Art. 25*
(b)   in case of non-delivery, if the seller does not deliver the goods within the additional period of time fixed by the buyer in accordance with paragraph (1) of Article 47 or declares that he will not deliver within the period so fixed.
(2)   However, in cases where the seller has delivered the goods, the buyer loses the right to declare the contract avoided unless he does so:
(a)   in respect of late delivery, within a reasonable time after he has become aware that delivery has been made;
(b)   in respect of any breach other than late delivery, within a reasonable time:
   (i)   after he knew or ought to have known of the breach;
   (ii)   after the expiration of any additional period of time fixed by the buyer in accordance with paragraph (1) of Article 47, or after the seller has declared that he will not perform his obligations within such an additional period; or

(iii)   after the expiration of any additional period of time indicated by the seller in accordance with paragraph (2) of Article 48, or after the buyer has declared that he will not accept performance.

Article 50 [Buyer's Right to Keep Non-Conforming Goods and Reduce Price]

If the goods do not conform with the contract and whether or not the price has already been paid, the buyer may reduce the price in the same proportion as the value that the goods actually delivered had at the time of the delivery bears to the value that conforming goods would have had at that time. However, if the seller remedies any failure to perform his obligations in accordance with Article 37 or Article 48 or if the buyer refuses to accept performance by the seller in accordance with those articles, the buyer may not reduce the price.

Article 51 [Partial Delivery]

(1)   If the seller delivers only a part of the goods or if only a part of the goods delivered is in conformity with the contract, Articles 46 to 50 apply in respect of the part which is missing or which does not conform.

(2)   The buyer may declare the contract avoided in its entirety only if the failure to make delivery completely or in conformity with the contract amounts to a fundamental breach of the contract.

Article 52 [Early Delivery and Excess Delivery]

(1)   If the seller delivers the goods before the date fixed, the buyer may take delivery or refuse to take delivery.

(2)   If the seller delivers a quantity of goods greater than that provided for in the contract, the buyer may take delivery or refuse to take delivery of the excess quantity. If the buyer takes delivery of all or part of the excess quantity, he must pay for it at the contract rate.

CHAPTER III - OBLIGATIONS OF THE BUYER

Article 53 [Primary Obligations]

The buyer must pay the price for the goods and take delivery of them as required by the contract and this Convention.

Section I. Payment of the Price

Article 54 [Payment and Payment Formalities]

The buyer's obligation to pay the price includes taking such steps and complying with such formalities as may be required under the contract or any laws and regulations to enable payment to be made.

Article 55 [Determination of Price]

Where a contract has been validly concluded but does not expressly or implicitly fix or make provision for determining the price, the parties are considered, in the absence of any indication to the contrary, to have impliedly made reference to the price generally charged at the time of the conclusion of the contract for such goods sold under comparable circumstances in the trade concerned.

Article 56 [Price Fixed According to Weight]

If the price is fixed according to the weight of the goods, in case of doubt it is to be determined by the net weight.

Article 57 [Place of Payment]

(1)   If the buyer is not bound to pay the price at any other particular place, he must pay it to the seller:

(a)   at the seller's place of business; or

(b)   if the payment is to be made against the handing over of the goods or of documents, at the place where the handing over takes place.

(2)   The seller must bear any increases in the expenses incidental to payment which is caused by a change in his place of business subsequent to the conclusion of the contract.

Article 58 [Time of Payment]

(1) If the buyer is not bound to pay the price at any other specific time, he must pay it when the seller places either the goods or documents controlling their disposition at the buyer's disposal in accordance with the contract and this Convention. The seller may make such payment a condition for handing over the goods or documents.

(2) If the contract involves carriage of the goods, the seller may dispatch the goods on terms whereby the goods, or documents controlling their disposition, will not be handed over to the buyer except against payment of the price.

(3) The buyer is not bound to pay the price until he has had an opportunity to examine the goods, unless the procedures for delivery or payment agreed upon by the parties are inconsistent with his having such an opportunity.

Article 59 [Payment Due Without Formal Demand]

The buyer must pay the price on the date fixed by or determinable from the contract and this Convention without the need for any request or compliance with any formality on the part of the seller.

Section II. Taking Delivery
Article 60 [Buyer's Obligation to Take Delivery]

The buyer's obligation to take delivery consists:

(a) in doing all the acts which could reasonably be expected of him in order to enable the seller to make delivery; and

(b) in taking over the goods.

Section III. Remedies for Breach of Contract by the Buyer
Article 61 [Seller's Remedies in the Event of Buyer's Breach]

(1) If the buyer fails to perform any of his obligations under the contract or this Convention, the seller may:

(a) exercise the rights provided in Articles 62 to 65;

(b) claim damages as provided in Articles 74 to 77.

(2) The seller is not deprived of any right he may have to claim damages by exercising his right to other remedies.

(3) No period of grace may be granted to the buyer by a court or arbitral tribunal when the seller resorts to a remedy for breach of contract.

Article 62 [Priority of the Right to Require Performance]

The seller may require the buyer to pay the price, take delivery or perform his other obligations, unless the seller has resorted to a remedy which is inconsistent with this requirement.

Article 63 [Additional Time Limit for Performance]

(1) The seller may fix an additional period of time of reasonable length for performance by the buyer of his obligations.

(2) Unless the seller has received notice from the buyer that he will not perform within the period so fixed, the seller may not, during that period, resort to any remedy for breach of contract. However, the seller is not deprived thereby of any right he may have to claim damages for delay in performance.

Article 64 [Seller's Right to Avoid]

(1) The seller may declare the contract avoided:

(a) if the failure by the buyer to perform any of his obligations under the contract or this Convention amounts to a fundamental breach of contract; or

(b) if the buyer does not, within the additional period of time fixed by the seller in accordance with paragraph (1) of Article 63, perform his obligation to pay the price or take delivery of the goods or if he declares that he will not do so within the period so fixed.

(2) However, in cases where the buyer has paid the price, the seller loses the right to declare the contract avoided unless he does so:

(a) in respect of late performance by the buyer, before the seller has become aware that performance has been rendered; or

(b) in respect of any breach other than late performance by the buyer, within a reasonable time:

   (i)   after the seller knew or ought to have known of the breach; or

   (ii) after the expiration of any additional period of time fixed by the seller in accordance with paragraph (1) or Article 63, or after the buyer has declared that he will not perform his obligations within such an additional period.

Article 65 [Right and Obligation to Make Specifications]

(1) If under the contract the buyer is to specify the form, measurement or other features of the goods and he fails to make such specification either on the date agreed upon or within a reasonable time after receipt of a request from the seller, the seller may, without prejudice to any other rights he may have, make the specification himself in accordance with the requirements of the buyer that may be known to him.

(2) If the seller makes the specification himself, he must inform the buyer of the details thereof and must fix a reasonable time within which the buyer may make a different specification. If, after receipt of such a communication, the buyer fails to do so within the time so fixed, the specification made by the seller is binding.

CHAPTER IV - PASSING OF RISK
Article 66 [General Rule]

Loss of or damage to the goods after the risk has passed to the buyer does not discharge him from his obligation to pay the price, unless the loss or damage is due to an act or omission of the seller.

Article 67 [Passing of Risk in the Absence of INCOTERM Specification]

(1) If the contract of sale involves carriage of the goods and the seller is not bound to hand them over at a particular place, the risk passes to the buyer when the goods are handed over to the first carrier for transmission to the buyer in accordance with the contract of sale. If the seller is bound to hand the goods over to a carrier at a particular place, the risk does not pass to the buyer until the goods are handed over to the carrier at that place. The fact that the seller is authorized to retain documents controlling the disposition of the goods does not affect the passage of the risk.

(2) Nevertheless, the risk does not pass to the buyer until the goods are clearly identified to the contract, whether by markings on the goods, by shipping documents, by notice given to the buyer or otherwise.

Article 68 [Goods Sold in Transit]

The risk in respect of goods sold in transit passes to the buyer from the time of the conclusion of the contract. However, if the circumstances so indicate, the risk is assumed by the buyer from the time the goods were handed over to the carrier who issued the documents embodying the contract of carriage. Nevertheless, if at the time of the conclusion of the contract of sale the seller knew or ought to have known that the goods had been lost or damaged and did not disclose this to the buyer, the loss or damage is at the risk of the seller.

Article 69 [Passing of Risk When Goods Are Delivered]

(1) In cases not within Articles 67 and 68, the risk passes to the buyer when he takes over the goods or, if he does not do so in due time, from the time when the goods are placed at his disposal and he commits a breach of contract by failing to take delivery.

(2) However, if the buyer is bound to take over the goods at a place other than a place of business of the seller, the risk passes when delivery is due and the buyer is aware of the fact that the goods are placed at his disposal at that place.

(3) If the contract relates to goods not then identified, the goods are considered not to be placed at the disposal of the buyer until they are clearly identified to the contract.

Article 70 [Seller's Breach Unconnected to Loss of Goods]
If the seller has committed a fundamental breach of contract, Articles 67, 68 and 69 do not impair the remedies available to the buyer on account of the breach.

CHAPTER V - PROVISIONS COMMON TO THE OBLIGATIONS OF THE SELLER AND OF THE BUYER
Section I. Anticipatory Breach and Instalment Contracts
Article 71 [Anticipated Problems Prior to Performance]
(1)   A party may suspend the performance of his obligations if, after the conclusion of the contract, it becomes apparent that the other party will not perform a substantial part of his obligations as a result of:
(a)   a serious deficiency in his ability to perform or in his creditworthiness; or
(b)   his conduct in preparing to perform or in performing the contract.
(2)   If the seller has already dispatched the goods before the grounds described in the preceding paragraph become evident, he may prevent the handing over of the goods to the buyer even though the buyer holds a document which entitles him to obtain them. The present paragraph relates only to the rights in the goods as between the buyer and the seller.
(3)   A party suspending performance, whether before or after dispatch of the goods, must immediately give notice of the suspension to the other party and must continue with performance if the other party provides adequate assurance of his performance.

Article 72 [Preventive Avoidance for Anticipatory Breach]
(1)   If prior to the date for performance of the contract it is clear that one of the parties will commit a fundamental breach of contract, the other party may declare the contract avoided.
(2)   If time allows, the party intending to declare the contract avoided must give reasonable notice to the other party in order to permit him to provide adequate assurance of his performance.
(3)   The requirements of the preceding paragraph do not apply if the other party has declared that he will not perform his obligations.

Article 73 [Problems with Installment Contracts]
(1)   In the case of a contract for delivery of goods by instalments, if the failure of one party to perform any of his obligations in respect of any instalment constitutes a fundamental breach of contract with respect to that instalment, the other party may declare the contract avoided with respect to that instalment.
(2)   If one party's failure to perform any of his obligations in respect of any instalment gives the other party good grounds to conclude that a fundamental breach of contract will occur with respect to future instalments, he may declare the contract avoided for the future, provided that he does so within a reasonable time.
(3)   A buyer who declares the contract avoided in respect of any delivery may, at the same time, declare it avoided in respect of deliveries already made or of future deliveries if, by reason of their interdependence, those deliveries could not be used for the purpose contemplated by the parties at the time of the conclusion of the contract.

Section II. Damages
Article 74 [Calculation of Damages]
Damages for breach of contract by one party consist of a sum equal to the loss, including loss of profit, suffered by the other party as a consequence of the breach. Such damages may not exceed the loss which the party in breach foresaw or ought to have foreseen at the time of the conclusion of the contract, in the light of the facts and matters of which he then knew or ought to have known, as a possible consequence of the breach of contract.

Article 75 [Cover Transaction]
If the contract is avoided and if, in a reasonable manner and within a reasonable time after avoidance, the buyer has bought goods in replacement or the seller has resold the goods, the

party claiming damages may recover the difference between the contract price and the price in the substitute transaction as well as any further damages recoverable under Article 74.

Article 76 [Difference Between Contract Price and Current Price as Damage]
(1)   If the contract is avoided and there is a current price for the goods, the party claiming damages may, if he has not made a purchase or resale under Article 75, recover the difference between the price fixed by the contract and the current price at the time of avoidance as well as any further damages recoverable under Article 74. If, however, the party claiming damages has avoided the contract after taking over the goods, the current price at the time of such taking over shall be applied instead of the current price at the time of avoidance.
(2)   For the purposes of the preceding paragraph, the current price is the price prevailing at the place where delivery of the goods should have been made or, if there is no current price at that place, the price at such other place as serves as a reasonable substitute, making due allowance for differences in the cost of transporting the goods.

Article 77 [Obligation to Mitigate Losses]
A party who relies on a breach of contract must take such measures as are reasonable in the circumstances to mitigate the loss, including loss of profit, resulting from the breach. If he fails to take such measures, the party in breach may claim a reduction in the damages in the amount by which the loss should have been mitigated.

Section III. Interest
Article 78 [Interest Separate from Damages]
If a party fails to pay the price or any other sum that is in arrears, the other party is entitled to interest on it, without prejudice to any claim for damages recoverable under Article 74.

Section IV. Exemptions
Article 79 [Force Majeure and Third Party Failure]
(1)   A party is not liable for a failure to perform any of his obligations if he proves that the failure was due to an impediment beyond his control and that he could not reasonably be expected to have taken the impediment into account at the time of the conclusion of the contract or to have avoided or overcome it or its consequences.
(2)   If the party's failure is due to the failure by a third person whom he has engaged to perform the whole or a part of the contract, that party is exempt from liability only if:
(a)   he is exempt under the preceding paragraph; and
(b)   the person whom he has so engaged would be so exempt if the provisions of that paragraph were applied to him.
(3)   The exemption provided by this Article has effect for the period during which the impediment exists.
(4)   The party who fails to perform must give notice to the other party of the impediment and its effect on his ability to perform. If the notice is not received by the other party within a reasonable time after the party who fails to perform knew or ought to have known of the impediment, he is liable for damages resulting from such non-receipt.
(5)   Nothing in this Article prevents either party from exercising any right other than to claim damages under this Convention.

Article 80 [Detrimental Act or Omission by the Promisee]
A party may not rely on a failure of the other party to perform, to the extent that such failure was caused by the first party's act or omission.

Section V. Effects of Avoidance
Article 81 [Some Contractual Obligations Survive Avoidance]
(1)   Avoidance of the contract releases both parties from their [primary] obligations under it, subject to any damages which may be due. Avoidance does not affect any provision of the con-

tract for the settlement of disputes or any other provision of the contract governing the rights and obligations of the parties consequent upon the avoidance of the contract.

(2) A party who has performed the contract either wholly or in part may claim restitution from the other party of whatever the first party has supplied or paid under the contract. If both parties are bound to make restitution, they must do so concurrently.

Article 82 [Right to Substitute Goods Requires Restitution of Non-Conforming Goods]

(1) The buyer loses the right to declare the contract avoided or to require the seller to deliver substitute goods if it is impossible for him to make restitution of the goods substantially in the condition in which he received them.

(2) The preceding paragraph does not apply:

(a) if the impossibility of making restitution of the goods or of making restitution of the goods substantially in the condition in which the buyer received them is not due to his act or omission;

(b) if the goods or part of the goods have perished or deteriorated as a result of the examination provided for in Article 38; or

(c) if the goods or part of the goods have been sold in the normal course of business or have been consumed or transformed by the buyer in the course normal use before he discovered or ought to have discovered the lack of conformity.

Article 83 [Independence of Different Remedies]

A buyer who has lost the right to declare the contract avoided or to require the seller to deliver substitute goods in accordance with Article 82 retains all other remedies under the contract and this Convention.

Article 84 [Mutual Restitution of Benefits After Avoidance]

(1) If the seller is bound to refund the price, he must also pay interest on it, from the date on which the price was paid.

(2) The buyer must account to the seller for all benefits which he has derived from the goods or part of them:

(a) if he must make restitution of the goods or part of them; or

(b) if it is impossible for him to make restitution of all or part of the goods or to make restitution of all or part of the goods substantially in the condition in which he received them, but he has nevertheless declared the contract avoided or required the seller to deliver substitute goods.

Section VI. Preservation of the Goods

Article 85 [Preservation by the Seller]

If the buyer is in delay in taking delivery of the goods or, where payment of the price and delivery of the goods are to be made concurrently, if he fails to pay the price, and the seller is either in possession of the goods or otherwise able to control their disposition, the seller must take such steps as are reasonable in the circumstances to preserve them. He is entitled to retain them until he has been reimbursed his reasonable expenses by the buyer.

Article 86 [Preservation by the Buyer]

(1) If the buyer has received the goods and intends to exercise any right under the contract or this Convention to reject them, he must take such steps to preserve them as are reasonable in the circumstances. He is entitled to retain them until he has been reimbursed his reasonable expenses by the seller.

(2) If goods dispatched to the buyer have been placed at his disposal at their destination and he exercises the right to reject them, he must take possession of them on behalf of the seller, provided that this can be done without payment of the price and without unreasonable inconvenience or unreasonable expense. This provision does not apply if the seller or a person authorized to take charge of the goods on his behalf is present at the destination. If the buyer takes possession of the goods under this paragraph, his rights and obligations are governed by the preceding paragraph.

Article 87 [Preservation by Third Parties]

A party who is bound to take steps to preserve the goods may deposit them in a warehouse of a third person at the expense of the other party provided that the expense incurred is not unreasonable.

Article 88 [Self-Help Sale]

(1)   A party who is bound to preserve the goods in accordance with Article 85 or 86 may sell them by any appropriate means if there has been an unreasonable delay by the other party in taking possession of the goods or in taking them back or in paying the price or the cost of preservation, provided that reasonable notice of the intention to sell has been given to the other party.

(2)   If the goods are subject to rapid deterioration or their preservation would involve unreasonable expense, a party who is bound to preserve the goods in accordance with Article 85 or 86 must take reasonable measures to sell them. To the extent possible he must give notice to the other party of his intention to sell.

(3)   A party selling the goods has the right to retain out of the proceeds of sale an amount equal to the reasonable expenses of preserving the goods and of selling them. He must account to the other party for the balance.

PART IV – FINAL PROVISIONS

Article 89 [Depository]

The Secretary-General of the United Nations is hereby designated as the depositary for this Convention.

Article 90 [Priority of Preceding Conventions]

This Convention does not prevail over any international agreement which has already been or may be entered into and which contains provisions concerning the matters governed by this Convention, provided that the parties have their places of business in States parties to such agreement.

Article 91 [Signature, Ratification, Accession]

(1)   This Convention is open for signature at the concluding meeting of the United Nations Conference on Contracts for the International Sale of Goods and will remain open for signature by all States at the Headquarters of the United Nations, New York until 30 September 1981.

(2)   This Convention is subject to ratification, acceptance or approval by the signatory States.

(3)   This Convention is open for accession by all States which are not signatory States as from the date it is open for signature.

(4)   Instruments of ratification, acceptance, approval and accession are to be deposited with the Secretary-General of the United Nations.

Article 92 [Reservation Against Part II or Part III of the Convention]

(1)   A Contracting State may declare at the time of signature, ratification, acceptance, approval or accession that it will not be bound by Part II of this Convention or that it will not be bound by Part III of this Convention.

(2)   A Contracting State which makes a declaration in accordance with the preceding paragraph in respect of Part II or Part III of this Convention is not to be considered a Contracting State within paragraph (1) of Article 1 of this Convention in respect of matters governed by the Part to which the declaration applies.

Article 93 [Federal State Clause]

(1)   If a Contracting State has two or more territorial units in which, according to its constitution, different systems of law are applicable in relation to the matters dealt with in this Convention, it may, at the time of signature, ratification, acceptance, approval or accession, declare that this Convention is to extend to all its territorial units or only to one or more of them, and may amend its declaration by submitting another declaration at any time.

(2)   These declarations are to be notified to the depositary and are to state expressly the territorial units to which the Convention extends.

(3)   If, by virtue of a declaration under this article, this Convention extends to one or more but not all of the territorial units of a Contracting State, and if the place of business of a party is located in that State, this place of business, for the purposes of this Convention, is considered not to be in a Contracting State, unless it is in a territorial unit to which the Convention extends.
(4)   If a Contracting State makes no declaration under paragraph (1) of this article, the Convention is to extend to all territorial units of that State.

Article 94 [Regional Harmonization]

(1)   Two or more Contracting States which have the same or closely related legal rules on matters governed by this Convention may at any time declare that the Convention is not to apply to contracts of sale or to their formation where the parties have their places of business in those States. Such declarations may be made jointly or by reciprocal unilateral declarations.
(2)   A Contracting State which has the same or closely related legal rules on matters governed by this Convention as one or more non-Contracting States may at any time declare that the Convention is not to apply to contracts of sale or to their formation where the parties have their places of business in those States.
(3)   If a State which is the object of a declaration under the preceding paragraph subsequently becomes a Contracting State, the declaration made will, as from the date on which the Convention enters into force in respect of the new Contracting State, have the effect of a declaration made under paragraph (1), provided that the new Contracting State joins in such declaration or makes a reciprocal unilateral declaration.

Article 95 [Reservation Against Article 1(1)(b) of the Convention]   ← U.S. did

Any State may declare at the time of the deposit of its instrument of ratification, acceptance, approval or accession that it will not be bound by subparagraph (1)(b) of Article 1 of this Convention.

Article 96 [Reservation Against Unwritten Contracts]

A Contracting State whose legislation requires contracts of sale to be concluded in or evidenced by writing may at any time make a declaration in accordance with Article 12 that any provision of Article 11, Article 29, or Part II of this Convention, that allows a contract of sale or its modification or termination by agreement or any offer, acceptance, or other indication of intention to be made in any form other than in writing, does not apply where any party has his place of business in that State.

Article 97 [Formal Requirements for Declarations and Reservations]

(1)   Declarations made under this Convention at the time of signature are subject to confirmation upon ratification, acceptance or approval.
(2)   Declarations and confirmations of declarations are to be in writing and be formally notified to the depositary.
(3)   A declaration takes effect simultaneously with the entry into force of this Convention in respect of the State concerned. However, a declaration of which the depositary receives formal notification after such entry into force takes effect on the first day of the month following the expiration of six months after the date of its receipt by the depositary. Reciprocal unilateral declarations under Article 94 take effect on the first day of the month following the expiration of six months after the receipt of the latest declaration by the depositary.
(4)   Any State which makes a declaration under this Convention may withdraw it at any time by a formal notification in writing addressed to the depositary. Such withdrawal is to take effect on the first day of the month following the expiration of six months after the date of the receipt of the notification by the depositary.
(5)   A withdrawal of a declaration made under Article 94 renders inoperative, as from the date on which the withdrawal takes effect, any reciprocal declaration made by another State under that article.

Article 98 [Prohibition of Other Reservations]

No reservations are permitted except those expressly authorized in this Convention.

Article 99 [Entry into Force]

(1)   This Convention enters into force, subject to the provisions of paragraph (6) of this article, on the first day of the month following the expiration of twelve months after the date of deposit of the tenth instrument of ratification, acceptance, approval or accession, including an instrument which contains a declaration made under Article 92.

(2)   When a State ratifies, accepts, approves or accedes to this Convention after the deposit of the tenth instrument of ratification, acceptance, approval or accession, this Convention, with the exception of the Part excluded, enters into force in respect of that State, subject to the provisions of paragraph (6) of this article, on the first day of the month following the expiration of twelve months after the date of the deposit of its instrument of ratification, acceptance, approval or accession.

(3)   A State which ratifies, accepts, approves or accedes to this Convention and is a party to either or both the Convention relating to a Uniform Law on the Formation of Contracts for the International Sale of Goods done at The Hague on 1 July 1964 (1964 Hague Formation Convention) and the Convention relating to a Uniform Law on the International Sale of Goods done at The Hague on 1 July 1964 (1964 Hague Sales Convention) shall at the same time denounce, as the case may be, either or both the 1964 Hague Sales Convention and the 1964 Hague Formation Convention by notifying the Government of the Netherlands to that effect.

(4)   A State party to the 1964 Hague Sales Convention which ratifies, accepts, approves or accedes to the present Convention and declares or has declared under Article 52 that it will not be bound by Part II of this Convention shall at the time of ratification, acceptance, approval or accession denounce the 1964 Hague Sales Convention by notifying the Government of the Netherlands to that effect.

(5)   A State party to the 1964 Hague Formation Convention which ratifies, accepts, approves or accedes to the present Convention and declares or has declared under Article 92 that it will not be bound by Part III of this Convention shall at the time of ratification, acceptance, approval or accession denounce the 1964 Hague Formation Convention by notifying the Government of the Netherlands to that effect.

(6)   For the purpose of this article, ratifications, acceptances, approvals and accessions in respect of this Convention by States parties to the 1964 Hague Formation Convention or to the 1964 Hague Sales Convention shall not be effective until such denunciations as may be required on the part of those States in respect of the latter two Conventions have themselves become effective. The depositary of this Convention shall consult with the Government of the Netherlands, as the depositary of the 1964 Conventions, so as to ensure necessary co-ordination in this respect.

Article 100 [Temporal Application]

(1)   This Convention applies to the formation of a contract only when the proposal for concluding the contract is made on or after the date when the Convention enters into force in respect of the Contracting States referred to in subparagraph (1)(a) or the Contracting State referred to in subparagraph (1)(b) of Article 1.

(2)   This Convention applies only to contracts concluded on or after the date when the Convention enters into force in respect of the Contracting States referred to in subparagraph (1)(a) or the Contracting State referred to in subparagraph (1)(b) of Article 1.

Article 101 [Denounciation]

(1)   A Contracting State may denounce this Convention, or Part II or Part III of the Convention, by a formal notification in writing addressed to the depositary.

(2)   The denunciation takes effect on the first day of the month following the expiration of twelve months after the notification is received by the depositary. Where a longer period for the

denunciation to take effect is specified in the notification, the denunciation takes effect upon the expiration of such longer period after the notification is received by the depositary.

DONE at Vienna, this day of eleventh day of April, one thousand nine hundred and eighty, in a single original, of which the Arabic, Chinese, English, French, Russian and Spanish texts are equally authentic.
IN WITNESS WHEREOF the undersigned plenipotentiaries, being duly authorized by their respective Governments, have signed this Convention.

Entry into force: 1 January 1988
Ratifications and binding effect as of July 2013: *U.K. hasn't ratified*

No.	Country	Entry into Force	Reservations
1	Albania	1 June 2010	
2	Argentina	1 Jan 1988	Art. 96
3	Armenia	1 Jan 2010	Art. 94, Art. 96
4	Australia	1 April 1989	Art. 93
5	Austria	1 Jan 1989	
6	Belarus	1 Nov 1990	Art. 96
7	Belgium	1 Nov 1997	
8	Benin	1 Aug 2012	
9	Bosnia-Herzegovina	6 March 1992	
10	Brazil	1 April 2014	
11	Bulgaria	1 Aug 1991	
12	Burundi	1 Oct 1999	
13	Canada	1 May 1992	
14	Chile	1 March 1991	Art. 96
15	China	1 Jan 1988	Art. 95
16	Colombia	1 Aug 2002	
17	Croatia	8 Oct 1991	
18	Cuba	1 Dec 1995	
19	Cyprus	1 April 2006	
20	Czech Republic	1 Jan 1993	Art. 95
21	Denmark	1 March 1990	Art. 92 (II) and Art. 94, Art. 93
22	Dominican Republic	1 July 2011	
23	Ecuador	1 Feb 1993	
24	Egypt	1 Jan 1988	
25	El Salvador	1 Dec 2007	
26	Estonia	1 Oct 1994	Art. 96
27	Finland	1 Jan 1989	Art. 92 (II) and Art. 94
28	France	1 Jan 1988	
29	Gabon	1 Jan 2006	
30	Georgia	1 Sept 1995	
31	Germany	1 Jan 1991	
32	Greece	1 Feb 1999	

33	Guinea	1 Feb 1992	
34	Honduras	1 Nov 2003	
35	Hungary	1 Jan 1988	Art. 96
36	Iceland	1 June 2002	
37	Iraq	1 April 1991	
38	Israel	1 Feb 2003	
39	Italy	1 Jan 1988	
40	Japan	1 Aug 2009	
41	Korea	1 March 2005	
42	Kyrgyzstan	1 June 2000	
43	Latvia	1 Aug 1998	
44	Lebanon	1 Dec 2009	
45	Lesotho	1 Jan 1988	
46	Liberia	1 Oct 2006	
47	Lithuania	1 Feb 1996	Art. 96
48	Luxembourg	1 Feb 1998	
49	Macedonia	17 Nov 1991	
50	Mauritania	1 Sept 2000	
51	Mexico	1 Jan 1989	
52	Moldova	1 Nov 1995	
53	Mongolia	1 Jan 1999	
54	Montenegro	3 June 2006	
55	Netherlands	1 Jan 1992	
56	New Zealand	1 Oct 1995	Art. 93
57	Norway	1 Aug 1989	Art. 92 (II) and Art. 94
58	Paraguay	1 Feb 2007	
59	Peru	1 April 2000	
60	Poland	1 June 1996	
61	Romania	1 June 1992	
62	Russian Federation	1 Sept 1991	Art. 96
63	Saint Vincent & Grenadines	1 Oct 2001	
64	San Marino	1 March 2013	
65	Serbia	27 April 1992	
66	Singapore	1 March 1996	Art. 95
67	Slovakia	1 Jan 1993	Art. 95
68	Slovenia	25 June 1991	
69	Spain	1 Aug 1991	
70	Sweden	1 Jan 1989	Art. 92 (II) and Art. 94
71	Switzerland	1 March 1991	
72	Syria	1 Jan 1988	
73	Turkey	1 Aug 2011	
74	Uganda	1 March 1993	

75	Ukraine	1 Feb 1991	Art. 96
76	United States of America	1 Jan 1988	Art. 95
77	Uruguay	1 Feb 2000	
78	Uzbekistan	1 Dec 1997	
79	Zambia	1 Jan 1988	

1974 UN CONVENTION ON THE LIMITATION PERIOD IN THE INTERNATIONAL SALE OF GOODS[1]

(as amended by the Protocol amending the Convention on the Limitation Period in the International Sale of Goods)

Preamble

THE STATES PARTIES TO THE PRESENT CONVENTION,

CONSIDERING that international trade is an important factor in the promotion of friendly relations amongst States,

BELIEVING that the adoption of uniform rules governing the limitation period in the international sale of goods would facilitate the development of world trade,

HAVE AGREED as follows:

Part I. Substantive Provisions

SPHERE OF APPLICATION

Article 1

(1) This Convention shall determine when claims of a buyer and a seller against each other arising from a contract of international sale of goods or relating to its breach, termination or invalidity can no longer be exercised by reason of the expiration of a period of time. Such a period of time is hereinafter referred to as "the limitation period".

(2) This Convention shall not affect a particular time-limit within which one party is required, as a condition for the acquisition or exercise of his claim, to give notice to the other party or perform any act other than the institution of legal proceedings.

(3) In this Convention:

(a) "buyer", "seller" and "party" mean persons who buy or sell, or agree to buy or sell, goods, and the successors to and assigns of their rights or obligations under the contract of sale;

(b) "creditor" means a party who asserts a claim, whether or not such a claim is for a sum of money;

(c) "debtor" means a party against whom a creditor asserts a claim;

(d) "breach of contract" means the failure of a party to perform the contract or any performance not in conformity with the contract;

(e) "legal proceedings" includes judicial, arbitral and administrative proceedings;

(f) "person" includes corporation, company, partnership, association or entity, whether private or public, which can sue or be sued;

(g) "writing" includes telegram and telex;

(h) "year" means a year according to the Gregorian calendar.

Article 2

For the purposes of this Convention:

(a) a contract of sale of goods shall be considered international if, at the time of the conclusion of the contract, the buyer and the seller have their places of business in different States;

---

1   © United Nations, 1511 UNTS 99, all rights reserved.

(b) the fact that the parties have their places of business in different States shall be disregarded whenever this fact does not appear either from the contract or from any dealings between, or from information disclosed by, the parties at any time before or at the conclusion of the contract;

(c) where a party to a contract of sale of goods has places of business in more than one State, the place of business shall be that which has the closest relationship to the contract and its performance, having regard to the circumstances known to or contemplated by the parties at the time of the conclusion of the contract;

(d) where a party does not have a place of business, reference shall be made to his habitual residence;

(e) neither the nationality of the parties nor the civil or commercial character of the parties or of the contract shall be taken into consideration.

Article 3[1]

(1) This Convention shall apply only

(a) if, at the time of the conclusion of the contract, the places of business of the parties to a contract of international sale of goods are in Contracting States; or

(b) if the rules of private international law make the law of a Contracting State applicable to the contract of sale.

(2) This Convention shall not apply when the parties have expressly excluded its application.

Article 4[2]

This Convention shall not apply to sales:

(a) of goods bought for personal, family or household use, unless the seller, at any time before or at the conclusion of the contract, neither knew nor ought to have known that the goods were bought for any such use;

(b) by auction;

(c) on execution or otherwise by authority of law;

(d) of stocks, shares, investment securities, negotiable instruments or money;

(e) of ships, vessels, hovercraft or aircraft;

(f) of electricity.

Article 5

This Convention shall not apply to claims based upon:

(a) death of, or personal injury to, any person;

(b) nuclear damage caused by the goods sold;

(c) a lien, mortgage or other security interest in property;

(d) a judgement or award made in legal proceedings;

(e) a document on which direct enforcement or execution can be obtained in accordance with the law of the place where such enforcement or execution is sought;

---

1   Text as amended in accordance with Article I of the 1980 Protocol. States that make a declaration under Article 36 bis (Article XII of the 1980 Protocol) will be bound by Article 3 as originally adopted in the Limitation Convention, 1974. Article 3 as originally adopted reads as follows:
"Article 3
(1) This Convention shall apply only if, at the time of the conclusion of the contract, the places of business of the parties to a contract of international sale of goods are in Contracting States.
(2) Unless this Convention provides otherwise, it shall apply irrespective of the law which would otherwise be applicable by virtue of the rules of private international law.
(3) This Convention shall not apply when the parties have expressly excluded its application."

2   Text of paragraphs (a) and (e) as amended in accordance with Article II of the 1980 Protocol. Paragraphs (a) and (e) of Article 4 as originally adopted in the Limitation Convention, 1974, prior to its amendment under the 1980 Protocol, read as follows:
"(a)   of goods bought for personal, family or household use;
(e)   of ships, vessels, or aircraft;".

(f)   a bill of exchange, cheque or promissory note.

Article 6

(1)   This Convention shall not apply to contracts in which the preponderant part of the obligations of the seller consists in the supply of labour or other services.

(2)   Contracts for the supply of goods to be manufactured or produced shall be considered to be sales, unless the party who orders the goods undertakes to supply a substantial part of the materials necessary for such manufacture or production.

Article 7

In the interpretation and application of the provisions of this Convention, regard shall be had to its international character and to the need to promote uniformity.

THE DURATION AND COMMENCEMENT OF THE LIMITATION PERIOD

Article 8

The limitation period shall be four years.

Article 9

(1)   Subject to the provisions of Articles 10, 11 and 12 the limitation period shall commence on the date [on] which the claim accrues.

(2)   The commencement of the limitation period shall not be postponed by:

(a)   a requirement that the party be given a notice as described in paragraph 2 of Article 1, or

(b)   a provision in an arbitration agreement that no right shall arise until an arbitration award has been made.

Article 10

(1)   A claim arising from a breach of contract shall accrue on the date on which such breach occurs.

(2)   A claim arising from a defect or other lack of conformity shall accrue on the date on which the goods are actually handed over to, or their tender is refused by, the buyer.

(3)   A claim based on fraud committed before or at the time of the conclusion of the contract or during its performance shall accrue on the date on which the fraud was or reasonably could have been discovered.

Article 11

If the seller has given an express undertaking relating to the goods which is stated to have effect for a certain period of time, whether expressed in terms of a specific period of time or otherwise, the limitation period in respect of any claim, arising from the undertaking shall commence on the date on which the buyer notifies the seller of the fact on which the claim is based, but not later than on the date of the expiration of the period of the undertaking.

Article 12

(1)   If, in circumstances provided for by the law applicable to the contract, one party is entitled to declare the contract terminated before the time for performance is due, and exercises this right, the limitation period in respect of a claim based on any such circumstances shall commence on the date on which the declaration is made to the other party. If the contract is not declared to be terminated before performance becomes due, the limitation period shall commence on the date on which performance is due.

(2)   The limitation period in respect of a claim arising out of a breach by one party of a contract for the delivery of or payment for goods by instalments shall, in relation to each separate instalment, commence on the date on which the particular breach occurs. If, under the law applicable to the contract, one party is entitled to declare the contract terminated by reason of such breach, and exercises this right, the limitation period in respect of all relevant instalments shall commence on the date on which the declaration is made to the other party.

CESSATION AND EXTENSION OF THE LIMITATION PERIOD
Article 13
The limitation period shall cease to run when the creditor performs any act which, under the law of the court where the proceedings are instituted, is recognized as commencing judicial proceedings against the debtor or as asserting his claim in such proceedings already instituted against the debtor, for the purpose of obtaining satisfaction or recognition of his claim.

Article 14
1.   Where the parties have agreed to submit to arbitration, the limitation period shall cease to run when either party commences arbitral proceedings in the manner provided for in the arbitration agreement or by the law applicable to such proceedings.
2.   In the absence of any such provision, arbitral proceedings shall be deemed to commence on the date on which a request that the claim in dispute be referred to arbitration is delivered at the habitual residence or place of business of the other party or, if he has no such residence or place of business, then at his last known residence or place of business.

Article 15
In any legal proceedings other than those mentioned in Articles 13 and 14, including legal proceedings commenced upon the occurrence of:
(a)   the death or incapacity of the debtor,
(b)   the bankruptcy or any state of insolvency affecting the whole of the property of the debtor, or
(c)   the dissolution or liquidation of a corporation, company, partnership, association or entity when it is the debtor, the limitation period shall cease to run when the creditor asserts his claim in such proceedings for the purpose of obtaining satisfaction or recognition of the claim, subject to the law governing the proceedings.

Article 16
For the purposes of Articles 13, 14 and 15, any act performed by way of counterclaim shall be deemed to have been performed on the same date as the act performed in relation to the claim against which the counterclaim is raised, provided that both the claim and the counterclaim relate to the same contract or to several contracts concluded in the course of the same transaction.

Article 17
(1)   Where a claim has been asserted in legal proceedings within the limitation period in accordance with Article 13, 14, 15 or 16, but such legal proceedings have ended without a decision binding on the merits of the claim, the limitation period shall be deemed to have continued to run.
(2)   If, at the time such legal proceedings ended, the limitation period has expired or has less than one year to run, the creditor shall be entitled to a period of one year from the date on which the legal proceedings ended.

Article 18
(1)   Where legal proceedings have been commenced against one debtor, the limitation period prescribed in this Convention shall cease to run against any other party jointly and severally liable with the debtor, provided that the creditor informs such party in writing within that period that the proceedings have been commenced.
(2)   Where legal proceedings have been commenced by a subpurchaser against the buyer, the limitation period prescribed in this Convention shall cease to run in relation to the buyer's claim over against the seller, if the buyer informs the seller in writing within that period that the proceedings have been commenced.
(3)   Where the legal proceedings referred to in paragraphs 1 and 2 of this Article have ended, the limitation period in respect of the claim of the creditor or the buyer against the party jointly and severally liable or against the seller shall be deemed not to have ceased running by virtue of paragraphs 1 and 2 of this article, but the creditor or the buyer shall be entitled to an additional

year from the date on which the legal proceedings ended, if at that time the limitation period had expired or had less than one year to run.

Article 19
Where the creditor performs, in the State in which the debtor has his place of business and before the expiration of the limitation period, any act, other than the acts described in Articles 13, 14, 15 and 16, which under the law of that State has the effect of recommencing a limitation period, a new limitation period of four years shall commence on the date prescribed by that law.

Article 20
(1)   Where the debtor, before the expiration of the limitation period, acknowledges in writing his obligation to the creditor, a new limitation period of four years shall commence to run from the date of such acknowledgement.
(2)   Payment of interest or partial performance of an obligation by the debtor shall have the same effect as an acknowledgement under paragraph 1 of this Article if it can reasonably be inferred from such payment or performance that the debtor acknowledges that obligation.

Article 21
Where, as a result of a circumstance which is beyond the control of the creditor and which he could neither avoid nor overcome, the creditor has been prevented from causing the limitation period to cease to run, the limitation period shall be extended so as not to expire before the expiration of one year from the date on which the relevant circumstance ceased to exist.

MODIFICATION OF THE LIMITATION PERIOD BY THE PARTIES
Article 22
(1)   The limitation period cannot be modified or affected by any declaration or agreement between the parties, except in the cases provided for in paragraph 2 of this article.
(2)   The debtor may at any time during the running of the limitation period extend the period by a declaration in writing to the creditor. This declaration may be renewed.
(3)   The provisions of this Article shall not affect the validity of a clause in the contract of sale which stipulates that arbitral proceedings shall be commenced within a shorter period of limitation than that prescribed by this Convention, provided that such clause is valid under the law applicable to the contract of sale.

GENERAL LIMIT OF THE LIMITATION PERIOD
Article 23
Notwithstanding the provisions of this Convention, a limitation period shall in any event expire not later than ten years from the date on which it commenced to run under Articles 9, 10, 11 and 12 of this Convention.

CONSEQUENCES OF THE EXPIRATION OF THE LIMITATION PERIOD
Article 24
Expiration of the limitation period shall be taken into consideration in any legal proceedings only if invoked by a party to such proceedings.

Article 25
(1)   Subject to the provisions of paragraph 2 of this Article and of Article 24, no claim shall be recognized or enforced in any legal proceedings commenced after the expiration of the limitation period.
(2)   Notwithstanding the expiration of the limitation period, one party may rely on his claim as a defence or for the purpose of set-off against a claim asserted by the other party, provided that in the latter case this may only be done:
(a)   if both claims relate to the same contract or to several contracts concluded in the course of the same transaction; or
(b)   if the claims could have been set-off at any time before the expiration of the limitation period.

Article 26

Where the debtor performs his obligation after the expiration of the limitation period, he shall not on that ground be entitled in any way to claim restitution even if he did not know at the time when he performed his obligation that the limitation period had expired.

Article 27

The expiration of the limitation period with respect to a principal debt shall have the same effect with respect to an obligation to pay interest on that debt.

CALCULATION OF THE PERIOD

Article 28

(1)   The limitation period shall be calculated in such a way that it shall expire at the end of the day which corresponds to the date on which the period commenced to run. If there is no such corresponding date, the period shall expire at the end of the last day of the last month of the limitation period.

(2)   The limitation period shall be calculated by reference to the date of the place where the legal proceedings are instituted.

Article 29

Where the last day of the limitation period falls on an official holiday or other dies non juridicus precluding the appropriate legal action in the jurisdiction where the creditor institutes legal proceedings or asserts a claim as envisaged in Article 13, 14 or 15, the limitation period shall be extended so as not to expire until the end of the first day following that official holiday or dies non juridicus on which such proceedings could be instituted or on which such a claim could be asserted in that jurisdiction.

INTERNATIONAL EFFECT

Article 30

The acts and circumstances referred to in Articles 13 through 19 which have taken place in one Contracting State shall have effect for the purposes of this Convention in another Contracting State, provided that the creditor has taken all reasonable steps to ensure that the debtor is informed of the relevant act or circumstances as soon as possible.

Part II. Implementation [...]

Part III. Declarations and Reservations [...]

Article 35

A Contracting State may declare, at the time of the deposit of its instrument of ratification or accession, that it will not apply the provisions of this Convention to actions for annulment of the contract.

Article 36

Any State may declare, at the time of the deposit of its instrument of ratification or accession, that it shall not be compelled to apply the provisions of Article 24 of this Convention.

Article 36 bis (Article XII of the Protocol)

Any State may declare at the time of the deposit of its instrument of accession or its notification under Article 43 bis that it will not be bound by the amendments to Article 3 made by Article I of the 1980 Protocol.[1] A declaration made under this Article shall be in writing and be formally notified to the depositary.

---

1   Such a State will then be bound by Article 3 of the unamended Convention. For its text, see footnote under Article 3.

Article 37[1]

This Convention shall not prevail over any international agreement which has already been or may be entered into and which contains provisions concerning the matters governed by this Convention, provided that the seller and buyer have their places of business in States parties to such agreement.

Article 38

(1)   A Contracting State which is a party to an existing convention relating to the international sale of goods may declare, at the time of the deposit of its instrument of ratification or accession, that it will apply this Convention exclusively to contracts of international sale of goods as defined in such existing convention.

(2)   Such declaration shall cease to be effective on the first day of the month following the expiration of twelve months after a new convention on the international sale of goods, concluded under the auspices of the United Nations, shall have entered into force.

Article 39

No reservation other than those made in accordance with Articles 34, 35, 36, 36 bis and 38 shall be permitted. [...]

Part IV. Final Clauses [...]

III. Explanatory Note by the UNCITRAL Secretariat on the Convention on the Limitation Period in the International Sale of Goods and the Protocol Amending the Convention on the Limitation Period in the International Sale of Goods

This note has been prepared by the secretariat of the United Nations Commission on International Trade Law for informational purposes; it is not an official commentary on the Convention. [...]

A. Introduction

1.   The Convention on the Limitation Period in the International Sale of Goods (New York, 1974) provides uniform international legal rules governing the period of time within which a party under a contract for the international sale of goods must commence legal proceedings against the other party to assert a claim arising from the contract or relating to its breach, termination or invalidity. This period is referred to in the Convention as the "limitation period". The basic aims of the limitation period are to prevent the institution of legal proceedings at such a late date that the evidence relating to the claim is likely to be unreliable or lost and to protect against the uncertainty and injustice that would result if a party were to remain exposed to unasserted claims for an extensive period of time.

2.   The Limitation Convention grew out of the work of the United Nations Commission on International Trade Law (UNCITRAL) towards the harmonization and unification of international sales law, which also resulted in the United Nations Convention on Contracts for the International Sale of Goods (Vienna, 1980) (hereinafter referred to as the "United Nations Sales Convention"). During that work it was observed that, while most legal systems limited or prescribed a claim from being asserted after the lapse of a specified period of time, numerous disparities existed among legal systems with respect to the conceptual basis for doing so. As a result there were disparities in the length of the period and in the rules governing the limitation or prescription of claims after that period. Those disparities created difficulties in the enforcement of claims arising from international sales transactions, and thus burdened international trade.

---

1   Text as amended in accordance with Article V of the Protocol. Article 37 as originally adopted in the Limitation Convention, 1974, prior to its amendment under the 1980 Protocol, read as follows:

"*Article 37*

This Convention shall not prevail over conventions already entered into or which may be entered into, and which contain provisions concerning the matters covered by this Convention, provided that the seller and buyer have their places of business in States parties to such a convention."

3.   In view of those problems UNCITRAL decided to prepare uniform international legal rules on the limitation period in the international sale of goods. On the basis of a draft Convention prepared by UNCITRAL, a diplomatic conference convened in New York by the General Assembly adopted the Limitation Convention on 14 June 1974.

4.   The Limitation Convention was amended by a Protocol adopted in 1980 by the diplomatic conference that adopted the United Nations Sales Convention, in order to harmonize the Limitation Convention with the latter Convention, in particular, with regard to scope of application and admissible declarations. As a result, the scope of application of the amended Limitation Convention and that of the United Nations Sales Convention are identical.

5.   The Limitation Convention entered into force on 1 August 1988. As of 1 October 2011, 29 States are parties to the unamended Convention and 21 of those 29 States are parties to the amended Convention. The current updated status of the Convention is available on the UNCITRAL website. Authoritative information on the status of the Convention, as well as on related declarations, including with respect to territorial application and succession of States, may be found on the United Nations Treaty Collection on the Internet.

B. Scope of Application

6.   The Convention applies to contracts for the sale of goods between parties whose places of business are in different States if both of those States are Contracting States. Under the 1980 Protocol the Convention also applies if the rules of private international law make the law of a Contracting State applicable to the contract. However, in becoming a party to the Protocol a State may declare that it will not be bound by that provision. Each Contracting State must apply the Convention to contracts concluded on or after the date of the entry into force of the Convention.

7.   The application of the Convention is excluded in certain situations. Firstly, the Convention will not apply if the parties to a sales contract expressly exclude its application. This provision gives effect to the basic principle of freedom of contract in the international sale of goods. Secondly, the Convention will not apply in certain cases where matters covered by the Convention are governed by other Conventions. Thirdly, Contracting States are permitted to deposit declarations excluding the application of the Convention in the following situations: two or more Contracting States may exclude the application of the Convention to contracts between parties having their places of business in those States when the States apply to those contracts the same or closely related legal rules. So far, one State has made that declaration. In addition, a State may exclude the application of the Convention to actions for annulment of the contract. No State has thus far availed itself of such a declaration.

8.   Since the Convention applies only in respect of international sales contracts, it clarifies whether contracts involving certain services are covered. A contract for the supply of goods to be manufactured or produced is considered to be a sales contract unless the party who orders the goods undertakes to supply a substantial part of the materials necessary for their manufacture or production. Furthermore, when the preponderant part of the obligations of the party who furnishes the goods consists in the supply of labour or other services, the Convention does not apply.

9.   The Convention contains a list of types of sales that are excluded from the Convention, either because of the purpose of the sale (goods bought for personal, family or household use (under the 1980 Protocol sales of those goods are covered by the Convention if the seller could not have known that they were bought for such use)), the nature of the sale (sales by auction, on execution or otherwise by law) or the nature of the goods (stocks, shares, investment securities, negotiable instruments, money, ships, vessels, aircraft or electricity (the 1980 Protocol adds hovercraft)).

10.   The Convention makes it clear that it applies only to the usual type of commercial claims based on contract. It specifically excludes claims based on death or personal injury; nuclear damage; a lien, mortgage or other security interest; a judgment or award; a document on which direct enforcement or execution can be obtained; and a bill of exchange, cheque or promissory note. The limitation periods for those claims are generally subject to particular rules and it

would not necessarily be appropriate to apply in respect of those claims the rules applicable to ordinary commercial contractual claims.

C. Duration and Commencement of Limitation Period

11.   The duration of the limitation period under the Convention is four years. The period cannot be modified by agreement of the parties, but it can be extended by a written declaration of the debtor during the running of the period. Also, the contract of sale may stipulate a shorter period for the commencement of arbitral proceedings, if the stipulation is valid under the law applicable to the contract. Rules are provided as to how the limitation period should be calculated.

12.   A limitation period of four years' duration was thought to accomplish the aims of the limitation period and yet to provide an adequate period of time to enable a party to an international sales contract to assert his claim against the other party. Circumstances where an extension or recommencement of the limitation period would be justified are dealt with in particular provisions of the Convention.

13.   With respect to the time when the limitation period commences to run, the basic rule is that it commences on the date on which the claim accrues. The Convention establishes when claims for breach of contract, for defects in the goods or other lack of conformity and for fraud are deemed to accrue. Special rules are provided for the commencement of the limitation period in two particular cases: where the seller has given the buyer an express undertaking (such as a warranty or guarantee) relating to the goods which is stated to have effect for a certain period of time, and where a party terminates the contract before the time for performance is due. Rules are also provided in respect of claims arising from the breach of an instalment contract and claims based on circumstances giving rise to a termination of an instalment contract.

D. Cessation and Extension of Limitation Period

14.   Having established the time of commencement and the length of the limitation period, the Convention sets forth rules concerning the cessation of the period. The period ceases to run when the claimant commences judicial or arbitral proceedings against the debtor, or when he asserts his claim in existing proceedings. A counterclaim is deemed to have been asserted on the same date as the date when the proceedings in which the counterclaim is asserted were commenced, if the counterclaim and the claim against which it is raised relate to the same contract or to several contracts concluded in the course of the same transaction.

15.   Judicial or arbitral proceedings commenced by a claimant within the limitation period might terminate without a binding decision on the merits of the claim, for example, because the court or arbitral tribunal lacks jurisdiction or because of a procedural defect. The creditor would normally be able to pursue his claim by commencing new proceedings. Thus, the Convention provides that if the original proceedings end without a binding decision on the merits the limitation period will be deemed to have continued to run. However, by the time the original proceedings have ended, the limitation period might have expired, or there might remain insufficient time for the claimant to commence new proceedings. To protect the claimant in those cases the Convention grants him an additional period of one year to commence new proceedings.

16.   The Convention contains rules to resolve in a uniform manner questions concerning the running of the limitation period in two particular cases. Firstly, it provides that where legal proceedings have been commenced against one party to the sales contract, the limitation period ceases to run against a person jointly and severally liable with him if the claimant informs that person in writing within the limitation period that the proceedings have been commenced. Secondly, it provides that where proceedings have been commenced against a buyer by a party who purchased the goods from him, the limitation period ceases to run in respect of the buyer's recourse claim against the seller if the buyer informs the seller in writing within the limitation period that the proceedings against the buyer have been commenced. Where the proceedings in either of those two cases have ended, the limitation period in respect of the claim against the jointly and severally liable person or against the seller will be deemed to have con-

tinued to run without interruption, but there will be an additional year to commence new proceedings if at that time the limitation period has expired or has less than a year to run.

17.   One effect of the provision mentioned above relating to the buyer is to enable him to await the outcome of the claim against him before commencing an action against the seller. This enables the buyer to avoid the trouble and expense of instituting proceedings against the seller and the disruption of their good business relationship if it turns out that the claim against the buyer was not successful.

18.   Under the Convention the limitation period recommences in two cases: if the creditor performs in the debtor's State an act that, under the law of that State, has the effect of recommencing a limitation period, or if the debtor acknowledges in writing his obligation to the creditor or pays interest or partially performs the obligation from which his acknowledgement can be inferred.

19.   The Convention protects a creditor who was prevented from taking the necessary acts to stop the running of the limitation period in extreme cases. It provides that when the creditor could not take those acts as a result of a circumstance beyond his control and which he could neither avoid nor overcome, the limitation period will be extended so as to expire one year after the date when the circumstance ceased to exist.

E. Overall Limit of Limitation Period

20.   Since the limitation period may, under the circumstances noted above, be extended or recommence, the Convention establishes an overall time period of 10 years, from the date on which the limitation period originally commenced to run, beyond which no legal proceedings to assert the claim may be commenced under any circumstances. The theory behind that provision is that enabling proceedings to be brought after that time would be inconsistent with the aims of the Convention in providing a definite limitation period.

F. Consequences of Expiration of Limitation Period

21.   The principal consequence of the expiration of the limitation period is that no claim will be recognized or enforced in legal proceedings commenced thereafter. The expiration of the limitation period will not be taken into consideration in legal proceedings unless it is invoked by a party to the proceedings. However, in light of views expressed at the diplomatic conference that adopted the Convention that the limitation or prescription of actions was a matter of public policy and that a court should be able to take the expiration of the limitation period into account on its own initiative, a Contracting State is permitted to declare that it will not apply that provision. No State has thus far made such a declaration.

22.   Even after the limitation period has expired a party can in certain situations raise his claim as a defence to or set-off against a claim asserted by the other party.

G. Other Provisions and Final Clauses [...]

H. Complementary Texts

27.   The Limitation Convention is complemented by the United Nations Convention on Contracts for the International Sale of Goods (the United Nations Sales Convention, also known as "CISG"). Adopted by a diplomatic conference on 11 April 1980, the United Nations Sales Convention establishes a comprehensive code of legal rules governing the formation of contracts for the international sale of goods, the obligations of the buyer and seller, remedies for breach of contract and other aspects of the contract.

28.   The Limitation Convention is also complemented, with respect to the use of electronic communications, by the United Nations Convention on the Use of Electronic Communications in International Contracts, 2005 (the Electronic Communications Convention). The Electronic Communications Convention aims at facilitating the use of electronic communications in international trade by assuring that contracts concluded and other communications exchanged electronically are as valid and enforceable as their traditional paper-based equivalents. In particular, certain formal requirements contained in widely adopted international trade law treaties may hinder the legal recognition of the use of electronic communications. The Electronic Communications Con-

vention is an enabling treaty whose effect is to remove those formal obstacles by establishing the requirements for functional equivalence between electronic and written form.

Ratifications and binding effect:

No.	Country	Ratification only of the 1974 Convention	Ratification also of the 1980 Protocol
1	Argentina		1 Aug 1988
2	Belarus	1 Aug 1997	
3	Belgium		1 Mar 2009
4	Benin	1 Feb 2012	
5	Bosnia and Herzegovina	6 March 1992	
6	Burundi	1 Apr 1999	
7	Cuba	1 June 1995	
8	Czech Republic		1 Jan 1993
9	Dominican Republic	1 Feb 2011	
10	Egypt		1 Aug 1988
11	Ghana	1 Aug 1988	
12	Guinea		1 Aug 1991
13	Hungary		1 Aug 1988
14	Liberia		1 Apr 2004
15	Mexico		1 Aug 1988
16	Montenegro		6 Aug 2012
17	Norway	1 Aug 1988	
18	Paraguay	1 Mar 2004	
19	Poland		1 Dec 2005
20	Moldova	1 Mar 1998	
21	Romania		1 Nov 1992
22	Serbia	27 Apr 1992	
23	Slovakia		1 Jan 1993
24	Slovenia		1 Mar 1996
25	Uganda		1 Sep 1992
26	Ukraine	1 Apr 1994	
27	United States of America		1 Dec 1994
28	Uruguay		1 Nov 1997
29	Zambia		1 Aug 1988

2005 UNITED NATIONS CONVENTION ON THE USE OF ELECTRONIC COMMUNICATIONS IN INTERNATIONAL CONTRACTS[1]

THE STATES PARTIES TO THIS CONVENTION,
REAFFIRMING their belief that international trade on the basis of equality and mutual benefit is an important element in promoting friendly relations among States,

---

1   © United Nations, G.A. Res. 60/21, U.N. Doc. A/RES/60/21 (9 December 2005); all rights reserved.

NOTING that the increased use of electronic communications improves the efficiency of commercial activities, enhances trade connections and allows new access opportunities for previously remote parties and markets, thus playing a fundamental role in promoting trade and economic development, both domestically and internationally,

CONSIDERING that problems created by uncertainty as to the legal value of the use of electronic communications in international contracts constitute an obstacle to international trade,

CONVINCED that the adoption of uniform rules to remove obstacles to the use of electronic communications in international contracts, including obstacles that might result from the operation of existing international trade law instruments, would enhance legal certainty and commercial predictability for international contracts and help States gain access to modern trade routes,

BEING OF THE OPINION that uniform rules should respect the freedom of parties to choose appropriate media and technologies, taking account of the principles of technological neutrality and functional equivalence, to the extent that the means chosen by the parties comply with the purpose of the relevant rules of law,

DESIRING to provide a common solution to remove legal obstacles to the use of electronic communications in a manner acceptable to States with different legal, social and economic systems,

HAVE AGREED as follows:

CHAPTER I. SPHERE OF APPLICATION
Article 1 - Scope of Application

1.   This Convention applies to the use of electronic communications in connection with the formation or performance of a contract between parties whose places of business are in different States.

2.   The fact that the parties have their places of business in different States is to be disregarded whenever this fact does not appear either from the contract or from any dealings between the parties or from information disclosed by the parties at any time before or at the conclusion of the contract.

3.   Neither the nationality of the parties nor the civil or commercial character of the parties or of the contract is to be taken into consideration in determining the application of this Convention.

Article 2 - Exclusions

1.   This Convention does not apply to electronic communications relating to any of the following:
(a)   Contracts concluded for personal, family or household purposes;
(b)   (i)   Transactions on a regulated exchange;
        (ii)   foreign exchange transactions;
        (iii)   inter-bank payment systems, inter-bank payment agreements or clearance and settlement systems relating to securities or other financial assets or instruments;
        (iv)   the transfer of security rights in sale, loan or holding of or agreement to repurchase securities or other financial assets or instruments held with an intermediary.

2.   This Convention does not apply to bills of exchange, promissory notes, consignment notes, bills of lading, warehouse receipts or any transferable document or instrument that entitles the bearer or beneficiary to claim the delivery of goods or the payment of a sum of money.

Article 3 - Party Autonomy

The parties may exclude the application of this Convention or derogate from or vary the effect of any of its provisions.

CHAPTER II. GENERAL PROVISIONS
Article 4 - Definitions

For the purposes of this Convention:
(a)   "Communication" means any statement, declaration, demand, notice or request, including an offer and the acceptance of an offer, that the parties are required to make or choose to make in connection with the formation or performance of a contract;

(b)   "Electronic communication" means any communication that the parties make by means of data messages;

(c)   "Data message" means information generated, sent, received or stored by electronic, magnetic, optical or similar means, including, but not limited to, electronic data interchange, electronic mail, telegram, telex or telecopy;

(d)   "Originator" of an electronic communication means a party by whom, or on whose behalf, the electronic communication has been sent or generated prior to storage, if any, but it does not include a party acting as an intermediary with respect to that electronic communication;

(e)   "Addressee" of an electronic communication means a party who is intended by the originator to receive the electronic communication, but does not include a party acting as an intermediary with respect to that electronic communication;

(f)   "Information system" means a system for generating, sending, receiving, storing or otherwise processing data messages;

(g)   "Automated message system" means a computer program or an electronic or other automated means used to initiate an action or respond to data messages or performances in whole or in part, without review or intervention by a natural person each time an action is initiated or a response is generated by the system;

(h)   "Place of business" means any place where a party maintains a non-transitory establishment to pursue an economic activity other than the temporary provision of goods or services out of a specific location.

Article 5 - Interpretation

1.   In the interpretation of this Convention, regard is to be had to its international character and to the need to promote uniformity in its application and the observance of good faith in international trade.

2.   Questions concerning matters governed by this Convention which are not expressly settled in it are to be settled in conformity with the general principles on which it is based or, in the absence of such principles, in conformity with the law applicable by virtue of the rules of private international law.

Article 6 - Location of the Parties

1.   For the purposes of this Convention, a party's place of business is presumed to be the location indicated by that party, unless another party demonstrates that the party making the indication does not have a place of business at that location.

2.   If a party has not indicated a place of business and has more than one place of business, then the place of business for the purposes of this Convention is that which has the closest relationship to the relevant contract, having regard to the circumstances known to or contemplated by the parties at any time before or at the conclusion of the contract.

3.   If a natural person does not have a place of business, reference is to be made to the person's habitual residence.

4.   A location is not a place of business merely because that is:

(a)   where equipment and technology supporting an information system used by a party in connection with the formation of a contract are located; or

(b)   where the information system may be accessed by other parties.

5.   The sole fact that a party makes use of a domain name or electronic mail address connected to a specific country does not create a presumption that its place of business is located in that country.

Article 7 - Information Requirements

Nothing in this Convention affects the application of any rule of law that may require the parties to disclose their identities, places of business or other information, or relieves a party from the legal consequences of making inaccurate, incomplete or false statements in that regard.

CHAPTER III. USE OF ELECTRONIC COMMUNICATIONS IN INTERNATIONAL CONTRACTS
Article 8 - Legal Recognition of Electronic Communications
1.   A communication or a contract shall not be denied validity or enforceability on the sole ground that it is in the form of an electronic communication.
2.   Nothing in this Convention requires a party to use or accept electronic communications, but a party's agreement to do so may be inferred from the party's conduct.

Article 9 - Form Requirements
1.   Nothing in this Convention requires a communication or a contract to be made or evidenced in any particular form.
2.   Where the law requires that a communication or a contract should be in writing, or provides consequences for the absence of a writing, that requirement is met by an electronic communication if the information contained therein is accessible so as to be usable for subsequent reference. 3.   Where the law requires that a communication or a contract should be signed by a party, or provides consequences for the absence of a signature, that requirement is met in relation to an electronic communication if:
(a)   A method is used to identify the party and to indicate that party's intention in respect of the information contained in the electronic communication; and
(b)   The method used is either:
    (i)   As reliable as appropriate for the purpose for which the electronic communication was generated or communicated, in the light of all the circumstances, including any relevant agreement; or
    (ii)   Proven in fact to have fulfilled the functions described in subparagraph (a) above, by itself or together with further evidence.
4.   Where the law requires that a communication or a contract should be made available or retained in its original form, or provides consequences for the absence of an original, that requirement is met in relation to an electronic communication if:
(a)   There exists a reliable assurance as to the integrity of the information it contains from the time when it was first generated in its final form, as an electronic communication or otherwise; and
(b)   Where it is required that the information it contains be made available, that information is capable of being displayed to the person to whom it is to be made available.
5.   For the purposes of paragraph 4 (a):
(a)   The criteria for assessing integrity shall be whether the information has remained complete and unaltered, apart from the addition of any endorsement and any change that arises in the normal course of communication, storage and display; and
(b)   The standard of reliability required shall be assessed in the light of the purpose for which the information was generated and in the light of all the relevant circumstances.

Article 10 - Time and Place of Dispatch and Receipt of Electronic Communications
1.   The time of dispatch of an electronic communication is the time when it leaves an information system under the control of the originator or of the party who sent it on behalf of the originator or, if the electronic communication has not left an information system under the control of the originator or of the party who sent it on behalf of the originator, the time when the electronic communication is received.
2.   The time of receipt of an electronic communication is the time when it becomes capable of being retrieved by the addressee at an electronic address designated by the addressee. The time of receipt of an electronic communication at another electronic address of the addressee is the time when it becomes capable of being retrieved by the addressee at that address and the addressee becomes aware that the electronic communication has been sent to that address. An electronic communication is presumed to be capable of being retrieved by the addressee when it reaches the addressee's electronic address.

3.   An electronic communication is deemed to be dispatched at the place where the originator has its place of business and is deemed to be received at the place where the addressee has
its place of business, as determined in accordance with Article 6.
4.   Paragraph 2 of this Article applies notwithstanding that the place where the information
system supporting an electronic address is located may be different from the place where the
electronic communication is deemed to be received under paragraph 3 of this article.

Article 11 - Invitations to Make Offers

A proposal to conclude a contract made through one or more electronic communications
which is not addressed to one or more specific parties, but is generally accessible to parties making use of information systems, including proposals that make use of interactive applications
for the placement of orders through such information systems, is to be considered as an invitation to make offers, unless it clearly indicates the intention of the party making the proposal to
be bound in case of acceptance.

Article 12 - Use of Automated Message Systems for Contract Formation

A contract formed by the interaction of an automated message system and a natural person, or
by the interaction of automated message systems, shall not be denied validity or enforceability
on the sole ground that no natural person reviewed or intervened in each of the individual
actions carried out by the automated message systems or the resulting contract.

Article 13 - Availability of Contract Terms

Nothing in this Convention affects the application of any rule of law that may require a party
that negotiates some or all of the terms of a contract through the exchange of electronic communications to make available to the other party those electronic communications which contain the contractual terms in a particular manner, or relieves a party from the legal consequences of its failure to do so.

Article 14 - Error in Electronic Communications

1.   Where a natural person makes an input error in an electronic communication exchanged
with the automated message system of another party and the automated message system
does not provide the person with an opportunity to correct the error, that person, or the party
on whose behalf that person was acting, has the right to withdraw the portion of the electronic
communication in which the input error was made if:
(a)   The person, or the party on whose behalf that person was acting, notifies the other party of
       the error as soon as possible after having learned of the error and indicates that he or she
       made an error in the electronic communication; and
(b)   The person, or the party on whose behalf that person was acting, has not used or received
       any material benefit or value from the goods or services, if any, received from the other party.
2.   Nothing in this Article affects the application of any rule of law that may govern the consequences of any error other than as provided for in paragraph 1.

CHAPTER IV. FINAL PROVISIONS [...]

Article 17 - Participation by Regional Economic Integration Organizations

1.   A regional economic integration organization that is constituted by sovereign States and has
competence over certain matters governed by this Convention may similarly sign, ratify, accept,
approve or accede to this Convention. The regional economic integration organization shall in that
case have the rights and obligations of a Contracting State, to the extent that that organization has
competence over matters governed by this Convention. Where the number of Contracting States
is relevant in this Convention, the regional economic integration organization shall not count as a
Contracting State in addition to its member States that are Contracting States.
2.   The regional economic integration organization shall, at the time of signature, ratification,
acceptance, approval or accession, make a declaration to the depositary specifying the matters
governed by this Convention in respect of which competence has been transferred to that
organization by its member States. The regional economic integration organization shall

promptly notify the depositary of any changes to the distribution of competence, including new transfers of competence, specified in the declaration under this paragraph.

3.   Any reference to a "Contracting State" or "Contracting States" in this Convention applies equally to a regional economic integration organization where the context so requires.

4.   This Convention shall not prevail over any conflicting rules of any regional economic integration organization as applicable to parties whose respective places of business are located in States members of any such organization, as set out by declaration made in accordance with Article 21. [...]

Article 19 - Declarations on the Scope of Application

1.   Any Contracting State may declare, in accordance with Article 21, that it will apply this Convention only:

(a)   When the States referred to in Article 1, paragraph 1, are Contracting States to this Convention; or

(b)   When the parties have agreed that it applies.

2.   Any Contracting State may exclude from the scope of application of this Convention the matters it specifies in a declaration made in accordance with Article 21.

Article 20 - Communications Exchanged Under Other International Conventions

1.   The provisions of this Convention apply to the use of electronic communications in connection with the formation or performance of a contract to which any of the following international conventions, to which a Contracting State to this Convention is or may become a Contracting State, apply:

- Convention on the Recognition and Enforcement of Foreign Arbitral Awards (New York, 10 June 1958);
- Convention on the Limitation Period in the International Sale of Goods (New York, 14 June 1974) and Protocol thereto (Vienna, 11 April 1980);
- United Nations Convention on Contracts for the International Sale of Goods (Vienna, 11 April 1980);
- United Nations Convention on the Liability of Operators of Transport Terminals in International Trade (Vienna, 19 April 1991);
- United Nations Convention on Independent Guarantees and Stand-by Letters of Credit (New York, 11 December 1995);
- United Nations Convention on the Assignment of Receivables in International Trade (New York, 12 December 2001).

2.   The provisions of this Convention apply further to electronic communications in connection with the formation or performance of a contract to which another international convention, treaty or agreement not specifically referred to in paragraph 1 of this article, and to which a Contracting State to this Convention is or may become a Contracting State, applies, unless the State has declared, in accordance with Article 21, that it will not be bound by this paragraph.

3.   A State that makes a declaration pursuant to paragraph 2 of this Article may also declare that it will nevertheless apply the provisions of this Convention to the use of electronic communications in connection with the formation or performance of any contract to which a specified international convention, treaty or agreement applies to which the State is or may become a Contracting State.

4.   Any State may declare that it will not apply the provisions of this Convention to the use of electronic communications in connection with the formation or performance of a contract to which any international convention, treaty or agreement specified in that State's declaration, to which the State is or may become a Contracting State, applies, including any of the conventions referred to in paragraph 1 of this article, even if such State has not excluded the application of paragraph 2 of this Article by a declaration made in accordance with Article 21.

Article 21 - Procedure and Effects of Declarations
1.   Declarations under Article 17, paragraph 4, Article 19, paragraphs 1 and 2, and Article 20, paragraphs 2, 3 and 4, may be made at any time. Declarations made at the time of signature are subject to confirmation upon ratification, acceptance or approval.
2.   Declarations and their confirmations are to be in writing and to be formally notified to the depositary.
3.   A declaration takes effect simultaneously with the entry into force of this Convention in respect of the State concerned. However, a declaration of which the depositary receives formal notification after such entry into force takes effect on the first day of the month following the expiration of six months after the date of its receipt by the depositary.
4.   Any State that makes a declaration under this Convention may modify or withdraw it at any time by a formal notification in writing addressed to the depositary. The modification or withdrawal is to take effect on the first day of the month following the expiration of six months after the date of the receipt of the notification by the depositary.

Article 22 - Reservations
No reservations may be made under this Convention. [...]

DONE at New York this twenty-third day of November two thousand and five, in a single original, of which the Arabic, Chinese, English, French, Russian and Spanish texts are equally authentic.
IN WITNESS WHEREOF the undersigned plenipotentiaries, being duly authorized by their respective Governments, have signed this Convention.

Entry into force: 1 March 2013
Ratifications to date: Dominican Republic (2012), Honduras (2010), Singapore (2010)[1]

---

1   As of June 2012, the Convention has been signed but not yet ratified by Central African Republic, China, Colombia, Iran, Korea, Lebanon, Madagascar, Montenegro, Panama, Paraguay, Philippines, Russian Federation, Saudi Arabia, Senegal, Sierra Leone, and Sri Lanka.

UNIFORM COMMERCIAL CODE[1]

---

1   © 2012 by The American Law Institute and the National Conference of Commissioners on Uniform State Laws; reproduced, published and distributed with permission of the Permanent Editorial Board for the Uniform Commercial Code. All rights reserved.

ARTICLE 1 - GENERAL PROVISIONS
PART 1. GENERAL PROVISIONS
§ 1-101. Short Titles
(a)   This [Act] may be cited as the Uniform Commercial Code.
(b)   This Article may be cited as Uniform Commercial Code-General Provisions.

§ 1-102. Scope of Article
This Article applies to a transaction to the extent that it is governed by another Article of [the Uniform Commercial Code].

§ 1-103. Construction of [Uniform Commercial Code] to Promote its Purposes and Policies: Applicability of Supplemental Principles of Law
(a)   [The Uniform Commercial Code] must be liberally construed and applied to promote its underlying purposes and policies, which are: (1) to simplify, clarify, and modernize the law governing commercial transactions; (2) to permit the continued expansion of commercial practices through custom, usage, and agreement of the parties; and (3) to make uniform the law among the various jurisdictions.
(b)   Unless displaced by the particular provisions of [the Uniform Commercial Code], the principles of law and equity, including the law merchant and the law relative to capacity to contract, principal and agent, estoppel, fraud, misrepresentation, duress, coercion, mistake, bankruptcy, and other validating or invalidating cause supplement its provisions.

§ 1-104. Construction Against Implied Repeal
[The Uniform Commercial Code] being a general act intended as a unified coverage of its subject matter, no part of it shall be deemed to be impliedly repealed by subsequent legislation if such construction can reasonably be avoided.

§ 1-105. Severability
If any provision or clause of [the Uniform Commercial Code] or its application to any person or circumstance is held invalid, the invalidity does not affect other provisions or applications of [the Uniform Commercial Code] which can be given effect without the invalid provision or application, and to this end the provisions of [the Uniform Commercial Code] are severable.

§ 1-106. Use of Singular and Plural; Gender
In [the Uniform Commercial Code], unless the statutory context otherwise requires: (1) words in the singular number include the plural, and those in the plural include the singular; and (2) words of any gender also refer to any other gender.

§ 1-107. Section Captions
Section captions are part of [the Uniform Commercial Code].

§ 1-108. Relation to Electronic Signatures in Global and National Commerce Act
This Article modifies, limits, and supersedes the federal Electronic Signatures in Global and National Commerce Act, 15 U.S.C. Section 7001 et seq., except that nothing in this Article modifies, limits, or supersedes Section 7001(c) of that Act or authorizes electronic delivery of any of the notices described in Section 7003(b) of that Act.

PART 2. GENERAL DEFINITIONS AND PRINCIPLES OF INTERPRETATION
§ 1-201. General Definitions
(a)   Unless the context otherwise requires, words or phrases defined in this section, or in the additional definitions contained in other articles of [the Uniform Commercial Code] that apply to particular articles or parts thereof, have the meanings stated.
(b)   Subject to definitions contained in other articles of [the Uniform Commercial Code] that apply to particular articles or parts thereof:
(1)   "Action", in the sense of a judicial proceeding, includes recoupment, counterclaim, set-off, suit in equity, and any other proceeding in which rights are determined.

(2)   "Aggrieved party" means a party entitled to pursue a remedy.

(3)   "Agreement", as distinguished from "contract", means the bargain of the parties in fact, as found in their language or inferred from other circumstances, including course of performance, course of dealing, or usage of trade as provided in Section 1-303.

(4)   "Bank" means a person engaged in the business of banking and includes a savings bank, savings and loan association, credit union, and trust company.

(5)   "Bearer" means a person in possession of a negotiable instrument, document of title, or certificated security that is payable to bearer or indorsed in blank.

(6)   "Bill of lading" means a document evidencing the receipt of goods for shipment issued by a person engaged in the business of transporting or forwarding goods.

(7)   "Branch" includes a separately incorporated foreign branch of a bank.

(8)   "Burden of establishing" a fact means the burden of persuading the trier of fact that the existence of the fact is more probable than its nonexistence.

(9)   "Buyer in ordinary course of business" means a person that buys goods in good faith, without knowledge that the sale violates the rights of another person in the goods, and in the ordinary course from a person, other than a pawnbroker, in the business of selling goods of that kind. A person buys goods in the ordinary course if the sale to the person comports with the usual or customary practices in the kind of business in which the seller is engaged or with the seller's own usual or customary practices. A person that sells oil, gas, or other minerals at the wellhead or minehead is a person in the business of selling goods of that kind. A buyer in ordinary course of business may buy for cash, by exchange of other property, or on secured or unsecured credit, and may acquire goods or documents of title under a preexisting contract for sale. Only a buyer that takes possession of the goods or has a right to recover the goods from the seller under Article 2 may be a buyer in ordinary course of business. "Buyer in ordinary course of business" does not include a person that acquires goods in a transfer in bulk or as security for or in total or partial satisfaction of a money debt.

(10)   "Conspicuous", with reference to a term, means so written, displayed, or presented that a reasonable person against which it is to operate ought to have noticed it. Whether a term is "conspicuous" or not is a decision for the court. Conspicuous terms include the following: (A) a heading in capitals equal to or greater in size than the surrounding text, or in contrasting type, font, or color to the surrounding text of the same or lesser size; and (B) language in the body of a record or display in larger type than the surrounding text, or in contrasting type, font, or color to the surrounding text of the same size, or set off from surrounding text of the same size by symbols or other marks that call attention to the language.

(11)   "Consumer" means an individual who enters into a transaction primarily for personal, family, or household purposes.

(12)   "Contract", as distinguished from "agreement", means the total legal obligation that results from the parties' agreement as determined by [the Uniform Commercial Code] as supplemented by any other applicable laws.

(13)   "Creditor" includes a general creditor, a secured creditor, a lien creditor, and any representative of creditors, including an assignee for the benefit of creditors, a trustee in bankruptcy, a receiver in equity, and an executor or administrator of an insolvent debtor's or assignor's estate.

(14)   "Defendant" includes a person in the position of defendant in a counterclaim, cross-claim, or third-party claim.

(15)   "Delivery", with respect to an instrument, document of title, or chattel paper, means voluntary transfer of possession.

(16)   "Document of title" includes bill of lading, dock warrant, dock receipt, warehouse receipt or order for the delivery of goods, and also any other document which in the regular course of business or financing is treated as adequately evidencing that the person in possession of it is entitled to receive, hold, and dispose of the document and the goods it covers. To be

a document of title, a document must purport to be issued by or addressed to a bailee and purport to cover goods in the bailee's possession which are either identified or are fungible portions of an identified mass.

(17) "Fault" means a default, breach, or wrongful act or omission.

(18) "Fungible goods" means: (A) goods of which any unit, by nature or usage of trade, is the equivalent of any other like unit; or (B) goods that by agreement are treated as equivalent.

(19) "Genuine" means free of forgery or counterfeiting.

(20) "Good faith," except as otherwise provided in Article 5, means honesty in fact and the observance of reasonable commercial standards of fair dealing.

(21) "Holder" means: (A) the person in possession of a negotiable instrument that is payable either to bearer or to an identified person that is the person in possession; or (B) the person in possession of a document of title if the goods are deliverable either to bearer or to the order of the person in possession.

(22) "Insolvency proceeding" includes an assignment for the benefit of creditors or other proceeding intended to liquidate or rehabilitate the estate of the person involved.

(23) "Insolvent" means: (A) having generally ceased to pay debts in the ordinary course of business other than as a result of bona fide dispute; (B) being unable to pay debts as they become due; or (C) being insolvent within the meaning of federal bankruptcy law.

(24) "Money" means a medium of exchange currently authorized or adopted by a domestic or foreign government. The term includes a monetary unit of account established by an intergovernmental organization or by agreement between two or more countries.

(25) "Organization" means a person other than an individual.

(26) "Party", as distinguished from "third party", means a person that has engaged in a transaction or made an agreement subject to [the Uniform Commercial Code].

(27) "Person" means an individual, corporation, business trust, estate, trust, partnership, limited liability company, association, joint venture, government, governmental subdivision, agency, or instrumentality, public corporation, or any other legal or commercial entity.

(28) "Present value" means the amount as of a date certain of one or more sums payable in the future, discounted to the date certain by use of either an interest rate specified by the parties if that rate is not manifestly unreasonable at the time the transaction is entered into or, if an interest rate is not so specified, a commercially reasonable rate that takes into account the facts and circumstances at the time the transaction is entered into.

(29) "Purchase" means taking by sale, lease, discount, negotiation, mortgage, pledge, lien, security interest, issue or reissue, gift, or any other voluntary transaction creating an interest in property.

(30) "Purchaser" means a person that takes by purchase.

(31) "Record" means information that is inscribed on a tangible medium or that is stored in an electronic or other medium and is retrievable in perceivable form.

(32) "Remedy" means any remedial right to which an aggrieved party is entitled with or without resort to a tribunal.

(33) "Representative" means a person empowered to act for another, including an agent, an officer of a corporation or association, and a trustee, executor, or administrator of an estate.

(34) "Right" includes remedy.

(35) "Security interest" means an interest in personal property or fixtures which secures payment or performance of an obligation. "Security interest" includes any interest of a consignor and a buyer of accounts, chattel paper, a payment intangible, or a promissory note in a transaction that is subject to Article 9. "Security interest" does not include the special property interest of a buyer of goods on identification of those goods to a contract for sale under Section 2-505, the right of a seller or lessor of goods under Article 2 or 2A to retain or acquire possession of the goods is not a "security interest", but a seller or lessor may also acquire a "security interest" by complying with Article 9. The retention or reservation of title by a seller of goods notwithstanding shipment or delivery to the buyer under Section 2-

401 is limited in effect to a reservation of a "security interest." Whether a transaction in the form of a lease creates a "security interest" is determined pursuant to Section 1-203.

(36) "Send" in connection with a writing, record, or notice means: (A) to deposit in the mail or deliver for transmission by any other usual means of communication with postage or cost of transmission provided for and properly addressed and, in the case of an instrument, to an address specified thereon or otherwise agreed, or if there be none to any address reasonable under the circumstances; or (B) in any other way to cause to be received any record or notice within the time it would have arrived if properly sent.

(37) "Signed" includes using any symbol executed or adopted with present intention to adopt or accept a writing.

(38) "State" means a State of the United States, the District of Columbia, Puerto Rico, the United States Virgin Islands, or any territory or insular possession subject to the jurisdiction of the United States.

(39) "Surety" includes a guarantor or other secondary obligor.

(40) "Term" means a portion of an agreement that relates to a particular matter.

(41) "Unauthorized signature" means a signature made without actual, implied, or apparent authority. The term includes a forgery.

(42) "Warehouse receipt" means a receipt issued by a person engaged in the business of storing goods for hire.

(43) "Writing" includes printing, typewriting, or any other intentional reduction to tangible form. "Written" has a corresponding meaning.

§ 1-202. Notice; Knowledge

(a)   Subject to subsection (f), a person has "notice" of a fact if the person: (1) has actual knowledge of it; (2) has received a notice or notification of it; or (3) from all the facts and circumstances known to the person at the time in question, has reason to know that it exists.

(b)   "Knowledge" means actual knowledge. "Knows" has a corresponding meaning.

(c)   "Discover", "learn", or words of similar import refer to knowledge rather than to reason to know.

(d)   A person "notifies" or "gives" a notice or notification to another person by taking such steps as may be reasonably required to inform the other person in ordinary course, whether or not the other person actually comes to know of it.

(e)   Subject to subsection (f), a person "receives" a notice or notification when: (1) it comes to that person's attention; or (2) it is duly delivered in a form reasonable under the circumstances at the place of business through which the contract was made or at another location held out by that person as the place for receipt of such communications.

(f)   Notice, knowledge, or a notice or notification received by an organization is effective for a particular transaction from the time it is brought to the attention of the individual conducting that transaction and, in any event, from the time it would have been brought to the individual's attention if the organization had exercised due diligence. An organization exercises due diligence if it maintains reasonable routines for communicating significant information to the person conducting the transaction and there is reasonable compliance with the routines. Due diligence does not require an individual acting for the organization to communicate information unless the communication is part of the individual's regular duties or the individual has reason to know of the transaction and that the transaction would be materially affected by the information.

§ 1-203. Lease Distinguished from Security Interest

(a)   Whether a transaction in the form of a lease creates a lease or security interest is determined by the facts of each case.

(b)   A transaction in the form of a lease creates a security interest if the consideration that the lessee is to pay the lessor for the right to possession and use of the goods is an obligation for the term of the lease and is not subject to termination by the lessee, and: (1) the original term of the lease is equal to or greater than the remaining economic life of the goods; (2) the lessee is bound to renew the lease for the remaining economic life of the goods or is bound to become the owner of the goods; (3) the lessee has an option to renew the lease for the remaining economic life of the goods for no additional consideration or for nominal additional consideration upon compliance with the lease agreement; or (4) the lessee has an option to become the owner of the goods for no additional consideration or for nominal additional consideration upon compliance with the lease agreement.

(c)   A transaction in the form of a lease does not create a security interest merely because: (1) the present value of the consideration the lessee is obligated to pay the lessor for the right to possession and use of the goods is substantially equal to or is greater than the fair market value of the goods at the time the lease is entered into; (2) the lessee assumes risk of loss of the goods; (3) the lessee agrees to pay, with respect to the goods, taxes, insurance, filing, recording, or registration fees, or service or maintenance costs; (4) the lessee has an option to renew the lease or to become the owner of the goods; (5) the lessee has an option to renew the lease for a fixed rent that is equal to or greater than the reasonably predictable fair market rent for the use of the goods for the term of the renewal at the time the option is to be performed; or (6) the lessee has an option to become the owner of the goods for a fixed price that is equal to or greater than the reasonably predictable fair market value of the goods at the time the option is to be performed.

(d)   Additional consideration is nominal if it is less than the lessee's reasonably predictable cost of performing under the lease agreement if the option is not exercised. Additional consideration is not nominal if: (1) when the option to renew the lease is granted to the lessee, the rent is stated to be the fair market rent for the use of the goods for the term of the renewal determined at the time the option is to be performed; or (2) when the option to become the owner of the goods is granted to the lessee, the price is stated to be the fair market value of the goods determined at the time the option is to be performed.

(e)   The "remaining economic life of the goods" and "reasonably predictable" fair market rent, fair market value, or cost of performing under the lease agreement must be determined with reference to the facts and circumstances at the time the transaction is entered into.

§ 1-204. Value

Except as otherwise provided in Articles 3, 4, [and] 5, [and 6], a person gives value for rights if the person acquires them: (1) in return for a binding commitment to extend credit or for the extension of immediately available credit, whether or not drawn upon and whether or not a chargeback is provided for in the event of difficulties in collection; (2) as security for, or in total or partial satisfaction of, a preexisting claim; (3) by accepting delivery under a preexisting contract for purchase; or (4) in return for any consideration sufficient to support a simple contract.

§ 1-205. Reasonable Time; Seasonableness

(a)   Whether a time for taking an action required by [the Uniform Commercial Code] is reasonable depends on the nature, purpose, and circumstances of the action.

(b)   An action is taken seasonably if it is taken at or within the time agreed or, if no time is agreed, at or within a reasonable time.

§ 1-206. Presumptions

Whenever [the Uniform Commercial Code] creates a "presumption" with respect to a fact, or provides that a fact is "presumed," the trier of fact must find the existence of the fact unless and until evidence is introduced that supports a finding of its nonexistence.

PART 3. TERRITORIAL APPLICABILITY AND GENERAL RULES

§ 1-301. Territorial Applicability; Parties' Power to Choose Applicable Law

(a)   In this section:

(1)   "Domestic transaction" means a transaction other than an international transaction.

(2)   "International transaction" means a transaction that bears a reasonable relation to a country other than the United States.

(b)   This section applies to a transaction to the extent that it is governed by another article of the [Uniform Commercial Code].
(c)   Except as otherwise provided in this section:
(1)   an agreement by parties to a domestic transaction that any or all of their rights and obliga-tions are to be determined by the law of this State or of another State is effective, whether or not the transaction bears a relation to the State designated; and
(2)   an agreement by parties to an international transaction that any or all of their rights and obligations are to be determined by the law of this State or of another State or country is effective, whether or not the transaction bears a relation to the State or country designated.
(d)   In the absence of an agreement effective under subsection (c), and except as provided in subsections (e) and (g), the rights and obligations of the parties are determined by the law that would be selected by application of this State's conflict of laws principles.
(e)   If one of the parties to a transaction is a consumer, the following rules apply:
(1)   An agreement referred to in subsection (c) is not effective unless the transaction bears a reasonable relation to the State or country designated.
(2)   Application of the law of the State or country determined pursuant to subsection (c) or (d) may not deprive the consumer of the protection of any rule of law governing a matter within the scope of this section, which both is protective of consumers and may not be va-ried by agreement: (A) of the State or country in which the consumer principally resides, unless subparagraph (B) applies; or (B) if the transaction is a sale of goods, of the State or country in which the consumer both makes the contract and takes delivery of those goods, if such State or country is not the State or country in which the consumer principally resi-des.
(f)   An agreement otherwise effective under subsection (c) is not effective to the extent that application of the law of the State or country designated would be contrary to a fundamental policy of the State or country whose law would govern in the absence of agreement under sub-section (d).
(g)   To the extent that [the Uniform Commercial Code] governs a transaction, if one of the fol-lowing provisions of [the Uniform Commercial Code] specifies the applicable law, that provision governs and a contrary agreement is effective only to the extent permitted by the law so spe-cified: (1) Section 2-402; (2) Sections 2A-105 and 2A-106; (3) Section 4-102; (4) Section 4A-507; (5) Section 5-116; [(6) Section 6-103;] (7) Section 8-110; (8) Sections 9-301 through 9-307.

§ 1-302. Variation by Agreement
(a)   Except as otherwise provided in subsection (b) or elsewhere in [the Uniform Commercial Code], the effect of provisions of [the Uniform Commercial Code] may be varied by agreement.
(b)   The obligations of good faith, diligence, reasonableness, and care prescribed by [the Uni-form Commercial Code] may not be disclaimed by agreement. The parties, by agreement, may determine the standards by which the performance of those obligations is to be measured if those standards are not manifestly unreasonable. Whenever [the Uniform Commercial Code] requires an action to be taken within a reasonable time, a time that is not manifestly unreason-able may be fixed by agreement.
(c)   The presence in certain provisions of [the Uniform Commercial Code] of the phrase "unless otherwise agreed", or words of similar import, does not imply that the effect of other provisions may not be varied by agreement under this section.

§ 1-303. Course of Performance, Course of Dealing, and Usage of Trade
(a)   A "course of performance" is a sequence of conduct between the parties to a particular transaction that exists if: (1) the agreement of the parties with respect to the transaction involves repeated occasions for performance by a party; and (2) the other party, with knowledge of the nature of the performance and opportunity for objection to it, accepts the performance or acquiesces in it without objection.

(b)   A "course of dealing" is a sequence of conduct concerning previous transactions between the parties to a particular transaction that is fairly to be regarded as establishing a common basis of understanding for interpreting their expressions and other conduct.

(c)   A "usage of trade" is any practice or method of dealing having such regularity of observance in a place, vocation, or trade as to justify an expectation that it will be observed with respect to the transaction in question. The existence and scope of such a usage must be proved as facts. If it is established that such a usage is embodied in a trade code or similar record, the interpretation of the record is a question of law.

(d)   A course of performance or course of dealing between the parties or usage of trade in the vocation or trade in which they are engaged or of which they are or should be aware is relevant in ascertaining the meaning of the parties' agreement, may give particular meaning to specific terms of the agreement, and may supplement or qualify the terms of the agreement. A usage of trade applicable in the place in which part of the performance under the agreement is to occur may be so utilized as to that part of the performance.

(e)   Except as otherwise provided in subsection (f), the express terms of an agreement and any applicable course of performance, course of dealing, or usage of trade must be construed whenever reasonable as consistent with each other. If such a construction is unreasonable: (1) express terms prevail over course of performance, course of dealing, and usage of trade; (2) course of performance prevails over course of dealing and usage of trade; and (3) course of dealing prevails over usage of trade.

(f)   Subject to Section 2-209, a course of performance is relevant to show a waiver or modification of any term inconsistent with the course of performance.

(g)   Evidence of a relevant usage of trade offered by one party is not admissible unless that party has given the other party notice that the court finds sufficient to prevent unfair surprise to the other party.

§ 1-304. Obligation of Good Faith

Every contract or duty within [the Uniform Commercial Code] imposes an obligation of good faith in its performance and enforcement.

§ 1-305. Remedies to Be Liberally Administered

(a)   The remedies provided by [the Uniform Commercial Code] must be liberally administered to the end that the aggrieved party may be put in as good a position as if the other party had fully performed but neither consequential or special damages nor penal damages may be had except as specifically provided in [the Uniform Commercial Code] or by other rule of law.

(b)   Any right or obligation declared by [the Uniform Commercial Code] is enforceable by action unless the provision declaring it specifies a different and limited effect.

§ 1-306. Waiver or Renunciation of Claim or Right After Breach

A claim or right arising out of an alleged breach may be discharged in whole or in part without consideration by agreement of the aggrieved party in an authenticated record.

§ 1-307. Prima Facie Evidence by Third-Party Documents

A document in due form purporting to be a bill of lading, policy or certificate of insurance, official weigher's or inspector's certificate, consular invoice, or any other document authorized or required by the contract to be issued by a third party is prima facie evidence of its own authenticity and genuineness and of the facts stated in the document by the third party.

§ 1-308. Performance or Acceptance Under Reservation of Rights

(a)   A party that with explicit reservation of rights performs or promises performance or assents to performance in a manner demanded or offered by the other party does not thereby prejudice the rights reserved. Such words as "without prejudice," "under protest," or the like are sufficient.

(b)   Subsection (a) does not apply to an accord and satisfaction.

§ 1-309. Option to Accelerate at Will

A term providing that one party or that party's successor in interest may accelerate payment or performance or require collateral or additional collateral "at will" or when the party "deems itself insecure," or words of similar import, means that the party has power to do so only if that party in good faith believes that the prospect of payment or performance is impaired. The burden of establishing lack of good faith is on the party against which the power has been exercised.

§ 1-310. Subordinated Obligations

An obligation may be issued as subordinated to performance of another obligation of the person obligated, or a creditor may subordinate its right to performance of an obligation by agreement with either the person obligated or another creditor of the person obligated. Subordination does not create a security interest as against either the common debtor or a subordinated creditor.

ARTICLE 2 - SALES

PART 1. SHORT TITLE, GENERAL CONSTRUCTION AND SUBJECT MATTER

§ 2-101. Short Title

This Article shall be known and may be cited as Uniform Commercial Code-Sales.

§ 2-102. Scope; Certain Security and Other Transactions Excluded From this Article

Unless the context otherwise requires, this Article applies to transactions in goods; it does not apply to any transaction which although in the form of an unconditional contract to sell or present sale is intended to operate only as a security transaction nor does this Article impair or repeal any statute regulating sales to consumers, farmers or other specified classes of buyers.

§ 2-103. Definitions and Index of Definitions

(1) In this Article unless the context otherwise requires
(a) "Buyer" means a person that buys or contracts to buy goods.
(b) "Conspicuous", with reference to a term, means so written, displayed, or presented that a reasonable person against which it is to operate ought to have noticed it. A term in an electronic record intended to evoke a response by an electronic agent is conspicuous if it is presented in a form that would enable a reasonably configured electronic agent to take it into account or react to it without review of the record by an individual. Whether a term is "conspicuous" or not is a decision for the court. Conspicuous terms include the following:
  (i)   for a person:
  (A) a heading in capitals equal to or greater in size than the surrounding text, or in contrasting type, font, or color to the surrounding text of the same or lesser size; and
  (B) language in the body of a record or display in larger type than the surrounding text, or in contrasting type, font, or color to the surrounding text of the same size, or set off from surrounding text of the same size by symbols or other marks that call attention to the language; and
  (ii) for a person or an electronic agent, a term that is so placed in a record or display that the person or electronic agent may not proceed without taking action with respect to the particular term.
(c) "Consumer" means an individual who buys or contracts to buy goods that, at the time of contracting, are intended by the individual to be used primarily for personal, family, or household purposes.
(d) "Consumer contract" means a contract between a merchant seller and a consumer.
(e) "Delivery" means the voluntary transfer of physical possession or control of goods.
(f) "Electronic" means relating to technology having electrical, digital, magnetic, wireless, optical, electromagnetic, or similar capabilities.
(g) "Electronic agent" means a computer program or an electronic or other automated means used independently to initiate an action or respond to electronic records or performances in whole or in part, without review or action by an individual.

(h)   "Electronic record" means a record created, generated, sent, communicated, received, or stored by electronic means.

(i)   "Foreign exchange transaction" means a transaction in which one party agrees to deliver a quantity of a specified money or unit of account in consideration of the other party's agreement to deliver another quantity of a different money or unit of account either currently or at a future date, and in which delivery is to be through funds transfer, book entry accounting, or other form of payment order, or other agreed means to transfer a credit balance. The term includes a transaction of this type involving two or more moneys and spot, forward, option, or other products derived from underlying moneys and any combination of these transactions. The term does not include a transaction involving two or more moneys in which one or both of the parties is obligated to make physical delivery, at the time of contracting or in the future, of banknotes, coins, or other form of legal tender or specie. [...]

(j)   "Good faith" means honesty in fact and the observance of reasonable commercial standards of fair dealing.
       Legislative Note: The definition of "good faith" should not be adopted if the jurisdiction has enacted this definition as part of Article 1.

(k)   "Goods" means all things that are movable at the time of identification to a contract for sale. The term includes future goods, specially manufactured goods, the unborn young of animals, growing crops, and other identified things attached to realty as described in Section 2-107. The term does not include information, the money in which the price is to be paid, investment securities under Article 8, the subject matter of foreign exchange transactions, or choses in action.

(l)   "Receipt of goods" means taking physical possession of goods.

(m) "Record" means information that is inscribed on a tangible medium or that is stored in an electronic or other medium and is retrievable in perceivable form.
       Legislative Note: The definition of "record" should not be adopted if the jurisdiction has enacted revised Article 1.

(n)   "Remedial promise" means a promise by the seller to repair or replace goods or to refund all or part of the price of goods upon the happening of a specified event.

(o)   "Seller" means a person that sells or contracts to sell goods.

(p)   "Sign" means, with present intent to authenticate or adopt a record:
       (i) to execute or adopt a tangible symbol; or
       (ii) to attach to or logically associate with the record an electronic sound, symbol, or process.

(2)   Other definitions applying to this Article or to specified Parts thereof, and the sections in which they appear are:
       "Acceptance". Section 2-606.
       "Between merchants". Section 2-104.
       "Cancellation". Section 2-106(4).
       "Commercial unit". Section 2-105.
       "Conforming to contract". Section 2-106.
       "Contract for sale". Section 2-106.
       "Cover". Section 2-712.
       "Entrusting". Section 2-403.
       "Financing agency". Section 2-104.
       "Future Goods". Section 2-105.
       "Goods". Section 2-103.
       "Identification". Section 2-501.
       "Installment contract". Section 2-612.
       "Lot". Section 2-105.
       "Merchant". Section 2-104.
       "Person in position of Seller". Section 2-707.

"Present sale". Section 2-106.
"Sale". Section 2-106.
"Sale on approval". Section 2-326.
"Sale or return". Section 2-326.
"Termination". Section 2-106.
(3) "Control" as provided in Section 7-106 and the following definitions in other Articles apply to this Article:
"Check". Section 3-104(f).
"Consignee". Section 7-102(3).
"Consignor". Section 7-102(4).
"Consumer Goods". Section 9-102(a)(23).
"Dishonor". Section 3-502.
"Draft". Section 3-104(e).
"Honor". Section 5-102(a)(8).
"Injunction against honor". Section 5-109(b).
"Letter of credit". Section 5-102(a)(10).
(4) In addition Article 1 contains general definitions and principles of construction and interpretation applicable throughout this Article.

§ 2-104. Definitions: "Merchant"; "Between Merchants"; "Financing Agency"

(1) "Merchant" means a person that deals in goods of the kind or otherwise holds itself out by occupation as having knowledge or skill peculiar to the practices or goods involved in the transaction or to which the knowledge or skill may be attributed by the person's employment of an agent or broker or other intermediary that holds itself out by occupation as having the knowledge or skill.
(2) "Financing agency" means a bank, finance company or other person that in the ordinary course of business makes advances against goods or documents of title or that by arrangement with either the seller or the buyer intervenes in ordinary course to make or collect payment due or claimed under the contract for sale, as by purchasing or paying the seller's draft or making advances against it or by merely taking it for collection whether or not documents of title accompany or are associated with the draft. The term includes also a bank or other person that similarly intervenes between persons that are in the position of seller and buyer in respect to the goods (Section 2-707).
(3) "Between Merchants" means in any transaction with respect to which both parties are chargeable with the knowledge or skill of merchants.

§ 2-105. Definitions: Transferability; "Future" Goods; "Lot"; "Commercial Unit"

(1) Goods must be both existing and identified before any interest in them may pass. Goods that are not both existing and identified are "future" goods. A purported present sale of future goods or of any interest therein operates as a contract to sell.
(2) There may be a sale of a part interest in existing identified goods.
(3) An undivided share in an identified bulk of fungible goods is sufficiently identified to be sold although the quantity of the bulk is not determined. Any agreed proportion of the bulk or any quantity thereof agreed upon by number, weight, or other measure may to the extent of the seller's interest in the bulk be sold to the buyer that then becomes an owner in common.
(4) "Lot" means a parcel or a single article which is the subject matter of a separate sale or delivery, whether or not it is sufficient to perform the contract.
(5) "Commercial unit" means such a unit of goods as by commercial usage is a single whole for purposes of sale and division of which materially impairs its character or value on the market or in use. A commercial unit may be a single article (as a machine) or a set of articles (as a suite of furniture or an assortment of sizes) or a quantity (as a bale, gross, or carload) or any other unit treated in use or in the relevant market as a single whole.

§ 2-106. Definitions: "Contract"; "Agreement"; "Contract for sale"; "Sale"; "Present sale"; "Conforming" to Contract; "Termination"; "Cancellation"

(1) In this Article unless the context otherwise requires "contract" and "agreement" are limited to those relating to the present or future sale of goods. "Contract for sale" includes both a present sale of goods and a contract to sell goods at a future time. A "sale" consists in the passing of title from the seller to the buyer for a price (Section 2-401). A "present sale" means a sale which is accomplished by the making of the contract.

(2) Goods or conduct including any part of a performance are "conforming" or conform to the contract when they are in accordance with the obligations under the contract.

(3) "Termination" occurs when either party pursuant to a power created by agreement or law puts an end to the contract otherwise than for its breach. On "termination" all obligations which are still executory on both sides are discharged but any right based on prior breach or performance survives.

(4) "Cancellation" occurs when either party puts an end to the contract for breach by the other and its effect is the same as that of "termination" except that the cancelling party also retains any remedy for breach of the whole contract or any unperformed balance.

§ 2-107. Goods to Be Severed From Realty: Recording

(1) A contract for the sale of minerals or the like (including oil and gas) or a structure or its materials to be removed from realty is a contract for the sale of goods within this Article if they are to be severed by the seller but until severance a purported present sale thereof which is not effective as a transfer of an interest in land is effective only as a contract to sell.

(2) A contract for the sale apart from the land of growing crops or other things attached to realty and capable of severance without material harm thereto but not described in subsection (1) or of timber to be cut is a contract for the sale of goods within this Article whether the subject matter is to be severed by the buyer or by the seller even though it forms part of the realty at the time of contracting, and the parties can by identification effect a present sale before severance.

(3) The provisions of this section are subject to any third party rights provided by the law relating to realty records, and the contract for sale may be executed and recorded as a document transferring an interest in land and shall then constitute notice to third parties of the buyer's rights under the contract for sale.

§ 2-108. Transactions Subject to Other Law

(1) A transaction subject to this Article is also subject to any applicable:

(a) [list any certificate of title statutes of this State covering automobiles, trailers, mobile homes, boats, farm tractors, or the like], except with respect to the rights of a buyer in ordinary course of business under Section 2-403(2) which arise before a certificate of title covering the goods is effective in the name of any other buyer;

(b) rule of law that establishes a different rule for consumers; or

(c) statute of this state applicable to the transaction, such as a statute dealing with:

    (i) the sale or lease of agricultural products;

    (ii) the transfer of human blood, blood products, tissues, or parts;

    (iii) the consignment or transfer by artists of works of art or fine prints;

    (iv) distribution agreements, franchises, and other relationships through which goods are sold;

    (v) the misbranding or adulteration of food products or drugs; and

    (vi) dealers in particular products, such as automobiles, motorized wheelchairs, agricultural equipment, and hearing aids.

(2) Except for the rights of a buyer in ordinary course of business under subsection (1)(a), in the event of a conflict between this Article and a law referred to in subsection (1), that law governs.

(3) For purposes of this article, failure to comply with a law referred to in subsection (1) has only the effect specified in that law.

(4)   This Article modifies, limits, and supersedes the federal Electronic Signatures in Global and National Commerce Act, 15 U.S.C. Section 7001 et seq., except that nothing in this Article modifies, limits, or supersedes Section 7001(c) of that Act or authorizes electronic delivery of any of the notices described in Section 7003(b) of that Act.

PART 2. FORM, FORMATION AND READJUSTMENT OF CONTRACT
§ 2-201. Formal Requirements; Statute of Frauds

(1)   A contract for the sale of goods for the price of $5,000 or more is not enforceable by way of action or defense unless there is some record sufficient to indicate that a contract for sale has been made between the parties and signed by the party against which enforcement is sought or by the party's authorized agent or broker. A record is not insufficient because it omits or incorrectly states a term agreed upon but the contract is not enforceable under this subsection beyond the quantity of goods shown in the record.

(2)   Between merchants if within a reasonable time a record in confirmation of the contract and sufficient against the sender is received and the party receiving it has reason to know its contents, it satisfies the requirements of subsection (1) against the recipient unless notice of objection to its contents is given in a record within 10 days after it is received.

(3)   A contract that does not satisfy the requirements of subsection (1) but which is valid in other respects is enforceable:

(a)   if the goods are to be specially manufactured for the buyer and are not suitable for sale to others in the ordinary course of the seller's business and the seller, before notice of repudiation is received and under circumstances that reasonably indicate that the goods are for the buyer, has made either a substantial beginning of their manufacture or commitments for their procurement;

(b)   if the party against which enforcement is sought admits in the party's pleading, or in the party's testimony or otherwise under oath that a contract for sale was made, but the contract is not enforceable under this paragraph beyond the quantity of goods admitted; or

(c)   with respect to goods for which payment has been made and accepted or which have been received and accepted (Sec. 2-606).

(4)   A contract that is enforceable under this section is not unenforceable merely because it is not capable of being performed within one year or any other period after its making.

§ 2-202. Final Expression in a Record: Parol or Extrinsic Evidence

(1)   Terms with respect to which the confirmatory records of the parties agree or which are otherwise set forth in a record intended by the parties as a final expression of their agreement with respect to such terms as are included therein may not be contradicted by evidence of any prior agreement or of a contemporaneous oral agreement but may be supplemented by evidence of:

(a)   course of performance, course of dealing, or usage of trade (Section 1-303); and

(b)   consistent additional terms unless the court finds the record to have been intended also as a complete and exclusive statement of the terms of the agreement.

(2)   Terms in a record may be explained by evidence of course of performance, course of dealing, or usage of trade without a preliminary determination by the court that the language used is ambiguous. [...]

§ 2-204. Formation in General

(1)   A contract for sale of goods may be made in any manner sufficient to show agreement, including offer and acceptance, conduct by both parties which recognizes the existence of a contract, the interaction of electronic agents, and the interaction of an electronic agent and an individual.

(2)   An agreement sufficient to constitute a contract for sale may be found even if the moment of its making is undetermined.

(3)   Even if one or more terms are left open, a contract for sale does not fail for indefiniteness if the parties have intended to make a contract and there is a reasonably certain basis for giving an appropriate remedy.

(4) Except as otherwise provided in Sections 2-211 through 2-213, the following rules apply:
(a) A contract may be formed by the interaction of electronic agents of the parties, even if no individual was aware of or reviewed the electronic agents' actions or the resulting terms and agreements.
(b) A contract may be formed by the interaction of an electronic agent and an individual acting on the individual's own behalf or for another person. A contract is formed if the individual takes actions that the individual is free to refuse to take or makes a statement, and the individual has reason to know that the actions or statement will:
      (i)   cause the electronic agent to complete the transaction or performance; or
      (ii) indicate acceptance of an offer, regardless of other expressions or actions by the individual to which the electronic agent cannot react.

§ 2-205. Firm Offers

An offer by a merchant to buy or sell goods in a signed record that by its terms gives assurance that it will be held open is not revocable, for lack of consideration, during the time stated or if no time is stated for a reasonable time, but in no event may such period of irrevocability exceed three months; but in no event may the period of irrevocability exceed three months. Any such term of assurance in a form supplied by the offeree must be separately signed by the offeror.

§ 2-206. Offer and Acceptance in Formation of Contract

(1) Unless otherwise unambiguously indicated by the language or circumstances
(a) an offer to make a contract shall be construed as inviting acceptance in any manner and by any medium reasonable in the circumstances:
(b) an order or other offer to buy goods for prompt or current shipment shall be construed as inviting acceptance either by a prompt promise to ship or by the prompt or current shipment of conforming or nonconforming goods, but the shipment of nonconforming goods is not an acceptance if the seller seasonably notifies the buyer that the shipment is offered only as an accommodation to the buyer.
(2) If the beginning of a requested performance is a reasonable mode of acceptance, an offeror that is not notified of acceptance within a reasonable time may treat the offer as having lapsed before acceptance.
(3) A definite and seasonable expression of acceptance in a record operates as an acceptance even if it contains terms additional to or different from the offer.

§ 2-207. Terms of Contract; Effect of Confirmation

Subject to Section 2-202, if (i) conduct by both parties recognizes the existence of a contract although their records do not otherwise establish a contract, (ii) a contract is formed by an offer and acceptance, or (iii) a contract formed in any manner is confirmed by a record that contains terms additional to or different from those in the contract being confirmed, the terms of the contract are:
(a) terms that appear in the records of both parties;
(b) terms, whether in a record or not, to which both parties agree; and
(c) terms supplied or incorporated under any provision of this Act. [...]

§ 2-209. Modification, Rescission and Waiver

(1) An agreement modifying a contract within this Article needs no consideration to be binding.
(2) An agreement in a signed record which excludes modification or rescission except by a signed record may not be otherwise modified or rescinded, but except as between merchants such a requirement in a form supplied by the merchant must be separately signed by the other party.
(3) The requirements of Section 2-201 must be satisfied if the contract as modified is within its provisions.
(4) Although an attempt at modification or rescission does not satisfy the requirements of subsection (2) or (3), it may operate as a waiver.

(5)   A party that has made a waiver affecting an executory portion of a contract may retract the waiver by reasonable notification received by the other party that strict performance will be required of any term waived, unless the retraction would be unjust in view of a material change of position in reliance on the waiver.

§ 2-210. Delegation of Performance; Assignment of Rights

(1)   If the seller or buyer assigns rights under a contract, the following rules apply:

(a)   Subject to paragraph (b) and except as otherwise provided in Section 9-406 or as otherwise agreed, all rights of the seller or the buyer may be assigned unless the assignment would materially change the duty of the other party, increase materially the burden or risk imposed on that party by the contract, or impair materially that party's chance of obtaining return performance. A right to damages for breach of the whole contract or a right arising out of the assignor's due performance of its entire obligation may be assigned despite an agreement otherwise.

(b)   The creation, attachment, perfection, or enforcement of a security interest in the seller's interest under a contract is not an assignment that materially changes the duty of or materially increases the burden or risk imposed on the buyer or materially impairs the buyer's chance of obtaining return performance under paragraph (a) unless, and only to the extent that, enforcement of the security interest results in a delegation of a material performance of the seller. Even in that event, the creation, attachment, perfection, and enforcement of the security interest remain effective. However, the seller is liable to the buyer for damages caused by the delegation to the extent that the damages could not reasonably be prevented by the buyer, and a court may grant other appropriate relief, including cancellation of the contract or an injunction against enforcement of the security interest or consummation of the enforcement.

(2)   If the seller or buyer delegates performance of its duties under a contract, the following rules apply:

(a)   A party may perform its duties through a delegate unless otherwise agreed or unless the other party has a substantial interest in having the original promisor perform or control the acts required by the contract. Delegation of performance does not relieve the delegating party of any duty to perform or liability for breach.

(b)   Acceptance of a delegation of duties by the assignee constitutes a promise to perform those duties. The promise is enforceable by either the assignor or the other party to the original contract.

(c)   The other party may treat any delegation of duties as creating reasonable grounds for insecurity and may without prejudice to its rights against the assignor demand assurances from the assignee under Section 2–609.

(d)   A contractual term prohibiting the delegation of duties otherwise delegable under paragraph (a) is enforceable, and an attempted delegation is not effective.

(3)   An assignment of "the contract" or of "all my rights under the contract" or an assignment in similar general terms is an assignment of rights and unless the language or the circumstances, as in an assignment for security, indicate the contrary, it is also a delegation of performance of the duties of the assignor.

(4)   Unless the circumstances indicate the contrary, a prohibition of assignment of "the contract" is to be construed as barring only the delegation to the assignee of the assignor's performance.

§ 2-211. Legal Recognition of Electronic Contracts, Records, and Signatures

(1)   A record or signature may not be denied legal effect or enforceability solely because it is in electronic form.

(2)   A contract may not be denied legal effect or enforceability solely because an electronic record was used in its formation.

(3)   This Article does not require a record or signature to be created, generated, sent, communicated, received, stored, or otherwise processed by electronic means or in electronic form.

(4)   A contract formed by the interaction of an individual and an electronic agent under Section 2-204(4)(b) does not include terms provided by the individual if the individual had reason to know that the agent could not react to the terms as provided.

§ 2-212. Attribution
An electronic record or electronic signature is attributable to a person if it was the act of the person or the person's electronic agent or the person is otherwise legally bound by the act.

§ 2-213. Electronic Communication
(1)   If the receipt of an electronic communication has a legal effect, it has that effect even if no individual is aware of its receipt.
(2)   Receipt of an electronic acknowledgment of an electronic communication establishes that the communication was received but, in itself, does not establish that the content sent corresponds to the content received.

PART 3. GENERAL OBLIGATION AND CONSTRUCTION OF CONTRACT
§ 2-301. General Obligations of Parties
The obligation of the seller is to transfer and deliver and that of the buyer is to accept and pay in accordance with the contract.

§ 2-302. Unconscionable Contract or Term
(1)   If the court as a matter of law finds the contract or any term of the contract to have been unconscionable at the time it was made the court may refuse to enforce the contract, or it may enforce the remainder of the contract without the unconscionable term, or it may so limit the application of any unconscionable term as to avoid any unconscionable result.
(2)   If it is claimed or appears to the court that the contract or any term thereof may be unconscionable the parties shall be afforded a reasonable opportunity to present evidence as to its commercial setting, purpose, and effect to aid the court in making the determination.

§ 2-303. Allocation or Division of Risks
Where this Article allocates a risk or a burden as between the parties "unless otherwise agreed", the agreement may not only shift the allocation but may also divide the risk or burden.

§ 2-304. Price Payable in Money, Goods, Realty, or Otherwise
(1)   The price may be made payable in money or otherwise. If it is payable in whole or in part in goods each party is a seller of the goods that the party is to transfer.
(2)   Even if all or part of the price is payable in an interest in real property the transfer of the goods and the seller's obligations with reference to them are subject to this Article, but not the transfer of the interest in real property or the transferor's obligations in connection therewith.

§ 2-305. Open Price Term
(1)   The parties if they so intend may conclude a contract for sale even if the price is not settled. In such a case the price is a reasonable price at the time for delivery if:
(a)   nothing is said as to price;
(b)   the price is left to be agreed by the parties and they fail to agree; or
(c)   the price is to be fixed in terms of some agreed market or other standard as set or recorded by a third person or agency and it is not so set or recorded.
(2)   A price to be fixed by the seller or by the buyer means a price to be fixed in good faith.
(3)   If a price left to be fixed otherwise than by agreement of the parties fails to be fixed through fault of one party the other may at the party's option treat the contract as cancelled or the party may fix a reasonable price.
(4)   If, however, the parties intend not to be bound unless the price is fixed or agreed and it is not fixed or agreed there is no contract. In such a case the buyer must return any goods already received or if unable to do so must pay their reasonable value at the time of delivery and the seller must return any portion of the price paid on account.

§ 2-306. Output, Requirements and Exclusive Dealings

(1)   A term which measures the quantity by the output of the seller or the requirements of the buyer means such actual output or requirements as may occur in good faith, except that no quantity unreasonably disproportionate to any stated estimate or in the absence of a stated estimate to any normal or otherwise comparable prior output or requirements may be tendered or demanded.

(2)   A lawful agreement by either the seller or the buyer for exclusive dealing in the kind of goods concerned imposes unless otherwise agreed an obligation by the seller to use best efforts to supply the goods and by the buyer to use best efforts to promote their sale.

§ 2-307. Delivery in Single Lot or Several Lots

Unless otherwise agreed all goods called for by a contract for sale must be tendered in a single delivery and payment is due only on such tender but where the circumstances give either party the right to make or demand delivery in lots the price if it can be apportioned may be demanded for each lot.

§ 2-308. Absence of Specified Place for Delivery

Unless otherwise agreed
(a)   the place for delivery of goods is the seller's place of business or if none, the seller's residence; but
(b)   in a contract for sale of identified goods which to the knowledge of the parties at the time of contracting are in some other place, that place is the place for their delivery; and
(c)   documents of title may be delivered through customary banking channels.

§ 2-309. Absence of Specific Time Provisions; Notice of Termination

(1)   The time for shipment or delivery or any other action under a contract if not provided in this Article or agreed upon shall be a reasonable time.

(2)   If the contract provides for successive performances but is indefinite in duration, it is valid for a reasonable time but unless otherwise agreed may be terminated at any time by either party.

(3)   Termination of a contract by one party except on the happening of an agreed event requires that reasonable notification be received by the other party and an agreement dispensing with notification is invalid if its operation would be unconscionable. A term specifying standards for the nature and timing of notice is enforceable if the standards are not manifestly unreasonable.

§ 2-310. Open Time for Payment or Running of Credit; Authority to Ship Under Reservation

Unless otherwise agreed
(a)   payment is due at the time and place at which the buyer is to receive the goods even though the place of shipment is the place of delivery;
(b)   if the seller is required or authorized to send the goods, the seller may ship them under reservation, and may tender the documents of title, but the buyer may inspect the goods after their arrival before payment is due unless the inspection is inconsistent with the terms of the contract (Section 2-513);
(c)   if tender of delivery is agreed to be made by way of documents of title otherwise than by paragraph (b), then payment is due regardless of where the goods are to be received (i) at the time and place at which the buyer is to receive delivery of the tangible documents, or (ii) at the time the buyer is to receive delivery of the electronic documents and at the seller's place of business or if none, the seller's residence; and
(d)   if the seller is required or authorized to ship the goods on credit the credit period runs from the time of shipment but postdating the invoice or delaying its dispatch will correspondingly delay the starting of the credit period.

§ 2-311. Options and Cooperation Respecting Performance

(1)   An agreement for sale which is otherwise sufficiently definite (Section 2-204 (3)) to be a contract is not made invalid by the fact that it leaves particulars of performance to be specified

by one of the parties. Any such specification must be made in good faith and within limits set by commercial reasonableness.

(2)   Unless otherwise agreed, specifications relating to assortment of the goods are at the buyer's option and specifications or arrangements relating to shipment are at the seller's option.

(3)   If the specification would materially affect the other party's performance but is not season-ably made or if one party's cooperation is necessary to the agreed performance of the other but is not seasonably forthcoming, the other party in addition to all other remedies:

(a)   is excused for any resulting delay in that party's performance; and

(b)   may also either proceed to perform in any reasonable manner or after the time for a mate-rial part of that party's performance treat the failure to specify or to cooperate as a breach by failure to deliver or accept the goods.

§ 2-312. Warranty of Title and Against Infringement; Buyer's Obligation Against Infringement

(1)   Subject to subsection (3), there is in a contract for sale a warranty by the seller that:

(a)   the title conveyed shall be good and its transfer rightful and shall not unreasonably expose the buyer to litigation because of any colorable claim to or interest in the goods; and

(b)   the goods shall be delivered free from any security interest or other lien or encumbrance of which the buyer at the time of contracting has no knowledge.

(2)   Unless otherwise agreed, a seller that is a merchant regularly dealing in goods of the kind warrants that the goods shall be delivered free of the rightful claim of any third person by way of infringement or the like but a buyer that furnishes specifications to the seller must hold the seller harmless against any such claim that arises out of compliance with the specifications.

(3)   A warranty under this section may be disclaimed or modified only by specific language or by circumstances that give the buyer reason to know that the seller does not claim title, that the seller is purporting to sell only the right or title as the seller or a third person may have, or that the seller is selling subject to any claims of infringement or the like.

§ 2-313. Express Warranties by Affirmation, Promise, Description, Sample

(1)   In this section, "immediate buyer" means a buyer that enters into a contract with the seller.

(2)   Express warranties by the seller to the immediate buyer are created as follows:

(a)   Any affirmation of fact or promise made by the seller which relates to the goods and be-comes part of the basis of the bargain creates an express warranty that the goods shall conform to the affirmation or promise.

(b)   Any description of the goods which is made part of the basis of the bargain creates an ex-press warranty that the goods shall conform to the description.

(c)   Any sample or model that is made part of the basis of the bargain creates an express warranty that the whole of the goods shall conform to the sample or model.

(3)   It is not necessary to the creation of an express warranty that the seller use formal words such as "warrant" or "guarantee" or that the seller have a specific intention to make a warranty, but an affirmation merely of the value of the goods or a statement purporting to be merely the seller's opinion or commendation of the goods does not create a warranty.

(4)   Any remedial promise made by the seller to the immediate buyer creates an obligation that the promise will be performed upon the happening of the specified event.

§ 2-313A Obligation to Remote Purchaser Created by Record Packaged With or Accompanying Goods

(1)   In this section:

(a)   "Immediate buyer" means a buyer that enters into a contract with the seller.

(b)   "Remote purchaser" means a person that buys or leases goods from an immediate buyer or other person in the normal chain of distribution.

(2)   This section applies only to new goods and goods sold or leased as new goods in a trans-action of purchase in the normal chain of distribution.

(3)   If in a record packaged with or accompanying the goods the seller makes an affirmation of fact or promise that relates to the goods, provides a description that relates to the goods, or

makes a remedial promise, and the seller reasonably expects the record to be, and the record is, furnished to the remote purchaser, the seller has an obligation to the remote purchaser that:
(a) the goods will conform to the affirmation of fact, promise, or description unless a reasonable person in the position of the remote purchaser would not believe that the affirmation of fact, promise, or description created an obligation; and
(b) the seller will perform the remedial promise.
(4) It is not necessary to the creation of an obligation under this section that the seller use formal words such as "warrant" or "guarantee" or that the seller have a specific intention to undertake an obligation, but an affirmation merely of the value of the goods or a statement purporting to be merely the seller's opinion or commendation of the goods does not create an obligation.
(5) The following rules apply to the remedies for breach of an obligation created under this section:
(a) The seller may modify or limit the remedies available to the remote purchaser if the modification or limitation is furnished to the remote purchaser no later than the time of purchase or if the modification or limitation is contained in the record that contains the affirmation of fact, promise, or description.
(b) Subject to a modification or limitation of remedy, a seller in breach is liable for incidental or consequential damages under Section 2-715, but not for lost profits.
(c) The remote purchaser may recover as damages for breach of a seller's obligation arising under subsection (3) the loss resulting in the ordinary course of events as determined in any reasonable manner.
(6) An obligation that is not a remedial promise is breached if the goods did not conform to the affirmation of fact, promise, or description creating the obligation when the goods left the seller's control.

§ 2-313B Obligation to Remote Purchaser Created by Communication to the Public
(1) In this section:
(a) "Immediate buyer" means a buyer that enters into a contract with the seller.
(b) "Remote purchaser" means a person that buys or leases goods from an immediate buyer or other person in the normal chain of distribution.
(2) This section applies only to new goods and goods sold or leased as new goods in a transaction of purchase in the normal chain of distribution.
(3) If in an advertisement or a similar communication to the public a seller makes an affirmation of fact or promise that relates to the goods, provides a description that relates to the goods, or makes a remedial promise, and the remote purchaser enters into a transaction of purchase with knowledge of and with the expectation that the goods will conform to the affirmation of fact, promise, or description, or that the seller will perform the remedial promise, the seller has an obligation to the remote purchaser that:
(a) the goods will conform to the affirmation of fact, promise, or description unless a reasonable person in the position of the remote purchaser would not believe that the affirmation of fact, promise, or description created an obligation; and
(b) the seller will perform the remedial promise.
(4) It is not necessary to the creation of an obligation under this section that the seller use formal words such as "warrant" or "guarantee" or that the seller have a specific intention to undertake an obligation, but an affirmation merely of the value of the goods or a statement purporting to be merely the seller's opinion or commendation of the goods does not create an obligation.
(5) The following rules apply to the remedies for breach of an obligation created under this section:
(a) The seller may modify or limit the remedies available to the remote purchaser if the modification or limitation is furnished to the remote purchaser no later than the time of purchase. The modification or limitation may be furnished as part of the communication that contains the affirmation of fact, promise, or description.

(b)   Subject to a modification or limitation of remedy, a seller in breach is liable for incidental or consequential damages under Section 2-715, but not for lost profits.
(c)   The remote purchaser may recover as damages for breach of a seller's obligation arising under subsection (3) the loss resulting in the ordinary course of events as determined in any reasonable manner.
(6)   An obligation that is not a remedial promise is breached if the goods did not conform to the affirmation of fact, promise, or description creating the obligation when the goods left the seller's control.

§ 2-314. Implied Warranty: Merchantability; Usage of Trade

(1)   Unless excluded or modified (Section 2-316), a warranty that the goods shall be merchantable is implied in a contract for their sale if the seller is a merchant with respect to goods of that kind. Under this section the serving for value of food or drink to be consumed either on the premises or elsewhere is a sale.
(2)   Goods to be merchantable must be at least such as:
(a)   pass without objection in the trade under the contract description;
(b)   in the case of fungible goods, are of fair average quality within the description;
(c)   are fit for the ordinary purposes for which goods of that description are used;
(d)   run, within the variations permitted by the agreement, of even kind, quality and quantity within each unit and among all units involved;
(e)   are adequately contained, packaged, and labeled as the agreement may require; and
(f)   conform to the promise or affirmations of fact made on the container or label if any.
(3)   Unless excluded or modified (Section 2-316) other implied warranties may arise from course of dealing or usage of trade.

§ 2-315. Implied Warranty: Fitness for Particular Purpose

Where the seller at the time of contracting has reason to know any particular purpose for which the goods are required and that the buyer is relying on the seller's skill or judgment to select or furnish suitable goods, there is unless excluded or modified under the next section an implied warranty that the goods shall be fit for such purpose.

§ 2-316. Exclusion or Modification of Warranties

(1)   Words or conduct relevant to the creation of an express warranty and words or conduct tending to negate or limit warranty shall be construed wherever reasonable as consistent with each other; but subject to Section 2-202, negation or limitation is inoperative to the extent that such construction is unreasonable.
(2)   Subject to subsection (3), to exclude or modify the implied warranty of merchantability or any part of it in a consumer contract the language must be in a record, be conspicuous, and state "The seller undertakes no responsibility for the quality of the goods except as otherwise provided in this contract," and in any other contract the language must mention merchantability and in case of a record must be conspicuous. Subject to subsection (3), to exclude or modify the implied warranty of fitness, the exclusion must be in a record and be conspicuous. Language to exclude all implied warranties of fitness in a consumer contract must state "The seller assumes no responsibility that the goods will be fit for any particular purpose for which you may be buying these goods, except as otherwise provided in the contract," and in any other contract the language is sufficient if it states, for example, that "There are no warranties that extend beyond the description on the face hereof." Language that satisfies the requirements of this subsection for the exclusion or modification of a warranty in a consumer contract also satisfies the requirements for any other contract.
(3)   Notwithstanding subsection (2)
(a)   unless the circumstances indicate otherwise, all implied warranties are excluded by expressions like "as is", "with all faults" or other language that in common understanding calls the buyer's attention to the exclusion of warranties, makes plain that there is no implied warranty, and, in a consumer contract evidenced by a record, is set forth conspicuously in the record;

(b)   if the buyer before entering into the contract has examined the goods or the sample or model as fully as desired or has refused to examine the goods after a demand by the seller there is no implied warranty with regard to defects that an examination in the circumstances should have revealed to the buyer; and

(c)   an implied warranty may also be excluded or modified by course of dealing or course of performance or usage of trade.

(4)   Remedies for breach of warranty may be limited in accordance with Sections 2-718 and 2-719.

§ 2-317. Cumulation and Conflict of Warranties Express or Implied

Warranties whether express or implied shall be construed as consistent with each other and as cumulative, but if such construction is unreasonable the intention of the parties shall determine which warranty is dominant. In ascertaining that intention the following rules apply:

(a)   Exact or technical specifications displace an inconsistent sample or model or general language of description.

(b)   A sample from an existing bulk displaces inconsistent general language of description.

(c)   Express warranties displace inconsistent implied warranties other than an implied warranty of fitness for a particular purpose.

§ 2-318. Third Party Beneficiaries of Warranties Express or Implied

(1)   In this section:

(a)   "Immediate buyer" means a buyer that enters into a contract with the seller.

(b)   "Remote purchaser" means a person that buys or leases goods from an immediate buyer or other person in the normal chain of distribution.

Alternative A to subsection (2)

A seller's warranty to an immediate buyer, whether express or implied, a seller's remedial promise to an immediate buyer, or a seller's obligation to a remote purchaser under Section 2-313A or 2-313B extends to any individual who is in the family or household of the immediate buyer or the remote purchaser or who is a guest in the home of either if it is reasonable to expect that the person may use, consume, or be affected by the goods and who is injured in person by breach of the warranty, remedial promise, or obligation. A seller may not exclude or limit the operation of this section.

Alternative B to subsection (2)

A seller's warranty to an immediate buyer, whether express or implied, a seller's remedial promise to an immediate buyer, or a seller's obligation to a remote purchaser under Section 2-313A or 2-313B extends to any individual who may reasonably be expected to use, consume, or be affected by the goods and who is injured in person by breach of the warranty, remedial promise, or obligation. A seller may not exclude or limit the operation of this section.

Alternative C to subsection (2)

A seller's warranty to an immediate buyer, whether express or implied, a seller's remedial promise to an immediate buyer, or a seller's obligation to a remote purchaser under Section 2-313A or 2-313B extends to any person that may reasonably be expected to use, consume, or be affected by the goods and that is injured by breach of the warranty, remedial promise, or obligation. A seller may not exclude or limit the operation of this section with respect to injury to the person of an individual to whom the warranty, remedial promise, or obligation extends. [...]

§ 2-325. "Letter of Credit" Term; "Confirmed Credit"

If the parties agree that the primary method of payment will be by letter of credit, the following rules apply:

(a)   The buyer's obligation to pay is suspended by seasonable delivery to the seller of a letter of credit issued or confirmed by a financing agency of good repute in which the issuer and any confirmer undertake to pay against presentation of documents that evidence delivery of the goods.

(b) Failure of a party seasonably to furnish a letter of credit as agreed is a breach of the contract for sale.
(c) If the letter of credit is dishonored or repudiated, the seller, on seasonable notification, may require payment directly from the buyer.

§ 2-326. Sale on Approval and Sale or Return; Consignment Sales and Rights of Creditors

(1) Unless otherwise agreed, if delivered goods may be returned by the buyer even if they conform to the contract, the transaction is:
(a) a "sale on approval" if the goods are delivered primarily for use; and
(b) a "sale or return" if the goods are delivered primarily for resale.
(2) Goods held on approval are not subject to the claims of the buyer's creditors until acceptance; goods held on sale or return are subject to such claims while in the buyer's possession.
(3) Any "or return" term of a contract for sale is to be treated as a separate contract for sale under Section 2-201 and as contradicting the sale aspect of the contract under Section 2-202.

§ 2-327. Special Incidents of Sale on Approval and Sale or Return

(1) Under a sale on approval unless otherwise agreed
(a) although the goods are identified to the contract the risk of loss and the title do not pass to the buyer until acceptance; and
(b) use of the goods consistent with the purpose of trial is not acceptance but failure seasonably to notify the seller of election to return the goods is acceptance, and if the goods conform to the contract acceptance of any part is acceptance of the whole; and
(c) after due notification of election to return, the return is at the seller's risk and expense but a merchant buyer must follow any reasonable instructions.
(2) Under a sale or return unless otherwise agreed
(a) the option to return extends to the whole or any commercial unit of the goods while in substantially their original condition, but must be exercised seasonably; and
(b) the return is at the buyer's risk and expense.

§ 2-328. Sale by Auction

(1) In a sale by auction, if goods are put up in lots each lot is the subject of a separate sale.
(2) A sale by auction is complete when the auctioneer so announces by the fall of the hammer or in other customary manner. If a bid is made during the process of completing the sale but before a prior bid is accepted, the auctioneer has discretion to reopen the bidding or to declare the goods sold under the prior bid.
(3) A sale by auction is subject to the seller's right to withdraw the goods unless at the time the goods are put up or during the course of the auction it is announced in express terms that the right to withdraw the goods is not reserved. In an auction in which the right to withdraw the goods is reserved, the auctioneer may withdraw the goods at any time until completion of the sale is announced by the auctioneer. In an auction in which the right to withdraw the goods is not reserved, after the auctioneer calls for bids on an article or lot, the article or lot may not be withdrawn unless no bid is made within a reasonable time. In either case a bidder may retract a bid until the auctioneer's announcement of completion of the sale, but a bidder's retraction does not revive any previous bid.
(4) If the auctioneer knowingly receives a bid on the seller's behalf or the seller makes or procures such a bid, and notice has not been given that liberty for such bidding is reserved, the buyer may at the buyer's option avoid the sale or take the goods at the price of the last good faith bid prior to the completion of the sale. This subsection shall not apply to any bid at an auction required by law.

PART 4. TITLE, CREDITORS AND GOOD FAITH PURCHASERS

§ 2-401. Passing of Title; Reservation for Security; Limited Application of this Section

Each provision of this Article with regard to the rights, obligations and remedies of the seller, the buyer, purchasers or other third parties applies irrespective of title to the goods except where the provision refers to such title. Insofar as situations are not covered by the other provisions of this Article and matters concerning title become material the following rules apply:

(1)   Title to goods cannot pass under a contract for sale prior to their identification to the contract (Section 2-501), and unless otherwise explicitly agreed the buyer acquires by their identification a special property as limited by this Act. Any retention or reservation by the seller of the title (property) in goods shipped or delivered to the buyer is limited in effect to a reservation of a security interest. Subject to these provisions and to the provisions of Article 9, title to goods passes from the seller to the buyer in any manner and on any conditions explicitly agreed on by the parties.

(2)   Unless otherwise explicitly agreed title passes to the buyer at the time and place at which the seller completes performance with reference to the physical delivery of the goods, despite any reservation of a security interest and even though a document of title is to be delivered at a different time or place; and in particular and despite any reservation of a security interest by the bill of lading

(a)   if the contract requires or authorizes the seller to send the goods to the buyer but does not require the seller to deliver them at destination, title passes to the buyer at the time and place of shipment; but

(b)   if the contract requires delivery at destination, title passes on tender there.

(3)   Unless otherwise explicitly agreed where delivery is to be made without moving the goods,

(a)   if the seller is to deliver a tangible document of title, title passes at the time when and the place where he delivers such documents and if the seller is to deliver an electronic document of title, title passes when the seller delivers the document; or

(b)   if the goods are at the time of contracting already identified and no documents of title are to be delivered, title passes at the time and place of contracting.

(4)   A rejection or other refusal by the buyer to receive or retain the goods, whether or not justified, or a justified revocation of acceptance revests title to the goods in the seller. Such revesting occurs by operation of law and is not a "sale".

§ 2-402. Rights of Seller's Creditors Against Sold Goods

(1)   Except as provided in subsections (2) and (3), rights of unsecured creditors of the seller with respect to goods which have been identified to a contract for sale are subject to the buyer's rights to recover the goods under this Article (Sections 2-502 and 2-716).

(2)   A creditor of the seller may treat a sale or an identification of goods to a contract for sale as void if as against him a retention of possession by the seller is fraudulent under any rule of law of the state where the goods are situated, except that retention of possession in good faith and current course of trade by a merchant-seller for a commercially reasonable time after a sale or identification is not fraudulent.

(3)   Nothing in this Article shall be deemed to impair the rights of creditors of the seller

(a)   under the provisions of the Article on Secured Transactions (Article 9); or

(b)   where identification to the contract or delivery is made not in current course of trade but in satisfaction of or as security for a pre-existing claim for money, security or the like and is made under circumstances which under any rule of law of the state where the goods are situated would apart from this Article constitute the transaction a fraudulent transfer or voidable preference.

§ 2-403. Power to Transfer; Good Faith Purchase of Goods; "Entrusting"

(1)   A purchaser of goods acquires all title which his transferor had or had power to transfer except that a purchaser of a limited interest acquires rights only to the extent of the interest purchased. A person with voidable title has power to transfer a good title to a good faith purchaser for value. When goods have been delivered under a transaction of purchase the purchaser has such power even though

(a)   the transferor was deceived as to the identity of the purchaser, or

(b)   the delivery was in exchange for a check which is later dishonored, or

(c)   it was agreed that the transaction was to be a "cash sale", or
(d)   the delivery was procured through fraud punishable as larcenous under the criminal law.
(2)   Any entrusting of possession of goods to a merchant that deals in goods of that kind gives him power to transfer all rights of the entruster to a buyer in ordinary course of business.
(3)   "Entrusting" includes any delivery and any acquiescence in retention of possession regardless of any condition expressed between the parties to the delivery or acquiescence and regardless of whether the procurement of the entrusting or the possessor's disposition of the goods have been such as to be larcenous under the criminal law.
[Note: If a state adopts the repealer of Article 6-Bulk Transfers (Alternative A), subsec. (4) should read as follows:]
(4)   The rights of other purchasers of goods and of lien creditors are governed by the Articles on Secured Transactions (Article 9) and Documents of Title (Article 7).
[Note: If a state adopts Revised Article 6-Bulk Sales (Alternative B), subsec. (4) should read as follows:]
(4)   The rights of other purchasers of goods and of lien creditors are governed by the Articles on Secured Transactions (Article 9), Bulk Sales (Article 6) and Documents of Title (Article 7).

PART 5. PERFORMANCE
§ 2-501. Insurable Interest in Goods; Manner of Identification of Goods
(1)   The buyer obtains a special property and an insurable interest in goods by identification of existing goods as goods to which the contract refers even though the goods so identified are non-conforming and he has an option to return or reject them. Such identification can be made at any time and in any manner explicitly agreed to by the parties. In the absence of explicit agreement identification occurs
(a)   when the contract is made if it is for the sale of goods already existing and identified;
(b)   if the contract is for the sale of future goods other than those described in paragraph (c), when goods are shipped, marked or otherwise designated by the seller as goods to which the contract refers;
(c)   when the crops are planted or otherwise become growing crops or the young are conceived if the contract is for the sale of unborn young to be born within twelve months after contracting or for the sale of crops to be harvested within twelve months or the next normal harvest reason after contracting whichever is longer.
(2)   The seller retains an insurable interest in goods so long as title to or any security interest in the goods remains in him and where the identification is by the seller alone he may until default or insolvency or notification to the buyer that the identification is final substitute other goods for those identified.
(3)   Nothing in this section impairs any insurable interest recognized under any other statute or rule of law.

§ 2-502. Buyer's Right to Goods on Seller's Repudiation, Failure to Deliver or Insolvency
(1)   Subject to subsections (2) and (3) and even though the goods have not been shipped a buyer who has paid a part or all of the price of goods in which he has a special property under the provisions of the immediately preceding section may on making and keeping good a tender of any unpaid portion of their price recover them from the seller if:
(a)   in the case of goods bought for personal, family, or household purposes, the seller repudiates or fails to deliver as required by the contract; or
(b)   in other cases, the seller becomes insolvent within ten days after receipt of the first installment on their price.
(2)   The buyer's right to recover the goods under subsection (1)(a) vests upon acquisition of a special property, even if the seller had not then repudiated or failed to deliver.
(3)   If the identification creating his special property has been made by the buyer he acquires the right to recover the goods only if they conform to the contract for sale.

§ 2-503. Manner of Seller's Tender of Delivery

(1)   Tender of delivery requires that the seller put and hold conforming goods at the buyer's disposition and give the buyer any notification reasonably necessary to enable him to take delivery. The manner, time and place for tender are determined by the agreement and this Article, and in particular

(a)   tender must be at a reasonable hour, and if it is of goods they must be kept available for the period reasonably necessary to enable the buyer to take possession; but

(b)   unless otherwise agreed the buyer must furnish facilities reasonably suited to the receipt of the goods.

(2)   Where the case is within the next section respecting shipment tender requires that the seller comply with its provisions.

(3)   Where the seller is required to deliver at a particular destination tender requires that he comply with subsection (1) and also in any appropriate case tender documents as described in subsections (4) and (5) of this section.

(4)   Where goods are in the possession of a bailee and are to be delivered without being moved

(a)   tender requires that the seller either tender a negotiable document of title covering such goods or procure acknowledgment by the bailee of the buyer's right to possession of the goods; but

(b)   tender to the buyer of a non-negotiable document of title or of a record directing the bailee to deliver is sufficient tender unless the buyer seasonably objects, and except as otherwise provided in Article 9 receipt by the bailee of notification of the buyer's rights fixes those rights as against the bailee and all third persons; but risk of loss of the goods and of any failure by the bailee to honor the non-negotiable document of title or to obey the direction remains on the seller until the buyer has had a reasonable time to present the document or direction, and a refusal by the bailee to honor the document or to obey the direction defeats the tender.

(5)   Where the contract requires the seller to deliver documents

(a)   he must tender all such documents in correct form, except as provided in this Article with respect to bills of lading in a set (subsection (2) of Section 2-323); and

(b)   tender through customary banking channels is sufficient and dishonor of a draft accompanying or associated with the documents constitutes non-acceptance or rejection.

§ 2-504. Shipment by Seller

Where the seller is required or authorized to send the goods to the buyer and the contract does not require him to deliver them at a particular destination, then unless otherwise agreed he must

(a)   put the goods in the possession of such a carrier and make such a contract for their transportation as may be reasonable having regard to the nature of the goods and other circumstances of the case; and

(b)   obtain and promptly deliver or tender in due form any document necessary to enable the buyer to obtain possession of the goods or otherwise required by the agreement or by usage of trade; and

(c)   promptly notify the buyer of the shipment.

Failure to notify the buyer under paragraph (c) or to make a proper contract under paragraph (a) is a ground for rejection only if material delay or loss ensues.

§ 2-505. Seller's Shipment Under Reservation

(1)   Where the seller has identified goods to the contract by or before shipment:

(a)   his procurement of a negotiable bill of lading to his own order or otherwise reserves in him a security interest in the goods. His procurement of the bill to the order of a financing agency or of the buyer indicates in addition only the seller's expectation of transferring that interest to the person named.

(b) a non-negotiable bill of lading to himself or his nominee reserves possession of the goods as security but except in a case of conditional delivery (subsection (2) of Section 2-507) a non-negotiable bill of lading naming the buyer as consignee reserves no security interest even though the seller retains possession or control of the bill of lading.

(2)   When shipment by the seller with reservation of a security interest is in violation of the contract for sale it constitutes an improper contract for transportation within the preceding section but impairs neither the rights given to the buyer by shipment and identification of the goods to the contract nor the seller's powers as a holder of a negotiable document of title.

§ 2-506. Rights of Financing Agency

(1)   A financing agency by paying or purchasing for value a draft which relates to a shipment of goods acquires to the extent of the payment or purchase and in addition to its own rights under the draft and any document of title securing it any rights of the shipper in the goods including the right to stop delivery and the shipper's right to have the draft honored by the buyer.

(2)   The right to reimbursement of a financing agency which has in good faith honored or purchased the draft under commitment to or authority from the buyer is not impaired by subsequent discovery of defects with reference to any relevant document which was apparently regular.

§ 2-507. Effect of Seller's Tender; Delivery on Condition

(1)   Tender of delivery is a condition to the buyer's duty to accept the goods and, unless otherwise agreed, to his duty to pay for them. Tender entitles the seller to acceptance of the goods and to payment according to the contract.

(2)   Where payment is due and demanded on the delivery to the buyer of goods or documents of title, his right as against the seller to retain or dispose of them is conditional upon his making the payment due.

§ 2-508. Cure by Seller of Improper Tender or Delivery; Replacement

(1)   Where any tender or delivery by the seller is rejected because non-conforming and the time for performance has not yet expired, the seller may seasonably notify the buyer of his intention to cure and may then within the contract time make a conforming delivery.

(2)   Where the buyer rejects a non-conforming tender which the seller had reasonable grounds to believe would be acceptable with or without money allowance the seller may if he seasonably notifies the buyer have a further reasonable time to substitute a conforming tender.

§ 2-509. Risk of Loss in the Absence of Breach

(1)   Where the contract requires or authorizes the seller to ship the goods by carrier
(a)   if it does not require him to deliver them at a particular destination, the risk of loss passes to the buyer when the goods are duly delivered to the carrier even though the shipment is under reservation (Section 2-505); but
(b)   if it does require him to deliver them at a particular destination and the goods are there duly tendered while in the possession of the carrier, the risk of loss passes to the buyer when the goods are there duly so tendered as to enable the buyer to take delivery.

(2)   Where the goods are held by a bailee to be delivered without being moved, the risk of loss passes to the buyer
(a)   on his receipt of possession or control of a negotiable document of title covering the goods; or
(b)   on acknowledgment by the bailee of the buyer's right to possession of the goods; or
(c)   after his receipt of possession or control of a non-negotiable document of title or other direction to deliver in a record, as provided in subsection (4)(b) of Section 2-503.

(3)   In any case not within subsection (1) or (2), the risk of loss passes to the buyer on his receipt of the goods if the seller is a merchant; otherwise the risk passes to the buyer on tender of delivery.

(4)   The provisions of this section are subject to contrary agreement of the parties and to the provisions of this Article on sale on approval (Section 2-327) and on effect of breach on risk of loss (Section 2-510).

§ 2-510. Effect of Breach on Risk of Loss
(1)   Where a tender or delivery of goods so fails to conform to the contract as to give a right of rejection the risk of their loss remains on the seller until cure or acceptance.
(2)   Where the buyer rightfully revokes acceptance he may to the extent of any deficiency in his effective insurance coverage treat the risk of loss as having rested on the seller from the beginning.
(3)   Where the buyer as to conforming goods already identified to the contract for sale repudiates or is otherwise in breach before risk of their loss has passed to him, the seller may to the extent of any deficiency in his effective insurance coverage treat the risk of loss as resting on the buyer for a commercially reasonable time.

§ 2-511. Tender of Payment by Buyer; Payment by Check
(1)   Unless otherwise agreed tender of payment is a condition to the seller's duty to tender and complete any delivery.
(2)   Tender of payment is sufficient when made by any means or in any manner current in the ordinary course of business unless the seller demands payment in legal tender and gives any extension of time reasonably necessary to procure it.
(3)   Subject to the provisions of this Act on the effect of an instrument on an obligation (Section 3-802), payment by check is conditional and is defeated as between the parties by dishonor of the check on due presentment.

§ 2-512. Payment by Buyer Before Inspection
(1)   Where the contract requires payment before inspection non-conformity of the goods does not excuse the buyer from so making payment unless
(a)   the non-conformity appears without inspection; or
(b)   despite tender of the required documents the circumstances would justify injunction against honor under this Act (Section 5-109(b)).
(2)   Payment pursuant to subsection (1) does not constitute an acceptance of goods or impair the buyer's right to inspect or any of his remedies.

§ 2-513. Buyer's Right to Inspection of Goods
(1)   Unless otherwise agreed and subject to subsection (3), where goods are tendered or delivered or identified to the contract for sale, the buyer has a right before payment or acceptance to inspect them at any reasonable place and time and in any reasonable manner. When the seller is required or authorized to send the goods to the buyer, the inspection may be after their arrival.
(2)   Expenses of inspection must be borne by the buyer but may be recovered from the seller if the goods do not conform and are rejected.
(3)   Unless otherwise agreed and subject to the provisions of this Article on C.I.F. contracts (subsection (3) of Section 2-321), the buyer is not entitled to inspect the goods before payment of the price when the contract provides
(a)   for delivery "C.O.D." or on other like terms; or
(b)   for payment against documents of title, except where such payment is due only after the goods are to become available for inspection.
(4)   A place or method of inspection fixed by the parties is presumed to be exclusive but unless otherwise expressly agreed it does not postpone identification or shift the place for delivery or for passing the risk of loss. If compliance becomes impossible, inspection shall be as provided in this section unless the place or method fixed was clearly intended as an indispensable condition failure of which avoids the contract.

§ 2-514. When Documents Deliverable on Acceptance; When on Payment
Unless otherwise agreed documents against which a draft is drawn are to be delivered to the drawee on acceptance of the draft if it is payable more than three days after presentment; otherwise, only on payment.

§ 2-515. Preserving Evidence of Goods in Dispute

In furtherance of the adjustment of any claim or dispute
(a)   either party on reasonable notification to the other and for the purpose of ascertaining the facts and preserving evidence has the right to inspect, test and sample the goods including such of them as may be in the possession or control of the other; and
(b)   the parties may agree to a third party inspection or survey to determine the conformity or condition of the goods and may agree that the findings shall be binding upon them in any subsequent litigation or adjustment.

PART 6. BREACH, REPUDIATION AND EXCUSE

§ 2-601. Buyer's Rights on Improper Delivery

Subject to the provisions of this Article on breach in installment contracts (Section 2-612) and unless otherwise agreed under the sections on contractual limitations of remedy (Sections 2-718 and 2-719), if the goods or the tender of delivery fail in any respect to conform to the contract, the buyer may *Perfect tender rule*
(a)   reject the whole; or
(b)   accept the whole; or
(c)   accept any commercial unit or units and reject the rest.

§ 2-602. Manner and Effect of Rightful Rejection

(1)   Rejection of goods must be within a reasonable time after their delivery or tender. It is ineffective unless the buyer seasonably notifies the seller.
(2)   Subject to the provisions of the two following sections on rejected goods (Sections 2-603 and 2-604),
(a)   after rejection any exercise of ownership by the buyer with respect to any commercial unit is wrongful as against the seller; and
(b)   if the buyer has before rejection taken physical possession of goods in which he does not have a security interest under the provisions of this Article (subsection (3) of Section 2-711), he is under a duty after rejection to hold them with reasonable care at the seller's disposition for a time sufficient to permit the seller to remove them; but
(c)   the buyer has no further obligations with regard to goods rightfully rejected.
(3)   The seller's rights with respect to goods wrongfully rejected are governed by the provisions of this Article on seller's remedies in general (Section 2-703).

§ 2-603. Merchant Buyer's Duties as to Rightfully Rejected Goods

(1)   Subject to any security interest in the buyer (subsection (3) of Section 2-711), when the seller has no agent or place of business at the market of rejection a merchant buyer is under a duty after rejection of goods in his possession or control to follow any reasonable instructions received from the seller with respect to the goods and in the absence of such instructions to make reasonable efforts to sell them for the seller's account if they are perishable or threaten to decline in value speedily. Instructions are not reasonable if on demand indemnity for expenses is not forthcoming.
(2)   When the buyer sells goods under subsection (1), he is entitled to reimbursement from the seller or out of the proceeds for reasonable expenses of caring for and selling them, and if the expenses include no selling commission then to such commission as is usual in the trade or if there is none to a reasonable sum not exceeding ten per cent on the gross proceeds.
(3)   In complying with this section the buyer is held only to good faith and good faith conduct hereunder is neither acceptance nor conversion nor the basis of an action for damages.

§ 2-604. Buyer's Options as to Salvage of Rightfully Rejected Goods

Subject to the provisions of the immediately preceding section on perishables if the seller gives no instructions within a reasonable time after notification of rejection the buyer may store the rejected goods for the seller's account or reship them to him or resell them for the seller's account with reimbursement as provided in the preceding section. Such action is not acceptance or conversion.

§ 2-605. Waiver of Buyer's Objections by Failure to Particularize

(1)   The buyer's failure to state in connection with rejection a particular defect which is ascertainable by reasonable inspection precludes him from relying on the unstated defect to justify rejection or to establish breach
(a)   where the seller could have cured it if stated seasonably; or
(b)   between merchants when the seller has after rejection made a request in writing for a full and final written statement of all defects on which the buyer proposes to rely.
(2)   Payment against documents made without reservation of rights precludes recovery of the payment for defects apparent in the documents.

§ 2-606. What Constitutes Acceptance of Goods

(1)   Acceptance of goods occurs when the buyer
(a)   after a reasonable opportunity to inspect the goods signifies to the seller that the goods are conforming or that he will take or retain them in spite of their non-conformity; or
(b)   fails to make an effective rejection (subsection (1) of Section 2-602), but such acceptance does not occur until the buyer has had a reasonable opportunity to inspect them; or
(c)   does any act inconsistent with the seller's ownership; but if such act is wrongful as against the seller it is an acceptance only if ratified by him.
(2)   Acceptance of a part of any commercial unit is acceptance of that entire unit.

§ 2-607. Effect of Acceptance; Notice of Breach; Burden of Establishing Breach After Acceptance; Notice of Claim or Litigation to Person Answerable Over

(1)   The buyer must pay at the contract rate for any goods accepted.
(2)   Acceptance of goods by the buyer precludes rejection of the goods accepted and if made with knowledge of a non-conformity cannot be revoked because of it unless the acceptance was on the reasonable assumption that the non-conformity would be seasonably cured but acceptance does not of itself impair any other remedy provided by this Article for non-conformity.
(3)   Where a tender has been accepted
(a)   the buyer must within a reasonable time after he discovers or should have discovered any breach notify the seller of breach or be barred from any remedy; and
(b)   if the claim is one for infringement or the like (subsection (3) of Section 2-312) and the buyer is sued as a result of such a breach he must so notify the seller within a reasonable time after he receives notice of the litigation or be barred from any remedy over for liability established by the litigation.
(4)   The burden is on the buyer to establish any breach with respect to the goods accepted.
(5)   Where the buyer is sued for breach of a warranty or other obligation for which his seller is answerable over
(a)   he may give his seller written notice of the litigation. If the notice states that the seller may come in and defend and that if the seller does not do so he will be bound in any action against him by his buyer by any determination of fact common to the two litigations, then unless the seller after seasonable receipt of the notice does come in and defend he is so bound.
(b)   if the claim is one for infringement or the like (subsection (3) of Section 2-312) the original seller may demand in writing that his buyer turn over to him control of the litigation including settlement or else be barred from any remedy over and if he also agrees to bear all expense and to satisfy any adverse judgment, then unless the buyer after seasonable receipt of the demand does turn over control the buyer is so barred.
(6)   The provisions of subsections (3), (4) and (5) apply to any obligation of a buyer to hold the seller harmless against infringement or the like (subsection (3) of Section 2-312).

§ 2-608. Revocation of Acceptance in Whole or in Part

(1)   The buyer may revoke his acceptance of a lot or commercial unit whose non-conformity substantially impairs its value to him if he has accepted it

(a)   on the reasonable assumption that its non-conformity would be cured and it has not been seasonably cured; or

(b)   without discovery of such non-conformity if his acceptance was reasonably induced either by the difficulty of discovery before acceptance or by the seller's assurances.

(2)   Revocation of acceptance must occur within a reasonable time after the buyer discovers or should have discovered the ground for it and before any substantial change in condition of the goods which is not caused by their own defects. It is not effective until the buyer notifies the seller of it.

(3)   A buyer who so revokes has the same rights and duties with regard to the goods involved as if he had rejected them.

(4)   If a buyer uses the goods after a rightful rejection or justifiable revocation of acceptance, the following rules apply:

(a)   Any use by the buyer that is unreasonable under the circumstances is wrongful as against the seller and is an acceptance only if ratified by the seller.

(b)   Any use of the goods that is reasonable under the circumstances is not wrongful as against the seller and is not an acceptance, but in an appropriate case the buyer is obligated to the seller for the value of the use to the buyer.

§ 2-609. Right to Adequate Assurance of Performance

(1)   A contract for sale imposes an obligation on each party that the other's expectation of receiving due performance will not be impaired. When reasonable grounds for insecurity arise with respect to the performance of either party the other may in writing demand adequate assurance of due performance and until he receives such assurance may if commercially reasonable suspend any performance for which he has not already received the agreed return.

(2)   Between merchants the reasonableness of grounds for insecurity and the adequacy of any assurance offered shall be determined according to commercial standards.

(3)   Acceptance of any improper delivery or payment does not prejudice the aggrieved party's right to demand adequate assurance of future performance.

(4)   After receipt of a justified demand failure to provide within a reasonable time not exceeding thirty days such assurance of due performance
as is adequate under the circumstances of the particular case is a repudiation of the contract.

§ 2-610. Anticipatory Repudiation

When either party repudiates the contract with respect to a performance not yet due the loss of which will substantially impair the value of the contract to the other, the aggrieved party may

(a)   for a commercially reasonable time await performance by the repudiating party; or

(b)   resort to any remedy for breach (Section 2-703 or Section 2-711), even though he has notified the repudiating party that he would await the latter's performance and has urged retraction; and

(c)   in either case suspend his own performance or proceed in accordance with the provisions of this Article on the seller's right to identify goods to the contract notwithstanding breach or to salvage unfinished goods (Section 2-704).

§ 2-611. Retraction of Anticipatory Repudiation

(1)   Until the repudiating party's next performance is due he can retract his repudiation unless the aggrieved party has since the repudiation cancelled or materially changed his position or otherwise indicated that he considers the repudiation final.

(2)   Retraction may be by any method which clearly indicates to the aggrieved party that the repudiating party intends to perform, but must include any assurance justifiably demanded under the provisions of this Article (Section 2-609).

(3)   Retraction reinstates the repudiating party's rights under the contract with due excuse and allowance to the aggrieved party for any delay occasioned by the repudiation.

§ 2-612. "Installment Contract"; Breach

(1)   An "installment contract" is one which requires or authorizes the delivery of goods in separate lots to be separately accepted, even though the contract contains a clause "each delivery is a separate contract" or its equivalent.

(2)   The buyer may reject any installment which is non-conforming if the non-conformity substantially impairs the value of that installment and cannot be cured or if the non-conformity is a defect in the required documents; but if the non-conformity does not fall within subsection (3) and the seller gives adequate assurance of its cure the buyer must accept that installment.

(3)   Whenever non-conformity or default with respect to one or more installments substantially impairs the value of the whole contract there is a breach of the whole. But the aggrieved party reinstates the contract if he accepts a non-conforming installment without seasonably notifying of cancellation or if he brings an action with respect only to past installments or demands performance as to future installments.

§ 2-613. Casualty to Identified Goods

Where the contract requires for its performance goods identified when the contract is made, and the goods suffer casualty without fault of either party before the risk of loss passes to the buyer, or in a proper case under a "no arrival, no sale" term (Section 2-324) then

(a)   if the loss is total the contract is avoided; and

(b)   if the loss is partial or the goods have so deteriorated as no longer to conform to the contract the buyer may nevertheless demand inspection and at his option either treat the contract as avoided or accept the goods with due allowance from the contract price for the deterioration or the deficiency in quantity but without further right against the seller.

§ 2-614. Substituted Performance

(1)   Where without fault of either party the agreed berthing, loading, or unloading facilities fail or an agreed type of carrier becomes unavailable or the agreed manner of delivery otherwise becomes commercially impracticable but a commercially reasonable substitute is available, such substitute performance must be tendered and accepted.

(2)   If the agreed means or manner of payment fails because of domestic or foreign governmental regulation, the seller may withhold or stop delivery unless the buyer provides a means or manner of payment which is commercially a substantial equivalent. If delivery has already been taken, payment by the means or in the manner provided by the regulation discharges the buyer's obligation unless the regulation is discriminatory, oppressive or predatory.

§ 2-615. Excuse by Failure of Presupposed Conditions

Except so far as a seller may have assumed a greater obligation and subject to the preceding section on substituted performance:

(a)   Delay in delivery or non-delivery in whole or in part by a seller that complies with paragraphs (b) and (c) is not a breach of his duty under a contract for sale if performance as agreed has been made impracticable by the occurrence of a contingency the non-occurrence of which was a basic assumption on which the contract was made or by compliance in good faith with any applicable foreign or domestic governmental regulation or order whether or not it later proves to be invalid.

(b)   Where the causes mentioned in paragraph (a) affect only a part of the seller's capacity to perform, he must allocate production and deliveries among his customers but may at his option include regular customers not then under contract as well as his own requirements for further manufacture. He may so allocate in any manner which is fair and reasonable.

(c)   The seller must notify the buyer seasonably that there will be delay or non-delivery and, when allocation is required under paragraph (b), of the estimated quota thus made available for the buyer.

§ 2-616. Procedure on Notice Claiming Excuse
(1)   Where the buyer receives notification of a material or indefinite delay or an allocation justi-fied under the preceding section he may by written notification to the seller as to any delivery concerned, and where the prospective deficiency substantially impairs the value of the whole contract under the provisions of this Article relating to breach of installment contracts (Section 2-612), then also as to the whole,
(a)   terminate and thereby discharge any unexecuted portion of the contract; or
(b)   modify the contract by agreeing to take his available quota in substitution.
(2)   If after receipt of such notification from the seller the buyer fails so to modify the contract within a reasonable time not exceeding thirty days the contract lapses with respect to any deliveries affected.
(3)   The provisions of this section may not be negated by agreement except in so far as the sel-ler has assumed a greater obligation under the preceding sections.

PART 7. REMEDIES
§ 2-701. Remedies for Breach of Collateral Contracts Not Impaired
Remedies for breach of any obligation or promise collateral or ancillary to a contract for sale are not impaired by the provisions of this Article.

§ 2-702. Seller's Remedies on Discovery of Buyer's Insolvency
(1)   Where the seller discovers the buyer to be insolvent he may refuse delivery except for cash including payment for all goods theretofore delivered under the contract, and stop delivery under this Article (Section 2-705).
(2)   Where the seller discovers that the buyer has received goods on credit while insolvent, the seller may reclaim the goods upon demand made within a reasonable time after the buyer's re-ceipt of the goods. Except as provided in this subsection, the seller may not base a right to reclaim goods on the buyer's fraudulent or innocent misrepresentation of solvency or of intent to pay.
(3)   The seller's right to reclaim under subsection (2) is subject to the rights of a buyer in ordina-ry course of business or other good-faith purchaser for value under Section 2-403. Successful reclamation of goods excludes all other remedies with respect to them.

§ 2-703. Seller's Remedies in General
(1)   A breach of contract by the buyer includes the buyer's wrongful rejection or wrongful attempt to revoke acceptance of goods, wrongful failure to perform a contractual obligation, failure to make a payment when due, and repudiation.
(2)   If the buyer is in breach of contract the seller, to the extent provided for by this Act or other law, may:
(a)   withhold delivery of such goods;
(b)   stop delivery of the goods under Section 2-705;
(c)   proceed under Section 2-704 with respect to goods unidentified to the contract or un-finished;
(d)   reclaim the goods under Section 2-507(2) or 2-702(2);
(e)   require payment directly from the buyer under Section 2-325(c);
(f)   cancel;
(g)   resell and recover damages under Section 2-706;
(h)   recover damages for non-acceptance or repudiation under (Section 2-708(1) or in a proper case the price (Section 2-709);
(j)   recover the price under Section 2-709;
(k)   obtain specific performance under Section 2-716;
(l)   recover liquidated damages under Section 2-718;
(m) in other cases, recover damages in any manner that is reasonable under the circumstances.
(3)   If the buyer becomes insolvent, the seller may:
(a)   withhold delivery under Section 2-702(1);
(b)   stop delivery of the goods under Section 2-705;

(c)   reclaim the goods under Section 2-702(2).

§ 2-704. Seller's Right to Identify Goods to the Contract Notwithstanding Breach or to Salvage Unfinished Goods

(1)   An aggrieved seller under the preceding section may

(a)   identify to the contract conforming goods not already identified if at the time he learned of the breach they are in his possession or control;

(b)   treat as the subject of resale goods which have demonstrably been intended for the particular contract even though those goods are unfinished.

(2)   Where the goods are unfinished an aggrieved seller may in the exercise of reasonable commercial judgment for the purposes of avoiding loss and of effective realization either complete the manufacture and wholly identify the goods to the contract or cease manufacture and resell for scrap or salvage value or proceed in any other reasonable manner.

§ 2-705. Seller's Stoppage of Delivery in Transit or Otherwise

(1)   The seller may stop delivery of goods in the possession of a carrier or other bailee when he discovers the buyer to be insolvent (Section 2-702) or if the buyer repudiates or fails to make a payment due before delivery or if for any other reason the seller has a right to withhold or reclaim the goods.

(2)   As against such buyer the seller may stop delivery until

(a)   receipt of the goods by the buyer; or

(b)   acknowledgment to the buyer by any bailee of the goods except a carrier that the bailee holds the goods for the buyer; or

(c)   such acknowledgment to the buyer by a carrier by reshipment or as a warehouse; or

(d)   negotiation to the buyer of any negotiable document of title covering the goods.

(3)(a) To stop delivery the seller must so notify as to enable the bailee by reasonable diligence to prevent delivery of the goods.

(b)   After such notification the bailee must hold and deliver the goods according to the directions of the seller but the seller is liable to the bailee for any ensuing charges or damages.

(c)   If a negotiable document of title has been issued for goods the bailee is not obliged to obey a notification to stop until surrender of possession or control of the document.

(d)   A carrier that has issued a non-negotiable bill of lading is not obliged to obey a notification to stop received from a person other than the consignor.

§ 2-706. Seller's Resale Including Contract for Resale

(1)   Under the conditions stated in Section 2-703 on seller's remedies, the seller may resell the goods concerned or the undelivered balance thereof. Where the resale is made in good faith and in a commercially reasonable manner the seller may recover the difference between the resale price and the contract price together with any incidental damages allowed under the provisions of this Article (Section 2-710), but less expenses saved in consequence of the buyer's breach.

(2)   Except as otherwise provided in subsection (3) or unless otherwise agreed resale may be at public or private sale including sale by way of one or more contracts to sell or of identification to an existing contract of the seller. Sale may be as a unit or in parcels and at any time and place and on any terms but every aspect of the sale including the method, manner, time, place and terms must be commercially reasonable. The resale must be reasonably identified as referring to the broken contract, but it is not necessary that the goods be in existence or that any or all of them have been identified to the contract before the breach.

(3)   Where the resale is at private sale the seller must give the buyer reasonable notification of his intention to resell.

(4)   Where the resale is at public sale

(a)   only identified goods can be sold except where there is a recognized market for a public sale of futures in goods of the kind; and

(b) it must be made at a usual place or market for public sale if one is reasonably available and except in the case of goods which are perishable or threaten to decline in value speedily the seller must give the buyer reasonable notice of the time and place of the resale; and

(c) if the goods are not to be within the view of those attending the sale the notification of sale must state the place where the goods are located and provide for their reasonable inspection by prospective bidders; and

(d) the seller may buy.

(5) A purchaser that buys in good faith at a resale takes the goods free of any rights of the original buyer even though the seller fails to comply with one or more of the requirements of this section.

(6) The seller is not accountable to the buyer for any profit made on any resale. A person in the position of a seller (Section 2-707) or a buyer that has rightfully rejected or justifiably revoked acceptance must account for any excess over the amount of his security interest, as hereinafter defined (subsection (3) of Section 2-711).

§ 2-707. "Person in the Position of a Seller"

(1) A "person in the position of a seller" includes as against a principal an agent that has paid or become responsible for the price of goods on behalf of his principal or anyone that otherwise holds a security interest or other right in goods similar to that of a seller.

(2) A person in the position of a seller has the same remedies as a seller under this Article.

§ 2-708. Seller's Damages for Non-Acceptance or Repudiation

(1) Subject to subsection (2) and to Section 2-723:

(a) the measure of damages for nonacceptance by the buyer is the difference between the contract price and the market price at the time and place for tender together with any incidental or consequential damages provided in Section 2-710, but less expenses saved in consequence of the buyer's breach; and

(b) the measure of damages for repudiation by the buyer is the difference between the con- tract price and the market price at the place for tender at the expiration of a commercially reasonable time after the seller learned of the repudiation, but no later than the time stated in paragraph (a), together with any incidental or consequential damages provided in Sec- tion 2-710, less expenses saved in consequence of the buyer's breach.

(2) If the measure of damages provided in subsection (1) is inadequate to put the seller in as good a position as performance would have done then the measure of damages is the profit (including reasonable overhead) which the seller would have made from full performance by the buyer, together with any incidental damages provided in this Article (Section 2-710), due allowance for costs reasonably incurred and due credit for payments or proceeds of resale.

§ 2-709. Action for the Price

(1) When the buyer fails to pay the price as it becomes due the seller may recover, together with any incidental damages under the next section, the price

(a) of goods accepted or of conforming goods lost or damaged within a commercially reason- able time after risk of their loss has passed to the buyer; and

(b) of goods identified to the contract if the seller is unable after reasonable effort to resell them at a reasonable price or the circumstances reasonably indicate that such effort will be unavailing.

(2) Where the seller sues for the price he must hold for the buyer any goods which have been identified to the contract and are still in his control except that if resale becomes possible he may resell them at any time prior to the collection of the judgment. The net proceeds of any such resale must be credited to the buyer and payment of the judgment entitles him to any goods not resold.

(3) After the buyer has wrongfully rejected or revoked acceptance of the goods or has failed to make a payment due or has repudiated (Section 2-610), a seller that is held not entitled to the

price under this section shall nevertheless be awarded damages for non-acceptance under the preceding section.

§ 2-710. Seller's Incidental Damages

(1)   Incidental damages to an aggrieved seller include any commercially reasonable charges, expenses or commissions incurred in stopping delivery, in the transportation, care and custody of goods after the buyer's breach, in connection with return or resale of the goods or otherwise resulting from the breach.

(2)   Consequential damages resulting from the buyer's breach include any loss resulting from general or particular requirements and needs of which the buyer at the time of contracting had reason to know and which could not reasonably be prevented by resale or otherwise.

(3)   In a consumer contract, a seller may not recover consequential damages from a consumer.

§ 2-711. Buyer's Remedies in General; Buyer's Security Interest in Rejected Goods

(1)   A breach of contract by the seller includes the seller's wrongful failure to deliver or to perform a contractual obligation, making of a nonconforming tender of delivery or performance, and repudiation.

(2)   If the seller is in breach of contract under subsection (1), the buyer, to the extent provided for by this Act or other law, may:

(a)   in the case of rightful cancellation, rightful rejection, or justifiable revocation of acceptance, recover so much of the price as has been paid;

(b)   deduct damages from any part of the price still due under Section 2-717;

(c)   cancel;

(d)   cover and have damages under Section 2-712 as to all goods affected whether or not they have been identified to the contract;

(e)   recover damages for non-delivery or repudiation under Section 2-713;

(f)   recover damages for breach with regard to accepted goods or breach with regard to a remedial promise under Section 2-714;

(g)   recover identified goods under Section 2-502;

(h)   obtain specific performance or obtain the goods by replevin or similar remedy under Section 2-716;

(i)   recover liquidated damages under Section 2-718;

(j)   in other cases, recover damages in any manner that is reasonable under the circumstances.

(3)   On rightful rejection or justifiable revocation of acceptance a buyer has a security interest in goods in his possession or control for any payments made on their price and any expenses reasonably incurred in their inspection, receipt, transportation, care and custody and may hold such goods and resell them in like manner as an aggrieved seller (Section 2-706).

§ 2-712. "Cover"; Buyer's Procurement of Substitute Goods

(1)   If the seller wrongfully fails to deliver or repudiates or the buyer rightfully rejects or justifiably revokes acceptance, the buyer may "cover" by making in good faith and without unreasonable delay any reasonable purchase of or contract to purchase goods in substitution for those due from the seller.

(2)   The buyer may recover from the seller as damages the difference between the cost of cover and the contract price together with any incidental or consequential damages as hereinafter defined (Section 2-715), but less expenses saved in consequence of the seller's breach.

(3)   Failure of the buyer to effect cover within this section does not bar him from any other remedy.

§ 2-713. Buyer's Damages for Non-Delivery or Repudiation

(1)   Subject to Section 2-723, if the seller wrongfully fails to deliver or repudiates or the buyer rightfully rejects or justifiably revokes acceptance:

(a)   the measure of damages in the case of wrongful failure to deliver by the seller or rightful rejection or justifiable revocation of acceptance by the buyer is the difference between the market price at the time for tender under the contract and the contract price together with any incidental or consequential damages under Section 2-715, but less expenses saved in consequence of the seller's breach; and

(b)   the measure of damages for repudiation by the seller is the difference between the market price at the expiration of a commercially reasonable time after the buyer learned of the repudiation, but no later than the time stated in paragraph (a), and the contract price together with any incidental or consequential damages provided in this Article (Section 2–715), less expenses saved in consequence of the seller's breach.

(2)   Market price is to be determined as of the place for tender or, in cases of rejection after arrival or revocation of acceptance, as of the place of arrival.

§ 2-714. Buyer's Damages for Breach in Regard to Accepted Goods

(1)   Where the buyer has accepted goods and given notification (subsection (3) of Section 2-607) he may recover as damages for any non-conformity of tender the loss resulting in the ordinary course of events from the seller's breach as determined in any manner which is reasonable.

(2)   The measure of damages for breach of warranty is the difference at the time and place of acceptance between the value of the goods accepted and the value they would have had if they had been as warranted, unless special circumstances show proximate damages of a different amount.

(3)   In a proper case any incidental and consequential damages under the next section may also be recovered.

§ 2-715. Buyer's Incidental and Consequential Damages

(1)   Incidental damages resulting from the seller's breach include expenses reasonably incurred in inspection, receipt, transportation and care and custody of goods rightfully rejected, any commercially reasonable charges, expenses or commissions in connection with effecting cover and any other reasonable expense incident to the delay or other breach.

(2)   Consequential damages resulting from the seller's breach include

(a)   any loss resulting from general or particular requirements and needs of which the seller at the time of contracting had reason to know and which could not reasonably be prevented by cover or otherwise; and

(b)   injury to person or property proximately resulting from any breach of warranty.

§ 2-716. Buyer's Right to Specific Performance or Replevin

(1)   Specific performance may be decreed if the goods are unique or in other proper circumstances. In a contract other than a consumer contract, specific performance may be decreed if the parties have agreed to that remedy. However, even if the parties agree to specific performance, specific performance may not be decreed if the breaching party's sole remaining contractual obligation is the payment of money.

(2)   The decree for specific performance may include such terms and conditions as to payment of the price, damages, or other relief as the court may deem just.

(3)   The buyer has a right of replevin or similar remedy for goods identified to the contract if after reasonable effort the buyer is unable to effect cover for such goods or the circumstances reasonably indicate that such effort will be unavailing or if the goods have been shipped under reservation and satisfaction of the security interest in them has been made or tendered.

(4)   The buyer's right under subsection (3) vests upon acquisition of a special property, even if the seller had not then repudiated or failed to deliver.

§ 2-717. Deduction of Damages from the Price

The buyer on notifying the seller of his intention to do so may deduct all or any part of the damages resulting from any breach of the contract from any part of the price still due under the same contract.

§ 2-718. Liquidation or Limitation of Damages; Deposits

(1)   Damages for breach by either party may be liquidated in the agreement but only at an amount which is reasonable in the light of the anticipated or actual harm caused by the breach, the difficulties of proof of loss, and the inconvenience or non-feasibility of otherwise obtaining

an adequate remedy. Section 2-719 determines the enforceability of a term that limits but does not liquidate damages.

(2)   If the seller justifiably withholds delivery of goods or stops performance because of the buyer's breach or insolvency, the buyer is entitled to restitution of any amount by which the sum of the buyer's payments exceeds the amount to which the seller is entitled by virtue of terms liquidating the seller's damages in accordance with subsection (1)

(a)   the amount to which the seller is entitled by virtue of terms liquidating the seller's damages in accordance with subsection (1), or

(b)   in the absence of such terms, twenty per cent of the value of the total performance for which the buyer is obligated under the contract or $500, whichever is smaller.

(3)   The buyer's right to restitution under subsection (2) is subject to offset to the extent that the seller establishes:

(a)   a right to recover damages under the provisions of this Article other than subsection (1), and

(b)   the amount or value of any benefits received by the buyer directly or indirectly by reason of the contract.

(4)   Where a seller has received payment in goods their reasonable value or the proceeds of their resale shall be treated as payments for the purposes of subsection (2); but if the seller has notice of the buyer's breach before reselling goods received in part performance, his resale is subject to the conditions laid down in this Article on resale by an aggrieved seller (Section 2-706).

§ 2-719. Contractual Modification or Limitation of Remedy

(1)   Subject to the provisions of subsections (2) and (3) of this section and of the preceding section on liquidation and limitation of damages,

(a)   the agreement may provide for remedies in addition to or in substitution for those provided in this Article and may limit or alter the measure of damages recoverable under this Article, as by limiting the buyer's remedies to return of the goods and repayment of the price or to repair and replacement of non-conforming goods or parts; and

(b)   resort to a remedy as provided is optional unless the remedy is expressly agreed to be exclusive, in which case it is the sole remedy.

(2)   Where circumstances cause an exclusive or limited remedy to fail of its essential purpose, remedy may be had as provided in this Act.

(3)   Consequential damages may be limited or excluded unless the limitation or exclusion is unconscionable. Limitation of consequential damages for injury to the person in the case of consumer goods is prima facie unconscionable but limitation of damages where the loss is commercial is not.

§ 2-720. Effect of "Cancellation" or "Rescission" on Claims for Antecedent Breach

Unless the contrary intention clearly appears, expressions of "cancellation" or "rescission" of the contract or the like shall not be construed as a renunciation or discharge of any claim in damages for an antecedent breach.

§ 2-721. Remedies for Fraud

Remedies for material misrepresentation or fraud include all remedies available under this Article for non-fraudulent breach. Neither rescission or a claim for rescission of the contract for sale nor rejection or return of the goods shall bar or be deemed inconsistent with a claim for damages or other remedy.

§ 2-722. Who Can Sue Third Parties for Injury to Goods

Where a third party so deals with goods which have been identified to a contract for sale as to cause actionable injury to a party to that contract

(a)   a right of action against the third party is in either party to the contract for sale that has title to or a security interest or a special property or an insurable interest in the goods; and if the goods have been destroyed or converted a right of action is also in the party that either bore the risk of loss under the contract for sale or has since the injury assumed that risk as against the other;

(b) if at the time of the injury the party plaintiff did not bear the risk of loss as against the other party to the contract for sale and there is no arrangement between them for disposition of the recovery, his suit or settlement is, subject to his own interest, as a fiduciary for the other party to the contract;

(c) either party may with the consent of the other sue for the benefit of which it may concern.

§ 2-723. Proof of Market Price: Time and Place

(1) If evidence of a price prevailing at the times or places described in this Article is not readily available the price prevailing within any reasonable time before or after the time described or at any other place which in commercial judgment or under usage of trade would serve as a reasonable substitute for the one described may be used, making any proper allowance for the cost of transporting the goods to or from such other place.

(2) Evidence of a relevant price prevailing at a time or place other than the one described in this Article offered by one party is not admissible unless and until he has given the other party such notice as the court finds sufficient to prevent unfair surprise.

§ 2-724. Admissibility of Market Quotations

Whenever the prevailing price or value of any goods regularly bought and sold in any established commodity market is in issue, reports in official publications or trade journals or in newspapers or periodicals of general circulation published as the reports of such market shall be admissible in evidence. The circumstances of the preparation of such a report may be shown to affect its weight but not its admissibility.

§ 2-725. Statute of Limitations in Contracts for Sale

(1) Except as otherwise provided in this section, an action for breach of any contract for sale must be commenced within the later of four years after the right of action has accrued under subsection (2) or (3) or one year after the breach was or should have been discovered, but no longer than five years after the right of action accrued. By the original agreement the parties may reduce the period of limitation to not less than one year but may not extend it. However, in a consumer contract, the period of limitation may not be reduced.

(2) Except as otherwise provided in subsection (3), the following rules apply:

(a) Except as otherwise provided in this subsection, a right of action for breach of a contract accrues when the breach occurs, even if the aggrieved party did not have knowledge of the breach.

(b) For breach of a contract by repudiation, a right of action accrues at the earlier of when the aggrieved party elects to treat the repudiation as a breach or when a commercially reasonable time for awaiting performance has expired.

(c) For breach of a remedial promise, a right of action accrues when the remedial promise is not performed when performance is due.

(d) In an action by a buyer against a person that is answerable over to the buyer for a claim asserted against the buyer, the buyer's right of action against the person answerable over accrues at the time the claim was originally asserted against the buyer.

(3) If a breach of a warranty arising under Section 2-312, 2-313(2), 2-314, or 2-315, or a breach of an obligation, other than a remedial promise, arising under Section 2-313A or 2-313B, is claimed, the following rules apply:

(a) Except as otherwise provided in paragraph (c), a right of action for breach of a warranty arising under Section 2-313(2), 2-314, or 2-315 accrues when the seller has tendered delivery to the immediate buyer, as defined in Section 2-313, and has completed performance of any agreed installation or assembly of the goods.

(b) Except as otherwise provided in paragraph (c), a right of action for breach of an obligation, other than a remedial promise, arising under Section 2-313A or 2-313B accrues when the remote purchaser, as defined in Section 2-313A or 2-313B, receives the goods.

(c) If a warranty arising under Section 2-313(2) or an obligation, other than a remedial promise, arising under Section 2-313A or 2-313B explicitly extends to future performance of the goods and discovery of the breach must await the time for performance, the right of action accrues when the immediate buyer as defined in Section 2-313 or the remote purchaser as defined in Section 2-313A or 2-313B discovers or should have discovered the breach.

(d) A right of action for breach of warranty arising under Section 2-312 accrues when the aggrieved party discovers or should have discovered the breach. However, an action for breach of the warranty of non-infringement may not be commenced more than six years after tender of delivery of the goods to the aggrieved party.

(4) Where an action commenced within the time limited by subsection (1) is so terminated as to leave available a remedy by another action for the same breach such other action may be commenced after the expiration of the time limited and within six months after the termination of the first action unless the termination resulted from voluntary discontinuance or from dismissal for failure or neglect to prosecute.

(5) This section does not alter the law on tolling of the statute of limitations nor does it apply to causes of action which have accrued before this Act becomes effective.

ARTICLE 7 - DOCUMENTS OF TITLE
PART 1. GENERAL
§ 7-101. Short Title

This Article may be cited as Uniform Commercial Code-Documents of Title.

§ 7-102. Definitions and Index of Definitions

(a) In this Article, unless the context otherwise requires:

(1) "Bailee" means a person that by a warehouse receipt, bill of lading, or other document of title acknowledges possession of goods and contracts to deliver them.

(2) "Carrier" means a person that issues a bill of lading.

(3) "Consignee" means a person named in a bill of lading to which or to whose order the bill promises delivery.

(4) "Consignor" means a person named in a bill of lading as the person from which the goods have been received for shipment.

(5) "Delivery order" means a record that contains an order to deliver goods directed to a warehouse, carrier, or other person that in the ordinary course of business issues warehouse receipts or bills of lading.

(6) "Good faith" means honesty in fact and the observance of reasonable commercial standards of fair dealing.

(7) "Goods" means all things that are treated as movable for the purposes of a contract for storage or transportation.

(8) "Issuer" means a bailee that issues a document of title or, in the case of an unaccepted delivery order, the person that orders the possessor of goods to deliver. The term includes a person for which an agent or employee purports to act in issuing a document if the agent or employee has real or apparent authority to issue documents, even if the issuer did not receive any goods, the goods were misdescribed, or in any other respect the agent or employee violated the issuer's instructions.

(9) "Person entitled under the document" means the holder, in the case of a negotiable document of title, or the person to which delivery of the goods is to be made by the terms of, or pursuant to instructions in a record under, a nonnegotiable document of title.

(10) "Record" means information that is inscribed on a tangible medium or that is stored in an electronic or other medium and is retrievable in perceivable form.

(11) "Sign" means, with present intent to authenticate or adopt a record:
    (A) to execute or adopt a tangible symbol; or
    (B) to attach to or logically associate with the record an electronic sound, symbol, or process.

(12) "Shipper" means a person that enters into a contract of transportation with a carrier.

(13) "Warehouse" means a person engaged in the business of storing goods for hire.

(b) Definitions in other articles applying to this Article and the sections in which they appear are:

(1) "Contract for sale", Section 2-106.

(2) "Lessee in ordinary course of business", Section 2A-103.

(3) "Receipt" of goods, Section 2-103.

(c) In addition, Article 1 contains general definitions and principles of construction and interpretation applicable throughout this article.

§ 7-103. Relation of Article to Treaty or Statute

(a) This Article is subject to any treaty or statute of the United States or a regulatory statute of this State to the extent the treaty, statute, or regulatory statute is applicable.

(b) This Article does not repeal or modify any law prescribing the form or contents of a document of title or the services or facilities to be afforded by a bailee, or otherwise regulating a bailee's businesses in respects not specifically treated in this article. However, violation of these laws does not affect the status of a document of title that otherwise complies with the definition of a document of title.

(c) This [Act] modifies, limits, and supersedes the federal Electronic Signatures in Global and National Commerce Act (15 U.S.C. Section 7001, et. seq.) but does not modify, limit, or supersede Section 101(c) of that act (15 U.S.C. Section 7001(c)) or authorize electronic delivery of any of the notices described in Section 103(b) of that act (15 U.S.C. Section 7003(b)).

(d) To the extent there is a conflict between the Uniform Electronic Transactions Act and this article, this Article governs.

§ 7-104. Negotiable and Non-Negotiable Document of Title

(a) A document of title is negotiable if by its terms the goods are to be delivered to bearer or to the order of a named person.

(b) A document of title other than one described in subsection (a) is non-negotiable. A bill of lading that states that the goods are consigned to a named person is not made negotiable by a provision that the goods are to be delivered only against an order in a record signed by the same or another named person.

(c) A document of title is non-negotiable if, at the time it is issued, the document has a conspicuous legend, however expressed, that it is non-negotiable.

§ 7-105. Reissuance in Alternative Medium

(a) Upon request of a person entitled under an electronic document of title, the issuer of the electronic document may issue a tangible document of title as a substitute for the electronic document if:

(1) the person entitled under the electronic document surrenders control of the document to the issuer; and

(2) the tangible document when issued contains a statement that it is issued in substitution for the electronic document.

(b) Upon issuance of a tangible document of title in substitution for an electronic document of title in accordance with subsection (a):

(1) the electronic document ceases to have any effect or validity; and

(2) the person that procured issuance of the tangible document warrants to all subsequent persons entitled under the tangible document that the warrantor was a person entitled under the electronic document when the warrantor surrendered control of the electronic document to the issuer.

(c) Upon request of a person entitled under a tangible document of title, the issuer of the tangible document may issue an electronic document of title as a substitute for the tangible document if:

(1) the person entitled under the tangible document surrenders possession of the document to the issuer; and

(2)   the electronic document when issued contains a statement that it is issued in substitution for the tangible document.

(d)   Upon issuance of the electronic document of title in substitution for a tangible document of title in accordance with subsection (c):

(1)   the tangible document ceases to have any effect or validity; and

(2)   the person that procured issuance of the electronic document warrants to all subsequent persons entitled under the electronic document that the warrantor was a person entitled under the tangible document when the warrantor surrendered possession of the tangible document to the issuer.

§ 7-106. Control of Electronic Document of Title

(a)   A person has control of an electronic document of title if a system employed for evidencing the transfer of interests in the electronic document reliably establishes that person as the person to which the electronic document was issued or transferred.

(b)   A system satisfies subsection (a), and a person is deemed to have control of an electronic document of title, if the document is created, stored, and assigned in such a manner that:

(1)   a single authoritative copy of the document exists which is unique, identifiable, and, except as otherwise provided in paragraphs (4), (5), and (6), unalterable;

(2)   the authoritative copy identifies the person asserting control as:

(A)   the person to which the document was issued; or

(B)   if the authoritative copy indicates that the document has been transferred, the person to which the document was most recently transferred;

(3)   the authoritative copy is communicated to and maintained by the person asserting control or its designated custodian;

(4)   copies or amendments that add or change an identified assignee of the authoritative copy can be made only with the consent of the person asserting control;

(5)   each copy of the authoritative copy and any copy of a copy is readily identifiable as a copy that is not the authoritative copy; and

(6)   any amendment of the authoritative copy is readily identifiable as authorized or unauthorized.

PART 2. WAREHOUSE RECEIPTS: SPECIAL PROVISIONS

§ 7-201. Person That May Issue a Warehouse Receipt; Storage Under Bond

(a)   A warehouse receipt may be issued by any warehouse.

(b)   If goods, including distilled spirits and agricultural commodities, are stored under a statute requiring a bond against withdrawal or a license for the issuance of receipts in the nature of warehouse receipts, a receipt issued for the goods is deemed to be a warehouse receipt even if issued by a person that is the owner of the goods and is not a warehouse.

§ 7-202. Form of Warehouse Receipt

(a)   A warehouse receipt need not be in any particular form.

(b)   Unless a warehouse receipt provides for each of the following, the warehouse is liable for damages caused to a person injured by its omission:

(1)   the location of the warehouse facility where the goods are stored;

(2)   the date of issue of the receipt;

(3)   the unique identification code of the receipt;

(4)   a statement whether the goods received will be delivered to the bearer, to a named person, or to a named person or its order;

(5)   the rate of storage and handling charges, but if goods are stored under a field warehousing arrangement, a statement of that fact is sufficient on a nonnegotiable receipt;

(6)   a description of the goods or the packages containing them;

(7)   the signature of the warehouse or its agent;

(8)   if the receipt is issued for goods that the warehouse owns, either solely, jointly, or in common with others, the fact of that ownership; and

(9)   a statement of the amount of advances made and of liabilities incurred for which the warehouse claims a lien or security interest, but if the precise amount of advances made or of
liabilities incurred is, at the time of the issue of the receipt, unknown to the warehouse or to
its agent that issued the receipt, a statement of the fact that advances have been made or
liabilities incurred and the purpose of the advances or liabilities is sufficient.
(c)   A warehouse may insert in its receipt any terms that are not contrary to [the Uniform Commercial Code] and do not impair its obligation of delivery under Section 7-403 or its duty of care
under Section 7-204. Any contrary provisions are ineffective.

§ 7-203. Liability for Nonreceipt or Misdescription
A party to or purchaser for value in good faith of a document of title, other than a bill of lading,
that relies upon the description of the goods in the document may recover from the issuer
damages caused by the nonreceipt or misdescription of the goods, except to the extent that:
(1)   the document conspicuously indicates that the issuer does not know whether all or part of
the goods in fact were received or conform to the description, such as a case in which the description is in terms of marks or labels or kind, quantity, or condition, or the receipt or description
is qualified by "contents, condition, and quality unknown", "said to contain", or words of similar
import, if the indication is true; or
(2)   the party or purchaser otherwise has notice of the nonreceipt or misdescription.

§ 7-204. Duty of Care; Contractual Limitation of Warehouse's Liability
(a)   A warehouse is liable for damages for loss of or injury to the goods caused by its failure to
exercise care with regard to the goods that a reasonably careful person would exercise under
similar circumstances. However, unless otherwise agreed, the warehouse is not liable for damages that could not have been avoided by the exercise of that care.
(b)   Damages may be limited by a term in the warehouse receipt or storage agreement
limiting the amount of liability in case of loss or damage beyond which the warehouse is not
liable. Such a limitation is not effective with respect to the warehouse's liability for conversion to
its own use. The warehouse's liability, on request of the bailor in a record at the time of signing
such storage agreement or within a reasonable time after receipt of the warehouse receipt, may
be increased on part or all of the goods covered by the storage agreement or the warehouse
receipt. In this event, increased rates may be charged based on an increased valuation of the
goods.
(c)   Reasonable provisions as to the time and manner of presenting claims and commencing
actions based on the bailment may be included in the warehouse receipt or storage agreement.
(d)   This section does not impair or repeal [Insert reference to any statute that imposes a higher
responsibility upon the warehouse or invalidates contractual limitations that would be permissible under this Article.]

§ 7-205. Title Under Warehouse Receipt Defeated in Certain Cases
A buyer in ordinary course of business of fungible goods goods and delivered by a warehouse
that is also in the business of buying and selling such goods takes the goods free of any claim
under a warehouse receipt even if the receipt is negotiable and has been duly negotiated.

§ 7-206. Termination of Storage at Warehouse's Option
(a)   A warehouse, by giving notice to the person on whose account the goods are held and
any other person known to claim an interest in the goods, may require payment of any charges
and removal of the goods from the warehouse at the termination of the period of storage fixed
by the document of title or, if a period is not fixed, within a stated period not less than 30 days
after the warehouse gives notice. If the goods are not removed before the date specified in the
notice, the warehouse may sell them pursuant to Section 7-210.
(b)   If a warehouse in good faith believes that goods are about to deteriorate or decline in
value to less than the amount of its lien within the time provided in subsection (a) and Section
7-210, the warehouse may specify in the notice given under subsection (a) any reasonable

shorter time for removal of the goods and, if the goods are not removed, may sell them at public sale held not less than one week after a single advertisement or posting.

(c)   If, as a result of a quality or condition of the goods of which the warehouse did not have notice at the time of deposit, the goods are a hazard to other property, the warehouse facilities, or other persons, the warehouse may sell the goods at public or private sale without advertisement or posting on reasonable notification to all persons known to claim an interest in the goods. If the warehouse, after a reasonable effort, is unable to sell the goods, it may dispose of them in any lawful manner and does not incur liability by reason of that disposition.

(d)   A warehouse shall deliver the goods to any person entitled to them under this Article upon due demand made at any time before sale or other disposition under this section.

(e)   A warehouse may satisfy its lien from the proceeds of any sale or disposition under this section but shall hold the balance for delivery on the demand of any person to which the warehouse would have been bound to deliver the goods.

§ 7-207. Goods Must Be Kept Separate; Fungible Goods

(a)   Unless the warehouse receipt provides otherwise, a warehouse shall keep separate the goods covered by each receipt so as to permit at all times identification and delivery of those goods. However, different lots of fungible goods may be commingled.

(b)   If different lots of fungible goods are commingled, the good are owned in common by the persons entitled thereto and the warehouse is severally liable to each owner for that owner's share. If, because of overissue, a mass of fungible goods is insufficient to meet all the receipts the warehouse has issued against it, the persons entitled include all holders to which overissued receipts have been duly negotiated.

§ 7-208. Altered Warehouse Receipts

If a blank in a negotiable tangible warehouse receipt has been filled in without authority, a good faith purchaser for value and without notice of the lack of authority may treat the insertion as authorized. Any other unauthorized alteration leaves any tangible or electronic warehouse receipt enforceable against the issuer according to its original tenor.

§ 7-209. Lien of Warehouse

(a)   A warehouse has a lien against the bailor on the goods covered by a warehouse receipt or storage agreement or on the proceeds thereof in its possession for charges for storage or transportation, including demurrage and terminal charges, insurance, labor, or other charges, present or future, in relation to the goods, and for expenses necessary for preservation of the goods or reasonably incurred in their sale pursuant to law. If the person on whose account the goods are held is liable for similar charges or expenses in relation to other goods whenever deposited and it is stated in the warehouse receipt or storage agreement that a lien is claimed for charges and expenses in relation to other goods, the warehouse also has a lien against the goods covered by the warehouse receipt or storage agreement or on the proceeds thereof in its possession for those charges and expenses, whether or not the other goods have been delivered by the warehouse. However, as against a person to which a negotiable warehouse receipt is duly negotiated, a warehouse's lien is limited to charges in an amount or at a rate specified in the warehouse receipt or, if no charges are so specified, to a reasonable charge for storage of the specific goods covered by the receipt subsequent to the date of the receipt.

(b)   The warehouse may also reserve a security interest under Article 9 against the bailor for the maximum amount specified on the receipt for charges other than those specified in subsection (a), such as for money advanced and interest. A security interest is governed by Article 9.

(c)   A warehouse's lien for charges and expenses under subsection (a) or a security interest under subsection (b) is also effective against any person that so entrusted the bailor with possession of the goods that a pledge of them by the bailor to a good faith purchaser for value would have been valid. However, the lien or security interest is not effective against a person that before issuance of a document of title had a legal interest or a perfected security interest in the goods and that did not:

(1)   deliver or entrust the goods or any document covering the goods to the bailor or the bailor's nominee with actual or apparent authority to ship, store, or sell; or with power to obtain delivery under Section 7-403; or with power of disposition under Sections 2-403, 2A-304(2), 2A-305(2) or 9-320 or other statute or rule of law; or

(2)   acquiesce in the procurement by the bailor or its nominee of any document.

(d)   A warehouse's lien on household goods for charges and expenses in relation to the goods under subsection (a) is also effective against all persons if the depositor was the legal possessor of the goods at the time of deposit. In this subsection, "household goods" means furniture, furnishings, or personal effects used by the depositor in a dwelling.

(e)   A warehouse loses its lien on any goods that it voluntarily delivers or unjustifiably refuses to deliver.

§ 7-210. Enforcement of Warehouse's Lien

(a)   Except as otherwise provided in subsection (b), a warehouse's lien may be enforced by public or private sale of the goods, in bulk or in packages, at any time or place and on any terms that are commercially reasonable, after notifying all persons known to claim an interest in the goods. The notification must include a statement of the amount due, the nature of the proposed sale, and the time and place of any public sale. The fact that a better price could have been obtained by a sale at a different time or in a different method from that selected by the warehouse is not of itself sufficient to establish that the sale was not made in a commercially reasonable manner. The warehouse has sold in a commercially reasonable manner if the warehouse sells the goods in the usual manner in any recognized market therefor, sells at the price current in that market at the time of the sale, or has otherwise sold in conformity with commercially reasonable practices among dealers in the type of goods sold. A sale of more goods than apparently necessary to be offered to ensure satisfaction of the obligation is not commercially reasonable, except in cases covered by the preceding sentence.

(b)   A warehouse's lien on goods, other than goods stored by a merchant in the course of its business, may be enforced only if the following requirements are satisfied:

(1)   All persons known to claim an interest in the goods must be notified.

(2)   The notification must include an itemized statement of the claim, a description of the goods subject to the lien, a demand for payment within a specified time not less than 10 days after receipt of the notification, and a conspicuous statement that unless the claim is paid within that time the goods will be advertised for sale and sold by auction at a specified time and place.

(3)   The sale must conform to the terms of the notification.

(4)   The sale must be held at the nearest suitable place to where the goods are held or stored.

(5)   After the expiration of the time given in the notification, an advertisement of the sale must be published once a week for two weeks consecutively in a newspaper of general circulation where the sale is to be held. The advertisement must include a description of the goods, the name of the person on whose account the goods are being held, and the time and place of the sale. The sale must take place at least 15 days after the first publication. If there is no newspaper of general circulation where the sale is to be held, the advertisement must be posted at least 10 days before the sale in not less than six conspicuous places in the neighborhood of the proposed sale.

(c)   Before any sale pursuant to this section, any person claiming a right in the goods may pay the amount necessary to satisfy the lien and the reasonable expenses incurred in complying with this section. In that event, the goods may not be sold but must be retained by the warehouse subject to the terms of the receipt and this article.

(d)   A warehouse may buy at any public sale held pursuant to this section.

(e)   A purchaser in good faith of goods sold to enforce a warehouse's lien takes the goods free of any rights of persons against which the lien was valid, despite the warehouse's noncompliance with this section.

(f)   A warehouse may satisfy its lien from the proceeds of any sale pursuant to this section but shall hold the balance, if any, for delivery on demand to any person to which the warehouse would have been bound to deliver the goods.

(g)   The rights provided by this section are in addition to all other rights allowed by law to a creditor against a debtor.

(h)   If a lien is on goods stored by a merchant in the course of its business, the lien may be enforced in accordance with subsection (a) or (b).

(i)   A warehouse is liable for damages caused by failure to comply with the requirements for sale under this section and, in case of willful violation, is liable for conversion.

PART 3. BILLS OF LADING: SPECIAL PROVISIONS
§ 7-301. Liability for Non-Receipt or Misdescription; "Said to Contain";
"Shipper's Load and Count"; Improper Handling

(a)   A consignee of a nonnegotiable bill of lading which has given value in good faith, or a holder to which a negotiable bill has been duly negotiated, relying upon the description of the goods in the bill or upon the date shown in the bill, may recover from the issuer damages caused by the misdating of the bill or the nonreceipt or misdescription of the goods, except to the extent that the document of title indicates that the issuer does not know whether any part or all of the goods in fact were received or conform to the description, such as in a case in which the description is in terms of marks or labels or kind, quantity, or condition or the receipt or description is qualified by "contents or condition of contents of packages unknown", "said to contain", "shipper's weight, load and count," or words of similar import, if that indication is true.

(b)   If goods are loaded by the issuer of the bill of lading, the issuer shall count the packages of goods if shipped in packages and ascertain the kind and quantity if shipped in bulk and words such as "shipper's weight, load and count," or words of similar import indicating that the description was made by the shipper are ineffective except as to goods concealed by packages.

(c)   If bulk goods are loaded by a shipper that makes available to the issuer of the bill of lading adequate facilities for weighing those goods, the issuer shall ascertain the kind and quantity within a reasonable time after receiving the shipper's request in a record to do so. In that case, "shipper's weight" or words of similar import are ineffective.

(d)   The issuer, by including in the bill of lading the words "shipper's weight, load and count," or words of similar import, may indicate that the goods were loaded by the shipper, and, if that statement is true, the issuer is not liable for damages caused by the improper loading. However, omission of such words does not imply liability for damages caused by improper loading.

(e)   A shipper guarantees to the issuer the accuracy at the time of shipment of the description, marks, labels, number, kind, quantity, condition, and weight, as furnished by the shipper, and the shipper shall indemnify the issuer against damage caused by inaccuracies in those particulars. This right of the issuer to that indemnity does not limit its responsibility or liability under the contract of carriage to any person other than the shipper.

§ 7-302. Through Bills of Lading and Similar Documents of Title

(a)   The issuer of a through bill of lading or other document of title embodying an undertaking to be performed in part by a person acting as its agent or by a performing carrier is liable to any person entitled to recover on the document for any breach by the other person or the performing carrier of its obligation under the document. However, to the extent that the bill covers an undertaking to be performed overseas or in territory not contiguous to the continental United States or an undertaking including matters other than transportation, this liability for breach by the other person or the performing carrier may be varied by agreement of the parties.

(b)   If goods covered by a through bill of lading or other document of title embodying an undertaking to be performed in part by a person other than the issuer are received by that person, the person is subject, with respect to its own performance while the goods are in its possession, to the obligation of the issuer. The person's obligation is discharged by delivery of the goods to another person pursuant to the document and does not include liability for breach by any other person or by the issuer.

(c)   The issuer of a through bill of lading or other document of title described in subsection (a) is entitled to recover from the performing carrier, or other person in possession of the goods when the breach of the obligation under the document occurred:

(1)   the amount it may be required to pay to any person entitled to recover on the document for the breach, as may be evidenced by any receipt, judgment, or transcript of judgment, and;

(2)   the amount of any expense reasonably incurred by the issuer in defending any action commenced by any person entitled to recover on the document for the breach.

§ 7-303. Diversion; Reconsignment; Change of Instructions

(a)   Unless the bill of lading otherwise provides, a carrier may deliver the goods to a person or destination other than that stated in the bill or may otherwise dispose of the goods, without liability for misdelivery, on instructions from:

(1)   the holder of a negotiable bill;

(2)   the consignor on a nonnegotiable bill even if the consignee has given contrary instructions;

(3)   the consignee on a nonnegotiable bill in the absence of contrary instructions from the consignor, if the goods have arrived at the billed destination or if the consignee is in possession of the tangible bill or in control of the electronic bill; or

(4)   the consignee on a nonnegotiable bill, if the consignee is entitled as against the consignor to dispose of the goods.

(b)   Unless instructions described in subsection (a) are included in a negotiable bill of lading, a person to which the bill is duly negotiated may hold the bailee according to the original terms.

§ 7-304. Tangible Bills of Lading in a Set

(a)   Except as customary in international transportation, a tangible bill of lading may not be issued in a set of parts. The issuer is liable for damages caused by violation of this subsection.

(b)   If a tangible bill of lading is lawfully issued in a set of parts, each of which contains an identification code and is expressed to be valid only if the goods have not been delivered against any other part, the whole of the parts constitutes one bill.

(c)   If a tangible negotiable bill of lading is lawfully issued in a set of parts and different parts are negotiated to different persons, the title of the holder to which the first due negotiation is made prevails as to both the document of title and the goods even if any later holder may have received the goods from the carrier in good faith and discharged the carrier's obligation by surrendering its part.

(d)   A person that negotiates or transfers a single part of a tangible bill of lading issued in a set is liable to holders of that part as if it were the whole set.

(e)   The bailee is obliged to deliver in accordance with Part 4 against the first presented part of a tangible bill of lading lawfully issued in a set. Delivery in this manner discharges the bailee's obligation on the whole bill.

§ 7-305. Destination Bills

(a)   Instead of issuing a bill of lading to the consignor at the place of shipment, a carrier, at the request of the consignor, may procure the bill to be issued at destination or at any other place designated in the request.

(b)   Upon request of any person entitled as against a carrier to control the goods while in transit and on surrender of possession or control of any outstanding bill of lading or other receipt covering the goods, the issuer, subject to Section 7-105, may procure a substitute bill to be issued at any place designated in the request.

§ 7-306. Altered Bills of Lading

An unauthorized alteration or filling in of a blank in a bill of lading leaves the bill enforceable according to its original tenor.

7-307. Lien of Carrier

(a)   A carrier has a lien on the goods covered by a bill of lading or on the proceeds thereof in its possession for charges after the date of the carrier's receipt of the goods for storage or transportation, including demurrage and terminal charges, and for expenses necessary for preservation of the goods incident to their transportation or reasonably incurred in their sale pursuant to law. However, against a purchaser for value of a negotiable bill of lading, a carrier's lien is limited to charges stated in the bill or the applicable tariffs or, if no charges are stated, a reasonable charge.
(b)   A lien for charges and expenses under subsection (a) on goods that the carrier was required by law to receive for transportation is effective against the consignor or any person entitled to the goods unless the carrier had notice that the consignor lacked authority to subject the goods to those charges and expenses. Any other lien under subsection (a) is effective against the consignor and any person that permitted the bailor to have control or possession of the goods unless the carrier had notice that the bailor lacked authority.
(c)   A carrier loses its lien on any goods that it voluntarily delivers or unjustifiably refuses to deliver.

§ 7-308. Enforcement of Carrier's Lien

(a) A carrier's lien on goods may be enforced by public or private sale of the goods, in bulk or in packages, at any time or place and on any terms that are commercially reasonable, after notifying all persons known to claim an interest in the goods. The notification must include a statement of the amount due, the nature of the proposed sale, and the time and place of any public sale. The fact that a better price could have been obtained by a sale at a different time or in a different method from that selected by the carrier is not of itself sufficient to establish that the sale was not made in a commercially reasonable manner. The carrier has sold goods in a commercially reasonable manner if the carrier sells the goods in the usual manner in any recognized market therefor, sells at the price current in that market at the time of the sale, or has otherwise sold in conformity with commercially reasonable practices among dealers in the type of goods sold. A sale of more goods than apparently necessary to be offered to ensure satisfaction of the obligation is not commercially reasonable, except in cases covered by the preceding sentence.
(b)   Before any sale pursuant to this section, any person claiming a right in the goods may pay the amount necessary to satisfy the lien and the reasonable expenses incurred in complying with this section. In that event, the goods may not be sold but must be retained by the carrier, subject to the terms of the bill of lading and this article.
(c)   A carrier may buy at any public sale pursuant to this section.
(d)   A purchaser in good faith of goods sold to enforce a carrier's lien takes the goods free of any rights of persons against which the lien was valid, despite the carrier's noncompliance with this section.
(e)   A carrier may satisfy its lien from the proceeds of any sale pursuant to this section but shall hold the balance, if any, for delivery on demand to any person to which the carrier would have been bound to deliver the goods.
(f) The rights provided by this section are in addition to all other rights allowed by law to a creditor against a debtor.
(g)   A carrier's lien may be enforced pursuant to either subsection (a) or the procedure set forth in Section 7-210(b).
(h)   A carrier is liable for damages caused by failure to comply with the requirements for sale under this section and, in case of willful violation, is liable for conversion.

§ 7-309. Duty of Care; Contractual Limitation of Carrier's Liability

(a)   A carrier that issues a bill of lading, whether negotiable or nonnegotiable, shall exercise the degree of care in relation to the goods which a reasonably careful person would exercise under similar circumstances. This subsection does not affect any statute, regulation, or rule of law that imposes liability upon a common carrier for damages not caused by its negligence.
(b)   Damages may be limited by a term in the bill of lading or in a transportation agreement that the carrier's liability may not exceed a value stated in the bill or transportation agreement if

the carrier's rates are dependent upon value and the consignor is afforded an opportunity to declare a higher value and the consignor is advised of the opportunity. However, such a limitation is not effective with respect to the carrier's liability for conversion to its own use.

(c)   Reasonable provisions as to the time and manner of presenting claims and commencing actions based on the shipment may be included in a bill of lading or a transportation agreement.

PART 4. WAREHOUSE RECEIPTS AND BILLS OF LADING: GENERAL OBLIGATIONS
§ 7-401. Irregularities in Issue of Receipt or Bill or Conduct of Issuer
The obligations imposed by this Article on an issuer apply to a document of title even if:

(1)   the document does not comply with the requirements of this Article or of any other statute, rule, or regulation regarding its issue, form, or content;

(2)   the issuer violated laws regulating the conduct of its business;

(3)   the goods covered by the document were owned by the bailee when the document was issued; or

(4)   the person issuing the document is not a warehouse but the document purports to be a warehouse receipt.

§ 7-402. Duplicate Document of Title; Overissue
A duplicate or any other document of title purporting to cover goods already represented by an outstanding document of the same issuer does not confer any right in the goods, except as provided in the case of tangible bills of lading in a set of parts, overissue of documents for fungible goods, substitutes for lost, stolen, or destroyed documents, or substitute documents issued pursuant to Section 7-105. The issuer is liable for damages caused by its overissue or failure to identify a duplicate document by a conspicuous notation.

§ 7-403. Obligation of Warehouse or Carrier to Deliver; Excuse
(a)   A bailee shall deliver the goods to a person entitled under a document of title if the person complies with subsections (b) and (c), unless and to the extent that the bailee establishes any of the following:

(1)   delivery of the goods to a person whose receipt was rightful as against the claimant;

(2)   damage to or delay, loss, or destruction of the goods for which the bailee is not liable;

(3)   previous sale or other disposition of the goods in lawful enforcement of a lien or on a warehouse's lawful termination of storage;

(4)   the exercise by a seller of its right to stop delivery pursuant to Section 2-705 or by a lessor of its right to stop delivery pursuant to Section 2A-526;

(5)   a diversion, reconsignment, or other disposition pursuant to Section 7-303;

(6)   release, satisfaction, or any other fact affording a personal defense against the claimant; or

(7)   any other lawful excuse.

(b)   A person claiming goods covered by a document of title shall satisfy the bailee's lien if the bailee so requests or the bailee is prohibited by law from delivering the goods until the charges are paid.

(c)   Unless a person claiming the goods is one against which the document of title does not confer a right under Section 7-503(a):

(1)   the person claiming under a document shall surrender possession or control of any outstanding negotiable document covering the goods for cancellation or indication of partial deliveries; and

(2)   the bailee shall cancel the document or conspicuously indicate in the document the partial delivery or be liable to any person to which the document is duly negotiated.

§ 7-404. No Liability for Good Faith Delivery Pursuant to Document of Title
A bailee that in good faith has received goods and delivered or otherwise disposed of the goods according to the terms of a document of title or pursuant to this Article is not liable for the goods even if:

(1)   the person from which the bailee received the goods did not have authority to procure the document or to dispose of the goods; or

(2)   the person to which the bailee delivered the goods did not have authority to receive the goods.

PART 5. WAREHOUSE RECEIPTS AND BILLS OF LADING: NEGOTIATION AND TRANSFER
§ 7-501. Form of Negotiation and Requirements of Due Negotiation

(a)   The following rules apply to a negotiable tangible document of title:

(1)   If the document's original terms run to the order of a named person, the document is nego-tiated by the named person's indorsement and delivery. After the named person's indorse-ment in blank or to bearer, any person may negotiate the document by delivery alone.

(2)   If the document's original terms run to bearer, it is negotiated by delivery alone.

(3)   If the document's original terms run to the order of a named person and it is delivered to the named person, the effect is the same as if the document had been negotiated.

(4)   Negotiation of the document after it has been indorsed to a named person requires in-dorsement by the named person as well as delivery.

(5)   A document is duly negotiated if it is negotiated in the manner stated in this subsection to a holder that purchases it in good faith, without notice of any defense against or claim to it on the part of any person, and for value, unless it is established that the negotiation is not in the regular course of business or financing or involves receiving the document in settle-ment or payment of a monetary obligation.

(b)   The following rules apply to a negotiable electronic document of title:

(1)   If the document's original terms run to the order of a named person or to bearer, the docu-ment is negotiated by delivery of the document to another person. Indorsement by the named person is not required to negotiate the document.

(2)   If the document's original terms run to the order of a named person and the named person has control of the document, the effect is the same as if the document had been negotiated.

(3)   A document is duly negotiated if it is negotiated in the manner stated in this subsection to a holder that purchases it in good faith, without notice of any defense against or claim to it on the part of any person, and for value, unless it is established that the negotiation is not in the regular course of business or financing or involves taking delivery of the document in settlement or payment of a monetary obligation.

(c)   Indorsement of a nonnegotiable document of title neither makes it negotiable nor adds to the transferee's rights.

(d)   The naming in a negotiable bill of lading of a person to be notified of the arrival of the goods does not limit the negotiability of the bill or constitute notice to a purchaser of the bill of any interest of that person in the goods.

§ 7-502. Rights Acquired by Due Negotiation

(a)   Subject to Sections 7-205 and 7-503, a holder to which a negotiable document of title has been duly negotiated acquires thereby:

(1)   title to the document;

(2)   title to the goods;

(3)   all rights accruing under the law of agency or estoppel, including rights to goods delivered to the bailee after the document was issued; and

(4)   the direct obligation of the issuer to hold or deliver the goods according to the terms of the document free of any defense or claim by the issuer except those arising under the terms of the document or under this article. In the case of a delivery order, the bailee's obligation accrues only upon the bailee's acceptance of the delivery order and the obligation acqui-red by the holder is that the issuer and any indorser will procure the acceptance of the bailee.

(b)   Subject to Section 7-503, title and rights acquired by due negotiation are not defeated by any stoppage of the goods represented by the document of title or by surrender of the goods by the bailee and are not impaired even if:

(1)   the due negotiation or any prior due negotiation constituted a breach of duty;

(2)   any person has been deprived of possession of a negotiable tangible document or control of a negotiable electronic document by misrepresentation, fraud, accident, mistake, duress, loss, theft, or conversion; or

(3)   a previous sale or other transfer of the goods or document has been made to a third person.

§ 7-503. Document of Title to Goods Defeated in Certain Cases

(a)   A document of title confers no right in goods against a person that before issuance of the document had a legal interest or a perfected security interest in the goods and that did not:

(1)   deliver or entrust the goods or any document covering the goods to the bailor or the bailor's nominee with actual or apparent authority to ship, store, or sell; with power to obtain delivery under Section 7-403; or with power of disposition under Section 2-403, 2A-304(2), 2A-305(2), or 9-320 or other statute or rule of law; or

(2)   acquiesce in the procurement by the bailor or its nominee of any document.

(b)   Title to goods based upon an unaccepted delivery order is subject to the rights of any person to which a negotiable warehouse receipt or bill of lading covering the goods has been duly negotiated. That title may be defeated under Section 7-504 to the same extent as the rights of the issuer or a transferee from the issuer.

(c)   Title to goods based upon a bill of lading issued to a freight forwarder is subject to the rights of any person to which a bill issued by the freight forwarder is duly negotiated. However, delivery by the carrier in accordance with Part 4 pursuant to its own bill of lading discharges the carrier's obligation to deliver.

§ 7-504. Rights Acquired in the Absence of Due Negotiation; Effect of Diversion; Stoppage of Delivery

(a)   A transferee of a document of title, whether negotiable or non-negotiable, to which the document has been delivered but not duly negotiated, acquires the title and rights that its transferor had or had actual authority to convey.

(b)   In the case of a non-negotiable document of title, until but not after the bailee receives notice of the transfer, the rights of the transferee may be defeated:

(1)   by those creditors of the transferor that could treat the transfer as void under Section 2-402 or 2A-308;

(2)   by a buyer from the transferor in ordinary course of business if the bailee has delivered the goods to the buyer or received notification of the buyer's rights;

(3)   by a lessee from the transferor in ordinary course of business if the bailee has delivered the goods to the lessee or received notification of the lessee's rights; or

(4)   as against the bailee, by good faith dealings of the bailee with the transferor.

(c)   A diversion or other change of shipping instructions by the consignor in a non-negotiable bill of lading which causes the bailee not to deliver the goods to the consignee defeats the consignee's title to the goods if the goods have been delivered to a buyer in ordinary course of business or a lessee in ordinary course of business and in any event defeats the consignee's rights against the bailee.

(d)   Delivery of the goods pursuant to a non-negotiable document of title may be stopped by a seller under Section 2-705 or a lessor under Section 2A-526, subject to the requirements of due notification in those sections. A bailee honoring the seller's or lessor's instructions is entitled to be indemnified by the seller or lessor against any resulting loss or expense.

§ 7-505. Indorser Not a Guarantor for Other Parties

The indorsement of a tangible document of title issued by a bailee does not make the indorser liable for any default by the bailee or previous indorsers.

§ 7-506. Delivery Without Indorsement: Right to Compel Indorsement

The transferee of a negotiable tangible document of title has a specifically enforceable right to have its transferor supply any necessary indorsement, but the transfer becomes a negotiation only as of the time the indorsement is supplied.

7-507. Warranties on Negotiation or Transfer of Document of Title

If a person negotiates or delivers a document of title for value, otherwise than as a mere intermediary under Section 7-508, unless otherwise agreed, the transferor warrants to its immediate purchaser only in addition to any warranty made in selling or leasing the goods that:
(1)   the document is genuine;
(2)   the transferor does not have knowledge of any fact that would impair the document's validity or worth; and
(3)   the negotiation or delivery is rightful and fully effective with respect to the title to the document and the goods it represents.

§ 7-508. Warranties of Collecting Bank as to Documents of Title

A collecting bank or other intermediary known to be entrusted with documents of title on behalf of another or with collection of a draft or other claim against delivery of documents warrants by the delivery of the documents only its own good faith and authority even if the collecting bank or other intermediary has purchased or made advances against the claim or draft to be collected.

§ 7-509. Adequate Compliance With Commercial Contract

Whether a document of title is adequate to fulfill the obligations of a contract for sale, a contract for lease, or the conditions of a letter of credit is determined by Article 2, 2A, or 5.

PART 6. WAREHOUSE RECEIPTS AND BILLS OF LADING: MISCELLANEOUS PROVISIONS

§ 7-601. Lost, Stolen, or Destroyed Documents of Title

(a)   If a document of title is lost, stolen, or destroyed, a court may order delivery of the goods or issuance of a substitute document and the bailee may without liability to any person comply with the order. If the document was negotiable, a court may not order delivery of the goods or issuance of a substitute document without the claimant's posting security unless it finds that any person that may suffer loss as a result of non-surrender of possession or control of the document is adequately protected against the loss. If the document was nonnegotiable, the court may require security. The court may also order payment of the bailee's reasonable costs and attorney's fees in any action under this subsection.
(b)   A bailee that without court order delivers goods to a person claiming under a missing negotiable document of title is liable to any person injured thereby. If the delivery is not in good faith, the bailee is liable for conversion. Delivery in good faith is not conversion if the claimant posts security with the bailee in an amount at least double the value of the goods at the time of posting to indemnify any person injured by the delivery which files a notice of claim within one year after the delivery.

§ 7-602. Attachment of Goods Covered by a Negotiable Document

Unless a document of title was originally issued upon delivery of the goods by a person that did not have power to dispose of them, a lien does not attach by virtue of any judicial process to goods in the possession of a bailee for which a negotiable document of title is outstanding unless possession or control of the document is first surrendered to the bailee or the document's negotiation is enjoined. The bailee may not be compelled to deliver the goods pursuant to process until possession or control of the document is surrendered to the bailee or to the court. A purchaser of the document for value without notice of the process or injunction takes free of the lien imposed by judicial process.

§ 7-603. Conflicting Claims; Interpleader

If more than one person claims title to or possession of the goods, the bailee is excused from delivery until the bailee has a reasonable time to ascertain the validity of the adverse claims or to commence an action for interpleader. The bailee may assert an interpleader either in defending an action for nondelivery of the goods or by original action.

PART 7. MISCELLANEOUS PROVISIONS [...]

ARTICLE 9 - SECURED TRANSACTIONS
PART 1. GENERAL PROVISIONS
Subpart 1. Short Title, Definitions, and General Concepts
§ 9-101. Short Title
This Article may be cited as Uniform Commercial Code-Secured Transactions.

§ 9-102. Definitions and Index of Definitions
(a)   In this article:
(1)   "Accession" means goods that are physically united with other goods in such a manner that the identity of the original goods is not lost.
(2)   "Account", except as used in "account for", means a right to payment of a monetary obligation, whether or not earned by performance, (i) for property that has been or is to be sold, leased, licensed, assigned, or otherwise disposed of, (ii) for services rendered or to be rendered, (iii) for a policy of insurance issued or to be issued, (iv) for a secondary obligation incurred or to be incurred, (v) for energy provided or to be provided, (vi) for the use or hire of a vessel under a charter or other contract, (vii) arising out of the use of a credit or charge card or information contained on or for use with the card, or (viii) as winnings in a lottery or other game of chance operated or sponsored by a State, governmental unit of a State, or person licensed or authorized to operate the game by a State or governmental unit of a State. The term includes health-care-insurance receivables. The term does not include (i) rights to payment evidenced by chattel paper or an instrument, (ii) commercial tort claims, (iii) deposit accounts, (iv) investment property, (v) letter-of-credit rights or letters of credit, or (vi) rights to payment for money or funds advanced or sold, other than rights arising out of the use of a credit or charge card or information contained on or for use with the card.
(3)   "Account debtor" means a person obligated on an account, chattel paper, or general intangible. The term does not include persons obligated to pay a negotiable instrument, even if the instrument constitutes part of chattel paper.
(4)   "Accounting", except as used in "accounting for", means a record:
      (A)   authenticated by a secured party;
      (B)   indicating the aggregate unpaid secured obligations as of a date not more than 35 days earlier or 35 days later than the date of the record; and
      (C)   identifying the components of the obligations in reasonable detail.
(5)   "Agricultural lien" means an interest, other than a security interest, in farm products:
      (A)   which secures payment or performance of an obligation for:
            (i)   goods or services furnished in connection with a debtor's farming operation; or
            (ii)   rent on real property leased by a debtor in connection with its farming operation;
      (B)   which is created by statute in favor of a person that:
            (i)   in the ordinary course of its business furnished goods or services to a debtor in connection with a debtor's farming operation; or
            (ii)   leased real property to a debtor in connection with the debtor's farming operation; and
      (C)   whose effectiveness does not depend on the person's possession of the personal property.
(6)   "As-extracted collateral" means:
      (A)   oil, gas, or other minerals that are subject to a security interest that:
            (i)   is created by a debtor having an interest in the minerals before extraction; and
            (ii)   attaches to the minerals as extracted; or
      (B)   accounts arising out of the sale at the wellhead or minehead of oil, gas, or other minerals in which the debtor had an interest before extraction.
(7)   "Authenticate" means:
      (A)   to sign; or

      (B)   to execute or otherwise adopt a symbol, or encrypt or similarly process a record in whole or in part, with the present intent of the authenticating person to identify the person and adopt or accept a record.

(8)   "Bank" means an organization that is engaged in the business of banking. The term includes savings banks, savings and loan associations, credit unions, and trust companies.

(9)   "Cash proceeds" means proceeds that are money, checks, deposit accounts, or the like.

(10) "Certificate of title" means a certificate of title with respect to which a statute provides for the security interest in question to be indicated on the certificate as a condition or result of the security interest's obtaining priority over the rights of a lien creditor with respect to the collateral.

(11) "Chattel paper" means a record or records that evidence both a monetary obligation and a security interest in specific goods, a security interest in specific goods and software used in the goods, a security interest in specific goods and license of software used in the goods, a lease of specific goods, or a lease of specific goods and license of software used in the goods. In this paragraph, "monetary obligation" means a monetary obligation secured by the goods or owed under a lease of the goods and includes a monetary obligation with respect to software used in the goods. The term does not include (i) charters or other contracts involving the use or hire of a vessel or (ii) records that evidence a right to payment arising out of the use of a credit or charge card or information contained on or for use with the card. If a transaction is evidenced by records that include an instrument or series of instruments, the group of records taken together constitutes chattel paper.

(12) "Collateral" means the property subject to a security interest or agricultural lien. The term includes:

      (A)   proceeds to which a security interest attaches;

      (B)   accounts, chattel paper, payment intangibles, and promissory notes that have been sold; and

      (C)   goods that are the subject of a consignment.

(13) "Commercial tort claim" means a claim arising in tort with respect to which:

      (A)   the claimant is an organization; or

      (B)   the claimant is an individual and the claim:

         (i)   arose in the course of the claimant's business or profession; and

         (ii) does not include damages arising out of personal injury to or the death of an individual.

(14) "Commodity account" means an account maintained by a commodity intermediary in which a commodity contract is carried for a commodity customer.

(15) "Commodity contract" means a commodity futures contract, an option on a commodity futures contract, a commodity option, or another contract if the contract or option is:

      (A)   traded on or subject to the rules of a board of trade that has been designated as a contract market for such a contract pursuant to federal commodities laws; or

      (B)   traded on a foreign commodity board of trade, exchange, or market, and is carried on the books of a commodity intermediary for a commodity customer.

(16) "Commodity customer" means a person for which a commodity intermediary carries a commodity contract on its books.

(17) "Commodity intermediary" means a person that:

      (A)   is registered as a futures commission merchant under federal commodities law; or

      (B)   in the ordinary course of its business provides clearance or settlement services for a board of trade that has been designated as a contract market pursuant to federal commodities law.

(18) "Communicate" means:

      (A)   to send a written or other tangible record;

      (B)   to transmit a record by any means agreed upon by the persons sending and receiving the record; or

    (C)   in the case of transmission of a record to or by a filing office, to transmit a record by any means prescribed by filing-office rule.

(19) "Consignee" means a merchant to which goods are delivered in a consignment.

(20) "Consignment" means a transaction, regardless of its form, in which a person delivers goods to a merchant for the purpose of sale and:
    (A) the merchant:
        (i)   deals in goods of that kind under a name other than the name of the person making delivery;
        (ii)   is not an auctioneer; and
        (iii) is not generally known by its creditors to be substantially engaged in selling the goods of others;
    (B) with respect to each delivery, the aggregate value of the goods is $1,000 or more at the time of delivery;
    (C) the goods are not consumer goods immediately before delivery; and
    (D) the transaction does not create a security interest that secures an obligation.

(21) "Consignor" means a person that delivers goods to a consignee in a consignment.

(22) "Consumer debtor" means a debtor in a consumer transaction.

(23) "Consumer goods" means goods that are used or bought for use primarily for personal, family, or household purposes.

(24) "Consumer-goods transaction" means a consumer transaction in which:
    (A) an individual incurs an obligation primarily for personal, family, or household purposes; and
    (B) a security interest in consumer goods secures the obligation.

(25) "Consumer obligor" means an obligor who is an individual and who incurred the obligation as part of a transaction entered into primarily for personal, family, or household purposes.

(26) "Consumer transaction" means a transaction in which (i) an individual incurs an obligation primarily for personal, family, or household purposes, (ii) a security interest secures the obligation, and (iii) the collateral is held or acquired primarily for personal, family, or household purposes. The term includes consumer-goods transactions.

(27) "Continuation statement" means an amendment of a financing statement which:
    (A) identifies, by its file number, the initial financing statement to which it relates; and
    (B) indicates that it is a continuation statement for, or that it is filed to continue the effectiveness of, the identified financing statement.

(28) "Debtor" means:
    (A) a person having an interest, other than a security interest or other lien, in the collateral, whether or not the person is an obligor;
    (B) a seller of accounts, chattel paper, payment intangibles, or promissory notes; or
    (C) a consignee.

(29) "Deposit account" means a demand, time, savings, passbook, or similar account maintained with a bank. The term does not include investment property or accounts evidenced by an instrument.

(30) "Document" means a document of title or a receipt of the type described in Section 7-201(2).

(31) "Electronic chattel paper" means chattel paper evidenced by a record or records consisting of information stored in an electronic medium.

(32) "Encumbrance" means a right, other than an ownership interest, in real property. The term includes mortgages and other liens on real property.

(33) "Equipment" means goods other than inventory, farm products, or consumer goods.

(34) "Farm products" means goods, other than standing timber, with respect to which the debtor is engaged in a farming operation and which are:
    (A) crops grown, growing, or to be grown, including:
        (i)   crops produced on trees, vines, and bushes; and

(ii)   aquatic goods produced in aquacultural operations;
(B)   livestock, born or unborn, including aquatic goods produced in aquacultural operations;
(C)   supplies used or produced in a farming operation; or
(D)   products of crops or livestock in their unmanufactured states.

(35) "Farming operation" means raising, cultivating, propagating, fattening, grazing, or any other farming, livestock, or aquacultural operation.

(36) "File number" means the number assigned to an initial financing statement pursuant to Section 9-519(a).

(37) "Filing office" means an office designated in Section 9-501 as the place to file a financing statement.

(38) "Filing-office rule" means a rule adopted pursuant to Section 9-526.

(39) "Financing statement" means a record or records composed of an initial financing statement and any filed record relating to the initial financing statement.

(40) "Fixture filing" means the filing of a financing statement covering goods that are or are to become fixtures and satisfying Section 9-502(a) and (b). The term includes the filing of a financing statement covering goods of a transmitting utility which are or are to become fixtures.

(41) "Fixtures" means goods that have become so related to particular real property that an interest in them arises under real property law.

(42) "General intangible" means any personal property, including things in action, other than accounts, chattel paper, commercial tort claims, deposit accounts, documents, goods, instruments, investment property, letter-of-credit rights, letters of credit, money, and oil, gas, or other minerals before extraction. The term includes payment intangibles and software.

(43) "Good faith" means honesty in fact and the observance of reasonable commercial standards of fair dealing.

(44) "Goods" means all things that are movable when a security interest attaches. The term includes (i) fixtures, (ii) standing timber that is to be cut and removed under a conveyance or contract for sale, (iii) the unborn young of animals, (iv) crops grown, growing, or to be grown, even if the crops are produced on trees, vines, or bushes, and (v) manufactured homes. The term also includes a computer program embedded in goods and any supporting information provided in connection with a transaction relating to the program if (i) the program is associated with the goods in such a manner that it customarily is considered part of the goods, or (ii) by becoming the owner of the goods, a person acquires a right to use the program in connection with the goods. The term does not include a computer program embedded in goods that consist solely of the medium in which the program is embedded. The term also does not include accounts, chattel paper, commercial tort claims, deposit accounts, documents, general intangibles, instruments, investment property, letter-of-credit rights, letters of credit, money, or oil, gas, or other minerals before extraction.

(45) "Governmental unit" means a subdivision, agency, department, county, parish, municipality, or other unit of the government of the United States, a State, or a foreign country. The term includes an organization having a separate corporate existence if the organization is eligible to issue debt on which interest is exempt from income taxation under the laws of the United States.

(46) "Health-care-insurance receivable" means an interest in or claim under a policy of insurance which is a right to payment of a monetary obligation for health-care goods or services provided.

(47) "Instrument" means a negotiable instrument or any other writing that evidences a right to the payment of a monetary obligation, is not itself a security agreement or lease, and is of a type that in ordinary course of business is transferred by delivery with any necessary indorsement or assignment. The term does not include (i) investment property, (ii) letters of credit, or (iii) writings that evidence a right to payment arising out of the use of a credit or charge card or information contained on or for use with the card.

(48) "Inventory" means goods, other than farm products, which:
  (A) are leased by a person as lessor;
  (B) are held by a person for sale or lease or to be furnished under a contract of service;
  (C) are furnished by a person under a contract of service; or
  (D) consist of raw materials, work in process, or materials used or consumed in a business.
(49) "Investment property" means a security, whether certificated or uncertificated, security entitlement, securities account, commodity contract, or commodity account.
(50) "Jurisdiction of organization", with respect to a registered organization, means the jurisdiction under whose law the organization is organized.
(51) "Letter-of-credit right" means a right to payment or performance under a letter of credit, whether or not the beneficiary has demanded or is at the time entitled to demand payment or performance. The term does not include the right of a beneficiary to demand payment or performance under a letter of credit.
(52) "Lien creditor" means:
  (A) a creditor that has acquired a lien on the property involved by attachment, levy, or the like;
  (B) an assignee for benefit of creditors from the time of assignment;
  (C) a trustee in bankruptcy from the date of the filing of the petition; or
  (D) a receiver in equity from the time of appointment.
(53) "Manufactured home" means a structure, transportable in one or more sections, which, in the traveling mode, is eight body feet or more in width or 40 body feet or more in length, or, when erected on site, is 320 or more square feet, and which is built on a permanent chassis and designed to be used as a dwelling with or without a permanent foundation when connected to the required utilities, and includes the plumbing, heating, air-conditioning, and electrical systems contained therein. The term includes any structure that meets all of the requirements of this paragraph except the size requirements and with respect to which the manufacturer voluntarily files a certification required by the United States Secretary of Housing and Urban Development and complies with the standards established under Title 42 of the United States Code.
(54) "Manufactured-home transaction" means a secured transaction:
  (A) that creates a purchase-money security interest in a manufactured home, other than a manufactured home held as inventory; or
  (B) in which a manufactured home, other than a manufactured home held as inventory, is the primary collateral.
(55) "Mortgage" means a consensual interest in real property, including fixtures, which secures payment or performance of an obligation.
(56) "New debtor" means a person that becomes bound as debtor under Section 9-203(d) by a security agreement previously entered into by another person.
(57) "New value" means (i) money, (ii) money's worth in property, services, or new credit, or (iii) release by a transferee of an interest in property previously transferred to the transferee. The term does not include an obligation substituted for another obligation.
(58) "Noncash proceeds" means proceeds other than cash proceeds.
(59) "Obligor" means a person that, with respect to an obligation secured by a security interest in or an agricultural lien on the collateral, (i) owes payment or other performance of the obligation, (ii) has provided property other than the collateral to secure payment or other performance of the obligation, or (iii) is otherwise accountable in whole or in part for payment or other performance of the obligation. The term does not include issuers or nominated persons under a letter of credit.
(60) "Original debtor", except as used in Section 9-310(c), means a person that, as debtor, entered into a security agreement to which a new debtor has become bound under Section 9-203(d).

(61) "Payment intangible" means a general intangible under which the account debtor's principal obligation is a monetary obligation.

(62) "Person related to", with respect to an individual, means:
(A) the spouse of the individual;
(B) a brother, brother-in-law, sister, or sister-in-law of the individual;
(C) an ancestor or lineal descendant of the individual or the individual's spouse; or
(D) any other relative, by blood or marriage, of the individual or the individual's spouse who shares the same home with the individual.

(63) "Person related to", with respect to an organization, means:
(A) a person directly or indirectly controlling, controlled by, or under common control with the organization;
(B) an officer or director of, or a person performing similar functions with respect to, the organization;
(C) an officer or director of, or a person performing similar functions with respect to, a person described in subparagraph (A);
(D) the spouse of an individual described in subparagraph (A), (B), or (C); or
(E) an individual who is related by blood or marriage to an individual described in subparagraph (A), (B), (C), or (D) and shares the same home with the individual.

(64) "Proceeds", except as used in Section 9-609(b), means the following property:
(A) whatever is acquired upon the sale, lease, license, exchange, or other disposition of collateral;
(B) whatever is collected on, or distributed on account of, collateral;
(C) rights arising out of collateral;
(D) to the extent of the value of collateral, claims arising out of the loss, nonconformity, or interference with the use of, defects or infringement of rights in, or damage to, the collateral; or
(E) to the extent of the value of collateral and to the extent payable to the debtor or the secured party, insurance payable by reason of the loss or nonconformity of, defects or infringement of rights in, or damage to, the collateral.

(65) "Promissory note" means an instrument that evidences a promise to pay a monetary obligation, does not evidence an order to pay, and does not contain an acknowledgment by a bank that the bank has received for deposit a sum of money or funds.

(66) "Proposal" means a record authenticated by a secured party which includes the terms on which the secured party is willing to accept collateral in full or partial satisfaction of the obligation it secures pursuant to Sections 9-620, 9-621, and 9-622.

(67) "Public-finance transaction" means a secured transaction in connection with which:
(A) debt securities are issued;
(B) all or a portion of the securities issued have an initial stated maturity of at least 20 years; and
(C) the debtor, obligor, secured party, account debtor or other person obligated on collateral, assignor or assignee of a secured obligation, or assignor or assignee of a security interest is a State or a governmental unit of a State.

(68) "Pursuant to commitment", with respect to an advance made or other value given by a secured party, means pursuant to the secured party's obligation, whether or not a subsequent event of default or other event not within the secured party's control has relieved or may relieve the secured party from its obligation.

(69) "Record", except as used in "for record", "of record", "record or legal title", and "record owner", means information that is inscribed on a tangible medium or which is stored in an electronic or other medium and is retrievable in perceivable form.

(70) "Registered organization" means an organization organized solely under the law of a single State or the United States and as to which the State or the United States must maintain a public record showing the organization to have been organized.

(71) "Secondary obligor" means an obligor to the extent that:
  (A) the obligor's obligation is secondary; or
  (B) the obligor has a right of recourse with respect to an obligation secured by collateral against the debtor, another obligor, or property of either.
(72) "Secured party" means:
  (A) a person in whose favor a security interest is created or provided for under a security agreement, whether or not any obligation to be secured is outstanding;
  (B) a person that holds an agricultural lien;
  (C) a consignor;
  (D) a person to which accounts, chattel paper, payment intangibles, or promissory notes have been sold;
  (E) a trustee, indenture trustee, agent, collateral agent, or other representative in whose favor a security interest or agricultural lien is created or provided for; or
  (F) a person that holds a security interest arising under Section 2-401, 2-505, 2-711(3), 2A-508(5), 4-210, or 5-118.
(73) "Security agreement" means an agreement that creates or provides for a security interest.
(74) "Send", in connection with a record or notification, means:
  (A) to deposit in the mail, deliver for transmission, or transmit by any other usual means of communication, with postage or cost of transmission provided for, addressed to any address reasonable under the circumstances; or
  (B) to cause the record or notification to be received within the time that it would have been received if properly sent under subparagraph (A).
(75) "Software" means a computer program and any supporting information provided in connection with a transaction relating to the program. The term does not include a computer program that is included in the definition of goods.
(76) "State" means a State of the United States, the District of Columbia, Puerto Rico, the United States Virgin Islands, or any territory or insular possession subject to the jurisdiction of the United States.
(77) "Supporting obligation" means a letter-of-credit right or secondary obligation that supports the payment or performance of an account, chattel paper, a document, a general intangible, an instrument, or investment property.
(78) "Tangible chattel paper" means chattel paper evidenced by a record or records consisting of information that is inscribed on a tangible medium.
(79) "Termination statement" means an amendment of a financing statement which:
  (A) identifies, by its file number, the initial financing statement to which it relates; and
  (B) indicates either that it is a termination statement or that the identified financing statement is no longer effective.
(80) "Transmitting utility" means a person primarily engaged in the business of:
  (A) operating a railroad, subway, street railway, or trolley bus;
  (B) transmitting communications electrically, electromagnetically, or by light;
  (C) transmitting goods by pipeline or sewer; or
  (D) transmitting or producing and transmitting electricity, steam, gas, or water.
(b) [Definitions in other articles.] The following definitions in other articles apply to this article:
  "Applicant" Section 5-102.
  "Beneficiary" Section 5-102.
  "Broker" Section 8-102.
  "Certificated security" Section 8-102.
  "Check" Section 3-104.
  "Clearing corporation" Section 8-102.
  "Contract for sale" Section 2-106.
  "Customer" Section 4-104.
  "Entitlement holder" Section 8-102.

"Financial asset" Section 8-102.
"Holder in due course" Section 3-302.
"Issuer" (with respect to a letter of credit or letter-of-credit right) Section 5-102.
"Issuer" (with respect to a security) Section 8-201.
"Issuer" (with respect to documents of title) Section 7-102.
"Lease" Section 2A-103.
"Lease agreement" Section 2A-103.
"Lease contract" Section 2A-103.
"Leasehold interest" Section 2A-103.
"Lessee" Section 2A-103.
"Lessee in ordinary course of business" Section 2A-103.
"Lessor" Section 2A-103.
"Lessor's residual interest" Section 2A-103.
"Letter of credit" Section 5-102.
"Merchant" Section 2-104.
"Negotiable instrument" Section 3-104.
"Nominated person" Section 5-102.
"Note" Section 3-104.
"Proceeds of a letter of credit" Section 5-114.
"Prove" Section 3-103.
"Sale" Section 2-106.
"Securities account" Section 8-501.
"Securities intermediary" Section 8-102.
"Security" Section 8-102.
"Security certificate" Section 8-102.
"Security entitlement" Section 8-102.
"Uncertificated security" Section 8-102.

(c) [Article 1 definitions and principles.] Article 1 contains general definitions and principles of construction and interpretation applicable throughout this article.

§ 9-103. Purchase-Money Security Interest; Application of Payments; Burden of Establishing
(a) [Definitions.] In this section:
(1) "purchase-money collateral" means goods or software that secures a purchase-money obligation incurred with respect to that collateral; and
(2) "purchase-money obligation" means an obligation of an obligor incurred as all or part of the price of the collateral or for value given to enable the debtor to acquire rights in or the use of the collateral if the value is in fact so used.

(b) [Purchase-money security interest in goods.] A security interest in goods is a purchase-money security interest:
(1) to the extent that the goods are purchase-money collateral with respect to that security interest;
(2) if the security interest is in inventory that is or was purchase-money collateral, also to the extent that the security interest secures a purchase- money obligation incurred with respect to other inventory in which the secured party holds or held a purchase-money security interest; and
(3) also to the extent that the security interest secures a purchase-money obligation incurred with respect to software in which the secured party holds or held a purchase-money security interest.

(c) [Purchase-money security interest in software.] A security interest in software is a purchase-money security interest to the extent that the security interest also secures a purchase-money obligation incurred with respect to goods in which the secured party holds or held a purchase-money security interest if:

(1)   the debtor acquired its interest in the software in an integrated transaction in which it acquired an interest in the goods; and

(2)   the debtor acquired its interest in the software for the principal purpose of using the software in the goods.

(d)   [Consignor's inventory purchase-money security interest.] The security interest of a consignor in goods that are the subject of a consignment is a purchase-money security interest in inventory.

(e)   [Application of payment in non-consumer-goods transaction.] In a transaction other than a consumer-goods transaction, if the extent to which a security interest is a purchase-money security interest depends on the application of a payment to a particular obligation, the payment must be applied:

(1)   in accordance with any reasonable method of application to which the parties agree;

(2)   in the absence of the parties' agreement to a reasonable method, in accordance with any intention of the obligor manifested at or before the time of payment; or

(3)   in the absence of an agreement to a reasonable method and a timely manifestation of the obligor's intention, in the following order:

(A)   to obligations that are not secured; and

(B)   if more than one obligation is secured, to obligations secured by purchase-money security interests in the order in which those obligations were incurred.

(f)   [No loss of status of purchase-money security interest in non-consumer-goods transaction.] In a transaction other than a consumer-goods transaction, a purchase-money security interest does not lose its status as such, even if:

(1)   the purchase-money collateral also secures an obligation that is not a purchase-money obligation;

(2)   collateral that is not purchase-money collateral also secures the purchase-money obligation; or

(3)   the purchase-money obligation has been renewed, refinanced, consolidated, or restructured.

(g)   [Burden of proof in non-consumer-goods transaction.] In a transaction other than a consumer-goods transaction, a secured party claiming a purchase- money security interest has the burden of establishing the extent to which the security interest is a purchase-money security interest.

(h)   [Non-consumer-goods transactions; no inference.] The limitation of the rules in subsections (e), (f), and (g) to transactions other than consumer-goods transactions is intended to leave to the court the determination of the proper rules in consumer-goods transactions. The court may not infer from that limitation the nature of the proper rule in consumer-goods transactions and may continue to apply established approaches.

§ 9-104. Control of Deposit Account

(a)   [Requirements for control.] A secured party has control of a deposit account if:

(1)   the secured party is the bank with which the deposit account is maintained;

(2)   the debtor, secured party, and bank have agreed in an authenticated record that the bank will comply with instructions originated by the secured party directing disposition of the funds in the deposit account without further consent by the debtor; or

(3)   the secured party becomes the bank's customer with respect to the deposit account.

(b)   [Debtor's right to direct disposition.] A secured party that has satisfied subsection (a) has control, even if the debtor retains the right to direct the disposition of funds from the deposit account.

§ 9-105. Control of Electronic Chattel Paper

A secured party has control of electronic chattel paper if the record or records comprising the chattel paper are created, stored, and assigned in such a manner that:

(1)   a single authoritative copy of the record or records exists which is unique, identifiable and, except as otherwise provided in paragraphs (4), (5), and (6), unalterable;

(2)   the authoritative copy identifies the secured party as the assignee of the record or records;

(3)   the authoritative copy is communicated to and maintained by the secured party or its designated custodian;

(4)   copies or revisions that add or change an identified assignee of the authoritative copy can be made only with the participation of the secured party;

(5)   each copy of the authoritative copy and any copy of a copy is readily identifiable as a copy that is not the authoritative copy; and

(6)   any revision of the authoritative copy is readily identifiable as an authorized or unauthorized revision.

§ 9-106. Control of Investment Property

(a)   [Control under Section 8-106.] A person has control of a certificated security, uncertificated security, or security entitlement as provided in Section 8-106.

(b)   [Control of commodity contract.] A secured party has control of a commodity contract if:

(1)   the secured party is the commodity intermediary with which the commodity contract is carried; or

(2)   the commodity customer, secured party, and commodity intermediary have agreed that the commodity intermediary will apply any value distributed on account of the commodity contract as directed by the secured party without further consent by the commodity customer.

(c)   [Effect of control of securities account or commodity account.] A secured party having control of all security entitlements or commodity contracts carried in a securities account or commodity account has control over the securities account or commodity account.

§ 9-107. Control of Letter-of-Credit Right

A secured party has control of a letter-of-credit right to the extent of any right to payment or performance by the issuer or any nominated person if the issuer or nominated person has consented to an assignment of proceeds of the letter of credit under Section 5-114(c) or otherwise applicable law or practice.

§ 9-108. Sufficiency of Description

(a)   [Sufficiency of description.] Except as otherwise provided in subsections (c), (d), and (e), a description of personal or real property is sufficient, whether or not it is specific, if it reasonably identifies what is described.

(b)   [Examples of reasonable identification.] Except as otherwise provided in subsection (d), a description of collateral reasonably identifies the collateral if it identifies the collateral by:

(1)   specific listing;

(2)   category;

(3)   except as otherwise provided in subsection (e), a type of collateral defined in [the Uniform Commercial Code];

(4)   quantity;

(5)   computational or allocational formula or procedure; or

(6)   except as otherwise provided in subsection (c), any other method, if the identity of the collateral is objectively determinable.

(c)   [Supergeneric description not sufficient.] A description of collateral as "all the debtor's assets" or "all the debtor's personal property" or using words of similar import does not reasonably identify the collateral.

(d)   [Investment property.] Except as otherwise provided in subsection (e), a description of a security entitlement, securities account, or commodity account is sufficient if it describes:

(1)   the collateral by those terms or as investment property; or

(2)   the underlying financial asset or commodity contract.

(e)   [When description by type insufficient.] A description only by type of collateral defined in [the Uniform Commercial Code] is an insufficient description of:

(1)   a commercial tort claim; or

(2)   in a consumer transaction, consumer goods, a security entitlement, a securities account, or a commodity account.

Subpart 2. Applicability of Article
§ 9-109. Scope

(a) [General scope of article.] Except as otherwise provided in subsections (c) and (d), this Article applies to:

(1) a transaction, regardless of its form, that creates a security interest in personal property or fixtures by contract;

(2) an agricultural lien;

(3) a sale of accounts, chattel paper, payment intangibles, or promissory notes;

(4) a consignment;

(5) a security interest arising under Section 2-401, 2-505, 2-711(3), or 2A-508(5), as provided in Section 9-110; and

(6) a security interest arising under Section 4-210 or 5-118.

(b) [Security interest in secured obligation.] The application of this Article to a security interest in a secured obligation is not affected by the fact that the obligation is itself secured by a transaction or interest to which this Article does not apply.

(c) [Extent to which Article does not apply.] This Article does not apply to the extent that:

(1) a statute, regulation, or treaty of the United States preempts this article;

(2) another statute of this State expressly governs the creation, perfection, priority, or enforcement of a security interest created by this State or a governmental unit of this State;

(3) a statute of another State, a foreign country, or a governmental unit of another State or a foreign country, other than a statute generally applicable to security interests, expressly governs creation, perfection, priority, or enforcement of a security interest created by the State, country, or governmental unit; or

(4) the rights of a transferee beneficiary or nominated person under a letter of credit are independent and superior under Section 5-114.

(d) [Inapplicability of article.] This Article does not apply to:

(1) a landlord's lien, other than an agricultural lien;

(2) a lien, other than an agricultural lien, given by statute or other rule of law for services or materials, but Section 9-333 applies with respect to priority of the lien;

(3) an assignment of a claim for wages, salary, or other compensation of an employee;

(4) a sale of accounts, chattel paper, payment intangibles, or promissory notes as part of a sale of the business out of which they arose;

(5) an assignment of accounts, chattel paper, payment intangibles, or promissory notes which is for the purpose of collection only;

(6) an assignment of a right to payment under a contract to an assignee that is also obligated to perform under the contract;

(7) an assignment of a single account, payment intangible, or promissory note to an assignee in full or partial satisfaction of a preexisting indebtedness;

(8) a transfer of an interest in or an assignment of a claim under a policy of insurance, other than an assignment by or to a health-care provider of a health-care-insurance receivable and any subsequent assignment of the right to payment, but Sections 9-315 and 9-322 apply with respect to proceeds and priorities in proceeds;

(9) an assignment of a right represented by a judgment, other than a judgment taken on a right to payment that was collateral;

(10) a right of recoupment or set-off, but:

    (A) Section 9-340 applies with respect to the effectiveness of rights of recoupment or set-off against deposit accounts; and

    (B) Section 9-404 applies with respect to defenses or claims of an account debtor;

(11) the creation or transfer of an interest in or lien on real property, including a lease or rents thereunder, except to the extent that provision is made for:

    (A) liens on real property in Sections 9-203 and 9-308;

    (B) fixtures in Section 9-334;

(C) fixture filings in Sections 9-501, 9-502, 9-512, 9-516, and 9-519; and
(D) security agreements covering personal and real property in Section 9-604;
(12) an assignment of a claim arising in tort, other than a commercial tort claim, but Sections 9-315 and 9-322 apply with respect to proceeds and priorities in proceeds; or
(13) an assignment of a deposit account in a consumer transaction, but Sections 9-315 and 9-322 apply with respect to proceeds and priorities in proceeds.

§ 9-110. Security Interests Arising under Article 2 or 2A

A security interest arising under Section 2-401, 2-505, 2-711(3), or 2A-508(5) is subject to this article. However, until the debtor obtains possession of the goods:
(1) the security interest is enforceable, even if Section 9-203(b)(3) has not been satisfied;
(2) filing is not required to perfect the security interest;
(3) the rights of the secured party after default by the debtor are governed by Article 2 or 2A; and
(4) the security interest has priority over a conflicting security interest created by the debtor.

PART 2. EFFECTIVENESS OF SECURITY AGREEMENT; ATTACHMENT OF SECURITY INTEREST; RIGHTS OF PARTIES TO SECURITY AGREEMENT

Subpart 1. Effectiveness and Attachment

§ 9-201. General Effectiveness of Security Agreement

(a) [General effectiveness.] Except as otherwise provided in [the Uniform Commercial Code], a security agreement is effective according to its terms between the parties, against purchasers of the collateral, and against creditors.
(b) [Applicable consumer laws and other law.] A transaction subject to this Article is subject to any applicable rule of law which establishes a different rule for consumers and [insert reference to (i) any other statute or regulation that regulates the rates, charges, agreements, and practices for loans, credit sales, or other extensions of credit and (ii) any consumer-protection statute or regulation].
(c) [Other applicable law controls.] In case of conflict between this Article and a rule of law, statute, or regulation described in subsection (b), the rule of law, statute, or regulation controls. Failure to comply with a statute or regulation described in subsection (b) has only the effect the statute or regulation specifies.
(d) [Further deference to other applicable law.] This Article does not:
(1) validate any rate, charge, agreement, or practice that violates a rule of law, statute, or regulation described in subsection (b); or
(2) extend the application of the rule of law, statute, or regulation to a transaction not otherwise subject to it.

§ 9-202. Title to Collateral Immaterial

Except as otherwise provided with respect to consignments or sales of accounts, chattel paper, payment intangibles, or promissory notes, the provisions of this Article with regard to rights and obligations apply whether title to collateral is in the secured party or the debtor.

§ 9-203. Attachment and Enforceability of Security Interest; Proceeds; Supporting Obligations; Formal Requisites

(a) [Attachment.] A security interest attaches to collateral when it becomes enforceable against the debtor with respect to the collateral, unless an agreement expressly postpones the time of attachment.
(b) [Enforceability.] Except as otherwise provided in subsections (c) through (i), a security interest is enforceable against the debtor and third parties with respect to the collateral only if :
(1) value has been given;
(2) the debtor has rights in the collateral or the power to transfer rights in the collateral to a secured party; and
(3) one of the following conditions is met:

(A) the debtor has authenticated a security agreement that provides a description of the collateral and, if the security interest covers timber to be cut, a description of the land concerned;

(B) the collateral is not a certificated security and is in the possession of the secured party under Section 9-313 pursuant to the debtor's security agreement;

(C) the collateral is a certificated security in registered form and the security certificate has been delivered to the secured party under Section 8-301 pursuant to the debtor's security agreement; or

(D) the collateral is deposit accounts, electronic chattel paper, investment property, or letter-of-credit rights, and the secured party has control under Section 9-104, 9-105, 9-106, or 9-107 pursuant to the debtor's security agreement.

(c) [Other UCC provisions.] Subsection (b) is subject to Section 4-210 on the security interest of a collecting bank, Section 5-118 on the security interest of a letter-of-credit issuer or nominated person, Section 9-110 on a security interest arising under Article 2 or 2A, and Section 9-206 on security interests in investment property.

(d) [When person becomes bound by another person's security agreement.] A person becomes bound as debtor by a security agreement entered into by another person if, by operation of law other than this Article or by contract:

(1) the security agreement becomes effective to create a security interest in the person's property; or

(2) the person becomes generally obligated for the obligations of the other person, including the obligation secured under the security agreement, and acquires or succeeds to all or substantially all of the assets of the other person.

(e) [Effect of new debtor becoming bound.] If a new debtor becomes bound as debtor by a security agreement entered into by another person:

(1) the agreement satisfies subsection (b)(3) with respect to existing or after-acquired property of the new debtor to the extent the property is described in the agreement; and

(2) another agreement is not necessary to make a security interest in the property enforceable.

(f) [Proceeds and supporting obligations.] The attachment of a security interest in collateral gives the secured party the rights to proceeds provided by Section 9-315 and is also attachment of a security interest in a supporting obligation for the collateral.

(g) [Lien securing right to payment.] The attachment of a security interest in a right to payment or performance secured by a security interest or other lien on personal or real property is also attachment of a security interest in the security interest, mortgage, or other lien.

(h) [Security entitlement carried in securities account.] The attachment of a security interest in a securities account is also attachment of a security interest in the security entitlements carried in the securities account.

(i) [Commodity contracts carried in commodity account.] The attachment of a security interest in a commodity account is also attachment of a security interest in the commodity contracts carried in the commodity account.

§ 9-204. After-Acquired Property; Future Advances

(a) [After-acquired collateral.] Except as otherwise provided in subsection (b), a security agreement may create or provide for a security interest in after-acquired collateral.

(b) [When after-acquired property clause not effective.] A security interest does not attach under a term constituting an after-acquired property clause to:

(1) consumer goods, other than an accession when given as additional security, unless the debtor acquires rights in them within 10 days after the secured party gives value; or

(2) a commercial tort claim.

(c) [Future advances and other value.] A security agreement may provide that collateral secures, or that accounts, chattel paper, payment intangibles, or promissory notes are sold in connection with, future advances or other value, whether or not the advances or value are given pursuant to commitment.

§ 9-205. Use or Disposition of Collateral Permissible

(a) [When security interest not invalid or fraudulent.] A security interest is not invalid or fraudulent against creditors solely because:

(1) the debtor has the right or ability to:

    (A) use, commingle, or dispose of all or part of the collateral, including returned or repossessed goods;

    (B) collect, compromise, enforce, or otherwise deal with collateral;

    (C) accept the return of collateral or make repossessions; or

    (D) use, commingle, or dispose of proceeds; or

(2) the secured party fails to require the debtor to account for proceeds or replace collateral.

(b) [Requirements of possession not relaxed.] This section does not relax the requirements of possession if attachment, perfection, or enforcement of a security interest depends upon possession of the collateral by the secured party.

§ 9-206. Security Interest Arising in Purchase or Delivery of Financial Asset

(a) [Security interest when person buys through securities intermediary.] A security interest in favor of a securities intermediary attaches to a person's security entitlement if:

(1) the person buys a financial asset through the securities intermediary in a transaction in which the person is obligated to pay the purchase price to the securities intermediary at the time of the purchase; and

(2) the securities intermediary credits the financial asset to the buyer's securities account before the buyer pays the securities intermediary.

(b) [Security interest secures obligation to pay for financial asset.] The security interest described in subsection (a) secures the person's obligation to pay for the financial asset.

(c) [Security interest in payment against delivery transaction.] A security interest in favor of a person that delivers a certificated security or other financial asset represented by a writing attaches to the security or other financial asset if:

(1) the security or other financial asset:

    (A) in the ordinary course of business is transferred by delivery with any necessary indorsement or assignment; and

    (B) is delivered under an agreement between persons in the business of dealing with such securities or financial assets; and

(2) the agreement calls for delivery against payment.

(d) [Security interest secures obligation to pay for delivery.] The security interest described in subsection (c) secures the obligation to make payment for the delivery.

Subpart 2. Rights and Duties

§ 9-207. Rights and Duties of Secured Party Having Possession or Control of Collateral

(a) [Duty of care when secured party in possession.] Except as otherwise provided in subsection (d), a secured party shall use reasonable care in the custody and preservation of collateral in the secured party's possession. In the case of chattel paper or an instrument, reasonable care includes taking necessary steps to preserve rights against prior parties unless otherwise agreed.

(b) [Expenses, risks, duties, and rights when secured party in possession.] Except as otherwise provided in subsection (d), if a secured party has possession of collateral:

(1) reasonable expenses, including the cost of insurance and payment of taxes or other charges, incurred in the custody, preservation, use, or operation of the collateral are chargeable to the debtor and are secured by the collateral;

(2) the risk of accidental loss or damage is on the debtor to the extent of a deficiency in any effective insurance coverage;

(3) the secured party shall keep the collateral identifiable, but fungible collateral may be commingled; and

(4) the secured party may use or operate the collateral:
  (A) for the purpose of preserving the collateral or its value;
  (B) as permitted by an order of a court having competent jurisdiction; or
  (C) except in the case of consumer goods, in the manner and to the extent agreed by the
       debtor.
(c) [Duties and rights when secured party in possession or control.] Except as otherwise provided in subsection (d), a secured party having possession of collateral or control of collateral
under Section 9-104, 9-105, 9-106, or 9-107:
(1) may hold as additional security any proceeds, except money or funds, received from the
     collateral;
(2) shall apply money or funds received from the collateral to reduce the secured obligation,
     unless remitted to the debtor; and
(3) may create a security interest in the collateral.
(d) [Buyer of certain rights to payment.] If the secured party is a buyer of accounts, chattel
paper, payment intangibles, or promissory notes or a consignor:
(1) subsection (a) does not apply unless the secured party is entitled under an agreement:
  (A) to charge back uncollected collateral; or
  (B) otherwise to full or limited recourse against the debtor or a secondary obligor based
       on the nonpayment or other default of an account debtor or other obligor on the col-
       lateral; and
(2) subsections (b) and (c) do not apply.

§ 9-208. Additional Duties of Secured Party Having Control of Collateral
(a) [Applicability of section.] This section applies to cases in which there is no outstanding secured obligation and the secured party is not committed to make advances, incur obligations,
or otherwise give value.
(b) [Duties of secured party after receiving demand from debtor.] Within 10 days after receiving an authenticated demand by the debtor:
(1) a secured party having control of a deposit account under Section 9-104(a)(2) shall send to
     the bank with which the deposit account is maintained an authenticated statement that
     releases the bank from any further obligation to comply with instructions originated by the
     secured party;
(2) a secured party having control of a deposit account under Section 9-104(a)(3) shall:
  (A) pay the debtor the balance on deposit in the deposit account; or
  (B) transfer the balance on deposit into a deposit account in the debtor's name;
(3) a secured party, other than a buyer, having control of electronic chattel paper under Sec-
     tion 9-105 shall:
  (A) communicate the authoritative copy of the electronic chattel paper to the debtor or
       its designated custodian;
  (B) if the debtor designates a custodian that is the designated custodian with which the
       authoritative copy of the electronic chattel paper is maintained for the secured party,
       communicate to the custodian an authenticated record releasing the designated cus-
       todian from any further obligation to comply with instructions originated by the secu-
       red party and instructing the custodian to comply with instructions originated by the
       debtor; and
  (C) take appropriate action to enable the debtor or its designated custodian to make co-
       pies of or revisions to the authoritative copy which add or change an identified assig-
       nee of the authoritative copy without the consent of the secured party;
(4) a secured party having control of investment property under Section 8-106(d)(2) or 9-
     106(b) shall send to the securities intermediary or commodity intermediary with which the
     security entitlement or commodity contract is maintained an authenticated record that
     releases the securities intermediary or commodity intermediary from any further obligation
     to comply with entitlement orders or directions originated by the secured party;

(5)   a secured party having control of a letter-of-credit right under Section 9-107 shall send to each person having an unfulfilled obligation to pay or deliver proceeds of the letter of credit to the secured party an authenticated release from any further obligation to pay or deliver proceeds of the letter of credit to the secured party.

§ 9-209. Duties of Secured Party If Account Debtor Has Been Notified of Assignment

(a)   [Applicability of section.] Except as otherwise provided in subsection (c), this section applies if:

(1)   there is no outstanding secured obligation; and

(2)   the secured party is not committed to make advances, incur obligations, or otherwise give value.

(b)   [Duties of secured party after receiving demand from debtor.] Within 10 days after receiving an authenticated demand by the debtor, a secured party shall send to an account debtor that has received notification of an assignment to the secured party as assignee under Section 9-406(a) an authenticated record that releases the account debtor from any further obligation to the secured party.

(c)   [Inapplicability to sales.] This section does not apply to an assignment constituting the sale of an account, chattel paper, or payment intangible.

§ 9-210. Request for Accounting; Request Regarding List of Collateral or Statement of Account

(a)   [Definitions.] In this section:

(1)   "Request" means a record of a type described in paragraph (2), (3), or (4).

(2)   "Request for an accounting" means a record authenticated by a debtor requesting that the recipient provide an accounting of the unpaid obligations secured by collateral and reasonably identifying the transaction or relationship that is the subject of the request.

(3)   "Request regarding a list of collateral" means a record authenticated by a debtor requesting that the recipient approve or correct a list of what the debtor believes to be the collateral securing an obligation and reasonably identifying the transaction or relationship that is the subject of the request.

(4)   "Request regarding a statement of account" means a record authenticated by a debtor requesting that the recipient approve or correct a statement indicating what the debtor believes to be the aggregate amount of unpaid obligations secured by collateral as of a specified date and reasonably identifying the transaction or relationship that is the subject of the request.

(b)   [Duty to respond to requests.] Subject to subsections (c), (d), (e), and (f), a secured party, other than a buyer of accounts, chattel paper, payment intangibles, or promissory notes or a consignor, shall comply with a request within 14 days after receipt:

(1)   in the case of a request for an accounting, by authenticating and sending to the debtor an accounting; and

(2)   in the case of a request regarding a list of collateral or a request regarding a statement of account, by authenticating and sending to the debtor an approval or correction.

(c)   [Request regarding list of collateral; statement concerning type of collateral.] A secured party that claims a security interest in all of a particular type of collateral owned by the debtor may comply with a request regarding a list of collateral by sending to the debtor an authenticated record including a statement to that effect within 14 days after receipt.

(d)   [Request regarding list of collateral; no interest claimed.] A person that receives a request regarding a list of collateral, claims no interest in the collateral when it receives the request, and claimed an interest in the collateral at an earlier time shall comply with the request within 14 days after receipt by sending to the debtor an authenticated record:

(1)   disclaiming any interest in the collateral; and

(2)   if known to the recipient, providing the name and mailing address of any assignee of or successor to the recipient's interest in the collateral.

(e)   [Request for accounting or regarding statement of account; no interest in obligation claimed.] A person that receives a request for an accounting or a request regarding a statement of

account, claims no interest in the obligations when it receives the request, and claimed an interest in the obligations at an earlier time shall comply with the request within 14 days after receipt by sending to the debtor an authenticated record:
(1)   disclaiming any interest in the obligations; and
(2)   if known to the recipient, providing the name and mailing address of any assignee of or successor to the recipient's interest in the obligations.
(f)   [Charges for responses.] A debtor is entitled without charge to one response to a request under this section during any six-month period. The secured party may require payment of a charge not exceeding $25 for each additional response.

PART 3. PERFECTION AND PRIORITY
Subpart 1. Law Governing Perfection and Priority
§ 9-301. Law Governing Perfection and Priority of Security Interests
Except as otherwise provided in Sections 9-303 through 9-306, the following rules determine the law governing perfection, the effect of perfection or nonperfection, and the priority of a security interest in collateral:
(1)   Except as otherwise provided in this section, while a debtor is located in a jurisdiction, the local law of that jurisdiction governs perfection, the effect of perfection or nonperfection, and the priority of a security interest in collateral.
(2)   While collateral is located in a jurisdiction, the local law of that jurisdiction governs perfection, the effect of perfection or nonperfection, and the priority of a possessory security interest in that collateral.
(3)   Except as otherwise provided in paragraph (4), while negotiable documents, goods, instruments, money, or tangible chattel paper is located in a jurisdiction, the local law of that jurisdiction governs:
(A)   perfection of a security interest in the goods by filing a fixture filing;
(B)   perfection of a security interest in timber to be cut; and
(C)   the effect of perfection or nonperfection and the priority of a nonpossessory security interest in the collateral.
(4)   The local law of the jurisdiction in which the wellhead or minehead is located governs perfection, the effect of perfection or nonperfection, and the priority of a security interest in as-extracted collateral.

§ 9-302. Law Governing Perfection and Priority of Agricultural Liens
While farm products are located in a jurisdiction, the local law of that jurisdiction governs perfection, the effect of perfection or nonperfection, and the priority of an agricultural lien on the farm products.

§ 9-303. Law Governing Perfection and Priority of Security Interests
in Goods Covered by a Certificate of Title
(a)   [Applicability of section.] This section applies to goods covered by a certificate of title, even if there is no other relationship between the jurisdiction under whose certificate of title the goods are covered and the goods or the debtor.
(b)   [When goods covered by certificate of title.] Goods become covered by a certificate of title when a valid application for the certificate of title and the applicable fee are delivered to the appropriate authority. Goods cease to be covered by a certificate of title at the earlier of the time the certificate of title ceases to be effective under the law of the issuing jurisdiction or the time the goods become covered subsequently by a certificate of title issued by another jurisdiction.
(c)   [Applicable law.] The local law of the jurisdiction under whose certificate of title the goods are covered governs perfection, the effect of perfection or nonperfection, and the priority of a security interest in goods covered by a certificate of title from the time the goods become covered by the certificate of title until the goods cease to be covered by the certificate of title.

§ 9-304. Law Governing Perfection and Priority of Security Interests in Deposit Accounts

(a) [Law of bank's jurisdiction governs.] The local law of a bank's jurisdiction governs perfection, the effect of perfection or nonperfection, and the priority of a security interest in a deposit account maintained with that bank.

(b) [Bank's jurisdiction.] The following rules determine a bank's jurisdiction for purposes of this part:

(1) If an agreement between the bank and the debtor governing the deposit account expressly provides that a particular jurisdiction is the bank's jurisdiction for purposes of this part, this article, or [the Uniform Commercial Code], that jurisdiction is the bank's jurisdiction.

(2) If paragraph (1) does not apply and an agreement between the bank and its customer governing the deposit account expressly provides that the agreement is governed by the law of a particular jurisdiction, that jurisdiction is the bank's jurisdiction.

(3) If neither paragraph (1) nor paragraph (2) applies and an agreement between the bank and its customer governing the deposit account expressly provides that the deposit account is maintained at an office in a particular jurisdiction, that jurisdiction is the bank's jurisdiction.

(4) If none of the preceding paragraphs applies, the bank's jurisdiction is the jurisdiction in which the office identified in an account statement as the office serving the customer's account is located.

(5) If none of the preceding paragraphs applies, the bank's jurisdiction is the jurisdiction in which the chief executive office of the bank is located.

§ 9-305. Law Governing Perfection and Priority of Security Interests in Investment Property

(a) [Governing law: general rules.] Except as otherwise provided in subsection (c), the following rules apply:

(1) While a security certificate is located in a jurisdiction, the local law of that jurisdiction governs perfection, the effect of perfection or nonperfection, and the priority of a security interest in the certificated security represented thereby.

(2) The local law of the issuer's jurisdiction as specified in Section 8-110(d) governs perfection, the effect of perfection or nonperfection, and the priority of a security interest in an uncertificated security.

(3) The local law of the securities intermediary's jurisdiction as specified in Section 8-110(e) governs perfection, the effect of perfection or nonperfection, and the priority of a security interest in a security entitlement or securities account.

(4) The local law of the commodity intermediary's jurisdiction governs perfection, the effect of perfection or nonperfection, and the priority of a security interest in a commodity contract or commodity account.

(b) [Commodity intermediary's jurisdiction.] The following rules determine a commodity intermediary's jurisdiction for purposes of this part:

(1) If an agreement between the commodity intermediary and commodity customer governing the commodity account expressly provides that a particular jurisdiction is the commodity intermediary's jurisdiction for purposes of this part, this article, or [the Uniform Commercial Code], that jurisdiction is the commodity intermediary's jurisdiction.

(2) If paragraph (1) does not apply and an agreement between the commodity intermediary and commodity customer governing the commodity account expressly provides that the agreement is governed by the law of a particular jurisdiction, that jurisdiction is the commodity intermediary's jurisdiction.

(3) If neither paragraph (1) nor paragraph (2) applies and an agreement between the commodity intermediary and commodity customer governing the commodity account expressly provides that the commodity account is maintained at an office in a particular jurisdiction, that jurisdiction is the commodity intermediary's jurisdiction.

(4) If none of the preceding paragraphs applies, the commodity intermediary's jurisdiction is the jurisdiction in which the office identified in an account statement as the office serving the commodity customer's account is located.

(5)   If none of the preceding paragraphs applies, the commodity intermediary's jurisdiction is the jurisdiction in which the chief executive office of the commodity intermediary is located.

(c)   [When perfection governed by law of jurisdiction where debtor located.] The local law of the jurisdiction in which the debtor is located governs:

(1)   perfection of a security interest in investment property by filing;

(2)   automatic perfection of a security interest in investment property created by a broker or securities intermediary; and

(3)   automatic perfection of a security interest in a commodity contract or commodity account created bya commodity intermediary.

§ 9-306. Law Governing Perfection and Priority of Security Interests in Letter-of-Credit Rights

(a)   [Governing law: issuer's or nominated person's jurisdiction.] Subject to subsection (c), the local law of the issuer's jurisdiction or a nominated person's jurisdiction governs perfection, the effect of perfection or nonperfection, and the priority of a security interest in a letter-of-credit right if the issuer's jurisdiction or nominated person's jurisdiction is a State.

(b)   [Issuer's or nominated person's jurisdiction.] For purposes of this part, an issuer's jurisdiction or nominated person's jurisdiction is the jurisdiction whose law governs the liability of the issuer or nominated person with respect to the letter-of-credit right as provided in Section 5-116.

(c)   [When section not applicable.] This section does not apply to a security interest that is perfected only under Section 9-308(d).

§ 9-307. Location of Debtor

(a)   ["Place of business."] In this section, "place of business" means a place where a debtor conducts its affairs.

(b)   [Debtor's location: general rules.] Except as otherwise provided in this section, the following rules determine a debtor's location:

(1)   A debtor who is an individual is located at the individual's principal residence.

(2)   A debtor that is an organization and has only one place of business is located at its place of business.

(3)   A debtor that is an organization and has more than one place of business is located at its chief executive office.

(c)   [Limitation of applicability of subsection (b).] Subsection (b) applies only if a debtor's residence, place of business, or chief executive office, as applicable, is located in a jurisdiction whose law generally requires information concerning the existence of a nonpossessory security interest to be made generally available in a filing, recording, or registration system as a condition or result of the security interest's obtaining priority over the rights of a lien creditor with respect to the collateral. If subsection (b) does not apply, the debtor is located in the District of Columbia.

(d)   [Continuation of location: cessation of existence, etc.] A person that ceases to exist, have a residence, or have a place of business continues to be located in the jurisdiction specified by subsections (b) and (c).

(e)   [Location of registered organization organized under State law.] A registered organization that is organized under the law of a State is located in that State.

(f)   [Location of registered organization organized under federal law; bank branches and agencies.] Except as otherwise provided in subsection (i), a registered organization that is organized under the law of the United States and a branch or agency of a bank that is not organized under the law of the United States or a State are located:

(1)   in the State that the law of the United States designates, if the law designates a State of location;

(2)   in the State that the registered organization, branch, or agency designates, if the law of the United States authorizes the registered organization, branch, or agency to designate its State of location; or

(3)   in the District of Columbia, if neither paragraph (1) nor paragraph (2) applies.

(g) [Continuation of location: change in status of registered organization.] A registered organization continues to be located in the jurisdiction specified by subsection (e) or (f) notwithstanding:
(1) the suspension, revocation, forfeiture, or lapse of the registered organization's status as
such in its jurisdiction of organization; or
(2) the dissolution, winding up, or cancellation of the existence of the registered organization.
(h) [Location of United States.] The United States is located in the District of Columbia.
(i) [Location of foreign bank branch or agency if licensed in only one state.] A branch or agency of a bank that is not organized under the law of the United States or a State is located in the
State in which the branch or agency is licensed, if all branches and agencies of the bank are
licensed in only one State.
(j) [Location of foreign air carrier.] A foreign air carrier under the Federal Aviation Act of 1958,
as amended, is located at the designated office of the agent upon which service of process may
be made on behalf of the carrier.
(k) [Section applies only to this part.] This section applies only for purposes of this part.

Subpart 2. Perfection
§ 9-308. When Security Interest or Agricultural Lien Is Perfected; Continuity of Perfection
(a) [Perfection of security interest.] Except as otherwise provided in this section and Section 9-
309, a security interest is perfected if it has attached and all of the applicable requirements for
perfection in Sections 9-310 through 9-316 have been satisfied. A security interest is perfected
when it attaches if the applicable requirements are satisfied before the security interest
attaches.
(b) [Perfection of agricultural lien.] An agricultural lien is perfected if it has become effective
and all of the applicable requirements for perfection in Section 9-310 have been satisfied. An
agricultural lien is perfected when it becomes effective if the applicable requirements are satisfied before the agricultural lien becomes effective.
(c) [Continuous perfection; perfection by different methods.] A security interest or
agricultural lien is perfected continuously if it is originally perfected by one method under this
Article and is later perfected by another method under this article, without an intermediate
period when it was unperfected.
(d) [Supporting obligation.] Perfection of a security interest in collateral also perfects a security
interest in a supporting obligation for the collateral.
(e) [Lien securing right to payment.] Perfection of a security interest in a right to payment or
performance also perfects a security interest in a security interest, mortgage, or other lien on
personal or real property securing the right.
(f) [Security entitlement carried in securities account.] Perfection of a security interest in a
securities account also perfects a security interest in the security entitlements carried in the
securities account.
(g) [Commodity contract carried in commodity account.] Perfection of a security interest in a
commodity account also perfects a security interest in the commodity contracts carried in the
commodity account.

§ 9-309. Security Interest Perfected upon Attachment
The following security interests are perfected when they attach:
(1) a purchase-money security interest in consumer goods, except as otherwise provided in
Section 9-311(b) with respect to consumer goods that are subject to a statute or treaty described in Section 9-311(a);
(2) an assignment of accounts or payment intangibles which does not by itself or in conjunction with other assignments to the same assignee transfer a significant part of the assignor's
outstanding accounts or payment intangibles;
(3) a sale of a payment intangible;
(4) a sale of a promissory note;
(5) a security interest created by the assignment of a health-care-insurance receivable to the
provider of the health-care goods or services;

(6)   a security interest arising under Section 2-401, 2-505, 2-711(3), or 2A-508(5), until the debtor obtains possession of the collateral;
(7)   a security interest of a collecting bank arising under Section 4-210;
(8)   a security interest of an issuer or nominated person arising under Section 5-118;
(9)   a security interest arising in the delivery of a financial asset under Section 9-206(c);
(10) a security interest in investment property created by a broker or securities intermediary;
(11) a security interest in a commodity contract or a commodity account created by a commodity intermediary;
(12) an assignment for the benefit of all creditors of the transferor and subsequent transfers by the assignee thereunder; and
(13) a security interest created by an assignment of a beneficial interest in a decedent's estate.

§ 9-310. When Filing Required to Perfect Security Interest or Agricultural Lien; Security Interests and Agricultural Liens to Which Filing Provisions Do Not Apply

(a)   [General rule: perfection by filing.] Except as otherwise provided in subsection (b) and Section 9-312(b), a financing statement must be filed to perfect all security interests and agricultural liens.
(b)   [Exceptions: filing not necessary.] The filing of a financing statement is not necessary to perfect a security interest:
(1)   that is perfected under Section 9-308(d), (e), (f), or (g);
(2)   that is perfected under Section 9-309 when it attaches;
(3)   in property subject to a statute, regulation, or treaty described in Section 9-311(a);
(4)   in goods in possession of a bailee which is perfected under Section 9-312(d)(1) or (2);
(5)   in certificated securities, documents, goods, or instruments which is perfected without filing or possession under Section 9-312(e), (f), or (g);
(6)   in collateral in the secured party's possession under Section 9-313;
(7)   in a certificated security which is perfected by delivery of the security certificate to the secured party under Section 9-313;
(8)   in deposit accounts, electronic chattel paper, investment property, or letter-of-credit rights which is perfected by control under Section 9-314;
(9)   in proceeds which is perfected under Section 9-315; or
(10) that is perfected under Section 9-316.
(c)   [Assignment of perfected security interest.] If a secured party assigns a perfected security interest or agricultural lien, a filing under this Article is not required to continue the perfected status of the security interest against creditors of and transferees from the original debtor.

§ 9-311. Perfection of Security Interests in Property Subject to Certain Statutes, Regulations, and Treaties

(a)   [Security interest subject to other law.] Except as otherwise provided in subsection (d), the filing of a financing statement is not necessary or effective to perfect a security interest in property subject to:
(1)   a statute, regulation, or treaty of the United States whose requirements for a security interest's obtaining priority over the rights of a lien creditor with respect to the property preempt Section 9-310(a);
(2)   [list any certificate-of-title statute covering automobiles, trailers, mobile homes, boats, farm tractors, or the like, which provides for a security interest to be indicated on the certificate as a condition or result of perfection, and any non-Uniform Commercial Code central filing statute]; or
(3)   a certificate-of-title statute of another jurisdiction which provides for a security interest to be indicated on the certificate as a condition or result of the security interest's obtaining priority over the rights of a lien creditor with respect to the property.
(b)   [Compliance with other law.] Compliance with the requirements of a statute, regulation, or treaty described in subsection (a) for obtaining priority over the rights of a lien creditor is equivalent to the filing of a financing statement under this article. Except as otherwise provided in sub-

section (d) and Sections 9-313 and 9-316(d) and (e) for goods covered by a certificate of title, a security interest in property subject to a statute, regulation, or treaty described in subsection (a) may be perfected only by compliance with those requirements, and a security interest so perfected remains perfected notwithstanding a change in the use or transfer of possession of the collateral.

(c) [Duration and renewal of perfection.] Except as otherwise provided in subsection (d) and Section 9-316(d) and (e), duration and renewal of perfection of a security interest perfected by compliance with the requirements prescribed by a statute, regulation, or treaty described in subsection (a) are governed by the statute, regulation, or treaty. In other respects, the security interest is subject to this article.

(d) [Inapplicability to certain inventory.] During any period in which collateral subject to a statute specified in subsection (a)(2) is inventory held for sale or lease by a person or leased by that person as lessor and that person is in the business of selling goods of that kind, this section does not apply to a security interest in that collateral created by that person.

§ 9-312. Perfection of Security Interests in Chattel Paper, Deposit Accounts, Documents, Goods
Covered by Documents, Instruments, Investment Property, Letter-of-credit Rights, and Money;
Perfection by Permissive Filing; Temporary Perfection Without Filing or Transfer of Possession

(a) [Perfection by filing permitted.] A security interest in chattel paper, negotiable documents, instruments, or investment property may be perfected by filing.

(b) [Control or possession of certain collateral.] Except as otherwise provided in Section 9-315(c) and (d) for proceeds:

(1) a security interest in a deposit account may be perfected only by control under Section 9-314;

(2) and except as otherwise provided in Section 9-308(d), a security interest in a letter-of-credit right may be perfected only by control under Section 9-314; and

(3) a security interest in money may be perfected only by the secured party's taking possession under Section 9-313.

(c) [Goods covered by negotiable document.] While goods are in the possession of a bailee that has issued a negotiable document covering the goods:

(1) a security interest in the goods may be perfected by perfecting a security interest in the document; and

(2) a security interest perfected in the document has priority over any security interest that becomes perfected in the goods by another method during that time.

(d) [Goods covered by non-negotiable document.] While goods are in the possession of a bailee that has issued a non-negotiable document covering the goods, a security interest in the goods may be perfected by:

(1) issuance of a document in the name of the secured party;

(2) the bailee's receipt of notification of the secured party's interest; or

(3) filing as to the goods.

(e) [Temporary perfection: new value.] A security interest in certificated securities, negotiable documents, or instruments is perfected without filing or the taking of possession or control for a period of 20 days from the time it attaches to the extent that it arises for new value given under an authenticated security agreement.

(f) [Temporary perfection: goods or documents made available to debtor.] A perfected security interest in a negotiable document or goods in possession of a bailee, other than one that has issued a negotiable document for the goods, remains perfected for 20 days without filing if the secured party makes available to the debtor the goods or documents representing the goods for the purpose of:

(1) ultimate sale or exchange; or

(2) loading, unloading, storing, shipping, transshipping, manufacturing, processing, or otherwise dealing with them in a manner preliminary to their sale or exchange.

(g) [Temporary perfection: delivery of security certificate or instrument to debtor.] A perfected security interest in a certificated security or instrument remains perfected for 20 days without filing if the secured party delivers the security certificate or instrument to the debtor for the purpose of:
(1) ultimate sale or exchange; or
(2) presentation, collection, enforcement, renewal, or registration of transfer.
(h) [Expiration of temporary perfection.] After the 20-day period specified in subsection (e), (f), or (g) expires, perfection depends upon compliance with this article.

§ 9-313. When Possession by or Delivery to Secured Party Perfects Security Interest Without Filing
(a) [Perfection by possession or delivery.] Except as otherwise provided in subsection (b), a secured party may perfect a security interest in negotiable documents, goods, instruments, money, or tangible chattel paper by taking possession of the collateral. A secured party may perfect a security interest in certificated securities by taking delivery of the certificated securities under Section 8-301.
(b) [Goods covered by certificate of title.] With respect to goods covered by a certificate of title issued by this State, a secured party may perfect a security interest in the goods by taking possession of the goods only in the circumstances described in Section 9-316(d).
(c) [Collateral in possession of person other than debtor.] With respect to collateral other than certificated securities and goods covered by a document, a secured party takes possession of collateral in the possession of a person other than the debtor, the secured party, or a lessee of the collateral from the debtor in the ordinary course of the debtor's business, when:
(1) the person in possession authenticates a record acknowledging that it holds possession of the collateral for the secured party's benefit; or
(2) the person takes possession of the collateral after having authenticated a record acknowledging that it will hold possession of collateral for the secured party's benefit.
(d) [Time of perfection by possession; continuation of perfection.] If perfection of a security interest depends upon possession of the collateral by a secured party, perfection occurs no earlier than the time the secured party takes possession and continues only while the secured party retains possession.
(e) [Time of perfection by delivery; continuation of perfection.] A security interest in a certificated security in registered form is perfected by delivery when delivery of the certificated security occurs under Section 8-301 and remains perfected by delivery until the debtor obtains possession of the security certificate.
(f) [Acknowledgment not required.] A person in possession of collateral is not required to acknowledge that it holds possession for a secured party's benefit.
(g) [Effectiveness of acknowledgment; no duties or confirmation.] If a person acknowledges that it holds possession for the secured party's benefit:
(1) the acknowledgment is effective under subsection (c) or Section 8-301(a), even if the acknowledgment violates the rights of a debtor; and
(2) unless the person otherwise agrees or law other than this Article otherwise provides, the person does not owe any duty to the secured party and is not required to confirm the acknowledgment to another person.
(h) [Secured party's delivery to person other than debtor.] A secured party having possession of collateral does not relinquish possession by delivering the collateral to a person other than the debtor or a lessee of the collateral from the debtor in the ordinary course of the debtor's business if the person was instructed before the delivery or is instructed contemporaneously with the delivery:
(1) to hold possession of the collateral for the secured party's benefit; or
(2) to redeliver the collateral to the secured party.
(i) [Effect of delivery under subsection (h); no duties or confirmation.] A secured party does not relinquish possession, even if a delivery under subsection (h) violates the rights of a debtor. A person to which collateral is delivered under subsection (h) does not owe any duty to the

secured party and is not required to confirm the delivery to another person unless the person otherwise agrees or law other than this Article otherwise provides.

§ 9-314. Perfection by Control

(a) [Perfection by control.] A security interest in investment property, deposit accounts, letter-of-credit rights, or electronic chattel paper may be perfected by control of the collateral under Section 9-104, 9-105, 9-106, or 9-107.

(b) [Specified collateral: time of perfection by control; continuation of perfection.] A security interest in deposit accounts, electronic chattel paper, or letter-of-credit rights is perfected by control under Section 9-104, 9-105, or 9-107 when the secured party obtains control and remains perfected by control only while the secured party retains control.

(c) [Investment property: time of perfection by control; continuation of perfection.] A security interest in investment property is perfected by control under Section 9-106 from the time the secured party obtains control and remains perfected by control until:

(1) the secured party does not have control; and

(2) one of the following occurs:

    (A) if the collateral is a certificated security, the debtor has or acquires possession of the security certificate;

    (B) if the collateral is an uncertificated security, the issuer has registered or registers the debtor as the registered owner; or

    (C) if the collateral is a security entitlement, the debtor is or becomes the entitlement holder.

§ 9-315. Secured Party's Rights on Disposition of Collateral and in Proceeds

(a) [Disposition of collateral: continuation of security interest or agricultural lien; proceeds.] Except as otherwise provided in this Article and in Section 2-403(2):

(1) a security interest or agricultural lien continues in collateral notwithstanding sale, lease, license, exchange, or other disposition thereof unless the secured party authorized the disposition free of the security interest or agricultural lien; and

(2) a security interest attaches to any identifiable proceeds of collateral.

(b) [When commingled proceeds identifiable.] Proceeds that are commingled with other property are identifiable proceeds:

(1) if the proceeds are goods, to the extent provided by Section 9-336; and

(2) if the proceeds are not goods, to the extent that the secured party identifies the proceeds by a method of tracing, including application of equitable principles, that is permitted under law other than this Article with respect to commingled property of the type involved.

(c) [Perfection of security interest in proceeds.] A security interest in proceeds is a perfected security interest if the security interest in the original collateral was perfected.

(d) [Continuation of perfection.] A perfected security interest in proceeds becomes unperfected on the 21st day after the security interest attaches to the proceeds unless:

(1) the following conditions are satisfied:

    (A) a filed financing statement covers the original collateral;

    (B) the proceeds are collateral in which a security interest may be perfected by filing in the office in which the financing statement has been filed; and

    (C) the proceeds are not acquired with cash proceeds;

(2) the proceeds are identifiable cash proceeds; or

(3) the security interest in the proceeds is perfected other than under subsection (c) when the security interest attaches to the proceeds or within 20 days thereafter.

(e) [When perfected security interest in proceeds becomes unperfected.] If a filed financing statement covers the original collateral, a security interest in proceeds which remains perfected under subsection (d)(1) becomes unperfected at the later of:

(1) when the effectiveness of the filed financing statement lapses under Section 9-515 or is terminated under Section 9-513; or

(2)   the 21st day after the security interest attaches to the proceeds.

§ 9-316. *Continued Perfection of Security Interest Following Change in Governing Law*
(a)   [General rule: effect on perfection of change in governing law.] A security interest perfected pursuant to the law of the jurisdiction designated in Section 9-301(1) or 9-305(c) remains perfected until the earliest of:
(1)   the time perfection would have ceased under the law of that jurisdiction;
(2)   the expiration of four months after a change of the debtor's location to another jurisdiction; or
(3)   the expiration of one year after a transfer of collateral to a person that thereby becomes a debtor and is located in another jurisdiction.
(b)   [Security interest perfected or unperfected under law of new jurisdiction.] If a security interest described in subsection (a) becomes perfected under the law of the other jurisdiction before the earliest time or event described in that subsection, it remains perfected thereafter. If the security interest does not become perfected under the law of the other jurisdiction before the earliest time or event, it becomes unperfected and is deemed never to have been perfected as against a purchaser of the collateral for value.
(c)   [Possessory security interest in collateral moved to new jurisdiction.] A possessory security interest in collateral, other than goods covered by a certificate of title and as-extracted collateral consisting of goods, remains continuously perfected if:
(1)   the collateral is located in one jurisdiction and subject to a security interest perfected under the law of that jurisdiction;
(2)   thereafter the collateral is brought into another jurisdiction; and
(3)   upon entry into the other jurisdiction, the security interest is perfected under the law of the other jurisdiction.
(d)   [Goods covered by certificate of title from this state.] Except as otherwise provided in subsection (e), a security interest in goods covered by a certificate of title which is perfected by any method under the law of another jurisdiction when the goods become covered by a certificate of title from this State remains perfected until the security interest would have become unperfected under the law of the other jurisdiction had the goods not become so covered.
(e)   [When subsection (d) security interest becomes unperfected against purchasers.] A security interest described in subsection (d) becomes unperfected as against a purchaser of the goods for value and is deemed never to have been perfected as against a purchaser of the goods for value if the applicable requirements for perfection under Section 9-311(b) or 9-313 are not satisfied before the earlier of:
(1)   the time the security interest would have become unperfected under the law of the other jurisdiction had the goods not become covered by a certificate of title from this State; or
(2)   the expiration of four months after the goods had become so covered.
(f)   [Change in jurisdiction of bank, issuer, nominated person, securities intermediary, or commodity intermediary.] A security interest in deposit accounts, letter-of-credit rights, or investment property which is perfected under the law of the bank's jurisdiction, the issuer's jurisdiction, a nominated person's jurisdiction, the securities intermediary's jurisdiction, or the commodity intermediary's jurisdiction, as applicable, remains perfected until the earlier of:
(1)   the time the security interest would have become unperfected under the law of that jurisdiction; or
(2)   the expiration of four months after a change of the applicable jurisdiction to another jurisdiction.
(g)   [Subsection (f) security interest perfected or unperfected under law of new jurisdiction.] If a security interest described in subsection (f) becomes perfected under the law of the other jurisdiction before the earlier of the time or the end of the period described in that subsection, it remains perfected thereafter. If the security interest does not become perfected under the law of the other jurisdiction before the earlier of that time or the end of that period, it becomes unper-

fected and is deemed never to have been perfected as against a purchaser of the collateral for value.

Subpart 3. Priority

§ 9-317. Interests That Take Priority over or Take Free of Security Interest or Agricultural Lien

(a) [Conflicting security interests and rights of lien creditors.] A security interest or agricultural lien is subordinate to the rights of:

(1) a person entitled to priority under Section 9-322; and

(2) except as otherwise provided in subsection (e), a person that becomes a lien creditor before the earlier of the time:

　　(A) the security interest or agricultural lien is perfected; or

　　(B) one of the conditions specified in Section 9-203(b)(3) is met and a financing statement covering the collateral is filed.

(b) [Buyers that receive delivery.] Except as otherwise provided in subsection (e), a buyer, other than a secured party, of tangible chattel paper, documents, goods, instruments, or a security certificate takes free of a security interest or agricultural lien if the buyer gives value and receives delivery of the collateral without knowledge of the security interest or agricultural lien and before it is perfected.

(c) [Lessees that receive delivery.] Except as otherwise provided in subsection (e), a lessee of goods takes free of a security interest or agricultural lien if the lessee gives value and receives delivery of the collateral without knowledge of the security interest or agricultural lien and before it is perfected.

(d) [Licensees and buyers of certain collateral.] A licensee of a general intangible or a buyer, other than a secured party, of accounts, electronic chattel paper, general intangibles, or investment property other than a certificated security takes free of a security interest if the licensee or buyer gives value without knowledge of the security interest and before it is perfected.

(e) [Purchase-money security interest.] Except as otherwise provided in Sections 9-320 and 9-321, if a person files a financing statement with respect to a purchase-money security interest before or within 20 days after the debtor receives delivery of the collateral, the security interest takes priority over the rights of a buyer, lessee, or lien creditor which arise between the time the security interest attaches and the time of filing.

§ 9-318. No Interest Retained in Right to Payment That Is Sold;
Rights and Title of Seller of Account or Chattel Paper with Respect to Creditors and Purchasers

(a) [Seller retains no interest.] A debtor that has sold an account, chattel paper, payment intangible, or promissory note does not retain a legal or equitable interest in the collateral sold.

(b) [Deemed rights of debtor if buyer's security interest unperfected.] For purposes of determining the rights of creditors of, and purchasers for value of an account or chattel paper from, a debtor that has sold an account or chattel paper, while the buyer's security interest is unperfected, the debtor is deemed to have rights and title to the account or chattel paper identical to those the debtor sold.

§ 9-319. Rights and Title of Consignee with Respect to Creditors and Purchasers

(a) [Consignee has consignor's rights.] Except as otherwise provided in subsection (b), for purposes of determining the rights of creditors of, and purchasers for value of goods from, a consignee, while the goods are in the possession of the consignee, the consignee is deemed to have rights and title to the goods identical to those the consignor had or had power to transfer.

(b) [Applicability of other law.] For purposes of determining the rights of a creditor of a consignee, law other than this Article determines the rights and title of a consignee while goods are in the consignee's possession if, under this part, a perfected security interest held by the consignor would have priority over the rights of the creditor.

§ 9-320. Buyer of Goods

(a) [Buyer in ordinary course of business.] Except as otherwise provided in subsection (e), a buyer in ordinary course of business, other than a person buying farm products from a person engaged in farming operations, takes free of a security interest created by the buyer's seller, even if the security interest is perfected and the buyer knows of its existence.

(b) [Buyer of consumer goods.] Except as otherwise provided in subsection (e), a buyer of goods from a person who used or bought the goods for use primarily for personal, family, or household purposes takes free of a security interest, even if perfected, if the buyer buys:

(1) without knowledge of the security interest;

(2) for value;

(3) primarily for the buyer's personal, family, or household purposes; and

(4) before the filing of a financing statement covering the goods.

(c) [Effectiveness of filing for subsection (b).] To the extent that it affects the priority of a security interest over a buyer of goods under subsection (b), the period of effectiveness of a filing made in the jurisdiction in which the seller is located is governed by Section 9-316(a) and (b).

(d) [Buyer in ordinary course of business at wellhead or minehead.] A buyer in ordinary course of business buying oil, gas, or other minerals at the wellhead or minehead or after extraction takes free of an interest arising out of an encumbrance.

(e) [Possessory security interest not affected.] Subsections (a) and (b) do not affect a security interest in goods in the possession of the secured party under Section 9-313.

§ 9-321. Licensee of General Intangible and Lessee of Goods in Ordinary Course of Business

(a) ["Licensee in ordinary course of business."] In this section, "licensee in ordinary course of business" means a person that becomes a licensee of a general intangible in good faith, without knowledge that the license violates the rights of another person in the general intangible, and in the ordinary course from a person in the business of licensing general intangibles of that kind. A person becomes a licensee in the ordinary course if the license to the person comports with the usual or customary practices in the kind of business in which the licensor is engaged or with the licensor's own usual or customary practices.

(b) [Rights of licensee in ordinary course of business.] A licensee in ordinary course of business takes its rights under a nonexclusive license free of a security interest in the general intangible created by the licensor, even if the security interest is perfected and the licensee knows of its existence.

(c) [Rights of lessee in ordinary course of business.] A lessee in ordinary course of business takes its leasehold interest free of a security interest in the goods created by the lessor, even if the security interest is perfected and the lessee knows of its existence.

§ 9-322. Priorities among Conflicting Security Interests in and Agricultural Liens on Same Collateral

(a) [General priority rules.] Except as otherwise provided in this section, priority among conflicting security interests and agricultural liens in the same collateral is determined according to the following rules:

(1) Conflicting perfected security interests and agricultural liens rank according to priority in time of filing or perfection. Priority dates from the earlier of the time a filing covering the collateral is first made or the security interest or agricultural lien is first perfected, if there is no period thereafter when there is neither filing nor perfection.

(2) A perfected security interest or agricultural lien has priority over a conflicting unperfected security interest or agricultural lien.

(3) The first security interest or agricultural lien to attach or become effective has priority if conflicting security interests and agricultural liens are unperfected.

(b) [Time of perfection: proceeds and supporting obligations.] For the purposes of subsection (a)(1):

(1) the time of filing or perfection as to a security interest in collateral is also the time of filing or perfection as to a security interest in proceeds; and

(2) the time of filing or perfection as to a security interest in collateral supported by a supporting obligation is also the time of filing or perfection as to a security interest in the supporting obligation.

(c) [Special priority rules: proceeds and supporting obligations.] Except as otherwise provided in subsection (f), a security interest in collateral which qualifies for priority over a conflicting security interest under Section 9-327, 9-328, 9-329, 9-330, or 9-331 also has priority over a conflicting security interest in:

(1) any supporting obligation for the collateral; and

(2) proceeds of the collateral if:

    (A) the security interest in proceeds is perfected;

    (B) the proceeds are cash proceeds or of the same type as the collateral; and

    (C) in the case of proceeds that are proceeds of proceeds, all intervening proceeds are cash proceeds, proceeds of the same type as the collateral, or an account relating to the collateral.

(d) [First-to-file priority rule for certain collateral.] Subject to subsection (e) and except as otherwise provided in subsection (f), if a security interest in chattel paper, deposit accounts, negotiable documents, instruments, investment property, or letter-of-credit rights is perfected by a method other than filing, conflicting perfected security interests in proceeds of the collateral rank according to priority in time of filing.

(e) [Applicability of subsection (d).] Subsection (d) applies only if the proceeds of the collateral are not cash proceeds, chattel paper, negotiable documents, instruments, investment property, or letter-of-credit rights.

(f) [Limitations on subsections (a) through (e).] Subsections (a) through (e) are subject to:

(1) subsection (g) and the other provisions of this part;

(2) Section 4-210 with respect to a security interest of a collecting bank;

(3) Section 5-118 with respect to a security interest of an issuer or nominated person; and

(4) Section 9-110 with respect to a security interest arising under Article 2 or 2A.

(g) [Priority under agricultural lien statute.] A perfected agricultural lien on collateral has priority over a conflicting security interest in or agricultural lien on the same collateral if the statute creating the agricultural lien so provides.

§ 9-323. Future Advances

(a) [When priority based on time of advance.] Except as otherwise provided in subsection (c), for purposes of determining the priority of a perfected security interest under Section 9-322(a)(1), perfection of the security interest dates from the time an advance is made to the extent that the security interest secures an advance that:

(1) is made while the security interest is perfected only:

    (A) under Section 9-309 when it attaches; or

    (B) temporarily under Section 9-312(e), (f), or (g); and

(2) is not made pursuant to a commitment entered into before or while the security interest is perfected by a method other than under Section 9-309 or 9-312(e), (f), or (g).

(b) [Lien creditor.] Except as otherwise provided in subsection (c), a security interest is subordinate to the rights of a person that becomes a lien creditor to the extent that the security interest secures an advance made more than 45 days after the person becomes a lien creditor unless the advance is made:

(1) without knowledge of the lien; or

(2) pursuant to a commitment entered into without knowledge of the lien.

(c) [Buyer of receivables.] Subsections (a) and (b) do not apply to a security interest held by a secured party that is a buyer of accounts, chattel paper, payment intangibles, or promissory notes or a consignor.

(d) [Buyer of goods.] Except as otherwise provided in subsection (e), a buyer of goods other than a buyer in ordinary course of business takes free of a security interest to the extent that it secures advances made after the earlier of:

(1)   the time the secured party acquires knowledge of the buyer's purchase; or
(2)   45 days after the purchase.
(e)   [Advances made pursuant to commitment: priority of buyer of goods.] Subsection (d) does not apply if the advance is made pursuant to a commitment entered into without knowledge of the buyer's purchase and before the expiration of the 45-day period.
(f)   [Lessee of goods.] Except as otherwise provided in subsection (g), a lessee of goods, other than a lessee in ordinary course of business, takes the leasehold interest free of a security interest to the extent that it secures advances made after the earlier of:
(1)   the time the secured party acquires knowledge of the lease; or
(2)   45 days after the lease contract becomes enforceable.
(g)   [Advances made pursuant to commitment: priority of lessee of goods.] Subsection (f) does not apply if the advance is made pursuant to a commitment entered into without knowledge of the lease and before the expiration of the 45-day period.

§ 9-324. Priority of Purchase-Money Security Interests

(a)   [General rule: purchase-money priority.] Except as otherwise provided in subsection (g), a perfected purchase-money security interest in goods other than inventory or livestock has priority over a conflicting security interest in the same goods, and, except as otherwise provided in Section 9-327, a perfected security interest in its identifiable proceeds also has priority, if the purchase-money security interest is perfected when the debtor receives possession of the collateral or within 20 days thereafter.
(b)   [Inventory purchase-money priority.] Subject to subsection (c) and except as otherwise provided in subsection (g), a perfected purchase-money security interest in inventory has priority over a conflicting security interest in the same inventory, has priority over a conflicting security interest in chattel paper or an instrument constituting proceeds of the inventory and in proceeds of the chattel paper, if so provided in Section 9-330, and, except as otherwise provided in Section 9-327, also has priority in identifiable cash proceeds of the inventory to the extent the identifiable cash proceeds are received on or before the delivery of the inventory to a buyer, if:
(1)   the purchase-money security interest is perfected when the debtor receives possession of the inventory;
(2)   the purchase-money secured party sends an authenticated notification to the holder of the conflicting security interest;
(3)   the holder of the conflicting security interest receives the notification within five years before the debtor receives possession of the inventory; and
(4)   the notification states that the person sending the notification has or expects to acquire a purchase-money security interest in inventory of the debtor and describes the inventory.
(c)   [Holders of conflicting inventory security interests to be notified.] Subsections (b)(2) through (4) apply only if the holder of the conflicting security interest had filed a financing statement covering the same types of inventory:
(1)   if the purchase-money security interest is perfected by filing, before the date of the filing; or
(2)   if the purchase-money security interest is temporarily perfected without filing or possession under Section 9-312(f), before the beginning of the 20-day period thereunder.
(d)   [Livestock purchase-money priority.] Subject to subsection (e) and except as otherwise provided in subsection (g), a perfected purchase-money security interest in livestock that are farm products has priority over a conflicting security interest in the same livestock, and, except as otherwise provided in Section 9-327, a perfected security interest in their identifiable proceeds and identifiable products in their unmanufactured states also has priority, if:
(1)   the purchase-money security interest is perfected when the debtor receives possession of the livestock;
(2)   the purchase-money secured party sends an authenticated notification to the holder of the conflicting security interest;
(3)   the holder of the conflicting security interest receives the notification within six months before the debtor receives possession of the livestock; and

(4) the notification states that the person sending the notification has or expects to acquire a purchase-money security interest in livestock of the debtor and describes the livestock.
(e) [Holders of conflicting livestock security interests to be notified.] Subsections (d)(2) through (4) apply only if the holder of the conflicting security interest had filed a financing statement covering the same types of livestock:
(1) if the purchase-money security interest is perfected by filing, before the date of the filing; or
(2) if the purchase-money security interest is temporarily perfected without filing or possession under Section 9-312(f), before the beginning of the 20-day period thereunder.
(f) [Software purchase-money priority.] Except as otherwise provided in subsection (g), a perfected purchase-money security interest in software has priority over a conflicting security interest in the same collateral, and, except as otherwise provided in Section 9-327, a perfected security interest in its identifiable proceeds also has priority, to the extent that the purchase-money security interest in the goods in which the software was acquired for use has priority in the goods and proceeds of the goods under this section.
(g) [Conflicting purchase-money security interests.] If more than one security interest qualifies for priority in the same collateral under subsection (a), (b), (d), or (f):
(1) a security interest securing an obligation incurred as all or part of the price of the collateral has priority over a security interest securing an obligation incurred for value given to enable the debtor to acquire rights in or the use of collateral; and
(2) in all other cases, Section 9-322(a) applies to the qualifying security interests.

§ 9-325. Priority of Security Interests in Transferred Collateral

(a) [Subordination of security interest in transferred collateral.] Except as otherwise provided in subsection (b), a security interest created by a debtor is subordinate to a security interest in the same collateral created by another person if:
(1) the debtor acquired the collateral subject to the security interest created by the other person;
(2) the security interest created by the other person was perfected when the debtor acquired the collateral; and
(3) there is no period thereafter when the security interest is unperfected.
(b) [Limitation of subsection (a) subordination.] Subsection (a) subordinates a security interest only if the security interest:
(1) otherwise would have priority solely under Section 9-322(a) or 9-324; or
(2) arose solely under Section 2-711(3) or 2A-508(5).

§ 9-326. Priority of Security Interests Created by New Debtor

(a) [Subordination of security interest created by new debtor.] Subject to subsection (b), a security interest created by a new debtor which is perfected by a filed financing statement that is effective solely under Section 9-508 in collateral in which a new debtor has or acquires rights is subordinate to a security interest in the same collateral which is perfected other than by a filed financing statement that is effective solely under Section 9-508.
(b) [Priority under other provisions; multiple original debtors.] The other provisions of this part determine the priority among conflicting security interests in the same collateral perfected by filed financing statements that are effective solely under Section 9-508. However, if the security agreements to which a new debtor became bound as debtor were not entered into by the same original debtor, the conflicting security interests rank according to priority in time of the new debtor's having become bound.

§ 9-327. Priority of Security Interests in Deposit Account

The following rules govern priority among conflicting security interests in the same deposit account:
(1) A security interest held by a secured party having control of the deposit account under Section 9-104 has priority over a conflicting security interest held by a secured party that does not have control.

(2)   Except as otherwise provided in paragraphs (3) and (4), security interests perfected by control under Section 9-314 rank according to priority in time of obtaining control.
(3)   Except as otherwise provided in paragraph (4), a security interest held by the bank with which the deposit account is maintained has priority over a conflicting security interest held by another secured party.
(4)   A security interest perfected by control under Section 9-104(a)(3) has priority over a security interest held by the bank with which the deposit account is maintained.

§ 9-328. Priority of Security Interests in Investment Property
The following rules govern priority among conflicting security interests in the same investment property:
(1)   A security interest held by a secured party having control of investment property under Section 9-106 has priority over a security interest held by a secured party that does not have control of the investment property.
(2)   Except as otherwise provided in paragraphs (3) and (4), conflicting security interests held by secured parties each of which has control under Section 9-106 rank according to priority in time of:
(A)   if the collateral is a security, obtaining control;
(B)   if the collateral is a security entitlement carried in a securities account and:
    (i)   if the secured party obtained control under Section 8-106(d)(1), the secured party's becoming the person for which the securities account is maintained;
    (ii)   if the secured party obtained control under Section 8-106(d)(2), the securities intermediary's agreement to comply with the secured party's entitlement orders with respect to security entitlements carried or to be carried in the securities account; or
    (iii) if the secured party obtained control through another person under Section 8-106 (d)(3), the time on which priority would be based under this paragraph if the other person were the secured party; or
(C)   if the collateral is a commodity contract carried with a commodity intermediary, the satisfaction of the requirement for control specified in Section 9-106(b)(2) with respect to commodity contracts carried or to be carried with the commodity intermediary.
(3)   A security interest held by a securities intermediary in a security entitlement or a securities account maintained with the securities intermediary has priority over a conflicting security interest held by another secured party.
(4)   A security interest held by a commodity intermediary in a commodity contract or a commodity account maintained with the commodity intermediary has priority over a conflicting security interest held by another secured party.
(5)   A security interest in a certificated security in registered form which is perfected by taking delivery under Section 9-313(a) and not by control under Section 9-314 has priority over a conflicting security interest perfected by a method other than control.
(6)   Conflicting security interests created by a broker, securities intermediary, or commodity intermediary which are perfected without control under Section 9-106 rank equally.
(7)   In all other cases, priority among conflicting security interests in investment property is governed by Sections 9-322 and 9-323.

§ 9-329. Priority of Security Interests in Letter-of-Credit Right
The following rules govern priority among conflicting security interests in the same letter-of-credit right:
(1)   A security interest held by a secured party having control of the letter-of-credit right under Section 9-107 has priority to the extent of its control over a conflicting security interest held by a secured party that does not have control.
(2)   Security interests perfected by control under Section 9-314 rank according to priority in time of obtaining control.

§ 9-330. Priority of Purchaser of Chattel Paper or Instrument

(a) [Purchaser's priority: security interest claimed merely as proceeds.] A purchaser of chattel paper has priority over a security interest in the chattel paper which is claimed merely as proceeds of inventory subject to a security interest if:

(1)   in good faith and in the ordinary course of the purchaser's business, the purchaser gives new value and takes possession of the chattel paper or obtains control of the chattel paper under Section 9-105; and

(2)   the chattel paper does not indicate that it has been assigned to an identified assignee other than the purchaser.

(b) [Purchaser's priority: other security interests.] A purchaser of chattel paper has priority over a security interest in the chattel paper which is claimed other than merely as proceeds of inventory subject to a security interest if the purchaser gives new value and takes possession of the chattel paper or obtains control of the chattel paper under Section 9-105 in good faith, in the ordinary course of the purchaser's business, and without knowledge that the purchase violates the rights of the secured party.

(c) [Chattel paper purchaser's priority in proceeds.] Except as otherwise provided in Section 9-327, a purchaser having priority in chattel paper under subsection (a) or (b) also has priority in proceeds of the chattel paper to the extent that:

(1)   Section 9-322 provides for priority in the proceeds; or

(2)   the proceeds consist of the specific goods covered by the chattel paper or cash proceeds of the specific goods, even if the purchaser's security interest in the proceeds is unperfected.

(d) [Instrument purchaser's priority.] Except as otherwise provided in Section 9-331(a), a purchaser of an instrument has priority over a security interest in the instrument perfected by a method other than possession if the purchaser gives value and takes possession of the instrument in good faith and without knowledge that the purchase violates the rights of the secured party.

(e) [Holder of purchase-money security interest gives new value.] For purposes of subsections (a) and (b), the holder of a purchase-money security interest in inventory gives new value for chattel paper constituting proceeds of the inventory.

(f) [Indication of assignment gives knowledge.] For purposes of subsections (b) and (d), if chattel paper or an instrument indicates that it has been assigned to an identified secured party other than the purchaser, a purchaser of the chattel paper or instrument has knowledge that the purchase violates the rights of the secured party.

§ 9-331. Priority of Rights of Purchasers of Instruments, Documents, and Securities under Other Articles; Priority of Interests in Financial Assets and Security Entitlements under Article 8

(a) [Rights under Articles 3, 7, and 8 not limited.] This Article does not limit the rights of a holder in due course of a negotiable instrument, a holder to which a negotiable document of title has been duly negotiated, or a protected purchaser of a security. These holders or purchasers take priority over an earlier security interest, even if perfected, to the extent provided in Articles 3, 7, and 8.

(b) [Protection under Article 8.] This Article does not limit the rights of or impose liability on a person to the extent that the person is protected against the assertion of a claim under Article 8.

(c) [Filing not notice.] Filing under this Article does not constitute notice of a claim or defense to the holders, or purchasers, or persons described in subsections (a) and (b).

§ 9-332. Transfer of Money; Transfer of Funds from Deposit Account

(a) [Transferee of money.] A transferee of money takes the money free of a security interest unless the transferee acts in collusion with the debtor in violating the rights of the secured party.

(b) [Transferee of funds from deposit account.] A transferee of funds from a deposit account takes the funds free of a security interest in the deposit account unless the transferee acts in collusion with the debtor in violating the rights of the secured party.

§ 9-333. Priority of Certain Liens Arising by Operation of Law

(a) ["Possessory lien."] In this section, "possessory lien" means an interest, other than a security interest or an agricultural lien:

(1) which secures payment or performance of an obligation for services or materials furnished with respect to goods by a person in the ordinary course of the person's business;

(2) which is created by statute or rule of law in favor of the person; and

(3) whose effectiveness depends on the person's possession of the goods.

(b) [Priority of possessory lien.] A possessory lien on goods has priority over a security interest in the goods unless the lien is created by a statute that expressly provides otherwise.

§ 9-334. Priority of Security Interests in Fixtures and Crops

(a) [Security interest in fixtures under this article.] A security interest under this Article may be created in goods that are fixtures or may continue in goods that become fixtures. A security interest does not exist under this Article in ordinary building materials incorporated into an improvement on land.

(b) [Security interest in fixtures under real-property law.] This Article does not prevent creation of an encumbrance upon fixtures under real property law.

(c) [General rule: subordination of security interest in fixtures.] In cases not governed by subsections (d) through (h), a security interest in fixtures is subordinate to a conflicting interest of an encumbrancer or owner of the related real property other than the debtor.

(d) [Fixtures purchase-money priority.] Except as otherwise provided in subsection (h), a perfected security interest in fixtures has priority over a conflicting interest of an encumbrancer or owner of the real property if the debtor has an interest of record in or is in possession of the real property and:

(1) the security interest is a purchase-money security interest;

(2) the interest of the encumbrancer or owner arises before the goods become fixtures; and

(3) the security interest is perfected by a fixture filing before the goods become fixtures or within 20 days thereafter.

(e) [Priority of security interest in fixtures over interests in real property.] A perfected security interest in fixtures has priority over a conflicting interest of an encumbrancer or owner of the real property if:

(1) the debtor has an interest of record in the real property or is in possession of the real property and the security interest:

(A) is perfected by a fixture filing before the interest of the encumbrancer or owner is of record; and

(B) has priority over any conflicting interest of a predecessor in title of the encumbrancer or owner;

(2) before the goods become fixtures, the security interest is perfected by any method permitted by this Article and the fixtures are readily removable:

(A) factory or office machines;

(B) equipment that is not primarily used or leased for use in the operation of the real property; or

(C) replacements of domestic appliances that are consumer goods;

(3) the conflicting interest is a lien on the real property obtained by legal or equitable proceedings after the security interest was perfected by any method permitted by this article; or

(4) the security interest is:

(A) created in a manufactured home in a manufactured-home transaction; and

(B) perfected pursuant to a statute described in Section 9-311(a)(2).

(f) [Priority based on consent, disclaimer, or right to remove.] A security interest in fixtures, whether or not perfected, has priority over a conflicting interest of an encumbrancer or owner of the real property if:

(1) the encumbrancer or owner has, in an authenticated record, consented to the security interest or disclaimed an interest in the goods as fixtures; or

(2)   the debtor has a right to remove the goods as against the encumbrancer or owner.

(g)   [Continuation of paragraph (f)(2) priority.] The priority of the security interest under paragraph (f)(2) continues for a reasonable time if the debtor's right to remove the goods as against the encumbrancer or owner terminates.

(h)   [Priority of construction mortgage.] A mortgage is a construction mortgage to the extent that it secures an obligation incurred for the construction of an improvement on land, including the acquisition cost of the land, if a recorded record of the mortgage so indicates. Except as otherwise provided in subsections (e) and (f), a security interest in fixtures is subordinate to a construction mortgage if a record of the mortgage is recorded before the goods become fixtures and the goods become fixtures before the completion of the construction. A mortgage has this priority to the same extent as a construction mortgage to the extent that it is given to refinance a construction mortgage.

(i)   [Priority of security interest in crops.] A perfected security interest in crops growing on real property has priority over a conflicting interest of an encumbrancer or owner of the real property if the debtor has an interest of record in or is in possession of the real property.

(j)   [Subsection (i) prevails.] Subsection (i) prevails over any inconsistent provisions of the following statutes: [List here any statutes containing provisions inconsistent with subsection (i).]

§ 9-335. Accessions

(a)   [Creation of security interest in accession.] A security interest may be created in an accession and continues in collateral that becomes an accession.

(b)   [Perfection of security interest.] If a security interest is perfected when the collateral becomes an accession, the security interest remains perfected in the collateral.

(c)   [Priority of security interest.] Except as otherwise provided in subsection (d), the other provisions of this part determine the priority of a security interest in an accession.

(d)   [Compliance with certificate-of-title statute.] A security interest in an accession is subordinate to a security interest in the whole which is perfected by compliance with the requirements of a certificate-of-title statute under Section 9-311(b).

(e)   [Removal of accession after default.] After default, subject to Part 6, a secured party may remove an accession from other goods if the security interest in the accession has priority over the claims of every person having an interest in the whole.

(f)   [Reimbursement following removal.] A secured party that removes an accession from other goods under subsection (e) shall promptly reimburse any holder of a security interest or other lien on, or owner of, the whole or of the other goods, other than the debtor, for the cost of repair of any physical injury to the whole or the other goods. The secured party need not reimburse the holder or owner for any diminution in value of the whole or the other goods caused by the absence of the accession removed or by any necessity for replacing it. A person entitled to reimbursement may refuse permission to remove until the secured party gives adequate assurance for the performance of the obligation to reimburse.

§ 9-336. Commingled Goods

(a)   ["Commingled goods."] In this section, "commingled goods" means goods that are physically united with other goods in such a manner that their identity is lost in a product or mass.

(b)   [No security interest in commingled goods as such.] A security interest does not exist in commingled goods as such. However, a security interest may attach to a product or mass that results when goods become commingled goods.

(c)   [Attachment of security interest to product or mass.] If collateral becomes commingled goods, a security interest attaches to the product or mass.

(d)   [Perfection of security interest.] If a security interest in collateral is perfected before the collateral becomes commingled goods, the security interest that attaches to the product or mass under subsection (c) is perfected.

(e) [Priority of security interest.] Except as otherwise provided in subsection (f), the other provisions of this part determine the priority of a security interest that attaches to the product or mass under subsection (c).

(f) [Conflicting security interests in product or mass] If more than one security interest attaches to the product or mass under subsection (c), the following rules determine priority:

(1) A security interest that is perfected under subsection (d) has priority over a security interest that is unperfected at the time the collateral becomes commingled goods.

(2) If more than one security interest is perfected under subsection (d), the security interests rank equally in proportion to the value of the collateral at the time it became commingled goods.

§ 9-337. Priority of Security Interests in Goods Covered by Certificate of Title

If, while a security interest in goods is perfected by any method under the law of another jurisdiction, this State issues a certificate of title that does not show that the goods are subject to the security interest or contain a statement that they may be subject to security interests not shown on the certificate:

(1) a buyer of the goods, other than a person in the business of selling goods of that kind, takes free of the security interest if the buyer gives value and receives delivery of the goods after issuance of the certificate and without knowledge of the security interest; and

(2) the security interest is subordinate to a conflicting security interest in the goods that attaches, and is perfected under Section 9-311(b), after issuance of the certificate and without the conflicting secured party's knowledge of the security interest.

§ 9-338. Priority of Security Interest or Agricultural Lien Perfected by Filed Financing Statement Providing Certain Incorrect Information

If a security interest or agricultural lien is perfected by a filed financing statement providing information described in Section 9-516(b)(5) which is incorrect at the time the financing statement is filed:

(1) the security interest or agricultural lien is subordinate to a conflicting perfected security interest in the collateral to the extent that the holder of the conflicting security interest gives value in reasonable reliance upon the incorrect information; and

(2) a purchaser, other than a secured party, of the collateral takes free of the security interest or agricultural lien to the extent that, in reasonable reliance upon the incorrect information, the purchaser gives value and, in the case of chattel paper, documents, goods, instruments, or a security certificate, receives delivery of the collateral.

§ 9-339. Priority Subject to Subordination

This Article does not preclude subordination by agreement by a person entitled to priority.

Subpart 4. Rights of Bank

§ 9-340. Effectiveness of Right of Recoupment or Set-off Against Deposit Account

(a) [Exercise of recoupment or set-off.] Except as otherwise provided in subsection (c), a bank with which a deposit account is maintained may exercise any right of recoupment or set-off against a secured party that holds a security interest in the deposit account.

(b) [Recoupment or setoff not affected by security interest.] Except as otherwise provided in subsection (c), the application of this Article to a security interest in a deposit account does not affect a right of recoupment or set-off of the secured party as to a deposit account maintained with the secured party.

(c) [When set-off ineffective.] The exercise by a bank of a set-off against a deposit account is ineffective against a secured party that holds a security interest in the deposit account which is perfected by control under Section 9-104(a)(3), if the set-off is based on a claim against the debtor.

§ 9-341. Bank's Rights and Duties with Respect to Deposit Account

Except as otherwise provided in Section 9-340(c), and unless the bank otherwise agrees in an authenticated record, a bank's rights and duties with respect to a deposit account maintained with the bank are not terminated, suspended, or modified by:

(1)   the creation, attachment, or perfection of a security interest in the deposit account;
(2)   the bank's knowledge of the security interest; or
(3)   the bank's receipt of instructions from the secured party.

§ 9-342. Bank's Right to Refuse to Enter into or Disclose Existence of Control Agreement

This Article does not require a bank to enter into an agreement of the kind described in Section 9-104(a)(2), even if its customer so requests or directs. A bank that has entered into such an agreement is not required to confirm the existence of the agreement to another person unless requested to do so by its customer.

PART 4. RIGHTS OF THIRD PARTIES

§ 9-401. Alienability of Debtor's Rights

(a)   [Other law governs alienability; exceptions.] Except as otherwise provided in subsection (b) and Sections 9-406, 9-407, 9-408, and 9-409, whether a debtor's rights in collateral may be voluntarily or involuntarily transferred is governed by law other than this article.
(b)   [Agreement does not prevent transfer.] An agreement between the debtor and secured party which prohibits a transfer of the debtor's rights in collateral or makes the transfer a default does not prevent the transfer from taking effect.

§ 9-402. Secured Party Not Obligated on Contract of Debtor or in Tort

The existence of a security interest, agricultural lien, or authority given to a debtor to dispose of or use collateral, without more, does not subject a secured party to liability in contract or tort for the debtor's acts or omissions.

§ 9-403. Agreement Not to Assert Defenses Against Assignee

(a)   ["Value."] In this section, "value" has the meaning provided in Section 3-303(a).
(b)   [Agreement not to assert claim or defense.] Except as otherwise provided in this section, an agreement between an account debtor and an assignor not to assert against an assignee any claim or defense that the account debtor may have against the assignor is enforceable by an assignee that takes an assignment:
(1)   for value;
(2)   in good faith;
(3)   without notice of a claim of a property or possessory right to the property assigned; and
(4)   without notice of a defense or claim in recoupment of the type that may be asserted against a person entitled to enforce a negotiable instrument under Section 3-305(a).
(c)   [When subsection (b) not applicable.] Subsection (b) does not apply to defenses of a type that may be asserted against a holder in due course of a negotiable instrument under Section 3-305(b).
(d)   [Omission of required statement in consumer transaction.] In a consumer transaction, if a record evidences the account debtor's obligation, law other than this Article requires that the record include a statement to the effect that the rights of an assignee are subject to claims or defenses that the account debtor could assert against the original obligee, and the record does not include such a statement:
(1)   the record has the same effect as if the record included such a statement; and
(2)   the account debtor may assert against an assignee those claims and defenses that would have been available if the record included such a statement.
(e)   [Rule for individual under other law.] This section is subject to law other than this Article which establishes a different rule for an account debtor who is an individual and who incurred the obligation primarily for personal, family, or household purposes.
(f)   [Other law not displaced.] Except as otherwise provided in subsection (d), this section does not displace law other than this Article which gives effect to an agreement by an account debtor not to assert a claim or defense against an assignee.

§ 9-404. Rights Acquired by Assignee; Claims and Defenses Against Assignee
(a)   [Assignee's rights subject to terms, claims, and defenses; exceptions.] Unless an account debtor has made an enforceable agreement not to assert defenses or claims, and subject to subsections (b) through (e), the rights of an assignee are subject to:
(1)   all terms of the agreement between the account debtor and assignor and any defense or claim in recoupment arising from the transaction that gave rise to the contract; and
(2)   any other defense or claim of the account debtor against the assignor which accrues before the account debtor receives a notification of the assignment authenticated by the assignor or the assignee.
(b)   [Account debtor's claim reduces amount owed to assignee.] Subject to subsection (c) and except as otherwise provided in subsection (d), the claim of an account debtor against an assignor may be asserted against an assignee under subsection (a) only to reduce the amount the account debtor owes.
(c)   [Rule for individual under other law.] This section is subject to law other than this Article which establishes a different rule for an account debtor who is an individual and who incurred the obligation primarily for personal, family, or household purposes.
(d)   [Omission of required statement in consumer transaction.] In a consumer transaction, if a record evidences the account debtor's obligation, law other than this Article requires that the record include a statement to the effect that the account debtor's recovery against an assignee with respect to claims and defenses against the assignor may not exceed amounts paid by the account debtor under the record, and the record does not include such a statement, the extent to which a claim of an account debtor against the assignor may be asserted against an assignee is determined as if the record included such a statement.
(e)   [Inapplicability to health-care-insurance receivable.] This section does not apply to an assignment of a health-care-insurance receivable.

§ 9-405. Modification of Assigned Contract
(a)   [Effect of modification on assignee.] A modification of or substitution for an assigned contract is effective against an assignee if made in good faith. The assignee acquires corresponding rights under the modified or substituted contract. The assignment may provide that the modification or substitution is a breach of contract by the assignor. This subsection is subject to subsections (b) through (d).
(b)   [Applicability of subsection (a).] Subsection (a) applies to the extent that:
(1)   the right to payment or a part thereof under an assigned contract has not been fully earned by performance; or
(2)   the right to payment or a part thereof has been fully earned by performance and the account debtor has not received notification of the assignment under Section 9-406(a).
(c)   [Rule for individual under other law.] This section is subject to law other than this Article which establishes a different rule for an account debtor who is an individual and who incurred the obligation primarily for personal, family, or household purposes.
(d)   [Inapplicability to health-care-insurance receivable.] This section does not apply to an assignment of a health-care-insurance receivable.

§ 9-406. Discharge of Account Debtor; Notification of Assignment; Identification and Proof of Assignment; Restrictions on Assignment of Accounts, Chattel Paper, Payment Intangibles, and Promissory Notes Ineffective
(a)   [Discharge of account debtor; effect of notification.] Subject to subsections (b) through (i), an account debtor on an account, chattel paper, or a payment intangible may discharge its obligation by paying the assignor until, but not after, the account debtor receives a notification, authenticated by the assignor or the assignee, that the amount due or to become due has been assigned and that payment is to be made to the assignee. After receipt of the notification, the account debtor may discharge its obligation by paying the assignee and may not discharge the obligation by paying the assignor.

(b) [When notification ineffective.] Subject to subsection (h), notification is ineffective under subsection (a):

(1) if it does not reasonably identify the rights assigned;

(2) to the extent that an agreement between an account debtor and a seller of a payment intangible limits the account debtor's duty to pay a person other than the seller and the limitation is effective under law other than this article; or

(3) at the option of an account debtor, if the notification notifies the account debtor to make less than the full amount of any installment or other periodic payment to the assignee, even if:

    (A) only a portion of the account, chattel paper, or payment intangible has been assigned to that assignee;

    (B) a portion has been assigned to another assignee; or

    (C) the account debtor knows that the assignment to that assignee is limited.

(c) [Proof of assignment.] Subject to subsection (h), if requested by the account debtor, an assignee shall seasonably furnish reasonable proof that the assignment has been made. Unless the assignee complies, the account debtor may discharge its obligation by paying the assignor, even if the account debtor has received a notification under subsection (a).

(d) [Term restricting assignment generally ineffective.] Except as otherwise provided in subsection (e) and Sections 2A-303 and 9-407, and subject to subsection (h), a term in an agreement between an account debtor and an assignor or in a promissory note is ineffective to the extent that it:

(1) prohibits, restricts, or requires the consent of the account debtor or person obligated on the promissory note to the assignment or transfer of, or the creation, attachment, perfection, or enforcement of a security interest in, the account, chattel paper, payment intangible, or promissory note; or

(2) provides that the assignment or transfer or the creation, attachment, perfection, or enforcement of the security interest may give rise to a default, breach, right of recoupment, claim, defense, termination, right of termination, or remedy under the account, chattel paper, payment intangible, or promissory note.

(e) [Inapplicability of subsection (d) to certain sales.] Subsection (d) does not apply to the sale of a payment intangible or promissory note.

(f) [Legal restrictions on assignment generally ineffective.] Except as otherwise provided in Sections 2A-303 and 9-407 and subject to subsections (h) and (i), a rule of law, statute, or regulation that prohibits, restricts, or requires the consent of a government, governmental body or official, or account debtor to the assignment or transfer of, or creation of a security interest in, an account or chattel paper is ineffective to the extent that the rule of law, statute, or regulation:

(1) prohibits, restricts, or requires the consent of the government, governmental body or official, or account debtor to the assignment or transfer of, or the creation, attachment, perfection, or enforcement of a security interest in the account or chattel paper; or

(2) provides that the creation, attachment, perfection, or enforcement of the security interest may give rise to a default, breach, right of recoupment, claim, defense, termination, right of termination, or remedy under the account or chattel paper.

(g) [Subsection (b)(3) not waivable.] Subject to subsection (h), an account debtor may not waive or vary its option under subsection (b)(3).

(h) [Rule for individual under other law.] This section is subject to law other than this Article which establishes a different rule for an account debtor who is an individual and who incurred the obligation primarily for personal, family, or household purposes.

(i) [Inapplicability to health-care-insurance receivable.] This section does not apply to an assignment of a health-care-insurance receivable.

(j) [Section prevails over specified inconsistent law.] This section prevails over any inconsistent provisions of the following statutes, rules, and regulations: [List here any statutes, rules, and regulations containing provisions inconsistent with this section.]

§ 9-407. Restrictions on Creation or Enforcement of Security Interest
in Leasehold Interest or in Lessor's Residual Interest

(a) [Term restricting assignment generally ineffective.] Except as otherwise provided in subsection (b), a term in a lease agreement is ineffective to the extent that it:

(1) prohibits, restricts, or requires the consent of a party to the lease to the the assignment or transfer of, or the creation, attachment, perfection, or enforcement of a security interest in an interest of a party under the lease contract or in the lessor's residual interest in the goods; or

(2) provides that the assignment or transfer or the creation, attachment, perfection, or enforcement of the security interest may give rise to a default, breach, right of recoupment, claim, defense, termination, right of termination, or remedy under the lease.

(b) [Effectiveness of certain terms.] Except as otherwise provided in Section 2A-303(7), a term described in subsection (a)(2) is effective to the extent that there is:

(1) a transfer by the lessee of the lessee's right of possession or use of the goods in violation of the term; or

(2) a delegation of a material performance of either party to the lease contract in violation of the term.

(c) [Security interest not material impairment.] The creation, attachment, perfection, or enforcement of a security interest in the lessor's interest under the lease contract or the lessor's residual interest in the goods is not a transfer that materially impairs the lessee's prospect of obtaining return performance or materially changes the duty of or materially increases the burden or risk imposed on the lessee within the purview of Section 2A-303(4) unless, and then only to the extent that, enforcement actually results in a delegation of material performance of the lessor.

§ 9-408. Restrictions on Assignment of Promissory Notes, Health-Care-Insurance Receivables,
and Certain General Intangibles Ineffective

(a) [Term restricting assignment generally ineffective.] Except as otherwise provided in subsection (b), a term in a promissory note or in an agreement between an account debtor and a debtor which relates to a health-care-insurance receivable or a general intangible, including a contract, permit, license, or franchise, and which term prohibits, restricts, or requires the consent of the person obligated on the promissory note or the account debtor to, the assignment or transfer of, or creation, attachment, or perfection of a security interest in, the promissory note, health-care-insurance receivable, or general intangible, is ineffective to the extent that the term:

(1) would impair the creation, attachment, or perfection of a security interest; or

(2) provides that the assignment or transfer or the creation, attachment, or perfection of the security interest may give rise to a default, breach, right of recoupment, claim, defense, termination, right of termination, or remedy under the promissory note, health-care-insurance receivable, or general intangible.

(b) [Applicability of subsection (a) to sales of certain rights to payment.] Subsection (a) applies to a security interest in a payment intangible or promissory note only if the security interest arises out of a sale of the payment intangible or promissory note.

(c) [Legal restrictions on assignment generally ineffective.] A rule of law, statute, or regulation that prohibits, restricts, or requires the consent of a government, governmental body or official, person obligated on a promissory note, or account debtor to the assignment or transfer of, or creation of a security interest in, a promissory note, health-care-insurance receivable, or general intangible, including a contract, permit, license, or franchise between an account debtor and a debtor, is ineffective to the extent that the rule of law, statute, or regulation:

(1) would impair the creation, attachment, or perfection of a security interest; or

(2) provides that the the the assignment or transfer or creation, attachment, or perfection of the security interest may give rise to a default, breach, right of recoupment, claim, defense, termination, right of termination, or remedy under the promissory note, health-care-insurance receivable, or general intangible.

(d) [Limitation on ineffectiveness under subsections (a) and (c).] To the extent that a term in a promissory note or in an agreement between an account debtor and a debtor which relates to a health-care-insurance receivable or general intangible or a rule of law, statute, or regulation described in subsection (c) would be effective under law other than this Article but is ineffective under subsection (a) or (c), the creation, attachment, or perfection of a security interest in the promissory note, health-care-insurance receivable, or general intangible:

(1) is not enforceable against the person obligated on the promissory note or the account debtor;

(2) does not impose a duty or obligation on the person obligated on the promissory note or the account debtor;

(3) does not require the person obligated on the promissory note or the account debtor to recognize the security interest, pay or render performance to the secured party, or accept payment or performance from the secured party;

(4) does not entitle the secured party to use or assign the debtor's rights under the promissory note, health-care-insurance receivable, or general intangible, including any related information or materials furnished to the debtor in the transaction giving rise to the promissory note, health-care-insurance receivable, or general intangible;

(5) does not entitle the secured party to use, assign, possess, or have access to any trade secrets or confidential information of the person obligated on the promissory note or the account debtor; and

(6) does not entitle the secured party to enforce the security interest in the promissory note, health-care-insurance receivable, or general intangible.

(e) [Section prevails over specified inconsistent law.] This section prevails over any inconsistent provisions of the following statutes, rules, and regulations: [List here any statutes, rules, and regulations containing provisions inconsistent with this section.]

§ 9-409. Restrictions on Assignment of Letter-of-Credit Rights Ineffective

(a) [Term or law restricting assignment generally ineffective.] A term in a letter of credit or a rule of law, statute, regulation, custom, or practice applicable to the letter of credit which prohibits, restricts, or requires the consent of an applicant, issuer, or nominated person to a beneficiary's assignment of or creation of a security interest in a letter-of-credit right is ineffective to the extent that the term or rule of law, statute, regulation, custom, or practice:

(1) would impair the creation, attachment, or perfection of a security interest in the letter-of-credit right; or

(2) provides that the creation, attachment, or perfection of the security interest may give rise to a default, breach, right of recoupment, claim, defense, termination, right of termination, or remedy under the letter-of-credit right.

(b) [Limitation on ineffectiveness under subsection (a).] To the extent that a term in a letter of credit is ineffective under subsection (a) but would be effective under law other than this Article or a custom or practice applicable to the letter of credit, to the transfer of a right to draw or otherwise demand performance under the letter of credit, or to the assignment of a right to proceeds of the letter of credit, the creation, attachment, or perfection of a security interest in the letter-of-credit right:

(1) is not enforceable against the applicant, issuer, nominated person, or transferee beneficiary;

(2) imposes no duties or obligations on the applicant, issuer, nominated person, or transferee beneficiary; and

(3) does not require the applicant, issuer, nominated person, or transferee beneficiary to recognize the security interest, pay or render performance to the secured party, or accept payment or other performance from the secured party.

PART 5. FILING
Subpart 1. Filing Office; Contents and Effectiveness of Financing Statement
§ 9-501. Filing Office

(a)   [Filing offices.] Except as otherwise provided in subsection (b), if the local law of this State governs perfection of a security interest or agricultural lien, the office in which to file a financing statement to perfect the security interest or agricultural lien is:

(1)   the office designated for the filing or recording of a record of a mortgage on the related real property, if:

(A)   the collateral is as-extracted collateral or timber to be cut; or

(B)   the financing statement is filed as a fixture filing and the collateral is goods that are or are to become fixtures; or

(2)   the office of [or any office duly authorized by [ ]], in all other cases, including a case in which the collateral is goods that are or are to become fixtures and the financing statement is not filed as a fixture filing.

(b)   [Filing office for transmitting utilities.] The office in which to file a financing statement to perfect a security interest in collateral, including fixtures, of a transmitting utility is the office of [ ]. The financing statement also constitutes a fixture filing as to the collateral indicated in the financing statement which is or is to become fixtures.

§ 9-502. Contents of Financing Statement; Record of Mortgage as Financing Statement; Time of Filing Financing Statement

(a)   [Sufficiency of financing statement.] Subject to subsection (b), a financing statement is sufficient only if it:

(1)   provides the name of the debtor;

(2)   provides the name of the secured party or a representative of the secured party; and

(3)   indicates the collateral covered by the financing statement.

(b)   [Real-property-related financing statements.] Except as otherwise provided in Section 9-501(b), to be sufficient, a financing statement that covers as-extracted collateral or timber to be cut, or which is filed as a fixture filing and covers goods that are or are to become fixtures, must satisfy subsection (a) and also:

(1)   indicate that it covers this type of collateral;

(2)   indicate that it is to be filed [for record] in the real property records;

(3)   provide a description of the real property to which the collateral is related [sufficient to give constructive notice of a mortgage under the law of this State if the description were contained in a record of the mortgage of the real property]; and

(4)   if the debtor does not have an interest of record in the real property, provide the name of a record owner.

(c)   [Record of mortgage as financing statement.] A record of a mortgage is effective, from the date of recording, as a financing statement filed as a fixture filing or as a financing statement covering as-extracted collateral or timber to be cut only if:

(1)   the record indicates the goods or accounts that it covers;

(2)   the goods are or are to become fixtures related to the real property described in the record or the collateral is related to the real property described in the record and is as-extracted collateral or timber to be cut;

(3)   the record satisfies the requirements for a financing statement in this section other than an indication that it is to be filed in the real property records; and

(4)   the record is [duly] recorded.

(d)   [Filing before security agreement or attachment.] A financing statement may be filed before a security agreement is made or a security interest otherwise attaches.

§ 9-503. Name of Debtor and Secured Party

(a)   [Sufficiency of debtor's name.] A financing statement sufficiently provides the name of the debtor:

(1) if the debtor is a registered organization, only if the financing statement provides the name of the debtor indicated on the public record of the debtor's jurisdiction of organization which shows the debtor to have been organized;

(2) if the debtor is a decedent's estate, only if the financing statement provides the name of the decedent and indicates that the debtor is an estate;

(3) if the debtor is a trust or a trustee acting with respect to property held in trust, only if the financing statement:

    (A) provides the name specified for the trust in its organic documents or, if no name is specified, provides the name of the settlor and additional information sufficient to distinguish the debtor from other trusts having one or more of the same settlors; and

    (B) indicates, in the debtor's name or otherwise, that the debtor is a trust or is a trustee acting with respect to property held in trust; and

(4) in other cases:

    (A) if the debtor has a name, only if it provides the individual or organizational name of the debtor; and

    (B) if the debtor does not have a name, only if it provides the names of the partners, members, associates, or other persons comprising the debtor.

(b) [Additional debtor-related information.] A financing statement that provides the name of the debtor in accordance with subsection (a) is not rendered ineffective by the absence of:

(1) a trade name or other name of the debtor; or

(2) unless required under subsection (a)(4)(B), names of partners, members, associates, or other persons comprising the debtor.

(c) [Debtor's trade name insufficient.] A financing statement that provides only the debtor's trade name does not sufficiently provide the name of the debtor.

(d) [Representative capacity.] Failure to indicate the representative capacity of a secured party or representative of a secured party does not affect the sufficiency of a financing statement.

(e) [Multiple debtors and secured parties.] A financing statement may provide the name of more than one debtor and the name of more than one secured party.

§ 9-504. Indication of Collateral

A financing statement sufficiently indicates the collateral that it covers if the financing statement provides:

(1) a description of the collateral pursuant to Section 9-108; or

(2) an indication that the financing statement covers all assets or all personal property.

§ 9-505. Filing and Compliance with Other Statutes and Treaties for Consignments, Leases, Other Bailments, and Other Transactions

(a) [Use of terms other than "debtor" and "secured party."] A consignor, lessor, or other bailor of goods, a licensor, or a buyer of a payment intangible or promissory note may file a financing statement, or may comply with a statute or treaty described in Section 9-311(a), using the terms "consignor", "consignee", "lessor", "lessee", "bailor", "bailee", "licensor", "licensee", "owner", "registered owner", "buyer", "seller", or words of similar import, instead of the terms "secured party" and "debtor".

(b) [Effect of financing statement under subsection (a).] This part applies to the filing of a financing statement under subsection (a) and, as appropriate, to compliance that is equivalent to filing a financing statement under Section 9-311(b), but the filing or compliance is not of itself a factor in determining whether the collateral secures an obligation. If it is determined for another reason that the collateral secures an obligation, a security interest held by the consignor, lessor, bailor, licensor, owner, or buyer which attaches to the collateral is perfected by the filing or compliance.

§ 9-506. Effect of Errors or Omissions

(a) [Minor errors and omissions.] A financing statement substantially satisfying the requirements of this part is effective, even if it has minor errors or omissions, unless the errors or omissions make the financing statement seriously misleading.

(b) [Financing statement seriously misleading.] Except as otherwise provided in subsection (c), a financing statement that fails sufficiently to provide the name of the debtor in accordance with Section 9-503(a) is seriously misleading.

(c) [Financing statement not seriously misleading.] If a search of the records of the filing office under the debtor's correct name, using the filing office's standard search logic, if any, would disclose a financing statement that fails sufficiently to provide the name of the debtor in accordance with Section 9-503(a), the name provided does not make the financing statement seriously misleading.

(d) ["Debtor's correct name."] For purposes of Section 9-508(b), the "debtor's correct name" in subsection (c) means the correct name of the new debtor.

§ 9-507. Effect of Certain Events on Effectiveness of Financing Statement

(a) [Disposition.] A filed financing statement remains effective with respect to collateral that is sold, exchanged, leased, licensed, or otherwise disposed of and in which a security interest or agricultural lien continues, even if the secured party knows of or consents to the disposition.

(b) [Information becoming seriously misleading.] Except as otherwise provided in subsection (c) and Section 9-508, a financing statement is not rendered ineffective if, after the financing statement is filed, the information provided in the financing statement becomes seriously misleading under Section 9-506.

(c) [Change in debtor's name.] If a debtor so changes its name that a filed financing statement becomes seriously misleading under Section 9-506:

(1) the financing statement is effective to perfect a security interest in collateral acquired by the debtor before, or within four months after, the change; and

(2) the financing statement is not effective to perfect a security interest in collateral acquired by the debtor more than four months after the change, unless an amendment to the financing statement which renders the financing statement not seriously misleading is filed within four months after the change.

§ 9-508. Effectiveness of Financing Statement If New Debtor Becomes Bound by Security Agreement

(a) [Financing statement naming original debtor.] Except as otherwise provided in this section, a filed financing statement naming an original debtor is effective to perfect a security interest in collateral in which a new debtor has or acquires rights to the extent that the financing statement would have been effective had the original debtor acquired rights in the collateral.

(b) [Financing statement becoming seriously misleading.] If the difference between the name of the original debtor and that of the new debtor causes a filed financing statement that is effective under subsection (a) to be seriously misleading under Section 9-506:

(1) the financing statement is effective to perfect a security interest in collateral acquired by the new debtor before, and within four months after, the new debtor becomes bound under Section 9-203(d); and

(2) the financing statement is not effective to perfect a security interest in collateral acquired by the new debtor more than four months after the new debtor becomes bound under Section 9-203(d) unless an initial financing statement providing the name of the new debtor is filed before the expiration of that time.

(c) [When section not applicable.] This section does not apply to collateral as to which a filed financing statement remains effective against the new debtor under Section 9-507(a).

§ 9-509. Persons Entitled to File a Record

(a) [Person entitled to file record.] A person may file an initial financing statement, amendment that adds collateral covered by a financing statement, or amendment that adds a debtor to a financing statement only if:

(1) the debtor authorizes the filing in an authenticated record or pursuant to subsection (b) or (c); or

(2) the person holds an agricultural lien that has become effective at the time of filing and the financing statement covers only collateral in which the person holds an agricultural lien.

(b) [Security agreement as authorization.] By authenticating or becoming bound as debtor by a security agreement, a debtor or new debtor authorizes the filing of an initial financing statement, and an amendment, covering:
(1)   the collateral described in the security agreement; and
(2)   property that becomes collateral under Section 9-315(a)(2), whether or not the security agreement expressly covers proceeds.
(c) [Acquisition of collateral as authorization.] By acquiring collateral in which a security interest or agricultural lien continues under Section 9-315(a)(1), a debtor authorizes the filing of an initial financing statement, and an amendment, covering the collateral and property that becomes collateral under Section 9-315(a)(2).
(d) [Person entitled to file certain amendments.] A person may file an amendment other than an amendment that adds collateral covered by a financing statement or an amendment that adds a debtor to a financing statement only if:
(1)   the secured party of record authorizes the filing; or
(2)   the amendment is a termination statement for a financing statement as to which the secured party of record has failed to file or send a termination statement as required by Section 9-513(a) or (c), the debtor authorizes the filing, and the termination statement indicates that the debtor authorized it to be filed.
(e) [Multiple secured parties of record.] If there is more than one secured party of record for a financing statement, each secured party of record may authorize the filing of an amendment under subsection (d).

§ 9-510. Effectiveness of Filed Record

(a) [Filed record effective if authorized.] A filed record is effective only to the extent that it was filed by a person that may file it under Section 9-509.
(b) [Authorization by one secured party of record.] A record authorized by one secured party of record does not affect the financing statement with respect to another secured party of record.
(c) [Continuation statement not timely filed.] A continuation statement that is not filed within the six-month period prescribed by Section 9-515(d) is ineffective.

§ 9-511. Secured Party of Record

(a) [Secured party of record.] A secured party of record with respect to a financing statement is a person whose name is provided as the name of the secured party or a representative of the secured party in an initial financing statement that has been filed. If an initial financing statement is filed under Section 9-514(a), the assignee named in the initial financing statement is the secured party of record with respect to the financing statement.
(b) [Amendment naming secured party of record.] If an amendment of a financing statement which provides the name of a person as a secured party or a representative of a secured party is filed, the person named in the amendment is a secured party of record. If an amendment is filed under Section 9-514(b), the assignee named in the amendment is a secured party of record.
(c) [Amendment deleting secured party of record.] A person remains a secured party of record until the filing of an amendment of the financing statement which deletes the person.

§ 9-512. Amendment of Financing Statement
[Alternative A]

(a) [Amendment of information in financing statement.] Subject to Section 9-509, a person may add or delete collateral covered by, continue or terminate the effectiveness of, or, subject to subsection (e), otherwise amend the information provided in, a financing statement by filing an amendment that:
(1)   identifies, by its file number, the initial financing statement to which the amendment relates; and
(2)   if the amendment relates to an initial financing statement filed [or recorded] in a filing office described in Section 9-501(a)(1), provides the information specified in Section 9-502(b).

[Alternative B]

(a) [Amendment of information in financing statement.] Subject to Section 9-509, a person may add or delete collateral covered by, continue or terminate the effectiveness of, or, subject to subsection (e), otherwise amend the information provided in, a financing statement by filing an amendment that:

(1) identifies, by its file number, the initial financing statement to which the amendment relates; and

(2) if the amendment relates to an initial financing statement filed [or recorded] in a filing office described in Section 9-501(a)(1), provides the date [and time] that the initial financing statement was filed [or recorded] and the information specified in Section 9-502(b).

[End of Alternatives]

(b) [Period of effectiveness not affected.] Except as otherwise provided in Section 9-515, the filing of an amendment does not extend the period of effectiveness of the financing statement.

(c) [Effectiveness of amendment adding collateral.] A financing statement that is amended by an amendment that adds collateral is effective as to the added collateral only from the date of the filing of the amendment.

(d) [Effectiveness of amendment adding debtor.] A financing statement that is amended by an amendment that adds a debtor is effective as to the added debtor only from the date of the filing of the amendment.

(e) [Certain amendments ineffective.] An amendment is ineffective to the extent it:

(1) purports to delete all debtors and fails to provide the name of a debtor to be covered by the financing statement; or

(2) purports to delete all secured parties of record and fails to provide the name of a new secured party of record.

§ 9-513. Termination Statement

(a) [Consumer goods.] A secured party shall cause the secured party of record for a financing statement to file a termination statement for the financing statement if the financing statement covers consumer goods and:

(1) there is no obligation secured by the collateral covered by the financing statement and no commitment to make an advance, incur an obligation, or otherwise give value; or

(2) the debtor did not authorize the filing of the initial financing statement.

(b) [Time for compliance with subsection (a).] To comply with subsection (a), a secured party shall cause the secured party of record to file the termination statement:

(1) within one month after there is no obligation secured by the collateral covered by the financing statement and no commitment to make an advance, incur an obligation, or otherwise give value; or

(2) if earlier, within 20 days after the secured party receives an authenticated demand from a debtor.

(c) [Other collateral.] In cases not governed by subsection (a), within 20 days after a secured party receives an authenticated demand from a debtor, the secured party shall cause the secured party of record for a financing statement to send to the debtor a termination statement for the financing statement or file the termination statement in the filing office if:

(1) except in the case of a financing statement covering accounts or chattel paper that has been sold or goods that are the subject of a consignment, there is no obligation secured by the collateral covered by the financing statement and no commitment to make an advance, incur an obligation, or otherwise give value;

(2) the financing statement covers accounts or chattel paper that has been sold but as to which the account debtor or other person obligated has discharged its obligation;

(3) the financing statement covers goods that were the subject of a consignment to the debtor but are not in the debtor's possession; or

(4) the debtor did not authorize the filing of the initial financing statement.

(d) [Effect of filing termination statement.] Except as otherwise provided in Section 9-510, upon the filing of a termination statement with the filing office, the financing statement to which the termination statement relates ceases to be effective. Except as otherwise provided in Section 9-510, for purposes of Sections 9-519(g), 9-522(a), and 9-523(c), the filing with the filing office of a termination statement relating to a financing statement that indicates that the debtor is a transmitting utility also causes the effectiveness of the financing statement to lapse.

§ 9-514. Assignment of Powers of Secured Party of Record

(a) [Assignment reflected on initial financing statement.] Except as otherwise provided in subsection (c), an initial financing statement may reflect an assignment of all of the secured party's power to authorize an amendment to the financing statement by providing the name and mailing address of the assignee as the name and address of the secured party.

(b) [Assignment of filed financing statement.] Except as otherwise provided in subsection (c), a secured party of record may assign of record all or part of its power to authorize an amendment to a financing statement by filing in the filing office an amendment of the financing statement which:

(1) identifies, by its file number, the initial financing statement to which it relates;

(2) provides the name of the assignor; and

(3) provides the name and mailing address of the assignee.

(c) [Assignment of record of mortgage.] An assignment of record of a security interest in a fixture covered by a record of a mortgage which is effective as a financing statement filed as a fixture filing under Section 9-502(c) may be made only by an assignment of record of the mortgage in the manner provided by law of this State other than [the Uniform Commercial Code].

§ 9-515. Duration and Effectiveness of Financing Statement; Effect of Lapsed Financing Statement

(a) [Five-year effectiveness.] Except as otherwise provided in subsections (b), (e), (f), and (g), a filed financing statement is effective for a period of five years after the date of filing.

(b) [Public-finance or manufactured-home transaction.] Except as otherwise provided in subsections (e), (f), and (g), an initial financing statement filed in connection with a public-finance transaction or manufactured-home transaction is effective for a period of 30 years after the date of filing if it indicates that it is filed in connection with a public-finance transaction or manufactured-home transaction.

(c) [Lapse and continuation of financing statement.] The effectiveness of a filed financing statement lapses on the expiration of the period of its effectiveness unless before the lapse a continuation statement is filed pursuant to subsection (d). Upon lapse, a financing statement ceases to be effective and any security interest or agricultural lien that was perfected by the financing statement becomes unperfected, unless the security interest is perfected otherwise. If the security interest or agricultural lien becomes unperfected upon lapse, it is deemed never to have been perfected as against a purchaser of the collateral for value.

(d) [When continuation statement may be filed.] A continuation statement may be filed only within six months before the expiration of the five-year period specified in subsection (a) or the 30-year period specified in subsection (b), whichever is applicable.

(e) [Effect of filing continuation statement.] Except as otherwise provided in Section 9-510, upon timely filing of a continuation statement, the effectiveness of the initial financing statement continues for a period of five years commencing on the day on which the financing statement would have become ineffective in the absence of the filing. Upon the expiration of the five-year period, the financing statement lapses in the same manner as provided in subsection (c), unless, before the lapse, another continuation statement is filed pursuant to subsection (d). Succeeding continuation statements may be filed in the same manner to continue the effectiveness of the initial financing statement.

(f) [Transmitting utility financing statement.] If a debtor is a transmitting utility and a filed financing statement so indicates, the financing statement is effective until a termination statement is filed.

(g) [Record of mortgage as financing statement.] A record of a mortgage that is effective as a financing statement filed as a fixture filing under Section 9-502(c) remains effective as a financing statement filed as a fixture filing until the mortgage is released or satisfied of record or its effectiveness otherwise terminates as to the real property.

§ 9-516. What Constitutes Filing; Effectiveness of Filing

(a) [What constitutes filing.] Except as otherwise provided in subsection (b), communication of a record to a filing office and tender of the filing fee or acceptance of the record by the filing office constitutes filing.

(b) [Refusal to accept record; filing does not occur.] Filing does not occur with respect to a record that a filing office refuses to accept because:

(1) the record is not communicated by a method or medium of communication authorized by the filing office;

(2) an amount equal to or greater than the applicable filing fee is not tendered;

(3) the filing office is unable to index the record because:

    (A) in the case of an initial financing statement, the record does not provide a name for the debtor;

    (B) in the case of an amendment or correction statement, the record:

        (i) does not identify the initial financing statement as required by Section 9-512 or 9-518, as applicable; or

        (ii) identifies an initial financing statement whose effectiveness has lapsed under Section 9-515;

    (C) in the case of an initial financing statement that provides the name of a debtor identified as an individual or an amendment that provides a name of a debtor identified as an individual which was not previously provided in the financing statement to which the record relates, the record does not identify the debtor's last name; or

    (D) in the case of a record filed [or recorded] in the filing office described in Section 9-501 (a)(1), the record does not provide a sufficient description of the real property to which it relates;

(4) in the case of an initial financing statement or an amendment that adds a secured party of record, the record does not provide a name and mailing address for the secured party of record;

(5) in the case of an initial financing statement or an amendment that provides a name of a debtor which was not previously provided in the financing statement to which the amendment relates, the record does not:

    (A) provide a mailing address for the debtor;

    (B) indicate whether the debtor is an individual or an organization; or

    (C) if the financing statement indicates that the debtor is an organization, provide:

        (i) a type of organization for the debtor;

        (ii) a jurisdiction of organization for the debtor; or

        (iii) an organizational identification number for the debtor or indicate that the debtor has none;

(6) in the case of an assignment reflected in an initial financing statement under Section 9-514(a) or an amendment filed under Section 9-514(b), the record does not provide a name and mailing address for the assignee; or

(7) in the case of a continuation statement, the record is not filed within the six-month period prescribed by Section 9-515(d).

(c) [Rules applicable to subsection (b).] For purposes of subsection (b):

(1) a record does not provide information if the filing office is unable to read or decipher the information; and

(2) a record that does not indicate that it is an amendment or identify an initial financing statement to which it relates, as required by Section 9-512, 9-514, or 9-518, is an initial financing statement.

(d) [Refusal to accept record; record effective as filed record.] A record that is communicated to the filing office with tender of the filing fee, but which the filing office refuses to accept for a reason other than one set forth in subsection (b), is effective as a filed record except as against a purchaser of the collateral which gives value in reasonable reliance upon the absence of the record from the files.

§ 9-517. Effect of Indexing Errors

The failure of the filing office to index a record correctly does not affect the effectiveness of the filed record.

§ 9-518. Claim Concerning Inaccurate or Wrongfully Filed Record

(a) [Correction statement.] A person may file in the filing office a correction statement with respect to a record indexed there under the person's name if the person believes that the record is inaccurate or was wrongfully filed.

[Alternative A]

(b) [Sufficiency of correction statement.] A correction statement must:
(1) identify the record to which it relates by the file number assigned to the initial financing statement to which the record relates;
(2) indicate that it is a correction statement; and
(3) provide the basis for the person's belief that the record is inaccurate and indicate the manner in which the person believes the record should be amended to cure any inaccuracy or provide the basis for the person's belief that the record was wrongfully filed.

[Alternative B]

(b) [Sufficiency of correction statement.] A correction statement must:
(1) identify the record to which it relates by:
   (A) the file number assigned to the initial financing statement to which the record relates; and
   (B) if the correction statement relates to a record filed [or recorded] in a filing office described in Section 9-501(a)(1), the date [and time] that the initial financing statement was filed [or recorded] and the information specified in Section 9-502(b);
(2) indicate that it is a correction statement; and
(3) provide the basis for the person's belief that the record is inaccurate and indicate the manner in which the person believes the record should be amended to cure any inaccuracy or provide the basis for the person's belief that the record was wrongfully filed.

[End of Alternatives]

(c) [Record not affected by correction statement.] The filing of a correction statement does not affect the effectiveness of an initial financing statement or other filed record.

Subpart 2. Duties and Operation of Filing Office
§ 9-519. Numbering, Maintaining, and Indexing Records;
Communicating Information Provided in Records

(a) [Filing office duties.] For each record filed in a filing office, the filing office shall:
(1) assign a unique number to the filed record;
(2) create a record that bears the number assigned to the filed record and the date and time of filing;
(3) maintain the filed record for public inspection; and
(4) index the filed record in accordance with subsections (c), (d), and (e).
(b) [File number.] A file number [assigned after January 1, 2002,] must include a digit that:
(1) is mathematically derived from or related to the other digits of the file number; and
(2) aids the filing office in determining whether a number communicated as the file number includes a single-digit or transpositional error.
(c) [Indexing: general.] Except as otherwise provided in subsections (d) and (e), the filing office shall:
(1) index an initial financing statement according to the name of the debtor and index all filed records relating to the initial financing statement in a manner that associates with one an-

other an initial financing statement and all filed records relating to the initial financing statement; and

(2)   index a record that provides a name of a debtor which was not previously provided in the financing statement to which the record relates also according to the name that was not previously provided.

(d)   [Indexing: real-property-related financing statement.] If a financing statement is filed as a fixture filing or covers as-extracted collateral or timber to be cut, [it must be filed for record and] the filing office shall index it:

(1)   under the names of the debtor and of each owner of record shown on the financing state-ment as if they were the mortgagors under a mortgage of the real property described; and

(2)   to the extent that the law of this State provides for indexing of records of mortgages under the name of the mortgagee, under the name of the secured party as if the secured party were the mortgagee thereunder, or, if indexing is by description, as if the financing state-ment were a record of a mortgage of the real property described.

(e)   [Indexing: real-property-related assignment.] If a financing statement is filed as a fixture filing or covers as-extracted collateral or timber to be cut, the filing office shall index an assign-ment filed under Section 9-514(a) or an amendment filed under Section 9-514(b):

(1)   under the name of the assignor as grantor; and

(2)   to the extent that the law of this State provides for indexing a record of the assignment of a mortgage under the name of the assignee, under the name of the assignee.

[Alternative A]

(f)   [Retrieval and association capability.] The filing office shall maintain a capability:

(1)   to retrieve a record by the name of the debtor and by the file number assigned to the initial financing statement to which the record relates; and

(2)   to associate and retrieve with one another an initial financing statement and each filed record relating to the initial financing statement.

[Alternative B]

(f)   [Retrieval and association capability.] The filing office shall maintain a capability:

(1)   to retrieve a record by the name of the debtor and:

(A)   if the filing office is described in Section 9-501(a)(1), by the file number assigned to the initial financing statement to which the record relates and the date [and time] that the record was filed [or recorded]; or

(B)   if the filing office is described in Section 9-501(a)(2), by the file number assigned to the initial financing statement to which the record relates; and

(2)   to associate and retrieve with one another an initial financing statement and each filed record relating to the initial financing statement.

[End of Alternatives]

(g)   [Removal of debtor's name.] The filing office may not remove a debtor's name from the index until one year after the effectiveness of a financing statement naming the debtor lapses under Section 9-515 with respect to all secured parties of record.

(h)   [Timeliness of filing office performance.] The filing office shall perform the acts required by subsections (a) through (e) at the time and in the manner prescribed by filing-office rule, but not later than two business days after the filing office receives the record in question.

[(i)   [Inapplicability to real-property-related filing office.] [Subsections] [(b)] [and] [(h)] do[es] not apply to a filing office described in Section 9-501(a)(1).]

§ 9-520. Acceptance and Refusal to Accept Record

(a)   [Mandatory refusal to accept record.] A filing office shall refuse to accept a record for filing for a reason set forth in Section 9-516(b) and may refuse to accept a record for filing only for a reason set forth in Section 9-516(b).

(b)   [Communication concerning refusal.] If a filing office refuses to accept a record for filing, it shall communicate to the person that presented the record the fact of and reason for the refusal and the date and time the record would have been filed had the filing office accepted it. The communication must be made at the time and in the manner prescribed by filing-office rule but [, in the case of a filing office described in Section 9-501(a)(2),] in no event more than two business days after the filing office receives the record.

(c) [When filed financing statement effective.] A filed financing statement satisfying Section 9-502(a) and (b) is effective, even if the filing office is required to refuse to accept it for filing under subsection (a). However, Section 9-338 applies to a filed financing statement providing information described in Section 9-516(b)(5) which is incorrect at the time the financing statement is filed.

(d) [Separate application to multiple debtors.] If a record communicated to a filing office provides information that relates to more than one debtor, this part applies as to each debtor separately.

§ 9-521. Uniform Form of Written Financing Statement and Amendment

(a) [Initial financing statement form.] A filing office that accepts written records may not refuse to accept a written initial financing statement in the following form and format except for a reason set forth in Section 9-516(b): [...]

(b) [Amendment form.] A filing office that accepts written records may not refuse to accept a written record in the following form and format except for a reason set forth in Section 9-516(b): [...]

§ 9-522. Maintenance and Destruction of Records
[Alternative A]

(a) [Post-lapse maintenance and retrieval of information.] The filing office shall maintain a record of the information provided in a filed financing statement for at least one year after the effectiveness of the financing statement has lapsed under Section 9-515 with respect to all secured parties of record. The record must be retrievable by using the name of the debtor and by using the file number assigned to the initial financing statement to which the record relates.

[Alternative B]

(a) [Post-lapse maintenance and retrieval of information.] The filing office shall maintain a record of the information provided in a filed financing statement for at least one year after the effectiveness of the financing statement has lapsed under Section 9-515 with respect to all secured parties of record. The record must be retrievable by using the name of the debtor and:

(1) if the record was filed [or recorded] in the filing office described in Section 9-501(a)(1), by using the file number assigned to the initial financing statement to which the record relates and the date [and time] that the record was filed [or recorded]; or

(2) if the record was filed in the filing office described in Section 9-501(a)(2), by using the file number assigned to the initial financing statement to which the record relates.

[End of Alternatives]

(b) [Destruction of written records.] Except to the extent that a statute governing disposition of public records provides otherwise, the filing office immediately may destroy any written record evidencing a financing statement. However, if the filing office destroys a written record, it shall maintain another record of the financing statement which complies with subsection (a).

§ 9-523. Information from Filing Office; Sale or License of Records

(a) [Acknowledgment of filing written record.] If a person that files a written record requests an acknowledgment of the filing, the filing office shall send to the person an image of the record showing the number assigned to the record pursuant to Section 9-519(a)(1) and the date and time of the filing of the record. However, if the person furnishes a copy of the record to the filing office, the filing office may instead:

(1) note upon the copy the number assigned to the record pursuant to Section 9-519(a)(1) and the date and time of the filing of the record; and

(2) send the copy to the person.

(b) [Acknowledgment of filing other record.] If a person files a record other than a written record, the filing office shall communicate to the person an acknowledgment that provides:

(1) the information in the record;

(2) the number assigned to the record pursuant to Section 9-519(a)(1); and

(3) the date and time of the filing of the record.
(c) [Communication of requested information.] The filing office shall communicate or otherwise make available in a record the following information to any person that requests it:
(1) whether there is on file on a date and time specified by the filing office, but not a date earlier than three business days before the filing office receives the request, any financing statement that:
 (A) designates a particular debtor [or, if the request so states, designates a particular debtor at the address specified in the request];
 (B) has not lapsed under Section 9-515 with respect to all secured parties of record; and
 (C) if the request so states, has lapsed under Section 9-515 and a record of which is maintained by the filing office under Section 9-522(a);
(2) the date and time of filing of each financing statement; and
(3) the information provided in each financing statement.
(d) [Medium for communicating information.] In complying with its duty under subsection (c), the filing office may communicate information in any medium. However, if requested, the filing office shall communicate information by issuing [its written certificate] [a record that can be admitted into evidence in the courts of this State without extrinsic evidence of its authenticity].
(e) [Timeliness of filing office performance.] The filing office shall perform the acts required by subsections (a) through (d) at the time and in the manner prescribed by filing-office rule, but not later than two business days after the filing office receives the request.
(f) [Public availability of records.] At least weekly, the [insert appropriate official or governmental agency] [filing office] shall offer to sell or license to the public on a nonexclusive basis, in bulk, copies of all records filed in it under this part, in every medium from time to time available to the filing office.

§ 9-524. Delay by Filing Office
Delay by the filing office beyond a time limit prescribed by this part is excused if:
(1) the delay is caused by interruption of communication or computer facilities, war, emergency conditions, failure of equipment, or other circumstances beyond control of the filing office; and
(2) the filing office exercises reasonable diligence under the circumstances.

§ 9-525. Fees
(a) [Initial financing statement or other record: general rule.] Except as otherwise provided in subsection (e), the fee for filing and indexing a record under this part, other than an initial financing statement of the kind described in subsection (b), is [the amount specified in subsection (c), if applicable, plus]: [...]

§ 9-526. Filing-Office Rules
(a) [Adoption of filing-office rules.] The [insert appropriate governmental official or agency] shall adopt and publish rules to implement this article. The filing-office rules must be:
(1) consistent with this article; and
(2) adopted and published in accordance with the [insert any applicable state administrative procedure act].
(b) [Harmonization of rules.] To keep the filing-office rules and practices of the filing office in harmony with the rules and practices of filing offices in other jurisdictions that enact substantially this part, and to keep the technology used by the filing office compatible with the technology used by filing offices in other jurisdictions that enact substantially this part, the [insert appropriate governmental official or agency], so far as is consistent with the purposes, policies, and provisions of this article, in adopting, amending, and repealing filing-office rules, shall:
(1) consult with filing offices in other jurisdictions that enact substantially this part; and
(2) consult the most recent version of the Model Rules promulgated by the International Association of Corporate Administrators or any successor organization; and
(3) take into consideration the rules and practices of, and the technology used by, filing offices in other jurisdictions that enact substantially this part.

§ 9-527. Duty to Report

The [insert appropriate governmental official or agency] shall report [annually on or before _____] to the [Governor and Legislature] on the operation of the filing office. The report must contain a statement of the extent to which:

(1)   the filing-office rules are not in harmony with the rules of filing offices in other jurisdictions that enact substantially this part and the reasons for these variations; and
(2)   the filing-office rules are not in harmony with the most recent version of the Model Rules promulgated by the International Association of Corporate Administrators, or any successor organization, and the reasons for these variations.

PART 6. DEFAULT

Subpart 1. Default and Enforcement of Security Interest

§ 9-601. Rights after Default; Judicial Enforcement; Consignor or Buyer of Accounts, Chattel Paper, Payment Intangibles, or Promissory Notes

(a)   [Rights of secured party after default.] After default, a secured party has the rights provided in this part and, except as otherwise provided in Section 9-602, those provided by agreement of the parties. A secured party:
(1)   may reduce a claim to judgment, foreclose, or otherwise enforce the claim, security interest, or agricultural lien by any available judicial procedure; and
(2)   if the collateral is documents, may proceed either as to the documents or as to the goods they cover.
(b)   [Rights and duties of secured party in possession or control.] A secured party in possession of collateral or control of collateral under Section 9-104, 9-105, 9-106, or 9-107 has the rights and duties provided in Section 9-207.
(c)   [Rights cumulative; simultaneous exercise.] The rights under subsections (a) and (b) are cumulative and may be exercised simultaneously.
(d)   [Rights of debtor and obligor.] Except as otherwise provided in subsection (g) and Section 9-605, after default, a debtor and an obligor have the rights provided in this part and by agreement of the parties.
(e)   [Lien of levy after judgment.] If a secured party has reduced its claim to judgment, the lien of any levy that may be made upon the collateral by virtue of an execution based upon the judgment relates back to the earliest of:
(1)   the date of perfection of the security interest or agricultural lien in the collateral;
(2)   the date of filing a financing statement covering the collateral; or
(3)   any date specified in a statute under which the agricultural lien was created.
(f)   [Execution sale.] A sale pursuant to an execution is a foreclosure of the security interest or agricultural lien by judicial procedure within the meaning of this section. A secured party may purchase at the sale and thereafter hold the collateral free of any other requirements of this article.
(g)   [Consignor or buyer of certain rights to payment.] Except as otherwise provided in Section 9-607(c), this part imposes no duties upon a secured party that is a consignor or is a buyer of accounts, chattel paper, payment intangibles, or promissory notes.

§ 9-602. Waiver and Variance of Rights and Duties

Except as otherwise provided in Section 9-624, to the extent that they give rights to a debtor or obligor and impose duties on a secured party, the debtor or obligor may not waive or vary the rules stated in the following listed sections:
(1)   Section 9-207(b)(4)(C), which deals with use and operation of the collateral by the secured party;
(2)   Section 9-210, which deals with requests for an accounting and requests concerning a list of collateral and statement of account;
(3)   Section 9-607(c), which deals with collection and enforcement of collateral;

(4)   Sections 9-608(a) and 9-615(c) to the extent that they deal with application or payment of noncash proceeds of collection, enforcement, or disposition;
(5)   Sections 9-608(a) and 9-615(d) to the extent that they require accounting for or payment of surplus proceeds of collateral;
(6)   Section 9-609 to the extent that it imposes upon a secured party that takes possession of collateral without judicial process the duty to do so without breach of the peace;
(7)   Sections 9-610(b), 9-611, 9-613, and 9-614, which deal with disposition of collateral;
(8)   Section 9-615(f), which deals with calculation of a deficiency or surplus when a disposition is made to the secured party, a person related to the secured party, or a secondary obligor;
(9)   Section 9-616, which deals with explanation of the calculation of a surplus or deficiency;
(10) Sections 9-620, 9-621, and 9-622, which deal with acceptance of collateral in satisfaction of obligation;
(11) Section 9-623, which deals with redemption of collateral;
(12) Section 9-624, which deals with permissible waivers; and
(13) Sections 9-625 and 9-626, which deal with the secured party's liability for failure to comply with this article.

§ 9-603. Agreement on Standards Concerning Rights and Duties

(a)   [Agreed standards.] The parties may determine by agreement the standards measuring the fulfillment of the rights of a debtor or obligor and the duties of a secured party under a rule stated in Section 9-602 if the standards are not manifestly unreasonable.
(b)   [Agreed standards inapplicable to breach of peace.] Subsection (a) does not apply to the duty under Section 9-609 to refrain from breaching the peace.

§ 9-604. Procedure If Security Agreement Covers Real Property or Fixtures

(a)   [Enforcement: personal and real property.] If a security agreement covers both personal and real property, a secured party may proceed:
(1)   under this part as to the personal property without prejudicing any rights with respect to the real property; or
(2)   as to both the personal property and the real property in accordance with the rights with respect to the real property, in which case the other provisions of this part do not apply.
(b)   [Enforcement: fixtures.] Subject to subsection (c), if a security agreement covers goods that are or become fixtures, a secured party may proceed:
(1)   under this part; or
(2)   in accordance with the rights with respect to real property, in which case the other provisions of this part do not apply.
(c)   [Removal of fixtures.] Subject to the other provisions of this part, if a secured party holding a security interest in fixtures has priority over all owners and encumbrancers of the real property, the secured party, after default, may remove the collateral from the real property.
(d)   [Injury caused by removal.] A secured party that removes collateral shall promptly reimburse any encumbrancer or owner of the real property, other than the debtor, for the cost of repair of any physical injury caused by the removal. The secured party need not reimburse the encumbrancer or owner for any diminution in value of the real property caused by the absence of the goods removed or by any necessity of replacing them. A person entitled to reimbursement may refuse permission to remove until the secured party gives adequate assurance for the performance of the obligation to reimburse.

§ 9-605. Unknown Debtor or Secondary Obligor

A secured party does not owe a duty based on its status as secured party:
(1)   to a person that is a debtor or obligor, unless the secured party knows:
(A)   that the person is a debtor or obligor;
(B)   the identity of the person; and
(C)   how to communicate with the person; or

(2) to a secured party or lienholder that has filed a financing statement against a person, unless the secured party knows:
(A) that the person is a debtor; and
(B) the identity of the person.

§ 9-606. Time of Default for Agricultural Lien

For purposes of this part, a default occurs in connection with an agricultural lien at the time the secured party becomes entitled to enforce the lien in accordance with the statute under which it was created.

§ 9-607. Collection and Enforcement by Secured Party

(a) [Collection and enforcement generally.] If so agreed, and in any event after default, a secured party:
(1) may notify an account debtor or other person obligated on collateral to make payment or otherwise render performance to or for the benefit of the secured party;
(2) may take any proceeds to which the secured party is entitled under Section 9-315;
(3) may enforce the obligations of an account debtor or other person obligated on collateral and exercise the rights of the debtor with respect to the obligation of the account debtor or other person obligated on collateral to make payment or otherwise render performance to the debtor, and with respect to any property that secures the obligations of the account debtor or other person obligated on the collateral;
(4) if it holds a security interest in a deposit account perfected by control under Section 9-104 (a)(1), may apply the balance of the deposit account to the obligation secured by the deposit account; and
(5) if it holds a security interest in a deposit account perfected by control under Section 9-104 (a)(2) or (3), may instruct the bank to pay the balance of the deposit account to or for the benefit of the secured party.
(b) [Nonjudicial enforcement of mortgage.] If necessary to enable a secured party to exercise under subsection (a)(3) the right of a debtor to enforce a mortgage nonjudicially, the secured party may record in the office in which a record of the mortgage is recorded:
(1) a copy of the security agreement that creates or provides for a security interest in the obligation secured by the mortgage; and
(2) the secured party's sworn affidavit in recordable form stating that:
(A) a default has occurred; and
(B) the secured party is entitled to enforce the mortgage nonjudicially.
(c) [Commercially reasonable collection and enforcement.] A secured party shall proceed in a commercially reasonable manner if the secured party:
(1) undertakes to collect from or enforce an obligation of an account debtor or other person obligated on collateral; and
(2) is entitled to charge back uncollected collateral or otherwise to full or limited recourse against the debtor or a secondary obligor.
(d) [Expenses of collection and enforcement.] A secured party may deduct from the collections made pursuant to subsection (c) reasonable expenses of collection and enforcement, including reasonable attorney's fees and legal expenses incurred by the secured party.
(e) [Duties to secured party not affected.] This section does not determine whether an account debtor, bank, or other person obligated on collateral owes a duty to a secured party.

§ 9-608. Application of Proceeds of Collection or Enforcement;
Liability for Deficiency and Right to Surplus

(a) [Application of proceeds, surplus, and deficiency if obligation secured.] If a security interest or agricultural lien secures payment or performance of an obligation, the following rules apply:
(1) A secured party shall apply or pay over for application the cash proceeds of collection or enforcement under Section 9-607 in the following order to:

(A) the reasonable expenses of collection and enforcement and, to the extent provided for by agreement and not prohibited by law, reasonable attorney's fees and legal expenses incurred by the secured party;

(B) the satisfaction of obligations secured by the security interest or agricultural lien under which the collection or enforcement is made; and

(C) the satisfaction of obligations secured by any subordinate security interest in or other lien on the collateral subject to the security interest or agricultural lien under which the collection or enforcement is made if the secured party receives an authenticated demand for proceeds before distribution of the proceeds is completed.

(2) If requested by a secured party, a holder of a subordinate security interest or other lien shall furnish reasonable proof of the interest or lien within a reasonable time. Unless the holder complies, the secured party need not comply with the holder's demand under paragraph (1)(C).

(3) A secured party need not apply or pay over for application noncash proceeds of collection and enforcement under Section 9-607 unless the failure to do so would be commercially unreasonable. A secured party that applies or pays over for application noncash proceeds shall do so in a commercially reasonable manner.

(4) A secured party shall account to and pay a debtor for any surplus, and the obligor is liable for any deficiency.

(b) [No surplus or deficiency in sales of certain rights to payment.] If the underlying transaction is a sale of accounts, chattel paper, payment intangibles, or promissory notes, the debtor is not entitled to any surplus, and the obligor is not liable for any deficiency.

§ 9-609. Secured Party's Right to Take Possession after Default

(a) [Possession; rendering equipment unusable; disposition on debtor's premises.] After default, a secured party:

(1) may take possession of the collateral; and

(2) without removal, may render equipment unusable and dispose of collateral on a debtor's premises under Section 9-610.

(b) [Judicial and nonjudicial process.] A secured party may proceed under subsection (a):

(1) pursuant to judicial process; or

(2) without judicial process, if it proceeds without breach of the peace.

(c) [Assembly of collateral.] If so agreed, and in any event after default, a secured party may re-quire the debtor to assemble the collateral and make it available to the secured party at a place to be designated by the secured party which is reasonably convenient to both parties.

§ 9-610. Disposition of Collateral after Default

(a) [Disposition after default.] After default, a secured party may sell, lease, license, or otherwise dispose of any or all of the collateral in its present condition or following any commercially rea-sonable preparation or processing.

(b) [Commercially reasonable disposition.] Every aspect of a disposition of collateral, including the method, manner, time, place, and other terms, must be commercially reasonable. If com-mercially reasonable, a secured party may dispose of collateral by public or private proceedings, by one or more contracts, as a unit or in parcels, and at any time and place and on any terms.

(c) [Purchase by secured party.] A secured party may purchase collateral:

(1) at a public disposition; or

(2) at a private disposition only if the collateral is of a kind that is customarily sold on a recogni-zed market or the subject of widely distributed standard price quotations.

(d) [Warranties on disposition.] A contract for sale, lease, license, or other disposition includes the warranties relating to title, possession, quiet enjoyment, and the like which by operation of law accompany a voluntary disposition of property of the kind subject to the contract.

(e) [Disclaimer of warranties.] A secured party may disclaim or modify warranties under sub-section (d):

(1) in a manner that would be effective to disclaim or modify the warranties in a voluntary dis-
     position of property of the kind subject to the contract of disposition; or
(2) by communicating to the purchaser a record evidencing the contract for disposition and
     including an express disclaimer or modification of the warranties.
(f) [Record sufficient to disclaim warranties.] A record is sufficient to disclaim warranties under
subsection (e) if it indicates "There is no warranty relating to title, possession, quiet enjoyment,
or the like in this disposition" or uses words of similar import.

§ 9-611. Notification Before Disposition of Collateral

(a) ["Notification date."] In this section, "notification date" means the earlier of the date on
which:
(1) a secured party sends to the debtor and any secondary obligor an authenticated notifica-
     tion of disposition; or
(2) the debtor and any secondary obligor waive the right to notification.
(b) [Notification of disposition required.] Except as otherwise provided in subsection (d), a secured party that disposes of collateral under Section 9-610 shall send to the persons specified in
subsection (c) a reasonable authenticated notification of disposition.
(c) [Persons to be notified.] To comply with subsection (b), the secured party shall send an authenticated notification of disposition to:
(1) the debtor;
(2) any secondary obligor; and
(3) if the collateral is other than consumer goods:
     (A) any other person from which the secured party has received, before the notification
          date, an authenticated notification of a claim of an interest in the collateral;
     (B) any other secured party or lienholder that, 10 days before the notification date, held a
          security interest in or other lien on the collateral perfected by the filing of a financing
          statement that:
          (i)   identified the collateral;
          (ii) was indexed under the debtor's name as of that date; and
          (iii) was filed in the office in which to file a financing statement against the debtor
                covering the collateral as of that date; and
     (C) any other secured party that, 10 days before the notification date, held a security inte-
          rest in the collateral perfected by compliance with a statute, regulation, or treaty des-
          cribed in Section 9-311(a).
(d) [Subsection (b) inapplicable: perishable collateral; recognized market.] Subsection (b) does
not apply if the collateral is perishable or threatens to decline speedily in value or is of a type
customarily sold on a recognized market.
(e) [Compliance with subsection (c)(3)(B).] A secured party complies with the requirement for
notification prescribed by subsection (c)(3)(B) if:
(1) not later than 20 days or earlier than 30 days before the notification date, the secured party
     requests, in a commercially reasonable manner, information concerning financing state-
     ments indexed under the debtor's name in the office indicated in subsection (c)(3)(B); and
(2) before the notification date, the secured party:
     (A) did not receive a response to the request for information; or
     (B) received a response to the request for information and sent an authenticated notifica-
          tion of disposition to each secured party or other lienholder named in that response
          whose financing statement covered the collateral.

§ 9-612. Timeliness of Notification Before Disposition of Collateral

(a) [Reasonable time is question of fact.] Except as otherwise provided in subsection (b), whether a notification is sent within a reasonable time is a question of fact.
(b) [10-day period sufficient in non-consumer transaction.] In a transaction other than a consumer transaction, a notification of disposition sent after default and 10 days or more before the

earliest time of disposition set forth in the notification is sent within a reasonable time before the disposition.

§ 9-613. *Contents and Form of Notification Before Disposition of Collateral: General*
Except in a consumer-goods transaction, the following rules apply:
(1)   The contents of a notification of disposition are sufficient if the notification:
(A)   describes the debtor and the secured party;
(B)   describes the collateral that is the subject of the intended disposition;
(C)   states the method of intended disposition;
(D)   states that the debtor is entitled to an accounting of the unpaid indebtedness and states the charge, if any, for an accounting; and
(E)   states the time and place of a public disposition or the time after which any other disposition is to be made.
(2)   Whether the contents of a notification that lacks any of the information specified in paragraph (1) are nevertheless sufficient is a question of fact.
(3)   The contents of a notification providing substantially the information specified in paragraph (1) are sufficient, even if the notification includes: (A) information not specified by that paragraph; or (B) minor errors that are not seriously misleading.
(4)   A particular phrasing of the notification is not required.
(5)   The following form of notification and the form appearing in Section 9-614(3), when completed, each provides sufficient information:

NOTIFICATION OF DISPOSITION OF COLLATERAL

To: [Name of debtor, obligor, or other person to which the notification is sent]
From: [Name, address, and telephone number of secured party]
Name of Debtor(s): [Include only if debtor(s) are not an addressee]
[For a public disposition:]
We will sell [or lease or license, as applicable] the [describe collateral] [to the highest qualified bidder] in public as follows:
Day and Date: _____
Time: _____
Place: _____
[For a private disposition:]
We will sell [or lease or license, as applicable] the [describe collateral] privately sometime after [day and date].
You are entitled to an accounting of the unpaid indebtedness secured by the property that we intend to sell [or lease or license, as applicable] [for a charge of $ _____].
You may request an accounting by calling us at [telephone number] [End of Form]

§ 9-614. *Contents and Form of Notification Before Disposition of Collateral:*
Consumer-Goods Transaction
In a consumer-goods transaction, the following rules apply:
(1)   A notification of disposition must provide the following information:
(A)   the information specified in Section 9-613(1);
(B)   a description of any liability for a deficiency of the person to which the notification is sent;
(C)   a telephone number from which the amount that must be paid to the secured party to redeem the collateral under Section 9-623 is available; and
(D)   a telephone number or mailing address from which additional information concerning the disposition and the obligation secured is available.
(2)   A particular phrasing of the notification is not required.
(3)   The following form of notification, when completed, provides sufficient information:

[Name and address of secured party]
[Date]

NOTICE OF OUR PLAN TO SELL PROPERTY

[Name and address of any obligor who is also a debtor]
Subject: [Identification of Transaction]
We have your [describe collateral], because you broke promises in our agreement.
[For a public disposition:]
We will sell [describe collateral] at public sale. A sale could include a lease or license. The sale will be held as follows:

Date: _____
Time: _____
Place: _____

You may attend the sale and bring bidders if you want.
[For a private disposition:]
We will sell [describe collateral] at private sale sometime after [date]. A sale could include a lease or license.

The money that we get from the sale (after paying our costs) will reduce the amount you owe. If we get less money than you owe, you [will or will not, as applicable]] still owe us the difference. If we get more money than you owe, you will get the extra money, unless we must pay it to someone else.

You can get the property back at any time before we sell it by paying us the full amount you owe (not just the past due payments), including our expenses. To learn the exact amount you must pay, call us at [telephone number]].

If you want us to explain to you in writing how we have figured the amount that you owe us, you may call us at " [telephone number]] [or write us at [secured party's address]] and request a written explanation. [We will charge you $ _____ for the explanation if we sent you another written explanation of the amount you owe us within the last six months.]

If you need more information about the sale call us at [telephone number]] [or write us at [secured party's address]].

We are sending this notice to the following other people who have an interest in [describe collateral] or who owe money under your agreement:

[Names of all other debtors and obligors, if any] [End of Form]

(4) A notification in the form of paragraph (3) is sufficient, even if additional information appears at the end of the form.

(5) A notification in the form of paragraph (3) is sufficient, even if it includes errors in information not required by paragraph (1), unless the error is misleading with respect to rights arising under this article.

(6) If a notification under this section is not in the form of paragraph (3), law other than this Article determines the effect of including information not required by paragraph (1).

§ 9-615. Application of Proceeds of Disposition; Liability for Deficiency and Right to Surplus

(a) [Application of proceeds.] A secured party shall apply or pay over for application the cash proceeds of disposition under Section 9-610 in the following order to:

(1) the reasonable expenses of retaking, holding, preparing for disposition, processing, and disposing, and, to the extent provided for by agreement and not prohibited by law, reasonable attorney's fees and legal expenses incurred by the secured party;

(2) the satisfaction of obligations secured by the security interest or agricultural lien under which the disposition is made;

(3) the satisfaction of obligations secured by any subordinate security interest in or other subordinate lien on the collateral if:

(A) the secured party receives from the holder of the subordinate security interest or other lien an authenticated demand for proceeds before distribution of the proceeds is completed; and

(B) in a case in which a consignor has an interest in the collateral, the subordinate security interest or other lien is senior to the interest of the consignor; and

(4) a secured party that is a consignor of the collateral if the secured party receives from the consignor an authenticated demand for proceeds before distribution of the proceeds is completed.

(b) [Proof of subordinate interest.] If requested by a secured party, a holder of a subordinate security interest or other lien shall furnish reasonable proof of the interest or lien within a reasonable time. Unless the holder does so, the secured party need not comply with the holder's demand under subsection (a)(3).

(c) [Application of noncash proceeds.] A secured party need not apply or pay over for application noncash proceeds of disposition under Section 9-610 unless the failure to do so would be commercially unreasonable. A secured party that applies or pays over for application noncash proceeds shall do so in a commercially reasonable manner.

(d) [Surplus or deficiency if obligation secured.] If the security interest under which a disposition is made secures payment or performance of an obligation, after making the payments and applications required by subsection (a) and permitted by subsection (c):

(1) unless subsection (a)(4) requires the secured party to apply or pay over cash proceeds to a consignor, the secured party shall account to and pay a debtor for any surplus; and

(2) the obligor is liable for any deficiency.

(e) [No surplus or deficiency in sales of certain rights to payment.] If the underlying transaction is a sale of accounts, chattel paper, payment intangibles, or promissory notes:

(1) the debtor is not entitled to any surplus; and

(2) the obligor is not liable for any deficiency.

(f) [Calculation of surplus or deficiency in disposition to person related to secured party.] The surplus or deficiency following a disposition is calculated based on the amount of proceeds that would have been realized in a disposition complying with this part to a transferee other than the secured party, a person related to the secured party, or a secondary obligor if:

(1) the transferee in the disposition is the secured party, a person related to the secured party, or a secondary obligor; and

(2) the amount of proceeds of the disposition is significantly below the range of proceeds that a complying disposition to a person other than the secured party, a person related to the secured party, or a secondary obligor would have brought.

(g) [Cash proceeds received by junior secured party.] A secured party that receives cash proceeds of a disposition in good faith and without knowledge that the receipt violates the rights of the holder of a security interest or other lien that is not subordinate to the security interest or agricultural lien under which the disposition is made:

(1) takes the cash proceeds free of the security interest or other lien;

(2) is not obligated to apply the proceeds of the disposition to the satisfaction of obligations secured by the security interest or other lien; and

(3) is not obligated to account to or pay the holder of the security interest or other lien for any surplus.

§ 9-616. Explanation of Calculation of Surplus or Deficiency

(a) [Definitions.] In this section:

(1) "Explanation" means a writing that:

(A) states the amount of the surplus or deficiency;

(B) provides an explanation in accordance with subsection (c) of how the secured party calculated the surplus or deficiency;

(C) states, if applicable, that future debits, credits, charges, including additional credit service charges or interest, rebates, and expenses may affect the amount of the surplus or deficiency; and

(D) provides a telephone number or mailing address from which additional information concerning the transaction is available.

(2)   "Request" means a record:
    (A)   authenticated by a debtor or consumer obligor;
    (B)   requesting that the recipient provide an explanation; and
    (C)   sent after disposition of the collateral under Section 9-610.
(b)   [Explanation of calculation.] In a consumer-goods transaction in which the debtor is entitled to a surplus or a consumer obligor is liable for a deficiency under Section 9-615, the secured
party shall:
(1)   send an explanation to the debtor or consumer obligor, as applicable, after the disposition
    and:
    (A)   before or when the secured party accounts to the debtor and pays any surplus or first
        makes written demand on the consumer obligor after the disposition for payment of
        the deficiency; and
    (B)   within 14 days after receipt of a request; or
(2)   in the case of a consumer obligor who is liable for a deficiency, within 14 days after receipt
    of a request, send to the consumer obligor a record waiving the secured party's right to a
    deficiency.
(c)   [Required information.] To comply with subsection (a)(1)(B), a writing must provide the following information in the following order:
(1)   the aggregate amount of obligations secured by the security interest under which the dis-
    position was made, and, if the amount reflects a rebate of unearned interest or credit ser-
    vice charge, an indication of that fact, calculated as of a specified date:
    (A)   if the secured party takes or receives possession of the collateral after default, not
        more than 35 days before the secured party takes or receives possession; or
    (B)   if the secured party takes or receives possession of the collateral before default or does
        not take possession of the collateral, not more than 35 days before the disposition;
(2)   the amount of proceeds of the disposition;
(3)   the aggregate amount of the obligations after deducting the amount of proceeds;
(4)   the amount, in the aggregate or by type, and types of expenses, including expenses of re-
    taking, holding, preparing for disposition, processing, and disposing of the collateral, and
    attorney's fees secured by the collateral which are known to the secured party and relate to
    the current disposition;
(5)   the amount, in the aggregate or by type, and types of credits, including rebates of interest
    or credit service charges, to which the obligor is known to be entitled and which are not
    reflected in the amount in paragraph (1); and
(6)   the amount of the surplus or deficiency.
(d)   [Substantial compliance.] A particular phrasing of the explanation is not required. An explanation complying substantially with the requirements of subsection (a) is sufficient, even if it includes minor errors that are not seriously misleading.
(e)   [Charges for responses.] A debtor or consumer obligor is entitled without charge to one
response to a request under this section during any six-month period in which the secured party did not send to the debtor or consumer obligor an explanation pursuant to subsection (b)(1).
The secured party may require payment of a charge not exceeding $25 for each additional
response.

§ 9-617. Rights of Transferee of Collateral

(a)   [Effects of disposition.] A secured party's disposition of collateral after default:
(1)   transfers to a transferee for value all of the debtor's rights in the collateral;
(2)   discharges the security interest under which the disposition is made; and
(3)   discharges any subordinate security interest or other subordinate lien [other than liens
    created under [cite acts or statutes providing for liens, if any, that are not to be discharged]].
(b)   [Rights of good-faith transferee.] A transferee that acts in good faith takes free of the rights
and interests described in subsection (a), even if the secured party fails to comply with this
Article or the requirements of any judicial proceeding.

(c) [Rights of other transferee.] If a transferee does not take free of the rights and interests described in subsection (a), the transferee takes the collateral subject to:
(1) the debtor's rights in the collateral;
(2) the security interest or agricultural lien under which the disposition is made; and
(3) any other security interest or other lien.

§ 9-618. Rights and Duties of Certain Secondary Obligors

(a) [Rights and duties of secondary obligor.] A secondary obligor acquires the rights and becomes obligated to perform the duties of the secured party after the secondary obligor:
(1) receives an assignment of a secured obligation from the secured party;
(2) receives a transfer of collateral from the secured party and agrees to accept the rights and assume the duties of the secured party; or
(3) is subrogated to the rights of a secured party with respect to collateral.
(b) [Effect of assignment, transfer, or subrogation.] An assignment, transfer, or subrogation described in subsection (a):
(1) is not a disposition of collateral under Section 9-610; and
(2) relieves the secured party of further duties under this article.

§ 9-619. Transfer of Record or Legal Title

(a) ["Transfer statement."] In this section, "transfer statement" means a record authenticated by a secured party stating:
(1) that the debtor has defaulted in connection with an obligation secured by specified collateral;
(2) that the secured party has exercised its post-default remedies with respect to the collateral;
(3) that, by reason of the exercise, a transferee has acquired the rights of the debtor in the collateral; and
(4) the name and mailing address of the secured party, debtor, and transferee.
(b) [Effect of transfer statement.] A transfer statement entitles the transferee to the transfer of record of all rights of the debtor in the collateral specified in the statement in any official filing, recording, registration, or certificate-of-title system covering the collateral. If a transfer statement is presented with the applicable fee and request form to the official or office responsible for maintaining the system, the official or office shall:
(1) accept the transfer statement;
(2) promptly amend its records to reflect the transfer; and
(3) if applicable, issue a new appropriate certificate of title in the name of the transferee.
(c) [Transfer not a disposition; no relief of secured party's duties.] A transfer of the record or legal title to collateral to a secured party under subsection (b) or otherwise is not of itself a disposition of collateral under this Article and does not of itself relieve the secured party of its duties under this article.

§ 9-620. Acceptance of Collateral in Full or Partial Satisfaction of Obligation; Compulsory Disposition of Collateral

(a) [Conditions to acceptance in satisfaction.] Except as otherwise provided in subsection (g), a secured party may accept collateral in full or partial satisfaction of the obligation it secures only if:
(1) the debtor consents to the acceptance under subsection (c);
(2) the secured party does not receive, within the time set forth in subsection (d), a notification of objection to the proposal authenticated by:
    (A) a person to which the secured party was required to send a proposal under Section 9-621; or
    (B) any other person, other than the debtor, holding an interest in the collateral subordinate to the security interest that is the subject of the proposal;
(3) if the collateral is consumer goods, the collateral is not in the possession of the debtor when the debtor consents to the acceptance; and

(4)   subsection (e) does not require the secured party to dispose of the collateral or the debtor waives the requirement pursuant to Section 9-624.

(b)   [Purported acceptance ineffective.] A purported or apparent acceptance of collateral under this section is ineffective unless:

(1)   the secured party consents to the acceptance in an authenticated record or sends a pro-posal to the debtor; and

(2)   the conditions of subsection (a) are met.

(c)   [Debtor's consent.] For purposes of this section:

(1)   a debtor consents to an acceptance of collateral in partial satisfaction of the obligation it secures only if the debtor agrees to the terms of the acceptance in a record authenticated after default; and

(2)   a debtor consents to an acceptance of collateral in full satisfaction of the obligation it se-cures only if the debtor agrees to the terms of the acceptance in a record authenticated after default or the secured party:

    (A)   sends to the debtor after default a proposal that is unconditional or subject only to a condition that collateral not in the possession of the secured party be preserved or maintained;

    (B)   in the proposal, proposes to accept collateral in full satisfaction of the obligation it se-cures; and

    (C)   does not receive a notification of objection authenticated by the debtor within 20 days after the proposal is sent.

(d)   [Effectiveness of notification.] To be effective under subsection (a)(2), a notification of objection must be received by the secured party:

(1)   in the case of a person to which the proposal was sent pursuant to Section 9-621, within 20 days after notification was sent to that person; and

(2)   in other cases:

    (A)   within 20 days after the last notification was sent pursuant to Section 9-621; or

    (B)   if a notification was not sent, before the debtor consents to the acceptance under sub-section (c).

(e)   [Mandatory disposition of consumer goods.] A secured party that has taken possession of collateral shall dispose of the collateral pursuant to Section 9-610 within the time specified in subsection (f) if:

(1)   60 percent of the cash price has been paid in the case of a purchase-money security inte-rest in consumer goods; or

(2)   60 percent of the principal amount of the obligation secured has been paid in the case of a non-purchase-money security interest in consumer goods.

(f)   [Compliance with mandatory disposition requirement.] To comply with subsection (e), the secured party shall dispose of the collateral:

(1)   within 90 days after taking possession; or

(2)   within any longer period to which the debtor and all secondary obligors have agreed in an agreement to that effect entered into and authenticated after default.

(g)   [No partial satisfaction in consumer transaction.] In a consumer transaction, a secured party may not accept collateral in partial satisfaction of the obligation it secures.

§ 9-621. Notification of Proposal to Accept Collateral

(a)   [Persons to which proposal to be sent.] A secured party that desires to accept collateral in full or partial satisfaction of the obligation it secures shall send its proposal to:

(1)   any person from which the secured party has received, before the debtor consented to the acceptance, an authenticated notification of a claim of an interest in the collateral;

(2)   any other secured party or lienholder that, 10 days before the debtor consented to the acceptance, held a security interest in or other lien on the collateral perfected by the filing of a financing statement that:

    (A)   identified the collateral;

    (B)   was indexed under the debtor's name as of that date; and
    (C)   was filed in the office or offices in which to file a financing statement against the deb-
         tor covering the collateral as of that date; and
(3)   any other secured party that, 10 days before the debtor consented to the acceptance, held
     a security interest in the collateral perfected by compliance with a statute, regulation, or
     treaty described in Section 9-311(a).
(b)   [Proposal to be sent to secondary obligor in partial satisfaction.] A secured party that desires to accept collateral in partial satisfaction of the obligation it secures shall send its proposal to
any secondary obligor in addition to the persons described in subsection (a).

§ 9-622. Effect of Acceptance of Collateral
(a)   [Effect of acceptance.] A secured party's acceptance of collateral in full or partial
satisfaction of the obligation it secures:
(1)   discharges the obligation to the extent consented to by the debtor;
(2)   transfers to the secured party all of a debtor's rights in the collateral;
(3)   discharges the security interest or agricultural lien that is the subject of the debtor's
     consent and any subordinate security interest or other subordinate lien; and
(4)   terminates any other subordinate interest.
(b)   [Discharge of subordinate interest notwithstanding noncompliance.] A subordinate interest is discharged or terminated under subsection (a), even if the secured party fails to comply
with this article.

§ 9-623. Right to Redeem Collateral
(a)   [Persons that may redeem.] A debtor, any secondary obligor, or any other secured party or
lienholder may redeem collateral.
(b)   [Requirements for redemption.] To redeem collateral, a person shall tender:
(1)   fulfillment of all obligations secured by the collateral; and
(2)   the reasonable expenses and attorney's fees described in Section 9-615(a)(1).
(c)   [When redemption may occur.] A redemption may occur at any time before a secured
party:
(1)   has collected collateral under Section 9-607;
(2)   has disposed of collateral or entered into a contract for its disposition under Section 9-610; or
(3)   has accepted collateral in full or partial satisfaction of the obligation it secures under Sec-
     tion 9-622.

§ 9-624. Waiver
(a)   [Waiver of disposition notification.] A debtor or secondary obligor may waive the right to
notification of disposition of collateral under Section 9-611 only by an agreement to that effect
entered into and authenticated after default.
(b)   [Waiver of mandatory disposition.] A debtor may waive the right to require disposition of
collateral under Section 9-620(e) only by an agreement to that effect entered into and authenticated after default.
(c)   [Waiver of redemption right.] Except in a consumer-goods transaction, a debtor or secondary obligor may waive the right to redeem collateral under Section 9-623 only by an agreement to that effect entered into and authenticated after default.

Subpart 2. Non-Compliance with Article
§ 9-625. Remedies for Secured Party's Failure to Comply with Article
(a)   [Judicial orders concerning non-compliance.] If it is established that a secured party is not
proceeding in accordance with this article, a court may order or restrain collection, enforcement,
or disposition of collateral on appropriate terms and conditions.
(b)   [Damages for non-compliance.] Subject to subsections (c), (d), and (f), a person is liable for
damages in the amount of any loss caused by a failure to comply with this article. Loss caused
by a failure to comply may include loss resulting from the debtor's inability to obtain, or increased costs of, alternative financing.

(c) [Persons entitled to recover damages; statutory damages in consumer-goods transaction.] Except as otherwise provided in Section 9-628:

(1) a person that, at the time of the failure, was a debtor, was an obligor, or held a security interest in or other lien on the collateral may recover damages under subsection (b) for its loss; and

(2) if the collateral is consumer goods, a person that was a debtor or a secondary obligor at the time a secured party failed to comply with this part may recover for that failure in any event an amount not less than the credit service charge plus 10 percent of the principal amount of the obligation or the time-price differential plus 10 percent of the cash price.

(d) [Recovery when deficiency eliminated or reduced.] A debtor whose deficiency is eliminated under Section 9-626 may recover damages for the loss of any surplus. However, a debtor or secondary obligor whose deficiency is eliminated or reduced under Section 9-626 may not otherwise recover under subsection (b) for noncompliance with the provisions of this part relating to collection, enforcement, disposition, or acceptance.

(e) [Statutory damages: non-compliance with specified provisions.] In addition to any damages recoverable under subsection (b), the debtor, consumer obligor, or person named as a debtor in a filed record, as applicable, may recover $500 in each case from a person that:

(1) fails to comply with Section 9-208;

(2) fails to comply with Section 9-209;

(3) files a record that the person is not entitled to file under Section 9-509(a);

(4) fails to cause the secured party of record to file or send a termination statement as required by Section 9-513(a) or (c);

(5) fails to comply with Section 9-616(b)(1) and whose failure is part of a pattern, or consistent with a practice, of noncompliance; or

(6) fails to comply with Section 9-616(b)(2).

(f) [Statutory damages: non-compliance with Section 9-210.] A debtor or consumer obligor may recover damages under subsection (b) and, in addition, $500 in each case from a person that, without reasonable cause, fails to comply with a request under Section 9-210. A recipient of a request under Section 9-210 which never claimed an interest in the collateral or obligations that are the subject of a request under that section has a reasonable excuse for failure to comply with the request within the meaning of this subsection.

(g) [Limitation of security interest: non-compliance with Section 9-210.] If a secured party fails to comply with a request regarding a list of collateral or a statement of account under Section 9-210, the secured party may claim a security interest only as shown in the list or statement included in the request as against a person that is reasonably misled by the failure.

§ 9-626. Action in Which Deficiency or Surplus Is in Issue

(a) [Applicable rules if amount of deficiency or surplus in issue.] In an action arising from a transaction, other than a consumer transaction, in which the amount of a deficiency or surplus is in issue, the following rules apply:

(1) A secured party need not prove compliance with the provisions of this part relating to collection, enforcement, disposition, or acceptance unless the debtor or a secondary obligor places the secured party's compliance in issue.

(2) If the secured party's compliance is placed in issue, the secured party has the burden of establishing that the collection, enforcement, disposition, or acceptance was conducted in accordance with this part.

(3) Except as otherwise provided in Section 9-628, if a secured party fails to prove that the collection, enforcement, disposition, or acceptance was conducted in accordance with the provisions of this part relating to collection, enforcement, disposition, or acceptance, the liability of a debtor or a secondary obligor for a deficiency is limited to an amount by which the sum of the secured obligation, expenses, and attorney's fees exceeds the greater of:

(A) the proceeds of the collection, enforcement, disposition, or acceptance; or

     (B) the amount of proceeds that would have been realized had the noncomplying secured party proceeded in accordance with the provisions of this part relating to collection, enforcement, disposition, or acceptance.

(4) For purposes of paragraph (3)(B), the amount of proceeds that would have been realized is equal to the sum of the secured obligation, expenses, and attorney's fees unless the secured party proves that the amount is less than that sum.

(5) If a deficiency or surplus is calculated under Section 9-615(f), the debtor or obligor has the burden of establishing that the amount of proceeds of the disposition is significantly below the range of prices that a complying disposition to a person other than the secured party, a person related to the secured party, or a secondary obligor would have brought.

(b) [Non-consumer transactions; no inference.] The limitation of the rules in subsection (a) to transactions other than consumer transactions is intended to leave to the court the determination of the proper rules in consumer transactions. The court may not infer from that limitation the nature of the proper rule in consumer transactions and may continue to apply established approaches.

§ 9-627. Determination of Whether Conduct Was Commercially Reasonable

(a) [Greater amount obtainable under other circumstances; no preclusion of commercial reasonableness.] The fact that a greater amount could have been obtained by a collection, enforcement, disposition, or acceptance at a different time or in a different method from that selected by the secured party is not of itself sufficient to preclude the secured party from establishing that the collection, enforcement, disposition, or acceptance was made in a commercially reasonable manner.

(b) [Dispositions that are commercially reasonable.] A disposition of collateral is made in a commercially reasonable manner if the disposition is made:

(1) in the usual manner on any recognized market;

(2) at the price current in any recognized market at the time of the disposition; or

(3) otherwise in conformity with reasonable commercial practices among dealers in the type of property that was the subject of the disposition.

(c) [Approval by court or on behalf of creditors.] A collection, enforcement, disposition, or acceptance is commercially reasonable if it has been approved:

(1) in a judicial proceeding;

(2) by a bona fide creditors' committee;

(3) by a representative of creditors; or

(4) by an assignee for the benefit of creditors.

(d) [Approval under subsection (c) not necessary; absence of approval has no effect.] Approval under subsection (c) need not be obtained, and lack of approval does not mean that the collection, enforcement, disposition, or acceptance is not commercially reasonable.

§ 9-628. Non-Liability and Limitation on Liability of Secured Party; Liability of Secondary Obligor

(a) [Limitation of liability of secured party for non-compliance with article.] Unless a secured party knows that a person is a debtor or obligor, knows the identity of the person, and knows how to communicate with the person:

(1) the secured party is not liable to the person, or to a secured party or lienholder that has filed a financing statement against the person, for failure to comply with this article; and

(2) the secured party's failure to comply with this Article does not affect the liability of the person for a deficiency.

(b) [Limitation of liability based on status as secured party.] A secured party is not liable because of its status as secured party:

(1) to a person that is a debtor or obligor, unless the secured party knows:

     (A) that the person is a debtor or obligor;

     (B) the identity of the person; and

     (C) how to communicate with the person; or

(2) to a secured party or lienholder that has filed a financing statement against a person, unless the secured party knows:
    (A) that the person is a debtor; and
    (B) the identity of the person.
(c) [Limitation of liability if reasonable belief that transaction not a consumer-goods transaction or consumer transaction.] A secured party is not liable to any person, and a person's liability for a deficiency is not affected, because of any act or omission arising out of the secured party's reasonable belief that a transaction is not a consumer-goods transaction or a consumer transaction or that goods are not consumer goods, if the secured party's belief is based on its reasonable reliance on:
(1) a debtor's representation concerning the purpose for which collateral was to be used, acquired, or held; or
(2) an obligor's representation concerning the purpose for which a secured obligation was incurred.
(d) [Limitation of liability for statutory damages.] A secured party is not liable to any person under Section 9-625(c)(2) for its failure to comply with Section 9-616.
(e) [Limitation of multiple liability for statutory damages.] A secured party is not liable under Section 9-625(c)(2) more than once with respect to any one secured obligation.

Part 7. Transition
§ 9-701. Effective Date
This [Act] takes effect on July 1, 2001. [...]

2004 UNIDROIT PRINCIPLES OF INTERNATIONAL COMMERCIAL CONTRACTS[1]

Preamble (Purpose of the Principles)
These Principles set forth general rules for international commercial contracts.
They shall be applied when the parties have agreed that their contract be governed by them.[2]
They may be applied when the parties have agreed that their contract be governed by general principles of law, the *lex mercatoria* or the like.
They may be applied when the parties have not chosen any law to govern their contract.
They may be used to interpret or supplement international uniform law instruments.
They may be used to interpret or supplement domestic law.
They may serve as a model for national and international legislators.

CHAPTER 1 — GENERAL PROVISIONS
Article 1.1 (Freedom of Contract)
The parties are free to enter into a contract and to determine its content.

Article 1.2 (No Form Required)
Nothing in these Principles requires a contract, statement or any other act to be made in or evidenced by a particular form. It may be proved by any means, including witnesses.

---

1   © International Institute for the Unification of Private Law.
2   Parties wishing to provide that their agreement be governed by the Principles might use the following words, adding any desired exceptions or modifications:
    "This contract shall be governed by the UNIDROIT Principles (2004) [except as to Articles …]".
    Parties wishing to provide in addition for the application of the law of a particular jurisdiction might use the following words:
    "This contract shall be governed by the UNIDROIT Principles (2004) [except as to Articles…], supplemented when necessary by the law of [jurisdiction X].

Article 1.3 (Binding Character of Contract)

A contract validly entered into is binding upon the parties. It can only be modified or terminated in accordance with its terms or by agreement or as otherwise provided in these Principles.

Article 1.4 (Mandatory Rules)

Nothing in these Principles shall restrict the application of mandatory rules, whether of national, international or supranational origin, which are applicable in accordance with the relevant rules of private international law.

Article 1.5 (Exclusion or Modification by the Parties)

The parties may exclude the application of these Principles or derogate from or vary the effect of any of their provisions, except as otherwise provided in the Principles.

Article 1.6 (Interpretation and Supplementation of the Principles)

(1)   In the interpretation of these Principles, regard is to be had to their international character and to their purposes including the need to promote uniformity in their application.
(2)   Issues within the scope of these Principles but not expressly settled by them are as far as possible to be settled in accordance with their underlying general principles.

Article 1.7 (Good Faith and Fair Dealing)

(1)   Each party must act in accordance with good faith and fair dealing in international trade.
(2)   The parties may not exclude or limit this duty.

Article 1.8 (Inconsistent Behaviour)

A party cannot act inconsistently with an understanding it has caused the other party to have and upon which that other party reasonably has acted in reliance to its detriment.

Article 1.9 (Usages and Practices)

(1)   The parties are bound by any usage to which they have agreed and by any practices which they have established between themselves.
(2)   The parties are bound by a usage that is widely known to and regularly observed in international trade by parties in the particular trade concerned except where the application of such a usage would be unreasonable.

Article 1.10 (Notice)

(1)   Where notice is required it may be given by any means appropriate to the circumstances.
(2)   A notice is effective when it reaches the person to whom it is given.
(3)   For the purpose of paragraph (2) a notice "reaches" a person when given to that person orally or delivered at that person's place of business or mailing address.
(4)   For the purpose of this Article "notice" includes a declaration, demand, request or any other communication of intention.

Article 1.11 (Definitions)

In these Principles
−   "court" includes an arbitral tribunal;
−   where a party has more than one place of business the relevant "place of business" is that which has the closest relationship to the contract and its performance, having regard to the circumstances known to or contemplated by the parties at any time before or at the conclusion of the contract;
−   "obligor" refers to the party who is to perform an obligation and "obligee" refers to the party who is entitled to performance of that obligation;
−   "writing" means any mode of communication that preserves a record of the information contained therein and is capable of being reproduced in tangible form.

Article 1.12 (Computation of Time Set by Parties)

(1)   Official holidays or non-business days occurring during a period set by parties for an act to be performed are included in calculating the period.

(2)   However, if the last day of the period is an official holiday or a non-business day at the place of business of the party to perform the act, the period is extended until the first business day which follows, unless the circumstances indicate otherwise.
(3)   The relevant time zone is that of the place of business of the party setting the time, unless the circumstances indicate otherwise.

CHAPTER 2 — FORMATION AND AUTHORITY OF AGENTS
Section 1: Formation
Article 2.1.1 (Manner of Formation)
A contract may be concluded either by the acceptance of an offer or by conduct of the parties that is sufficient to show agreement.

Article 2.1.2 (Definition of Offer)
A proposal for concluding a contract constitutes an offer if it is sufficiently definite and indicates the intention of the offeror to be bound in case of acceptance.

Article 2.1.3 (Withdrawal of Offer)
(1)   An offer becomes effective when it reaches the offeree.
(2)   An offer, even if it is irrevocable, may be withdrawn if the withdrawal reaches the offeree before or at the same time as the offer.

Article 2.1.4 (Revocation of Offer)
(1)   Until a contract is concluded an offer may be revoked if the revocation reaches the offeree before it has dispatched an acceptance.
(2)   However, an offer cannot be revoked
(a)   if it indicates, whether by stating a fixed time for acceptance or otherwise, that it is irrevoc-able; or
(b)   if it was reasonable for the offeree to rely on the offer as being irrevocable and the offeree has acted in reliance on the offer.

Article 2.1.5 (Rejection of Offer)
An offer is terminated when a rejection reaches the offeror.

Article 2.1.6 (Mode of Acceptance)
(1)   A statement made by or other conduct of the offeree indicating assent to an offer is an acceptance. Silence or inactivity does not in itself amount to acceptance.
(2)   An acceptance of an offer becomes effective when the indication of assent reaches the offeror.
(3)   However, if by virtue of the offer or as a result of practices which the parties have established between themselves or of usage, the offeree may indicate assent by performing an act without notice to the offeror, the acceptance is effective when the act is performed.

Article 2.1.7 (Time of Acceptance)
An offer must be accepted within the time the offeror has fixed or, if no time is fixed, within a reasonable time having regard to the circumstances, including the rapidity of the means of communication employed by the offeror. An oral offer must be accepted immediately unless the circumstances indicate otherwise.

Article 2.1.8 (Acceptance Within a Fixed Period of Time)
A period of acceptance fixed by the offeror begins to run from the time that the offer is dispatched. A time indicated in the offer is deemed to be the time of dispatch unless the circumstances indicate otherwise.

Article 2.1.9 (Late Acceptance. Delay in Transmission)
(1)   A late acceptance is nevertheless effective as an acceptance if without undue delay the offeror so informs the offeree or gives notice to that effect.

(2)   If a communication containing a late acceptance shows that it has been sent in such circumstances that if its transmission had been normal it would have reached the offeror in due
time, the late acceptance is effective as an acceptance unless, without undue delay, the offeror
informs the offeree that it considers the offer as having lapsed.

Article 2.1.10 (Withdrawal of Acceptance)
An acceptance may be withdrawn if the withdrawal reaches the offeror before or at the same
time as the acceptance would have become effective.

Article 2.1.11 (Modified Acceptance)
(1)   A reply to an offer which purports to be an acceptance but contains additions, limitations
or other modifications is a rejection of the offer and constitutes a counter-offer.
(2)   However, a reply to an offer which purports to be an acceptance but contains additional or
different terms which do not materially alter the terms of the offer constitutes an acceptance,
unless the offeror, without undue delay, objects to the discrepancy. If the offeror does not object, the terms of the contract are the terms of the offer with the modifications contained in the
acceptance.

Article 2.1.12 (Writings in Confirmation)
If a writing which is sent within a reasonable time after the conclusion of the contract and which
purports to be a confirmation of the contract contains additional or different terms, such terms
become part of the contract, unless they materially alter the contract or the recipient, without
undue delay, objects to the discrepancy.

Article 2.1.13 (Conclusion of Contract Dependent on Agreement on Specific Matters
or in a Particular Form)
Where in the course of negotiations one of the parties insists that the contract is not concluded
until there is agreement on specific matters or in a particular form, no contract is concluded
before agreement is reached on those matters or in that form.

Article 2.1.14 (Contract with Terms Deliberately Left Open)
(1)   If the parties intend to conclude a contract, the fact that they intentionally leave a term to
be agreed upon in further negotiations or to be determined by a third person does not prevent
a contract from coming into existence.
(2)   The existence of the contract is not affected by the fact that subsequently
(a)   the parties reach no agreement on the term; or
(b)   the third person does not determine the term,
provided that there is an alternative means of rendering the term definite that is reasonable in
the circumstances, having regard to the intention of the parties.

Article 2.1.15 (Negotiations in Bad Faith)
(1)   A party is free to negotiate and is not liable for failure to reach an agreement.
(2)   However, a party who negotiates or breaks off negotiations in bad faith is liable for the
losses caused to the other party.
(3)   It is bad faith, in particular, for a party to enter into or continue negotiations when intending not to reach an agreement with the other party.

Article 2.1.16 (Duty of Confidentiality)
Where information is given as confidential by one party in the course of negotiations, the other
party is under a duty not to disclose that information or to use it improperly for its own purposes, whether or not a contract is subsequently concluded. Where appropriate, the remedy for
breach of that duty may include compensation based on the benefit received by the other
party.

Article 2.1.17 (Merger Clauses)
A contract in writing which contains a clause indicating that the writing completely embodies
the terms on which the parties have agreed cannot be contradicted or supplemented by evi-

dence of prior statements or agreements. However, such statements or agreements may be used to interpret the writing.

Article 2.1.18 (Modification in a Particular Form)
A contract in writing which contains a clause requiring any modification or termination by agreement to be in a particular form may not be otherwise modified or terminated. However, a party may be precluded by its conduct from asserting such a clause to the extent that the other party has reasonably acted in reliance on that conduct.

Article 2.1.19 (Contracting under Standard Terms)
(1)   Where one party or both parties use standard terms in concluding a contract, the general rules on formation apply, subject to Articles 2.1.20 - 2.1.22.
(2)   Standard terms are provisions which are prepared in advance for general and repeated use by one party and which are actually used without negotiation with the other party.

Article 2.1.20 (Surprising Terms)
(1)   No term contained in standard terms which is of such a character that the other party could not reasonably have expected it, is effective unless it has been expressly accepted by that party.
(2)   In determining whether a term is of such a character regard shall be had to its content, language and presentation.

Article 2.1.21 (Conflict Between Standard Terms and Non-standard Terms)
In case of conflict between a standard term and a term which is not a standard term the latter prevails.

Article 2.1.22 (Battle of Forms)
Where both parties use standard terms and reach agreement except on those terms, a contract is concluded on the basis of the agreed terms and of any standard terms which are common in substance unless one party clearly indicates in advance, or later and without undue delay informs the other party, that it does not intend to be bound by such a contract.

Section 2: Authority of Agents
Article 2.2.1 (Scope of the Section)
(1)   This Section governs the authority of a person ("the agent"), to affect the legal relations of another person ("the principal"), by or with respect to a contract with a third party, whether the agent acts in its own name or in that of the principal.
(2)   It governs only the relations between the principal or the agent on the one hand, and the third party on the other.
(3)   It does not govern an agent's authority conferred by law or the authority of an agent appointed by a public or judicial authority.

Article 2.2.2 (Establishment and Scope of the Authority of the Agent)
(1)   The principal's grant of authority to an agent may be express or implied.
(2)   The agent has authority to perform all acts necessary in the circumstances to achieve the purposes for which the authority was granted.

Article 2.2.3 (Agency Disclosed)
(1)   Where an agent acts within the scope of its authority and the third party knew or ought to have known that the agent was acting as an agent, the acts of the agent shall directly affect the legal relations between the principal and the third party and no legal relation is created between the agent and the third party.
(2)   However, the acts of the agent shall affect only the relations between the agent and the third party, where the agent with the consent of the principal undertakes to become the party to the contract.

Article 2.2.4 (Agency Undisclosed)

(1)   Where an agent acts within the scope of its authority and the third party neither knew nor ought to have known that the agent was acting as an agent, the acts of the agent shall affect only the relations between the agent and the third party.

(2)   However, where such an agent, when contracting with the third party on behalf of a business, represents itself to be the owner of that business, the third party, upon discovery of the real owner of the business, may exercise also against the latter the rights it has against the agent.

Article 2.2.5 (Agent Acting Without or Exceeding its Authority)

(1)   Where an agent acts without authority or exceeds its authority, its acts do not affect the legal relations between the principal and the third party.

(2)   However, where the principal causes the third party reasonably to believe that the agent has authority to act on behalf of the principal and that the agent is acting within the scope of that authority, the principal may not invoke against the third party the lack of authority of the agent.

Article 2.2.6 (Liability of Agent Acting Without or Exceeding its Authority)

(1)   An agent that acts without authority or exceeds its authority is, failing ratification by the principal, liable for damages that will place the third party in the same position as if the agent had acted with authority and not exceeded its authority.

(2)   However, the agent is not liable if the third party knew or ought to have known that the agent had no authority or was exceeding its authority.

Article 2.2.7 (Conflict of Interests)

(1)   If a contract concluded by an agent involves the agent in a conflict of interests with the principal of which the third party knew or ought to have known, the principal may avoid the contract. The right to avoid is subject to Articles 3.12 and 3.14 to 3.17.

(2)   However, the principal may not avoid the contract

(a)   if the principal had consented to, or knew or ought to have known of, the agent's involvement in the conflict of interests; or

(b)   if the agent had disclosed the conflict of interests to the principal and the latter had not objected within a reasonable time.

Article 2.2.8 (Sub-Agency)

An agent has implied authority to appoint a sub-agent to perform acts which it is not reasonable to expect the agent to perform itself. The rules of this Section apply to the sub-agency.

Article 2.2.9 (Ratification)

(1)   An act by an agent that acts without authority or exceeds its authority may be ratified by the principal. On ratification the act produces the same effects as if it had initially been carried out with authority.

(2)   The third party may by notice to the principal specify a reasonable period of time for ratification. If the principal does not ratify within that period of time it can no longer do so.

(3)   If, at the time of the agent's act, the third party neither knew nor ought to have known of the lack of authority, it may, at any time before ratification, by notice to the principal indicate its refusal to become bound by a ratification.

Article 2.2.10 (Termination of Authority)

(1)   Termination of authority is not effective in relation to the third party unless the third party knew or ought to have known of it.

(2)   Notwithstanding the termination of its authority, an agent remains authorised to perform the acts that are necessary to prevent harm to the principal's interests.

CHAPTER 3 — VALIDITY

Article 3.1 (Matters Not Covered)

These Principles do not deal with invalidity arising from

(a)   lack of capacity;

(b)   immorality or illegality.

Article 3.2 (Validity of Mere Agreement)

A contract is concluded, modified or terminated by the mere agreement of the parties, without any further requirement.

Article 3.3 (Initial Impossibility)

(1)   The mere fact that at the time of the conclusion of the contract the performance of the obligation assumed was impossible does not affect the validity of the contract.

(2)   The mere fact that at the time of the conclusion of the contract a party was not entitled to dispose of the assets to which the contract relates does not affect the validity of the contract.

Article 3.4 (Definition of Mistake)

Mistake is an erroneous assumption relating to facts or to law existing when the contract was concluded.

Article 3.5 (Relevant Mistake)

(1)   A party may only avoid the contract for mistake if, when the contract was concluded, the mistake was of such importance that a reasonable person in the same situation as the party in error would only have concluded the contract on materially different terms or would not have concluded it at all if the true state of affairs had been known, and

(a)   the other party made the same mistake, or caused the mistake, or knew or ought to have known of the mistake and it was contrary to reasonable commercial standards of fair dealing to leave the mistaken party in error; or

(b)   the other party had not at the time of avoidance reasonably acted in reliance on the contract.

(2)   However, a party may not avoid the contract if

(a)   it was grossly negligent in committing the mistake; or

(b)   the mistake relates to a matter in regard to which the risk of mistake was assumed or, having regard to the circumstances, should be borne by the mistaken party.

Article 3.6 (Error in Expression or Transmission)

An error occurring in the expression or transmission of a declaration is considered to be a mistake of the person from whom the declaration emanated.

Article 3.7 (Remedies for Non-performance)

A party is not entitled to avoid the contract on the ground of mistake if the circumstances on which that party relies afford, or could have afforded, a remedy for non-performance.

Article 3.8 (Fraud)

A party may avoid the contract when it has been led to conclude the contract by the other party's fraudulent representation, including language or practices, or fraudulent non-disclosure of circumstances which, according to reasonable commercial standards of fair dealing, the latter party should have disclosed.

Article 3.9 (Threat)

A party may avoid the contract when it has been led to conclude the contract by the other party's unjustified threat which, having regard to the circumstances, is so imminent and serious as to leave the first party no reasonable alternative. In particular, a threat is unjustified if the act or omission with which a party has been threatened is wrongful in itself, or it is wrongful to use it as a means to obtain the conclusion of the contract.

Article 3.10 (Gross Disparity)

(1)   A party may avoid the contract or an individual term of it if, at the time of the conclusion of the contract, the contract or term unjustifiably gave the other party an excessive advantage. Regard is to be had, among other factors, to

(a)   the fact that the other party has taken unfair advantage of the first party's dependence, economic distress or urgent needs, or of its improvidence, ignorance, inexperience or lack of bargaining skill, and

(b)   the nature and purpose of the contract.
(2)   Upon the request of the party entitled to avoidance, a court may adapt the contract or term in order to make it accord with reasonable commercial standards of fair dealing.
(3)   A court may also adapt the contract or term upon the request of the party receiving notice of avoidance, provided that that party informs the other party of its request promptly after receiving such notice and before the other party has reasonably acted in reliance on it. The provisions of Article 3.13(2) apply accordingly.

Article 3.11 (Third Persons)

(1)   Where fraud, threat, gross disparity or a party's mistake is imputable to, or is known or ought to be known by, a third person for whose acts the other party is responsible, the contract may be avoided under the same conditions as if the behaviour or knowledge had been that of the party itself.
(2)   Where fraud, threat or gross disparity is imputable to a third person for whose acts the other party is not responsible, the contract may be avoided if that party knew or ought to have known of the fraud, threat or disparity, or has not at the time of avoidance reasonably acted in reliance on the contract.

Article 3.12 (Confirmation)

If the party entitled to avoid the contract expressly or impliedly confirms the contract after the period of time for giving notice of avoidance has begun to run, avoidance of the contract is excluded.

Article 3.13 (Loss of Right to Avoid)

(1)   If a party is entitled to avoid the contract for mistake but the other party declares itself willing to perform or performs the contract as it was understood by the party entitled to avoidance, the contract is considered to have been concluded as the latter party understood it. The other party must make such a declaration or render such performance promptly after having been informed of the manner in which the party entitled to avoidance had understood the contract and before that party has reasonably acted in reliance on a notice of avoidance.
(2)   After such a declaration or performance the right to avoidance is lost and any earlier notice of avoidance is ineffective.

Article 3.14 (Notice of Avoidance)

The right of a party to avoid the contract is exercised by notice to the other party.

Article 3.15 (Time Limits)

(1)   Notice of avoidance shall be given within a reasonable time, having regard to the circumstances, after the avoiding party knew or could not have been unaware of the relevant facts or became capable of acting freely.
(2)   Where an individual term of the contract may be avoided by a party under Article 3.10, the period of time for giving notice of avoidance begins to run when that term is asserted by the other party.

Article 3.16 (Partial Avoidance)

Where a ground of avoidance affects only individual terms of the contract, the effect of avoidance is limited to those terms unless, having regard to the circumstances, it is unreasonable to uphold the remaining contract.

Article 3.17 (Retroactive Effect of Avoidance)

(1)   Avoidance takes effect retroactively.
(2)   On avoidance either party may claim restitution of whatever it has supplied under the contract or the part of it avoided, provided that it concurrently makes restitution of whatever it has received under the contract or the part of it avoided or, if it cannot make restitution in kind, it makes an allowance for what it has received.

Article 3.18 (Damages)
Irrespective of whether or not the contract has been avoided, the party who knew or ought to have known of the ground for avoidance is liable for damages so as to put the other party in the same position in which it would have been if it had not concluded the contract.

Article 3.19 (Mandatory Character of the Provisions)
The provisions of this Chapter are mandatory, except insofar as they relate to the binding force of mere agreement, initial impossibility or mistake.

Article 3.20 (Unilateral Declarations)
The provisions of this Chapter apply with appropriate adaptations to any communication of intention addressed by one party to the other.

CHAPTER 4 — INTERPRETATION
Article 4.1 (Intention of the Parties)
(1)   A contract shall be interpreted according to the common intention of the parties.
(2)   If such an intention cannot be established, the contract shall be interpreted according to the meaning that reasonable persons of the same kind as the parties would give to it in the same circumstances.

Article 4.2 (Interpretation of Statements and Other Conduct)
(1)   The statements and other conduct of a party shall be interpreted according to that party's intention if the other party knew or could not have been unaware of that intention.
(2)   If the preceding paragraph is not applicable, such statements and other conduct shall be interpreted according to the meaning that a reasonable person of the same kind as the other party would give to it in the same circumstances.

Article 4.3 (Relevant Circumstances)
In applying Articles 4.1 and 4.2, regard shall be had to all the circumstances, including
(a)   preliminary negotiations between the parties;
(b)   practices which the parties have established between themselves;
(c)   the conduct of the parties subsequent to the conclusion of the contract;
(d)   the nature and purpose of the contract;
(e)   the meaning commonly given to terms and expressions in the trade concerned;
(f)   usages.

Article 4.4 (Reference to Contract or Statement as a Whole)
Terms and expressions shall be interpreted in the light of the whole contract or statement in which they appear.

Article 4.5 (All Terms to Be Given Effect)
Contract terms shall be interpreted so as to give effect to all the terms rather than to deprive some of them of effect.

Article 4.6 (Contra Proferentem Rule)
If contract terms supplied by one party are unclear, an interpretation against that party is preferred.

Article 4.7 (Linguistic Discrepancies)
Where a contract is drawn up in two or more language versions which are equally authoritative there is, in case of discrepancy between the versions, a preference for the interpretation according to a version in which the contract was originally drawn up.

Article 4.8 (Supplying an Omitted Term)
(1)   Where the parties to a contract have not agreed with respect to a term which is important for a determination of their rights and duties, a term which is appropriate in the circumstances shall be supplied.
(2)   In determining what is an appropriate term regard shall be had, among other factors, to
(a)   the intention of the parties;
(b)   the nature and purpose of the contract;

(c)   good faith and fair dealing;
(d)   reasonableness.

CHAPTER 5 — CONTENT AND THIRD PARTY RIGHTS
Section 1: Content
Article 5.1.1 (Express and Implied Obligations)
The contractual obligations of the parties may be express or implied.

Article 5.1.2 (Implied Obligations)
Implied obligations stem from
(a)   the nature and purpose of the contract;
(b)   practices established between the parties and usages;
(c)   good faith and fair dealing;
(d)   reasonableness.

Article 5.1.3 (Co-operation Between the Parties)
Each party shall cooperate with the other party when such co-operation may reasonably be expected for the performance of that party's obligations.

Article 5.1.4 (Duty to Achieve a Specific Result. Duty of Best Efforts)
(1)   To the extent that an obligation of a party involves a duty to achieve a specific result, that party is bound to achieve that result.
(2)   To the extent that an obligation of a party involves a duty of best efforts in the performance of an activity, that party is bound to make such efforts as would be made by a reasonable person of the same kind in the same circumstances.

Article 5.1.5 (Determination of Kind of Duty Involved)
In determining the extent to which an obligation of a party involves a duty of best efforts in the performance of an activity or a duty to achieve a specific result, regard shall be had, among other factors, to
(a)   the way in which the obligation is expressed in the contract;
(b)   the contractual price and other terms of the contract;
(c)   the degree of risk normally involved in achieving the expected result;
(d)   the ability of the other party to influence the performance of the obligation.

Article 5.1.6 (Determination of Quality of Performance)
Where the quality of performance is neither fixed by, nor determinable from, the contract a party is bound to render a performance of a quality that is reasonable and not less than average in the circumstances.

Article 5.1.7 (Price Determination)
(1)   Where a contract does not fix or make provision for determining the price, the parties are considered, in the absence of any indication to the contrary, to have made reference to the price generally charged at the time of the conclusion of the contract for such performance in comparable circumstances in the trade concerned or, if no such price is available, to a reasonable price.
(2)   Where the price is to be determined by one party and that determination is manifestly unreasonable, a reasonable price shall be substituted notwithstanding any contract term to the contrary.
(3)   Where the price is to be fixed by a third person, and that person cannot or will not do so, the price shall be a reasonable price.
(4)   Where the price is to be fixed by reference to factors which do not exist or have ceased to exist or to be accessible, the nearest equivalent factor shall be treated as a substitute.

Article 5.1.8 (Contract for an Indefinite Period)
A contract for an indefinite period may be ended by either party by giving notice a reasonable time in advance.

Article 5.1.9 (Release by Agreement)

(1)   An obligee may release its right by agreement with the obligor.

(2)   An offer to release a right gratuitously shall be deemed accepted if the obligor does not reject the offer without delay after having become aware of it.

Section 2: Third Party Rights

Article 5.2.1 (Contracts in Favour of Third Parties)

(1)   The parties (the "promisor" and the "promisee") may confer by express or implied agreement a right on a third party (the "beneficiary").

(2)   The existence and content of the beneficiary's right against the promisor are determined by the agreement of the parties and are subject to any conditions or other limitations under the agreement.

Article 5.2.2 (Third Party Identifiable)

The beneficiary must be identifiable with adequate certainty by the contract but need not be in existence at the time the contract is made.

Article 5.2.3 (Exclusion and Limitation Clauses)

The conferment of rights in the beneficiary includes the right to invoke a clause in the contract which excludes or limits the liability of the beneficiary.

Article 5.2.4 (Defences)

The promisor may assert against the beneficiary all defences which the promisor could assert against the promisee.

Article 5.2.5 (Revocation)

The parties may modify or revoke the rights conferred by the contract on the beneficiary until the beneficiary has accepted them or reasonably acted in reliance on them.

Article 5.2.6 (Renunciation)

The beneficiary may renounce a right conferred on it.

CHAPTER 6 — PERFORMANCE
Section 1: Performance in General

Article 6.1.1 (Time of Performance)

A party must perform its obligations:

(a)   if a time is fixed by or determinable from the contract, at that time;

(b)   if a period of time is fixed by or determinable from the contract, at any time within that period unless circumstances indicate that the other party is to choose a time;

(c)   in any other case, within a reasonable time after the conclusion of the contract.

Article 6.1.2 (Performance at One Time or in Instalments)

In cases under Article 6.1.1(b) or (c), a party must perform its obligations at one time if that performance can be rendered at one time and the circumstances do not indicate otherwise.

Article 6.1.3 (Partial Performance)

(1)   The obligee may reject an offer to perform in part at the time performance is due, whether or not such offer is coupled with an assurance as to the balance of the performance, unless the obligee has no legitimate interest in so doing.

(2)   Additional expenses caused to the obligee by partial performance are to be borne by the obligor without prejudice to any other remedy.

Article 6.1.4 (Order of Performance)

(1)   To the extent that the performances of the parties can be rendered simultaneously, the parties are bound to render them simultaneously unless the circumstances indicate otherwise.

(2)   To the extent that the performance of only one party requires a period of time, that party is bound to render its performance first, unless the circumstances indicate otherwise.

Article 6.1.5 (Earlier Performance)
(1)   The obligee may reject an earlier performance unless it has no legitimate interest in so doing.
(2)   Acceptance by a party of an earlier performance does not affect the time for the performance of its own obligations if that time has been fixed irrespective of the performance of the other party's obligations.
(3)   Additional expenses caused to the obligee by earlier performance are to be borne by the obligor, without prejudice to any other remedy.

Article 6.1.6 (Place of Performance)
(1)   If the place of performance is neither fixed by, nor determinable from, the contract, a party is to perform:
(a)   a monetary obligation, at the obligee's place of business;
(b)   any other obligation, at its own place of business.
(2)   A party must bear any increase in the expenses incidental to performance which is caused by a change in its place of business subsequent to the conclusion of the contract.

Article 6.1.7 (Payment by Cheque or Other Instrument)
(1)   Payment may be made in any form used in the ordinary course of business at the place for payment.
(2)   However, an obligee who accepts, either by virtue of paragraph (1) or voluntarily, a cheque, any other order to pay or a promise to pay, is presumed to do so only on condition that it will be honoured.

Article 6.1.8 (Payment by Funds Transfer)
(1)   Unless the obligee has indicated a particular account, payment may be made by a transfer to any of the financial institutions in which the obligee has made it known that it has an account.
(2)   In case of payment by a transfer the obligation of the obligor is discharged when the transfer to the obligee's financial institution becomes effective.

Article 6.1.9 (Currency of Payment)
(1)   If a monetary obligation is expressed in a currency other than that of the place for payment, it may be paid by the obligor in the currency of the place for payment unless
(a)   that currency is not freely convertible; or
(b)   the parties have agreed that payment should be made only in the currency in which the monetary obligation is expressed.
(2)   If it is impossible for the obligor to make payment in the currency in which the monetary obligation is expressed, the obligee may require payment in the currency of the place for payment, even in the case referred to in paragraph (1)(b).
(3)   Payment in the currency of the place for payment is to be made according to the applicable rate of exchange prevailing there when payment is due.
(4)   However, if the obligor has not paid at the time when payment is due, the obligee may require payment according to the applicable rate of exchange prevailing either when payment is due or at the time of actual payment.

Article 6.1.10 (Currency Not Expressed)
Where a monetary obligation is not expressed in a particular currency, payment must be made in the currency of the place where payment is to be made.

Article 6.1.11 (Costs of Performance)
Each party shall bear the costs of performance of its obligations.

Article 6.1.12 (Imputation of Payments)
(1)   An obligor owing several monetary obligations to the same obligee may specify at the time of payment the debt to which it intends the payment to be applied. However, the payment discharges first any expenses, then interest due and finally the principal.

(2)   If the obligor makes no such specification, the obligee may, within a reasonable time after payment, declare to the obligor the obligation to which it imputes the payment, provided that the obligation is due and undisputed.

(3)   In the absence of imputation under paragraphs (1) or (2), payment is imputed to that obligation which satisfies one of the following criteria in the order indicated:

(a)   an obligation which is due or which is the first to fall due;

(b)   the obligation for which the obligee has least security;

(c)   the obligation which is the most burdensome for the obligor;

(d)   the obligation which has arisen first.

If none of the preceding criteria applies, payment is imputed to all the obligations proportionally.

Article 6.1.13 (Imputation of Non-Monetary Obligations)

Article 6.1.12 applies with appropriate adaptations to the imputation of performance of non-monetary obligations.

Article 6.1.14 (Application for Public Permission)

Where the law of a State requires a public permission affecting the validity of the contract or its performance and neither that law nor the circumstances indicate otherwise

(a)   if only one party has its place of business in that State, that party shall take the measures necessary to obtain the permission;

(b)   in any other case the party whose performance requires permission shall take the necessary measures.

Article 6.1.15 (Procedure in Applying for Permission)

(1)   The party required to take the measures necessary to obtain the permission shall do so without undue delay and shall bear any expenses incurred.

(2)   That party shall whenever appropriate give the other party notice of the grant or refusal of such permission without undue delay.

Article 6.1.16 (Permission Neither Granted Nor Refused)

(1)   If, notwithstanding the fact that the party responsible has taken all measures required, permission is neither granted nor refused within an agreed period or, where no period has been agreed, within a reasonable time from the conclusion of the contract, either party is entitled to terminate the contract.

(2)   Where the permission affects some terms only, paragraph (1) does not apply if, having regard to the circumstances, it is reasonable to uphold the remaining contract even if the permission is refused.

Article 6.1.17 (Permission Refused)

(1)   The refusal of a permission affecting the validity of the contract renders the contract void. If the refusal affects the validity of some terms only, only such terms are void if, having regard to the circumstances, it is reasonable to uphold the remaining contract.

(2)   Where the refusal of a permission renders the performance of the contract impossible in whole or in part, the rules on non-performance apply.

Section 2: Hardship

Article 6.2.1 (Contract to Be Observed)

Where the performance of a contract becomes more onerous for one of the parties, that party is nevertheless bound to perform its obligations subject to the following provisions on hardship.

Article 6.2.2 (Definition of Hardship)

There is hardship where the occurrence of events fundamentally alters the equilibrium of the contract either because the cost of a party's performance has increased or because the value of the performance a party receives has diminished, and

(a)   the events occur or become known to the disadvantaged party after the conclusion of the contract;

(b)   the events could not reasonably have been taken into account by the disadvantaged party at the time of the conclusion of the contract;
(c)   the events are beyond the control of the disadvantaged party; and
(d)   the risk of the events was not assumed by the disadvantaged party.

Article 6.2.3 (Effects of Hardship)

(1)   In case of hardship the disadvantaged party is entitled to request renegotiations. The request shall be made without undue delay and shall indicate the grounds on which it is based.
(2)   The request for renegotiation does not in itself entitle the disadvantaged party to withhold performance.
(3)   Upon failure to reach agreement within a reasonable time either party may resort to the court.
(4)   If the court finds hardship it may, if reasonable,
(a)   terminate the contract at a date and on terms to be fixed, or
(b)   adapt the contract with a view to restoring its equilibrium.

CHAPTER 7 — NON-PERFORMANCE
Section 1: Non-Performance in General
Article 7.1.1 (Non-Performance Defined)

Non-performance is failure by a party to perform any of its obligations under the contract, including defective performance or late performance.

Article 7.1.2 (Interference by the Other Party)

A party may not rely on the non-performance of the other party to the extent that such non-performance was caused by the first party's act or omission or by another event as to which the first party bears the risk.

Article 7.1.3 (Withholding Performance)

(1)   Where the parties are to perform simultaneously, either party may withhold performance until the other party tenders its performance.
(2)   Where the parties are to perform consecutively, the party that is to perform later may withhold its performance until the first party has performed.

Article 7.1.4 (Cure by Non-Performing Party)

(1)   The non-performing party may, at its own expense, cure any nonperformance, provided that
(a)   without undue delay, it gives notice indicating the proposed manner and timing of the cure;
(b)   cure is appropriate in the circumstances;
(c)   the aggrieved party has no legitimate interest in refusing cure; and
(d)   cure is effected promptly.
(2)   The right to cure is not precluded by notice of termination.
(3)   Upon effective notice of cure, rights of the aggrieved party that are inconsistent with the non-performing party's performance are suspended until the time for cure has expired.
(4)   The aggrieved party may withhold performance pending cure.
(5)   Notwithstanding cure, the aggrieved party retains the right to claim damages for delay as well as for any harm caused or not prevented by the cure.

Article 7.1.5 (Additional Period for Performance)

(1)   In a case of non-performance the aggrieved party may by notice to the other party allow an additional period of time for performance.
(2)   During the additional period the aggrieved party may withhold performance of its own reciprocal obligations and may claim damages but may not resort to any other remedy. If it receives notice from the other party that the latter will not perform within that period, or if upon expiry of that period due performance has not been made, the aggrieved party may resort to any of the remedies that may be available under this Chapter.
(3)   Where in a case of delay in performance which is not fundamental the aggrieved party has given notice allowing an additional period of time of reasonable length, it may terminate the

contract at the end of that period. If the additional period allowed is not of reasonable length it shall be extended to a reasonable length. The aggrieved party may in its notice provide that if the other party fails to perform within the period allowed by the notice the contract shall automatically terminate.

(4)   Paragraph (3) does not apply where the obligation which has not been performed is only a minor part of the contractual obligation of the non-performing party.

Article 7.1.6 (Exemption Clauses)

A clause which limits or excludes one party's liability for non-performance or which permits one party to render performance substantially different from what the other party reasonably expected may not be invoked if it would be grossly unfair to do so, having regard to the purpose of the contract.

Article 7.1.7 (Force Majeure)

(1)   Non-performance by a party is excused if that party proves that the nonperformance was due to an impediment beyond its control and that it could not reasonably be expected to have taken the impediment into account at the time of the conclusion of the contract or to have avoided or overcome it or its consequences.

(2)   When the impediment is only temporary, the excuse shall have effect for such period as is reasonable having regard to the effect of the impediment on the performance of the contract.

(3)   The party who fails to perform must give notice to the other party of the impediment and its effect on its ability to perform. If the notice is not received by the other party within a reasonable time after the party who fails to perform knew or ought to have known of the impediment, it is liable for damages resulting from such non-receipt.

(4)   Nothing in this Article prevents a party from exercising a right to terminate the contract or to withhold performance or request interest on money due.

Section 2: Right to Performance

Article 7.2.1 (Performance of Monetary Obligation)

Where a party who is obliged to pay money does not do so, the other party may require payment.

Article 7.2.2 (Performance of Non-Monetary Obligation)

Where a party who owes an obligation other than one to pay money does not perform, the other party may require performance, unless

(a)   performance is impossible in law or in fact;
(b)   performance or, where relevant, enforcement is unreasonably burdensome or expensive;
(c)   the party entitled to performance may reasonably obtain performance from another source;
(d)   performance is of an exclusively personal character; or
(e)   the party entitled to performance does not require performance within a reasonable time after it has, or ought to have, become aware of the non-performance.

Article 7.2.3 (Repair and Replacement of Defective Performance)

The right to performance includes in appropriate cases the right to require repair, replacement, or other cure of defective performance. The provisions of Articles 7.2.1 and 7.2.2 apply accordingly.

Article 7.2.4 (Judicial Penalty)

(1)   Where the court orders a party to perform, it may also direct that this party pay a penalty if it does not comply with the order.

(2)   The penalty shall be paid to the aggrieved party unless mandatory provisions of the law of the forum provide otherwise. Payment of the penalty to the aggrieved party does not exclude any claim for damages.

Article 7.2.5 (Change of Remedy)

(1)   An aggrieved party who has required performance of a non-monetary obligation and who has not received performance within a period fixed or otherwise within a reasonable period of time may invoke any other remedy.

(2)   Where the decision of a court for performance of a non-monetary obligation cannot be enforced, the aggrieved party may invoke any other remedy.

Section 3: Termination
Article 7.3.1 (Right to Terminate the Contract)
(1)   A party may terminate the contract where the failure of the other party to perform an obligation under the contract amounts to a fundamental non-performance.
(2)   In determining whether a failure to perform an obligation amounts to a fundamental non-performance regard shall be had, in particular, to whether
(a)   the non-performance substantially deprives the aggrieved party of what it was entitled to expect under the contract unless the other party did not foresee and could not reasonably have foreseen such result;
(b)   strict compliance with the obligation which has not been performed is of essence under the contract;
(c)   the non-performance is intentional or reckless;
(d)   the non-performance gives the aggrieved party reason to believe that it cannot rely on the other party's future performance;
(e)   the non-performing party will suffer disproportionate loss as a result of the preparation or performance if the contract is terminated.
(3)   In the case of delay the aggrieved party may also terminate the contract if the other party fails to perform before the time allowed it under Article 7.1.5 has expired.

Article 7.3.2 (Notice of Termination)
(1)   The right of a party to terminate the contract is exercised by notice to the other party.
(2)   If performance has been offered late or otherwise does not conform to the contract the aggrieved party will lose its right to terminate the contract unless it gives notice to the other party within a reasonable time after it has or ought to have become aware of the offer or of the non-conforming performance.

Article 7.3.3 (Anticipatory Non-Performance)
Where prior to the date for performance by one of the parties it is clear that there will be a fundamental non-performance by that party, the other party may terminate the contract.

Article 7.3.4 (Adequate Assurance of Due Performance)
A party who reasonably believes that there will be a fundamental non-performance by the other party may demand adequate assurance of due performance and may meanwhile withhold its own performance. Where this assurance is not provided within a reasonable time the party demanding it may terminate the contract.

Article 7.3.5 (Effects of Termination in General)
(1)   Termination of the contract releases both parties from their obligation to effect and to receive future performance.
(2)   Termination does not preclude a claim for damages for non-performance.
(3)   Termination does not affect any provision in the contract for the settlement of disputes or any other term of the contract which is to operate even after termination.

Article 7.3.6 (Restitution)
(1)   On termination of the contract either party may claim restitution of whatever it has supplied, provided that such party concurrently makes restitution of whatever it has received. If restitution in kind is not possible or appropriate allowance should be made in money whenever reasonable.
(2)   However, if performance of the contract has extended over a period of time and the contract is divisible, such restitution can only be claimed for the period after termination has taken effect.

Section 4: Damages
Article 7.4.1 (Right to Damages)
Any non-performance gives the aggrieved party a right to damages either exclusively or in conjunction with any other remedies except where the non-performance is excused under these Principles.

Article 7.4.2 (Full Compensation)
(1)   The aggrieved party is entitled to full compensation for harm sustained as a result of the non-performance. Such harm includes both any loss which it suffered and any gain of which it was deprived, taking into account any gain to the aggrieved party resulting from its avoidance of cost or harm.
(2)   Such harm may be non-pecuniary and includes, for instance, physical suffering or emotional distress.

Article 7.4.3 (Certainty of Harm)
(1)   Compensation is due only for harm, including future harm, that is established with a reasonable degree of certainty.
(2)   Compensation may be due for the loss of a chance in proportion to the probability of its occurrence.
(3)   Where the amount of damages cannot be established with a sufficient degree of certainty, the assessment is at the discretion of the court.

Article 7.4.4 (Foreseeability of Harm)
The non-performing party is liable only for harm which it foresaw or could reasonably have foreseen at the time of the conclusion of the contract as being likely to result from its non-performance.

Article 7.4.5 (Proof of Harm in Case of Replacement Transaction)
Where the aggrieved party has terminated the contract and has made a replacement transaction within a reasonable time and in a reasonable manner it may recover the difference between the contract price and the price of the replacement transaction as well as damages for any further harm.

Article 7.4.6 (Proof of Harm by Current Price)
(1)   Where the aggrieved party has terminated the contract and has not made a replacement transaction but there is a current price for the performance contracted for, it may recover the difference between the contract price and the price current at the time the contract is terminated as well as damages for any further harm.
(2)   Current price is the price generally charged for goods delivered or services rendered in comparable circumstances at the place where the contract should have been performed or, if there is no current price at that place, the current price at such other place that appears reasonable to take as a reference.

Article 7.4.7 (Harm Due in Part to Aggrieved Party)
Where the harm is due in part to an act or omission of the aggrieved party or to another event as to which that party bears the risk, the amount of damages shall be reduced to the extent that these factors have contributed to the harm, having regard to the conduct of each of the parties.

Article 7.4.8 (Mitigation of Harm)
(1)   The non-performing party is not liable for harm suffered by the aggrieved party to the extent that the harm could have been reduced by the latter party's taking reasonable steps.
(2)   The aggrieved party is entitled to recover any expenses reasonably incurred in attempting to reduce the harm.

Article 7.4.9 (Interest for Failure to Pay Money)
(1)   If a party does not pay a sum of money when it falls due the aggrieved party is entitled to interest upon that sum from the time when payment is due to the time of payment whether or not the non-payment is excused.

(2)   The rate of interest shall be the average bank short-term lending rate to prime borrowers prevailing for the currency of payment at the place for payment, or where no such rate exists at that place, then the same rate in the State of the currency of payment. In the absence of such a rate at either place the rate of interest shall be the appropriate rate fixed by the law of the State of the currency of payment.

(3)   The aggrieved party is entitled to additional damages if the non-payment caused it a greater harm.

Article 7.4.10 (Interest on Damages)

Unless otherwise agreed, interest on damages for non-performance of non-monetary obligations accrues as from the time of non-performance.

Article 7.4.11 (Manner of Monetary Redress)

(1)   Damages are to be paid in a lump sum. However, they may be payable in instalments where the nature of the harm makes this appropriate.

(2)   Damages to be paid in instalments may be indexed.

Article 7.4.12 (Currency in Which to Assess Damages)

Damages are to be assessed either in the currency in which the monetary obligation was expressed or in the currency in which the harm was suffered, whichever is more appropriate.

Article 7.4.13 (Agreed Payment for Non-Performance)

(1)   Where the contract provides that a party who does not perform is to pay a specified sum to the aggrieved party for such non-performance, the aggrieved party is entitled to that sum irrespective of its actual harm.

(2)   However, notwithstanding any agreement to the contrary the specified sum may be reduced to a reasonable amount where it is grossly excessive in relation to the harm resulting from the non-performance and to the other circumstances.

CHAPTER 8 — SET-OFF

Article 8.1 (Conditions of Set-off)

(1)   Where two parties owe each other money or other performances of the same kind, either of them ("the first party") may set off its obligation against that of its obligee ("the other party") if at the time of set-off,

(a)   the first party is entitled to perform its obligation;

(b)   the other party's obligation is ascertained as to its existence and amount and performance is due.

(2)   If the obligations of both parties arise from the same contract, the first party may also set off its obligation against an obligation of the other party which is not ascertained as to its existence or to its amount.

Article 8.2 (Foreign Currency Set-off)

Where the obligations are to pay money in different currencies, the right of set-off may be exercised, provided that both currencies are freely convertible and the parties have not agreed that the first party shall pay only in a specified currency.

Article 8.3 (Set-off by Notice)

The right of set-off is exercised by notice to the other party.

Article 8.4 (Content of Notice)

(1)   The notice must specify the obligations to which it relates.

(2)   If the notice does not specify the obligation against which set-off is exercised, the other party may, within a reasonable time, declare to the first party the obligation to which set-off relates. If no such declaration is made, the set-off will relate to all the obligations proportionally.

Article 8.5 (Effect of Set-off)

(1)   Set-off discharges the obligations.

(2)   If obligations differ in amount, set-off discharges the obligations up to the amount of the lesser obligation.
(3)   Set-off takes effect as from the time of notice.

CHAPTER 9 — ASSIGNMENT OF RIGHTS, TRANSFER OF OBLIGATIONS, ASSIGNMENT OF CONTRACTS
Section 1: Assignment of Rights
Article 9.1.1 (Definitions)

"Assignment of a right" means the transfer by agreement from one person (the "assignor") to another person (the "assignee"), including transfer by way of security, of the assignor's right to payment of a monetary sum or other performance from a third person ("the obligor").

Article 9.1.2 (Exclusions)

This Section does not apply to transfers made under the special rules governing the transfers:
(a)   of instruments such as negotiable instruments, documents of title or financial instruments, or
(b)   of rights in the course of transferring a business.

Article 9.1.3 (Assignability of Non-Monetary Rights)

A right to non-monetary performance may be assigned only if the assignment does not render the obligation significantly more burdensome.

Article 9.1.4 (Partial Assignment)

(1)   A right to the payment of a monetary sum may be assigned partially.
(2)   A right to other performance may be assigned partially only if it is divisible, and the assignment does not render the obligation significantly more burdensome.

Article 9.1.5 (Future Rights)

A future right is deemed to be transferred at the time of the agreement, provided the right, when it comes into existence, can be identified as the right to which the assignment relates.

Article 9.1.6 (Rights Assigned Without Individual Specification)

A number of rights may be assigned without individual specification, provided such rights can be identified as rights to which the assignment relates at the time of the assignment or when they come into existence.

Article 9.1.7 (Agreement Between Assignor and Assignee Sufficient)

(1)   A right is assigned by mere agreement between the assignor and the assignee, without notice to the obligor.
(2)   The consent of the obligor is not required unless the obligation in the circumstances is of an essentially personal character.

Article 9.1.8 (Obligor's Additional Costs)

The obligor has a right to be compensated by the assignor or the assignee for any additional costs caused by the assignment.

Article 9.1.9 (Non-Assignment Clauses)

(1)   The assignment of a right to the payment of a monetary sum is effective notwithstanding an agreement between the assignor and the obligor limiting or prohibiting such an assignment. However, the assignor may be liable to the obligor for breach of contract.
(2)   The assignment of a right to other performance is ineffective if it is contrary to an agreement between the assignor and the obligor limiting or prohibiting the assignment. Nevertheless, the assignment is effective if the assignee, at the time of the assignment, neither knew nor ought to have known of the agreement. The assignor may then be liable to the obligor for breach of contract.

Article 9.1.10 (Notice to the Obligor)

(1)   Until the obligor receives a notice of the assignment from either the assignor or the assignee, it is discharged by paying the assignor.

(2)   After the obligor receives such a notice, it is discharged only by paying the assignee.

Article 9.1.11 (Successive Assignments)

If the same right has been assigned by the same assignor to two or more successive assignees, the obligor is discharged by paying according to the order in which the notices were received.

Article 9.1.12 (Adequate Proof of Assignment)

(1)   If notice of the assignment is given by the assignee, the obligor may request the assignee to provide within a reasonable time adequate proof that the assignment has been made.

(2)   Until adequate proof is provided, the obligor may withhold payment.

(3)   Unless adequate proof is provided, notice is not effective.

(4)   Adequate proof includes, but is not limited to, any writing emanating from the assignor and indicating that the assignment has taken place.

Article 9.1.13 (Defences and Rights of Set-off)

(1)   The obligor may assert against the assignee all defences that the obligor could assert against the assignor.

(2)   The obligor may exercise against the assignee any right of set-off available to the obligor against the assignor up to the time notice of assignment was received.

Article 9.1.14 (Rights Related to the Right Assigned)

The assignment of a right transfers to the assignee:

(a)   all the assignor's rights to payment or other performance under the contract in respect of the right assigned, and

(b)   all rights securing performance of the right assigned.

Article 9.1.15 (Undertakings of the Assignor)

The assignor undertakes towards the assignee, except as otherwise disclosed to the assignee, that:

(a)   the assigned right exists at the time of the assignment, unless the right is a future right;

(b)   the assignor is entitled to assign the right;

(c)   the right has not been previously assigned to another assignee, and it is free from any right or claim from a third party;

(d)   the obligor does not have any defences;

(e)   neither the obligor nor the assignor has given notice of set-off concerning the assigned right and will not give any such notice;

(f)   the assignor will reimburse the assignee for any payment received from the obligor before notice of the assignment was given.

Section 2: Transfer of Obligations

Article 9.2.1 (Modes of Transfer)

An obligation to pay money or render other performance may be transferred from one person (the "original obligor") to another person (the "new obligor") either

(a)   by an agreement between the original obligor and the new obligor subject to Article 9.2.3, or

(b)   by an agreement between the obligee and the new obligor, by which the new obligor assumes the obligation.

Article 9.2.2 (Exclusion)

This Section does not apply to transfers of obligations made under the special rules governing transfers of obligations in the course of transferring a business.

Article 9.2.3 (Requirement of Obligee's Consent to Transfer)

The transfer of an obligation by an agreement between the original obligor and the new obligor requires the consent of the obligee.

Article 9.2.4 (Advance Consent of Obligee)
(1)   The obligee may give its consent in advance.
(2)   If the obligee has given its consent in advance, the transfer of the obligation becomes effective when a notice of the transfer is given to the obligee or when the obligee acknowledges it.

Article 9.2.5 (Discharge of Original Obligor)
(1)   The obligee may discharge the original obligor.
(2)   The obligee may also retain the original obligor as an obligor in case the new obligor does not perform properly.
(3)   Otherwise the original obligor and the new obligor are jointly and severally liable.

Article 9.2.6 (Third Party Performance)
(1)   Without the obligee's consent, the obligor may contract with another person that this person will perform the obligation in place of the obligor, unless the obligation in the circumstances has an essentially personal character.
(2)   The obligee retains its claim against the obligor.

Article 9.2.7 (Defences and Rights of Set-off)
(1)   The new obligor may assert against the obligee all defences which the original obligor could assert against the obligee.
(2)   The new obligor may not exercise against the obligee any right of set-off available to the original obligor against the obligee.

Article 9.2.8 (Rights Related to the Obligation Transferred)
(1)   The obligee may assert against the new obligor all its rights to payment or other performance under the contract in respect of the obligation transferred.
(2)   If the original obligor is discharged under Article 9.2.5(1), a security granted by any person other than the new obligor for the performance of the obligation is discharged, unless that other person agrees that it should continue to be available to the obligee.
(3)   Discharge of the original obligor also extends to any security of the original obligor given to the obligee for the performance of the obligation, unless the security is over an asset which is transferred as part of a transaction between the original obligor and the new obligor.

Section 3: Assignment of Contracts
Article 9.3.1 (Definitions)
"Assignment of a contract" means the transfer by agreement from one person (the "assignor") to another person (the "assignee") of the assignor's rights and obligations arising out of a contract with another person (the "other party").

Article 9.3.2 (Exclusion)
This Section does not apply to the assignment of contracts made under the special rules governing transfers of contracts in the course of transferring a business.

Article 9.3.3 (Requirement of Consent of the Other Party)
The assignment of a contract requires the consent of the other party.

Article 9.3.4 (Advance Consent of the Other Party)
(1)   The other party may give its consent in advance.
(2) If the other party has given its consent in advance, the assignment of the contract becomes effective when a notice of the assignment is given to the other party or when the other party acknowledges it.

Article 9.3.5 (Discharge of the Assignor)
(1)   The other party may discharge the assignor.
(2)   The other party may also retain the assignor as an obligor in case the assignee does not perform properly.

(3) Otherwise the assignor and the assignee are jointly and severally liable.

Article 9.3.6 (Defences and Rights of Set-off)
(1) To the extent that the assignment of a contract involves an assignment of rights, Article 9.1.13 applies accordingly.
(2) To the extent that the assignment of a contract involves a transfer of obligations, Article 9.2.7 applies accordingly.

Article 9.3.7 (Rights Transferred with the Contract)
(1) To the extent that the assignment of a contract involves an assignment of rights, Article 9.1.14 applies accordingly.
(2) To the extent that the assignment of a contract involves a transfer of obligations, Article 9.2.8 applies accordingly.

CHAPTER 10 — LIMITATION PERIODS

Article 10.1 (Scope of the Chapter)
(1) The exercise of rights governed by these Principles is barred by the expiration of a period of time, referred to as "limitation period", according to the rules of this Chapter.
(2) This Chapter does not govern the time within which one party is required under these Principles, as a condition for the acquisition or exercise of its right, to give notice to the other party or to perform any act other than the institution of legal proceedings.

Article 10.2 (Limitation Periods)
(1) The general limitation period is three years beginning on the day after the day the obligee knows or ought to know the facts as a result of which the obligee's right can be exercised.
(2) In any event, the maximum limitation period is ten years beginning on the day after the day the right can be exercised.

Article 10.3 (Modification of Limitation Periods by the Parties)
(1) The parties may modify the limitation periods.
(2) However they may not
(a) shorten the general limitation period to less than one year;
(b) shorten the maximum limitation period to less than four years;
(c) extend the maximum limitation period to more than fifteen years.

Article 10.4 (New Limitation Period by Acknowledgement)
(1) Where the obligor before the expiration of the general limitation period acknowledges the right of the obligee, a new general limitation period begins on the day after the day of the acknowledgement.
(2) The maximum limitation period does not begin to run again, but may be exceeded by the beginning of a new general limitation period under Art. 10.2(1).

Article 10.5 (Suspension by Judicial Proceedings)
(1) The running of the limitation period is suspended
(a) when the obligee performs any act, by commencing judicial proceedings or in judicial proceedings already instituted, that is recognised by the law of the court as asserting the obligee's right against the obligor;
(b) in the case of the obligor's insolvency when the obligee has asserted its rights in the insolvency proceedings; or
(c) in the case of proceedings for dissolution of the entity which is the obligor when the obligee has asserted its rights in the dissolution proceedings.
(2) Suspension lasts until a final decision has been issued or until the proceedings have been otherwise terminated.

Article 10.6 (Suspension by Arbitral Proceedings)
(1) The running of the limitation period is suspended when the obligee performs any act, by commencing arbitral proceedings or in arbitral proceedings already instituted, that is recogni-

sed by the law of the arbitral tribunal as asserting the obligee's right against the obligor. In the absence of regulations for arbitral proceedings or provisions determining the exact date of the commencement of arbitral proceedings, the proceedings are deemed to commence on the date on which a request that the right in dispute should be adjudicated reaches the obligor.
(2) Suspension lasts until a binding decision has been issued or until the proceedings have been otherwise terminated.

Article 10.7 (Alternative Dispute Resolution)

The provisions of Articles 10.5 and 10.6 apply with appropriate modifications to other proceedings whereby the parties request a third person to assist them in their attempt to reach an amicable settlement of their dispute.

Article 10.8 (Suspension in Case of Force Majeure, Death or Incapacity)

(1) Where the obligee has been prevented by an impediment that is beyond its control and that it could neither avoid nor overcome, from causing a limitation period to cease to run under the preceding articles, the general limitation period is suspended so as not to expire before one year after the relevant impediment has ceased to exist.
(2) Where the impediment consists of the incapacity or death of the obligee or obligor, suspension ceases when a representative for the incapacitated or deceased party or its estate has been appointed or a successor has inherited the respective party's position. The additional one-year period under paragraph (1) applies accordingly.

Article 10.9 (The Effects of Expiration of Limitation Period)

(1) The expiration of the limitation period does not extinguish the right.
(2) For the expiration of the limitation period to have effect, the obligor must assert it as a defence.
(3) A right may still be relied on as a defence even though the expiration of the limitation period for that right has been asserted.

Article 10.10 (Right of Set-off)

The obligee may exercise the right of set-off until the obligor has asserted the expiration of the limitation period.

Article 10.11 (Restitution)

Where there has been performance in order to discharge an obligation, there is no right of restitution merely because the limitation period has expired.

2009 EU DRAFT COMMON FRAME OF REFERENCE[1]

Table of Contents

---

1   © Study Group on a European Civil Code and the Research Group on EC Private Law (Acquis Group).

BOOK I GENERAL PROVISIONS

I. – 1:101: Intended Field of Application

(1)   These rules are intended to be used primarily in relation to contracts and other juridical acts, contractual and non-contractual rights and obligations and related property matters.

(2)   They are not intended to be used, or used without modification or supplementation, in relation to rights and obligations of a public law nature or, except where otherwise provided, in relation to:

(a)   the status or legal capacity of natural persons;

(b)   wills and succession;

(c)   family relationships, including matrimonial and similar relationships;

(d)   bills of exchange, cheques and promissory notes and other negotiable instruments;

(e)   employment relationships;

(f)   the ownership of, or rights in security over, immovable property;

(g)   the creation, capacity, internal organisation, regulation or dissolution of companies and other bodies corporate or unincorporated;

(h)   matters relating primarily to procedure or enforcement.

(3)   Further restrictions on intended fields of application are contained in later Books.

I. – 1:102: Interpretation and Development

(1)   These rules are to be interpreted and developed autonomously and in accordance with their objectives and the principles underlying them.

(2)   They are to be read in the light of any applicable instruments guaranteeing human rights and fundamental freedoms and any applicable constitutional laws.

(3)   In their interpretation and development regard should be had to the need to promote:

(a)   uniformity of application;

(b)   good faith and fair dealing; and

(c)   legal certainty.

(4)   Issues within the scope of the rules but not expressly settled by them are so far as possible to be settled in accordance with the principles underlying them.

(5)   Where there is a general rule and a special rule applying to a particular situation within the scope of the general rule, the special rule prevails in any case of conflict.

I. – 1:103: Good Faith and Fair Dealing

(1)   The expression "good faith and fair dealing" refers to a standard of conduct characterised by honesty, openness and consideration for the interests of the other party to the transaction or relationship in question.

(2)   It is, in particular, contrary to good faith and fair dealing for a party to act inconsistently with that party's prior statements or conduct when the other party has reasonably relied on them to that other party's detriment.

I. – 1:104: Reasonableness

Reasonableness is to be objectively ascertained, having regard to the nature and purpose of what is being done, to the circumstances of the case and to any relevant usages and practices.

I. – 1:105: "Consumer" and "Business"

(1)   A "consumer" means any natural person who is acting primarily for purposes which are not related to his or her trade, business or profession.

(2)   A "business" means any natural or legal person, irrespective of whether publicly or privately owned, who is acting for purposes relating to the person's self-employed trade, work or profession, even if the person does not intend to make a profit in the course of the activity.

(3)   A person who is within both of the preceding paragraphs is regarded as falling exclusively within paragraph (1) in relation to a rule which would provide protection for that person if that person were a consumer, and otherwise as falling exclusively within paragraph (2).

I. – 1:106: "In Writing" and Similar Expressions

(1)   For the purposes of these rules, a statement is "in writing" if it is in textual form and in characters which are directly legible from paper or another tangible durable medium.

(2)   "Textual form" means a text which is expressed in alphabetical or other intelligible characters by means of any support which permits reading, recording of the information contained in the text and its reproduction in tangible form.

(3)   "Durable medium" means any material on which information is stored so that it is accessible for future reference for a period of time adequate to the purposes of the information, and which allows the unchanged reproduction of this information.

I. – 1:107: "Signature" and Similar Expressions

(1)   A reference to a person's signature includes a reference to that person's handwritten signature, electronic signature or advanced electronic signature, and references to anything being signed by a person are to be construed accordingly.

(2)   A "handwritten signature" means the name of, or sign representing, a person written by that person's own hand for the purpose of authentication.

(3)   An "electronic signature" means data in electronic form which are attached to or logically associated with other electronic data, and which serve as a method of authentication.

(4)   An "advanced electronic signature" means an electronic signature which is:

(a)   uniquely linked to the signatory;

(b)   capable of identifying the signatory;

(c)   created using means which can be maintained under the signatory's sole control; and

(d)   linked to the data to which it relates in such a manner that any subsequent change of the data is detectable.

(5)   In this Article, "electronic" means relating to technology with electrical, digital, magnetic, wireless, optical, electromagnetic, or similar capabilities.

I. – 1:108: Definitions in Annex

(1)   The definitions in the Annex apply for all the purposes of these rules unless the context otherwise requires.

(2)   Where a word is defined, other grammatical forms of the word have a corresponding meaning.

I. – 1:109: Notice

(1)   This Article applies in relation to the giving of notice for any purpose under these rules. "Notice" includes the communication of information or of a juridical act.

(2)   The notice may be given by any means appropriate to the circumstances.

(3)   The notice becomes effective when it reaches the addressee, unless it provides for a delayed effect.

(4)   The notice reaches the addressee:

(a)   when it is delivered to the addressee;

(b)   when it is delivered to the addressee's place of business or, where there is no such place of business or the notice does not relate to a business matter, to the addressee's habitual residence;

(c)   in the case of a notice transmitted by electronic means, when it can be accessed by the addressee; or

(d)   when it is otherwise made available to the addressee at such a place and in such a way that the addressee could reasonably be expected to obtain access to it without undue delay.

(5)   The notice has no effect if a revocation of it reaches the addressee before or at the same time as the notice.

(6)   Any reference in these rules to a notice given by or to a person includes a notice given by or to an agent of that person who has authority to give or receive it.

(7)   In relations between a business and a consumer the parties may not, to the detriment of the consumer, exclude the rule in paragraph (4)(c) or derogate from or vary its effects.

I. – 1:110: Computation of Time

(1)   The provisions of this Article apply in relation to the computation of time for any purpose under these rules.

(2)   Subject to the following provisions of this Article:

(a)   a period expressed in hours starts at the beginning of the first hour and ends with the expiry of the last hour of the period;

(b)   a period expressed in days starts at the beginning of the first hour of the first day and ends with the expiry of the last hour of the last day of the period;

(c)   a period expressed in weeks, months or years starts at the beginning of the first hour of the first day of the period, and ends with the expiry of the last hour of whichever day in the last week, month or year is the same day of the week, or falls on the same date, as the day from which the period runs; with the qualification that if, in a period expressed in months or in years, the day on which the period should expire does not occur in the last month, it ends with the expiry of the last hour of the last day of that month;

(d)   if a period includes part of a month, the month is considered to have thirty days for the purpose of calculating the length of the part.

(3)   Where a period is to be calculated from a specified event or action, then:

(a)   if the period is expressed in hours, the hour during which the event occurs or the action takes place is not considered to fall within the period in question; and

(b)   if the period is expressed in days, weeks, months or years, the day during which the event occurs or the action takes place is not considered to fall within the period in question.

(4)   Where a period is to be calculated from a specified time, then:

(a)   if the period is expressed in hours, the first hour of the period is considered to begin at the specified time; and

(b)   if the period is expressed in days, weeks, months or years, the day during which the specified time arrives is not considered to fall within the period in question.

(5)   The periods concerned include Saturdays, Sundays and public holidays, save where these are expressly excepted or where the periods are expressed in working days.

(6)   Where the last day of a period expressed otherwise than in hours is a Saturday, Sunday or public holiday at the place where a prescribed act is to be done, the period ends with the expiry of the last hour of the following working day. This provision does not apply to periods calculated retroactively from a given date or event.

(7)   Any period of two days or more is regarded as including at least two working days.

(8)   Where a person sends another person a document which sets a period of time within which the addressee has to reply or take other action but does not state when the period is to begin, then, in the absence of indications to the contrary, the period is calculated from the date stated as the date of the document or, if no date is stated, from the moment the document reaches the addressee.

(9) In this Article:
(a) "public holiday" with reference to a member state, or part of a member state, of the European Union means any day designated as such for that state or part in a list published in the official journal; and
(b) "working days" means all days other than Saturdays, Sundays and public holidays.

BOOK II CONTRACTS AND OTHER JURIDICAL ACTS
Chapter 1: General Provisions
II. – 1:101: Meaning of "Contract" and "Juridical Act"

(1) A contract is an agreement which is intended to give rise to a binding legal relationship or to have some other legal effect. It is a bilateral or multilateral juridical act.
(2) A juridical act is any statement or agreement, whether express or implied from conduct, which is intended to have legal effect as such. It may be unilateral, bilateral or multilateral.

II. – 1:102: Party Autonomy

(1) Parties are free to make a contract or other juridical act and to determine its contents, subject to any applicable mandatory rules.
(2) Parties may exclude the application of any of the following rules relating to contracts or other juridical acts, or the rights and obligations arising from them, or derogate from or vary their effects, except as otherwise provided.
(3) A provision to the effect that parties may not exclude the application of a rule or derogate from or vary its effects does not prevent a party from waiving a right which has already arisen and of which that party is aware.

II. – 1:103: Binding Effect

(1) A valid contract is binding on the parties.
(2) A valid unilateral undertaking is binding on the person giving it if it is intended to be legally binding without acceptance.
(3) This Article does not prevent modification or termination of any resulting right or obligation by agreement between the debtor and creditor or as provided by law.

II. – 1:104: Usages and Practices

(1) The parties to a contract are bound by any usage to which they have agreed and by any practice they have established between themselves.
(2) The parties are bound by a usage which would be considered generally applicable by persons in the same situation as the parties, except where the application of such usage would be unreasonable.
(3) This Article applies to other juridical acts with any necessary adaptations.

II. – 1:105: Imputed Knowledge etc.

If a person who with a party's assent was involved in making a contract or other juridical act or in exercising a right or performing an obligation under it:
(a) knew or foresaw a fact, or is treated as having knowledge or foresight of a fact; or
(b) acted intentionally or with any other relevant state of mind this knowledge, foresight or state of mind is imputed to the party.

II. – 1:106: Form

(1) A contract or other juridical act need not be concluded, made or evidenced in writing nor is it subject to any other requirement as to form.
(2) Where a contract or other juridical act is invalid only by reason of noncompliance with a particular requirement as to form, one party (the first party) is liable for any loss suffered by the other (the second party) by acting in the mistaken, but reasonable, belief that it was valid if the first party:
(a) knew it was invalid;
(b) knew or could reasonably be expected to know that the second party was acting to that party's potential prejudice in the mistaken belief that it was valid; and

(c)   contrary to good faith and fair dealing, allowed the second party to continue so acting.

II. – 1:107: Mixed Contracts

(1)   For the purposes of this Article a mixed contract is a contract which contains:

(a)   parts falling within two or more of the categories of contracts regulated specifically in these rules; or

(b)   a part falling within one such category and another part falling within the category of contracts governed only by the rules applicable to contracts generally.

(2)   Where a contract is a mixed contract then, unless this is contrary to the nature and purpose of the contract, the rules applicable to each relevant category apply, with any appropriate adaptations, to the corresponding part of the contract and the rights and obligations arising from it.

(3)   Paragraph (2) does not apply where:

(a)   a rule provides that a mixed contract is to be regarded as falling primarily within one category; or

(b)   in a case not covered by the preceding sub-paragraph, one part of a mixed contract is in fact so predominant that it would be unreasonable not to regard the contract as falling primarily within one category.

(4)   In cases covered by paragraph (3) the rules applicable to the category into which the contract primarily falls (the primary category) apply to the contract and the rights and obligations arising from it. However, rules applicable to any elements of the contract falling within another category apply with any appropriate adaptations so far as is necessary to regulate those elements and provided that they do not conflict with the rules applicable to the primary category.

(5)   Nothing in this Article prevents the application of any mandatory rules.

II. – 1:108: Partial Invalidity or Ineffectiveness

Where only part of a contract or other juridical act is invalid or ineffective, the remaining part continues in effect if it can reasonably be maintained without the invalid or ineffective part.

II. – 1:109: Standard Terms

A "standard term" is a term which has been formulated in advance for several transactions involving different parties and which has not been individually negotiated by the parties.

II. – 1:110: Terms "Not Individually Negotiated"

(1)   A term supplied by one party is not individually negotiated if the other party has not been able to influence its content, in particular because it has been drafted in advance, whether or not as part of standard terms.

(2)   If one party supplies a selection of terms to the other party, a term will not be regarded as individually negotiated merely because the other party chooses that term from that selection.

(3)   If it is disputed whether a term supplied by one party as part of standard terms has since been individually negotiated, that party bears the burden of proving that it has been.

(4)   In a contract between a business and a consumer, the business bears the burden of proving that a term supplied by the business has been individually negotiated.

(5)   In contracts between a business and a consumer, terms drafted by a third person are considered to have been supplied by the business, unless the consumer introduced them to the contract.

Chapter 2: Non-Discrimination

II. – 2:101: Right Not to Be Discriminated Against

A person has a right not to be discriminated against on the grounds of sex or ethnic or racial origin in relation to a contract or other juridical act the object of which is to provide access to, or supply, goods, other assets or services which are available to the public.

II. – 2:102: Meaning of Discrimination

(1)   "Discrimination" means any conduct whereby, or situation where, on grounds such as those mentioned in the preceding Article:

(a)   one person is treated less favourably than another person is, has been or would be treated in a comparable situation; or
(b)   an apparently neutral provision, criterion or practice would place one group of persons at a particular disadvantage when compared to a different group of persons.
(2)   Discrimination also includes harassment on grounds such as those mentioned in the preceding Article. "Harassment" means unwanted conduct (including conduct of a sexual nature) which violates a person's dignity, particularly when such conduct creates an intimidating, hostile, degrading, humiliating or offensive environment, or which aims to do so.
(3)   Any instruction to discriminate also amounts to discrimination.

II. – 2:103: Exception

Unequal treatment which is justified by a legitimate aim does not amount to discrimination if the means used to achieve that aim are appropriate and necessary.

II. – 2:104: Remedies

(1)   If a person is discriminated against contrary to II. – 2:101 (Right not to be discriminated against) then, without prejudice to any remedy which may be available under Book VI (Non-contractual liability for damage caused to another), the remedies for non-performance of an obligation under Book III, Chapter 3 (including damages for economic and non-economic loss) are available.
(2)   Any remedy granted should be proportionate to the injury or anticipated injury; the dissuasive effect of remedies may be taken into account.

II. – 2:105: Burden of Proof

(1)   If a person who considers himself or herself discriminated against on one of the grounds mentioned in II. – 2:101 (Right not to be discriminated against) establishes, before a court or another competent authority, facts from which it may be presumed that there has been such discrimination, it falls on the other party to prove that there has been no such discrimination.
(2)   Paragraph (1) does not apply to proceedings in which it is for the court or another competent authority to investigate the facts of the case.

Chapter 3: Marketing and Pre-Contractual Duties
Section 1: Information Duties
II. – 3:101: Duty to Disclose Information about Goods, Other Assets and Services

(1)   Before the conclusion of a contract for the supply of goods, other assets or services by a business to another person, the business has a duty to disclose to the other person such information concerning the goods, other assets or services to be supplied as the other person can reasonably expect, taking into account the standards of quality and performance which would be normal under the circumstances.
(2)   In assessing what information the other person can reasonably expect to be disclosed, the test to be applied, if the other person is also a business, is whether the failure to provide the information would deviate from good commercial practice.

II. – 3:102: Specific Duties for Businesses Marketing to Consumers

(1)   Where a business is marketing goods, other assets or services to a consumer, the business has a duty not to give misleading information. Information is misleading if it misrepresents or omits material facts which the average consumer could expect to be given for an informed decision on whether to take steps towards the conclusion of a contract. In assessing what an average consumer could expect to be given, account is to be taken of all the circumstances and of the limitations of the communication medium employed.
(2)   Where a business uses a commercial communication which gives the impression to consumers that it contains all the relevant information necessary to make a decision about concluding a contract, the business has a duty to ensure that the communication in fact contains all the relevant information. Where it is not already apparent from the context of the commercial communication, the information to be provided comprises:

(a) the main characteristics of the goods, other assets or services, the identity and address, if relevant, of the business, the price, and any available right of withdrawal;

(b) peculiarities related to payment, delivery, performance and complaint handling, if they depart from the requirements of professional diligence; and

(c) the language to be used for communications between the parties after the conclusion of the contract, if this differs from the language of the commercial communication.

(3) A duty to provide information under this Article is not fulfilled unless all the information to be provided is provided in the same language.

II. – 3:103: Duty to Provide Information When Concluding Contract with a Consumer Who Is at a Particular Disadvantage

(1) In the case of transactions that place the consumer at a significant informational disadvantage because of the technical medium used for contracting, the physical distance between business and consumer, or the nature of the transaction, the business has a duty, as appropriate in the circumstances, to provide clear information about the main characteristics of any goods, other assets or services to be supplied, the price, the address and identity of the business with which the consumer is transacting, the terms of the contract, the rights and obligations of both contracting parties, and any available right of withdrawal or redress procedures. This information must be provided a reasonable time before the conclusion of the contract. The information on the right of withdrawal must, as appropriate in the circumstances, also be adequate in the sense of II. – 5:104 (Adequate information on the right to withdraw).

(2) Where more specific information duties are provided for specific situations, these take precedence over the general information duty under paragraph (1).

(3) The business bears the burden of proof that it has provided the information required by this Article.

II. – 3:104: Information Duties in Real Time Distance Communication

(1) When initiating real time distance communication with a consumer, a business has a duty to provide at the outset explicit information on its name and the commercial purpose of the contact.

(2) Real time distance communication means direct and immediate distance communication of such a type that one party can interrupt the other in the course of the communication. It includes telephone and electronic means such as voice over internet protocol and internet related chat, but does not include communication by electronic mail.

(3) The business bears the burden of proof that the consumer has received the information required under paragraph (1).

(4) If a business has failed to comply with the duty under paragraph (1) and a contract has been concluded as a result of the communication, the other party has a right to withdraw from the contract by giving notice to the business within the period specified in II. – 5:103 (Withdrawal period).

(5) A business is liable to the consumer for any loss caused by a breach of the duty under paragraph (1).

II. – 3:105: Formation by Electronic Means

(1) If a contract is to be concluded by electronic means and without individual communication, a business has a duty to provide information about the following matters before the other party makes or accepts an offer:

(a) the technical steps to be taken in order to conclude the contract;

(b) whether or not a contract document will be filed by the business and whether it will be accessible;

(c) the technical means for identifying and correcting input errors before the other party makes or accepts an offer;

(d) the languages offered for the conclusion of the contract;

(e) any contract terms used.

(2)   The business has a duty to ensure that the contract terms referred to in paragraph (1)(e) are available in textual form.
(3)   If a business has failed to comply with the duty under paragraph (1) and a contract has been concluded in the circumstances there stated, the other party has a right to withdraw from the contract by giving notice to the business within the period specified in II. – 5:103 (Withdrawal period).
(4)   A business is liable to the consumer for any loss caused by a breach of the duty under paragraph (1).

II. – 3:106: Clarity and Form of Information

(1)   A duty to provide information imposed on a business under this Chapter is not fulfilled unless the requirements of this Article are satisfied.
(2)   The information must be clear and precise, and expressed in plain and intelligible language.
(3)   Where rules for specific contracts require information to be provided on a durable medium or in another particular form it must be provided in that way.
(4)   In the case of contracts between a business and a consumer concluded at a distance, information about the main characteristics of any goods, other assets or services to be supplied, the price, the address and identity of the business with which the consumer is transacting, the terms of the contract, the rights and obligations of both contracting parties, and any available redress procedures, as may be appropriate in the particular case, must be confirmed in textual form on a durable medium at the time of conclusion of the contract. The information on the right of withdrawal must also be adequate in the sense of II. – 5:104 (Adequate information on the right to withdraw).

II. – 3:107: Information about Price and Additional Charges

Where under this Chapter a business has a duty to provide information about price, the duty is not fulfilled unless what is provided:
(a)   includes information about any deposits payable, delivery charges and any additional taxes and duties where these may be indicated separately;
(b)   if an exact price cannot be indicated, gives such information on the basis for the calculation as will enable the consumer to verify the price; and
(c)   if the price is not payable in one sum, includes information about the payment schedule.

II. – 3:108: Information about Address and Identity of Business

(1)   Where under this Chapter a business has a duty to provide information about its address and identity, the duty is not fulfilled unless the information includes:
(a)   the name of the business;
(b)   any trading names relevant to the contract in question;
(c)   the registration number in any official register, and the name of that register;
(d)   the geographical address of the business;
(e)   contact details;
(f)   where the business has a representative in the consumer's state of residence, the address and identity of that representative;
(g)   where the activity of the business is subject to an authorisation scheme, the particulars of the relevant supervisory authority; and
(h)   where the business exercises an activity which is subject to VAT, the relevant VAT identification number.
(2)   For the purpose of II. – 3:103 (Duty to provide information when concluding contract with a consumer who is at a particular disadvantage), the address and identity of the business include only the information indicated in paragraph (1)(a), (c), (d) and (e).

II. – 3:109: Remedies for Breach of Information Duties

(1)   If a business has a duty under II. – 3:103 (Duty to provide information when concluding contract with a consumer who is at a particular disadvantage) to provide information to a con-

sumer before the conclusion of a contract from which the consumer has the right to withdraw, the withdrawal period does not commence until all this information has been provided. Regardless of this, the right of withdrawal lapses after one year from the time of the conclusion of the contract.

(2)   If a business has failed to comply with any duty imposed by the preceding Articles of this Section and a contract has been concluded, the business has such obligations under the contract as the other party has reasonably expected as a consequence of the absence or incorrectness of the information. Remedies provided under Book III, Chapter 3 apply to non-performance of these obligations.

(3)   Whether or not a contract is concluded, a business which has failed to comply with any duty imposed by the preceding Articles of this Section is liable for any loss caused to the other party to the transaction by such failure. This paragraph does not apply to the extent that a remedy is available for non-performance of a contractual obligation under the preceding paragraph.

(4)   The remedies provided under this Article are without prejudice to any remedy which may be available under II. – 7:201 (Mistake).

(5)   In relations between a business and a consumer the parties may not, to the detriment of the consumer, exclude the application of this Article or derogate from or vary its effects.

Section 2: Duty to Prevent Input Errors and Acknowledge Receipt
II. – 3:201: Correction of Input Errors

(1)   A business which intends to conclude a contract by making available electronic means without individual communication for concluding it has a duty to make available to the other party appropriate, effective and accessible technical means for identifying and correcting input errors before the other party makes or accepts an offer.

(2)   Where a person concludes a contract in error because of a failure by a business to comply with the duty under paragraph (1) the business is liable for any loss caused to that person by such failure. This is without prejudice to any remedy which may be available under II. – 7:201 (Mistake).

(3)   In relations between a business and a consumer the parties may not, to the detriment of the consumer, exclude the application of this Article or derogate from or vary its effects.

II. – 3:202: Acknowledgement of Receipt

(1)   A business which offers the facility to conclude a contract by electronic means and without individual communication has a duty to acknowledge by electronic means the receipt of an offer or an acceptance by the other party.

(2)   If the other party does not receive the acknowledgement without undue delay, that other party may revoke the offer or withdraw from the contract.

(3)   The business is liable for any loss caused to the other party by a breach of the duty under paragraph (1).

(4)   In relations between a business and a consumer the parties may not, to the detriment of the consumer, exclude the application of this Article or derogate from or vary its effects.

Section 3: Negotiation and Confidentiality Duties
II. – 3:301: Negotiations Contrary to Good Faith and Fair Dealing

(1)   A person is free to negotiate and is not liable for failure to reach an agreement.

(2)   A person who is engaged in negotiations has a duty to negotiate in accordance with good faith and fair dealing and not to break off negotiations contrary to good faith and fair dealing. This duty may not be excluded or limited by contract.

(3)   A person who is in breach of the duty is liable for any loss caused to the other party by the breach.

(4)   It is contrary to good faith and fair dealing, in particular, for a person to enter into or continue negotiations with no real intention of reaching an agreement with the other party.

II. – 3:302: Breach of Confidentiality
(1)   If confidential information is given by one party in the course of negotiations, the other party is under a duty not to disclose that information or use it for that party's own purposes whether or not a contract is subsequently concluded.
(2)   In this Article, "confidential information" means information which, either from its nature or the circumstances in which it was obtained, the party receiving the information knows or could reasonably be expected to know is confidential to the other party.
(3)   A party who reasonably anticipates a breach of the duty may obtain a court order prohibiting it.
(4)   A party who is in breach of the duty is liable for any loss caused to the other party by the breach and may be ordered to pay over to the other party any benefit obtained by the breach.

Section 4: Unsolicited Goods or Services
II. – 3:401: No Obligation Arising from Failure to Respond
(1)   If a business delivers unsolicited goods to, or performs unsolicited services for, a consumer:
(a)   no contract arises from the consumer's failure to respond or from any other action or inaction by the consumer in relation to the goods and services; and
(b)   no non-contractual obligation arises from the consumer's acquisition, retention, rejection or use of the goods or receipt of benefit from the services.
(2)   Sub-paragraph (b) of the preceding paragraph does not apply if the goods or services were supplied:
(a)   by way of benevolent intervention in another's affairs; or
(b)   in error or in such other circumstances that there is a right to reversal of an unjustified enrichment.
(3)   This Article is subject to the rules on delivery of excess quantity under a contract for the sale of goods.
(4)   For the purposes of paragraph (1) delivery occurs when the consumer obtains physical control over the goods.

Section 5: Damages for Breach of Duty under this Chapter
II. – 3:501: Liability for Damages
(1)   Where any rule in this Chapter makes a person liable for loss caused to another person by a breach of a duty, the other person has a right to damages for that loss.
(2)   The rules on III. – 3:704 (Loss attributable to creditor) and III. – 3:705 (Reduction of loss) apply with the adaptation that the reference to non-performance of the obligation is to be taken as a reference to breach of the duty.

Chapter 4: Formation
Section 1: General Provisions
II. – 4:101: Requirements for the Conclusion of a Contract
A contract is concluded, without any further requirement, if the parties:
(a)   intend to enter into a binding legal relationship or bring about some other legal effect; and
(b)   reach a sufficient agreement.

II. – 4:102: How Intention Is Determined
The intention of a party to enter into a binding legal relationship or bring about some other legal effect is to be determined from the party's statements or conduct as they were reasonably understood by the other party.

II. – 4:103: Sufficient Agreement
(1)   Agreement is sufficient if:
(a)   the terms of the contract have been sufficiently defined by the parties for the contract to be given effect; or
(b)   the terms of the contract, or the rights and obligations of the parties under it, can be otherwise sufficiently determined for the contract to be given effect.

(2) If one of the parties refuses to conclude a contract unless the parties have agreed on some specific matter, there is no contract unless agreement on that matter has been reached.

II. – 4:104: Merger Clause

(1) If a contract document contains an individually negotiated term stating that the document embodies all the terms of the contract (a merger clause), any prior statements, undertakings or agreements which are not embodied in the document do not form part of the contract.

(2) If the merger clause is not individually negotiated it establishes only a presumption that the parties intended that their prior statements, undertakings or agreements were not to form part of the contract. This rule may not be excluded or restricted.

(3) The parties' prior statements may be used to interpret the contract. This rule may not be excluded or restricted except by an individually negotiated term.

(4) A party may by statements or conduct be precluded from asserting a merger clause to the extent that the other party has reasonably relied on such statements or conduct.

II. – 4:105: Modification in Certain Form Only

(1) A term in a contract requiring any agreement to modify its terms, or to terminate the relationship resulting from it, to be in a certain form establishes only a presumption that any such agreement is not intended to be legally binding unless it is in that form.

(2) A party may by statements or conduct be precluded from asserting such a term to the extent that the other party has reasonably relied on such statements or conduct.

Section 2: Offer and Acceptance
II. – 4:201: Offer

(1) A proposal amounts to an offer if:
(a) it is intended to result in a contract if the other party accepts it; and
(b) it contains sufficiently definite terms to form a contract.
(2) An offer may be made to one or more specific persons or to the public.
(3) A proposal to supply goods from stock, or a service, at a stated price made by a business in a public advertisement or a catalogue, or by a display of goods, is treated, unless the circumstances indicate otherwise, as an offer to supply at that price until the stock of goods, or the business's capacity to supply the service, is exhausted.

II. – 4:202: Revocation of Offer

(1) An offer may be revoked if the revocation reaches the offeree before the offeree has dispatched an acceptance or, in cases of acceptance by conduct, before the contract has been concluded.

(2) An offer made to the public can be revoked by the same means as were used to make the offer.

(3) However, a revocation of an offer is ineffective if:
(a) the offer indicates that it is irrevocable;
(b) the offer states a fixed time for its acceptance; or
(c) it was reasonable for the offeree to rely on the offer as being irrevocable and the offeree has acted in reliance on the offer.

(4) Paragraph (3) does not apply to an offer if the offeror would have a right under any rule in Books II to IV to withdraw from a contract resulting from its acceptance. The parties may not, to the detriment of the offeror, exclude the application of this rule or derogate from or vary its effects.

II. – 4:203: Rejection of Offer

When a rejection of an offer reaches the offeror, the offer lapses.

II. – 4:204: Acceptance

(1) Any form of statement or conduct by the offeree is an acceptance if it indicates assent to the offer.

(2) Silence or inactivity does not in itself amount to acceptance.

II. – 4:205: Time of Conclusion of the Contract

(1) If an acceptance has been dispatched by the offeree the contract is concluded when the acceptance reaches the offeror.
(2) In the case of acceptance by conduct, the contract is concluded when notice of the conduct reaches the offeror.
(3) If by virtue of the offer, of practices which the parties have established between themselves, or of a usage, the offeree may accept the offer by doing an act without notice to the offeror, the contract is concluded when the offeree begins to do the act.

II. – 4:206: Time Limit for Acceptance

(1) An acceptance of an offer is effective only if it reaches the offeror within the time fixed by the offeror.
(2) If no time has been fixed by the offeror the acceptance is effective only if it reaches the offeror within a reasonable time.
(3) Where an offer may be accepted by performing an act without notice to the offeror, the acceptance is effective only if the act is performed within the time for acceptance fixed by the offeror or, if no such time is fixed, within a reasonable time.

II. – 4:207: Late Acceptance

(1) A late acceptance is nonetheless effective as an acceptance if without undue delay the offeror informs the offeree that it is treated as an effective acceptance.
(2) If a letter or other communication containing a late acceptance shows that it has been dispatched in such circumstances that if its transmission had been normal it would have reached the offeror in due time, the late acceptance is effective as an acceptance unless, without undue delay, the offeror informs the offeree that the offer is considered to have lapsed.

II. – 4:208: Modified Acceptance

(1) A reply by the offeree which states or implies additional or different terms which materially alter the terms of the offer is a rejection and a new offer.
(2) A reply which gives a definite assent to an offer operates as an acceptance even if it states or implies additional or different terms, provided these do not materially alter the terms of the offer. The additional or different terms then become part of the contract.
(3) However, such a reply is treated as a rejection of the offer if:
(a) the offer expressly limits acceptance to the terms of the offer;
(b) the offeror objects to the additional or different terms without undue delay; or
(c) the offeree makes the acceptance conditional upon the offeror's assent to the additional or different terms, and the assent does not reach the offeree within a reasonable time.

II. – 4:209: Conflicting Standard Terms

(1) If the parties have reached agreement except that the offer and acceptance refer to conflicting standard terms, a contract is nonetheless formed. The standard terms form part of the contract to the extent that they are common in substance.
(2) However, no contract is formed if one party:
(a) has indicated in advance, explicitly, and not by way of standard terms, an intention not to be bound by a contract on the basis of paragraph (1); or
(b) without undue delay, informs the other party of such an intention.

II. – 4:210: Formal Confirmation of Contract Between Businesses

If businesses have concluded a contract but have not embodied it in a final document, and one without undue delay sends the other a notice in textual form on a durable medium which purports to be a confirmation of the contract but which contains additional or different terms, such terms become part of the contract unless:
(a) the terms materially alter the terms of the contract; or

(b)   the addressee objects to them without undue delay.

II. – 4:211: Contracts Not Concluded Through Offer and Acceptance
The rules in this Section apply with appropriate adaptations even though the process of conclusion of a contract cannot be analysed into offer and acceptance.

Section 3: Other Juridical Acts
II. – 4:301: Requirements for a Unilateral Juridical Act
The requirements for a unilateral juridical act are:
(a)   that the party doing the act intends to be legally bound or to achieve the relevant legal effect;
(b)   that the act is sufficiently certain; and
(c)   that notice of the act reaches the person to whom it is addressed or, if the act is addressed to the public, the act is made public by advertisement, public notice or otherwise.

II. – 4:302: How Intention Is Determined
The intention of a party to be legally bound or to achieve the relevant legal effect is to be determined from the party's statements or conduct as they were reasonably understood by the person to whom the act is addressed.

II. – 4:303: Right or Benefit May Be Rejected
Where a unilateral juridical act confers a right or benefit on the person to whom it is addressed, that person may reject it by notice to the maker of the act, provided that is done without undue delay and before the right or benefit has been expressly or impliedly accepted. On such rejection, the right or benefit is treated as never having accrued.

Chapter 5: Right of Withdrawal
Section 1: Exercise and Effect
II. – 5:101: Scope and Mandatory Nature
(1)   The provisions in this Section apply where under any rule in Books II to IV a party has a right to withdraw from a contract within a certain period.
(2)   The parties may not, to the detriment of the entitled party, exclude the application of the rules in this Chapter or derogate from or vary their effects.

II. – 5:102: Exercise of Right to Withdraw
(1)   A right to withdraw is exercised by notice to the other party. No reasons need to be given.
(2)   Returning the subject matter of the contract is considered a notice of withdrawal unless the circumstances indicate otherwise.

II. – 5:103: Withdrawal Period
(1)   A right to withdraw may be exercised at any time after the conclusion of the contract and before the end of the withdrawal period.
(2)   The withdrawal period ends fourteen days after the latest of the following times;
(a)   the time of conclusion of the contract;
(b)   the time when the entitled party receives from the other party adequate information on the right to withdraw; or
(c)   if the subject matter of the contract is the delivery of goods, the time when the goods are received.
(3)   The withdrawal period ends no later than one year after the time of conclusion of the contract.
(4)   A notice of withdrawal is timely if dispatched before the end of the withdrawal period.

II. – 5:104: Adequate Information on the Right to Withdraw
Adequate information on the right to withdraw requires that the right is appropriately brought to the entitled party's attention, and that the information provides, in textual form on a durable medium and in clear and comprehensible language, information about how the right may be exercised, the withdrawal period, and the name and address of the person to whom the withdrawal is to be communicated.

II. – 5:105: Effects of Withdrawal

(1)   Withdrawal terminates the contractual relationship and the obligations of both parties under the contract.
(2)   The restitutionary effects of such termination are governed by the rules in Book III, Chapter 3, Section 5, Sub-section 4 (Restitution) as modified by this Article, unless the contract provides otherwise in favour of the withdrawing party.
(3)   Where the withdrawing party has made a payment under the contract, the business has an obligation to return the payment without undue delay, and in any case not later than thirty days after the withdrawal becomes effective.
(4)   The withdrawing party is not liable to pay:
(a)   for any diminution in the value of anything received under the contract caused by inspection and testing;
(b)   for any destruction or loss of, or damage to, anything received under the contract, provided the withdrawing party used reasonable care to prevent such destruction, loss or damage.
(5)   The withdrawing party is liable for any diminution in value caused by normal use, unless that party had not received adequate notice of the right of withdrawal.
(6)   Except as provided in this Article, the withdrawing party does not incur any liability through the exercise of the right of withdrawal.
(7)   If a consumer exercises a right to withdraw from a contract after a business has made use of a contractual right to supply something of equivalent quality and price in case what was ordered is unavailable, the business must bear the cost of returning what the consumer has received under the contract.

II. – 5:106: Linked Contracts

(1)   If a consumer exercises a right of withdrawal from a contract for the supply of goods, other assets or services by a business, the effects of withdrawal extend to any linked contract.
(2)   Where a contract is partially or exclusively financed by a credit contract, they form linked contracts, in particular:
(a)   if the business supplying goods, other assets or services finances the consumer's performance;
(b)   if a third party which finances the consumer's performance uses the services of the business for preparing or concluding the credit contract;
(c)   if the credit contract refers to specific goods, assets or services to be financed with this credit, and if this link between both contracts was suggested by the supplier of the goods, other assets or services, or by the supplier of credit; or
(d)   if there is a similar economic link.
(3)   The provisions of II. – 5:105 (Effects of withdrawal) apply accordingly to the linked contract.
(4)   Paragraph (1) does not apply to credit contracts financing the contracts mentioned in paragraph (2)(f) of the following Article.

Section 2: Particular Rights of Withdrawal

II. – 5:201: Contracts Negotiated Away from Business Premises

(1)   A consumer is entitled to withdraw from a contract under which a business supplies goods, other assets or services, including financial services, to the consumer, or is granted a personal security by the consumer, if the consumer's offer or acceptance was expressed away from the business premises.
(2)   Paragraph (1) does not apply to:
(a)   a contract concluded by means of an automatic vending machine or automated commercial premises;
(b)   a contract concluded with telecommunications operators through the use of public payphones;
(c)   a contract for the construction and sale of immovable property or relating to other immovable property rights, except for rental;

(d) a contract for the supply of foodstuffs, beverages or other goods intended for everyday consumption supplied to the home, residence or workplace of the consumer by regular roundsmen;

(e) a contract concluded by means of distance communication, but outside of an organised distance sales or service-provision scheme run by the supplier;

(f) a contract for the supply of goods, other assets or services whose price depends on fluctuations in the financial market outside the supplier's control, which may occur during the withdrawal period;

(g) a contract concluded at an auction;

(h) travel and baggage insurance policies or similar short-term insurance policies of less than one month's duration.

(3) If the business has exclusively used means of distance communication for concluding the contract, paragraph (1) also does not apply if the contract is for:

(a) the supply of accommodation, transport, catering or leisure services, where the business undertakes, when the contract is concluded, to supply these services on a specific date or within a specific period;

(b) the supply of services other than financial services if performance has begun, at the consumer's express and informed request, before the end of the withdrawal period referred to in II. – 5:103 (Withdrawal period) paragraph (1);

(c) the supply of goods made to the consumer's specifications or clearly personalised or which, by reason of their nature, cannot be returned or are liable to deteriorate or expire rapidly;

(d) the supply of audio or video recordings or computer software
(i)   which were unsealed by the consumer, or
(ii)   which can be downloaded or reproduced for permanent use, in case of supply by electronic means;

(e) the supply of newspapers, periodicals and magazines;

(f) gaming and lottery services.

(4) With regard to financial services, paragraph (1) also does not apply to contracts that have been fully performed by both parties, at the consumer's express request, before the consumer exercises his or her right of withdrawal.

II. – 5:202: Timeshare Contracts

(1) A consumer who acquires a right to use immovable property under a timeshare contract with a business is entitled to withdraw from the contract.

(2) Where a consumer exercises the right of withdrawal under paragraph (1), the contract may require the consumer to reimburse those expenses which:

(a) have been incurred as a result of the conclusion of and withdrawal from the contract;

(b) correspond to legal formalities which must be completed before the end of the period referred to in II. – 5:103 (Withdrawal period) paragraph (1);

(c) are reasonable and appropriate;

(d) are expressly mentioned in the contract; and

(e) are in conformity with any applicable rules on such expenses.

The consumer is not obliged to reimburse any expenses when exercising the right of withdrawal in the situation covered by paragraph (1) of II. – 3:109 (Remedies for breach of information duties).

(3) The business must not demand or accept any advance payment by the consumer during the period in which the latter may exercise the right of withdrawal. The business is obliged to return any such payment received.

Chapter 6: Representation
II. – 6:101: Scope

(1) This Chapter applies to the external relationships created by acts of representation – that is to say, the relationships between:

(a)   the principal and the third party; and
(b)   the representative and the third party.
(2)   It applies also to situations where a person purports to be a representative without actually being a representative.
(3)   It does not apply to the internal relationship between the representative and the principal.

II. – 6:102: Definitions

(1)   A "representative" is a person who has authority to affect directly the legal position of another person, the principal, in relation to a third party by acting on behalf of the principal.
(2)   The "authority" of a representative is the power to affect the principal's legal position.
(3)   The "authorisation" of the representative is the granting or maintaining of the authority.
(4)   "Acting without authority" includes acting beyond the scope of the authority granted.
(5)   A "third party", in this Chapter, includes the representative who, when acting for the principal, also acts in a personal capacity as the other party to the transaction.

II. – 6:103: Authorisation

(1)   The authority of a representative may be granted by the principal or by the law.
(2)   The principal's authorisation may be express or implied.
(3)   If a person causes a third party reasonably and in good faith to believe that the person has authorised a representative to perform certain acts, the person is treated as a principal who has so authorised the apparent representative.

II. – 6:104: Scope of Authority

(1)   The scope of the representative's authority is determined by the grant.
(2)   The representative has authority to perform all incidental acts necessary to achieve the purposes for which the authority was granted.
(3)   A representative has authority to delegate authority to another person (the delegate) to do acts on behalf of the principal which it is not reasonable to expect the representative to do personally. The rules of this Chapter apply to acts done by the delegate.

II. – 6:105: When Representative's Act Affects Principal's Legal Position

When the representative acts:
(a)   in the name of a principal or otherwise in such a way as to indicate to the third party an intention to affect the legal position of a principal; and
(b)   within the scope of the representative's authority,
the act affects the legal position of the principal in relation to the third party as if it had been done by the principal. It does not as such give rise to any legal relation between the representative and the third party.

II. – 6:106: Representative Acting in Own Name

When the representative, despite having authority, does an act in the representative's own name or otherwise in such a way as not to indicate to the third party an intention to affect the legal position of a principal, the act affects the legal position of the representative in relation to the third party as if done by the representative in a personal capacity. It does not as such affect the legal position of the principal in relation to the third party unless this is specifically provided for by any rule of law.

II. – 6:107: Person Purporting to Act as Representative but Not Having Authority

(1)   When a person acts in the name of a principal or otherwise in such a way as to indicate to the third party an intention to affect the legal position of a principal but acts without authority, the act does not affect the legal position of the purported principal or, save as provided in paragraph (2), give rise to legal relations between the unauthorised person and the third party.
(2)   Failing ratification by the purported principal, the person is liable to pay the third party such damages as will place the third party in the same position as if the person had acted with authority.
(3)   Paragraph (2) does not apply if the third party knew or could reasonably be expected to have known of the lack of authority.

II. – 6:108: Unidentified Principal

If a representative acts for a principal whose identity is to be revealed later, but fails to reveal that identity within a reasonable time after a request by the third party, the representative is treated as having acted in a personal capacity.

II. – 6:109: Conflict of Interest

(1)   If an act done by a representative involves the representative in a conflict of interest of which the third party knew or could reasonably be expected to have known, the principal may avoid the act according to the provisions of II. – 7:209(Notice of avoidance) to II. – 7:213 (Partial avoidance).

(2)   There is presumed to be a conflict of interest where:

(a)   the representative also acted as representative for the third party; or

(b)   the transaction was with the representative in a personal capacity.

(3)   However, the principal may not avoid the act:

(a)   if the representative acted with the principal's prior consent; or

(b)   if the representative had disclosed the conflict of interest to the principal and the principal did not object within a reasonable time;

(c)   if the principal otherwise knew, or could reasonably be expected to have known, of the representative's involvement in the conflict of interest and did not object within a reasonable time; or

(d)   if, for any other reason, the representative was entitled as against the principal to do the act by virtue of IV. D. – 5:101 (Self-contracting) or IV. D. – 5:102 (Double mandate).

II. – 6:110: Several Representatives

Where several representatives have authority to act for the same principal, each of them may act separately.

II. – 6:111: Ratification

(1)   Where a person purports to act as a representative but acts without authority, the purported principal may ratify the act.

(2)   Upon ratification, the act is considered as having been done with authority, without prejudice to the rights of other persons.

(3)   The third party who knows that an act was done without authority may by notice to the purported principal specify a reasonable period of time for ratification. If the act is not ratified within that period ratification is no longer possible.

II. – 6:112: Effect of Ending or Restriction of Authorisation

(1)   The authority of a representative continues in relation to a third party who knew of the authority notwithstanding the ending or restriction of the representative's authorisation until the third party knows or can reasonably be expected to know of the ending or restriction.

(2)   Where the principal is under an obligation to the third party not to end or restrict the representative's authorisation, the authority of a representative continues notwithstanding an ending or restriction of the authorisation even if the third party knows of the ending or restriction.

(3)   The third party can reasonably be expected to know of the ending or restriction if, in particular, it has been communicated or publicised in the same way as the granting of the authority was originally communicated or publicised.

(4)   Notwithstanding the ending of authorisation, the representative continues to have authority for a reasonable time to perform those acts which are necessary to protect the interests of the principal or the principal's successors.

Chapter 7: Grounds of Invalidity
Section 1: General Provisions
II. – 7:101: Scope

(1)   This Chapter deals with the effects of:

(a)   mistake, fraud, threats, or unfair exploitation; and

(b)   infringement of fundamental principles or mandatory rules.
(2)   It does not deal with lack of capacity.
(3)   It applies in relation to contracts and, with any necessary adaptations, other juridical acts.

II. – 7:102: Initial Impossibility or Lack of Right or Authority to Dispose

A contract is not invalid, in whole or in part, merely because at the time it is concluded performance of any obligation assumed is impossible, or because a party has no right or authority to dispose of any assets to which the contract relates.

Section 2: Vitiated Consent or Intention
II. – 7:201: Mistake

(1)   A party may avoid a contract for mistake of fact or law existing when the contract was concluded if:
(a)   the party, but for the mistake, would not have concluded the contract or would have done so only on fundamentally different terms and the other party knew or could reasonably be expected to have known this; and
(b)   the other party;
      (i)   caused the mistake;
      (ii)   caused the contract to be concluded in mistake by leaving the mistaken party in error, contrary to good faith and fair dealing, when the other party knew or could reasonably be expected to have known of the mistake;
      (iii) caused the contract to be concluded in mistake by failing to comply with a pre-contractual information duty or a duty to make available a means of correcting input errors; or
      (iv)   made the same mistake.
(2)   However a party may not avoid the contract for mistake if:
(a)   the mistake was inexcusable in the circumstances; or
(b)   the risk of the mistake was assumed, or in the circumstances should be borne, by that party.

II. – 7:202: Inaccuracy in Communication May Be Treated as Mistake

An inaccuracy in the expression or transmission of a statement is treated as a mistake of the person who made or sent the statement.

II. – 7:203: Adaptation of Contract in Case of Mistake

(1)   If a party is entitled to avoid the contract for mistake but the other party performs, or indicates a willingness to perform, the obligations under the contract as it was understood by the party entitled to avoid it, the contract is treated as having been concluded as that party understood it. This applies only if the other party performs, or indicates a willingness to perform, without undue delay after being informed of the manner in which the party entitled to avoid it understood the contract and before that party acts in reliance on any notice of avoidance.
(2)   After such performance or indication the right to avoid is lost and any earlier notice of avoidance is ineffective.
(3)   Where both parties have made the same mistake, the court may at the request of either party bring the contract into accordance with what might reasonably have been agreed had the mistake not occurred.

II. – 7:204: Liability for Loss Caused by Reliance on Incorrect Information

(1)   A party who has concluded a contract in reasonable reliance on incorrect information given by the other party in the course of negotiations has a right to damages for loss suffered as a result if the provider of the information:
(a)   believed the information to be incorrect or had no reasonable grounds for believing it to be correct; and
(b)   knew or could reasonably be expected to have known that the recipient would rely on the information in deciding whether or not to conclude the contract on the agreed terms.

(2)   This Article applies even if there is no right to avoid the contract.

II. – 7:205: Fraud

(1)   A party may avoid a contract when the other party has induced the conclusion of the contract by fraudulent misrepresentation, whether by words or conduct, or fraudulent non-disclosure of any information which good faith and fair dealing, or any pre-contractual information duty, required that party to disclose.

(2)   A misrepresentation is fraudulent if it is made with knowledge or belief that the representation is false and is intended to induce the recipient to make a mistake. A non-disclosure is fraudulent if it is intended to induce the person from whom the information is withheld to make a mistake.

(3)   In determining whether good faith and fair dealing required a party to disclose particular information, regard should be had to all the circumstances, including:

(a)   whether the party had special expertise;

(b)   the cost to the party of acquiring the relevant information;

(c)   whether the other party could reasonably acquire the information by other means; and

(d)   the apparent importance of the information to the other party.

II. – 7:206: Coercion or Threats

(1)   A party may avoid a contract when the other party has induced the conclusion of the contract by coercion or by the threat of an imminent and serious harm which it is wrongful to inflict, or wrongful to use as a means to obtain the conclusion of the contract.

(2)   A threat is not regarded as inducing the contract if in the circumstances the threatened party had a reasonable alternative.

II. – 7:207: Unfair Exploitation

(1)   A party may avoid a contract if, at the time of the conclusion of the contract:

(a)   the party was dependent on or had a relationship of trust with the other party, was in economic distress or had urgent needs, was improvident, ignorant, inexperienced or lacking in bargaining skill; and

(b)   the other party knew or could reasonably be expected to have known this and, given the circumstances and purpose of the contract, exploited the first party's situation by taking an excessive benefit or grossly unfair advantage.

(2)   Upon the request of the party entitled to avoidance, a court may if it is appropriate adapt the contract in order to bring it into accordance with what might have been agreed had the requirements of good faith and fair dealing been observed.

(3)   A court may similarly adapt the contract upon the request of a party receiving notice of avoidance for unfair exploitation, provided that this party informs the party who gave the notice without undue delay after receiving it and before that party has acted in reliance on it.

II. – 7:208: Third Persons

(1)   Where a third person for whose acts a party is responsible or who with a party's assent is involved in the making of a contract:

(a)   causes a mistake, or knows of or could reasonably be expected to know of a mistake; or

(b)   is guilty of fraud, coercion, threats or unfair exploitation, remedies under this Section are available as if the behaviour or knowledge had been that of the party.

(2)   Where a third person for whose acts a party is not responsible and who does not have the party's assent to be involved in the making of a contract is guilty of fraud, coercion, threats or unfair exploitation, remedies under this Section are available if the party knew or could reasonably be expected to have known of the relevant facts, or at the time of avoidance has not acted in reliance on the contract.

II. – 7:209: Notice of Avoidance

Avoidance under this Section is effected by notice to the other party.

II. – 7:210: Time
A notice of avoidance under this Section is ineffective unless given within a reasonable time, with due regard to the circumstances, after the avoiding party knew or could reasonably be expected to have known of the relevant facts or became capable of acting freely.

II. – 7:211: Confirmation
If a party who is entitled to avoid a contract under this Section confirms it, expressly or impliedly, after the period of time for giving notice of avoidance has begun to run, avoidance is excluded.

II. – 7:212: Effects of Avoidance
(1)   A contract which may be avoided under this Section is valid until avoided but, once avoided, is retrospectively invalid from the beginning.
(2)   The question whether either party has a right to the return of whatever has been transferred or supplied under a contract which has been avoided under this Section, or a monetary equivalent, is regulated by the rules on unjustified enrichment.
(3)   The effect of avoidance under this Section on the ownership of property which has been transferred under the avoided contract is governed by the rules on the transfer of property.

II. – 7:213: Partial Avoidance
If a ground of avoidance under this Section affects only particular terms of a contract, the effect of an avoidance is limited to those terms unless, giving due consideration to all the circumstances of the case, it is unreasonable to uphold the remaining contract.

II. – 7:214: Damages for Loss
(1)   A party who has the right to avoid a contract under this Section (or who had such a right before it was lost by the effect of time limits or confirmation) is entitled, whether or not the contract is avoided, to damages from the other party for any loss suffered as a result of the mistake, fraud, coercion, threats or unfair exploitation, provided that the other party knew or could reasonably be expected to have known of the ground for avoidance.
(2)   The damages recoverable are such as to place the aggrieved party as nearly as possible in the position in which that party would have been if the contract had not been concluded, with the further limitation that, if the party does not avoid the contract, the damages are not to exceed the loss caused by the mistake, fraud, coercion, threats or unfair exploitation.
(3)   In other respects the rules on damages for non-performance of a contractual obligation apply with any appropriate adaptation.

II. – 7:215: Exclusion or Restriction of Remedies
(1)   Remedies for fraud, coercion, threats and unfair exploitation cannot be excluded or restricted.
(2)   Remedies for mistake may be excluded or restricted unless the exclusion or restriction is contrary to good faith and fair dealing.

II. – 7:216: Overlapping Remedies
A party who is entitled to a remedy under this Section in circumstances which afford that party a remedy for non-performance may pursue either remedy.

Section 3: Infringement of Fundamental Principles or Mandatory Rules
II. – 7:301: Contracts Infringing Fundamental Principles
A contract is void to the extent that:
(a)   it infringes a principle recognised as fundamental in the laws of the Member States of the European Union; and
(b)   nullity is required to give effect to that principle.

II. – 7:302: Contracts Infringing Mandatory Rules
(1)   Where a contract is not void under the preceding Article but infringes a mandatory rule of law, the effects of that infringement on the validity of the contract are the effects, if any, expressly prescribed by that mandatory rule.

(2)   Where the mandatory rule does not expressly prescribe the effects of an infringement on the validity of a contract, a court may:
(a)   declare the contract to be valid;
(b)   avoid the contract, with retrospective effect, in whole or in part; or
(c)   modify the contract or its effects.
(3)   A decision reached under paragraph (2) should be an appropriate and proportional response to the infringement, having regard to all relevant circumstances, including:
(a)   the purpose of the rule which has been infringed;
(b)   the category of persons for whose protection the rule exists;
(c)   any sanction that may be imposed under the rule infringed;
(d)   the seriousness of the infringement;
(e)   whether the infringement was intentional; and
(f)   the closeness of the relationship between the infringement and the contract.

II. – 7:303: Effects of Nullity or Avoidance

(1)   The question whether either party has a right to the return of whatever has been transferred or supplied under a contract, or part of a contract, which is void or has been avoided under this Section, or a monetary equivalent, is regulated by the rules on unjustified enrichment.
(2)   The effect of nullity or avoidance under this Section on the ownership of property which has been transferred under the void or avoided contract, or part of a contract, is governed by the rules on the transfer of property.
(3)   This Article is subject to the powers of the court to modify the contract or its effects.

II. – 7:304: Damages for Loss

(1)   A party to a contract which is void or avoided, in whole or in part, under this Section is entitled to damages from the other party for any loss suffered as a result of the invalidity, provided that the first party did not know and could not reasonably be expected to have known, and the other party knew or could reasonably be expected to have known, of the infringement.
(2)   The damages recoverable are such as to place the aggrieved party as nearly as possible in the position in which that party would have been if the contract had not been concluded or the infringing term had not been included.

Chapter 8: Interpretation
Section 1: Interpretation of Contracts
II. – 8:101: General Rules

(1)   A contract is to be interpreted according to the common intention of the parties even if this differs from the literal meaning of the words.
(2)   If one party intended the contract, or a term or expression used in it, to have a particular meaning, and at the time of the conclusion of the contract the other party was aware, or could reasonably be expected to have been aware, of the first party's intention, the contract is to be interpreted in the way intended by the first party.
(3)   The contract is, however, to be interpreted according to the meaning which a reasonable person would give to it:
(a)   if an intention cannot be established under the preceding paragraphs; or
(b)   if the question arises with a person, not being a party to the contract or a person who by law has no better rights than such a party, who has reasonably and in good faith relied on the contract's apparent meaning.

II. – 8:102: Relevant Matters

(1)   In interpreting the contract, regard may be had, in particular, to:
(a)   the circumstances in which it was concluded, including the preliminary negotiations;
(b)   the conduct of the parties, even subsequent to the conclusion of the contract;

(c)   the interpretation which has already been given by the parties to terms or expressions which are the same as, or similar to, those used in the contract and the practices they have established between themselves;

(d)   the meaning commonly given to such terms or expressions in the branch of activity concerned and the interpretation such terms or expressions may already have received;

(e)   the nature and purpose of the contract;

(f)   usages; and

(g)   good faith and fair dealing.

(2)   In a question with a person, not being a party to the contract or a person such as an assignee who by law has no better rights than such a party, who has reasonably and in good faith relied on the contract's apparent meaning, regard may be had to the circumstances mentioned in sub-paragraphs (a) to (c) above only to the extent that those circumstances were known to, or could reasonably be expected to have been known to, that person.

II. – 8:103: Interpretation Against Supplier of Term or Dominant Party

(1)   Where there is doubt about the meaning of a term not individually negotiated, an interpretation of the term against the party who supplied it is to be preferred.

(2)   Where there is doubt about the meaning of any other term, and that term has been established under the dominant influence of one party, an interpretation of the term against that party is to be preferred.

II. – 8:104: Preference for Negotiated Terms

Terms which have been individually negotiated take preference over those which have not.

II. – 8:105: Reference to Contract as a Whole

Terms and expressions are to be interpreted in the light of the whole contract in which they appear.

II. – 8:106: Preference for Interpretation Which Gives Terms Effect

An interpretation which renders the terms of the contract lawful, or effective, is to be preferred to one which would not.

II. – 8:107: Linguistic Discrepancies

Where a contract document is in two or more language versions none of which is stated to be authoritative, there is, in case of discrepancy between the versions, a preference for the interpretation according to the version in which the contract was originally drawn up.

Section 2: Interpretation of Other Juridical Acts
II. – 8:201: General Rules

(1)   A unilateral juridical act is to be interpreted in the way in which it could reasonably be expected to be understood by the person to whom it is addressed.

(2)   If the person making the juridical act intended the act, or a term or expression used in it, to have a particular meaning, and at the time of the act the person to whom it was addressed was aware, or could reasonably be expected to have been aware, of the first person's intention, the act is to be interpreted in the way intended by the first person.

(3)   The act is, however, to be interpreted according to the meaning which a reasonable person would give to it:

(a)   if neither paragraph (1) nor paragraph (2) applies; or

(b)   if the question arises with a person, not being the addressee or a person who by law has no better rights than the addressee, who has reasonably and in good faith relied on the contract's apparent meaning.

II. – 8:202: Application of Other Rules by Analogy

The provisions of Section 1, apart from its first Article, apply with appropriate adaptations to the interpretation of a juridical act other than a contract.

Chapter 9: Contents and Effects of Contracts
Section 1: Contents
II. – 9:101: Terms of a Contract

(1)   The terms of a contract may be derived from the express or tacit agreement of the parties, from rules of law or from practices established between the parties or usages.

(2)   Where it is necessary to provide for a matter which the parties have not foreseen or provided for, a court may imply an additional term, having regard in particular to:

(a)   the nature and purpose of the contract;

(b)   the circumstances in which the contract was concluded; and

(c)   the requirements of good faith and fair dealing.

(3)   Any term implied under paragraph (2) should, where possible, be such as to give effect to what the parties, had they provided for the matter, would probably have agreed.

(4)   Paragraph (2) does not apply if the parties have deliberately left a matter unprovided for, accepting the consequences of so doing.

II. – 9:102: Certain Pre-Contractual Statements Regarded as Contract Terms

(1)   A statement made by one party before a contract is concluded is regarded as a term of the contract if the other party reasonably understood it as being made on the basis that it would form part of the contract terms if a contract were concluded. In assessing whether the other party was reasonable in understanding the statement in that way account may be taken of:

(a)   the apparent importance of the statement to the other party;

(b)   whether the party was making the statement in the course of business; and

(c)   the relative expertise of the parties.

(2)   If one of the parties to a contract is a business and before the contract is concluded makes a statement, either to the other party or publicly, about the specific characteristics of what is to be supplied by that business under the contract, the statement is regarded as a term of the contract unless:

(a)   the other party was aware when the contract was concluded, or could reasonably be expected to have been so aware, that the statement was incorrect or could not otherwise be relied on as such a term; or

(b)   the other party's decision to conclude the contract was not influenced by the statement.

(3)   For the purposes of paragraph (2), a statement made by a person engaged in advertising or marketing on behalf of the business is treated as being made by the business.

(4)   Where the other party is a consumer then, for the purposes of paragraph (2), a public statement made by or on behalf of a producer or other person in earlier links of the business chain between the producer and the consumer is treated as being made by the business unless the business, at the time of conclusion of the contract, did not know and could not reasonably be expected to have known of it.

(5)   In the circumstances covered by paragraph (4) a business which at the time of conclusion of the contract did not know and could not reasonably be expected to have known that the statement was incorrect has a right to be indemnified by the person making the statement for any liability incurred as a result of that paragraph.

(6)   In relations between a business and a consumer the parties may not, to the detriment of the consumer, exclude the application of this Article or derogate from or vary its effects.

II. – 9:103: Terms Not Individually Negotiated

(1)   Terms supplied by one party and not individually negotiated may be invoked against the other party only if the other party was aware of them, or if the party supplying the terms took reasonable steps to draw the other party's attention to them, before or when the contract was concluded.

(2)   If a contract is to be concluded by electronic means, the party supplying any terms which have not been individually negotiated may invoke them against the other party only if they are made available to the other party in textual form.

(3) For the purposes of this Article
(a) "not individually negotiated" has the meaning given by II. – 1:110 (Terms "not individually negotiated"); and
(b) terms are not sufficiently brought to the other party's attention by a mere reference to them in a contract document, even if that party signs the document.

II. – 9:104: Determination of Price

Where the amount of the price payable under a contract cannot be determined from the terms agreed by the parties, from any other applicable rule of law or from usages or practices, the price payable is the price normally charged in comparable circumstances at the time of the conclusion of the contract or, if no such price is available, a reasonable price.

II. – 9:105: Unilateral Determination by a Party

Where the price or any other contractual term is to be determined by one party and that party's determination is grossly unreasonable then, notwithstanding any provision in the contract to the contrary, a reasonable price or other term is substituted.

II. – 9:106: Determination by a Third Person

(1) Where a third person is to determine the price or any other contractual term and cannot or will not do so, a court may, unless this is inconsistent with the terms of the contract, appoint another person to determine it.
(2) If a price or other term determined by a third person is grossly unreasonable, a reasonable price or term is substituted.

II. – 9:107: Reference to a Non-Existent Factor

Where the price or any other contractual term is to be determined by reference to a factor which does not exist or has ceased to exist or to be accessible, the nearest equivalent factor is substituted unless this would be unreasonable in the circumstances, in which case a reasonable price or other term is substituted.

II. – 9:108: Quality

Where the quality of anything to be supplied or provided under the contract cannot be determined from the terms agreed by the parties, from any other applicable rule of law or from usages or practices, the quality required is the quality which the recipient could reasonably expect in the circumstances.

II. – 9:109: Language

Where the language to be used for communications relating to the contract or the rights or obligations arising from it cannot be determined from the terms agreed by the parties, from any other applicable rule of law or from usages or practices, the language to be used is that used for the conclusion of the contract.

Section 2: Simulation
II. – 9:201: Effect of Simulation

(1) When the parties have concluded a contract or an apparent contract and have deliberately done so in such a way that it has an apparent effect different from the effect which the parties intend it to have, the parties' true intention prevails.
(2) However, the apparent effect prevails in relation to a person, not being a party to the contract or apparent contract or a person who by law has no better rights than such a party, who has reasonably and in good faith relied on the apparent effect.

Section 3: Effect of Stipulation in Favour of a Third Party
II. – 9:301: Basic Rules

(1) The parties to a contract may, by the contract, confer a right or other benefit on a third party. The third party need not be in existence or identified at the time the contract is concluded.
(2) The nature and content of the third party's right or benefit are determined by the contract and are subject to any conditions or other limitations under the contract.

(3)   The benefit conferred may take the form of an exclusion or limitation of the third party's liability to one of the contracting parties.

II. – 9:302: Rights, Remedies and Defences

Where one of the contracting parties is bound to render a performance to the third party under the contract, then, in the absence of provision to the contrary in the contract:

(a)   the third party has the same rights to performance and remedies for non-performance as if the contracting party was bound to render the performance under a binding unilateral undertaking in favour of the third party; and

(b)   the contracting party may assert against the third party all defences which the contracting party could assert against the other party to the contract.

II. – 9:303: Rejection or Revocation of Benefit

(1)   The third party may reject the right or benefit by notice to either of the contracting parties, if that is done without undue delay after being notified of the right or benefit and before it has been expressly or impliedly accepted. On such rejection, the right or benefit is treated as never having accrued to the third party.

(2)   The contracting parties may remove or modify the contractual term conferring the right or benefit if this is done before either of them has given the third party notice that the right or benefit has been conferred. The contract determines whether and by whom and in what circumstances the right or benefit can be revoked or modified after that time.

(3)   Even if the right or benefit conferred is by virtue of the contract revocable or subject to modification, the right to revoke or modify is lost if the parties have, or the party having the right to revoke or modify has, led the third party to believe that it is not revocable or subject to modification and if the third party has reasonably acted in reliance on it.

Section 4: Unfair Terms
II. – 9:401: Mandatory Nature of Following Provisions

The parties may not exclude the application of the provisions in this Section or derogate from or vary their effects.

II. – 9:402: Duty of Transparency in Terms Not Individually Negotiated

(1)   A person who supplies terms which have not been individually negotiated has a duty to ensure that they are drafted and communicated in plain, intelligible language.

(2)   In a contract between a business and a consumer a term which has been supplied by the business in breach of the duty of transparency imposed by paragraph (1) may on that ground alone be considered unfair.

II. – 9:403: Meaning of "Unfair" in Contracts Between a Business and a Consumer

In a contract between a business and a consumer, a term [which has not been individually negotiated] is unfair for the purposes of this Section if it is supplied by the business and if it significantly disadvantages the consumer, contrary to good faith and fair dealing.

II. – 9:404: Meaning of "Unfair" in Contracts Between Non-Business Parties

In a contract between parties neither of whom is a business, a term is unfair for the purposes of this Section only if it is a term forming part of standard terms supplied by one party and significantly disadvantages the other party, contrary to good faith and fair dealing.

II. – 9:405: Meaning of "Unfair" in Contracts Between Businesses

A term in a contract between businesses is unfair for the purposes of this Section only if it is a term forming part of standard terms supplied by one party and of such a nature that its use grossly deviates from good commercial practice, contrary to good faith and fair dealing.

II. – 9:406: Exclusions from Unfairness Test

(1)   Contract terms are not subjected to an unfairness test under this Section if they are based on:

(a)   provisions of the applicable law;

(b)   international conventions to which the Member States are parties, or to which the Euro-
      pean Union is a party; or
(c)   these rules.
(2)   For contract terms which are drafted in plain and intelligible language, the unfairness test
extends neither to the definition of the main subject matter of the contract, nor to the adequacy
of the price to be paid.

II. – 9:407: Factors to Be Taken into Account in Assessing Unfairness

(1)   When assessing the unfairness of a contractual term for the purposes of this Section,
regard is to be had to the duty of transparency under II. – 9:402 (Duty of transparency in terms
not individually negotiated), to the nature of what is to be provided under the contract, to the
circumstances prevailing during the conclusion of the contract, to the other terms of the
contract and to the terms of any other contract on which the contract depends.
(2)   For the purposes of II. – 9:403 (Meaning of "unfair" in contracts between a business and a
consumer) the circumstances prevailing during the conclusion of the contract include the extent to which the consumer was given a real opportunity to become acquainted with the term
before the conclusion of the contract.

II. – 9:408: Effects of Unfair Terms

(1)   A term which is unfair under this Section is not binding on the party who did not supply it.
(2)   If the contract can reasonably be maintained without the unfair term, the other terms
remain binding on the parties.

II. – 9:409: Exclusive Jurisdiction Clauses

(1)   A term in a contract between a business and a consumer is unfair for the purposes of this
Section if it is supplied by the business and if it confers exclusive jurisdiction for all disputes
arising under the contract on the court for the place where the business is domiciled.
(2)   Paragraph (1) does not apply if the chosen court is also the court for the place where the
consumer is domiciled.

II. – 9:410: Terms Which Are Presumed to Be Unfair in Contracts Between a Business and a Consumer

(1)   A term in a contract between a business and a consumer is presumed to be unfair for the
purposes of this Section if it is supplied by the business and if it:
(a)   excludes or limits the liability of a business for death or personal injury caused to a con-
      sumer through an act or omission of that business;
(b)   inappropriately excludes or limits the remedies, including any right to set-off, available to
      the consumer against the business or a third party for non-performance by the business of
      obligations under the contract;
(c)   makes binding on a consumer an obligation which is subject to a condition the fulfilment
      of which depends solely on the intention of the business;
(d)   permits a business to keep money paid by a consumer if the latter decides not to conclude
      the contract, or perform obligations under it, without providing for the consumer to
      receive compensation of an equivalent amount from the business in the reverse situation;
(e)   requires a consumer who fails to perform his or her obligations to pay a disproportionately
      high amount of damages;
(f)   entitles a business to withdraw from or terminate the contractual relationship on a discre-
      tionary basis without giving the same right to the consumer, or entitles a business to keep
      money paid for services not yet supplied in the case where the business withdraws from or
      terminates the contractual relationship;
(g)   enables a business to terminate a contractual relationship of indeterminate duration with-
      out reasonable notice, except where there are serious grounds for doing so; this does not
      affect terms in financial services contracts where there is a valid reason, provided that the
      supplier is required to inform the other contracting party thereof immediately;
(h)   automatically extends a contract of fixed duration unless the consumer indicates other-
      wise, in cases where such terms provide for an unreasonably early deadline;

(i)   enables a business to alter the terms of the contract unilaterally without a valid reason which is specified in the contract; this does not affect terms under which a supplier of financial services reserves the right to change the rate of interest to be paid by, or to, the consumer, or the amount of other charges for financial services without notice where there is a valid reason, provided that the supplier is required to inform the consumer at the earliest opportunity and that the consumer is free to terminate the contractual relationship with immediate effect; neither does it affect terms under which a business reserves the right to alter unilaterally the conditions of a contract of indeterminate duration, provided that the business is required to inform the consumer with reasonable notice, and that the consumer is free to terminate the contractual relationship;

(j)   enables a business to alter unilaterally without a valid reason any characteristics of the goods, other assets or services to be provided;

(k)   provides that the price of goods or other assets is to be determined at the time of delivery or supply, or allows a business to increase the price without giving the consumer the right to withdraw if the increased price is too high in relation to the price agreed at the conclusion of the contract; this does not affect price-indexation clauses, where lawful, provided that the method by which prices vary is explicitly described;

(l)   gives a business the right to determine whether the goods, other assets or services supplied are in conformity with the contract, or gives the business the exclusive right to interpret any term of the contract;

(m)   limits the obligation of a business to respect commitments undertaken by its agents, or makes its commitments subject to compliance with a particular formality;

(n)   obliges a consumer to fulfil all his or her obligations where the business fails to fulfil its own;

(o)   allows a business to transfer its rights and obligations under the contract without the consumer's consent, if this could reduce the guarantees available to the consumer;

(p)   excludes or restricts a consumer's right to take legal action or to exercise any other remedy, in particular by referring the consumer to arbitration proceedings which are not covered by legal provisions, by unduly restricting the evidence available to the consumer, or by shifting a burden of proof on to the consumer;

(q)   allows a business, where what has been ordered is unavailable, to supply an equivalent without having expressly informed the consumer of this possibility and of the fact that the business must bear the cost of returning what the consumer has received under the contract if the consumer exercises a right to withdraw.

(2)   Subparagraphs (g), (i) and (k) do not apply to:

(a)   transactions in transferable securities, financial instruments and other products or services where the price is linked to fluctuations in a stock exchange quotation or index or a financial market rate beyond the control of the business;

(b)   contracts for the purchase or sale of foreign currency, traveller's cheques or international money orders denominated in foreign currency.

BOOK III OBLIGATIONS AND CORRESPONDING RIGHTS
Chapter 1: General
III. – 1:101: Scope of Book

This Book applies, except as otherwise provided, to all obligations within the scope of these rules, whether they are contractual or not, and to corresponding rights to performance.

III. – 1:102: Definitions

(1)   An obligation is a duty to perform which one party to a legal relationship, the debtor, owes to another party, the creditor.

(2)   Performance of an obligation is the doing by the debtor of what is to be done under the obligation or the not doing by the debtor of what is not to be done.

(3) Non-performance of an obligation is any failure to perform the obligation, whether or not excused, and includes delayed performance and any other performance which is not in accordance with the terms regulating the obligation.

(4) An obligation is reciprocal in relation to another obligation if:

(a) performance of the obligation is due in exchange for performance of the other obligation;

(b) it is an obligation to facilitate or accept performance of the other obligation; or

(c) it is so clearly connected to the other obligation or its subject matter that performance of the one can reasonably be regarded as dependent on performance of the other.

(5) The terms regulating an obligation may be derived from a contract or other juridical act, the law or a legally binding usage or practice, or a court order; and similarly for the terms regulating a right.

III. – 1:103: Good Faith and Fair Dealing

(1) A person has a duty to act in accordance with good faith and fair dealing in performing an obligation, in exercising a right to performance, in pursuing or defending a remedy for non-performance, or in exercising a right to terminate an obligation or contractual relationship.

(2) The duty may not be excluded or limited by contract or other juridical act.

(3) Breach of the duty does not give rise directly to the remedies for nonperformance of an obligation but may preclude the person in breach from exercising or relying on a right, remedy or defence which that person would otherwise have.

III. – 1:104: Co-operation

The debtor and creditor are obliged to co-operate with each other when and to the extent that this can reasonably be expected for the performance of the debtor's obligation.

III. – 1:105: Non-Discrimination

Chapter 2 (Non-discrimination) of Book II applies with appropriate adaptations to:

(a) the performance of any obligation to provide access to, or supply, goods, other assets or services which are available to members of the public;

(b) the exercise of a right to performance of any such obligation or the pursuing or defending of any remedy for non-performance of any such obligation; and

(c) the exercise of a right to terminate any such obligation.

III. – 1:106: Conditional Rights and Obligations

(1) The terms regulating a right, obligation or contractual relationship may provide that it is conditional upon the occurrence of an uncertain future event, so that it takes effect only if the event occurs (suspensive condition) or comes to an end if the event occurs (resolutive condition).

(2) Upon fulfilment of a suspensive condition, the relevant right, obligation or relationship takes effect.

(3) Upon fulfilment of a resolutive condition, the relevant right, obligation or relationship comes to an end.

(4) When a party, contrary to the duty of good faith and fair dealing or the obligation to co-operate, interferes with events so as to bring about the fulfilment or non-fulfilment of a condition to that party's advantage, the other party may treat the condition as not having been fulfilled or as having been fulfilled as the case may be.

(5) When a contractual obligation or relationship comes to an end on the fulfilment of a resolutive condition any restitutionary effects are regulated by the rules in Chapter 3, Section 5, Subsection 4 (Restitution) with appropriate adaptations.

III. – 1:107: Time-Limited Rights and Obligations

(1) The terms regulating a right, obligation or contractual relationship may provide that it is to take effect from or end at a specified time, after a specified period of time or on the occurrence of an event which is certain to occur.

(2) It will take effect or come to an end at the time or on the event without further steps having to be taken.

(3)   When a contractual obligation or relationship comes to an end under this Article any restitutionary effects are regulated by the rules in Chapter 3, Section 5, Sub-section 4 (Restitution) with appropriate adaptations.

III. – 1:108: Variation or Termination by Agreement

(1)   A right, obligation or contractual relationship may be varied or terminated by agreement at any time.

(2)   Where the parties do not regulate the effects of termination, then:

(a)   it has prospective effect only and does not affect any right to damages, or a stipulated payment, for non-performance of any obligation performance of which was due before termination;

(b)   it does not affect any provision for the settlement of disputes or any other provision which is to operate even after termination; and

(c)   in the case of a contractual obligation or relationship any restitutionary effects are regulated by the rules in Chapter 3, Section 5, Sub-section 4 (Restitution) with appropriate adaptations.

III. – 1:109: Variation or Termination by Notice

(1)   A right, obligation or contractual relationship may be varied or terminated by notice by either party where this is provided for by the terms regulating it.

(2)   Where, in a case involving continuous or periodic performance of a contractual obligation, the terms of the contract do not say when the contractual relationship is to end or say that it will never end, it may be terminated by either party by giving a reasonable period of notice. In assessing whether a period of notice is reasonable, regard may be had to the interval between performances or counter-performances.

(3)   Where the parties do not regulate the effects of termination, then:

(a)   it has prospective effect only and does not affect any right to damages, or a stipulated payment, for non-performance of any obligation performance of which was due before termination;

(b)   it does not affect any provision for the settlement of disputes or any other provision which is to operate even after termination; and

(c)   in the case of a contractual obligation or relationship any restitutionary effects are regulated by the rules in Chapter 3, Section 5, Sub-section 4 (Restitution) with appropriate adaptations.

III. – 1:110: Variation or Termination by Court on a Change of Circumstances

(1)   An obligation must be performed even if performance has become more onerous, whether because the cost of performance has increased or because the value of what is to be received in return has diminished.

(2)   If, however, performance of a contractual obligation or of an obligation arising from a unilateral juridical act becomes so onerous because of an exceptional change of circumstances that it would be manifestly unjust to hold the debtor to the obligation a court may:

(a)   vary the obligation in order to make it reasonable and equitable in the new circumstances; or

(b)   terminate the obligation at a date and on terms to be determined by the court.

(3)   Paragraph (2) applies only if:

(a)   the change of circumstances occurred after the time when the obligation was incurred;

(b)   the debtor did not at that time take into account, and could not reasonably be expected to have taken into account, the possibility or scale of that change of circumstances;

(c)   the debtor did not assume, and cannot reasonably be regarded as having assumed, the risk of that change of circumstances; and

(d)   the debtor has attempted, reasonably and in good faith, to achieve by negotiation a reasonable and equitable adjustment of the terms regulating the obligation.

III. – 1:111: Tacit Prolongation

Where a contract provides for continuous or repeated performance of obligations for a definite period and the obligations continue to be performed by both parties after that period has expired, the contract becomes a contract for an indefinite period, unless the circumstances are inconsistent with the tacit consent of the parties to such prolongation.

Chapter 2: Performance

III. – 2:101: Place of Performance

(1) If the place of performance of an obligation cannot be otherwise determined from the terms regulating the obligation it is:
(a) in the case of a monetary obligation, the creditor's place of business;
(b) in the case of any other obligation, the debtor's place of business.
(2) For the purposes of the preceding paragraph:
(a) if a party has more than one place of business, the place of business is that which has the closest relationship to the obligation; and
(b) if a party does not have a place of business, or the obligation does not relate to a business matter, the habitual residence is substituted.
(3) If, in a case to which paragraph (1) applies, a party causes any increase in the expenses incidental to performance by a change in place of business or habitual residence subsequent to the time when the obligation was incurred, that party is obliged to bear the increase.

III. – 2:102: Time of Performance

(1) If the time at which, or a period of time within which, an obligation is to be performed cannot otherwise be determined from the terms regulating the obligation it must be performed within a reasonable time after it arises.
(2) If a period of time within which the obligation is to be performed can be determined from the terms regulating the obligation, the obligation may be performed at any time within that period chosen by the debtor unless the circumstances of the case indicate that the creditor is to choose the time.
(3) Unless the parties have agreed otherwise, a business must perform the obligations incurred under a contract concluded at a distance for the supply of goods, other assets or services to a consumer no later than 30 days after the contract was concluded.
(4) If a business has an obligation to reimburse money received from a consumer for goods, other assets or services supplied, the reimbursement must be made as soon as possible and in any case no later than 30 days after the obligation arose.

III. – 2:103: Early Performance

(1) A creditor may reject an offer to perform before performance is due unless the early performance would not cause the creditor unreasonable prejudice.
(2) A creditor's acceptance of early performance does not affect the time fixed for the performance by the creditor of any reciprocal obligation.

III. – 2:104: Order of Performance

If the order of performance of reciprocal obligations cannot be otherwise determined from the terms regulating the obligations then, to the extent that the obligations can be performed simultaneously, the parties are bound to perform simultaneously unless the circumstances indicate otherwise.

III. – 2:105: Alternative Obligations or Methods of Performance

(1) Where a debtor is bound to perform one of two or more obligations, or to perform an obligation in one of two or more ways, the choice belongs to the debtor, unless the terms regulating the obligations or obligation provide otherwise.
(2) If the party who is to make the choice fails to choose by the time when performance is due, then:

(a)　if the delay amounts to a fundamental non-performance, the right to choose passes to the other party;

(b)　if the delay does not amount to a fundamental non-performance, the other party may give a notice fixing an additional period of reasonable length within which the party to choose is required to do so. If the latter still fails to do so, the right to choose passes to the other party.

III. – 2:106: Performance Entrusted to Another

A debtor who entrusts performance of an obligation to another person remains responsible for performance.

III. – 2:107: Performance by a Third Person

(1)　Where personal performance by the debtor is not required by the terms regulating the obligation, the creditor cannot refuse performance by a third person if:

(a)　the third person acts with the assent of the debtor; or

(b)　the third person has a legitimate interest in performing and the debtor has failed to perform or it is clear that the debtor will not perform at the time performance is due.

(2)　Performance by a third person in accordance with paragraph (1) discharges the debtor except to the extent that the third person takes over the creditor's right by assignment or subrogation.

(3)　Where personal performance by the debtor is not required and the creditor accepts performance of the debtor's obligation by a third party in circumstances not covered by paragraph (1) the debtor is discharged but the creditor is liable to the debtor for any loss caused by that acceptance.

III. – 2:108: Method of Payment

(1)　Payment of money due may be made by any method used in the ordinary course of business.

(2)　A creditor who accepts a cheque or other order to pay or a promise to pay is presumed to do so only on condition that it will be honoured. The creditor may not enforce the original obligation to pay unless the order or promise is not honoured.

III. – 2:109: Currency of Payment

(1)　The debtor and the creditor may agree that payment is to be made only in a specified currency.

(2)　In the absence of such agreement, a sum of money expressed in a currency other than that of the place where payment is due may be paid in the currency of that place according to the rate of exchange prevailing there at the time when payment is due.

(3)　If, in a case falling within the preceding paragraph, the debtor has not paid at the time when payment is due, the creditor may require payment in the currency of the place where payment is due according to the rate of exchange prevailing there either at the time when payment is due or at the time of actual payment.

(4)　Where a monetary obligation is not expressed in a particular currency, payment must be made in the currency of the place where payment is to be made.

III. – 2:110: Imputation of Performance

(1)　Where a debtor has to perform several obligations of the same nature and makes a performance which does not suffice to extinguish all of the obligations, then subject to paragraph (5), the debtor may at the time of performance notify the creditor of the obligation to which the performance is to be imputed.

(2)　If the debtor does not make such a notification the creditor may, within a reasonable time and by notifying the debtor, impute the performance to one of the obligations.

(3)　An imputation under paragraph (2) is not effective if it is to an obligation which is not yet due, or is illegal, or is disputed.

(4)　In the absence of an effective imputation by either party, and subject to the following paragraph, the performance is imputed to that obligation which satisfies one of the following criteria in the sequence indicated:

(a)　the obligation which is due or is the first to fall due;

(b)   the obligation for which the creditor has the least security;
(c)   the obligation which is the most burdensome for the debtor;
(d)   the obligation which has arisen first.
If none of the preceding criteria applies, the performance is imputed proportionately to all the obligations.
(5)   In the case of a monetary obligation, a payment by the debtor is to be imputed, first, to expenses, secondly, to interest, and thirdly, to principal, unless the creditor makes a different imputation.

III. – 2:111: Property Not Accepted

(1)   A person who has an obligation to deliver or return corporeal property other than money and who is left in possession of the property because of the creditor's failure to accept or retake the property, has an ancillary obligation to take reasonable steps to protect and preserve it.
(2)   The debtor may obtain discharge from the obligation to deliver or return and from the ancillary obligation mentioned in the preceding paragraph:
(a)   by depositing the property on reasonable terms with a third person to be held to the order of the creditor, and notifying the creditor of this; or
(b)   by selling the property on reasonable terms after notice to the creditor, and paying the net proceeds to the creditor.
(3)   Where, however, the property is liable to rapid deterioration or its preservation is unreasonably expensive, the debtor has an obligation to take reasonable steps to dispose of it. The debtor may obtain discharge from the obligation to deliver or return by paying the net proceeds to the creditor.
(4)   The debtor left in possession is entitled to be reimbursed or to retain out of the proceeds of sale any costs reasonably incurred.

III. – 2:112: Money Not Accepted

(1)   Where a creditor fails to accept money properly tendered by the debtor, the debtor may after notice to the creditor obtain discharge from the obligation to pay by depositing the money to the order of the creditor in accordance with the law of the place where payment is due.
(2)   Paragraph (1) applies, with appropriate adaptations, to money properly tendered by a third party in circumstances where the creditor is not entitled to refuse such performance.

III. – 2:113: Costs and Formalities of Performance

(1)   The costs of performing an obligation are borne by the debtor.
(2)   In the case of a monetary obligation the debtor's obligation to pay includes taking such steps and complying with such formalities as may be necessary to enable payment to be made.

III. – 2:114: Extinctive Effect of Performance

Full performance extinguishes the obligation if it is:
(a)   in accordance with the terms regulating the obligation; or
(b)   of such a type as by law to afford the debtor a good discharge.

Chapter 3: Remedies for Non-Performance
Section 1: General
III. – 3:101: Remedies Available

(1)   If an obligation is not performed by the debtor and the non-performance is not excused, the creditor may resort to any of the remedies set out in this Chapter.
(2)   If the debtor's non-performance is excused, the creditor may resort to any of those remedies except enforcing specific performance and damages.
(3)   The creditor may not resort to any of those remedies to the extent that the creditor caused the debtor's non-performance

III. – 3:102: Cumulation of Remedies

Remedies which are not incompatible may be cumulated. In particular, a creditor is not deprived of the right to damages by resorting to any other remedy.

III. – 3:103: Notice Fixing Additional Period for Performance
(1)   In any case of non-performance of an obligation the creditor may by notice to the debtor allow an additional period of time for performance.
(2)   During the additional period the creditor may withhold performance of the creditor's reciprocal obligations and may claim damages, but may not resort to any other remedy.
(3)   If the creditor receives notice from the debtor that the debtor will not perform within that period, or if upon expiry of that period due performance has not been made, the creditor may resort to any available remedy.

III. – 3:104: Excuse Due to an Impediment
(1)   A debtor's non-performance of an obligation is excused if it is due to an impediment beyond the debtor's control and if the debtor could not reasonably be expected to have avoided or overcome the impediment or its consequences.
(2)   Where the obligation arose out of a contract or other juridical act, nonperformance is not excused if the debtor could reasonably be expected to have taken the impediment into account at the time when the obligation was incurred.
(3)   Where the excusing impediment is only temporary the excuse has effect for the period during which the impediment exists. However, if the delay amounts to a fundamental non-performance, the creditor may treat it as such.
(4)   Where the excusing impediment is permanent the obligation is extinguished. Any reciprocal obligation is also extinguished. In the case of contractual obligations any restitutionary effects of extinction are regulated by the rules in Chapter 3, Section 5, Sub-section 4 (Restitution) with appropriate adaptations.
(5)   The debtor has a duty to ensure that notice of the impediment and of its effect on the ability to perform reaches the creditor within a reasonable time after the debtor knew or could reasonably be expected to have known of these circumstances. The creditor is entitled to damages for any loss resulting from the non-receipt of such notice.

III. – 3:105: Term Excluding or Restricting Remedies
(1)   A term of a contract or other juridical act which purports to exclude or restrict liability to pay damages for personal injury (including fatal injury) caused intentionally or by gross negligence is void.
(2)   A term excluding or restricting a remedy for non-performance of an obligation, even if valid and otherwise effective, having regard in particular to the rules on unfair contract terms in Book II, Chapter 9, Section 4, may nevertheless not be invoked if it would be contrary to good faith and fair dealing to do so.

III. – 3:106: Notices Relating to Non-Performance
(1)   If the creditor gives notice to the debtor because of the debtor's nonperformance of an obligation or because such non-performance is anticipated, and the notice is properly dispatched or given, a delay or inaccuracy in the transmission of the notice or its failure to arrive does not prevent it from having effect.
(2) The notice has effect from the time at which it would have arrived in normal circumstances.

III. – 3:107: Failure to Notify Non-Conformity
(1)   If, in the case of an obligation to supply goods, other assets or services, the debtor supplies goods, other assets or services which are not in conformity with the terms regulating the obligation, the creditor may not rely on the lack of conformity unless the creditor gives notice to the debtor within a reasonable time specifying the nature of the lack of conformity.
(2)   The reasonable time runs from the time when the goods or other assets are supplied or the service is completed or from the time, if it is later, when the creditor discovered or could reasonably be expected to have discovered the non-conformity.

(3)   The debtor is not entitled to rely on paragraph (1) if the failure relates to facts which the debtor knew or could reasonably be expected to have known and which the debtor did not disclose to the creditor.
(4)   This Article does not apply where the creditor is a consumer.

III. – 3:108: Business Unable to Fulfil Consumer's Order by Distance Communication
(1)   Where a business is unable to perform its obligations under a contract concluded with a consumer by means of distance communication, it is obliged to inform the consumer immediately and refund any sums paid by the consumer without undue delay and in any case within 30 days. The consumer's remedies for non-performance remain unaffected.
(2)   The parties may not, to the detriment of the consumer, exclude the application of this Article or derogate from or vary its effects.

Section 2: Cure by Debtor of Non-Conforming Performance
III. – 3:201: Scope
This Section applies where a debtor's performance does not conform to the terms regulating the obligation.

III. – 3:202: Cure by Debtor: General Rules
(1)   The debtor may make a new and conforming tender if that can be done within the time allowed for performance.
(2)   If the debtor cannot make a new and conforming tender within the time allowed for performance but, promptly after being notified of the lack of conformity, offers to cure it within a reasonable time and at the debtor's own expense, the creditor may not pursue any remedy for non-performance, other than withholding performance, before allowing the debtor a reasonable period in which to attempt to cure the nonconformity.
(3)   Paragraph (2) is subject to the provisions of the following Article.

III. – 3:203: When Creditor Need Not Allow Debtor an Opportunity to Cure
The creditor need not, under paragraph (2) of the preceding Article, allow the debtor a period in which to attempt cure if:
(a)   failure to perform a contractual obligation within the time allowed for performance amounts to a fundamental non-performance;
(b)   the creditor has reason to believe that the debtor's performance was made with knowledge of the non-conformity and was not in accordance with good faith and fair dealing;
(c)   the creditor has reason to believe that the debtor will be unable to effect the cure within a reasonable time and without significant inconvenience to the creditor or other prejudice to the creditor's legitimate interests; or
(d)   cure would be inappropriate in the circumstances.

III. – 3:204: Consequences of Allowing Debtor Opportunity to Cure
(1)   During the period allowed for cure the creditor may withhold performance of the creditor's reciprocal obligations, but may not resort to any other remedy.
(2)   If the debtor fails to effect cure within the time allowed, the creditor may resort to any available remedy.
(3)   Notwithstanding cure, the creditor retains the right to damages for any loss caused by the debtor's initial or subsequent non-performance or by the process of effecting cure.

III. – 3:205: Return of Replaced Item
(1)   Where the debtor has, whether voluntarily or in compliance with an order under III. – 3:302 (Enforcement of non-monetary obligations), remedied a non-conforming performance by replacement, the debtor has a right and an obligation to take back the replaced item at the debtor's expense.
(2)   The creditor is not liable to pay for any use made of the replaced item in the period prior to the replacement.

Section 3: Right to Enforce Performance
III. – 3:301: Enforcement of Monetary Obligations
(1)   The creditor is entitled to recover money payment of which is due.

(2)   Where the creditor has not yet performed the reciprocal obligation for which payment will be due and it is clear that the debtor in the monetary obligation will be unwilling to receive performance, the creditor may nonetheless proceed with performance and may recover payment unless:

(a)   the creditor could have made a reasonable substitute transaction without significant effort or expense; or

(b)   performance would be unreasonable in the circumstances.

III. – 3:302: Enforcement of Non-Monetary Obligations
(1)   The creditor is entitled to enforce specific performance of an obligation other than one to pay money.

(2)   Specific performance includes the remedying free of charge of a performance which is not in conformity with the terms regulating the obligation.

(3)   Specific performance cannot, however, be enforced where:

(a)   performance would be unlawful or impossible;

(b)   performance would be unreasonably burdensome or expensive; or

(c)   performance would be of such a personal character that it would be unreasonable to enforce it.

(4)   The creditor loses the right to enforce specific performance if performance is not requested within a reasonable time after the creditor has become, or could reasonably be expected to have become, aware of the non-performance.

(5)   The creditor cannot recover damages for loss or a stipulated payment for non-performance to the extent that the creditor has increased the loss or the amount of the payment by insisting unreasonably on specific performance in circumstances where the creditor could have made a reasonable substitute transaction without significant effort or expense.

III. – 3:303: Damages Not Precluded
The fact that a right to enforce specific performance is excluded under the preceding Article does not preclude a claim for damages.

Section 4: Withholding Performance
III. – 3:401: Right to Withhold Performance of Reciprocal Obligation
(1)   A creditor who is to perform a reciprocal obligation at the same time as, or after, the debtor performs has a right to withhold performance of the reciprocal obligation until the debtor has tendered performance or has performed.

(2)   A creditor who is to perform a reciprocal obligation before the debtor performs and who reasonably believes that there will be non-performance by the debtor when the debtor's performance becomes due may withhold performance of the reciprocal obligation for as long as the reasonable belief continues. However, the right to withhold performance is lost if the debtor gives an adequate assurance of due performance.

(3)   A creditor who withholds performance in the situation mentioned in paragraph (2) has a duty to give notice of that fact to the debtor as soon as is reasonably practicable and is liable for any loss caused to the debtor by a breach of that duty.

(4)   The performance which may be withheld under this Article is the whole or part of the performance as may be reasonable in the circumstances.

Section 5: Termination
III. – 3:501: Scope and Definition
(1)   This Section applies only to contractual obligations and contractual relationships.

(2)   In this Section "termination" means the termination of the contractual relationship in whole or in part and "terminate" has a corresponding meaning.

Sub-section 1: Grounds for Termination
III. – 3:502: Termination for Fundamental Non-Performance

(1) A creditor may terminate if the debtor's non-performance of a contractual obligation is fundamental.

(2) A non-performance of a contractual obligation is fundamental if:

(a) it substantially deprives the creditor of what the creditor was entitled to expect under the contract, as applied to the whole or relevant part of the performance, unless at the time of conclusion of the contract the debtor did not foresee and could not reasonably be expected to have foreseen that result; or

(b) it is intentional or reckless and gives the creditor reason to believe that the debtor's future performance cannot be relied on.

III. – 3:503: Termination After Notice Fixing Additional Time for Performance

(1) A creditor may terminate in a case of delay in performance of a contractual obligation which is not in itself fundamental if the creditor gives a notice fixing an additional period of time of reasonable length for performance and the debtor does not perform within that period.

(2) If the period fixed is unreasonably short, the creditor may terminate only after a reasonable period from the time of the notice.

III. – 3:504: Termination for Anticipated Non-Performance

A creditor may terminate before performance of a contractual obligation is due if the debtor has declared that there will be a non-performance of the obligation, or it is otherwise clear that there will be such a non-performance, and if the non-performance would have been fundamental.

III. – 3:505: Termination for Inadequate Assurance of Performance

A creditor who reasonably believes that there will be a fundamental nonperformance of a contractual obligation by the debtor may terminate if the creditor demands an adequate assurance of due performance and no such assurance is provided within a reasonable time.

Sub-section 2: Scope, Exercise and Loss of Right to Terminate
III. – 3:506: Scope of Right to Terminate

(1) Where the debtor's obligations under the contract are not divisible the creditor may only terminate the contractual relationship as a whole.

(2) Where the debtor's obligations under the contract are to be performed in separate parts or are otherwise divisible, then:

(a) if there is a ground for termination under this Section of a part to which a counter-performance can be apportioned, the creditor may terminate the contractual relationship so far as it relates to that part;

(b) the creditor may terminate the contractual relationship as a whole only if the creditor cannot reasonably be expected to accept performance of the other parts or there is a ground for termination in relation to the contractual relationship as a whole.

III. – 3:507: Notice of Termination

(1) A right to terminate under this Section is exercised by notice to the debtor.

(2) Where a notice under III. – 3:503 (Termination after notice fixing additional time for performance) provides for automatic termination if the debtor does not perform within the period fixed by the notice, termination takes effect after that period or a reasonable length of time from the giving of notice (whichever is longer) without further notice.

III. – 3:508: Loss of Right to Terminate

(1) If performance has been tendered late or a tendered performance otherwise does not conform to the contract the creditor loses the right to terminate under this Section unless notice of termination is given within a reasonable time.

(2) Where the creditor has given the debtor a period of time to cure the non-performance under III. – 3:202 (Cure by debtor: general rules) the time mentioned in paragraph (1) begins to

run from the expiry of that period. In other cases that time begins to run from the time when the creditor has become, or could reasonably be expected to have become, aware of the tender or the non-conformity.

(3)   A creditor loses a right to terminate by notice under III. – 3:503 (Termination after notice fixing additional time for performance), III. – 3:504 (Termination for anticipated non-performance) or III. – 3:505 (Termination for inadequate assurance of performance) unless the creditor gives notice of termination within a reasonable time after the right has arisen.

Sub-section 3: Effects of Termination
III. – 3:509: Effect on Obligations Under the Contract

(1)   On termination under this Section, the outstanding obligations or relevant part of the outstanding obligations of the parties under the contract come to an end.

(2)   Termination does not, however, affect any provision of the contract for the settlement of disputes or other provision which is to operate even after termination.

(3)   A creditor who terminates under this Section retains existing rights to damages or a stipulated payment for non-performance and in addition has the same right to damages or a stipulated payment for non-performance as the creditor would have had if there had been non-performance of the now extinguished obligations of the debtor. In relation to such extinguished obligations the creditor is not regarded as having caused or contributed to the loss merely by exercising the right to terminate.

Sub-section 4: Restitution
III. – 3:510: Restitution of Benefits Received by Performance

(1)   On termination under this Section a party (the recipient) who has received any benefit by the other's performance of obligations under the terminated contractual relationship or terminated part of the contractual relationship is obliged to return it. Where both parties have obligations to return, the obligations are reciprocal.

(2)   If the performance was a payment of money, the amount received is to be repaid.

(3)   To the extent that the benefit (not being money) is transferable, it is to be returned by transferring it. However, if a transfer would cause unreasonable effort or expense, the benefit may be returned by paying its value.

(4)   To the extent that the benefit is not transferable it is to be returned by paying its value in accordance with III. – 3:512 (Payment of value of benefit).

(5)   The obligation to return a benefit extends to any natural or legal fruits received from the benefit.

III. – 3:511: When Restitution Not Required

(1)   There is no obligation to make restitution under this Sub-section to the extent that conforming performance by one party has been met by conforming performance by the other.

(2)   The terminating party may elect to treat performance as non-conforming if what was received by that party is of no, or fundamentally reduced, value to that party because of the other party's non-performance.

(3)   Restitution under this Sub-section is not required where the contract was gratuitous.

III. – 3:512: Payment of Value of Benefit

(1)   The recipient is obliged to:

(a)   pay the value (at the time of performance) of a benefit which is not transferable or which ceases to be transferable before the time when it is to be returned; and

(b)   pay recompense for any reduction in the value of a returnable benefit as a result of a change in the condition of the benefit between the time of receipt and the time when it is to be returned.

(2)   Where there was an agreed price the value of the benefit is that proportion of the price which the value of the actual performance bears to the value of the promised performance. Where no price was agreed the value of the benefit is the sum of money which a willing and

capable provider and a willing and capable recipient, knowing of any non-conformity, would lawfully have agreed.

(3)   The recipient's liability to pay the value of a benefit is reduced to the extent that as a result of a non-performance of an obligation owed by the other party to the recipient:

(a)   the benefit cannot be returned in essentially the same condition as when it was received; or

(b)   the recipient is compelled without compensation either to dispose of it or to sustain a disadvantage in order to preserve it.

(4)   The recipient's liability to pay the value of a benefit is likewise reduced to the extent that it cannot be returned in the same condition as when it was received as a result of conduct of the recipient in the reasonable, but mistaken, belief that there was no non-conformity.

III. – 3:513: Use and Improvements

(1)   The recipient is obliged to pay a reasonable amount for any use which the recipient makes of the benefit except in so far as the recipient is liable under III. – 3:512 (Payment of value of benefit) paragraph (1) in respect of that use.

(2)   A recipient who has improved a benefit which the recipient is obliged under this Section to return has a right to payment of the value of improvements if the other party can readily obtain that value by dealing with the benefit unless:

(a)   the improvement was a non-performance of an obligation owed by the recipient to the other party; or

(b)   the recipient made the improvement when the recipient knew or could reasonably be expected to know that the benefit would have to be returned.

III. – 3:514: Liabilities Arising after Time When Return Due

(1)   The recipient is obliged to:

(a)   pay the value (at the time of performance) of a benefit which ceases to be transferable after the time when its return was due; and

(b)   pay recompense for any reduction in the value of a returnable benefit as a result of a change in the condition of the benefit after the time when its return was due.

(2)   If the benefit is disposed of after the time when return was due, the value to be paid is the value of any proceeds, if this is greater.

(3)   Other liabilities arising from non-performance of an obligation to return a benefit are unaffected.

Section 6: Price Reduction
III. – 3:601: Right to Reduce Price

(1)   A creditor who accepts a performance not conforming to the terms regulating the obligation may reduce the price. The reduction is to be proportionate to the decrease in the value of what was received by virtue of the performance at the time it was made compared to the value of what would have been received by virtue of a conforming performance.

(2)   A creditor who is entitled to reduce the price under the preceding paragraph and who has already paid a sum exceeding the reduced price may recover the excess from the debtor.

(3)   A creditor who reduces the price cannot also recover damages for the loss thereby compensated but remains entitled to damages for any further loss suffered.

(4)   This Article applies with appropriate adaptations to a reciprocal obligation of the creditor other than an obligation to pay a price.

Section 7: Damages and Interest
III. – 3:701: Right to Damages

(1)   The creditor is entitled to damages for loss caused by the debtor's nonperformance of an obligation, unless the non-performance is excused.

(2)   The loss for which damages are recoverable includes future loss which is reasonably likely to occur.

(3)   "Loss" includes economic and non-economic loss. "Economic loss" includes loss of income or profit, burdens incurred and a reduction in the value of property. "Non-economic loss" includes pain and suffering and impairment of the quality of life.

III. – 3:702: General Measure of Damages

The general measure of damages for loss caused by non-performance of an obligation is such sum as will put the creditor as nearly as possible into the position in which the creditor would have been if the obligation had been duly performed. Such damages cover loss which the creditor has suffered and gain of which the creditor has been deprived.

III. – 3:703: Foreseeability

The debtor in an obligation which arises from a contract or other juridical act is liable only for loss which the debtor foresaw or could reasonably be expected to have foreseen at the time when the obligation was incurred as a likely result of the non-performance, unless the non-performance was intentional, reckless or grossly negligent.

III. – 3:704: Loss Attributable to Creditor

The debtor is not liable for loss suffered by the creditor to the extent that the creditor contributed to the non-performance or its effects.

III. – 3:705: Reduction of Loss

(1)   The debtor is not liable for loss suffered by the creditor to the extent that the creditor could have reduced the loss by taking reasonable steps.
(2)   The creditor is entitled to recover any expenses reasonably incurred in attempting to reduce the loss.

III. – 3:706: Substitute Transaction

A creditor who has terminated a contractual relationship in whole or in part under Section 5 and has made a substitute transaction within a reasonable time and in a reasonable manner may, in so far as entitled to damages, recover the difference between the value of what would have been payable under the terminated relationship and the value of what is payable under the substitute transaction, as well as damages for any further loss.

III. – 3:707: Current Price

Where the creditor has terminated a contractual relationship in whole or in part under Section 5 and has not made a substitute transaction but there is a current price for the performance, the creditor may, in so far as entitled to damages, recover the difference between the contract price and the price current at the time of termination as well as damages for any further loss.

III. – 3:708: Interest on Late Payments

(1)   If payment of a sum of money is delayed, whether or not the nonperformance is excused, the creditor is entitled to interest on that sum from the time when payment is due to the time of payment at the average commercial bank short-term lending rate to prime borrowers prevailing for the currency of payment at the place where payment is due.
(2)   The creditor may in addition recover damages for any further loss.

III. – 3:709: When Interest to Be Added to Capital

(1)   Interest payable according to the preceding Article is added to the outstanding capital every 12 months.
(2)   Paragraph (1) of this Article does not apply if the parties have provided for interest upon delay in payment.

III. – 3:710: Interest in Commercial Contracts

(1)   If a business delays the payment of a price due under a contract for the supply of goods, other assets or services without being excused under III. – 3:104 (Excuse due to an impediment), interest is due at the rate specified in paragraph (4), unless a higher interest rate is applicable.

(2)   Interest at the rate specified in paragraph (4) starts to run on the day which follows the date or the end of the period for payment provided in the contract. If there is no such date or period, interest at that rate starts to run:
(a)   30 days after the date when the debtor receives the invoice or an equivalent request for payment; or
(b)   30 days after the date of receipt of the goods or services, if the date under (a) is earlier or uncertain, or if it is uncertain whether the debtor has received an invoice or equivalent request for payment.
(3)   If conformity of goods or services to the contract is to be ascertained by way of acceptance or verification, the 30 day period under paragraph (2)(b) starts to run on the date of acceptance or verification.
(4)   The interest rate for delayed payment is the interest rate applied by the European Central Bank to its most recent main refinancing operation carried out before the first calendar day of the half-year in question ("the reference rate"), plus seven percentage points. For the currency of a Member State which is not participating in the third stage of economic and monetary union, the reference rate is the equivalent rate set by its national central bank.
(5)   The creditor may in addition recover damages for any further loss.

III. – 3:711: Unfair Terms Relating to Interest
(1)   A term whereby a business pays interest from a date later than that specified in the preceding Article paragraph (2) (a) and (b) and paragraph (3), or at a rate lower than that specified in paragraph (4), is not binding to the extent that this would be unfair.
(2)   A term whereby a debtor is allowed to pay the price for goods, other assets or services later than the time when interest starts to run under the preceding Article paragraph (2)(a) and (b) and paragraph (3) does not deprive the creditor of interest to the extent that this would be unfair.
(3)   Something is unfair for the purposes of this Article if it grossly deviates from good commercial practice, contrary to good faith and fair dealing.

III. – 3:712: Stipulated Payment for Non-Performance
(1)   Where the terms regulating an obligation provide that a debtor who fails to perform the obligation is to pay a specified sum to the creditor for such non-performance, the creditor is entitled to that sum irrespective of the actual loss.
(2)   However, despite any provision to the contrary, the sum so specified in a contract or other juridical act may be reduced to a reasonable amount where it is grossly excessive in relation to the loss resulting from the non-performance and the other circumstances.

III. – 3:713: Currency by Which Damages to Be Measured
Damages are to be measured by the currency which most appropriately reflects the creditor's loss.

Chapter 4: Plurality of Debtors and Creditors
Section 1: Plurality of Debtors
III. – 4:101: Scope of Section
This Section applies where two or more debtors are bound to perform one obligation.

III. – 4:102: Solidary, Divided and Joint Obligations
(1)   An obligation is solidary when each debtor is bound to perform the obligation in full and the creditor may require performance from any of them until full performance has been received.
(2)   An obligation is divided when each debtor is bound to perform only part of the obligation and the creditor may claim from each debtor only performance of that debtor's part.
(3)   An obligation is joint when the debtors are bound to perform the obligation together and the creditor may require performance only from all of them together.

III. – 4:103: When Different Types of Obligation Arise
(1)   Whether an obligation is solidary, divided or joint depends on the terms regulating the obligation.

(2)   If the terms do not determine the question, the liability of two or more debtors to perform the same obligation is solidary. Liability is solidary in particular where two or more persons are liable for the same damage.

(3)   The fact that the debtors are not liable on the same terms or grounds does not prevent solidarity.

III. – 4:104: Liability Under Divided Obligations

Debtors bound by a divided obligation are liable in equal shares.

III. – 4:105: Joint Obligations: Special Rule When Money Claimed for Non-Performance

Notwithstanding III. – 4:102 (Solidary, divided and joint obligations) paragraph (3), when money is claimed for non-performance of a joint obligation, the debtors have solidary liability for payment to the creditor.

III. – 4:106: Apportionment Between Solidary Debtors

(1)   As between themselves, solidary debtors are liable in equal shares.

(2)   If two or more debtors have solidary liability for the same damage, their share of liability as between themselves is equal unless different shares of liability are more appropriate having regard to all the circumstances of the case and in particular to fault or to the extent to which a source of danger for which one of them was responsible contributed to the occurrence or extent of the damage.

III. – 4:107: Recourse Between Solidary Debtors

(1)   A solidary debtor who has performed more than that debtor's share has a right to recover the excess from any of the other debtors to the extent of each debtor's unperformed share, together with a share of any costs reasonably incurred.

(2)   A solidary debtor to whom paragraph (1) applies may also, subject to any prior right and interest of the creditor, exercise the rights and actions of the creditor, including any supporting security rights, to recover the excess from any of the other debtors to the extent of each debtor's unperformed share.

(3)   If a solidary debtor who has performed more than that debtor's share is unable, despite all reasonable efforts, to recover contribution from another solidary debtor, the share of the others, including the one who has performed, is increased proportionally.

III. – 4:108: Performance, Set-off and Merger in Solidary Obligations

(1)   Performance or set-off by a solidary debtor or set-off by the creditor against one solidary debtor discharges the other debtors in relation to the creditor to the extent of the performance or set-off.

(2)   Merger of debts between a solidary debtor and the creditor discharges the other debtors only for the share of the debtor concerned.

III. – 4:109: Release or Settlement in Solidary Obligations

(1)   When the creditor releases, or reaches a settlement with, one solidary debtor, the other debtors are discharged of liability for the share of that debtor.

(2)   As between solidary debtors, the debtor who is discharged from that debtor's share is discharged only to the extent of the share at the time of the discharge and not from any supplementary share for which that debtor may subsequently become liable under III. – 4:107 (Recourse between solidary debtors) paragraph (3).

(3)   When the debtors have solidary liability for the same damage the discharge under paragraph (1) extends only so far as is necessary to prevent the creditor from recovering more than full reparation and the other debtors retain their rights of recourse against the released or settling debtor to the extent of that debtor's unperformed share.

III. – 4:110: Effect of Judgment in Solidary Obligations

A decision by a court as to the liability to the creditor of one solidary debtor does not affect:

(a)   the liability to the creditor of the other solidary debtors; or

(b)   the rights of recourse between the solidary debtors under III. – 4:107 (Recourse between solidary debtors).

III. – 4:111: Prescription in Solidary Obligations

Prescription of the creditor's right to performance against one solidary debtor does not affect:
(a)   the liability to the creditor of the other solidary debtors; or
(b)   the rights of recourse between the solidary debtors under III. – 4:107 (Recourse between solidary debtors).

III. – 4:112: Opposability of Other Defences in Solidary Obligations

(1)   A solidary debtor may invoke against the creditor any defence which another solidary debtor can invoke, other than a defence personal to that other debtor. Invoking the defence has no effect with regard to the other solidary debtors.
(2)   A debtor from whom contribution is claimed may invoke against the claimant any personal defence that that debtor could have invoked against the creditor.

Section 2: Plurality of Creditors

III. – 4:201: Scope of Section

This Section applies where two or more creditors have a right to performance under one obligation.

III. – 4:202: Solidary, Divided and Joint Rights

(1)   A right to performance is solidary when any of the creditors may require full performance from the debtor and the debtor may perform to any of the creditors.
(2)   A right to performance is divided when each creditor may require performance only of that creditor's share and the debtor owes each creditor only that creditor's share.
(3)   A right to performance is joint when any creditor may require performance only for the benefit of all the creditors and the debtor must perform to all the creditors.

III. – 4:203: When Different Types of Right Arise

(1)   Whether a right to performance is solidary, divided or communal depends on the terms regulating the right.
(2)   If the terms do not determine the question, the right of co-creditors is divided.

III. – 4:204: Apportionment in Cases of Divided Rights

In the case of divided rights the creditors have equal shares.

III. – 4:205: Difficulties of Performing in Cases of Joint Rights

If one of the creditors who have joint rights to performance refuses to accept, or is unable to receive, the performance, the debtor may obtain discharge from the obligation by depositing the property or money with a third party according to III. – 2:111 (Property not accepted) or III. – 2:112 (Money not accepted).

III. – 4:206: Apportionment in Cases of Solidary Rights

(1)   In the case of solidary rights the creditors have equal shares.
(2)   A creditor who has received more than that creditor's share has an obligation to transfer the excess to the other creditors to the extent of their respective shares.

III. – 4:207: Regime of Solidary Rights

(1)   A release granted to the debtor by one of the solidary creditors has no effect on the other solidary creditors.
(2)   The rules of III. – 4:108 (Performance, set-off and merger in solidary obligations), III. – 4:110 (Effect of judgment in solidary obligations), III. – 4:111 (Prescription in solidary obligations) and III. – 4:112 (Opposability of other defences in solidary obligations) paragraph (1) apply, with appropriate adaptations, to solidary rights to performance.

Chapter 5: Change of Parties
Section 1: Assignment of Rights
Sub-section 1: General
III. – 5:101: Scope of Section

(1)   This Section applies to the assignment, by a contract or other juridical act, of a right to performance of an obligation.

(2)   It does not apply to the transfer of a financial instrument or investment security where such transfer is required to be by entry in a register maintained by or for the issuer or where there are other requirements for transfer or restrictions on transfer.

III. – 5:102: Definitions

(1)   An "assignment" of a right is the transfer of the right from one person (the "assignor") to another person (the "assignee").

(2)   An "act of assignment" is a contract or other juridical act which is intended to effect a transfer of the right.

(3)   Where part of a right is assigned, any reference in this Section to a right includes a reference to the assigned part of the right.

III. – 5:103: Priority of Provisions on Proprietary Securities and Trusts

(1)   In relation to assignments for purposes of security, the provisions of Book IX apply and have priority over the provisions in this Chapter.

(2)   In relation to assignments for purposes of a trust, or to or from a trust, the provisions of Book X apply and have priority over the provisions in this Chapter.

Sub-section 2: Requirements for Assignment
III. – 5:104: Basic Requirements

(1)   The requirements for an assignment of a right to performance are that:
(a)   the right exists;
(b)   the right is assignable;
(c)   the person purporting to assign the right has the right or authority to transfer it;
(d)   the assignee is entitled as against the assignor to the transfer by virtue of a contract or other juridical act, a court order or a rule of law; and
(e)   there is a valid act of assignment of the right.

(2)   The entitlement referred to in paragraph (1)(d) need not precede the act of assignment.

(3)   The same contract or other juridical act may operate as the conferment of an entitlement and as the act of assignment.

(4)   Neither notice to the debtor nor the consent of the debtor to the assignment is required.

III. – 5:105: Assignability: General Rule

(1)   All rights to performance are assignable except where otherwise provided by law.

(2)   A right to performance which is by law accessory to another right is not assignable separately from that right.

III. – 5:106: Future and Unspecified Rights

(1)   A future right to performance may be the subject of an act of assignment but the transfer of the right depends on its coming into existence and being identifiable as the right to which the act of assignment relates.

(2)   A number of rights to performance may be assigned without individual specification if, at the time when the assignment is to take place in relation to them, they are identifiable as rights to which the act of assignment relates.

III. – 5:107: Assignability in Part

(1)   A right to performance of a monetary obligation may be assigned in part.
(2)   A right to performance of a non-monetary obligation may be assigned in part only if:
(a)   the debtor consents to the assignment; or

(b)   the right is divisible and the assignment does not render the obligation significantly more
       burdensome.
(3)   Where a right is assigned in part the assignor is liable to the debtor for any increased costs
which the debtor thereby incurs.

III. – 5:108: Assignability: Effect of Contractual Prohibition
(1)   A contractual prohibition of, or restriction on, the assignment of a right does not affect the
assignability of the right.
(2)   However, where a right is assigned in breach of such a prohibition or restriction:
(a)   the debtor may perform in favour of the assignor and is discharged by so doing; and
(b)   the debtor retains all rights of set-off against the assignor as if the right had not been assigned.
(3)   Paragraph (2) does not apply if:
(a)   the debtor has consented to the assignment;
(b)   the debtor has caused the assignee to believe on reasonable grounds that there was no
       such prohibition or restriction; or
(c)   the assigned right is a right to payment for the provision of goods or services.
(4)   The fact that a right is assignable notwithstanding a contractual prohibition or restriction
does not affect the assignor's liability to the debtor for any breach of the prohibition or restriction.

III. – 5:109: Assignability: Rights Personal to the Creditor
(1)   A right is not assignable if it is a right to a performance which the debtor, by reason of the
nature of the performance or the relationship between the debtor and the creditor, could not
reasonably be required to render to anyone except that creditor.
(2)   Paragraph (1) does not apply if the debtor has consented to the assignment.

III. – 5:110: Act of Assignment: Formation and Validity
(1)   Subject to paragraphs (2) and (3), the rules of Book II on the formation and validity of contracts and other juridical acts apply to acts of assignment.
(2)   The rules of Book IV.H on the formation and validity of contracts of donation apply to gratuitous acts of assignment.
(3)   The rules of Book IX on the formation and validity of security agreements apply to acts of
assignment for purposes of security.

III. – 5:111: Right or Authority to Assign
The requirement of right or authority in III. – 5:104 (Basic requirements) paragraph (1)(c) need
not be satisfied at the time of the act of assignment but has to be satisfied at the time the
assignment is to take place.

Sub-section 3: Undertakings by Assignor
III. – 5:112: Undertakings by Assignor
(1)   The undertakings in paragraphs (2) to (6) are included in the act of assignment unless the
act of assignment or the circumstances indicate otherwise.
(2)   The assignor undertakes that:
(a)   the assigned right exists or will exist at the time when the assignment is to take effect;
(b)   the assignor is entitled to assign the right or will be so entitled at the time when the assign-
       ment is to take effect.
(c)   the debtor has no defences against an assertion of the right;
(d)   the right will not be affected by any right of set-off available as between the assignor and
       the debtor; and
(e)   the right has not been the subject of a prior assignment to another assignee and is not
       subject to any right in security in favour of any other person or to any other incumbrance.
(3)   The assignor undertakes that any terms of a contract or other juridical act which have been
disclosed to the assignee as terms regulating the right have not been modified and are not
affected by any undisclosed agreement as to their meaning or effect which would be
prejudicial to the assignee.

(4)   The assignor undertakes that the terms of any contract or other juridical act from which the right arises will not be modified without the consent of the assignee unless the modification is provided for in the act of assignment or is one which is made in good faith and is of a nature to which the assignee could not reasonably object.

(5)   The assignor undertakes not to conclude or grant any subsequent act of assignment of the same right which could lead to another person obtaining priority over the assignee.

(6)   The assignor undertakes to transfer to the assignee, or to take such steps as are necessary to complete the transfer of, all transferable rights intended to secure the performance which are not already transferred by the assignment, and to transfer the proceeds of any non-transferable rights intended to secure the performance.

(7)   The assignor does not represent that the debtor has, or will have, the ability to pay.

Sub-section 4: Effects of Assignment
III. – 5:113: New Creditor

As soon as the assignment takes place the assignor ceases to be the creditor and the assignee becomes the creditor in relation to the right assigned.

III. – 5:114: When Assignment Takes Place

(1)   An assignment takes place when the requirements of III. – 5:104 (Basic requirements) are satisfied, or at such later time as the act of assignment may provide.

(2)   However, an assignment of a right which was a future right at the time of the act of assignment is regarded as having taken place when all requirements other than those dependent on the existence of the right were satisfied.

(3)   Where the requirements of III. – 5:104 (Basic requirements) are satisfied in relation to successive acts of assignment at the same time, the earliest act of assignment takes effect unless it provides otherwise.

III. – 5:115: Rights Transferred to Assignee

(1)   The assignment of a right to performance transfers to the assignee not only the primary right but also all accessory rights and transferable supporting security rights.

(2)   Where the assignment of a right to performance of a contractual obligation is associated with the substitution of the assignee as debtor in respect of any obligation owed by the assignor under the same contract, this Article takes effect subject to III. – 5:302 (Transfer of contractual position).

III. – 5:116: Effect on Defences and Rights of Set-off

(1)   The debtor may invoke against the assignee all substantive and procedural defences to a claim based on the assigned right which the debtor could have invoked against the assignor.

(2)   The debtor may not, however, invoke a defence against the assignee:

(a)   if the debtor has caused the assignee to believe that there was no such defence; or

(b)   if the defence is based on breach by the assignor of a prohibition or restriction on assignment.

(3)   The debtor may invoke against the assignee all rights of set-off which would have been available against the assignor in respect of rights against the assignor:

(a)   existing at the time when the debtor could no longer obtain a discharge by performing to the assignor; or

(b)   closely connected with the assigned right.

III. – 5:117: Effect on Place of Performance

(1)   Where the assigned right relates to an obligation to pay money at a particular place, the assignee may require payment at any place within the same country or, if that country is a Member State of the European Union, at any place within the European Union, but the assignor is liable to the debtor for any increased costs which the debtor incurs by reason of any change in the place of performance.

(2)   Where the assigned right relates to a non-monetary obligation to be performed at a particular place, the assignee may not require performance at any other place.

III. – 5:118: Effect of Initial Invalidity, Subsequent Avoidance, Withdrawal, Termination and Revocation

(1) This Article applies where the assignee's entitlement for the purposes of III. – 5:104 (Basic requirements) paragraph (1)(d) arises from a contract or other juridical act (the underlying contract or other juridical act) whether or not it is followed by a separate act of assignment for the purposes of paragraph (1)(e) of that Article.

(2) Where the underlying contract or other juridical act is void from the beginning, no assignment takes place.

(3) Where, after an assignment has taken place, the underlying contract or other juridical act is avoided under Book II, Chapter 7, the right is treated as never having passed to the assignee (retroactive effect on assignment).

(4) Where, after an assignment has taken place, the underlying contract or other juridical act is withdrawn in the sense of Book II, Chapter 5, or the contractual relationship is terminated under any rule of Book III, or a donation is revoked in the sense of Book IV. H Chapter 4, there is no retroactive effect on the assignment.

(5) This Article does not affect any right to recover based on other provisions of these model rules.

Sub-section 5: Protection of Debtor

III. – 5:119: Performance to Person Who Is Not the Creditor

(1) The debtor is discharged by performing to the assignor so long as the debtor has not received a notice of assignment from either the assignor or the assignee and does not know that the assignor is no longer entitled to receive performance.

(2) Notwithstanding that the person identified as the assignee in a notice of assignment received from the assignor is not the creditor, the debtor is discharged by performing in good faith to that person.

(3) Notwithstanding that the person identified as the assignee in a notice of assignment received from a person claiming to be the assignee is not the creditor, the debtor is discharged by performing to that person if the creditor has caused the debtor reasonably and in good faith to believe that the right has been assigned to that person.

III. – 5:120: Adequate Proof of Assignment

(1) A debtor who believes on reasonable grounds that the right has been assigned but who has not received a notice of assignment, may request the person who is believed to have assigned the right to provide a notice of assignment or a confirmation that the right has not been assigned or that the assignor is still entitled to receive payment.

(2) A debtor who has received a notice of assignment which is not in textual form on a durable medium or which does not give adequate information about the assigned right or the name and address of the assignee may request the person giving the notice to provide a new notice which satisfies these requirements.

(3) A debtor who has received a notice of assignment from the assignee but not from the assignor may request the assignee to provide reliable evidence of the assignment. Reliable evidence includes, but is not limited to, any statement in textual form on a durable medium emanating from the assignor indicating that the right has been assigned.

(4) A debtor who has made a request under this Article may withhold performance until the request is met.

Sub-section 6: Priority Rules

III. – 5:121: Competition Between Successive Assignees

(1) Where there are successive purported assignments by the same person of the same right to performance the purported assignee whose assignment is first notified to the debtor has priority over any earlier assignee if at the time of the later assignment the assignee under that assignment neither knew nor could reasonably be expected to have known of the earlier assignment.

(2) The debtor is discharged by paying the first to notify even if aware of competing demands.

III. – 5:122: Competition Between Assignee and Assignor Receiving Proceeds
Where the debtor is discharged under III. – 5:108 (Assignability: effect of contractual prohibition) paragraph (2)(a) or III. – 5:119 (Performance to person who is not the creditor) paragraph (1), the assignee's right against the assignor to the proceeds has priority over the right of a competing claimant so long as the proceeds are held by the assignor and are reasonably identifiable from the other assets of the assignor.

Section 2: Substitution and Addition of Debtors
III. – 5:201: Scope
This Section applies only to the substitution or addition of a new debtor by agreement.

III. – 5:202: Types of Substitution or Addition
(1) A new debtor may be substituted or added:
(a) in such a way that the original debtor is discharged (complete substitution of new debtor);
(b) in such a way that the original debtor is retained as a debtor in case the new debtor does not perform properly (incomplete substitution of new debtor); or
(c) in such a way that the original debtor and the new debtor have solidary liability (addition of new debtor).
(2) If it is clear that there is a new debtor but not clear what type of substitution or addition was intended, the original debtor and the new debtor have solidary liability.

III. – 5:203: Consent of Creditor
(1) The consent of the creditor is required for the substitution of a new debtor, whether complete or incomplete.
(2) The consent of the creditor to the substitution of a new debtor may be given in advance. In such a case the substitution takes effect only when the creditor is given notice by the new debtor of the agreement between the new and the original debtor.
(3) The consent of the creditor is not required for the addition of a new debtor but the creditor, by notice to the new debtor, can reject the right conferred against the new debtor if that is done without undue delay after being informed of the right and before it has been expressly or impliedly accepted. On such rejection the right is treated as never having been conferred.

III. – 5:204: Complete Substitution
A third person may undertake with the agreement of the creditor and the original debtor to be completely substituted as debtor, with the effect that the original debtor is discharged.

III. – 5:205: Effects of Complete Substitution on Defences, Set-off and Security Rights
(1) The new debtor may invoke against the creditor all defences which the original debtor could have invoked against the creditor.
(2) The new debtor may not exercise against the creditor any right of set-off available to the original debtor against the creditor.
(3) The new debtor cannot invoke against the creditor any rights or defences arising from the relationship between the new debtor and the original debtor.
(4) The discharge of the original debtor also extends to any personal or proprietary security provided by the original debtor to the creditor for the performance of the obligation, unless the security is over an asset which is transferred to the new debtor as part of a transaction between the original and the new debtor.
(5) Upon discharge of the original debtor, a security granted by any person other than the new debtor for the performance of the obligation is released, unless that other person agrees that it should continue to be available to the creditor.

III. – 5:206: Incomplete Substitution
A third person may agree with the creditor and with the original debtor to be incompletely substituted as debtor, with the effect that the original debtor is retained as a debtor in case the original debtor does not perform properly.

III. – 5:207: Effects of Incomplete Substitution
(1)   The effects of an incomplete substitution on defences and set-off are the same as the effects of a complete substitution.
(2)   To the extent that the original debtor is not discharged, any personal or proprietary security provided for the performance of that debtor's obligations is unaffected by the substitution.
(3)   So far as not inconsistent with paragraphs (1) and (2) the liability of the original debtor is governed by the rules on the liability of a provider of dependent personal security with subsidiary liability.

III. – 5:208: Addition of New Debtor
A third person may agree with the debtor to be added as a debtor, with the effect that the original debtor and the new debtor have solidary liability.

III. – 5:209: Effects of Addition of New Debtor
(1)   Where there is a contract between the new debtor and the creditor, or a separate unilateral juridical act by the new debtor in favour of the creditor, whereby the new debtor is added as a debtor, the new debtor cannot invoke against the creditor any rights or defences arising from the relationship between the new debtor and the original debtor. Where there is no such contract or unilateral juridical act the new debtor can invoke against the creditor any ground of invalidity affecting the agreement with the original debtor.
(2)   So far as not inconsistent with paragraph (1), the rules of Book III, Chapter 4, Section 1 (Plurality of debtors) apply.

Section 3: Transfer of Contractual Position
III. – 5:301: Scope
This Section applies only to transfers by agreement.

III. – 5:302: Transfer of Contractual Position
(1)   A party to a contractual relationship may agree with a third person, with the consent of the other party to the contractual relationship, that that person is to be substituted as a party to the relationship.
(2)   The consent of the other party may be given in advance. In such a case the transfer takes effect only when that party is given notice of it.
(3)   To the extent that the substitution of the third person involves a transfer of rights, the provisions of Section 1 of this Chapter on the assignment of rights apply; to the extent that obligations are transferred, the provisions of Section 2 of this Chapter on the substitution of a new debtor apply.

Section 4: Transfer of Rights and Obligations on Agent's Insolvency
III. – 5:401: Principal's Option to Take over Rights in Case of Agent's Insolvency
(1)   This Article applies where an agent has concluded a contract with a third party on the instructions of and on behalf of a principal but has done so in such a way that the agent, and not the principal, is a party to the contract.
(2)   If the agent becomes insolvent the principal may by notice to the third party and to the agent take over the rights of the agent under the contract in relation to the third party.
(3)   The third party may invoke against the principal any defence which the third party could have invoked against the agent and has all the other protections which would be available if the rights had been voluntarily assigned by the agent to the principal.

III. – 5:402: Third Party's Counter-Option
Where the principal has taken over the rights of the agent under the preceding Article, the third party may by notice to the principal and the agent opt to exercise against the principal the rights which the third party has against the agent, subject to any defences which the agent has against the third party.

Chapter 6: Set-Off and Merger
Section 1: Set-off
III. – 6:101: Definition and Scope
(1) "Set-off" is the process by which a person may use a right to performance held against another person to extinguish in whole or in part an obligation owed to that person.
(2) This Chapter does not apply to set-off in insolvency.

III. – 6:102: Requirements for Set-off
If two parties owe each other obligations of the same kind, either party may set off that party's right against the other party's right, if and to the extent that, at the time of set-off:
(a) the performance of the first party is due or, even if it is not due, the first party can oblige the other party to accept performance;
(b) the performance of the other party is due; and
(c) each party has authority to dispose of that party's right for the purpose of the set-off.

III. – 6:103: Unascertained Rights
(1) A debtor may not set off a right which is unascertained as to its existence or value unless the set-off will not prejudice the interests of the creditor.
(2) Where the rights of both parties arise from the same legal relationship it is presumed that the creditor's interests will not be prejudiced.

III. – 6:104: Foreign Currency Set-off
Where parties owe each other money in different currencies, each party may set off that party's right against the other party's right, unless the parties have agreed that the party declaring set-off is to pay exclusively in a specified currency.

III. – 6:105: Set-off by Notice
Set-off is effected by notice to the other party.

III. – 6:106: Two or More Rights and Obligations
(1) Where the party giving notice of set-off has two or more rights against the other party, the notice is effective only if it identifies the right to which it relates.
(2) Where the party giving notice of set-off has to perform two or more obligations towards the other party, the rules on imputation of performance apply with appropriate adaptations.

III. – 6:107: Effect of Set-off
Set-off extinguishes the obligations, as far as they are coextensive, as from the time of notice.

III. – 6:108: Exclusion of Right of Set-off
Set-off cannot be effected:
(a) where it is excluded by agreement;
(b) against a right to the extent that that right is not capable of attachment; and
(c) against a right arising from an intentional wrongful act.

Section 2: Merger of Debts
III. – 6:201: Extinction of Obligations by Merger
(1) An obligation is extinguished if the same person becomes debtor and creditor in the same capacity.
(2) Paragraph (1) does not, however, apply if the effect would be to deprive a third person of a right.

Chapter 7: Prescription
Section 1: General Provision
III. – 7:101: Rights Subject to Prescription
A right to performance of an obligation is subject to prescription by the expiry of a period of time in accordance with the rules in this Chapter.

Section 2: Periods of Prescription and Their Commencement
III. – 7:201: General Period
The general period of prescription is three years.

III. – 7:202: Period for a Right Established by Legal Proceedings
(1)   The period of prescription for a right established by judgment is ten years.
(2)   The same applies to a right established by an arbitral award or other instrument which is enforceable as if it were a judgment.
III. – 7:203: Commencement
(1)   The general period of prescription begins to run from the time when the debtor has to effect performance or, in the case of a right to damages, from the time of the act which gives rise to the right.
(2)   Where the debtor is under a continuing obligation to do or refrain from doing something, the general period of prescription begins to run with each breach of the obligation.
(3)   The period of prescription set out in III. – 7:202 (Period for a right established by legal proceedings) begins to run from the time when the judgment or arbitral award obtains the effect of res judicata, or the other instrument becomes enforceable, though not before the debtor has to effect performance.

Section 3: Extension of Period
III. – 7:301: Suspension in Case of Ignorance
The running of the period of prescription is suspended as long as the creditor does not know of, and could not reasonably be expected to know of:
(a)   the identity of the debtor; or
(b)   the facts giving rise to the right including, in the case of a right to damages, the type of damage.
III. – 7:302: Suspension in Case of Judicial and Other Proceedings
(1)   The running of the period of prescription is suspended from the time when judicial proceedings to assert the right are begun.
(2)   Suspension lasts until a decision has been made which has the effect of res judicata, or until the case has been otherwise disposed of. Where the proceedings end within the last six months of the prescription period without a decision on the merits, the period of prescription does not expire before six months have passed after the time when the proceedings ended.
(3)   These provisions apply, with appropriate adaptations, to arbitration proceedings, to mediation proceedings, to proceedings whereby an issue between two parties is referred to a third party for a binding decision and to all other proceedings initiated with the aim of obtaining a decision relating to the right.
(4)   Mediation proceedings mean structured proceedings whereby two or more parties to a dispute attempt to reach an agreement on the settlement of their dispute with the assistance of a mediator.
III. – 7:303: Suspension in Case of Impediment Beyond Creditor's Control
(1)   The running of the period of prescription is suspended as long as the creditor is prevented from pursuing proceedings to assert the right by an impediment which is beyond the creditor's control and which the creditor could not reasonably have been expected to avoid or overcome.
(2)   Paragraph (1) applies only if the impediment arises, or subsists, within the last six months of the prescription period.
(3)   Where the duration or nature of the impediment is such that it would be unreasonable to expect the creditor to take proceedings to assert the right within the part of the period of prescription which has still to run after the suspension comes to an end, the period of prescription does not expire before six months have passed after the time when the impediment was removed.
(4)   In this Article an impediment includes a psychological impediment.

III. – 7:304: Postponement of Expiry in Case of Negotiations
If the parties negotiate about the right, or about circumstances from which a claim relating to the right might arise, the period of prescription does not expire before one year has passed since the last communication made in the negotiations.

III. – 7:305: Postponement of Expiry in Case of Incapacity
(1)   If a person subject to an incapacity is without a representative, the period of prescription of a right held by or against that person does not expire before one year has passed after either the incapacity has ended or a representative has been appointed.
(2)   The period of prescription of rights between a person subject to an incapacity and that person's representative does not expire before one year has passed after either the incapacity has ended or a new representative has been appointed.

III. – 7:306: Postponement of Expiry: Deceased's Estate
Where the creditor or debtor has died, the period of prescription of a right held by or against the deceased's estate does not expire before one year has passed after the right can be enforced by or against an heir, or by or against a representative of the estate.

III. – 7:307: Maximum Length of Period
The period of prescription cannot be extended, by suspension of its running or postponement of its expiry under this Chapter, to more than ten years or, in case of rights to damages for personal injuries, to more than thirty years. This does not apply to suspension under III. – 7:302 (Suspension in case of judicial and other proceedings).

Section 4: Renewal of Period
III. – 7:401: Renewal by Acknowledgement
(1)   If the debtor acknowledges the right, vis-à-vis the creditor, by part payment, payment of interest, giving of security, or in any other manner, a new period of prescription begins to run.
(2)   The new period is the general period of prescription, regardless of whether the right was originally subject to the general period of prescription or the ten year period under III. – 7:202 (Period for a right established by legal proceedings). In the latter case, however, this Article does not operate so as to shorten the ten year period.

III. – 7:402: Renewal by Attempted Execution
The ten year period of prescription laid down in III. – 7:202 (Period for a right established by legal proceedings) begins to run again with each reasonable attempt at execution undertaken by the creditor.

Section 5: Effects of Prescription
III. – 7:501: General Effect
(1)   After expiry of the period of prescription the debtor is entitled to refuse performance.
(2)   Whatever has been paid or transferred by the debtor in performance of the obligation may not be reclaimed merely because the period of prescription had expired.

III. – 7:502: Effect on Ancillary Rights
The period of prescription for a right to payment of interest, and other rights of an ancillary nature, expires not later than the period for the principal right.

III. – 7:503: Effect on Set-off
A right in relation to which the period of prescription has expired may nonetheless be set off, unless the debtor has invoked prescription previously or does so within two months of notification of set-off.

Section 6: Modification by Agreement
III. – 7:601: Agreements Concerning Prescription
(1)   The requirements for prescription may be modified by agreement between the parties, in particular by either shortening or lengthening the periods of prescription.

(2)   The period of prescription may not, however, be reduced to less than one year or extended to more than thirty years after the time of commencement set out in III. – 7:203 (Commencement).

Book IV Specific Contracts and the Rights and Obligations Arising from Them
Part A. Sales
Chapter 1: Scope and Definitions
Section 1: Scope
IV. A. – 1:101: Contracts Covered

(1)   This Part of Book IV applies to contracts for the sale of goods and associated consumer guarantees.
(2)   It applies with appropriate adaptations to:
(a)   contracts for the sale of electricity;
(b)   contracts for the sale of stocks, shares, investment securities and negotiable instruments;
(c)   contracts for the sale of other forms of incorporeal property, including rights to the performance of obligations, industrial and intellectual property rights and other transferable rights;
(d)   contracts conferring, in exchange for a price, rights in information or data, including software and databases;
(e)   contracts for the barter of goods or any of the other assets mentioned above.
(3)   It does not apply to contracts for the sale or barter of immovable property or rights in immovable property.

IV. A. – 1:102: Goods to Be Manufactured or Produced

A contract under which one party undertakes, for a price, to manufacture or produce goods for the other party and to transfer their ownership to the other party is to be considered as primarily a contract for the sale of the goods.

Section 2: Definitions
IV. A. – 1:201: Goods

In this Part of Book IV:
(a)   the word "goods" includes goods which at the time of the conclusion of the contract do not yet exist; and
(b)   references to goods, other than in IV. A. – 1:101 (Contracts covered) itself, are to be taken as referring also to the other assets mentioned in paragraph (2) of that Article.

IV. A. – 1:202: Contract for Sale

A contract for the "sale" of goods is a contract under which one party, the seller, undertakes to another party, the buyer, to transfer the ownership of the goods to the buyer, or to a third person, either immediately on conclusion of the contract or at some future time, and the buyer undertakes to pay the price.

IV. A. – 1:203: Contract for Barter

(1)   A contract for the "barter" of goods is a contract under which each party undertakes to transfer the ownership of goods, either immediately on conclusion of the contract or at some future time, in return for the transfer of ownership of other goods.
(2)   Each party is considered to be the buyer with respect to the goods to be received and the seller with respect to the goods or assets to be transferred.

IV. A. – 1:204: Consumer Contract for Sale

For the purpose of this Part of Book IV, a consumer contract for sale is a contract for sale in which the seller is a business and the buyer is a consumer.

Chapter 2: Obligations of the Seller
Section 1: Overview
IV. A. – 2:101: Overview of Obligations of the Seller

The seller must:
(a) transfer the ownership of the goods;
(b) deliver the goods;
(c) transfer such documents representing or relating to the goods as may be required by the contract; and
(d) ensure that the goods conform to the contract.

Section 2: Delivery of the Goods
IV. A. – 2:201: Delivery

(1) The seller fulfils the obligation to deliver by making the goods, or where it is agreed that the seller need only deliver documents representing the goods, the documents, available to the buyer.
(2) If the contract involves carriage of the goods by a carrier or series of carriers, the seller fulfils the obligation to deliver by handing over the goods to the first carrier for transmission to the buyer and by transferring to the buyer any document necessary to enable the buyer to take over the goods from the carrier holding the goods.
(3) In this Article, any reference to the buyer includes a third person to whom delivery is to be made in accordance with the contract.

IV. A. – 2:202: Place and Time for Delivery

(1) The place and time for delivery are determined by III. – 2:101 (Place of performance) and III. – 2:102 (Time of performance) as modified by this Article.
(2) If the performance of the obligation to deliver requires the transfer of documents representing the goods, the seller must transfer them at such a time and place and in such a form as is required by the contract.
(3) If in a consumer contract for sale the contract involves carriage of goods by a carrier or a series of carriers and the consumer is given a time for delivery, the goods must be received from the last carrier or made available for collection from that carrier by that time.

IV. A. – 2:203: Cure in Case of Early Delivery

(1) If the seller has delivered goods before the time for delivery, the seller may, up to that time, deliver any missing part or make up any deficiency in the quantity of the goods delivered, or deliver goods in replacement of any non-conforming goods delivered or otherwise remedy any lack of conformity in the goods delivered, provided that the exercise of this right does not cause the buyer unreasonable inconvenience or unreasonable expense.
(2) If the seller has transferred documents before the time required by the contract, the seller may, up to that time, cure any lack of conformity in the documents, provided that the exercise of this right does not cause the buyer unreasonable inconvenience or unreasonable expense.
(3) This Article does not preclude the buyer from claiming damages, in accordance with Book III, Chapter 3, Section 7 (Damages and interest), for any loss not remedied by the seller's cure.

IV. A. – 2:204: Carriage of the Goods

(1) If the contract requires the seller to arrange for carriage of the goods, the seller must make such contracts as are necessary for carriage to the place fixed by means of transportation appropriate in the circumstances and according to the usual terms for such transportation.
(2) If the seller, in accordance with the contract, hands over the goods to a carrier and if the goods are not clearly identified to the contract by markings on the goods, by shipping documents or otherwise, the seller must give the buyer notice of the consignment specifying the goods.
(3) If the contract does not require the seller to effect insurance in respect of the carriage of the goods, the seller must, at the buyer's request, provide the buyer with all available information necessary to enable the buyer to effect such insurance.

Section 3: Conformity of the Goods
IV. A. – 2:301: Conformity with the Contract
The goods do not conform with the contract unless they:
(a)   are of the quantity, quality and description required by the contract;
(b)   are contained or packaged in the manner required by the contract;
(c)   are supplied along with any accessories, installation instructions or other instructions required by the contract; and
(d)   comply with the remaining Articles of this Section.

IV. A. – 2:302: Fitness for Purpose, Qualities, Packaging
The goods must:
(a)   be fit for any particular purpose made known to the seller at the time of the conclusion of
the contract, except where the circumstances show that the buyer did not rely, or that it was unreasonable for the buyer to rely, on the seller's skill and judgement;
(b)   be fit for the purposes for which goods of the same description would ordinarily be used;
(c)   possess the qualities of goods which the seller held out to the buyer as a sample or model;
(d)   be contained or packaged in the manner usual for such goods or, where there is no such
manner, in a manner adequate to preserve and protect the goods;
(e)   be supplied along with such accessories, installation instructions or other instructions as
the buyer may reasonably expect to receive; and
(f)   possess such qualities and performance capabilities as the buyer may reasonably expect.

IV. A. – 2:303: Statements by Third Persons
The goods must possess the qualities and performance capabilities held out in any statement
on the specific characteristics of the goods made about them by a person in earlier links of the
business chain, the producer or the producer's representative which forms part of the terms of
the contract by virtue of II. – 9:102 (Certain pre-contractual statements regarded as contract
terms).

IV. A. – 2:304: Incorrect Installation Under a Consumer Contract for Sale
Where goods supplied under a consumer contract for sale are incorrectly installed, any lack of
conformity resulting from the incorrect installation is regarded as a lack of conformity of the
goods if:
(a)   the goods were installed by the seller or under the seller's responsibility; or
(b)   the goods were intended to be installed by the consumer and the incorrect installation
was due to a shortcoming in the installation instructions.

IV. A. – 2:305: Third Party Rights or Claims in General
The goods must be free from any right or reasonably well founded claim of a third party. However, if such a right or claim is based on industrial property or other intellectual property, the
seller's obligation is governed by the following Article.

IV. A. – 2:306: Third Party Rights or Claims Based on Industrial Property or Other Intellectual Property
(1)   The goods must be free from any right or claim of a third party which is based on
industrial property or other intellectual property and of which at the time of the conclusion of
the contract the seller knew or could reasonably be expected to have known.
(2)   However, paragraph (1) does not apply where the right or claim results from the seller's
compliance with technical drawings, designs, formulae or other such specifications furnished by
the buyer.

IV. A. – 2:307: Buyer's Knowledge of Lack of Conformity
(1)   The seller is not liable under IV. A. – 2:302 (Fitness for purpose, qualities, packaging), IV. A. –
2:305 (Third party rights or claims in general) or IV. A. – 2:306 (Third party rights or claims based
on industrial property or other intellectual property) if, at the time of the conclusion of the contract, the buyer knew or could reasonably be assumed to have known of the lack of conformity.

(2)　The seller is not liable under IV. A. – 2:304 (Incorrect installation under a consumer contract for sale) sub-paragraph (b) if, at the time of the conclusion of the contract, the buyer knew or could reasonably be assumed to have known of the shortcoming in the installation instructions.

IV. A. – 2:308: Relevant Time for Establishing Conformity

(1)　The seller is liable for any lack of conformity which exists at the time when the risk passes to the buyer, even if the lack of conformity becomes apparent only after that time.

(2)　In a consumer contract for sale, any lack of conformity which becomes apparent within six months of the time when risk passes to the buyer is presumed to have existed at that time unless this is incompatible with the nature of the goods or the nature of the lack of conformity.

(3)　In a case governed by IV. A. – 2:304 (Incorrect installation under a consumer contract for sale) any reference in paragraphs (1) or (2) to the time when risk passes to the buyer is to be read as a reference to the time when the installation is complete.

IV. A. – 2:309: Limits on Derogation from Conformity Rights in a Consumer Contract for Sale

In a consumer contract for sale, any contractual term or agreement concluded with the seller before a lack of conformity is brought to the seller's attention which directly or indirectly waives or restricts the rights resulting from the seller's obligation to ensure that the goods conform to the contract is not binding on the consumer.

Chapter 3: Obligations of the Buyer

IV. A. – 3:101: Main Obligations of the Buyer

The buyer must:

(a)　pay the price;

(b)　take delivery of the goods; and

(c)　take over documents representing or relating to the goods as may be required by the contract.

IV. A. – 3:102: Determination of Form, Measurement or Other Features

(1)　If under the contract the buyer is to specify the form, measurement or other features of the goods, or the time or manner of their delivery, and fails to make such specification either within the time agreed upon or within a reasonable time after receipt of a request from the seller, the seller may, without prejudice to any other rights, make the specification in accordance with any requirements of the buyer that may be known to the seller.

(2)　A seller who makes such a specification must inform the buyer of the details of the specification and must fix a reasonable time within which the buyer may make a different specification. If, after receipt of such a communication, the buyer fails to do so within the time so fixed, the specification made by the seller is binding.

IV. A. – 3:103: Price Fixed by Weight

If the price is fixed according to the weight of the goods, in case of doubt it is to be determined by the net weight.

IV. A. – 3:104: Taking Delivery

The buyer fulfils the obligation to take delivery by:

(a)　doing all the acts which could reasonably be expected in order to enable the seller to perform the obligation to deliver; and

(b)　taking over the goods, or the documents representing the goods, as required by the contract.

IV. A. – 3:105: Early Delivery and Delivery of Excess Quantity

(1)　If the seller delivers all or part of the goods before the time fixed, the buyer may take delivery or, except where acceptance of the tender would not unreasonably prejudice the buyer's interests, refuse to take delivery.

(2)　If the seller delivers a quantity of goods greater than that provided for by the contract, the buyer may retain or refuse the excess quantity.

(3)　If the buyer retains the excess quantity it is regarded as having been supplied under the contract and must be paid for at the contractual rate.

(4)   In a consumer contract for sale paragraph (3) does not apply if the buyer believes on reasonable grounds that the seller has delivered the excess quantity intentionally and without
error, knowing that it had not been ordered. In such a case the rules on unsolicited goods apply.

Chapter 4: Remedies
Section 1: Limits on Derogation
IV. A. – 4:101: Limits on Derogation from Remedies for Non-Conformity
in a Consumer Contract for Sale

In a consumer contract for sale, any contractual term or agreement concluded with the seller
before a lack of conformity is brought to the seller's attention which directly or indirectly waives
or restricts the remedies of the buyer provided in Book III, Chapter 3 (Remedies for Non-performance), as modified in this Chapter, in respect of the lack of conformity is not binding on the
consumer.

Section 2: Modifications of Buyer's Remedies for Lack of Conformity
IV. A. – 4:201: Termination by Consumer for Lack of Conformity

In a consumer contract for sale, the buyer may terminate the contractual relationship for non-
performance under Book III, Chapter 3, Section 5 (Termination) in the case of any lack of conformity, unless the lack of conformity is minor.

IV. A. – 4:202: Limitation of Liability for Damages of Non-Business Sellers

(1)   If the seller is a natural person acting for purposes not related to that person's trade, business or profession, the buyer is not entitled to damages for lack of conformity exceeding the
contract price.
(2)   The seller is not entitled to rely on paragraph (1) if the lack of conformity relates to facts of
which the seller, at the time when the risk passed to the buyer, knew or could reasonably be
expected to have known and which the seller did not disclose to the buyer before that time.

Section 3: Requirements of Examination and Notification
IV. A. – 4:301: Examination of the Goods

(1)   The buyer should examine the goods, or cause them to be examined, within as short a
period as is reasonable in the circumstances. Failure to do so may result in the buyer losing,
under III. – 3:107 (Failure to notify non-conformity) as supplemented by IV. A. – 4:302 (Notification of lack of conformity), the right to rely on the lack of conformity.
(2)   If the contract involves carriage of the goods, examination may be deferred until after the
goods have arrived at their destination.
(3)   If the goods are redirected in transit, or redispatched by the buyer before the buyer has
had a reasonable opportunity to examine them, and at the time of the conclusion of the
contract the seller knew or could reasonably be expected to have known of the possibility of
such redirection or redispatch, examination may be deferred until after the goods have arrived
at the new destination.
(4)   This Article does not apply to a consumer contract for sale.

IV. A. – 4:302: Notification of Lack of Conformity

(1)   In a contract between two businesses the rule in III. – 3:107 (Failure to notify non-conformity) requiring notification of a lack of conformity within a reasonable time is supplemented by
the following rules.
(2)   The buyer in any event loses the right to rely on a lack of conformity if the buyer does not
give the seller notice of the lack of conformity at the latest within two years from the time at
which the goods were actually handed over to the buyer in accordance with the contract.
(3)   If the parties have agreed that the goods must remain fit for a particular purpose or for
their ordinary purpose during a fixed period of time, the period for giving notice under
paragraph (2) does not expire before the end of the agreed period.

(4)   Paragraph (2) does not apply in respect of third party claims or rights pursuant to IV. A. – 2:305 (Third party rights or claims in general) and IV. A. – 2:306 (Third party rights or claims based on industrial property or other intellectual property) .

IV. A. – 4:303: Notification of Partial Delivery
The buyer does not have to notify the seller that not all the goods have been delivered, if the buyer has reason to believe that the remaining goods will be delivered.

IV. A. – 4:304: Seller's Knowledge of Lack of Conformity
The seller is not entitled to rely on the provisions of IV. A. – 4:301 (Examination of the goods) or IV. A. – 4:302 (Notification of lack of conformity) if the lack of conformity relates to facts of which the seller knew or could reasonably be expected to have known and which the seller did not disclose to the buyer.

Chapter 5: Passing of Risk
Section 1: General Provisions
IV. A. – 5:101: Effect of Passing of Risk
Loss of, or damage to, the goods after the risk has passed to the buyer does not discharge the buyer from the obligation to pay the price, unless the loss or damage is due to an act or omission of the seller.

IV. A. – 5:102: Time When Risk Passes
(1)   The risk passes when the buyer takes over the goods or the documents representing them.
(2)   However, if the contract relates to goods not then identified, the risk does not pass to the buyer until the goods are clearly identified to the contract, whether by markings on the goods, by shipping documents, by notice given to the buyer or otherwise.
(3)   The rule in paragraph (1) is subject to the Articles in Section 2 of this Chapter.

IV. A. – 5:103: Passing of Risk in a Consumer Contract for Sale
(1)   In a consumer contract for sale, the risk does not pass until the buyer takes over the goods.
(2)   Paragraph (1) does not apply if the buyer has failed to perform the obligation to take over the goods and the non-performance is not excused under III. – 3:104 (Excuse due to an impediment) in which case IV. A. – 5:201 (Goods placed at buyer's disposal) applies.
(3)   Except in so far as provided in the preceding paragraph, Section 2 of this Chapter does not apply to a consumer contract for sale.
(4)   The parties may not, to the detriment of the consumer, exclude the application of this Article or derogate from or vary its effects.

Section 2: Special Rules
IV. A. – 5:201: Goods Placed at Buyer's Disposal
(1)   If the goods are placed at the buyer's disposal and the buyer is aware of this, the risk passes to the buyer from the time when the goods should have been taken over, unless the buyer was entitled to withhold taking of delivery under III. – 3:401 (Right to withhold performance of reciprocal obligation).
(2)   If the goods are placed at the buyer's disposal at a place other than a place of business of the seller, the risk passes when delivery is due and the buyer is aware of the fact that the goods are placed at the buyer's disposal at that place.

IV. A. – 5:202: Carriage of the Goods
(1)   This Article applies to any contract of sale which involves carriage of goods.
(2)   If the seller is not bound to hand over the goods at a particular place, the risk passes to the buyer when the goods are handed over to the first carrier for transmission to the buyer in accordance with the contract.
(3)   If the seller is bound to hand over the goods to a carrier at a particular place, the risk does not pass to the buyer until the goods are handed over to the carrier at that place.

(4)   The fact that the seller is authorised to retain documents controlling the disposition of the goods does not affect the passing of the risk.

IV. A. – 5:203: Goods Sold in Transit

(1)   This Article applies to any contract of sale which involves goods sold in transit.

(2)   The risk passes to the buyer at the time the goods are handed over to the first carrier. However, if the circumstances so indicate, the risk passes to the buyer as from the time of the conclusion of the contract.

(3)   If at the time of the conclusion of the contract the seller knew or could reasonably be expected to have known that the goods had been lost or damaged and did not disclose this to the buyer, the loss or damage is at the risk of the seller.

Chapter 6: Consumer Goods Guarantees

IV. A. – 6:101: Definition of a Consumer Goods Guarantee

(1)   A consumer goods guarantee means any undertaking of a type mentioned in the following paragraph given to a consumer in connection with a consumer contract for the sale of goods:

(a)   by a producer or a person in later links of the business chain; or

(b)   by the seller in addition to the seller's obligations as seller of the goods.

(2)   The undertaking may be that:

(a)   apart from misuse, mistreatment or accident the goods will remain fit for their ordinary purpose for a specified period of time, or otherwise;

(b)   the goods will meet the specifications set out in the guarantee document or in associated advertising; or

(c)   subject to any conditions stated in the guarantee,

    (i)   the goods will be repaired or replaced;

    (ii)   the price paid for the goods will be reimbursed in whole or in part; or

    (iii) some other remedy will be provided.

IV. A. – 6:102: Binding Nature of the Guarantee

(1)   A consumer goods guarantee, whether contractual or in the form of a unilateral undertaking, is binding in favour of the first buyer, and in the case of a unilateral undertaking is so binding without acceptance notwithstanding any provision to the contrary in the guarantee document or the associated advertising.

(2)   If not otherwise provided in the guarantee document, the guarantee is also binding without acceptance in favour of every owner of the goods within the duration of the guarantee.

(3)   Any requirement in the guarantee whereby it is conditional on the fulfilment by the guarantee holder of any formal requirement, such as registration or notification of purchase, is not binding on the consumer.

IV. A. – 6:103: Guarantee Document

(1)   A person who gives a consumer goods guarantee must (unless such a document has already been provided to the buyer) provide the buyer with a guarantee document which:

(a)   states that the buyer has legal rights which are not affected by the guarantee;

(b)   points out the advantages of the guarantee for the buyer in comparison with the conformity rules;

(c)   lists all the essential particulars necessary for making claims under the guarantee, notably:

–   the name and address of the guarantor;

–   the name and address of the person to whom any notification is to be made and the procedure by which the notification is to be made;

–   any territorial limitations to the guarantee;

(d)   is drafted in plain, intelligible language; and

(e)   is drafted in the same language as that in which the goods were offered.

(2)   The guarantee document must be in textual form on a durable medium and be available and accessible to the buyer.

(3)   The validity of the guarantee is not affected by any failure to comply with paragraphs (1) and (2), and accordingly the guarantee holder can still rely on the guarantee and require it to be honoured.

(4)   If the obligations under paragraphs (1) and (2) are not observed the guarantee holder may, without prejudice to any right to damages which may be available, require the guarantor to provide a guarantee document which conforms to those requirements.

(5)   The parties may not, to the detriment of the consumer, exclude the application of this Article or derogate from or vary its effects.

IV. A. – 6:104: Coverage of the Guarantee

If the guarantee document does not specify otherwise:

(a)   the period of the guarantee is 5 years or the estimated life-span of the goods, whichever is shorter;

(b)   the guarantor's obligations become effective if, for a reason other than misuse, mistreatment or accident, the goods at any time during the period of the guarantee become unfit for their ordinary purpose or cease to possess such qualities and performance capabilities as the guarantee holder may reasonably expect;

(c)   the guarantor is obliged, if the conditions of the guarantee are satisfied, to repair or replace the goods; and

(d)   all costs involved in invoking and performing the guarantee are to be borne by the guarantor.

IV. A. – 6:105: Guarantee Limited to Specific Parts

A consumer goods guarantee relating only to a specific part or specific parts of the goods must clearly indicate this limitation in the guarantee document; otherwise the limitation is not binding on the consumer.

IV. A. – 6:106: Exclusion or Limitation of the Guarantor's Liability

The guarantee may exclude or limit the guarantor's liability under the guarantee for any failure of or damage to the goods caused by failure to maintain the goods in accordance with instructions, provided that the exclusion or limitation is clearly set out in the guarantee document.

IV. A. – 6:107: Burden of Proof

(1)   Where the guarantee holder invokes a consumer goods guarantee within the period covered by the guarantee the burden of proof is on the guarantor that:

(a)   the goods met the specifications set out in the guarantee document or in associated advertisements; and

(b)   any failure of or damage to the goods is due to misuse, mistreatment, accident, failure to maintain, or other cause for which the guarantor is not responsible.

(2)   The parties may not, to the detriment of the consumer, exclude the application of this Article or derogate from or vary its effects.

IV. A. – 6:108: Prolongation of the Guarantee Period

(1)   If any defect or failure in the goods is remedied under the guarantee then the guarantee is prolonged for a period equal to the period during which the guarantee holder could not use the goods due to the defect or failure.

(2)   The parties may not, to the detriment of the consumer, exclude the application of this Article or derogate from or vary its effects.

Part B. Lease of Goods
Chapter 1: Scope of Application and General Provisions
IV. B. – 1:101: Lease of Goods

(1)   This Part of Book IV applies to contracts for the lease of goods.

(2)   A contract for the lease of goods is a contract under which one party, the lessor, undertakes to provide the other party, the lessee, with a temporary right of use of goods in exchange for rent. The rent may be in the form of money or other value.

(3)   This Part of Book IV does not apply to contracts where the parties have agreed that owner-ship will be transferred after a period with right of use even if the parties have described the contract as a lease.

(4)   The application of this Part of Book IV is not excluded by the fact that the contract has a financing purpose, the lessor has the role as a financing party, or the lessee has an option to be-come owner of the goods.

(5)   This Part of Book IV regulates only the contractual relationship arising from a contract for lease.

IV. B. – 1:102: Consumer Contract for the Lease of Goods

For the purpose of this Part of Book IV, a consumer contract for the lease of goods is a contract for the lease of goods in which the lessor is a business and the lessee is a consumer.

IV. B. – 1:103: Limits on Derogation from Conformity Rights in a Consumer Contract for Lease

In the case of a consumer contract for the lease of goods, any contractual term or agreement concluded with the lessor before a lack of conformity is brought to the lessor's attention which directly or indirectly waives or restricts the rights resulting from the lessor's obligation to ensure that the goods conform to the contract is not binding on the consumer.

IV. B. – 1:104: Limits on Derogation from Rules on Remedies in a Consumer Contract for Lease

(1)   In the case of a consumer contract for the lease of goods the parties may not, to the detri-ment of the consumer, exclude the application of the rules on remedies in Book III, Chapter 3, as modified in Chapters 3 and 6 of this Part, or derogate from or vary their effects.

(2)   Notwithstanding paragraph (1), the parties may agree on a limitation of the lessor's liability for loss related to the lessee's trade, business or profession. Such a term may not, however, be invoked if it would be contrary to good faith and fair dealing to do so.

Chapter 2: Lease Period

IV. B. – 2:101: Start of Lease Period

(1)   The lease period starts:
(a)   at the time determinable from the terms agreed by the parties;
(b)   if a time frame within which the lease period is to start can be determined, at any time chosen by the lessor within that time frame unless the circumstances of the case indicate that the lessee is to choose the time;
(c)   in any other case, a reasonable time after the conclusion of the contract, at the request of either party.

(2)   The lease period starts at the time when the lessee takes control of the goods if this is earlier than the starting time under paragraph (1).

IV. B. – 2:102: End of Lease Period

(1)   A definite lease period ends at the time determinable from the terms agreed by the parties. A definite lease period cannot be terminated unilaterally beforehand by giving notice.

(2)   An indefinite lease period ends at the time specified in a notice of termination given by either party.

(3)   A notice under paragraph (2) is effective only if the time specified in the notice of termina-tion is in compliance with the terms agreed by the parties or, if no period of notice can be deter-mined from such terms, a reasonable time after the notice has reached the other party.

IV. B. – 2:103: Tacit Prolongation

(1)   Where a contract for the lease of goods for a definite period is tacitly prolonged under III. – 1:111 (Tacit prolongation) and where the rent prior to prolongation was calculated so as to take into account amortisation of the cost of the goods by the lessee, the rent payable following pro-longation is limited to what is reasonable having regard to the amount already paid.

(2)   In the case of a consumer contract for the lease of goods the parties may not, to the detri-ment of the consumer, exclude the application of paragraph (1) or derogate from or vary its effects.

Chapter 3: Obligations of the Lessor
IV. B. – 3:101: Availability of the Goods

(1)   The lessor must make the goods available for the lessee's use at the start of the lease period and at the place determined by III. – 2:101 (Place of performance).

(2)   Notwithstanding the rule in the previous paragraph, the lessor must make the goods available for the lessee's use at the lessee's place of business or, as the case may be, at the lessee's habitual residence if the lessor, on the specifications of the lessee, acquires the goods from a supplier selected by the lessee.

(3)   The lessor must ensure that the goods remain available for the lessee's use throughout the lease period, free from any right or reasonably based claim of a third party which prevents or is otherwise likely to interfere with the lessee's use of the goods in accordance with the contract.

(4)   The lessor's obligations when the goods are lost or damaged during the lease period are regulated by IV. B. – 3:104 (Conformity of the goods during the lease period).

IV. B. – 3:102: Conformity with the Contract at the Start of the Lease Period

(1)   The lessor must ensure that the goods conform with the contract at the start of the lease period.

(2)   The goods do not conform with the contract unless they:

(a)   are of the quantity, quality and description required by the terms agreed by the parties;

(b)   are contained or packaged in the manner required by the terms agreed by the parties;

(c)   are supplied along with any accessories, installation instructions or other instructions required by the terms agreed by the parties; and

(d)   comply with the following Article.

IV. B. – 3:103: Fitness for Purpose, Qualities, Packaging etc.

The goods do not conform with the contract unless they:

(a)   are fit for any particular purpose made known to the lessor at the time of the conclusion of the contract, except where the circumstances show that the lessee did not rely, or that it was unreasonable for the lessee to rely, on the lessor's skill and judgement;

(b)   are fit for the purposes for which goods of the same description would ordinarily be used;

(c)   possess the qualities of goods which the lessor held out to the lessee as a sample or model;

(d)   are contained or packaged in the manner usual for such goods or, where there is no such manner, in a manner adequate to preserve and protect the goods;

(e)   are supplied along with such accessories, installation instructions or other instructions as the lessee could reasonably expect to receive; and

(f)   possess such qualities and performance capabilities as the lessee may reasonably expect.

IV. B. – 3:104: Conformity of the Goods During the Lease Period

(1)   The lessor must ensure that throughout the lease period, and subject to normal wear and tear, the goods:

(a)   remain of the quantity, quality and description required by the contract; and

(b)   remain fit for the purposes of the lease, even where this requires modifications to the goods.

(2)   Paragraph (1) does not apply where the rent is calculated so as to take into account the amortisation of the cost of the goods by the lessee.

(3)   Nothing in paragraph (1) affects the lessee's obligations under IV. B. – 5:104 (Handling the goods in accordance with the contract) paragraph (1)(c).

IV. B. – 3:105: Incorrect Installation Under a Consumer Contract for the Lease of Goods

Where, under a consumer contract for the lease of goods, the goods are incorrectly installed, any lack of conformity resulting from the incorrect installation is regarded as a lack of conformity of the goods if:

(a)   the goods were installed by the lessor or under the lessor's responsibility; or

(b)   the goods were intended to be installed by the consumer and the incorrect installation was due to shortcomings in the installation instructions.

IV. B. – 3:106: Obligations on Return of the Goods

The lessor must:

(a)   take all the steps which may reasonably be expected in order to enable the lessee to perform the obligation to return the goods; and

(b)   accept return of the goods as required by the contract.

Chapter 4: Remedies of the Lessee: Modifications of Normal Rules

IV. B. – 4:101: Lessee's Right to Have Lack of Conformity Remedied

(1)   The lessee may have any lack of conformity of the goods remedied, and recover any expenses reasonably incurred, to the extent that the lessee is entitled to enforce specific performance according to III. – 3:302 (Enforcement of non-monetary obligations).

(2)   Nothing in the preceding paragraph affects the lessor's right to cure the lack of conformity according to Book III, Chapter 3, Section 2.

IV. B. – 4:102: Rent Reduction

(1)   The lessee may reduce the rent for a period in which the value of the lessor's performance is decreased due to delay or lack of conformity, to the extent that the reduction in value is not caused by the lessee.

(2)   The rent may be reduced even for periods in which the lessor retains the right to perform or cure according to III. – 3:103 (Notice fixing additional time for performance), III. – 3:202 (Cure by debtor: general rules) paragraph (2) and III. – 3:204 (Consequences of allowing debtor opportunity to cure)).

(3)   Notwithstanding the rule in paragraph (1), the lessee may lose the right to reduce the rent for a period according to IV. B. – 4:103 (Notification of lack of conformity).

IV. B. – 4:103: Notification of Lack of Conformity

(1)   The lessee cannot resort to remedies for lack of conformity unless notification is given to the lessor. Where notification is not timely, the lack of conformity is disregarded for a period corresponding to the unreasonable delay. Notification is always considered timely where it is given within a reasonable time after the lessee has become, or could reasonably be expected to have become, aware of the lack of conformity.

(2)   When the lease period has ended the rules in III. – 3:107 (Failure to notify non-conformity) apply.

(3)   The lessor is not entitled to rely on the provisions of paragraphs (1) and (2) if the lack of conformity relates to facts of which the lessor knew or could reasonably be expected to have known and which the lessor did not disclose to the lessee.

IV. B. – 4:104: Remedies to Be Directed Towards Supplier of the Goods

(1)   This Article applies where:

(a)   the lessor, on the specifications of the lessee, acquires the goods from a supplier selected by the lessee;

(b)   the lessee, in providing the specifications for the goods and selecting the supplier, does not rely primarily on the skill and judgement of the lessor;

(c)   the lessee approves the terms of the supply contract;

(d)   the supplier's obligations under the supply contract are owed, by law or by contract, to the lessee as a party to the supply contract or as if the lessee were a party to that contract; and

(e)   the supplier's obligations owed to the lessee cannot be varied without the consent of the lessee.

(2)   The lessee has no right to enforce performance by the lessor, to reduce the rent or to damages or interest from the lessor, for late delivery or for lack of conformity, unless non-performance results from an act or omission of the lessor.

(3)   The provision in paragraph (2) does not preclude:

(a) any right of the lessee to reject the goods, to terminate the lease under Book III, Chapter 3, Section 5 (Termination) or, prior to acceptance of the goods, to withhold rent to the extent that the lessee could have resorted to these remedies as a party to the supply contract; or

(b) any remedy of the lessee where a third party right or reasonably based claim prevents, or is otherwise likely to interfere with, the lessee's continuous use of the goods in accordance with the contract.

(4) The lessee cannot terminate the lessee's contractual relationship with the supplier under the supply contract without the consent of the lessor.

Chapter 5: Obligations of the Lessee
IV. B. – 5:101: Obligation to Pay Rent

(1) The lessee must pay the rent.

(2) Where the rent cannot be determined from the terms agreed by the parties, from any other applicable rule of law or from usages or practices, it is a monetary sum determined in accordance with II. – 9:104 (Determination of price).

(3) The rent accrues from the start of the lease period.

IV. B. – 5:102: Time for Payment

Rent is payable:

(a) at the end of each period for which the rent is agreed;

(b) if the rent is not agreed for certain periods, at the expiry of a definite lease period; or

(c) if no definite lease period is agreed and the rent is not agreed for certain periods, at the end of reasonable intervals.

IV. B. – 5:103: Acceptance of Goods

The lessee must:

(a) take all steps reasonably to be expected in order to enable the lessor to perform the obligation to make the goods available at the start of the lease period; and

(b) take control of the goods as required by the contract.

IV. B. – 5:104: Handling the Goods in Accordance with the Contract

(1) The lessee must:

(a) observe the requirements and restrictions which follow from the terms agreed by the parties;

(b) handle the goods with the care which can reasonably be expected in the circumstances, taking into account the duration of the lease period, the purpose of the lease and the character of the goods; and

(c) take all measures which could ordinarily be expected to become necessary in order to preserve the normal standard and functioning of the goods, in so far as is reasonable, taking into account the duration of the lease period, the purpose of the lease and the character of the goods.

(2) Where the rent is calculated so as to take into account the amortisation of the cost of the goods by the lessee, the lessee must, during the lease period, keep the goods in the condition they were in at the start of the lease period, subject to any wear and tear which is normal for that kind of goods.

IV. B. – 5:105: Intervention to Avoid Danger or Damage to the Goods

(1) The lessee must take such measures for the maintenance and repair of the goods as would ordinarily be carried out by the lessor, if the measures are necessary to avoid danger or damage to the goods, and it is impossible or impracticable for the lessor, but not for the lessee, to ensure these measures are taken.

(2) The lessee has a right against the lessor to indemnification or, as the case may be, reimbursement in respect of an obligation or expenditure (whether of money or other assets) in so far as reasonably incurred for the purposes of the measures.

IV. B. – 5:106: Compensation for Maintenance and Improvements

(1)   The lessee has no right to compensation for maintenance of or improvements to the goods.

(2)   Paragraph (1) does not exclude or restrict any right the lessee may have to damages or any right the lessee may have under IV. B. – 4:101 (Lessee's right to have lack of conformity remedied), IV. B. – 5:105 (Intervention to avoid danger or damage to the goods) or Book VIII (Acquisition and loss of ownership of goods).

IV. B. – 5:107: Obligation to Inform

(1)   The lessee must inform the lessor of any damage or danger to the goods, and of any right or claim of a third party, if these circumstances would normally give rise to a need for action on the part of the lessor.

(2)   The lessee must inform the lessor under paragraph (1) within a reasonable time after the lessee first becomes aware of the circumstances and their character.

(3)   The lessee is presumed to be aware of the circumstances and their character if the lessee could reasonably be expected to be so aware.

IV. B. – 5:108: Repairs and Inspections of the Lessor

(1)   The lessee, if given reasonable notice where possible, must tolerate the carrying out by the lessor of repair work and other work on the goods which is necessary in order to preserve the goods, remove defects and prevent danger. This obligation does not preclude the lessee from reducing the rent in accordance with IV. B. – 4:102 (Rent reduction).

(2)   The lessee must tolerate the carrying out of work on the goods which does not fall under paragraph (1), unless there is good reason to object.

(3)   The lessee must tolerate inspection of the goods for the purposes indicated in paragraph (1). The lessee must also accept inspection of the goods by a prospective lessee during a reasonable period prior to expiry of the lease.

IV. B. – 5:109: Obligation to Return the Goods

At the end of the lease period the lessee must return the goods to the place where they were made available for the lessee.

Chapter 6: Remedies of the Lessor: Modifications of Normal Rules

IV. B. – 6:101: Limitation of Right to Enforce Payment of Future Rent

(1)   Where the lessee has taken control of the goods, the lessor may not enforce payment of future rent if the lessee wishes to return the goods and it would be reasonable for the lessor to accept their return.

(2)   The fact that a right to enforce specific performance is excluded under paragraph (1) does not preclude a claim for damages.

IV. B. – 6:102: Reduction of Liability in Consumer Contract for the Lease of Goods

(1)   In the case of a consumer contract for the lease of goods, the lessor's right to damages may be reduced to the extent that the loss is mitigated by insurance covering the goods, or to the extent that loss would have been mitigated by insurance, in circumstances where it is reasonable to expect the lessor to take out such insurance.

(2)   The rule in paragraph (1) applies in addition to the rules in Book III, Chapter 3, Section 7.

Chapter 7: New Parties and Sublease

IV. B. – 7:101: Change in Ownership and Substitution of Lessor

(1)   Where ownership passes from the lessor to a new owner, the new owner of the goods is substituted as a party to the lease if the lessee has possession of the goods at the time ownership passes. The former owner remains subsidiarily liable for the non-performance of the obligations under the contract for lease as a personal security provider.

(2)   A reversal of the passing of ownership puts the parties back in their original positions except as regards performance already rendered at the time of reversal.

(3)   The rules in the preceding paragraphs apply accordingly where the lessor has acted as holder of a right other than ownership.

IV. B. – 7:102: Assignment of Lessee's Rights to Performance

The lessee's rights to performance of the lessor's obligations under the contract for lease cannot be assigned without the lessor's consent.

IV. B. – 7:103: Sublease

(1)   The lessee may not sublease the goods without the lessor's consent.

(2)   If consent to a sublease is withheld without good reason, the lessee may terminate the lease by giving a reasonable period of notice.

(3)   In the case of a sublease, the lessee remains liable for the performance of the lessee's obligations under the contract for lease.

Part C. Services
Chapter 1: General Provisions
IV. C. – 1:101: Scope

(1)   This Part of Book IV applies:

(a)   to contracts under which one party, the service provider, undertakes to supply a service to the other party, the client, in exchange for a price; and

(b)   with appropriate adaptations, to contracts under which the service provider undertakes to supply a service to the client otherwise than in exchange for a price.

(2)   It applies in particular to contracts for construction, processing, storage, design, information or advice, and treatment.

IV. C. – 1:102: Exclusions

This Part does not apply to contracts in so far as they are for transport, insurance, the provision of a security or the supply of a financial product or a financial service.

IV. C. – 1:103: Priority Rules

In the case of any conflict:

(a)   the rules in Part IV. D. (Mandate) and Part IV. E. (Commercial agency, franchise and distributorship) prevail over the rules in this Part; and

(b)   the rules in Chapters 3 to 8 of this Part prevail over the rules in Chapter 2 of this Part.

Chapter 2: Rules Applying to Service Contracts in General
IV. C. – 2:101: Price

Where the service provider is a business, a price is payable unless the circumstances indicate otherwise.

IV. C. – 2:102: Pre-Contractual Duties to Warn

(1)   The service provider is under a pre-contractual duty to warn the client if the service provider becomes aware of a risk that the service requested:

(a)   may not achieve the result stated or envisaged by the client;

(b)   may damage other interests of the client; or

(c)   may become more expensive or take more time than reasonably expected by the client.

(2)   The duty to warn in paragraph (1) does not apply if the client:

(a)   already knows of the risks referred to in paragraph (1); or

(b)   could reasonably be expected to know of them.

(3)   If a risk referred to in paragraph (1) materialises and the service provider was in breach of the duty to warn of it, a subsequent change of the service by the service provider under IV. C. – 2:109 (Unilateral variation of the service contract) which is based on the materialisation of the risk is of no effect unless the service provider proves that the client, if duly warned, would have entered into a contract anyway. This is without prejudice to any other remedies, including remedies for mistake, which the client may have.

(4)   The client is under a pre-contractual duty to warn the service provider if the client becomes aware of unusual facts which are likely to cause the service to become more expensive or time-

consuming than expected by the service provider or to cause any danger to the service provider or others when performing the service.

(5)   If the facts referred to under paragraph (4) occur and the service provider was not duly warned, the service provider is entitled to:

(a)   damages for the loss the service provider sustained as a consequence of the failure to
      warn; and

(b)   an adjustment of the time allowed for performance of the service.

(6)   For the purpose of paragraph (1), the service provider is presumed to be aware of the risks
mentioned if they should be obvious from all the facts and circumstances known to the service
provider, considering the information which the service provider must collect about the result
stated or envisaged by the client and the circumstances in which the service is to be carried out.

(7)   For the purpose of paragraph (2)(b) the client cannot reasonably be expected to know of a
risk merely because the client was competent, or was advised by others who were competent,
in the relevant field, unless such other person acted as the agent of the client, in which case II. –
1:105 (Imputed knowledge etc.) applies.

(8)   For the purpose of paragraph (4), the client is presumed to be aware of the facts mentioned if they should be obvious from all the facts and circumstances known to the client without
investigation.

IV. C. – 2:103: Obligation to Co-operate

(1)   The obligation of co-operation requires in particular:

(a)   the client to answer reasonable requests by the service provider for information in so far as
      this may reasonably be considered necessary to enable the service provider to perform the
      obligations under the contract;

(b)   the client to give directions regarding the performance of the service in so far as this may
      reasonably be considered necessary to enable the service provider to perform the obliga-
      tions under the contract;

(c)   the client, in so far as the client is to obtain permits or licences, to obtain these at such time
      as may reasonably be considered necessary to enable the service provider to perform the
      obligations under the contract;

(d)   the service provider to give the client a reasonable opportunity to determine whether the
      service provider is performing the obligations under the contract; and

(e)   the parties to co-ordinate their respective efforts in so far as this may reasonably be consi-
      dered necessary to perform their respective obligations under the contract.

(2)   If the client fails to perform the obligations under paragraph (1)(a) or (b), the service provider may either withhold performance or base performance on the expectations, preferences
and priorities the client could reasonably be expected to have, given the information and directions which have been gathered, provided that the client is warned in accordance with IV. C. –
2:108 (Contractual obligation of the service provider to warn).

(3)   If the client fails to perform the obligations under paragraph (1) causing the service to become more expensive or to take more time than agreed on in the contract, the service provider
is entitled to:

(a)   damages for the loss the service provider sustained as a consequence of the non-perfor-
      mance; and

(b)   an adjustment of the time allowed for supplying the service.

IV. C. – 2:104: Subcontractors, Tools and Materials

(1)   The service provider may subcontract the performance of the service in whole or in part
without the client's consent, unless personal performance is required by the contract.

(2)   Any subcontractor so engaged by the service provider must be of adequate competence.

(3)   The service provider must ensure that any tools and materials used for the performance of
the service are in conformity with the contract and the applicable statutory rules, and fit to
achieve the particular purpose for which they are to be used.

(4)   In so far as subcontractors are nominated by the client or tools and materials are provided by the client, the responsibility of the service provider is governed by IV. C. – 2:107 (Directions of the client) and IV. C. – 2:108 (Contractual obligation of the service provider to warn).

IV. C. – 2:105: Obligation of Skill and Care

(1)   The service provider must perform the service:
(a)   with the care and skill which a reasonable service provider would exercise under the circumstances; and
(b)   in conformity with any statutory or other binding legal rules which are applicable to the service.
(2)   If the service provider professes a higher standard of care and skill the provider must exercise that care and skill.
(3)   If the service provider is, or purports to be, a member of a group of professional service providers for which standards have been set by a relevant authority or by that group itself, the service provider must exercise the care and skill expressed in those standards.
(4)   In determining the care and skill the client is entitled to expect, regard is to be had, among other things, to:
(a)   the nature, the magnitude, the frequency and the foreseeability of the risks involved in the performance of the service for the client;
(b)   if damage has occurred, the costs of any precautions which would have prevented that damage or similar damage from occurring;
(c)   whether the service provider is a business;
(d)   whether a price is payable and, if one is payable, its amount; and
(e)   the time reasonably available for the performance of the service.
(5)   The obligations under this Article require in particular the service provider to take reasonable precautions in order to prevent the occurrence of damage as a consequence of the performance of the service.

IV. C. – 2:106: Obligation to Achieve Result

(1)   The supplier of a service must achieve the specific result stated or envisaged by the client at the time of the conclusion of the contract,
provided that in the case of a result envisaged but not stated:
(a)   the result envisaged was one which the client could reasonably be expected to have envisaged; and
(b)   the client had no reason to believe that there was a substantial risk that the result would not be achieved by the service.
(2)   In so far as ownership of anything is transferred to the client under the service contract, it must be transferred free from any right or reasonably based claim of a third party. IV. A. – 2:305 (Third party rights or claims in general) and IV. A. – 2:306 (Third party rights or claims based on industrial property or other intellectual property) apply with any appropriate adaptations.

IV. C. – 2:107: Directions of the Client

(1)   The service provider must follow all timely directions of the client regarding the performance of the service, provided that the directions:
(a)   are part of the contract itself or are specified in any document to which the contract refers; or
(b)   result from the realisation of choices left to the client by the contract; or
(c)   result from the realisation of choices initially left open by the parties.
(2)   If non-performance of one or more of the obligations of the service provider under IV. C. – 2:105 (Obligation of skill and care) or IV. C. – 2:106 (Obligation to achieve result) is the consequence of following a direction which the service provider is obliged to follow under paragraph (1), the service provider is not liable under those Articles, provided that the client was duly warned under IV. C. – 2:108 (Contractual obligation of the service provider to warn).

(3)   If the service provider perceives a direction falling under paragraph (1) to be a variation of the contract under IV. C. – 2:109 (Unilateral variation of the service contract) the service provider must warn the client accordingly. Unless the client then revokes the direction without undue delay, the service provider must follow the direction and the direction has effect as a variation of the contract.

IV. C. – 2:108: Contractual Obligation of the Service Provider to Warn

(1)   The service provider must warn the client if the service provider becomes aware of a risk that the service requested:
(a)   may not achieve the result stated or envisaged by the client at the time of conclusion of the contract;
(b)   may damage other interests of the client; or
(c)   may become more expensive or take more time than agreed on in the contract either as a result of following information or directions given by the client or collected in preparation for performance, or as a result of the occurrence of any other risk.
(2)   The service provider must take reasonable measures to ensure that the client understands the content of the warning.
(3)   The obligation to warn in paragraph (1) does not apply if the client:
(a)   already knows of the risks referred to in paragraph (1); or
(b)   could reasonably be expected to know of them.
(4)   If a risk referred to in paragraph (1) materialises and the service provider did not perform the obligation to warn the client of it, a notice of variation by the service provider under IV. C. – 2:109 (Unilateral variation of the service contract) based on the materialisation of that risk is without effect.
(5)   For the purpose of paragraph (1), the service provider is presumed to be aware of the risks mentioned if they should be obvious from all the facts and circumstances known to the service provider without investigation.
(6)   For the purpose of paragraph (3)(b), the client cannot reasonably be expected to know of a risk merely because the client was competent, or was advised by others who were competent, in the relevant field, unless such other person acted as the agent of the client, in which case II. – 1:105 (Imputed knowledge etc.) applies.

IV. C. – 2:109: Unilateral Variation of the Service Contract

(1)   Without prejudice to the client's right to terminate under IV. C. – 2:111 (Client's right to terminate), either party may, by notice to the other party, change the service to be provided, if such a change is reasonable taking into account:
(a)   the result to be achieved;
(b)   the interests of the client;
(c)   the interests of the service provider; and
(d)   the circumstances at the time of the change.
(2)   A change is regarded as reasonable only if it is:
(a)   necessary in order to enable the service provider to act in accordance with IV. C. – 2:105 (Obligation of skill and care) or, as the case may be, IV. C. – 2:106 (Obligation to achieve result);
(b)   the consequence of a direction given in accordance with paragraph (1) of IV. C. – 2:107 (Directions of the client) and not revoked without undue delay after receipt of a warning in accordance with paragraph (3) of that Article;
(c)   a reasonable response to a warning from the service provider under IV. C. – 2:108 (Contractual obligation of the service provider to warn); or
(d)   required by a change of circumstances which would justify a variation of the service provider's obligations under III. – 1:110 (Variation or termination by court on a change of circumstances).

(3)   Any additional price due as a result of the change has to be reasonable and is to be determined using the same methods of calculation as were used to establish the original price for the service.

(4)   In so far as the service is reduced, the loss of profit, the expenses saved and any possibility that the service provider may be able to use the released capacity for other purposes are to be taken into account in the calculation of the price due as a result of the change.

(5)   A change of the service may lead to an adjustment of the time of performance proportionate to the extra work required in relation to the work originally required for the performance of the service and the time span determined for performance of the service.

IV. C. – 2:110: Client's Obligation to Notify Anticipated Non-Conformity

(1)   The client must notify the service provider if the client becomes aware during the period for performance of the service that the service provider will fail to perform the obligation under IV. C. – 2:106 (Obligation to achieve result).

(2)   The client is presumed to be so aware if from all the facts and circumstances known to the client without investigation the client has reason to be so aware.

(3)   If a non-performance of the obligation under paragraph (1) causes the service to become more expensive or to take more time than agreed on in the contract, the service provider is entitled to:

(a)   damages for the loss the service provider sustains as a consequence of that failure; and

(b)   an adjustment of the time allowed for performance of the service.

IV. C. – 2:111: Client's Right to Terminate

(1)   The client may terminate the contractual relationship at any time by giving notice to the service provider.

(2)   The effects of termination are governed by III. – 1:109 (Variation or termination by notice) paragraph (3).

(3)   When the client was justified in terminating the relationship no damages are payable for so doing.

(4)   When the client was not justified in terminating the relationship, the termination is nevertheless effective but, the service provider has a right to damages in accordance with the rules in Book III.

(5)   For the purposes of this Article, the client is justified in terminating the relationship if the client:

(a)   was entitled to terminate the relationship under the express terms of the contract and observed any requirements laid down in the contract for doing so;

(b)   was entitled to terminate the relationship under Book III, Chapter 3, Section 5 (Termination); or

(c)   was entitled to terminate the relationship under III. – 1:109 (Variation or termination by notice) paragraph (2) and gave a reasonable period of notice as required by that provision.

Chapter 3: Construction
IV. C. – 3:101: Scope

(1)   This Chapter applies to contracts under which one party, the constructor, undertakes to construct a building or other immovable structure, or to materially alter an existing building or other immovable structure, following a design provided by the client.

(2)   It applies with appropriate adaptations to contracts under which the constructor undertakes:

(a)   to construct a movable or incorporeal thing, following a design provided by the client; or

(b)   to construct a building or other immovable structure, to materially alter an existing building or other immovable structure, or to construct a movable or incorporeal thing, following a design provided by the constructor.

IV. C. – 3:102: Obligation of Client to Co-operate

The obligation of co-operation requires in particular the client to:

(a)   provide access to the site where the construction has to take place in so far as this may reasonably be considered necessary to enable the constructor to perform the obligations under the contract; and
(b)   provide the components, materials and tools, in so far as they must be provided by the client, at such time as may reasonably be considered necessary to enable the constructor to perform the obligations under the contract.

IV. C. – 3:103: Obligation to Prevent Damage to Structure
The constructor must take reasonable precautions in order to prevent any damage to the structure.

IV. C. – 3:104: Conformity
(1)   The constructor must ensure that the structure is of the quality and description required by the contract. Where more than one structure is to be made, the quantity also must be in conformity with the contract.
(2)   The structure does not conform to the contract unless it is:
(a)   fit for any particular purpose expressly or impliedly made known to the constructor at the time of the conclusion of the contract or at the time of any variation in accordance with IV. C. – 2:109 (Unilateral variation of the service contract) pertaining to the issue in question; and
(b)   fit for the particular purpose or purposes for which a structure of the same description would ordinarily be used.
(3)   The client is not entitled to invoke a remedy for non-conformity if a direction provided by the client under IV. C. – 2:107 (Directions of the client) is the cause of the non-conformity and the constructor performed the obligation to warn pursuant to IV. C. – 2:108 (Contractual obligation of the service provider to warn).

IV. C. – 3:105: Inspection, Supervision and Acceptance
(1)   The client may inspect or supervise the tools and materials used in the construction process, the process of construction and the resulting structure in a reasonable manner and at any reasonable time, but is not bound to do so.
(2)   If the parties agree that the constructor has to present certain elements of the tools and materials used, the process or the resulting structure to the client for acceptance, the constructor may not proceed with the construction before having been allowed by the client to do so.
(3)   Absence of, or inadequate, inspection, supervision or acceptance does not relieve the constructor wholly or partially from liability. This rule also applies when the client is under a contractual obligation to inspect, supervise or accept the structure or the construction of it.

IV. C. – 3:106: Handing-Over of the Structure
(1)   If the constructor regards the structure, or any part of it which is fit for independent use, as sufficiently completed and wishes to transfer control over it to the client, the client must accept such control within a reasonable time after being notified. The client may refuse to accept the control when the structure, or the relevant part of it, does not conform to the contract and such non-conformity makes it unfit for use.
(2)   Acceptance by the client of the control over the structure does not relieve the constructor wholly or partially from liability. This rule also applies when the client is under a contractual obligation to inspect, supervise or accept the structure or the construction of it.
(3)   This Article does not apply if, under the contract, control is not to be transferred to the client.

IV. C. – 3:107: Payment of the Price
(1)   The price or a proportionate part of it is payable when the constructor transfers the control of the structure or a part of it to the client in accordance with the preceding Article.
(2)   However, where work remains to be done under the contract on the structure or relevant part of it after such transfer the client may withhold such part of the price as is reasonable until the work is completed.

(3)   If, under the contract, control is not to be transferred to the client, the price is payable when the work has been completed, the constructor has so informed the client and the client has had a chance to inspect the structure.

IV. C. – 3:108: Risks

(1)   This Article applies if the structure is destroyed or damaged due to an event which the constructor could not have avoided or overcome and the constructor cannot be held accountable for the destruction or damage.

(2)   In this Article the "relevant time" is:

(a)   where the control of the structure is to be transferred to the client, the time when such control has been, or should have been, transferred in accordance with IV. C. – 3:106 (Handing-over of the structure);

(b)   in other cases, the time when the work has been completed and the constructor has so informed the client.

(3)   When the situation mentioned in paragraph (1) has been caused by an event occurring before the relevant time and it is still possible to perform:

(a)   the constructor still has to perform or, as the case may be, perform again;

(b)   the client is only obliged to pay for the constructor's performance under (a);

(c)   the time for performance is extended in accordance with paragraph (6) of IV. C. – 2:109 (Unilateral variation of the service contract);

(d)   the rules of III. – 3:104 (Excuse due to an impediment) may apply to the constructor's original performance; and

(e)   the constructor is not obliged to compensate the client for losses to materials provided by the client.

(4)   When the situation mentioned in paragraph (1) has been caused by an event occurring before the relevant time, and it is no longer possible to perform:

(a)   the client does not have to pay for the service rendered;

(b)   the rules of III. – 3:104 (Excuse due to an impediment) may apply to the constructor's performance; and

(c)   the constructor is not obliged to compensate the client for losses to materials provided by the client, but is obliged to return the structure or what remains of it to the client.

(5)   When the situation mentioned in paragraph (1) has been caused by an event occurring after the relevant time:

(a)   the constructor does not have to perform again; and

(b)   the client remains obliged to pay the price.

Chapter 4: Processing
IV. C. – 4:101: Scope

(1)   This Chapter applies to contracts under which one party, the processor, undertakes to perform a service on an existing movable or incorporeal thing or to an immovable structure for another party, the client. It does not, however, apply to construction work on an existing building or other immovable structure.

(2)   This Chapter applies in particular to contracts under which the processor undertakes to repair, maintain or clean an existing movable or incorporeal thing or immovable structure.

IV. C. – 4:102: Obligation of Client to Co-operate

The obligation to co-operate requires in particular the client to:

(a)   hand over the thing or to give the control of it to the processor, or to give access to the site where the service is to be performed in so far as may reasonably be considered necessary to enable the processor to perform the obligations under the contract; and

(b)   in so far as they must be provided by the client, provide the components, materials and tools in time to enable the processor to perform the obligations under the contract.

IV. C. – 4:103: Obligation to Prevent Damage to Thing Being Processed

The processor must take reasonable precautions in order to prevent any damage to the thing being processed.

IV. C. – 4:104: Inspection and Supervision

(1)   If the service is to be performed at a site provided by the client, the client may inspect or supervise the tools and material used, the performance of the service and the thing on which the service is performed in a reasonable manner and at any reasonable time, but is not bound to do so.

(2)   Absence of, or inadequate inspection or supervision does not relieve the processor wholly or partially from liability. This rule also applies when the client is under a contractual obligation to accept, inspect or supervise the processing of the thing.

IV. C. – 4:105: Return of the Thing Processed

(1)   If the processor regards the service as sufficiently completed and wishes to return the thing or the control of it to the client, the client must accept such return or control within a reasonable time after being notified. The client may refuse to accept the return or control when the thing is not fit for use in accordance with the particular purpose for which the client had the service performed, provided that such purpose was made known to the processor or that the processor otherwise has reason to know of it.

(2)   The processor must return the thing or the control of it within a reasonable time after being so requested by the client.

(3)   Acceptance by the client of the return of the thing or the control of it does not relieve the processor wholly or partially from liability for nonperformance.

(4)   If, by virtue of the rules on the acquisition of property, the processor has become the owner of the thing, or a share in it, as a consequence of the performance of the obligations under the contract, the processor must transfer ownership of the thing or share when the thing is returned.

IV. C. – 4:106: Payment of the Price

(1)   The price is payable when the processor transfers the thing or the control of it to the client in accordance with IV. C. – 4:105 (Return of the thing processed) or the client, without being entitled to do so, refuses to accept the return of the thing.

(2)   However, where work remains to be done under the contract on the thing after such transfer or refusal the client may withhold such part of the price as is reasonable until the work is completed.

(3)   If, under the contract, the thing or the control of it is not to be transferred to the client, the price is payable when the work has been completed and the processor has so informed the client.

IV. C. – 4:107: Risks

(1)   This Article applies if the thing is destroyed or damaged due to an event which the processor could not have avoided or overcome and the processor cannot be held accountable for the destruction or damage.

(2)   If, prior to the event mentioned in paragraph (1), the processor had indicated that the processor regarded the service as sufficiently completed and that the processor wished to return the thing or the control of it to the client:

(a)   the processor is not required to perform again; and

(b)   the client must pay the price.

The price is due when the processor returns the remains of the thing, if any, or the client indicates that the client does not want the remains. In the latter case, the processor may dispose of the remains at the client's expense. This provision does not apply if the client was entitled to refuse the return of the thing under paragraph (1) of IV. C. – 4:105 (Return of the thing processed).

(3)   If the parties had agreed that the processor would be paid for each period which has elapsed, the client is obliged to pay the price for each period which has elapsed before the event mentioned in paragraph (1) occurred.

(4)   If, after the event mentioned in paragraph (1), performance of the obligations under the contract is still possible for the processor:

(a)   the processor still has to perform or, as the case may be, perform again;

(b)   the client is only obliged to pay for the processor's performance under (a); the processor's entitlement to a price under paragraph (3) is not affected by this provision;

(c)   the client is obliged to compensate the processor for the costs the processor has to incur in order to acquire materials replacing the materials supplied by the client, unless the client on being so requested by the processor supplies these materials; and

(d)   if need be, the time for performance is extended in accordance with paragraph (6) of IV. C. – 2:109 (Unilateral variation of the service contract).

This paragraph is without prejudice to the client's right to terminate the contractual relationship under IV. C. – 2:111 (Client's right to terminate).

(5)   If, in the situation mentioned in paragraph (1), performance of the obligations under the contract is no longer possible for the processor:

(a)   the client does not have to pay for the service rendered; the processor's entitlement to a price under paragraph (3) is not affected by this provision; and

(b)   the processor is obliged to return to the client the thing and the materials supplied by the client or what remains of them, unless the client indicates that the client does not want the remains. In the latter case, the processor may dispose of the remains at the client's expense.

IV. C. – 4:108: Limitation of Liability

In a contract between two businesses, a term restricting the processor's liability for non-performance to the value of the thing, had the service been performed correctly, is presumed to be fair for the purposes of II. – 9:405 (Meaning of "unfair" in contracts between businesses) except to the extent that it restricts liability for damage caused intentionally or by way of grossly negligent behaviour on the part of the processor or any person for whose actions the processor is responsible.

Chapter 5: Storage
IV. C. – 5:101: Scope

(1)   This Chapter applies to contracts under which one party, the storer, undertakes to store a movable or incorporeal thing for another party, the client.

(2)   This Chapter does not apply to the storage of:

(a)   immovable structures;

(b)   movable or incorporeal things during transportation; and

(c)   money or securities (except in the circumstances mentioned in paragraph (7) of IV. C. – 5:110 (Liability of the hotel-keeper)) or rights.

IV. C. – 5:102: Storage Place and Subcontractors

(1)   The storer, in so far as the storer provides the storage place, must provide a place fit for storing the thing in such a manner that the thing can be returned in the condition the client may expect.

(2)   The storer may not subcontract the performance of the service without the client's consent.

IV. C. – 5:103: Protection and Use of the Thing Stored

(1)   The storer must take reasonable precautions in order to prevent unnecessary deterioration, decay or depreciation of the thing stored.

(2)   The storer may use the thing handed over for storage only if the client has agreed to such use.

IV. C. – 5:104: Return of the Thing Stored

(1)   Without prejudice to any other obligation to return the thing, the storer must return the thing at the agreed time or, where the contractual relationship is terminated before the agreed time, within a reasonable time after being so requested by the client.

(2)   The client must accept the return of the thing when the storage obligation comes to an end and when acceptance of return is properly requested by the storer.

(3)   Acceptance by the client of the return of the thing does not relieve the storer wholly or partially from liability for non-performance.

(4)   If the client fails to accept the return of the thing at the time provided under paragraph (2), the storer has the right to sell the thing in accordance with III. – 2:111 (Property not accepted), provided that the storer has given the client reasonable warning of the storer's intention to do so. (5)   If, during storage, the thing bears fruit, the storer must hand this fruit over when the thing is returned to the client.

(6)   If, by virtue of the rules on the acquisition of ownership, the storer has become the owner of the thing, the storer must return a thing of the same kind and the same quality and quantity and transfer ownership of that thing. This Article applies with appropriate adaptations to the substituted thing.

(7)   This Article applies with appropriate adaptations if a third party who has the right or authority to receive the thing requests its return.

IV. C. – 5:105: Conformity

(1)   The storage of the thing does not conform with the contract unless the thing is returned in the same condition as it was in when handed over to the storer.

(2)   If, given the nature of the thing or the contract, it cannot reasonably be expected that the thing is returned in the same condition, the storage of the thing does not conform with the contract if the thing is not returned in such condition as the client could reasonably expect.

(3)   If, given the nature of the thing or the contract, it cannot reasonably be expected that the same thing is returned, the storage of the thing does not conform with the contract if the thing which is returned is not in the same condition as the thing which was handed over for storage, or if it is not of the same kind, quality and quantity, or if ownership of the thing is not transferred in accordance with paragraph (6) of IV. C. – 5:104 (Return of the thing stored).

IV. C. – 5:106: Payment of the Price

(1)   The price is payable at the time when the thing is returned to the client in accordance with IV. C. – 5:104 (Return of the thing stored) or the client, without being entitled to do so, refuses to accept the return of the thing.

(2)   The storer may withhold the thing until the client pays the price. III. – 3:401 (Right to withhold performance of reciprocal obligation) applies accordingly.

IV. C. – 5:107: Post-Storage Obligation to Inform

After the ending of the storage, the storer must inform the client of:

(a)   any damage which has occurred to the thing during storage; and

(b)   the necessary precautions which the client must take before using or transporting the thing, unless the client could reasonably be expected to be aware of the need for such precautions.

IV. C. – 5:108: Risks

(1)   This Article applies if the thing is destroyed or damaged due to an event which the storer could not have avoided or overcome and if the storer cannot be held accountable for the destruction or damage.

(2)   If, prior to the event, the storer had notified the client that the client was required to accept the return of the thing, the client must pay the price. The price is due when the storer returns the remains of the thing, if any, or the client indicates to the storer that the client does not want those remains.

(3)   If, prior to the event, the storer had not notified the client that the client was required to accept the return of the thing:
(a)   if the parties had agreed that the storer would be paid for each period of time which has elapsed, the client must pay the price for each period which has elapsed before the event occurred;
(b)   if further performance of the obligations under the contract is still possible for the storer, the storer is required to continue performance, without prejudice to the client's right to terminate the contractual relationship under IV. C. – 2:111 (Client's right to terminate);
(c)   if performance of the obligations under the contract is no longer possible for the storer the client does not have to pay for the service rendered except to the extent that the storer is entitled to a price under subparagraph (a); and the storer must return to the client the remains of the thing unless the client indicates that the client does not want those remains.
(4)   If the client indicates to the storer that the client does not want the remains of the thing, the storer may dispose of the remains at the client's expense.

IV. C. – 5:109: Limitation of Liability
In a contract between two businesses, a term restricting the storer's liability for non-performance to the value of the thing is presumed to be fair for the purposes of II. – 9:405 (Meaning of "unfair" in contracts between businesses), except to the extent that it restricts liability for damage caused intentionally or by way of grossly negligent conduct on the part of the storer or any person for whose actions the storer is responsible.

IV. C. – 5:110: Liability of the Hotel-Keeper
(1)   A hotel-keeper is liable as a storer for any damage to, or destruction or loss of, a thing brought to the hotel by any guest who stays at the hotel and has sleeping accommodation there.
(2)   For the purposes of paragraph (1) a thing is regarded as brought to the hotel:
(a)   if it is at the hotel during the time when the guest has the use of sleeping accommodation there;
(b)   if the hotel-keeper or a person for whose actions the hotel-keeper is responsible takes charge of it outside the hotel during the period for which the guest has the use of the sleeping accommodation at the hotel; or
(c)   if the hotel-keeper or a person for whose actions the hotel-keeper is responsible takes charge of it whether at the hotel or outside it during a reasonable period preceding or following the time when the guest has the use of sleeping accommodation at the hotel.
(3)   The hotel-keeper is not liable in so far as the damage, destruction or loss is caused by:
(a)   a guest or any person accompanying, employed by or visiting the guest;
(b)   an impediment beyond the hotel-keeper's control; or
(c)   the nature of the thing.
(4)   A term excluding or limiting the liability of the hotel-keeper is unfair for the purposes of Book II, Chapter 9, Section 4 if it excludes or limits liability in a case where the hotel-keeper, or a person for whose actions the hotel-keeper is responsible, causes the damage, destruction or loss intentionally or by way of grossly negligent conduct.
(5)   Except where the damage, destruction or loss is caused intentionally or by way of grossly negligent conduct of the hotel-keeper or a person for whose actions the hotel-keeper is responsible, the guest is required to inform the hotel-keeper of the damage, destruction or loss without undue delay. If the guest fails to inform the hotel-keeper without undue delay, the hotel-keeper is not liable.
(6)   The hotel-keeper has the right to withhold any thing referred to in paragraph (1) until the guest has satisfied any right the hotel-keeper has against the guest with respect to accommodation, food, drink and solicited services performed for the guest in the hotel-keeper's professional capacity.
(7)   This Article does not apply if and to the extent that a separate storage contract is concluded between the hotel-keeper and any guest for any thing brought to the hotel. A separate

storage contract is concluded if a thing is handed over for storage to, and accepted for storage by, the hotel-keeper.

Chapter 6: Design
IV. C. – 6:101: Scope
(1)   This Chapter applies to contracts under which one party, the designer, undertakes to design for another party, the client:
(a)   an immovable structure which is to be constructed by or on behalf of the client; or
(b)   a movable or incorporeal thing or service which is to be constructed or performed by or on behalf of the client.
(2)   A contract under which one party undertakes to design and to supply a service which consists of carrying out the design is to be considered as primarily a contract for the supply of the subsequent service.

IV. C. – 6:102: Pre-contractual Duty to Warn
The designer's pre-contractual duty to warn requires in particular the designer to warn the client in so far as the designer lacks special expertise in specific problems which require the involvement of specialists.

IV. C. – 6:103: Obligation of Skill and Care
The designer's obligation of skill and care requires in particular the designer to:
(a)   attune the design work to the work of other designers who contracted with the client, to enable there to be an efficient performance of all services involved;
(b)   integrate the work of other designers which is necessary to ensure that the design will conform to the contract;
(c)   include any information for the interpretation of the design which is necessary for a user of the design of average competence (or a specific user made known to the designer at the conclusion of the contract) to give effect to the design;
(d)   enable the user of the design to give effect to the design without violation of public law rules or interference based on justified third-party rights of which the designer knows or could reasonably be expected to know; and
(e)   provide a design which allows economic and technically efficient realisation.

IV. C. – 6:104: Conformity
(1)   The design does not conform to the contract unless it enables the user of the design to achieve a specific result by carrying out the design with the skill and care which could reasonably be expected.
(2)   The client is not entitled to invoke a remedy for non-conformity if a direction provided by the client under IV. C. – 2:107 (Directions of the client) is the cause of the non-conformity and the designer performed the obligation to warn under IV. C. – 2:108 (Contractual obligation of the service provider to warn).

IV. C. – 6:105: Handing Over of the Design
(1)   In so far as the designer regards the design, or a part of it which is fit for carrying out independently from the completion of the rest of the design, as sufficiently completed and wishes to transfer the design to the client, the client must accept it within a reasonable time after being notified.
(2)   The client may refuse to accept the design when it, or the relevant part of it, does not conform to the contract and such non-conformity amounts to a fundamental non-performance.

IV. C. – 6:106: Records
(1)   After performance of both parties' other contractual obligations, the designer must, on request by the client, hand over all relevant documents or copies of them.
(2)   The designer must store, for a reasonable time, relevant documents which are not handed over. Before destroying the documents, the designer must offer them again to the client.

IV. C. – 6:107: Limitation of Liability

In contracts between two businesses, a term restricting the designer's liability for non-performance to the value of the structure, thing or service which is to be constructed or performed by or on behalf of the client following the design, is presumed to be fair for the purposes of II. – 9:405 (Meaning of "unfair" in contracts between businesses) except to the extent that it restricts liability for damage caused intentionally or by grossly negligent conduct on the part of the designer or any person for whose actions the designer is responsible.

Chapter 7: Information and Advice
IV. C. – 7:101: Scope

(1) This Chapter applies to contracts under which one party, the provider, undertakes to provide information or advice to another party, the client.
(2) This Chapter does not apply in relation to treatment in so far as Chapter 8 (Treatment) contains more specific rules on the obligation to inform.
(3) In the remainder of this Chapter any reference to information includes a reference to advice.

IV. C. – 7:102: Obligation to Collect Preliminary Data

(1) The provider must, in so far as this may reasonably be considered necessary for the performance of the service, collect data about:
(a) the particular purpose for which the client requires the information;
(b) the client's preferences and priorities in relation to the information;
(c) the decision the client can be expected to make on the basis of the information; and
(d) the personal situation of the client.
(2) In case the information is intended to be passed on to a group of persons, the data to be collected must relate to the purposes, preferences, priorities and personal situations that can reasonably be expected from individuals within such a group.
(3) In so far as the provider must obtain data from the client, the provider must explain what the client is required to supply.

IV. C. – 7:103: Obligation to Acquire and Use Expert Knowledge

The provider must acquire and use the expert knowledge to which the provider has or should have access as a professional information provider or adviser, in so far as this may reasonably be considered necessary for the performance of the service.

IV. C. – 7:104: Obligation of Skill and Care

(1) The provider's obligation of skill and care requires in particular the provider to:
(a) take reasonable measures to ensure that the client understands the content of the information;
(b) act with the care and skill that a reasonable information provider would demonstrate under the circumstances when providing evaluative information; and
(c) in any case where the client is expected to make a decision on the basis of the information, inform the client of the risks involved, in so far as such risks could reasonably be expected to influence the client's decision.
(2) When the provider expressly or impliedly undertakes to provide the client with a recommendation to enable the client to make a subsequent decision, the provider must:
(a) base the recommendation on a skilful analysis of the expert knowledge to be collected in relation to the purposes, priorities, preferences and personal situation of the client;
(b) inform the client of alternatives the provider can personally provide relating to the subsequent decision and of their advantages and risks, as compared with those of the recommended decision; and
(c) inform the client of other alternatives the provider cannot personally provide, unless the provider expressly informs the client that only a limited range of alternatives is offered or this is apparent from the situation.

IV. C. – 7:105: Conformity

(1)   The provider must provide information which is of the quantity, quality and description required by the contract.

(2)   The factual information provided by the information provider to the client must be a correct description of the actual situation described.

IV. C. – 7:106: Records

In so far as this may reasonably be considered necessary, having regard to the interest of the client, the provider must keep records regarding the information provided in accordance with this Chapter and make such records or excerpts from them available to the client on reasonable request.

IV. C. – 7:107: Conflict of Interest

(1)   When the provider expressly or impliedly undertakes to provide the client with a recommendation to enable the client to make a subsequent decision, the provider must disclose any possible conflict of interest which might influence the performance of the provider's obligations.

(2)   So long as the contractual obligations have not been completely performed, the provider may not enter into a relationship with another party which may give rise to a possible conflict with the interests of the client, without full disclosure to the client and the client's explicit or implicit consent.

IV. C. – 7:108: Influence of Ability of the Client

(1)   The involvement in the supply of the service of other persons on the client's behalf or the mere competence of the client does not relieve the provider of any obligation under this Chapter.

(2)   The provider is relieved of those obligations if the client already has knowledge of the information or if the client has reason to know of the information.

(3)   For the purpose of paragraph (2), the client has reason to know if the information should be obvious to the client without investigation.

IV. C. – 7:109: Causation

If the provider knows or could reasonably be expected to know that a subsequent decision will be based on the information to be provided, and if the client makes such a decision and suffers loss as a result, any non-performance of an obligation under the contract by the provider is presumed to have caused the loss if the client proves that, if the provider had provided all information required, it would have been reasonable for the client to have seriously considered making an alternative decision.

Chapter 8: Treatment

IV. C. – 8:101: Scope

(1)   This Chapter applies to contracts under which one party, the treatment provider, undertakes to provide medical treatment for another party, the patient.

(2)   It applies with appropriate adaptations to contracts under which the treatment provider undertakes to provide any other service in order to change the physical or mental condition of a person.

(3)   Where the patient is not the contracting party, the patient is regarded as a third party on whom the contract confers rights corresponding to the obligations of the treatment provider imposed by this Chapter.

IV. C. – 8:102: Preliminary Assessment

The treatment provider must, in so far as this may reasonably be considered necessary for the performance of the service:

(a)   interview the patient about the patient's health condition, symptoms, previous illnesses, allergies, previous or other current treatment and the patient's preferences and priorities in relation to the treatment;

(b)   carry out the examinations necessary to diagnose the health condition of the patient; and

(c)   consult with any other treatment providers involved in the treatment of the patient.

IV. C. – 8:103: Obligations Regarding Instruments, Medicines, Materials, Installations and Premises

(1)   The treatment provider must use instruments, medicines, materials, installations and premises which are of at least the quality demanded by accepted and sound professional practice, which conform to applicable statutory rules, and which are fit to achieve the particular purpose for which they are to be used.

(2)   The parties may not, to the detriment of the patient, exclude the application of this Article or derogate from or vary its effects.

IV. C. – 8:104: Obligation of Skill and Care

(1)   The treatment provider's obligation of skill and care requires in particular the treatment provider to provide the patient with the care and skill which a reasonable treatment provider exercising and professing care and skill would demonstrate under the given circumstances.

(2)   If the treatment provider lacks the experience or skill to treat the patient with the required degree of skill and care, the treatment provider must refer the patient to a treatment provider who can.

(3)   The parties may not, to the detriment of the patient, exclude the application of this Article or derogate from or vary its effects.

IV. C. – 8:105: Obligation to Inform

(1)   The treatment provider must, in order to give the patient a free choice regarding treatment, inform the patient about, in particular:
(a)   the patient's existing state of health;
(b)   the nature of the proposed treatment;
(c)   the advantages of the proposed treatment;
(d)   the risks of the proposed treatment;
(e)   the alternatives to the proposed treatment, and their advantages and risks as compared to those of the proposed treatment; and
(f)   the consequences of not having treatment.

(2)   The treatment provider must, in any case, inform the patient about any risk or alternative which might reasonably influence the patient's decision on whether to give consent to the proposed treatment or not. It is presumed that a risk might reasonably influence that decision if its materialisation would lead to serious detriment to the patient. Unless otherwise provided, the obligation to inform is subject to the provisions of Chapter 7 (Information and Advice).

(3)   The information must be provided in a way understandable to the patient.

IV. C. – 8:106: Obligation to Inform in Case of Unnecessary or Experimental Treatment

(1)   If the treatment is not necessary for the preservation or improvement of the patient's health, the treatment provider must disclose all known risks.

(2)   If the treatment is experimental, the treatment provider must disclose all information regarding the objectives of the experiment, the nature of the treatment, its advantages and risks and the alternatives, even if only potential.

(3)   The parties may not, to the detriment of the patient, exclude the application of this Article or derogate from or vary its effects.

IV. C. – 8:107: Exceptions to the Obligation to Inform

(1)   Information which would normally have to be provided by virtue of the obligation to inform may be withheld from the patient:
(a)   if there are objective reasons to believe that it would seriously and negatively influence the patient's health or life; or
(b)   if the patient expressly states a wish not to be informed, provided that the non-disclosure of the information does not endanger the health or safety of third parties.

(2)   The obligation to inform need not be performed where treatment must be provided in an emergency. In such a case the treatment provider must, so far as possible, provide the information later.

IV. C. – 8:108: Obligation Not to Treat Without Consent

(1) The treatment provider must not carry out treatment unless the patient has given prior informed consent to it.

(2) The patient may revoke consent at any time.

(3) In so far as the patient is incapable of giving consent, the treatment provider must not carry out treatment unless:

(a) informed consent has been obtained from a person or institution legally entitled to take decisions regarding the treatment on behalf of the patient; or

(b) any rules or procedures enabling treatment to be lawfully given without such consent have been complied with; or

(c) the treatment must be provided in an emergency.

(4) In the situation described in paragraph (3), the treatment provider must not carry out treatment without considering, so far as possible, the opinion of the incapable patient with regard to the treatment and any such opinion expressed by the patient before becoming incapable.

(5) In the situation described in paragraph (3), the treatment provider may carry out only such treatment as is intended to improve the health condition of the patient.

(6) In the situation described in paragraph (2) of IV. C. – 8:106 (Obligation to inform in case of unnecessary or experimental treatment), consent must be given in an express and specific way.

(7) The parties may not, to the detriment of the patient, exclude the application of this Article or derogate from or vary its effects.

IV. C. – 8:109: Records

(1) The treatment provider must create adequate records of the treatment. Such records must include, in particular, information collected in any preliminary interviews, examinations or consultations, information regarding the consent of the patient and information regarding the treatment performed.

(2) The treatment provider must, on reasonable request:

(a) give the patient, or if the patient is incapable of giving consent, the person or institution legally entitled to take decisions on behalf of the patient, access to the records; and

(b) answer, in so far as reasonable, questions regarding the interpretation of the records.

(3) If the patient has suffered injury and claims that it is a result of non-performance by the treatment provider of the obligation of skill and care and the treatment provider fails to comply with paragraph (2), non-performance of the obligation of skill and care and a causal link between such non-performance and the injury are presumed.

(4) The treatment provider must keep the records, and give information about their interpretation, during a reasonable time of at least 10 years after the treatment has ended, depending on the usefulness of these records for the patient or the patient's heirs or representatives and for future treatments. Records which can reasonably be expected to be important after the reasonable time must be kept by the treatment provider after that time. If for any reason the treatment provider ceases activity, the records must be deposited or delivered to the patient for future consultation.

(5) The parties may not, to the detriment of the patient, exclude the application of paragraphs (1) to (4) or derogate from or vary their effects.

(6) The treatment provider may not disclose information about the patient or other persons involved in the patient's treatment to third parties unless disclosure is necessary in order to protect third parties or the public interest. The treatment provider may use the records in an anonymous way for statistical, educational or scientific purposes.

IV. C. – 8:110: Remedies for Non-Performance

With regard to any non-performance of an obligation under a contract for treatment, Book III, Chapter 3 (Remedies for Non-performance) and IV. C. – 2:111 (Client's right to terminate) apply with the following adaptations:

(a) the treatment provider may not withhold performance or terminate the contractual relationship under that Chapter if this would seriously endanger the health of the patient; and

(b)   in so far as the treatment provider has the right to withhold performance or to terminate the contractual relationship and is planning to exercise that right, the treatment provider must refer the patient to another treatment provider.

IV. C. – 8:111: Obligations of Treatment-Providing Organisations
(1)   If, in the process of performance of the obligations under the treatment contract, activities take place in a hospital or on the premises of another treatment-providing organisation, and the hospital or that other treatment-providing organisation is not a party to the treatment contract, it must make clear to the patient that it is not the contracting party.
(2)   Where the treatment provider cannot be identified, the hospital or treatment-providing organisation in which the treatment took place is treated as the treatment provider unless the hospital or treatment-providing organisation informs the patient, within a reasonable time, of the identity of the treatment provider.
(3)   The parties may not, to the detriment of the patient, exclude the application of this Article or derogate from or vary its effects.

Part D. Mandate Contracts
Chapter 1: General Provisions
IV. D. – 1:101: Scope
(1)   This Part of Book IV applies to contracts and other juridical acts under which a person, the agent, is authorised and instructed (mandated) by another person, the principal:
(a)   to conclude a contract between the principal and a third party or otherwise directly affect the legal position of the principal in relation to a third party;
(b)   to conclude a contract with a third party, or do another juridical act in relation to a third party, on behalf of the principal but in such a way that the agent and not the principal is a party to the contract or other juridical act; or
(c)   to take steps which are meant to lead to, or facilitate, the conclusion of a contract between the principal and a third party or the doing of another juridical act which would affect the legal position of the principal in relation to a third party.
(2)   It applies where the agent undertakes to act on behalf of, and in accordance with the instructions of, the principal and, with appropriate adaptations, where the agent is merely authorised but does not undertake to act, but nevertheless does act.
(3)   It applies where the agent is to be paid a price and, with appropriate adaptations, where the agent is not to be paid a price.
(4)   It applies only to the internal relationship between the principal and the agent (the mandate relationship). It does not apply to the relationship between the principal and the third party or the relationship (if any) between the agent and the third party.
(5)   Contracts to which this Part applies and to which Part C (Services) also applies are to be regarded as falling primarily under this Part.
(6)   This Part does not apply to contracts pertaining to investment services and activities as defined by Directive 2004/39/EC, OJ 2004 L 145/1, as subsequently amended or replaced.

IV. D. – 1:102: Definitions
In this Part;
(a)   the 'mandate' of the agent is the authorisation and instruction given by the principal as modified by any subsequent direction;
(b)   the 'mandate contract' is the contract under which the agent is authorised and instructed to act, and any reference to the mandate contract includes a reference to any other juridical act by which the agent is authorised and instructed to act;
(c)   the 'prospective contract' is the contract the agent is authorised and instructed to conclude, negotiate or facilitate, and any reference to the prospective contract includes a reference to any other juridical act which the agent is authorised and instructed to do, negotiate or facilitate;

(d)   a mandate for direct representation is a mandate under which the agent is to act in the name of the principal, or otherwise in such a way as to indicate an intention to affect the principal's legal position;

(e)   a mandate for indirect representation is a mandate under which the agent is to act in the agent's own name or otherwise in such a way as not to indicate an intention to affect the principal's legal position;

(f)   a "direction" is a decision by the principal pertaining to the performance of the obligations under the mandate contract or to the contents of the prospective contract that is given at the time the mandate contract is concluded or, in accordance with the mandate, at a later moment;

(g)   the "third party" is the party with whom the prospective contract is to be concluded, negotiated or facilitated by the agent;

(h)   the "revocation" of the mandate of the agent is the recall by the principal of the mandate, so that it no longer has effect.

IV. D. – 1:103: Duration of the Mandate Contract

A mandate contract may be concluded:

(a)   for an indefinite period of time;

(b)   for a fixed period; or

(c)   for a particular task.

IV. D. – 1:104: Revocation of the Mandate

(1)   Unless the following Article applies, the mandate of the agent can be revoked by the principal at any time by giving notice to the agent.

(2)   The termination of the mandate relationship has the effect of a revocation of the mandate of the agent.

(3)   The parties may not, to the detriment of the principal, exclude the application of this Article or derogate from or vary its effects, unless the requirements of the following Article are met.

IV. D. – 1:105: Irrevocable Mandate

(1)   In derogation of the preceding Article, the mandate of the agent cannot be revoked by the principal if the mandate is given:

(a)   in order to safeguard a legitimate interest of the agent other than the interest in the payment of the price; or

(b)   in the common interest of the parties to another legal relationship, whether or not these parties are all parties to the mandate contract, and the irrevocability of the mandate of the agent is meant to properly safeguard the interest of one or more of these parties.

(2)   The mandate may nevertheless be revoked if:

(a)   the mandate is irrevocable under paragraph (1)(a) and:

   (i)   the contractual relationship from which the legitimate interest of the agent originates is terminated for non-performance by the agent; or

   (ii)   there is a fundamental non-performance by the agent of the obligations under the mandate contract; or

   (iii) there is an extraordinary and serious reason for the principal to terminate under IV. D. – 6:103 (Termination by principal for extraordinary and serious reason); or

(b)   the mandate is irrevocable under paragraph (1)(b) and:

   (i)   the parties in whose interest the mandate is irrevocable have agreed to the revocation of the mandate;

   (ii)   the relationship referred to in paragraph (1)(b) is terminated;

   (iii) the agent commits a fundamental non-performance of the obligations under the mandate contract, provided that the agent is replaced without undue delay by another agent in conformity with the terms regulating the legal relationship between the principal and the other party or parties; or

   (iv)   there is an extraordinary and serious reason for the principal to terminate under IV. D. – 6:103 (Termination by principal for extraordinary and serious reason), provided that the agent is replaced without undue delay by another agent in conformity with the terms regulating the legal relationship between the principal and the other party or parties.

(3) Where the revocation of the mandate is not allowed under this Article, a notice of revocation is without effect.

(4) This Article does not apply if the mandate relationship is terminated under Chapter 7 of this Part.

Chapter 2: Main Obligations of the Principal

IV. D. – 2:101: Obligation to Co-operate

The obligation to co-operate under III. – 1:104 (Co-operation) requires the principal in particular to:

(a) answer requests by the agent for information in so far as such information is needed to allow the agent to perform the obligations under the mandate contract;

(b) give a direction regarding the performance of the obligations under the mandate contract in so far as this is required under the mandate contract or follows from a request for a direction under IV. D. – 4:102 (Request for a direction).

IV. D. – 2:102: Price

(1) The principal must pay a price if the agent performs the obligations under the mandate contract in the course of a business, unless the principal expected and could reasonably have expected the agent to perform the obligations otherwise than in exchange for a price.

(2) The price is payable when the mandated task has been completed and the agent has given account of that to the principal.

(3) If the parties had agreed on payment of a price for services rendered, the mandate relationship has terminated and the mandated task has not been completed, the price is payable as of the moment the agent has given account of the performance of the obligations under the mandate contract.

(4) When the mandate is for the conclusion of a prospective contract and the principal has concluded the prospective contract directly or another person appointed by the principal has concluded the prospective contract on the principal's behalf, the agent is entitled to the price or a proportionate part of it if the conclusion of the prospective contract can be attributed in full or in part to the agent's performance of the obligations under the mandate contract.

(5) When the mandate is for the conclusion of a prospective contract and the prospective contract is concluded after the mandate relationship has terminated, the principal must pay the price if payment of a price based solely on the conclusion of the prospective contract was agreed and:

(a) the conclusion of the prospective contract is mainly the result of the agent's efforts; and

(b) the prospective contract is concluded within a reasonable period after the mandate relationship has terminated.

IV. D. – 2:103: Expenses Incurred by Agent

(1) When the agent is entitled to a price, the price is presumed to include the reimbursement of the expenses the agent has incurred in the performance of the obligations under the mandate contract.

(2) When the agent is not entitled to a price or when the parties have agreed that the expenses will be paid separately, the principal must reimburse the agent for the expenses the agent has incurred in the performance of the obligations under the mandate contract, when and in so far as the agent acted reasonably when incurring the expenses.

(3) The agent is entitled to reimbursement of expenses under paragraph (2) as from the time when the expenses are incurred and the agent has given account of the expenses.

(4) If the mandate relationship has terminated and the result on which the agent's remuneration is dependent is not achieved, the agent is entitled to reimbursement of reasonable expenses the agent has incurred in the performance of the obligations under the mandate contract. Paragraph (3) applies accordingly.

Chapter 3: Performance by the Agent
Section 1: Main Obligations of Agent
IV. D. – 3:101: Obligation to Act in Accordance with Mandate

At all stages of the mandate relationship the agent must act in accordance with the mandate.

IV. D. – 3:102: Obligation to Act in Interests of Principal

(1)   The agent must act in accordance with the interests of the principal, in so far as these have been communicated to the agent or the agent could reasonably be expected to be aware of them.

(2)   Where the agent is not sufficiently aware of the principal's interests to enable the agent to properly perform the obligations under the mandate contract, the agent must request information from the principal.

IV. D. – 3:103: Obligation of Skill and Care

(1)   The agent has an obligation to perform the obligations under the mandate contract with the care and skill that the principal is entitled to expect under the circumstances.

(2)   If the agent professes a higher standard of care and skill the agent has an obligation to exercise that care and skill.

(3)   If the agent is, or purports to be, a member of a group of professional agents for which standards exist that have been set by a relevant authority or by that group itself, the agent must exercise the care and skill expressed in these standards.

(4)   In determining the care and skill the principal is entitled to expect, regard is to be had, among other things, to:

(a)   the nature, the magnitude, the frequency and the foreseeability of the risks involved in the performance of the obligations;

(b)   whether the obligations are performed by a non-professional or gratuitously;

(c)   the amount of the remuneration for the performance of the obligations; and

(d)   the time reasonably available for the performance of the obligations.

Section 2: Consequences of Acting Beyond Mandate
IV. D. – 3:201: Acting Beyond Mandate

(1)   The agent may act in a way not covered by the mandate if:

(a)   the agent has reasonable ground for so acting on behalf of the principal;

(b)   the agent does not have a reasonable opportunity to discover the principal's wishes in the particular circumstances; and

(c)   the agent does not know and could not reasonably be expected to know that the act in the particular circumstances is against the principal's wishes.

(2)   An act within paragraph (1) has the same consequences as between the agent and the principal as an act covered by the mandate.

IV. D. – 3:202: Consequences of Ratification

Where, in circumstances not covered by the preceding Article, an agent has acted beyond the mandate in concluding a contract on behalf of the principal, ratification of that contract by the principal absolves the agent from liability to the principal, unless the principal without undue delay after ratification notifies the agent that the principal reserves remedies for the non-performance by the agent.

Section 3: Mandate Normally Not Exclusive
IV. D. – 3:301: Exclusivity Not Presumed

The principal is free to conclude, negotiate or facilitate the prospective contract directly or to appoint another agent to do so.

IV. D. – 3:302: Subcontracting

(1)   The agent may subcontract the performance of the obligations under the mandate contract in whole or in part without the principal's consent, unless personal performance is required by the contract.

(2)   Any subcontractor so engaged by the agent must be of adequate competence.

(3)   In accordance with III. – 2:106 (Performance entrusted to another) the agent remains responsible for performance.

Section 4: Obligation to Inform Principal

IV. D. – 3:401: Information About Progress of Performance

During the performance of the obligations under the mandate contract the agent must in so far as is reasonable under the circumstances inform the principal of the existence of, and the progress in, the negotiations or other steps leading to the possible conclusion or facilitation of the prospective contract.

IV. D. – 3:402: Accounting to the Principal

(1)   The agent must without undue delay inform the principal of the completion of the mandated task.
(2)   The agent must give an account to the principal:
(a)   of the manner in which the obligations under the mandate contract have been performed; and
(b)   of money spent or received or expenses incurred by the agent in performing those obligations.
(3)   Paragraph (2) applies with appropriate modifications if the mandate relationship is terminated in accordance with Chapters 6 and 7 and the obligations under the mandate contract have not been fully performed.

IV. D. – 3:403: Communication of Identity of Third Party

(1)   An agent who concludes the prospective contract with a third party must communicate the name and address of the third party to the principal on the principal's demand.
(2)   In the case of a mandate for indirect representation paragraph (1) applies only if the agent has become insolvent.

Chapter 4: Directions and Changes

Section 1: Directions

IV. D. – 4:101: Directions Given by Principal

(1)   The principal is entitled to give directions to the agent.
(2)   The agent must follow directions by the principal.
(3)   The agent must warn the principal if the direction:
(a)   has the effect that the performance of the obligations under the mandate contract would become significantly more expensive or take significantly more time than agreed upon in the mandate contract; or
(b)   is inconsistent with the purpose of the mandate contract or may otherwise be detrimental to the interests of the principal.
(4)   Unless the principal revokes the direction without undue delay after having been so warned by the agent, the direction is to be regarded as a change of the mandate contract under IV. D. – 4:201 (Changes of the mandate contract).

IV. D. – 4:102: Request for a Direction

(1)   The agent must ask for a direction on obtaining information which requires the principal to make a decision pertaining to the performance of the obligations under the mandate contract or the content of the prospective contract.
(2)   The agent must ask for a direction if the mandated task is the conclusion of a prospective contract and the mandate contract does not determine whether the mandate is for direct representation or indirect representation.

IV. D. – 4:103: Consequences of Failure to Give a Direction

(1)   If the principal fails to give a direction when required to do so under the mandate contract or under paragraph (1) of IV. D. – 4:102 (Request for a direction), the agent may, in so far as relevant, resort to any of the remedies under Book III, Chapter 3 (Remedies for Non-performance) or base performance upon the expectations, preferences and priorities the principal might reasonably be expected to have, given the information and directions that have been gathered.

(2)   Where the agent bases performance upon the expectations, preferences and priorities the principal might reasonably be expected to have, the agent has a right to a proportionate adjustment of the price and of the time allowed or required for the conclusion of the prospective contract.

(3)   If the principal fails to give a direction under paragraph (2) of IV. D. – 4:102 (Request for a direction), the agent may choose direct representation or indirect representation or may withhold performance under III. – 3:401 (Right to withhold performance of reciprocal obligation).

(4)   The adjusted price that is to be paid under paragraph (2) must be reasonable and is to be determined using the same methods of calculation as were used to establish the original price for the performance of the obligations under the mandate contract.

IV. D. – 4:104: No Time to Ask or Wait for Direction

(1)   If the agent is required to ask for a direction under IV. D. – 4:102 (Request for a direction) but needs to act before being able to contact the principal and to ask for a direction, or needs to act before the direction is given, the agent may base performance upon the expectations, preferences and priorities the principal might reasonably be expected to have, given the information and directions that have been gathered.

(2)   In the situation referred to in paragraph (1), the agent has a right to a proportionate adjustment of the price and of the time allowed or required for the performance of the obligations under the mandate contract in so far as such an adjustment is reasonable given the circumstances of the case.

Section 2: Changes of the Mandate Contract
IV. D. – 4:201: Changes of the Mandate Contract

(1)   The mandate contract is changed if the principal:
(a)   significantly changes the mandate of the agent;
(b)   does not revoke a direction without undue delay after having been warned in accordance with paragraph (3) of IV. D. – 4:101 (Directions given by principal).

(2)   In the case of a change of the mandate contract under paragraph (1) the agent is entitled:
(a)   to a proportionate adjustment of the price and of the time allowed or required for the performance of the obligations under the mandate contract; or
(b)   to damages in accordance with III. – 3:702 (General measure of damages) to put the agent as nearly as possible into the position in which the agent would have been if the mandate contract had not been changed.

(3)   In the case of a change of the mandate contract under paragraph (1) the agent may also terminate the mandate relationship by giving notice of termination for an extraordinary and serious reason under IV. D. – 6:105 (Termination by agent for extraordinary and serious reason), unless the change is minor or is to the agent's advantage.

(4)   The adjusted price that is to be paid under paragraph (2)(a) must be reasonable and is to be determined using the same methods of calculation as were used to establish the original price for the performance of the obligations under the mandate contract.

Chapter 5: Conflicts of Interests
IV. D. – 5:101: Self-Contracting

(1)   The agent may not become the principal's counterparty to the prospective contract.
(2)   The agent may nevertheless become the counterparty if:
(a)   this is agreed by the parties in the mandate contract;
(b)   the agent has disclosed an intention to become the counterparty and:
      (i)   the principal subsequently expresses consent; or
      (ii) the principal does not object to the agent becoming the counterparty after having been requested to indicate consent or a refusal of consent;
(c)   the principal otherwise knew, or could reasonably be expected to have known, of the agent becoming the counterparty and the principal did not object within a reasonable time; or

(d) the content of the prospective contract is so precisely determined in the mandate contract that there is no risk that the interests of the principal may be disregarded.

(3) If the principal is a consumer, the agent may only become the counterparty if:

(a) the agent has disclosed that information and the principal has given express consent to the agent becoming the counterparty to the particular prospective contract; or

(b) the content of the prospective contract is so precisely determined in the mandate contract that there is no risk that the interests of the principal may be disregarded.

(4) The parties may not, to the detriment of the principal, exclude the application of paragraph (3) or derogate from or vary its effects.

(5) If the agent has become the counterparty, the agent is not entitled to a price for services rendered as an agent.

IV. D. – 5:102: Double Mandate

(1) The agent may not act as the agent of both the principal and the principal's counterparty to the prospective contract.

(2) The agent may nevertheless act as the agent of both the principal and the counterparty if:

(a) this is agreed by the parties in the mandate contract;

(b) the agent has disclosed an intention to act as the agent of the counterparty and the principal:

(i) subsequently expresses consent; or

(ii) does not object to the agent acting as the agent of the counterparty after having been requested to indicate consent or a refusal of consent;

(c) the principal otherwise knew, or could reasonably be expected to have known, of the agent acting as the agent of the counterparty and the principal did not object within a reasonable time; or

(d) the content of the prospective contract is so precisely determined in the mandate contract that there is no risk that the interests of the principal may be disregarded.

(3) If the principal is a consumer, the agent may only act as the agent of both the principal and of the counterparty if:

(a) the agent has disclosed that information and the principal has given express consent to the agent acting also as the agent of the counterparty to the particular prospective contract; or

(b) the content of the prospective contract is so precisely determined in the mandate contract that there is no risk that the interests of the principal may be disregarded.

(4) The parties may not, to the detriment of the principal, exclude the application of paragraph (3) or derogate from or vary its effects.

(5) If and in so far as the agent has acted in accordance with the previous paragraphs, the agent is entitled to the price.

Chapter 6: Termination by Notice Other than for Non-Performance

IV. D. – 6:101: Termination by Notice in General

(1) Either party may terminate the mandate relationship at any time by giving notice to the other.

(2) For the purposes of paragraph (1), a revocation of the mandate of the agent is treated as termination.

(3) Termination of the mandate relationship is not effective if the mandate of the agent is irrevocable under IV. D. – 1:105 (Irrevocable mandate).

(4) The effects of termination are governed by III. – 1:109 (Variation or termination by notice) paragraph (3).

(5) When the party giving the notice was justified in terminating the relationship no damages are payable for so doing.

(6) When the party giving the notice was not justified in terminating the relationship, the termination is nevertheless effective but the other party is entitled to damages in accordance with the rules in Book III.

(7)   For the purposes of this Article the party giving the notice is justified in terminating the relationship if that party:
(a)   was entitled to terminate the relationship under the express terms of the contract and observed any requirements laid down in the contract for doing so;
(b)   was entitled to terminate the relationship under Book III, Chapter 3, Section 5 (Termination); or
(c)   was entitled to terminate the relationship under any other Article of the present Chapter and observed any requirements laid down in such Article for doing so.

IV. D. – 6:102: Termination by Principal When Relationship Is to Last for Indefinite Period or When Mandate Is for a Particular Task

(1)   The principal may terminate the mandate relationship at any time by giving notice of reasonable length if the mandate contract has been concluded for an indefinite period or for a particular task.
(2)   Paragraph (1) does not apply if the mandate is irrevocable.
(3)   The parties may not, to the detriment of the principal, exclude the application of this Article or derogate from or vary its effects, unless the conditions set out under IV. D. – 1:105 (Irrevocable mandate) are met.

IV. D. – 6:103: Termination by Principal for Extraordinary and Serious Reason

(1)   The principal may terminate the mandate relationship by giving notice for extraordinary and serious reason.
(2)   No period of notice is required.
(3)   For the purposes of this Article, the death or incapacity of the person who, at the time of conclusion of the mandate contract, the parties had intended to perform the agent's obligations under the mandate contract, constitutes an extraordinary and serious reason.
(4)   This Article applies with appropriate adaptations if the successors of the principal terminate the mandate relationship in accordance with IV. D. – 7:102 (Death of the principal).
(5)   The parties may not, to the detriment of the principal or the principal's successors, exclude the application of this Article or derogate from or vary its effects.

IV. D. – 6:104: Termination by Agent When Relationship Is to Last for Indefinite Period or When it Is Gratuitous

(1)   The agent may terminate the mandate relationship at any time by giving notice of reasonable length if the mandate contract has been concluded for an indefinite period.
(2)   The agent may terminate the mandate relationship by giving notice of reasonable length if the agent is to represent the principal otherwise than in exchange for a price.
(3)   The parties may not, to the detriment of the agent, exclude the application of paragraph (1) of this Article or derogate from or vary its effects.

IV. D. – 6:105: Termination by Agent for Extraordinary and Serious Reason

(1)   The agent may terminate the mandate relationship by giving notice for extraordinary and serious reason.
(2)   No period of notice is required.
(3)   For the purposes of this Article an extraordinary and serious reason includes:
(a)   a change of the mandate contract under IV. D. – 4:201 (Changes of the mandate contract);
(b)   the death or incapacity of the principal; and
(c)   the death or incapacity of the person who, at the time of conclusion of the mandate contract, the parties had intended to perform the agent's obligations under the mandate contract.
(4)   The parties may not, to the detriment of the agent, exclude the application of this Article or derogate from or vary its effects.

Chapter 7: Other Grounds for Termination
IV. D. – 7:101: Conclusion of Prospective Contract by Principal or Other Agent

(1)   If the mandate contract was concluded solely for the conclusion of a specific prospective contract the mandate relationship terminates when the principal or another agent appointed by the principal has concluded the prospective contract.

(2)   In such a case, the conclusion of the prospective contract is treated as a notice under IV. D. – 6:101 (Termination by notice in general).

IV. D. – 7:102: Death of the Principal

(1)   The death of the principal does not end the mandate relationship.

(2)   Both the agent and the successors of the principal may terminate the mandate relationship by giving notice of termination for extraordinary and serious reason under IV. D. – 6:103 (Termination by principal for extraordinary and serious reason) or IV. D. – 6:105 (Termination by agent for extraordinary and serious reason).

IV. D. – 7:103: Death of the Agent

(1)   The death of the agent ends the mandate relationship.

(2)   The expenses and any other payments due at the time of death remain payable.

Part E. Commercial Agency, Franchise and Distributorship
Chapter 1: General Provisions
Section 1: Scope
IV. E. – 1:101: Contracts Covered

(1)   This Part of Book IV applies to contracts for the establishment and regulation of a commercial agency, franchise or distributorship and with appropriate adaptations to other contracts under which a party engaged in business independently is to use skills and efforts to bring another party's products on to the market.

(2)   In this Part, "products" includes goods and services.

Section 2: Other General Provisions
IV. E. – 1:201: Priority Rules

In the case of any conflict:

(a)   the rules in this Part prevail over the rules in Part D (Mandate); and

(b)   the rules in Chapters 3 to 5 of this Part prevail over the rules in Chapter 2 of this Part.

Chapter 2: Rules Applying to All Contracts Within the Scope of this Part
Section 1: Pre-Contractual
IV. E. – 2:101: Pre-contractual Information Duty

A party who is engaged in negotiations for a contract within the scope of this Part has a duty to provide the other party, a reasonable time before the contract is concluded and so far as required by good commercial practice, with such information as is sufficient to enable the other party to decide on a reasonably informed basis whether or not to enter into a contract of the type and on the terms under consideration.

Section 2: Obligations of the Parties
IV. E. – 2:201: Co-operation

The parties to a contract within the scope of this Part of Book IV must collaborate actively and loyally and co-ordinate their respective efforts in order to achieve the objectives of the contract.

IV. E. – 2:202: Information During the Performance

During the period of the contractual relationship each party must provide the other in due time with all the information which the first party has and the second party needs in order to achieve the objectives of the contract.

IV. E. – 2:203: Confidentiality

(1)   A party who receives confidential information from the other must keep such information confidential and must not disclose the information to third parties either during or after the period of the contractual relationship.

(2)   A party who receives confidential information from the other must not use such information for purposes other than the objectives of the contract.

(3)   Any information which a party already possessed or which has been disclosed to the general public, and any information which must necessarily be disclosed to customers as a result of the operation of the business is not regarded as confidential information for this purpose.

Section 3: Termination of Contractual Relationship
IV. E. – 2:301: Contract for a Definite Period

A party is free not to renew a contract for a definite period. If a party has given notice in due time that it wishes to renew the contract, the contract will be renewed for an indefinite period unless the other party gives that party notice, not later than a reasonable time before the expiry of the contract period, that it is not to be renewed.

IV. E. – 2:302: Contract for an Indefinite Period

(1)   Either party to a contract for an indefinite period may terminate the contractual relationship by giving notice to the other.

(2)   If the notice provides for termination after a period of reasonable length no damages are payable under IV. E. – 2:303 (Damages for termination with inadequate notice). If the notice provides for immediate termination or termination after a period which is not of reasonable length damages are payable under that Article.

(3)   Whether a period of notice is of reasonable length depends, among other factors, on:

(a)   the time the contractual relationship has lasted;

(b)   reasonable investments made;

(c)   the time it will take to find a reasonable alternative; and

(d)   usages.

(4)   A period of notice of one month for each year during which the contractual relationship has lasted, with a maximum of 36 months, is presumed to be reasonable.

(5)   The period of notice for the principal, the franchisor or the supplier is to be no shorter than one month for the first year, two months for the second, three months for the third, four months for the fourth, five months for the fifth and six months for the sixth and subsequent years during which the contractual relationship has lasted. Parties may not exclude the application of this provision or derogate from or vary its effects.

(6)   Agreements on longer periods than those laid down in paragraphs (4) and (5) are valid provided that the agreed period to be observed by the principal, franchisor or supplier is no shorter than that to be observed by the commercial agent, the franchisee or the distributor.

(7)   In relation to contracts within the scope of this Part, the rules in this Article replace those in paragraph (2) of III. – 1:109 (Variation or termination by notice). Paragraph (3) of that Article governs the effects of termination.

IV. E. – 2:303: Damages for Termination with Inadequate Notice

(1)   Where a party terminates a contractual relationship under IV. E. – 2:302 (Contract for an indefinite period) but does not give a reasonable period of notice the other party is entitled to damages.

(2)   The general measure of damages is such sum as corresponds to the benefit which the other party would have obtained during the extra period for which the relationship would have lasted if a reasonable period of notice had been given.

(3)   The yearly benefit is presumed to be equal to the average benefit which the aggrieved party has obtained from the contract during the previous 3 years or, if the contractual relationship has lasted for a shorter period, during that period.

(4)   The general rules on damages for non-performance in Book III, Chapter 3, Section 7 apply with any appropriate adaptations.

IV. E. – 2:304: Termination for Non-Performance
(1)   Any term of a contract within the scope of this Part whereby a party may terminate the contractual relationship for non-performance which is not fundamental is without effect.
(2)   The parties may not exclude the application of this Article or derogate from or vary its effects.

IV. E. – 2:305: Indemnity for Goodwill
(1)   When the contractual relationship comes to an end for any reason (including termination by either party for fundamental non-performance), a party is entitled to an indemnity from the other party for goodwill if and to the extent that:
(a)   the first party has significantly increased the other party's volume of business and the other party continues to derive substantial benefits from that business; and
(b)   the payment of the indemnity is reasonable.
(2)   The grant of an indemnity does not prevent a party from seeking damages under IV. E. – 2:303 (Damages for termination with inadequate notice).

IV. E. – 2:306: Stock, Spare Parts and Materials
If the contract is avoided, or the contractual relationship terminated, by either party, the party whose products are being brought on to the market must repurchase the other party's remaining stock, spare parts and materials at a reasonable price, unless the other party can reasonably resell them.

Section 4: Other General Provisions
IV. E. – 2:401: Right of Retention
In order to secure its rights to remuneration, compensation, damages and indemnity the party who is bringing the products on to the market has a right of retention over the movables of the other party which are in its possession as a result of the contract, until the other party has performed its obligations.

IV. E. – 2:402: Signed Document Available on Request
(1)   Each party is entitled to receive from the other, on request, a signed statement in textual form on a durable medium setting out the terms of the contract.
(2)   The parties may not exclude the application of this Article or derogate from or vary its effects.

Chapter 3: Commercial Agency
Section 1: General
IV. E. – 3:101: Scope
This Chapter applies to contracts under which one party, the commercial agent, agrees to act on a continuing basis as a self-employed intermediary to negotiate or to conclude contracts on behalf of another party, the principal, and the principal agrees to remunerate the agent for those activities.

Section 2: Obligations of the Commercial Agent
IV. E. – 3:201: Negotiate and Conclude Contracts
The commercial agent must make reasonable efforts to negotiate contracts on behalf of the principal and to conclude the contracts which the agent was instructed to conclude.

IV. E. – 3:202: Instructions
The commercial agent must follow the principal's reasonable instructions, provided they do not substantially affect the agent's independence.

IV. E. – 3:203: Information by Agent During the Performance
The obligation to inform requires the commercial agent in particular to provide the principal with information concerning:
(a)   contracts negotiated or concluded;
(b)   market conditions;

(c)   the solvency of and other characteristics relating to clients.

IV. E. – 3:204: Accounting

(1)   The commercial agent must maintain proper accounts relating to the contracts negotiated or concluded on behalf of the principal.

(2)   If the agent represents more than one principal, the agent must maintain independent accounts for each principal.

(3)   If the principal has important reasons to doubt that the agent maintains proper accounts, the agent must allow an independent accountant to have reasonable access to the agent's books upon the principal's request. The principal must pay for the services of the independent accountant.

Section 3: Obligations of the Principal

IV. E. – 3:301: Commission During the Agency

(1)   The commercial agent is entitled to commission on any contract concluded with a client during the period covered by the agency, if:

(a)   the contract has been concluded
- (i)   as a result of the commercial agent's efforts;
- (ii)   with a third party whom the commercial agent has previously acquired as a client for contracts of the same kind; or
- (iii)   with a client belonging to a certain geographical area or group of clients with which the commercial agent was entrusted; and

(b)   either
- (i)   the principal has or should have performed the principal's obligations under the contract; or
- (ii)   the client has performed the client's obligations under the contract or justifiably withholds performance.

(2)   The parties may not, to the detriment of the commercial agent, exclude the application of paragraph (1)(b)(ii) or derogate from or vary its effects.

IV. E. – 3:302: Commission After the Agency Has Ended

(1)   The commercial agent is entitled to commission on any contract concluded with a client after the agency has ended, if:

(a)   either
- (i)   the contract with the client is mainly the result of the commercial agent's efforts during the period covered by the agency contract, and the contract with the client was concluded within a reasonable period after the agency ended; or
- (ii)   the requirements of paragraph (1) of IV. E. – 3:301 (Commission during the agency) would have been satisfied except that the contract with the client was not concluded during the period of the agency, and the client's offer reached the principal or the commercial agent before the agency ended; and

(b)   either
- (i)   the principal has or should have performed the principal's obligations under the contract; or
- (ii)   the client has performed the client's obligations under the contract or justifiably withholds the client's performance.

(2)   The parties may not, to the detriment of the commercial agent, exclude the application of paragraph (1)(b)(ii) or derogate from or vary its effects.

IV. E. – 3:303: Conflicting Entitlements of Successive Agents

The commercial agent is not entitled to the commission referred to in IV. E. – 3:301 (Commission during the agency) if a previous commercial agent is entitled to that commission under IV.E– 3:302 (Commission after the agency has ended), unless it is reasonable that the commission is shared between the two commercial agents.

IV. E. – 3:304: When Commission Is to Be Paid

(1)   The principal must pay the commercial agent's commission not later than the last day of the month following the quarter in which the agent became entitled to it.

(2)   The parties may not, to the detriment of the commercial agent, exclude the application of this Article or derogate from or vary its effects.

IV. E. – 3:305: Entitlement to Commission Extinguished

(1)   A contract term whereby the commercial agent's entitlement to commission on a contract concluded with a client is extinguished is valid only if and to the extent that it provides for extinction on the basis that the client's contractual obligations are not performed for a reason for which the principal is not accountable.

(2)   Upon the extinguishing of the commercial agent's entitlement to commission, the commercial agent must refund any commission already received.

(3)   The parties may not, to the detriment of the commercial agent, exclude the application of paragraph (1) or derogate from or vary its effects.

IV. E. – 3:306: Remuneration

Any remuneration which wholly or partially depends upon the number or value of contracts is presumed to be commission within the meaning of this Chapter.

IV. E. – 3:307: Information by Principal During the Performance

The obligation to inform requires the principal in particular to provide the commercial agent with information concerning:

(a)   characteristics of the goods or services; and

(b)   prices and conditions of sale or purchase.

IV. E. – 3:308: Information on Acceptance, Rejection and Non-performance

(1)   The principal must inform the commercial agent, within a reasonable period, of:

(a)   the principal's acceptance or rejection of a contract which the commercial agent has negotiated on the principal's behalf; and

(b)   any non-performance of obligations under a contract which the commercial agent has negotiated or concluded on the principal's behalf.

(2)   The parties may not, to the detriment of the commercial agent, exclude the application of this Article or derogate from or vary its effects.

IV. E. – 3:309: Warning of Decreased Volume of Contracts

(1)   The principal must warn the commercial agent within a reasonable time when the principal foresees that the volume of contracts that the principal will be able to conclude will be significantly lower than the commercial agent could reasonably have expected.

(2)   For the purpose of paragraph (1) the principal is presumed to foresee what the principal could reasonably be expected to foresee.

(3)   The parties may not, to the detriment of the commercial agent, exclude the application of this Article or derogate from or vary its effects.

IV. E. – 3:310: Information on Commission

(1)   The principal must supply the commercial agent in reasonable time with a statement of the commission to which the commercial agent is entitled. This statement must set out how the amount of the commission has been calculated.

(2)   For the purpose of calculating commission, the principal must provide the commercial agent upon request with an extract from the principal's books.

(3)   The parties may not, to the detriment of the commercial agent, exclude the application of this Article or derogate from or vary its effects.

IV. E. – 3:311: Accounting

(1)   The principal must maintain proper accounts relating to the contracts negotiated or concluded by the commercial agent.

(2)   If the principal has more than one commercial agent, the principal must maintain independent accounts for each commercial agent.
(3)   The principal must allow an independent accountant to have reasonable access to the
principal's books upon the commercial agent's request, if:
(a)   the principal does not comply with the principal's obligations under paragraphs (1) or (2) of
      IV. E. – 3:310 (Information on commission); or
(b)   the commercial agent has important reasons to doubt that the principal maintains proper
      accounts.

IV. E. – 3:312: Amount of Indemnity

(1)   The commercial agent is entitled to an indemnity for goodwill on the basis of IV. E. – 2:305
(Indemnity for goodwill) amounting to:
(a)   the average commission on contracts with new clients and on the increased volume of
      business with existing clients calculated for the last 12 months, multiplied by:
(b)   the number of years the principal is likely to continue to derive benefits from these con-
      tracts in the future.
(2)   The resulting indemnity must be amended to take account of:
(a)   the probable attrition of clients, based on the average rate of migration in the commercial
      agent's territory; and
(b)   the discount required for early payment, based on average interest rates.
(3)   In any case, the indemnity must not exceed one year's remuneration, calculated from the
commercial agent's average annual remuneration over the preceding five years or, if the contractual relationship has been in existence for less than five years, from the average during the
period in question.
(4)   The parties may not, to the detriment of the commercial agent, exclude the application of
this Article or derogate from or vary its effects.

IV. E. – 3:313: Del Credere Clause

(1)   An agreement whereby the commercial agent guarantees that a client will pay the price of
the products forming the subject-matter of the contract which the commercial agent has negotiated or concluded (del credere clause) is valid only if and to the extent that the agreement:
(a)   is in textual form on a durable medium;
(b)   covers particular contracts which were negotiated or concluded by the commercial agent
      or such contracts with particular clients who are specified in the agreement; and
(c)   is reasonable with regard to the interests of the parties.
(2)   The commercial agent is entitled to be paid a commission of a reasonable amount on contracts to which the del credere guarantee applies (del credere commission).

Chapter 4: Franchise
Section 1: General
IV. E. – 4:101: Scope

This Chapter applies to contracts under which one party (the franchisor) grants the other party
(the franchisee), in exchange for remuneration, the right to conduct a business (franchise business) within the franchisor's network for the purposes of supplying certain products on the franchisee's behalf and in the franchisee's name, and under which the franchisee has the right and
the obligation to use the franchisor's tradename or trademark or other intellectual property
rights, know-how and business method.

IV. E. – 4:102: Pre-contractual information

(1)   The duty under IV. E. – 2:101 (Pre-contractual information duty) requires the franchisor in
particular to provide the franchisee with adequate and timely information concerning:
(a)   the franchisor's company and experience;
(b)   the relevant intellectual property rights;
(c)   the characteristics of the relevant know-how;
(d)   the commercial sector and the market conditions;

(e)   the particular franchise method and its operation;
(f)   the structure and extent of the franchise network;
(g)   the fees, royalties or any other periodical payments; and
(h)   the terms of the contract.
(2)   Even if the franchisor's non-compliance with paragraph (1) does not give rise to a mistake for which the contract could be avoided under II. – 7:201 (Mistake), the franchisee may recover damages in accordance with paragraphs (2) and (3) of II. – 7:214 (Damages for loss), unless the franchisor had reason to believe that the information was adequate or had been given in reasonable time.
(3)   The parties may not exclude the application of this Article or derogate from or vary its effects.

IV. E. – 4:103: Co-operation
The parties to a contract within the scope of this Chapter may not exclude the application of IV. E. – 2:201 (Co-operation) or derogate from or vary its effects.

Section 2: Obligations of the Franchisor
IV. E. – 4:201: Intellectual Property Rights
(1)   The franchisor must grant the franchisee a right to use the intellectual property rights to the extent necessary to operate the franchise business.
(2)   The franchisor must make reasonable efforts to ensure the undisturbed and continuous use of the intellectual property rights.
(3)   The parties may not exclude the application of this Article or derogate from or vary its effects.

IV. E. – 4:202: Know-how
(1)   Throughout the duration of the contractual relationship the franchisor must provide the franchisee with the know-how which is necessary to operate the franchise business.
(2)   The parties may not exclude the application of this Article or derogate from or vary its effects.

IV. E. – 4:203: Assistance
(1)   The franchisor must provide the franchisee with assistance in the form of training courses, guidance and advice, in so far as necessary for the operation of the franchise business, without additional charge for the franchisee.
(2)   The franchisor must provide further assistance, in so far as reasonably requested by the franchisee, at a reasonable cost.

IV. E. – 4:204: Supply
(1)   When the franchisee is obliged to obtain the products from the franchisor, or from a supplier designated by the franchisor, the franchisor must ensure that the products ordered by the franchisee are supplied within a reasonable time, in so far as practicable and provided that the order is reasonable.
(2)   Paragraph (1) also applies to cases where the franchisee, although not legally obliged to obtain the products from the franchisor or from a supplier designated by the franchisor, is in fact required to do so.
(3)   The parties may not exclude the application of this Article or derogate from or vary its effects.

IV. E. – 4:205: Information by Franchisor During the Performance
The obligation to inform requires the franchisor in particular to provide the franchisee with information concerning:
(a)   market conditions;
(b)   commercial results of the franchise network;
(c)   characteristics of the products;
(d)   prices and terms for the supply of products;
(e)   any recommended prices and terms for the re-supply of products to customers;
(f)   relevant communication between the franchisor and customers in the territory; and

(g)   advertising campaigns.

IV. E. – 4:206: Warning of Decreased Supply Capacity

(1)   When the franchisee is obliged to obtain the products from the franchisor, or from a supplier designated by the franchisor, the franchisor must warn the franchisee within a reasonable time when the franchisor foresees that the franchisor's supply capacity or the supply capacity of the designated suppliers will be significantly less than the franchisee had reason to expect.

(2)   For the purpose of paragraph (1) the franchisor is presumed to foresee what the franchisor could reasonably be expected to foresee.

(3)   Paragraph (1) also applies to cases where the franchisee, although not legally obliged to obtain the products from the franchisor or from a supplier designated by the franchisor, is in fact required to do so.

(4)   The parties may not, to the detriment of the franchisee, exclude the application of this Article or derogate from or vary its effects.

IV. E. – 4:207: Reputation of Network and Advertising

(1)   The franchisor must make reasonable efforts to promote and maintain the reputation of the franchise network.

(2)   In particular, the franchisor must design and co-ordinate the appropriate advertising campaigns aiming at the promotion of the franchise network.

(3)   The activities of promotion and maintenance of the reputation of the franchise network are to be carried out without additional charge to the franchisee.

Section 3: Obligations of the Franchisee
IV. E. – 4:301: Fees, Royalties and Other Periodical Payments

(1)   The franchisee must pay to the franchisor fees, royalties or other periodical payments agreed upon in the contract.

(2)   If fees, royalties or any other periodical payments are to be determined unilaterally by the franchisor, II. – 9:105 (Unilateral determination by a party) applies.

IV. E. – 4:302: Information by Franchisee During the Performance

The obligation under IV. E. – 2:202 ((Information during the performance) requires the franchisee in particular to provide the franchisor with information concerning:

(a)   claims brought or threatened by third parties in relation to the franchisor's intellectual property rights; and

(b)   infringements by third parties of the franchisor's intellectual property rights.

IV. E. – 4:303: Business Method and Instructions

(1)   The franchisee must make reasonable efforts to operate the franchise business according to the business method of the franchisor.

(2)   The franchisee must follow the franchisor's reasonable instructions in relation to the business method and the maintenance of the reputation of the network.

(3)   The franchisee must take reasonable care not to harm the franchise network.

(4)   The parties may not exclude the application of this Article or derogate from or vary its effects.

IV. E. – 4:304: Inspection

(1)   The franchisee must grant the franchisor reasonable access to the franchisee's premises to enable the franchisor to check that the franchisee is complying with the franchisor's business method and instructions.

(2)   The franchise must grant the franchisor reasonable access to the accounting books of the franchisee.

Chapter 5: Distributorship
Section 1: General
IV. E. – 5:101: Scope and Definitions

(1)   This Chapter applies to contracts (distribution contracts) under which one party, the supplier, agrees to supply the other party, the distributor, with products on a continuing basis and the distributor agrees to purchase them, or to take and pay for them, and to supply them to others in the distributor's name and on the distributor's behalf.

(2)   An exclusive distribution contract is a distribution contract under which the supplier agrees to supply products to only one distributor within a certain territory or to a certain group of customers.

(3)   A selective distribution contract is a distribution contract under which the supplier agrees to supply products, either directly or indirectly, only to distributors selected on the basis of specified criteria.

(4)   An exclusive purchasing contract is a distribution contract under which the distributor agrees to purchase, or to take and pay for, products only from the supplier or from a party designated by the supplier.

Section 2: Obligations of the Supplier
IV. E. – 5:201: Obligation to Supply

The supplier must supply the products ordered by the distributor in so far as it is practicable and provided that the order is reasonable.

IV. E. – 5:202: Information by Supplier During the Performance

The obligation under IV. E. – 2:202 (Information during the performance) requires the supplier to provide the distributor with information concerning:

(a)   the characteristics of the products;
(b)   the prices and terms for the supply of the products;
(c)   any recommended prices and terms for the re-supply of the products to customers;
(d)   any relevant communication between the supplier and customers; and
(e)   any advertising campaigns relevant to the operation of the business.

IV. E. – 5:203: Warning by Supplier of Decreased Supply Capacity

(1)   The supplier must warn the distributor within a reasonable time when the supplier foresees that the supplier's supply capacity will be significantly less than the distributor had reason to expect.

(2)   For the purpose of paragraph (1) the supplier is presumed to foresee what the supplier could reasonably be expected to foresee.

(3)   In exclusive purchasing contracts, the parties may not exclude the application of this Article or derogate from or vary its effects.

IV. E. – 5:204: Advertising Materials

The supplier must provide the distributor at a reasonable price with all the advertising materials the supplier has which are needed for the proper distribution and promotion of the products.

IV. E. – 5:205: The Reputation of the Products

The supplier must make reasonable efforts not to damage the reputation of the products.

Section 3: Obligations of the Distributor
IV. E. – 5:301: Obligation to Distribute

In exclusive distribution contracts and selective distribution contracts the distributor must, so far as practicable, make reasonable efforts to promote the products.

IV. E. – 5:302: Information by Distributor During the Performance

In exclusive distribution contracts and selective distribution contracts, the obligation under IV. E. – 2:202 (Information during the performance) requires the distributor to provide the supplier with information concerning:

(a) claims brought or threatened by third parties in relation to the supplier's intellectual property rights; and
(b) infringements by third parties of the supplier's intellectual property rights.

IV. E. – 5:303: Warning by Distributor of Decreased Requirements

(1) In exclusive distribution contracts and selective distribution contracts, the distributor must
warn the supplier within a reasonable time when the distributor foresees that the distributor's
requirements will be significantly less than the supplier had reason to expect.
(2) For the purpose of paragraph (1) the distributor is presumed to foresee what the distributor could reasonably be expected to foresee.

IV. E. – 5:304: Instructions

In exclusive distribution contracts and selective distribution contracts, the distributor must follow reasonable instructions from the supplier which are designed to secure the proper distribution of the products or to maintain the reputation or the distinctiveness of the products.

IV. E. – 5:305: Inspection

In exclusive distribution contracts and selective distribution contracts, the distributor must provide the supplier with reasonable access to the distributor's premises to enable the supplier to
check that the distributor is complying with the standards agreed upon in the contract and with
reasonable instructions given.

IV. E. – 5:306: The Reputation of the Products

In exclusive distribution contracts and selective distribution contracts, the distributor must
make reasonable efforts not to damage the reputation of the products.

Part F. Loan Contracts

IV.F. – 1:101: Scope

(1) This Part of Book IV applies to loan contracts other than:
(a) those under which a business lends to a consumer; and
(b) those where the loan is made for the purchase or maintenance of immovable property.
(2) A loan contract is a contract by which one party, the lender, is obliged to provide the other
party, the borrower, with credit of any amount for a definite or indefinite period (the loan period), in the form of a monetary loan or of an overdraft facility and by which the borrower is obliged to repay the money obtained under the credit, whether or not the borrower is obliged to
pay interest or any other kind of remuneration the parties have agreed upon.
(3) A monetary loan is a fixed sum of money which is lent to the borrower and which the borrower agrees to repay either by fixed instalments or by paying the whole sum at the end of the
loan period.
(4) An overdraft facility is an option for the borrower to withdraw funds on a fluctuating, limited basis from the borrower's current account in excess of the current balance in the account.
Unless otherwise determined, an overdraft facility has a revolving character meaning that the
borrower has the possibility to use this facility over and over again.
(5) A contract is not a loan contract merely because it provides for the time of payment of an
obligation to pay money to be deferred, unless it requires the borrower to pay interest or any
other charge in addition to the price.
(6) The parties may however agree that money due under an existing obligation to pay money will in future be due under a loan contract.

IV.F. – 1:102: Main Obligation of the Lender

(1) The lender is obliged to provide the borrower with credit for the amount, in the manner
and for the period determinable from the contract.
(2) If a period of time within which the obligation is to be performed cannot be determined
from the terms regulating the obligation, the lender is obliged to make the credit available a
reasonable time after the borrower's demand.

IV.F. – 1:103: Obligation of the Borrower to Take up Loan
(1)   Where the credit takes the form of a monetary loan, the borrower is obliged to take up the loan in the manner and for the period determinable from the contract.
(2)   If the time the borrower is to take up the loan is not determinable from the contract, the borrower is obliged to take up the loan a reasonable time after the lender's demand.

IV.F. – 1:104: Interest
(1)   The borrower is obliged to pay interest or any other kind of remuneration according to the terms of the contract.
(2)   If the contract does not specify the interest payable, interest is payable unless both parties are consumers.
(3)   Interest accrues day by day from the date the borrower takes up the monetary loan or makes use of the overdraft facility but is payable at the end of the loan period or annually, whichever occurs earlier.
(4)   Interest payable according to the preceding paragraph is added to the outstanding capital every 12 months.

IV.F. – 1:105: Purpose of the Credit
If the contract restricts use of the credit to a specific purpose, the borrower is obliged, within a reasonable time after the lender's demand, to provide information necessary to enable the lender to verify its use.

IV.F. – 1:106: Repayment and Termination
(1)   The borrower is obliged to repay the money obtained under the credit in the manner and at the time determinable from the loan contract. If the time the borrower is to repay the money is not determinable from the contract, the borrower is obliged to repay it a reasonable time after the lender's demand.
(2)   The borrower can, by repayment, terminate an overdraft at will.
(3)   The borrower can, by repayment, terminate a loan at any time if under the loan contract the borrower does not have to pay interest or any other kind of remuneration which depends on the duration of the credit.
(4)   The borrower can, by repayment, terminate at any time the loan under any other type of loan contract with a specified duration. Parties cannot exclude the application of this rule or derogate from or vary its effects.
(5)   Where the loan contract has a specified duration of more than 1 year and provides for a fixed interest rate the borrower can terminate by early repayment under paragraph (4) only on giving the lender three months notice.
(6)   On early termination under paragraphs (4) or (5) the borrower is obliged to pay all interest due up to the date of repayment and to indemnify the lender for any loss caused by the early termination.
(7)   If the loan contract has an unspecified duration then, without prejudice to the borrower's rights under paragraphs (2) and (3), either party can terminate the relationship by giving the other a reasonable period of notice. II. – 1:109 (Variation or termination by notice) applies.

Part G. Personal Security
Chapter 1: Common Rules
IV. G. – 1:101: Definitions
For the purposes of this Part:
(a)   a "dependent personal security" is an obligation by a security provider which is assumed in favour of a creditor in order to secure a right to performance of a present or future obligation of the debtor owed to the creditor and performance of which is due only if, and to the extent that, performance of the latter obligation is due;
(b)   an "independent personal security" is an obligation by a security provider which is assumed in favour of a creditor for the purposes of security and which is expressly or impliedly declared not to depend upon another person's obligation owed to the creditor;

(c)   the "security provider" is the person who assumes the obligations towards the creditor for the purposes of security;

(d)   the "debtor" is the person who owes the secured obligation, if any, to the creditor, and, in provisions relating to purported obligations, includes an apparent debtor;

(e)   a "co-debtorship for security purposes" is an obligation owed by two or more debtors in which one of the debtors, the security provider, assumes the obligation primarily for purposes of security towards the creditor;

(f)   a "global security" is a dependent personal security which is assumed in order to secure a right to performance of all the debtor's obligations towards the creditor or a right to payment of the debit balance of a current account or a security of a similar extent;

(g)   "proprietary security" covers security rights in all kinds of assets, whether movable or immovable, corporeal or incorporeal; and

(h)   the "secured obligation" is the obligation the right to the performance of which is secured.

IV. G. – 1:102: Scope

(1)   This Part applies to any type of voluntarily assumed personal security and, in particular, to:

(a)   dependent personal securities, including those assumed by binding comfort letters;

(b)   independent personal securities, including those assumed by stand-by letters of credit; and

(c)   co-debtorship for security purposes.

(2)   This Part does not apply to insurance contracts. In the case of a guarantee insurance, this Part applies only if and in so far as the insurer has issued a document containing a personal security in favour of the creditor.

(3)   This Part does not affect the rules on the aval and the security endorsement of negotiable instruments, but does apply to security for obligations resulting from such an aval or security endorsement.

IV. G. – 1:103: Creditor's Acceptance

(1)   If the parties intend to create the security by contract, the creditor is regarded as accepting an offer of security as soon as the offer reaches the creditor, unless the offer requires express acceptance, or the creditor without undue delay rejects it or reserves time for consideration.

(2)   A personal security can also be assumed by a unilateral undertaking intended to be legally binding without acceptance. The rules of this Part apply with any appropriate adaptations.

IV. G. – 1:104: Co-debtorship for Security Purposes

A co-debtorship for security purposes is subject to the rules of Chapters 1 and 4 and, subsidiarily, to the rules in Book III, Chapter 4, Section 1 (Plurality of debtors).

IV. G. – 1:105: Several Security Providers: Solidary Liability Towards Creditor

(1)   To the extent that several providers of personal security have secured the right to performance of the same obligation or the same part of an obligation or have assumed their undertakings for the same security purpose, each security provider assumes within the limits of that security provider's undertaking to the creditor solidary liability together with the other security providers. This rule also applies if these security providers in assuming their securities have acted independently.

(2)   Paragraph (1) applies with appropriate adaptations if proprietary security has been provided by the debtor or a third person in addition to the personal security.

IV. G. – 1:106: Several Security Providers: Internal Recourse

(1)   In the cases covered by the preceding Article recourse between several providers of personal security or between providers of personal security and of proprietary security is governed by III. – 4:107 (Recourse between solidary debtors), subject to the following paragraphs.

(2)   Subject to paragraph (8), the proportionate share of each security provider for the purposes of that Article is determined according to the rules in paragraphs (3) to (7).

(3)   Unless the security providers have otherwise agreed, as between themselves each security provider is liable in the same proportion that the maximum risk assumed by that secu-

rity provider bore to the total of the maximum risks assumed by all the security providers. The relevant time is that of the creation of the last security.

(4)   For personal security, the maximum risk is determined by the agreed maximum amount of the security. In the absence of an agreed maximum amount, the value of the secured right or, if a current account has been secured, the credit limit is decisive. If a secured current account does not have a credit limit, its final balance is decisive.

(5)   For proprietary security, the maximum risk is determined by the agreed maximum amount of the security. In the absence of an agreed maximum amount, the value of the assets serving as security is decisive.

(6)   If the maximum amount in the case of paragraph (4) first sentence or the maximum amount or the value, respectively, in the case of paragraph (5) is higher than the value of the secured right at the time of creation of the last security, the latter determines the maximum risk.

(7)   In the case of an unlimited personal security securing an unlimited credit the maximum risk of other limited personal or proprietary security rights which exceed the final balance of the secured credit is limited to the latter.

(8)   The rules in paragraphs (3) to (7) do not apply to proprietary security provided by the debtor and to security providers who, at the time when the creditor was satisfied, were not liable towards the latter.

IV. G. – 1:107: Several Security Providers: Recourse Against Debtor

(1)   Any security provider who has satisfied a right of recourse of another security provider is subrogated to this extent to the other security provider's rights against the debtor as acquired under IV. G. – 2:113 (Security provider's rights after performance) paragraphs (1) and (3), including proprietary security rights granted by the debtor. IV. G. – 2:110 (Reduction of creditor's rights) applies with appropriate adaptations.

(2)   Where a security provider has recourse against the debtor by virtue of the rights acquired under IV. G. – 2:113 (Security provider's rights after performance) paragraphs (1) and (3) or under the preceding paragraph, including proprietary security rights granted by the debtor, every security provider is entitled to a proportionate share, as defined in IV. G. – 1:106 (Several security providers: internal recourse) paragraph (2) and III. – 4:107 (Recourse between solidary debtors), of the benefits recovered from the debtor. IV. G. – 2:110 (Reduction of creditor's rights) applies with appropriate adaptations.

(3)   Unless expressly stated to the contrary, the preceding rules do not apply to proprietary security provided by the debtor.

IV. G. – 1:108: Subsidiary Application of Rules on Solidary Debtors

If and in so far as the provisions of this Part do not apply, the rules on plurality of debtors in III. – 4:107 (Recourse between solidary debtors) to III. – 4:112 (Opposability of other defences in solidary obligations) are subsidiarily applicable.

Chapter 2: Dependent Personal Security

IV. G. – 2:101: Presumption for Dependent Personal Security

(1)   Any undertaking to pay, to render any other performance or to pay damages to the creditor by way of security is presumed to give rise to a dependent personal security, unless the creditor shows that it was agreed otherwise.

(2)   A binding comfort letter is presumed to give rise to a dependent personal security.

IV. G. – 2:102: Dependence of Security Provider's Obligation

(1)   Whether and to what extent performance of the obligation of the provider of a dependent personal security is due, depends upon whether and to what extent performance of the debtor's obligation to the creditor is due.

(2)   The security provider's obligation does not exceed the debtor's obligation. This rule does not apply if the debtor's obligations are reduced or discharged:

(a)   in an insolvency proceeding;

(b) in any other way caused by the debtor's inability to perform because of insolvency; or

(c) by virtue of law due to events affecting the person of the debtor.

(3) Except in the case of a global security, if an amount has not been fixed for the security and cannot be determined from the agreement of the parties, the security provider's obligation is limited to the value of the secured right at the time the security became effective.

(4) Except in the case of a global security, any agreement between the creditor and the debtor to make performance of the secured obligation due earlier, or to make the obligation more onerous by changing the conditions on which performance is due, or to increase its amount, does not affect the security provider's obligation if the agreement was concluded after the security provider's obligation became effective.

IV. G. – 2:103: Debtor's Defences Available to the Security Provider

(1) As against the creditor, the security provider may invoke any defence of the debtor with respect to the secured obligation, even if the defence is no longer available to the debtor due to acts or omissions of the debtor occurring after the security became effective.

(2) The security provider is entitled to refuse to perform the security obligation if:

(a) the debtor is entitled to withdraw from the contract with the creditor under Book II, Chapter 5 (Right of withdrawal).

(b) the debtor has a right to withhold performance under III. – 3:401 (Right to withhold performance of reciprocal obligation); or

(c) the debtor is entitled to terminate the debtor's contractual relationship with the creditor under Book III, Chapter 3, Section 5 (Termination).

(3) The security provider may not invoke the lack of capacity of the debtor, whether a natural person or a legal entity, or the non-existence of the debtor, if a legal entity, if the relevant facts were known to the security provider at the time when the security became effective.

(4) As long as the debtor is entitled to avoid the contract from which the secured obligation arises on a ground other than those mentioned in the preceding paragraph and has not exercised that right, the security provider is entitled to refuse performance.

(5) The preceding paragraph applies with appropriate adaptations if the secured obligation is subject to set-off.

IV. G. – 2:104: Coverage of Security

(1) The security covers, within its maximum amount, if any, not only the principal secured obligation, but also the debtor's ancillary obligations towards the creditor, especially:

(a) contractual interest and interest due by law on delay in payment;

(b) damages, a penalty or an agreed payment for non-performance by the debtor; and

(c) the reasonable costs of extra-judicial recovery of those items.

(2) The costs of legal proceedings and enforcement proceedings against the debtor are covered, provided the security provider had been informed about the creditor's intention to undertake such proceedings in sufficient time to enable the security provider to avert those costs.

(3) A global security covers only obligations which originated in contracts between the debtor and the creditor.

IV. G. – 2:105: Solidary Liability of Security Provider

Unless otherwise agreed, the liability of the debtor and the security provider is solidary and, accordingly, the creditor has the choice of claiming solidary performance from the debtor or, within the limits of the security, from the security provider.

IV. G. – 2:106: Subsidiary Liability of Security Provider

(1) If so agreed, the security provider may invoke as against the creditor the subsidiary character of the security provider's liability. A binding comfort letter is presumed to establish only subsidiary liability.

(2) Subject to paragraph (3), before demanding performance from the security provider, the creditor must have undertaken appropriate attempts to obtain satisfaction from the debtor and

other security providers, if any, securing the same obligation under a personal or proprietary security establishing solidary liability.

(3)   The creditor is not required to attempt to obtain satisfaction from the debtor and any other security provider according to the preceding paragraph if and in so far as it is obviously impossible or exceedingly difficult to obtain satisfaction from the person concerned. This exception applies, in particular, if and in so far as an insolvency or equivalent proceeding has been opened against the person concerned or opening of such a proceeding has failed due to insufficient assets, unless a proprietary security provided by that person and for the same obligation is available.

IV. G. – 2:107: Requirement of Notification by Creditor

(1)   The creditor is required to notify the security provider without undue delay in case of a non-performance by, or inability to pay of, the debtor as well as of an extension of maturity; this notification must include information about the secured amounts of the principal obligation, interest and other ancillary obligations owed by the debtor on the date of the notification. An additional notification of a new event of non-performance need not be given before three months have expired since the previous notification. No notification is required if an event of non-performance merely relates to ancillary obligations of the debtor, unless the total amount of all non-performed secured obligations has reached five percent of the outstanding amount of the secured obligation.

(2)   In addition, in the case of a global security, the creditor is required to notify the security provider of any agreed increase:

(a)   whenever such increase, starting from the creation of the security, reaches 20 percent of the amount that was so secured at that time; and

(b)   whenever the secured amount is further increased by 20 percent compared with the secured amount at the date when the last information according to this paragraph was or should have been given.

(3)   Paragraphs (1) and (2) do not apply, if and in so far as the security provider knows or could reasonably be expected to know the required information.

(4)   If the creditor omits or delays any notification required by this Article the creditor's rights against the security provider are reduced by the extent necessary to prevent the latter from suffering any loss as a result of the omission or delay.

IV. G. – 2:108: Time Limit for Resort to Security

(1)   If a time limit has been agreed, directly or indirectly, for resort to a security establishing solidary liability for the security provider, the latter is no longer liable after expiration of the agreed time limit. However, the security provider remains liable if the creditor had requested performance from the security provider after maturity of the secured obligation but before expiration of the time limit for the security.

(2)   If a time limit has been agreed, directly or indirectly, for resort to a security establishing subsidiary liability for the security provider, the latter is no longer liable after the expiration of the agreed time limit. However, the security provider remains liable if the creditor:

(a)   after maturity of the secured obligation, but before expiration of the time limit, has informed the security provider of an intention to demand performance of the security and of the commencement of appropriate attempts to obtain satisfaction as required according to IV. G. – 2:106 (Subsidiary liability of security provider) paragraphs (2) and (3); and

(b)   informs the security provider every six months about the status of these attempts, if so demanded by the security provider.

(3)   If performance of the secured obligations falls due upon, or within 14 days before, expiration of the time limit of the security, the request for performance or the information according to paragraphs (1) and (2) may be given earlier than provided for in paragraphs (1) and (2), but no more than 14 days before expiration of the time limit of the security.

(4)   If the creditor has taken due measures according to the preceding paragraphs, the security provider's maximum liability is restricted to the amount of the secured obligations as defined in

IV. G. – 2:104 (Coverage of security) paragraphs (1) and (2). The relevant time is that at which the agreed time limit expires.

IV. G. – 2:109: Limiting Security Without Time Limit

(1)   Where the scope of a security is not limited to obligations arising, or obligations performance of which falls due, within an agreed time limit, the scope of the security may be limited by any party giving notice of at least three months to the other party. The preceding sentence does not apply if the security is restricted to cover specific obligations or obligations arising from specific contracts.

(2)   By virtue of the notice, the scope of the security is limited to the secured principal obligations performance of which is due at the date at which the limitation becomes effective and any secured ancillary obligations as defined in IV. G. – 2:104 (Coverage of security) paragraphs (1) and (2).

IV. G. – 2:110: Reduction of Creditor's Rights

(1)   If and in so far as due to the creditor's conduct the security provider cannot be subrogated to the creditor's rights against the debtor and to the creditor's personal and proprietary security rights granted by third persons, or cannot be fully reimbursed from the debtor or from third party security providers, if any, the creditor's rights against the security provider are reduced by the extent necessary to prevent the latter from suffering any loss as a result of the creditor's conduct. The security provider has a corresponding right to recover from the creditor if the security provider has already performed.

(2)   Paragraph (1) applies only if the creditor's conduct falls short of the standard of care which could be expected of persons managing their affairs with reasonable prudence.

IV. G. – 2:111: Debtor's Relief for the Security Provider

(1)   A security provider who has provided a security at the debtor's request or with the debtor's express or presumed consent may request relief by the debtor:
(a)   if the debtor has not performed the secured obligation when performance became due;
(b)   if the debtor is unable to pay or has suffered a substantial diminution of assets; or
(c)   if the creditor has brought an action on the security against the security provider.
(2)   Relief may be granted by furnishing adequate security.

IV. G. – 2:112: Notification and Request by Security Provider Before Performance

(1)   Before performance to the creditor, the security provider is required to notify the debtor and request information about the outstanding amount of the secured obligation and any defences or counterclaims against it.

(2)   If the security provider fails to comply with the requirements in paragraph (1) or neglects to raise defences communicated by the debtor or known to the security provider from other sources, the security provider's rights to recover from the debtor under IV. G. – 2:113 (Security provider's rights after performance) are reduced by the extent necessary to prevent loss to the debtor as a result of such failure or neglect.

(3)   The security provider's rights against the creditor remain unaffected.

IV. G. – 2:113: Security Provider's Rights after Performance

(1)   The security provider has a right to reimbursement from the debtor if and in so far as the security provider has performed the security obligation. In addition the security provider is subrogated to the extent indicated in the preceding sentence to the creditor's rights against the debtor. The right to reimbursement and rights acquired by subrogation are concurrent.

(2)   In case of part performance, the creditor's remaining partial rights against the debtor have priority over the rights to which the security provider has been subrogated.

(3)   By virtue of the subrogation under paragraph (1), dependent and independent personal and proprietary security rights are transferred by operation of law to the security provider notwithstanding any contractual restriction or exclusion of transferability agreed by the debtor.

Rights against other security providers can be exercised only within the limits of IV. G. – 1:106 (Several security providers: internal recourse).
(4) Where the debtor due to incapacity is not liable to the creditor but the security provider is nonetheless bound by, and performs, the security obligation, the security provider's right to re-imbursement from the debtor is limited to the extent of the debtor's enrichment by the transaction with the creditor. This rule applies also if a debtor legal entity has not come into existence.

Chapter 3: Independent Personal Security
IV. G. – 3:101: Scope
(1) The independence of a security is not prejudiced by a mere general reference to an underlying obligation (including a personal security).
(2) The provisions of this Chapter also apply to standby letters of credit.

IV. G. – 3:102: Notification to Debtor by Security Provider
(1) The security provider is required:
(a) to notify the debtor immediately if a demand for performance is received and to state whether or not, in the view of the security provider, performance falls to be made;
(b) to notify the debtor immediately if performance has been made in accordance with a demand; and
(c) to notify the debtor immediately if performance has been refused notwithstanding a demand and to state the reasons for the refusal.
(2) If the security provider fails to comply with the requirements in paragraph (1) the security provider's rights against the debtor under IV. G. – 3:109 (Security provider's rights after performance) are reduced by the extent necessary to prevent loss to the debtor as a result of such failure.

IV. G. – 3:103: Performance by Security Provider
(1) The security provider is obliged to perform only if there is, in textual form, a demand for performance which complies exactly with the terms set out in the contract or other juridical act creating the security.
(2) Unless otherwise agreed, the security provider may invoke defences which the security provider has against the creditor.
(3) The security provider must without undue delay and at the latest within seven days of receipt, in textual form, of a demand for performance:
(a) perform in accordance with the demand; or
(b) inform the creditor of a refusal to perform, stating the reasons for the refusal.

IV. G. – 3:104: Independent Personal Security on First Demand
(1) An independent personal security which is expressed as being due upon first demand or which is in such terms that this can unequivocally be inferred, is governed by the rules in the preceding Article, except as provided in the two following paragraphs.
(2) The security provider is obliged to perform only if the creditor's demand is supported by a declaration in textual form by the creditor which expressly confirms that any condition upon which performance of the security becomes due is fulfilled.
(3) Paragraph (2) of the preceding Article does not apply.

IV. G. – 3:105: Manifestly Abusive or Fraudulent Demand
(1) A security provider is not obliged to comply with a demand for performance if it is proved by present evidence that the demand is manifestly abusive or fraudulent.
(2) If the requirements of the preceding paragraph are fulfilled, the debtor may prohibit:
(a) performance by the security provider; and
(b) issuance or utilisation of a demand for performance by the creditor.

IV. G. – 3:106: Security Provider's Right to Reclaim
(1) The security provider has the right to reclaim the benefits received by the creditor if:
(a) the conditions for the creditor's demand were not or subsequently ceased to be fulfilled; or

(b)   the creditor's demand was manifestly abusive or fraudulent.
(2)   The security provider's right to reclaim benefits is subject to the rules in Book VII (Unjustified Enrichment).

IV. G. – 3:107: Security With or Without Time Limits

(1)   If a time limit has been agreed, directly or indirectly, for the resort to a security, the security provider exceptionally remains liable even after expiration of the time limit, provided the creditor had demanded performance according to IV. G. – 3:103 (Performance by security provider) paragraph (1) or IV. G. – 3:104 (Independent personal security on first demand) at a time when the creditor was entitled to do so and before expiration of the time limit for the security. IV. G. – 2:108 (Time limit for resort to security) paragraph (3) applies with appropriate adaptations. The security provider's maximum liability is restricted to the amount which the creditor could have demanded as of the date when the time limit expired.
(2)   Where a security does not have an agreed time limit, the security provider may set such a time limit by giving notice of at least three months to the other party. The security provider's liability is restricted to the amount which the creditor could have demanded as of the date set by the security provider. The preceding sentences do not apply if the security is given for specific purposes.

IV. G. – 3:108: Transfer of Security Right

(1)   The creditor's right to performance by the security provider can be assigned or otherwise transferred.
(2)   However, in the case of an independent personal security on first demand, the right to performance cannot be assigned or otherwise transferred and the demand for performance can be made only by the original creditor, unless the security provides otherwise. This does not prevent transfer of the proceeds of the security.

IV. G. – 3:109: Security Provider's Rights after Performance

IV. G. – 2:113 (Security provider's rights after performance) applies with appropriate adaptations to the rights which the security provider may exercise after performance.

Chapter 4: Special Rules for Personal Security of Consumers
IV. G. – 4:101: Scope of Application

(1)   Subject to paragraph (2), this Chapter applies when a security is provided by a consumer.
(2)   This Chapter is not applicable if:
(a)   the creditor is also a consumer; or
(b)   the consumer security provider is able to exercise substantial influence upon the debtor where the debtor is not a natural person.

IV. G. – 4:102: Applicable Rules

(1)   A personal security subject to this Chapter is governed by the rules of Chapters 1 and 2, except as otherwise provided in this Chapter.
(2)   The parties may not, to the detriment of a security provider, exclude the application of the rules of this Chapter or derogate from or vary their effects.

IV. G. – 4:103: Creditor's Pre-Contractual Duties

(1)   Before a security is granted, the creditor has a duty to explain to the intending security provider:
(a)   the general effect of the intended security; and
(b)   the special risks to which the security provider may according to the information accessible to the creditor be exposed in view of the financial situation of the debtor.
(2)   If the creditor knows or has reason to know that due to a relationship of trust and confidence between the debtor and the security provider there is a significant risk that the security provider is not acting freely or with adequate information, the creditor has a duty to ascertain that the security provider has received independent advice.

(3)   If the information or independent advice required by the preceding paragraphs is not given at least five days before the security provider signs the offer of security or the contract creating the security, the offer can be revoked or the contract avoided by the security provider within a reasonable time after receipt of the information or the independent advice. For this purpose five days is regarded as a reasonable time unless the circumstances suggest otherwise.
(4)   If contrary to paragraph (1) or (2) no information or independent advice is given, the offer can be revoked or the contract avoided by the security provider at any time.
(5)   If the security provider revokes the offer or avoids the contract according to the preceding paragraphs, the return of benefits received by the parties is governed by Book VII (Unjustified Enrichment).

IV. G. – 4:104: Form

The contract of security must be in textual form on a durable medium and must be signed by the security provider. A contract of security which does not comply with the requirements of the preceding sentence is void.

IV. G. – 4:105: Nature of Security Provider's Liability

Where this Chapter applies:
(a)   an agreement purporting to create a security without a maximum amount, whether a global security or not, is considered as creating a dependent security with a fixed amount to be determined according to IV. G. – 2:102 (Dependence of security provider's obligation) paragraph (3);
(b)   the liability of a provider of dependent security is subsidiary within the meaning of IV. G. – 2:106 (Subsidiary liability of security provider), unless expressly agreed otherwise; and
(c)   in an agreement purporting to create an independent security, the declaration that it does not depend upon another person's obligation owed to the creditor is disregarded, and accordingly a dependent security is considered as having been created, provided the other requirements of such a security are met.

IV. G. – 4:106: Creditor's Obligations of Annual Information

(1)   Subject to the debtor's consent, the creditor has to inform the security provider annually about the secured amounts of the principal obligation, interest and other ancillary obligations owed by the debtor on the date of the information. The debtor's consent, once given, is irrevocable.
(2)   IV. G. – 2:107 (Requirement of notification by creditor) paragraphs (3) and (4) apply with appropriate adaptations.

IV. G. – 4:107: Limiting Security with Time Limit

(1)   A security provider who has provided a security whose scope is limited to obligations arising, or obligations performance of which falls due, within an agreed time limit may three years after the security became effective limit its effects by giving notice of at least three months to the creditor. The preceding sentence does not apply if the security is restricted to cover specific obligations or obligations arising from specific contracts. The creditor has to inform the debtor immediately on receipt of a notice of limitation of the security by the security provider.
(2)   By virtue of the notice, the scope of the security is limited according to IV. G. – 2:109 (Limiting security without time limit) paragraph (2).

Part H. Donation
Chapter 1: Scope and General Provisions
Section 1: Scope and Definitions
IV. H. – 1:101: Contracts Covered

(1)   This Part of Book IV applies to contracts for the donation of goods.
(2)   A contract for the donation of goods is a contract under which one party, the donor, gratuitously undertakes to transfer the ownership of goods to another party, the donee, and does so with an intention to benefit the donee.

IV. H. – 1:102: Future Goods and Goods to Be Manufactured or Produced

(1)   In this Part of Book IV the word "goods" includes goods which at the time of the conclusion of the contract do not yet exist or are to be acquired by the donor.

(2)   A contract under which one party undertakes gratuitously, and with an intention to benefit the other party, to manufacture or produce goods for the other party and to transfer their ownership to the other party is to be regarded as primarily a contract for the donation of the goods.

IV. H. – 1:103: Application to Other Assets

(1)   This Part applies with appropriate adaptations to:
(a)   contracts for the donation of money;
(b)   contracts for the donation of electricity;
(c)   contracts for the donation of stocks, shares, investment securities and negotiable instruments;
(d)   contracts for the donation of other forms of incorporeal property, including rights to the performance of obligations, industrial and intellectual property rights and other transferable rights;
(e)   contracts gratuitously conferring rights in information or data, including software and databases.

(2)   This Part does not apply to contracts for the donation of immovable property or rights in immovable property.

IV. H. – 1:104: Application to Unilateral Undertakings and Immediate Donations

This Part applies with appropriate adaptations where the donor gratuitously, with an intention to benefit the donee:
(a)   unilaterally undertakes to transfer the ownership of goods to the donee; or
(b)   immediately transfers the ownership of goods to the donee.

Iv. H. – 1:105: Donations Due or Conditional on Death

(1)   This Part does not apply where:
(a)   performance of the obligation to transfer is due only on the donor's death;
(b)   the transfer or obligation to transfer is subject to the suspensive condition of the donor's death; or
(c)   the transfer or obligation to transfer is made subject to the resolutive condition of the donee predeceasing the donor.

(2)   Paragraph (1) does not apply if the donor renders performance or waives the condition before the donor's death.

Section 2: Gratuitousness and Intention to Benefit

IV. H. – 1:201: Gratuitousness

An undertaking to transfer is gratuitous if it is done without reward.

IV. H. – 1:202: Transactions Which Are Not Entirely Gratuitous

(1)   If the party undertaking to transfer receives or is entitled to some reward and the transaction is thereby not entirely gratuitous the contract is regarded primarily as a contract for the donation of goods if:
(a)   this party undertakes to transfer with an intention inter alia to benefit the other party; and
(b)   the values to be conferred by the performances are regarded by both parties as not substantially equivalent.

(2)   If the contract coming under paragraph (1) is void or avoided under these rules but would not be under general rules, III. – 1:110 (Variation or termination by court on a change of circumstances) applies with appropriate adaptations.

(3)   If in a case within paragraph (1) a party exercises a right to revoke under this Part, IV. H. – 4:103 (Consequences of revocation) applies to the whole contractual relationship. The other party may prevent the effects of revocation by offering a reasonable reward within a reasonable time after revocation.

IV. H. – 1:203: Intention to Benefit

A donor may be regarded as intending to benefit the donee notwithstanding that the donor:
(a)   is under a moral obligation to transfer; or
(b)   has a promotional purpose.

Chapter 2: Formation and Validity

IV. H. – 2:101: Form Requirements

A contract for the donation of goods is not valid unless the undertaking of the donor is in textual form on a durable medium signed by the donor. An electronic signature which is not an advanced signature in the sense of I. – 1:107 ("Signature" and similar expressions) paragraph 4, does not suffice in this regard.

IV. H. – 2:102: Exceptions to the Form Requirements

The preceding Article does not apply:
(a)   in the case of an immediate delivery of the goods to the donee or an equivalent to such delivery, regardless of whether ownership is transferred;
(b)   if the donation is made by a business;
(c)   if the undertaking of the donor is declared in a public statement broadcast in the radio or television or published in print and is not excessive in the circumstances.

IV. H. – 2:103: Mistake

A donor may avoid the contract if it was concluded because of a mistake of fact or law although the requirements of II. – 7:201 (Mistake) paragraph (1)(b) are not satisfied.

IV. H. – 2:104: Unfair Exploitation

A donor, who was dependent on, or was the more vulnerable party in a relationship of trust with, the donee, may avoid the contract under II. – 7:207 (Unfair exploitation) unless the donee proves that the donee did not exploit the donor's situation by taking an excessive benefit or grossly unfair advantage.

Chapter 3: Obligations and Remedies

Section 1: Obligations of the Donor

IV. H. – 3:101: Obligations in General

(1)   The donor must:
(a)   deliver goods which conform with the contract; and
(b)   transfer the ownership in the goods as required by the contract.
(2)   This Section applies with appropriate adaptations to fruits acquired from the time when the obligation to deliver is due.

IV. H. – 3:102: Conformity of the Goods

(1)   The goods do not conform with the contract if they do not possess the qualities which the donee could reasonably expect unless the donee knew of the lack of quality or could reason- ably be expected to have known of it when the contract was concluded.
(2)   In determining what qualities the donee could reasonably expect, regard is to be had, among other things, to:
(a)   the gratuitous nature of the contract;
(b)   the purpose of the contract of donation known by, or obvious to, the donee;
(c)   whether the transfer or delivery of the goods was immediate;
(d)   the value of the goods; and
(e)   whether the donor was a business.
(3)   The goods do not conform to the contract if they are not of a quantity, quality or descrip- tion provided for by the terms of the contract.

IV. H. – 3:103: Third Party Rights or Claims

The goods do not conform with the contract if they are not free from any right or reasonably well founded claim of a third party unless the donee knew or could reasonably expected to have known of the third party's right or claim.

Section 2: Remedies of the Donee
IV. H. – 3:201: Application of General Rules

If the donor fails to perform any of the donor's obligations under the contract, the donee has the remedies provided for in Book III, Chapter 3 (Remedies for non-performance) unless otherwise provided in this Section.

IV. H. – 3:202: Restricted Right to Enforce Performance

(1)   If the goods do not conform with the contract, the donee may not require replacement or repair under III. – 3:302 (Enforcement of non-monetary obligations).
(2)   The donee may not enforce performance under III. – 3:302 (Enforcement of non-monetary obligations) in the case of goods which are to be acquired by the donor.

IV. H. – 3:203: Restitution in Case of Termination

If the donee terminates the contract under Book III, Chapter 3, Section 5 (Termination), III. – 3:511 (When restitution not required) paragraph (3) does not apply.

IV. H. – 3:204: Exclusion of the Right to Damages in Case of Impediment

(1)   A donee's right to damages is excluded if the donor's non-performance is due to an impediment and if the donor could not reasonably be expected to have avoided or overcome the impediment or its consequences.
(2)   III. – 3:104 (Excuse due to an impediment) paragraphs (3) and (5) apply correspondingly.
(3)   In determining what impediment or consequences the donor could reasonably be expected to have avoided or overcome regard is to be had to the gratuitous nature of the contract.
(4)   This Article does not affect liability under Book VI (Non-contractual liability arising out of damage caused to another).

IV. H. – 3:205: Measure of Damages

(1)   Damages cover loss suffered by the donee acting in the reasonable belief that the donor would fulfil the obligations.
(2)   A supplementary sum of damages may be awarded by the court if it is seen as just and reasonable in the circumstances.
(3)   In determining what is just and reasonable under paragraph (2), regard is to be had, among other things and apart from the gratuitous nature of the contract:
(a)   the declarations and acts of the parties;
(b)   the donor's purpose in making the donation; and
(c)   the reasonable expectations of the donee.
(4)   The total amount of damages under this Article may not exceed such a sum as will put the aggrieved party as nearly as possible into the position in which it would have been if the donor's obligations under the contract had been duly performed.
(5)   This Article does not affect liability under Book VI (Non-contractual liability arising out of damage caused to another).

IV. H. – 3:206: Delay in Payment of Money

If payment of a sum of money is delayed, the donee is entitled to interest under III. – 3:708 (Interest on late payments) unless the non-performance is excused under III. – 3:104 (Excuse due to an impediment) or the donee's right to damages is excluded under IV. H. – 3:204 (Exclusion of the right to damages in case of impediment).

Section 3: Obligations of the Donee
IV. H. – 3:301: Obligations to Take Delivery and Accept Transfer

(1)   The donee must take delivery and accept the transfer of ownership.

(2)   The donee performs the obligation to take delivery and accept transfer by carrying out all the acts which could reasonably be expected of the donee in order to enable the donor to perform the obligations to deliver and transfer.

Section 4: Remedies of the Donor
IV. H. – 3:401: Application of General Rules

If the donee fails to perform any of the donee's obligations under the contract, the donor has the remedies provided for in III. – 2:111 (Property not accepted), III. – 2:112 (Money not accepted) and Book III, Chapter 3 (Remedies for non-performance).

Chapter 4: Revocation by the Donor
Section 1: Revocation in General
IV. H. – 4:101: Irrevocability and its Exceptions

Contracts for the donation of goods are revocable only if a right to revoke is
(a)   conferred by the terms of the contract; or
(b)   provided for under the rules in this Chapter.

IV. H. – 4:102: Exercise and Scope of the Right to Revoke

(1)   The donor's right to revoke is to be exercised by giving notice to the donee.
(2)   A declaration of partial revocation is to be understood as a revocation of the whole contract for the donation of goods, if, giving due consideration to all the circumstances of the case, it is unreasonable to uphold the remaining parts.

IV. H. – 4:103: Consequences of Revocation

(1)   On revocation under this Chapter, the outstanding obligations of the parties under the contract come to an end. In the case of a partial revocation, the relevant part of the outstanding obligations comes to an end.
(2)   On revocation under this Chapter, the donee is obliged to return the goods. Chapters 5 and 6 of Book VII (Unjustified enrichment) apply with appropriate adaptations, unless otherwise provided in this Chapter.

IV. H. – 4:104: Time Limits

The right to revoke under this Chapter expires if notice of revocation is not given within a reasonable time, with due regard to the circumstances, after the donor knew or could reasonably be expected to have known of the relevant facts.

Section 2: Rights of the Donor to Revoke
IV. H. – 4:201: Ingratitude of the Donee

(1)   A contract for the donation of goods may be revoked if the donee is guilty of gross ingratitude by intentionally committing a serious wrong against the donor.
(2)   Revocation under this Article is excluded if the donor knowing the relevant facts forgives the donee.
(3)   For the purpose of paragraph (1) a reasonable time under IV.H–4:104 (Time limits) is at least one year. If the donor dies before the reasonable time has expired, the running of the period is suspended until the person entitled to revoke knows or can reasonably be expected to know of the relevant facts.
(4)   For the purpose of paragraph (1) the defence of disenrichment under VII. – 6:101 (Disenrichment) does not apply.

IV. H. – 4:202: Impoverishment of the Donor

(1)   A contract for the donation of goods may be revoked if the donor is not in a position to maintain himself or herself out of his or her own patrimony or income.
(2)   The donor is not in a position to maintain himself or herself if:
(a)   he or she would be entitled to maintenance from another if that other were in a position to provide the maintenance; or
(b)   he or she is entitled to social assistance.

(3)   The right to revoke is suspended if the donee maintains the donor to the extent that the latter is or would be entitled to under paragraph (2).
(4)   A donor who is not in a position to maintain himself or herself in the sense of paragraph (1) or who will imminently be in that situation may withhold performance of any obligations under the contract which have not yet been performed. Paragraph (3) applies correspondingly to the right to withhold performance. If the donor withholds performance, the donee may terminate the contractual relationship.
(5)   This Article applies also when the donor's ability to meet maintenance obligations established by rule of law or by court order, or the existence of those obligations, is dependent on effective revocation of a donation.
(6)   The right to revoke under this Article may not be restricted or excluded by the parties.

IV. H. – 4:203: Residual Right to Revoke

(1)   A contract for the donation of goods may also be revoked to the extent that other essential circumstances upon which it was based have materially changed after the conclusion of the contract, provided that as a result of that change:
(a)   the benefit to the donee is manifestly inappropriate or excessive; or
(b)   it is manifestly unjust to hold the donor to the donation.
(2)   Paragraph (1) applies only if:
(a)   the change of circumstances was not so foreseeable at the time of the conclusion of the contract that the donor could reasonably have been expected to provide for it; and
(b)   the risk of that change of circumstances was not assumed by the donor.

Book V Benevolent Intervention in Another's Affairs
Chapter 1: Scope
V. – 1:101: Intervention to Benefit Another

(1)   This Book applies where a person, the intervener, acts with the predominant intention of benefiting another, the principal, and:
(a)   the intervener has a reasonable ground for acting; or
(b)   the principal approves the act without such undue delay as would adversely affect the intervener.
(2)   The intervener does not have a reasonable ground for acting if the intervener:
(a)   has a reasonable opportunity to discover the principal's wishes but does not do so; or
(b)   knows or can reasonably be expected to know that the intervention is against the principal's wishes.

V. – 1:102: Intervention to Perform Another's Duty

Where an intervener acts to perform another person's duty, the performance of which is due and urgently required as a matter of overriding public interest, and the intervener acts with the predominant intention of benefiting the recipient of the performance, the person whose duty the intervener acts to perform is a principal to whom this Book applies.

V. – 1:103: Exclusions

This Book does not apply where the intervener:
(a)   is authorised to act under a contractual or other obligation to the principal;
(b)   is authorised, other than under this Book, to act independently of the principal's consent; or
(c)   is under an obligation to a third party to act.

Chapter 2: Duties of Intervener
V. – 2:101: Duties During Intervention

(1)   During the intervention, the intervener must:
(a)   act with reasonable care;
(b)   except in relation to a principal within V. – 1:102 (Intervention to perform another's duty), act in a manner which the intervener knows or can reasonably be expected to assume accords with the principal's wishes; and

(c)   so far as possible and reasonable, inform the principal about the intervention and seek the principal's consent to further acts.

(2)   The intervention may not be discontinued without good reason.

V. – 2:102: Reparation for Damage Caused by Breach of Duty

(1)   The intervener is liable to make reparation to the principal for damage caused by breach of a duty set out in this Chapter if the damage resulted from a risk which the intervener created, increased or intentionally perpetuated.

(2)   The intervener's liability is reduced or excluded in so far as this is fair and reasonable, having regard to, among other things, the intervener's reasons for acting.

(3)   An intervener who at the time of intervening lacks full legal capacity is liable to make reparation only in so far as that intervener is also liable to make reparation under Book VI (Non-contractual liability arising out of damage caused to another).

V. – 2:103: Obligations After Intervention

(1)   After intervening the intervener must without undue delay report and account to the principal and hand over anything obtained as a result of the intervention.

(2)   If at the time of intervening the intervener lacks full legal capacity, the obligation to hand over is subject to the defence which would be available under VII. – 6:101 (Disenrichment).

(3)   The remedies for non-performance in Book III, Chapter 3 apply but with the modification that any liability to pay damages or interest is subject to the qualifications in paragraphs (2) and (3) of the preceding Article.

Chapter 3: Rights and Authority of Intervener

V. – 3:101: Right to Indemnification or Reimbursement

The intervener has a right against the principal for indemnification or, as the case may be, reimbursement in respect of an obligation or expenditure (whether of money or other assets) in so far as reasonably incurred for the purposes of the intervention.

V. – 3:102: Right to Remuneration

(1)   The intervener has a right to remuneration in so far as the intervention is reasonable and undertaken in the course of the intervener's profession or trade.

(2)   The remuneration due is the amount, so far as reasonable, which is ordinarily paid at the time and place of intervention in order to obtain a performance of the kind undertaken. If there is no such amount a reasonable remuneration is due.

V. – 3:103: Right to Reparation

An intervener who acts to protect the principal, or the principal's property or interests, against danger has a right against the principal for reparation for loss caused as a result of personal injury or property damage suffered in acting, if:

(a)   the intervention created or significantly increased the risk of such injury or damage; and

(b)   that risk, so far as foreseeable, was in reasonable proportion to the risk to the principal.

V. – 3:104: Reduction or Exclusion of Intervener's Rights

(1)   The intervener's rights are reduced or excluded in so far as the intervener at the time of acting did not want to demand indemnification, reimbursement, remuneration or reparation, as the case may be.

(2)   These rights are also reduced or excluded in so far as this is fair and reasonable, having regard among other things to whether the intervener acted to protect the principal in a situation of joint danger, whether the liability of the principal would be excessive and whether the intervener could reasonably be expected to obtain appropriate redress from another.

V. – 3:105: Obligation of Third Person to Indemnify or Reimburse the Principal

If the intervener acts to protect the principal from damage, a person who would be accountable under Book VI (Non-contractual liability arising out of damage caused to another) for the causation of such damage to the principal is obliged to indemnify or, as the case may be, reimburse the principal's liability to the intervener.

V. – 3:106: Authority of Intervener to Act as Representative of the Principal
(1)   The intervener may conclude legal transactions or perform other juridical acts as a representative of the principal in so far as this may reasonably be expected to benefit the principal.
(2)   However, a unilateral juridical act by the intervener as a representative of the principal has no effect if the person to whom it is addressed rejects the act without undue delay.

Book VI Non-Contractual Liability Arising Out of Damage Caused to Another
Chapter 1: Fundamental Provisions
VI. – 1:101: Basic Rule
(1)   A person who suffers legally relevant damage has a right to reparation from a person who caused the damage intentionally or negligently or is otherwise accountable for the causation of the damage.
(2)   Where a person has not caused legally relevant damage intentionally or negligently that person is accountable for the causation of legally relevant damage only if Chapter 3 so provides.

VI. – 1:102: Prevention
Where legally relevant damage is impending, this Book confers on a person who would suffer the damage a right to prevent it. This right is against a person who would be accountable for the causation of the damage if it occurred.

VI. – 1:103: Scope of Application
VI. – 1:101 (Basic rule) and VI. – 1:102 (Prevention):
(a)   apply only in accordance with the following provisions of this Book;
(b)   apply to both legal and natural persons, unless otherwise stated;
(c)   do not apply in so far as their application would contradict the purpose of other private law rules; and
(d)   do not affect remedies available on other legal grounds.

Chapter 2: Legally Relevant Damage
Section 1: General
VI. – 2:101: Meaning of Legally Relevant Damage
(1)   Loss, whether economic or non-economic, or injury is legally relevant damage if:
(a)   one of the following rules of this Chapter so provides;
(b)   the loss or injury results from a violation of a right otherwise conferred by the law; or
(c)   the loss or injury results from a violation of an interest worthy of legal protection.
(2)   In any case covered only by sub-paragraphs (b) or (c) of paragraph (1) loss or injury constitutes legally relevant damage only if it would be fair and reasonable for there to be a right to reparation or prevention, as the case may be, under VI. – 1:101 (Basic rule) or VI. – 1:102 (Prevention).
(3)   In considering whether it would be fair and reasonable for there to be a right to reparation or prevention regard is to be had to the ground of accountability, to the nature and proximity of the damage or impending damage, to the reasonable expectations of the person who suffers or would suffer the damage, and to considerations of public policy.
(4)   In this Book:
(a)   economic loss includes loss of income or profit, burdens incurred and a reduction in the value of property;
(b)   non-economic loss includes pain and suffering and impairment of the quality of life.

Section 2: Particular Instances of Legally Relevant Damage
VI. – 2:201: Personal Injury and Consequential Loss
(1)   Loss caused to a natural person as a result of injury to his or her body or health and the injury as such are legally relevant damage.
(2)   In this Book:

(a)   such loss includes the costs of health care including expenses reasonably incurred for the care of the injured person by those close to him or her; and
(b)   personal injury includes injury to mental health only if it amounts to a medical condition.

VI. – 2:202: Loss Suffered by Third Persons as a Result of Another's Personal Injury or Death

(1)   Non-economic loss caused to a natural person as a result of another's personal injury or death is legally relevant damage if at the time of injury that person is in a particularly close personal relationship to the injured person.
(2)   Where a person has been fatally injured:
(a)   legally relevant damage caused to the deceased on account of the injury to the time of death becomes legally relevant damage to the deceased's successors;
(b)   reasonable funeral expenses are legally relevant damage to the person incurring them; and
(c)   loss of maintenance is legally relevant damage to a natural person whom the deceased maintained or, had death not occurred, would have maintained under statutory provisions or to whom the deceased provided care and financial support.

VI. – 2:203: Infringement of Dignity, Liberty and Privacy

(1)   Loss caused to a natural person as a result of infringement of his or her right to respect for his or her dignity, such as the rights to liberty and privacy, and the injury as such are legally relevant damage.
(2)   Loss caused to a person as a result of injury to that person's reputation and the injury as such are also legally relevant damage if national law so provides.

VI. – 2:204: Loss upon Communication of Incorrect Information about Another

Loss caused to a person as a result of the communication of information about that person which the person communicating the information knows or could reasonably be expected to know is incorrect is legally relevant damage.

VI. – 2:205: Loss upon Breach of Confidence

Loss caused to a person as a result of the communication of information which, either from its nature or the circumstances in which it was obtained, the person communicating the information knows or could reasonably be expected to know is confidential to the person suffering the loss is legally relevant damage.

VI. – 2:206: Loss upon Infringement of Property or Lawful Possession

(1)   Loss caused to a person as a result of an infringement of that person's property right or lawful possession of a movable or immovable thing is legally relevant damage.
(2)   In this Article:
(a)   loss includes being deprived of the use of property;
(b)   infringement of a property right includes destruction of or physical damage to the subject-matter of the right (property damage), disposition of the right, interference with its use and other disturbance of the exercise of the right.

VI. – 2:207: Loss upon Reliance on Incorrect Advice or Information

Loss caused to a person as a result of making a decision in reasonable reliance on incorrect advice or information is legally relevant damage if:
(a)   the advice or information is provided by a person in pursuit of a profession or in the course of trade; and
(b)   the provider knew or could reasonably be expected to have known that the recipient would rely on the advice or information in making a decision of the kind made.

VI. – 2:208: Loss upon Unlawful Impairment of Business

(1)   Loss caused to a person as a result of an unlawful impairment of that person's exercise of a profession or conduct of a trade is legally relevant damage.

(2)   Loss caused to a consumer as a result of unfair competition is also legally relevant damage if Community or national law so provides.

VI. – 2:209: Burdens Incurred by the State upon Environmental Impairment

Burdens incurred by the State or designated competent authorities in restoring substantially impaired natural elements constituting the environment, such as air, water, soil, flora and fauna, are legally relevant damage to the State or the authorities concerned.

VI. – 2:210: Loss upon Fraudulent Misrepresentation

(1)   Without prejudice to the other provisions of this Section loss caused to a person as a result of another's fraudulent misrepresentation, whether by words or conduct, is legally relevant damage.
(2)   A misrepresentation is fraudulent if it is made with knowledge or belief that the representation is false and it is intended to induce the recipient to make a mistake.

VI. – 2:211: Loss upon Inducement of Non-Performance of Obligation

Without prejudice to the other provisions of this Section, loss caused to a person as a result of another's inducement of the non-performance of an obligation by a third person is legally relevant damage only if:
(a)   the obligation was owed to the person sustaining the loss; and
(b)   the person inducing the non-performance:
    (i)   intended the third person to fail to perform the obligation, and
    (ii)   did not act in legitimate protection of the inducing person's own interest.

Chapter 3: Accountability
Section 1: Intention and Negligence
VI. – 3:101: Intention

A person causes legally relevant damage intentionally when that person causes such damage either:
(a)   meaning to cause damage of the type caused; or
(b)   by conduct which that person means to do, knowing that such damage, or damage of that type, will or will almost certainly be caused.

VI. – 3:102: Negligence

A person causes legally relevant damage negligently when that person causes the damage by conduct which either:
(a)   does not meet the particular standard of care provided by a statutory provision whose purpose is the protection of the person suffering the damage from that damage; or
(b)   does not otherwise amount to such care as could be expected from a reasonably careful person in the circumstances of the case.

VI. – 3:103: Persons Under Eighteen

(1)   A person under eighteen years of age is accountable for causing legally relevant damage according to VI. – 3:102 (Negligence) sub-paragraph (b) only in so far as that person does not exercise such care as could be expected from a reasonably careful person of the same age in the circumstances of the case.
(2)   A person under seven years of age is not accountable for causing damage intentionally or negligently.
(3)   However, paragraphs (1) and (2) do not apply to the extent that:
(a)   the person suffering the damage cannot obtain reparation under this Book from another; and
(b)   liability to make reparation would be equitable having regard to the financial means of the parties and all other circumstances of the case.

VI. – 3:104: Accountability for Damage Caused by Children or Supervised Persons

(1)   Parents or other persons obliged by law to provide parental care for a person under fourteen years of age are accountable for the causation of legally relevant damage where that per-

son under age caused the damage by conduct that would constitute intentional or negligent conduct if it were the conduct of an adult.

(2)   An institution or other body obliged to supervise a person is accountable for the causation of legally relevant damage suffered by a third party when:

(a)   the damage is personal injury, loss within VI. – 2:202 (Loss suffered by third persons as a result of another's personal injury or death) or property damage;

(b)   the person whom the institution or other body is obliged to supervise caused that damage intentionally or negligently or, in the case of a person under eighteen, by conduct that would constitute intention or negligence if it were the conduct of an adult; and

(c)   the person whom the institution or other body is obliged to supervise is a person likely to cause damage of that type.

(3)   However, a person is not accountable under this Article for the causation of damage if that person shows that there was no defective supervision of the person causing the damage.

Section 2: Accountability Without Intention or Negligence
VI. – 3:201: Accountability for Damage Caused by Employees and Representatives

(1)   A person who employs or similarly engages another is accountable for the causation of legally relevant damage suffered by a third person when the person employed or engaged:

(a)   caused the damage in the course of the employment or engagement; and

(b)   caused the damage intentionally or negligently, or is otherwise accountable for the causation of the damage.

(2)   Paragraph (1) applies correspondingly to a legal person in relation to a representative causing damage in the course of their engagement. A representative is a person who is authorised to effect juridical acts on behalf of the legal person by its constitution.

VI. – 3:202: Accountability for Damage Caused by the Unsafe State of an Immovable

(1)   A person who independently exercises control over an immovable is accountable for the causation of personal injury and consequential loss, loss within VI. – 2:202 (Loss suffered by third persons as a result of another's personal injury or death), and loss resulting from property damage (other than to the immovable itself) by a state of the immovable which does not ensure such safety as a person in or near the immovable is entitled to expect having regard to the circumstances including:

(a)   the nature of the immovable;

(b)   the access to the immovable; and

(c)   the cost of avoiding the immovable being in that state.

(2)   A person exercises independent control over an immovable if that person exercises such control that it is reasonable to impose a duty on that person to prevent legally relevant damage within the scope of this Article.

(3)   The owner of the immovable is to be regarded as independently exercising control, unless the owner shows that another independently exercises control.

VI. – 3:203: Accountability for Damage Caused by Animals

A keeper of an animal is accountable for the causation by the animal of personal injury and consequential loss, loss within VI. – 2:202 (Loss suffered by third persons as a result of another's personal injury or death), and loss resulting from property damage.

VI. – 3:204: Accountability for Damage Caused by Defective Products

(1)   The producer of a product is accountable for the causation of personal injury and consequential loss, loss within VI. – 2:202 (Loss suffered by third persons as a result of another's personal injury or death), and, in relation to consumers, loss resulting from property damage (other than to the product itself) by a defect in the product.

(2)   A person who imported the product into the European Economic Area for sale, hire, leasing or distribution in the course of that person's business is accountable correspondingly.

(3)   A supplier of the product is accountable correspondingly if:

(a) the producer cannot be identified; or
(b) in the case of an imported product, the product does not indicate the identity of the importer (whether or not the producer's name is indicated), unless the supplier informs the person suffering the damage, within a reasonable time, of the identity of the producer or the person who supplied that supplier with the product.
(4) A person is not accountable under this Article for the causation of damage if that person shows that:
(a) that person did not put the product into circulation;
(b) it is probable that the defect which caused the damage did not exist at the time when that person put the product into circulation;
(c) that person neither manufactured the product for sale or distribution for economic purpose nor manufactured or distributed it in the course of business;
(d) the defect is due to the product's compliance with mandatory regulations issued by public authorities;
(e) the state of scientific and technical knowledge at the time that person put the product into circulation did not enable the existence of the defect to be discovered; or
(f) in the case of a manufacturer of a component, the defect is attributable to:
    (i) the design of the product into which the component has been fitted; or
    (ii) instructions given by the manufacturer of the product.
(5) "Producer" means:
(a) in the case of a finished product or a component, the manufacturer;
(b) in the case of raw material, the person who abstracts or wins it; and
(c) any person who, by putting a name, trade mark or other distinguishing feature on the product, gives the impression of being its producer.
(6) "Product" means a movable, even if incorporated into another movable or an immovable, or electricity.
(7) A product is defective if it does not provide the safety which a person is entitled to expect, having regard to the circumstances including:
(a) the presentation of the product;
(b) the use to which it could reasonably be expected that the product would be put; and
(c) the time when the product was put into circulation, but a product is not defective merely because a better product is subsequently put into circulation.

VI. – 3:205: Accountability for Damage Caused by Motor Vehicles

(1) A keeper of a motor vehicle is accountable for the causation of personal injury and consequential loss, loss within VI. – 2:202 (Loss suffered by third persons as a result of another's personal injury or death), and loss resulting from property damage (other than to the vehicle and its freight) in a traffic accident which results from the use of the vehicle.
(2) "Motor vehicle" means any vehicle intended for travel on land and propelled by mechanical power, but not running on rails, and any trailer, whether or not coupled.

VI. – 3:206: Accountability for Damage Caused by Dangerous Substances or Emissions

(1) A keeper of a substance or an operator of an installation is accountable for the causation by that substance or by emissions from that installation of personal injury and consequential loss, loss within VI. – 2:202 (Loss suffered by third persons as a result of another's personal injury or death), loss resulting from property damage, and burdens within VI. – 2:209 (Burdens incurred by the State upon environmental impairment), if:
(a) having regard to their quantity and attributes, at the time of the emission, or, failing an emission, at the time of contact with the substance it is very likely that the substance or emission will cause such damage unless adequately controlled; and
(b) the damage results from the realisation of that danger.
(2) "Substance" includes chemicals (whether solid, liquid or gaseous). Microorganisms are to be treated like substances.

(3) "Emission" includes:
(a) the release or escape of substances;
(b) the conduction of electricity;
(c) heat, light and other radiation;
(d) noise and other vibrations; and
(e) other incorporeal impact on the environment.
(4) "Installation" includes a mobile installation and an installation under construction or not in use.
(5) However, a person is not accountable for the causation of damage under this Article if that person:
(a) does not keep the substance or operate the installation for purposes related to that person's trade, business or profession; or
(b) shows that there was no failure to comply with statutory standards of control of the substance or management of the installation.

VI. – 3:207: Other Accountability for the Causation of Legally Relevant Damage
A person is also accountable for the causation of legally relevant damage if national law so provides where it:
(a) relates to a source of danger which is not within VI. – 3:104 (Accountability for damage caused by children or supervised persons) to VI. – 3:205 (Accountability for damage caused by motor vehicles);
(b) relates to substances or emissions; or
(c) disapplies VI. – 3:204 (Accountability for damage caused by defective products) paragraph (4)(e).

VI. – 3:208: Abandonment
For the purposes of this section, a person remains accountable for an immovable, vehicle, substance or installation which that person abandons until another exercises independent control over it or becomes its keeper or operator. This applies correspondingly, so far as reasonable, in respect of a keeper of an animal.

Chapter 4: Causation
VI. – 4:101: General Rule
(1) A person causes legally relevant damage to another if the damage is to be regarded as a consequence of that person's conduct or the source of danger for which that person is responsible.
(2) In cases of personal injury or death the injured person's predisposition with respect to the type or extent of the injury sustained is to be disregarded.

VI. – 4:102: Collaboration
A person who participates with, instigates or materially assists another in causing legally relevant damage is to be regarded as causing that damage.

VI. – 4:103: Alternative Causes
Where legally relevant damage may have been caused by any one or more of a number of occurrences for which different persons are accountable and it is established that the damage was caused by one of these occurrences but not which one, each person who is accountable for any of the occurrences is rebuttably presumed to have caused that damage.

Chapter 5: Defences
Section 1: Consent or Conduct of the Person Suffering the Damage
VI. – 5:101: Consent and Acting at Own Risk
(1) A person has a defence if the person suffering the damage validly consents to the legally relevant damage and is aware or could reasonably be expected to be aware of the consequences of that consent.

(2)   The same applies if the person suffering the damage, knowing the risk of damage of the type caused, voluntarily takes that risk and is to be regarded as accepting it.

VI. – 5:102: Contributory Fault and Accountability

(1)   Where the fault of the person suffering the damage contributes to the occurrence or extent of legally relevant damage, reparation is to be reduced according to the degree of such fault.

(2)   However, no regard is to be had to:

(a)   an insubstantial fault of the person suffering the damage;

(b)   fault or accountability whose contribution to the causation of the damage is insubstantial;

(c)   the injured person's want of care contributing to that person's personal injury caused by a motor vehicle in a traffic accident, unless that want of care constitutes profound failure to take such care as is manifestly required in the circumstances.

(3)   Paragraphs (1) and (2) apply correspondingly where the fault of a person for whom the person suffering the damage is responsible within the scope of VI. – 3:201 (Accountability for damage caused by employees and representatives) contributes to the occurrence or extent of the damage.

(4)   Compensation is to be reduced likewise if and in so far as any other source of danger for which the person suffering the damage is responsible under Chapter 3 (Accountability) contributes to the occurrence or extent of the damage.

VI. – 5:103: Damage Caused by a Criminal to a Collaborator

Legally relevant damage caused unintentionally in the course of committing a criminal offence to another person participating or otherwise collaborating in the offence does not give rise to a right to reparation if this would be contrary to public policy.

Section 2: Interests of Accountable Persons or Third Parties
VI. – 5:201: Authority Conferred by Law

A person has a defence if legally relevant damage is caused with authority conferred by law.

VI. – 5:202: Self-Defence, Benevolent Intervention and Necessity

(1)   A person has a defence if that person causes legally relevant damage in reasonable protection of a right or of an interest worthy of legal protection of that person or a third person if the person suffering the legally relevant damage is accountable for endangering the right or interest protected. For the purposes of this paragraph VI. – 3:103 (Persons under eighteen) is to be disregarded.

(2)   The same applies to legally relevant damage caused by a benevolent intervener to a principal without breach of the intervener's duties.

(3)   Where a person causes legally relevant damage to the patrimony of another in a situation of imminent danger to life, body, health or liberty in order to save the person causing the damage or a third person from that danger and the danger could not be eliminated without causing the damage, the person causing the damage is not liable to make reparation beyond providing reasonable recompense.

VI. – 5:203: Protection of Public Interest

A person has a defence if legally relevant damage is caused in necessary protection of values fundamental to a democratic society, in particular where damage is caused by dissemination of information in the media.

Section 3: Inability to Control
VI. – 5:301: Mental Incompetence

(1)   A person who is mentally incompetent at the time of conduct causing legally relevant damage is liable only if this is equitable, having regard to the mentally incompetent person's financial means and all the other circumstances of the case. Liability is limited to reasonable recompense.

(2)   A person is to be regarded as mentally incompetent if that person lacks sufficient insight into the nature of his or her conduct, unless the lack of sufficient insight is the temporary result of his or her own misconduct.

VI. – 5:302: Event Beyond Control

A person has a defence if legally relevant damage is caused by an abnormal event which cannot be averted by any reasonable measure and which is not to be regarded as that person's risk.

Section 4: Contractual Exclusion and Restriction of Liability

VI. – 5:401: Contractual Exclusion and Restriction of Liability

(1)   Liability for causing legally relevant damage intentionally cannot be excluded or restricted.

(2)   Liability for causing legally relevant damage as a result of a profound failure to take such care as is manifestly required in the circumstances cannot be excluded or restricted:

(a)   in respect of personal injury (including fatal injury); or

(b)   if the exclusion or restriction is otherwise illegal or contrary to good faith and fair dealing.

(3)   Liability for damage for the causation of which a person is accountable under VI. – 3:204 (Accountability for damage caused by defective products) cannot be restricted or excluded.

(4)   Other liability under this Book can be excluded or restricted unless statute provides otherwise.

Section 5: Loss Within VI. – 2:202 (Loss Suffered by Third Persons
as a Result of Another's Personal Injury or Death)

VI. – 5:501: Extension of Defences Against the Injured Person to Third Persons

A defence which may be asserted against a person's right of reparation in respect of that person's personal injury or, if death had not occurred, could have been asserted, may also be asserted against a person suffering loss within VI. – 2:202 (Loss suffered by third persons as a result of another's personal injury or death).

Chapter 6: Remedies

Section 1: Reparation in General

VI. – 6:101: Aim and Forms of Reparation

(1)   Reparation is to reinstate the person suffering the legally relevant damage in the position that person would have been in had the legally relevant damage not occurred.

(2)   Reparation may be in money (compensation) or otherwise, as is most appropriate, having regard to the kind and extent of damage suffered and all the other circumstances of the case.

(3)   Where a tangible object is damaged, compensation equal to its depreciation of value is to be awarded instead of the cost of its repair if the cost of repair unreasonably exceeds the depreciation of value. This rule applies to animals only if appropriate, having regard to the purpose for which the animal was kept.

(4)   As an alternative to reinstatement under paragraph (1), but only where this is reasonable, reparation may take the form of recovery from the person accountable for the causation of the legally relevant damage of any advantage obtained by the latter in connection with causing the damage.

VI. – 6:102: De Minimis Rule

Trivial damage is to be disregarded.

VI. – 6:103: Equalisation of Benefits

(1)   Benefits arising to the person suffering legally relevant damage as a result of the damaging event are to be disregarded unless it would be fair and reasonable to take them into account.

(2)   In deciding whether it would be fair and reasonable to take the benefits into account, regard shall be had to the kind of damage sustained, the nature of the accountability of the person causing the damage and, where the benefits are conferred by a third person, the purpose of conferring those benefits.

VI. – 6:104: Multiple Persons Suffering Damage

Where multiple persons suffer legally relevant damage and reparation to one person will also make reparation to another, Book III, Chapter 4, Section 2 (Plurality of creditors) applies with appropriate adaptation to their rights to reparation.

VI. – 6:105: Solidary Liability

Where several persons are liable for the same legally relevant damage, they are liable solidarily.

VI. – 6:106: Assignment of Right to Reparation

The person suffering the damage may assign a right to reparation, including a right to reparation for non-economic loss.

Section 2: Compensation

VI. – 6:201: Right of Election

The person suffering the damage may choose whether or not to spend compensation on the reinstatement of the damaged interest.

VI. – 6:202: Reduction of Liability

Where it is fair and reasonable to do so, a person may be relieved of liability to compensate, either wholly or in part, if, where the damage is not caused intentionally, liability in full would be disproportionate to the accountability of the person causing the damage or the extent of the damage or the means to prevent it.

VI. – 6:203: Capitalisation and Quantification

(1)   Compensation is to be awarded as a lump sum unless a good reason requires periodical payment.

(2)   National law determines how compensation for personal injury and non-economic loss is to be quantified.

VI. – 6:204: Compensation for Injury as Such

Injury as such is to be compensated independent of compensation for economic or non-economic loss.

Section 3: Prevention

VI. – 6:301: Right to Prevention

(1)   The right to prevention exists only in so far as:

(a)   reparation would not be an adequate alternative remedy; and

(b)   it is reasonable for the person who would be accountable for the causation of the damage to prevent it from occurring.

(2)   Where the source of danger is an object or an animal and it is not reasonably possible for the endangered person to avoid the danger the right to prevention includes a right to have the source of danger removed.

VI. – 6:302: Liability for Loss in Preventing Damage

A person who has reasonably incurred expenditure or sustained other loss in order to prevent that person from suffering an impending damage, or in order to limit the extent or severity of damage suffered, has a right to compensation from the person who would have been accountable for the causation of the damage.

Chapter 7: Ancillary Rules

VI. – 7:101: National Constitutional Laws

The provisions of this Book are to be interpreted and applied in a manner compatible with the constitutional law of the court.

VI. – 7:102: Statutory Provisions

National law determines what legal provisions are statutory provisions.

VI. – 7:103: Public Law Functions and Court Proceedings

This Book does not govern the liability of a person or body arising from the exercise or omission to exercise public law functions or from performing duties during court proceedings.

VI. – 7:104: Liability of Employees, Employers, Trade Unions and Employers' Associations
This Book does not govern the liability of:
(a)   employees (whether to co-employees, employers or third parties) arising in the course of employment;
(b)   employers to employees arising in the course of employment; and
(c)   trade unions and employers' associations arising in the course of an industrial dispute.

VI. – 7:105: Reduction or Exclusion of Liability to Indemnified Persons
If a person is entitled from another source to reparation, whether in full or in part, for that person's damage, in particular from an insurer, fund or other body, national law determines whether or not by virtue of that entitlement liability under this Book is limited or excluded.

Book VII Unjustified Enrichment
Chapter 1: General
VII. – 1:101: Basic Rule
(1)   A person who obtains an unjustified enrichment which is attributable to another's disadvantage is obliged to that other to reverse the enrichment.
(2)   This rule applies only in accordance with the following provisions of this Book.

Chapter 2: When Enrichment Is Unjustified
VII. – 2:101: Circumstances in Which an Enrichment Is Unjustified
(1)   An enrichment is unjustified unless:
(a)   the enriched person is entitled as against the disadvantaged person to the enrichment by virtue of a contract or other juridical act, a court order or a rule of law; or
(b)   the disadvantaged person consented freely and without error to the disadvantage.
(2)   If the contract or other juridical act, court order or rule of law referred to in paragraph (1)(a) is void or avoided or otherwise rendered ineffective retrospectively, the enriched person is not entitled to the enrichment on that basis.
(3)   However, the enriched person is to be regarded as entitled to an enrichment by virtue of a rule of law only if the policy of that rule is that the enriched person is to retain the value of the enrichment.
(4)   An enrichment is also unjustified if:
(a)   the disadvantaged person conferred it:
    (i)   for a purpose which is not achieved; or
    (ii)   with an expectation which is not realised;
(b)   the enriched person knew of, or could reasonably be expected to know of, the purpose or expectation; and
(c)   the enriched person accepted or could reasonably be assumed to have accepted that the enrichment must be reversed in such circumstances.

VII. – 2:102: Performance of Obligation to Third Person
Where the enriched person obtains the enrichment as a result of the disadvantaged person performing an obligation or a supposed obligation owed by the disadvantaged person to a third person, the enrichment is justified if:
(a)   the disadvantaged person performed freely; or
(b)   the enrichment was merely the incidental result of performance of the obligation.

VII. – 2:103: Consenting or Performing Freely
(1)   If the disadvantaged person's consent is affected by incapacity, fraud, coercion, threats or unfair exploitation, the disadvantaged person does not consent freely.
(2)   If the obligation which is performed is ineffective because of incapacity, fraud, coercion threats or unfair exploitation, the disadvantaged person does not perform freely.

Chapter 3: Enrichment and Disadvantage
VII. – 3:101: Enrichment

(1)   A person is enriched by:
(a)   an increase in assets or a decrease in liabilities;
(b)   receiving a service or having work done; or
(c)   use of another's assets.
(2)   In determining whether and to what extent a person obtains an enrichment, no regard is to be had to any disadvantage which that person sustains in exchange for or after the enrichment.

VII. – 3:102: Disadvantage

(1)   A person is disadvantaged by:
(a)   a decrease in assets or an increase in liabilities;
(b)   rendering a service or doing work; or
(c)   another's use of that person's assets.
(2)   In determining whether and to what extent a person sustains a disadvantage, no regard is to be had to any enrichment which that person obtains in exchange for or after the disadvantage.

Chapter 4: Attribution
VII. – 4:101: Instances of Attribution

An enrichment is attributable to another's disadvantage in particular where:
(a)   an asset of that other is transferred to the enriched person by that other;
(b)   a service is rendered to or work is done for the enriched person by that other;
(c)   the enriched person uses that other's asset, especially where the enriched person infringes the disadvantaged person's rights or legally protected interests;
(d)   an asset of the enriched person is improved by that other; or
(e)   the enriched person is discharged from a liability by that other.

VII. – 4:102: Intermediaries

Where one party to a juridical act is an authorised intermediary indirectly representing a principal, any enrichment or disadvantage of the principal which results from the juridical act, or from a performance of obligations under it, is to be regarded as an enrichment or disadvantage of the intermediary.

VII. – 4:103: Debtor's Performance to a Non-Creditor; Onward Transfer in Good Faith

(1)   An enrichment is also attributable to another's disadvantage where a debtor confers the enrichment on the enriched person and as a result the disadvantaged person loses a right against the debtor to the same or a like enrichment.
(2)   Paragraph (1) applies in particular where a person who is obliged to the disadvantaged person to reverse an unjustified enrichment transfers it to a third person in circumstances in which the debtor has a defence under VII. – 6:101 (Disenrichment).

VII. – 4:104: Ratification of Debtor's Performance to a Non-Creditor

(1)   Where a debtor purports to discharge a debt by paying a third person, the creditor may ratify that act.
(2)   Ratification extinguishes the creditor's right against the debtor to the extent of the payment with the effect that the third person's enrichment is attributable to the creditor's loss of the claim against the debtor.
(3)   As between the creditor and the third person, ratification does not amount to consent to the loss of the creditor's right against the debtor.
(4)   This Article applies correspondingly to performances of non-monetary obligations.
(5)   Other rules may exclude the application of this Article if an insolvency or equivalent proceeding has been opened against the debtor before the creditor ratifies.

VII. – 4:105: Attribution Resulting from an Act of an Intervener

(1)   An enrichment is also attributable to another's disadvantage where a third person uses an asset of the disadvantaged person without authority so that the disadvantaged person is deprived of the asset and it accrues to the enriched person.

(2)   Paragraph (1) applies in particular where, as a result of an intervener's interference with or disposition of goods, the disadvantaged person ceases to be owner of the goods and the enriched person becomes owner, whether by juridical act or rule of law.

VII. – 4:106: Ratification of Intervener's Acts

(1)   A person entitled to an asset may ratify the act of an intervener who purports to dispose of or otherwise uses that asset in a juridical act with a third person.

(2)   The ratified act has the same effect as a juridical act by an authorised intermediary. As between the person ratifying and the intervener, ratification does not amount to consent to the intervener's use of the asset.

VII. – 4:107: Where Type or Value Not Identical

An enrichment may be attributable to another's disadvantage even though the enrichment and disadvantage are not of the same type or value.

Chapter 5: Reversal of Enrichment

VII. – 5:101: Transferable Enrichment

(1)   Where the enrichment consists of a transferable asset, the enriched person reverses the enrichment by transferring the asset to the disadvantaged person.

(2)   Instead of transferring the asset, the enriched person may choose to reverse the enrichment by paying its monetary value to the disadvantaged person if a transfer would cause the enriched person unreasonable effort or expense.

(3)   If the enriched person is no longer able to transfer the asset, the enriched person reverses the enrichment by paying its monetary value to the disadvantaged person.

(4)   However, to the extent that the enriched person has obtained a substitute in exchange, the substitute is the enrichment to be reversed if:

(a)   the enriched person is in good faith at the time of disposal or loss and the enriched person so chooses; or

(b)   the enriched person is not in good faith at the time of disposal or loss, the disadvantaged person so chooses and the choice is not inequitable.

(5)   The enriched person is in good faith if that person neither knew nor could reasonably be expected to know that the enrichment was or was likely to become unjustified.

VII. – 5:102: Non-Transferable Enrichment

(1)   Where the enrichment does not consist of a transferable asset, the enriched person reverses the enrichment by paying its monetary value to the disadvantaged person.

(2)   The enriched person is not liable to pay more than any saving if the enriched person:

(a)   did not consent to the enrichment; or

(b)   was in good faith.

(3)   However, where the enrichment was obtained under an agreement which fixed a price or value for the enrichment, the enriched person is at least liable to pay that sum if the agreement was void or voidable for reasons which were not material to the fixing of the price.

(4)   Paragraph (3) does not apply so as to increase liability beyond the monetary value of the enrichment.

VII. – 5:103: Monetary Value of an Enrichment; Saving

(1)   The monetary value of an enrichment is the sum of money which a provider and a recipient with a real intention of reaching an agreement would lawfully have agreed as its price. Expenditure of a service provider which the agreement would require the recipient to reimburse is to be regarded as part of the price.

(2)   A saving is the decrease in assets or increase in liabilities which the enriched person would have sustained if the enrichment had not been obtained.

VII. – 5:104: Fruits and Use of an Enrichment
(1)   Reversal of the enrichment extends to the fruits and use of the enrichment or, if less, any saving resulting from the fruits or use.
(2)   However, if the enriched person obtains the fruits or use in bad faith, reversal of the enrichment extends to the fruits and use even if the saving is less than the value of the fruits or use.

Chapter 6: Defences
VII. – 6:101: Disenrichment
(1)   The enriched person is not liable to reverse the enrichment to the extent that the enriched person has sustained a disadvantage by disposing of the enrichment or otherwise (disenrichment), unless the enriched person would have been disenriched even if the enrichment had not been obtained.
(2)   However, a disenrichment is to be disregarded to the extent that:
(a)   the enriched person has obtained a substitute;
(b)   the enriched person was not in good faith at the time of disenrichment, unless:
    (i)   the disadvantaged person would also have been disenriched even if the enrichment had been reversed; or
    (ii)   the enriched person was in good faith at the time of enrichment, the disenrichment was sustained before performance of the obligation to reverse the enrichment was due and the disenrichment resulted from the realisation of a risk for which the enriched person is not to be regarded as responsible; or
(c)   paragraph (3) of VII. – 5:102 (Non-transferable enrichment) applies.
(3)   Where the enriched person has a defence under this Article as against the disadvantaged person as a result of a disposal to a third person, any right of the disadvantaged person against that third person is unaffected.

VII. – 6:102: Juridical Acts in Good Faith with Third Parties
The enriched person is also not liable to reverse the enrichment if:
(a)   in exchange for that enrichment the enriched person confers another enrichment on a third person; and
(b)   the enriched person is still in good faith at that time.

VII. – 6:103: Illegality
Where a contract or other juridical act under which an enrichment is obtained is void or avoided because of an infringement of a fundamental principle (II. – 7:301 (Contracts infringing fundamental principles)) or mandatory rule of law, the enriched person is not liable to reverse the enrichment to the extent that the reversal would contravene the policy underlying the principle or rule.

Chapter 7: Relation to Other Legal Rules
VII. – 7:101: Other Private Law Rights to Recover
(1)   The legal consequences of an enrichment which is obtained by virtue of a contract or other juridical act are governed by other rules if those rules grant or exclude a right to reversal of an enrichment, whether on withdrawal, termination, price reduction or otherwise.
(2)   This Book does not address the proprietary effect of a right to reversal of an enrichment.
(3)   This Book does not affect any other right to recover arising under contractual or other rules of private law.

VII. – 7:102: Concurrent Obligations
(1)   Where the disadvantaged person has both:
(a)   a claim under this Book for reversal of an unjustified enrichment; and
(b)   (i)   a claim for reparation for the disadvantage (whether against the enriched person or a third party); or

(ii) a right to recover under other rules of private law as a result of the unjustified enrichment,

the satisfaction of one of the claims reduces the other claim by the same amount.

(2) The same applies where a person uses an asset of the disadvantaged person so that it
accrues to another and under this Book:

(a) the user is liable to the disadvantaged person in respect of the use of the asset; and

(b) the recipient is liable to the disadvantaged person in respect of the increase in assets.

VII. – 7:103: Public Law Claims

This Book does not determine whether it applies to enrichments which a person or body
obtains or confers in the exercise of public law functions.

Book VIII Acquisition and Loss of Ownership of Goods
Chapter 1: General Provisions

Section 1: Scope of Application and Relation to Other Provisions
VIII. – 1:101: Scope of Application

(1) This Book applies to the acquisition, loss and protection of ownership of goods and to specific related issues.

(2) This Book does not apply to the acquisition or loss of ownership of goods by:

(a) universal succession, in particular under the law of succession and under company law;

(b) expropriation and forfeiture;

(c) separation from movable or immovable property;

(d) division of co-ownership, unless provided by VIII. – 2:306 (Delivery out of the bulk) or VIII. –
5:202 (Commingling);

(e) survivorship or accrual, unless covered by Chapter 5 of this Book;

(f) real subrogation, unless covered by Chapter 5 of this Book;

(g) occupation;

(h) finding; or

(i) abandonment.

(3) This Book applies to the acquisition and loss of ownership of goods by extrajudicial enforcement in the sense of Book IX or the equivalent. It may be applied, with appropriate adaptations, to the acquisition and loss of ownership of goods by judicial or equivalent enforcement.

(4) This Book does not apply to:

(a) company shares or documents embodying the right to an asset or to the performance of
an obligation, except documents containing the undertaking to deliver goods for the purposes of VIII. – 2:105 (Equivalents to delivery) paragraph (4); or

(b) electricity.

(5) This Book applies, with appropriate adaptations, to banknotes and coins that are current
legal tender.

VIII. – 1:102: Registration of Goods

(1) Whether ownership and the transfer of ownership in certain categories of goods may be or
have to be registered in a public register is determined by national law.

(2) The effects of such registration, as determined by national law, have priority over the respective rules of this Book.

VIII. – 1:103: Priority of Other Provisions

(1) In relation to a transfer, or retention, of ownership for purposes of security, the provisions of
Book IX apply and have priority over the provisions in this Book.

(2) In relation to a transfer of ownership for purposes of a trust, or to or from a trust, the provisions of Book X apply and have priority over the provisions in this Book.

VIII. – 1:104: Application of Rules of Books I to III

Where, under the provisions of this Book, proprietary effects are determined by an agreement,
Books I to III apply, where appropriate.

Section 2: Definitions
VIII. – 1:201: Goods
"Goods" means corporeal movables. It includes ships, vessels, hovercraft or aircraft, space objects, animals, liquids and gases.

VIII. – 1:202: Ownership
"Ownership" is the most comprehensive right a person, the "owner", can have over property, including the exclusive right, so far as consistent with applicable laws or rights granted by the owner, to use, enjoy, modify, destroy, dispose of and recover the property.

VIII. – 1:203: Co-Ownership
Where "co-ownership" is created under this Book, this means that two or more co-owners own undivided shares in the whole goods and each co-owner can dispose of that co-owner's share by acting alone, unless otherwise provided by the parties.

VIII. – 1:204: Limited Proprietary Rights
Limited proprietary rights in the sense of this Book are:
(a)   security rights if characterised or treated as proprietary rights by Book IX or by national law;
(b)   rights to use if characterised or treated as proprietary rights by other provisions of these model rules or by national law;
(c)   rights to acquire in the sense of VIII. – 2:307 (Contingent right of transferee under retention of ownership) or if characterised or treated as proprietary rights by other provisions of these model rules or by national law;
(d)   trust-related rights if characterised or treated as proprietary rights by Book X or by national law.

VIII. – 1:205: Possession
(1)   Possession, in relation to goods, means having direct physical control or indirect physical control over the goods.
(2)   Direct physical control is physical control which is exercised by the possessor personally or through a possession-agent exercising such control on behalf of the possessor (direct possession).
(3)   Indirect physical control is physical control which is exercised by means of another person, a limited-right-possessor (indirect possession).

VIII. – 1:206: Possession by Owner-Possessor
An "owner-possessor" is a person who exercises direct or indirect physical control over the goods with the intention of doing so as, or as if, an owner.

VIII. – 1:207: Possession by Limited-Right-Possessor
(1)   A "limited-right-possessor" is a person who exercises physical control over the goods either:
(a)   with the intention of doing so in that person's own interest, and under a specific legal relationship with the owner-possessor which gives the limited-right-possessor the right to possess the goods; or
(b)   with the intention of doing so to the order of the owner-possessor, and under a specific contractual relationship with the owner-possessor which gives the limited-right-possessor a right to retain the goods until any charges or costs have been paid by the owner-possessor.
(2)   A limited-right-possessor may have direct physical control or indirect physical control over the goods.

VIII. – 1:208: Possession Through a Possession-Agent
(1)   A "possession-agent" is a person:
(a)   who exercises direct physical control over the goods on behalf of an owner-possessor or limited-right-possessor without the intention and specific legal relationship required under VIII. – 1:207 (Possession by limited-right-possessor) paragraph (1); and
(b)   to whom the owner-possessor or limited-right-possessor may give binding instructions as to the use of the goods in the interest of the owner-possessor or limited-right-possessor.

(2)   A possession-agent may, in particular, be:
(a)   an employee of the owner-possessor or limited-right-possessor or a person exercising a similar function; or
(b)   a person who is given physical control over the goods by the owner-possessor or limited-right-possessor for practical reasons.
(3)   A person is also a possession-agent where that person is accidentally in a position to exercise, and does exercise, direct physical control over the goods for an owner-possessor or limited-right-possessor.

Section 3: Further General Rules
VIII. – 1:301: Transferability

(1)   All goods are transferable except where provided otherwise by law. A limitation or prohibition of the transfer of goods by a contract or other juridical act does not affect the transferability of the goods.
(2)   Whether or to what extent uncollected fruits of, and accessories or appurtenances to, goods or immovable assets are transferable separately is regulated by national law. Chapter 5 remains unaffected.

Chapter 2: Transfer of Ownership Based on the Transferor's Right or Authority
Section 1: Requirements for Transfer under this Chapter
VIII. – 2:101: Requirements for the Transfer of Ownership in General

(1)   The transfer of ownership of goods under this Chapter requires that:
(a)   the goods exist;
(b)   the goods are transferable;
(c)   the transferor has the right or authority to transfer the ownership;
(d)   the transferee is entitled as against the transferor to the transfer of ownership by virtue of a contract or other juridical act, a court order or a rule of law; and
(e)   there is an agreement as to the time ownership is to pass and the conditions of this agreement are met, or, in the absence of such agreement, delivery or an equivalent to delivery.
(2)   For the purposes of paragraph (1)(e) the delivery or equivalent to delivery must be based on, or referable to, the entitlement under the contract or other juridical act, court order or rule of law.
(3)   Where the contract or other juridical act, court order or rule of law defines the goods in generic terms, ownership can pass only when the goods are identified to it. Where goods form part of an identified bulk, VIII. – 2:305 (Transfer of goods forming part of a bulk) applies.
(4)   Paragraph (1)(e) does not apply where ownership passes under a court order or rule of law at the time determined in it.

VIII. – 2:102: Transferor's Right or Authority

(1)   Where the transferor lacks a right or authority to transfer ownership at the time ownership is to pass, the transfer takes place when the right is obtained or the person having the right or authority to transfer has ratified the transfer at a later time.
(2)   Upon ratification the transfer produces the same effects as if it had initially been carried out with authority. However, proprietary rights acquired by other persons before ratification remain unaffected.

VIII. – 2:103: Agreement as to the Time Ownership Is to Pass

The point in time when ownership passes may be determined by party agreement, except where registration is necessary to acquire ownership under national law.

VIII. – 2:104: Delivery

(1)   For the purposes of this Book, delivery of the goods takes place when the transferor gives up and the transferee obtains possession of the goods in the sense of VIII. – 1:205 (Possession).
(2)   If the contract or other juridical act, court order or rule of law involves carriage of the goods by a carrier or a series of carriers, delivery of the goods takes place when the transferor's obligation to deliver is fulfilled and the carrier or the transferee obtains possession of the goods.

VIII. – 2:105: Equivalents to Delivery

(1) Where the goods are already in the possession of the transferee, the retention of the goods on the coming into effect of the entitlement under the contract or other juridical act, court order or rule of law has the same effect as delivery.

(2) Where a third person possesses the goods for the transferor, the same effect as delivery is achieved when the third party receives the transferor's notice of the ownership being transferred to the transferee, or at a later time if so stated in the notice. The same applies where notice is given to a possession-agent in the sense of VIII. – 1:208 (Possession through possession-agent).

(3) The same effect as delivery of the goods is achieved when the transferor gives up and the transferee obtains possession of means enabling the transferee to obtain possession of the goods.

(4) Where a person exercising physical control over goods issues a document containing an undertaking to deliver the goods to the current holder of the document, the transfer of that document is equivalent to delivery of the goods. The document may be an electronic one.

Section 2: Effects

VIII. – 2:201: Effects of the Transfer of Ownership

(1) At the time determined by Section 1, ownership passes within the limits of the transferor's right or authority to dispose, with effect between the parties and with effect against third persons.

(2) The transfer of ownership does not affect rights and obligations between the parties based on the terms of a contract or other juridical act, court order or rule of law, such as:

(a) a right resulting from the passing of risk;

(b) a right to withhold performance;

(c) a right to fruits or benefits, or an obligation to cover costs and charges; or

(d) a right to use or an obligation not to use or otherwise deal with the goods.

(3) The transfer of ownership does not affect rights of or against third parties under other rules of law, such as:

(a) any right of the transferor's creditors to treat the transfer as ineffective arising from the law of insolvency or similar provisions; or

(b) a right to claim reparation under Book VI (Non-contractual liability arising out of damage caused to another) from a third party damaging the goods.

(4) Where ownership has been transferred but the transferor still has a right to withhold delivery of the goods (paragraph (2)(b)), terminating the contractual relationship while exercising the right to withhold performance has retroactive proprietary effect in the sense of the following Article.

VIII. – 2:202: Effect of Initial Invalidity, Subsequent Avoidance, Withdrawal, Termination and Revocation

(1) Where the underlying contract or other juridical act is invalid from the beginning, a transfer of ownership does not take place.

(2) Where, after ownership has been transferred, the underlying contract or other juridical act is avoided under Book II, Chapter 7, ownership is treated as never having passed to the transferee (retroactive proprietary effect).

(3) Where ownership must be re-transferred as a consequence of withdrawal in the sense of Book II, Chapter 5, or termination in the sense of Book III, Chapter 3, or revocation of a donation in the sense of Book IV.H, there is no retroactive proprietary effect nor is ownership re-transferred immediately. VIII. – 2:201 (Effects of the transfer of ownership) paragraph (4) remains unaffected.

(4) This Article does not affect any right to recover the goods based on other provisions of these model rules.

VIII. – 2:203: Transfer Subject to Condition

(1) Where the parties agreed on a transfer subject to a resolutive condition, ownership is re-transferred immediately upon the fulfilment of that condition, subject to the limits of the re-transferor's right or authority to dispose at that time. A retroactive proprietary effect of the re-transfer cannot be achieved by party agreement.

(2) Where the contract or other juridical act entitling to the transfer of ownership is subject to a suspensive condition, ownership passes when the condition is fulfilled.

Section 3: Special Constellations
VIII. – 2:301: Multiple Transfers
(1) Where there are several purported transfers of the same goods by the transferor, ownership is acquired by the transferee who first fulfils all the requirements of Section 1 and, in the case of a later transferee, who neither knew nor could reasonably be expected to know of the earlier entitlement of the other transferee.

(2) A later transferee who first fulfils all the requirements of Section 1 but is not in good faith in the sense of paragraph (1) must restore the goods to the transferor. The transferor's entitlement to recovery of the goods from that transferee may also be exercised by the first transferee.

VIII. – 2:302: Indirect Representation
(1) Where an agent acting under a mandate for indirect representation within the meaning of IV. D. – 1:102 (Definitions) acquires goods from a third party on behalf of the principal, the principal directly acquires the ownership of the goods (representation for acquisition).

(2) Where an agent acting under a mandate for indirect representation within the meaning of IV. D. – 1:102 (Definitions) transfers goods on behalf of the principal to a third party, the third party directly acquires the ownership of the goods (representation for alienation).

(3) The acquisition of ownership of the goods by the principal (paragraph (1)) or by the third party (paragraph (2)) takes place when:

(a) the agent has authority to transfer or receive the goods on behalf of the principal;

(b) there is an entitlement to transfer by virtue of a contract or other juridical act, a court order or a rule of law between the agent and the third party; and

(c) there has been an agreement as to the time ownership is to pass or delivery or an equivalent to delivery in the sense of VIII. – 2:101 (Requirements for the transfer of ownership in general) paragraph (1)(e) between the third party and the agent.

VIII. – 2:303: Passing of Ownership in Case of Direct Delivery in a Chain of Transactions
Where there is a chain of contracts or other juridical acts, court orders or entitlements based on a rule of law for the transfer of ownership of the same goods and delivery or an equivalent to delivery is effected directly between two parties within this chain, ownership passes to the recipient with effect as if it had been transferred from each preceding member of the chain to the next.

VIII. – 2:304: Passing of Ownership of Unsolicited Goods
(1) If a business delivers unsolicited goods to a consumer, the consumer acquires ownership subject to the business's right or authority to transfer ownership. The consumer may reject the acquisition of ownership; for these purposes, II. – 4:303 (Right or benefit may be rejected) applies by way of analogy.

(2) The exceptions provided for in II. – 3:401 (No obligation arising from failure to respond) paragraphs (2) and (3) apply accordingly.

(3) For the purposes of this Article delivery occurs when the consumer obtains physical control over the goods.

VIII. – 2:305: Transfer of Goods Forming Part of a Bulk
(1) For the purposes of this Chapter, "bulk" means a mass or mixture of fungible goods which is identified as contained in a defined space or area.

(2) If the transfer of a specified quantity of an identified bulk fails to take effect because the goods have not yet been identified in the sense of VIII. – 2:101 (Requirements for the transfer of ownership in general) paragraph (3), the transferee acquires co-ownership in the bulk.

(3) The undivided share of the transferee in the bulk at any time is such share as the quantity of goods to which the transferee is entitled out of the bulk as against the transferor bears to the quantity of the goods in the bulk at that time.

(4)   Where the sum of the quantities to which the transferees are entitled as against the trans-feror and, if relevant, of the quantity of the transferor exceeds the total quantity contained in the bulk because the bulk has diminished, the diminution of the bulk is first attributed to the transferor, before being attributed to the transferees in proportion to their individual shares.

(5)   Where the transferor purports to transfer more than the total quantity contained in the bulk, the quantity in excess of the total quantity of the bulk to which a transferee is entitled as against the transferor is reflected in the transferee's undivided share in the bulk only if the trans-feree, acquiring for value, neither knew nor could reasonably be expected to know of this excess. Where, as a result of such purported transfer of a quantity in excess of the bulk to a transferee in good faith and for value, the sum of the quantities to which the transferees are entitled as against the transferor exceeds the total quantity contained in the bulk, the lack of quantity is attributed to the transferees in proportion to their individual shares.

VIII. – 2:306: Delivery out of the Bulk

(1)   Each transferee can take delivery of a quantity corresponding to the transferee's undivided share and acquires ownership of that quantity by taking delivery.

(2)   Where the delivered quantity exceeds the quantity corresponding to the transferee's undi-vided share, the transferee acquires ownership of the excess quantity only if the transferee, acquiring for value, neither knew nor could reasonably be expected to know of possible nega-tive consequences of this excess for the other transferees.

VIII. – 2:307: Contingent Right of Transferee Under Retention of Ownership

Where the transferor retains ownership of the goods for the purposes of a "retention of owner-ship device" in the sense of IX. – 1:103 (Retention of ownership devices: scope), the transferee's right to pay the price under the terms of the contract and the transferee's right to acquire ownership upon payment have effect against the transferor's creditors.

Chapter 3: Good Faith Acquisition of Ownership
VIII. – 3:101: Good Faith Acquisition Through a Person Without Right
or Authority to Transfer Ownership

(1)   Where the person purporting to transfer the ownership (the transferor) has no right or au-thority to transfer ownership of the goods, the transferee nevertheless acquires and the former owner loses ownership provided that:
(a)   the requirements set out in VIII. – 2:101 (Requirements for the transfer of ownership in ge-neral) paragraphs (1)(a), (1)(b), (1)(d), (2) and (3) are fulfilled;
(b)   the requirement of delivery or an equivalent to delivery as set out in VIII. – 2:101 (Require-ments for the transfer of ownership in general) paragraph (1)(e) is fulfilled;
(c)   the transferee acquires the goods for value; and
(d)   the transferee neither knew nor could reasonably be expected to know that the transferor had no right or authority to transfer ownership of the goods at the time ownership would pass under VIII. – 2:101 (Requirements for the transfer of ownership in general). The facts from which it follows that the transferee could not reasonably be expected to know of the transferor's lack of right or authority have to be proved by the transferee.

(2)   Good faith acquisition in the sense of paragraph (1) does not take place with regard to stolen goods, unless the transferee acquired the goods from a transferor acting in the ordinary course of business. Good faith acquisition of stolen cultural objects in the sense of VIII. – 4:102 (Cultural objects) is impossible.

(3)   Where the transferee is already in possession of the goods, good faith acquisition will take place only if the transferee obtained possession from the transferor.

VIII. – 3:102: Good Faith Acquisition of Ownership Free of Limited Proprietary Rights

(1)   Where the goods are encumbered with a limited proprietary right of a third person and the transferor has no right or authority to dispose of the goods free of the third person's right, the transferee nevertheless acquires ownership free of this right provided that:

(a)   the transferee acquires ownership in a manner provided for in Chapter 2 or the preceding Article;
(b)   the requirement of delivery or an equivalent to delivery as set out in VIII. – 2:101 (Requirements for the transfer of ownership in general) paragraph (1)(e) is fulfilled;
(c)   the transferee acquires the goods for value; and
(d)   the transferee neither knew nor could reasonably be expected to know that the transferor had no right or authority to transfer ownership of the goods free of the third person's right at the time ownership passes. The facts from which it follows that the transferee could not reasonably be expected to know of the transferor's lack of right or authority have to be proved by the transferee.
(2)   Paragraphs (2) and (3) of the preceding Article apply for the purposes of this Article.
(3)   Where the goods are transferred by notice as provided for in VIII. – 2:105 (Equivalents to delivery) paragraph (2), the notified person's limited proprietary rights in the goods are not extinguished.
(4)   For the purposes of the application of this Article to proprietary security rights, IX. – 6:102 (Loss of proprietary security due to good faith acquisition of ownership) paragraph (2) applies in addition to this Article.

Chapter 4: Acquisition of Ownership by Continuous Possession

Section 1: Requirements for Acquisition of Ownership by Continuous Possession

VIII. – 4:101: Basic Rule

(1)   An owner-possessor acquires ownership by continuous possession of goods:
(a)   for a period of ten years, provided that the possessor, throughout the whole period, possesses in good faith; or
(b)   for a period of thirty years.
(2)   For the purposes of paragraph (1)(a):
(a)   a person possesses in good faith if, and only if, the person possesses in the belief of being the owner and is reasonably justified in that belief; and
(b)   good faith of the possessor is presumed.
(3)   Acquisition of ownership by continuous possession is excluded for a person who obtained possession by stealing the goods.

VIII. – 4:102: Cultural Objects

(1)   Under this Chapter, acquisition of ownership of goods qualifying as a "cultural object" in the sense of Article 1 (1) of Council Directive 93/7/EEC, regardless of whether the cultural object has been unlawfully removed before or after 1 January 1993, or not removed from the territory of a Member State at all, requires continuous possession of the goods:
(a)   for a period of 30 years, provided that the possessor, throughout the whole period, possesses in good faith; or
(b)   for a period of 50 years.
(2)   Member States may adopt or maintain in force more stringent provisions to ensure a higher level of protection for the owner of cultural objects in the sense of this paragraph or in the sense of national or international regulations.

VIII. – 4:103: Continuous Possession

(1)   Involuntary loss of possession does not exclude continuous possession for the purpose of VIII. – 4:101 (Basic rule), provided that possession is recovered within one year or an action which leads to such recovery is instituted within one year.
(2)   Where the owner-possessor is in possession of the goods at the beginning and at the end of the period there is a presumption of continuous possession for the whole period.

Section 2: Additional Provisions as to the Period Required for Acquisition of Ownership
VIII. – 4:201: Extension in Case of Incapacity
(1)   If an owner who is subject to an incapacity is without a representative when the period required for the acquisition of ownership by another by continuous possession would begin to
run, the commencement of the period against that person is suspended until either the incapacity has ended or a representative has been appointed.
(2)   If the running of the period has already begun before incapacity occurred, the period does
not expire before one year has passed after either incapacity has ended or a representative has
been appointed.
(3)   The running of the period is suspended where the owner is a person subject to an incapacity and the owner-possessor is that person's representative, as long as this relationship lasts.
The period does not expire before one year has passed after either the incapacity has ended or
a new representative has been appointed.

VIII. – 4:202: Extension in Case of Impediment Beyond Owner's Control
(1)   The running of the period is suspended as long as the owner is prevented from exercising
the right to recover the goods by an impediment which is beyond the owner's control and
which the owner could not reasonably have been expected to avoid or overcome. The mere
fact that the owner does not know where the goods are does not cause suspension under this
Article.
(2)   Paragraph (1) applies only if the impediment arises, or subsists, within the last six months of
the period.
(3)   Where the duration or nature of the impediment is such that it would be unreasonable to
expect the owner to take proceedings to assert the right to recover the goods within the part of
the period which has still to run after the suspension comes to an end, the period does not
expire before six months have passed after the time when the impediment was removed.

VIII. – 4:203: Extension and Renewal in Case of Judicial and Other Proceedings
(1)   The running of the period is suspended from the time when judicial proceedings are
begun against the owner-possessor or a person exercising physical control for the owner-possessor, by or on behalf of the owner, contesting the owner-possessor's ownership or possession.
Suspension lasts until a decision has been made which has the effect of res judicata or until the
case has otherwise been disposed of. Suspension has effect only in relation to the parties to the
judicial proceedings and persons on whose behalf the parties act.
(2)   Suspension under paragraph (1) is to be disregarded when the action is dismissed or
otherwise unsuccessful. Where the action is dismissed because of incompetence of the court,
the period does not expire before six months have passed from this decision.
(3)   Where the action is successful, a new period begins to run from the day when the effect of
res judicata occurs or the case has otherwise been disposed of in favour of the owner.
(4)   These provisions apply, with appropriate adaptations, to arbitration proceedings and to all
other proceedings initiated with the aim of obtaining an instrument which is enforceable as if it
were a judgment.
VIII. – 4:204: Postponement of Expiry in Case of Negotiations
If the owner and the owner-possessor or a person exercising physical control for the owner-possessor negotiate about the right of ownership, or about circumstances from which acquisition
of ownership by the owner-possessor may arise, the period does not expire before six months
have passed since the last communication made in the negotiations.

VIII. – 4:205: Ending of Period in Case of Acknowledgement
The period ends when the owner-possessor, or a person exercising physical control for the
owner-possessor, acknowledges the owner's right to the goods. A new period begins to run
when the former owner-possessor continues to exercise direct or indirect physical control with
the intention of doing so as, or as if, an owner.

VIII. – 4:206: Period of a Predecessor to Be Taken into Account

(1)   Where one person succeeds another in owner-possession and the requirements set out in this Chapter are fulfilled cumulatively by the predecessor and the successor in possession, the period of the predecessor is taken into account in favour of the successor.

(2)   A successor in good faith may take into account the period of a predecessor in bad faith only for acquisition under VIII. – 4:101 (Basic rule) paragraph (1)(b).

Section 3: Effects of Acquisition of Ownership by Continuous Possession
VIII. – 4:301: Acquisition of Ownership

(1)   Upon expiry of the period required for the acquisition of ownership by continuous possession the original owner loses and the owner-possessor acquires ownership.

(2)   When the owner-possessor knows or can reasonably be expected to know that the goods are encumbered with a limited proprietary right of a third person, this right continues to exist as long as this right is not itself extinguished by expiry of the respective period, or a period of 30 years (VIII. – 4:101 (Basic rule) paragraph (1)(b)) or 50 years (VIII. – 4:102 (Cultural objects) paragraph (1)(b)) has passed.

VIII. – 4:302: Extinction of Rights under Rules on Unjustified Enrichment and Non-contractual Liability for Damage

Upon acquisition of ownership, the original owner loses all rights to recover the goods and all rights to payment of the monetary value of the goods or for any future use of the goods under the provisions on unjustified enrichment (Book VII) and non-contractual liability for damage (Book VI).

Chapter 5: Production, Combination and Commingling
Section 1: General Provisions
VIII. – 5:101: Party Autonomy and Relation to Other Provisions

(1)   The consequences of production, combination or commingling can be regulated by party agreement. The provisions of Section 2 apply where production, combination or commingling takes place:

(a)   without the consent of the owner of the material; or

(b)   with the consent of the owner of the material, but without a party agreement as to the proprietary consequences.

(2)   An agreement in the sense of paragraph (1) may provide for:

(a)   proprietary rights as recognised by this Book; and

(b)   a right to payment or other performance.

(3)   The effects of production, combination and commingling as to goods subject to a retention of ownership device are regulated by Book IX.

(4)   Proprietary security rights created under Section 2 of this Chapter are subject to the provisions on proprietary security rights in Book IX, unless provided otherwise in Section 2. Proprietary security rights created by a party agreement under paragraph (1) are subject to the provisions on proprietary security rights in Book IX except as provided otherwise by VIII. – 5:204 (Additional provisions as to proprietary security rights) paragraph (3).

(5)   This Chapter does not affect the applicability of the rules on non-contractual liability for damage (Book VI). The rules on benevolent intervention in another's affairs (Book V) have priority over the provisions of this Chapter.

Section 2: Default Rules and Supplementary Provisions
VIII. – 5:201: Production

(1)   Where one person, by contributing labour, produces new goods out of material owned by another person, the producer becomes owner of the new goods and the owner of the material is entitled, against the producer, to payment equal to the value of the material at the moment of production, secured by a proprietary security right in the new goods.

(2)   Paragraph (1) does not apply where:

(a)   the labour contribution is of minor importance; or

(b)   the producer knows that the material is owned by another person and that the owner of the material does not consent to the production, unless the value of the labour is much higher than the value of the material.

(3)   In the cases covered by paragraph (2) and in cases where no new goods are produced, ownership remains with the owner of the material or, where there is more than one such owner, the attribution of ownership is determined by application of VIII. – 5:202 (Commingling) or VIII. – 5:203 (Combination). The person contributing labour is entitled to the reversal of any enrichment subject to the provisions of Book VII. For the purposes of this paragraph, VII. – 2:101 (Circumstances in which an enrichment is unjustified) paragraph (1)(b) does not exclude the entitlement of a person contributing labour to a reversal of the enrichment.

VIII. – 5:202: Commingling

(1)   Where goods owned by different persons are commingled in the sense that it is impossible or economically unreasonable to separate the resulting mass or mixture into its original constituents, but it is possible and economically reasonable to separate the mass or mixture into proportionate quantities, these persons become co-owners of the resulting mass or mixture, each for a share proportionate to the value of the respective part at the moment of commingling.

(2)   Each co-owner can separate a quantity equivalent to that co-owner's undivided share out of the mass or mixture.

VIII. – 5:203: Combination

(1)   This Article applies where goods owned by different persons are combined in the sense that separation would be impossible or economically unreasonable.

(2)   Where one of the component parts is to be regarded as the principal part, the owner of that part acquires sole ownership of the whole, and the owner or the owners of the subordinate parts are entitled, against the sole owner, to payment subject to sentence 2, secured by a proprietary security right in the combined goods. The amount due under sentence 1 is calculated according to the rules on unjustified enrichment (Book VII); or, where the owner of the principal part effects the combination, is equal to the value of the respective subordinate part at the moment of combination.

(3)   Where none of the component parts is to be regarded as the principal part, the owners of the component parts become co-owners of the whole, each for a share proportionate to the value of the respective part at the moment of combination. If, in the case of more than two component parts, one component part is of minimal importance in relation to other parts, the owner of this part is entitled, against the co-owners, only to payment proportionate to the value of the respective part at the moment of combination, secured by a proprietary security right in the combined goods.

(4)   Paragraph (2) does not apply where the person who owns the principal part effects the combination, knowing that a subordinate part is owned by another person and that the owner of the subordinate part does not consent to combination, unless the value of the principal part is much higher than the value of the subordinate part. The owners of the component parts become co-owners, the shares of the owners of subordinate parts being equal to the value of their respective parts at the moment of combination.

VIII. – 5:204: Additional Provisions as to Proprietary Security Rights

(1)   A proprietary security right created under the preceding Articles on production and combination is effective against third persons without requiring possession by, or registration of, the former owner of the material or of the component part.

(2)   If the proprietary security right in the new or combined goods is extinguished by a third party's good faith acquisition (Chapter 3), the security right extends to the proceeds of the sale. Paragraph (1) applies accordingly.

(3)   A proprietary security right created under the preceding Articles on production and combination takes priority over any other security right which has previously been created, by the pro-

ducer or by the owner of the principal part, in the new or combined goods. The same applies to equivalent security rights created by agreement between the former owner of the material and the producer, or between the former owner of the subordinate part and the owner of the principal part.

Chapter 6: Protection of Ownership and Protection of Possession
Section 1: Protection of Ownership
VIII. – 6:101: Protection of Ownership

(1) The owner is entitled to obtain or recover possession of the goods from any person exercising physical control over these goods, unless this person has a right to possess the goods in the sense of VIII. – 1:207 (Possession by limited-right-possessor) in relation to the owner.

(2) Where another person interferes with the owner's rights as owner or where such interference is imminent, the owner is entitled to a declaration of ownership and to a protection order.

(3) A protection order is an order which, as the circumstances may require:

(a) prohibits imminent future interference;

(b) orders the cessation of existing interference;

(c) orders the removal of traces of past interference.

VIII. – 6:102: Recovery of Goods after Transfer Based on Invalid or Avoided Contract or Other Juridical Act

(1) Where goods are or have been transferred based on a contract or other juridical act which is invalid or avoided, the transferor may exercise the right of recovery under paragraph (1) of the preceding Article in order to recover physical control of the goods.

(2) Where the obligation of the transferee to restore the goods to the transferor, after a transfer based on an invalid or avoided contract or other juridical act, is one of two reciprocal obligations which have to be performed simultaneously, the transferee may, in accordance with III. – 3:401 (Right to withhold performance of reciprocal obligation), withhold performance of the obligation to restore the goods until the transferor has tendered performance of, or has performed, the transferor's reciprocal obligation.

(3) The preceding paragraphs also apply where the transfer was based on a contract or other juridical act subject to a resolutive condition in the sense of VIII. – 2:203 (Transfer subject to condition) paragraph (1) and this condition is fulfilled.

Section 2: Protection of Mere Possession
VIII. – 6:201: Definition of Unlawful Dispossession and Interference

A person depriving the possessor of possession or interfering with that possession acts "unlawfully" under this Section if the person acts without the consent of the possessor and the dispossession or interference is not permitted by law.

VIII. – 6:202: Self-Help of Possessor

(1) A possessor or a third person may resort to self-help against another person who unlawfully deprives the possessor of possession of the goods, or who otherwise unlawfully interferes with that possession, or whose act of unlawful dispossession or interference is imminent.

(2) The means of self-help are limited to such immediate and proportionate action as is necessary to regain the goods or to stop or prevent the dispossession or interference.

(3) Under the restrictions of paragraphs (1) and (2) self-help may also be directed against an indirect owner-possessor who unlawfully deprives the limited-right-possessor of possession or interferes with that possession in violation of the specific legal relationship between owner-possessor and limited-right-possessor. This rule applies equally to an indirect limited-right-possessor who unlawfully deprives the other limited-right-possessor of possession or interferes with that possession.

(4) Where a person in the exercise of a right of self-help conferred by this Article causes legally relevant damage to the person depriving the possessor of possession or interfering with that possession, VI. – 5:202 (Self-defence, benevolent intervention and necessity) applies.

VIII. – 6:203: Entitlement to Recover as Protection of Mere Possession

(1)   Where another person unlawfully deprives an owner-possessor or a limited-right-posses-sor of possession, the possessor is, within the period of one year, entitled to recover the goods, irrespective of who has the right or better position in terms of VIII. – 6:301 (Entitlement to re-cover in case of better possession) to possess the goods. The period of one year starts to run at the time of dispossession.

(2)   The right to recover may also be directed against an indirect owner-possessor who unlaw-fully deprives the limited-right-possessor of possession in violation of the specific legal relation-ship between them. This rule applies equally to an indirect limited-right-possessor who unlaw-fully deprives the other limited-right-possessor of possession.

(3)   The right to recover is excluded if the person seeking to exercise it unlawfully deprived the other person of possession within the last year.

(4)   Where the other person in the sense of paragraph (1) invokes an alleged right or better position in terms of VIII. – 6:301 (Entitlement to recover in case of better possession) to possess the goods as a defence or counter-claim, the obligation to return the goods according to para-graph (1) may be replaced by an obligation to hand the goods over to the court or other com-petent public authority, or to a third person pursuant to an order of the competent authority.

VIII. – 6:204: Entitlement to Protection Order to Protect Mere Possession

(1)   Where another person unlawfully interferes with the possession of goods or such interfe-rence or an unlawful dispossession is imminent, the owner-possessor or the limited-right-pos-sessor is, within the period of one year, entitled to a protection order under VIII. – 6:101 (Protec-tion of ownership) paragraph (3), irrespective of who has the right or better position in terms of VIII. – 6:301 (Entitlement to recover in case of better possession) to possess, use or otherwise deal with the goods. The period of one year starts to run from the time when the interference began or, in cases of repeated interferences, from the time when the last interference began.

(2)   The protection order may also be directed against an indirect owner-possessor who unlaw-fully interferes with the possession of a limited-right-possessor in violation of the specific legal relationship between them. This rule applies equally to an indirect limited-right-possessor who unlawfully interferes with the possession of a subsidiary limited-right-possessor in violation of the specific legal relationship between them.

(3)   Where the other person in the sense of paragraph (1) invokes an alleged right or better position to possess, use or otherwise deal with the goods as a defence or counter-claim, the court order may be suspended until, or replaced by, a decision on the existence of such alleged right or better position.

Section 3: Protection of Better Possession

VIII. – 6:301: Entitlement to Recover in Case of Better Possession

(1)   A former owner-possessor or former limited-right possessor is entitled to recover posses-sion of the goods from another person exercising physical control over them if the former pos-session was "better" than the current possession of the other person in the sense of paragraph (2).

(2)   The former possession is "better" than the current possession if the former possessor is in good faith and has a right to possess, while the other person has no right to possess, the goods. Where both persons are in good faith and have a right to possess the goods, the right derived from the owner prevails over a right derived from an owner-possessor who is not the owner; if this does not apply, the older rightful possession prevails. Where both persons are in good faith, but neither has a right to possess the goods, the current possession prevails.

VIII. – 6:302: Entitlement to Protection Order in Case of Better Possession

Where another person interferes with the possession, or such interference or a dispossession is imminent, the owner-possessor or the limited-right-possessor who is in good faith is entitled to a protection order under VIII. – 6:101 (Protection of ownership) paragraph (3), unless the other person would, in case of dispossession, have a better possession in the sense of VIII. – 6:301 (Entitlement to recover in case of better possession) paragraph (2), or the third person has a better right to use or otherwise deal with the goods than the owner-possessor or limited-right-possessor.

Section 4: Other Remedies
VIII. – 6:401: Non-Contractual Liability
The owner and the limited-right-possessor are entitled to reparation for an infringement of their right of ownership or their right to possess the goods under the terms of VI. – 2:206 (Loss upon infringement of property or lawful possession).

Chapter 7: Consequential Questions on Restitution of Goods
VIII. – 7:101: Scope
(1)   This Chapter applies where the situations covered by the subsequent Articles occur while the goods are possessed by a person against whom, at that time, the owner is entitled to obtain or recover possession of the goods.
(2)   Where the requirements for the application of Book V are fulfilled, the provisions of that Book apply and have priority over the provisions of this Chapter.
(3)   The provisions of Chapter 5 have priority over the provisions of this Chapter.

VIII. – 7:102: Loss of, or Damage to, the Goods During Possession
(1)   Where the goods are lost, are destroyed or deteriorate during possession in the sense of VIII. – 7:101 (Scope of application), the rights of the owner resulting from such loss or damage are determined by Book VI.
(2)   For the purposes of this Article, intention or negligence as to possessing the goods despite the owner's entitlement to obtain or recover possession suffice to establish accountability in the sense of Book VI, Chapter 3.

VIII. – 7:103: Fruits From, Use of, and Other Benefits Derived from the Goods During Possession
Where the possessor obtains fruits from, makes use of, or derives other benefits from the goods during possession in the sense of VIII. – 7:101 (Scope of application), the rights of the owner resulting from such benefits are determined by Book VII.

VIII. – 7:104: Expenditure on, or Parts Added to, the Goods During Possession
(1)   Where the possessor incurs expenditure on, or adds parts to, the goods during possession in the sense of VIII. – 7:101 (Scope of application), the rights of the possessor to reimbursement of such expenditure or for such addition are determined by Book VII.
(2)   The possessor is entitled to retain the goods in order to secure the rights referred to in paragraph (1). Sentence 1 does not apply where the possessor knows of the owner's entitlement to obtain or recover possession at the time when expenditure is incurred on, or parts are added to, the goods.

Book IX Proprietary Security in Movable Assets
Chapter 1: General Rules
Section 1: Scope
IX. – 1:101: General Rule
(1)   This Book applies to the following rights in movable property based upon contracts for proprietary security:
(a)   security rights; and
(b)   ownership retained under retention of ownership devices.
(2)   The rules of this Book on security rights apply with appropriate adaptations to:
(a)   rights under a trust for security purposes;
(b)   security rights in movable assets created by unilateral juridical acts; and
(c)   security rights in movable assets implied by patrimonial law, if and in so far as this is compatible with the purpose of the law.

IX. – 1:102: Security Right in Movable Asset

(1)   A security right in a movable asset is any limited proprietary right in the asset which entitles the secured creditor to preferential satisfaction of the secured right from the encumbered asset.

(2)   The term security right includes:

(a)   limited proprietary rights of a type which is generally recognised as designed to serve as proprietary security, especially the pledge;

(b)   limited proprietary rights, however named, that are based upon a contract for proprietary security and that are either intended by the parties to entitle the secured creditor to preferential satisfaction of the secured right from the encumbered asset or have this effect under the contract; and

(c)   other rights which are regarded as security rights under the rules of this Book, such as the right referred to in IX. – 2:114 (Right of retention of possession) and the rights covered by paragraph (3).

(3)   A transfer or purported transfer of ownership of a movable asset which is made, on the basis of a contract for proprietary security, with the intention or the effect of securing satisfaction of a secured right can create only a security right in the asset for the transferee.

(4)   Paragraph (3) applies in particular to:

(a)   a security transfer of ownership of corporeal assets;

(b)   a security assignment;

(c)   a sale and lease-back; and

(d)   a sale and resale.

IX. – 1:103: Retention of Ownership Devices: Scope

(1)   There is a "retention of ownership device" when ownership is retained by the owner of supplied assets in order to secure a right to performance of an obligation.

(2)   The term retention of ownership device includes:

(a)   retention of ownership by a seller under a contract of sale;

(b)   ownership of the supplier under a contract of hire-purchase;

(c)   ownership of the leased assets under a contract of leasing, provided that according to the terms of the contract the lessee at the expiration of the lease period has an option to acquire ownership of, or a right to continue to use, the leased asset without payment or for merely nominal payment (financial leasing); and

(d)   ownership of the supplier under a contract of consignment with the intention or the effect of fulfilling a security purpose.

IX. – 1:104: Retention of Ownership Devices: Applicable Rules

(1)   Retention of ownership devices are subject to the following rules on security rights, unless specifically provided otherwise:

(a)   IX. – 2:104 (Specific issues of transferability, existence and specification) paragraphs (2) to (4);

(b)   Chapter 2, Sections 3 and 4;

(c)   Chapters 3 to 6; and

(d)   Chapter 7, Section 1.

(2)   When applying rules on security rights to retention of ownership devices, the following adaptations apply:

(a)   references to the encumbered assets refer to the assets supplied under a contract of sale, hire-purchase, leasing or consignment, respectively;

(b)   in retention of ownership under contracts of sale, references to the secured creditor are to be understood as referring to the seller, and references to the security provider as referring to the buyer;

(c)   in retention of ownership devices under contracts of hire-purchase, references to the secured creditor are to be understood as referring to the supplier, and references to the security provider as referring to the hire-purchaser;

(d) in retention of ownership devices under contracts of financial leasing, references to the se-cured creditor are to be understood as referring to the lessor, and references to the security provider as referring to the lessee; and

(e) in retention of ownership devices under contracts of consignment, references to the secu-red creditor are to be understood as referring to the supplier, and references to the security provider as referring to the consignee.

IX. – 1:105: Exclusions

(1) This Book does not apply to security rights for micro-credits, if and in so far as national legis-lation of the place where the security provider's business or residence is located contains speci-fic protective rules for the security provider.

(2) The rules of an international Convention dealing with a subject-matter regulated in this Book and binding upon a member state are presumed to have for that member state prece-dence over the rules of this Book.

Section 2: Definitions
IX. – 1:201: Definitions

(1) For the purposes of this Book the following definitions apply.

(2) An "accessory" is a corporeal asset that is or becomes closely connected with or part of a movable or an immovable, provided it is possible and economically reasonable to separate the accessory without damage from the movable or immovable.

(3) "Acquisition finance devices" cover:

(a) retention of ownership devices;

(b) where ownership of the sold assets has been transferred to the buyer, those security rights in the sold asset which secure the right:

    (i) of the seller to payment of the purchase price for the encumbered asset under a con-tract of sale;

    (ii) of a lender to repayment of a loan granted to the buyer for payment of the purchase price for the encumbered asset, if and in so far as this payment is actually made to the seller; and

(c) rights of third persons to whom any of the rights under sub-paragraph (a) or (b) has been transferred as security for a credit covered by sub-paragraphs (a) or (b).

(4) A "contract for proprietary security" is a contract under which:

(a) a security provider undertakes to grant a security right to the secured creditor;

(b) a secured creditor is entitled to retain a security right when transferring ownership to the transferee who is regarded as security provider; or

(c) a seller, lessor or other supplier of assets is entitled to retain ownership of the supplied assets in order to secure its rights to performance.

(5) "Default" means:

(a) any non-performance by the debtor of the obligation covered by the security; and

(b) any other event or set of circumstances agreed by the secured creditor and the security provider as entitling the secured creditor to have recourse to the security.

(6) "Financial assets" are financial instruments and rights to the payment of money.

(7) "Financial instruments" are:

(a) share certificates and equivalent securities as well as bonds and equivalent debt instru-ments, if these are negotiable;

(b) any other securities which are dealt in and which give the right to acquire any such finan-cial instruments or which give rise to cash settlements, except instruments of payment;

(c) share rights in collective investment undertakings;

(d) money market instruments; and

(e) rights in or relating to the instruments covered by sub-paragraphs (a) to (d).

(8) "Intangibles" means incorporeal assets and includes uncertificated and indirectly held securities and the undivided share of a co-owner in corporeal assets or in a bulk or a fund.

(9) "Ownership" for the purposes of these rules covers ownership of movable corporeal assets and of intangible assets.

(10) A "possessory security right" is a security right that requires possession of the encumbered corporeal asset by the secured creditor or another person (except the debtor) holding for the secured creditor.

(11) "Proceeds" is every value derived from an encumbered asset, such as:

(a) value realised by sale or other disposition or by collection;

(b) damages or insurance payments in respect of defects, damage or loss;

(c) civil and natural fruits, including distributions; and

(d) proceeds of proceeds.

(12) The "secured creditor" may be the creditor of the secured right or a third person who may hold the security right in that person's own name for the creditor, especially as a trustee.

(13) The "security provider" may be the debtor of the obligation to be covered by the security right or a third person.

Chapter 2: Creation and Coverage
Section 1: Creation of Security Rights
Subsection 1: General Provisions
IX. – 2:101: Methods of Creation of Security Rights

A security right in a movable asset may be created:

(a) by the security provider granting the security right to the secured creditor;

(b) by the secured creditor retaining the security right when transferring ownership of the asset to the security provider; or

(c) by the secured creditor relying on a right of retention of possession.

IX. – 2:102: Requirements for Creation of Security Rights in General

The creation of a security right in a movable asset requires that:

(a) the asset exists;

(b) the asset is transferable;

(c) the secured right exists; and

(d) the additional requirements for the creation of a security right by granting, by retention or on the basis of a right of retention of possession are fulfilled.

IX. – 2:103: Possessory and Non-Possessory Security Rights

Unless otherwise agreed by the parties, the creation of a security right by contract does not require possession of the encumbered asset by the secured creditor.

IX. – 2:104: Specific Issues of Transferability, Existence and Specification

(1) A security right can be created in a right to performance other than a right to the payment of money, even if this right is not transferable, provided that it can be transformed into a right to the payment of money.

(2) A security right can be created in an asset, even if its owner had agreed not to transfer or to encumber the asset. This rule applies also to a right to performance, whether contractual or not, unless it is non-assignable by virtue of III. – 5:109 (Assignability: rights personal to the creditor) paragraph (1)).

(3) If the parties purport to create a security right in a future, generic or untransferable asset, the security right arises only if and when the asset comes into existence, is specified or becomes transferable. Paragraph (2) remains unaffected.

(4) Paragraph (3) sentence 1 applies with appropriate adaptations to the creation of security rights in a conditional right, including the rights covered by that paragraph. A security right may be created in a present conditional right, especially in the right of a transferee under a conditional transfer of ownership.

(5) Paragraph (3) sentence 1 applies with appropriate adaptations to the creation of security rights for secured rights which are future or only conditional.

Subsection 2: Granting of Security Right
IX. – 2:105: Requirements for Granting of Security Right

In addition to the requirements under Subsection 1, the creation of a security right in a movable asset by granting requires that:
(a)   the asset to be encumbered is specified by the parties;
(b)   the security provider has the right or authority to grant a security right in the asset;
(c)   the secured creditor is entitled as against the security provider to the granting of a security right on the basis of the contract for proprietary security; and
(d)   the secured creditor and the security provider agree on the granting of a security right to the secured creditor.

IX. – 2:106: Time When Security Right Is Created by Granting

Subject to IX. – 2:110 (Delayed creation), the security right is created by granting at the time when the requirements set out in the preceding Article are fulfilled, unless the parties have agreed on another time of creation.

IX. – 2:107: Granting of Security Right by Consumer

(1)   The creation of a security right by a consumer security provider by granting is only valid within the following limits:
(a)   the assets to be encumbered must be identified individually; and
(b)   an asset not yet owned by the consumer upon conclusion of the contract for proprietary security (apart from the rights to payment covered by paragraph (2)) can only be encumbered as security for a credit to be used for the acquisition of the asset by the consumer.
(2)   Rights to payment of future salary, pensions or equivalent income cannot be encumbered in so far as they serve the satisfaction of the living expenses of the consumer security provider and his or her family.

IX. – 2:108: Good Faith Acquisition of Security Right

(1)   Even where the security provider has no right or authority to dispose of a corporeal asset, the secured creditor nevertheless acquires a security right in it, provided that:
(a)   the asset or a negotiable document to bearer on the asset is in the security provider's possession or, if so required, the asset is registered in an international or national register of ownership as owned by the security provider at the time the security right is to be created; and
(b)   the secured creditor does not know and cannot reasonably be expected to know that the security provider has no right or authority to grant a security right in the asset at the time the security right is to be created.
(2)   For the purposes of paragraph (1)(b), a secured creditor acquiring a security right in an asset that is subject to a retention of ownership device which is registered under Chapter 3 Section 3 against the security provider is regarded as knowing that the latter has no right or authority to grant a security right in the asset.
(3)   Good faith acquisition of a security right is excluded for an asset that was stolen from the owner or the person holding for the owner.

IX. – 2:109: Good Faith Acquisition of Security Right in Encumbered Corporeal Asset

(1)   Where a corporeal asset is encumbered with a security right or another limited proprietary right and the security provider has no right or authority to dispose of the asset free from the third person's limited proprietary right, a secured creditor nevertheless acquires a security right free from that other right, provided that:
(a)   the requirements of paragraph (1)(a) of the preceding Article are met; and
(b)   the secured creditor does not know nor can reasonably be expected to know that the security provider has no right or authority to grant a security right in disregard of the third person's limited proprietary right at the time the security right is to be created.
(2)   For the purposes of paragraph (1)(b), a secured creditor acquiring a security right in the encumbered asset is regarded as knowing that the security provider has no right or authority to

grant a security right in the asset in disregard of the existing security right if this right is registered under Chapter 3, Section 3 against the security provider.
(3)   Where the requirements of paragraph (1) are not met but the requirements of the preceding Article are met, the secured creditor obtains a security right in the encumbered assets. The
priority between this security right and the prior encumbrance is determined according to the
general provisions.

IX. – 2:110: Delayed Creation

In assets for which at the time when the security right would have been created according to IX.
– 2:106 (Time when security right is created by granting) the requirements of IX. – 2:107 (Granting of security right by consumer) and IX. – 2:108 (Good faith acquisition of security right) have
not yet been met, a security right automatically arises as soon as the events indicated in the preceding provisions have occurred.

IX. – 2:111: Security Right in Cash, Negotiable Instruments and Documents

A security right in cash, negotiable instruments and documents to bearer may be created free
from any earlier rights, even if the requirements of IX. – 2:105 (Requirements for granting of
security right) sub-paragraph (b), IX. – 2:108 (Good faith acquisition of security right) and IX. –
2:109 (Good faith acquisition of security right in an encumbered corporeal asset) are not met,
provided that direct possession of these assets is transferred to the secured creditor.

IX. – 2:112: General Matters of Property Law

Rules on general matters of property law in Book VIII, Chapter 2 apply for the purposes of this
Book with appropriate adaptations.

Subsection 3: Retention of Security Right
IX. – 2:113: Requirements for Retention of Security Right

(1)   In addition to the requirements under Subsection 1, the creation of a security right in a
movable asset by retention requires that:
(a)   the secured creditor is entitled as against the transferee to the retention of a security right
      by virtue of the contract for proprietary security; and
(b)   the secured creditor transfers its ownership in the asset to be encumbered by the retained
      security right to the transferee.
(2)   The security right is created by retention at the time when all the requirements set out in
the preceding paragraph are fulfilled.
(3)   The transferee is regarded as the security provider for the purposes of the application of
the rules of this Book.

Subsection 4: Right of Retention of Possession
IX. – 2:114: Right of Retention of Possession

Where under a contract or rule of law a person is entitled as against the owner of an asset to retain possession of the asset as security for a right to performance, this right of retention of possession gives rise to a possessory security right.

Section 2: Creation of Retention of Ownership Devices
IX. – 2:201: Retention of Ownership Devices

(1)   A retention of ownership device arises in the cases set out in IX. – 1:103 (Retention of
ownership devices: scope) paragraph (2) if:
(a)   the seller, supplier or lessor is the owner of the supplied asset or acts with authority in rela-
      tion to this asset;
(b)   the asset is specified in the contract for proprietary security;
(c)   the secured right exists; and
(d)   the seller, supplier or lessor retains ownership.
(2)   Ownership is also retained for the purposes of paragraph (1)(d) where there is a transfer
subject to the suspensive condition that the obligation covered is performed.

Section 3: Creation of Security Rights in Specific Types of Assets
IX. – 2:301: Encumbrance of Right to Payment of Money
(1)   The encumbrance of a right to payment of money is also subject to the following special rules.
(2)   The provisions of Book III, Chapter 5 apply with appropriate adaptations, except III. – 5:108 (Assignability: effect of contractual prohibition) paragraphs (2) and (3) and III. – 5:121 (Competition between successive assignees).
(3)   A right to payment held by the security provider against the secured creditor may be encumbered by the security provider also in favour of the secured creditor.
(4)   A security right encumbering a right to payment extends to any personal or proprietary security right securing this right to payment.

IX. – 2:302: Security Rights in Shares of a Company
(1)   Possession of negotiable certificates of shares of a company which are directly held is regarded as possession of the shares.
(2)   Shares of companies which do not meet the requirements of paragraph (1), whether or not they are registered, cannot be subject to a possessory security right.
(3)   Security rights in shares of companies extend to dividends, bonus shares and other assets which the shareholder derives from the shares but are limited to the financial value of the shares and such assets.

IX. – 2:303: Security Rights in Bonds
Paragraphs (1) and (2) of the preceding Article apply also to bonds.

IX. – 2:304: Negotiable Documents of Title and Negotiable Instruments
(1)   If and as long as a negotiable document of title covers goods, a security right in the document covers also the goods.
(2)   For negotiable instruments, a security right in the instrument covers also the right embodied in the instrument.
(3)   Possession of a negotiable document of title or a negotiable instrument is regarded as possession of the goods covered by the document of title or the right embodied in the instrument.

IX. – 2:305: Security Right in an Accessory
(1)   A security right may be created in an asset that, at the time of creation, is an accessory to a movable or an immovable. If the rules applicable to immovable property so provide, the security right may also be created according to the rules governing immovable property.
(2)   A security right in goods continues even if the encumbered asset subsequently becomes an accessory to a movable or an immovable.

IX. – 2:306: Proceeds of the Originally Encumbered Assets
(1)   A security right extends to rights to payment due to a defect in, damage to, or loss of the originally encumbered asset, including insurance proceeds.
(2)   A possessory security right extends to civil and natural fruits of the originally encumbered assets unless the parties agree otherwise.
(3)   Other proceeds of the originally encumbered assets are covered only if the parties so agree.

IX. – 2:307: Use of Encumbered Goods for Production or Combination
(1)   Where encumbered materials owned by the security provider are used for the production of new goods, the secured creditor's security right may be extended by party agreement:
(a)   to the products; and
(b)   to the right to payment to which the security provider as former owner of the material is entitled by virtue of the production against the producer according to VIII. – 5:201 (Production).
(2)   The preceding paragraph applies accordingly if goods are combined in such a way that separation would be impossible or economically unreasonable for the purposes of VIII. – 5:203 (Combination).

(3)   The issue whether a former owner of material other than the holder of a retention of ownership device acquires a security right by operation of law as the result of production or combination involving the material, and the effectiveness and priority of this security right are governed by Book VIII, Chapter 5. If these security rights are created by party agreement, they are subject to the provisions of Book IX, but enjoy superpriority according to VIII. – 5:204 (Additional provisions as to proprietary security rights) paragraph (3).

(4)   In the case of paragraph (1)(b), the right of the secured creditor, as the former holder of an encumbrance in the material, extends to the security rights mentioned in paragraph (3).

IX. – 2:308: Use of Goods Subject to a Retention of Ownership Device for Production or Combination

(1)   The rules of Book VIII, Chapter 5 (Production, combination and commingling) apply to the consequences of production or combination of goods subject to a retention of ownership device; references to the owner of these goods are to be understood as references to the buyer, hire-purchaser, lessee or consignee.

(2)   Where materials subject to a retention of ownership device are used for the production of new goods, the seller, supplier or lessor may acquire a security right by party agreement:

(a)   in the products; and

(b)   in the right to payment to which the buyer, hire-purchaser, lessee or consignee is entitled against the producer according to VIII. – 5:201 (Production) on the basis of being regarded as the former owner of the material according to paragraph (1).

(3)   The preceding paragraph applies accordingly if the goods are combined.

(4)   In the case of paragraph (2)(b), the right of the seller, supplier or lessor extends to the security rights in the products or combined goods acquired by the buyer, hire-purchaser, lessee or consignee as a result of the production or combination.

IX. – 2:309: Commingling of Assets Subject to Proprietary Security

(1)   Where encumbered goods are commingled in such a way that it is impossible or economically unreasonable to separate the resulting mass or mixture into its original constituents, but it is possible and economically reasonable to separate the mass or mixture into proportionate quantities, the security rights that had encumbered the goods continue as encumbrances of the rights which the former owners of the goods have in the resulting mass or mixture by virtue of VIII. – 5:202 (Commingling) paragraph (1); this encumbrance is limited to a share proportionate to the value of the respective goods at the moment of commingling.

(2)   Where the goods that are commingled as set out in the preceding paragraph were subject to a retention of ownership device, VIII. – 5:202 (Commingling) paragraph (1) applies with the proviso that the rights of the holder of the retention of ownership device are continued in a share of the resulting mass or mixture proportionate to the value of the respective goods at the moment of commingling.

(3)   Any secured creditor is entitled to exercise the security provider's right to separate a quantity equivalent to that co-owner's undivided share out of the mass or mixture (VIII. – 5:202 (Commingling) paragraph (2)).

(4)   If encumbered financial assets held by the secured creditor are commingled by the latter in a fund, the security provider is entitled to a share in the fund. Paragraph (1) applies with appropriate adaptations.

(5) If in the cases covered by paragraphs (1), (2) and (4) the assets of the mass or fund do not suffice to satisfy all co-owners, VIII. – 2:305 (Transfer of goods forming part of a bulk) paragraphs (4) and (5) apply accordingly.

Section 4: Coverage of Security

IX. – 2:401: Secured Rights

(1)   The security covers, within its maximum amount, if any, not only the principal secured right, but also the ancillary rights of the creditor against the debtor, especially rights to payment of:

(a)   contractual and default interest;

(b)   damages, a penalty or an agreed sum for non-performance by the debtor; and

(c)   the reasonable costs of extra-judicial recovery of those items.
(2)   The right to payment of the reasonable costs of legal proceedings and enforcement proceedings against the security provider and against the debtor, if different from the security provider, is covered, provided the security provider had been informed about the creditor's intention to undertake such proceedings in sufficient time to enable the security provider to avert
those costs.
(3)   A global security covers only rights which originated in contracts between the debtor and
the creditor.

Chapter 3: Effectiveness as Against Third Persons
Section 1: General Rules
IX. – 3:101: Effectiveness as Against Third Persons

(1)   A security right created according to Chapter 2 has no effects against the following classes
of third persons:
(a)   holders of proprietary rights, including effective security rights, in the encumbered asset;
(b)   a creditor who has started to bring execution against those assets and who, under the
applicable law, has obtained a position providing protection against a subsequent execution; and
(c)   the insolvency administrator of the security provider, unless, subject to exceptions, the requirements of this Chapter are met.
(2)   Where a security right that is effective against third persons according to the provisions of
this Chapter is extended by virtue of the provisions of this Book without a need for an agreement to this effect to assets other than the assets that were originally encumbered, the extension of the security right is not subject to the requirements of this Chapter.
(3)   A security right that had been acquired by a good faith acquisition in disregard of a retention of ownership device or an earlier security right in the asset to be encumbered is effective
against the holder of the retention of ownership device or the holder of the earlier security right
even if the requirements of this Chapter are not met. The effectiveness of the security right that
had been acquired by a good faith acquisition against other third persons remains subject to
the other rules of this Chapter.

IX. – 3:102: Methods of Achieving Effectiveness

(1)   For security rights in all types of assets, effectiveness may be achieved by registration of the
security right pursuant to Section 3.
(2)   Effectiveness can also be achieved pursuant to Section 2:
(a)   in the case of corporeal assets, by the secured creditor holding possession of the encumbered assets; or
(b)   in the case of certain intangible assets, by the secured creditor exercising control over the
encumbered assets.

IX. – 3:103: Security Right Made Effective by Several Methods

(1)   If a security right has been made effective by registration, possession or control, it may be
made effective also by any of the other methods. Where the effects diverge, the stronger effects
of a chosen method prevail.
(2)   The preceding rules also apply if a security right that is exempted from the requirements of
this Chapter is also made effective by registration, possession or control.

IX. – 3:104: Change of Method

If the method for achieving effectiveness is changed, effectiveness is continuous, provided the requirements of the new method are met immediately upon termination of the preceding method.

IX. – 3:105: Security Right in an Accessory to an Immovable

A security right in an accessory to an immovable may upon accession also be made effective by
registration or annotation in a land register, provided this is authorised by the law governing
the land register.

IX. – 3:106: Security Right in Commingled Assets
(1)   Where a corporeal asset, which is encumbered with an effective security right, is comming-led, the security right in the corresponding share of the bulk according to IX. – 2:309 (Comming-ling of assets subject to proprietary security) remains effective.
(2)   The preceding paragraph applies with appropriate adaptations if financial assets are com-mingled in a fund.

IX. – 3:107: Registration of Acquisition Finance Devices
(1)   An acquisition finance device is effective only if registered.
(2)   If registration is effected within 35 days after delivery of the supplied asset, the acquisition finance device is effective from the date of creation.
(3)   If registration takes place later than 35 days after delivery, the acquisition finance device be-comes effective only at the time of registration and does not enjoy superpriority under IX. – 4:102 (Superpriority).
(4)   Where a credit for assets supplied to a consumer is secured by an acquisition finance de-vice, this proprietary security is effective without registration. This exception does not apply to security rights in proceeds and other assets different from the supplied asset.

IX. – 3:108: Importation of Encumbered Asset
If an encumbered asset is brought from a country outside the European Union into this area, any pre-existing security right which is effective remains effective if the requirements laid down in this Chapter are fulfilled within three months.

Section 2: Possession or Control by Creditor
IX. – 3:201: Possession
Security rights in encumbered corporeal assets can be made effective by the secured creditor holding possession:
(a)   if the secured creditor or an agent (other than the security provider) acting for the secured creditor exercises direct physical control over the encumbered assets;
(b)   where the encumbered assets are held by a third person (other than the security provider), if the third person has agreed with the secured creditor to hold the encumbered assets only for the latter; or
(c)   where the encumbered assets are jointly held by the secured creditor and the security pro-vider or where a third person holds the encumbered assets for both parties, if in either case the security provider has no access to the encumbered assets without the secured creditor's express consent.

IX. – 3:202: Negotiable Documents of Title and Negotiable Instruments
(1)   Possession of a negotiable document of title or negotiable instrument is also sufficient for the effectiveness of a security right in the goods covered by the document of title or in the right embodied in the instrument.
(2)   The security right in the goods covered by the document of title according to paragraph (1) is not affected if the covered assets are relinquished to the security provider or another person for a period of up to ten days against a duly dated formal trust receipt and for the purpose of loading or unloading, sale or exchange or other dealing with the goods except the creation of a competing security right.

IX. – 3:203: Certificated Shares and Bonds
Paragraph (1) of the preceding Article applies with appropriate adaptations to possession of directly held certificates of shares of companies, if negotiable, and directly held bond certificates.

IX. – 3:204: Control over Financial Assets
(1)   Security rights can be made effective by the secured creditor exercising control over:
(a)   financial assets which are entered into book accounts held by a financial institution (inter-mediated financial assets); and

(b) non-intermediated financial instruments registered in a register maintained by or for the issuer or which under national law is determinative of title.
(2) The secured creditor exercises control over the assets mentioned in paragraph (1)(a), if:
(a) the secured creditor with the assent of the security provider has instructed the financial institution administering the book account not to admit dispositions by the security provider without the secured creditor's consent;
(b) the assets are held by the financial institution for the secured creditor in a special account; or
(c) the financial institution is the secured creditor.
(3) The preceding paragraph applies with appropriate adaptations to the exercise of control by the secured creditor over the assets mentioned in paragraph (1)(b).
(4) The satisfaction of the requirements of paragraphs (2) and (3) must be evidenced in writing or recording by electronic means or any other durable medium.

Section 3: Registration
Subsection 1: Operation of the Register of Proprietary Security
IX. – 3:301: European Register of Proprietary Security; Other Systems of Registration or Notation
(1) A registration that is required or allowed for any security right or retention of ownership device under the rules of this Book is to be effected in a European register of proprietary security, subject to paragraph (2).
(2) Where systems of registration or notation on title certificates for security rights in specific types of assets exist, the effectiveness of a security right to be registered or noted in these systems depends upon compliance with any mandatory rules applicable for these systems. For systems established under the national law of a member state, this rule is subject to IX. – 3:312 (Transitional provision in relation to entries in other systems of registration or notation under national law).
(3) An entry of security rights in financial instruments into a register maintained by or for the issuer of financial instruments or which under national law is determinative of title is not regarded as registration for the purposes of this Section but may constitute control if the requirements of IX. – 3:204 (Control over financial assets) paragraph (3) are complied with.

IX. – 3:302: Structure and Operation of the Register
(1) The European register of proprietary security is to operate as a personal folio system, allowing entries concerning security rights to be filed against identified security providers.
(2) The register is to operate electronically and to be directly accessible for its users in an online format.

IX. – 3:303: Retention of Ownership Devices and Security Rights
(1) For the purposes of the European register of proprietary security no distinction is made between retention of ownership devices and security rights.
(2) Any reference in this Section to security rights includes retention of ownership devices.

IX. – 3:304: Authentication as Requirement for Declarations to the Register
(1) Any declaration to the online register, such as filing, amending or deleting an entry in the register or a declaration of consent, requires authentication by the person making the declaration.
(2) Authentication requires:
(a) the use of log-in information which is issued to individual users of the online register after an initial enrolment in the register during which the identity and the contact details of the user are verified; or
(b) the use of secure online identity verification systems of general application, if such systems are brought into operation at a European or member state level.

Subsection 2: Entries in the Register
IX. – 3:305: Entries to Be Made by Secured Creditor and Advance Filing
(1)   Entries in the register can be made directly by the secured creditor.
(2)   Entries can be made before or after the security right referred to has been created or the contract for proprietary security has been concluded.

IX. – 3:306: Minimum Content of the Entry in the Register
(1)   An entry can be entered into the register only if:
(a)   it is made in respect of an identified security provider;
(b)   it contains a minimum declaration as to the encumbered assets;
(c)   it is indicated by one or several references to a list of categories of assets to which category the encumbered assets belong;
(d)   the requirements of consent are fulfilled; and
(e)   it is accompanied by a declaration of the creditor that the latter assumes liability for damage caused to the security provider or third persons by a wrongful registration.
(2)   For the purposes of paragraph (1)(b) a declaration that the creditor is to take security over the security provider's assets or is to retain ownership as security is sufficient.

IX. – 3:307: Additional Content of the Entry
An entry in the register may include the following additional content:
(a)   additional information provided by the creditor in relation to the encumbered assets or the content of the security right;
(b)   a date at which the entry is to expire provided that it is before the end of the regular period of expiry of five years; and
(c)   a maximum amount of the security.

IX. – 3:308: Information Appearing on the Register
In respect of each entry the following information appears on the register and is accessible to any user:
(a)   the name and contact details of the security provider;
(b)   the name and contact details of the creditor;
(c)   the time the entry was made;
(d)   the minimum content of the entry under IX. – 3:306 (Minimum content of the entry in the register) paragraph (1)(b) and (c); and
(e)   any additional content of the entry under IX. – 3:307 (Additional content of the entry) sub-paragraphs (a) to (c).

IX. – 3:309: Required Consent of the Security Provider
(1)   An entry in the register can be made only if the security provider has consented to it by declaration to the register. Any such consent can be freely terminated by the security provider by declaration to the register. A termination of consent does not affect entries that have been entered before the termination of the consent is declared to the register.
(2)   The secured creditor may demand from the security provider a declaration of consent to an entry to the extent that such a consent is necessary to cover the security rights created in the contract for proprietary security.
(3)   This Article does not affect the validity, terms and effects of any of the security provider's agreements with the secured creditor other than the declaration of consent to the register.

IX. – 3:310: Identity of Security Provider, Description of Encumbered Assets
and Effectiveness of Registration
(1)   If under the rules in this Book the effectiveness or priority of a security right encumbering assets of a certain security provider depends upon registration, an entry in the register according to this Subsection suffices only if:
(a)   the entry is filed against the correct security provider;

(b)   the creditor's declaration as to the encumbered assets as appearing on the register covers the assets encumbered by the security right;
(c)   the encumbered assets actually belong to the category or categories of assets indicated in the entry; and
(d)   the creditor's declaration is in an official language of the European Union. The creditor may add translations.
(2)   For the purposes of paragraph (1)(b):
(a)   the entry is effective in respect of fruits, products, proceeds and any other assets different from the original assets serving as security only if these assets are also covered by the creditor's declaration as to the encumbered assets; and
(b)   a description identifying individual assets is not necessary.
(3)   The creditor making the entry bears the risk that:
(a)   the description of the encumbered assets, the translation of this description or the indication of the category or categories of encumbered assets is wrong; and
(b)   the entry is filed against a wrong person.

IX. – 3:311: Amendments of Entries

(1)   The creditor may amend any of the creditor's entries after filing.
(2)   An amendment to an entry can only be entered into the register if:
(a)   it is made in respect of a specific entry;
(b)   it contains a declaration as to the content of the amendment; and
(c)   it is accompanied by a declaration of the creditor that the latter assumes liability for damage caused to the security provider or third persons by a wrongful amendment to the original entry.
(3)   In case of an amendment, the register preserves and shows both the original text and the amendment as such, including the time the amendment was made.
(4)   An amendment to an entry is effective only if it does not extend the creditor's rights. In particular, an amendment can have the effect of limiting the creditor's rights, especially by subordinating the creditor's rights to another creditor's rights, by indicating a transfer of the security right to another creditor, by limiting the scope of assets covered according to the content of the creditor's declaration as to the encumbered assets or by setting or predating a date of expiry of the entry.
(5)   An extension of the creditor's rights is effective only if contained in a new entry.

IX. – 3:312: Transitional Provision in Relation to Entries in Other Systems of Registration or Notation Under National Law

(1)   Where a security right is registered or noted in another system of registration or notation on title certificates under the national law of a member state, as long as such systems are still in operation for security rights in specific types of assets, an entry reiterating the content of that registration or notation, including the time of the registration or notation, is to be entered into the European register of proprietary security against the security provider by the body operating the other system. An entry in the European register of proprietary security is required for the effectiveness of the registration or notation under this Book.
(2)   For purposes of priority according to Chapter 4, the time of registration or notation in the national system is decisive.

IX. – 3:313: Automated Certification of Entry to Creditor and Security Provider

After an entry or an amendment to an entry has been filed, a certificate to that effect is to be communicated automatically to the creditor and the security provider.

IX. – 3:314: Third Person Acting as Agent of the Creditor

(1)   As an additional content of the entry made by the secured creditor, the latter may identify a third person acting as agent of the creditor, whose name and contact details will appear on the register instead of those of the creditor. In such a situation, the entry can be entered into the

register only if in addition to the requirements of the preceding Articles being satisfied this third person has also consented to it according to IX. – 3:309 (Required consent of the security provider) paragraphs (1) and (3), applied with appropriate adaptations.

(2)   By a declaration to the register that is subject to IX. – 3:309 (Required consent of the security provider) paragraphs (1) and (3), applied with appropriate adaptations, a secured creditor may authorise a third person to make declarations to the register on the secured creditor's behalf.

(3)   Where a third person acting as agent for the secured creditor is identified in the entry, the secured creditor and the third person are liable as solidary debtors for all obligations of secured creditors under this Section.

Subsection 3: Protection of the Security Provider
IX. – 3:315: Security Provider's Right to Deletion or Amendment of Entry

The security provider is entitled against the secured creditor to deletion or amendment of an entry if and in so far as no corresponding security right exists.

IX. – 3:316: Review of Contested Entries by Registration Office

(1)   The security provider may apply for the assistance of the registration office in the assertion of the right to demand deletion or amendment of an entry from the secured creditor.

(2)   On the security provider's application, the registration office asks the secured creditor whether the latter agrees to the security provider's demand.

(3)   If the secured creditor does not object within two months of being asked by the registration office according to paragraph (2), the entry is deleted or amended according to the security provider's demand.

(4)   If the secured creditor objects within the time limit of paragraph (3), the entry is marked as contested to the extent of the security provider's demand.

(5)   The entry remains marked as contested until:
(a)   the security provider withdraws the application by declaration to the registration office;
(b)   the secured creditor agrees to the security provider's demand by declaration made to the registration office;
(c)   the secured creditor deletes the entry; or
(d)   a final decision is rendered on the security provider's demand by a competent court.

Subsection 4: Accessing and Searching the Register
IX. – 3:317: Access to the Register for Searching Purposes

Access to the register for searching purposes is open to anyone, subject to the payment of fees; it does not depend upon a consent by the security provider or the secured creditor.

IX. – 3:318: Searching the Register

The register can be searched for entries filed against individual security providers or for entries containing specified descriptions of the encumbered assets.

Subsection 5: Registered Creditors' Duty to Answer Requests for Information
IX. – 3:319: Duty to Give Information

(1)   Any registered secured creditor has a duty to answer requests for information by inquirers concerning the security right covered by the entry and the encumbered assets if these requests are made with the security provider's approval.

(2)   The request must be in an official language of the member state of the European Union where the place of business or incorporation or the residence of the secured creditor is situated or in English.

(3)   The request must be answered within fourteen days after the request, including the security provider's approval, has been received by the secured creditor.

(4)   The secured creditor's duty to answer requests for information by inquirers according to the preceding paragraphs is owed both to the inquirer and to the security provider. To both parties, the secured creditor is liable in damages for any loss caused by breach of the duty.

IX. – 3:320: Content of the Information

(1)   Requests for information under the preceding Article must be answered by the secured creditor giving information concerning the existence of a security right in specific assets at the time when the information is given.

(2)   The information may be given by:

(a)   stating specifically whether the assets concerned are encumbered in favour of the secured creditor; or

(b)   forwarding the relevant parts of the agreements between security provider and secured creditor covering the providing or retention of proprietary security.

(3)   Where the security right has been transferred, the person registered as the secured creditor must disclose the name and contact details of the transferee.

(4)   The information must be given in an official language of the member state of the European Union where the place of business or incorporation or the residence of the secured creditor is situated or in English.

(5)   No information needs to be given:

(a)   if it is apparent directly from the entry that the asset concerned is not encumbered, provided that the entry complies with the requirements of paragraph (4); or

(b)   if the secured creditor had already answered a request for information by the same inquirer in relation to the same asset within the past three months and the information given is still correct.

(6)   These provisions do not affect the secured creditor's obligation to give information concerning the obligation covered by the security under IX. – 5:401 (Secured creditor's obligation to give information about secured right) or any equivalent obligation owed to the debtor of the obligation covered by the security and the consequences of a non-performance of these obligations.

IX. – 3:321: Consequences of Correct Information Given by Secured Creditor

(1)   If the secured creditor correctly informs the inquirer under this Subsection that the assets concerned are not encumbered, a security right in these assets which is subsequently created in favour of the secured creditor cannot enjoy priority conferred by the original entry over security rights of the inquirer. This rule applies only if the security rights of the inquirer are acquired by the latter within three months after the request for information had been made.

(2)   If the secured creditor correctly informs the inquirer under this Subsection that the assets concerned are encumbered, the inquirer cannot acquire a proprietary right in the encumbered assets free of the encumbrance in favour of the secured creditor even if that would otherwise be possible under the principles of good faith acquisition.

IX. – 3:322: Consequences of Incorrect Information Given by Secured Creditor

(1)   If the secured creditor incorrectly informs the inquirer under this Subsection that the assets concerned are not encumbered, the inquirer may within three months acquire a proprietary right in these assets free of any encumbrance in favour of the secured creditor on the basis of a good faith acquisition in spite of the entry in the register covering the secured creditor's rights.

(2)   If the secured creditor incorrectly informs the inquirer under this Subsection that the assets concerned are encumbered, and the inquirer nevertheless acquires a proprietary security right in the assets concerned from the security provider, IX. – 3:321 (Consequences of correct information given by secured creditor) paragraph (1) first sentence applies with appropriate adaptations.

IX. – 3:323: Consequences of Failure to Give Information

(1)   If the secured creditor fails to answer the request for information under IX. – 3:319 (Duty to give information) and IX. – 3:320 (Content of the information) or incorrectly answers that its security rights in the assets concerned have been transferred, the inquirer is to be treated as if the secured creditor had given the information that the assets concerned are not encumbered. IX. – 3:321 (Consequences of correct information given by secured creditor) paragraph (1) or IX.

– 3:322 (Consequences of incorrect information given by secured creditor) paragraph (1), respectively, apply with appropriate adaptations.

(2)   If the secured creditor delays in answering the request for information under IX. – 3:319 (Duty to give information) and IX. – 3:320 (Content of the information), the preceding paragraph applies if a proprietary right is created in favour of or acquired by the inquirer before the secured creditor answers the request for information.

IX. – 3:324: Form of Requests and Information

The request for information under this Subsection and the answer must be in textual form. Both may be made via an electronic means of communication provided by the register, in which case a certification of the inquiry or the answer is to be communicated by the register to the inquirer or the secured creditor, respectively, serving as proof of receipt of the inquiry or of the answer by the other party.

Subsection 6: Duration, Renewal and Deletion of Entries
IX. – 3:325: Duration

(1)   An entry expires five years after it has been entered into the register or at the date of expiry indicated in the entry.

(2)   Once an entry expires, it no longer appears on the register and is no longer directly accessible for any user. It ceases to have any effect under this Section. The content of the entry is kept for reference purposes in the archives of the registration office.

IX. – 3:326: Renewal

(1) Unless a date of expiry has been included in the entry, an entry may be renewed before the end of the regular period of expiry for an additional period of five years.

(2) The renewal of an entry is effected by a declaration of the secured creditor to the register.

IX. – 3:327: Deletion

(1)   The secured creditor may at any time delete the entry by declaration to the register.

(2)   For the consequences of a declaration according to the preceding paragraph, IX. – 3:325 (Duration) paragraph (2) is applicable with appropriate adaptations.

Subsection 7: Transfer of the Security Right or of the Encumbered Asset
IX. – 3:328: Transfer of the Security Right: General Rules

(1)   Where the security right is transferred, it remains effective by virtue of the original entry.

(2)   Even if there is no declaration indicating the transfer under IX. – 3:329 (Transfer of the security right: declaration indicating the transfer), the transferee is bound under Subsection 5 in the same way as a secured creditor from the moment of the transfer.

(3)   The transferor is liable towards the transferee for any damage caused by its conduct in relation to the entry, as well as to amendments and deletions thereof from the moment of the transfer of the security right until a declaration indicating the transfer is filed or until the transferor declares its consent to such a declaration under IX. – 3:329 (Transfer of the security right: declaration indicating the transfer) paragraph (4)).

IX. – 3:329: Transfer of the Security Right: Declaration Indicating the Transfer

(1)   Where the security right is transferred, the original entry may be amended by a declaration indicating the transfer.

(2)   The declaration indicating the transfer is subject to IX. – 3:311 (Amendments of entries) and any additional rules as laid down in this Article.

(3)   The declaration indicating the transfer can be entered into the register only if:

(a)   it is made in respect of a specific entry;

(b)   it indicates the security rights to be transferred;

(c)   it identifies the transferee; and

(d)   it is accompanied by a declaration of the person making the amendment that the latter assumes liability for damage caused to the secured creditor or third persons by a wrongful entry.

(4)   The declaration indicating the transfer may be filed by the transferor or, with the transferor's consent, by the transferee.

(5)   On the basis and to the extent of the transfer of the security right, the security provider is
entitled as against the transferor to the filing of a declaration indicating the transfer and the
transferee is entitled to a declaration of consent by the transferor according to the preceding
paragraph. IX. – 3:316 (Review of contested entries by registration office) applies with appropriate adaptations to the assertion of these rights.

(6)   Once the declaration indicating the transfer is filed, the original entry is amended accordingly and is no longer regarded as covering the security rights indicated as having been transferred.

(7)   Once the declaration indicating the transfer is filed, a new entry is automatically filed
against the security provider reiterating the content of the original entry and stating that the
security rights indicated are transferred to the transferee.

(8)   The transferee assumes the position of the secured creditor in respect of the new entry for
all purposes under this Section. In respect of the security rights indicated as transferred, the new
entry preserves the priority conferred by the original entry.

IX. – 3:330: Transfer of the Encumbered Asset: General Rules

(1)   Ownership of the encumbered asset may be transferred subject to the existing security
right without a new entry being filed in the register.

(2)   The continuation of effectiveness and the priority of the security right in the encumbered
asset by virtue of the original entry in the register are governed by IX. – 5:303 (Transfer of encumbered asset).

(3)   For the purposes of this Section, the transferee assumes the position of the security provider in respect of the security right in the transferred assets from the moment of the transfer.

(4)   The preceding paragraphs apply with appropriate adaptations where the rights of a buyer,
hire-purchaser, lessee or consignee in or relating to the supplied assets are transferred subject
to an existing retention of ownership device.

IX. – 3:331: Transfer of the Encumbered Asset: Declaration of Transfer

(1)   A transferee acquiring ownership of an encumbered asset subject to an existing security
right has a duty to enter in the register an entry against itself indicating the transfer, unless such
a declaration has already been entered by the secured creditor.

(2)   The transferee is liable towards the secured creditor holding a security right in the transferred asset for damage resulting from a breach of the duty under the preceding paragraph.

(3)   The declaration of transfer can be entered by the transferee or the secured creditor if:

(a)   it is made in respect of an identified security provider as transferee;

(b)   it indicates the identity of an identified security provider as transferor;

(c)   it contains a minimum declaration as to the transferred asset;

(d)   it is indicated by one or several references to a list of categories of assets to which category
the transferred asset belongs; and

(e)   it is accompanied by a declaration of the person making the declaration of transfer that the
latter assumes liability for any damage caused to the transferee, the secured creditor or
third persons by a wrongful entry.

(4)   The preceding paragraphs apply with appropriate adaptations where the rights of a buyer,
hire-purchaser, lessee or consignee in or relating to the supplied assets are transferred subject
to an existing retention of ownership device.

Subsection 8: Costs
IX. – 3:332: Distribution of Costs

(1)   As between the parties:

(a)   each party has to bear the costs of its enrolment or admission to a secure online identity
verification system; and

(b)   the security provider has to bear any other costs reasonably incurred by the secured credi-
      tor in connection with the registration.
(2)   The costs of inquiries and of answers to such inquires are to be borne by the inquirer.

Subsection 9: Security Rights Created Before Establishment of Register
IX. – 3:333: Security Rights Created Before Establishment of Register
(1)   Security rights that were effective before the European register of proprietary security started
to operate do not require registration under this Section in order to remain effective thereafter.
(2)   If the security rights were registered or noted in any system of registration or notation on
title certificates under the national law of a member state, an entry reiterating the content of
that registration or notation, including the date of registration or notation, is to be entered in
the European register of proprietary security against the security provider by the body
operating the other register once this register is established.

Chapter 4: Priority
IX. – 4:101: Priority: General Rules
(1)   Subject to exceptions, the priority between several security rights and between a security
right and other limited proprietary rights in the same asset is determined according to the order
of the relevant time.
(2)   The relevant time is:
(a)   for security rights, the time of registration according to Chapter 3, Section 3, if any, or the
      time at which the security right has otherwise become effective according to the other
      rules of Chapter 3, whichever is earlier;
(b)   for other limited proprietary rights, the time of creation.
(3)   An effective security right has priority over an ineffective security right, even if the latter was
created earlier.
(4)   The ranking of two or more security rights which are ineffective is determined by the time
of their creation.
(5)   Subject to IX. – 4:108 (Change of ranking), a security right that had been acquired by a
good faith acquisition in an asset subject to a retention of ownership device or in disregard of
an earlier encumbrance in the same asset always has priority over the retention of ownership
device or earlier security right.

IX. – 4:102: Superpriority
(1)   An acquisition finance device that is effective against third persons according to the rules
of Chapter 3 takes priority over any security right or other limited proprietary right created by
the security provider.
(2)   A security right in financial assets made effective by control according to IX. – 3:204
(Control over financial assets) or by possession takes priority over any other security right or
other limited proprietary right in the same asset. If control is created for different secured
creditors, IX. – 4:101 (Priority: general rules) paragraphs (1) and (2)(a) apply.
(3)   A security right based upon a right of retention of possession according to IX. – 2:114 (Right
of retention of possession) takes priority over any other right in the retained asset.
(4)   The preceding paragraphs are subject to IX. – 4:101 (Priority: general rules) paragraph (5)
and IX. – 4:108 (Change of ranking).

IX. – 4:103: Continuation of Priority
(1)   Priority is not affected if the encumbered asset:
(a)   becomes an accessory to a movable asset; or
(b)   is used for the production of new goods, or is commingled or combined with other assets,
      provided that the security right extends to the security provider's rights in the asset resul-
      ting from the production, commingling or combination.
(2)   Paragraph (1)(a) also applies if a movable asset becomes an accessory to an immovable,
unless the law governing the immovable determines otherwise.

IX. – 4:104: Fruits and Proceeds: General Rules

(1)   Security rights in fruits and proceeds of the following types of assets preserve the priority of the security right in the encumbered original assets:
(a)   fruits and proceeds of the same kind as the assets that were originally encumbered;
(b)   rights to payment due to defects in, damage to, or loss of the assets that were originally encumbered, including insurance proceeds; and
(c)   fruits and proceeds that are covered by the registration of the security right in the assets that were originally encumbered.
(2)   In cases not covered by paragraph (1), the priority of security rights in fruits and proceeds is determined according to the general rules laid down in IX. – 4:101 (Priority: general rules) and IX. – 4:102 (Superpriority).

IX. – 4:105: Fruits and Proceeds: Exceptions

(1)   Security rights in fruits and proceeds of assets that are subject to an acquisition finance device or are covered by VIII. – 5:204 (Additional provisions as to proprietary security rights) paragraph (3) do not enjoy the superpriority of the security right in the assets that were originally encumbered.
(2)   The preceding paragraph does not affect the superpriority of security rights in:
(a)   rights to payment due to defects in, damage to, or loss of the assets that were originally encumbered, including insurance proceeds; and
(b)   proceeds of the sale of the assets that were originally encumbered.

IX. – 4:106: Importation of Encumbered Asset

If an encumbered asset is brought from a country outside the European Union into this area, the priority of a security right which was effective before removal of the encumbered asset into the European Union and which fulfils the conditions of IX. – 3:108 (Importation of encumbered asset) is preserved.

IX. – 4:107: Priority of Execution Creditor

For the purpose of determining priority, an execution creditor is regarded as holding an effective security right as from the moment of bringing an execution against specific assets if all preconditions for execution proceedings against these assets according to the procedural rules of the place of execution are fulfilled.

IX. – 4:108: Change of Ranking

(1)   The priority between a security right and other security rights as well as other limited proprietary rights in the same asset may be changed by an agreement in textual form between the holders of all rights that would be affected by the change of ranking.
(2)   A third person acquiring a security right or a limited proprietary right that has been negatively affected by a change of ranking is bound only if the entry for the security right in the European register of proprietary security has been amended accordingly or if the third person at the time of the transfer knew or had reason to know of the change of ranking.

Chapter 5: Predefault Rules

Section 1: General Principles

IX. – 5:101: General Principles

(1)   The security provider and the secured creditor are free to determine their mutual relationship with respect to the encumbered asset, except as otherwise provided in these rules.
(2)   Any agreement concluded before default and providing for the appropriation of the encumbered assets by the secured creditor or having this effect, is void, unless expressly provided otherwise. This paragraph does not apply to retention of ownership devices.

Section 2: Encumbered Assets

IX. – 5:201: Care and Insurance of the Encumbered Assets

(1)   The party who is in possession of the encumbered assets has an obligation to keep them identifiable from assets owned by others and must preserve and maintain them with reasonable care.

(2)   The other party is entitled to inspect the encumbered assets at any reasonable time.

(3)   The security provider has an obligation to insure the encumbered assets against such risks as are usually insured against by a prudent owner at the location of the assets. Upon request of the secured creditor, the security provider must furnish proof of the insurance coverage. If there is no or only insufficient insurance coverage or no proof of it, the secured creditor is entitled to take out sufficient insurance and to add any expenses to the obligation covered by the security.

Subsection 1: Security Provider's Rights and Obligations

IX. – 5:202: Rights in General

If and as long as the security provider is entitled to possession of the encumbered assets, the security provider is entitled to make use of them in a reasonable manner.

IX. – 5:203: Use of Encumbered Industrial Material

A security provider in possession of encumbered industrial material, such as raw material or semi-finished products, may apply such material for production, unless expressly prohibited.

IX. – 5:204: Dispositions of Encumbered Assets by Traders and Manufacturers

(1)   A security provider acting in the ordinary course of its business as a trader or manufacturer may dispose of the following types of encumbered assets free of any security right if they are in the security provider's possession:

(a)   assets designated for sale and lease and industrial material (inventory); and

(b)   products of industrial material.

(2)   A trader or manufacturer may not dispose of items of its encumbered equipment, unless expressly so authorised by the secured creditor.

IX. – 5:205: Unauthorised Use or Disposition

(1)   A security provider in possession of the encumbered assets has an obligation to the secured creditor not to use or dispose of them in breach of the limits imposed by the preceding Articles of this Subsection.

(2)   In addition to liability for damages for non-performance of the obligation referred to in paragraph (1), the security provider who is in breach of those limits is obliged to account to the secured creditor for the value derived from the use or the proceeds of the disposition and to pay the resulting amount, but only up to the amount of the secured right that would otherwise remain unsatisfied.

Subsection 2: Secured Creditor's Rights and Obligations

IX. – 5:206: Limited Right of Use

A secured creditor who is in possession or control of the encumbered assets is not entitled to use the assets, unless and in so far as proper use is indispensable for their up-keep and preservation.

IX. – 5:207: Banks Entitled to Dispose of Financial Assets

(1)   Banks and equivalent financial institutions holding financial assets as secured creditors are entitled to use, appropriate and dispose of the encumbered assets, provided this is expressly agreed.

(2)   Upon satisfaction of the secured right, the secured creditor is only obliged to transfer financial assets of the same kind, quality and value to the security provider.

IX. – 5:208: Appropriation of Civil Fruits

If the security right extends to civil fruits of the assets that were originally encumbered, the secured creditor is entitled to collect and to apply money received as civil fruits to reduce the secured right even before it has become due.

Section 3: Change of Parties
IX. – 5:301: Transfer of the Secured Right

(1)   If a secured right is transferred to another creditor, the security right also passes to that creditor.

(2)   The transferor is obliged to inform the transferee of any security right securing the transferred right.

(3)   Effectiveness of the security right against third persons is achieved:

(a)   by virtue of the original registration according to IX. – 3:328 (Transfer of the security right: general rules) paragraph (1);

(b)   if either possession or control of the encumbered asset is transferred to the transferee;

(c)   if the transferor agrees to hold possession or control for the transferee; or

(d)   if the security right had been effective without observation of any requirements under Chapter 3.

(4)   If the security right remains effective, its priority is not affected by the transfer.

IX. – 5:302: Partial Transfer of the Secured Right

If the secured right is divided into parts held by different persons as the result of a transfer of a part of the secured right or of a transfer of the whole secured right to different transferees each acquiring a part only:

(a)   each holder of a part of the secured right is entitled to a part of the security right in proportion to the nominal amount of its part of the secured right; and

(b)   the effectiveness of the security rights of each holder of a part of the secured right is to be determined individually; possession or control of the encumbered asset may be held by one holder of a part of the secured right for the others also.

IX. – 5:303: Transfer of Encumbered Asset

(1)   Where ownership of an encumbered asset is transferred to another person, neither the existence nor the effectiveness against third persons of a security right in the asset is affected. As of the time of the transfer, the transferee is regarded as the security provider.

(2)   The preceding paragraph does not apply if the transferor acted with authority to dispose of the encumbered asset free of the encumbrance or if the transferee acquires the asset free of the encumbrance on the basis of a good faith acquisition.

(3)   Security rights which before transfer of ownership of the encumbered asset had been created for secured creditors in future assets of the new owner do not have priority over security rights encumbering the transferred asset at the time of the transfer.

(4)   The preceding paragraphs apply with appropriate adaptations where there is a transfer of the rights of a buyer, hire-purchaser, lessee or consignee in or relating to the supplied assets subject to an existing retention of ownership device.

Section 4: Secured Creditor's Obligation to Give Information about Secured Right
IX. – 5:401: Secured Creditor's Obligation to Give Information about Secured Right

(1)   The security provider has a right to, and the secured creditor has an obligation to provide on request by the security provider, information concerning the amount of the obligation covered by the security. The security provider can require this information to be given to a third person.

(2)   If the security provider is not the debtor of the obligation covered by the security, the security provider's right under the preceding Article depends upon the debtor's approval.

Chapter 6: Termination
IX. – 6:101: Instances of Termination of Proprietary Security

(1)   A security right is terminated if, and in so far as:

(a)   the security provider and secured creditor so agree;

(b)   the secured creditor waives the security right, such a waiver being presumed where the secured creditor returns possession of the encumbered asset to the security provider;

(c)   the encumbered asset ceases to exist;

(d)   ownership of the encumbered asset is acquired by the secured creditor;

(e)   ownership in the encumbered asset is acquired by a third person free from the security right; or

(f)   any other provision so provides or this consequence is implied, such as where the debtor and creditor of the secured right become identical, especially by inheritance or merger.

(2)   A security right is also terminated if the secured right ceases to exist entirely, especially if a right to payment is fully satisfied by payment to the secured creditor, unless the security right with the secured right passes to another person who has made payment to the secured creditor.

(3)   Paragraph (1)(a) to (c), (e) and (f) and paragraph (2) apply with appropriate adaptations to the termination of a retention of ownership device. A retention of ownership device is also terminated if the rights of the buyer, hire-purchaser, lessee or consignee in or relating to the supplied assets under the contract of sale, hire-purchase, financial leasing or consignment cease to exist.

IX. – 6:102: Loss of Proprietary Security Due to Good Faith Acquisition of Ownership

(1)   Whether a security right is lost due to good faith acquisition of ownership of the encumbered asset by a third person free from a security right is determined by VIII. – 3:102 (Good faith acquisition of ownership free of limited proprietary rights).

(2)   For the purposes of VIII. – 3:102 (Good faith acquisition of ownership free of limited proprietary rights) paragraph (1)(d) sentence 1, a transferee is regarded as knowing that the transferor has no right or authority to transfer ownership free from the security right if this right is registered under Chapter 3, Section 3 unless:

(a)   the transferor acts in the ordinary course of its business; or

(b)   the entry is filed against a security provider different from the transferor.

(3)   Whether a retention of ownership device is lost due to good faith acquisition of ownership of the supplied asset by a third person is determined by VIII. – 3:101 (Good faith acquisition through a person without right or authority to transfer ownership). Paragraph (2) above applies with appropriate adaptations.

IX. – 6:103: Prescription of the Secured Right

A security right can be enforced even if the secured right is prescribed and up to two years after the debtor of the secured right has invoked this prescription as against its creditor.

IX. – 6:104: Consequences of Termination

(1)   The full or partial termination of a security right implies the corresponding termination of the encumbrance of the asset concerned.

(2)   If and in so far as a security right is terminated, the secured creditor is no longer entitled to possession or control of the asset that was encumbered as against its owner. For the right to deletion of an entry in the European register of proprietary security, IX. – 3:315 (Security provider's right to have entry deleted or amended) applies.

(3)   The secured creditor is obliged to inform any third person holding the encumbered assets of the removal of the encumbrance and, if the third person holds the assets for the secured creditor's account, to ask the security provider for instructions.

(4)   Where in the case of an encumbered right to payment notice of the encumbrance had been given to the third party debtor, the secured creditor is obliged to notify the debtor of the removal of the encumbrance.

(5)   If and in so far as a retention of ownership device is terminated, the seller's, supplier's or lessor's ownership of the supplied assets is no longer subject to the rules of this Book. An acquisition of ownership of the supplied assets by the buyer, hire-purchaser, lessee or consignee or the latter's right to use the supplied assets is subject to an agreement of the parties. For the right to deletion of an entry in the European register of proprietary security, paragraph (2) second sentence applies.

IX. – 6:105: Secured Creditor Liable to Account for Proceeds
Upon termination of the security right, the secured creditor is liable to account for any proceeds from the encumbered assets, whether or not it has received, used or consumed them, and to transfer them to the security provider.

IX. – 6:106: Recourse of Third Party Security Provider
(1) If a security provider who is not the debtor of the secured right (a third party security provider), pays the outstanding amount of the obligation covered by the security, IV. G. – 2:113 (Security provider's rights after performance), IV. G. – 1:106 (Several security providers: internal recourse) and IV. G. – 1:107 (Several security providers: recourse against debtor) apply with appropriate adaptations.
(2) A security provider other than the debtor has as against the debtor the same position as a person who has provided dependent personal security.

Chapter 7: Default and Enforcement
Section 1: General Rules
IX. – 7:101: Secured Creditor's Rights after Default
(1) After an event of default, and provided that any additional conditions agreed by the parties are fulfilled, a secured creditor may exercise the rights under this Chapter.
(2) If a third person listed in IX. – 3:101 (Effectiveness as against third persons) paragraph (1) and fulfilling the requirements of that provision is involved, a secured creditor may exercise the rights under this Chapter only if the security right is effective according to the rules of Book IX Chapter 3. If no such third person is involved, it is sufficient that the security right has been validly created. The provisions on priority remain unaffected.

IX. – 7:102: Mandatory Rules
As between the enforcing secured creditor and the security provider, the rules of this Chapter are mandatory, unless otherwise provided.

IX. – 7:103: Extra-Judicial and Judicial Enforcement
(1) Unless otherwise agreed, the secured creditor may carry out extra-judicial enforcement of the security right.
(2) A security right in an asset of a consumer can only be enforced by a court or other competent authority, unless after default the consumer security provider has agreed to extra-judicial enforcement.
(3) In the case of retention of ownership devices the parties may not agree to exclude extra-judicial enforcement and paragraph (2) does not apply.
(4) Enforcement is to be undertaken by the secured creditor in a commercially reasonable way and as far as possible in cooperation with the security provider and, where applicable, any third person involved.

IX. – 7:104: Right to Seek Court Assistance and Damages
Any party or third person whose rights are violated by enforcement measures or by resistance to justified enforcement measures may:
(a) call upon a competent court or other authority, which must decide expeditiously, to order the party responsible to act in accordance with the provisions of this Chapter; and
(b) claim damages from the party responsible.

IX. – 7:105: Predefault Agreement on Appropriation of Encumbered Assets
(1) Any agreement concluded before default providing for the transfer of ownership of the encumbered assets to the secured creditor after default, or having this effect, is void.
(2) Paragraph (1) does not apply:
(a) if the encumbered asset is a fungible asset that is traded on a recognised market with published prices; or
(b) if the parties agree in advance on some other method which allows a ready determination of a reasonable market price.

(3)   Paragraph (2)(b) does not apply to a consumer security provider.

(4)   Where appropriation is allowed, the secured creditor is entitled to appropriate encumbered assets only for the value of their recognised or agreed market price at the date of appropriation. The security provider is entitled to any surplus over the obligations covered by the security right. The debtor remains liable for any deficit.

(5)   This Article does not apply to retention of ownership devices.

IX. – 7:106: Security Provider's Right of Redemption

(1)   Even after default, if the outstanding amount of the obligation covered by the security right is paid, the security provider may require the secured creditor to terminate the exercise of the rights under this Chapter and to return possession of the encumbered asset.

(2)   The security provider's rights under paragraph (1) may no longer be exercised if:

(a)   in the case of an enforcement under Section 2, the encumbered asset has been appropriated or sold or the secured creditor has concluded a binding contract to sell the asset to a third person; or

(b)   in the case of exercising the rights under Section 3, the holder of the retention of ownership device has terminated the relationship arising under the contract of sale, hire-purchase, financial leasing or consignment.

IX. – 7:107: Enforcement Notice to Consumer

(1)   A secured creditor may exercise the rights under this Chapter against a consumer security provider only if the secured creditor delivers at least ten days before enforcement is to begin an enforcement notice in textual form to the security provider and, if the latter is not the debtor, also to the debtor, if the debtor also is a consumer.

(2)   The enforcement notice must:

(a)   unequivocally designate the obligation covered by the security right and state the amount that is due by the end of the day before the notice is sent;

(b)   state that any other condition for enforcement agreed by the parties has been fulfilled;

(c)   state that the secured creditor intends to enforce the security and identify those encumbered assets against which the secured creditor intends to enforce it; and

(d)   be signed by or on behalf of the secured creditor.

(3)   The notice must be in an official language of the consumer's place of residence.

IX. – 7:108: Solidary Liability of Several Security Providers

(1)   To the extent that several proprietary security rights have been created covering the same obligation or the same part of an obligation, the creditor may seek satisfaction from any, several or all of these security rights. IV. G. – 1:105 (Several security providers: solidary liability towards creditor) applies accordingly.

(2)   Paragraph (1) applies with appropriate adaptations if, in addition to one or more proprietary security rights, personal security has been granted by one or more persons.

IX. – 7:109: Rights of Recourse of Third Party Security Provider

If the obligation covered by the security right is satisfied by enforcement against the assets of a security provider who is not the debtor, the rights of recourse between several providers of proprietary security or between providers of proprietary security and personal security as well as recourse against the debtor are governed by IV. G. – 2:113 (Security provider's rights after performance), IV. G. – 1:106 (Several security providers: internal recourse) and IV. G. – 1:107 (Several security providers: recourse against debtor), applied with appropriate adaptations.

Section 2: Enforcement of Security Rights
Subsection 1: Extra-judicial Enforcement: Rules Preparatory to Realisation
IX. – 7:201: Creditor's Right to Possession of Corporeal Asset

(1)   The secured creditor is not entitled to take possession of an encumbered corporeal asset, unless:

(a)   the security provider consents at the time when the secured creditor exercises this right; or

(b) the security provider had agreed to the secured creditor's right to take possession and neither the security provider nor the actual holder objects at the time when the secured creditor exercises this right.

(2) In enforcements against a consumer, the right to take possession according to paragraph (1) does not arise until ten days have elapsed since an enforcement notice has been served.

(3) Unless it indicates otherwise, a consent or agreement to the taking of possession according to paragraph (1) covers the right to enter the security provider's or other holder's premises for the purpose of exercising the right to take possession.

IX. – 7:202: Creditor's Right to Immobilise and to Preserve Encumbered Asset

(1) The secured creditor is entitled to take any steps necessary to immobilise the encumbered asset, to prevent unauthorised use or disposition of it, and to protect it physically. Paragraphs (1) to (3) of the preceding Article apply with appropriate adaptations.

(2) The secured creditor is entitled:

(a) to take reasonable steps to preserve, maintain and insure the encumbered asset and to obtain reimbursement for such actions from the security provider;

(b) to lease the encumbered asset to a third party for the purpose of preserving its value; or

(c) to take any other protective measures agreed with the security provider.

IX. – 7:203: Intervention of Court or Other Authority

(1) The secured creditor may apply to the competent court or other authority for an order to obtain possession of or access to the encumbered asset, if the security provider or a third person in possession of the asset refuses delivery to or access by the secured creditor.

(2) Upon application by either party, a court or other authority may order the taking of any of the protective measures mentioned in the preceding Article.

IX. – 7:204: Encumbrance of a Right to Payment

(1) Where the encumbered asset is a right entitling the security provider to payment from a third party debtor, the secured creditor may exercise the rights under this Chapter only if the secured creditor:

(a) sends to the third party debtor:

(i) where the security provider is a consumer, a copy of an enforcement notice complying with all the requirements of IX. – 7:107 (Enforcement notice to consumer); and

(ii) in other cases, an enforcement notice complying with paragraph (2)(a) and (d) of that Article; and

(b) informs the third party debtor as precisely as possible in the circumstances of the nature, amount and maturity of the security provider's right to payment against the third party debtor.

(2) The third party debtor is obliged to inform the enforcing secured creditor about the amount and maturity of competing rights of other secured creditors known to the third party debtor.

IX. – 7:205: Negotiable Instrument

(1) IX. – 7:201 (Creditor's right to possession of corporeal asset), IX. – 7:202 (Creditor's right to immobilise and to preserve encumbered asset) and IX. – 7:203 (Intervention of court or other authority) apply to the taking of possession of a negotiable instrument as such.

(2) IX. – 7:204 (Encumbrance of a right to payment) does not apply to negotiable instruments.

IX. – 7:206: Negotiable Document of Title

The preceding Article applies also to the taking of possession of a negotiable document of title.

Subsection 2: Extra-Judicial Enforcement: Realisation of Encumbered Asset
IX. – 7:207: General Rule on Realisation

(1) The secured creditor is entitled to realise the encumbered asset in order to apply the proceeds towards satisfaction of the secured right:

(a)   by sale of the encumbered asset according to IX. – 7:211 (Sale by public or private auction or by private sale), unless agreed otherwise by the parties;
(b)   by leasing the encumbered asset to a third person and collecting the fruits;
(c)   by appropriation according to IX. – 7:216 (Appropriation of encumbered asset by secured creditor); or
(d)   by exercising the methods of realisation (collection, sale or appropriation) for rights to payment and negotiable instruments according to IX. – 7:214 (Realisation of security in right to payment or in negotiable instrument).
(2)   Where an enforcement notice is required under IX. – 7:107 (Enforcement notice to consumer), paragraph (1) applies only if ten days have elapsed since the delivery of that notice.
(3)   The secured creditor may appoint a private agent or apply to a competent court officer to undertake all or some of the steps for realisation of the encumbered assets.

IX. – 7:208: Notice of Extra-Judicial Disposition

(1)   A secured creditor may exercise its right to dispose of the encumbered asset only if the secured creditor gives notice of its intention to do so.
(2)   Paragraph (1) does not apply if the encumbered asset is perishable or may otherwise speedily decline in value or is a fungible asset that is traded on a recognised market with published prices.

IX. – 7:209: Addressees of the Notice

The notice required by the preceding Article must be given:
(a)   to the security provider, the debtor (if different from the security provider) and other persons who, to the knowledge of the secured creditor, are liable for the obligation covered by the security; and
(b)   to the following persons with rights in the encumbered asset:
(i)   other secured creditors who have registered such rights;
(ii)   persons who were in possession or control of the encumbered asset when enforcement commenced; and
(iii) other persons who were actually known to the secured creditor to have a right in the encumbered asset.

IX. – 7:210: Time and Contents of Notice

(1)   The notice required by IX. – 7:208 (Notice of extra-judicial disposition) must be given in due time. A notice that reaches its addressees at least ten days before the disposition is regarded as given in due time.
(2)   The notice must indicate:
(a)   the place and time of the planned disposition;
(b)   a reasonable description of the encumbered asset to be disposed of;
(c)   any minimum price for the disposition of the encumbered asset and payment terms; and
(d)   the right of the security provider, of the debtor and of other interested persons to avert disposition of the encumbered asset by payment of the outstanding amount of the obligation covered by the security.
(3)   The notice must be in a language that can be expected to inform its addressees.

IX. – 7:211: Sale by Public or Private Auction or by Private Sale

(1)   Realisation of all or parts of the encumbered assets by sale may be by an officially supervised auction (public auction) or by an auction to which the public is invited (private auction).
(2)   Realisation of all or parts of the encumbered assets by sale may be by private sale, if so agreed by the parties or if there is a published market price for the encumbered asset.
(3)   The details of the arrangements to be made under the preceding paragraphs can be fixed by the secured creditor.
(4)   If the transfer is subject to pre-existing prior rights and upon demand, the secured creditor must disclose to the purchaser the relevant details.

(5)   If the secured creditor acquires the encumbered asset in a sale by public or private auction, the sale may be set aside by the security provider within a period of ten days after the auction.
(6)   Where the owner of the encumbered asset participates as buyer in a realisation of the encumbered asset according to this Article, the sale operates as an agreement to release encumbrances of the asset.

IX. – 7:212: Commercially Reasonable Price

(1)   The secured creditor must realise a commercially reasonable price for the encumbered asset.
(2)   If there is a recognised market which is easily accessible for the secured creditor, a price is commercially reasonable if it corresponds to the market price at the time of the sale, having due regard to any special features of the encumbered asset.
(3)   If the preceding paragraph does not apply, a price is commercially reasonable if the secured creditor took such steps as could be expected to be taken in the circumstances.
(4)   If the sale is by private sale, the security provider may demand that the creditor communicates to the security provider the expected price or price range. If the security provider can show that it is likely that this price range is significantly below what might reasonably be achieved at a private or public auction, the security provider may demand that the secured creditor arrange for a private or a public auction. Subject to paragraph (5) of the preceding Article, a price achieved in this way is binding upon the parties.

IX. – 7:213: Buyer's Rights in the Assets after Realisation by Sale

(1)   The buyer acquires rights in the sold assets free of the rights of:
(a)   the security provider;
(b)   the enforcing secured creditor;
(c)   junior secured creditors, whether holders of security rights or retention of ownership devices; and
(d)   holders of other limited proprietary rights with lower priority than the enforcing secured creditor's rights.
(2)   The following rights in the sold assets remain in existence after the transfer, unless the enforcing secured creditor acted with authority to dispose of the encumbered assets free of these rights or the buyer acquires in good faith according to IX. – 6:102 (Loss of proprietary security due to good faith acquisition of ownership):
(a)   rights of senior secured creditors, whether holders of security rights or retention of ownership devices; and
(b)   other limited proprietary rights with higher priority.
(3)   The buyer's position is not affected by any failure to comply with notice requirements under this Chapter or by any other violation of procedural provisions under this Chapter for the auction or private sale.
(4)   If the secured creditor or the security provider participates in the realisation by sale as buyer, the preceding paragraphs apply with appropriate adaptations with respect to the effects of the sale.

IX. – 7:214: Realisation of Security in Right to Payment or in Negotiable Instrument

(1)   Where the encumbered asset is a right to payment or a negotiable instrument, the secured creditor may collect the outstanding performance from the third party debtor or may sell and assign or appropriate the right to payment or the negotiable instrument.
(2)   If there are other security rights in the encumbered right to payment or the negotiable instrument which enjoy priority, the secured creditor is not entitled as against these senior secured creditors to collect the encumbered right to payment or to the negotiable instrument.
(3)   The third party debtor, except a debtor under a negotiable instrument, may refuse to pay unless the secured creditor sends a notice indicating the amount duet, supported by adequate proof.

(4)   The secured creditor may also collect or otherwise enforce any personal or proprietary se-curity right to which the security in the right to payment extends according to IX. – 2:301 (Encumbrance of right to payment of money) paragraph (4).

IX. – 7:215: Distribution of Proceeds

(1)   The proceeds of any extra-judicial enforcement of an encumbered asset according to the preceding provisions are to be distributed by the secured creditor in the following order.
(2)   First, the secured creditor who has enforced may apply the proceeds for the satisfaction of the secured right including the expenses incurred for enforcement.
(3)   Second, any secured creditor whose proprietary security has a lower priority than the enforcing secured creditor's right is entitled to receive any remaining proceeds after any deductions according to paragraph (2) up to the amount of the obligation covered by this secured creditor's security. If there are several junior secured creditors, the remaining proceeds are distributed in accordance with the order of priority between their rights. The preceding sentences apply with appropriate adaptations to holders of other limited proprietary rights with lower priority than the enforcing secured creditor's rights; instead of an obligation covered by the security, the value of these limited proprietary rights is decisive.
(4)   Third, any remaining proceeds after any deductions according to paragraphs (2) and (3) must be repaid to the security provider.
(5)   No secured creditor may receive more than any maximum amount that has been agreed or registered for that creditor's security right. This limit does not apply to reasonable expenses incurred for enforcement.

IX. – 7:216: Appropriation of Encumbered Asset by Secured Creditor

The secured creditor may accept the encumbered assets in total or partial satisfaction of the secured right under the following conditions:
(a)   the secured creditor must give advance notice of the intention to acquire all or parts of the encumbered assets in total or partial satisfaction of the secured right, specifying the relevant details;
(b)   the proposal must be sent to the persons specified in IX. – 7:209 (Addressees of the notice);
(c)   the conditions of IX. – 7:210 (Time and contents of notice) paragraphs (1), (2) (b) and (d) and (3) and IX. – 7:212 (Commercially reasonable price) paragraph (1), applied with appropriate adaptations, must be fulfilled;
(d)   the proposal must indicate the secured amount owed as of the end of business on the day before the proposal is sent and the amount of the right that is proposed to be satisfied by accepting the encumbered asset; and
(e)   no addressee objects to this proposal in writing within ten days after the proposal has been received by every addressee.

Subsection 3: Judicial Enforcement
IX. – 7:217: Applicable Rules

(1)   Judicial enforcement is to be undertaken according to the procedural rules of the member state where enforcement by a court or other competent authority is sought by the secured creditor.
(2)   The secured creditor may apply to the court or other competent authority to exercise any of the rights under the preceding Subsections. These rights may be exercised by the court or other competent authority regardless of whether they are under the preceding Subsections dependent upon or excluded by a party agreement or a consent or the absence of an objection of the security provider or other persons.

Section 3: Rules for Retention of Ownership Devices
IX. – 7:301: Consequences of Default under Retention of Ownership Devices

(1)   The holder of a retention of ownership device exercises the rights under the retention of ownership device by termination of the contractual relationship under a contract of sale, hire-

purchase, financial leasing or consignment according to the general rules of Book III, Chapter 3, Section 5.

(2)   Any rights in the supplied asset that were transferred or created by the buyer, hire-purchaser, lessee or consignee will terminate, unless:

(a)   the latter had been authorised to create or transfer such rights;

(b)   the transferee is protected by IX. – 2:108 (Good faith acquisition of security right) to IX. – 2:111 (Security right in cash, negotiable instruments and documents) or IX. – 6:102 (Loss of proprietary security due to good faith acquisition of ownership); or

(c)   the rights of the transferee exceptionally enjoy priority over the rights of the holder of the retention of ownership device.

(3)   On resale or re-leasing, the holder of the retention of ownership device is entitled to any surplus over the original price for the supplied assets which may be realised.

(4)   A third party to whom the retention of ownership device has been transferred by agreement or by law is entitled to the rights under paragraphs (1) to (3).

IX. – 7:302: Possession, Immobilisation and Preservation

IX. – 7:201 (Creditor's right to possession of corporeal asset), IX. – 7:202 (Creditor's right to immobilise and to preserve encumbered asset) and IX. – 7:203 (Intervention of court or other authority) apply in relation to retention of ownership devices with the adaptations set out in IX. – 1:104 (Retention of ownership devices: applicable rules) paragraph (2).

Book X Trusts
Chapter 1: Fundamental Provisions
Section 1: Scope and Relation to Other Rules
X. – 1:101: Trusts to Which this Book Applies

(1)   This Book applies to trusts created under Chapter 2 (Constitution of trusts).

(2)   With appropriate modifications this Book also applies to trusts:

(a)   constituted by:

(i)   a declaration to that effect set out in an enactment; or

(ii)   a court order with prospective effect; or

(b)   arising by operation of law set out in an enactment relating to a matter not determined by these rules.

(3)   In this Book, "court" includes a public officer or body, if authorised to act under the applicable national law, but does not include an arbitral tribunal.

X. – 1:102: Priority of the Law of Proprietary Securities

In relation to trusts for security purposes, this Book is subject to the application of the rules in Book IX (Proprietary security in movable assets).

Section 2: Definition, Special Legal Effects and Parties
X. – 1:201: Definition of a Trust

A trust is a legal relationship in which a trustee is obliged to administer or dispose of one or more assets (the trust fund) in accordance with the terms governing the relationship (trust terms) to benefit a beneficiary or advance public benefit purposes.

X. – 1:202: Special Legal Effects of a Trust

(1)   A trust takes effect in accordance with the rules in Chapter 10 (Relations to third parties) with the effect that the trust fund is to be regarded as a patrimony distinct from the personal patrimony of the trustee and any other patrimonies vested in or managed by the trustee.

(2)   In particular (and except for some reason other than merely that the trust fund is vested in the trustee):

(a)   the personal creditors of the trustee may not have recourse to the trust fund, whether by execution or by means of insolvency proceedings;

(b)   the trust fund is not subject to rules allocating property rights on the basis of matrimonial or family relationships; and

(c)   the trustee's successors are not entitled to benefit from the trust fund on the trustee's death.

X. – 1:203: Parties to a Trust

(1)   The truster is a person who constitutes or intends to constitute a trust by juridical act.

(2)   The trustee is the person in whom the trust fund becomes or remains vested when the trust is created or subsequently on or after appointment and who has the obligation set out in X. – 1:201 (Definition of a trust).

(3)   A beneficiary is a person who, according to the trust terms, has either a right to benefit or an eligibility for benefit from the trust fund.

(4)   A trust auxiliary is a person who, according to the trust terms, has a power to appoint or remove a trustee or to consent to a trustee's resignation.

(5)   Except as otherwise provided for by this Book:

(a)   a truster may also be a trustee or a beneficiary;

(b)   a trustee may also be a beneficiary; and

(c)   any of those parties to a trust may also be a trust auxiliary.

(6)   In this Book a person's "successor" is the heir or representative who under the law of succession becomes entitled to that person's personal patrimony on that person's death. Where the context permits, a reference to a party (or former party) to a trust is a reference to that person's successor if that person has died.

X. – 1:204: Plurality of Trustees

(1)   Where there are several trustees, the trust is solidary.

(2)   Where trust assets are vested in several trustees together, their co-ownership is joint.

X. – 1:205: Persons Entitled to Enforce Performance of Trustee's Obligations

(1)   A beneficiary has a right to performance of the trustee's obligations so far as they relate to that beneficiary's right to benefit or eligibility for benefit.

(2)   The persons who may enforce performance of the trustee's obligations under a trust to advance public benefit purposes are:

(a)   any public officer or body having that function; and

(b)   any other person having sufficient interest in the performance of the obligations.

(3)   A trustee may enforce performance of the obligations of a co-trustee.

X. – 1:206: Right to Benefit and Eligibility for Benefit

(1)   A person has a right to benefit if the trust terms require the trustee in given circumstances to dispose of all or part of the trust fund so as to confer a benefit on that person.

(2)   A person has an eligibility for benefit if the trust terms permit the trustee in given circumstances to dispose of all or part of the trust fund so as to confer a benefit on that person, but whether or not that person is to obtain a benefit depends on an exercise of discretion by the trustee or another.

(3)   A beneficiary's eligibility for benefit becomes a right to benefit if the trustee gives the beneficiary notice of a decision to confer benefit on that beneficiary in accordance with the trust terms governing that eligibility.

(4)   In this Book "benefit" does not include the exercise by a trustee of a right of recourse to the trust fund.

Section 3: Modifications of and Additions to General Rules
X. – 1:301: Extended Meaning of Gratuitous

(1)   In this Book "gratuitous" means done or provided without reward.

(2)   A juridical act or a benefit is also regarded as gratuitous in this Book if, considering the value of the rights created by the juridical act or the benefit provided, the value of the reward is so trivial that fairness requires it to be disregarded.

X. – 1:302: Notice
(1)   Where this Book requires notice to be given to a person, but it is not reasonably practical to do so, notice may be given instead to the court.
(2)   Where there are several trustees, a requirement to give notice to the trustees is satisfied by giving notice to any one of them, but a notice relating to a change in trustees must be given to a trustee who will continue to be a trustee after the change takes effect.

X. – 1:303: Mandatory Nature of Rules
The rules of this Book are mandatory, except as otherwise provided.

Chapter 2: Constitution of Trusts
Section 1: Basic Rules on Constitution by Juridical Act
X. – 2:101: Requirements for Constitution
A trust is constituted in relation to a fund vested in the truster, without any further requirement, if:
(a)   the truster declares an intention to constitute a trust in relation to that fund;
(b)   the declaration satisfies the requirements set out in X. – 2:201 (Requirements for a declaration); and
(c)   either X. – 2:102 (Constitution by transfer) or X. – 2:103 (Constitution without transfer) applies.

X. – 2:102: Constitution by Transfer
(1)   If the other requirements for constitution are satisfied, a trust is constituted when in implementation of the declaration the fund is transferred to a person who agrees to be a trustee or is identified in the declaration as a person who is or is to be a trustee.
(2)   The rules on contracts for donation apply analogously to an agreement between truster and intended trustee for the transfer of the fund in the truster's lifetime.
(3)   Where the truster has made a binding unilateral undertaking to constitute a trust to a person who is intended to be a trustee of the fund, that person is a trustee of the right to performance of the obligation created by the undertaking, unless that right is rejected.

X. – 2:103: Constitution Without Transfer
(1)   If the other requirements for constitution are satisfied, a trust is constituted by the declaration alone, without a transfer, if:
(a)   the declaration indicates that the truster is to be a sole trustee;
(b)   the declaration is testamentary and does not provide for a trustee; or
(c)   (i)   the truster does all of the acts required of the truster to transfer the fund to the intended trustee,
       (ii)   the intended trustee does not or cannot accept the fund, and
       (iii) the declaration does not provide otherwise.
(2)   When a trust is constituted under paragraph (1), the truster becomes a trustee.

Section 2: Declaration
X. – 2:201: Requirements for a Declaration
(1)   The requirements referred to in Section 1 (Basic rules on constitution by juridical act) for a declaration of an intention to constitute a trust are that:
(a)   the declaration is made by the truster or a person who has authority to make it on the truster's behalf; and
(b)   the declaration complies with any requirement as to form set out in X. – 2:203 (Formal requirements for declaration).
(2)   No notice or publication of the declaration to any party is required.

X. – 2:202: Mode of Declaration
(1)   A person declares an intention to constitute a trust when that person by statements or conduct indicates an intention that the person in whom the fund is or is to be vested is to be legally bound as a trustee.

(2)   In determining whether one or more statements contained in a testamentary or other instrument determining rights over an asset amount to a declaration of an intention to constitute a trust in relation to that asset, an interpretation of those statements which gives effect to their entirety is to be preferred.

X. – 2:203: Formal Requirements for Declaration

(1)   Where the transfer of a fund requires the making of an instrument by the transferor, the declaration of an intention to constitute a trust is of no effect unless contained in the instrument of transfer or made in the same or an equivalent form.

(2)   A declaration that the truster is to be the sole trustee is of no effect unless made in the same form as a unilateral undertaking to donate.

(3)   Where the trust is to be created on the death of the maker of the declaration, the declaration is of no effect unless made by testamentary instrument.

X. – 2:204: Revocation or Variation of Declaration

(1)   The maker of a declaration may revoke or vary the declaration or a term of the declaration at any time before the trust is constituted.

(2)   A revocation or variation is of no effect unless it satisfies the formality requirements, if any, which applied to the declaration.

(3)   However, a declaration or term set out in an instrument may be revoked by substantially destroying or defacing that instrument, so far as it relates to that declaration or term, if the applicable national rules permit a statement intended to have legal effect contained in such an instrument to be revoked by that means.

X. – 2:205: Effects When Declaration Does Not Satisfy Requirements

If the fund is transferred to the intended trustee in implementation of a declaration which does not satisfy the requirements of X. – 2:201 (Requirements for a declaration), the transferee takes the fund on the terms of a trust to re-transfer the fund to the truster.

Section 3: Refusal of Trust and Rejection of Right to Benefit
X. – 2:301: Right of Trustee to Refuse the Trust

(1)   If a person has become a trustee without agreeing to act when a trust is constituted, that person may refuse to act as a trustee by notice to:

(a)   the truster; or

(b)   any co-trustee who has full legal capacity and agrees to act as a trustee.

(2)   Refusal may take the form of either a rejection of all the rights which have vested or a disclaimer of the whole trust, but operates as both a rejection and a disclaimer.

(3)   A refusal may not be revoked.

(4)   Where a person reasonably incurs costs in order to refuse, that person has a right to be reimbursed by any co-trustees who accept the trust fund and agree to act or, if there are no such co-trustees, the truster.

(5)   Where a sole trustee refuses or there is no co-trustee who accepts the trust fund and agrees to act, the truster becomes a trustee of the fund in accordance with X. – 2:103 (Constitution without transfer) paragraph (1)(c), unless the declaration of the intention to constitute a trust provides
otherwise.

(6)   Subject to the previous paragraphs of this Article, the requirements for a refusal and its effects are determined by the application or analogous application of II. – 4:303 (Right or benefit may be rejected).

X. – 2:302: Rejection of Right to Benefit or Eligibility for Benefit

A beneficiary's right under II. – 4:303 (Right or benefit may be rejected) to reject a right to benefit or an eligibility for benefit is exercised by giving notice to the trustees.

Section 4: Additional Rules for Particular Instances
X. – 2:401: Whether Donation or Trust
(1)   Where a person transfers an asset to another gratuitously and it is uncertain whether or to what extent the transferor intends to donate the asset or to constitute a trust in respect of it for the benefit of the transferor, it is presumed that the transferor intends:
(a)   to donate to the transferee, if this would be consistent with the relationship between the parties and past or concurrent dealings of the transferor;
(b)   in any other case, that the transferee be a trustee for the benefit of the transferor.
(2)   A presumption in paragraph (1) may be rebutted (and the alternative intention in paragraph (1) established) by showing that at the time of transfer the transferor did not or, as the case may be, did intend to dispose of the asset for the exclusive benefit of the transferee.
(3)   Paragraphs (1) and (2) apply correspondingly where the transfer is to several transferees (including where the transfer is to the transferor and another).
(4)   Where it is shown or presumed that the transferor intends to dispose of the fund for the benefit of a transferee only in part, or for the benefit of one transferee, but not a co–transferee, the transferor is to be regarded as intending to constitute a trust for the benefit of the transferee to that extent.

X. – 2:402: Priority of Rules of Succession Law
Where the trust is to take effect on the truster's death, the trust is subject to the prior application of those rules of succession law which determine:
(a)   how the deceased's estate is to be disposed of in satisfaction of the funeral costs and debts of the deceased; and
(b)(i) whether the truster was free to dispose of any part of the fund,
(ii)   whether any person has a claim in respect of any part of the fund by reason of a family or other connection to the deceased, and
(iii) how such claims are to be satisfied.

X. – 2:403: Trust in Respect of Right to Legacy Pending Transfer of Legacy
Where a truster declares that a legatee is to be a trustee in relation to a legacy from the truster and that declaration satisfies the requirements set out in X. – 2:201 (Requirements for a declaration), but the legacy has not yet been transferred, the legatee is a trustee of the right against the truster's successor which arises in respect of the legacy on the truster's death.

Chapter 3: Trust Fund
Section 1: Requirements for the Initial Trust Fund
X. – 3:101: Trust Fund
(1)   Trust assets, whether or not of the same kind, form a single trust fund if they are vested in the same trustees and either:
(a)   the trust terms relating to the assets indicate that they form a single fund or require them to be administered together; or
(b)   separate trusts relating to the assets are merged in performance of the obligations under those trusts.
(2)   Where trusts are constituted at the same time, on the same terms, and with the same trustees, the trust assets form a single trust fund unless the trust terms provide otherwise.
(3)   In this Book "part of the trust fund" means a share of the trust fund, a specific asset or share of an asset in the fund, or a specific amount to be provided out of the fund.

X. – 3:102: Permissible Trust Assets
Trust assets may consist of proprietary or other rights, so far as these are transferable.

X. – 3:103: Ascertainability and Segregation of the Trust Fund
(1)   A trust is only created in relation to a fund in so far as, at the time the trust is to come into effect,

(a)   the fund is sufficiently defined in the trust terms or the assets forming the fund are other-
      wise ascertainable; and
(b)   the fund is segregated from other assets.
(2)   A declaration of intention to create a trust in relation to an unsegregated fund is to be regarded, so far as the other terms of the declaration permit, as a declaration of an intention to
create a trust of the entire mixture containing the fund on the terms that:
(a)   the trustee is obliged to segregate the intended trust fund; and
(b)   until the fund is segregated, the rights and obligations envisaged by the terms of the
      declaration apply in relation to a corresponding part of the mixture.

Section 2: Changes to the Trust Fund
X. – 3:201: Additions to the Trust Fund
(1)   After a trust is created, an asset which is capable of being a trust asset becomes part of the
trust fund if it is acquired by a trustee:
(a)   in performance of the obligations under the trust;
(b)   as an addition to or by making use of the trust fund;
(c)   by making use of information or an opportunity obtained in the capacity of trustee, if the
      use is not in accordance with the terms of the trust; or
(d)   when or after the trustee disposed of that asset otherwise than in accordance with the
      terms of the trust.
(2)   Where there are several trustees, an asset may become part of the trust fund in
accordance with this Article without being acquired by all of them.

X. – 3:202: Subtractions from the Trust Fund
(1)   An asset ceases to be part of the trust fund when it ceases to be vested in a person who is
under the obligation set out in X. – 1:201 (Definition of a trust).
(2)   Where there are several trustees, an asset remains part of the trust fund so long as it is
vested in at least one of the trustees in that capacity.

X. – 3:203: Mixing of the Trust Fund with Other Assets
(1)   If trust assets are mixed with other assets vested in the trustee in such a way that the trust assets cease to be identifiable, a trust arises in respect of the mixture and VIII. – 5:202 (Commingling)
applies analogously, as if each patrimony had a different owner, so as to determine the share of
the mixture which is to be administered and disposed of in accordance with the original trust.
(2)   If the other assets are the personal patrimony of the trustee, any diminution in the mixture
is to be allocated to the trustee's personal share.

X. – 3:204: Loss or Exhaustion of Trust Fund
(1)   A trust ends when the trust fund has been completely disposed of in performance of the
obligations under the trust or for any other reason there ceases to be a trust fund.
(2)   Where the trustee is liable to reinstate the trust fund as a result of nonperformance of
obligations under the trust, the trust revives if the trust fund is reinstated.

Chapter 4: Trust Terms and Invalidity
Section 1: Trust Terms
X. – 4:101: Interpretation
Without prejudice to the other rules on the interpretation of unilateral juridical acts, if the meaning of a trust term cannot otherwise be established, interpretations to be preferred are those
which:
(a)   give effect to the entirety of the words and expressions used;
(b)   prevent reasonable conduct of a trustee from amounting to a non-performance;
(c)   prevent or best reduce any incompleteness in provision for disposal of the trust fund; and
(d)   confer on the truster a right to benefit or enlarge such right, if the trust is constituted gratuitously in the truster's lifetime and the truster has or may have reserved such a right.

X. – 4:102: Incomplete Disposal of the Trust Fund

(1)   To the extent that the trust terms and the rules of this Book do not otherwise dispose of the trust fund in circumstances which have arisen, the trust fund is to be disposed of for the benefit of the truster.

(2)   However, if the incomplete disposal of the trust fund arises because effect cannot be given to a trust for advancement of a public benefit purpose or because performance of the obligations under such a trust does not exhaust the trust fund, the trust fund is to be disposed of for the advancement of the public benefit purpose which most closely resembles the original purpose.

X. – 4:103: Ascertainability of Beneficiaries

(1)   A trust term which purports to confer a right to benefit is valid only if the beneficiary is sufficiently identified by the truster or is otherwise ascertainable at the time the benefit is due.

(2)   A trust term which permits a trustee to benefit those members of a class of persons which the trustee or a third person selects is valid only if, at the time the selection is permitted, it can be determined with reasonable certainty whether any given person is a member of that class.

(3)   A person may be a beneficiary notwithstanding that that person comes into existence only after the trust is created.

X. – 4:104: Ascertainability of Right to Benefit or Eligibility for Benefit

(1)   A right to benefit or eligibility for benefit is valid only in so far as the benefit is sufficiently defined in the trust terms or is otherwise ascertainable at the time the benefit is due or to be conferred.

(2)   If the benefit to be conferred is not ascertainable only because a third party cannot or does not make a choice, the trustees may make that choice unless the trust terms provide otherwise.

X. – 4:105: Trusts to Pay Creditors

A trust for the purpose of paying a debt, or for the benefit of a creditor as such, takes effect as a trust to benefit the debtor by a performance of the debtor's obligation discharging the debtor.

Section 2: Invalidity
X. – 4:201: Avoidance by the Truster

Without prejudice to other necessary adaptations, Book II Chapter 7 (Grounds of invalidity) is modified as follows in its application to trusts constituted gratuitously in the truster's lifetime:

(a)   the truster may avoid the trust or a trust term if the trust was constituted or the term included because of a mistake of fact or law, regardless of whether the requirements of II. – 7:201 (Mistake) paragraph (1)(b) are satisfied;

(b)   a truster who was dependent on, or was the more vulnerable party in a relationship of trust with, a beneficiary may avoid the trust or a trust term in so far as it provides for benefit to that beneficiary unless that beneficiary proves that the beneficiary did not exploit the truster's situation by taking an excessive benefit or grossly unfair advantage;

(c)   the reasonable time for giving notice of avoidance (II. – 7:210 (Time)) does not commence so long as:

(i)   the truster exercises an exclusive right to benefit from the income; or

(ii)   the trust fund consists of one or more rights to benefit which are not yet due; and

(d)   where sub-paragraph (c)(i) applies, acceptance of benefit is not to be regarded as an implied confirmation of the trust.

X. – 4:202: Protection of Trustees and Third Parties after Avoidance

(1)   The trustee's title to the trust fund is unaffected by avoidance.

(2)   Unless the trustee knew or could reasonably be expected to know that the trust or trust term might be avoided:

(a)   a trustee is not liable in respect of any administration or disposition of the trust fund which was in accordance with the terms of the trust before the trust was avoided;

(b)   a trustee may invoke against the person entitled to benefit as a result of avoidance defences which the trustee could have invoked against the beneficiary who had a right to that
benefit before avoidance; and
(c)   a trustee retains any right of recourse to the trust fund which arose before avoidance.
(3)   Avoidance of the trust does not affect the rights of a third party who before avoidance
acquired a beneficiary's right to benefit, or a security right or other limited right in that right to
benefit, if:
(a)   the third party neither knew nor had reason to know that the trust or trust term could be
avoided; and
(b)   the disposition is not gratuitous.

X. – 4:203: Unenforceable Trust Purposes
(1)   A trust which is for a purpose other than to benefit beneficiaries or to advance public benefit purposes takes effect as a trust for the truster.
(2)   The trustee has a revocable authority to dispose of the trust fund in accordance with the
original trust for the advancement of the unenforceable purpose in so far as:
(a)   advancement of that purpose does not infringe a fundamental principle or mandatory rule
and is not contrary to the public interest;
(b)   it can be determined with reasonable certainty whether any given disposal of the trust
fund is or is not for its advancement; and
(c)   the disposal is not manifestly disproportionate to any likely benefit from that disposal.

Chapter 5: Trustee Decision-Making and Powers
Section 1: Trustee Decision-Making
X. – 5:101: Trustee Discretion
(1)   Subject to the obligations of a trustee under this Book and exceptions provided for by
other rules, the trustees are free to determine whether, when and how the exercise of their
powers and discretions is best suited to performing their obligations under the trust.
(2)   Except in so far as the trust terms or other rules provide otherwise, the trustees are not
bound by, and are not to regard themselves as bound by, any directions or wishes of any of the
parties to the trust or other persons.
(3)   The trustees are not obliged to disclose the reasons for the exercise of their discretion unless the trust is for the advancement of a public benefit purpose or the trust terms provide
otherwise.

X. – 5:102: Decision-Making by Several Trustees
If there are several trustees, their powers and discretions are exercised by simple majority decision unless the trust terms or other rules of this Book provide otherwise.

X. – 5:103: Conflict of Interest in Exercise of Power or Discretion
Unless the trust terms provide otherwise, a trustee may not participate in a decision to exercise
or not to exercise a power or discretion if the effect of the decision is to confer, confirm, or
enlarge a right to benefit or eligibility for benefit in favour of the trustee.

Section 2: Powers of a Trustee
Sub-section 1: General Rules
X. – 5:201: Powers in General
(1)   Except where restricted by the trust terms or other rules of this Book, a trustee may do any
act in performance of the obligations under the trust which:
(a)   an owner of the fund might lawfully do; or
(b)   a person might be authorised to do on behalf of another.
(2)   Subject to restrictions or modifications in the trust terms, the other Articles of this Section
provide for the powers of a trustee in particular cases.

X. – 5:202: Restriction in Case of Minimum Number of Trustees
(1)   Where there are fewer trustees than a minimum required by the trust terms or these rules, the trustees may only exercise:
(a)   a power to appoint trustees;
(b)   the right to apply to court for assistance;
(c)   a right under X. – 6:201 (Right of reimbursement and indemnification out of the trust fund); and
(d)   any other right or power of a trustee to the extent that its exercise is:
    (i)   expressly provided for in the circumstances by the trust terms;
    (ii)   necessary for the preservation of the trust fund; or
    (iii) necessary for the satisfaction of trust debts whose performance is due or impending.
(2)   If the trust is constituted by a transfer to at least two trustees the minimum number of trustees is two, unless the trust terms provide otherwise.

Sub-section 2: Particular Powers of a Trustee
X. – 5:203: Power to Authorise Agent
(1)   The trustees may authorise an agent to act on behalf of the trustees and, subject to the restrictions set out in the following Articles of this Section, may entrust to another performance of obligations under the trust.
(2)   Several trustees may authorise one of them to act on their behalf.
(3)   However, personal performance by a trustee is required for decisions as to whether or how to exercise:
(a)   a discretion to confer benefit on a beneficiary or to choose a public benefit purpose to be advanced or its manner of advancement;
(b)   a power to change the trustees; or
(c)   a power to delegate performance of obligations under the trust.
(4)   A person to whom performance of an obligation is entrusted has the same obligations as a trustee, so far as they relate to that performance.
(5)   A trustee is obliged not to conclude, without good reason, a contract of mandate which is not in writing or which includes the following terms:
(a)   a term conferring an irrevocable mandate;
(b)   terms excluding the obligations of an agent set out in Book IV. D., Chapter 3, Section 1 (Main obligations of agent) or modifying them to the detriment of the principal;
(c)   a term permitting the agent to subcontract;
(d)   terms permitting a conflict of interest on the part of the agent;
(e)   a term excluding or restricting the agent's liability to the principal for non-performance.
(6)   The trustees are obliged to keep the performance of the agent under review and, if required in the circumstances, give a direction to the agent or terminate the mandate relationship.

X. – 5:204: Power to Transfer Title to Person Undertaking to Be a Trustee
(1)   The trustees may transfer trust assets to a person who undertakes to be a trustee in relation to the assets and to dispose of them as the original trustees direct and in default of any such direction to transfer them back to the original trustees on demand.
(2)   The recipient must be:
(a)   a person who gives such undertakings in the course of business;
(b)   a legal person controlled by the trustees; or
(c)   a legal person designated in an enactment as eligible to carry out such a trust obligation or satisfying requirements set out therein for this purpose.
(3)   X. – 5:203 (Power to authorise agent) paragraphs (5) and (6) apply correspondingly.

X. – 5:205: Power to Transfer Physical Control to a Storer

(1)   The trustees may place trust assets and documents relating to those assets in the physical control of a person who undertakes to keep the trust assets safe and to deliver them back to the trustees on demand.

(2)   X. – 5:204 (Power to transfer title to person undertaking to be a trustee) paragraphs (2) and (3) apply correspondingly.

X. – 5:206: Power to Delegate

A trustee may entrust to another the performance of any of the trustee's obligations under the trust and the exercise of any of the trustee's powers, including the exercise of a discretion, authority to dispose of trust assets and the power to delegate, but remains responsible for performance in accordance with III. – 2:106 (Performance entrusted to another).

X. – 5:207: Power to Select Investments

In so far as the trustees are obliged to invest the trust fund, the trustees may invest in any form of investment and determine the particular manner of investment which is best suited to fulfil that obligation.

X. – 5:208: Power to Submit Trust Accounts for Audit

Where appropriate, a trustee may submit the trust accounts for an audit by an independent and competent auditor.

Chapter 6: Obligations and Rights of Trustees and Trust Auxiliaries
Section 1: Obligations of a Trustee
Sub-section 1: General Rules
X. – 6:101: General Obligation of a Trustee

(1)   A trustee is obliged to administer the trust fund and exercise any power to dispose of the fund as a prudent manager of another's affairs for the benefit of the beneficiaries or the advancement of the public benefit purposes, in accordance with the law and the trust terms.

(2)   In particular, a trustee is obliged to act with the required care and skill, fairly and in good faith.

(3)   Except in so far as the trust terms provide otherwise:

(a)   these obligations include the particular obligations set out in X. – 6:102 (Required care and skill) and the following sub-section; and

(b) an administration or disposal of the trust fund is of benefit to a beneficiary only if it is for that person's economic benefit.

X. – 6:102: Required Care and Skill

(1)   A trustee is required to act with the care and skill which can be expected of a reasonably competent and careful person managing another's affairs, having regard to whether the trustee has a right to remuneration.

(2)   If the trustee is acting in the course of a profession, the trustee must act with the care and skill that is expected of a member of that profession.

Sub-section 2: Particular Obligations of a Trustee
X. – 6:103: Obligations to Segregate, Safeguard and Insure

(1)   A trustee is obliged to keep the trust fund segregated from other patrimony and to keep the trust assets safe.

(2)   In particular, a trustee may not invest in assets which are especially at risk of misappropriation unless particular care is taken for their safekeeping. Where the asset is a document embodying a right to a performance which is owed to whoever is the holder of the document, such care is taken if the document is placed in a storer's safekeeping in accordance with X. – 5:205 (Power to transfer physical control to a storer).

(3)   So far as it is possible and appropriate to do so, the trustee is obliged to insure the trust assets against loss.

X. – 6:104: Obligation to Inform and Report

(1)   A trustee is obliged to inform a beneficiary who has a right to benefit of the existence of the trust and that beneficiary's right.

(2)   A trustee is obliged to make reasonable efforts to inform a beneficiary who has an eligibility for benefit of the existence of the trust and that beneficiary's eligibility.

(3)   In determining what efforts are reasonable for the purposes of paragraph (2), regard is to be had to:

(a)   whether the expense required is proportionate to the value of the benefit which might be conferred on that beneficiary;

(b)   whether the beneficiary is a member of a class whose members the trustee is required to benefit; and

(c)   the practicalities of identifying and communicating with the beneficiary.

(4)   So far as appropriate, a trustee is obliged to make available information about the state and investment of the trust fund, trust debts, and disposals of trust assets and their proceeds.

X. – 6:105: Obligation to Keep Trust Accounts

A trustee is obliged to keep accounts in respect of the trust funds (trust accounts).

X. – 6:106: Obligation to Permit Inspection and Copying of Trust Documents

(1)   A trustee must permit a beneficiary or other person entitled to enforce performance of the obligations under the trust to inspect the trust documents and to make copies of them at that person's own expense.

(2)   Paragraph (1) does not apply to:

(a)   the opinions of a legal adviser relating to actual or contemplated legal proceedings by the trustees in that capacity against the person seeking inspection; and evidence gathered for such proceedings;

(b)   communications between the trustees and other beneficiaries and any other communications whose disclosure would result in a breach of confidence owed by the trustees in that capacity to another.

(3)   The trustees may refuse inspection and copying of trust documents so far as these relate to information which is confidential to the trustees in that capacity if the beneficiary does not provide adequate assurance that the confidentiality will be maintained.

(4)   Unless the trust is for the advancement of public benefit purposes, the trustees may also refuse inspection and copying of documents so far as the documents disclose the reasons for the trustees' decision to exercise or not to exercise a discretion, the deliberations of the trustees which preceded that decision, and material relevant to the deliberations.

(5)   The trust terms may enlarge the rights of inspection and copying which are provided for by this Article.

(6)   In this Book "trust documents" are:

(a)   any documents containing the truster's declaration of intentions relating to the trust (whether or not intended to be binding) and any juridical act or court order varying the trust terms;

(b)   minutes of meetings of the trustees;

(c)   records made and notices and other communications in writing received by a trustee in that capacity, including the opinions of a legal adviser engaged by a trustee at the trust fund's expense;

(d)   any documents containing juridical acts concluded or made by the trustees;

(e)   receipts for disposal of trust assets; and

(f)   the trust accounts.

X. – 6:107: Obligation to Invest

(1)   A trustee is obliged to invest the trust fund, so far as available for investment, and in particular:

(a)   to dispose of assets which ordinarily neither produce income nor increase in value and to invest the proceeds;

(b) to take professional advice on investment of the fund, if the trustees lack the expertise required for the efficient and prudent investment of funds of the size and nature of the trust fund;
(c) to make a spread of investments in which overall:
(i) the risks of failure or loss of particular investments are diversified; and
(ii) the expected gain significantly outweighs the potential failure or loss;
unless the trust fund is so small that a spread of investments is inappropriate; and
(d) to review at appropriate intervals the suitableness of retaining or changing the investments.
(2) A trustee is not obliged to invest assets:
(a) which are imminently required for transfer to or use by a beneficiary or for satisfaction of a
trust debt; or
(b) whose investment would otherwise impede the trustees in carrying out their other obligations under this Book.
(3) The obligation to invest does not authorise a trustee to dispose of trust assets which according to the trust terms are to be retained by the trustees or transferred in kind to a beneficiary.

X. – 6:108: Obligation Not to Acquire Trust Assets or Trust Creditors' Rights
(1) A trustee is obliged not to purchase a trust asset or the right of a trust creditor against the
trustees, whether personally or by means of an agent.
(2) A contract for the sale of a trust asset which is concluded as a result of non-performance of
this obligation may be avoided by any other party to the trust or any person entitled to enforce
performance of the obligations under the trust.
(3) The right to avoid is in addition to any remedy for non-performance.
(4) This Article applies with appropriate modifications to other contracts for the acquisition or
use of a trust asset or a right corresponding to a trust debt.

X. – 6:109: Obligation Not to Obtain Unauthorised Enrichment or Advantage
(1) A trustee is obliged not to make use of the trust fund, or information or an opportunity obtained in the capacity of trustee, to obtain an enrichment unless that use is authorised by the
trust terms.
(2) A trustee may not set off a right to performance from a beneficiary, which is owed to the
trustee in a personal capacity, against that beneficiary's right to benefit.

X. – 6:110: Obligations Regarding Co-Trustees
A trustee is obliged to:
(a) cooperate with co-trustees in performing the obligations under the trust; and
(b) take appropriate action if a trustee knows or has reason to suspect that:
(i) a co-trustee has failed to perform any obligation under, or arising out of, the trust, or such
non-performance is impending; and
(ii) the non-performance is likely to result or have resulted in loss to the trust fund.

Section 2: Rights of a Trustee
X. – 6:201: Right to Reimbursement and Indemnification out of the Trust Fund
A trustee has a right to reimbursement or indemnification out of the trust fund in respect of expenditure and trust debts which the trustee incurs in performance of the obligations under the
trust.

X. – 6:202: Right to Remuneration out of the Trust Fund
(1) A trustee has a right to such remuneration out of the trust fund as is provided for by the
trust terms.
(2) Unless this is inconsistent with the trust terms, a trustee who acts as a trustee in the course
of a profession has a right to reasonable remuneration out of the trust fund for work done in
performance of the obligations under the trust.
(3) Paragraph (2) does not apply if:
(a) the trustee, in the capacity of beneficiary, is entitled to significant benefit from the trust
fund; or

(b)   the trust was created as a result of a contract between the trustee and the truster; or

(c)   the trust is for the advancement of public benefit purposes.

X. – 6:203: Rights in Respect of Unauthorised Acquisitions

(1)   This Article applies where:

(a)   a trustee acquires an asset or other enrichment as a result of a non-performance of an obligation under the trust; and

(b)   the asset becomes part of the trust fund or the enrichment is added to the trust fund in performance of an obligation to disgorge.

(2)   The trustee has a right to reimbursement or indemnification for any expenditure or obligation which it was necessary to incur to make the acquisition. If the trustee previously satisfied in full or in part a liability under X. – 7:201 (Liability of trustee to reinstate the trust fund), the trustee has a right to reimbursement from the trust fund to the extent that after the acquisition the trust fund is more than reinstated.

(3)   The trustee also has a right to reasonable remuneration if:

(a)   the acquisition was made in good faith to increase the trust fund; and

(b)   the trustee would be entitled to remuneration under X. – 6:202 (Right to remuneration out of the trust fund) paragraph (2)(b) if the acquisition had been in performance of an obligation under the trust.

(4)   If the acquisition resulted from a non-performance of the obligation under X. – 6:109 (Obligation not to obtain unauthorised enrichment or advantage) to which a beneficiary validly consented, the trustee may waive the rights under paragraphs (2) and (3) and take over the consenting beneficiary's right to benefit from the acquisition.

(5)   A trustee is not entitled under this Article to more than the value of the acquisition.

X. – 6:204: Corresponding Rights Against Beneficiaries

(1)   Where the right of a trustee under X. – 6:201 (Right to reimbursement and indemnification out of the trust fund) exceeds the trust fund, the trustee may recover the excess from the beneficiaries.

(2)   The liability of a beneficiary under paragraph (1) is:

(a)   limited to the enrichment which that beneficiary has obtained in accordance with the trust terms; and

(b)   subject to the defence of disenrichment, VII. – 6:101 (Disenrichment) applying with appropriate adaptations.

(3)   The right to recover under paragraph (1) ends six months after the right to reimbursement or indemnification has arisen.

X. – 6:205: Right to Insure Against Personal Liability at Trust Fund's Expense

(1)   A trustee has a right to reimbursement or indemnification out of the trust fund in respect of expenditure or a debt which the trustee reasonably incurs to obtain insurance against liability under X. – 7:201 (Liability of trustee to reinstate the trust fund).

(2)   Paragraph (1) does not apply in so far as:

(a)   the trustee has a right to remuneration for performing the obligations under the trust; or

(b)   the insurance is against liability arising out of a non-performance which is intentional or grossly negligent.

Section 3: Obligations of a Trust Auxiliary
X. – 6:301: Obligations of a Trust Auxiliary

(1)   A trust auxiliary is obliged to disclose the identity of the trustees if this information is known to the trust auxiliary and is not otherwise apparent.

(2)   In deciding whether to exercise a power a trust auxiliary is obliged:

(a)   to act in good faith; and

(b)   not to obtain an enrichment which is not authorised by the trust terms.

Chapter 7: Remedies for Non-Performance
Section 1: Specific Performance, Judicial Review and Ancillary Remedies
X. – 7:101: Specific Performance
(1)   The enforcement of specific performance of an obligation under the trust includes the prevention of a trustee from disposing of or otherwise dealing with a trust asset otherwise than in accordance with the terms of the trust.
(2)   Specific performance cannot be enforced if performance requires a trustee to exercise a discretion.

X. – 7:102: Judicial Review
(1)   On the application of a party to the trust or a person entitled to enforce performance of an obligation under the trust, a court may review a decision of the trustees or a trust auxiliary whether or how to exercise a power or discretion conferred on them by the trust terms or this Book.
(2)   A former trustee who has been removed by the trustees or a trust auxiliary without the trustee's consent has a corresponding right to judicial review of that decision.
(3)   A court may avoid a decision of the trustees or a trust auxiliary which is irrational or grossly unreasonable, motivated by irrelevant or improper considerations, or otherwise an abuse of power or outside the powers of the trustees or the trust auxiliary.

X. – 7:103: Further Remedies
Other rules may provide for:
(a)   accounts and inquiries concerning the trust fund and its administration and disposal, as directed by court order;
(b)   payment or transfer into court of money or other assets in the trust fund;
(c)   the appointment by court order of a receiver to administer a trust fund;
(d)   the exercise of rights and powers of a trustee by a public officer or body, in particular in relation to trusts to advance public benefit purposes;
(e)   suspension of the rights and powers of the trustees to administer and dispose of the fund;
in cases of actual or suspected non-performance of the obligations under the trust.

Section 2: Reparation and Disgorgement of Unauthorised Enrichment
X. – 7:201: Liability of Trustee to Reinstate the Trust Fund
(1)   A trustee is liable to reinstate the trust fund in respect of loss caused to the trust fund by non-performance of any obligation under, or arising out of, the trust, if the non-performance:
(a)   is not excused; and
(b)   results from the trustee's failure to exercise the required care and skill.
(2)   However, a person is liable under paragraph (1) only if that person knew, or it was manifest, that that person was a trustee.
(3)   A trustee is not liable merely because a co-trustee, an agent or other person entrusted with performance, or an authorised recipient of trust assets has caused loss to the trust fund.
(4)   Paragraph (3) does not prejudice any liability of the trustee arising:
(a)   under paragraph (1) out of the trustee's own non-performance of an obligation under the trust, in particular:
   (i)   an obligation to act with the required care and skill when choosing to appoint or engage that person and agreeing the terms of the engagement; or
   (ii)   the obligation to keep the performance of that person under review and, if required in the circumstances, to take measures to protect the trust fund; or
(b)   out of delegation of performance (X. – 5:206 (Power to delegate));
(c)   under VI. – 3:201 (Accountability for damage caused by employees and representatives); or
(d)   because the trustee induced, assisted or collaborated in that person's non-performance.
(5)   III. – 3:702 (General measure of damages) applies with appropriate adaptations to determine the measure of reinstatement.
(6)   The following rights of a trustee are suspended until the trustee has completely reinstated the trust fund:

(a)   any right of recourse to the trust fund; and
(b)   any right to benefit which the trustee has in the capacity of beneficiary.
(7)   This Article is subject to the trust terms.

X. – 7:202: Liability of Trustee to Compensate a Beneficiary

(1)   A trustee who is liable under X. – 7:201 (Liability of trustee to reinstate the trust fund) is also obliged to compensate a beneficiary who, despite reinstatement of the trust fund, does not obtain a benefit to which that beneficiary was entitled or, if there had been no failure of performance, would have been entitled under the trust terms.
(2)   The beneficiary has the same right to compensation as arises from non-performance of a contractual obligation.
(3)   This Article is subject to the trust terms.

X. – 7:203: Disgorgement of Unauthorised Enrichment

Where a trustee obtains an enrichment as a result of non-performance of the obligation under X. – 6:109 (Obligation not to obtain unauthorised enrichment or advantage) and that enrichment does not become part of the trust fund under X. – 3:201 (Additions to the trust fund), the trustee is obliged to add the enrichment to the trust fund or, if that is not possible, to add its monetary value.

Section 3: Defences
X. – 7:301: Consent of Beneficiary to Non-Performance

(1)   A trustee has a defence to liability to the extent that reinstatement, compensation or disgorgement would benefit a beneficiary who validly consented to the non-performance.
(2)   A beneficiary consents to a non-performance when that beneficiary agrees to conduct of the trustee which amounts to a non-performance and either:
(a)   the beneficiary knew that such conduct would amount to a nonperformance; or
(b)   it was manifest that such conduct would amount to a non-performance.
(3)   Paragraph (1) applies whether or not the non-performance enriched or disadvantaged the beneficiary who consented.
(4)   Where a beneficiary participates in the non-performance in the capacity of trustee, paragraph (1) applies in relation to any co-trustees who are liable. A right of recourse between the solidary debtors as regards any residual liability to reinstate the trust fund or compensate a beneficiary is unaffected.
(5)   A consent is not valid if it results from a mistake which was caused by false information given by the trustee or the trustee's non-performance of an obligation to inform.

X. – 7:302: Prescription

The general period of prescription for a right to performance of an obligation under a trust does not begin to run against a beneficiary until benefit to that beneficiary is due.

X. – 7:303 Protection of the Trustee

(1)   A trustee is discharged by performing to a person who, after reasonable inquiry, appears to be entitled to the benefit conferred.
(2)   The right of the beneficiary who was entitled to the benefit against the recipient of the benefit arising under Book VII (Unjustified enrichment) is unaffected.

Section 4: Solidary Liability and Forfeiture
X. – 7:401: Solidary Liability

(1)   Where several trustees are liable in respect of the same non-performance, their liability is solidary.
(2)   As between the solidary debtors themselves, the shares of liability are in proportion to each debtor's relative responsibility for the non-performance, having regard to each debtor's skills and experience as a trustee.

(3)   A debtor's relative responsibility for a non-performance to which that debtor consented is not reduced merely because that debtor took no active part in bringing it about.

X. – 7:402: Forfeiture of Collaborating Beneficiary's Right to Benefit

(1)   Where a beneficiary collaborated in a trustee's non-performance, a court may order on the application of that trustee or another beneficiary that the right to benefit of the beneficiary who collaborated be forfeited.

(2)   The right to benefit of a beneficiary who validly consented to the nonperformance, but did not collaborate in it, may be forfeited only to the extent that the beneficiary has been enriched by the non-performance.

(3)   To the extent that a beneficiary's right to benefit is forfeited under this Article, benefit which is otherwise due to that beneficiary is to be applied so as to satisfy the trustee's liability until either the liability is extinguished or the right to benefit is exhausted.

Chapter 8: Change of Trustees or Trust Auxiliary
Section 1: General Rules on Change of Trustees
X. – 8:101: Powers to Change Trustees in General

(1)   After the creation of a trust, a person may be appointed a trustee and a trustee may resign or be removed:
(a)   in accordance with a power:
    (i)   under the trust terms or
    (ii)   conferred on the trustees by this Section; or
(b)   by court order under this Section.

(2)   The exercise of a power within paragraph (1)(a) is of no effect unless it is in writing. The same applies to a binding direction to trustees regarding the exercise of such a power.

(3)   An exercise of a power under the trust terms by a person who is not also a continuing trustee does not take effect until notice is given to the continuing trustees.

(4)   The resignation or removal of a sole trustee is effective only if a substitute trustee is appointed at the same time.

X. – 8:102: Powers to Change Trustees Conferred on Trustees

(1)   The powers conferred by this Section on trustees may only be exercised:
(a)   by unanimous decision; and
(b)   if in the circumstances a trust auxiliary does not have a corresponding power or the trust auxiliary cannot or does not exercise such a power within a reasonable period after a request to do so by the trustees.

(2)   Subject to paragraph (1), the trustees are obliged to exercise their powers under this Section in accordance with any joint direction by the beneficiaries if the beneficiaries have a joint right to terminate the trust in respect of the whole fund.

(3)   The trust terms may modify or exclude the powers conferred by this Section on trustees.

Section 2: Appointment of Trustees
X. – 8:201: General Restrictions on Appointments

(1)   An appointment of a person as trustee is of no effect if:
(a)   it is manifest that the co-trustees would have power to remove that person, if appointed, on grounds of that person's inability, refusal to act, or unsuitability;
(b)   the person appointed does not agree to act as trustee; or
(c)   the appointment exceeds a maximum number of trustees provided for by the trust terms.

(2)   A provision in the trust terms that there is to be only one trustee takes effect as a maximum of two.

X. – 8:202: Appointment by Trust Auxiliary or Trustees

(1)   The trustees may appoint one or more additional trustees.

(2)   The continuing trustees may appoint a substitute trustee for a person who has ceased to be a trustee.

(3) Unless the trust terms provide otherwise, a self-appointment by a trust auxiliary is of no effect.

X. – 8:203: Appointment by Court Order

On the application of any party to the trust or any person entitled to enforce performance of an obligation under the trust, a court may appoint:
(a)   a substitute trustee for a person who has ceased to be a trustee, or
(b)   one or more additional trustees,
if in the circumstances:
(i)   no one else is able and willing to exercise a power to appoint; and
(ii)   the appointment is likely to promote the efficient and prudent administration and disposal of the trust fund in accordance with the trust terms.

Section 3: Resignation of Trustees
X. – 8:301: Resignation with Consent of Trust Auxiliary or Co-Trustees

(1) A trust auxiliary who may appoint a substitute trustee in the event of the trustee's resignation may consent to a resignation.
(2) A trust auxiliary may consent to a resignation without the consent of the continuing trustees only if a substitute trustee is appointed at the same time.
(3) The continuing trustees may consent to a resignation.
(4) A trustee may only resign with the consent of a trust auxiliary or co-trustees if after resignation there will be at least two continuing trustees or a special trustee.
(5) Special trustees, for the purposes of this Book, are:
(a) any public officer or body having the function of acting as a trustee; and
(b) any legal persons designated as such in an enactment or satisfying requirements set out in an enactment for this purpose.

X. – 8:302: Resignation with Approval of Court

A court may approve the resignation of a trustee who cannot otherwise resign if it is fair to release the trustee from obligations under the trust, having regard in particular to whether after resignation an efficient and prudent administration and disposal of the trust fund in accordance with the trust terms can be secured.

Section 4: Removal of Trustees
X. – 8:401: Removal by Trust Auxiliary or Co-Trustees

(1) Where a court might remove a trustee on grounds of inability, refusal to act, or unsuitability, the continuing trustees may remove that trustee.
(2) The removal of a trustee by a trust auxiliary or the trustees does not take effect until notice of the removal is given to the trustee who is to be removed.

X. – 8:402: Removal by Court Order

On the application of any party to the trust, a court may remove a trustee without that trustee's consent and regardless of the trust terms if it is inappropriate for the trustee to remain a trustee, in particular on grounds of the trustee's:
(a)   inability;
(b)   actual or anticipated material non-performance of any obligation under, or arising out of, the trust;
(c)   unsuitability;
(d)   permanent or recurrent fundamental disagreement with co-trustees on a matter requiring a unanimous decision of the trustees; or
(e)   other interests which substantially conflict with performance of the obligations under, or arising out of, the trust.

Section 5: Effect of Change of Trustees
X. – 8:501: Effect on Trustees' Obligations and Rights
(1)   A person who is appointed a trustee becomes bound by the trust and acquires the corresponding rights and powers. Subject to the following paragraphs of this Article, a trustee who resigns or is removed is released from the trust and loses those rights and powers.
(2)   The obligation to cooperate with co-trustees does not end until the expiry of a reasonable period after resignation or removal.
(3)   A former trustee's right of recourse to the trust fund takes effect as a right against the continuing trustees. A right to reimbursement, indemnification or remuneration by a beneficiary is unaffected.
(4)   A former trustee remains bound by:
(a)   the obligation in X. – 6:109 (Obligation not to obtain unauthorised enrichment or advantage);
(b)   trust debts; and
(c)   obligations arising from non-performance.

X. – 8:502: Vesting and Divesting of Trust Assets
(1)   Title to a trust asset vests in a person on appointment as a trustee, without a court order to that effect, if that title is:
(a)   capable of transfer by agreement between a transferor and a transferee without the necessity for any further act of transfer or formality; or
(b)   regarded under the applicable national law as vested in the trustees as a body.
(2)   The vesting of an asset in a person who is appointed a trustee does not divest any continuing trustees.
(3)   A person who resigns or is removed as a trustee is divested correspondingly.

X. – 8:503: Transmission of Trust Documents
A continuing or substitute trustee is entitled to the delivery up of trust documents in the possession of a former trustee. The person in possession has the right to make and retain copies at that person's own expense.

X. – 8:504: Effect of Death or Dissolution of Trustee
(1)   Where one of several trustees dies or a corporate trustee is dissolved, the trust fund remains vested in the continuing trustees. This applies to the exclusion of any person succeeding to a deceased or dissolved trustee's other patrimony.
(2)   Where a sole trustee dies, the deceased trustee's successors become trustees and accordingly:
(a)   the trustee's successors become subject to the trust and acquire the corresponding rights and powers;
(b)   the trustee's successors become liable for trust debts incurred by the deceased trustee to the extent of the deceased trustee's estate; and
(c)   the trust fund vests in the trustee's successors, but the trustee's successors may only exercise the powers set out in X. – 5:202 (Restriction in case of minimum number of trustees) paragraph (1), regardless of the number of successors.
(3)   A trustee's testamentary disposition of the trust fund is of no effect, but the trust terms may confer a testamentary power to appoint a trustee.
(4)   Obligations arising from non-performance devolve on the deceased trustee's successor.

Section 6: Death or Dissolution of Trust Auxiliary
X. – 8:601: Effect of Death or Dissolution of Trust Auxiliary
A power of a trust auxiliary ends when the trust auxiliary dies or is dissolved, but the trust terms may permit a testamentary exercise of the power.

Chapter 9: Termination and Variation of Trusts and Transfer of Rights to Benefit
Section 1: Termination
Sub-section 1: General Rules on Termination
X. – 9:101: Modes of Termination

A trust in respect of a fund or part of a fund may be terminated:
(a)   by a truster or beneficiaries in accordance with a right provided for by the trust terms;
(b)   by a truster in accordance with X. – 9:103 (Right of truster to terminate a gratuitous trust);
(c)   by a beneficiary in accordance with X. – 9:104 (Right of beneficiaries to terminate);
(d)   by a trustee under X. – 9:108 (Termination by trustee);
(e)   by merger of rights and obligations under X. – 9:109 (Merger of right and obligation).

X. – 9:102: Effect of Termination on Trustee's Liabilities

(1)   To the extent that the trust is terminated the trustee is discharged.
(2)   Unless the parties concerned agree otherwise, termination of the trust does not release a trustee from liability:
(a)   to a beneficiary arising out of the trustee's non-performance of any obligation under, or arising out of, the trust; or
(b)   to a trust creditor.

Sub-section 2: Termination by Truster or Beneficiaries
X. – 9:103: Right of Truster to Terminate a Gratuitous Trust

(1)   Except as provided for by paragraphs (2) and (3), a truster has no implied right to terminate a trust or a trust term merely because the trust was constituted gratuitously, irrespective of whether:
(a)   the trust was constituted without a transfer by the truster;
(b)   the truster reserved a right to benefit during the truster's lifetime.
(2)   A truster may terminate a gratuitously constituted trust, or a term of such a trust, which is for the benefit of a person who does not yet exist.
(3)   A truster may terminate a gratuitously constituted trust for the benefit of another to the same extent that the truster might have revoked a donation to that beneficiary if the benefit had been conferred by way of donation.

X. – 9:104: Right of Beneficiaries to Terminate

(1)   A beneficiary of full legal capacity may terminate the trust in respect of a fund or part of the fund which is for that beneficiary's exclusive benefit.
(2)   If each is of full legal capacity, several beneficiaries have a corresponding joint right to terminate the trust in respect of a fund or part of the fund which is for the exclusive benefit of those beneficiaries.
(3)   A trust may not be terminated in respect of part of the fund if this would adversely affect the trust in respect of the rest of the fund for the benefit of other beneficiaries or for the advancement of public benefit purposes.

X. – 9:105: Meaning of "Exclusive Benefit"

(1)   A fund or part of a fund is to be regarded as for a beneficiary's exclusive benefit if all of that capital and all of the future income from that capital can only be disposed of in accordance with the trust terms for the benefit of that beneficiary or that beneficiary's estate.
(2)   For the purposes of paragraph (1) the possibility that the beneficiary might give a consent, or might fail to exercise a right adverse to that beneficiary's own benefit, is to be disregarded.

X. – 9:106: Notice of Termination and its Effects

(1)   A truster or beneficiary exercises a right to terminate by giving notice in writing to the trustees.
(2)   A trust or part of a trust which is terminated by the truster takes effect from that time as a trust for the benefit of the truster.
(3)   Where a beneficiary, exercising a right to terminate, instructs the trustee to transfer to someone other than the beneficiary, notice of termination vests in that person the right to benefit from the fund or part of the fund which is to be transferred.

(4)　Unless the transfer is impossible or unlawful, the trustee is obliged to transfer the fund or part of the fund in accordance with the notice of termination and without delay. The obligation to transfer supersedes the obligation to administer and dispose of the fund or part in accordance with the trust terms.

(5)　If a transfer is impossible because it would require the grant of an undivided share in an asset for which undivided shares are not allowed, the trustee is obliged:

(a)　to divide the asset and transfer the divided share, so far as this is possible and reasonable; and otherwise

(b)　to sell the asset, if this is possible, and transfer the corresponding share of the proceeds.

(6)　The trust is terminated when and to the extent that the required transfer is made.

X. – 9:107: Trustee's Right to Withhold

(1)　A trustee may withhold such part of the fund which is to be transferred as is needed to satisfy:

(a)　trust debts;

(b)　the trustee's accrued rights of recourse to the fund; and

(c)　the costs of transfer and of any required division or sale of an asset, so far as those debts, rights and costs are allocated to the part of the fund which is to be transferred.

(2)　The right to withhold ends if the person exercising the right to terminate pays compensation for the debts, rights and costs allocated to the part of the fund which is to be transferred.

Sub-section 3: Other Modes of Termination
X. – 9:108: Termination by Trustee

(1)　Where a beneficiary has a right to terminate a trust under X. – 9:104 (Right of beneficiaries to terminate) paragraph (1), a trustee may give a notice to that beneficiary requiring that beneficiary to exercise that right within a period of reasonable length fixed by the notice. If the beneficiary fails to do so within that period, the trustee may terminate the trust by a transfer to that beneficiary. The beneficiary is obliged to accept the transfer.

(2)　A trustee may also terminate the trust by payment of money or transfer of other assets of the trust fund into court where other rules so provide.

X. – 9:109: Merger of Right and Obligation

(1)　A trust ends when the sole trustee is also the sole beneficiary and the trust fund is for that beneficiary's exclusive benefit.

(2)　Where there are several trustees, paragraph (1) applies correspondingly only if they have a joint right to benefit.

(3)　If a trust subsists in relation to the beneficiary's right to benefit or the right to benefit is encumbered with a security right or other limited right, the trustee remains bound by that trust or encumbrance.

Section 2: Variation
X. – 9:201: Variation by Truster or Beneficiary

(1)　The trust terms may be varied by a truster or beneficiary in accordance with:

(a)　a right provided for by the trust terms;

(b)　the right provided for by paragraph (2).

(2)　A truster or beneficiary who has a right to terminate a trust has a corresponding right to vary the trust terms so far as they relate to the fund or part of the fund in respect of which the trust might be terminated.

(3)　The exercise by several beneficiaries of a joint right to vary the trust terms requires their agreement to that effect.

(4)　A variation which is to take effect from the death of the person exercising the right to vary is of no effect unless it is made by testamentary instrument.

(5)　A variation does not take effect until notice in writing is given to the trustees.

X. – 9:202: Variation by Court Order of Administrative Trust Terms
(1)   On the application of any party to the trust or any person entitled to enforce performance of obligations under the trust, a court may vary a trust term relating to the administration of the trust fund if the variation is likely to promote a more efficient and prudent administration of the fund.
(2)   A variation under paragraph (1) may not significantly affect the operation of the trust terms governing its disposal unless the court also has power to vary those terms under one of the following Articles.

X. – 9:203: Variation by Court Order of Trusts for Beneficiaries
(1)   On the application of any party to the trust or any person who would benefit if the term to be varied were removed, a court may vary a trust term which confers a right to benefit or eligibility for benefit on a person who:
(a)   does not yet exist; or
(b)   does not presently conform to a description, such as membership of a class, on which the right depends.
(2)   The same applies where the trust term confers a right to benefit or eligibility for benefit at a remote time in the future or which is conditional on the occurrence of an improbable event.

X. – 9:204: Variation by Court Order of Trusts for Public Benefit Purposes
(1)   On the application of any party to the trust or any person entitled to enforce performance of obligations under the trust, a court may vary a trust term which provides for the advancement of a public benefit purpose if, as a result of a change of circumstances, the advancement of the particular purpose provided for by the trust term cannot be regarded as a suitable and effective use of resources.
(2)   A variation under paragraph (2) must be in favour of such general or particular public benefit purposes as the truster would probably have chosen if the truster had constituted the trust after the change in circumstances.

Section 3: Transfer of Right to Benefit
X. – 9:301: Transfer by Juridical Act of Right to Benefit
(1)   Subject to the other paragraphs of this Article, the transfer by juridical act of a right to benefit is governed by Book III Chapter 5 Section 1 (Assignment of rights).
(2)   A gratuitous transfer is of no effect unless it is made in writing.
(3)   A transfer which is to take effect on the death of the transferor takes effect only in accordance with the applicable law of succession.

Chapter 10: Relations to Third Parties
Section 1: General Provisions on Creditors
X.–10:101: Basic Rule on Creditors
(1)   A person to whom a trustee owes a trust debt (a trust creditor) may satisfy that person's right out of the trust fund (in accordance with X. – 10:202 (Rights of trust creditors in relation to the trust fund)), but other creditors may not except in so far as these rules provide otherwise.
(2)   Paragraph (1) does not affect any right of a creditor of a party to a trust to invoke a right of that party relating to the trust fund.

X.–10:102: Definition of Trust Debt
(1)   An obligation is a trust debt if it is incurred by the trustee:
(a)   as the owner for the time being of a trust asset;
(b)   for the purposes of, and in accordance with the terms of, the trust;
(c)   in the capacity of trustee and by a contract or other juridical act which is not gratuitous, unless the creditor knew or could reasonably be expected to know that the obligation was not incurred in accordance with the terms of the trust;
(d)   as a result of an act or omission in the administration or disposition of the trust fund or the performance of a trust debt; or
(e)   otherwise materially in connection with the trust patrimony.

(2)   The obligations of trustees to reimburse, indemnify or remunerate a former trustee or an intended trustee who has exercised a right of refusal are also trust debts.
(3)   Other obligations of a trustee are not trust debts.

Section 2: Trust Creditors
X.–10:201: Rights of Trust Creditors Against the Trustee
(1)   A trustee is personally liable to satisfy trust debts.
(2)   Unless the trustee and the trust creditor agree otherwise:
(a)   liability is not limited to the value of the trust fund at the time the trust creditor's right to performance is enforced; and
(b)   subject to the rules on change of trustees, liability does not end if the trust fund ceases to be vested in the trustee.
(3)   A party to a contract is not to be treated as agreeing to exclude or limit liability merely because the other party discloses that that other party is concluding the contract in the capacity of trustee.

X.–10:202: Rights of Trust Creditors in Relation to the Trust Fund
A trust creditor may satisfy a right out of the trust fund:
(a)   to enforce performance of a trustee's personal liability under X. – 10:201 (Rights of trust creditors against the trustee); or
(b)   in the exercise of a security right in trust assets.

X.–10:203: Protection of the Truster and Beneficiaries
A truster or beneficiary is not in that capacity liable to a trust creditor.

Section 3: Trust Debtors
X.–10:301: Right to Enforce Performance of Trust Debtor's Obligation
(1)   Where a trustee has a right to performance and that right is a trust asset, the right to enforce performance of the obligation of the debtor (the trust debtor) accrues to the trustee.
(2)   Paragraph (1) does not affect:
(a)   a beneficiary's right to performance by the trustee of obligations under the trust in respect of the right against the trust debtor; or
(b)   procedural rules which allow a beneficiary to be a party to legal proceedings against the trust debtor to which the trustee is also a party.

X.–10:302: Set-off
A trustee's right against a trust debtor may only be set off against:
(a)   a right corresponding to a trust debt; or
(b)   a beneficiary's right to benefit out of the trust fund.

X.–10:303: Discharge of Trust Debtor
The discharge of a trust debtor by a trustee is of no effect if:
(a)   the discharge is not in performance of the trustee's obligations under the trust; and
(b)(i) the discharge is gratuitous; or
(ii)   the debtor knows or has reason to know that the discharge is not in performance of the trustee's obligations under the trust.

Section 4: Acquirers of Trust Assets and Rights Encumbering Trust Assets
X.–10:401: Liability of Donees and Bad Faith Acquirers
(1)   Where a trustee transfers a trust asset to another and the transfer is not in accordance with the terms of the trust, the transferee takes the asset subject to the trust if:
(a)   the transfer is gratuitous; or
(b)   the transferee knows or could reasonably be expected to know that the transfer is by a trustee and is not in accordance with the terms of the trust.
(2)   A transferee on whom a trust is imposed under paragraph (1) has a corresponding right to a return of any benefit conferred in exchange.

(3) The trust imposed under paragraph (1) is extinguished if:
(a) benefit which was provided by the transferee in exchange is disposed of in performance of an obligation under the trust; or
(b) the trustee or a third party satisfies an obligation to reinstate the trust fund.
(4) A transferee can reasonably be expected to know a matter if:
(a) it would have been apparent from a reasonably careful investigation; and
(b) having regard to the nature and value of the asset, the nature and costs of such investigation, and commercial practice, it is fair and reasonable to expect a transferee in the circumstances to make that investigation.
(5) This Article applies correspondingly where a trustee creates a security right or other limited right in a trust asset in favour of another.

Section 5: Other Rules on Liability and Protection of Third Parties
X.–10:501: Liability for Inducing or Assisting Misapplication of the Trust Fund
(1) Non–contractual liability arising out of damage caused to another by virtue of VI. – 2:211 (Loss upon inducement of non-performance of obligation) is modified as provided for by paragraph (2).
(2) A person who intentionally induces a trustee's non-performance of an obligation under the trust, or intentionally assists such non-performance, is solidarily liable with that trustee, if the trustee is liable to reinstate the trust fund.

X.–10:502: Protection of Third Parties Dealing with Trustees
(1) A contract which a trustee concludes as a result of a non-performance of an obligation under the trust with a person who is not a party to a trust is not void or avoidable for that reason.
(2) In favour of a person who is not a party to the trust and as against a trustee, a person who has no knowledge of the true facts may rely on the apparent effect of a trust document and the truth of a statement contained in it.

Annex Definitions
(General notes. These definitions are introduced by I. – 1:108 (Definitions in Annex) which provides that they apply for all the purposes of these rules unless the context otherwise requires and that, where a word is defined, other grammatical forms of the word have a corresponding meaning. For the convenience of the user, where a definition is taken from or derived from a particular Article a reference to that Article is added in brackets after the definition. The list also includes some terms which are frequently used in the rules but which are not defined in any Article. It does not include definitions which do not contain any legal concept but which are only drafting devices for the purposes of a particular Article or group of Articles.)

Accessory An "accessory", in relation to proprietary security, is a corporeal asset that is or becomes closely connected with, or part of, a movable or an immovable, provided it is possible and economically reasonable to separate the accessory without damage from the movable or immovable. (IX. – 1:201)

Acquisition finance device An "acquisition finance device" is (a) a retention of ownership device; (b) where ownership of a sold asset has been transferred to the buyer, those security rights in the asset which secure the right (i) of the seller to payment of the purchase price or (ii) of a lender to repayment of a loan granted to the buyer for payment of the purchase price, if and in so far as this payment is actually made to the seller; and (c) a right of a third person to whom any of the rights under (a) or (b) has been transferred as security for a credit covered by (a) or (b). (IX. – 1:201(3))

Advanced electronic signature An "advanced electronic signature" is an electronic signature which is (a) uniquely linked to the signatory (b) capable of identifying the signatory (c) created using means which can be maintained under the signatory's sole control; and (d) linked to the data to which it relates in such a manner that any subsequent change of the data is detectable. (I. – 1:108(4))

Act of assignment An "act of assignment" of a right is a contract or other juridical act which is intended to effect a transfer of the right. (III. – 5:102(2))

Agent An "agent" is a person who is authorised to act for another.

Assets "Assets" means anything of economic value, including property; rights having a monetary value; and goodwill.

Assignment "Assignment", in relation to a right, means the transfer of the right by one person, the "assignor", to another, "the assignee". (III. – 5:102(1))

Authorisation "Authorisation" is the granting or maintaining of authority. (II. – 6:102(3))

Authority "Authority", in relation to a representative acting for a principal, is the power to affect the principal's legal position. (II. – 6:102(2))

Avoidance "Avoidance" of a juridical act or legal relationship is the process whereby a party or, as the case may be, a court invokes a ground of invalidity so as to make the act or relationship, which has been valid until that point, retrospectively ineffective from the beginning.

Barter, contract for A contract for the "barter" of goods is a contract under which each party undertakes to transfer the ownership of goods, either immediately on conclusion of the contract or at some future time, in return for the transfer of ownership of other goods. (IV. A. – 1:203)

Beneficiary A "beneficiary", in relation to a trust, is a person who, according to the trust terms, has either a right to benefit or an eligibility for benefit from the trust fund. (X. – 1:203(3))

Benevolent intervention in another's affairs "Benevolent intervention in another's affairs" is the process whereby a person, the intervener, acts with the predominant intention of benefiting another, the principal, but without being authorised or bound to do so. (V. – 1:101)

Business "Business" means any natural or legal person, irrespective of whether publicly or privately owned, who is acting for purposes relating to the person's self-employed trade, work or profession, even if the person does not intend to make a profit in the course of the activity. (I. – 1:106(2))

Claim A "claim" is a demand for something based on the assertion of a right.

Claimant A "claimant" is a person who makes, or who has grounds for making, a claim.

Co-debtorship for security purposes A "co-debtorship for security purposes" is an obligation owed by two or more debtors in which one of the debtors, the security provider, assumes the obligation primarily for purposes of security towards the creditor. (IV. G. – 1:101(e))

Commercial agency A "commercial agency" is the legal relationship arising from a contract under which one party, the commercial agent, agrees to act on a continuing basis as a self-employed intermediary to negotiate or to conclude contracts on behalf of another party, the principal, and the principal agrees to remunerate the agent for those activities. (IV. E. – 3:101)

Compensation "Compensation" means reparation in money. (VI. – 6:101(2))

Complete substitution of debtor There is complete substitution of a debtor when a third person is substituted as debtor with the effect that the original debtor is discharged. (III. – 5:203)

Condition A "condition" is a provision which makes a legal relationship or effect depend on the occurrence or non-occurrence of an uncertain future event. A condition may be suspensive or resolutive. (III. – 1:106)

Conduct "Conduct" means voluntary behaviour of any kind, verbal or nonverbal: it includes a single act or a number of acts, behaviour of a negative or passive nature (such as accepting something without protest or not doing something) and behaviour of a continuing or intermittent nature (such as exercising control over something).

Confidential information "Confidential information" means information which, either from its nature or the circumstances in which it was obtained, the party receiving the information knows or could reasonably be expected to know is confidential to the other party. (II. – 2:302(2))

Construction, contract for A contract for construction is a contract under which one party, the constructor, undertakes to construct something for another party, the client, or to materially alter an existing building or other immovable structure for a client. (IV.C–3:101)

Consumer A "consumer" means any natural person who is acting primarily for purposes which are not related to his or her trade, business or profession. (I. – 1:106(1))

Consumer contract for sale A "consumer contract for sale" is a contract for sale in which the seller is a business and the buyer is a consumer. (IV. A. – 1:204)

Contract A "contract" is an agreement which is intended to give rise to a binding legal relationship or to have some other legal effect. It is a bilateral or multilateral juridical act. (II. – 1:101(1))

Contractual obligation A "contractual obligation" is an obligation which arises from a contract, whether from an express term or an implied term or by operation of a rule of law imposing an obligation on a contracting party as such.

Contractual relationship A "contractual relationship" is a legal relationship resulting from a contract.

Co-ownership "Co-ownership", when created under Book VIII, means that two or more co-owners own undivided shares in the whole and each coowner can dispose of that co-owner's share by acting alone, unless otherwise provided by the parties. (Cf. VIII. – 1:203)

Corporeal "Corporeal", in relation to property, means having a physical existence in solid, liquid or gaseous form.

Costs "Costs" includes expenses.

Counter-performance A "counter-performance" is a performance which is due in exchange for another performance.

Court "Court" includes an arbitral tribunal.

Creditor A "creditor" is a person who has a right to performance of an obligation, whether monetary or non-monetary, by another person, the debtor.

Damage "Damage" means any type of detrimental effect.

Damages "Damages" means a sum of money to which a person may be entitled, or which a person may be awarded by a court, as compensation for some specified type of damage.

Debtor A "debtor" is a person who has an obligation, whether monetary or non-monetary, to another person, the creditor.

Default "Default", in relation to proprietary security, means any non-performance by the debtor of the obligation covered by the security; and any other event or set of circumstances agreed by the secured creditor and the security provider as entitling the secured creditor to have recourse to the security. (IX. – 1:201(5))

Defence A "defence" to a claim is a legal objection or a factual argument, other than a mere denial of an element which the claimant has to prove which, if well-founded, defeats the claim in whole or in part.

Delivery "Delivery" to a person, for the purposes of any obligation to deliver goods, means transferring possession of the goods to that person or taking such steps to transfer possession as are required by the terms regulating the obligation. For the purposes of Book VIII (Acquisition and loss of ownership of goods) delivery of the goods takes place only when the transferor gives up and the transferee obtains possession of the goods: if the contract or other juridical act, court order or rule of law under which the transferee is entitled to the transfer of ownership involves carriage of the goods by a carrier or a series of carriers, delivery of the goods takes place when the transferor's obligation to deliver is fulfilled and the carrier or the transferee obtains possession of the goods. (VIII. – 2:104)

Dependent personal security A "dependent personal security" is an obligation by a security provider which is assumed in favour of a creditor in order to secure a present or future obligation of the debtor owed to the creditor and performance of which is due only if, and to the extent that, performance of the latter obligation is due. (IV. G. – 1:101(a))

Design, contract for A contract for design is a contract under which one party, the designer, undertakes to design for another party, the client, an immovable structure which is to be constructed by or on behalf of the client or a movable or incorporeal thing or service which is to be constructed or performed by or on behalf of the client. (IV. C.- 6:101)

Direct physical control Direct physical control is physical control which is exercised by the possessor personally or through a possession-agent exercising such control on behalf of the possessor (direct possession). (VIII. – 1:205)

Discrimination "Discrimination" means any conduct whereby, or situation where, on grounds such as sex or ethnic or racial origin, (a) one person is treated less favourably than another person is, has been or would be treated in a comparable situation; or (b) an apparently neutral provision, criterion or practice would place one group of persons at a particular disadvantage when compared to a different group of persons. (II. – 2:102(1))

Distribution contract A "distribution contract" is a contract under which one party, the supplier, agrees to supply the other party, the distributor, with products on a continuing basis and the distributor agrees to purchase them, or to take and pay for them, and to supply them to others in the distributor's name and on the distributor's behalf. (IV. E. – 5:101(1))

Distributorship A "distributorship" is the legal relationship arising from a distribution contract.

Divided obligation An obligation owed by two or more debtors is a "divided obligation" when each debtor is bound to render only part of the performance and the creditor may require from each debtor only that debtor's part. (III. – 4:102(2))

Divided right A right to performance held by two or more creditors is a "divided right" when the debtor owes each creditor only that creditor's share and each creditor may require performance only of that creditor's share. (III. – 4:202(2))

Donation, contract for A contract for the donation of goods is a contract under which one party, the donor, gratuitously undertakes to transfer the ownership of goods to another party, the donee, and does so with an intention to benefit the donee. (IV. H. – 1:101)

Durable medium A "durable medium" means any material on which information is stored so that it is accessible for future reference for a period of time adequate to the purposes of the information, and which allows the unchanged reproduction of this information. (I. – 1:107(3))

Duty A person has a "duty" to do something if the person is bound to do it or expected to do it according to an applicable normative standard of conduct. A duty may or may not be owed to a specific creditor. A duty is not necessarily an aspect of a legal relationship. There is not necessarily a sanction for breach of a duty. All obligations are duties, but not all duties are obligations.

Economic loss See "Loss".

Electronic "Electronic" means relating to technology with electrical, digital, magnetic, wireless, optical, electromagnetic, or similar capabilities.

Electronic signature An "electronic signature" means data in electronic form which are attached to, or logically associated with, other data and which serve as a method of authentication. (I. – 1:108(3))

Financial assets "Financial assets" are financial instruments and rights to the payment of money. (IX. – 1:201(6))

Financial instruments "Financial instruments" are (a) share certificates and equivalent securities as well as bonds and equivalent debt instruments, if these are negotiable (b) any other securities which are dealt in and which give the right to acquire any such financial instruments or which give rise to cash settlements, except instruments of payment (c) share rights in collective investment undertakings (d) money market instruments and (e) rights in or relating to the foregoing instruments. (IX. – 1:201(7))

Franchise A "franchise" is the legal relationship arising from a contract under which one party, the franchisor, grants the other party, the franchisee, in exchange for remuneration, the right to conduct a business (franchise business) within the franchisor's network for the purposes of supplying certain products on the franchisee's behalf and in the franchisee's name, and whereby the franchisee has the right and the obligation to use the franchisor's trade name or trademark or other intellectual property rights, know-how and business method. (IV. E. – 4:101)

Fraudulent A misrepresentation is fraudulent if it is made with knowledge or belief that it is false and is intended to induce the recipient to make a mistake to the recipient's prejudice. A non-disclosure is fraudulent if it is intended to induce the person from whom the information is withheld to make a mistake to that person's prejudice. (II. – 7:205(2))

Fundamental non-performance A non-performance of a contractual obligation is fundamental if (a) it substantially deprives the creditor of what the creditor was entitled to expect under the contract, as applied to the whole or relevant part of the performance, unless at the time of conclusion of the contract the debtor did not foresee and could not reasonably be expected to have foreseen that result or (b) it is intentional or reckless and gives the creditor reason to believe that the debtor's future performance cannot be relied on. (III. – 3:502(2))

Global security A "global security" is a security which is assumed in order to secure all the debtor's obligations towards the creditor or the debit balance of a current account or a security of a similar extent. (IV.G. – 1:101(f)

Good faith "Good faith" is a mental attitude characterised by honesty and an absence of knowledge that an apparent situation is not the true situation.

Good faith and fair dealing "Good faith and fair dealing" is a standard of conduct characterised by honesty, openness and consideration for the interests of the other party to the transaction or relationship in question. (I. – 1:103)

Goods "Goods" means corporeal movables. It includes ships, vessels, hovercraft or aircraft, space objects, animals, liquids and gases. See also "movables".

Gross negligence There is "gross negligence" if a person is guilty of a profound failure to take such care as is self-evidently required in the circumstances.

Handwritten signature A "handwritten signature" means the name of, or sign representing, a person written by that person's own hand for the purpose of authentication. (I. – 1:108(2))

Harassment "Harassment" means unwanted conduct (including conduct of a sexual nature) which violates a person's dignity, particularly when such conduct creates an intimidating, hostile, degrading, humiliating or offensive environment, or which aims to do so. (II. – 2:102(2))

Immovable property "Immovable property" means land and anything so attached to land as not to be subject to change of place by usual human action.

Incomplete substitution of debtor There is incomplete substitution of a debtor when a third person is substituted as debtor with the effect that the original debtor is retained as a debtor in case the original debtor does not perform properly. (III. – 5:205)

Incorporeal "Incorporeal", in relation to property, means not having a physical existence in solid, liquid or gaseous form.

Indemnify To "indemnify" means to make such payment to a person as will ensure that that person suffers no loss.

Independent personal security An "independent personal security" is an obligation by a security provider which is assumed in favour of a creditor for the purposes of security and which is expressly or impliedly declared not to depend upon another person's obligation owed to the creditor. (IV.G.– 1:101(b))

Indirect physical control Indirect physical control is physical control which is exercised by means of another person, a limited-right-possessor (indirect possession). (VIII. – 1:205)

Individually negotiated See "not individually negotiated" and II. – 1:110.

Ineffective "Ineffective" in relation to a contract or other juridical act means having no effect, whether that state of affairs is temporary or permanent, general or restricted.

Insolvency proceeding An "insolvency proceeding" means a collective judicial or administrative proceeding, including an interim proceeding, in which the assets and affairs of a person who is, or who is believed to be, insolvent are subject to control or supervision by a court or other competent authority for the purpose of reorganisation or liquidation.

Intangibles "Intangibles", in relation to proprietary security, means incorporeal assets and includes uncertificated and indirectly held securities and the undivided share of a co-owner in corporeal assets or in a bulk or a fund. (IX. – 1:201(8))

Interest "Interest" means simple interest without any assumption that it will be capitalised from time to time.

Invalid "Invalid" in relation to a juridical act or legal relationship means that the act or relationship is void or has been avoided.

Joint obligation An obligation owed by two or more debtors is a "joint obligation" when all the debtors are bound to render the performance together and the creditor may require it only from all of them. (III. – 4:102(3))

Joint right A right to performance held by two or more creditors is a "joint right" when the debtor must perform to all the creditors and any creditor may require performance only for the benefit of all. (III. – 4:202(3))

Juridical act A "juridical act" is any statement or agreement, whether express or implied from conduct, which is intended to have legal effect as such. It may be unilateral, bilateral or multilateral. (II. – 1:101(2))

Keeper A keeper, in relation to an animal, vehicle or substance, is the person who has the beneficial use or physical control of it for that person's own benefit and who exercises the right to control it or its use.

Lease A "lease" is the legal relationship arising from a contract under which one party, the lessor, undertakes to provide the other party, the lessee, with a temporary right of use in exchange for rent. (IV. B. – 1:101)

Limited proprietary rights Limited proprietary rights are such rights of the following character as are characterised or treated as proprietary rights by any provision of these model rules or by national law:– (a) security rights (b) rights to use (c) rights to acquire (including a right to acquire in the sense of VIII. – 2:307 (Contingent right of transferee under retention of ownership)) and (d) trust-related rights. (VIII. – 1:204)

Limited-right-possessor A "limited-right-possessor", in relation to goods, is a person who exercises physical control over the goods either (a) with the intention of doing so in that person's own interest, and under a specific legal relationship with the owner-possessor which gives the limitedright-possessor the right to possess the goods or (b) with the intention of doing so to the order of the owner-possessor, and under a specific contractual relationship with the owner-possessor which gives the limited-right-possessor a right to retain the goods until any charges or costs have been paid by the owner-possessor. (VIII. – 1:207)

Loan contract A loan contract is a contract by which one party, the lender, is obliged to provide the other party, the borrower, with credit of any amount for a definite or indefinite period (the loan period), in the form of a monetary loan or of an overdraft facility and by which the borrower is obliged to repay the money obtained under the credit, whether or not the borrower is obliged to pay interest or any other kind of remuneration the parties have agreed upon. (IV. F.– 1:101(2))

Loss "Loss" includes economic and non-economic loss. "Economic loss" includes loss of income or profit, burdens incurred and a reduction in the value of property. "Non-economic loss" includes pain and suffering and impairment of the quality of life. (III. – 3:701(3) and VI. – 2:101(4))

Mandate The "mandate" of an agent is the authorisation and instruction given by the principal, as modified by any subsequent direction, in relation to the facilitation, negotiation or conclusion of a contract or other juridical act with a third party. (IV. D. – 1:102(1)(a))

Mandate for direct representation A "mandate for direct representation" is a mandate under which the agent is to act in the name of the principal, or otherwise in such a way as to indicate an intention to affect the principal's legal position directly. (IV. D. – 1:102(1)(d))

Mandate for indirect representation A "mandate for indirect representation" is a mandate under which the agent is to act in the agent's own name or otherwise in such a way as not to indicate an intention to affect the principal's legal position directly. (IV. D. – 1:102(1)(e))

Merger of debts A "merger of debts" means that the attributes of debtor and creditor are united in the same person in the same capacity. (III. – 6:201)

Merger clause A "merger clause" is a term in a contract document stating that the document embodies all the terms of the contract. (II. – 4:104)

Monetary loan A monetary loan is a fixed sum of money which is lent to the borrower and which the borrower agrees to repay either by fixed instalments or by paying the whole sum at the end of the loan period. (IV. F. – 1:101(3))

Motor vehicle "Motor vehicle" means any vehicle intended for travel on land and propelled by mechanical power, but not running on rails, and any trailer, whether or not coupled. (VI. – 3:205(2))

Movables "Movables" means corporeal and incorporeal property other than immovable property.

Negligence There is "negligence" if a person does not meet the standard of care which could reasonably be expected in the circumstances.

Non-economic loss See "Loss".

Non-performance "Non-performance", in relation to an obligation, means any failure to perform the obligation, whether or not excused. It includes delayed performance and defective performance. (III. – 1:101(3))

Notice "Notice" includes the communication of information or of a juridical act. (I. – 1:105)

Not individually negotiated A term supplied by one party is not individually negotiated if the other party has not been able to influence its content, in particular because it has been drafted in advance, whether or not as part of standard terms. (II. – 1:110)

Obligation An obligation is a duty to perform which one party to a legal relationship, the debtor, owes to another party, the creditor. (III. – 1:101(1))

Overdraft facility An "overdraft facility" is an option for the borrower to withdraw funds on a fluctuating, limited basis from the borrower's current account in excess of the current balance in the account. (IV. F.– 1:101(4))

Owner-possessor An "owner-possessor", in relation to goods, is a person who exercises physical control over the goods with the intention of doing so as, or as if, an owner. ((VIII. – 1:206)

Ownership "Ownership" is the most comprehensive right a person, the owner, can have over property, including the exclusive right, so far as consistent with applicable laws or rights granted by the owner, to use, enjoy, modify, destroy, dispose of and recover the property. (VIII. – 1:202)

Performance "Performance", in relation to an obligation, is the doing by the debtor of what is to be done under the obligation or the not doing by the debtor of what is not to be done. (III. – 1:101(2))

Person "Person" means a natural or legal person.

Physical control "Physical control", in relation to goods, means direct physical control or indirect physical control. (Cf. VIII. – 1:205)

Possession Possession, in relation to goods, means having physical control over the goods. (VIII. – 1:205)

Possession-agent A "possession-agent", in relation to goods, is a person (such as an employee) who exercises direct physical control over the goods on behalf of an owner-possessor or limited-right-possessor (without the intention and specific legal relationship required for that person to be a limited-right-possessor); and to whom the owner-possessor or limited-right-possessor may give binding instructions as to the use of the goods in the interest of the owner-possessor or limited-rightpossessor. A person is also a possession-agent where that person is accidentally in a position to exercise, and does exercise, direct physical control over the goods for an owner-possessor or limited-rightpossessor. (VIII. – 1:208)

Possessory security right A "possessory security right" is a security right that requires possession of the encumbered corporeal asset by the secured creditor or another person (except the debtor) holding for the secured creditor. (IX. – 1:201(10))

Prescription "Prescription", in relation to the right to performance of an obligation, is the legal effect whereby the lapse of a prescribed period of time entitles the debtor to refuse performance.

Presumption A "presumption" means that the existence of a known fact or state of affairs allows the deduction that something else should be held true, until the contrary is demonstrated.

Price The "price" is what is due by the debtor under a monetary obligation, in exchange for something supplied or provided, expressed in a currency which the law recognises as such.

Proceeds "Proceeds", in relation to proprietary security, is every value derived from an encumbered asset, such as value realised by sale, collection or other disposition; damages or insurance payments in respect of defects, damage or loss; civil and natural fruits, including distributions; and proceeds of proceeds. (IX. – 1:201(11))

Processing, contract for A contract for processing is a contract under which one party, the processor, undertakes to perform a service on an existing movable or incorporeal thing or to an immovable structure for another party, the client (except where the service is construction work on an existing building or other immovable structure). (IV. C. – 4:101)

Producer "Producer" includes, in the case of something made, the maker or manufacturer; in the case of raw material, the person who abstracts or wins it; and in the case of something grown, bred or raised, the grower, breeder or raiser. A special definition applies for the purposes of VI. – 3:204.

Property "Property" means anything which can be owned: it may be movable or immovable, corporeal or incorporeal.

Proprietary security A "proprietary security" covers security rights in all kinds of assets, whether movable or immovable, corporeal or incorporeal. (IV.G. – 1:101(g))

Proprietary security, contract for A "contract for proprietary security" is a contract under which a security provider undertakes to grant a security right to the secured creditor; or a secured creditor is entitled to retain a security right when transferring ownership; or a seller, lessor or other supplier of assets is entitled to retain ownership of the supplied assets in order to secure its rights to performance. (IX. – 1:201(4))

Public holiday A "public holiday" with reference to a member state, or part of a member state, of the European Union means any day designated as such for that state or part in a list published in the official journal. (I. – 1:110(9))

Ratify "Ratify" means confirm with legal effect.

Reasonable What is "reasonable" is to be objectively ascertained, having regard to the nature and purpose of what is being done, to the circumstances of the case and to any relevant usages and practices. (I. – 1:104)

Reciprocal An obligation is reciprocal in relation to another obligation if (a) performance of the obligation is due in exchange for performance of the other obligation; (b) it is an obligation to facilitate or accept performance of the other obligation; or (c) it is so clearly connected to the other obligation or its subject matter that performance of the one can reasonably be regarded as dependent on performance of the other. (III. – 1:101(4))

Recklessness A person is "reckless" if the person knows of an obvious and serious risk of proceeding in a certain way but nonetheless voluntarily proceeds without caring whether or not the risk materialises.

Rent "Rent" is the money or other value which is due in exchange for a temporary right of use. (IV. B. – 1:101)

Reparation "Reparation" means compensation or another appropriate measure to reinstate the person suffering damage in the position that person would have been in had the damage not occurred. (VI. – 6:101)

Representative A "representative" is a person who has authority to affect the legal position of another person, the principal, in relation to a third party by acting in the name of the principal or otherwise in such a way as to indicate an intention to affect the principal's legal position directly. (II. – 6:102(1))

Requirement A "requirement" is something which is needed before a particular result follows or a particular right can be exercised.

Resolutive A condition is "resolutive" if it causes a legal relationship or effect to come to an end when the condition is satisfied. (III. – 1:106)

Retention of ownership device There is a retention of ownership device when ownership is retained by the owner of supplied assets in order to secure a right to performance of an obligation. (IX. – 1:103)

Revocation "Revocation", means (a) in relation to a juridical act, its recall by a person or persons having the power to recall it, so that it no longer has effect and (b) in relation to something conferred or transferred, its recall, by a person or persons having power to recall it, so that it comes back or must be returned to the person who conferred it or transferred it.

Right "Right", depending on the context, may mean (a) the correlative of an obligation or liability (as in "a significant imbalance in the parties' rights and obligations arising under the contract"); (b) a proprietary right (such as the right of ownership); (c) a personality right (as in a right to respect for dignity, or a right to liberty and privacy); (d) a legally conferred power to bring about a particular result (as in "the right to avoid" a contract); (e) an entitlement to a particular remedy (as in a right to have performance of a contractual obligation judicially ordered) or (f) an entitlement to do or not to do something affecting another person's legal position without exposure to adverse consequences (as in a "right to withhold performance of the reciprocal obligation").

Sale, contract for A contract for the "sale" of goods or other assets is a contract under which one party, the seller, undertakes to another party, the buyer, to transfer the ownership of the goods or other assets to the buyer, or to a third person, either immediately on conclusion of the contract or at some future time, and the buyer undertakes to pay the price. (IV.A. – 1:202)

Security right in movable asset A security right in a movable asset is any limited proprietary right in the asset which entitles the secured creditor to preferential satisfaction of the secured right from the encumbered asset. (IX. – 1:102(1))

Services, contract for A contract for services is a contract under which one party, the service provider, undertakes to supply a service to the other party, the client. (IV. C. – 1:101)

Set-off "Set-off" is the process by which a person may use a right to performance held against another person to extinguish in whole or in part an obligation owed to that person. (III. – 6:101)

Signature "Signature" includes a handwritten signature, an electronic signature or an advanced electronic signature. (I. – 1:108(2))

Solidary obligation An obligation owed by two or more debtors is a "solidary obligation" when all the debtors are bound to render one and the same performance and the creditor may require it from any one of them until there has been full performance. (III. – 4:102(1))

Solidary right A right to performance held by two or more creditors is a "solidary right" when any of the creditors may require full performance from the debtor and the debtor may render performance to any of the creditors. (III. – 4:202(1))

Standard terms "Standard terms" are terms which have been formulated in advance for several transactions involving different parties, and which have not been individually negotiated by the parties. (II. – 1:109)

Storage, contract for A contract for storage is a contract under which one party, the storer, undertakes to store a movable or incorporeal thing for another party, the client. (IV. C. – 5:101)

Subrogation "Subrogation", in relation to rights, is the process by which a person who has made a payment or other performance to another person acquires by operation of law that person's rights against a third person.

Substitution of debtor "Substitution" of a debtor is the process whereby, with the agreement of the creditor, a third party is substituted completely or incompletely for the debtor, the contract remaining in force. (III. – 5:202) See also "complete substitution of debtor" and "incomplete substitution of debtor".

Supply To "supply" goods or other assets means to make them available to another person, whether by sale, gift, barter, lease or other means: to "supply" services means to provide them to another person, whether or not for a price. Unless otherwise stated, "supply" covers the supply of goods, other assets and services.

Suspensive A condition is "suspensive" if it prevents a legal relationship or effect from coming into existence until the condition is satisfied. (III. – 1:106)

Tacit prolongation "Tacit prolongation" is the process whereby, when a contract provides for continuous or repeated performance of obligations for a definite period and the obligations continue to be performed by both parties after that period has expired, the contract becomes a contract for an indefinite period, unless the circumstances are inconsistent with the tacit consent of the parties to such prolongation. (III. – 1:111)

Term "Term" means any provision, express or implied, of a contract or other juridical act, of a law, of a court order or of a legally binding usage or practice: it includes a condition.

Termination "Termination", in relation to an existing right, obligation or legal relationship, means bringing it to an end with prospective effect except in so far as otherwise provided.

Textual form In "textual form", in relation to a statement, means expressed in alphabetical or other intelligible characters by means of any support which permits reading, recording of the information contained in the statement and its reproduction in tangible form. (I. – 1:107(2))

Transfer of contractual position "Transfer of contractual position" is the process whereby, with the agreement of all three parties, a new party replaces an existing party to a contract, taking over the rights, obligations and entire contractual position of that party. (III. – 5:302)

Treatment, contract for A contract for treatment is a contract under which one party, the treatment provider, undertakes to provide medical treatment for another party, the patient, or to provide any other service in order to change the physical or mental condition of a person. (IV. C. – 8:101)

Trust A "trust" is a legal relationship in which a trustee is obliged to administer or dispose of one or more assets (the trust fund) in accordance with the terms governing the relationship (trust terms) to benefit a beneficiary or advance public benefit purposes. (X. – 1:201)

Trustee A "trustee" is a person in whom a trust fund becomes or remains vested when the trust is created or subsequently on or after appointment and who has the obligation set out in the definition of "trust" above. (X. – 1:203(2))

Truster A "truster" is a person who constitutes or intends to constitute a trust by juridical act. (X. – 1:203(1))

Unjustified enrichment An "unjustified enrichment" is an enrichment which is not legally justified.

Valid "Valid", in relation to a juridical act or legal relationship, means that the act or relationship is not void and has not been avoided.

Void "Void", in relation to a juridical act or legal relationship, means that the act or relationship is automatically of no effect from the beginning.

Voidable "Voidable", in relation to a juridical act or legal relationship, means that the act or relationship is subject to a defect which renders it liable to be avoided and hence rendered retrospectively of no effect.

Withdraw A right to "withdraw" from a contract or other juridical act is a right, exercisable only within a limited period, to terminate the legal relationship arising from the contract or other juridical act, without having to give any reason for so doing and without incurring any liability for non-performance of the obligations arising from that contract or juridical act. (II. – 5:101 to II. – 5:105)

Withholding performance "Withholding performance", as a remedy for non-performance of a contractual obligation, means that one party to a contract may decline to render due counter-performance until the other party has tendered performance or has performed. (III. – 3:401)

Working days "Working days" means all days other than Saturdays, Sundays and public holidays. (I. – 1:110(9)(b))

Writing In "writing" means in textual form, on paper or another durable medium and in directly legible characters. (I. – 1:107(1))

INCOTERMS 2010[1]

1 Two New Incoterms Rules – DAT and DAP – Have Replaced
the Incoterms 2000 Rules DAF, DES, DEQ and DDU

The number of Incoterms® rules has been reduced from 13 to 11. This has been achieved by substituting two new rules that may be used irrespective of the agreed mode of transport – DAT, Delivered at Terminal, and DAP, Delivered at Place – for the Incoterms® 2000 rules DAF, DES, DEQ and DDU.

Under both new rules, delivery occurs at a named destination: in DAT, at the buyer's disposal unloaded from the arriving vehicle (as under the former DEQ rule); in DAP, likewise at the buyer's disposal, but ready for unloading (as under the former DAF, DES and DDU rules).

The new rules make the Incoterms® 2000 rules DES and DEQ superfluous. The named terminal in DAT may well be in a port, and DAT can therefore safely be used in cases where the Incoterms® 2000 rule DEQ once was. Likewise, the arriving "vehicle" under DAP may well be a ship and the named place of destination may well be a port: consequently, DAP can safely be used in cases where the Incoterms® 2000 rule DES once was. These new rules, like their predecessors, are "delivered", with the seller bearing all the costs (other than those related to import clearance, where applicable) and risks involved in bringing the goods to the named place of destination.

2 Classification of the 11 Incoterms® 2010 Rules

The 11 Incoterms® 2010 rules are presented in two distinct classes:

Rules for Any Mode or Modes of Transport

EXW	EX WORKS
FCA	FREE CARRIER
CPT	CARRIAGE PAID TO
CIP	CARRIAGE AND INSURANCE PAID TO
DAT	DELIVERED AT TERMINAL
DAP	DELIVERED AT PLACE
DDP	DELIVERED DUTY PAID

1   © International Chamber of Commerce (ICC), reproduced with permission. For detailed information please visit http://www.iccwbo.org/incoterms/.

[handwritten margin note: buyer's choice to buy insurance]

Rules for Sea and Inland Waterway Transport

FAS	FREE ALONGSIDE SHIP	*[handwritten: risk passes prior to loading, but at dock]*
FOB	FREE ON BOARD	*[handwritten: risk passes when loaded on to ship]*
CFR	COST AND FREIGHT	
CIF	COST INSURANCE AND FREIGHT	*[handwritten: see LPT]*

The first class includes the seven Incoterms® 2010 rules that can be used irrespective of the mode of transport selected and irrespective of whether one or more than one mode of transport is employed. EXW, FCA, CPT, CIP, DAT, DAP and DDP belong to this class. They can be used even when there is no maritime transport at all. It is important to remember, however, that these rules can be used in cases where a ship is used for part of the carriage.

In the second class of Incoterms® 2010 rules, the point of delivery and the place to which the goods are carried to the buyer are *both* ports, hence the label "sea and inland waterway" rules. FAS, FOB, CFR and CIF belong to this class. Under the last three Incoterms rules, all mention of the ship's rail as the point of delivery has been omitted in preference for the goods being delivered when they are "on board" the vessel. This more closely reflects modern commercial reality and avoids the rather dated image of the risk swinging to and fro across an imaginary perpendicular line.

3 Rules for Domestic and International Trade

Incoterms® rules have traditionally been used in *international* sale contracts where goods pass across national borders. In various areas of the world, however, trade blocs, like the European Union, have made border formalities between different countries less significant. Consequently, the subtitle of the Incoterms® 2010 rules formally recognizes that they are available for application to both international and domestic sale contracts. As a result, the Incoterms® 2010 rules clearly state in a number of places that the obligation to comply with export/import formalities exists only where applicable.

Two developments have persuaded the ICC that a movement in this direction is timely. Firstly, traders commonly use Incoterms® rules for purely domestic sale contracts. The second reason is the greater willingness in the United States to use Incoterms® rules in domestic trade rather than the former Uniform Commercial Code shipment and delivery terms.

4 Guidance Notes

Before each Incoterms® 2010 rule you will find a Guidance Note. The Guidance Notes explain the fundamentals of each Incoterms® rule, such as when it should be used, when risk passes, and how costs are allocated between seller and buyer. The Guidance Notes are not part of the actual Incoterms® 2010 rules, but are intended to help the user accurately and efficiently steer towards the appropriate Incoterms® rule for a particular transaction.

5 Electronic Communication

Previous versions of Incoterms® rules have specified those documents that could be replaced by EDI messages. Articles A1/B1 of the Incoterms® 2010 rules, however, now give electronic means of communication the same effect as paper communication, as long as the parties so agree or where customary. This formulation facilitates the evolution of new electronic procedures throughout the lifetime of the Incoterms® 2010 rules.

6 Insurance Cover

The Incoterms® 2010 rules are the first version of the Incoterms® rules since the revision of the Institute Cargo Clauses and take account of alterations made to those clauses. The Incoterms® 2010 rules place information duties relating to insurance in articles A3/B3, which deal with contracts of carriage and insurance. These provisions have been moved from the more generic articles found in articles A10/B10 of the Incoterms® 2000 rules. The language in articles A3/B3 relating to insurance has also been altered with a view to clarifying the parties' obligations in this regard.

7 Security-Related Clearances and Information Required for Such Clearances

There is heightened concern nowadays about security in the movement of goods, requiring verification that the goods do not pose a threat to life or property for reasons other than their inherent nature. Therefore, the Incoterms® 2010 rules have allocated obligations between the buyer and seller to obtain or to render assistance in obtaining security-related clearances, such as chain-of-custody information, in articles A2/B2 and A10/B10 of various Incoterms® rules.

8 Terminal Handling Charges

Under Incoterms® rules CPT, CIP, CFR, CIF, DAT, DAP, and DDP, the seller must make arrangements for the carriage of the goods to the agreed destination. While the freight is paid by the seller, it is actually *paid for by the buyer* as freight costs are normally included by the seller in the total selling price. The carriage costs will sometimes include the costs of handling and moving the goods within port or container terminal facilities and the carrier or terminal operator may well charge these costs to the buyer who receives the goods. In these circumstances, the buyer will want to avoid paying for the same service twice: once to the seller as part of the total selling price and once independently to the carrier or the terminal operator. The Incoterms® 2010 rules seek to avoid this happening by clearly allocating such costs in articles A6/B6 of the relevant Incoterms rules.

9 String Sales

In the sale of commodities, as opposed to the sale of manufactured goods, cargo is frequently sold several times during transit "down a string". When this happens, a seller in the middle of the string does not "ship" the goods because these have already been shipped by the first seller in the string. The seller in the middle of the string therefore performs its obligations towards its buyer not by shipping the goods, but by "procuring" goods that have been shipped. For clarification purposes, Incoterms® 2010 rules include the obligation to "procure goods shipped" as an alternative to the obligation to ship goods in the relevant Incoterms rules.

Part 2 - Documentary Credit

1930 GENEVA CONVENTION PROVIDING A UNIFORM LAW FOR BILLS OF EXCHANGE AND PROMISSORY NOTES[1]

TITLE I - Bills of Exchange
CHAPTER I - Issue and Form of a Bill of Exchange
Article 1

A bill of exchange contains:
1. The term 'bill of exchange' inserted in the body of the instrument and expressed in the language employed in drawing up the instrument;
2. An unconditional order to pay a determinate sum of money;
3. The name of the person who is to pay (drawee);
4. A statement of the time of payment;
5. A statement of the place where payment is to be made;
6. The name of the person to whom or to whose order payment is to be made;
7. A statement of the date and of the place where the bill is issued;
8. The signature of the person who issues the bill (drawer).

Article 2

An instrument in which any of the requirements mentioned in the preceding Article is wanting is invalid as a bill of exchange, except in the cases specified in the following paragraphs:

A bill of exchange in which the time of payment is not specified is deemed to be payable at sight.

In default of special mention, the place specified beside the name of the drawee is deemed to be the place of payment, and at the same time the place of the domicile of the drawee.

A bill of exchange which does not mention the place of its issue is deemed to have been drawn in the place mentioned beside the name of the drawer.

Article 3

A bill of exchange may be drawn payable to drawer's order. It may be drawn on the drawer himself. It may be drawn for account of a third person.

Article 4

A bill of exchange may be payable at the domicile of a third person either in the locality where the drawee has his domicile or in another locality.

Article 5

When a bill of exchange is payable at sight, or at a fixed period after sight, the drawer may stipulate that the sum payable shall bear interest. In the case of any other bill of exchange, this stipulation is deemed not to be written.

The rate of interest must be specified in the bill; in default of such specification, the stipulation shall be deemed not to be written.

Interest runs from the date of the bill of exchange, unless some other date is specified.

Article 6

When the sum payable by a bill of exchange is expressed in words and also in figures, and there is a discrepancy between the two, the sum denoted by the words is the amount payable.

---

[1]   League of Nations Treaty Series Vol. 143, p. 257. The more modern *1988 UN Convention on International Bills of Exchange and International Promissory Notes* has not entered into force as of June 2012. It requires at least 10 ratifications and has so far been ratified by 5 States (Guinea, Mexico, Honduras, Gabon, and Liberia) and signed by 3 more (Canada, USA, Russian Federation).

Where the sum payable by a bill of exchange is expressed more than once in words or more than once in figures, and there is a discrepancy, the smaller sum is the sum payable.

Article 7
If a bill of exchange bears signatures of persons incapable of binding themselves by a bill of exchange, or forged signatures, or signatures of fictitious persons, or signatures which for any other reason cannot bind the persons who signed the bill of exchange or on whose behalf it was signed, the obligations of the other persons who signed it are none the less valid.

Article 8
Whosoever puts his signature on a bill of exchange as representing a person for whom he had no power to act is bound himself as a party to the bill and, if he pays, has the same rights as the person for whom he purported to act. The same rule applies to a representative who has exceeded his powers.

Article 9
The drawer guarantees both acceptance and payment. He may release himself from guaranteeing acceptance- every stipulation by which he releases himself from the guarantee of payment is deemed not to be written (non écrite).

Article 10
If a bill of exchange, which was incomplete when issued, has been completed otherwise than in accordance with the agreements entered into, the non-observance of such agreements may not be set up against the holder unless he has acquired the bill of exchange in bad faith or, in acquiring it, has been guilty of gross negligence.

CHAPTER II - Endorsement
Article 11
Every bill of exchange, even if not expressly drawn to order, may be transferred by means of endorsement.

When the drawer has inserted in a bill of exchange the words 'not to order' or an equivalent expression, the instrument can only be transferred according to the form, and with the effects of an ordinary assignment.

The bill may be endorsed even in favour of the drawee, whether he has accepted or not, or of the drawer, or of any other party to the bill. These persons may re-endorse the bill.

Article 12
An endorsement must be unconditional. Any condition to which it is made subject is deemed not to be written (non écrite). A partial endorsement is null and void. An endorsement 'to bearer' is equivalent to an endorsement in blank.

Article 13
An endorsement must be written on the bill of exchange or on a slip affixed thereto (allonge). It must be signed by the endorser.

The endorsement may leave the beneficiary unspecified or may consist simply of the signature of the endorser (endorsement in blank). In the latter case, the endorsement, to be valid, must be written on the back of the bill of exchange or on the slip attached thereto (allonge).

Article 14
An endorsement transfers all the rights arising out of a bill of exchange. If the endorsement is in blank, the holder may:
1. Fill up the blank either with his own name or with the name of some other person;
2. Re-endorse the bill in blank, or to some other person;
3. Transfer the bill to a third person without filling up the blank, and without endorsing it.

Article 15

In the absence of any contrary stipulation, the endorser guarantees acceptance and payment. He may prohibit any further endorsement; in this case, he gives no guarantee to the persons to whom the bill is subsequently endorsed.

Article 16

The possessor of a bill of exchange is deemed to be the lawful holder if he establishes his title to the bill through an uninterrupted series of endorsements, even if the last endorsement is in blank. In this connection, cancelled endorsements are deemed not to be written (non écrits). When an endorsement in blank is followed by another endorsement, the person who signed this last endorsement is deemed to have acquired the bill by the endorsement in blank.

Where a person has been dispossessed of a bill of exchanged, in any manner whatsoever, the holder who establishes his right thereto in the manner mentioned in the preceding paragraph is not bound to give up the bill unless he has acquired it in bad faith, or unless in acquiring it he has been guilty of gross negligence.

Article 17

Persons sued on a bill of exchange cannot set up against the holder defences founded on their personal relations with the drawer or with previous holders, unless the holder, in acquiring the bill, has knowingly acted to the detriment of the debtor.

Article 18

When an endorsement contains the statements 'value in collection' ('valeur en recouvrement'), 'for collection' ('pour encaissement'), 'by procuration' ('par procuration') or any other phrase implying a simple mandate, the holder may exercise all rights arising out of the bill of exchange, but he can only endorse it in his capacity as agent.

In this case, the parties liable can only set up against the holder defences which could be set up against the endorser.

The mandate contained in an endorsement by procuration does not terminate by reason of the death of the party giving the mandate or by reason of his becoming legally incapable.

Article 19

When an endorsement contains the statements 'value in security' ('valeur en garantie'), 'value in pledge' ('valeur en gage'), or any other statement implying a pledge, the holder may exercise all the rights arising out of the bill of exchange, but an endorsement by him has the effects only of an endorsement by an agent.

The parties liable cannot set up against the holder defences founded on their personal relations with the endorser, unless the holder, in receiving the bill, has knowingly acted to the detriment of the debtor.

Article 20

An endorsement after maturity has the same effects as an endorsement before maturity. Nevertheless an endorsement after protest for non-payment, or after the expiration of the limit of time fixed for drawing up the protest, operates only as an ordinary assignment.

Failing proof to the contrary, an endorsement without date is deemed to have been placed on the bill before the expiration of the limit of time fixed for drawing up the protest.

CHAPTER III - Acceptance
Article 21

Until maturity, a bill of exchange may be presented to the drawee for acceptance at his domicile. either by the holder or by a person who is merely in possession of the bill.

Article 22

In any bill of exchange, the drawer may stipulate that it shall be presented for acceptance with or without fixing a limit of time for presentment.

Except in the case of a bill payable at the address of a third party or in a locality other than that of the domicile of the drawee, or, except in the case of a bill drawn payable at a fixed period after sight, the drawer may prohibit presentment for acceptance.

He may al so stipulate that presentment for acceptance shall not take place before a named date.

Unless the drawer has prohibited acceptance, every endorser may stipulate that the bill shall be presented for acceptance, with or without fixing a limit of time for presentment.

Article 23

Bills of exchange payable at a fixed period after sight must be presented for acceptance within one year of their date. The drawer may abridge or extend this period. These periods may be abridged by the endorsers.

Article 24

The drawee may demand that a bill shall be presented to him a second time on the day after the first presentment. Parties interested are not allowed to set up that this demand has not been complied with unless this request is mentioned in the protest.

The holder is not obliged to surrender to the drawee a bill presented for acceptance.

Article 25

An acceptance is written on the bill of exchange. It is expressed by the word 'accepted' or any other equivalent term. It is signed by the drawee. The simple signature of the drawee on the face of the bill constitutes an acceptance.

When the bill is payable at a certain time after sight, or when it must be presented for acceptance within a certain limit of time in accordance with a special stipulation the acceptance must be dated as of the day when the acceptance is given unless the holder requires it shall be dated as of the day of presentment. If it is undated, the holder, in order to preserve his right of recourse against the endorsers and the drawer, must authenticate the omission by a protest drawn up within the proper time.

Article 26

An acceptance is unconditional, but the drawee may restrict it to part of the sum payable. t Every other modification introduced by an acceptance into the tenor of the bill of exchange operates as a refusal to accept. Nevertheless, the acceptor is bound according to the terms of his acceptance.

Article 27

When the drawer of a bill has indicated a place of payment other than the domicile of the drawee without specifying a third party at whose address payment must be made, the drawee may name such third party at the time of acceptance. In default of this indication, the acceptor is deemed to have undertaken to pay the bill himself at the place of payment.

If a bill is payable at the domicile of the drawee, the latter may in his acceptance indicate an address in the same place where payment is to be made.

Article 28

By accepting, the drawee undertakes to pay the bill of exchange at its maturity. In default of payment, the holder, even if he is the drawer, has a direct action on the bill of exchange against the acceptor for all that can be demanded in accordance with Articles 48 and 49.

Article 29

Where the drawee who has put his acceptance on a bill has cancelled it before restoring the bill, acceptance is deemed to be refused. Failing proof to the contrary, the cancellation is deemed to have taken place before the bill was restored.

Nevertheless, if the drawee has notified his acceptance in writing to the holder or to any party who has signed the bill, he is liable to such parties according to the terms of his acceptance.

CHAPTER IV - 'Avals'
Article 30
Payment of a bill of exchange may be guaranteed by an 'aval' as to the whole or part of its amount.

This guarantee may be given by a third person or even by a person who has signed as a party to the bill.

Article 31
The 'aval' is given either on the bill itself or on an 'allonge'.

It is expressed by the words 'good as aval'('bon pour aval') or by any other equivalent formula. It is signed by the giver of the 'aval'.

It is deemed to be constituted by the mere signature of the giver of the 'aval' placed on the face of the bill, except in the case of the signature of the drawee or of the drawer.

An 'aval' must specify for whose account it is given. In default of this it is deemed to be given for the drawer.

Article 32
The giver of an 'aval' is bound in the same manner as the person for whom he has become guarantor.

His undertaking is valid even when the liability which he has guaranteed is inoperative for any reason other than defect of form.

He has, when he pays a bill of exchange, the rights arising out of the bill of exchange against the person guaranteed and against those who are liable to the latter on the bill of exchange.

CHAPTER V - Maturity
Article 33
A bill of exchange may be drawn payable:
-   at sight;
-   at a fixed period after sight;
-   at a fixed period after date;
-   at a fixed date.

Bills of exchange at other maturities or payable by instalments are null and void.

Article 34
A bill of exchange at sight is payable on presentment. It must be presented for payment within a year of its date. The drawer may abridge or extend this period. These periods may be abridged by the endorsers.

The drawer may prescribe that a bill of exchange payable at sight must not be presented for payment before a named date. In this case, the period for presentation begins from the said date.

Article 35
The maturity of a bill of exchange payable at a fixed period after sight is determined either by the date of the acceptance or by the date of the protest.

In the absence of the protest, an undated acceptance is deemed, so far as regards the acceptor, to have been given on the last day of the limit of time for presentment for acceptance.

Article 36
Where a bill of exchange is drawn at one or more months after date or after sight, the bill matures on the corresponding date of the month when payment must be made. If there be no corresponding date, the bill matures on the last day of this month.

When a bill of exchange is drawn at one or more months and a-half after date or sight, entire months must first be calculated.

If the maturity is fixed at the commencement, in the middle (mid-January or mid-February, etc.,) or at the end of the month, the first, fifteenth or last day of the month is to be understood.

The expressions 'eight days' or 'fifteen days' indicate not one or two weeks, but a period of eight or fifteen actual days.

The expression 'half-month' means a period of fifteen days.

Article 37

When a bill of exchange is payable on a fixed day in a place where the calendar is different from the calendar in the place of issue, the day of maturity is deemed to be fixed according to the calendar of the place of payment.

When a bill of exchange drawn between two places having different calendars is payable at a fixed period after date, the day of issue is referred to the corresponding day of the calendar in the place of payment, and the maturity is fixed accordingly.

The time for presenting bills of exchange is calculated in accordance with the rules of the preceding paragraph.

These rules do not apply if a stipulation in the bill or even the simple terms of the instrument indicate an intention to adopt some different rule.

Bills of exchange at other maturities or payable by instalments are null and void.

CHAPTER VI - Payment

Article 38

The holder of a bill of exchange payable on a fixed day or at a fixed period after date or after sight must present the bill for payment either on the day on which it is payable or on one of the two business days which follow.

The presentment of a bill of exchange at a clearing-house is equivalent to a presentment for payment.

Article 39

The drawee who pays a bill of exchange may require that it shall be given up to him receipted by the holder.

The holder may not refuse partial payment.

In case of partial payment the drawee may require that mention of this payment shall be made on the bill, and that a receipt therefor shall be given to him.

Article 40

The holder of a bill of exchange cannot be compelled to receive a payment thereof before maturity.

The drawee who pays before maturity does so at his own risk and peril. He who pays at maturity is validly discharged, unless he has been guilty of fraud or gross negligence. He is bound to verify the regularity of the series of endorsements, but not the signature of the endorsers.

Article 41

When a bill of exchange is drawn payable in a currency which is not that of the place of payment, the sum payable may be paid in the currency of the country, according to its value on the date of maturity. If the debtor is in default, the holder may at his option demand that the amount of the bill be paid in the currency of the country according to the rate on the day of maturity or the day of payment.

The usages of the place of payment determine the value of foreign currency. Nevertheless, the drawer may stipulate that the sum payable shall be calculated according to a rate expressed in the bill.

The foregoing rules shall not apply to the case in which the drawer has stipulated that payment must be made in a certain specified currency (stipulation for effective payment in foreign currency).

If the amount of the bill of exchange is specified in a currency having the same denomination, but a different value in the country of issue and the country of payment, reference is deemed to be made to the currency of the place of payment.

Article 42

When a bill of exchange e is not presented for payment within the limit of time fixed by Article 38, every debtor is authorised to deposit the amount with the competent authority at the charge, risk and peril of the holder.

CHAPTER VII - Recourse for Non-Acceptance or Non-Payment

Article 43

The holder may exercise his right of recourse against the endorsers, the drawer and the other parties liable:

At maturity: If payment has not been made;

Even before maturity;

1. If there has been total or partial refusal to accept;
2. In the event of the bankruptcy (faillite) of the drawee, whether he has accepted or not, or in the event of a stoppage of payment on his part, even when not declared by a judgement, or when execution has been levied against his goods without result;
3. In the event of the bankruptcy (faillite) of the drawer of a non-acceptable bill.

Article 44

Default of acceptance or on payment must be evidenced by an authentic act (protest for non-acceptance or non-payment).

Protest for non-acceptance must be made within the limit of time fixed for presentment for acceptance. If in the case contemplated by Article 24, paragraph 1, the first presentment takes place on the last day of that time, the protest may nevertheless be drawn up on the next day.

Protest for non-payment of a bill of exchange payable on a fixed day or at a fixed period after date or sight must be made on one of the two business days following the day on which the bill is payable. In the case of a bill payable at sight, the protest must be drawn up under the conditions specified in the foregoing paragraph for the drawing up of a protest for non-acceptance.

Protest for non-acceptance dispenses with presentment for payment and protest for non-payment.

If there is a stoppage of payment on the part of the drawee, whether he has accepted or not, or if execution has been levied against his goods without result, the holder cannot exercise his right of recourse until after presentment of the bill to the drawee for payment and after the protest has been drawn up.

If the drawee, whether he accepted or not, is declared bankrupt (faillite déclarée), or in the event of the declared bankruptcy of the drawer of a non-acceptable bill, the production of the judgement declaring the bankruptcy suffices to enable the holder to exercise his right of re-course.

Article 45

The holder must give notice of non-acceptance or non-payment to his endorser and to the drawer within the four business days which follow the day for protest or, in case of a stipulation 'retour sans frais', the day for presentment. Every endorser must, within the two business days following the day on which he receives notice, notify his endorser of the notice he has received, mentioning the names and addresses of those who have given the previous notices, and so on through the series until the drawer is reached. The periods mentioned above run from the receipt of the preceding notice.

When, in conformity with the preceding paragraph, notice is given to a person who has signed a bill of exchange, the same notice must be given within the same limit of time to his avaliseur.

Where an endorser either has not specified his address or has specified it in an illegible manner, it is sufficient that notice should be given to the preceding endorser.

A person who must give notice may give it in any form whatever, even by simply returning the bill of exchange.

He must prove that he has given notice within the time allowed. This time-limit shall be regarded as having been observed if a letter giving the notice has been posted within the prescribed time.

A person who does not give notice within the limit of time mentioned above does not forfeit his rights. He is responsible for the injury, if any, caused by his negligence, but the damages shall not exceed the amount of the bill of exchange.

Article 46

The drawer, an endorser, or a person guaranteeing payment by aval (avaliseur) may, by the stipulation 'retour sans frais', 'sans protet', or any other equivalent expression written on the instrument and signed, release the holder from having a protest of non-acceptance or non-payment drawn up in order to exercise his right of recourse.

This stipulation does not release the holder from presenting the bill within the prescribed time, or from the notices he has to give. The burden of proving the non-observance of the limits of time lies on the person who seeks to set it up against the holder.

If the stipulation is written by the drawer, it is operative in respect of all persons who have signed the bill; if it is written by an endorser or an avaliseur, it is operative only in respect of such endorser or avaliseur. If, in spite of the stipulation written by the drawer, the holder has the protest drawn up, he must bear the expenses thereof. When the stipulation emanates from an endorser or avaliseur, the costs of the protest, if one is drawn up, may be recovered from all the persons who have signed the bill.

Article 47

All drawers, acceptors, endorsers or guarantors by aval of a bill of exchange are jointly and severally liable to the holder. The holder has the right of proceeding against all these persons individually or collectively without being required to observe the order in which they have become bound.

The same right is possessed by any person signing the bill who has taken it up and paid it.

Proceedings against one of the parties liable do not prevent proceedings against the others, even though they may be subsequent to the party first proceeded against.

Article 48

The holder may recover from the person against whom he exercises his right of recourse:
1.   The amount of the unaccepted or unpaid bill of exchange with interest, if interest has been stipulated for;
2.   Interest at the rate of 6 per cent from the date of maturity;
3.   The expenses of protest and of the notices given as well as other expenses.
If the right of recourse is exercised before maturity, the amount of the bill shall be subject to a discount. This discount shall be calculated according to the official rate of discount (bank-rate) ruling on the date when recourse is exercised at the place of domicile of the holder.

Article 49

A party who takes up and pays a bill of exchange can recover from the parties liable to him:
1.   The entire sum which he has paid;
2.   Interest on the said sum calculated at the rate of 6 per cent, starting from the day when he made payment;
3.   Any expenses which he has incurred.

Article 50

Every party liable against whom a right of recourse is or may be exercised, can require against payment, that the bill shall be given up to him with the protest and a receipted account.

Every endorser who has taken up and paid a bill of exchange may cancel his own endorsement and those of subsequent endorsers.

Article 51

In the case of the exercise of the right of recourse after a partial acceptance, the party who pays the sum in respect of which the bill has not been accepted can require that this payment shall be specified on the bill and that he shall be given a receipt therefor. The holder must also give him a certified copy of the bill, together with the protest, in order to enable subsequent recourse to be exercised.

Article 52

Every person having the right of recourse may, in the absence of agreement to the contrary, reimburse himself by means of a fresh bill (redraft) to be drawn at sight on one of the parties liable to him and payable at the domicile of that party.

The redraft includes, in addition to the sums mentioned in Articles 48 and 49, brokerage and the cost of stamping the redraft.

If the redraft is drawn by the holder, the sum payable is fixed according to the rate for a sight bill drawn at the place where the original bill was payable upon the party liable at the place of his domicile. If the redraft is drawn by an endorser, the sum payable is fixed according to the rate for a sight bill drawn at the place where the drawer of the redraft is domiciled upon the place of domicile of the party liable.

Article 53

After the expiration of the limits of time fixed:

For the presentment of a bill of exchange drawn at sight or at a fixed period after sight;

For drawing up the protest for non-acceptance or non-payment;

For presentment for payment in the case of a stipulation retour sans frais, the holder loses his rights of recourse against the endorsers, against the drawer and against the other parties liable, with the exception of the acceptor.

In default of presentment for acceptance within the limit of time stipulated by the drawer, the holder loses his right of recourse for non-payment, as well as for non-acceptance, unless it appears from the terms of the stipulation that the drawer only meant to release himself from the guarantee of acceptance.

If the stipulation for a limit of time for presentment is contained in an endorsement, the endorser alone can avail himself of it.

Article 54

Should the presentment of the bill of exchange or the drawing up of the protest within the prescribed limits of time be prevented by an insurmountable obstacle (legal prohibition (prescription légale) by any State or other case of vis major), these limits of time shall be extended. The holder is bound to give notice without delay of the case of vis major to his endorser and to specify this notice, which he must date and sign, on the bill or on an allonge; in other respects the provisions of Article 45 shall apply.

When vis major has terminated the holder must without delay present the bill of exchange for acceptance or payment and, if need be, draw up the protest. If vis major continues to operate beyond thirty days after maturity, recourse may be exercised, and neither presentment nor the drawing up of a protest shall be necessary.

In the case of bills of exchange drawn at sight or at a fixed period after sight, the time-limit of thirty days shall run from the date on which the holder, even before the expiration of the time for presentment, has given notice of vis major to his endorser. In the case of bill of exchange drawn at a certain time after sight, the above time-limit of thirty days shall be added to the period after sight specified in the bill of exchange.

Facts which are purely personal to the holder or to the person whom he has entrusted with the presentment of the bill or drawing up of the bill or drawing up of the protest are not deemed to constitute cases of vis major.

CHAPTER VIII - Intervention for Honour
I. General Provisions
Article 55

The drawer, an endorser, or a person giving an aval may specify a person who is to accept or pay in case of need.

A bill of exchange may, subject as hereinafter mentioned, be accepted or paid by a person who intervenes for the honour of any debtor against whom a right of recourse exists.

The person intervening may be a third party, even the drawee, or, save the acceptor, a party already liable on the bill of exchange.

The person intervening is bound to give, within two business days, notice of his intervention to the party for whose honour he has intervened. In default, he is responsible for the injury, if any, due to his negligence, but the damages shall not exceed the amount of the bill of exchange.

2. Acceptance by Intervention (for Honour)
Article 56

There may be acceptance by intervention in all cases where the holder has a right of recourse before maturity on a bill which is capable of acceptance.

When the bill of exchange indicates a person who is designated to accept or pay it in case of need at the place of payment, the holder may not exercise his rights of recourse before maturity against the person naming such referee in case of need and against subsequent signatories, unless he has presented the bill of exchange to the referee in case of need and until, if acceptance is refused by the latter, this refusal has been authenticated by a protest.

In other cases of intervention the holder may refuse an acceptance by intervention. Nevertheless, if he allows it, he loses his right of recourse before maturity against the person on whose behalf such acceptance was given and against subsequent signatories.

Article 57

Acceptance by intervention is specified on the bill of exchange. It is signed by the person intervening. It mentions the person for whose honour it has been given and, in default of such mention, the acceptance is deemed to have been given for the honour of the drawer.

Article 58

The acceptor by intervention is liable to the holder and to the endorsers subsequent to the party for whose honour he intervened, in the same manner as such party.

Notwithstanding an acceptance by intervention, the party for whose honour it has been given and the parties liable to him may require the holder, in exchange for payment of the sum mentioned in Article 48, to deliver the bill, the protest, and a receipted account, if any.

3. Payment by Intervention
Article 59

Payment by intervention may take place in all cases where, either at maturity or before maturity, the holder has a right of recourse on the bill.

Payment must include the whole amount payable by the party for whose honour it is made.

It must be made at the latest on the day following the last day allowed for drawing up the protest for non-payment.

Article 60

If a bill of exchange has been accepted by persons intervening who are domiciled in the place of payment, or if persons domiciled therein have been named as referees in case of need, the holder must present the bill to all these persons and, if necessary, have a protest for non-payment drawn up at latest on the day following the last day allowed for drawing up the protest.

In default of protest within this limit of time, the party who has named the referee in case of need, or for whose account the bill has been accepted, and the subsequent endorsers are discharged.

Article 61

The holder who refuses payment by intervention loses his right of recourse against any persons who would have been discharged thereby.

Article 62

Payment by intervention must be authenticated by a receipt given on the bill of exchange mentioning the person for whose honour payment has been made. In default of such mention, payment is deemed to have been made for the honour of the drawer.

The bill of exchange and the protest, if any, must be given up to the person paying by intervention.

Article 63

The person paying by intervention acquires the rights arising out of the bill of exchange against the party for whose honour he has paid and against persons who are liable to the latter on the bill of exchange. Nevertheless, he cannot re-endorse the bill of exchange.

Endorsers subsequent to the party for whose honour payment has been made are discharged.

In case of competition for payment by intervention, the payment which effects the greater number of releases has the preference. Any person who, with a knowledge of the facts, intervenes in a manner contrary to this rule, loses his right of recourse against those who would have been discharged.

CHAPTER IX - Parts of a Set and Copies
1. Parts of a Set
Article 64

A bill of exchange can be drawn in a set of two or more identical parts. These parts must be numbered in the body of the instrument itself; in default, each part is considered as a separate bill of exchange.

Every holder of a bill which does not specify that it has been drawn as a sole bill may, at his own expense, require the delivery of two or more parts. For this purpose he must apply to his immediate endorser, who is bound to assist him in proceeding against his own endorser, and so on in the series until the drawer is reached. The endorsers are bound to reproduce their endorsements on the new parts of the set.

Article 65

Payment made on one part of a set operates as a discharge, even though there is no stipulation that this payment annuls the effect on the other parts. Nevertheless, the drawee is liable on each accepted part which he has not recovered.

An endorser who has transferred parts of a set to different persons, as well as subsequent endorsers, are liable on all the parts bearing their signature which have not been restored.

Article 66

A party who has sent one part for acceptance must indicate on the other parts the name of the person in whose hands this part is to be found. That person is bound to give it up to the lawful holder of another part.

If he refuses, the holder cannot exercise his right of recourse until he has had a protest drawn us specifying:

1. That the part sent for acceptance has not been given up to him on demand;
2. that acceptance or payment could not be obtained on another of parts.

2. Copies
Article 67

Every holder of a bill of exchange has the right to make copies of it. A copy must reproduce the original exactly, with the endorsements and all other statements to be found therein. It must specify where the copy ends. It may be endorsed and guaranteed by aval in the same manner and with the same effects as the original.

Article 68

A copy must specify the person in possession of the original instrument. The latter is bound to hand over the said instrument to the lawful holder of the copy.

If he refuses, the holder may not exercise his right of recourse against the persons who have endorsed the copy or guaranteed it by aval until he has had a protest drawn up specifying that the original has not been given up to him on his demand.

Where the original instrument, after the last endorsement before the making of the copy contains a clause 'commencing from here an endorsement is only valid if made on the copy' or some equivalent formula, a subsequent endorsement on the original is null and void.

CHAPTER X - Alterations
Article 69

In case of alteration of the text of a bill of exchange, parties who have signed subsequent to the alteration are bound according to the terms of the altered text; parties who have signed before the alteration are bound according to the terms of the original text.

CHAPTER XI - Limitation of Actions
Article 70

All actions arising out of a bill of exchange against the acceptor are barred after three years, reckoned from the date of maturity.

Actions by the holder against the endorsers and against the drawer are barred after one year from the date of a protest drawn up within proper time, or from the date of maturity where there is a stipulation retour sans frais.

Actions by endorsers against each other and against the drawer are barred after six months, reckoned from the day when the endorser took up and paid the bill or from the day when he himself was sued.

Article 71

Interruption of the period of limitation is only effective against the person in respect of whom the period has been interrupted.

CHAPTER XII - General Provisions
Article 72

Payment of a bill of exchange which falls due on a legal holiday (jour férié légal) cannot be demanded until the next business day. So, too, all other proceedings relating to a bill of exchange, in particular presentment for acceptance and protest, can only be taken on a business day.

Where any of these proceedings must be taken within a certain limit of time the last day of which is a legal holiday (jour férié légal), the limit of time is extended until the first business day which follows the expiration of that time. Intermediate holidays (jours fériés) are included in computing limits of time.

Article 73

Legal or contractual limits of time do not include the day on which the period commences.

Article 74

No days of grace, whether legal or judicial, are permitted.

TITLE II - Promissory Notes
Article 75

A promissory note contains:
1.   The term 'promissory note' inserted in the body of the instrument and expressed in the language employed in drawing up the instrument;
2.   An unconditional promise to pay a determinate sum of money;
3.   A statement of the time of payment;
4.   A statement of the place where payment is to be made;
5.   The name of the person to whom or to whose order payment is to be made;
6.   A statement of the date and of the place where the promissory note is issued;

7.   The signature of the person who issues the instrument (maker).

Article 76
An instrument in which any of the requirements mentioned in the preceding Article are wanting is invalid as a promissory note except in the cases specified in the following paragraphs.

A promissory note in which the time of payment is not specified is deemed to be payable at sight.

In default of special mention, the place where the instrument is made is deemed to be the place of payment and at the same time the place of the domicile of the maker.

A promissory note which does not mention the place of its issue is deemed to have been made in the place mentioned beside the name of the maker.

Article 77
The following provisions relating to bills of exchange apply to promissory notes so far as they are not inconsistent with the nature of these instruments, viz:
-    Endorsement (Article 11 to 20);
-    Time of payment (Articles 33 to 37);
-    Payment (Articles 38 to 42);
-    Recourse in case of non-payment (Articles 43 to 50, 52 to 54);
-    Payment by intervention (Articles 55, 59 to 63);
-    Copies (Articles 67 and 68);
-    Alterations (Article 69);
-    Limitation of actions (Articles 70 and 71);
-    Holidays, computation of limits of time and prohibition of days of grace (Articles 72, 73 and 74).

The following provisions are also applicable to a promissory note: The provisions concerning a bill of exchange payable at the address of a third party or in a locality other than that of the domicile of the drawee (Articles 4 and 27): stipulation for interest (Article 5); discrepancies as regards the sum payable (Article 6); the consequences of signature under the conditions mentioned in Article 7, the consequences of signature by a person who acts without authority or who exceeds his authority (Article 8); and provisions concerning a bill of exchange in blank (Article 10).

The following provisions are also applicable to a promissory note: Provisions relating to guarantee by aval (Articles 30-32); in the case provided for in Article 31, last paragraph, if the aval does not specify on whose behalf it has been given, it is deemed to have been given on behalf of the maker of the promissory note.

Article 78
The maker of a promissory note is bound in the same manner as an acceptor of a bill of exchange.

Promissory notes payable at a certain time after sight must be presented for the visa of the maker within the limits of time fixed by Article 23. The limit of time runs from the date of which marks the commencement of the period of time after sight. [...]

Entry into Force: 1 January 1934
Ratification and Binding Effect as of July 2013: Austria (1934), Azerbaijan (2000), Belarus (1998), Belgium (1934), Brazil (1942), Denmark (1934), Finland (1934), France (1936), Germany (1934), Greece (1934), Hungary (1964), Italy (1934), Japan (1934), Kazakhstan (1995), Kyrgyzstan (2003), Lithuania (1997), Luxembourg (1963), Monaco (1934), Netherlands (1934), Norway (1934), Poland (1936), Portugal (1934), Sweden (1934), Switzerland (1934), Ukraine (1999), USSR (1936).

UNIFORM CUSTOMS AND PRACTICE FOR DOCUMENTARY CREDITS ("UCP 600")[1]

Article 1 Application of UCP

The Uniform Customs and Practice for Documentary Credits, 2007 Revision, ICC Publication no. 600 ("UCP") are rules that apply to any documentary credit ("credit") (including, to the extent to which they may be applicable, any standby letter of credit) when the text of the credit expressly indicates that it is subject to these rules. They are binding on all parties thereto unless expressly modified or excluded by the credit.

Article 2 Definitions

For the purpose of these rules:

Advising bank means the bank that advises the credit at the request of the issuing bank.

Applicant means the party on whose request the credit is issued.

Banking day means a day on which a bank is regularly open at the place at which an act subject to these rules is to be performed.

Beneficiary means the party in whose favour a credit is issued.

Complying presentation means a presentation that is in accordance with the terms and conditions of the credit, the applicable provisions of these rules and international standard banking practice.

Confirmation means a definite undertaking of the confirming bank, in addition to that of the issuing bank, to honour or negotiate a complying presentation.

Confirming bank means the bank that adds its confirmation to a credit upon the issuing bank's authorization or request.

Credit means any arrangement, however named or described, that is irrevocable and thereby constitutes a definite undertaking of the issuing bank to honour a complying presentation.

Honour means:

a. to pay at sight if the credit is available by sight payment.

b. to incur a deferred payment undertaking and pay at maturity if the credit is available by deferred payment.

c. to accept a bill of exchange ("draft") drawn by the beneficiary and pay at maturity if the credit is available by acceptance.

Issuing bank means the bank that issues a credit at the request of an applicant or on its own behalf.

Negotiation means the purchase by the nominated bank of drafts (drawn on a bank other than the nominated bank) and/or documents under a complying presentation, by advancing or agreeing to advance funds to the beneficiary on or before the banking day on which reimbursement is due to the nominated bank.

Nominated bank means the bank with which the credit is available or any bank in the case of a credit available with any bank.

Presentation means either the delivery of documents under a credit to the issuing bank or nominated bank or the documents so delivered.

Presenter means a beneficiary, bank or other party that makes a presentation.

Article 3 Interpretations

For the purpose of these rules:

Where applicable, words in the singular include the plural and in the plural include the singular.

A credit is irrevocable even if there is no indication to that effect.

A document may be signed by handwriting, facsimile signature, perforated signature, stamp, symbol or any other mechanical or electronic method of authentication.

---

1   © International Chamber of Commerce, Paris.

A requirement for a document to be legalized, visaed, certified or similar will be satisfied by any signature, mark, stamp or label on the document which appears to satisfy that requirement.

Branches of a bank in different countries are considered to be separate banks.

Terms such as "first class", "well known", "qualified", "independent", "official", "competent" or "local" used to describe the issuer of a document allow any issuer except the beneficiary to issue that document.

Unless required to be used in a document, words such as "prompt", "immediately" or "as soon as possible" will be disregarded.

The expression "on or about" or similar will be interpreted as a stipulation that an event is to occur during a period of five calendar days before until five calendar days after the specified date, both start and end dates included.

The words "to", "until", "till", "from" and "between" when used to determine a period of shipment include the date or dates mentioned, and the words "before" and "after" exclude the date mentioned.

The words "from" and "after" when used to determine a maturity date exclude the date mentioned.

The terms "first half" and "second half" of a month shall be construed respectively as the 1st to the 15th and the 16th to the last day of the month, all dates inclusive.

The terms "beginning", "middle" and "end" of a month shall be construed respectively as the 1st to the 10th, the 11th to the 20th and the 21st to the last day of the month, all dates inclusive.

Article 4 Credits v. Contracts *principal of independence*

a. A credit by its nature is a separate transaction from the sale or other contract on which it may be based. Banks are in no way concerned with or bound by such contract, even if any reference whatsoever to it is included in the credit. Consequently, the undertaking of a bank to honour, to negotiate or to fulfil any other obligation under the credit is not subject to claims or defences by the applicant resulting from its relationships with the issuing bank or the beneficiary.

A beneficiary can in no case avail itself of the contractual relationships existing between banks or between the applicant and the issuing bank.

b. An issuing bank should discourage any attempt by the applicant to include, as an integral part of the credit, copies of the underlying contract, proforma invoice and the like.

Article 5 Documents v. Goods, Services or Performance

Banks deal with documents and not with goods, services or performance to which the documents may relate.

Article 6 Availability, Expiry Date and Place for Presentation

a. A credit must state the bank with which it is available or whether it is available with any bank.

A credit available with a nominated bank is also available with the issuing bank.

b. A credit must state whether it is available by sight payment, deferred payment, acceptance or negotiation.

c. A credit must not be issued available by a draft drawn on the applicant.

d. **i.** A credit must state an expiry date for presentation. An expiry date stated for honour or negotiation will be deemed to be an expiry date for presentation.

ii. The place of the bank with which the credit is available is the place for presentation. The place for presentation under a credit available with any bank is that of any bank. A place for presentation other than that of the issuing bank is in addition to the place of the issuing bank.

e. Except as provided in sub-article 29 (a), a presentation by or on behalf of the beneficiary must be made on or before the expiry date.

Article 7 Issuing Bank Undertaking -obligations

a.   Provided that the <u>stipulated documents are presented</u> to the nominated bank or to the issuing bank and that they <u>constitute a complying presentation</u>, the <u>issuing bank must honour</u> <u>if the credit is available by</u>:

  i. sight payment, deferred payment or acceptance with the issuing bank;
  ii. sight payment with a nominated bank and that nominated bank does not pay;
  iii. deferred payment with a nominated bank and that nominated bank does not incur its deferred payment undertaking or, having incurred its deferred payment undertaking, does not pay at maturity;
  iv. acceptance with a nominated bank and that nominated bank does not accept a draft drawn on it or, having accepted a draft drawn on it, does not pay at maturity;
  v. negotiation with a nominated bank and that nominated bank does not negotiate.

b.   An issuing bank is irrevocably bound to honour as of the time it issues the credit.

c.   An issuing bank undertakes to reimburse a nominated bank that has honoured or negotiated a complying presentation and forwarded the documents to the issuing bank. Reimbursement for the amount of a complying presentation under a credit available by acceptance or deferred payment is due at maturity, whether or not the nominated bank prepaid or purchased before maturity. An issuing bank's undertaking to reimburse a nominated bank is independent of the issuing bank's undertaking to the beneficiary.

Article 8 Confirming Bank Undertaking

a.   Provided that the <u>stipulated documents</u> are <u>presented</u> to the confirming bank or <u>to any</u> <u>other nominated bank</u> and that they <u>constitute a complying presentation</u>, the <u>confirming bank</u> must:

  i. <u>honour, if the credit is available by</u>
    aa. sight payment, deferred payment or acceptance with the confirming bank;
    bb. sight payment with another nominated bank and that nominated bank does not pay;
    cc. deferred payment with another nominated bank and that nominated bank does not incur its deferred payment undertaking or, having incurred its deferred payment undertaking, does not pay at maturity;
    dd. acceptance with another nominated bank and that nominated bank does not accept a draft drawn on it or, having accepted a draft drawn on it, does not pay at maturity;
    ee. negotiation with another nominated bank and that nominated bank does not negotiate.
  ii. <u>negotiate, without recourse, if the credit is available by negotiation with the confirming</u> <u>bank.</u>

b.   A confirming bank is irrevocably bound to honour or negotiate as of the time it adds its confirmation to the credit.

c.   A confirming bank undertakes to reimburse another nominated bank that has honoured or negotiated a complying presentation and forwarded the documents to the confirming bank. Reimbursement for the amount of a complying presentation under a credit available by acceptance or deferred payment is due at maturity, whether or not another nominated bank prepaid or purchased before maturity. A confirming bank's undertaking to reimburse another nominated bank is independent of the confirming bank's undertaking to the beneficiary.

d.   If a bank is authorized or requested by the issuing bank to confirm a credit but is not prepared to do so, it must inform the issuing bank without delay and may advise the credit without confirmation.

Article 9 Advising of Credits and Amendments

a.   A credit and any amendment may be advised to a beneficiary through an advising bank. An advising bank that is not a confirming bank advises the credit and any amendment without any undertaking to honour or negotiate.

b. By advising the credit or amendment, the advising bank signifies that it has satisfied itself as to the apparent authenticity of the credit or amendment and that the advice accurately reflects the terms and conditions of the credit or amendment received.

c. An advising bank may utilize the services of another bank ("second advising bank") to advise the credit and any amendment to the beneficiary. By advising the credit or amendment, the second advising bank signifies that it has satisfied itself as to the apparent authenticity of the advice it has received and that the advice accurately reflects the terms and conditions of the credit or amendment received.

d. A bank utilizing the services of an advising bank or second advising bank to advise a credit must use the same bank to advise any amendment thereto.

e. If a bank is requested to advise a credit or amendment but elects not to do so, it must so inform, without delay, the bank from which the credit, amendment or advice has been received.

f. If a bank is requested to advise a credit or amendment but cannot satisfy itself as to the apparent authenticity of the credit, the amendment or the advice, it must so inform, without delay, the bank from which the instructions appear to have been received. If the advising bank or second advising bank elects nonetheless to advise the credit or amendment, it must inform the beneficiary or second advising bank that it has not been able to satisfy itself as to the apparent authenticity of the credit, the amendment or the advice.

Article 10 Amendments

a. Except as otherwise provided by Article 38, a credit can neither be amended nor cancelled without the agreement of the issuing bank, the confirming bank, if any, and the beneficiary.

b. An issuing bank is irrevocably bound by an amendment as of the time it issues the amendment. A confirming bank may extend its confirmation to an amendment and will be irrevocably bound as of the time it advises the amendment. A confirming bank may, however, choose to advise an amendment without extending its confirmation and, if so, it must inform the issuing bank without delay and inform the beneficiary in its advice.

c. The terms and conditions of the original credit (or a credit incorporating previously accepted amendments) will remain in force for the beneficiary until the beneficiary communicates its acceptance of the amendment to the bank that advised such amendment. The beneficiary should give notification of acceptance or rejection of an amendment. If the beneficiary fails to give such notification, a presentation that complies with the credit and to any not yet accepted amendment will be deemed to be notification of acceptance by the beneficiary of such amendment. As of that moment the credit will be amended.

d. A bank that advises an amendment should inform the bank from which it received the amendment of any notification of acceptance or rejection.

e. Partial acceptance of an amendment is not allowed and will be deemed to be notification of rejection of the amendment.

f. A provision in an amendment to the effect that the amendment shall enter into force unless rejected by the beneficiary within a certain time shall be disregarded.

Article 11 Teletransmitted and Pre-Advised Credits and Amendments

a. An authenticated teletransmission of a credit or amendment will be deemed to be the operative credit or amendment, and any subsequent mail confirmation shall be disregarded.

If a teletransmission states "full details to follow" (or words of similar effect), or states that the mail confirmation is to be the operative credit or amendment, then the teletransmission will not be deemed to be the operative credit or amendment. The issuing bank must then issue the operative credit or amendment without delay in terms not inconsistent with the teletransmission.

b. A preliminary advice of the issuance of a credit or amendment ("pre-advice") shall only be sent if the issuing bank is prepared to issue the operative credit or amendment. An issuing bank that sends a pre-advice is irrevocably committed to issue the operative credit or amendment, without delay, in terms not inconsistent with the pre-advice.

Article 12 Nomination

a. Unless a nominated bank is the confirming bank, an authorization to honour or negotiate does not impose any obligation on that nominated bank to honour or negotiate, except when expressly agreed to by that nominated bank and so communicated to the beneficiary.

b. By nominating a bank to accept a draft or incur a deferred payment undertaking, an issuing bank authorizes that nominated bank to prepay or purchase a draft accepted or a deferred payment undertaking incurred by that nominated bank.

c. Receipt or examination and forwarding of documents by a nominated bank that is not a confirming bank does not make that nominated bank liable to honour or negotiate, nor does it constitute honour or negotiation.

Article 13 Bank-to-Bank Reimbursement Arrangements

a. If a credit states that reimbursement is to be obtained by a nominated bank ("claiming bank") claiming on another party ("reimbursing bank"), the credit must state if the reimbursement is subject to the ICC rules for bank-to-bank reimbursements in effect on the date of issuance of the credit.

b. If a credit does not state that reimbursement is subject to the ICC rules for bank-to-bank reimbursements, the following apply:

i. An issuing bank must provide a reimbursing bank with a reimbursement authorization that conforms with the availability stated in the credit. The reimbursement authorization should not be subject to an expiry date.

ii. A claiming bank shall not be required to supply a reimbursing bank with a certificate of compliance with the terms and conditions of the credit.

iii. An issuing bank will be responsible for any loss of interest, together with any expenses incurred, if reimbursement is not provided on first demand by a reimbursing bank in accordance with the terms and conditions of the credit.

iv. A reimbursing bank's charges are for the account of the issuing bank. However, if the charges are for the account of the beneficiary, it is the responsibility of an issuing bank to so indicate in the credit and in the reimbursement authorization. If a reimbursing bank's charges are for the account of the beneficiary, they shall be deducted from the amount due to a claiming bank when reimbursement is made. If no reimbursement is made, the reimbursing bank's charges remain the obligation of the issuing bank.

c. An issuing bank is not relieved of any of its obligations to provide reimbursement if reimbursement is not made by a reimbursing bank on first demand.

Article 14 Standard for Examination of Documents

a. A nominated bank acting on its nomination, a confirming bank, if any, and the issuing bank must examine a presentation to determine, on the basis of the documents alone, whether or not the documents appear on their face to constitute a complying presentation.

b. A nominated bank acting on its nomination, a confirming bank, if any, and the issuing bank shall each have a maximum of five banking days following the day of presentation to determine if a presentation is complying. This period is not curtailed or otherwise affected by the occurrence on or after the date of presentation of any expiry date or last day for presentation.

c. A presentation including one or more original transport documents subject to articles 19, 20, 21, 22, 23, 24 or 25 must be made by or on behalf of the beneficiary not later than 21 calendar days after the date of shipment as described in these rules, but in any event not later than the expiry date of the credit.

d. Data in a document, when read in context with the credit, the document itself and international standard banking practice, need not be identical to, but must not conflict with, data in that document, any other stipulated document or the credit.

e. In documents other than the commercial invoice, the description of the goods, services or performance, if stated, may be in general terms not conflicting with their description in the credit.

f.   If a credit requires presentation of a document other than a transport document, insurance document or commercial invoice, without stipulating by whom the document is to be issued or its data content, banks will accept the document as presented if its content appears to fulfil the function of the required document and otherwise complies with sub-article 14 (d).

g.   A document presented but not required by the credit will be disregarded and may be returned to the presenter. *see art. 4*

h.   If a credit contains a condition without stipulating the document to indicate compliance with the condition, banks will deem such condition as not stated and will disregard it.

i.   A document may be dated prior to the issuance date of the credit, but must not be dated later than its date of presentation.

j.   When the addresses of the beneficiary and the applicant appear in any stipulated document, they need not be the same as those stated in the credit or in any other stipulated document, but must be within the same country as the respective addresses mentioned in the credit. Contact details (telefax, telephone, email and the like) stated as part of the beneficiary's and the applicant's address will be disregarded. However, when the address and contact details of the applicant appear as part of the consignee or notify party details on a transport document subject to articles 19, 20, 21, 22, 23, 24 or 25, they must be as stated in the credit.

k.   The shipper or consignor of the goods indicated on any document need not be the beneficiary of the credit.

l.   A transport document may be issued by any party other than a carrier, owner, master or charterer provided that the transport document meets the requirements of articles 19, 20, 21, 22, 23 or 24 of these rules.

Article 15 Complying Presentation

a.   When an issuing bank determines that a presentation is complying, it must honour.

b.   When a confirming bank determines that a presentation is complying, it must honour or negotiate and forward the documents to the issuing bank.

c.   When a nominated bank determines that a presentation is complying and honours or negotiates, it must forward the documents to the confirming bank or issuing bank.

Article 16 Discrepant Documents, Waiver and Notice

a.   When a nominated bank acting on its nomination, a confirming bank, if any, or the issuing bank determines that a presentation does not comply, it may refuse to honour or negotiate.

b.   When an issuing bank determines that a presentation does not comply, it may in its sole judgement approach the applicant for a waiver of the discrepancies. This does not, however, extend the period mentioned in sub-article 14 (b).

c.   When a nominated bank acting on its nomination, a confirming bank, if any, or the issuing bank decides to refuse to honour or negotiate, it must give a single notice to that effect to the presenter.

The notice must state:

i. that the bank is refusing to honour or negotiate; and

ii. each discrepancy in respect of which the bank refuses to honour or negotiate; and

iii.   aa.   that the bank is holding the documents pending further instructions from the presenter; or

bb.   that the issuing bank is holding the documents until it receives a waiver from the applicant and agrees to accept it, or receives further instructions from the presenter prior to agreeing to accept a waiver; or

cc.   that the bank is returning the documents; or

dd.   that the bank is acting in accordance with instructions previously received from the presenter.

d.   The notice required in sub-article 16 (c) must be given by telecommunication or, if that is not possible, by other expeditious means no later than the close of the fifth banking day following the day of presentation.

e. A nominated bank acting on its nomination, a confirming bank, if any, or the issuing bank may, after providing notice required by sub-article 16 (c) (iii) (a) or (b), return the documents to the presenter at any time.

f. If an issuing bank or a confirming bank fails to act in accordance with the provisions of this article, it shall be precluded from claiming that the documents do not constitute a complying presentation.

g. When an issuing bank refuses to honour or a confirming bank refuses to honour or negotiate and has given notice to that effect in accordance with this article, it shall then be entitled to claim a refund, with interest, of any reimbursement made.

Article 17 Original Documents and Copies

a. At least one original of each document stipulated in the credit must be presented.

b. A bank shall treat as an original any document bearing an apparently original signature, mark, stamp, or label of the issuer of the document, unless the document itself indicates that it is not an original.

c. Unless a document indicates otherwise, a bank will also accept a document as original if it:
i. appears to be written, typed, perforated or stamped by the document issuer's hand; or
ii. appears to be on the document issuer's original stationery; or
iii. states that it is original, unless the statement appears not to apply to the document presented.

d. If a credit requires presentation of copies of documents, presentation of either originals or copies is permitted.

e. If a credit requires presentation of multiple documents by using terms such as "in duplicate", "in two fold" or "in two copies", this will be satisfied by the presentation of at least one original and the remaining number in copies, except when the document itself indicates otherwise.

Article 18 Commercial Invoice

a. A commercial invoice:
i. must appear to have been issued by the beneficiary (except as provided in Article 38);
ii. must be made out in the name of the applicant (except as provided in sub-article 38 (g));
iii. must be made out in the same currency as the credit; and
iv. need not be signed.

b. A nominated bank acting on its nomination, a confirming bank, if any, or the issuing bank may accept a commercial invoice issued for an amount in excess of the amount permitted by the credit, and its decision will be binding upon all parties, provided the bank in question has not honoured or negotiated for an amount in excess of that permitted by the credit.

c. The description of the goods, services or performance in a commercial invoice must correspond with that appearing in the credit.

Article 19 Transport Document Covering at Least Two Different Modes of Transport

a. A transport document covering at least two different modes of transport (multimodal or combined transport document), however named, must appear to:
i. indicate the name of the carrier and be signed by:
-      the carrier or a named agent for or on behalf of the carrier, or
-      the master or a named agent for or on behalf of the master.
Any signature by the carrier, master or agent must be identified as that of the carrier, master or agent.
Any signature by an agent must indicate whether the agent has signed for or on behalf of the carrier or for or on behalf of the master.
ii. indicate that the goods have been dispatched, taken in charge or shipped on board at the place stated in the credit, by:
-      pre-printed wording, or

- a stamp or notation indicating the date on which the goods have been dispatched, taken in charge or shipped on board.

The date of issuance of the transport document will be deemed to be the date of dispatch, taking in charge or shipped on board, and the date of shipment. However, if the transport document indicates, by stamp or notation, a date of dispatch, taking in charge or shipped on board, this date will be deemed to be the date of shipment.

iii. indicate the place of dispatch, taking in charge or shipment and the place of final destination stated in the credit, even if:

aa. the transport document states, in addition, a different place of dispatch, taking in charge or shipment or place of final destination, or

bb. the transport document contains the indication "intended" or similar qualification in relation to the vessel, port of loading or port of discharge.

iv. be the sole original transport document or, if issued in more than one original, be the full set as indicated on the transport document.

v. contain terms and conditions of carriage or make reference to another source containing the terms and conditions of carriage (short form or blank back transport document). Contents of terms and conditions of carriage will not be examined.

vi. contain no indication that it is subject to a charter party.

b.   For the purpose of this article, transhipment means unloading from one means of conveyance and reloading to another means of conveyance (whether or not in different modes of transport) during the carriage from the place of dispatch, taking in charge or shipment to the place of final destination stated in the credit.

c.   **i.** A transport document may indicate that the goods will or may be transhipped provided that the entire carriage is covered by one and the same transport document.

ii. A transport document indicating that transhipment will or may take place is acceptable, even if the credit prohibits transhipment.

Article 20 Bill of Lading

a.   A bill of lading, however named, must appear to:

i. indicate the name of the carrier and be signed by:

- the carrier or a named agent for or on behalf of the carrier, or
- the master or a named agent for or on behalf of the master.

Any signature by the carrier, master or agent must be identified as that of the carrier, master or agent.

Any signature by an agent must indicate whether the agent has signed for or on behalf of the carrier or for or on behalf of the master.

ii. indicate that the goods have been shipped on board a named vessel at the port of loading stated in the credit by:

- pre-printed wording, or
- an on board notation indicating the date on which the goods have been shipped on board.

The date of issuance of the bill of lading will be deemed to be the date of shipment unless the bill of lading contains an on board notation indicating the date of shipment, in which case the date stated in the on board notation will be deemed to be the date of shipment.

If the bill of lading contains the indication "intended vessel" or similar qualification in relation to the name of the vessel, an on board notation indicating the date of shipment and the name of the actual vessel is required.

iii. indicate shipment from the port of loading to the port of discharge stated in the credit.

If the bill of lading does not indicate the port of loading stated in the credit as the port of loading, or if it contains the indication "intended" or similar qualification in relation to the port of loading, an on board notation indicating the port of loading as stated in the credit, the date of shipment and the name of the vessel is required. This provision applies even when loading on board or shipment on a named vessel is indicated by preprinted wording on the bill of lading.

iv. be the sole original bill of lading or, if issued in more than one original, be the full set as indicated on the bill of lading.

v. contain terms and conditions of carriage or make reference to another source containing the terms and conditions of carriage (short form or blank back bill of lading). Contents of terms and conditions of carriage will not be examined.

vi. contain no indication that it is subject to a charter party.

b. For the purpose of this article, transhipment means unloading from one vessel and re-loading to another vessel during the carriage from the port of loading to the port of discharge stated in the credit.

c. **i.** A bill of lading may indicate that the goods will or may be transshipped provided that the entire carriage is covered by one and the same bill of lading.

ii. A bill of lading indicating that transhipment will or may take place is acceptable, even if the credit prohibits transhipment, if the goods have been shipped in a container, trailer or LASH barge as evidenced by the bill of lading.

d. Clauses in a bill of lading stating that the carrier reserves the right to tranship will be disregarded.

Article 21 Non-Negotiable Sea Waybill

a. A non-negotiable sea waybill, however named, must appear to:

i. indicate the name of the carrier and be signed by:

- the carrier or a named agent for or on behalf of the carrier, or
- the master or a named agent for or on behalf of the master.

Any signature by the carrier, master or agent must be identified as that of the carrier, master or agent.

Any signature by an agent must indicate whether the agent has signed for or on behalf of the carrier or for or on behalf of the master.

ii. indicate that the goods have been shipped on board a named vessel at the port of loading stated in the credit by:

- pre-printed wording, or
- an on board notation indicating the date on which the goods have been shipped on board.

The date of issuance of the non-negotiable sea waybill will be deemed to be the date of shipment unless the non-negotiable sea waybill contains an on board notation indicating the date of shipment, in which case the date stated in the on board notation will be deemed to be the date of shipment.

If the non-negotiable sea waybill contains the indication "intended vessel" or similar qualification in relation to the name of the vessel, an on board notation indicating the date of shipment and the name of the actual vessel is required.

iii. indicate shipment from the port of loading to the port of discharge stated in the credit. If the non-negotiable sea waybill does not indicate the port of loading stated in the credit as the port of loading, or if it contains the indication "intended" or similar qualification in relation to the port of loading, an on board notation indicating the port of loading as stated in the credit, the date of shipment and the name of the vessel is required. This provision applies even when loading on board or shipment on a named vessel is indicated by pre-printed wording on the non-negotiable sea waybill.

iv. be the sole original non-negotiable sea waybill or, if issued in more than one original, be the full set as indicated on the non-negotiable sea waybill.

v. contain terms and conditions of carriage or make reference to another source containing the terms and conditions of carriage (short form or blank back non-negotiable sea waybill). Contents of terms and conditions of carriage will not be examined.

vi. contain no indication that it is subject to a charter party.

b.   For the purpose of this article, transhipment means unloading from one vessel and re-loading to another vessel during the carriage from the port of loading to the port of discharge stated in the credit.

c.   **i.** A non-negotiable sea waybill may indicate that the goods will or may be transhipped provided that the entire carriage is covered by one and the same non-negotiable sea waybill.

ii. A non-negotiable sea waybill indicating that transhipment will or may take place is acceptable, even if the credit prohibits transhipment, if the goods have been shipped in a container, trailer or LASH barge as evidenced by the non-negotiable sea waybill.

d.   Clauses in a non-negotiable sea waybill stating that the carrier reserves the right to tranship will be disregarded.

Article 22 Charter Party Bill of Lading

a.   A bill of lading, however named, containing an indication that it is subject to a charter party (charter party bill of lading), must appear to:

i. be signed by:
-       the master or a named agent for or on behalf of the master, or
-       the owner or a named agent for or on behalf of the owner, or
-       the charterer or a named agent for or on behalf of the charterer.

Any signature by the master, owner, charterer or agent must be identified as that of the master, owner, charterer or agent.

Any signature by an agent must indicate whether the agent has signed for or on behalf of the master, owner or charterer.

An agent signing for or on behalf of the owner or charterer must indicate the name of the owner or charterer.

ii. indicate that the goods have been shipped on board a named vessel at the port of loading stated in the credit by:
-       pre-printed wording, or
-       an on board notation indicating the date on which the goods have been shipped on board.

The date of issuance of the charter party bill of lading will be deemed to be the date of shipment unless the charter party bill of lading contains an on board notation indicating the date of shipment, in which case the date stated in the on board notation will be deemed to be the date of shipment.

iii. indicate shipment from the port of loading to the port of discharge stated in the credit. The port of discharge may also be shown as a range of ports or a geographical area, as stated in the credit.

iv. be the sole original charter party bill of lading or, if issued in more than one original, be the full set as indicated on the charter party bill of lading.

b.   A bank will not examine charter party contracts, even if they are required to be presented by the terms of the credit.

Article 23 Air Transport Document

a.   An air transport document, however named, must appear to:

i. indicate the name of the carrier and be signed by:
-       the carrier, or
-       a named agent for or on behalf of the carrier.

Any signature by the carrier or agent must be identified as that of the carrier or agent.

Any signature by an agent must indicate that the agent has signed for or on behalf of the carrier.

ii. indicate that the goods have been accepted for carriage.

iii. indicate the date of issuance. This date will be deemed to be the date of shipment unless the air transport document contains a specific notation of the actual date of shipment, in which case the date stated in the notation will be deemed to be the date of shipment.

Any other information appearing on the air transport document relative to the flight number and date will not be considered in determining the date of shipment.

iv. indicate the airport of departure and the airport of destination stated in the credit.

v. be the original for consignor or shipper, even if the credit stipulates a full set of originals.

vi. contain terms and conditions of carriage or make reference to another source containing the terms and conditions of carriage. Contents of terms and conditions of carriage will not be examined.

b. For the purpose of this article, transhipment means unloading from one aircraft and reloading to another aircraft during the carriage from the airport of departure to the airport of destination stated in the credit.

c.   **i.** An air transport document may indicate that the goods will or may be transhipped, provided that the entire carriage is covered by one and the same air transport document.

ii. An air transport document indicating that transhipment will or may take place is acceptable, even if the credit prohibits transhipment.

Article 24 Road, Rail or Inland Waterway Transport Documents

a. A road, rail or inland waterway transport document, however named, must appear to:

i. indicate the name of the carrier and:

- be signed by the carrier or a named agent for or on behalf of the carrier, or
- indicate receipt of the goods by signature, stamp or notation by the carrier or a named agent for or on behalf of the carrier.

Any signature, stamp or notation of receipt of the goods by the carrier or agent must be identified as that of the carrier or agent.

Any signature, stamp or notation of receipt of the goods by the agent must indicate that the agent has signed or acted for or on behalf of the carrier.

If a rail transport document does not identify the carrier, any signature or stamp of the railway company will be accepted as evidence of the document being signed by the carrier.

ii. indicate the date of shipment or the date the goods have been received for shipment, dispatch or carriage at the place stated in the credit. Unless the transport document contains a dated reception stamp, an indication of the date of receipt or a date of shipment, the date of issuance of the transport document will be deemed to be the date of shipment.

iii. indicate the place of shipment and the place of destination stated in the credit.

b.   **i.** A road transport document must appear to be the original for consignor or shipper or bear no marking indicating for whom the document has been prepared.

ii. A rail transport document marked "duplicate" will be accepted as an original.

iii. A rail or inland waterway transport document will be accepted as an original whether marked as an original or not.

c. In the absence of an indication on the transport document as to the number of originals issued, the number presented will be deemed to constitute a full set.

d. For the purpose of this article, transhipment means unloading from one means of conveyance and reloading to another means of conveyance, within the same mode of transport, during the carriage from the place of shipment, dispatch or carriage to the place of destination stated in the credit.

e.   **i.** A road, rail or inland waterway transport document may indicate that the goods will or may be transhipped provided that the entire carriage is covered by one and the same transport document.

ii. A road, rail or inland waterway transport document indicating that transhipment will or may take place is acceptable, even if the credit prohibits transhipment.

Article 25 Courier Receipt, Post Receipt or Certificate of Posting

a. A courier receipt, however named, evidencing receipt of goods for transport, must appear to:

i. indicate the name of the courier service and be stamped or signed by the named courier service at the place from which the credit states the goods are to be shipped; and

ii. indicate a date of pick-up or of receipt or wording to this effect. This date will be deemed to be the date of shipment.

b. A requirement that courier charges are to be paid or prepaid may be satisfied by a transport document issued by a courier service evidencing that courier charges are for the account of a party other than the consignee.

c. A post receipt or certificate of posting, however named, evidencing receipt of goods for transport, must appear to be stamped or signed and dated at the place from which the credit states the goods are to be shipped. This date will be deemed to be the date of shipment.

Article 26 "On Deck", "Shipper's Load and Count", "Said by Shipper to Contain" and Charges Additional to Freight

a. A transport document must not indicate that the goods are or will be loaded on deck. A clause on a transport document stating that the goods may be loaded on deck is acceptable.

b. A transport document bearing a clause such as "shipper's load and count" and "said by shipper to contain" is acceptable.

c. A transport document may bear a reference, by stamp or otherwise, to charges additional to the freight.

Article 27 Clean Transport Document

A bank will only accept a clean transport document. A clean transport document is one bearing no clause or notation expressly declaring a defective condition of the goods or their packaging.

The word "clean" need not appear on a transport document, even if a credit has a requirement for that transport document to be "clean on board".

Article 28 Insurance Document and Coverage

a. An insurance document, such as an insurance policy, an insurance certificate or a declaration under an open cover, must appear to be issued and signed by an insurance company, an underwriter or their agents or their proxies.

Any signature by an agent or proxy must indicate whether the agent or proxy has signed for or on behalf of the insurance company or underwriter.

b. When the insurance document indicates that it has been issued in more than one original, all originals must be presented.

c. Cover notes will not be accepted.

d. An insurance policy is acceptable in lieu of an insurance certificate or a declaration under an open cover.

e. The date of the insurance document must be no later than the date of shipment, unless it appears from the insurance document that the cover is effective from a date not later than the date of shipment.

f. **i.** The insurance document must indicate the amount of insurance coverage and be in the same currency as the credit.

ii. A requirement in the credit for insurance coverage to be for a percentage of the value of the goods, of the invoice value or similar is deemed to be the minimum amount of coverage required.

If there is no indication in the credit of the insurance coverage required, the amount of insurance coverage must be at least 110% of the CIF or CIP value of the goods.

When the CIF or CIP value cannot be determined from the documents, the amount of insurance coverage must be calculated on the basis of the amount for which honour or negotiation is requested or the gross value of the goods as shown on the invoice, whichever is greater.

iii. The insurance document must indicate that risks are covered at least between the place of taking in charge or shipment and the place of discharge or final destination as stated in the credit.

g.   A credit should state the type of insurance required and, if any, the additional risks to be covered. An insurance document will be accepted without regard to any risks that are not covered if the credit uses imprecise terms such as "usual risks" or "customary risks".
h.   When a credit requires insurance against "all risks" and an insurance document is presented containing any "all risks" notation or clause, whether or not bearing the heading "all risks", the insurance document will be accepted without regard to any risks stated to be excluded.
i.   An insurance document may contain reference to any exclusion clause.
j.   An insurance document may indicate that the cover is subject to a franchise or excess (deductible).

Article 29 Extension of Expiry Date or Last Day for Presentation

a.   If the expiry date of a credit or the last day for presentation falls on a day when the bank to which presentation is to be made is closed for reasons other than those referred to in Article 36, the expiry date or the last day for presentation, as the case may be, will be extended to the first following banking day.
b.   If presentation is made on the first following banking day, a nominated bank must provide the issuing bank or confirming bank with a statement on its covering schedule that the presentation was made within the time limits extended in accordance with sub-article 29 (a).
c.   The latest date for shipment will not be extended as a result of sub-article 29 (a).

Article 30 Tolerance in Credit Amount, Quantity and Unit Prices

a.   The words "about" or "approximately" used in connection with the amount of the credit or the quantity or the unit price stated in the credit are to be construed as allowing a tolerance not to exceed 10% more or 10% less than the amount, the quantity or the unit price to which they refer.
b.   A tolerance not to exceed 5% more or 5% less than the quantity of the goods is allowed, provided the credit does not state the quantity in terms of a stipulated number of packing units or individual items and the total amount of the drawings does not exceed the amount of the credit.
c.   Even when partial shipments are not allowed, a tolerance not to exceed 5% less than the amount of the credit is allowed, provided that the quantity of the goods, if stated in the credit, is shipped in full and a unit price, if stated in the credit, is not reduced or that sub-article 30 (b) is not applicable. This tolerance does not apply when the credit stipulates a specific tolerance or uses the expressions referred to in sub-article 30 (a).

Article 31 Partial Drawings or Shipments

a.   Partial drawings or shipments are allowed.
b.   A presentation consisting of more than one set of transport documents evidencing shipment commencing on the same means of conveyance and for the same journey, provided they indicate the same destination, will not be regarded as covering a partial shipment, even if they indicate different dates of shipment or different ports of loading, places of taking in charge or dispatch. If the presentation consists of more than one set of transport documents, the latest date of shipment as evidenced on any of the sets of transport documents will be regarded as the date of shipment.
A presentation consisting of one or more sets of transport documents evidencing shipment on more than one means of conveyance within the same mode of transport will be regarded as covering a partial shipment, even if the means of conveyance leave on the same day for the same destination.
c.   A presentation consisting of more than one courier receipt, post receipt or certificate of posting will not be regarded as a partial shipment if the courier receipts, post receipts or certificates of posting appear to have been stamped or signed by the same courier or postal service at the same place and date and for the same destination.

Article 32 Instalment Drawings or Shipments

If a drawing or shipment by instalments within given periods is stipulated in the credit and any instalment is not drawn or shipped within the period allowed for that instalment, the credit ceases to be available for that and any subsequent instalment.

Article 33 Hours of Presentation

A bank has no obligation to accept a presentation outside of its banking hours.

Article 34 Disclaimer on Effectiveness of Documents

A bank assumes no liability or responsibility for the form, sufficiency, accuracy, genuineness, falsification or legal effect of any document, or for the general or particular conditions stipulated in a document or superimposed thereon; nor does it assume any liability or responsibility for the description, quantity, weight, quality, condition, packing, delivery, value or existence of the goods, services or other performance represented by any document, or for the good faith or acts or omissions, solvency, performance or standing of the consignor, the carrier, the forwarder, the consignee or the insurer of the goods or any other person.

Article 35 Disclaimer on Transmission and Translation

A bank assumes no liability or responsibility for the consequences arising out of delay, loss in transit, mutilation or other errors arising in the transmission of any messages or delivery of letters or documents, when such messages, letters or documents are transmitted or sent according to the requirements stated in the credit, or when the bank may have taken the initiative in the choice of the delivery service in the absence of such instructions in the credit.

If a nominated bank determines that a presentation is complying and forwards the documents to the issuing bank or confirming bank, whether or not the nominated bank has honoured or negotiated, an issuing bank or confirming bank must honour or negotiate, or reimburse that nominated bank, even when the documents have been lost in transit between the nominated bank and the issuing bank or confirming bank, or between the confirming bank and the issuing bank.

A bank assumes no liability or responsibility for errors in translation or interpretation of technical terms and may transmit credit terms without translating them.

Article 36 Force Majeure

A bank assumes no liability or responsibility for the consequences arising out of the interruption of its business by Acts of God, riots, civil commotions, insurrections, wars, acts of terrorism, or by any strikes or lockouts or any other causes beyond its control.

A bank will not, upon resumption of its business, honour or negotiate under a credit that expired during such interruption of its business.

Article 37 Disclaimer for Acts of an Instructed Party

a.   A bank utilizing the services of another bank for the purpose of giving effect to the instructions of the applicant does so for the account and at the risk of the applicant.

b.   An issuing bank or advising bank assumes no liability or responsibility should the instructions it transmits to another bank not be carried out, even if it has taken the initiative in the choice of that other bank.

c.   A bank instructing another bank to perform services is liable for any commissions, fees, costs or expenses ("charges") incurred by that bank in connection with its instructions.

If a credit states that charges are for the account of the beneficiary and charges cannot be collected or deducted from proceeds, the issuing bank remains liable for payment of charges.

A credit or amendment should not stipulate that the advising to a beneficiary is conditional upon the receipt by the advising bank or second advising bank of its charges.

d.   The applicant shall be bound by and liable to indemnify a bank against all obligations and responsibilities imposed by foreign laws and usages.

Article 38 Transferable Credits

a. A bank is under no obligation to transfer a credit except to the extent and in the manner expressly consented to by that bank.

b. For the purpose of this article:

Transferable credit means a credit that specifically states it is "transferable". A transferable credit may be made available in whole or in part to another beneficiary ("second beneficiary") at the request of the beneficiary ("first beneficiary").

Transferring bank means a nominated bank that transfers the credit or, in a credit available with any bank, a bank that is specifically authorized by the issuing bank to transfer and that transfers the credit. An issuing bank may be a transferring bank.

Transferred credit means a credit that has been made available by the transferring bank to a second beneficiary.

c. Unless otherwise agreed at the time of transfer, all charges (such as commissions, fees, costs or expenses) incurred in respect of a transfer must be paid by the first beneficiary.

d. A credit may be transferred in part to more than one second beneficiary provided partial drawings or shipments are allowed.

A transferred credit cannot be transferred at the request of a second beneficiary to any subsequent beneficiary. The first beneficiary is not considered to be a subsequent beneficiary.

e. Any request for transfer must indicate if and under what conditions amendments may be advised to the second beneficiary. The transferred credit must clearly indicate those conditions.

f. If a credit is transferred to more than one second beneficiary, rejection of an amendment by one or more second beneficiary does not invalidate the acceptance by any other second beneficiary, with respect to which the transferred credit will be amended accordingly. For any second beneficiary that rejected the amendment, the transferred credit will remain unamended.

g. The transferred credit must accurately reflect the terms and conditions of the credit, including confirmation, if any, with the exception of:
- the amount of the credit,
- any unit price stated therein,
- the expiry date,
- the period for presentation, or
- the latest shipment date or given period for shipment,

any or all of which may be reduced or curtailed.

The percentage for which insurance cover must be effected may be increased to provide the amount of cover stipulated in the credit or these articles.

The name of the first beneficiary may be substituted for that of the applicant in the credit. If the name of the applicant is specifically required by the credit to appear in any document other than the invoice, such requirement must be reflected in the transferred credit.

h. The first beneficiary has the right to substitute its own invoice and draft, if any, for those of a second beneficiary for an amount not in excess of that stipulated in the credit, and upon such substitution the first beneficiary can draw under the credit for the difference, if any, between its invoice and the invoice of a second beneficiary.

i. If the first beneficiary is to present its own invoice and draft, if any, but fails to do so on first demand, or if the invoices presented by the first beneficiary create discrepancies that did not exist in the presentation made by the second beneficiary and the first beneficiary fails to correct them on first demand, the transferring bank has the right to present the documents as received from the second beneficiary to the issuing bank, without further responsibility to the first beneficiary.

j. The first beneficiary may, in its request for transfer, indicate that honour or negotiation is to be effected to a second beneficiary at the place to which the credit has been transferred, up to and including the expiry date of the credit. This is without prejudice to the right of the first beneficiary in accordance with sub-article 38 (h).

k. Presentation of documents by or on behalf of a second beneficiary must be made to the transferring bank.

Article 39 Assignment of Proceeds

The fact that a credit is not stated to be transferable shall not affect the right of the beneficiary to assign any proceeds to which it may be or may become entitled under the credit, in accordance with the provisions of applicable law. This Article relates only to the assignment of proceeds and not to the assignment of the right to perform under the credit.

1995 UNITED NATIONS CONVENTION ON INDEPENDENT GUARANTEES AND STAND-BY LETTERS OF CREDIT[1]

[handwritten: never applies – not signed by U.S.]

CHAPTER I. SCOPE OF APPLICATION

Article 1 - Scope of Application

(1) This Convention applies to an international undertaking referred to in Article 2:

1   © United Nations, 2169 UNTS 163, all rights reserved.

(a) If the place of business of the guarantor/issuer at which the undertaking is issued is in a Contracting State, or

(b) If the rules of private international law lead to the application of the law of a Contracting State, unless the undertaking excludes the application of the Convention.

(2) This Convention applies also to an international letter of credit not falling within Article 2 if it expressly states that it is subject to this Convention.

(3) The provisions of articles 21 and 22 apply to international undertakings referred to in Article 2 independently of paragraph (1) of this article.

Article 2 - Undertaking

(1) For the purposes of this Convention, an undertaking is an independent commitment, known in international practice as an independent guarantee or as a stand-by letter of credit, given by a bank or other institution or person ("guarantor/issuer") to pay to the beneficiary a certain or determinable amount upon simple demand or upon demand accompanied by other documents, in conformity with the terms and any documentary conditions of the undertaking, indicating, or from which it is to be inferred, that payment is due because of a default in the performance of an obligation, or because of another contingency, or for money borrowed or advanced, or on account of any mature indebtedness undertaken by the principal/applicant or another person.

(2) The undertaking may be given:

(a) At the request or on the instruction of the customer ("principal/applicant") of the guarantor/issuer;

(b) On the instruction of another bank, institution or person ("instructing party") that acts at the request of the customer ("principal/applicant") of that instructing party; or

(c) On behalf of the guarantor/issuer itself.

(3) Payment may be stipulated in the undertaking to be made in any form, including:

(a) Payment in a specified currency or unit of account;

(b) Acceptance of a bill of exchange (draft);

(c) Payment on a deferred basis;

(d) Supply of a specified item of value.

(4) The undertaking may stipulate that the guarantor/issuer itself is the beneficiary when acting in favour of another person.

Article 3 - Independence of Undertaking

For the purposes of this Convention, an undertaking is independent where the guarantor/issuer's obligation to the beneficiary is not:

(a) Dependent upon the existence or validity of any underlying transaction, or upon any other undertaking (including stand-by letters of credit or independent guarantees to which confirmations or counter-guarantees relate); or

(b) Subject to any term or condition not appearing in the undertaking, or to any future, uncertain act or event except presentation of documents or another such act or event within a guarantor/issuer's sphere of operations.

Article 4 - Internationality of Undertaking

(1) An undertaking is international if the places of business, as specified in the undertaking, of any two of the following persons are in different States: guarantor/issuer, beneficiary, principal/applicant, instructing party, confirmer.

(2) For the purposes of the preceding paragraph:

(a) If the undertaking lists more than one place of business for a given person, the relevant place of business is that which has the closest relationship to the undertaking;

(b) If the undertaking does not specify a place of business for a given person but specifies its habitual residence, that residence is relevant for determining the international character of the undertaking.

CHAPTER II. INTERPRETATION

Article 5 - Principles of Interpretation

In the interpretation of this Convention, regard is to be had to its international character and to the need to promote uniformity in its application and the observance of good faith in the international practice of independent guarantees and stand-by letters of credit.

Article 6 - Definitions

For the purposes of this Convention and unless otherwise indicated in a provision of this Convention or required by the context:

(a)   "Undertaking" includes "counter-guarantee" and "confirmation of an undertaking";

(b)   "Guarantor/issuer" includes "counter-guarantor" and "confirmer";

(c)   "Counter-guarantee" means an undertaking given to the guarantor/issuer of another undertaking by its instructing party and providing for payment upon simple demand or upon demand accompanied by other documents, in conformity with the terms and any documentary conditions of the undertaking, indicating, or from which it is to be inferred, that payment under that other undertaking has been demanded from, or made by, the person issuing that other undertaking;

(d)   "Counter-guarantor" means the person issuing a counter-guarantee;

(e)   "Confirmation" of an undertaking means an undertaking added to that of the guarantor/issuer, and authorized by the guarantor/issuer, providing the beneficiary with the option of demanding payment from the confirmer instead of from the guarantor/issuer, upon simple demand or upon demand accompanied by other documents, in conformity with the terms and any documentary conditions of the confirmed undertaking, without prejudice to the beneficiary's right to demand payment from the guarantor/issuer;

(f)   "Confirmer" means the person adding a confirmation to an undertaking;

(g)   "Document" means a communication made in a form that provides a complete record thereof.

CHAPTER III. FORM AND CONTENT OF UNDERTAKING

Article 7 - Issuance, Form and Irrevocability of Undertaking

(1)   Issuance of an undertaking occurs when and where the undertaking leaves the sphere of control of the guarantor/issuer concerned.

(2)   An undertaking may be issued in any form which preserves a complete record of the text of the undertaking and provides authentication of its source by generally accepted means or by a procedure agreed upon by the guarantor/issuer and the beneficiary.

(3)   From the time of issuance of an undertaking, a demand for payment may be made in accordance with the terms and conditions of the undertaking, unless the undertaking stipulates a different time.

(4)   An undertaking is irrevocable upon issuance, unless it stipulates that it is revocable.

Article 8 - Amendment

(1)   An undertaking may not be amended except in the form stipulated in the undertaking or, failing such stipulation, in a form referred to in paragraph (2) of Article 7.

(2)   Unless otherwise stipulated in the undertaking or elsewhere agreed by the guarantor/issuer and the beneficiary, an undertaking is amended upon issuance of the amendment if the amendment has previously been authorized by the beneficiary.

(3)   Unless otherwise stipulated in the undertaking or elsewhere agreed by the guarantor/issuer and the beneficiary, where any amendment has not previously been authorized by the beneficiary, the undertaking is amended only when the guarantor/issuer receives a notice of acceptance of the amendment by the beneficiary in a form referred to in paragraph (2) of Article 7.

(4)   An amendment of an undertaking has no effect on the rights and obligations of the principal/applicant (or an instructing party) or of a confirmer of the undertaking unless such person consents to the amendment.

Article 9 - Transfer of Beneficiary's Right to Demand Payment
(1)   The beneficiary's right to demand payment may be transferred only if authorized in the undertaking, and only to the extent and in the manner authorized in the undertaking.
(2)   If an undertaking is designated as transferable without specifying whether or not the consent of the guarantor/issuer or another authorized person is required for the actual transfer, neither the guarantor/issuer nor any other authorized person is obliged to effect the transfer except to the extent and in the manner expressly consented to by it.

Article 10 - Assignment of Proceeds
(1)   Unless otherwise stipulated in the undertaking or elsewhere agreed by the guarantor/issuer and the beneficiary, the beneficiary may assign to another person any proceeds to which it may be, or may become, entitled under the undertaking.
(2)   If the guarantor/issuer or another person obliged to effect payment has received a notice originating from the beneficiary, in a form referred to in paragraph (2) of Article 7, of the beneficiary's irrevocable assignment, payment to the assignee discharges the obligor, to the extent of its payment, from its liability under the undertaking.

Article 11 - Cessation of Right to Demand Payment
(1)   The right of the beneficiary to demand payment under the undertaking ceases when:
(a)   The guarantor/issuer has received a statement by the beneficiary of release from liability in a form referred to in paragraph (2) of Article 7;
(b)   The beneficiary and the guarantor/issuer have agreed on the termination of the undertaking in the form stipulated in the undertaking or, failing such stipulation, in a form referred to in paragraph (2) of Article 7;
(c)   The amount available under the undertaking has been paid, unless the undertaking provides for the automatic renewal or for an automatic increase of the amount available or otherwise provides for continuation of the undertaking;
(d)   The validity period of the undertaking expires in accordance with the provisions of Article 12.
(2)   The undertaking may stipulate, or the guarantor/issuer and the beneficiary may agree elsewhere, that return of the document embodying the undertaking to the guarantor/issuer, or a procedure functionally equivalent to the return of the document in the case of the issuance of the undertaking in non-paper form, is required for the cessation of the right to demand payment, either alone or in conjunction with one of the events referred to in subparagraphs (a) and (b) of paragraph (1) of this article. However, in no case shall retention of any such document by the beneficiary after the right to demand payment ceases in accordance with subparagraph (c) or (d) of paragraph (1) of this Article preserve any rights of the beneficiary under the undertaking.

Article 12 - Expiry
The validity period of the undertaking expires:
(a)   At the expiry date, which may be a specified calendar date or the last day of a fixed period of time stipulated in the undertaking, provided that, if the expiry date is not a business day at the place of business of the guarantor/issuer at which the undertaking is issued, or of another person or at another place stipulated in the undertaking for presentation of the demand for payment, expiry occurs on the first business day which follows;
(b)   If expiry depends according to the undertaking on the occurrence of an act or event not within the guarantor/issuer's sphere of operations, when the guarantor/issuer is advised that the act or event has occurred by presentation of the document specified for that purpose in the undertaking or, if no such document is specified, of a certification by the beneficiary of the occurrence of the act or event;
(c)   If the undertaking does not state an expiry date, or if the act or event on which expiry is stated to depend has not yet been established by presentation of the required document and an expiry date has not been stated in addition, when six years have elapsed from the date of issuance of the undertaking.

CHAPTER IV. RIGHTS, OBLIGATIONS AND DEFENCES
Article 13 - Determination of Rights and Obligations
(1)   The rights and obligations of the guarantor/issuer and the beneficiary arising from the undertaking are determined by the terms and conditions set forth in the undertaking, including any rules, general conditions or usages specifically referred to therein, and by the provisions of this Convention.
(2)   In interpreting terms and conditions of the undertaking and in settling questions that are not addressed by the terms and conditions of the undertaking or by the provisions of this Convention, regard shall be had to generally accepted international rules and usages of independent guarantee or stand-by letter of credit practice.

Article 14 - Standard of Conduct and Liability of Guarantor/Issuer
(1)   In discharging its obligations under the undertaking and this Convention, the guarantor/issuer shall act in good faith and exercise reasonable care having due regard to generally accepted standards of international practice of independent guarantees or stand-by letters of credit.
(2)   A guarantor/issuer may not be exempted from liability for its failure to act in good faith or for any grossly negligent conduct.

Article 15 - Demand
(1)   Any demand for payment under the undertaking shall be made in a form referred to in paragraph (2) of Article 7 and in conformity with the terms and conditions of the undertaking.
(2)   Unless otherwise stipulated in the undertaking, the demand and any certification or other document required by the undertaking shall be presented, within the time that a demand for payment may be made, to the guarantor/issuer at the place where the undertaking was issued.
(3)   The beneficiary, when demanding payment, is deemed to certify that the demand is not in bad faith and that none of the elements referred to in subparagraphs (a), (b) and (c) of paragraph (1) of Article 19 are present.

Article 16 - Examination of Demand and Accompanying Documents
(1)   The guarantor/issuer shall examine the demand and any accompanying documents in accordance with the standard of conduct referred to in paragraph (1) of Article 14. In determining whether documents are in facial conformity with the terms and conditions of the undertaking, and are consistent with one another, the guarantor/issuer shall have due regard to the applicable international standard of independent guarantee or stand-by letter of credit practice.
(2)   Unless otherwise stipulated in the undertaking or elsewhere agreed by the guarantor/issuer and the beneficiary, the guarantor/issuer shall have reasonable time, but not more than seven business days following the day of receipt of the demand and any accompanying documents, in which to:
(a)   Examine the demand and any accompanying documents;
(b)   Decide whether or not to pay;
(c)   If the decision is not to pay, issue notice thereof to the beneficiary.
The notice referred to in subparagraph (c) above shall, unless otherwise stipulated in the undertaking or elsewhere agreed by the guarantor/issuer and the beneficiary, be made by teletransmission or, if that is not possible, by other expeditious means and indicate the reason for the decision not to pay.

Article 17 - Payment
(1)   Subject to Article 19, the guarantor/issuer shall pay against a demand made in accordance with the provisions of Article 15. Following a determination that a demand for payment so conforms, payment shall be made promptly, unless the undertaking stipulates payment on a deferred basis, in which case payment shall be made at the stipulated time.
(2)   Any payment against a demand that is not in accordance with the provisions of Article 15 does not prejudice the rights of the principal/applicant.

Article 18 - Set-off

Unless otherwise stipulated in the undertaking or elsewhere agreed by the guarantor/issuer and the beneficiary, the guarantor/issuer may discharge the payment obligation under the undertaking by availing itself of a right of set-off, except with any claim assigned to it by the principal/applicant or the instructing party.

Article 19 - Exception to Payment Obligation

(1)   If it is manifest and clear that:
(a)   Any document is not genuine or has been falsified;
(b)   No payment is due on the basis asserted in the demand and the supporting documents; or
(c)   Judging by the type and purpose of the undertaking, the demand has no conceivable basis, the guarantor/issuer, acting in good faith, has a right, as against the beneficiary, to withhold payment.

(2)   For the purposes of subparagraph (c) of paragraph (1) of this article, the following are types of situations in which a demand has no conceivable basis:
(a)   The contingency or risk against which the undertaking was designed to secure the beneficiary has undoubtedly not materialized;
(b)   The underlying obligation of the principal/applicant has been declared invalid by a court or arbitral tribunal, unless the undertaking indicates that such contingency falls within the risk to be covered by the undertaking;
(c)   The underlying obligation has undoubtedly been fulfilled to the satisfaction of the beneficiary;
(d)   Fulfilment of the underlying obligation has clearly been prevented by wilful misconduct of the beneficiary;
(e)   In the case of a demand under a counter-guarantee, the beneficiary of the counter-guarantee has made payment in bad faith as guarantor/issuer of the undertaking to which the counter-guarantee relates.

(3)   In the circumstances set out in subparagraphs (a), (b) and (c) of paragraph (1) of this article, the principal/applicant is entitled to provisional court measures in accordance with Article 20.

CHAPTER V. PROVISIONAL COURT MEASURES

Article 20 - Provisional Court Measures

(1)   Where, on an application by the principal/applicant or the instructing party, it is shown that there is a high probability that, with regard to a demand made, or expected to be made, by the beneficiary, one of the circumstances referred to in subparagraphs (a), (b) and (c) of paragraph (1) of Article 19 is present, the court, on the basis of immediately available strong evidence, may:
(a)   Issue a provisional order to the effect that the beneficiary does not receive payment, including an order that the guarantor/issuer hold the amount of the undertaking, or
(b)   Issue a provisional order to the effect that the proceeds of the undertaking paid to the beneficiary are blocked, taking into account whether in the absence of such an order the principal/applicant would be likely to suffer serious harm.

(2)   The court, when issuing a provisional order referred to in paragraph (1) of this article, may require the person applying therefor to furnish such form of security as the court deems appropriate.
(3)   The court may not issue a provisional order of the kind referred to in paragraph (1) of this Article based on any objection to payment other than those referred to in subparagraphs (a), (b) and (c) of paragraph (1) of Article 19, or use of the undertaking for a criminal purpose.

CHAPTER VI. CONFLICT OF LAWS

Article 21 - Choice of Applicable Law

The undertaking is governed by the law the choice of which is:
(a)   Stipulated in the undertaking or demonstrated by the terms and conditions of the undertaking; or
(b)   Agreed elsewhere by the guarantor/issuer and the beneficiary.

Article 22 - Determination of Applicable Law

Failing a choice of law in accordance with Article 21, the undertaking is governed by the law of the State where the guarantor/issuer has that place of business at which the undertaking was issued.

CHAPTER VII. FINAL CLAUSES

Article 23 - Depositary

The Secretary-General of the United Nations is the depositary of this Convention.

Article 24 - Signature, Ratification, Acceptance, Approval, Accession

(1)   This Convention is open for signature by all States at the Headquarters of the United Nations, New York, until 11 December 1997.
(2)   This Convention is subject to ratification, acceptance or approval by the signatory States.
(3)   This Convention is open to accession by all States which are not signatory States as from the date it is open for signature.
(4)   Instruments of ratification, acceptance, approval and accession are to be deposited with the Secretary-General of the United Nations.

Article 25 - Application to Territorial Units

(1)   If a State has two or more territorial units in which different systems of law are applicable in relation to the matters dealt with in this Convention, it may, at the time of signature, ratification, acceptance, approval or accession, declare that this Convention is to extend to all its territorial units or only one or more of them, and may at any time substitute another declaration for its earlier declaration.
(2)   These declarations are to state expressly the territorial units to which the Convention extends.
(3)   If, by virtue of a declaration under this article, this Convention does not extend to all territorial units of a State and the place of business of the guarantor/issuer or of the beneficiary is located in a territorial unit to which the Convention does not extend, this place of business is considered not to be in a Contracting State.
(4)   If a State makes no declaration under paragraph (1) of this article, the Convention is to extend to all territorial units of that State.

Article 26 - Effect of Declaration

(1)   Declarations made under Article 25 at the time of signature are subject to confirmation upon ratification, acceptance or approval.
(2)   Declarations and confirmations of declarations are to be in writing and to be formally notified to the depositary.
(3)   A declaration takes effect simultaneously with the entry into force of this Convention in respect of the State concerned. However, a declaration of which the depositary receives formal notification after such entry into force takes effect on the first day of the month following the expiration of six months after the date of its receipt by the depositary.
(4)   Any State which makes a declaration under Article 25 may withdraw it at any time by a formal notification in writing addressed to the depositary. Such withdrawal takes effect on the first day of the month following the expiration of six months after the date of the receipt of the notification of the depositary.

Article 27 - Reservations

No reservations may be made to this Convention.

Article 28 - Entry into Force

(1)   This Convention enters into force on the first day of the month following the expiration of one year from the date of the deposit of the fifth instrument of ratification, acceptance, approval or accession.
(2)   For each State which becomes a Contracting State to this Convention after the date of the deposit of the fifth instrument of ratification, acceptance, approval or accession, this Convention

enters into force on the first day of the month following the expiration of one year after the date of the deposit of the appropriate instrument on behalf of that State.

(3)   This Convention applies only to undertakings issued on or after the date when the Convention enters into force in respect of the Contracting State referred to in subparagraph (a) or the Contracting State referred to in subparagraph (b) of paragraph (1) of Article 1.

Article 29 - Denunciation

(1)   A Contracting State may denounce this Convention at any time by means of a notification in writing addressed to the depositary.

(2)   The denunciation takes effect on the first day of the month following the expiration of one year after the notification is received by the depositary. Where a longer period is specified in the notification, the denunciation takes effect upon the expiration of such longer period after the notification is received by the depositary.

DONE at New York, this eleventh day of December one thousand nine hundred and ninety-five, in a single original, of which the Arabic, Chinese, English, French, Russian and Spanish texts are equally authentic.

IN WITNESS WHEREOF the undersigned plenipotentiaries, being duly authorized by their respective Governments, have signed the present Convention.

Entry into force: 1 January 2000
Ratifications and binding effect: Belarus (2002), Ecuador (2000), El Salvador (2000), Gabon (2004), Kuwait (2000), Liberia (2005), Panama (2000), Tunisia (1998)[1]

INTERNATIONAL STANDBY PRACTICES (ISP98)[2]

RULE 1: GENERAL PROVISIONS
Scope, Application, Definitions, and Interpretation of These Rules

1.01 Scope and Application

(a)   These Rules are intended to be applied to standby letters of credit (including performance, financial, and direct pay standby letters of credit).

(b)   A standby letter of credit or other similar undertaking, however named or described, whether for domestic or international use, may be made subject to these Rules by express reference to them.

(c)   An undertaking subject to these Rules may expressly modify or exclude their application.

(d)   An undertaking subject to these Rules is hereinafter referred to as a "standby".

1.02 Relationship to Law and Other Rules

(a)   These Rules supplement the applicable law to the extent not prohibited by that law.

(b)   These Rules supersede conflicting provisions in any other rules of practice to which a standby letter of credit is also made subject.

1.03 Interpretative Principles

These Rules shall be interpreted as mercantile usage with regard for:

(a)   integrity of standbys as reliable and efficient undertakings to pay;

(b)   practice and terminology of banks and businesses in day-to-day transactions;

(c)   consistency within the worldwide system of banking operations and commerce; and

(d)   worldwide uniformity in their interpretation and application.

---

1   The United States of America signed the Convention in 1997 but so far have not ratified it.

2   © Institute of International Banking Law & Practice, Inc.

1.04 Effect of the Rules

Unless the context otherwise requires, or unless expressly modified or excluded, these Rules apply as terms and conditions incorporated into a standby, confirmation, advice, nomination, amendment, transfer, request for issuance, or other agreement of:

(i)   the issuer;
(ii) the beneficiary to the extent it uses the standby;
(iii) any advisor;
(iv) any confirmer;
(v)   any person nominated in the standby who acts or agrees to act; and
(vi) the applicant who authorizes issuance of the standby or otherwise agrees to the application of these Rules.

1.05 Exclusion of Matters Related to Due Issuance and Fraudulent or Abusive Drawing

These Rules do not define or otherwise provide for:

(a) power or authority to issue a standby;
(b) formal requirements for execution of a standby (e.g. a signed writing); or
(c) defenses to honour based on fraud, abuse, or similar matters.

These matters are left to applicable law.

General Principles

1.06 Nature of Standbys

(a)   A standby is an irrevocable, independent, documentary, and binding undertaking when issued and need not so state.

(b)   Because a standby is irrevocable, an issuer's obligations under a standby cannot be amended or cancelled by the issuer except as provided in the standby or as consented to by the person against whom the amendment or cancellation is asserted.

(c)   Because a standby is independent, the enforceability of an issuer's obligations under a standby does not depend on:

(i)   the issuer's right or ability to obtain reimbursement from the applicant;
(ii) the beneficiary's right to obtain payment from the applicant;
(iii) a reference in the standby to any reimbursement agreement or underlying transaction; or
(iv) the issuer's knowledge of performance or breach of any reimbursement agreement or underlying transaction.

(d)   Because a standby is documentary, an issuer's obligations depend on the presentation of documents and an examination of required documents on their face.

(e)   Because a standby or amendment is binding when issued, it is enforceable against an issuer whether or not the applicant authorized its issuance, the issuer received a fee, or the beneficiary received or relied on the standby or the amendment.

1.07 Independence of the Issuer-Beneficiary Relationship

An issuer's obligations toward the beneficiary are not affected by the issuer's rights and obligations toward the applicant under any applicable agreement, practice, or law.

1.08 Limits to Responsibilities

An issuer is not responsible for:

(a) performance or breach of any underlying transaction;
(b) accuracy, genuineness, or effect of any document presented under the standby;
(c) action or omission of others even if the other person is chosen by the issuer or nominated person; or
(d) observance of law or practice other than that chosen in the standby or applicable at the place of issuance.

Terminology
1.09 Defined Terms

In addition to the meanings given in standard banking practice and applicable law, the following terms have or include the meanings indicated below:

(a) Definitions

"Applicant" is a person who applies for issuance of a standby or for whose account it is issued, and includes (i) a person applying in its own name but for the account of another person or (ii) an issuer acting for its own account.

"Beneficiary" is a named person who is entitled to draw under a standby. See Rule 1.11(c)(ii).

"Business day" means a day on which the place of business at which the relevant act is to be performed is regularly open; and

"Banking day" means a day on which the relevant bank is regularly open at the place at which the relevant act is to be performed.

"Confirmer" is a person who, upon an issuer's nomination to do so, adds to the issuer's undertaking its own undertaking to honour a standby. See Rule 1.11(c)(i).

"Demand" means, depending on the context, either a request to honour a standby or a document that makes such request.

"Document" means a draft, demand, document of title, investment security, invoice, certificate of default, or any other representation of fact, law, right, or opinion, that upon presentation (whether in a paper or electronic medium), is capable of being examined for compliance with the terms and conditions of a standby.

"Drawing" means, depending on the context, either a demand presented or a demand honoured.

"Expiration date" means the latest day for a complying presentation provided in a standby.

"Person" includes a natural person, partnership, corporation, limited liability company, government agency, bank, trustee, and any other legal or commercial association or entity.

"Presentation" means, depending on the context, either the act of delivering documents for examination under a standby or the documents so delivered.

"Presenter" is a person who makes a presentation as or on behalf of a beneficiary or nominated person.

"Signature" includes any symbol executed or adopted by a person with a present intent to authenticate a document.

(b) Cross references

"Amendment"	—	Rule 2.06
"Advice"	—	Rule 2.05
"Approximately" ("About" or "Circa")	—	Rule 3.08(f)
"Assignment of Proceeds"	—	Rule 6.06
"Automatic amendment"	—	Rule 2.06(a)
"Copy"	—	Rule 4.15(d)
"Cover instructions"	—	Rule 5.08
"Honour"	—	Rule 2.01
"Issuer"	—	Rule 2.01
"Multiple presentations"	—	Rule 3.08(b)
"Nominated person"	—	Rule 2.04
"Non-documentary conditions"	—	Rule 4.11
"Original"	—	Rule 4.15(b) and (c)
"Partial drawing"	—	Rule 3.08(a)
"Standby"	—	Rule 1.01(d)
"Transfer"	—	Rule 6.01
"Transferee beneficiary"	—	Rule 1.11*(c)*(ii)
"Transfer by operation of law"	—	Rule 6.11

(c)   Electronic presentations

The following terms in a standby providing for or permitting electronic presentation shall have the following meanings unless the context otherwise requires:

"Electronic record" means:

(i)   a record (information that is inscribed on a tangible medium or that is stored in an electronic or other medium and is retrievable in perceivable form);

(ii)   communicated by electronic means to a system for receiving, storing, re-transmitting, or otherwise processing information (data, text, images, sounds, codes, computer programs, software, databases, and the like); and

(iii) capable of being authenticated and then examined for compliance with the terms and conditions of the standby.

"Authenticate" means to verify an electronic record by generally accepted procedure or methodology in commercial practice:

(i)   the identity of a sender or source, and

(ii)   the integrity of or errors in the transmission of information content.

The criteria for assessing the integrity of information in an electronic record is whether the information has remained complete and unaltered, apart from the addition of any endorsement and any change which arises in the normal course of communication, storage, and display.

"Electronic signature" means letters, characters, numbers, or other symbols in electronic form, attached to or logically associated with an electronic record that are executed or adopted by a party with present intent to authenticate an electronic record.

"Receipt" occurs when:

(i)   an electronic record enters in a form capable of being processed by the information system designated in the standby, or

(ii)   an issuer retrieves an electronic record sent to an information system other than that designated by the issuer.

1.10 Redundant or Otherwise Undesirable Terms

(a)   A standby should not or need not state that it is:

(i)   unconditional or abstract (if it does, it signifies merely that payment under it is conditioned solely on presentation of specified documents);

(ii)   absolute (if it does, it signifies merely that it is irrevocable);

(iii) primary (if it does, it signifies merely that it is the independent obligation of the issuer);

(iv)   payable from the issuer's own funds (if it does, it signifies merely that payment under it does not depend on the availability of applicant funds and is made to satisfy the issuer's own independent obligation);

(v)   clean or payable on demand (if it does, it signifies merely that it is payable upon presentation of a written demand or other documents specified in the standby).

(b)   A standby should not use the term "and/or" (if it does it means either or both).

(c)   The following terms have no single accepted meaning:

(i)   and shall be disregarded: "callable", "divisible", "fractionable", "indivisible", and "transmissible".

(ii)   and shall be disregarded unless their context gives them meaning: "assignable", "evergreen", "reinstate", and "revolving".

1.11 Interpretation of These Rules

(a)   These Rules are to be interpreted in the context of applicable standard practice.

(b)   In these Rules, "standby letter of credit" refers to the type of independent undertaking for which these Rules were intended, whereas "standby" refers to an undertaking subjected to these Rules.

(c)   Unless the context otherwise requires:

(i)   "Issuer" includes a "confirmer" as if the confirmer were a separate issuer and its confirmation were a separate standby issued for the account of the issuer;

(ii)   "Beneficiary" includes a person to whom the named beneficiary has effectively transferred drawing rights ("transferee beneficiary");

(iii) "Including" means "including but not limited to";

(iv)   "A or B" means "A or B or both"; "either A or B" means "A or B, but not both"; and "A and B" means "both A and B";

(v)   Words in the singular number include the plural, and in the plural include the singular; and

(vi)   Words of the neuter gender include any gender.

(d)(i)Use of the phrase "unless a standby otherwise states" or the like in a rule emphasizes that the text of the standby controls over the rule;

(ii)   Absence of such a phrase in other rules does not imply that other rules have priority over the text of the standby;

(iii) Addition of the term "expressly" or "clearly" to the phrase "unless a standby otherwise states" or the like emphasizes that the rule should be excluded or modified only by wording in the standby that is specific and unambiguous; and

(iv)   While the effect of all of these Rules may be varied by the text of the standby, variations of the effect of some of these Rules may disqualify the standby as an independent undertaking under applicable law.

(e)   The phrase "stated in the standby" or the like refers to the actual text of a standby (whether as issued or effectively amended) whereas the phrase "provided in the standby" or the like refers to both the text of the standby and these Rules as incorporated.

RULE 2: OBLIGATIONS
2.01 Undertaking to Honour by Issuer and Any Confirmer to Beneficiary

(a)   An issuer undertakes to the beneficiary to honour a presentation that appears on its face to comply with the terms and conditions of the standby in accordance with these Rules supplemented by standard standby practice.

(b)   An issuer honours a complying presentation made to it by paying the amount demanded of it at sight, unless the standby provides for honour:

(i)   by acceptance of a draft drawn by the beneficiary on the issuer, in which case the issuer honours by:
-    timely accepting the draft; and
-    thereafter paying the holder of the draft on presentation of the accepted draft on or after its maturity.

(ii)   by deferred payment of a demand made by the beneficiary on the issuer, in which case the issuer honours by:
-    timely incurring a deferred payment obligation; and
-    thereafter paying at maturity.

(iii) by negotiation, in which case the issuer honours by paying the amount demanded at sight without recourse.

(c)   An issuer acts in a timely manner if it pays at sight, accepts a draft, or undertakes a deferred payment obligation (or if it gives notice of dishonour) within the time permitted for examining the presentation and giving notice of dishonour.

(d)(i)A confirmer undertakes to honour a complying presentation made to it by paying the amount demanded of it at sight or, if the standby so states, by another method of honour consistent with the issuer's undertaking.

(ii)   If the confirmation permits presentation to the issuer, then the confirmer undertakes also to honour upon the issuer's wrongful dishonour by performing as if the presentation had been made to the confirmer.

(iii) If the standby permits presentation to the confirmer, then the issuer undertakes also to honour upon the confirmer's wrongful dishonour by performing as if the presentation had been made to the issuer.

(e)   An issuer honours by paying in immediately available funds in the currency designated in the standby unless the standby states it is payable by:

(i)   payment of a monetary unit of account, in which case the undertaking is to pay in that unit
       of account; or
(ii)   delivery of other items of value, in which case the undertaking is to deliver those items.

2.02 Obligation of Different Branches, Agencies, or Other Offices

For the purposes of these Rules, an issuer's branch, agency, or other office acting or undertaking
to act under a standby in a capacity other than as issuer is obligated in that capacity only and
shall be treated as a different person.

2.03 Conditions to Issuance

A standby is issued when it leaves an issuer's control unless it clearly specifies that it is not then
"issued" or "enforceable". Statements that a standby is not "available", "operative", "effective", or
the like do not affect its irrevocable and binding nature at the time it leaves the issuer's control.

2.04 Nomination

(a)   A standby may nominate a person to advise, receive a presentation, effect a transfer, confirm, pay, negotiate, incur a deferred payment obligation, or accept a draft.
(b)   Nomination does not obligate the nominated person to act except to the extent that the
nominated person undertakes to act.
(c)   A nominated person is not authorized to bind the person making the nomination.

2.05 Advice of Standby or Amendment

(a)   Unless an advice states otherwise, it signifies that:
(i)   the advisor has checked the apparent authenticity of the advised message in accordance
       with standard letter of credit practice; and
(ii)   the advice accurately reflects what has been received.
(b)   A person who is requested to advise a standby and decides not to do so should notify the
requesting party.

2.06 When an Amendment Is Authorized and Binding

(a)   If a standby expressly states that it is subject to "automatic amendment" by an increase or
decrease in the amount available, an extension of the expiration date, or the like, the amendment is effective automatically without any further notification or consent beyond that expressly provided for in the standby. (Such an amendment may also be referred to as becoming effective "without amendment".)
(b)   If there is no provision for automatic amendment, an amendment binds:
(i)   the issuer when it leaves the issuer's control; and
(ii)   the confirmer when it leaves the confirmer's control, unless the confirmer indicates that it
       does not confirm the amendment.
(c)   If there is no provision for automatic amendment:
(i)   the beneficiary must consent to the amendment for it to be binding;
(ii)   the beneficiary's consent must be made by an express communication to the person advi-
       sing the amendment unless the beneficiary presents documents which comply with the
       standby as amended and which would not comply with the standby prior to such amend-
       ment; and
(iii) an amendment does not require the applicant's consent to be binding on the issuer, the
       confirmer, or the beneficiary.
(d)   Consent to only part of an amendment is a rejection of the entire amendment.

2.07 Routing of Amendments

(a)   An issuer using another person to advise a standby must advise all amendments to that
person.
(b)   An amendment or cancellation of a standby does not affect the issuer's obligation to a nominated person that has acted within the scope of its nomination before receipt of notice of the
amendment or cancellation.

(c)   Non-extension of an automatically extendable (renewable) standby does not affect an issuer's obligation to a nominated person who has acted within the scope of its nomination before receipt of a notice of non-extension.

RULE 3: PRESENTATION

3.01 Complying Presentation Under a Standby

A standby should indicate the time, place and location within that place, person to whom, and medium in which presentation should be made. If so, presentation must be so made in order to comply. To the extent that a standby does not so indicate, presentation must be made in accordance with these Rules in order to be complying.

3.02 What Constitutes a Presentation?

The receipt of a document required by and presented under a standby constitutes a presentation requiring examination for compliance with the terms and conditions of the standby even if not all of the required documents have been presented.

3.03 Identification of Standby

(a)   A presentation must identify the standby under which the presentation is made.
(b)   A presentation may identify the standby by stating the complete reference number of the standby and the name and location of the issuer or by attaching the original or a copy of the standby.
(c)   If the issuer cannot determine from the face of a document received that it should be processed under a standby or cannot identify the standby to which it relates, presentation is deemed to have been made on the date of identification.

3.04 Where and to Whom Complying Presentation Made?

(a)   To comply, a presentation must be made at the place and any location at that place indicated in the standby or provided in these Rules.
(b)   If no place of presentation to the issuer is indicated in the standby, presentation to the issuer must be made at the place of business from which the standby was issued.
(c)   If a standby is confirmed, but no place for presentation is indicated in the confirmation, presentation for the purpose of obligating the confirmer (and the issuer) must be made at the place of business of the confirmer from which the confirmation was issued or to the issuer.
(d)   If no location at a place of presentation is indicated (such as department, floor, room, station, mail stop, post office box, or other location), presentation may be made to:
(i)   the general postal address indicated in the standby;
(ii)   any location at the place designated to receive deliveries of mail or documents; or
(iii) any person at the place of presentation actually or apparently authorized to receive it.

3.05 When Timely Presentation Made?

(a)   A presentation is timely if made at any time after issuance and before expiry on the expiration date.
(b)   A presentation made after the close of business at the place of presentation is deemed to have been made on the next business day.

3.06 Complying Medium of Presentation

(a)   To comply, a document must be presented in the medium indicated in the standby.
(b)   Where no medium is indicated, to comply a document must be presented as a paper document, unless only a demand is required, in which case:
(i)   a demand that is presented via S.W.I.F.T., tested telex, or other similar authenticated means by a beneficiary that is a S.W.I.F.T. participant or a bank complies; otherwise
(ii)   a demand that is not presented as a paper document does not comply unless the issuer permits, in its sole discretion, the use of that medium.
(c)   A document is not presented as a paper document if it is communicated by electronic means even if the issuer or nominated person receiving it generates a paper document from it.

(d)   Where presentation in an electronic medium is indicated, to comply a document must be presented as an electronic record capable of being authenticated by the issuer or nominated person to whom it is presented.

3.07 Separateness of Each Presentation

(a)   Making a non-complying presentation, withdrawing a presentation, or failing to make any one of a number of scheduled or permitted presentations does not waive or otherwise preju- dice the right to make another timely presentation or a timely re-presentation whether or not the standby prohibits partial or multiple drawings or presentations.
(b)   Wrongful dishonour of a complying presentation does not constitute dishonour of any other presentation under a standby or repudiation of the standby.
(c)   Honour of a non-complying presentation, with or without notice of its non-compliance, does not waive requirements of a standby for other presentations.

3.08 Partial Drawing and Multiple Presentations; Amount of Drawings

(a)   A presentation may be made for less than the full amount available ("partial drawing").
(b)   More than one presentation ("multiple presentations") may be made.
(c)   The statement "partial drawings prohibited" or a similar expression means that a presenta- tion must be for the full amount available.
(d)   The statement "multiple drawings prohibited" or a similar expression means that only one presentation may be made and honoured but that it may be for less than the full amount avail- able.
(e)   If a demand exceeds the amount available under the standby, the drawing is discrepant. Any document other than the demand stating an amount in excess of the amount demanded is not discrepant for that reason.
(f)   Use of "approximately", "about", "circa", or a similar word permits a tolerance not to exceed 10 per cent more or 10 per cent less of the amount to which such word refers.

3.09 Extend or Pay

A beneficiary's request to extend the expiration date of the standby or, alternatively, to pay the amount available under it:
(a)   is a presentation demanding payment under the standby, to be examined as such in accordance with these Rules; and
(b)   implies that the beneficiary:
(i)   consents to the amendment to extend the expiry date to the date requested;
(ii)   requests the issuer to exercise its discretion to seek the approval of the applicant and to issue that amendment;
(iii) upon issuance of that amendment, retracts its demand for payment; and
(iv)   consents to the maximum time available under these Rules for examination and notice of dishonour.

3.10 No Notice of Receipt of Presentation

An issuer is not required to notify the applicant of receipt of a presentation under the standby.

3.11 Issuer Waiver and Applicant Consent to Waiver of Presentation Rules

In addition to other discretionary provisions in a standby or these Rules, an issuer may, in its sole discretion, without notice to or consent of the applicant and without effect on the applicant's obligations to the issuer, waive:
(a)   the following Rules and any similar terms stated in the standby which are primarily for the issuer's benefit or operational convenience:
(i)   treatment of documents received, at the request of the presenter, as having been presen- ted at a later date (Rule 3.02);
(ii)   identification of a presentation to the standby under which it is presented (Rule 3.03(a));
(iii) where and to whom presentation is made (Rule 3.04(b), (c), and (d)), except the country of presentation stated in the standby; or

(iv) treatment of a presentation made after the close of business as if it were made on the next business day (Rule 3.05(b)).
(b)   the following Rule but not similar terms stated in the standby:
(i)   a required document dated after the date of its stated presentation (Rule 4.06); or
(ii) the requirement that a document issued by the beneficiary be in the language of the standby (Rule 4.04).
(c)   the following Rule relating to the operational integrity of the standby only in so far as the bank is in fact dealing with the true beneficiary:
-     acceptance of a demand in an electronic medium (Rule 3.06(b)).
Waiver by the confirmer requires the consent of the issuer with respect to paragraphs (b) and (c) of this Rule.

3.12 Original Standby Lost, Stolen, Mutilated, or Destroyed

(a)   If an original standby is lost, stolen, mutilated, or destroyed, the issuer need not replace it or waive any requirement that the original be presented under the standby.
(b)   If the issuer agrees to replace an original standby or to waive a requirement for its presentation, it may provide a replacement or copy to the beneficiary without affecting the applicant's obligations to the issuer to reimburse, but, if it does so, the issuer must mark the replacement or copy as such. The issuer may, in its sole discretion, require indemnities satisfactory to it from the beneficiary and assurances from nominated persons that no payment
has been made.

Closure on Expiry Date

3.13 Expiration Date on a Non-Business Day

(a)   If the last day for presentation stated in a standby (whether stated to be the expiration date or the date by which documents must be received) is not a business day of the issuer or nominated person where presentation is to be made, then presentation made there on the first following business day shall be deemed timely.
(b)   A nominated person to whom such a presentation is made must so notify the issuer.

3.14 Closure on a Business Day and Authorization of Another Reasonable Place for Presentation

(a)   If on the last business day for presentation the place for presentation stated in a standby is for any reason closed and presentation is not timely made because of the closure, then the last day for presentation is automatically extended to the day occurring thirty calendar days after the place for presentation re-opens for business, unless the standby otherwise provides.
(b)   Upon or in anticipation of closure of the place of presentation, an issuer may authorize another reasonable place for presentation in the standby or in a communication received by the beneficiary. If it does so, then
(i)   presentation must be made at that reasonable place; and
(ii) if the communication is received fewer than thirty calendar days before the last day for presentation and for that reason presentation is not timely made, the last day for presentation is automatically extended to the day occurring thirty calendar days after the last day for presentation.

RULE 4: EXAMINATION

4.01 Examination for Compliance

(a)   Demands for honour of a standby must comply with the terms and conditions of the standby.
(b)   Whether a presentation appears to comply is determined by examining the presentation on its face against the terms and conditions stated in the standby as interpreted and supplemented by these Rules which are to be read in the context of standard standby practice.

4.02 Non-Examination of Extraneous Documents

Documents presented which are not required by the standby need not be examined and, in any event, shall be disregarded for purposes of determining compliance of the presentation.

They may without responsibility be returned to the presenter or passed on with the other documents presented.

4.03 Examination for Inconsistency

An issuer or nominated person is required to examine documents for inconsistency with each other only to the extent provided in the standby.

4.04 Language of Documents

The language of all documents issued by the beneficiary is to be that of the standby.

4.05 Issuer of Documents

Any required document must be issued by the beneficiary unless the standby indicates that the document is to be issued by a third person or the document is of a type that standard standby practice requires to be issued by a third person.

4.06 Date of Documents

The issuance date of a required document may be earlier but not later than the date of its presentation.

4.07 Required Signature on a Document

(a) A required document need not be signed unless the standby indicates that the document must be signed or the document is of a type that standard standby practice requires be signed.
(b) A required signature may be made in any manner that corresponds to the medium in which the signed document is presented.
(c) Unless a standby specifies:
(i) the name of a person who must sign a document, any signature or authentication will be regarded as a complying signature.
(ii) the status of a person who must sign, no indication of status is necessary.
(d) If a standby specifies that a signature must be made by:
(i) a named natural person without requiring that the signer's status be identified, a signature complies that appears to be that of the named person;
(ii) a named legal person or government agency without identifying who is to sign on its behalf or its status, any signature complies that appears to have been made on behalf of the named legal person or government agency; or
(iii) a named natural person, legal person, or government agency requiring the status of the signer be indicated, a signature complies which appears to be that of the named natural person, legal person, or government agency and indicates its status.

4.08 Demand Document Implied

If a standby does not specify any required document, it will still be deemed to require a documentary demand for payment.

4.09 Identical Wording and Quotation Marks

If a standby requires:
(a) a statement without specifying precise wording, then the wording in the document presented must appear to convey the same meaning as that required by the standby;
(b) specified wording by the use of quotation marks, blocked wording, or an attached exhibit or form, the typographical errors in spelling, punctuation, spacing, or the like that are apparent when read in context are not required to be duplicated and blank lines or spaces for data may be completed in any manner not inconsistent with the standby; or
(c) specified wording by the use of quotation marks, blocked wording, or an attached exhibit or form, and also provides that the specified wording be "exact" or "identical", then the wording in the documents presented must duplicate the specified wording, including typographical errors in spelling, punctuation, spacing and the like, as well as blank lines and spaces for data must be exactly reproduced.

4.10 Applicant Approval

A standby should not specify that a required document be issued, signed, or counter-signed by the applicant. However, if the standby includes such a requirement, the issuer may not waive the requirement and is not responsible for the applicant's withholding of the document or signature.

4.11 Non-Documentary Terms or Conditions

(a)   A standby term or condition which is non-documentary must be disregarded whether or not it affects the issuer's obligation to treat a presentation as complying or to treat the standby as issued, amended, or terminated.

(b)   Terms or conditions are non-documentary if the standby does not require presentation of a document in which they are to be evidenced and if their fulfillment cannot be determined by the issuer from the issuer's own records or within the issuer's normal operations.

(c)   Determinations from the issuer's own records or within the issuer's normal operations include determinations of:

(i)   when, where, and how documents are presented or otherwise delivered to the issuer;

(ii)   when, where, and how communications affecting the standby are sent or received by the issuer, beneficiary, or any nominated person;

(iii)   amounts transferred into or out of accounts with the issuer; and

(iv)   amounts determinable from a published index (e.g. if a standby provides for determining amounts of interest accruing according to published interest rates).

(d)   An issuer need not re-compute a beneficiary's computations under a formula stated or referenced in a standby except to the extent that the standby so provides.

4.12 Formality of Statements in Documents

(a)   A required statement need not be accompanied by a solemnity, officialization, or any other formality.

(b)   If a standby provides for the addition of a formality to a required statement by the person making it without specifying form or content, the statement complies if it indicates that it was declared, averred, warranted, attested, sworn under oath, affirmed, certified, or the like.

(c)   If a standby provides for a statement to be witnessed by another person without specifying form or content, the witnessed statement complies if it appears to contain a signature of a person other than the beneficiary with an indication that the person is acting as a witness.

(d)   If a standby provides for a statement to be counter-signed, legalized, visaed, or the like by a person other than the beneficiary acting in a governmental, judicial, corporate, or other representative capacity without specifying form or content, the statement complies if it contains the signature of a person other than the beneficiary and includes an indication of that person's representative capacity and the organization on whose behalf the person has acted.

4.13 No Responsibility to Identify Beneficiary

Except to the extent that a standby requires presentation of an electronic record:

(a)   a person honouring a presentation has No obligation to the applicant to ascertain the identity of any person making a presentation or any assignee of proceeds;

(b)   payment to a named beneficiary, transferee, an acknowledged assignee, successor by operation of law, to an account or account number stated in the standby or in a cover instruction from the beneficiary or nominated person fulfils the obligation under the standby to effect payment.

4.14 Name of Acquired or Merged Issuer or Confirmer

If the issuer or confirmer is reorganized, merged, or changes its name, any required reference by name to the issuer or confirmer in the documents presented may be to it or its successor.

4.15 Original, Copy, and Multiple Documents

(a)   A presented document must be an original.

(b)   Presentation of an electronic record, where an electronic presentation is permitted or required, is deemed to be an "original".

(c)(i) A presented document is deemed to be an original unless it appears on its face to have been reproduced from an original.

(ii)   A document which appears to have been reproduced from an original is deemed to be an original if the signature or authentication appears to be original.

(d)   A standby that requires presentation of a "copy" permits presentation of either an original or copy unless the standby states that only a copy be presented or otherwise addresses the disposition of all originals.

(e)   If multiples of the same document are requested, only one must be an original unless:

(i)   "duplicate originals" or "multiple originals" are requested in which case all must be originals; or

(ii)   "two copies", "two-fold", or the like are requested in which case either originals or copies may be presented.

Standby Document Types

4.16 Demand for Payment

(a)   A demand for payment need not be separate from the beneficiary's statement or other required document.

(b)   If a separate demand is required, it must contain:

(i)   a demand for payment from the beneficiary directed to the issuer or nominated person;

(ii)   a date indicating when the demand was issued;

(iii) the amount demanded; and

(iv)   the beneficiary's signature.

(c)   A demand may be in the form of a draft or other instruction, order, or request to pay. If a standby requires presentation of a "draft" or "bill of exchange", that draft or bill of exchange need not be in negotiable form unless the standby so states.

4.17 Statement of Default or Other Drawing Event

If a standby requires a statement, certificate, or other recital of a default or other drawing event and does not specify content, the document complies if it contains:

(a)   a representation to the effect that payment is due because a drawing event described in the standby has occurred;

(b)   a date indicating when it was issued; and

(c)   the beneficiary's signature.

4.18 Negotiable Documents

If a standby requires presentation of a document that is transferable by endorsement and delivery without stating whether, how, or to whom endorsement must be made, then the document may be presented without endorsement, or, if endorsed, the endorsement may be in blank and, in any event, the document may be issued or negotiated with or without recourse.

4.19 Legal or Judicial Documents

If a standby requires presentation of a government-issued document, a court order, an arbitration award, or the like, a document or a copy is deemed to comply if it appears to be:

(i)   issued by a government agency, court, tribunal, or the like;

(ii)   suitably titled or named;

(iii) signed;

(iv)   dated; and

(v)   originally certified or authenticated by an official of a government agency, court, tribunal, or the like.

4.20 Other Documents

(a)   If a standby requires a document other than one whose content is specified in these Rules without specifying the issuer, data content, or wording, a document complies if it appears to be appropriately titled or to serve the function of that type of document under standard standby practice.

(b)   A document presented under a standby is to be examined in the context of standby practice under these Rules even if the document is of a type (such as a commercial invoice, transport documents, insurance documents or the like) for which the Uniform Customs and Practice for Documentary Credits contains detailed rules.

4.21 Request to Issue Separate Undertaking

If a standby requests that the beneficiary of the standby issue its own separate undertaking to another (whether or not the standby recites the text of that undertaking):

(a)   the beneficiary receives no rights other than its rights to draw under the standby even if the issuer pays a fee to the beneficiary for issuing the separate undertaking;

(b)   neither the separate undertaking nor any documents presented under it need be presented to the issuer; and

(c)   if originals or copies of the separate undertaking or documents presented under it are received by the issuer although not required to be presented as a condition to honour of the standby:

(i)   the issuer need not examine, and, in any event, shall disregard their compliance or consistency with the standby, with the beneficiary's demand under the standby, or with the beneficiary's separate undertaking; and

(ii)   the issuer may without responsibility return them to the presenter or forward them to the applicant with the presentation.

RULE 5: NOTICE, PRECLUSION, AND DISPOSITION OF DOCUMENTS
5.01 Timely Notice of Dishonour

(a)   Notice of dishonour must be given within a time after presentation of documents which is not unreasonable.

(i)   Notice given within three business days is deemed to be not unreasonable and beyond seven business days is deemed to be unreasonable.

(ii)   Whether the time within which notice is given is unreasonable does not depend upon an imminent deadline for presentation.

(iii) The time for calculating when notice of dishonour must be given begins on the business day following the business day of presentation.

(iv)   Unless a standby otherwise expressly states a shortened time within which notice of dishonour must be given, the issuer has no obligation to accelerate its examination of a presentation.

(b)(i)The means by which a notice of dishonour is to be given is by telecommunication, if available, and, if not, by another available means which allows for prompt notice.

(ii)   If notice of dishonour is received within the time permitted for giving the notice, then it is deemed to have been given by prompt means.

(c)   Notice of dishonour must be given to the person from whom the documents were received (whether the beneficiary, nominated person, or person other than a delivery person) except as otherwise requested by the presenter.

5.02 Statement of Grounds for Dishonour

A notice of dishonour shall state all discrepancies upon which dishonour is based.

5.03 Failure to Give Timely Notice of Dishonour

(a)   Failure to give notice of a discrepancy in a notice of dishonour within the time and by the means specified in the standby or these rules precludes assertion of that discrepancy in any document containing the discrepancy that is retained or re-presented, but does not preclude assertion of that discrepancy in any different presentation under the same or a separate standby.

(b)   Failure to give notice of dishonour or acceptance or acknowledgement that a deferred payment undertaking has been incurred obligates the issuer to pay at maturity.

5.04 Notice of Expiry

Failure to give notice that a presentation was made after the expiration date does not preclude dishonour for that reason.

5.05 Issuer Request for Applicant Waiver Without Request by Presenter

If the issuer decides that a presentation does not comply and if the presenter does not otherwise instruct, the issuer may, in its sole discretion, request the applicant to waive non-compliance or otherwise to authorize honour within the time available for giving notice of dishonour but without extending it. Obtaining the applicant's waiver does not obligate the issuer to waive non-compliance.

5.06 Issuer Request for Applicant Waiver upon Request of Presenter

If, after receipt of notice of dishonour, a presenter requests that the presented documents be forwarded to the issuer or that the issuer seek the applicant's waiver:
(a)   no person is obligated to forward the discrepant documents or seek the applicant's waiver;
(b)   the presentation to the issuer remains subject to these Rules unless departure from them is expressly consented to by the presenter; and
(c)   if the documents are forwarded or if a waiver is sought:
(i)   the presenter is precluded from objecting to the discrepancies notified to it by the issuer;
(ii)   the issuer is not relieved from examining the presentation under these Rules;
(iii) the issuer is not obligated to waive the discrepancy even if the applicant waives it; and
(iv) the issuer must hold the documents until it receives a response from the applicant or is requested by the presenter to return the documents, and if the issuer receives no such response or request within ten business days of its notice of dishonour, it may return the documents to the presenter.

5.07 Disposition of Documents

Dishonoured documents must be returned, held, or disposed of as reasonably instructed by the presenter. Failure to give notice of the disposition of documents in the notice of dishonour does not preclude the issuer from asserting any defense otherwise available to it against honour.

5.08 Cover Instructions/Transmittal Letter

(a)   Instructions accompanying a presentation made under a standby may be relied on to the extent that they are not contrary to the terms or conditions of the standby, the demand, or these Rules.
(b)   Representations made by a nominated person accompanying a presentation may be relied upon to the extent that they are not contrary to the terms or conditions of a standby or these Rules.
(c)   Notwithstanding receipt of instructions, an issuer or nominated person may pay, give notice, return the documents, or otherwise deal directly with the presenter.
(d)   A statement in the cover letter that the documents are discrepant does not relieve the issuer from examining the presentation for compliance.

5.09 Applicant Notice of Objection

(a)   An applicant must timely object to an issuer's honour of a noncomplying presentation by giving timely notice by prompt means.
(b)   An applicant acts timely if it objects to discrepancies by sending a notice to the issuer stating the discrepancies on which the objection is based within a time after the applicant's receipt of the documents which is not unreasonable.
(c)   Failure to give a timely notice of objection by prompt means precludes assertion by the applicant against the issuer of any discrepancy or other matter apparent on the face of the documents received by the applicant, but does not preclude assertion of that objection to any different presentation under the same or a different standby.

RULE 6: TRANSFER, ASSIGNMENT, AND TRANSFER BY OPERATION OF LAW
Transfer of Drawing Rights
6.01 Request to Transfer Drawing Rights

Where a beneficiary requests that an issuer or nominated person honour a drawing from another person as if that person were the beneficiary, these Rules on transfer of drawing rights ("transfer") apply.

6.02 When Drawing Rights Are Transferable

(a) A standby is not transferable unless it so states.

(b) A standby that states that it is transferable without further provision means that drawing rights:

(i) may be transferred in their entirety more than once;

(ii) may not be partially transferred; and

(iii) may not be transferred unless the issuer (including the confirmer) or another person specifically nominated in the standby agrees to and effects the transfer requested by the beneficiary.

6.03 Conditions to Transfer

An issuer of a transferable standby or a nominated person need not effect a transfer unless:

(a) it is satisfied as to the existence and authenticity of the original standby; and

(b) the beneficiary submits or fulfils:

(i) a request in a form acceptable to the issuer or nominated person including the effective date of the transfer and the name and address of the transferee;

(ii) the original standby;

(iii) verification of the signature of the person signing for the beneficiary;

(iv) verification of the authority of the person signing for the beneficiary;

(v) payment of the transfer fee; and

(vi) any other reasonable requirements.

6.04 Effect of Transfer on Required Documents

Where there has been a transfer of drawing rights in their entirety:

(a) a draft or demand must be signed by the transferee beneficiary; and

(b) the name of the transferee beneficiary may be used in place of the name of the transferor beneficiary in any other required document.

6.05 Reimbursement for Payment Based on a Transfer

An issuer or nominated person paying under a transfer pursuant to Rule 6.03*(a)*, *(b)*(i), and *(b)*(ii) is entitled to reimbursement as if it had made payment to the beneficiary.

Acknowledgement of Assignment of Proceeds
6.06 Assignment of Proceeds

Where an issuer or nominated person is asked to acknowledge a beneficiary's request to pay an assignee all or part of any proceeds of the beneficiary's drawing under the standby, these Rules on acknowledgement of an assignment of proceeds apply except where applicable law otherwise requires.

6.07 Request for Acknowledgement

(a) Unless applicable law otherwise requires, an issuer or nominated person

(i) is not obligated to give effect to an assignment of proceeds which it has not acknowledged; and

(ii) is not obligated to acknowledge the assignment.

(b) If an assignment is acknowledged:

(i) the acknowledgement confers no rights with respect to the standby to the assignee who is only entitled to the proceeds assigned, if any, and whose rights may be affected by amendment or cancellation; and

(ii) the rights of the assignee are subject to:

(a) the existence of any net proceeds payable to the beneficiary by the person making the acknowledgement;
(b) rights of nominated persons and transferee beneficiaries;
(c) rights of other acknowledged assignees; and
(d) any other rights or interests that may have priority under applicable law.

6.08 Conditions to Acknowledgement of Assignment of Proceeds
An issuer or nominated person may condition its acknowledgement on receipt of:
(a) the original standby for examination or notation;
(b) verification of the signature of the person signing for the beneficiary;
(c) verification of the authority of the person signing for the beneficiary;
(d) an irrevocable request signed by the beneficiary for acknowledgement of the assignment that includes statements, covenants, indemnities, and other provisions which may be contained in the issuer's or nominated person's required form requesting acknowledgement of assignment, such as:
(i) the identity of the affected drawings if the standby permits multiple drawings;
(ii) the full name, legal form, location, and mailing address of the beneficiary and the assignee;
(iii) details of any request affecting the method of payment or delivery of the standby proceeds;
(iv) limitation on partial assignments and prohibition of successive assignments;
(v) statements regarding the legality and relative priority of the assignment; or
(vi) right of recovery by the issuer or nominated person of any proceeds received by the assignee that are recoverable from the beneficiary;
(e) payment of a fee for the acknowledgement; and
(f) fulfilment of other reasonable requirements.

6.09 Conflicting Claims to Proceeds
If there are conflicting claims to proceeds, then payment to an acknowledged assignee may be suspended pending resolution of the conflict.

6.10 Reimbursement for Payment Based on an Assignment
An issuer or nominated person paying under an acknowledged assignment pursuant to Rule 6.08(a) and (b) is entitled to reimbursement as if it had made payment to the beneficiary. If the beneficiary is a bank, the acknowledgement may be based solely upon an authenticated communication.

Transfer by Operation of Law
6.11 Transferee by Operation of Law
Where an heir, personal representative, liquidator, trustee, receiver, successor corporation, or similar person who claims to be designated by law to succeed to the interests of a beneficiary presents documents in its own name as if it were the authorized transferee of the beneficiary, these Rules on transfer by operation of law apply.

6.12 Additional Document in Event of Drawing in Successor's Name
A claimed successor may be treated as if it were an authorized transferee of a beneficiary's drawing rights in their entirety if it presents an additional document or documents which appear to be issued by a public official or representative (including a judicial officer) and indicate:
(a) that the claimed successor is the survivor of a merger, consolidation, or similar action of a corporation, limited liability company, or other similar organization;
(b) that the claimed successor is authorized or appointed to act on behalf of the named beneficiary or its estate because of an insolvency proceeding;
(c) that the claimed successor is authorized or appointed to act on behalf of the named beneficiary because of death or incapacity; or
(d) that the name of the named beneficiary has been changed to that of the claimed successor.

6.13 Suspension of Obligations upon Presentation by Successor

An issuer or nominated person which receives a presentation from a claimed successor which complies in all respects except for the name of the beneficiary:

(a) may request in a manner satisfactory as to form and substance:

(i) a legal opinion;

(ii) an additional document referred to in Rule 6.12 (Additional document in event of drawing in successor's name) from a public official;

(iii) statements, covenants, and indemnities regarding the status of the claimed successor as successor by operation of law;

(iv) payment of fees reasonably related to these determinations; and

(v) anything which may be required for a transfer under Rule 6.03 (Conditions to transfer) or an acknowledgement of assignment of proceeds under Rule 6.08 (Conditions to acknowledgement of assignment of proceeds);

but such documentation shall not constitute a required document for purposes of expiry of the standby.

(b) Until the issuer or nominated person receives the requested documentation, its obligation to honour or give notice of dishonour is suspended, but any deadline for presentation of required documents is not thereby extended.

6.14 Reimbursement for Payment Based on a Transfer by Operation of Law

An issuer or nominated person paying under a transfer by operation of law pursuant to Rule 6.12 (Additional document in event of drawing in successor's name) is entitled to reimbursement as if it had made payment to the beneficiary.

RULE 7: CANCELLATION

7.01 When an Irrevocable Standby Is Cancelled or Terminated

A beneficiary's rights under a standby may not be cancelled without its consent. Consent may be evidenced in writing or by an action such as return of the original standby in a manner which implies that the beneficiary consents to cancellation. A beneficiary's consent to cancellation is irrevocable when communicated to the issuer.

7.02 Issuer's Discretion Regarding a Decision to Cancel

Before acceding to a beneficiary's authorization to cancel and treating the standby as cancelled for all purposes, an issuer may require in a manner satisfactory as to form and substance:

(a) the original standby;

(b) verification of the signature of the person signing for the beneficiary;

(c) verification of the authorization of the person signing for the beneficiary;

(d) a legal opinion;

(e) an irrevocable authority signed by the beneficiary for cancellation that includes statements, covenants, indemnities, and similar provisions contained in a required form;

(f) satisfaction that the obligation of any confirmer has been cancelled;

(g) satisfaction that there has not been a transfer or payment by any nominated person; and

(h) any other reasonable measure.

RULE 8: REIMBURSEMENT OBLIGATIONS

8.01 Right to Reimbursement

(a) Where payment is made against a complying presentation in accordance with these Rules, reimbursement must be made by:

(i) an applicant to an issuer requested to issue a standby; and

(ii) an issuer to a person nominated to honour or otherwise give value.

(b) An applicant must indemnify the issuer against all claims, obligations, and responsibilities (including attorney's fees) arising out of:

(i) the imposition of law or practice other than that chosen in the standby or applicable at the place of issuance;

(ii)   the fraud, forgery, or illegal action of others; or
(iii) the issuer's performance of the obligations of a confirmer that wrongfully dishonours a confirmation.
(c)   This Rule supplements any applicable agreement, course of dealing, practice, custom or usage providing for reimbursement or indemnification on lesser or other grounds.

8.02 Charges for Fees and Costs
(a)   An applicant must pay the issuer's charges and reimburse the issuer for any charges that the issuer is obligated to pay to persons nominated with the applicant's consent to advise, confirm, honour, negotiate, transfer, or to issue a separate undertaking.
(b)   An issuer is obligated to pay the charges of other persons:
(i)   if they are payable in accordance with the terms of the standby; or
(ii)   if they are the reasonable and customary fees and expenses of a person requested by the issuer to advise, honour, negotiate, transfer, or to issue a separate undertaking, and they are unrecovered and unrecoverable from the beneficiary or other presenter because no demand is made under the standby.

8.03 Refund of Reimbursement
A nominated person that obtains reimbursement before the issuer timely dishonours the presentation must refund the reimbursement with interest if the issuer dishonours. The refund does not preclude the nominated person's wrongful dishonour claims.

8.04 Bank-to-Bank Reimbursement
Any instruction or authorization to obtain reimbursement from another bank is subject to the International Chamber of Commerce standard rules for bank-to-bank reimbursements.

RULE 9: TIMING
9.01 Duration of Standby
A standby must:
(a)   contain an expiry date; or
(b)   permit the issuer to terminate the standby upon reasonable prior notice or payment.

9.02 Effect of Expiration on Nominated Person
The rights of a nominated person that acts within the scope of its nomination are not affected by the subsequent expiry of the standby.

9.03 Calculation of Time
(a)   A period of time within which an action must be taken under these Rules begins to run on the first business day following the business day when the action could have been undertaken at the place where the action should have been undertaken.
(b)   An extension period starts on the calendar day following the stated expiry date even if either day falls on a day when the issuer is closed.

9.04 Time of Day of Expiration
If no time of day is stated for expiration, it occurs at the close of business at the place of presentation.

9.05 Retention of Standby
Retention of the original standby does not preserve any rights under the standby after the right to demand payment ceases.

RULE 10: SYNDICATION/PARTICIPATION
10.01 Syndication
If a standby with more than one issuer does not state to whom presentation may be made, presentation may be made to any issuer with binding effect on all issuers.

10.02 Participation

(a)   Unless otherwise agreed between an applicant and an issuer, the issuer may sell participations in the issuer's rights against the applicant and any presenter and may disclose relevant applicant information in confidence to potential participants.

(b)   An issuer's sale of participations does not affect the obligations of the issuer under the standby or create any rights or obligations between the beneficiary and any participant.

UNIFORM RULES FOR DEMAND GUARANTEES (URDG 758)[1]

Article 1 - Application of URDG

a.   The Uniform Rules for Demand Guarantees ("URDG") apply to any demand guarantee or counter-guarantee that expressly indicates it is subject to them. They are binding on all parties to the demand guarantee or counter-guarantee except so far as the demand guarantee or counter-guarantee modifies or excludes them.

b.   Where, at the request of a counter-guarantor, a demand guarantee is issued subject to the URDG, the counter-guarantee shall also be subject to the URDG unless the counter-guarantee excludes the URDG. However, a demand guarantee does not become subject to the URDG merely because the counter-guarantee is subject to the URDG.

c.   Where, at the request or with the agreement of the instructing party, a demand guarantee or counter-guarantee is issued subject to the URDG, the instructing party is deemed to have accepted the rights and obligations expressly ascribed to it in these rules.

d.   Where a demand guarantee or counter-guarantee issued on or after 1 July 2010 states that it is subject to the URDG without stating whether the 1992 version or the 2010 revision is to apply or indicating the publication number, the demand guarantee or counter-guarantee shall be subject to the URDG 2010 revision.

Article 2 - Definitions

In these rules:

advising party means the party that advises the guarantee at the request of the guarantor;

applicant means the party indicated in the guarantee as having its obligation under the underlying relationship supported by the guarantee. The applicant may or may not be the instructing party;

application means the request for the issue of the guarantee;

authenticated, when applied to an electronic document, means that the party to whom that document is presented is able to verify the apparent identity of the sender and whether the data received have remained complete and unaltered;

beneficiary means the party in whose favour a guarantee is issued;

business day means a day on which the place of business where an act of a kind subject to these rules is to be performed is regularly open for the performance of such an act;

charges mean any commissions, fees, costs or expenses due to any party acting under a guarantee governed by these rules;

complying demand means a demand that meets the requirements of a complying presentation;

complying presentation under a guarantee means a presentation that is in accordance with, first, the terms and conditions of that guarantee, second, these rules so far as consistent with those terms and conditions and, third, in the absence of a relevant provision in the guarantee or these rules, international standard demand guarantee practice;

counter-guarantee means any signed undertaking, however named or described, that is given by the counter-guarantor to another party to procure the issue by that other party of a guarantee or another counter-guarantee, and that provides for payment upon the presentation of a complying demand under the counter-guarantee issued in favour of that party;

---

1   © International Chamber of Commerce, Paris.

counter-guarantor means the party issuing a counter-guarantee, whether in favour of a guarantor or another counter-guarantor, and includes a party acting for its own account;

demand means a signed document by the beneficiary demanding payment under a guarantee;

demand guarantee or **guarantee** means any signed undertaking, however named or described, providing for payment on presentation of a complying demand;

document means a signed or unsigned record of information, in paper or in electronic form, that is capable of being reproduced in tangible form by the person to whom it is presented. Under these rules, a document includes a demand and a supporting statement;

expiry means the expiry date or the expiry event or, if both are specified, the earlier of the two;

expiry date means the date specified in the guarantee on or before which a presentation may be made;

expiry event means an event which under the terms of the guarantee results in its expiry, whether immediately or within a specified time after the event occurs, for which purpose the event is deemed to occur only:

a.   when a document specified in the guarantee as indicating the occurrence of the event is presented to the guarantor, or

b.   if no such document is specified in the guarantee, when the occurrence of the event becomes determinable from the guarantor's own records.

guarantee, see demand guarantee;

guarantor means the party issuing a guarantee, and includes a party acting for its own account;

guarantor's own records means records of the guarantor showing amounts credited to or debited from accounts held with the guarantor, provided the record of those credits or debits enables the guarantor to identify the guarantee to which they relate;

instructing party means the party, other than the counter-guarantor, who gives instructions to issue a guarantee or counter-guarantee and is responsible for indemnifying the guarantor or, in the case of a counter-guarantee, the counter-guarantor. The instructing party may or may not be the applicant;

presentation means the delivery of a document under a guarantee to the guarantor or the document so delivered. It includes a presentation other than for a demand, for example, a presentation for the purpose of triggering the expiry of the guarantee or a variation of its amount;

presenter means a person who makes a presentation as or on behalf of the beneficiary or the applicant, as the case may be;

signed, when applied to a document, a guarantee or a counter-guarantee, means that an original of the same is signed by or on behalf of its issuer, whether by an electronic signature that can be authenticated by the party to whom that document, guarantee or counter-guarantee is presented or by handwriting, facsimile signature, perforated signature, stamp, symbol or other mechanical method;

supporting statement means the statement referred to in either Article 15 (a) or Article 15 (b);

underlying relationship means the contract, tender conditions or other relationship between the applicant and the beneficiary on which the guarantee is based.

Article 3 - Interpretation

In these rules;

a.   Branches of a guarantor in different countries are considered to be separate entities.

b.   Except where the context otherwise requires, a guarantee includes a counter-guarantee and any amendment to either, a guarantor includes a counter-guarantor, and a beneficiary includes the party in whose favour a counter-guarantee is issued.

c.   Any requirement for presentation of one or more originals or copies of an electronic document is satisfied by the presentation of one electronic document.

d.   When used with a date or dates to determine the start, end or duration of any period, the terms (I.) "from", "to", "until", "till" and "between", include; and (ii.) "before" and "after" exclude, the date or dates mentioned.

e.   The term "within", when used in connection with a period after a given date or event, excludes that date or the date of that event but includes the last date of that period.

f.   Terms such as "first class", "well-known", "qualified", "independent", "official", "competent" or "local" when used to describe the issuer of a document allow any issuer except the beneficiary or the applicant to issue that document.

Article 4 - Issue and Effectiveness

a.   A guarantee is issued when it leaves the control of the guarantor.

b.   A guarantee is irrevocable on issue even if it does not state this.

c.   The beneficiary may present a demand from the time of issue of the guarantee or such later time or event as the guarantee provides.

Article 5 - Independence of Guarantee and Counter-Guarantee

a.   A guarantee is by its nature independent of the underlying relationship and the application, and the guarantor is in no way concerned with or bound by such relationship. A reference in the guarantee to the underlying relationship for the purpose of identifying it does not change the independent nature of the guarantee. The undertaking of a guarantor to pay under the guarantee is not subject to claims or defences arising from any relationship other than a relationship between the guarantor and the beneficiary.

b.   A counter-guarantee is by its nature independent of the guarantee, the underlying relationship, the application and any other counter-guarantee to which it relates, and the counter-guarantor is in no way concerned with or bound by such relationship. A reference in the counter-guarantee to the underlying relationship for the purpose of identifying it does not change the independent nature of the counter-guarantee. The undertaking of a counter-guarantor to pay under the counter-guarantee is not subject to claims or defences arising from any relationship other than a relationship between the counter-guarantor and the guarantor or other counter-guarantor to whom the counter-guarantee is issued.

Article 6 - Documents v. Goods, Services or Performance

Guarantors deal with documents and not with goods, services or performance to which the documents may relate.

Article 7 - Non-Documentary Conditions

A guarantee should not contain a condition other than a date or the lapse of a period without specifying a document to indicate compliance with that condition. If the guarantee does not specify any such document and the fulfilment of the condition cannot be determined from the guarantor's own records or from an index specified in the guarantee, then the guarantor will deem such condition as not stated and will disregard it except for the purpose of determining whether data that may appear in a document specified in and presented under the guarantee do not conflict with data in the guarantee.

Article 8 - Content of Instructions and Guarantees

All instructions for the issue of guarantees and guarantees themselves should be clear and precise and should avoid excessive detail. It is recommended that all guarantees specify:

a.   the applicant;

b.   the beneficiary;

c.   the guarantor;

d.   a reference number or other information identifying the underlying relationship;

e.   a reference number or other information identifying the issued guarantee or in the case of a counter-guarantee, the issued counter-guarantee;

f.   the amount or maximum amount payable and the currency in which it is payable;

g.   the expiry of the guarantee;

h.   any terms for demanding payment;

i.   whether a demand or other document shall be presented in paper and/or electronic form;

j.   the language of any document specified in the guarantee; and

k.   the party liable for the payment of any charges.

Article 9 - Application Not Taken Up

Where, at the tame of receipt of the application, the guarantor is not prepared or is unable to issue the guarantee, the guarantor should without delay so inform the party that gave the guarantor its instructions.

Article 10 - Advising of Guarantee or Amendment

a.   A guarantee may be advised to a beneficiary through an advising party. By advising a guarantee, whether directly or by utilizing the services of another party ("second advising party"), the advising party signifies to the beneficiary and, if applicable, to the second advising party, that it has satisfied itself as to the apparent authenticity of the guarantee and that the advice accurately reflects the terms and conditions of the guarantee as received by the advising party.

b.   By advising a guarantee, the second advising party signifies to the beneficiary that it has satisfied itself as to the apparent authenticity of the advice it has received and that the advice accurately reflects the terms and conditions of the guarantee as received by the second advising party.

c.   An advising party or a second advising party advises a guarantee without any additional representation or any undertaking whatsoever to the beneficiary.

d.   If a party is requested to advise a guarantee or an amendment but is not prepared or is unable to do so, it should without delay so inform the party from whom it received that guarantee, amendment or advice.

e.   If a party is requested to advise a guarantee, and agrees to do so, but cannot satisfy itself as to the apparent authenticity of that guarantee or advice, it shall without delay so inform the party from whom the instructions appear to have been received. If the advising party or second advising party elects nonetheless to advise that guarantee, it shall inform the beneficiary or second advising party that it has not been able to satisfy itself as to the apparent authenticity of the guarantee or the advice.

f.   A guarantor using the services of an advising party or a second advising party, as well as an advising party using the services of a second advising party, to advise a guarantee should whenever possible use the same party to advise any amendment to that guarantee.

Article 11 - Amendments

a.   Where, at the time of receipt of instructions for the issue of an amendment to the guarantee, the guarantor for whatever reason is not prepared or is unable to issue that amendment, the guarantor shall without delay so inform the party that gave the guarantor its instructions.

b.   An amendment made without the beneficiary's agreement is not binding on the beneficiary. Nevertheless the guarantor is irrevocably bound by an amendment from the time it issues the amendment, unless and until the beneficiary rejects that amendment.

c.   Except where made in accordance with the terms of the guarantee, the beneficiary may reject an amendment of the guarantee at any time until it notifies its acceptance of the amendment or makes a presentation that complies only with the guarantee as amended.

d.   An advising party shall without delay inform the party from which it has received the amendment of the beneficiary's notification of acceptance or rejection of that amendment.

e.   Partial acceptance of an amendment is not allowed and will be deemed to be notification of rejection of the amendment.

f.   A provision in an amendment to the effect that the amendment shall take effect unless rejected within a certain time shall be disregarded.

Article 12 - Extent of Guarantor's Liability Under Guarantee

A guarantor is liable to the beneficiary only in accordance with, first, the terms and conditions of the guarantee and, second, these rules so far as consistent with those terms and conditions, up to the guarantee amount.

Article 13 - Variation of Amount of Guarantee

A guarantee may provide for the reduction or the increase of its amount on specified dates or on the occurrence of a specified event which under the terms of the guarantee results in the variation of its amount, and for this purpose the event is deemed to have occurred only:

a.   when a document specified in the guarantee as indicating the occurrence of the event is presented to the guarantor, or

b.   if no such document is specified in the guarantee, when the occurrence of the event becomes determinable from the guarantor's own records or from an index specified in the guarantee.

Article 14 - Presentation

a.   A presentation shall be made to the guarantor:

i.   at the place of issue, or such other place as is specified in the guarantee and,

ii.   on or before expiry.

b.   A presentation has to be complete unless it indicates that it is to be completed later. In that case, it shall be completed before expiry.

c.   Where the guarantee indicates that a presentation is to be made in electronic form, the guarantee should specify the format, the system for data delivery and the electronic address for that presentation. If the guarantee does not so specify, a document may be presented in any electronic format that allows it to be authenticated or in paper form. An electronic document that cannot be authenticated is deemed not to have been presented.

d.   Where the guarantee indicates that a presentation is to be made in paper form through a particular mode of delivery but does not expressly exclude the use of another mode, the use of another mode of delivery by the presenter shall be effective if the presentation is received at the place and by the time indicated in paragraph (a) of this article.

e.   Where the guarantee does not indicate whether a presentation is to be made in electronic or paper form, any presentation shall be made in paper form.

f.   Each presentation shall identify the guarantee under which it is made, such as by stating the guarantor's reference number for the guarantee. If it does not, the time for examination indicated in Article 20 shall start on the date of identification. Nothing in this paragraph shall result in an extension of the guarantee or limit the requirement in Article 15 (a) or (b) for any separately presented documents also to identify the demand to which they relate.

g.   Except where the guarantee otherwise provides, documents issued by or on behalf of the applicant or the beneficiary, including any demand or supporting statement, shall be in the language of the guarantee. Documents issued by any other person may be in any language.

Article 15 - Requirements for Demand

a.   A demand under the guarantee shall be supported by such other documents as the guarantee specifies, and in any event by a statement, by the beneficiary, indicating in what respect the applicant is in breach of its obligations under the underlying relationship. This statement may be in the demand or in a separate signed document accompanying or identifying the demand.

b.   A demand under the counter-guarantee shall in any event be supported by a statement, by the party to whom the counter-guarantee was issued, indicating that such party has received a complying demand under the guarantee or counter-guarantee issued by that party. This statement may be in the demand or in a separate signed document accompanying or identifying the demand.

c.   The requirement for a supporting statement in paragraph(a) or (b) of this Article applies except to the extent the guarantee or counter-guarantee expressly excludes this requirement. Exclusion terms such as "The supporting statement under Article 15[(a)] [(b)] is excluded" satisfy the requirement of this paragraph.

d.   Neither the demand nor the supporting statement may be dated before the date when the beneficiary is entitled to present a demand. Any other document may be dated before that date. Neither the demand, nor the supporting statement, nor any other document may be dated later than the date of its presentation.

Article 16 - Information About Demand

The guarantor shall without delay inform the instructing party or, where applicable, the counter-guarantor of any demand under the guarantee and of any request, as an alternative, to extend the expiry of the guarantee. The counter-guarantor shall without delay inform the instructing party of any demand under the counter-guarantee and of any request, as an alternative, to extend the expiry of the counter-guarantee.

Article 17 - Partial Demand and Multiple Demands; Amount of Demands

a.   A demand may be made for less than the full amount available ("partial demand").

b.   More than one demand ("multiple demands") may be made.

c.   The expression "multiple demands prohibited" or a similar expression means that only one demand covering all or part of the amount available may be made.

d.   Where the guarantee provides that only one demand may be made, and that demand is rejected, another demand can be made on or before expiry of the guarantee.

e.   A demand is a non-complying demand if:

i.   it is for more than the amount available under the guarantee, or

ii.   any supporting statement or other documents required by the guarantee indicate amounts that in total are less than the amount demanded.

Conversely, any supporting statement or other document indicating an amount that is more than the amount demanded does not make the demand a non-complying demand.

Article 18 - Separateness of Each Demand

a.   Making a demand that is not a complying demand or withdrawing a demand does not waive or otherwise prejudice the right to make another timely demand, whether or not the guarantee prohibits partial or multiple demands.

b.   Payment of a demand that is not a complying demand does not waive the requirement for other demands to be complying demands.

Article 19 - Examination

a.   The guarantor shall determine, on the basis of a presentation alone, whether it appears on its face to be a complying presentation.

b.   Data in a document required by the guarantee shall be examined in context with that document, the guarantee and these rules. Data need not be identical to, but shall not conflict with, data in that document, any other required document or the guarantee.

c.   If the guarantee requires presentation of a document without stipulating whether it needs to be signed, by whom it is to be issued or signed, or its data content, then:

i.   the guarantor will accept the document as presented if its content appears to fulfil the function of the document required by the guarantee and otherwise complies with Article 19 (b), and

ii.   if the document is signed, any signature will be accepted and no indication of name or position of the signatory is necessary.

d.   If a document that is not required by the guarantee or referred to in these rules is presented, it will be disregarded and may be returned to the presenter.

e.   The guarantor need not re-calculate a beneficiary's calculations under a formula stated or referenced in a guarantee.

f.   The guarantor shall consider a requirement for a document to be legalised, visaed, certified or similar as satisfied by any signature, mark, stamp or label on the document which appears to satisfy that requirement.

Article 20 - Time for Examination of Demand; Payment

a.   If a presentation of a demand does not indicate that it is to be completed later, the guarantor shall, within five business days following the day of presentation, examine that demand and determine if it is a complying demand. This period is not shortened or otherwise affected by the expiry of the guarantee on or after the date of presentation. However, if the presentation indicates that it is to be completed later, it need not be examined until it is completed.

b.   When the guarantor determines that a demand is complying, it shall pay.

c.   Payment is to be made at the branch or office of the guarantor or counter-guarantor that issued the guarantee or counter-guarantee or such other place as may be indicated in that guarantee or counter-guarantee ("place for payment").

Article 21 - Currency of Payment

a.   The guarantor shall pay a complying demand in the currency specified in the guarantee.

b.   If, on any date on which a payment is to be made under the guarantee:

i.   the guarantor is unable to make payment in the currency specified in the guarantee due to an impediment beyond its control; or

ii.   it is illegal under the law of the place for payment to make payment in the specified currency,

the guarantor shall make payment in the currency of the place for payment even if the guarantee indicates that payment can only be made in the currency specified in the guarantee. The instructing party or, in the case of a counter-guarantee, the counter-guarantor, shall be bound by a payment made in such currency. The guarantor or counter-guarantor may elect to be reimbursed either in the currency in which payment was made or in the currency specified in the guarantee or, as the case may be, the counter-guarantee.

c.   Payment or reimbursement in the currency of the place for payment under paragraph (b) is to be made according to the applicable rate of exchange prevailing there when payment or reimbursement is due. However, if the guarantor has not paid at the time when payment is due, the beneficiary may require payment according to the applicable rate of exchange prevailing either when payment was due or at the time of actual payment.

Article 22 - Transmission of Copies of Complying Demand

The guarantor shall without delay transmit a copy of the complying demand and of any related documents to the instructing party or, where applicable, to the counter-guarantor for transmission to the instructing party. However, neither the counter-guarantor nor the instructing party, as the case may be, may withhold payment or reimbursement pending such transmission.

Article 23 - Extend or Pay

a.   Where a complying demand includes, as an alternative, a request to extend the expiry, the guarantor may suspend payment for a period not exceeding 30 calendar days following its receipt of the demand.

b.   Where, following such suspension, the guarantor makes a complying demand under the counter-guarantee that includes, as an alternative, a request to extend the expiry, the counter-guarantor may suspend payment for a period not exceeding four calendar days less than the period during which payment of the demand under the guarantee was suspended.

c.   The guarantor shall without delay inform the instructing party or, in the case of a counter-guarantee, the counter-guarantor, of the period of suspension of payment under the guarantee. The counter-guarantor shall then inform the instructing party of such suspension and of any suspension of payment under the counter-guarantee. Complying with this Article satisfies the information duty under Article 16.

d.   The demand for payment is deemed to be withdrawn if the period of extension requested in that demand or otherwise agreed by the party making that demand is granted within the time provided under paragraph (a) or (b) of this article. If no such period of extension is granted, the complying demand shall be paid without the need to present any further demand.

e.   The guarantor or counter-guarantor may refuse to grant any extension even if instructed to do so and shall then pay.

f.   The guarantor or counter-guarantor shall without delay inform the party from whom it has received its instructions of its decision to extend under paragraph (d) or to pay.

g.   The guarantor and the counter-guarantor assume no liability for any payment suspended in accordance with this article.

Article 24 - Non-Complying Demand, Waiver and Notice

a.   When the guarantor determines that a demand under the guarantee is not a complying demand, it may reject that demand or, in its sole judgement, approach the instructing party, or in the case of a counter-guarantee, the counter-guarantor, for a waiver of the discrepancies.

b.   When the counter-guarantor determines that a demand under the counter-guarantee is not a complying demand, it may reject that demand or, in its sole judgement, approach the instructing party for a waiver of the discrepancies.

c.   Nothing in paragraphs (a) or (b) of this Article shall extend the period mentioned in Article 20 or dispense with the requirements of Article 16. Obtaining the waiver of the counter-guarantor or of the instructing party does not oblige the guarantor or the counter-guarantor to waive any discrepancy.

d.   When the guarantor rejects a demand, it shall give a single notice to that effect to the presenter of the demand. The notice shall state:

i.   that the guarantor is rejecting the demand, and

ii.   each discrepancy for which the guarantor rejects the demand.

e.   The notice required by paragraph (d) of this Article shall be sent without delay but not later than the close of the fifth business day following the day of presentation.

f.   A guarantor failing to act in accordance with paragraphs (d) or (e) of this Article shall be precluded from claiming that the demand and any related documents do not constitute a complying demand.

g.   The guarantor may at any time, after providing the notice required in paragraph (d) of this article, return any documents presented in paper form to the presenter and dispose of the electronic records in any manner that it considers appropriate without incurring any responsibility.

h.   For the purpose of paragraphs (d), (f) and (g) of this article, guarantor includes counter-guarantor.

Article 25 - Reduction and Termination

a.   The amount payable under the guarantee shall be reduced by any amount:

i.   paid under the guarantee,

ii.   resulting from the application of Article 13, or

iii.   indicated in the beneficiary's signed partial release from liability under the guarantee.

b.   Whether or not the guarantee document is returned to the guarantor, the guarantee shall terminate:

i.   on expiry,

ii.   when no amount remains payable under it, or

iii.   on presentation to the guarantor of the beneficiary's signed release from liability under the guarantee.

c.   If the guarantee or the counter-guarantee states neither an expiry date nor an expiry event, the guarantee shall terminate after the lapse of three years from the date of issue and the counter-guarantee shall terminate 30 calendar days after the guarantee terminates.

d.   If the expiry date of a guarantee falls on a day that is not a business day at the place for presentation of the demand, the expiry date is extended to the first following business day at that place.

e.   Where, to the knowledge of the guarantor, the guarantee terminates as a result of any of the reasons indicated in paragraph (b) above, but other than because of the advent of the expiry date, the guarantor shall without delay so inform the instructing party or, where applicable, the counter-guarantor and, in that case, the counter-guarantor shall so inform the instructing party.

Article 26 - Force Majeure

a.   In this article, "force majeure" means acts of God, riots, civil commotions, insurrections, wars, acts of terrorism or any causes beyond the control of the guarantor or counter-guarantor that interrupt its business as it relates to acts of a kind subject to these rules.

b.   Should the guarantee expire at a time when presentation or payment under that guarantee is prevented by force majeure:

i.   each of the guarantee and any counter-guarantee shall be extended for a period of 30 calendar days from the date on which it would otherwise have expired, and the guarantor shall as soon as practicable inform the instructing party or, in the case of a counter-guarantee, the counter-guarantor, of the force majeure and the extension, and the counter-guarantor shall so inform the instructing party;

ii.   the running of the time for examination under Article 20 of a presentation made but not yet examined before the force majeure shall be suspended until the resumption of the guarantor's business; and

iii.   a complying demand under the guarantee presented before the force majeure but not paid because of the force majeure shall be paid when the force majeure ceases even if that guarantee has expired, and in this situation the guarantor shall be entitled to present a demand under the counter-guarantee within 30 calendar days after cessation of the force majeure even if the counter-guarantee has expired.

c.   Should the counter-guarantee expire at a time when presentation or payment under that counter-guarantee is prevented by force majeure:

i.   the counter-guarantee shall be extended for a period of 30 calendar days from the date on which the counter-guarantor informs the guarantor of the cessation of the force majeure. The counter-guarantor shall then inform the instructing party of the force majeure and the extension;

ii.   the running of the time for examination under Article 20 of a presentation made but not yet examined before the force majeure shall be suspended until the resumption of the counter-guarantor's business; and

iii.   a complying demand under the counter-guarantee presented before the force majeure but not paid because of the force majeure shall be paid when the force majeure ceases even if that counter-guarantee has expired.

d.   The instructing party shall be bound by any extension, suspension or payment under this article.

e. The guarantor and the counter-guarantor assume no further liability for the consequences of the force majeure.

Article 27 - Disclaimer on Effectiveness of Documents

The guarantor assumes no liability or responsibility for:

a.   the form, sufficiency, accuracy, genuineness, falsification, or legal effect of any signature or document presented to it;

b.   the general or particular statements made in, or superimposed on, document presented to it;

c.   the description, quantity, weight, quality, condition, packing, delivery, value or existence of the goods, services or other performance or data represented by or referred to in any document presented to it; or

d.   the good faith, acts, omissions, solvency, performance or standing of any person issuing or referred to in any other capacity in any document presented to it.

Article 28 - Disclaimer on Transmission and Translation

a.   The guarantor assumes no liability or responsibility for the consequences of delay, loss in transit, mutilation or other errors arising in the transmission of any document, if that document is transmitted or sent according to the requirements stated in the guarantee, or when the guarantor may have taken the initiative in the choice of the delivery service in the absence of instructions to that effect.

b.   The guarantor assumes no liability or responsibility for errors in translation or interpretation of technical terms and may transmit all or any part of the guarantee text without translating it.

Article 29 - Disclaimer for Acts of Another Party

A guarantor using the services of another party for the purpose of giving effect to the instructions of an instructing party or counter-guarantor does so for the account and at the risk of that instructing party or counter-guarantor.

Article 30 - Limits on Exemption from Liability

Articles 27 to 29 shall not exempt a guarantor from liability or responsibility for its failure to act in good faith.

Article 31 - Indemnity for Foreign Laws and Usages

The instructing party or, in the case of a counter-guarantee, the counter-guarantor, shall indemnify the guarantor against all obligations and responsibilities imposed by foreign laws and usages, including where those foreign laws and usages impose terms into the guarantee or the counter-guarantee that override its specified terms. The instructing party shall indemnify the counter-guarantor that has indemnified the guarantor under this article.

Article 32 - Liability for Charges

a.   A party instructing another party to perform services under these rules is liable to pay that party's charges for carrying out its instructions.

b.   If a guarantee states that charges are for the account of the beneficiary and those charges cannot be collected, the instructing party is liable to pay those charges. If a counter-guarantee states that charges relating to the guarantee are for the account of the beneficiary and those charges cannot be collected, the counter-guarantor remains liable to the guarantor, and the instructing party to the counter-guarantor, to pay those charges.

c.   Neither the guarantor nor any advising party should stipulate that the guarantee, or any advice or amendment of it, is conditional upon the receipt by the guarantor or any advising party of its charges.

Article 33 - Transfer of Guarantee and Assignment of Proceeds

a.   A guarantee is transferable only if it specifically states that it is "transferable", in which case it may be transferred more than once for the full amount available at the time of transfer. A counter-guarantee is not transferable.

b.   Even if a guarantee specifically states that it is transferable, the guarantor is not obliged to give effect to a request to transfer that guarantee after its issue except to the extent and in the manner expressly consented to by the guarantor.

c.   A transferable guarantee means a guarantee that may be made available by the guarantor to a new beneficiary ("transferee") at the request of the existing beneficiary ("transferor").

d.   The following provisions apply to the transfer of a guarantee:

i.   a transferred guarantee shall include all amendments to which the transferor and guarantor have agreed as of the date of transfer; and

ii.   a guarantee can only be transferred where, in addition to the conditions stated in paragraphs (a), (b) and (d)(i) of this article, the transferor has provided a signed statement to the guarantor that the transferee has acquired the transferor's rights and obligations in the underlying relationship.

e.   Unless otherwise agreed at the time of transfer, the transferor shall pay all charges incurred for the transfer.

f.   Under a transferred guarantee, a demand and any supporting statement shall be signed by the transferee. Unless the guarantee provides otherwise, the name and the signature of the transferee may be used in place of the name and signature of the transferor in any other document.

g.   Whether or not the guarantee states that it is transferable, and subject to the provisions of the applicable law:

i.   the beneficiary may assign any proceeds to which it may be or may become entitled under the guarantee;

ii.   however, the guarantor shall not be obliged to pay an assignee of these proceeds unless the guarantor has agreed to do so.

Article 34 - Governing Law

a.   Unless otherwise provided in the guarantee, its governing law shall be that of the location of the guarantor's branch or office that issued the guarantee.

b.   Unless otherwise provided in the counter-guarantee, its governing law shall be that of the location of the counter-guarantor's branch or office that issued the counter-guarantee.

Article 35 - Jurisdiction

a.   Unless otherwise provided in the guarantee, any dispute between the guarantor and the beneficiary relating to the guarantee shall be settled exclusively by the competent court of the country of the location of the guarantor's branch or office that issued the guarantee.

b.   Unless otherwise provided in the counter-guarantee, any dispute between the counter-guarantor and the guarantor relating to the counter-guarantee shall be settled exclusively by the competent court of the country of the location of the counter-guarantor's branch or office that issued the counter-guarantee.

U.C.C. - ARTICLE 4A - FUNDS TRANSFER[1]

PART 1. SUBJECT MATTER AND DEFINITIONS

§ 4A-101. Short Title

This Article may be cited as Uniform Commercial Code—Funds Transfers.

§ 4A-102. Subject Matter

Except as otherwise provided in Section 4A-108, this Article applies to funds transfers defined in Section 4A-104.

§ 4A-103. Payment Order - Definitions

(a)   In this Article:

(1)   "Payment order" means an instruction of a sender to a receiving bank, transmitted orally, electronically, or in writing, to pay, or to cause another bank to pay, a fixed or determinable amount of money to a beneficiary if:

   (i)   the instruction does not state a condition to payment to the beneficiary other than time of payment,

   (ii)   the receiving bank is to be reimbursed by debiting an account of, or otherwise receiving payment from, the sender, and

   (iii) the instruction is transmitted by the sender directly to the receiving bank or to an agent, funds-transfer system, or communication system for transmittal to the receiving bank.

(2)   "Beneficiary" means the person to be paid by the beneficiary's bank.

(3)   "Beneficiary's bank" means the bank identified in a payment order in which an account of the beneficiary is to be credited pursuant to the order or which otherwise is to make payment to the beneficiary if the order does not provide for payment to an account.

(4)   "Receiving bank" means the bank to which the sender's instruction is addressed.

(5)   "Sender" means the person giving the instruction to the receiving bank.

(b)   If an instruction complying with subsection (a)(1) is to make more than one payment to a beneficiary, the instruction is a separate payment order with respect to each payment.

(c)   A payment order is issued when it is sent to the receiving bank.

---

1   © 2012 by The American Law Institute and the National Conference of Commissioners on Uniform State Laws; reproduced, published and distributed with permission of the Permanent Editorial Board for the Uniform Commercial Code. All rights reserved.

§ 4A-104. Funds Transfer - Definitions

In this Article:

(a) "Funds transfer" means the series of transactions, beginning with the originator's payment order, made for the purpose of making payment to the beneficiary of the order. The term includes any payment order issued by the originator's bank or an intermediary bank intended to carry out the originator's payment order. A funds transfer is completed by acceptance by the beneficiary's bank of a payment order for the benefit of the beneficiary of the originator's payment order.

(b) "Intermediary bank" means a receiving bank other than the originator's bank or the beneficiary's bank.

(c) "Originator" means the sender of the first payment order in a funds transfer.

(d) "Originator's bank" means (i) the receiving bank to which the payment order of the originator is issued if the originator is not a bank, or (ii) the originator if the originator is a bank.

§ 4A-105. Other Definitions

(a) In this Article:

(1) "Authorized account" means a deposit account of a customer in a bank designated by the customer as a source of payment of payment orders issued by the customer to the bank. If a customer does not so designate an account, any account of the customer is an authorized account if payment of a payment order from that account is not inconsistent with a restriction on the use of that account.

(2) "Bank" means a person engaged in the business of banking and includes a savings bank, savings and loan association, credit union, and trust company. A branch or separate office of a bank is a separate bank for purposes of this Article.

(3) "Customer" means a person, including a bank, having an account with a bank or from whom a bank has agreed to receive payment orders.

(4) "Funds-transfer business day" of a receiving bank means the part of a day during which the receiving bank is open for the receipt, processing, and transmittal of payment orders and cancellations and amendments of payment orders.

(5) "Funds-transfer system" means a wire transfer network, automated clearing house, or other communication system of a clearing house or other association of banks through which a payment order by a bank may be transmitted to the bank to which the order is addressed.

(6) [reserved]

(7) "Prove" with respect to a fact means to meet the burden of establishing the fact (Section 1-201(b)(8)).

(b) Other definitions applying to this Article and the sections in which they appear are:

"Acceptance" – Section 4A-209
"Beneficiary" – Section 4A-103
"Beneficiary's bank" – Section 4A-103
"Executed" – Section 4A-301
"Execution date" – Section 4A-301
"Funds transfer" – Section 4A-104
"Funds-transfer system rule" – Section 4A-501
"Intermediary bank" – Section 4A-104
"Originator" – Section 4A-104
"Originator's bank" – Section 4A-104
"Payment by beneficiary's bank to beneficiary" – Section 4A-405
"Payment by originator to beneficiary" – Section 4A-406
"Payment by sender to receiving bank" – Section 4A-403
"Payment date" – Section 4A-401
"Payment order" – Section 4A-103
"Receiving bank" – Section 4A-103
"Security procedure" – Section 4A-201

"Sender" – Section 4A-103
(c)   The following definitions in Article 4 apply to this Article:
       "Clearing house" – Section 4-104
       "Item" – Section 4-104
       "Suspends payments" – Section 4-104
(d)   In addition Article 1 contains general definitions and principles of construction and interpretation applicable throughout this Article.

§ 4A-106. Time Payment Order Is Received

(a)   The time of receipt of a payment order or communication cancelling or amending a payment order is determined by the rules applicable to receipt of a notice stated in Section 1-202. A
receiving bank may fix a cut-off time or times on a funds-transfer business day for the receipt
and processing of payment orders and communications cancelling or amending payment orders. Different cut-off times may apply to payment orders, cancellations, or amendments, or to
different categories of payment orders, cancellations, or amendments. A cut-off time may apply
to senders generally or different cut-off times may apply to different senders or categories of
payment orders. If a payment order or communication cancelling or amending a payment order is received after the close of a funds-transfer business day or after the appropriate cut-off
time on a funds-transfer business day, the receiving bank may treat the payment order or communication as received at the opening of the next funds-transfer business day.
(b)   If this Article refers to an execution date or payment date or states a day on which a receiving bank is required to take action, and the date or day does not fall on a funds-transfer business day, the next day that is a funds-transfer business day is treated as the date or day stated,
unless the contrary is stated in this Article.

§ 4A-107. Federal Reserve Regulations and Operating Circulars

Regulations of the Board of Governors of the Federal Reserve System and operating circulars of
the Federal Reserve Banks supersede any inconsistent provision of this Article to the extent of
the inconsistency.

§ 4A-108. Exclusion of Consumer Transactions Governed by Federal Law

This Article does not apply to a funds transfer any part of which is governed by the Electronic
Fund Transfer Act of 1978 (Title XX, Public Law 95-630, 92 Stat. 3728, 15 U.S.C. § 1693 et seq.) as
amended from time to time.

PART 2. ISSUE AND ACCEPTANCE OF PAYMENT ORDER

§ 4A-201. Security Procedure

"Security procedure" means a procedure established by agreement of a customer and a receiving bank for the purpose of (i) verifying that a payment order or communication amending or
cancelling a payment order is that of the customer, or (ii) detecting error in the transmission or
the content of the payment order or communication. A security procedure may require the use
of algorithms or other codes, identifying words or numbers, encryption, callback procedures, or
similar security devices. Comparison of a signature on a payment order or communication with
an authorized specimen signature of the customer is not by itself a security procedure.

§ 4A-202. Authorized and Verified Payment Orders

(a)   A payment order received by the receiving bank is the authorized order of the person
identified as sender if that person authorized the order or is otherwise bound by it under the
law of agency.
(b)   If a bank and its customer have agreed that the authenticity of payment orders issued to
the bank in the name of the customer as sender will be verified pursuant to a security procedure, a payment order received by the receiving bank is effective as the order of the customer,
whether or not authorized, if (i) the security procedure is a commercially reasonable method of
providing security against unauthorized payment orders, and (ii) the bank proves that it accepted the payment order in good faith and in compliance with the security procedure and any

written agreement or instruction of the customer restricting acceptance of payment orders issued in the name of the customer. The bank is not required to follow an instruction that violates a written agreement with the customer or notice of which is not received at a time and in a manner affording the bank a reasonable opportunity to act on it before the payment order is accepted.

(c)   Commercial reasonableness of a security procedure is a question of law to be determined by considering the wishes of the customer expressed to the bank, the circumstances of the customer known to the bank, including the size, type, and frequency of payment orders normally issued by the customer to the bank, alternative security procedures offered to the customer, and security procedures in general use by customers and receiving banks similarly situated. A security procedure is deemed to be commercially reasonable if (i) the security procedure was chosen by the customer after the bank offered, and the customer refused, a security procedure that was commercially reasonable for that customer, and (ii) the customer expressly agreed in writing to be bound by any payment order, whether or not authorized, issued in its name and accepted by the bank in compliance with the security procedure chosen by the customer.

(d)   The term "sender" in this Article includes the customer in whose name a payment order is issued if the order is the authorized order of the customer under subsection (a), or it is effective as the order of the customer under subsection (b).

(e)   This section applies to amendments and cancellations of payment orders to the same extent it applies to payment orders.

(f)   Except as provided in this section and in Section 4A-203(a)(1), rights and obligations arising under this section or Section 4A-203 may not be varied by agreement.

§ 4A-203. Unenforceability of Certain Verified Payment Orders

(a)   If an accepted payment order is not, under Section 4A-202(a), an authorized order of a customer identified as sender, but is effective as an order of the customer pursuant to Section 4A-202(b), the following rules apply:

(1)   By express written agreement, the receiving bank may limit the extent to which it is entitled to enforce or retain payment of the payment order.

(2)   The receiving bank is not entitled to enforce or retain payment of the payment order if the customer proves that the order was not caused, directly or indirectly, by a person (i) entrusted at any time with duties to act for the customer with respect to payment orders or the security procedure, or (ii) who obtained access to transmitting facilities of the customer or who obtained, from a source controlled by the customer and without authority of the receiving bank, information facilitating breach of the security procedure, regardless of how the information was obtained or whether the customer was at fault. Information includes any access device, computer software, or the like.

(b)   This section applies to amendments of payment orders to the same extent it applies to payment orders.

§ 4A-204. Refund of Payment and Duty of Customer to Report with Respect to Unauthorized Payment Order

(a)   If a receiving bank accepts a payment order issued in the name of its customer as sender which is (i) not authorized and not effective as the order of the customer under Section 4A-202, or (ii) not enforceable, in whole or in part, against the customer under Section 4A-203, the bank shall refund any payment of the payment order received from the customer to the extent the bank is not entitled to enforce payment and shall pay interest on the refundable amount calculated from the date the bank received payment to the date of the refund. However, the customer is not entitled to interest from the bank on the amount to be refunded if the customer fails to exercise ordinary care to determine that the order was not authorized by the customer and to notify the bank of the relevant facts within a reasonable time not exceeding 90 days after the date the customer received notification from the bank that the order was accepted or that the customer's account was debited with respect to the order. The bank is not entitled to any recovery from the customer on account of a failure by the customer to give notification as stated in this section.

(b)   Reasonable time under subsection (a) may be fixed by agreement as stated in Section 1-204(1), but the obligation of a receiving bank to refund payment as stated in subsection (a) may not otherwise be varied by agreement.

§ 4A-205. Erroneous Payment Orders

(a)   If an accepted payment order was transmitted pursuant to a security procedure for the detection of error and the payment order (i) erroneously instructed payment to a beneficiary not intended by the sender, (ii) erroneously instructed payment in an amount greater than the amount intended by the sender, or (iii) was an erroneously transmitted duplicate of a payment order previously sent by the sender, the following rules apply:

(1)   If the sender proves that the sender or a person acting on behalf of the sender pursuant to Section 4A-206 complied with the security procedure and that the error would have been detected if the receiving bank had also complied, the sender is not obliged to pay the order to the extent stated in paragraphs (2) and (3).

(2)   If the funds transfer is completed on the basis of an erroneous payment order described in clause (i) or (iii) of subsection (a), the sender is not obliged to pay the order and the receiving bank is entitled to recover from the beneficiary any amount paid to the beneficiary to the extent allowed by the law governing mistake and restitution.

(3)   If the funds transfer is completed on the basis of a payment order described in clause (ii) of subsection (a), the sender is not obliged to pay the order to the extent the amount received by the beneficiary is greater than the amount intended by the sender. In that case, the receiving bank is entitled to recover from the beneficiary the excess amount received to the extent allowed by the law governing mistake and restitution.

(b)   If (i) the sender of an erroneous payment order described in subsection (a) is not obliged to pay all or part of the order, and (ii) the sender receives notification from the receiving bank that the order was accepted by the bank or that the sender's account was debited with respect to the order, the sender has a duty to exercise ordinary care, on the basis of information available to the sender, to discover the error with respect to the order and to advise the bank of the relevant facts within a reasonable time, not exceeding 90 days, after the bank's notification was received by the sender. If the bank proves that the sender failed to perform that duty, the sender is liable to the bank for the loss the bank proves it incurred as a result of the failure, but the liability of the sender may not exceed the amount of the sender's order.

(c)   This section applies to amendments to payment orders to the same extent it applies to payment orders.

§ 4A-206. Transmission of Payment Order Through Funds-Transfer or Other Communication System

(a)   If a payment order addressed to a receiving bank is transmitted to a funds-transfer system or other third-party communication system for transmittal to the bank, the system is deemed to be an agent of the sender for the purpose of transmitting the payment order to the bank. If there is a discrepancy between the terms of the payment order transmitted to the system and the terms of the payment order transmitted by the system to the bank, the terms of the payment order of the sender are those transmitted by the system. This section does not apply to a funds-transfer system of the Federal Reserve Banks.

(b)   This section applies to cancellations and amendments of payment orders to the same extent it applies to payment orders.

§ 4A-207. Misdescription of Beneficiary

(a)   Subject to subsection (b), if, in a payment order received by the beneficiary's bank, the name, bank account number, or other identification of the beneficiary refers to a nonexistent or unidentifiable person or account, no person has rights as a beneficiary of the order and acceptance of the order cannot occur.

(b)   If a payment order received by the beneficiary's bank identifies the beneficiary both by name and by an identifying or bank account number and the name and number identify different persons, the following rules apply:

(1)   Except as otherwise provided in subsection (c), if the beneficiary's bank does not know that the name and number refer to different persons, it may rely on the number as the proper identification of the beneficiary of the order. The beneficiary's bank need not determine whether the name and number refer to the same person.

(2)   If the beneficiary's bank pays the person identified by name or knows that the name and number identify different persons, no person has rights as beneficiary except the person paid by the beneficiary's bank if that person was entitled to receive payment from the originator of the funds transfer. If no person has rights as beneficiary, acceptance of the order cannot occur.

(c)   If (i) a payment order described in subsection (b) is accepted, (ii) the originator's payment order described the beneficiary inconsistently by name and number, and (iii) the beneficiary's bank pays the person identified by number as permitted by subsection (b)(1), the following rules apply:

(1)   If the originator is a bank, the originator is obliged to pay its order.

(2)   If the originator is not a bank and proves that the person identified by number was not entitled to receive payment from the originator, the originator is not obliged to pay its order unless the originator's bank proves that the originator, before acceptance of the originator's order, had notice that payment of a payment order issued by the originator might be made by the beneficiary's bank on the basis of an identifying or bank account number even if it identifies a person different from the named beneficiary. Proof of notice may be made by any admissible evidence. The originator's bank satisfies the burden of proof if it proves that the originator, before the payment order was accepted, signed a writing stating the information to which the notice relates.

(d)   In a case governed by subsection (b)(1), if the beneficiary's bank rightfully pays the person identified by number and that person was not entitled to receive payment from the originator, the amount paid may be recovered from that person to the extent allowed by the law governing mistake and restitution as follows:

(1)   If the originator is obliged to pay its payment order as stated in subsection (c), the originator has the right to recover.

(2)   If the originator is not a bank and is not obliged to pay its payment order, the originator's bank has the right to recover.

§ 4A-208. Misdescription of Intermediary Bank or Beneficiary's Bank

(a)   This subsection applies to a payment order identifying an intermediary bank or the beneficiary's bank only by an identifying number.

(1)   The receiving bank may rely on the number as the proper identification of the intermediary or beneficiary's bank and need not determine whether the number identifies a bank.

(2)   The sender is obliged to compensate the receiving bank for any loss and expenses incurred by the receiving bank as a result of its reliance on the number in executing or attempting to execute the order.

(b)   This subsection applies to a payment order identifying an intermediary bank or the beneficiary's bank both by name and an identifying number if the name and number identify different persons.

(1)   If the sender is a bank, the receiving bank may rely on the number as the proper identification of the intermediary or beneficiary's bank if the receiving bank, when it executes the sender's order, does not know that the name and number identify different persons. The receiving bank need not determine whether the name and number refer to the same person or whether the number refers to a bank. The sender is obliged to compensate the receiving bank for any loss and expenses incurred by the receiving bank as a result of its reliance on the number in executing or attempting to execute the order.

(2)   If the sender is not a bank and the receiving bank proves that the sender, before the payment order was accepted, had notice that the receiving bank might rely on the number as the proper identification of the intermediary or beneficiary's bank even if it identifies a person different from the bank identified by name, the rights and obligations of the sender and the receiving bank are governed by subsection (b)(1), as though the sender were a bank. Proof of notice may be made by any admissible evidence. The receiving bank satisfies the burden of proof if it proves that the sender, before the payment order was accepted, signed a writing stating the information to which the notice relates.

(3)   Regardless of whether the sender is a bank, the receiving bank may rely on the name as the proper identification of the intermediary or beneficiary's bank if the receiving bank, at the time it executes the sender's order, does not know that the name and number identify different persons. The receiving bank need not determine whether the name and number refer to the same person.

(4)   If the receiving bank knows that the name and number identify different persons, reliance on either the name or the number in executing the sender's payment order is a breach of the obligation stated in Section 4A-302(a)(1).

§ 4A-209. Acceptance of Payment Order

(a)   Subject to subsection (d), a receiving bank other than the beneficiary's bank accepts a payment order when it executes the order.

(b)   Subject to subsections (c) and (d), a beneficiary's bank accepts a payment order at the earliest of the following times:

(1)   when the bank (i) pays the beneficiary as stated in Section 4A-405(a) or 4A-405(b), or (ii) notifies the beneficiary of receipt of the order or that the account of the beneficiary has been credited with respect to the order unless the notice indicates that the bank is rejecting the order or that funds with respect to the order may not be withdrawn or used until receipt of payment from the sender of the order;

(2)   when the bank receives payment of the entire amount of the sender's order pursuant to Section 4A-403(a)(1) or 4A-403(a)(2); or

(3)   the opening of the next funds-transfer business day of the bank following the payment date of the order if, at that time, the amount of the sender's order is fully covered by a withdrawable credit balance in an authorized account of the sender or the bank has otherwise received full payment from the sender, unless the order was rejected before that time or is rejected within (i) one hour after that time, or (ii) one hour after the opening of the next business day of the sender following the payment date if that time is later. If notice of rejection is received by the sender after the payment date and the authorized account of the sender does not bear interest, the bank is obliged to pay interest to the sender on the amount of the order for the number of days elapsing after the payment date to the day the sender receives notice or learns that the order was not accepted, counting that day as an elapsed day. If the withdrawable credit balance during that period falls below the amount of the order, the amount of interest payable is reduced accordingly.

(c)   Acceptance of a payment order cannot occur before the order is received by the receiving bank. Acceptance does not occur under subsection (b)(2) or (b)(3) if the beneficiary of the payment order does not have an account with the receiving bank, the account has been closed, or the receiving bank is not permitted by law to receive credits for the beneficiary's account.

(d)   A payment order issued to the originator's bank cannot be accepted until the payment date if the bank is the beneficiary's bank, or the execution date if the bank is not the beneficiary's bank. If the originator's bank executes the originator's payment order before the execution date or pays the beneficiary of the originator's payment order before the payment date and the payment order is subsequently canceled pursuant to Section 4A-211(b), the bank may recover from the beneficiary any payment received to the extent allowed by the law governing mistake and restitution.

§ 4A-210. Rejection of Payment Order

(a)   A payment order is rejected by the receiving bank by a notice of rejection transmitted to the sender orally, electronically, or in writing. A notice of rejection need not use any particular words and is sufficient if it indicates that the receiving bank is rejecting the order or will not execute or pay the order. Rejection is effective when the notice is given if transmission is by a means that is reasonable in the circumstances. If notice of rejection is given by a means that is not reasonable, rejection is effective when the notice is received. If an agreement of the sender and receiving bank establishes the means to be used to reject a payment order, (i) any means complying with the agreement is reasonable and (ii) any means not complying is not reasonable unless no significant delay in receipt of the notice resulted from the use of the noncomplying means.

(b)   This subsection applies if a receiving bank other than the beneficiary's bank fails to execute a payment order despite the existence on the execution date of a withdrawable credit balance in an authorized account of the sender sufficient to cover the order. If the sender does not receive notice of rejection of the order on the execution date and the authorized account of the sender does not bear interest, the bank is obliged to pay interest to the sender on the amount of the order for the number of days elapsing after the execution date to the earlier of the day the order is canceled pursuant to Section 4A-211(d) or the day the sender receives notice or learns that the order was not executed, counting the final day of the period as an elapsed day. If the withdrawable credit balance during that period falls below the amount of the order, the amount of interest is reduced accordingly.

(c)   If a receiving bank suspends payments, all unaccepted payment orders issued to it are deemed rejected at the time the bank suspends payments.

(d)   Acceptance of a payment order precludes a later rejection of the order. Rejection of a payment order precludes a later acceptance of the order.

§ 4A-211. Cancellation and Amendment of Payment Order

(a)   A communication of the sender of a payment order cancelling or amending the order may be transmitted to the receiving bank orally, electronically, or in writing. If a security procedure is in effect between the sender and the receiving bank, the communication is not effective to cancel or amend the order unless the communication is verified pursuant to the security procedure or the bank agrees to the cancellation or amendment.

(b)   Subject to subsection (a), a communication by the sender cancelling or amending a payment order is effective to cancel or amend the order if notice of the communication is received at a time and in a manner affording the receiving bank a reasonable opportunity to act on the communication before the bank accepts the payment order.

(c)   After a payment order has been accepted, cancellation or amendment of the order is not effective unless the receiving bank agrees or a funds-transfer system rule allows cancellation or amendment without agreement of the bank.

(1)   With respect to a payment order accepted by a receiving bank other than the beneficiary's bank, cancellation or amendment is not effective unless a conforming cancellation or amendment of the payment order issued by the receiving bank is also made.

(2)   With respect to a payment order accepted by the beneficiary's bank, cancellation or amendment is not effective unless the order was issued in execution of an unauthorized payment order, or because of a mistake by a sender in the funds transfer which resulted in the issuance of a payment order (i) that is a duplicate of a payment order previously issued by the sender, (ii) that orders payment to a beneficiary not entitled to receive payment from the originator, or (iii) that orders payment in an amount greater than the amount the beneficiary was entitled to receive from the originator. If the payment order is canceled or amended, the beneficiary's bank is entitled to recover from the beneficiary any amount paid to the beneficiary to the extent allowed by the law governing mistake and restitution.

(d)   An unaccepted payment order is canceled by operation of law at the close of the fifth funds-transfer business day of the receiving bank after the execution date or payment date of the order.

(e)   A canceled payment order cannot be accepted. If an accepted payment order is canceled, the acceptance is nullified and no person has any right or obligation based on the acceptance. Amendment of a payment order is deemed to be cancellation of the original order at the time of amendment and issue of a new payment order in the amended form at the same time.

(f)   Unless otherwise provided in an agreement of the parties or in a funds-transfer system rule, if the receiving bank, after accepting a payment order, agrees to cancellation or amendment of the order by the sender or is bound by a funds-transfer system rule allowing cancellation or amendment without the bank's agreement, the sender, whether or not cancellation or amendment is effective, is liable to the bank for any loss and expenses, including reasonable attorney's fees, incurred by the bank as a result of the cancellation or amendment or attempted cancellation or amendment.

(g)   A payment order is not revoked by the death or legal incapacity of the sender unless the receiving bank knows of the death or of an adjudication of incapacity by a court of competent jurisdiction and has reasonable opportunity to act before acceptance of the order.

(h)   A funds-transfer system rule is not effective to the extent it conflicts with subsection (c)(2).

§ 4A-212. Liability and Duty of Receiving Bank Regarding Unaccepted Payment Order

If a receiving bank fails to accept a payment order that it is obliged by express agreement to accept, the bank is liable for breach of the agreement to the extent provided in the agreement or in this Article, but does not otherwise have any duty to accept a payment order or, before acceptance, to take any action, or refrain from taking action, with respect to the order except as provided in this Article or by express agreement. Liability based on acceptance arises only when acceptance occurs as stated in Section 4A-209, and liability is limited to that provided in this Article. A receiving bank is not the agent of the sender or beneficiary of the payment order it accepts, or of any other party to the funds transfer, and the bank owes no duty to any party to the funds transfer except as provided in this Article or by express agreement.

PART 3. EXECUTION OF SENDER'S PAYMENT ORDER BY RECEIVING BANK
§ 4A-301. Execution and Execution Date

(a)   A payment order is "executed" by the receiving bank when it issues a payment order intended to carry out the payment order received by the bank. A payment order received by the beneficiary's bank can be accepted but cannot be executed.

(b)   "Execution date" of a payment order means the day on which the receiving bank may properly issue a payment order in execution of the sender's order. The execution date may be determined by instruction of the sender but cannot be earlier than the day the order is received and, unless otherwise determined, is the day the order is received. If the sender's instruction states a payment date, the execution date is the payment date or an earlier date on which execution is reasonably necessary to allow payment to the beneficiary on the payment date.

§ 4A-302. Obligations of Receiving Bank in Execution of Payment Order

(a)   Except as provided in subsections (b) through (d), if the receiving bank accepts a payment order pursuant to Section 4A-209(a), the bank has the following obligations in executing the order:

(1)   The receiving bank is obliged to issue, on the execution date, a payment order complying with the sender's order and to follow the sender's instructions concerning (i) any intermediary bank or funds-transfer system to be used in carrying out the funds transfer, or (ii) the means by which payment orders are to be transmitted in the funds transfer. If the originator's bank issues a payment order to an intermediary bank, the originator's bank is obliged to instruct the intermediary bank according to the instruction of the originator. An intermediary bank in the funds transfer is similarly bound by an instruction given to it by the sender of the payment order it accepts.

(2)   If the sender's instruction states that the funds transfer is to be carried out telephonically or by wire transfer or otherwise indicates that the funds transfer is to be carried out by the most expeditious means, the receiving bank is obliged to transmit its payment order by the most expeditious available means, and to instruct any intermediary bank accordingly. If a sender's instruction states a payment date, the receiving bank is obliged to transmit its payment order at a time and by means reasonably necessary to allow payment to the beneficiary on the payment date or as soon thereafter as is feasible.

(b)   Unless otherwise instructed, a receiving bank executing a payment order may (i) use any funds-transfer system if use of that system is reasonable in the circumstances, and (ii) issue a payment order to the beneficiary's bank or to an intermediary bank through which a payment order conforming to the sender's order can expeditiously be issued to the beneficiary's bank if the receiving bank exercises ordinary care in the selection of the intermediary bank. A receiving bank is not required to follow an instruction of the sender designating a funds-transfer system to be used in carrying out the funds transfer if the receiving bank, in good faith, determines that it is not feasible to follow the instruction or that following the instruction would unduly delay completion of the funds transfer.

(c)   Unless subsection (a)(2) applies or the receiving bank is otherwise instructed, the bank may execute a payment order by transmitting its payment order by first class mail or by any means reasonable in the circumstances. If the receiving bank is instructed to execute the sender's order by transmitting its payment order by a particular means, the receiving bank may issue its payment order by the means stated or by any means as expeditious as the means stated.

(d)   Unless instructed by the sender, (i) the receiving bank may not obtain payment of its charges for services and expenses in connection with the execution of the sender's order by issuing a payment order in an amount equal to the amount of the sender's order less the amount of the charges, and (ii) may not instruct a subsequent receiving bank to obtain payment of its charges in the same manner.

§ 4A-303. Erroneous Execution of Payment Order

(a)   A receiving bank that (i) executes the payment order of the sender by issuing a payment order in an amount greater than the amount of the sender's order, or (ii) issues a payment order in execution of the sender's order and then issues a duplicate order, is entitled to payment of the amount of the sender's order under Section 4A-402(c) if that subsection is otherwise satisfied. The bank is entitled to recover from the beneficiary of the erroneous order the excess payment received to the extent allowed by the law governing mistake and restitution.

(b)   A receiving bank that executes the payment order of the sender by issuing a payment order in an amount less than the amount of the sender's order is entitled to payment of the amount of the sender's order under Section 4A-402(c) if (i) that subsection is otherwise satisfied and (ii) the bank corrects its mistake by issuing an additional payment order for the benefit of the beneficiary of the sender's order. If the error is not corrected, the issuer of the erroneous order is entitled to receive or retain payment from the sender of the order it accepted only to the extent of the amount of the erroneous order. This subsection does not apply if the receiving bank executes the sender's payment order by issuing a payment order in an amount less than the amount of the sender's order for the purpose of obtaining payment of its charges for services and expenses pursuant to instruction of the sender.

(c)   If a receiving bank executes the payment order of the sender by issuing a payment order to a beneficiary different from the beneficiary of the sender's order and the funds transfer is completed on the basis of that error, the sender of the payment order that was erroneously executed and all previous senders in the funds transfer are not obliged to pay the payment orders they issued. The issuer of the erroneous order is entitled to recover from the beneficiary of the order the payment received to the extent allowed by the law governing mistake and restitution.

§ 4A-304. Duty of Sender to Report Erroneously Executed Payment Order

If the sender of a payment order that is erroneously executed as stated in Section 4A-303 receives notification from the receiving bank that the order was executed or that the sender's account was debited with respect to the order, the sender has a duty to exercise ordinary care to determine, on the basis of information available to the sender, that the order was erroneously executed and to notify the bank of the relevant facts within a reasonable time not exceeding 90 days after the notification from the bank was received by the sender. If the sender fails to perform that duty, the bank is not obliged to pay interest on any amount refundable to the sender under Section 4A-402(d) for the period before the bank learns of the execution error. The bank is not entitled to any recovery from the sender on account of a failure by the sender to perform the duty stated in this section.

§ 4A-305. Liability for Late or Improper Execution or Failure to Execute Payment Order

(a)   If a funds transfer is completed but execution of a payment order by the receiving bank in breach of Section 4A-302 results in delay in payment to the beneficiary, the bank is obliged to pay interest to either the originator or the beneficiary of the funds transfer for the period of delay caused by the improper execution. Except as provided in subsection (c), additional damages are not recoverable.

(b)   If execution of a payment order by a receiving bank in breach of Section 4A-302 results in (i) non-completion of the funds transfer, (ii) failure to use an intermediary bank designated by the originator, or (iii) issuance of a payment order that does not comply with the terms of the payment order of the originator, the bank is liable to the originator for its expenses in the funds transfer and for incidental expenses and interest losses, to the extent not covered by subsection (a), resulting from the improper execution. Except as provided in subsection (c), additional damages are not recoverable.

(c)   In addition to the amounts payable under subsections (a) and (b), damages, including consequential damages, are recoverable to the extent provided in an express written agreement of the receiving bank.

(d)   If a receiving bank fails to execute a payment order it was obliged by express agreement to execute, the receiving bank is liable to the sender for its expenses in the transaction and for incidental expenses and interest losses resulting from the failure to execute. Additional damages, including consequential damages, are recoverable to the extent provided in an express written agreement of the receiving bank, but are not otherwise recoverable.

(e)   Reasonable attorney's fees are recoverable if demand for compensation under subsection (a) or (b) is made and refused before an action is brought on the claim. If a claim is made for breach of an agreement under subsection (d) and the agreement does not provide for damages, reasonable attorney's fees are recoverable if demand for compensation under subsection (d) is made and refused before an action is brought on the claim.

(f)   Except as stated in this section, the liability of a receiving bank under subsections (a) and (b) may not be varied by agreement.

PART 4. PAYMENT

§ 4A-401. Payment Date

"Payment date" of a payment order means the day on which the amount of the order is payable to the beneficiary by the beneficiary's bank. The payment date may be determined by instruction of the sender but cannot be earlier than the day the order is received by the beneficiary's bank and, unless otherwise determined, is the day the order is received by the beneficiary's bank.

§ 4A-402. Obligation of Sender to Pay Receiving Bank

(a)   This section is subject to Sections 4A-205 and 4A-207.

(b)   With respect to a payment order issued to the beneficiary's bank, acceptance of the order by the bank obliges the sender to pay the bank the amount of the order, but payment is not due until the payment date of the order.

(c)   This subsection is subject to subsection (e) and to Section 4A-303. With respect to a payment order issued to a receiving bank other than the beneficiary's bank, acceptance of the order by the receiving bank obliges the sender to pay the bank the amount of the sender's order. Payment by the sender is not due until the execution date of the sender's order. The obligation of that sender to pay its payment order is excused if the funds transfer is not completed by acceptance by the beneficiary's bank of a payment order instructing payment to the beneficiary of that sender's payment order.

(d) If the sender of a payment order pays the order and was not obliged to pay all or part of the amount paid, the bank receiving payment is obliged to refund payment to the extent the sender was not obliged to pay. Except as provided in Sections 4A-204 and 4A-304, interest is payable on the refundable amount from the date of payment.

(e) If a funds transfer is not completed as stated in subsection (c) and an intermediary bank is obliged to refund payment as stated in subsection (d) but is unable to do so because not permitted by applicable law or because the bank suspends payments, a sender in the funds transfer that executed a payment order in compliance with an instruction, as stated in Section 4A-302(a)(1), to route the funds transfer through that intermediary bank is entitled to receive or retain payment from the sender of the payment order that it accepted. The first sender in the funds transfer that issued an instruction requiring routing through that intermediary bank is subrogated to the right of the bank that paid the intermediary bank to refund as stated in subsection (d).

(f) The right of the sender of a payment order to be excused from the obligation to pay the order as stated in subsection (c) or to receive refund under subsection (d) may not be varied by agreement.

§ 4A-403. Payment by Sender to Receiving Bank

(a) Payment of the sender's obligation under Section 4A-402 to pay the receiving bank occurs as follows:

(1) If the sender is a bank, payment occurs when the receiving bank receives final settlement of the obligation through a Federal Reserve Bank or through a funds-transfer system.

(2) If the sender is a bank and the sender (i) credited an account of the receiving bank with the sender, or (ii) caused an account of the receiving bank in another bank to be credited, payment occurs when the credit is withdrawn or, if not withdrawn, at midnight of the day on which the credit is withdrawable and the receiving bank learns of that fact.

(3) If the receiving bank debits an account of the sender with the receiving bank, payment occurs when the debit is made to the extent the debit is covered by a withdrawable credit balance in the account.

(b) If the sender and receiving bank are members of a funds-transfer system that nets obligations multilaterally among participants, the receiving bank receives final settlement when settlement is complete in accordance with the rules of the system. The obligation of the sender to pay the amount of a payment order transmitted through the funds-transfer system may be satisfied, to the extent permitted by the rules of the system, by setting off and applying against the sender's obligation the right of the sender to receive payment from the receiving bank of the amount of any other payment order transmitted to the sender by the receiving bank through the funds-transfer system. The aggregate balance of obligations owed by each sender to each receiving bank in the funds-transfer system may be satisfied, to the extent permitted by the rules of the system, by setting off and applying against that balance the aggregate balance of obligations owed to the sender by other members of the system. The aggregate balance is determined after the right of setoff stated in the second sentence of this subsection has been exercised.

(c) If two banks transmit payment orders to each other under an agreement that settlement of the obligations of each bank to the other under Section 4A-402 will be made at the end of the day or other period, the total amount owed with respect to all orders transmitted by one bank shall be set off against the total amount owed with respect to all orders transmitted by the other bank. To the extent of the setoff, each bank has made payment to the other.

(d) In a case not covered by subsection (a), the time when payment of the sender's obligation under Section 4A-402(b) or 4A-402(c) occurs is governed by applicable principles of law that determine when an obligation is satisfied.

§ 4A-404. Obligation of Beneficiary's Bank to Pay and Give Notice to Beneficiary

(a)   Subject to Sections 4A-211(e), 4A-405(d), and 4A-405(e), if a beneficiary's bank accepts a payment order, the bank is obliged to pay the amount of the order to the beneficiary of the order. Payment is due on the payment date of the order, but if acceptance occurs on the payment date after the close of the funds-transfer business day of the bank, payment is due on the next funds-transfer business day. If the bank refuses to pay after demand by the beneficiary and receipt of notice of particular circumstances that will give rise to consequential damages as a result of nonpayment, the beneficiary may recover damages resulting from the refusal to pay to the extent the bank had notice of the damages, unless the bank proves that it did not pay because of a reasonable doubt concerning the right of the beneficiary to payment.

(b)   If a payment order accepted by the beneficiary's bank instructs payment to an account of the beneficiary, the bank is obliged to notify the beneficiary of receipt of the order before midnight of the next funds-transfer business day following the payment date. If the payment order does not instruct payment to an account of the beneficiary, the bank is required to notify the beneficiary only if notice is required by the order. Notice may be given by first class mail or any other means reasonable in the circumstances. If the bank fails to give the required notice, the bank is obliged to pay interest to the beneficiary on the amount of the payment order from the day notice should have been given until the day the beneficiary learned of receipt of the payment order by the bank. No other damages are recoverable. Reasonable attorney's fees are also recoverable if demand for interest is made and refused before an action is brought on the claim.

(c)   The right of a beneficiary to receive payment and damages as stated in subsection (a) may not be varied by agreement or a funds-transfer system rule. The right of a beneficiary to be notified as stated in subsection (b) may be varied by agreement of the beneficiary or by a funds-transfer system rule if the beneficiary is notified of the rule before initiation of the funds transfer.

§ 4A-405. Payment by Beneficiary's Bank to Beneficiary

(a)   If the beneficiary's bank credits an account of the beneficiary of a payment order, payment of the bank's obligation under Section 4A-404(a) occurs when and to the extent (i) the beneficiary is notified of the right to withdraw the credit, (ii) the bank lawfully applies the credit to a debt of the beneficiary, or (iii) funds with respect to the order are otherwise made available to the beneficiary by the bank.

(b)   If the beneficiary's bank does not credit an account of the beneficiary of a payment order, the time when payment of the bank's obligation under Section 4A-404(a) occurs is governed by principles of law that determine when an obligation is satisfied.

(c)   Except as stated in subsections (d) and (e), if the beneficiary's bank pays the beneficiary of a payment order under a condition to payment or agreement of the beneficiary giving the bank the right to recover payment from the beneficiary if the bank does not receive payment of the order, the condition to payment or agreement is not enforceable.

(d)   A funds-transfer system rule may provide that payments made to beneficiaries of funds transfers made through the system are provisional until receipt of payment by the beneficiary's bank of the payment order it accepted. A beneficiary's bank that makes a payment that is provisional under the rule is entitled to refund from the beneficiary if (i) the rule requires that both the beneficiary and the originator be given notice of the provisional nature of the payment before the funds transfer is initiated, (ii) the beneficiary, the beneficiary's bank and the originator's bank agreed to be bound by the rule, and (iii) the beneficiary's bank did not receive payment of the payment order that it accepted. If the beneficiary is obliged to refund payment to the beneficiary's bank, acceptance of the payment order by the beneficiary's bank is nullified and no payment by the originator of the funds transfer to the beneficiary occurs under Section 4A-406.

(e)   This subsection applies to a funds transfer that includes a payment order transmitted over a funds-transfer system that (i) nets obligations multilaterally among participants, and (ii) has in effect a loss-sharing agreement among participants for the purpose of providing funds necessary to complete settlement of the obligations of one or more participants that do not meet their settlement obligations. If the beneficiary's bank in the funds transfer accepts a payment order and the system fails to complete settlement pursuant to its rules with respect to any payment order in the funds transfer, (i) the acceptance by the beneficiary's bank is nullified and no person has any right or obligation based on the acceptance, (ii) the beneficiary's bank is entitled to recover payment from the beneficiary, (iii) no payment by the originator to the beneficiary occurs under Section 4A-406, and (iv) subject to Section 4A-402(e), each sender in the funds transfer is excused from its obligation to pay its payment order under Section 4A-402(c) because the funds transfer has not been completed.

§ 4A-406. Payment by Originator to Beneficiary; Discharge of Underlying Obligation

(a)   Subject to Sections 4A-211(e), 4A-405(d), and 4A-405(e), the originator of a funds transfer pays the beneficiary of the originator's payment order (i) at the time a payment order for the benefit of the beneficiary is accepted by the beneficiary's bank in the funds transfer and (ii) in an amount equal to the amount of the order accepted by the beneficiary's bank, but not more than the amount of the originator's order.

(b)   If payment under subsection (a) is made to satisfy an obligation, the obligation is discharged to the same extent discharge would result from payment to the beneficiary of the same amount in money, unless (i) the payment under subsection (a) was made by a means prohibited by the contract of the beneficiary with respect to the obligation, (ii) the beneficiary, within a reasonable time after receiving notice of receipt of the order by the beneficiary's bank, notified the originator of the beneficiary's refusal of the payment, (iii) funds with respect to the order were not withdrawn by the beneficiary or applied to a debt of the beneficiary, and (iv) the beneficiary would suffer a loss that could reasonably have been avoided if payment had been made by a means complying with the contract. If payment by the originator does not result in discharge under this section, the originator is subrogated to the rights of the beneficiary to receive payment from the beneficiary's bank under Section 4A-404(a).

(c)   For the purpose of determining whether discharge of an obligation occurs under subsection (b), if the beneficiary's bank accepts a payment order in an amount equal to the amount of the originator's payment order less charges of one or more receiving banks in the funds transfer, payment to the beneficiary is deemed to be in the amount of the originator's order unless upon demand by the beneficiary the originator does not pay the beneficiary the amount of the deducted charges.

(d)   Rights of the originator or of the beneficiary of a funds transfer under this section may be varied only by agreement of the originator and the beneficiary.

PART 5. MISCELLANEOUS PROVISIONS

§ 4A-501. Variation by Agreement and Effect of Funds-Transfer System Rule

(a)   Except as otherwise provided in this Article, the rights and obligations of a party to a funds transfer may be varied by agreement of the affected party.

(b)   "Funds-transfer system rule" means a rule of an association of banks (i) governing transmission of payment orders by means of a funds-transfer system of the association or rights and obligations with respect to those orders, or (ii) to the extent the rule governs rights and obligations between banks that are parties to a funds transfer in which a Federal Reserve Bank, acting as an intermediary bank, sends a payment order to the beneficiary's bank. Except as otherwise provided in this Article, a funds-transfer system rule governing rights and obligations between participating banks using the system may be effective even if the rule conflicts with this Article and indirectly affects another party to the funds transfer who does not consent to the rule. A funds-transfer system rule may also govern rights and obligations of parties other than participating banks using the system to the extent stated in Sections 4A-404(c), 4A-405(d), and 4A-507(c).

§ 4A-502. Creditor Process Served on Receiving Bank; Set-off by Beneficiary's Bank

(a)   As used in this section, "creditor process" means levy, attachment, garnishment, notice of lien, sequestration, or similar process issued by or on behalf of a creditor or other claimant with respect to an account.

(b)   This subsection applies to creditor process with respect to an authorized account of the sender of a payment order if the creditor process is served on the receiving bank. For the purpose of determining rights with respect to the creditor process, if the receiving bank accepts the payment order the balance in the authorized account is deemed to be reduced by the amount of the payment order to the extent the bank did not otherwise receive payment of the order, unless the creditor process is served at a time and in a manner affording the bank a reasonable opportunity to act on it before the bank accepts the payment order.

(c)   If a beneficiary's bank has received a payment order for payment to the beneficiary's account in the bank, the following rules apply:

(1)   The bank may credit the beneficiary's account. The amount credited may be set off against an obligation owed by the beneficiary to the bank or may be applied to satisfy creditor process served on the bank with respect to the account.

(2)   The bank may credit the beneficiary's account and allow withdrawal of the amount credited unless creditor process with respect to the account is served at a time and in a manner affording the bank a reasonable opportunity to act to prevent withdrawal.

(3)   If creditor process with respect to the beneficiary's account has been served and the bank has had a reasonable opportunity to act on it, the bank may not reject the payment order except for a reason unrelated to the service of process.

(d)   Creditor process with respect to a payment by the originator to the beneficiary pursuant to a funds transfer may be served only on the beneficiary's bank with respect to the debt owed by that bank to the beneficiary. Any other bank served with the creditor process is not obliged to act with respect to the process.

§ 4A-503. Injunction or Restraining Order with Respect to Funds Transfer

For proper cause and in compliance with applicable law, a court may restrain (i) a person from issuing a payment order to initiate a funds transfer, (ii) an originator's bank from executing the payment order of the originator, or (iii) the beneficiary's bank from releasing funds to the beneficiary or the beneficiary from withdrawing the funds. A court may not otherwise restrain a person from issuing a payment order, paying or receiving payment of a payment order, or otherwise acting with respect to a funds transfer.

§ 4A-504. Order in Which Items and Payment Orders May Be Charged to Account; Order of Withdrawals from Account

(a)   If a receiving bank has received more than one payment order of the sender or one or more payment orders and other items that are payable from the sender's account, the bank may charge the sender's account with respect to the various orders and items in any sequence.

(b)   In determining whether a credit to an account has been withdrawn by the holder of the account or applied to a debt of the holder of the account, credits first made to the account are first withdrawn or applied.

§ 4A-505. Preclusion of Objection to Debit of Customer's Account

If a receiving bank has received payment from its customer with respect to a payment order issued in the name of the customer as sender and accepted by the bank, and the customer received notification reasonably identifying the order, the customer is precluded from asserting that the bank is not entitled to retain the payment unless the customer notifies the bank of the customer's objection to the payment within one year after the notification was received by the customer.

§ 4A-506. Rate of Interest

(a)   If, under this Article, a receiving bank is obliged to pay interest with respect to a payment order issued to the bank, the amount payable may be determined (i) by agreement of the sender and receiving bank, or (ii) by a funds-transfer system rule if the payment order is transmitted through a funds-transfer system.

(b)   If the amount of interest is not determined by an agreement or rule as stated in subsection (a), the amount is calculated by multiplying the applicable Federal Funds rate by the amount on which interest is payable, and then multiplying the product by the number of days for which interest is payable. The applicable Federal Funds rate is the average of the Federal Funds rates published by the Federal Reserve Bank of New York for each of the days for which interest is payable divided by 360. The Federal Funds rate for any day on which a published rate is not available is the same as the published rate for the next preceding day for which there is a published rate. If a receiving bank that accepted a payment order is required to refund payment to the sender of the order because the funds transfer was not completed, but the failure to complete was not due to any fault by the bank, the interest payable is reduced by a percentage equal to the reserve requirement on deposits of the receiving bank.

§ 4A-507. Choice of Law

(a)   The following rules apply unless the affected parties otherwise agree or subsection (c) applies:
(1)   The rights and obligations between the sender of a payment order and the receiving bank are governed by the law of the jurisdiction in which the receiving bank is located.
(2)   The rights and obligations between the beneficiary's bank and the beneficiary are governed by the law of the jurisdiction in which the beneficiary's bank is located.
(3)   The issue of when payment is made pursuant to a funds transfer by the originator to the beneficiary is governed by the law of the jurisdiction in which the beneficiary's bank is located.
(b)   If the parties described in each paragraph of subsection (a) have made an agreement selecting the law of a particular jurisdiction to govern rights and obligations between each other, the law of that jurisdiction governs those rights and obligations, whether or not the payment order or the funds transfer bears a reasonable relation to that jurisdiction.
(c)   A funds-transfer system rule may select the law of a particular jurisdiction to govern (i) rights and obligations between participating banks with respect to payment orders transmitted or processed through the system, or (ii) the rights and obligations of some or all parties to a funds transfer any part of which is carried out by means of the system. A choice of law made pursuant to clause (i) is binding on participating banks. A choice of law made pursuant to clause (ii) is binding on the originator, other sender, or a receiving bank having notice that the funds-transfer system might be used in the funds transfer and of the choice of law by the system when the originator, other sender, or receiving bank issued or accepted a payment order. The beneficiary of a funds transfer is bound by the choice of law if, when the funds transfer is initiated, the beneficiary has notice that the funds-transfer system might be used in the funds transfer and of the choice of law by the system. The law of a jurisdiction selected pursuant to this subsection may govern, whether or not that law bears a reasonable relation to the matter in issue.
(d)   In the event of inconsistency between an agreement under subsection (b) and a choice-of-law rule under subsection (c), the agreement under subsection (b) prevails.
(e)   If a funds transfer is made by use of more than one funds-transfer system and there is inconsistency between choice-of-law rules of the systems, the matter in issue is governed by the law of the selected jurisdiction that has the most significant relationship to the matter in issue.

U.C.C. - ARTICLE 5 - LETTERS OF CREDIT[1]

§ 5-101. Short Title

This Article shall be known and may be cited as Uniform Commercial Code-Letters of Credit.

§ 5-102. Definitions

(a)   In this article:

(1)   "Adviser" means a person who, at the request of the issuer, a confirmer, or another adviser, notifies or requests another adviser to notify the beneficiary that a letter of credit has been issued, confirmed, or amended.

(2)   "Applicant" means a person at whose request or for whose account a letter of credit is issued. The term includes a person who requests an issuer to issue a letter of credit on behalf of another if the person making the request undertakes an obligation to reimburse the issuer.

(3)   "Beneficiary" means a person who under the terms of a letter of credit is entitled to have its complying presentation honored. The term includes a person to whom drawing rights have been transferred under a transferable letter of credit.

(4)   "Confirmer" means a nominated person who undertakes, at the request or with the consent of the issuer, to honor a presentation under a letter of credit issued by another.

(5)   "Dishonor" of a letter of credit means failure timely to honor or to take an interim action, such as acceptance of a draft, that may be required by the letter of credit.

(6)   "Document" means a draft or other demand, document of title, investment security, certificate, invoice, or other record, statement, or representation of fact, law, right, or opinion (i) which is presented in a written or other medium permitted by the letter of credit or, unless prohibited by the letter of credit, by the standard practice referred to in Section 5-108(e) and (ii) which is capable of being examined for compliance with the terms and conditions of the letter of credit. A document may not be oral.

(7)   "Good faith" means honesty in fact in the conduct or transaction concerned.

(8)   "Honor" of a letter of credit means performance of the issuer's undertaking in the letter of credit to pay or deliver an item of value. Unless the letter of credit otherwise provides, "honor" occurs (i) upon payment,(ii) if the letter of credit provides for acceptance, upon acceptance of a draft and, at maturity, its payment, or(iii) if the letter of credit provides for incurring a deferred obligation, upon incurring the obligation and, at maturity, its performance.

(9)   "Issuer" means a bank or other person that issues a letter of credit, but does not include an individual who makes an engagement for personal, family, or household purposes.

(10) "Letter of credit" means a definite undertaking that satisfies the requirements of Section 5-104 by an issuer to a beneficiary at the request or for the account of an applicant or, in the case of a financial institution, to itself or for its own account, to honor a documentary presentation by payment or delivery of an item of value.

(11) "Nominated person" means a person whom the issuer (i) designates or authorizes to pay, accept, negotiate, or otherwise give value under a letter of credit and (ii) undertakes by agreement or custom and practice to reimburse.

(12) "Presentation" means delivery of a document to an issuer or nominated person for honor or giving of value under a letter of credit.

(13) "Presenter" means a person making a presentation as or on behalf of a beneficiary or nominated person.

(14) "Record" means information that is inscribed on a tangible medium, or that is stored in an electronic or other medium and is retrievable in perceivable form.

---

1   © 2012 by The American Law Institute and the National Conference of Commissioners on Uniform State Laws; reproduced, published and distributed with permission of the Permanent Editorial Board for the Uniform Commercial Code. All rights reserved.

(15) "Successor of a beneficiary" means a person who succeeds to substantially all of the rights of a beneficiary by operation of law, including a corporation with or into which the beneficiary has been merged or consolidated, an administrator, executor, personal representative, trustee in bankruptcy, debtor in possession, liquidator, and receiver.

(b) Definitions in other Articles applying to this Article and the sections in which they appear are:
"Accept" or "Acceptance" Section 3-409
"Value" Sections 3-303, 4-211

(c) Article 1 contains certain additional general definitions and principles of construction and interpretation applicable throughout this article.

§ 5-103. Scope

(a) This Article applies to letters of credit and to certain rights and obligations arising out of transactions involving letters of credit.

(b) The statement of a rule in this Article does not by itself require, imply, or negate application of the same or a different rule to a situation not provided for, or to a person not specified, in this article.

(c) With the exception of this subsection, subsections (a) and (d), Sections 5-102(a)(9) and (10), 5-106(d), and 5-114(d), and except to the extent prohibited in Sections 1-302 and 5-117(d), the effect of this Article may be varied by agreement or by a provision stated or incorporated by reference in an undertaking. A term in an agreement or undertaking generally excusing liability or generally limiting remedies for failure to perform obligations is not sufficient to vary obligations prescribed by this article.

(d) Rights and obligations of an issuer to a beneficiary or a nominated person under a letter of credit are independent of the existence, performance, or nonperformance of a contract or arrangement out of which the letter of credit arises or which underlies it, including contracts or arrangements between the issuer and the applicant and between the applicant and the beneficiary.

§ 5-104. Formal Requirements

A letter of credit, confirmation, advice, transfer, amendment, or cancellation may be issued in any form that is a record and is authenticated (i) by a signature or (ii) in accordance with the agreement of the parties or the standard practice referred to in Section 5-108(e).

§ 5-105. Consideration

Consideration is not required to issue, amend, transfer, or cancel a letter of credit, advice, or confirmation.

§ 5-106. Issuance, Amendment, Cancellation, and Duration

(a) A letter of credit is issued and becomes enforceable according to its terms against the issuer when the issuer sends or otherwise transmits it to the person requested to advise or to the beneficiary. A letter of credit is revocable only if it so provides.

(b) After a letter of credit is issued, rights and obligations of a beneficiary, applicant, confirmer, and issuer are not affected by an amendment or cancellation to which that person has not consented except to the extent the letter of credit provides that it is revocable or that the issuer may amend or cancel the letter of credit without that consent.

(c) If there is no stated expiration date or other provision that determines its duration, a letter of credit expires one year after its stated date of issuance or, if none is stated, after the date on which it is issued.

(d) A letter of credit that states that it is perpetual expires five years after its stated date of issuance, or if none is stated, after the date on which it is issued.

§ 5-107. Confirmer, Nominated Person, and Adviser

(a) A confirmer is directly obligated on a letter of credit and has the rights and obligations of an issuer to the extent of its confirmation. The confirmer also has rights against and obligations to the issuer as if the issuer were an applicant and the confirmer had issued the letter of credit at the request and for the account of the issuer.

(b)   A nominated person who is not a confirmer is not obligated to honor or otherwise give value for a presentation.

(c)   A person requested to advise may decline to act as an adviser. An adviser that is not a confirmer is not obligated to honor or give value for a presentation. An adviser undertakes to the issuer and to the beneficiary accurately to advise the terms of the letter of credit, confirmation, amendment, or advice received by that person and undertakes to the beneficiary to check the apparent authenticity of the request to advise. Even if the advice is inaccurate, the letter of credit, confirmation, or amendment is enforceable as issued.

(d)   A person who notifies a transferee beneficiary of the terms of a letter of credit, confirmation, amendment, or advice has the rights and obligations of an adviser under subsection (c). The terms in the notice to the transferee beneficiary may differ from the terms in any notice to the transferor beneficiary to the extent permitted by the letter of credit, confirmation, amendment, or advice received by the person who so notifies.

§ 5-108. Issuer's Rights and Obligations

(a)   Except as otherwise provided in Section 5-109, an issuer shall honor a presentation that, as determined by the standard practice referred to in subsection (e), appears on its face strictly to comply with the terms and conditions of the letter of credit. Except as otherwise provided in Section 5-113 and unless otherwise agreed with the applicant, an issuer shall dishonor a presentation that does not appear so to comply.

(b)   An issuer has a reasonable time after presentation, but not beyond the end of the seventh business day of the issuer after the day of its receipt of documents:

(1)   to honor,

(2)   if the letter of credit provides for honor to be completed more than seven business days after presentation, to accept a draft or incur a deferred obligation, or

(3)   to give notice to the presenter of discrepancies in the presentation.

(c)   Except as otherwise provided in subsection (d), an issuer is precluded from asserting as a basis for dishonor any discrepancy if timely notice is not given, or any discrepancy not stated in the notice if timely notice is given.

(d)   Failure to give the notice specified in subsection (b) or to mention fraud, forgery, or expiration in the notice does not preclude the issuer from asserting as a basis for dishonor fraud or forgery as described in Section 5-109(a) or expiration of the letter of credit before presentation.

(e)   An issuer shall observe standard practice of financial institutions that regularly issue letters of credit. Determination of the issuer's observance of the standard practice is a matter of interpretation for the court. The court shall offer the parties a reasonable opportunity to present evidence of the standard practice.

(f)   An issuer is not responsible for:

(1)   the performance or nonperformance of the underlying contract, arrangement, or transaction,

(2)   an act or omission of others, or

(3)   observance or knowledge of the usage of a particular trade other than the standard practice referred to in subsection (e).

(g)   If an undertaking constituting a letter of credit under Section 5-102(a)(10) contains nondocumentary conditions, an issuer shall disregard the nondocumentary conditions and treat them as if they were not stated.

(h)   An issuer that has dishonored a presentation shall return the documents or hold them at the disposal of, and send advice to that effect to, the presenter.

(i)   An issuer that has honored a presentation as permitted or required by this article:

(1)   is entitled to be reimbursed by the applicant in immediately available funds not later than the date of its payment of funds;

(2)   takes the documents free of claims of the beneficiary or presenter;

(3)   is precluded from asserting a right of recourse on a draft under Sections 3-414 and 3-415;

(4)   except as otherwise provided in Sections 5-110 and 5-117, is precluded from restitution of money paid or other value given by mistake to the extent the mistake concerns discrepancies in the documents or tender which are apparent on the face of the presentation; and

(5)   is discharged to the extent of its performance under the letter of credit unless the issuer honored a presentation in which a required signature of a beneficiary was forged.

§ 5-109. Fraud and Forgery

(a)   If a presentation is made that appears on its face strictly to comply with the terms and conditions of the letter of credit, but a required document is forged or materially fraudulent, or honor of the presentation would facilitate a material fraud by the beneficiary on the issuer or applicant:

(1)   the issuer shall honor the presentation, if honor is demanded by (i) a nominated person who has given value in good faith and without notice of forgery or material fraud, (ii) a confirmer who has honored its confirmation in good faith, (iii) a holder in due course of a draft drawn under the letter of credit which was taken after acceptance by the issuer or nominated person, or (iv) an assignee of the issuer's or nominated person's deferred obligation that was taken for value and without notice of forgery or material fraud after the obligation was incurred by the issuer or nominated person; and

(2)   the issuer, acting in good faith, may honor or dishonor the presentation in any other case.

(b)   If an applicant claims that a required document is forged or materially fraudulent or that honor of the presentation would facilitate a material fraud by the beneficiary on the issuer or applicant, a court of competent jurisdiction may temporarily or permanently enjoin the issuer from honoring a presentation or grant similar relief against the issuer or other persons only if the court finds that:

(1)   the relief is not prohibited under the law applicable to an accepted draft or deferred obligation incurred by the issuer;

(2)   a beneficiary, issuer, or nominated person who may be adversely affected is adequately protected against loss that it may suffer because the relief is granted;

(3)   all of the conditions to entitle a person to the relief under the law of this State have been met; and

(4)   on the basis of the information submitted to the court, the applicant is more likely than not to succeed under its claim of forgery or material fraud and the person demanding honor does not qualify for protection under subsection (a)(1).

§ 5-110. Warranties

(a)   If its presentation is honored, the beneficiary warrants:

(1)   to the issuer, any other person to whom presentation is made, and the applicant that there is no fraud or forgery of the kind described in Section 5-109(a); and

(2)   to the applicant that the drawing does not violate any agreement between the applicant and beneficiary or any other agreement intended by them to be augmented by the letter of credit.

(b)   The warranties in subsection (a) are in addition to warranties arising under Article 3, 4, 7, and 8 because of the presentation or transfer of documents covered by any of those articles.

§ 5-111. Remedies

(a)   If an issuer wrongfully dishonors or repudiates its obligation to pay money under a letter of credit before presentation, the beneficiary, successor, or nominated person presenting on its own behalf may recover from the issuer the amount that is the subject of the dishonor or repudiation. If the issuer's obligation under the letter of credit is not for the payment of money, the claimant may obtain specific performance or, at the claimant's election, recover an amount equal to the value of performance from the issuer. In either case, the claimant may also recover incidental but not consequential damages. The claimant is not obligated to take action to avoid damages that might be due from the issuer under this subsection. If, although not obligated to do so, the claimant avoids damages, the claimant's recovery from the issuer must be reduced by the amount of damages avoided. The issuer has the burden of proving the amount of damages avoided. In the case of repudiation the claimant need not present any document.

(b)   If an issuer wrongfully dishonors a draft or demand presented under a letter of credit or honors a draft or demand in breach of its obligation to the applicant, the applicant may recover damages resulting from the breach, including incidental but not consequential damages, less any amount saved as a result of the breach.

(c)   If an adviser or nominated person other than a confirmer breaches an obligation under this Article or an issuer breaches an obligation not covered in subsection (a) or (b), a person to whom the obligation is owed may recover damages resulting from the breach, including incidental but not consequential damages, less any amount saved as a result of the breach. To the extent of the confirmation, a confirmer has the liability of an issuer specified in this subsection and subsections (a) and (b).

(d)   An issuer, nominated person, or adviser who is found liable under subsection (a), (b), or (c) shall pay interest on the amount owed thereunder from the date of wrongful dishonor or other appropriate date.

(e)   Reasonable attorney's fees and other expenses of litigation must be awarded to the prevailing party in an action in which a remedy is sought under this article.

(f)   Damages that would otherwise be payable by a party for breach of an obligation under this Article may be liquidated by agreement or undertaking, but only in an amount or by a formula that is reasonable in light of the harm anticipated.

§ 5-112. Transfer of Letter of Credit

(a)   Except as otherwise provided in Section 5-113, unless a letter of credit provides that it is transferable, the right of a beneficiary to draw or otherwise demand performance under a letter of credit may not be transferred.

(b)   Even if a letter of credit provides that it is transferable, the issuer may refuse to recognize or carry out a transfer if:

(1)   the transfer would violate applicable law; or

(2)   the transferor or transferee has failed to comply with any requirement stated in the letter of credit or any other requirement relating to transfer imposed by the issuer which is within the standard practice referred to in Section 5-108(e) or is otherwise reasonable under the circumstances.

§ 5-113. Transfer by Operation of Law

(a)   A successor of a beneficiary may consent to amendments, sign and present documents, and receive payment or other items of value in the name of the beneficiary without disclosing its status as a successor.

(b)   A successor of a beneficiary may consent to amendments, sign and present documents, and receive payment or other items of value in its own name as the disclosed successor of the beneficiary. Except as otherwise provided in subsection (e), an issuer shall recognize a disclosed successor of a beneficiary as beneficiary in full substitution for its predecessor upon compliance with the requirements for recognition by the issuer of a transfer of drawing rights by operation of law under the standard practice referred to in Section 5-108(e) or, in the absence of such a practice, compliance with other reasonable procedures sufficient to protect the issuer.

(c)   An issuer is not obliged to determine whether a purported successor is a successor of a beneficiary or whether the signature of a purported successor is genuine or authorized.

(d)   Honor of a purported successor's apparently complying presentation under subsection (a) or (b) has the consequences specified in Section 5-108(i) even if the purported successor is not the successor of a beneficiary. Documents signed in the name of the beneficiary or of a disclosed successor by a person who is neither the beneficiary nor the successor of the beneficiary are forged documents for the purposes of Section 5-109.

(e)   An issuer whose rights of reimbursement are not covered by subsection (d) or substantially similar law and any confirmer or nominated person may decline to recognize a presentation under subsection (b).

(f)   A beneficiary whose name is changed after the issuance of a letter of credit has the same rights and obligations as a successor of a beneficiary under this section.

§ 5-114. Assignment of Proceeds

(a)   In this section, "proceeds of a letter of credit" means the cash, check, accepted draft, or other item of value paid or delivered upon honor or giving of value by the issuer or any nominated person under the letter of credit. The term does not include a beneficiary's drawing rights or documents presented by the beneficiary.

(b)   A beneficiary may assign its right to part or all of the proceeds of a letter of credit. The beneficiary may do so before presentation as a present assignment of its right to receive proceeds contingent upon its compliance with the terms and conditions of the letter of credit.

(c)   An issuer or nominated person need not recognize an assignment of proceeds of a letter of credit until it consents to the assignment.

(d)   An issuer or nominated person has no obligation to give or withhold its consent to an assignment of proceeds of a letter of credit, but consent may not be unreasonably withheld if the assignee possesses and exhibits the letter of credit and presentation of the letter of credit is a condition to honor.

(e)   Rights of a transferee beneficiary or nominated person are independent of the beneficiary's assignment of the proceeds of a letter of credit and are superior to the assignee's right to the proceeds.

(f)   Neither the rights recognized by this section between an assignee and an issuer, transferee beneficiary, or nominated person nor the issuer's or nominated person's payment of proceeds to an assignee or a third person affect the rights between the assignee and any person other than the issuer, transferee beneficiary, or nominated person. The mode of creating and perfecting a security interest in or granting an assignment of a beneficiary's rights to proceeds is governed by Article 9 or other law. Against persons other than the issuer, transferee beneficiary, or nominated person, the rights and obligations arising upon the creation of a security interest or other assignment of a beneficiary's right to proceeds and its perfection are governed by Article 9 or other law.

§ 5-115. Statute of Limitations

An action to enforce a right or obligation arising under this Article must be commenced within one year after the expiration date of the relevant letter of credit or one year after the [claim for relief] [cause of action] accrues, whichever occurs later. A [claim for relief] [cause of action] accrues when the breach occurs, regardless of the aggrieved party's lack of knowledge of the breach.

§ 5-116. Choice of Law and Forum

(a)   The liability of an issuer, nominated person, or adviser for action or omission is governed by the law of the jurisdiction chosen by an agreement in the form of a record signed or otherwise authenticated by the affected parties in the manner provided in Section 5-104 or by a provision in the person's letter of credit, confirmation, or other undertaking. The jurisdiction whose law is chosen need not bear any relation to the transaction.

(b)   Unless subsection (a) applies, the liability of an issuer, nominated person, or adviser for action or omission is governed by the law of the jurisdiction in which the person is located. The person is considered to be located at the address indicated in the person's undertaking. If more than one address is indicated, the person is considered to be located at the address from which the person's undertaking was issued. For the purpose of jurisdiction, choice of law, and recognition of interbranch letters of credit, but not enforcement of a judgment, all branches of a bank are considered separate juridical entities and a bank is considered to be located at the place where its relevant branch is considered to be located under this subsection.

(c)   Except as otherwise provided in this subsection, the liability of an issuer, nominated person, or adviser is governed by any rules of custom or practice, such as the Uniform Customs and Practice for Documentary Credits, to which the letter of credit, confirmation, or other undertaking is expressly made subject. If (i) this Article would govern the liability of an issuer, nominated person, or adviser under subsection (a) or (b), (ii) the relevant undertaking incorporates rules of custom or practice, and (iii) there is conflict between this Article and those rules as applied to that undertaking, those rules govern except to the extent of any conflict with the nonvariable provisions specified in Section 5-103(c).

(d)   If there is conflict between this Article and Article 3, 4, 4A, or 9, this Article governs.

(e)   The forum for settling disputes arising out of an undertaking within this Article may be chosen in the manner and with the binding effect that governing law may be chosen in accordance with subsection (a).

§ 5-117. Subrogation of Issuer, Applicant, and Nominated Person

(a)   An issuer that honors a beneficiary's presentation is subrogated to the rights of the beneficiary to the same extent as if the issuer were a secondary obligor of the underlying obligation owed to the beneficiary and of the applicant to the same extent as if the issuer were the secondary obligor of the underlying obligation owed to the applicant.

(b)   An applicant that reimburses an issuer is subrogated to the rights of the issuer against any beneficiary, presenter, or nominated person to the same extent as if the applicant were the secondary obligor of the obligations owed to the issuer and has the rights of subrogation of the issuer to the rights of the beneficiary stated in subsection (a).

(c)   A nominated person who pays or gives value against a draft or demand presented under a letter of credit is subrogated to the rights of:

(1)   the issuer against the applicant to the same extent as if the nominated person were a secondary obligor of the obligation owed to the issuer by the applicant;

(2)   the beneficiary to the same extent as if the nominated person were a secondary obligor of the underlying obligation owed to the beneficiary; and

(3)   the applicant to same extent as if the nominated person were a secondary obligor of the underlying obligation owed to the applicant.

(d)   Notwithstanding any agreement or term to the contrary, the rights of subrogation stated in subsections (a) and (b) do not arise until the issuer honors the letter of credit or otherwise pays and the rights in subsection (c) do not arise until the nominated person pays or otherwise gives value. Until then, the issuer, nominated person, and the applicant do not derive under this section present or prospective rights forming the basis of a claim, defense, or excuse.

§ 5-118. Security Interest of Issuer or Nominated Person

(a)   An issuer or nominated person has a security interest in a document presented under a letter of credit and any identifiable proceeds of the collateral to the extent that the issuer or nominated person honors or gives value for the presentation.

(b)   Subject to subsection (c), as long as and to the extent that an issuer or nominated person has not been reimbursed or has not otherwise recovered the value given with respect to a security interest in a document under subsection (a), the security interest continues and is subject to Article 9, but:

(1)   a security agreement is not necessary to make the security interest enforceable under Section 9-203(b)(3);

(2)   if the document is presented in a medium other than a written or other tangible medium, the security interest is perfected; and

(3)   if the document is presented in a written or other tangible medium and is not a certificated security, chattel paper, a document of title, an instrument, or a letter of credit, so long as the debtor does not have possession of the document, the security interest is perfected and has priority over a conflicting security interest in the document.

TRANSITION PROVISIONS [...]

Part III - Shipping

1924 INTERNATIONAL CONVENTION FOR THE UNIFICATION OF CERTAIN RULES OF LAW RELATING TO BILLS OF LADING ("Hague Rules")

The President of the German Republic, the President of the Argentine Republic, His Majesty the King of the Belgians, the President of the Republic of Chile, the President of the Republic of Cuba, His Majesty the King of Denmark and Iceland, His Majesty the King of Spain, the Head of the Estonian State, the President of the United States of America, the President of the Republic of Finland, the President of the French Republic, His Majesty the King of the United Kingdom of Great Britain and Ireland and of the British Dominions beyond the Seas, Emperor of India, His Most Supreme Highness the Governor of the Kingdom of Hungary, His Majesty the King of Italy, His Majesty the Emperor of Japan, the President of the Latvian Republic, the President of the Republic of Mexico, His Majesty the King of Norway, Her Majesty the Queen of the Netherlands, the President of the Republic of Peru, the President of the Polish Republic, the President of the Portuguese Republic, His Majesty the King of Romania, His Majesty the King of the Serbs, Croats and Slovenes, His Majesty the King of Sweden, and the President of the Republic of Uruguay, HAVING RECOGNIZED the utility of fixing by agreement certain uniform rules of law relating to bills of lading,

HAVE DECIDED to conclude a convention with this object and have appointed the following Plenipotentiaries:

WHO, duly authorized thereto, have agreed as follows:

Article 1 [Definitions]

In this Convention the following words are employed with the meanings set out below:

(a) "Carrier" includes the owner or the charterer who enters into a contract of carriage with a shipper.

(b) "Contract of carriage" applies only to contracts of carriage covered by a bill of lading or any similar document of title, in so far as such document relates to the carriage of goods by sea, including any bill of lading or any similar document as aforesaid issued under or pursuant to a charter party from the moment at which such bill of lading or similar document of title regulates the relations between a carrier and a holder of the same.

(c) "Goods" includes goods, wares, merchandise and articles of every kind whatsoever except live animals and cargo which by the contract of carriage in stated as being carried on deck and is so carried.

(d) "Ship" means any vessel used for the carriage of goods by sea.

(e) "Carriage of goods" covers the period from the time when the goods are loaded on to the time they are discharged from the ship.

Article 2 [Scope]

Subject to the provisions of Article 6, under every contract of carriage of goods by sea the carrier, in relation to the loading, handling, stowage, carriage, custody, care and discharge of such goods, shall be subject to the responsibilities and liabilities, and entitled to the rights and immunities hereinafter set forth.

Article 3 [Responsibilities of the Carrier]

1. The carrier shall be bound before and at the beginning of the voyage to exercise due diligence to:

(a) Make the ship seaworthy.

(b) Properly man, equip and supply the ship.

(c) Make the holds, refrigerating and cool chambers, and all other parts of the ship in which goods are carried, fit and safe for their reception, carriage and preservation.

2.   Subject to the provisions of Article 4, the carrier shall properly and carefully load, handle, stow, carry, keep, care for, and discharge the goods carried.

3.   After receiving the goods into his charge the carrier or the master or agent of the carrier shall, on demand of the shipper, issue to the shipper a bill of lading showing among other things:

(a)   The leading marks necessary for identification of the goods as the same are furnished in writing by the shipper before the loading of such goods starts, provided such marks are stamped or otherwise shown clearly upon the goods if uncovered, or on the cases or coverings in which such goods are contained, in such a manner as should ordinarily remain legible until the end of the voyage.

(b)   Either the number of packages or pieces, or the quantity, or weight, as the case may be, as furnished in writing by the shipper.

(c)   The apparent order and condition of the goods.

Provided that no carrier, master or agent of the carrier shall be bound to state or show in the bill of lading any marks, number, quantity, or weight which he has reasonable ground for suspecting not accurately to represent the goods actually received, or which he has had no reasonable means of checking.

4.   Such a bill of lading shall be prima facie evidence of the receipt by the carrier of the goods as therein described in accordance with paragraph 3(a), (b) and (c).

5.   The shipper shall be deemed to have guaranteed to the carrier the accuracy at the time of shipment of the marks, number, quantity and weight, as furnished by him, and the shipper shall indemnity the carrier against all loss, damages and expenses arising or resulting from inaccuracies in such particulars. The right of the carrier to such indemnity shall in no way limit his responsibility and liability under the contract of carriage to any person other than the shipper.

6.   Unless notice of loss or damage and the general nature of such loss or damage be given in writing to the carrier or his agent at the port of discharge before or at the time of the removal of the goods into the custody of the person entitled to delivery thereof under the contract of carriage, or if the loss or damage be not apparent, within three days, such removal shall be prima facie evidence of the delivery by the carrier of the goods as described in the bill of lading. If the loss or damage is not apparent, the notice must be given within three days of the delivery of the goods.

      The notice in writing need not be given if the state of the goods has, at the time of their receipt, been the subject of joint survey or inspection.

      In any event the carrier and the ship shall be discharged from all liability in respect of loss or damage unless suit is brought within one year after delivery of the goods or the date when the goods should have been delivered.

      In the case of any actual or apprehended loss or damage the carrier and the receiver shall give all reasonable facilities to each other for inspecting and tallying the goods.

7.   After the goods are loaded the bill of lading to be issued by the carrier, master, or agent of the carrier, to the shipper shall, if the shipper so demands, be a "shipped" bill of lading, provided that if the shipper shall have previously taken up any document of title to such goods, he shall surrender the same as against the issue of the "shipped" bill of lading, but at the option of the carrier such document of title may be noted at the port of shipment by the carrier, master, or agent with the name or names of the ship or ships upon which the goods have been shipped and the date or dates of shipment, and when so noted, if it shows the particulars mentioned in paragraph 3 of Article 3, shall for the purpose of this Article be deemed to constitute a "shipped" bill of lading.

8.   Any clause, covenant, or agreement in a contract of carriage relieving the carrier or the ship from liability for loss or damage to, or in connexion with, goods arising from negligence, fault, or failure in the duties and obligations provided in this Article or lessening such liability otherwise than as provided in this Convention, shall be null and void and of no effect. A benefit of insurance in favour of the carrier or similar clause shall be deemed to be a clause relieving the carrier from liability.

Article 4 [Limitations of Carrier Liability]

1. Neither the carrier nor the ship shall be liable for loss or damage arising or resulting from unseaworthiness unless caused by want of due diligence on the part of the carrier to make the ship seaworthy, and to secure that the ship is properly manned, equipped and supplied, and to make the holds, refrigerating and cool chambers and all other parts of the ship in which goods are carried fit and safe for their reception, carriage and preservation in accordance with the provisions of paragraph 1 of Article 3. Whenever loss or damage has resulted from unseaworthiness the burden of proving the exercise of due diligence shall be on the carrier or other person claiming exemption under this Article.

2. Neither the carrier nor the ship shall be responsible for loss or damage arising or resulting from:

(a) Act, neglect, or default of the master, mariner, pilot, or the servants of the carrier in the navigation or in the management of the ship.
(b) Fire, unless caused by the actual fault or privity of the carrier.
(c) Perils, dangers and accidents of the sea or other navigable waters.
(d) Act of God.
(e) Act of war.
(f) Act of public enemies.
(g) Arrest or restraint of princes, rulers or people, or seizure under legal process.
(h) Quarantine restrictions.
(i) Act or omission of the shipper or owner of the goods, his agent or representative.
(j) Strikes or lockouts or stoppage or restraint of labour from whatever cause, whether partial or general.
(k) Riots and civil commotions.
(l) Saving or attempting to save life or property at sea.
(m) Wastage in bulk or weight or any other loss or damage arising from inherent defect, quality or vice of the goods.
(n) Insufficiency of packing.
(o) Insufficiency or inadequacy of marks.
(p) Latent defects not discoverable by due diligence.
(q) Any other cause arising without the actual fault or privity of the carrier, or without the actual fault or neglect of the agents or servants of the carrier, but the burden of proof shall be on the person claiming the benefit of this exception to show that neither the actual fault or privity of the carrier nor the fault or neglect of the agents or servants of the carrier contributed to the loss or damage.

3. The shipper shall not be responsible for loss or damage sustained by the carrier or the ship arising or resulting from any cause without the act, fault or neglect of the shipper, his agents or his servants.

4. Any deviation in saving or attempting to save life or property at sea or any reasonable deviation shall not be deemed to be an infringement or breach of this Convention or of the contract of carriage, and the carrier shall not be liable for any loss or damage resulting therefrom.

5. Neither the carrier nor the ship shall in any event be or become liable for any loss or damage to or in connexion with goods in an amount exceeding 100 pounds sterling per package or unit, or the equivalent of that sum in other currency unless the nature and value of such goods have been declared by the shipper before shipment and inserted in the bill of lading.

This declaration if embodied in the bill of lading shall be prima facie evidence, but shall not be binding or conclusive on the carrier.

By agreement between the carrier, master or agent of the carrier and the shipper another maximum amount than that mentioned in this paragraph may be fixed, provided that such maximum shall not be less than the figure above named.

Neither the carrier nor the ship shall be responsible in any event for loss or damage to, or in connexion with, goods if the nature or value thereof has been knowingly misstated by the shipper in the bill of lading.

6.   Goods of an inflammable, explosive or dangerous nature to the shipment whereof the carrier, master or agent of the carrier has not consented with knowledge of their nature and character, may at any time before discharge be landed at any place, or destroyed or rendered innocuous by the carrier without compensation and the shipper of such goods shall be liable for all damage and expenses directly or indirectly arising out of or resulting from such shipment. If any such goods shipped with such knowledge and consent shall become a danger to the ship or cargo, they may in like manner be landed at any place, or destroyed or rendered innocuous by the carrier without liability on the part of the carrier except to general average, if any.

Article 5 [Priority of Provisions in the Bill of Lading]

A carrier shall be at liberty to surrender in whole or in part all or any of his rights and immunities or to increase any of his responsibilities and obligations under this Convention, provided such surrender or increase shall be embodied in the bill of lading issued to the shipper.

The provisions of this Convention shall not be applicable to charter parties, but if bills of lading are issued in the case of a ship under a charter party they shall comply with the terms of this Convention. Nothing in these rules shall be held to prevent the insertion in a bill of lading of any lawful provision regarding general average.

Article 6 [Priority of Contracts of Carriage]

Notwithstanding the provisions of the preceding Articles, a carrier, master or agent of the carrier and a shipper shall in regard to any particular goods be at liberty to enter into any agreement in any terms as to the responsibility and liability of the carrier for such goods, and as to the rights and immunities of the carrier in respect of such goods, or his obligation as to seaworthiness, so far as this stipulation is not contrary to public policy, or the care or diligence of his servants or agents in regard to the loading, handling, stowage, carriage, custody, care and discharge of the goods carried by sea, provided that in this case no bill of lading has been or shall be issued and that the terms agreed shall be embodied in a receipt which shall be a non-negotiable document and shall be marked as such.

Any agreement so entered into shall have full legal effect.

Provided that this Article shall not apply to ordinary commercial shipments made in the ordinary course of trade, but only to other shipments where the character or condition of the property to be carried or the circumstances, terms and conditions under which the carriage is to be performed are such as reasonably to justify a special agreement.

Article 7 [Priority of Other Agreements]

Nothing herein contained shall prevent a carrier or a shipper from entering into any agreement, stipulation, condition, reservation or exemption as to the responsibility and liability of the carrier or the ship for the loss or damage to, or in connexion with, the custody and care and handling of goods prior to the loading on, and subsequent to, the discharge from the ship on which the goods are carried by sea.

Article 8 [Priority of Statutory Provisions]

The provisions of this Convention shall not affect the rights and obligations of the carrier under any statute for the time being in force relating to the limitation of the liability of owners of sea-going vessels.

Article 9 [Monetary Units]

The monetary units mentioned in this Convention are to be taken to be gold value.

Those contracting States in which the pound sterling is not a monetary unit reserve to themselves the right of translating the sums indicated in this Convention in terms of pound sterling into terms of their own monetary system in round figures.

The national laws may reserve to the debtor the right of discharging his debt in national currency according to the rate of exchange prevailing on the day of the arrival of the ship at the port of discharge of the goods concerned.

Article 10 [Application to all Bills of Lading]

The provisions of this Convention shall apply to all bills of lading issued in any of the contracting States.

Article 11 [Ratification and Entry into Force]

After an interval of not more than two years from the day on which the Convention is signed, the Belgian Government shall place itself in communication with the Governments of the High Contracting Parties which have declared themselves prepared to ratify the Convention, with a view to deciding whether it shall be put into force. The ratifications shall be deposited at Brussels at a date to be fixed by agreement among the said Governments. The first deposit of ratifications shall be recorded in a procès- verbal signed by the representatives of the Powers which take part therein and by the Belgian Minister of Foreign Affairs.

The subsequent deposit of ratifications shall be made by means of a written notification, addressed to the Belgian Government and accompanied by the instrument of ratification.

A duly certified copy of the procès-verbal relating to the first deposit of ratifications, of the notifications referred to in the previous paragraph, and also of the instruments of ratification accompanying them, shall be immediately sent by the Belgian Government through the diplomatic channel to the Powers who have signed this Convention or who have acceded to it. In the cases contemplated in the preceding paragraph, the said Government shall inform them at the same time of the date on which it received the notification.

Article 12 [Accession]

Non-signatory States may accede to the present Convention whether or not they have been represented at the International Conference at Brussels.

A State which desires to accede shall notify its intention in writing to the Belgian Government, forwarding to it the document of accession, which shall be deposited in the archives of the said Government.

The Belgian Government shall immediately forward to all the States which have signed or acceded to the Convention a duly certified copy of the notification and of the act of accession, mentioning the date on which it received the notification.

Article 13 [Territorial Application]

The High Contracting Parties may at the time of signature, ratification or accession declare that their acceptance of the present Convention does not include any or all of the self-governing dominions, or of the colonies, overseas possessions, protectorates or territories under their sovereignty or authority, and they may subsequently accede separately on behalf of any self-governing dominion, colony, overseas possession, protectorate or territory excluded in their declaration. They may also denounce the Convention separately in accordance with its provisions in respect of any self-governing dominion, or any colony, overseas possession, protectorate or territory under their sovereignty or authority.

Article 14 [Entry into Force]

The present Convention shall take effect, in the case of the States which have taken part in the first deposit of ratifications, one year after the date of the protocol recording such deposit.

As respects the States which ratify subsequently or which accede, and also in cases in which the Convention is subsequently put into effect in accordance with Article 13, it shall take effect six months after the notifications specified in paragraph 2 of Article 11 and paragraph 2 of Article 12 have been received by the Belgian Government.

Article 15 [Denounciation]

In the event of one of the contracting States wishing to denounce the present Convention, the denunciation shall be notified in writing to the Belgian Government, which shall immediately communicate a duly certified copy of the notification to all the other States, informing them of the date on which it was received.

The denunciation shall only operate in respect of the State which made the notification, and on the expiry of one year after the notification has reached the Belgian Government.

Article 16 [Amendments]

Any one of the contracting States shall have the right to call for a fresh conference with a view to considering possible amendments.

A State which would exercise this right should notify its intention to the other States through the Belgian Government, which would make arrangements for convening the Conference.

DONE at Brussels, in a single copy, August 25th, 1924.

PROTOCOL OF SIGNATURE

At the time of signing the International Convention for the Unification of Certain Rules of Law relating to Bills of Lading the Plenipotentiaries whose signatures appear below have adopted this Protocol, which will have the same force and the same value as if its provisions were inserted in the text of the Convention to which it relates.

The High Contracting Parties may give effect to this Convention either by giving it the force of law or by including in their national legislation in a form appropriate to that legislation the rules adopted under this Convention.

They may reserve the right:

1. To prescribe that in the cases referred to in paragraph 2(c) to (p) of Article 4 the holder of a bill of lading shall be entitled to establish responsibility for loss or damage arising from the personal fault of the carrier or the fault of his servants which are not covered by paragraph (a).
2. To apply Article 6 in so far as the national coasting trade is concerned to all classes of goods without taking account of the restriction set out in the last paragraph of that Article.

DONE at Brussels, in single copy, August 25th, 1924.

Entry into force: 2 June 1931

Ratification and binding effect: Algeria, Angola, Antigua and Barbuda, Argentina, Bahamas, Barbados, Belize, Bolivia, Bosnia and Herzegovina, Congo, Croatia, Cuba, Cyprus, Fiji, Gambia, Ghana, Grenada, Guyana, Iran, Ireland, Israel, Ivory Coast, Jamaica, Kenya, Kiribati, Kuwait, Macedonia, Madagascar, Mauritius, Monaco, Montenegro, Nauru, Netherlands, Nigeria, Papua New Guinea, Paraguay, Peru, Portugal, St. Kitts and Nevis, St. Lucia, St. Vincent, Salomon Islands, Serbia, Seychelles, Slovenia, Somalia, Trinidad and Tobago, Turkey, Tuvalu, United Kingdom, United States of America[1]

THE HAGUE-VISBY RULES *not ratified by U.S.*
The Hague Rules as Amended by the Brussels Protocol 1968

Article I *see pg. 492*

In these Rules the following words are employed, with the meanings set out below:

(a) 'Carrier' includes the owner or the charterer who enters into a contract of carriage with a shipper.

(b) 'Contract of carriage' applies only to contracts of carriage covered by a bill of lading or any similar document of title, in so far as such document relates to the carriage of goods by sea, including any bill of lading or any similar document as aforesaid issued under or pursuant to a

---

1   The following countries apply parallel national laws without having ratified the Rules: India, Malaysia, Taiwan.

charter party from the moment at which such bill of lading or similar document of title regulates the relations between a carrier and a holder of the same.

(c)   'Goods' includes goods, wares, merchandise, and articles of every kind whatsoever except live animals and cargo which by the contract of carriage is stated as being carried on deck and is so carried.

(d)   'Ship' means any vessel used for the carriage of goods by sea.

(e)   'Carriage of goods' covers the period from the time when the goods are loaded on to the time they are discharged from the ship.

Article II

Subject to the provisions of Article VI, under every contract of carriage of goods by sea the carrier, in relation to the loading, handling, stowage, carriage, custody, care and discharge of such goods, shall be subject to the responsibilities and liabilities and entitled to the rights and immunities hereinafter set forth.

Article III [Responsibilities of the Carrier]

1.   The carrier shall be bound before and at the beginning of the voyage to exercise due diligence to:

(a)   Make the ship seaworthy;

(b)   Properly man, equip and supply the ship;

(c)   Make the holds, refrigerating and cool chambers, and all other parts of the ship in which goods are carried, fit and safe for their reception, carriage and preservation.

2.   Subject to the provisions of Article IV, the carrier shall properly and carefully load, handle, stow, carry, keep, care for, and discharge the goods carried.

3.   After receiving the goods into his charge the carrier or the master or agent of the carrier shall, on demand of the shipper, issue to the shipper a bill of lading showing among other things:

(a)   The leading marks necessary for identification of the goods as the same are furnished in writing by the shipper before the loading of such goods starts, provided such marks are stamped or otherwise shown clearly upon the goods if uncovered, or on the cases or coverings in which such goods are contained, in such a manner as should ordinarily remain legible until the end of the voyage.

(b)   Either the number of packages or pieces, or the quantity, or weight, as the case may be, as furnished in writing by the shipper.

(c)   The apparent order and condition of the goods.

Provided that no carrier, master or agent of the carrier shall be bound to state or show in the bill of lading any marks, number, quantity or weight which he has reasonable ground for suspecting not accurately to represent the goods actually received, or which he has had no reasonable means of checking.

4.   Such a bill of lading shall be prima facie evidence of the receipt by the carrier of the goods as therein described in accordance with paragraph 3 (a), (b) and (c). However, proof to the contrary shall not be admissible when the bill of lading has been transferred to a third party acting in good faith.

5.   The shipper shall be deemed to have guaranteed to the carrier the accuracy at the time of shipment of the marks, number, quantity and weight, as furnished by him, and the shipper shall indemnify the carrier against all loss, damages and expenses arising or resulting from inaccuracies in such particulars. The right of the carrier to such indemnity shall in no way limit his responsibility and liability under the contract of carriage to any person other than the shipper.

6.   Unless notice of loss or damage and the general nature of such loss or damage be given in writing to the carrier or his agent at the port of discharge before or at the time of the removal of the goods into the custody of the person entitled to delivery thereof under the contract of carriage, or, if the loss or damage be not apparent, within three days, such removal shall be prima facie evidence of the delivery by the carrier of the goods as described in the bill of lading.

The notice in writing need not be given if the state of the goods has, at the time of their receipt, been the subject of joint survey or inspection.

Subject to paragraph 6bis the carrier and the ship shall in any event be discharged from all liability whatsoever in respect of the goods, unless suit is brought within one year of their delivery or of the date when they should have been delivered. This period, may however, be extended if the parties so agree after the cause of action has arisen.

In the case of any actual or apprehended loss or damage the carrier and the receiver shall give all reasonable facilities to each other for inspecting and tallying the goods.

6bis. An action for indemnity against a third person may be brought even after the expiration of the year provided for in the preceding paragraph if brought within the time allowed by the law of the Court seized of the case. However, the time allowed shall be not less than three months, commencing from the day when the person bringing such action for indemnity has settled the claim or has been served with process in the action against himself.

7.   After the goods are loaded the bill of lading to be issued by the carrier, master, or agent of the carrier, to the shipper shall, if the shipper so demands be a 'shipped' bill of lading, provided that if the shipper shall have previously taken up any document of title to such goods, he shall surrender the same as against the issue of the 'shipped' bill of lading, but at the option of the carrier such document of title may be noted at the port of shipment by the carrier, master, or agent with the name or names of the ship or ships upon which the goods have been shipped and the date or dates of shipment, and when so noted, if it shows the particulars mentioned in paragraph 3 of Article III, shall for the purpose of this Article be deemed to constitute a 'shipped' bill of lading.

8.   Any clause, covenant, or agreement in a contract of carriage relieving the carrier or the ship from liability for loss or damage to, or in connection with, goods arising from negligence, fault, or failure in the duties and obligations provided in this Article or lessening such liability otherwise than as provided in these Rules, shall be null and void and of no effect. A benefit of insurance in favour of the carrier or similar clause shall be deemed to be a clause relieving the carrier from liability.

Article IV [Limitation of Carrier Liability]

1.   Neither the carrier nor the ship shall be liable for loss or damage arising or resulting from unseaworthiness unless caused by want of due diligence on the part of the carrier to make the ship seaworthy, and to secure that the ship is properly manned, equipped and supplied, and to make the holds, refrigerating and cool chambers and all other parts of the ship in which goods are carried fit and safe for their reception, carriage and preservation in accordance with the provisions of paragraph 1 of Article III. Whenever loss or damage has resulted from unseaworthiness the burden of proving the exercise of due diligence shall be on the carrier or other person claiming exemption under this article.

2.   Neither the carrier nor the ship shall be responsible for loss or damage arising or resulting from:

(a)   Act, neglect, or default of the master, mariner, pilot, or the servants of the carrier in the navigation or in the management of the ship.

(b)   Fire, unless caused by the actual fault or privity of the carrier.

(c)   Perils, dangers and accidents of the sea or other navigable waters.

(d)   Act of God.

(e)   Act of war.

(f)   Act of public enemies.

(g)   Arrest or restraint of princes, rulers or people, or seizure under legal process.

(h)   Quarantine restrictions.

(i)   Act or omission of the shipper or owner of the goods, his agent or representative.

(j)   Strikes or lockouts or stoppage or restraint of labour from whatever cause, whether partial or general.

(k)   Riots and civil commotions.

(l)   Saving or attempting to save life or property at sea.
(m) Wastage in bulk of weight or any other loss or damage arising from inherent defect, quality or vice of the goods.
(n)   Insufficiency of packing.
(o)   Insufficiency or inadequacy of marks.
(p)   Latent defects not discoverable by due diligence.
(q)   Any other cause arising without the actual fault or privity of the carrier, or without the fault or neglect of the agents or servants of the carrier, but the burden of proof shall be on the person claiming the benefit of this exception to show that neither the actual fault or privity of the carrier nor the fault or neglect of the agents or servants of the carrier contributed to the loss or damage.

3.   The shipper shall not be responsible for loss or damage sustained by the carrier or the ship arising or resulting from any cause without the act, fault or neglect of the shipper, his agents or his servants.

4.   Any deviation in saving or attempting to save life or property at sea or any reasonable deviation shall not be deemed to be an infringement or breach of these Rules or of the contract of carriage, and the carrier shall not be liable for any loss or damage resulting therefrom.

5.(a) Unless the nature and value of such goods have been declared by the shipper before shipment and inserted in the bill of lading, neither the carrier nor the ship shall in any event be or become liable for any loss or damage to or in connection with the goods in an amount exceeding the equivalent of 666.67 units of account per package or unit or units of account per kilo of gross weight of the goods lost or damaged, whichever is the higher.

(b)   The total amount recoverable shall be calculated by reference to the value of such goods at the place and time at which the goods are discharged from the ship in accordance with the contract or should have been so discharged.
      The value of the goods shall be fixed according to the commodity exchange price, or, if there be no such price, according to the current market price, or, if there be no commodity exchange price or current market price, by reference to the normal value of goods of the same kind and quality.

(c)   Where a container, pallet or similar article of transport is used to consolidate goods, the number of packages or units enumerated in the bill of lading as packed in such article of transport shall be deemed the number of packages or units for the purpose of this paragraph as far as these packages or units are concerned. Except as aforesaid such article of transport shall be considered the package or unit.

(d)   The unit of account mentioned in this Article is the special drawing right as defined by the International Monetary Fund. The amounts mentioned in sub-paragraph (a) of this paragraph shall be converted into national currency on the basis of the value of that currency on a date to be determined by the law of the Court seized of the case.

(e)   Neither the carrier nor the ship shall be entitled to the benefit of the limitation of liability provided for in this paragraph if it is proved that the damage resulted from an act or omission of the carrier done with intent to cause damage, or recklessly and with knowledge that damage would probably result.

(f)   The declaration mentioned in sub-paragraph (a) of this paragraph, if embodied in the bill of lading, shall be prima facie evidence, but shall not be binding or conclusive on the carrier.

(g)   By agreement between the carrier, master or agent of the carrier and the shipper other maximum amounts than those mentioned in sub-paragraph (a) of this paragraph may be fixed, provided that no maximum amount so fixed shall be less than the appropriate maximum mentioned in that sub-paragraph.

(h)   Neither the carrier nor the ship shall be responsible in any event for loss or damage to, or in connection with, goods if the nature or value thereof has been knowingly misstated by the shipper in the bill of lading.

6.   Goods of an inflammable, explosive or dangerous nature to the shipment whereof the carrier, master or agent of the carrier has not consented with knowledge of their nature and character, may at any time before discharge be landed at any place, or destroyed or rendered innocuous by the carrier without compensation and the shipper of such goods shall be liable for all damages and expenses directly or indirectly arising out of or resulting from such shipment. If any such goods shipped with such knowledge and consent shall become a danger to the ship or cargo, they may in like manner be landed at any place, or destroyed or rendered innocuous by the carrier without liability on the part of the carrier except to general average, if any.

Article IV bis

1.   The defences and limits of liability provided for in these Rules shall apply in any action against the carrier in respect of loss or damage to goods covered by a contract of carriage whether the action be founded in contract or in tort.

2.   If such an action is brought against a servant or agent of the carrier (such servant or agent not being an independent contractor), such servant or agent shall be entitled to avail himself of the defences and limits of liability which the carrier is entitled to invoke under these Rules.

3.   The aggregate of the amounts recoverable from the carrier, and such servants and agents, shall in no case exceed the limit provided for in these Rules.

4.   Nevertheless, a servant or agent of the carrier shall not be entitled to avail himself of the provisions of this article, if it is proved that the damage resulted from an act or omission of the servant or agent done with intent to cause damage or recklessly and with knowledge that damage would probably result.

Article V

A carrier shall be at liberty to surrender in whole or in part all or any of his rights and immunities or to increase any of his responsibilities and obligations under these Rules, provided such surrender or increase shall be embodied in the bill of lading issued to the shipper. The provisions of these Rules shall not be applicable to charter parties, but if bills of lading are issued in the case of a ship under a charter party they shall comply with the terms of these Rules. Nothing in these Rules shall be held to prevent the insertion in a bill of lading of any lawful provision regarding general average.

Article VI

Notwithstanding the provisions of the preceding articles, a carrier, master or agent of the carrier and a shipper shall in regard to any particular goods be at liberty to enter into any agreement in any terms as to the responsibility and liability of the carrier for such goods, and as to the rights and immunities of the carrier in respect of such goods, or his obligation as to seaworthiness, so far as this stipulation is not contrary to public policy, or the care or diligence of his servants or agents in regard to the loading, handling, stowage, carriage, custody, care and discharge of the goods carried by sea, provided that in this case no bill of lading has been or shall be issued and that the terms agreed shall be embodied in a receipt which shall be a non-negotiable document and shall be marked as such.

An agreement so entered into shall have full legal effect.

Provided that this Article shall not apply to ordinary commercial shipments made in the ordinary course of trade, but only to other shipments where the character or condition of the property to be carried or the circumstances, terms and conditions under which the carriage is to be performed are such as reasonably to justify a special agreement.

Article VII

Nothing herein contained shall prevent a carrier or a shipper from entering into any agreement, stipulation, condition, reservation or exemption as to the responsibility and liability of the carrier or the ship for the loss or damage to, or in connection with, the custody and care and handling of goods prior to the loading on, and subsequent to the discharge from, the ship on which the goods are carried by sea.

Article VIII

The provisions of these Rules shall not affect the rights and obligations of the carrier under any statute for the time being in force relating to the limitation of the liability of owners of sea-going vessels.

Article IX

These Rules shall not affect the provisions of any international Convention or national law governing liability for nuclear damage.

Article X [Scope of Application]

The provisions of these Rules shall apply to every bill of lading relating to the carriage of goods between ports in two different States if
(a)   the bill of lading is issued in a contracting State, or
(b)   the carriage is from a port in a contracting State, or
(c)   the contract contained in or evidenced by the bill of lading provides that these Rules or legislation of any State giving effect to them are to govern the contract;
whatever may be the nationality of the ship, the carrier, the shipper, the consignee, or any other interested person.

(The last two paragraphs of this Article are not reproduced. They require contracting States to apply the Rules to bills of lading mentioned in the Article and authorise them to apply the Rules to other bills of lading).

(Article 11 to 16 of the International Convention for the unification of certain rules of law relating to bills of lading signed at Brussels on August 25, 1974 are not reproduced. They deal with the coming into force of the Convention, procedure for ratification, accession and denunciation and the right to call for a fresh conference to consider amendments to the Rules contained in the Convention).

Entry into force: 1977
Ratification and binding effect: Australia, Belgium, Canada, Denmark, Ecuador, Finland, France, Greece, Italy, Japan, Latvia, Luxembourg, Netherlands, New Zealand, Norway, Poland, Singapore, Spain, Sri Lanka, Sweden, Switzerland, Syria, Tonga, United Kingdom[1]

1978 UNITED NATIONS CONVENTION ON THE CARRIAGE OF GOODS BY SEA ("Hamburg Rules")[2]

Preamble

THE STATES PARTIES TO THIS CONVENTION,
HAVING RECOGNIZED the desirability of determining by agreement certain rules relating to the carriage of goods by sea,
HAVE DECIDED to conclude a Convention for this purpose and have thereto agreed as follows:

PART I - GENERAL PROVISIONS

Article 1 Definitions

In this Convention:
1.   "Carrier" means any person by whom or in whose name a contract of carriage of goods by sea has been concluded with a shipper.
2.   "Actual carrier" means any person to whom the performance of the carriage of the goods, or of part of the carriage, has been entrusted by the carrier, and includes any other person to whom such performance has been entrusted.

---

1   The following countries apply parallel national rules without having ratified the Rules: Germany, Liberia.
2   © United Nations, 1695 UNTS p. 3, all rights reserved.

3.   "Shipper" means any person by whom or in whose name or on whose behalf a contract of carriage of goods by sea has been concluded with a carrier, or any person by whom or in whose name or on whose behalf the goods are actually delivered to the carrier in relation to the contract of carriage by sea.

4.   "Consignee" means the person entitled to take delivery of the goods.

5.   "Goods" includes live animals; where the goods are consolidated in a container, pallet or similar article of transport or where they are packed, "goods" includes such article of transport or packaging if supplied by the shipper.

6.   "Contract of carriage by sea" means any contract whereby the carrier undertakes against payment of freight to carry goods by sea from one port to another; however, a contract which involves carriage by sea and also carriage by some other means is deemed to be a contract of carriage by sea for the purposes of this Convention only in so far as it relates to the carriage by sea.

7.   "Bill of lading" means a document which evidences a contract of carriage by sea and the taking over or loading of the goods by the carrier, and by which the carrier undertakes to deliver the goods against surrender of the document. A provision in the document that the goods are to be delivered to the order of a named person, or to order, or to bearer, constitutes such an undertaking.

8.   "Writing" includes, inter alia, telegram and telex.

Article 2 Scope of Application

1.   The provisions of this Convention are applicable to all contracts of carriage by sea between two different States, if:

(a)   the port of loading as provided for in the contract of carriage by sea is located in a Contracting State, or

(b)   the port of discharge as provided for in the contract of carriage by sea is located in a Contracting State, or

(c)   one of the optional ports of discharge provided for in the contract of carriage by sea is the actual port of discharge and such port is located in a Contracting State, or

(d)   the bill of lading or other document evidencing the contract of carriage by sea is issued in a Contracting State, or

(e)   the bill of lading or other document evidencing the contract of carriage by sea provides that the provisions of this Convention or the legislation of any State giving effect to them are to govern the contract.

2.   The provisions of this Convention are applicable without regard to the nationality of the ship, the carrier, the actual carrier, the shipper, the consignee or any other interested person.

3.   The provisions of this Convention are not applicable to charter-parties. However, where a bill of lading is issued pursuant to a charter-party, the provisions of the Convention apply to such a bill of lading if it governs the relation between the carrier and the holder of the bill of lading, not being the charterer.

4.   If a contract provides for future carriage of goods in a series of shipments during an agreed period, the provisions of this Convention apply to each shipment. However, where a shipment is made under a charter-party, the provisions of paragraph 3 of this Article apply.

Article 3 Interpretation of the Convention

In the interpretation and application of the provisions of this Convention regard shall be had to its international character and to the need to promote uniformity.

PART II - LIABILITY OF THE CARRIER

Article 4 Period of Responsibility

1.   The responsibility of the carrier for the goods under this Convention covers the period during which the carrier is in charge of the goods at the port of loading, during the carriage and at the port of discharge.

2.   For the purpose of paragraph 1 of this article, the carrier is deemed to be in charge of the goods

(a) from the time he has taken over the goods from:
    (i) the shipper, or a person acting on his behalf; or
    (ii) an authority or other third party to whom, pursuant to law or regulations applicable at the port of loading, the goods must be handed over for shipment;
(b) until the time he has delivered the goods:
    (i) by handing over the goods to the consignee; or
    (ii) in cases where the consignee does not receive the goods from the carrier, by placing them at the disposal of the consignee in accordance with the contract or with the law or with the usage of the particular trade, applicable at the port of discharge; or
    (iii) by handing over the goods to an authority or other third party to whom, pursuant to law or regulations applicable at the port of discharge, the goods must be handed over.

3.   In paragraphs 1 and 2 of this article, reference to the carrier or to the consignee means, in addition to the carrier or the consignee, the servants or agents, respectively of the carrier or the consignee.

Article 5 Basis of Liability

1.   The carrier is liable for loss resulting from loss of or damage to the goods, as well as from delay in delivery, if the occurrence which caused the loss, damage or delay took place while the goods were in his charge as defined in Article 4, unless the carrier proves that he, his servants or agents took all measures that could reasonably be required to avoid the occurrence and its consequences.

2.   Delay in delivery occurs when the goods have not been delivered at the port of discharge provided for in the contract of carriage by sea within the time expressly agreed upon or, in the absence of such agreement, within the time which it would be reasonable to require of a diligent carrier, having regard to the circumstances of the case.

3.   The person entitled to make a claim for the loss of goods may treat the goods as lost if they have not been delivered as required by Article 4 within 60 consecutive days following the expiry of the time for delivery according to paragraph 2 of this article.

4.(a) The carrier is liable
    (i) for loss of or damage to the goods or delay in delivery caused by fire, if the claimant proves that the fire arose from fault or neglect on the part of the carrier, his servants or agents;
    (ii) for such loss, damage or delay in delivery which is proved by the claimant to have resulted from the fault or neglect of the carrier, his servants or agents, in taking all measures that could reasonably be required to put out the fire and avoid or mitigate its consequences.
(b) In case of fire on board the ship affecting the goods, if the claimant or the carrier so desires, a survey in accordance with shipping practices must be held into the cause and circumstances of the fire, and a copy of the surveyor's report shall be made available on demand to the carrier and the claimant.

5.   With respect to live animals, the carrier is not liable for loss, damage or delay in delivery resulting from any special risks inherent in that kind of carriage. If the carrier proves that he has complied with any special instructions given to him by the shipper respecting the animals and that, in the circumstances of the case, the loss, damage or delay in delivery could be attributed to such risks, it is presumed that the loss, damage or delay in delivery was so caused, unless there is proof that all or a part of the loss, damage or delay in delivery resulted from fault or neglect on the part of the carrier, his servants or agents.

6.   The carrier is not liable, except in general average, where loss, damage or delay in delivery resulted from measures to save life or from reasonable measures to save property at sea.

7.   Where fault or neglect on the part of the carrier, his servants or agents combines with another cause to produce loss, damage or delay in delivery the carrier is liable only to the extent that the loss, damage or delay in delivery is attributable to such fault or neglect, provided that the carrier proves the amount of the loss, damage or delay in delivery not attributable thereto.

Article 6 Limits of Liability

1.(a) The liability of the carrier for loss resulting from loss of or damage to goods according to the provisions of Article 5 is limited to an amount equivalent to 835 units of account per package or other shipping unit or 2.5 units of account per kilogramme of gross weight of the goods lost or damaged, whichever is the higher.

(b) The liability of the carrier for delay in delivery according to the provisions of Article 5 is limited to an amount equivalent to two and a half times the freight payable for the goods delayed, but not exceeding the total freight payable under the contract of carriage of goods by sea.

(c) In no case shall the aggregate liability of the carrier, under both subparagraphs (a) and (b) of this paragraph, exceed the limitation which would be established under subparagraph (a) of this paragraph for total loss of the goods with respect to which such liability was incurred.

2. For the purpose of calculating which amount is the higher in accordance with paragraph 1(a) of this article, the following rules apply:

(a) Where a container, pallet or similar article of transport is used to consolidate goods, the package or other shipping units enumerated in the bill of lading, if issued, or otherwise in any other document evidencing the contract of carriage by sea, as packed in such article of transport are deemed packages or shipping units. Except as aforesaid the goods in such article of transport are deemed one shipping unit.

(b) In cases where the article of transport itself has been lost or damaged, that article of transport, if not owned or otherwise supplied by the carrier, is considered one separate shipping unit.

3. Unit of account means the unit of account mentioned in Article 26.

4. By agreement between the carrier and the shipper, limits of liability exceeding those provided for in paragraph 1 may be fixed.

Article 7 Application to Non-contractual Claims

1. The defences and limits of liability provided for in this Convention apply in any action against the carrier in respect of loss or damage to the goods covered by the contract of carriage by sea, as well as of delay in delivery whether the action is founded in contract, in tort or otherwise.

2. If such an action is brought against a servant or agent of the carrier, such servant or agent, if he proves that he acted within the scope of his employment, is entitled to avail himself of the defences and limits of liability which the carrier is entitled to invoke under this Convention.

3. Except as provided in Article 8, the aggregate of the amounts recoverable from the carrier and from any persons referred to in paragraph 2 of this Article shall not exceed the limits of liability provided for in this Convention.

Article 8 Loss of Right to Limit Responsibility

1. The carrier is not entitled to the benefit of the limitation of liability provided for in Article 6 if it is proved that the loss, damage or delay in delivery resulted from an act or omission of the carrier done with the intent to cause such loss, damage or delay, or recklessly and with knowledge that such loss, damage or delay would probably result.

2. Notwithstanding the provisions of paragraph 2 of Article 7, a servant or agent of the carrier is not entitled to the benefit of the limitation of liability provided for in Article 6 if it is proved that the loss, damage or delay in delivery resulted from an act or omission of such servant or agent, done with the intent to cause such loss, damage or delay, or recklessly and with knowledge that such loss, damage or delay would probably result.

Article 9 Deck Cargo

1. The carrier is entitled to carry the goods on deck only if such carriage is in accordance with an agreement with the shipper or with the usage of the particular trade or is required by statutory rules or regulations.

2.   If the carrier and the shipper have agreed that the goods shall or may be carried on deck, the carrier must insert in the bill of lading or other document evidencing the contract of carriage by sea a statement to that effect. In the absence of such a statement the carrier has the burden of proving that an agreement for carriage on deck has been entered into; however, the carrier is not entitled to invoke such an agreement against a third party, including a consignee, who has acquired the bill of lading in good faith.

3.   Where the goods have been carried on deck contrary to the provisions of paragraph 1 of this Article or where the carrier may not under paragraph 2 of this Article invoke an agreement for carriage on deck, the carrier, notwithstanding the provisions of paragraph 1 of Article 5, is liable for loss of or damage to the goods, as well as for delay in delivery, resulting solely from the carriage on deck, and the extent of his liability is to be determined in accordance with the provisions of Article 6 or Article 8 of this Convention, as the case may be.

4.   Carriage of goods on deck contrary to express agreement for carriage under deck is deemed to be an act or omission of the carrier within the meaning of Article 8.

Article 10 Liability of the Carrier and Actual Carrier

1.   Where the performance of the carriage or part thereof has been entrusted to an actual carrier, whether or not in pursuance of a liberty under the contract of carriage by sea to do so, the carrier nevertheless remains responsible for the entire carriage according to the provisions of this Convention. The carrier is responsible, in relation to the carriage performed by the actual carrier, for the acts and omissions of the actual carrier and of his servants and agents acting within the scope of their employment.

2.   All the provisions of this Convention governing the responsibility of the carrier also apply to the responsibility of the actual carrier for the carriage performed by him. The provisions of paragraphs 2 and 3 of Article 7 and of paragraph 2 of Article 8 apply if an action is brought against a servant or agent of the actual carrier.

3.   Any special agreement under which the carrier assumes obligations not imposed by this Convention or waives rights conferred by this Convention affects the actual carrier only if agreed to by him expressly and in writing. Whether or not the actual carrier has so agreed, the carrier nevertheless remains bound by the obligations or waivers resulting from such special agreement.

4.   Where and to the extent that both the carrier and the actual carrier are liable, their liability is joint and several.

5.   The aggregate of the amounts recoverable from the carrier, the actual carrier and their servants and agents shall not exceed the limits of liability provided for in this Convention.

6.   Nothing in this Article shall prejudice any right of recourse as between the carrier and the actual carrier.

Article 11 Through Carriage

1.   Notwithstanding the provisions of paragraph 1 of Article 10, where a contract of carriage by sea provides explicitly that a specified part of the carriage covered by the said contract is to be performed by a named person other than the carrier, the contract may also provide that the carrier is not liable for loss, damage or delay in delivery caused by an occurrence which takes place while the goods are in the charge of the actual carrier during such part of the carriage. Nevertheless, any stipulation limiting or excluding such liability is without effect if no judicial proceedings can be instituted against the actual carrier in a court competent under paragraph 1 or 2 of Article 21. The burden of proving that any loss, damage or delay in delivery has been caused by such an occurrence rests upon the carrier.

2.   The actual carrier is responsible in accordance with the provisions of paragraph 2 of Article 10 for loss, damage or delay in delivery caused by an occurrence which takes place while the goods are in his charge.

PART III - LIABILITY OF THE SHIPPER

Article 12 General Rule

The shipper is not liable for loss sustained by the carrier or the actual carrier, or for damage sustained by the ship, unless such loss or damage was caused by the fault or neglect of the shipper, his servants or agents. Nor is any servant or agent of the shipper liable for such loss or damage unless the loss or damage was caused by fault or neglect on his part.

Article 13 Special Rules on Dangerous Goods

1.   The shipper must mark or label in a suitable manner dangerous goods as dangerous.
2.   Where the shipper hands over dangerous goods to the carrier or an actual carrier, as the case may be, the shipper must inform him of the dangerous character of the goods and, if necessary, of the precautions to be taken. If the shipper fails to do so and such carrier or actual carrier does not otherwise have knowledge of their dangerous character:
(a)   the shipper is liable to the carrier and any actual carrier for the loss resulting from the shipment of such goods, and
(b)   the goods may at any time be unloaded, destroyed or rendered innocuous, as the circumstances may require, without payment of compensation.
3.   The provisions of paragraph 2 of this Article may not be invoked by any person if during the carriage he has taken the goods in his charge with knowledge of their dangerous character.
4.   If, in cases where the provisions of paragraph 2, subparagraph (b), of this Article do not apply or may not be invoked, dangerous goods become an actual danger to life or property, they may be unloaded, destroyed or rendered innocuous, as the circumstances may require, without payment of compensation except where there is an obligation to contribute in general average or where the carrier is liable in accordance with the provisions of Article 5.

PART IV - TRANSPORT DOCUMENTS

Article 14 Issue of Bill of Lading

1.   When the carrier or the actual carrier takes the goods in his charge, the carrier must, on demand of the shipper, issue to the shipper a bill of lading.
2.   The bill of lading may be signed by a person having authority from the carrier. A bill of lading signed by the master of the ship carrying the goods is deemed to have been signed on behalf of the carrier.
3.   The signature on the bill of lading may be in handwriting, printed in facsimile, perforated, stamped, in symbols, or made by an other mechanical or electronic means, if not inconsistent with the law of the country where the bill of lading is issued.

Article 15 Contents of Bill of Lading

1.   The bill of lading must include, inter alia, the following particulars:
(a)   the general nature of the goods, the leading marks necessary for identification of the goods, an express statement, if applicable, as to the dangerous character of the goods, the number of packages or pieces, and the weight of the goods or their quantity otherwise expressed, all such particulars as furnished by the shipper;
(b)   the apparent condition of the goods;
(c)   the name and principal place of business of the carrier;
(d)   the name of the shipper;
(e)   the consignee if named by the shipper;
(f)   the port of loading under the contract of carriage by sea and the date on which the goods were taken over by the carrier at the port of loading;
(g)   the port of discharge under the contract of carriage by sea;
(h)   the number of originals of the bill of lading, if more than one;
(i)   the place of issuance of the bill of lading;
(j)   the signature of the carrier or a person acting on his behalf;
(k)   the freight to the extent payable by the consignee or other indication that freight is payable by him;

(l)   the statement referred to in paragraph 3 of Article 23;
(m) the statement, if applicable, that the goods shall or may be carried on deck;
(n)   the date or the period of delivery of the goods at the port of discharge if expressly agreed
       upon between the parties; and
(o)   any increased limit or limits of liability where agreed in accordance with paragraph 4 of
       Article 6.
2.   After the goods have been loaded on board, if the shipper so demands, the carrier must
issue to the shipper a "shipped" bill of lading which, in addition to the particulars required under
paragraph 1 of this article, must state that the goods are on board a named ship or ships, and
the date or dates of loading. If the carrier has previously issued to the shipper a bill of lading or
other document of title with respect to any of such goods, on request of the carrier, the shipper
must surrender such document in exchange for a "shipped" bill of lading. The carrier may
amend any previously issued document in order to meet the shipper's demand for a "shipped"
bill of lading if, as amended, such document includes all the information required to be contained in a "shipped" bill of lading.
3.   The absence in the bill of lading of one or more particulars referred to in this Article does
not affect the legal character of the document as a bill of lading provided that it nevertheless
meets the requirements set out in paragraph 7 of Article 1.

Article 16 Bills of Lading: Reservations and Evidentiary Effect
1.   If the bill of lading contains particulars concerning the general nature, leading marks, number of packages or pieces, weight or quantity of the goods which the carrier or other person
issuing the bill of lading on his behalf knows or has reasonable grounds to suspect do not accurately represent the goods actually taken over or, where a "shipped" bill of lading is issued, loaded, or if he had no reasonable means of checking such particulars, the carrier or such other
person must insert in the bill of lading a reservation specifying these inaccuracies, grounds of
suspicion or the absence of reasonable means of checking.
2.   If the carrier or other person issuing the bill of lading on his behalf fails to note on the bill of
lading the apparent condition of the goods, he is deemed to have noted on the bill of lading
that the goods were in apparent good condition.
3.   Except for particulars in respect of which and to the extent to which a reservation permitted under paragraph 1 of this Article has been entered:
(a)   the bill of lading is prima facie evidence of the taking over or, where a "shipped" bill of
       lading is issued, loading, by the carrier of the goods as described in the bill of lading; and
(b)   proof to the contrary by the carrier is not admissible if the bill of lading has been
       transferred to a third party, including a consignee, who in good faith has acted in reliance
       on the description of the goods therein.
4.   A bill of lading which does not, as provided in paragraph 1, subparagraph (k) of Article 15,
set forth the freight or otherwise indicate that freight is payable by the consignee or does not
set forth demurrage incurred at the port of loading payable by the consignee, is prima facie evidence that no freight or such demurrage is payable by him. However, proof to the contrary by
the carrier is not admissible when the bill of lading has been transferred to a third party, including a consignee, who in good faith has acted in reliance on the absence in the bill of lading of
any such indication.

Article 17 Guarantees by the Shipper
1.   The shipper is deemed to have guaranteed to the carrier the accuracy of particulars
relating to the general nature of the goods, their marks, number, weight and quantity as
furnished by him for insertion in the bill of lading. The shipper must indemnify the carrier
against the loss resulting from inaccuracies in such particulars. The shipper remains liable even if
the bill of lading has been transferred by him. The right of the carrier to such indemnity in no
way limits his liability under the contract of carriage by sea to any person other than the shipper.
2.   Any letter of guarantee or agreement by which the shipper undertakes to indemnify the
carrier against loss resulting from the issuance of the bill of lading by the carrier, or by a person

acting on his behalf, without entering a reservation relating to particulars furnished by the shipper for insertion in the bill of lading, or to the apparent condition of the goods, is void and of no effect as against any third party, including a consignee, to whom the bill of lading has been transferred.

3.   Such letter of guarantee or agreement is valid as against the shipper unless the carrier or the person acting on his behalf, by omitting the reservation referred to in paragraph 2 of this article, intends to defraud a third party, including a consignee, who acts in reliance on the description of the goods in the bill of lading. In the latter case, if the reservation omitted relates to particulars furnished by the shipper for insertion in the bill of lading, the carrier has no right of indemnity from the shipper pursuant to paragraph 1 of this article.

4.   In the case of intended fraud referred to in paragraph 3 of this Article the carrier is liable, without the benefit of the limitation of liability provided for in this Convention, for the loss incurred by a third party, including a consignee, because he has acted in reliance on the description of the goods in the bill of lading.

Article 18 Documents Other than Bills of Lading

Where a carrier issues a document other than a bill of lading to evidence the receipt of the goods to be carried, such a document is prima facie evidence of the conclusion of the contract of carriage by sea and the taking over by the carrier of the goods as therein described.

PART V - CLAIMS AND ACTIONS
Article 19 Notice of Loss, Damage or Delay

1.   Unless notice of loss or damage, specifying the general nature of such loss or damage, is given in writing by the consignee to the carrier not later than the working day after the day when the goods were handed over to the consignee, such handing over is prima facie evidence of the delivery by the carrier of the goods as described in the document of transport or, if no such document has been issued, in good condition.

2.   Where the loss or damage is not apparent, the provisions of paragraph 1 of this Article apply correspondingly if notice in writing is not given within 15 consecutive days after the day when the goods were handed over to the consignee.

3.   If the state of the goods at the time they were handed over to the consignee has been the subject of a joint survey or inspection by the parties, notice in writing need not be given of loss or damage ascertained during such survey or inspection.

4.   In the case of any actual or apprehended loss or damage the carrier and the consignee must give all reasonable facilities to each other for inspecting and tallying the goods.

5.   No compensation shall be payable for loss resulting from delay in delivery unless a notice has been given in writing to the carrier within 60 consecutive days after the day when the goods were handed over to the consignee.

6.   If the goods have been delivered by an actual carrier, any notice given under this Article to him shall have the same effect as if it had been given to the carrier, and any notice given to the carrier shall have effect as if given to such actual carrier.

7. Unless notice of loss or damage, specifying the general nature of the loss or damage, is given in writing by the carrier or actual carrier to the shipper not later than 90 consecutive days after the occurrence of such loss or damage or after the delivery of the goods in accordance with paragraph 2 of Article 4, whichever is later, the failure to give such notice is prima facie evidence that the carrier or the actual carrier has sustained no loss or damage due to the fault or neglect of the shipper, his servants or agents.

8.   For the purpose of this article, notice given to a person acting on the carrier's or the actual carrier's behalf, including the master or the officer in charge of the ship, or to a person acting on the shipper's behalf is deemed to have been given to the carrier, to the actual carrier or to the shipper, respectively.

Article 20 Limitation of Actions

1.   Any action relating to carriage of goods under this Convention is time-barred if judicial or arbitral proceedings have not been instituted within a period of two years.

2.   The limitation period commences on the day on which the carrier has delivered the goods or part thereof or, in cases where no goods have been delivered, on the last day on which the goods should have been delivered.

3.   The day on which the limitation period commences is not included in the period.

4.   The person against whom a claim is made may at any time during the running of the limitation period extend that period by a declaration in writing to the claimant. This period may be further extended by another declaration or declarations.

5.   An action for indemnity by a person held liable may be instituted even after the expiration of the limitation period provided for in the preceding paragraphs if instituted within the time allowed by the law of the State where proceedings are instituted. However, the time allowed shall not be less than 90 days commencing from the day when the person instituting such action for indemnity has settled the claim or has been served with process in the action against himself.

Article 21 Jurisdiction

1.   In judicial proceedings relating to carriage of goods under this Convention the plaintiff, at his option, may institute an action in a court which, according to the law of the State where the court is situated, is competent and within the jurisdiction of which is situated one of the following places:
(a)   the principal place of business or, in the absence thereof, the habitual residence of the defendant; or
(b)   the place where the contract was made provided that the defendant has there a place of business, branch or agency through which the contract was made; or
(c)   the port of loading or the port of discharge; or
(d)   any additional place designated for that purpose in the contract of carriage by sea.
2.(a) Notwithstanding the preceding provisions of this article, an action may be instituted in the courts of any port or place in a Contracting State at which the carrying vessel or any other vessel of the same ownership may have been arrested in accordance with applicable rules of the law of that State and of international law. However, in such a case, at the petition of the defendant, the claimant must remove the action, at his choice, to one of the jurisdictions referred to in paragraph 1 of this Article for the determination of the claim, but before such removal the defendant must furnish security sufficient to ensure payment of any judgement that may subsequently be awarded to the claimant in the action.
(b)   All questions relating to the sufficiency or otherwise of the security shall be determined by the court of the port or place of the arrest.
3.   No judicial proceedings relating to carriage of goods under this Convention may be instituted in a place not specified in paragraph 1 or 2 of this article. The provisions of this paragraph do not constitute an obstacle to the jurisdiction of the Contracting States for provisional or protective measures.
4.(a) Where an action has been instituted in a court competent under paragraph 1 or 2 of this Article or where judgement has been delivered by such a court, no new action may be started between the same parties on the same grounds unless the judgement of the court before which the first action was instituted is not enforceable in the country in which the new proceedings are instituted;
(b)   for the purpose of this Article the institution of measures with a view to obtaining enforcement of a judgement is not to be considered as the starting of a new action;
(c)   for the purpose of this article, the removal of an action to a different court within the same country, or to a court in another country, in accordance with paragraph 2(a) of this article, is not to be considered as the starting of a new action.

5.   Notwithstanding the provisions of the preceding paragraphs, an agreement made by the parties, after a claim under the contract of carriage by sea has arisen, which designates the place where the claimant may institute an action, is effective.

Article 22 Arbitration

1.   Subject to the provisions of this article, parties may provide by agreement evidenced in writing that any dispute that may arise relating to carriage of goods under this Convention shall be referred to arbitration.

2.   Where a charter-party contains a provision that disputes arising thereunder shall be referred to arbitration and a bill of lading issued pursuant to the charter-party does not contain a special annotation providing that such provision shall be binding upon the holder of the bill of lading, the carrier may not invoke such provision as against a holder having acquired the bill of lading in good faith.

3.   The arbitration proceedings shall, at the option of the claimant, be instituted at one of the following places:

(a)   a place in a State within whose territory is situated:
   (i)   the principal place of business of the defendant or, in the absence thereof, the habitual residence of the defendant; or
   (ii)   the place where the contract was made, provided that the defendant has there a place of business, branch or agency through which the contract was made; or
   (iii) the port of loading or the port of discharge; or
(b)   any place designated for that purpose in the arbitration clause or agreement.

4.   The arbitrator or arbitration tribunal shall apply the rules of this Convention.

5.   The provisions of paragraphs 3 and 4 of this Article are deemed to be part of every arbitration clause or agreement, and any term of such clause or agreement which is inconsistent therewith is null and void.

6.   Nothing in this Article affects the validity of an agreement relating to arbitration made by the parties after the claim under the contract of carriage by sea has arisen.

PART VI - SUPPLEMENTARY PROVISIONS

Article 23 Contractual Stipulations

1.   Any stipulation in a contract of carriage by sea, in a bill of lading, or in any other document evidencing the contract of carriage by sea is null and void to the extent that it derogates, directly or indirectly, from the provisions of this Convention. The nullity of such a stipulation does not affect the validity of the other provisions of the contract or document of which it forms a part. A clause assigning benefit of insurance of the goods in favour of the carrier, or any similar clause, is null and void.

2.   Notwithstanding the provisions of paragraph 1 of this article, a carrier may increase his responsibilities and obligations under this Convention.

3.   Where a bill of lading or any other document evidencing the contract of carriage by sea is issued, it must contain a statement that the carriage is subject to the provisions of this Convention which nullify any stipulation derogating therefrom to the detriment of the shipper or the consignee.

4.   Where the claimant in respect of the goods has incurred loss as a result of a stipulation which is null and void by virtue of the present article, or as a result of the omission of the statement referred to in paragraph 3 of this article, the carrier must pay compensation to the extent required in order to give the claimant compensation in accordance with the provisions of this Convention for any loss of or damage to the goods as well as for delay in delivery. The carrier must, in addition, pay compensation for costs incurred by the claimant for the purpose of exercising his right, provided that costs incurred in the action where the foregoing provision is invoked are to be determined in accordance with the law of the State where proceedings are instituted.

Article 24 General Average

1.   Nothing in this Convention shall prevent the application of provisions in the contract of carriage by sea or national law regarding the adjustment of general average.
2.   With the exception of Article 20, the provisions of this Convention relating to the liability of the carrier for loss of or damage to the goods also determine whether the consignee may refuse contribution in general average and the liability of the carrier to indemnify the consignee in respect of any such contribution made or any salvage paid.

Article 25 Other Conventions

1.   This Convention does not modify the rights or duties of the carrier, the actual carrier and their servants and agents, provided for in international conventions or national law relating to the limitation of liability of owners of seagoing ships.
2.   The provisions of articles 21 and 22 of this Convention do not prevent the application of the mandatory provisions of any other multilateral convention already in force at the date of this Convention [March 31, 1978] relating to matters dealt with in the said articles, provided that the dispute arises exclusively between parties having their principal place of business in States members of such other convention. However, this paragraph does not affect the application of paragraph 4 of Article 22 of this Convention.
3.   No liability shall arise under the provisions of this Convention for damage caused by a nuclear incident if the operator of a nuclear installation is liable for such damage:
(a)   under either the Paris Convention of 29 July 1960 on Third Party Liability in the Field of Nuclear Energy as amended by the Additional Protocol of 28 January 1964 or the Vienna Convention of 21 May 1963 on Civil Liability for Nuclear Damage, or
(b)   by virtue of national law governing the liability for such damage, provided that such law is in all respects as favourable to persons who may suffer damage as either the Paris or Vienna Conventions.
4.   No liability shall arise under the provisions of this Convention for any loss of or damage to or delay in delivery of luggage for which the carrier is responsible under any international convention or national law relating to the carriage of passengers and their luggage by sea.
5.   Nothing contained in this Convention prevents a Contracting State from applying any other international convention which is already in force at the date of this Convention and which applies mandatorily to contracts of carriage of goods primarily by a mode of transport other than transport by sea. This provision also applies to any subsequent revision or amendment of such international convention.

Article 26 Unit of Account

1.   The unit of account referred to in Article 6 of this Convention is the Special Drawing Right as defined by the International Monetary Fund. The amounts mentioned in Article 6 are to be converted into the national currency of a State according to the value of such currency at the date of judgement or the date agreed upon by the parties. The value of a national currency, in terms of the Special Drawing Right, of a Contracting State which is a member of the International Monetary Fund is to be calculated in accordance with the method of valuation applied by the International Monetary Fund in effect at the date in question for its operations and transactions. The value of a national currency in terms of the Special Drawing Right of a Contracting State which is not a member of the International Monetary Fund is to be calculated in a manner determined by that State.
2.   Nevertheless, those States which are not members of the International Monetary Fund and whose law does not permit the application of the provisions of paragraph 1 of this Article may, at the time of signature, or at the time of ratification, acceptance, approval or accession or at any time thereafter, declare that the limits of liability provided for in this Convention to be applied in their territories shall be fixed as:

12,500 monetary units per package or other shipping unit or 37.5 monetary units per kilogramme of gross weight of the goods.

3.   The monetary unit referred to in paragraph 2 of this Article corresponds to sixty-five and a half milligrammes of gold of millesimal fineness nine hundred. The conversion of the amounts referred to in paragraph 2 into the national currency is to be made according to the law of the State concerned.

4.   The calculation mentioned in the last sentence of paragraph 1 and the conversion mentioned in paragraph 3 of this Article is to be made in such a manner as to express in the national currency of the Contracting State as far as possible the same real value for the amounts in Article 6 as is expressed there in units of account. Contracting States must communicate to the depositary the manner of calculation pursuant to paragraph 1 of this article, or the result of the conversion mentioned in paragraph 3 of this article, as the case may be, at the time of signature or when depositing their instruments of ratification, acceptance, approval or accession, or when availing themselves of the option provided for in paragraph 2 of this Article and whenever there is a change in the manner of such calculation or in the result of such conversion.

PART VII - FINAL CLAUSES

Article 27 Depositary

The Secretary General of the United Nations is hereby designated as the depositary of this Convention.

Article 28 Signature, Ratification, Acceptance, Approval, Accession

1.   This Convention is open for signature by all States until 30 April 1979 at the Headquarters of the United Nations, New York.

2.   This Convention is subject to ratification, acceptance or approval by the signatory States.

3.   After 30 April 1979, this Convention will be open for accession by all States which are not signatory States.

4.   Instruments of ratification, acceptance, approval and accession are to be deposited with the Secretary-General of the United Nations.

Article 29 Reservations

No reservations may be made to this Convention.

Article 30 Entry into Force

1.   This Convention enters into force on the first day of the month following the expiration of one year from the date of deposit of the 20th instrument of ratification, acceptance, approval or accession.

2.   For each State which becomes a Contracting State to this Convention after the date of deposit of the 20th instrument of ratification, acceptance approval or accession, this Convention enters into force on the first day of the month following the expiration of one year after the deposit of the appropriate instrument on behalf of that State.

3.   Each Contracting State shall apply the provisions of this Convention to contracts of carriage by sea concluded on or after the date of the entry into force of this Convention in respect of that State.

Article 31 Denunciation of Other Conventions

1.   Upon becoming a Contracting State to this Convention, any State party to the International Convention for the Unification of Certain Rules relating to Bills of Lading signed at Brussels on 25 August 1924 (1924 Convention) must notify the Government of Belgium as the depositary of the 1924 Convention of its denunciation of the said Convention with a declaration that the denunciation is to take effect as from the date when this Convention enters into force in respect of that State.

2.   Upon the entry into force of this Convention under paragraph 1 of Article 30, the depositary of this Convention must notify the Government of Belgium as the depositary of the 1924 Convention of the date of such entry into force, and of the names of the Contracting States in respect of which the Convention has entered into force.

3.   The provisions of paragraphs 1 and 2 of this Article apply correspondingly in respect of States parties to the Protocol signed on 23 February 1968 to amend the International Convention

for the Unification of Certain Rules relating to Bills of Lading signed at Brussels on 25 August 1924.

4.   Notwithstanding Article 2 of this Convention, for the purposes of paragraph 1 of this article, a Contracting State may, if it deems it desirable, defer the denunciation of the 1924 Convention and of the 1924 Convention as modified by the 1968 Protocol for a maximum period of five years from the entry into force of this Convention. It will then notify the Government of Belgium of its intention. During this transitory period, it must apply to the Contracting States this Convention to the exclusion of any other one.

Article 32 Revision and Amendment

1.   At the request of not less than one-third of the Contracting States to this Convention, the depositary shall convene a conference of the Contracting States for revising or amending it.

2.   Any instrument of ratification, acceptance, approval or accession deposited after the entry into force of an amendment to this Convention, is deemed to apply to the Convention as amended.

Article 33 Revision of the Limitation Amounts and Unit of Account or Monetary Unit

1.   Notwithstanding the provisions of Article 32, a conference only for the purpose of altering the amount specified in Article 6 and paragraph 2 of Article 26, or of substituting either or both of the units defined in paragraphs 1 and 3 of Article 26 by other units is to be convened by the depositary in accordance with paragraph 2 of this article. An alteration of the amounts shall be made only because of a significant change in their real value.

2.   A revision conference is to be convened by the depositary when not less than one-fourth of the Contracting States so request.

3.   Any decision by the conference must be taken by a two-thirds majority of the participating States. The amendment is communicated by the depositary to all the Contracting States for acceptance and to all the States signatories of the Convention for information.

4.   Any amendment adopted enters into force on the first day of the month following one year after its acceptance by two-thirds of the Contracting States. Acceptance is to be effected by the deposit of a formal instrument to that effect, with the depositary.

5.   After entry into force of an amendment a Contracting State which has accepted the amendment is entitled to apply the Convention as amended in its relations with Contracting States which have not within six months after the adoption of the amendment notified the depositary that they are not bound by the amendment.

6.   Any instrument of ratification, acceptance, approval or accession deposited after the entry into force of an amendment to this Convention, is deemed to apply to the Convention as amended.

Article 34 Denunciation

1.   A Contracting State may denounce this Convention at any time by means of a notification in writing addressed to the depositary.

2.   The denunciation takes effect on the first day of the month following the expiration of one year after the notification is received by the depositary. Where a longer period is specified in the notification, the denunciation takes effect upon the expiration of such longer period after the notification is received by the depositary.

DONE at Hamburg, this thirty-first day of March one thousand nine hundred and seventy-eight, in a single original, of which the Arabic, Chinese, English, French, Russian and Spanish texts are equally authentic.

IN WITNESS WHEREOF the undersigned plenipotentiaries, being duly authorized by their respective Governments, have signed the present Convention.

COMMON UNDERSTANDING ADOPTED BY THE UNITED NATIONS CONFERENCE ON THE CAR-
RIAGE OF GOODS BY SEA
It is the common understanding that the liability of the carrier under this Convention is based
on the principle of presumed fault or neglect. This means that, as a rule, the burden of proof
rests on the carrier but, with respect to certain cases, the provisions of the Convention modify
this rule.

Entry into force: 1 November 1992
Ratifications and binding effect: Albania (2007), Austria (1994), Barbados (1992), Botswana
(1992), Burkina Faso (1992), Burundi (1999), Cameroon (1994), Chile (1992), Czech Republic
(1996), Dominican Republic (2008), Egypt (1992), Gambia (1997), Georgia (1997), Guinea (1992),
Hungary (1992), Jordan (2002), Kazakhstan (2009), Kenya (1992), Lebanon (1992), Lesotho
(1992), Liberia (2006), Malawi (1992), Morocco (1992), Nigeria (1992), Paraguay (2006), Romania
(1992), Senegal (1992), Sierra Leone (1992), St. Vincent and the Grenadines (2001), Syria (2003),
Tanzania (1992), Tunisia (1992), Uganda (1992), Zambia (1992)[1]

2009 UNITED NATIONS CONVENTION ON CONTRACTS FOR THE INTERNATIONAL CARRIAGE OF GOODS WHOLLY OR PARTLY BY SEA ("Rotterdam Rules")[2]

THE GENERAL ASSEMBLY,
RECALLING its resolution 2205 (XXI) of 17 December 1966, by which it established the United Nations
Commission on International Trade Law with a mandate to further the progressive harmonization and
unification of the law of international trade and in that respect to bear in mind the interests of all peoples,
in particular those of developing countries, in the extensive development of international trade,
CONCERNED that the current legal regime governing the international carriage of goods by sea lacks uniformity and fails to adequately take into account modern transport practices, including containerization,
door-to-door transport contracts and the use of electronic transport documents,
NOTING that the development of international trade on the basis of equality and mutual benefit is an important element in promoting friendly relations among States,
CONVINCED that the adoption of uniform rules to modernize and harmonize the rules that govern the
international carriage of goods involving a sea leg would enhance legal certainty, improve efficiency and
commercial predictability in the international carriage of goods and reduce legal obstacles to the flow of
international trade among all States,
BELIEVING that the adoption of uniform rules to govern international contracts of carriage wholly or partly
by sea will promote legal certainty, improve the efficiency of international carriage of goods and facilitate
new access opportunities for previously remote parties and markets, thus playing a fundamental role in
promoting trade and economic development, both domestically and internationally,
NOTING that shippers and carriers do not have the benefit of a binding and balanced universal regime to
support the operation of contracts of carriage involving various modes of transport,
RECALLING that, at its thirty-fourth and thirty-fifth sessions, in 2001 and 2002, the Commission decided to
prepare an international legislative instrument governing door-to-door transport operations that involve
a sea leg,
RECOGNIZING that all States and interested international organizations were invited to participate in the
preparation of the draft Convention on Contracts for the International Carriage of Goods Wholly or Partly
by Sea and in the forty-first session of the Commission, either as members or as observers, with a full opportunity to speak and make proposals,
NOTING WITH SATISFACTION that the text of the draft Convention was circulated for comment to all
States Members of the United Nations and intergovernmental organizations invited to attend the mee-

---

1   The following countries have signed but not yet ratified the Convention as of July 2013: Brazil, Democratic Repu-
     blic of Congo, Denmark, Ecuador, Finland, France, Germany, Ghana, Holy See, Madagascar, Mexico, Norway,
     Pakistan, Panama, Philippines, Portugal, Singapore, Slovakia, Sweden, United States of America, and Venezuela.
2   © United Nations, Doc. A/RES/63/122, all rights reserved.

tings of the Commission as observers, and that the comments received were before the Commission at its forty-first session,

TAKING NOTE WITH SATISFACTION of the decision of the Commission at its forty-first session to submit the draft Convention to the General Assembly for its consideration,

TAKING NOTE of the draft Convention approved by the Commission,

EXPRESSING ITS APPRECIATION to the Government of the Netherlands for its offer to host a signing ceremony for the Convention in Rotterdam,

1. COMMENDS the United Nations Commission on International Trade Law for preparing the draft Convention on Contracts for the International Carriage of Goods Wholly or Partly by Sea;

2. ADOPTS the United Nations Convention on Contracts for the International Carriage of Goods Wholly or Partly by Sea, contained in the annex to the present resolution;

3. AUTHORIZES a ceremony for the opening for signature to be held on 23 September 2009 in Rotterdam, the Netherlands, and recommends that the rules embodied in the Convention be known as the "Rotterdam Rules";

4. CALLS UPON all Governments to consider becoming party to the Convention.

67th plenary meeting 11 December 2008

Annex
UNITED NATIONS CONVENTION ON CONTRACTS FOR THE INTERNATIONAL CARRIAGE OF GOODS WHOLLY OR PARTLY BY SEA

THE STATES PARTIES TO THIS CONVENTION,

REAFFIRMING their belief that international trade on the basis of equality and mutual benefit is an important element in promoting friendly relations among States,

CONVINCED that the progressive harmonization and unification of international trade law, in reducing or removing legal obstacles to the flow of international trade, significantly contributes to universal economic cooperation among all States on a basis of equality, equity and common interest, and to the well-being of all peoples,

RECOGNIZING the significant contribution of the International Convention for the Unification of Certain Rules of Law relating to Bills of Lading, signed in Brussels on 25 August 1924, and its Protocols, and of the United Nations Convention on the Carriage of Goods by Sea, signed in Hamburg on 31 March 1978, to the harmonization of the law governing the carriage of goods by sea,

MINDFUL of the technological and commercial developments that have taken place since the adoption of those conventions and of the need to consolidate and modernize them,

Noting that shippers and carriers do not have the benefit of a binding universal regime to support the operation of contracts of maritime carriage involving other modes of transport,

BELIEVING that the adoption of uniform rules to govern international contracts of carriage wholly or partly by sea will promote legal certainty, improve the efficiency of international carriage of goods and facilitate new access opportunities for previously remote parties and markets, thus playing a fundamental role in promoting trade and economic development, both domestically and internationally,

HAVE AGREED as follows:

Chapter 1 General Provisions
Article 1 Definitions

For the purposes of this Convention:

1.   "Contract of carriage" means a contract in which a carrier, against the payment of freight, undertakes to carry goods from one place to another. The contract shall provide for carriage by sea and may provide for carriage by other modes of transport in addition to the sea carriage.

2.   "Volume contract" means a contract of carriage that provides for the carriage of a specified quantity of goods in a series of shipments during an agreed period of time. The specification of the quantity may include a minimum, a maximum or a certain range.

3.   "Liner transportation" means a transportation service that is offered to the public through publication or similar means and includes transportation by ships operating on a regular schedule between specified ports in accordance with publicly available timetables of sailing dates.

4.   "Non-liner transportation" means any transportation that is not liner transportation.

5.   "Carrier" means a person that enters into a contract of carriage with a shipper.

6.(a) "Performing party" means a person other than the carrier that performs or undertakes to perform any of the carrier's obligations under a contract of carriage with respect to the receipt, loading, handling, stowage, carriage, care, unloading or delivery of the goods, to the extent that such person acts, either directly or indirectly, at the carrier's request or under the carrier's supervision or control.

(b)   "Performing party" does not include any person that is retained, directly or indirectly, by a shipper, by a documentary shipper, by the controlling party or by the consignee instead of by the carrier.

7.   "Maritime performing party" means a performing party to the extent that it performs or undertakes to perform any of the carrier's obligations during the period between the arrival of the goods at the port of loading of a ship and their departure from the port of discharge of a ship. An inland carrier is a maritime performing party only if it performs or undertakes to perform its services exclusively within a port area.

8.   "Shipper" means a person that enters into a contract of carriage with a carrier.

9.   "Documentary shipper" means a person, other than the shipper, that accepts to be named as "shipper" in the transport document or electronic transport record.

10.   "Holder" means:

(a)   A person that is in possession of a negotiable transport document; and (i) if the document is an order document, is identified in it as the shipper or the consignee, or is the person to which the document is duly endorsed; or (ii) if the document is a blank endorsed order document or bearer document, is the bearer thereof; or

(b)   The person to which a negotiable electronic transport record has been issued or transferred in accordance with the procedures referred to in Article 9, paragraph 1.

11.   "Consignee" means a person entitled to delivery of the goods under a contract of carriage or a transport document or electronic transport record.

12.   "Right of control" of the goods means the right under the contract of carriage to give the carrier instructions in respect of the goods in accordance with chapter 10.

13.   "Controlling party" means the person that pursuant to Article 51 is entitled to exercise the right of control.

14.   "Transport document" means a document issued under a contract of carriage by the carrier that:

(a)   Evidences the carrier's or a performing party's receipt of goods under a contract of carriage; and

(b)   Evidences or contains a contract of carriage.

15.   "Negotiable transport document" means a transport document that indicates, by wording such as "to order" or "negotiable" or other appropriate wording recognized as having the same effect by the law applicable to the document, that the goods have been consigned to the order of the shipper, to the order of the consignee, or to bearer, and is not explicitly stated as being "non-negotiable" or "not negotiable".

16.   "Non-negotiable transport document" means a transport document that is not a negotiable transport document.

17.   "Electronic communication" means information generated, sent, received or stored by electronic, optical, digital or similar means with the result that the information communicated is accessible so as to be usable for subsequent reference.

18.   "Electronic transport record" means information in one or more messages issued by electronic communication under a contract of carriage by a carrier, including information logically associated with the electronic transport record by attachments or otherwise linked to the electronic transport record contemporaneously with or subsequent to its issue by the carrier, so as to become part of the electronic transport record, that:

(a)   Evidences the carrier's or a performing party's receipt of goods under a contract of carriage; and

(b)   Evidences or contains a contract of carriage.

19.   "Negotiable electronic transport record" means an electronic transport record:

(a)   That indicates, by wording such as "to order", or "negotiable", or other appropriate wording recognized as having the same effect by the law applicable to the record, that the goods have been consigned to the order of the shipper or to the order of the consignee, and is not explicitly stated as being "non-negotiable" or "not negotiable"; and

(b)   The use of which meets the requirements of Article 9, paragraph 1.

20.   "Non-negotiable electronic transport record" means an electronic transport record that is not a negotiable electronic transport record.

21.   The "issuance" of a negotiable electronic transport record means the issuance of the record in accordance with procedures that ensure that the record is subject to exclusive control from its creation until it ceases to have any effect or validity.

22.   The "transfer" of a negotiable electronic transport record means the transfer of exclusive control over the record.

23.   "Contract particulars" means any information relating to the contract of carriage or to the goods (including terms, notations, signatures and endorsements) that is in a transport document or an electronic transport record.

24.   "Goods" means the wares, merchandise, and articles of every kind whatsoever that a carrier undertakes to carry under a contract of carriage and includes the packing and any equipment and container not supplied by or on behalf of the carrier.

25.   "Ship" means any vessel used to carry goods by sea.

26.   "Container" means any type of container, transportable tank or flat, swapbody, or any similar unit load used to consolidate goods, and any equipment ancillary to such unit load.

27.   "Vehicle" means a road or railroad cargo vehicle.

28.   "Freight" means the remuneration payable to the carrier for the carriage of goods under a contract of carriage.

29.   "Domicile" means (a) a place where a company or other legal person or association of natural or legal persons has its (i) statutory seat or place of incorporation or central registered office, whichever is applicable, (ii) central administration or (iii) principal place of business, and (b) the habitual residence of a natural person.

30.   "Competent court" means a court in a Contracting State that, according to the rules on the internal allocation of jurisdiction among the courts of that State, may exercise jurisdiction over the dispute.

Article 2 Interpretation of this Convention

In the interpretation of this Convention, regard is to be had to its international character and to the need to promote uniformity in its application and the observance of good faith in international trade.

Article 3 Form Requirements

The notices, confirmation, consent, agreement, declaration and other communications referred to in articles 19, paragraph 2; 23, paragraphs 1 to 4; 36, subparagraphs 1 (b), (c) and (d); 40, sub-paragraph 4 (b); 44; 48, paragraph 3; 51, subparagraph 1 (b); 59, paragraph 1; 63; 66; 67, paragraph 2; 75, paragraph 4; and 80, paragraphs 2 and 5, shall be in writing. Electronic communications may be used for these purposes, provided that the use of such means is with the consent of the person by which it is communicated and of the person to which it is communicated.

Article 4 Applicability of Defences and Limits of Liability

1.   Any provision of this Convention that may provide a defence for, or limit the liability of, the carrier applies in any judicial or arbitral proceeding, whether founded in contract, in tort, or otherwise, that is instituted in respect of loss of, damage to, or delay in delivery of goods covered by a contract of carriage or for the breach of any other obligation under this Convention against:

(a)   The carrier or a maritime performing party;

(b)   The master, crew or any other person that performs services on board the ship; or

(c)   Employees of the carrier or a maritime performing party.

2.   Any provision of this Convention that may provide a defence for the shipper or the documentary shipper applies in any judicial or arbitral proceeding, whether founded in contract, in tort, or otherwise, that is instituted against the shipper, the documentary shipper, or their subcontractors, agents or employees.

Chapter 2 Scope of Application
Article 5 General Scope of Application

1.   Subject to Article 6, this Convention applies to contracts of carriage in which the place of receipt and the place of delivery are in different States, and the port of loading of a sea carriage and the port of discharge of the same sea carriage are in different States, if, according to the contract of carriage, any one of the following places is located in a Contracting State:
(a)   The place of receipt;
(b)   The port of loading;
(c)   The place of delivery; or
(d)   The port of discharge.

2.   This Convention applies without regard to the nationality of the vessel, the carrier, the performing parties, the shipper, the consignee, or any other interested parties.

Article 6 Specific Exclusions

1.   This Convention does not apply to the following contracts in liner transportation:
(a)   Charter parties; and
(b)   Other contracts for the use of a ship or of any space thereon.

2.   This Convention does not apply to contracts of carriage in non-liner transportation except when:
(a)   There is no charter party or other contract between the parties for the use of a ship or of any space thereon; and
(b)   A transport document or an electronic transport record is issued.

Article 7 Application to Certain Parties

Notwithstanding Article 6, this Convention applies as between the carrier and the consignee, controlling party or holder that is not an original party to the charter party or other contract of carriage excluded from the application of this Convention. However, this Convention does not apply as between the original parties to a contract of carriage excluded pursuant to Article 6.

Chapter 3 Electronic Transport Records
Article 8 Use and Effect of Electronic Transport Records

Subject to the requirements set out in this Convention:
(a)   Anything that is to be in or on a transport document under this Convention may be recorded in an electronic transport record, provided the issuance and subsequent use of an electronic transport record is with the consent of the carrier and the shipper; and
(b)   The issuance, exclusive control, or transfer of an electronic transport record has the same effect as the issuance, possession, or transfer of a transport document.

Article 9 Procedures for Use of Negotiable Electronic Transport Records

1.   The use of a negotiable electronic transport record shall be subject to procedures that provide for:
(a)   The method for the issuance and the transfer of that record to an intended holder;
(b)   An assurance that the negotiable electronic transport record retains its integrity;
(c)   The manner in which the holder is able to demonstrate that it is the holder; and
(d)   The manner of providing confirmation that delivery to the holder has been effected, or that, pursuant to articles 10, paragraph 2, or 47, subparagraphs 1 (a) (ii) and (c), the electronic transport record has ceased to have any effect or validity.

2.   The procedures in paragraph 1 of this Article shall be referred to in the contract particulars and be readily ascertainable.

Article 10 Replacement of Negotiable Transport Document or Negotiable Electronic Transport Record
1.   If a negotiable transport document has been issued and the carrier and the holder agree to replace that document by a negotiable electronic transport record:
(a)   The holder shall surrender the negotiable transport document, or all of them if more than one has been issued, to the carrier;
(b)   The carrier shall issue to the holder a negotiable electronic transport record that includes a statement that it replaces the negotiable transport document; and
(c)   The negotiable transport document ceases thereafter to have any effect or validity.
2.   If a negotiable electronic transport record has been issued and the carrier and the holder agree to replace that electronic transport record by a negotiable transport document:
(a)   The carrier shall issue to the holder, in place of the electronic transport record, a negotiable transport document that includes a statement that it replaces the negotiable electronic transport record; and
(b)   The electronic transport record ceases thereafter to have any effect or validity.

Chapter 4 Obligations of the Carrier
Article 11 Carriage and Delivery of the Goods
The carrier shall, subject to this Convention and in accordance with the terms of the contract of carriage, carry the goods to the place of destination and deliver them to the consignee.

Article 12 Period of Responsibility of the Carrier
1.   The period of responsibility of the carrier for the goods under this Convention begins when the carrier or a performing party receives the goods for carriage and ends when the goods are delivered.
2.(a) If the law or regulations of the place of receipt require the goods to be handed over to an authority or other third party from which the carrier may collect them, the period of responsibility of the carrier begins when the carrier collects the goods from the authority or other third party.
(b)   If the law or regulations of the place of delivery require the carrier to hand over the goods to an authority or other third party from which the consignee may collect them, the period of responsibility of the carrier ends when the carrier hands the goods over to the authority or other third party.
3.   For the purpose of determining the carrier's period of responsibility, the parties may agree on the time and location of receipt and delivery of the goods, but a provision in a contract of carriage is void to the extent that it provides that:
(a)   The time of receipt of the goods is subsequent to the beginning of their initial loading under the contract of carriage; or
(b)   The time of delivery of the goods is prior to the completion of their final unloading under the contract of carriage.

Article 13 Specific Obligations
1.   The carrier shall during the period of its responsibility as defined in Article 12, and subject to Article 26, properly and carefully receive, load, handle, stow, carry, keep, care for, unload and deliver the goods.
2.   Notwithstanding paragraph 1 of this article, and without prejudice to the other provisions in chapter 4 and to chapters 5 to 7, the carrier and the shipper may agree that the loading, handling, stowing or unloading of the goods is to be performed by the shipper, the documentary shipper or the consignee. Such an agreement shall be referred to in the contract particulars.

Article 14 Specific Obligations Applicable to the Voyage by Sea
The carrier is bound before, at the beginning of, and during the voyage by sea to exercise due diligence to:

(a) Make and keep the ship seaworthy;

(b) Properly crew, equip and supply the ship and keep the ship so crewed, equipped and supplied throughout the voyage; and

(c) Make and keep the holds and all other parts of the ship in which the goods are carried, and any containers supplied by the carrier in or upon which the goods are carried, fit and safe for their reception, carriage and preservation.

Article 15 Goods That May Become a Danger

Notwithstanding articles 11 and 13, the carrier or a performing party may decline to receive or to load, and may take such other measures as are reasonable, including unloading, destroying, or rendering goods harmless, if the goods are, or reasonably appear likely to become during the carrier's period of responsibility, an actual danger to persons, property or the environment.

Article 16 Sacrifice of the Goods During the Voyage by Sea

Notwithstanding articles 11, 13, and 14, the carrier or a performing party may sacrifice goods at sea when the sacrifice is reasonably made for the common safety or for the purpose of preserving from peril human life or other property involved in the common adventure.

Chapter 5 Liability of the Carrier for Loss, Damage or Delay

Article 17 Basis of Liability

1. The carrier is liable for loss of or damage to the goods, as well as for delay in delivery, if the claimant proves that the loss, damage, or delay, or the event or circumstance that caused or contributed to it took place during the period of the carrier's responsibility as defined in chapter 4.

2. The carrier is relieved of all or part of its liability pursuant to paragraph 1 of this Article if it proves that the cause or one of the causes of the loss, damage, or delay is not attributable to its fault or to the fault of any person referred to in Article 18.

3. The carrier is also relieved of all or part of its liability pursuant to paragraph 1 of this Article if, alternatively to proving the absence of fault as provided in paragraph 2 of this article, it proves that one or more of the following events or circumstances caused or contributed to the loss, damage, or delay:

(a) Act of God;

(b) Perils, dangers, and accidents of the sea or other navigable waters;

(c) War, hostilities, armed conflict, piracy, terrorism, riots, and civil commotions;

(d) Quarantine restrictions; interference by or impediments created by governments, public authorities, rulers, or people including detention, arrest, or seizure not attributable to the carrier or any person referred to in Article 18;

(e) Strikes, lockouts, stoppages, or restraints of labour;

(f) Fire on the ship;

(g) Latent defects not discoverable by due diligence;

(h) Act or omission of the shipper, the documentary shipper, the controlling party, or any other person for whose acts the shipper or the documentary shipper is liable pursuant to Article 33 or 34;

(i) Loading, handling, stowing, or unloading of the goods performed pursuant to an agreement in accordance with Article 13, paragraph 2, unless the carrier or a performing party performs such activity on behalf of the shipper, the documentary shipper or the consignee;

(j) Wastage in bulk or weight or any other loss or damage arising from inherent defect, quality, or vice of the goods;

(k) Insufficiency or defective condition of packing or marking not performed by or on behalf of the carrier;

(l) Saving or attempting to save life at sea;

(m) Reasonable measures to save or attempt to save property at sea;

(n) Reasonable measures to avoid or attempt to avoid damage to the environment; or

(o) Acts of the carrier in pursuance of the powers conferred by articles 15 and 16.

4.   Notwithstanding paragraph 3 of this article, the carrier is liable for all or part of the loss, damage, or delay:
(a)   If the claimant proves that the fault of the carrier or of a person referred to in Article 18 caused or contributed to the event or circumstance on which the carrier relies; or
(b)   If the claimant proves that an event or circumstance not listed in paragraph 3 of this Article contributed to the loss, damage, or delay, and the carrier cannot prove that this event or circumstance is not attributable to its fault or to the fault of any person referred to in Article 18.
5.   The carrier is also liable, notwithstanding paragraph 3 of this article, for all or part of the loss, damage, or delay if:
(a)   The claimant proves that the loss, damage, or delay was or was probably caused by or contributed to by (i) the unseaworthiness of the ship; (ii) the improper crewing, equipping, and supplying of the ship; or (iii) the fact that the holds or other parts of the ship in which the goods are carried, or any containers supplied by the carrier in or upon which the goods are carried, were not fit and safe for reception, carriage, and preservation of the goods; and
(b)   The carrier is unable to prove either that: (i) none of the events or circumstances referred to in subparagraph 5 (*a*) of this Article caused the loss, damage, or delay; or (ii) it complied with its obligation to exercise due diligence pursuant to Article 14.
6.   When the carrier is relieved of part of its liability pursuant to this article, the carrier is liable only for that part of the loss, damage or delay that is attributable to the event or circumstance for which it is liable pursuant to this article.

Article 18 Liability of the Carrier for Other Persons

The carrier is liable for the breach of its obligations under this Convention caused by the acts or omissions of:
(a)   Any performing party;
(b)   The master or crew of the ship;
(c)   Employees of the carrier or a performing party; or
(d)   Any other person that performs or undertakes to perform any of the carrier's obligations under the contract of carriage, to the extent that the person acts, either directly or indirectly, at the carrier's request or under the carrier's supervision or control.

Article 19 Liability of Maritime Performing Parties

1.   A maritime performing party is subject to the obligations and liabilities imposed on the carrier under this Convention and is entitled to the carrier's defences and limits of liability as provided for in this Convention if:
(*a*)   The maritime performing party received the goods for carriage in a Contracting State, or delivered them in a Contracting State, or performed its activities with respect to the goods in a port in a Contracting State; and
(*b*)   The occurrence that caused the loss, damage or delay took place: (i) during the period between the arrival of the goods at the port of loading of the ship and their departure from the port of discharge from the ship; (ii) while the maritime performing party had custody of the goods; or (iii) at any other time to the extent that it was participating in the performance of any of the activities contemplated by the contract of carriage.
2.   If the carrier agrees to assume obligations other than those imposed on the carrier under this Convention, or agrees that the limits of its liability are higher than the limits specified under this Convention, a maritime performing party is not bound by this agreement unless it expressly agrees to accept such obligations or such higher limits.
3.   A maritime performing party is liable for the breach of its obligations under this Convention caused by the acts or omissions of any person to which it has entrusted the performance of any of the carrier's obligations under the contract of carriage under the conditions set out in paragraph 1 of this article.
4.   Nothing in this Convention imposes liability on the master or crew of the ship or on an employee of the carrier or of a maritime performing party.

Article 20 Joint and Several Liability

1.   If the carrier and one or more maritime performing parties are liable for the loss of, damage to, or delay in delivery of the goods, their liability is joint and several but only up to the limits provided for under this Convention.

2.   Without prejudice to Article 61, the aggregate liability of all such persons shall not exceed the overall limits of liability under this Convention.

Article 21 Delay

Delay in delivery occurs when the goods are not delivered at the place of destination provided for in the contract of carriage within the time agreed.

Article 22 Calculation of Compensation

1.   Subject to Article 59, the compensation payable by the carrier for loss of or damage to the goods is calculated by reference to the value of such goods at the place and time of delivery established in accordance with Article 43.

2.   The value of the goods is fixed according to the commodity exchange price or, if there is no such price, according to their market price or, if there is no commodity exchange price or market price, by reference to the normal value of the goods of the same kind and quality at the place of delivery.

3.   In case of loss of or damage to the goods, the carrier is not liable for payment of any compensation beyond what is provided for in paragraphs 1 and 2 of this Article except when the carrier and the shipper have agreed to calculate compensation in a different manner within the limits of chapter 16.

Article 23 Notice in Case of Loss, Damage or Delay

1.   The carrier is presumed, in absence of proof to the contrary, to have delivered the goods according to their description in the contract particulars unless notice of loss of or damage to the goods, indicating the general nature of such loss or damage, was given to the carrier or the performing party that delivered the goods before or at the time of the delivery, or, if the loss or damage is not apparent, within seven working days at the place of delivery after the delivery of the goods.

2.   Failure to provide the notice referred to in this Article to the carrier or the performing party shall not affect the right to claim compensation for loss of or damage to the goods under this Convention, nor shall it affect the allocation of the burden of proof set out in Article 17.

3.   The notice referred to in this Article is not required in respect of loss or damage that is ascertained in a joint inspection of the goods by the person to which they have been delivered and the carrier or the maritime performing party against which liability is being asserted.

4.   No compensation in respect of delay is payable unless notice of loss due to delay was given to the carrier within twenty-one consecutive days of delivery of the goods.

5.   When the notice referred to in this Article is given to the performing party that delivered the goods, it has the same effect as if that notice was given to the carrier, and notice given to the carrier has the same effect as a notice given to a maritime performing party.

6.   In the case of any actual or apprehended loss or damage, the parties to the dispute shall give all reasonable facilities to each other for inspecting and tallying the goods and shall provide access to records and documents relevant to the carriage of the goods.

Chapter 6 Additional Provisions Relating to Particular Stages of Carriage

Article 24 Deviation

When pursuant to applicable law a deviation constitutes a breach of the carrier's obligations, such deviation of itself shall not deprive the carrier or a maritime performing party of any defence or limitation of this Convention, except to the extent provided in Article 61.

Article 25 Deck Cargo on Ships

1.   Goods may be carried on the deck of a ship only if:

(a)   Such carriage is required by law;

(b)   They are carried in or on containers or vehicles that are fit for deck carriage, and the decks are specially fitted to carry such containers or vehicles; or

(c)   The carriage on deck is in accordance with the contract of carriage, or the customs, usages or practices of the trade in question.

2.   The provisions of this Convention relating to the liability of the carrier apply to the loss of, damage to or delay in the delivery of goods carried on deck pursuant to paragraph 1 of this article, but the carrier is not liable for loss of or damage to such goods, or delay in their delivery, caused by the special risks involved in their carriage on deck when the goods are carried in accordance with subparagraphs 1 (a) or (c) of this article.

3.   If the goods have been carried on deck in cases other than those permitted pursuant to paragraph 1 of this article, the carrier is liable for loss of or damage to the goods or delay in their delivery that is exclusively caused by their carriage on deck, and is not entitled to the defences provided for in Article 17.

4.   The carrier is not entitled to invoke subparagraph 1 (c) of this Article against a third party that has acquired a negotiable transport document or a negotiable electronic transport record in good faith, unless the contract particulars state that the goods may be carried on deck.

5.   If the carrier and shipper expressly agreed that the goods would be carried under deck, the carrier is not entitled to the benefit of the limitation of liability for any loss of, damage to or delay in the delivery of the goods to the extent that such loss, damage, or delay resulted from their carriage on deck.

Article 26 Carriage Preceding or Subsequent to Sea Carriage

When loss of or damage to goods, or an event or circumstance causing a delay in their delivery, occurs during the carrier's period of responsibility but solely before their loading onto the ship or solely after their discharge from the ship, the provisions of this Convention do not prevail over those provisions of another international instrument that, at the time of such loss, damage or event or circumstance causing delay:

(a)   Pursuant to the provisions of such international instrument would have applied to all or any of the carrier's activities if the shipper had made a separate and direct contract with the carrier in respect of the particular stage of carriage where the loss of, or damage to goods, or an event or circumstance causing delay in their delivery occurred;

(b)   Specifically provide for the carrier's liability, limitation of liability, or time for suit; and

(c)   Cannot be departed from by contract either at all or to the detriment of the shipper under that instrument.

Chapter 7 Obligations of the Shipper to the Carrier

Article 27 Delivery for Carriage

1.   Unless otherwise agreed in the contract of carriage, the shipper shall deliver the goods ready for carriage. In any event, the shipper shall deliver the goods in such condition that they will withstand the intended carriage, including their loading, handling, stowing, lashing and securing, and unloading, and that they will not cause harm to persons or property.

2.   The shipper shall properly and carefully perform any obligation assumed under an agreement made pursuant to Article 13, paragraph 2.

3.   When a container is packed or a vehicle is loaded by the shipper, the shipper shall properly and carefully stow, lash and secure the contents in or on the container or vehicle, and in such a way that they will not cause harm to persons or property.

Article 28 Cooperation of the Shipper and the Carrier in Providing Information and Instructions

The carrier and the shipper shall respond to requests from each other to provide information and instructions required for the proper handling and carriage of the goods if the information is in the requested party's possession or the instructions are within the requested party's reasonable ability to provide and they are not otherwise reasonably available to the requesting party.

Article 29 Shipper's Obligation to Provide Information, Instructions and Documents

1.   The shipper shall provide to the carrier in a timely manner such information, instructions and documents relating to the goods that are not otherwise reasonably available to the carrier, and that are reasonably necessary:

(a)   For the proper handling and carriage of the goods, including precautions to be taken by the carrier or a performing party; and

(b)   For the carrier to comply with law, regulations or other requirements of public authorities in connection with the intended carriage, provided that the carrier notifies the shipper in a timely manner of the information, instructions and documents it requires.

2.   Nothing in this Article affects any specific obligation to provide certain information, instructions and documents related to the goods pursuant to law, regulations or other requirements of public authorities in connection with the intended carriage.

Article 30 Basis of Shipper's Liability to the Carrier

1.   The shipper is liable for loss or damage sustained by the carrier if the carrier proves that such loss or damage was caused by a breach of the shipper's obligations under this Convention.

2.   Except in respect of loss or damage caused by a breach by the shipper of its obligations pursuant to articles 31, paragraph 2, and 32, the shipper is relieved of all or part of its liability if the cause or one of the causes of the loss or damage is not attributable to its fault or to the fault of any person referred to in Article 34.

3.   When the shipper is relieved of part of its liability pursuant to this article, the shipper is liable only for that part of the loss or damage that is attributable to its fault or to the fault of any person referred to in Article 34.

Article 31 Information for Compilation of Contract Particulars

1.   The shipper shall provide to the carrier, in a timely manner, accurate information required for the compilation of the contract particulars and the issuance of the transport documents or electronic transport records, including the particulars referred to in Article 36, paragraph 1; the name of the party to be identified as the shipper in the contract particulars; the name of the consignee, if any; and the name of the person to whose order the transport document or electronic transport record is to be issued, if any.

2.   The shipper is deemed to have guaranteed the accuracy at the time of receipt by the carrier of the information that is provided according to paragraph 1 of this article. The shipper shall indemnify the carrier against loss or damage resulting from the inaccuracy of such information.

Article 32 Special Rules on Dangerous Goods

When goods by their nature or character are, or reasonably appear likely to become, a danger to persons, property or the environment:

(a)   The shipper shall inform the carrier of the dangerous nature or character of the goods in a timely manner before they are delivered to the carrier or a performing party. If the shipper fails to do so and the carrier or performing party does not otherwise have knowledge of their dangerous nature or character, the shipper is liable to the carrier for loss or damage resulting from such failure to inform; and

(b)   The shipper shall mark or label dangerous goods in accordance with any law, regulations or other requirements of public authorities that apply during any stage of the intended carriage of the goods. If the shipper fails to do so, it is liable to the carrier for loss or damage resulting from such failure.

Article 33 Assumption of Shipper's Rights and Obligations by the Documentary Shipper

1.   A documentary shipper is subject to the obligations and liabilities imposed on the shipper pursuant to this chapter and pursuant to Article 55, and is entitled to the shipper's rights and defences provided by this chapter and by chapter 13.

2.   Paragraph 1 of this Article does not affect the obligations, liabilities, rights or defences of the shipper.

Article 34 Liability of the Shipper for Other Persons

The shipper is liable for the breach of its obligations under this Convention caused by the acts or omissions of any person, including employees, agents and subcontractors, to which it has entrusted the performance of any of its obligations, but the shipper is not liable for acts or omissions of the carrier or a performing party acting on behalf of the carrier, to which the shipper has entrusted the performance of its obligations.

Chapter 8 Transport Documents and Electronic Transport Records

Article 35 Issuance of the Transport Document or the Electronic Transport Record

Unless the shipper and the carrier have agreed not to use a transport document or an electronic transport record, or it is the custom, usage or practice of the trade not to use one, upon delivery of the goods for carriage to the carrier or performing party, the shipper or, if the shipper consents, the documentary shipper, is entitled to obtain from the carrier, at the shipper's option:

(a)   A non-negotiable transport document or, subject to Article 8, subparagraph (a), a non-negotiable electronic transport record; or

(b)   An appropriate negotiable transport document or, subject to Article 8, subparagraph (*a*), a negotiable electronic transport record, unless the shipper and the carrier have agreed not to use a negotiable transport document or negotiable electronic transport record, or it is the custom, usage or practice of the trade not to use one.

Article 36 Contract Particulars

1.   The contract particulars in the transport document or electronic transport record referred to in Article 35 shall include the following information, as furnished by the shipper:

(a)   A description of the goods as appropriate for the transport;

(b)   The leading marks necessary for identification of the goods;

(c)   The number of packages or pieces, or the quantity of goods; and

(d)   The weight of the goods, if furnished by the shipper.

2.   The contract particulars in the transport document or electronic transport record referred to in Article 35 shall also include:

(a)   A statement of the apparent order and condition of the goods at the time the carrier or a performing party receives them for carriage;

(b)   The name and address of the carrier;

(c)   The date on which the carrier or a performing party received the goods, or on which the goods were loaded on board the ship, or on which the transport document or electronic transport record was issued; and

(d)   If the transport document is negotiable, the number of originals of the negotiable transport document, when more than one original is issued.

3.   The contract particulars in the transport document or electronic transport record referred to in Article 35 shall further include:

(a)   The name and address of the consignee, if named by the shipper;

(b)   The name of a ship, if specified in the contract of carriage;

(c)   The place of receipt and, if known to the carrier, the place of delivery; and

(d)   The port of loading and the port of discharge, if specified in the contract of carriage.

4.   For the purposes of this article, the phrase "apparent order and condition of the goods" in subparagraph 2 (*a*) of this Article refers to the order and condition of the goods based on:

(a)   A reasonable external inspection of the goods as packaged at the time the shipper delivers them to the carrier or a performing party; and

(b)   Any additional inspection that the carrier or a performing party actually performs before issuing the transport document or electronic transport record.

Article 37 Identity of the Carrier

1.   If a carrier is identified by name in the contract particulars, any other information in the transport document or electronic transport record relating to the identity of the carrier shall have no effect to the extent that it is inconsistent with that identification.

2.   If no person is identified in the contract particulars as the carrier as required pursuant to Article 36, subparagraph 2 (*b*), but the contract particulars indicate that the goods have been loaded on board a named ship, the registered owner of that ship is presumed to be the carrier, unless it proves that the ship was under a bareboat charter at the time of the carriage and it identifies this bareboat charterer and indicates its address, in which case this bareboat charterer is presumed to be the carrier. Alternatively, the registered owner may rebut the presumption of being the carrier by identifying the carrier and indicating its address. The bareboat charterer may rebut any presumption of being the carrier in the same manner.

3.   Nothing in this Article prevents the claimant from proving that any person other than a person identified in the contract particulars or pursuant to paragraph 2 of this Article is the carrier.

Article 38 Signature

1.   A transport document shall be signed by the carrier or a person acting on its behalf.

2.   An electronic transport record shall include the electronic signature of the carrier or a person acting on its behalf. Such electronic signature shall identify the signatory in relation to the electronic transport record and indicate the carrier's authorization of the electronic transport record.

Article 39 Deficiencies in the Contract Particulars

1.   The absence or inaccuracy of one or more of the contract particulars referred to in Article 36, paragraphs 1, 2 or 3, does not of itself affect the legal character or validity of the transport document or of the electronic transport record.

2.   If the contract particulars include the date but fail to indicate its significance, the date is deemed to be:

(a)   The date on which all of the goods indicated in the transport document or electronic transport record were loaded on board the ship, if the contract particulars indicate that the goods have been loaded on board a ship; or

(b)   The date on which the carrier or a performing party received the goods, if the contract particulars do not indicate that the goods have been loaded on board a ship.

3.   If the contract particulars fail to state the apparent order and condition of the goods at the time the carrier or a performing party receives them, the contract particulars are deemed to have stated that the goods were in apparent good order and condition at the time the carrier or a performing party received them.

Article 40 Qualifying the Information Relating to the Goods in the Contract Particulars

1.   The carrier shall qualify the information referred to in Article 36, paragraph 1, to indicate that the carrier does not assume responsibility for the accuracy of the information furnished by the shipper if:

(a)   The carrier has actual knowledge that any material statement in the transport document or electronic transport record is false or misleading; or

(b)   The carrier has reasonable grounds to believe that a material statement in the transport document or electronic transport record is false or misleading.

2.   Without prejudice to paragraph 1 of this article, the carrier may qualify the information referred to in Article 36, paragraph 1, in the circumstances and in the manner set out in paragraphs 3 and 4 of this Article to indicate that the carrier does not assume responsibility for the accuracy of the information furnished by the shipper.

3.   When the goods are not delivered for carriage to the carrier or a performing party in a closed container or vehicle, or when they are delivered in a closed container or vehicle and the carrier or a performing party actually inspects them, the carrier may qualify the information referred to in Article 36, paragraph 1, if:

(a)   The carrier had no physically practicable or commercially reasonable means of checking the information furnished by the shipper, in which case it may indicate which information it was unable to check; or

(b)   The carrier has reasonable grounds to believe the information furnished by the shipper to be inaccurate, in which case it may include a clause providing what it reasonably considers accurate information.

4.   When the goods are delivered for carriage to the carrier or a performing party in a closed container or vehicle, the carrier may qualify the information referred to in:

(a)   Article 36, subparagraphs 1 (a), (b), or (c), if:

    (i)   The goods inside the container or vehicle have not actually been inspected by the carrier or a performing party; and

    (ii)   Neither the carrier nor a performing party otherwise has actual knowledge of its contents before issuing the transport document or the electronic transport record; and

(b)   Article 36, subparagraph 1 (d), if:

    (i)   Neither the carrier nor a performing party weighed the container or vehicle, and the shipper and the carrier had not agreed prior to the shipment that the container or vehicle would be weighed and the weight would be included in the contract particulars; or

    (ii)   There was no physically practicable or commercially reasonable means of checking the weight of the container or vehicle.

Article 41 Evidentiary Effect of the Contract Particulars

Except to the extent that the contract particulars have been qualified in the circumstances and in the manner set out in Article 40:

(a)   A transport document or an electronic transport record is prima facie evidence of the carrier's receipt of the goods as stated in the contract particulars;

(b)   Proof to the contrary by the carrier in respect of any contract particulars shall not be admissible, when such contract particulars are included in:

    (i)   A negotiable transport document or a negotiable electronic transport record that is transferred to a third party acting in good faith; or

    (ii)   A non-negotiable transport document that indicates that it must be surrendered in order to obtain delivery of the goods and is transferred to the consignee acting in good faith;

(c)   Proof to the contrary by the carrier shall not be admissible against a consignee that in good faith has acted in reliance on any of the following contract particulars included in a non-negotiable transport document or a non-negotiable electronic transport record:

    (i)   The contract particulars referred to in Article 36, paragraph 1, when such contract particulars are furnished by the carrier;

    (ii)   The number, type and identifying numbers of the containers, but not the identifying numbers of the container seals; and

    (iii) The contract particulars referred to in Article 36, paragraph 2.

Article 42 "Freight Prepaid"

If the contract particulars contain the statement "freight prepaid" or a statement of a similar nature, the carrier cannot assert against the holder or the consignee the fact that the freight has not been paid. This Article does not apply if the holder or the consignee is also the shipper.

Chapter 9 Delivery of the Goods

Article 43 Obligation to Accept Delivery

When the goods have arrived at their destination, the consignee that demands delivery of the goods under the contract of carriage shall accept delivery of the goods at the time or within the time period and at the location agreed in the contract of carriage or, failing such agreement, at the time and location at which, having regard to the terms of the contract, the customs, usages or practices of the trade and the circumstances of the carriage, delivery could reasonably be expected.

Article 44 Obligation to Acknowledge Receipt

On request of the carrier or the performing party that delivers the goods, the consignee shall acknowledge receipt of the goods from the carrier or the performing party in the manner that is customary at the place of delivery. The carrier may refuse delivery if the consignee refuses to acknowledge such receipt.

Article 45 Delivery When No Negotiable Transport Document
or Negotiable Electronic Transport Record Is Issued

When neither a negotiable transport document nor a negotiable electronic transport record has been issued:

(a)   The carrier shall deliver the goods to the consignee at the time and location referred to in Article 43. The carrier may refuse delivery if the person claiming to be the consignee does not properly identify itself as the consignee on the request of the carrier;

(b)   If the name and address of the consignee are not referred to in the contract particulars, the controlling party shall prior to or upon the arrival of the goods at the place of destination advise the carrier of such name and address;

(c)   Without prejudice to Article 48, paragraph 1, if the goods are not deliverable because (i) the consignee, after having received a notice of arrival, does not, at the time or within the time period referred to in Article 43, claim delivery of the goods from the carrier after their arrival at the place of destination, (ii) the carrier refuses delivery because the person claiming to be the consignee does not properly identify itself as the consignee, or (iii) the carrier is, after reasonable effort, unable to locate the consignee in order to request delivery instructions, the carrier may so advise the controlling party and request instructions in respect of the delivery of the goods. If, after reasonable effort, the carrier is unable to locate the controlling party, the carrier may so advise the shipper and request instructions in respect of the delivery of the goods. If, after reasonable effort, the carrier is unable to locate the shipper, the carrier may so advise the documentary shipper and request instructions in respect of the delivery of the goods;

(d)   The carrier that delivers the goods upon instruction of the controlling party, the shipper or the documentary shipper pursuant to subparagraph (c) of this Article is discharged from its obligations to deliver the goods under the contract of carriage.

Article 46 Delivery When a Non-Negotiable Transport Document That Requires Surrender Is Issued

When a non-negotiable transport document has been issued that indicates that it shall be surrendered in order to obtain delivery of the goods:

(a)   The carrier shall deliver the goods at the time and location referred to in Article 43 to the consignee upon the consignee properly identifying itself on the request of the carrier and surrender of the non-negotiable document. The carrier may refuse delivery if the person claiming to be the consignee fails to properly identify itself on the request of the carrier, and shall refuse delivery if the non-negotiable document is not surrendered. If more than one original of the non-negotiable document has been issued, the surrender of one original will suffice and the other originals cease to have any effect or validity;

(b)   Without prejudice to Article 48, paragraph 1, if the goods are not deliverable because (i) the consignee, after having received a notice of arrival, does not, at the time or within the time period referred to in Article 43, claim delivery of the goods from the carrier after their arrival at the place of destination, (ii) the carrier refuses delivery because the person claiming to be the consignee does not properly identify itself as the consignee or does not surrender the document, or (iii) the carrier is, after reasonable effort, unable to locate the consignee in order to request delivery instructions, the carrier may so advise the shipper and request instructions in respect of the delivery of the goods. If, after reasonable effort, the carrier is unable to locate the shipper, the carrier may so advise the documentary shipper and request instructions in respect of the delivery of the goods;

(c)   The carrier that delivers the goods upon instruction of the shipper or the documentary shipper pursuant to subparagraph (b) of this Article is discharged from its obligation to deliver the goods under the contract of carriage, irrespective of whether the non-negotiable transport document has been surrendered to it.

Article 47 Delivery When a Negotiable Transport Document
or Negotiable Electronic Transport Record Is Issued

1.   When a negotiable transport document or a negotiable electronic transport record has been issued:

(a) The holder of the negotiable transport document or negotiable electronic transport record is entitled to claim delivery of the goods from the carrier after they have arrived at the place of destination, in which event the carrier shall deliver the goods at the time and location referred to in Article 43 to the holder:

   (i)   Upon surrender of the negotiable transport document and, if the holder is one of the persons referred to in Article 1, subparagraph 10 (a) (i), upon the holder properly identifying itself; or

   (ii) Upon demonstration by the holder, in accordance with the procedures referred to in Article 9, paragraph 1, that it is the holder of the negotiable electronic transport record;

(b) The carrier shall refuse delivery if the requirements of subparagraph (a) (i) or (a) (ii) of this paragraph are not met;

(c) If more than one original of the negotiable transport document has been issued, and the number of originals is stated in that document, the surrender of one original will suffice and the other originals cease to have any effect or validity. When a negotiable electronic transport record has been used, such electronic transport record ceases to have any effect or validity upon delivery to the holder in accordance with the procedures required by Article 9, paragraph 1.

2.   Without prejudice to Article 48, paragraph 1, if the negotiable transport document or the negotiable electronic transport record expressly states that the goods may be delivered without the surrender of the transport document or the electronic transport record, the following rules apply:

(a) If the goods are not deliverable because (i) the holder, after having received a notice of arrival, does not, at the time or within the time period referred to in Article 43, claim delivery of the goods from the carrier after their arrival at the place of destination, (ii) the carrier refuses delivery because the person claiming to be a holder does not properly identify itself as one of the persons referred to in Article 1, subparagraph 10 (*a*) (i), or (iii) the carrier is, after reasonable effort, unable to locate the holder in order to request delivery instructions, the carrier may so advise the shipper and request instructions in respect of the delivery of the goods. If, after reasonable effort, the carrier is unable to locate the shipper, the carrier may so advise the documentary shipper and request instructions in respect of the delivery of the goods;

(b) The carrier that delivers the goods upon instruction of the shipper or the documentary shipper in accordance with subparagraph 2 (a) of this Article is discharged from its obligation to deliver the goods under the contract of carriage to the holder, irrespective of whether the negotiable transport document has been surrendered to it, or the person claiming delivery under a negotiable electronic transport record has demonstrated, in accordance with the procedures referred to in Article 9, paragraph 1, that it is the holder;

(c) The person giving instructions under subparagraph 2 (a) of this Article shall indemnify the carrier against loss arising from its being held liable to the holder under subparagraph 2 (e) of this article. The carrier may refuse to follow those instructions if the person fails to provide adequate security as the carrier may reasonably request;

(d) A person that becomes a holder of the negotiable transport document or the negotiable electronic transport record after the carrier has delivered the goods pursuant to subparagraph 2 (b) of this article, but pursuant to contractual or other arrangements made before such delivery acquires rights against the carrier under the contract of carriage, other than the right to claim delivery of the goods;

(e) Notwithstanding subparagraphs 2 (*b*) and 2 (*d*) of this article, a holder that becomes a holder after such delivery, and that did not have and could not reasonably have had knowledge of such delivery at the time it became a holder, acquires the rights incorporated in the negotiable transport document or negotiable electronic transport record. When the contract particulars state the expected time of arrival of the goods, or indicate how to obtain information as to whether the goods have been delivered, it is presumed that the holder at the time that it became a holder had or could reasonably have had knowledge of the delivery of the goods.

Article 48 Goods Remaining Undelivered

1. For the purposes of this article, goods shall be deemed to have remained undelivered only if, after their arrival at the place of destination:
(a) The consignee does not accept delivery of the goods pursuant to this chapter at the time and location referred to in Article 43;
(b) The controlling party, the holder, the shipper or the documentary shipper cannot be found or does not give the carrier adequate instructions pursuant to articles 45, 46 and 47;
(c) The carrier is entitled or required to refuse delivery pursuant to articles 44, 45, 46 and 47;
(d) The carrier is not allowed to deliver the goods to the consignee pursuant to the law or regulations of the place at which delivery is requested; or
(e) The goods are otherwise undeliverable by the carrier.
2. Without prejudice to any other rights that the carrier may have against the shipper, controlling party or consignee, if the goods have remained undelivered, the carrier may, at the risk and expense of the person entitled to the goods, take such action in respect of the goods as circumstances may reasonably require, including:
(a) To store the goods at any suitable place;
(b) To unpack the goods if they are packed in containers or vehicles, or to act otherwise in respect of the goods, including by moving them; and
(c) To cause the goods to be sold or destroyed in accordance with the practices or pursuant to the law or regulations of the place where the goods are located at the time.
3. The carrier may exercise the rights under paragraph 2 of this Article only after it has given reasonable notice of the intended action under paragraph 2 of this Article to the person stated in the contract particulars as the person, if any, to be notified of the arrival of the goods at the place of destination, and to one of the following persons in the order indicated, if known to the carrier: the consignee, the controlling party or the shipper.
4. If the goods are sold pursuant to subparagraph 2 (c) of this article, the carrier shall hold the proceeds of the sale for the benefit of the person entitled to the goods, subject to the deduction of any costs incurred by the carrier and any other amounts that are due to the carrier in connection with the carriage of those goods.
5. The carrier shall not be liable for loss of or damage to goods that occurs during the time that they remain undelivered pursuant to this Article unless the claimant proves that such loss or damage resulted from the failure by the carrier to take steps that would have been reasonable in the circumstances to preserve the goods and that the carrier knew or ought to have known that the loss or damage to the goods would result from its failure to take such steps.

Article 49 Retention of Goods

Nothing in this Convention affects a right of the carrier or a performing party that may exist pursuant to the contract of carriage or the applicable law to retain the goods to secure the payment of sums due.

Chapter 10 Rights of the Controlling Party

Article 50 Exercise and Extent of Right of Control

1. The right of control may be exercised only by the controlling party and is limited to:
(a) The right to give or modify instructions in respect of the goods that do not constitute a variation of the contract of carriage;
(b) The right to obtain delivery of the goods at a scheduled port of call or, in respect of inland carriage, any place en route; and

(c)   The right to replace the consignee by any other person including the controlling party.
2.   The right of control exists during the entire period of responsibility of the carrier, as provided in Article 12, and ceases when that period expires.

Article 51 Identity of the Controlling Party and Transfer of the Right of Control

1.   Except in the cases referred to in paragraphs 2, 3 and 4 of this article:
(a)   The shipper is the controlling party unless the shipper, when the contract of carriage is concluded, designates the consignee, the documentary shipper or another person as the controlling party;
(b)   The controlling party is entitled to transfer the right of control to another person. The transfer becomes effective with respect to the carrier upon its notification of the transfer by the
transferor, and the transferee becomes the controlling party; and
(c)   The controlling party shall properly identify itself when it exercises the right of control.
2.   When a non-negotiable transport document has been issued that indicates that it shall be
surrendered in order to obtain delivery of the goods:
(a)   The shipper is the controlling party and may transfer the right of control to the consignee
named in the transport document by transferring the document to that person without
endorsement. If more than one original of the document was issued, all originals shall be
transferred in order to effect a transfer of the right of control; and
(b)   In order to exercise its right of control, the controlling party shall produce the document
and properly identify itself. If more than one original of the document was issued, all originals shall be produced, failing which the right of control cannot be exercised.
3.   When a negotiable transport document is issued:
(a)   The holder or, if more than one original of the negotiable transport document is issued, the
holder of all originals is the controlling party;
(b)   The holder may transfer the right of control by transferring the negotiable transport document to another person in accordance with Article 57. If more than one original of that
document was issued, all originals shall be transferred to that person in order to effect a
transfer of the right of control; and
(c)   In order to exercise the right of control, the holder shall produce the negotiable transport
document to the carrier, and if the holder is one of the persons referred to in Article 1, subparagraph 10 (a) (i), the holder shall properly identify itself. If more than one original of the
document was issued, all originals shall be produced, failing which the right of control cannot be exercised.
4.   When a negotiable electronic transport record is issued:
(a)   The holder is the controlling party;
(b)   The holder may transfer the right of control to another person by transferring the negotiable electronic transport record in accordance with the procedures referred to in Article 9,
paragraph 1; and
(c)   In order to exercise the right of control, the holder shall demonstrate, in accordance with
the procedures referred to in Article 9, paragraph 1, that it is the holder.

Article 52 Carrier's Execution of Instructions

1.   Subject to paragraphs 2 and 3 of this article, the carrier shall execute the instructions referred to in Article 50 if:
(a)   The person giving such instructions is entitled to exercise the right of control;
(b)   The instructions can reasonably be executed according to their terms at the moment that
they reach the carrier; and
(c)   The instructions will not interfere with the normal operations of the carrier, including its delivery practices.
2.   In any event, the controlling party shall reimburse the carrier for any reasonable additional
expense that the carrier may incur and shall indemnify the carrier against loss or damage that
the carrier may suffer as a result of diligently executing any instruction pursuant to this article,

including compensation that the carrier may become liable to pay for loss of or damage to other goods being carried.

3.   The carrier is entitled to obtain security from the controlling party for the amount of additional expense, loss or damage that the carrier reasonably expects will arise in connection with the execution of an instruction pursuant to this article. The carrier may refuse to carry out the instructions if no such security is provided.

4.   The carrier's liability for loss of or damage to the goods or for delay in delivery resulting from its failure to comply with the instructions of the controlling party in breach of its obligation pursuant to paragraph 1 of this Article shall be subject to articles 17 to 23, and the amount of the compensation payable by the carrier shall be subject to articles 59 to 61.

Article 53 Deemed Delivery

Goods that are delivered pursuant to an instruction in accordance with Article 52, paragraph 1, are deemed to be delivered at the place of destination, and the provisions of chapter 9 relating to such delivery apply to such goods.

Article 54 Variations to the Contract of Carriage

1.   The controlling party is the only person that may agree with the carrier to variations to the contract of carriage other than those referred to in Article 50, subparagraphs 1 (b) and (c).

2.   Variations to the contract of carriage, including those referred to in Article 50, subparagraphs 1 (b) and (c), shall be stated in a negotiable transport document or in a non-negotiable transport document that requires surrender, or incorporated in a negotiable electronic transport record, or, upon the request of the controlling party, shall be stated in a non-negotiable transport document or incorporated in a non-negotiable electronic transport record. If so stated or incorporated, such variations shall be signed in accordance with Article 38.

Article 55 Providing Additional Information, Instructions or Documents to Carrier

1.   The controlling party, on request of the carrier or a performing party, shall provide in a timely manner information, instructions or documents relating to the goods not yet provided by the shipper and not otherwise reasonably available to the carrier that the carrier may reasonably need to perform its obligations under the contract of carriage.

2.   If the carrier, after reasonable effort, is unable to locate the controlling party or the controlling party is unable to provide adequate information, instructions or documents to the carrier, the shipper shall provide them. If the carrier, after reasonable effort, is unable to locate the shipper, the documentary shipper shall provide such information, instructions or documents.

Article 56 Variation by Agreement

The parties to the contract of carriage may vary the effect of articles 50, subparagraphs 1 (b) and (c), 50, paragraph 2, and 52. The parties may also restrict or exclude the transferability of the right of control referred to in Article 51, subparagraph 1 (b).

Chapter 11 Transfer of Rights
Article 57 When a Negotiable Transport Document
or Negotiable Electronic Transport Record Is Issued

1.   When a negotiable transport document is issued, the holder may transfer the rights incorporated in the document by transferring it to another person:

(a)   Duly endorsed either to such other person or in blank, if an order document; or

(b)   Without endorsement, if: (i) a bearer document or a blank endorsed document; or (ii) a document made out to the order of a named person and the transfer is between the first holder and the named person.

2.   When a negotiable electronic transport record is issued, its holder may transfer the rights incorporated in it, whether it be made out to order or to the order of a named person, by transferring the electronic transport record in accordance with the procedures referred to in Article 9, paragraph 1.

Article 58 Liability of Holder

1.   Without prejudice to Article 55, a holder that is not the shipper and that does not exercise any right under the contract of carriage does not assume any liability under the contract of carriage solely by reason of being a holder.

2.   A holder that is not the shipper and that exercises any right under the contract of carriage assumes any liabilities imposed on it under the contract of carriage to the extent that such liabilities are incorporated in or ascertainable from the negotiable transport document or the negotiable electronic transport record.

3.   For the purposes of paragraphs 1 and 2 of this article, a holder that is not the shipper does not exercise any right under the contract of carriage solely because:

(a)   It agrees with the carrier, pursuant to Article 10, to replace a negotiable transport document by a negotiable electronic transport record or to replace a negotiable electronic transport record by a negotiable transport document; or

(b)   It transfers its rights pursuant to Article 57.

Chapter 12 Limits of Liability

Article 59 Limits of Liability

1.   Subject to articles 60 and 61, paragraph 1, the carrier's liability for breaches of its obligations under this Convention is limited to 875 units of account per package or other shipping unit, or 3 units of account per kilogram of the gross weight of the goods that are the subject of the claim or dispute, whichever amount is the higher, except when the value of the goods has been declared by the shipper and included in the contract particulars, or when a higher amount than the amount of limitation of liability set out in this Article has been agreed upon between the carrier and the shipper.

2.   When goods are carried in or on a container, pallet or similar article of transport used to consolidate goods, or in or on a vehicle, the packages or shipping units enumerated in the contract particulars as packed in or on such article of transport or vehicle are deemed packages or shipping units. If not so enumerated, the goods in or on such article of transport or vehicle are deemed one shipping unit.

3.   The unit of account referred to in this Article is the Special Drawing Right as defined by the International Monetary Fund. The amounts referred to in this Article are to be converted into the national currency of a State according to the value of such currency at the date of judgement or award or the date agreed upon by the parties. The value of a national currency, in terms of the Special Drawing Right, of a Contracting State that is a member of the International Monetary Fund is to be calculated in accordance with the method of valuation applied by the International Monetary Fund in effect at the date in question for its operations and transactions. The value of a national currency, in terms of the Special Drawing Right, of a Contracting State that is not a member of the International Monetary Fund is to be calculated in a manner to be determined by that State.

Article 60 Limits of Liability for Loss Caused by Delay

Subject to Article 61, paragraph 2, compensation for loss of or damage to the goods due to delay shall be calculated in accordance with Article 22 and liability for economic loss due to delay is limited to an amount equivalent to two and one-half times the freight payable on the goods delayed. The total amount payable pursuant to this Article and Article 59, paragraph 1, may not exceed the limit that would be established pursuant to Article 59, paragraph 1, in respect of the total loss of the goods concerned.

Article 61 Loss of the Benefit of Limitation of Liability

1.   Neither the carrier nor any of the persons referred to in Article 18 is entitled to the benefit of the limitation of liability as provided in Article 59, or as provided in the contract of carriage, if the claimant proves that the loss resulting from the breach of the carrier's obligation under this Convention was attributable to a personal act or omission of the person claiming a right to limit

done with the intent to cause such loss or recklessly and with knowledge that such loss would probably result.

2.   Neither the carrier nor any of the persons mentioned in Article 18 is entitled to the benefit of the limitation of liability as provided in Article 60 if the claimant proves that the delay in delivery resulted from a personal act or omission of the person claiming a right to limit done with the intent to cause the loss due to delay or recklessly and with knowledge that such loss would probably result.

Chapter 13 Time for Suit
Article 62 Period of Time for Suit

1.   No judicial or arbitral proceedings in respect of claims or disputes arising from a breach of an obligation under this Convention may be instituted after the expiration of a period of two years.

2.   The period referred to in paragraph 1 of this Article commences on the day on which the carrier has delivered the goods or, in cases in which no goods have been delivered or only part of the goods have been delivered, on the last day on which the goods should have been delivered. The day on which the period commences is not included in the period.

3.   Notwithstanding the expiration of the period set out in paragraph 1 of this article, one party may rely on its claim as a defence or for the purpose of set-off against a claim asserted by the other party.

Article 63 Extension of Time for Suit

The period provided in Article 62 shall not be subject to suspension or interruption, but the person against which a claim is made may at any time during the running of the period extend that period by a declaration to the claimant. This period may be further extended by another declaration or declarations.

Article 64 Action for Indemnity

An action for indemnity by a person held liable may be instituted after the expiration of the period provided in Article 62 if the indemnity action is instituted within the later of:

(a)   The time allowed by the applicable law in the jurisdiction where proceedings are instituted; or

(b)   Ninety days commencing from the day when the person instituting the action for indemnity has either settled the claim or been served with process in the action against itself, whichever is earlier.

Article 65 Actions Against the Person Identified as the Carrier

An action against the bareboat charterer or the person identified as the carrier pursuant to Article 37, paragraph 2, may be instituted after the expiration of the period provided in Article 62 if the action is instituted within the later of:

(a)   The time allowed by the applicable law in the jurisdiction where proceedings are instituted; or

(b)   Ninety days commencing from the day when the carrier has been identified, or the registered owner or bareboat charterer has rebutted the presumption that it is the carrier, pursuant to Article 37, paragraph 2.

Chapter 14 Jurisdiction
Article 66 Actions Against the Carrier

Unless the contract of carriage contains an exclusive choice of court agreement that complies with Article 67 or 72, the plaintiff has the right to institute judicial proceedings under this Convention against the carrier:

(a)   In a competent court within the jurisdiction of which is situated one of the following places:
(i)   The domicile of the carrier;
(ii)   The place of receipt agreed in the contract of carriage;
(iii) The place of delivery agreed in the contract of carriage; or
(iv) The port where the goods are initially loaded on a ship or the port where the goods are finally discharged from a ship; or

(b)   In a competent court or courts designated by an agreement between the shipper and the carrier for the purpose of deciding claims against the carrier that may arise under this Convention.

Article 67 Choice of Court Agreements

1.   The jurisdiction of a court chosen in accordance with Article 66, subparagraph b), is exclusive for disputes between the parties to the contract only if the parties so agree and the agreement conferring jurisdiction:
(a)   Is contained in a volume contract that clearly states the names and addresses of the parties and either (i) is individually negotiated or (ii) contains a prominent statement that there is an exclusive choice of court agreement and specifies the sections of the volume contract containing that agreement; and
(b)   Clearly designates the courts of one Contracting State or one or more specific courts of one Contracting State.
2.   A person that is not a party to the volume contract is bound by an exclusive choice of court agreement concluded in accordance with paragraph 1 of this Article only if:
(a)   The court is in one of the places designated in Article 66, subparagraph (a);
(b)   That agreement is contained in the transport document or electronic transport record;
(c)   That person is given timely and adequate notice of the court where the action shall be brought and that the jurisdiction of that court is exclusive; and
(d)   The law of the court seized recognizes that that person may be bound by the exclusive choice of court agreement.

Article 68 Actions Against the Maritime Performing Party

The plaintiff has the right to institute judicial proceedings under this Convention against the maritime performing party in a competent court within the jurisdiction of which is situated one of the following places:
(a)   The domicile of the maritime performing party; or
(b)   The port where the goods are received by the maritime performing party, the port where the goods are delivered by the maritime performing party or the port in which the maritime performing party performs its activities with respect to the goods.

Article 69 No Additional Bases of Jurisdiction

Subject to articles 71 and 72, no judicial proceedings under this Convention against the carrier or a maritime performing party may be instituted in a court not designated pursuant to Article 66 or 68.

Article 70 Arrest and Provisional or Protective Measures

Nothing in this Convention affects jurisdiction with regard to provisional or protective measures, including arrest. A court in a State in which a provisional or protective measure was taken does not have jurisdiction to determine the case upon its merits unless:
(a)   The requirements of this chapter are fulfilled; or
(b)   An international convention that applies in that State so provides.

Article 71 Consolidation and Removal of Actions

1.   Except when there is an exclusive choice of court agreement that is binding pursuant to Article 67 or 72, if a single action is brought against both the carrier and the maritime performing party arising out of a single occurrence, the action may be instituted only in a court designated pursuant to both Article 66 and Article 68. If there is no such court, such action may be instituted in a court designated pursuant to Article 68, subparagraph (b), if there is such a court.
2.   Except when there is an exclusive choice of court agreement that is binding pursuant to Article 67 or 72, a carrier or a maritime performing party that institutes an action seeking a declaration of non-liability or any other action that would deprive a person of its right to select the forum pursuant to Article 66 or 68 shall, at the request of the defendant, withdraw that action

once the defendant has chosen a court designated pursuant to Article 66 or 68, whichever is applicable, where the action may be recommenced.

Article 72 Agreement After a Dispute Has Arisen and Jurisdiction When the Defendant Has Entered an Appearance

1.   After a dispute has arisen, the parties to the dispute may agree to resolve it in any competent court.
2.   A competent court before which a defendant appears, without contesting jurisdiction in accordance with the rules of that court, has jurisdiction.

Article 73 Recognition and Enforcement

1.   A decision made in one Contracting State by a court having jurisdiction under this Convention shall be recognized and enforced in another Contracting State in accordance with the law of such latter Contracting State when both States have made a declaration in accordance with Article 74.
2.   A court may refuse recognition and enforcement based on the grounds for the refusal of recognition and enforcement available pursuant to its law.
3.   This chapter shall not affect the application of the rules of a regional economic integration organization that is a party to this Convention, as concerns the recognition or enforcement of judgements as between member States of the regional economic integration organization, whether adopted before or after this Convention.

Article 74 Application of Chapter 14

The provisions of this chapter shall bind only Contracting States that declare in accordance with Article 91 that they will be bound by them.

Chapter 15 Arbitration
Article 75 Arbitration Agreements

1.   Subject to this chapter, parties may agree that any dispute that may arise relating to the carriage of goods under this Convention shall be referred to arbitration.
2.   The arbitration proceedings shall, at the option of the person asserting a claim against the carrier, take place at:
(a)   Any place designated for that purpose in the arbitration agreement; or
(b)   Any other place situated in a State where any of the following places is located:
      (i)   The domicile of the carrier;
      (ii)   The place of receipt agreed in the contract of carriage;
      (iii) The place of delivery agreed in the contract of carriage; or
      (iv)   The port where the goods are initially loaded on a ship or the port where the goods are finally discharged from a ship.
3.   The designation of the place of arbitration in the agreement is binding for disputes between the parties to the agreement if the agreement is contained in a volume contract that clearly states the names and addresses of the parties and either:
(a)   Is individually negotiated; or
(b)   Contains a prominent statement that there is an arbitration agreement and specifies the sections of the volume contract containing the arbitration agreement.
4.   When an arbitration agreement has been concluded in accordance with paragraph 3 of this article, a person that is not a party to the volume contract is bound by the designation of the place of arbitration in that agreement only if:
(a)   The place of arbitration designated in the agreement is situated in one of the places referred to in subparagraph 2 (b) of this article;
(b)   The agreement is contained in the transport document or electronic transport record;
(c)   The person to be bound is given timely and adequate notice of the place of arbitration; and
(d)   Applicable law permits that person to be bound by the arbitration agreement.

5.   The provisions of paragraphs 1, 2, 3 and 4 of this Article are deemed to be part of every arbitration clause or agreement, and any term of such clause or agreement to the extent that it is inconsistent therewith is void.

Article 76 Arbitration Agreement in Non-Liner Transportation
1.   Nothing in this Convention affects the enforceability of an arbitration agreement in a contract of carriage in non-liner transportation to which this Convention or the provisions of this Convention apply by reason of:
(a)   The application of Article 7; or
(b)   The parties' voluntary incorporation of this Convention in a contract of carriage that would not otherwise be subject to this Convention.
2.   Notwithstanding paragraph 1 of this article, an arbitration agreement in a transport document or electronic transport record to which this Convention applies by reason of the application of Article 7 is subject to this chapter unless such a transport document or electronic transport record:
(a)   Identifies the parties to and the date of the charter party or other contract excluded from the application of this Convention by reason of the application of Article 6; and
(b)   Incorporates by specific reference the clause in the charter party or other contract that contains the terms of the arbitration agreement.

Article 77 Agreement to Arbitrate After a Dispute Has Arisen
Notwithstanding the provisions of this chapter and chapter 14, after a dispute has arisen the parties to the dispute may agree to resolve it by arbitration in any place.

Article 78 Application of Chapter 15
The provisions of this chapter shall bind only Contracting States that declare in accordance with Article 91 that they will be bound by them.

Chapter 16 Validity of Contractual Terms
Article 79 General Provisions
1.   Unless otherwise provided in this Convention, any term in a contract of carriage is void to the extent that it:
(a)   Directly or indirectly excludes or limits the obligations of the carrier or a maritime performing party under this Convention;
(b)   Directly or indirectly excludes or limits the liability of the carrier or a maritime performing party for breach of an obligation under this Convention; or
(c)   Assigns a benefit of insurance of the goods in favour of the carrier or a person referred to in Article 18.
2.   Unless otherwise provided in this Convention, any term in a contract of carriage is void to the extent that it:
(a)   Directly or indirectly excludes, limits or increases the obligations under this Convention of the shipper, consignee, controlling party, holder or documentary shipper; or
(b)   Directly or indirectly excludes, limits or increases the liability of the shipper, consignee, controlling party, holder or documentary shipper for breach of any of its obligations under this Convention.

Article 80 Special Rules for Volume Contracts
1.   Notwithstanding Article 79, as between the carrier and the shipper, a volume contract to which this Convention applies may provide for greater or lesser rights, obligations and liabilities than those imposed by this Convention.
2.   A derogation pursuant to paragraph 1 of this Article is binding only when:
(a)   The volume contract contains a prominent statement that it derogates from this Convention;
(b)   The volume contract is (i) individually negotiated or (ii) prominently specifies the sections of the volume contract containing the derogations;

(c)   The shipper is given an opportunity and notice of the opportunity to conclude a contract of carriage on terms and conditions that comply with this Convention without any derogation under this article; and

(d)   The derogation is neither (i) incorporated by reference from another document nor (ii) included in a contract of adhesion that is not subject to negotiation.

3.   A carrier's public schedule of prices and services, transport document, electronic transport record or similar document is not a volume contract pursuant to paragraph 1 of this article, but a volume contract may incorporate such documents by reference as terms of the contract.

4.   Paragraph 1 of this Article does not apply to rights and obligations provided in articles 14, subparagraphs (a) and (b), 29 and 32 or to liability arising from the breach thereof, nor does it apply to any liability arising from an act or omission referred to in Article 61.

5.   The terms of the volume contract that derogate from this Convention, if the volume contract satisfies the requirements of paragraph 2 of this article, apply between the carrier and any person other than the shipper provided that:

(a)   Such person received information that prominently states that the volume contract derogates from this Convention and gave its express consent to be bound by such derogations; and

(b)   Such consent is not solely set forth in a carrier's public schedule of prices and services, transport document or electronic transport record.

6.   The party claiming the benefit of the derogation bears the burden of proof that the conditions for derogation have been fulfilled.

Article 81 Special Rules for Live Animals and Certain Other Goods

Notwithstanding Article 79 and without prejudice to Article 80, the contract of carriage may exclude or limit the obligations or the liability of both the carrier and a maritime performing party if:

(a)   The goods are live animals, but any such exclusion or limitation will not be effective if the claimant proves that the loss of or damage to the goods, or delay in delivery, resulted from an act or omission of the carrier or of a person referred to in Article 18, done with the intent to cause such loss of or damage to the goods or such loss due to delay or done recklessly and with knowledge that such loss or damage or such loss due to delay would probably result; or

(b)   The character or condition of the goods or the circumstances and terms and conditions under which the carriage is to be performed are such as reasonably to justify a special agreement, provided that such contract of carriage is not related to ordinary commercial shipments made in the ordinary course of trade and that no negotiable transport document or negotiable electronic transport record is issued for the carriage of the goods.

Chapter 17 Matters Not Governed by this Convention

Article 82 International Conventions Governing the Carriage of Goods by Other Modes of Transport

Nothing in this Convention affects the application of any of the following international conventions in force at the time this Convention enters into force, including any future amendment to such conventions, that regulate the liability of the carrier for loss of or damage to the goods:

(a)   Any convention governing the carriage of goods by air to the extent that such convention according to its provisions applies to any part of the contract of carriage;

(b)   Any convention governing the carriage of goods by road to the extent that such convention according to its provisions applies to the carriage of goods that remain loaded on a road cargo vehicle carried on board a ship;

(c)   Any convention governing the carriage of goods by rail to the extent that such convention according to its provisions applies to carriage of goods by sea as a supplement to the carriage by rail; or

(d)   Any convention governing the carriage of goods by inland waterways to the extent that such convention according to its provisions applies to a carriage of goods without trans-shipment both by inland waterways and sea.

Article 83 Global Limitation of Liability
Nothing in this Convention affects the application of any international convention or national law regulating the global limitation of liability of vessel owners.

Article 84 General Average
Nothing in this Convention affects the application of terms in the contract of carriage or provisions of national law regarding the adjustment of general average.

Article 85 Passengers and Luggage
This Convention does not apply to a contract of carriage for passengers and their luggage.

Article 86 Damage Caused by Nuclear Incident
No liability arises under this Convention for damage caused by a nuclear incident if the operator of a nuclear installation is liable for such damage:
(a)   Under the Paris Convention on Third Party Liability in the Field of Nuclear Energy of 29 July 1960 as amended by the Additional Protocol of 28 January 1964 and by the Protocols of 16 November 1982 and 12 February 2004, the Vienna Convention on Civil Liability for Nuclear Damage of 21 May 1963 as amended by the Joint Protocol Relating to the Application of the Vienna Convention and the Paris Convention of 21 September 1988 and as amended by the Protocol to Amend the 1963 Vienna Convention on Civil Liability for Nuclear Damage of 12 September 1997, or the Convention on Supplementary Compensation for Nuclear Damage of 12 September 1997, including any amendment to these conventions and any future convention in respect of the liability of the operator of a nuclear installation for damage caused by a nuclear incident; or
(b)   Under national law applicable to the liability for such damage, provided that such law is in all respects as favourable to persons that may suffer damage as either the Paris or Vienna Conventions or the Convention on Supplementary Compensation for Nuclear Damage.

Chapter 18 Final Clauses
Article 87 Depositary
The Secretary-General of the United Nations is hereby designated as the depositary of this Convention.

Article 88 Signature, Ratification, Acceptance, Approval or Accession
1.   This Convention is open for signature by all States at Rotterdam, the Netherlands, on 23 September 2009, and thereafter at the Headquarters of the United Nations in New York.
2.   This Convention is subject to ratification, acceptance or approval by the signatory States.
3.   This Convention is open for accession by all States that are not signatory States as from the date it is open for signature.
4.   Instruments of ratification, acceptance, approval and accession are to be deposited with the Secretary-General of the United Nations.

Article 89 Denunciation of Other Conventions
1.   A State that ratifies, accepts, approves or accedes to this Convention and is a party to the International Convention for the Unification of certain Rules of Law relating to Bills of Lading signed at Brussels on 25 August 1924, to the Protocol to amend the International Convention for the Unification of certain Rules of Law relating to Bills of Lading, signed at Brussels on 23 February 1968, or to the Protocol to amend the International Convention for the Unification of certain Rules of Law relating to Bills of Lading as Modified by the Amending Protocol of 23 February 1968, signed at Brussels on 21 December 1979, shall at the same time denounce that Convention and the protocol or protocols thereto to which it is a party by notifying the Government of Belgium to that effect, with a declaration that the denunciation is to take effect as from the date when this Convention enters into force in respect of that State.
2.   A State that ratifies, accepts, approves or accedes to this Convention and is a party to the United Nations Convention on the Carriage of Goods by Sea concluded at Hamburg on 31 March 1978 shall at the same time denounce that Convention by notifying the Secretary-Gene-

ral of the United Nations to that effect, with a declaration that the denunciation is to take effect as from the date when this Convention enters into force in respect of that State.

3.   For the purposes of this article, ratifications, acceptances, approvals and accessions in respect of this Convention by States parties to the instruments listed in paragraphs 1 and 2 of this Article that are notified to the depositary after this Convention has entered into force are not effective until such denunciations as may be required on the part of those States in respect of these instruments have become effective. The depositary of this Convention shall consult with the Government of Belgium, as the depositary of the instruments referred to in paragraph 1 of this article, so as to ensure necessary coordination in this respect.

Article 90 Reservations
No reservation is permitted to this Convention.

Article 91 Procedure and Effect of Declarations
1.   The declarations permitted by articles 74 and 78 may be made at any time. The initial declarations permitted by Article 92, paragraph 1, and Article 93, paragraph 2, shall be made at the time of signature, ratification, acceptance, approval or accession. No other declaration is permitted under this Convention.

2.   Declarations made at the time of signature are subject to confirmation upon ratification, acceptance or approval.

3.   Declarations and their confirmations are to be in writing and to be formally notified to the depositary.

4.   A declaration takes effect simultaneously with the entry into force of this Convention in respect of the State concerned. However, a declaration of which the depositary receives formal notification after such entry into force takes effect on the first day of the month following the expiration of six months after the date of its receipt by the depositary.

5.   Any State that makes a declaration under this Convention may withdraw it at any time by a formal notification in writing addressed to the depositary. The withdrawal of a declaration, or its modification where permitted by this Convention, takes effect on the first day of the month following the expiration of six months after the date of the receipt of the notification by the depositary.

Article 92 Effect in Domestic Territorial Units
1.   If a Contracting State has two or more territorial units in which different systems of law are applicable in relation to the matters dealt with in this Convention, it may, at the time of signature, ratification, acceptance, approval or accession, declare that this Convention is to extend to all its territorial units or only to one or more of them, and may amend its declaration by submitting another declaration at any time.

2.   These declarations are to be notified to the depositary and are to state expressly the territorial units to which the Convention extends.

3.   When a Contracting State has declared pursuant to this Article that this Convention extends to one or more but not all of its territorial units, a place located in a territorial unit to which this Convention does not extend is not considered to be in a Contracting State for the purposes of this Convention.

4.   If a Contracting State makes no declaration pursuant to paragraph 1 of this article, the Convention is to extend to all territorial units of that State.

Article 93 Participation by Regional Economic Integration Organizations
1.   A regional economic integration organization that is constituted by sovereign States and has competence over certain matters governed by this Convention may similarly sign, ratify, accept, approve or accede to this Convention. The regional economic integration organization shall in that case have the rights and obligations of a Contracting State, to the extent that that organization has competence over matters governed by this Convention. When the number of Contracting States is relevant in this Convention, the regional economic integration organiza-

tion does not count as a Contracting State in addition to its member States which are Contracting States.
2.   The regional economic integration organization shall, at the time of signature, ratification, acceptance, approval or accession, make a declaration to the depositary specifying the matters governed by this Convention in respect of which competence has been transferred to that organization by its member States. The regional economic integration organization shall promptly notify the depositary of any changes to the distribution of competence, including new transfers of competence, specified in the declaration pursuant to this paragraph.
3.   Any reference to a "Contracting State" or "Contracting States" in this Convention applies equally to a regional economic integration organization when the context so requires.

Article 94 Entry into Force
1.   This Convention enters into force on the first day of the month following the expiration of one year after the date of deposit of the twentieth instrument of ratification, acceptance, approval or accession.
2.   For each State that becomes a Contracting State to this Convention after the date of the deposit of the twentieth instrument of ratification, acceptance, approval or accession, this Convention enters into force on the first day of the month following the expiration of one year after the deposit of the appropriate instrument on behalf of that State.
3.   Each Contracting State shall apply this Convention to contracts of carriage concluded on or after the date of the entry into force of this Convention in respect of that State.

Article 95 Revision and Amendment
1.   At the request of not less than one third of the Contracting States to this Convention, the Secretary-General of the United Nations shall convene a conference of the Contracting States for revising or amending it.
2.   Any instrument of ratification, acceptance, approval or accession deposited after the entry into force of an amendment to this Convention is deemed to apply to the Convention as amended.

Article 96 Denunciation of this Convention
1.   A Contracting State may denounce this Convention at any time by means of a notification in writing addressed to the depositary.
2.   The denunciation takes effect on the first day of the month following the expiration of one year after the notification is received by the depositary. If a longer period is specified in the notification, the denunciation takes effect upon the expiration of such longer period after the notification is received by the depositary.

DONE at New York, this eleventh day of December two thousand and eight, in a single original, of which the Arabic, Chinese, English, French, Russian and Spanish texts are equally authentic.
IN WITNESS WHEREOF the undersigned plenipotentiaries, being duly authorized by their respective Governments, have signed this Convention.

Entry into force: not yet in force
Ratification: Spain (2011), Togo (2012)[1]

---

1   The Convention has been signed but not yet ratified as of July 2013 by the following countries: Armenia, Cameroon, Congo, Democratic Republic of the Congo, Denmark, France, Gabon, Ghana, Greece, Guinea, Luxembourg, Madagascar, Mali, Netherlands, Niger, Nigeria, Norway, Norway, Poland, Senegal, Sweden, Switzerland, and the United States of America.

UNITED STATES CARRIAGE OF GOODS BY SEA ACT ("COGSA")
(16 April 1936)

§ 1300. Bills of Lading Subject to Chapter

Every bill of lading or similar document of title which is evidence of a contract for the carriage of goods by sea to or from ports of the United States, in foreign trade, shall have effect subject to the provisions of this chapter. (Apr. 16, 1936, ch. 229, § 1, 49 Stat. 1207.)

§ 1301. Definitions

When used in this chapter—

(a) The term "carrier" includes the owner or the charterer who enters into a contract of carriage with a shipper.

(b) The term "contract of carriage" applies only to contracts of carriage covered by a bill of lading or any similar document of title, insofar as such document relates to the carriage of goods by sea, including any bill of lading or any similar document as aforesaid issued under or pursuant to a charter party from the moment at which such bill of lading or similar document of title regulates the relations between a carrier and a holder of the same.

(c) The term "goods" includes goods, wares, merchandise, and articles of every kind whatsoever, except live animals and cargo which by the contract of carriage is stated as being carried on deck and is so carried.

(d) The term "ship" means any vessel used for the carriage of goods by sea.

(e) The term "carriage of goods" covers the period from the time when the goods are loaded on to the time when they are discharged from the ship. (Apr. 16, 1936, ch. 229, title I, § 1, 49 Stat. 1208.)

§ 1302. Duties and Rights of Carrier

Subject to the provisions of section 1306 of this Appendix, under every contract of carriage of goods by sea, the carrier in relation to the loading, handling, stowage, carriage, custody, care, and discharge of such goods, shall be subject to the responsibilities and liabilities and entitled to the rights and immunities set forth in sections 1303 and 1304 of this Appendix. (Apr. 16, 1936, ch. 229, title I, § 2, 49 Stat. 1208.)

§ 1303. Responsibilities and Liabilities of Carrier and Ship

(1) Seaworthiness

The carrier shall be bound, before and at the beginning of the voyage, to exercise due diligence to—

(a) Make the ship seaworthy;

(b) Properly man, equip, and supply the ship;

(c) Make the holds, refrigerating and cooling chambers, and all other parts of the ship in which goods are carried, fit and safe for their reception, carriage, and preservation.

(2) Cargo

The carrier shall properly and carefully load, handle, stow, carry, keep, care for, and discharge the goods carried.

(3) Contents of bill

After receiving the goods into his charge the carrier, or the master or agent of the carrier, shall, on demand of the shipper, issue to the shipper a bill of lading showing among other things—

(a) The leading marks necessary for identification of the goods as the same are furnished in writing by the shipper before the loading of such goods starts, provided such marks are stamped or otherwise shown clearly upon the goods if uncovered, or on the cases or coverings in which such goods are contained, in such a manner as should ordinarily remain legible until the end of the voyage.

(b) Either the number of packages or pieces, or the quantity or weight, as the case may be, as furnished in writing by the shipper.

(c) The apparent order and condition of the goods: Provided, That no carrier, master, or agent of the carrier, shall be bound to state or show in the bill of lading any marks, number, quantity, or weight which he has reasonable ground for suspecting not accurately to represent the goods actually received, or which he has had no reasonable means of checking.

(4)   Bill as prima facie evidence

Such a bill of lading shall be prima facie evidence of the receipt by the carrier of the goods as therein described in accordance with paragraphs (3)(a), (b), and (c), of this section: Provided, That nothing in this chapter shall be construed as repealing or limiting the application of any part of chapter 801 of title 49.

(5)   Guaranty of statements

The shipper shall be deemed to have guaranteed to the carrier the accuracy at the time of shipment of the marks, number, quantity, and weight, as furnished by him; and the shipper shall indemnify the carrier against all loss, damages, and expenses arising or resulting from inaccuracies in such particulars. The right of the carrier to such indemnity shall in no way limit his responsibility and liability under the contract of carriage to any person other than the shipper.

(6)   Notice of loss or damage; limitation of actions

Unless notice of loss or damage and the general nature of such loss or damage be given in writing to the carrier or his agent at the port of discharge before or at the time of the removal of the goods into the custody of the person entitled to delivery thereof under the contract of carriage, such removal shall be prima facie evidence of the delivery by the carrier of the goods as described in the bill of lading. If the loss or damage is not apparent, the notice must be given within three days of the delivery.

Said notice of loss or damage may be endorsed upon the receipt for the goods given by the person taking delivery thereof.

The notice in writing need not be given if the state of the goods has at the time of their receipt been the subject of joint survey or inspection.

In any event the carrier and the ship shall be discharged from all liability in respect of loss or damage unless suit is brought within one year after delivery of the goods or the date when the goods should have been delivered: Provided, That if a notice of loss or damage, either apparent or concealed, is not given as provided for in this section, that fact shall not affect or prejudice the right of the shipper to bring suit within one year after the delivery of the goods or the date when the goods should have been delivered.

In the case of any actual or apprehended loss or damage the carrier and the receiver shall give all reasonable facilities to each other for inspecting and tallying the goods.

(7)   "Shipped" bill of lading

After the goods are loaded the bill of lading to be issued by the carrier, master, or agent of the carrier to the shipper shall, if the shipper so demands, be a "shipped" bill of lading: Provided, That if the shipper shall have previously taken up any document of title to such goods, he shall surrender the same as against the issue of the "shipped" bill of lading, but at the option of the carrier such document of title may be noted at the port of shipment by the carrier, master, or agent with the name or names of the ship or ships upon which the goods have been shipped and the date or dates of shipment, and when so noted the same shall for the purpose of this section be deemed to constitute a "shipped" bill of lading.

(8)   Limitation of liability for negligence

Any clause, covenant, or agreement in a contract of carriage relieving the carrier or the ship from liability for loss or damage to or in connection with the goods, arising from negligence, fault, or failure in the duties and obligations provided in this section, or lessening such liability otherwise than as provided in this chapter, shall be null and void and of no effect. A benefit of insurance in favor of the carrier, or similar clause, shall be deemed to be a clause relieving the carrier from liability. (Apr. 16, 1936, ch. 229, title I, § 3, 49 Stat. 1208.)

§ 1304. Rights and Immunities of Carrier and Ship

(1)   Unseaworthiness

Neither the carrier nor the ship shall be liable for loss or damage arising or resulting from unseaworthiness unless caused by want of due diligence on the part of the carrier to make the ship seaworthy, and to secure that the ship is properly manned, equipped, and supplied, and to make the holds, refrigerating and cool chambers, and all other parts of the ship in which goods are carried fit and safe for their reception, carriage, and preservation in accordance with the provisions of paragraph (1) of section 1303 of this Appendix. Whenever loss or damage has resulted from unseaworthiness, the burden of proving the exercise of due diligence shall be on the carrier or other persons claiming exemption under this section.

(2)   Uncontrollable causes of loss

Neither the carrier nor the ship shall be responsible for loss or damage arising or resulting from—

(a)   Act, neglect, or default of the master, mariner, pilot, or the servants of the carrier in the navigation or in the management of the ship;

(b)   Fire, unless caused by the actual fault or privity of the carrier;

(c)   Perils, dangers, and accidents of the sea or other navigable waters;

(d)   Act of God;

(e)   Act of war;

(f)   Act of public enemies;

(g)   Arrest or restraint of princes, rulers, or people, or seizure under legal process;

(h)   Quarantine restrictions;

(i)   Act or omission of the shipper or owner of the goods, his agent or representative;

(j)   Strikes or lockouts or stoppage or restraint of labor from whatever cause, whether partial or general: Provided, That nothing herein contained shall be construed to relieve a carrier from responsibility for the carrier's own acts;

(k)   Riots and civil commotions;

(l)   Saving or attempting to save life or property at sea;

(m)   Wastage in bulk or weight or any other loss or damage arising from inherent defect, quality, or vice of the goods;

(n)   Insufficiency of packing;

(o)   Insufficiency or inadequacy of marks;

(p)   Latent defects not discoverable by due diligence; and

(q)   Any other cause arising without the actual fault and privity of the carrier and without the fault or neglect of the agents or servants of the carrier, but the burden of proof shall be on the person claiming the benefit of this exception to show that neither the actual fault or privity of the carrier nor the fault or neglect of the agents or servants of the carrier contributed to the loss or damage.

(3)   Freedom from negligence

The shipper shall not be responsible for loss or damage sustained by the carrier or the ship arising or resulting from any cause without the act, fault, or neglect of the shipper, his agents, or his servants.

(4)   Deviations

Any deviation in saving or attempting to save life or property at sea, or any reasonable deviation shall not be deemed to be an infringement or breach of this chapter or of the contract of carriage, and the carrier shall not be liable for any loss or damage resulting therefrom: Provided, however, That if the deviation is for the purpose of loading or unloading cargo or passengers it shall, prima facie, be regarded as unreasonable.

(5)   Amount of liability; valuation of cargo

Neither the carrier nor the ship shall in any event be or become liable for any loss or damage to or in connection with the transportation of goods in an amount exceeding $500 per package lawful money of the United States, or in case of goods not shipped in packages, per customary freight unit, or the equivalent of that sum in other currency, unless the nature and value of such goods have been declared by the shipper before shipment and inserted in the bill of lading. This declaration, if embodied in the bill of lading, shall be prima facie evidence, but shall not be conclusive on the carrier.

By agreement between the carrier, master, or agent of the carrier, and the shipper another maximum amount than that mentioned in this paragraph may be fixed: Provided, That such maximum shall not be less than the figure above named. In no event shall the carrier be liable for more than the amount of damage actually sustained.

Neither the carrier nor the ship shall be responsible in any event for loss or damage to or in connection with the transportation of the goods if the nature or value thereof has been knowingly and fraudulently misstated by the shipper in the bill of lading.

(6)   Inflammable, explosive, or dangerous cargo

Goods of an inflammable, explosive, or dangerous nature to the shipment whereof the carrier, master or agent of the carrier, has not consented with knowledge of their nature and character, may at any time before discharge be landed at any place or destroyed or rendered innocuous by the carrier without compensation, and the shipper of such goods shall be liable for all damages and expenses directly or indirectly arising out of or resulting from such shipment. If any such goods shipped with such knowledge and consent shall become a danger to the ship or cargo, they may in like manner be landed at any place, or destroyed or rendered innocuous by the carrier without liability on the part of the carrier except to general average, if any. (Apr. 16, 1936, ch. 229, title I, § 4, 49 Stat. 1210.)

§ 1305. Surrender of Rights; Increase of Liabilities; Charter Parties; General Average

A carrier shall be at liberty to surrender in whole or in part all or any of his rights and immunities or to increase any of his responsibilities and liabilities under this chapter, provided such surrender or increase shall be embodied in the bill of lading issued to the shipper.

The provisions of this chapter shall not be applicable to charter parties; but if bills of lading are issued in the case of a ship under a charter party, they shall comply with the terms of this chapter. Nothing in this chapter shall be held to prevent the insertion in a bill of lading of any lawful provision regarding general average. (Apr. 16, 1936, ch. 229, title I, § 5, 49 Stat. 1211.)

§ 1306. Special Agreement as to Particular Goods

Notwithstanding the provisions of sections 1303 to 1305 of this Appendix, a carrier, master or agent of the carrier, and a shipper shall, in regard to any particular goods be at liberty to enter into any agreement in any terms as to the responsibility and liability of the carrier for such goods, and as to the rights and immunities of the carrier in respect of such goods, or his obligation as to seaworthiness (so far as the stipulation regarding seaworthiness is not contrary to public policy), or the care or diligence of his servants or agents in regard to the loading, handling, stowage, carriage, custody, care, and discharge of the goods carried by sea: Provided, That in this case no bill of lading has been or shall be issued and that the terms agreed shall be embodied in a receipt which shall be a nonnegotiable document and shall be marked as such.

Any agreement so entered into shall have full legal effect: Provided, That this section shall not apply to ordinary commercial shipments made in the ordinary course of trade but only to other shipments where the character or condition of the property to be carried or the circumstances, terms, and conditions under which the carriage is to be performed are such as reasonably to justify a special agreement. (Apr. 16, 1936, ch. 229, title I, § 6, 49 Stat. 1211.)

§ 1307. Agreement as to Liability Prior to Loading or After Discharge

Nothing contained in this chapter shall prevent a carrier or a shipper from entering into any agreement, stipulation, condition, reservation, or exemption as to the responsibility and liability of the carrier or the ship for the loss or damage to or in connection with the custody and care and handling of goods prior to the loading on and subsequent to the discharge from the ship on which the goods are carried by sea. (Apr. 16, 1936, ch. 229, title I, § 7, 49 Stat. 1212.)

§ 1308. Rights and Liabilities Under Other Provisions

The provisions of this chapter shall not affect the rights and obligations of the carrier under the provisions of the Shipping Act, 1916 [46 App. U.S.C. 801 et seq.], or under the provisions of sections 4281 to 4289, inclusive, of the Revised Statutes of the United States [46 App. 181-188] or of any amendments thereto; or under the provisions of any other enactment for the time being in force relating to the limitation of the liability of the owners of seagoing vessels. (Apr. 16, 1936, ch. 229, title I, § 8, 49 Stat. 1212.)

§ 1309. Discrimination Between Competing Shippers

Nothing contained in this chapter shall be construed as permitting a common carrier by water to discriminate between competing shippers similarly placed in time and circumstances, either (a) with respect to their right to demand and receive bills of lading subject to the provisions of this chapter; or (b) when issuing such bills of lading, either in the surrender of any of the carrier's rights and immunities or in the increase of any of the carrier's responsibilities and liabilities pursuant to section 1305 of this Appendix; or (c) in any other way prohibited by the Shipping Act, 1916, as amended [46 App. U.S.C. 801 et seq.]. (Apr. 16, 1936, ch. 229, title II, § 9, 49 Stat. 1212.)

§ 1310. Weight of Bulk Cargo

Where under the customs of any trade the weight of any bulk cargo inserted in the bill of lading is a weight ascertained or accepted by a third party other than the carrier or the shipper, and the fact that the weight is so ascertained or accepted is stated in the bill of lading, then, notwithstanding anything in this chapter, the bill of lading shall not be deemed to be prima facie evidence against the carrier of the receipt of goods of the weight so inserted in the bill of lading, and the accuracy thereof at the time of shipment shall not be deemed to have been guaranteed by the shipper. (Apr. 16, 1936, ch. 229, title II, § 11, 49 Stat. 1212.)

§ 1311. Liabilities Before Loading and After Discharge; Effect on Other Laws

Nothing in this chapter shall be construed as superseding any part of sections 190 to 196 of this Appendix, or of any other law which would be applicable in the absence of this chapter, insofar as they relate to the duties, responsibilities, and liabilities of the ship or carrier prior to the time when the goods are loaded on or after the time they are discharged from the ship. (Apr. 16, 1936, ch. 229, title II, § 12, 49 Stat. 1212.)

§ 1312. Scope of Chapter; "United States"; "Foreign Trade"

This chapter shall apply to all contracts for carriage of goods by sea to or from ports of the United States in foreign trade. As used in this chapter the term "United States" includes its districts, territories, and possessions. The term "foreign trade" means the transportation of goods between the ports of the United States and ports of foreign countries. Nothing in this chapter shall be held to apply to contracts for carriage of goods by sea between any port of the United States or its possessions, and any other port of the United States or its possessions: Provided, however, That any bill of lading or similar document of title which is evidence of a contract for the carriage of goods by sea between such ports, containing an express statement that it shall be subject to the provisions of this chapter, shall be subjected hereto as fully as if subject hereto by the express provisions of this chapter: Provided further, That every bill of lading or similar document of title which is evidence of a contract for the carriage of goods by sea from ports of the United States, in foreign trade, shall contain a statement that it shall have effect subject to the provisions of this chapter. (Apr. 16, 1936, ch. 229, title II, § 13, 49 Stat. 1212; Proc. No. 2695, eff. July 4, 1946, 11 F.R. 7517, 60 Stat. 1352.)

§ 1313. Suspension of Provisions by President

Upon the certification of the Secretary of Transportation that the foreign commerce of the United States in its competition with that of foreign nations is prejudiced by the provisions, or any of them, of sections 1301 to 1308 of this Appendix, or by the laws of any foreign country or countries relating to the carriage of goods by sea, the President of the United States may, from time to time, by proclamation, suspend any or all provisions of said sections for such periods of time or indefinitely as may be designated in the proclamation. The President may at any time rescind such suspension of said sections, and any provisions thereof which may have been suspended shall thereby be reinstated and again apply to contracts thereafter made for the carriage of goods by sea. Any proclamation of suspension or rescission of any such suspension shall take effect on a date named therein, which date shall be not less than ten days from the issue of the proclamation.

Any contract for the carriage of goods by sea, subject to the provisions of this chapter, effective during any period when sections 1301 to 1308 of this Appendix, or any part thereof, are suspended, shall be subject to all provisions of law now or hereafter applicable to that part of said sections which may have thus been suspended. (Apr. 16, 1936, ch. 229, title II, § 14, 49 Stat. 1213; Pub. L. 97-31, § 12(146), Aug. 6, 1981, 95 Stat. 166.)

§ 1314. Effective Date; Retroactive Effect

This chapter shall take effect ninety days after April 16, 1936; but nothing in this chapter shall apply during a period not to exceed one year following April 16, 1936, to any contract for the carriage of goods by sea, made before April 16, 1936, nor to any bill of lading or similar document of title issued, whether before or after such date in pursuance of any such contract as aforesaid. (Apr. 16, 1936, ch. 229, title II, § 15, 49 Stat. 1213.)

§ 1315. Short Title

This chapter may be cited as the "Carriage of Goods by Sea Act."
(Apr. 16, 1936, ch. 229, title II, § 16, 49 Stat. 1213.)

CONVENTION FOR THE UNIFICATION OF CERTAIN RULES RELATING TO INTERNATIONAL CARRIAGE BY AIR ("Warsaw Convention")[1]
(12 October 1929)

CHAPTER I - SCOPE - DEFINITIONS
Article 1

1.   This Convention applies to all international carriage of persons, luggage or goods performed by aircraft for reward. It applies equally to gratuitous carriage by aircraft performed by an air transport undertaking.

2.   For the purposes of this Convention the expression "international carriage" means any carriage in which, according to the contract made by the parties, the place of departure and the place of destination, whether or not there be a break in the carriage or a transhipment, are situated either within the territories of two High Contracting Parties, or within the territory of a single High Contracting Party, if there is an agreed stopping place within a territory subject to the sovereignty, suzerainty, mandate or authority of another Power, even though that Power is not a party to this Convention. A carriage without such an agreed stopping place between territories subject to the sovereignty, suzerainty, mandate or authority of the same High Contracting Party is not deemed to be international for the purposes of this Convention.

3.   A carriage to be performed by several successive air carriers is deemed, for the purposes of this Convention, to be one undivided carriage, if it has been regarded by the parties as a single operation, whether it had been agreed upon under the form of a single contract or of a series of contracts, and it does not lose its international character merely because one contract or a series of contracts is to be performed entirely within a territory subject to the sovereignty, suzerainty, mandate or authority of the same High Contracting Party.

---

1   © International Civil Aviation Organization (ICAO), all rights reserved.

Article 2

1.   This Convention applies to carriage performed by the State or by legally constituted public bodies provided it falls within the conditions laid down in Article 1.

2.   This Convention does not apply to carriage performed under the terms of any international postal Convention.

CHAPTER II - DOCUMENTS OF CARRIAGE
Section I - Passenger Ticket
Article 3

1.   For the carriage of passengers the carrier must deliver a passenger ticket which shall contain the following particulars:-
(a)   the place and date of issue;
(b)   the place of departure and of destination;
(c)   the agreed stopping places, provided that the carrier may reserve the right to alter the stopping places in case of necessity, and that if he exercises that right, the alteration shall not have the effect of depriving the carriage of its international character;
(d)   the name and address of the carrier or carriers;
(e)   a statement that the carriage is subject to the rules relating to liability established by this Convention.

2.   The absence, irregularity or loss of the passenger ticket does not affect the existence or the validity of the contract of carriage, which shall none the less be subject to the rules of this Convention. Nevertheless, if the carrier accepts a passenger without a passenger ticket having been delivered he shall not be entitled to avail himself of those provisions of this Convention which exclude or limit his liability.

Section II - Luggage Ticket
Article 4

1.   For the carriage of luggage, other than small personal objects of which the passenger takes charge himself, the carrier must deliver a luggage ticket.

2.   The luggage ticket shall be made out in duplicate, one part for the passenger and the other part for the carrier.

3.   The luggage ticket shall contain the following particulars:-
(a)   the place and date of issue;
(b)   the place of departure and of destination;
(c)   the name and address of the carrier or carriers;
(d)   the number of the passenger ticket;
(e)   a statement that delivery of the luggage will be made to the bearer of the luggage ticket;
(f)   the number and weight of the packages;
(g)   the amount of the value declared in accordance with Article 22(2);
(h)   a statement that the carriage is subject to the rules relating to liability established by this Convention.

4.   The absence, irregularity or loss of the luggage ticket does not affect the existence or the validity of the contract of carriage, which shall none the less be subject to the rules of this Convention. Nevertheless, if the carrier accepts luggage without a luggage ticket having been delivered, or if the luggage ticket does not contain the particulars set out at (d), (f) and (h) above, the carrier shall not be entitled to avail himself of those provisions of the Convention which exclude or limit his liability.

Section III - Air Consignment Note
Article 5

1.   Every carrier of goods has the right to require the consignor to make out and hand over to him a document called an "air consignment note"; every consignor has the right to require the carrier to accept this document.

2.   The absence, irregularity or loss of this document does not affect the existence or the validity of the contract of carriage which shall, subject to the provisions of Article 9, be none the less governed by the rules of this Convention.

Article 6
1.   The air consignment note shall be made out by the consignor in three original parts and be handed over with the goods.
2.   The first part shall be marked "for the carrier," and shall be signed by the consignor. The second part shall be marked "for the consignee"; it shall be signed by the consignor and by the carrier and shall accompany the goods. The third part shall be signed by the carrier and handed by him to the consignor after the goods have been accepted.
3.   The carrier shall sign on acceptance of the goods.
4.   The signature of the carrier may be stamped; that of the consignor may be printed or stamped.
5.   If, at the request of the consignor, the carrier makes out the air consignment note, he shall be deemed, subject to proof to the contrary, to have done so on behalf of the consignor.

Article 7
The carrier of goods has the right to require the consignor to make out separate consignment notes when there is more than one package.

Article 8
The air consignment note shall contain the following particulars:-
(a)   the place and date of its execution;
(b)   the place of departure and of destination;
(c)   the agreed stopping places, provided that the carrier may reserve the right to alter the stopping places in case of necessity, and that if he exercises that right the alteration shall not have the effect of depriving the carriage of its international character;
(d)   the name and address of the consignor;
(e)   the name and address of the first carrier;
(f)   the name and address of the consignee, if the case so requires;
(g)   the nature of the goods;
(h)   the number of the packages, the method of packing and the particular marks or numbers upon them;
(i)   the weight, the quantity and the volume or dimensions of the goods;
(j)   the apparent condition of the goods and of the packing;
(k)   the freight, if it has been agreed upon, the date and place of payment, and the person who is to pay it;
(l)   if the goods are sent for payment on delivery, the price of the goods, and, if the case so requires, the amount of the expenses incurred;
(m)   the amount of the value declared in accordance with Article 22 (2);
(n)   the number of parts of the air consignment note;
(o)   the documents handed to the carrier to accompany the air consignment note;
(p)   the time fixed for the completion of the carriage and a brief note of the route to be followed, if these matters have been agreed upon;
(q)   a statement that the carriage is subject to the rules relating to liability established by this Convention.

Article 9
If the carrier accepts goods without an air consignment note having been made out, or if the air consignment note does not contain all the particulars set out in Article 8(a) to (i) inclusive and (q), the carrier shall not be entitled to avail himself of the provisions of this Convention which exclude or limit his liability.

Article 10
1.   The consignor is responsible for the correctness of the particulars and statements relating to the goods which he inserts in the air consignment note.

2.   The consignor will be liable for all damage suffered by the carrier or any other person by reason of the irregularity, incorrectness or incompleteness of the said particulars and statements.

Article 11

1.   The air consignment note is prima facie evidence of the conclusion of the contract, of the receipt of the goods and of the conditions of carriage.

2.   The statements in the air consignment note relating to the weight, dimensions and packing of the goods, as well as those relating to the number of packages, are prima facie evidence of the facts stated; those relating to the quantity, volume and condition of the goods do not constitute evidence against the carrier except so far as they both have been, and are stated in the air consignment note to have been, checked by him in the presence of the consignor, or relate to the apparent condition of the goods.

Article 12

1.   Subject to his liability to carry out all his obligations under the contract of carriage, the consignor has the right to dispose of the goods by withdrawing them at the aerodrome of departure or destination, or by stopping them in the course of the journey on any landing, or by calling for them to be delivered at the place of destination or in the course of the journey to a person other than the consignee named in the air consignment note, or by requiring them to be returned to the aerodrome of departure. He must not exercise this right of disposition in such a way as to prejudice the carrier or other consignors and he must repay any expenses occasioned by the exercise of this right.

2.   If it is impossible to carry out the orders of the consignor the carrier must so inform him forthwith.

3.   If the carrier obeys the orders of the consignor for the disposition of the goods without requiring the production of the part of the air consignment note delivered to the latter, he will be liable, without prejudice to his right of recovery from the consignor, for any damage which may be caused thereby to any person who is lawfully in possession of that part of the air consignment note.

4.   The right conferred on the consignor ceases at the moment when that of the consignee begins in accordance with Article 13. Nevertheless, if the consignee declines to accept the consignment note or the goods, or if he cannot be communicated with, the consignor resumes his right of disposition.

Article 13

1.   Except in the circumstances set out in the preceding Article, the consignee is entitled, on arrival of the goods at the place of destination, to require the carrier to hand over to him the air consignment note and to deliver the goods to him, on payment of the charges due and on complying with the conditions of carriage set out in the air consignment note.

2.   Unless it is otherwise agreed, it is the duty of the carrier to give notice to the consignee as soon as the goods arrive.

3.   If the carrier admits the loss of the goods, or if the goods have not arrived at the expiration of seven days after the date on which they ought to have arrived, the consignee is entitled to put into force against the carrier the rights which flow from the contract of carriage.

Article 14

The consignor and the consignee can respectively enforce all the rights given them by Articles 12 and 13, each in his own name, whether he is acting in his own interest or in the interest of another, provided that he carries out the obligations imposed by the contract.

Article 15

1.   Articles 12, 13 and 14 do not affect either the relations of the consignor or the consignee with each other or the mutual relations of third parties whose rights are derived either from the consignor or from the consignee.

2.   The provisions of Articles 12, 13 and 14 can only be varied by express provision in the air consignment note.

Article 16

1.   The consignor must furnish such information and attach to the air consignment note such documents as are necessary to meet the formalities of customs, octroi or police before the goods can be delivered to the consignee. The consignor is liable to the carrier for any damage occasioned by the absence, insufficiency or irregularity of any such information or documents, unless the damage is due to the fault of the carrier or his agents.

2.   The carrier is under no obligation to enquire into the correctness or sufficiency of such information or documents.

CHAPTER III - LIABILITY OF THE CARRIER

Article 17

The carrier is liable for damage sustained in the event of the death or wounding of a passenger or any other bodily injury suffered by a passenger, if the accident which caused the damage so sustained took place on board the aircraft or in the course of any of the operations of embarking or disembarking.

Article 18

1.   The carrier is liable for damage sustained in the event of the destruction or loss of, or of damage to, any registered luggage or any goods, if the occurrence which caused the damage so sustained took place during the carriage by air.

2.   The carriage by air within the meaning of the preceding paragraph comprises the period during which the luggage or goods are in charge of the carrier, whether in an aerodrome or on board an aircraft, or, in the case of a landing outside an aerodrome, in any place whatsoever.

3.   The period of the carriage by air does not extend to any carriage by land, by sea or by river performed outside an aerodrome. If, however, such a carriage takes place in the performance of a contract for carriage by air, for the purpose of loading, delivery or transshipment, any damage is presumed, subject to proof to the contrary, to have been the result of an event which took place during the carriage by air.

Article 19

The carrier is liable for damage occasioned by delay in the carriage by air of passengers, luggage or goods.

Article 20

1.   The carrier is not liable if he proves that he and his agents have taken all necessary measures to avoid the damage or that it was impossible for him or them to take such measures.

2.   In the carriage of goods and luggage the carrier is not liable if he proves that the damage was occasioned by negligent pilotage or negligence in the handling of the aircraft or in navigation and that, in all other respects, he and his agents have taken all necessary measures to avoid the damage.

Article 21

If the carrier proves that the damage was caused by or contributed to by the negligence of the injured person the Court may, in accordance with the provisions of its own law, exonerate the carrier wholly or partly from his liability.

Article 22

1.   In the carriage of passengers the liability of the carrier for each passenger is limited to the sum of 125,000 francs. Where, in accordance with the law of the Court seised of the case, damages may be awarded in the form of periodical payments, the equivalent capital value of the said payments shall not exceed 125,000 francs. Nevertheless, by special contract, the carrier and the passenger may agree to a higher limit of liability.

2.   In the carriage of registered luggage and of goods, the liability of the carrier is limited to a sum of 250 francs per kilogram, unless the consignor has made, at the time when the package was handed over to the carrier, a special declaration of the value at delivery and has paid a supplementary sum if the case so requires. In that case the carrier will be liable to pay a sum not ex-

ceeding the declared sum, unless he proves that that sum is greater than the actual value to the consignor at delivery.

3.   As regards objects of which the passenger takes charge himself the liability of the carrier is limited to 5,000 francs per passenger.

4.   The sums mentioned above shall be deemed to refer to the French franc consisting of 65 milligrams gold of millesimal fineness 900. These sums may be converted into any national currency in round figures.

Article 23

Any provision tending to relieve the carrier of liability or to fix a lower limit than that which is laid down in this Convention shall be null and void, but the nullity of any such provision does not involve the nullity of the whole contract, which shall remain subject to the provisions of this Convention.

Article 24

1.   In the cases covered by Articles 18 and 19 any action for damages, however founded, can only be brought subject to the conditions and limits set out in this Convention.

2.   In the cases covered by Article 17 the provisions of the preceding paragraph also apply, without prejudice to the questions as to who are the persons who have the right to bring suit and what are their respective rights.

Article 25

1.   The carrier shall not be entitled to avail himself of the provisions of this Convention which exclude or limit his liability, if the damage is caused by his wilful misconduct or by such default on his part as, in accordance with the law of the Court seised of the case, is considered to be equivalent to wilful misconduct.

2.   Similarly the carrier shall not be entitled to avail himself of the said provisions, if the damage is caused as aforesaid by any agent of the carrier acting within the scope of his employment.

Article 26

1.   Receipt by the person entitled to delivery of luggage or goods without complaint is prima facie evidence that the same have been delivered in good condition and in accordance with the document of carriage.

2.   In the case of damage, the person entitled to delivery must complain to the carrier forthwith after the discovery of the damage, and, at the latest, within three days from the date of receipt in the case of luggage and seven days from the date of receipt in the case of goods. In the case of delay the complaint must be made at the latest within fourteen days from the date on which the luggage or goods have been placed at his disposal.

3.   Every complaint must be made in writing upon the document of carriage or by separate notice in writing despatched within the times aforesaid.

4.   Failing complaint within the times aforesaid, no action shall lie against the carrier, save in the case of fraud on his part.

Article 27

In the case of the death of the person liable, an action for damages lies in accordance with the terms of this Convention against those legally representing his estate.

Article 28

1.   An action for damages must be brought, at the option of the plaintiff, in the territory of one of the High Contracting Parties, either before the Court having jurisdiction where the carrier is ordinarily resident, or has his principal place of business, or has an establishment by which the contract has been made or before the Court having jurisdiction at the place of destination.

2.   Questions of procedure shall be governed by the law of the Court seised of the case.

Article 29

1.   The right to damages shall be extinguished if an action is not brought within two years, reckoned from the date of arrival at the destination, or from the date on which the aircraft ought to have arrived, or from the date on which the carriage stopped.

2.   The method of calculating the period of limitation shall be determined by the law of the Court seised of the case.

Article 30

1.   In the case of carriage to be performed by various successive carriers and falling within the definition set out in the third paragraph of Article 1, each carrier who accepts passengers, luggage or goods is subjected to the rules set out in this Convention, and is deemed to be one of the contracting parties to the contract of carriage in so far as the contract deals with that part of the carriage which is performed under his supervision.

2.   In the case of carriage of this nature, the passenger or his representative can take action only against the carrier who performed the carriage during which the accident or the delay occurred, save in the case where, by express agreement, the first carrier has assumed liability for the whole journey.

3. A s regards luggage or goods, the passenger or consignor will have a right of action against the first carrier, and the passenger or consignee who is entitled to delivery will have a right of action against the last carrier, and further, each may take action against the carrier who performed the carriage during which the destruction, loss, damage or delay took place. These carriers will be jointly and severally liable to the passenger or to the consignor or consignee.

CHAPTER IV - PROVISIONS RELATING TO COMBINED CARRIAGE

Article 31

1.   In the case of combined carriage performed partly by air and partly by any other mode of carriage, the provisions of this Convention apply only to the carriage by air, provided that the carriage by air falls within the terms of Article 1.

2.   Nothing in this Convention shall prevent the parties in the case of combined carriage from inserting in the document of air carriage conditions relating to other modes of carriage, provided that the provisions of this Convention are observed as regards the carriage by air.

CHAPTER V - GENERAL AND FINAL PROVISIONS

Article 32

Any clause contained in the contract and all special agreements entered into before the damage occurred by which the parties purport to infringe the rules laid down by this Convention, whether by deciding the law to be applied, or by altering the rules as to jurisdiction, shall be null and void. Nevertheless for the carriage of goods arbitration clauses are allowed, subject to this Convention, if the arbitration is to take place within one of the jurisdictions referred to in the first paragraph of Article 28.

Article 33

Nothing contained in this Convention shall prevent the carrier either from refusing to enter into any contract of carriage, or from making regulations which do not conflict with the provisions of this Convention.

Article 34

This Convention does not apply to international carriage by air performed by way of experimental trial by air navigation undertakings with the view to the establishment of a regular line of air navigation, nor does it apply to carriage performed in extraordinary circumstances outside the normal scope of an air carrier's business.

Article 35

The expression "days" when used in this Convention means current days not working days.

Article 36

The Convention is drawn up in French in a single copy which shall remain deposited in the archives of the Ministry for Foreign Affairs of Poland and of which one duly certified copy shall be sent by the Polish Government to the Government of each of the High Contracting Parties.

Article 37

1.   This Convention shall be ratified. The instruments of ratification shall be deposited in the archives of the Ministry for Foreign Affairs of Poland, which will notify the deposit to the Government of each of the High Contracting Parties.

2.   As soon as this Convention shall have been ratified by five of the High Contracting Parties it shall come into force as between them on the ninetieth day after the deposit of the fifth ratification. Thereafter it shall come into force between the High Contracting Parties who shall have ratified and the High Contracting Party who deposits his instrument of ratification on the ninetieth day after the deposit.

3.   It shall be the duty of the Government of the Republic of Poland to notify to the Government of each of the High Contracting Parties the date on which this Convention comes into force as well as the date of the deposit of each ratification.

Article 38

1.   This Convention shall, after it has come into force, remain open for accession by any State.

2.   The accession shall be effected by a notification addressed to the Government of the Republic of Poland, which will inform the Government of each of the High Contracting Parties thereof.

3.   The accession shall take effect as from the ninetieth day after the notification made to the Government of the Republic of Poland.

Article 39

1.   Any one of the High Contracting Parties may denounce this Convention by a notification addressed to the Government of the Republic of Poland, which will at once inform the Government of each of the High Contracting Parties.

2.   Denunciation shall take effect six months after the notification of denunciation, and shall operate only as regards the Party who shall have proceeded to denunciation.

Article 40

1.   Any High Contracting Party may, at the time of signature or of deposit of ratification or of accession declare that the acceptance which he gives to this Convention does not apply to all or any of his colonies, protectorates, territories under mandate, or any other territory subject to his sovereignty or his authority, or any territory under his suzerainty.

2.   Accordingly any High Contracting Party may subsequently accede separately in the name of all or any of his colonies, protectorates, territories under mandate or any other territory subject to his sovereignty or to his authority or any territory under his suzerainty which has been thus excluded by his original declaration.

3.   Any High Contracting Party may denounce this Convention, in accordance with its provisions, separately or for all or any of his colonies, protectorates, territories under mandate or any other territory subject to his sovereignty or to his authority, or any other territory under his suzerainty.

Article 41

Any High Contracting Party shall be entitled not earlier than two years after the coming into force of this Convention to call for the assembling of a new international Conference in order to consider any improvements which may be made in this Convention. To this end he will communicate with the Government of the French Republic which will take the necessary measures to make preparations for such Conference.

This Convention done at Warsaw on the 12th October, 1929, shall remain open for signature until the 31st January, 1930.

Additional Protocol (With reference to Article 2)

The High Contracting Parties reserve to themselves the right to declare at the time of ratification or of accession that the first paragraph of Article 2 of this Convention shall not apply to international carriage by air performed directly by the State, its colonies, protectorates or mandated territories or by any other territory under its sovereignty, suzerainty or authority."

Entry into force: 13 February 1933
Ratifications and binding effect: 1929 Convention: 152 Member States; 1955 Hague Protocol to Amend the 1929 Convention (amendments not reproduced here): 137 Member States

CONVENTION FOR THE UNIFICATION OF CERTAIN RULES FOR INTERNATIONAL CARRIAGE BY AIR ("Montreal Convention")[1]
(28 May 1999)

THE STATES PARTIES TO THIS CONVENTION
RECOGNIZING the significant contribution of the Convention for the Unification of Certain Rules relating to International Carriage by Air signed in Warsaw on 12 October 1929, hereinafter referred to as the "Warsaw Convention", and other related instruments to the harmonization of private international air law;
RECOGNIZING the need to modernize and consolidate the Warsaw Convention and related instruments;
RECOGNIZING the importance of ensuring protection of the interests of consumers in international carriage by air and the need for equitable compensation based on the principle of restitution;
REAFFIRMING the desirability of an orderly development of international air transport operations and the smooth flow of passengers, baggage and cargo in accordance with the principles and objectives of the Convention on International Civil Aviation, done at Chicago on 7 December 1944;
CONVINCED that collective State action for further harmonization and codification of certain rules governing international carriage by air through a new Convention is the most adequate means of achieving an equitable balance of interests;
HAVE AGREED AS FOLLOWS:

Chapter 1 - General Provisions
Article 1 - Scope of Application

1.   This Convention applies to all international carriage of persons, baggage or cargo performed by aircraft for reward. It applies equally to gratuitous carriage by aircraft performed by an air transport undertaking.

2.   For the purposes of this Convention, the expression "international carriage" means any carriage in which, according to the agreement between the parties, the place of departure and the place of destination, whether or not there be a break in the carriage or a transhipment, are situated either within the territories of two States Parties, or within the territory of a single State Party if there is an agreed stopping place within the territory of another State, even if that State is not a State Party.

Carriage between two points within the territory of a single State Party without an agreed stopping place within the territory of another State is not international carriage for the purposes of this Convention.

3.   Carriage to be performed by several successive carriers is deemed, for the purposes of this Convention, to be one undivided carriage if it has been regarded by the parties as a single operation, whether it had been agreed upon under the form of a single contract or of a series of

---

1   © International Civil Aviation Organization (ICAO), Doc. 9740, all rights reserved. This Convention replaces the Warsaw Convention once ratified by all Contracting States.

contracts, and it does not lose its international character merely because one contract or a series of contracts is to be performed entirely within the territory of the same State.

4.   This Convention applies also to carriage as set out in Chapter V, subject to the terms contained therein.

Article 2 - Carriage Performed by State and Carriage of Postal Items

1.   This Convention applies to carriage performed by the State or by legally constituted public bodies provided it falls within the conditions laid down in Article 1.

2.   In the carriage of postal items, the carrier shall be liable only to the relevant postal administration in accordance with the rules applicable to the relationship between the carriers and the postal administrations.

3.   Except as provided in paragraph 2 of this Article, the provisions of this Convention shall not apply to the carriage of postal items.

Chapter II - Documentation and Duties of the Parties Relating to the Carriage of Passengers, Baggage and Cargo

Article 3 - Passengers and Baggage

1.   In respect of carriage of passengers, an individual or collective document of carriage shall be delivered containing:

(a)   an indication of the places of departure and destination;

(b)   if the places of departure and destination are within the territory of a single State Party, one or more agreed stopping places being within the territory of another State, an indication of at least one such stopping place.

2.   Any other means which preserves the information indicated in paragraph 1 may be substituted for the delivery of the document referred to in that paragraph. If any such other means is used, the carrier shall offer to deliver to the passenger a written statement of the information so preserved.

3.   The carrier shall deliver to the passenger a baggage identification tag for each piece of checked baggage.

4.   The passenger shall be given written notice to the effect that where this Convention is applicable it governs and may limit the liability of carriers in respect of death or injury and for destruction or loss of, or damage to, baggage, and for delay.

5.   Non-compliance with the provisions of the foregoing paragraphs shall not affect the existence or the validity of the contract of carriage, which shall, nonetheless, be subject to the rules of this Convention including those relating to limitation of liability.

Article 4 - Cargo

1.   In respect of the carriage of cargo, an air waybill shall be delivered.

2.   Any other means which preserves a record of the carriage to be performed may be substituted for the delivery of an air waybill. If such other means are used, the carrier shall, if so requested by the consignor, deliver to the consignor a cargo receipt permitting identification of the consignment and access to the information contained in the record preserved by such other means.

Article 5 - Contents of Air Waybill or Cargo Receipt

The air waybill or the cargo receipt shall include:

(a)   an indication of the places of departure and destination;

(b)   if the places of departure and destination are within the territory of a single State Party, one or more agreed stopping places being within the territory of another State, an indication of at least one such stopping place; and

(c)   an indication of the weight of the consignment.

Article 6 - Document Relating to the Nature of the Cargo

The consignor may be required, if necessary, to meet the formalities of customs, police and similar public authorities to deliver a document indicating the nature of the cargo. This provision creates for the carrier no duty, obligation or liability resulting therefrom.

Article 7 - Description of Air Waybill

1.   The air waybill shall be made out by the consignor in three original parts.
2.   The first part shall be marked "for the carrier"; it shall be signed by the consignor. The second part shall be marked "for the consignee"; it shall be signed by the consignor and by the carrier. The third part shall be signed by the carrier who shall hand it to the consignor after the cargo has been accepted.
3.   The signature of the carrier and that of the consignor may be printed or stamped.
4.   If, at the request of the consignor, the carrier makes out the air waybill, the carrier shall be deemed, subject to proof to the contrary, to have done so on behalf of the consignor.

Article 8 - Documentation for Multiple Packages

When there is more than one package:
(a)   the carrier of cargo has the right to require the consignor to make out separate air waybills;
(b)   the consignor has the right to require the carrier to deliver separate cargo receipts when the other means referred to in paragraph 2 of Article 4 are used.

Article 9 - Non-compliance with Documentary Requirements

Non-compliance with the provisions of Articles 4 to 8 shall not affect the existence or the validity of the contract of carriage, which shall, nonetheless, be subject to the rules of this Convention including those relating to limitation of liability.

Article 10 - Responsibility for Particulars of Documentation

1.   The consignor is responsible for the correctness of the particulars and statements relating to the cargo inserted by it or on its behalf in the air waybill or furnished by it or on its behalf to the carrier for insertion in the cargo receipt or for insertion in the record preserved by the other means referred to in paragraph 2 of Article 4. The foregoing shall also apply where the person acting on behalf of the consignor is also the agent of the carrier.
2.   The consignor shall indemnify the carrier against all damage suffered by it, or by any other person to whom the carrier is liable, by reason of the irregularity, incorrectness or incompleteness of the particulars and statements furnished by the consignor or on its behalf.
3.   Subject to the provisions of paragraphs 1 and 2 of this Article, the carrier shall indemnify the consignor against all damage suffered by it, or by any other person to whom the consignor is liable, by reason of the irregularity, incorrectness or incompleteness of the particulars and statements inserted by the carrier or on its behalf in the cargo receipt or in the record preserved by the other means referred to in paragraph 2 of Article 4.

Article 11 - Evidentiary Value of Documentation

1.   The air waybill or the cargo receipt is prima facie evidence of the conclusion of the contract, of the acceptance of the cargo and of the conditions of carriage mentioned therein.
2.   Any statements in the air waybill or the cargo receipt relating to the weight, dimensions and packing of the cargo, as well as those relating to the number of packages, are prima facie evidence of the facts stated; those relating to the quantity, volume and condition of the cargo do not constitute evidence against the carrier except so far as they both have been, and are stated in the air waybill or the cargo receipt to have been, checked by it in the presence of the consignor, or relate to the apparent condition of the cargo.

Article 12 - Right of Disposition of Cargo

1.   Subject to its liability to carry out all its obligations under the contract of carriage, the consignor has the right to dispose of the cargo by withdrawing it at the airport of departure or destination, or by stopping it in the course of the journey on any landing, or by calling for it to be

(a)   such damage was not due to the negligence or other wrongful act or omission of the carrier or its servants or agents; or

(b)   such damage was solely due to the negligence or other wrongful act or omission of a third party.

Article 22 - Limits of Liability in Relation to Delay, Baggage and Cargo

1.   In the case of damage caused by delay as specified in Article 19 in the carriage of persons, the liability of the carrier for each passenger is limited to 4,150 Special Drawing Rights.

2.   In the carriage of baggage, the liability of the carrier in the case of destruction, loss, damage or delay is limited to 1,000 Special Drawing Rights for each passenger unless the passenger has made, at the time when the checked baggage was handed over to the carrier, a special declaration of interest in delivery at destination and has paid a supplementary sum if the case so requires. In that case the carrier will be liable to pay a sum not exceeding the declared sum, unless it proves that the sum is greater than the passenger's actual interest in delivery at destination.

3.   In the carriage of cargo, the liability of the carrier in the case of destruction, loss, damage or delay is limited to a sum of 17 Special Drawing Rights per kilogram, unless the consignor has made, at the time when the package was handed over to the carrier, a special declaration of interest in delivery at destination and has paid a supplementary sum if the case so requires. In that case the carrier will be liable to pay a sum not exceeding the declared sum, unless it proves that the sum is greater than the consignor's actual interest in delivery at destination.

4. In the case of destruction, loss, damage or delay of part of the cargo, or of any object contained therein, the weight to be taken into consideration in determining the amount to which the carrier's liability is limited shall be only the total weight of the package or packages concerned.

Nevertheless, when the destruction, loss, damage or delay of a part of the cargo, or of an object contained therein, affects the value of other packages covered by the same air waybill, or the same receipt or, if they were not issued, by the same record preserved by the other means referred to in paragraph 2 of Article 4, the total weight of such package or packages shall also be taken into consideration in determining the limit of liability.

5.   The foregoing provisions of paragraphs 1 and 2 of this Article shall not apply if it is proved that the damage resulted from an act or omission of the carrier, its servants or agents, done with intent to cause damage or recklessly and with knowledge that damage would probably result; provided that, in the case of such act or omission of a servant or agent, it is also proved that such servant or agent was acting within the scope of its employment.

6.   The limits prescribed in Article 21 and in this Article shall not prevent the court from awarding, in accordance with its own law, in addition, the whole or part of the court costs and of the other expenses of the litigation incurred by the plaintiff, including interest. The foregoing provision shall not apply if the amount of the damages awarded, excluding court costs and other expenses of the litigation, does not exceed the sum which the carrier has offered in writing to the plaintiff within a period of six months from the date of the occurrence causing the damage, or before the commencement of the action, if that is later.

Article 23 - Conversion of Monetary Units

1.   The sums mentioned in terms of Special Drawing Right in this Convention shall be deemed to refer to the Special Drawing Right as defined by the International Monetary Fund. Conversion of the sums into national currencies shall, in case of judicial proceedings, be made according to the value of such currencies in terms of the Special Drawing Right at the date of the judgement. The value of a national currency, in terms of the Special Drawing Right, of a State Party which is a Member of the International Monetary Fund, shall be calculated in accordance with the method of valuation applied by the International Monetary Fund, in effect at the date of the judgement, for its operations and transactions. The value of a national currency, in terms of the Special Drawing Right, of a State Party which is not a Member of the International Monetary Fund, shall be calculated in a manner determined by that State.

2.   Nevertheless, those States which are not Members of the International Monetary Fund and whose law does not permit the application of the provisions of paragraph 1 of this Article may,

at the time of ratification or accession or at any time thereafter, declare that the limit of liability of the carrier prescribed in Article 21 is fixed at a sum of 1,500,000 monetary units per passenger in judicial proceedings in their territories; 62,500 monetary units per passenger with respect to paragraph 1 of Article 22; 15,000 monetary units per passenger with respect to paragraph 2 of Article 22; and 250 monetary units per kilogram with respect to paragraph 3 of Article 22. This monetary unit corresponds to sixty-five and a half milligrams of gold of millesimal fineness nine hundred. These sums may be converted into the national currency concerned in round figures. The conversion of these sums into national currency shall be made according to the law of the State concerned.

3.   The calculation mentioned in the last sentence of paragraph I of this Article and the conversion method mentioned in paragraph 2 of this Article shall be made in such manner as to express in the national currency of the State Party as far as possible the same real value for the amounts in Articles 21 and 22 as would result from the application of the first three sentences of paragraph 1 of this Article. States Parties shall communicate to the depositary the manner of calculation pursuant to paragraph 1 of this Article, or the result of the conversion in paragraph 2 of this Article as the case may be, when depositing an instrument of ratification, acceptance, approval of or accession to this Convention and whenever there is a change in either.

Article 24 - Review of Limits

1.   Without prejudice to the provisions of Article 25 of this Convention and subject to paragraph 2 below, the limits of liability prescribed in Articles 21, 22 and 23 shall be reviewed by the Depositary at five-year intervals, the first such review to take place at the end of the fifth year following the date of entry into force of this Convention, or if the Convention does not enter into force within five years of the date it is first open for signature, within the first year of its entry into force, by reference to an inflation factor which corresponds to the accumulated rate of inflation since the previous revision or in the first instance since the date of entry into force of the Convention. The measure of the rate of inflation to be used in determining the inflation factor shall be the weighted average of the annual rates of increase or decrease in the Consumer Price Indices of the States whose currencies comprise the Special Drawing Right mentioned in paragraph 1 of Article 23.

2.   If the review referred to in the preceding paragraph concludes that the inflation factor has exceeded 10 percent, the Depositary shall notify States Parties of a revision of the limits of liability. Any such revision shall become effective six months after its notification to the States Parties. If within three months after its notification to the States Parties a majority of the States Parties register their disapproval, the revision shall not become effective and the Depositary shall refer the matter to a meeting of the States Parties. The Depositary shall immediately notify all States Parties of the coming into force of any revision.

3.   Notwithstanding paragraph 1 of this Article, the procedure referred to in paragraph 2 of this Article shall be applied at any time provided that one-third of the States Parties express a desire to that effect and upon condition that the inflation factor referred to in paragraph 1 has exceeded 30 percent since the previous revision or since the date of entry into force of this Convention if there has been no previous revision. Subsequent reviews using the procedure described in paragraph 1 of this Article will take place at five-year intervals starting at the end of the fifth year following the date of the reviews under the present paragraph.

Article 25 - Stipulation on Limits

A carrier may stipulate that the contract of carriage shall be subject to higher limits of liability than those provided for in this Convention or to no limits of liability whatsoever.

Article 26 - Invalidity of Contractual Provisions

Any provision tending to relieve the carrier of liability or to fix a lower limit than that which is laid down in this Convention shall be null and void, but the nullity of any such provision does not involve the nullity of the whole contract, which shall remain subject to the provisions of this Convention.

Article 27 - Freedom to Contract

Nothing contained in this Convention shall prevent the carrier from refusing to enter into any contract of carriage, from waiving any defences available under the Convention, or from laying down conditions which do not conflict with the provisions of this Convention.

Article 28 - Advance Payments

In the case of aircraft accidents resulting in death or injury of passengers, the carrier shall, if required by its national law, make advance payments without delay to a natural person or persons who are entitled to claim compensation in order to meet the immediate economic needs of such persons. Such advance payments shall not constitute a recognition of liability and may be offset against any amounts subsequently paid as damages by the carrier.

Article 29 - Basis of Claims

In the carriage of passengers, baggage and cargo, any action for damages, however founded, whether under this Convention or in contract or in tort or otherwise, can only be brought subject to the conditions and such limits of liability as are set out in this Convention without prejudice to the question as to who are the persons who have the right to bring suit and what are their respective rights. In any such action, punitive, exemplary or any other non-compensatory damages shall not be recoverable.

Article 30 - Servants, Agents - Aggregation of Claims

1.   If an action is brought against a servant or agent of the carrier arising out of damage to which the Convention relates, such servant or agent, if they prove that they acted within the scope of their employment, shall be entitled to avail themselves of the conditions and limits of liability which the carrier itself is entitled to invoke under this Convention.

2.   The aggregate of the amounts recoverable from the carrier, its servants and agents, in that case, shall not exceed the said limits.

3.   Save in respect of the carriage of cargo, the provisions of paragraphs 1 and 2 of this Article shall not apply if it is proved that the damage resulted from an act or omission of the servant or agent done with intent to cause damage or recklessly and with knowledge that damage would probably result.

Article 31 - Timely Notice of Complaints

1.   Receipt by the person entitled to delivery of checked baggage or cargo without complaint is prima facie evidence that the same has been delivered in good condition and in accordance with the document of carriage or with the record preserved by the other means referred to in paragraph 2 of Article 3 and paragraph 2 of Article 4.

2.   In the case of damage, the person entitled to delivery must complain to the carrier forthwith after the discovery of the damage, and, at the latest, within seven days from the date of receipt in the case of checked baggage and fourteen days from the date of receipt in the case of cargo. In the case of delay, the complaint must be made at the latest within twenty-one days from the date on which the baggage or cargo have been placed at his or her disposal.

3.   Every complaint must be made in writing and given or dispatched within the times aforesaid.

4.   If no complaint is made within the times aforesaid, no action shall lie against the carrier, save in the case of fraud on its part.

Article 32 - Death of Person Liable

In the case of the death of the person liable, an action for damages lies in accordance with the terms of this Convention against those legally representing his or her estate.

Article 33 - Jurisdiction

1.   An action for damages must be brought, at the option of the plaintiff, in the territory of one of the States Parties, either before the court of the domicile of the carrier or of its principal place of business, or where it has a place of business through which the contract has been made or before the court at the place of destination.

2.   In respect of damage resulting from the death or injury of a passenger, an action may be brought before one of the courts mentioned in paragraph 1 of this Article, or in the territory of a State Party in which at the time of the accident the passenger has his or her principal and permanent residence and to or from which the carrier operates services for the carriage of passengers by air, either on its own aircraft or on another carrier's aircraft pursuant to a commercial agreement, and in which that carrier conducts its business of carriage of passengers by air from premises leased or owned by the carrier itself or by another carrier with which it has a commercial agreement.

3.   For the purposes of paragraph 2,

(a)   "commercial agreement" means an agreement, other than an agency agreement, made between carriers and relating to the provision of their joint services for carriage of passengers by air;

(b)   "principal and permanent residence" means the one fixed and permanent abode of the passenger at the time of the accident. The nationality of the passenger shall not be the determining factor in this regard.

4.   Questions of procedure shall be governed by the law of the court seized of the case.

Article 34 - Arbitration

1.   Subject to the provisions of this Article, the parties to the contract of carriage for cargo may stipulate that any dispute relating to the liability of the carrier under this Convention shall be settled by arbitration. Such agreement shall be in writing.

2.   The arbitration proceedings shall, at the option of the claimant, take place within one of the jurisdictions referred to in Article 33.

3.   The arbitrator or arbitration tribunal shall apply the provisions of this Convention.

4.   The provisions of paragraphs 2 and 3 of this Article shall be deemed to be part of every arbitration clause or agreement, and any term of such clause or agreement which is inconsistent therewith shall be null and void.

Article 35 - Limitation of Actions

1.   The right to damages shall be extinguished if an action is not brought within a period of two years, reckoned from the date of arrival at the destination, or from the date on which the aircraft ought to have arrived, or from the date on which the carriage stopped.

2.   The method of calculating that period shall be determined by the law of the court seized of the case.

Article 36 - Successive Carriage

1.   In the case of carriage to be performed by various successive carriers and falling within the definition set out in paragraph 3 of Article 1, each carrier which accepts passengers, baggage or cargo is subject to the rules set out in this Convention and is deemed to be one of the parties to the contract of carriage in so far as the contract deals with that part of the carriage which is performed under its supervision.

2.   In the case of carriage of this nature, the passenger or any person entitled to compensation in respect of him or her can take action only against the carrier which performed the carriage during which the accident or the delay occurred, save in the case where, by express agreement, the first carrier has assumed liability for the whole journey.

3.   As regards baggage or cargo, the passenger or consignor will have a right of action against the first carrier, and the passenger or consignee who is entitled to delivery will have a right of action against the last carrier, and further, each may take action against the carrier which performed the carriage during which the destruction, loss, damage or delay took place. These carriers will be jointly and severally liable to the passenger or to the consignor or consignee.

Article 37 - Right of Recourse Against Third Parties

Nothing in this Convention shall prejudice the question whether a person liable for damage in accordance with its provisions has a right of recourse against any other person.

Chapter IV - Combined Carriage
Article 38 - Combined Carriage

1.   In the case of combined carriage performed partly by air and partly by any other mode of carriage, the provisions of this Convention shall, subject to paragraph 4 of Article 18, apply only to the carriage by air, provided that the carriage by air falls within the terms of Article 1.

2.   Nothing in this Convention shall prevent the parties in the case of combined carriage from inserting in the document of air carriage conditions relating to other modes of carriage, provided that the provisions of this Convention are observed as regards the carriage by air.

Chapter V - Carriage by Air Performed by a Person Other than the Contracting Carrier
Article 39 - Contracting Carrier - Actual Carrier

The provisions of this Chapter apply when a person (hereinafter referred to as "the contracting carrier") as a principal makes a contract of carriage governed by this Convention with a passenger or consignor or with a person acting on behalf of the passenger or consignor, and another person (hereinafter referred to as "the actual carrier") performs, by virtue of authority from the contracting carrier, the whole or part of the carriage, but is not with respect to such part a successive carrier within the meaning of this Convention. Such authority shall be presumed in the absence of proof to the contrary.

Article 40 - Respective liability of contracting and actual carriers

If an actual carrier performs the whole or part of carriage which, according to the contract referred to in Article 39, is governed by this Convention, both the contracting carrier and the actual carrier shall, except as otherwise provided in this Chapter, be subject to the rules of this Convention, the former for the whole of the carriage contemplated in the contract, the latter solely for the carriage which it performs.

Article 41 - Mutual Liability

1.   The acts and omissions of the actual carrier and of its servants and agents acting within the scope of their employment shall, in relation to the carriage performed by the actual carrier, be deemed to be also those of the contracting carrier.

2.   The acts and omissions of the contracting carrier and of its servants and agents acting within the scope of their employment shall, in relation to the carriage performed by the actual carrier, be deemed to be also those of the actual carrier. Nevertheless, no such act or omission shall subject the actual carrier to liability exceeding the amounts referred to in Articles 21, 22, 23 and 24. Any special agreement under which the contracting carrier assumes obligations not imposed by this Convention or any waiver of rights or defences conferred by this Convention or any special declaration of interest in delivery at destination contemplated in Article 22 shall not affect the actual carrier unless agreed to by it.

Article 42 - Addressee of Complaints and Instructions

Any complaint to be made or instruction to be given under this Convention to the carrier shall have the same effect whether addressed to the contracting carrier or to the actual carrier. Nevertheless, instructions referred to in Article 12 shall only be effective if addressed to the contracting carrier.

Article 43 - Servants and Agents

In relation to the carriage performed by the actual carrier, any servant or agent of that carrier or of the contracting carrier shall, if they prove that they acted within the scope of their employment, be entitled to avail themselves of the conditions and limits of liability which are applicable under this Convention to the carrier whose servant or agent they are, unless it is proved that they acted in a manner that prevents the limits of liability from being invoked in accordance with this Convention.

Article 44 - Aggregation of Damages

In relation to the carriage performed by the actual carrier, the aggregate of the amounts recoverable from that carrier and the contracting carrier, and from their servants and agents acting within the scope of their employment, shall not exceed the highest amount which could be awarded against either the contracting carrier or the actual carrier under this Convention, but none of the persons mentioned shall be liable for a sum in excess of the limit applicable to that person.

Article 45 - Addressee of Claims

In relation to the carriage performed by the actual carrier, an action for damages may be brought, at the option of the plaintiff, against that carrier or the contracting carrier, or against both together or separately. If the action is brought against only one of those carriers, that carrier shall have the right to require the other carrier to be joined in the proceedings, the procedure and effects being governed by the law of the court seized of the case.

Article 46 - Additional Jurisdiction

Any action for damages contemplated in Article 45 must be brought, at the option of the plaintiff, in the territory of one of the States Parties, either before a court in which an action may be brought against the contracting carrier, as provided in Article 33, or before the court having jurisdiction at the place where the actual carrier has its domicile or its principal place of business.

Article 47 - Invalidity of Contractual Provisions

Any contractual provision tending to relieve the contracting carrier or the actual carrier of liability under this Chapter or to fix a lower limit than that which is applicable according to this Chapter shall be null and void, but the nullity of any such provision does not involve the nullity of the whole contract, which shall remain subject to the provisions of this Chapter.

Article 48 - Mutual Relations of Contracting and Actual Carriers

Except as provided in Article 45, nothing in this Chapter shall affect the rights and obligations of the carriers between themselves, including any right of recourse or indemnification.

Chapter VI - Other Provisions

Article 49 - Mandatory Application

Any clause contained in the contract of carriage and all special agreements entered into before the damage occurred by which the parties purport to infringe the rules laid down by this Convention, whether by deciding the law to be applied, or by altering the rules as to jurisdiction, shall be null and void.

Article 50 - Insurance

States Parties shall require their carriers to maintain adequate insurance covering their liability under this Convention. A carrier may be required by the State Party into which it operates to furnish evidence that it maintains adequate insurance covering its liability under this Convention.

Article 51 - Carriage Performed in Extraordinary Circumstances

The provisions of Articles 3 to 5, 7 and 8 relating to the documentation of carriage shall not apply in the case of carriage performed in extraordinary circumstances outside the normal scope of a carrier's business.

Article 52 - Definition of Days

The expression "days" when used in this Convention means calendar days, not working days.

Chapter VII - Final Clauses

Article 53 - Signature, Ratification and Entry into Force

1.   This Convention shall be open for signature in Montreal on 28 May 1999 by States participating in the International Conference on Air Law held at Montreal from 10 to 28 May 1999. After 28 May 1999, the Convention shall be open to all States for signature at the headquarters of the International Civil Aviation Organization in Montreal until it enters into force in accordance with paragraph 6 of this Article.

2.   This Convention shall similarly be open for signature by Regional Economic Integration Organisations. For the purpose of this Convention, a "Regional Economic Integration Organisation" means any organisation which is constituted by sovereign States of a given region which has competence in respect of certain matters governed by this Convention and has been

duly authorized to sign and to ratify, accept, approve or accede to this Convention. A reference to a "State Party" or "States Parties" in this Convention, otherwise than in paragraph 2 of Article 1, paragraph 1(b) of Article 3, paragraph (b) of Article 5, Articles 23, 33, 46 and paragraph (b) of Article 57, applies equally to a Regional Economic Integration Organisation. For the purpose of Article 24, the references to "a majority of the States Parties" and "one-third of the States Parties" shall not apply to a Regional Economic Integration Organisation.

3.   This Convention shall be subject to ratification by States and by Regional Economic Integration Organisations which have signed it.

4.   Any State or Regional Economic Integration Organisation which does not sign this Convention may accept, approve or accede to it at any time.

5.   Instruments of ratification, acceptance, approval or accession shall be deposited with the International Civil Aviation Organization, which is hereby designated the Depositary.

6.   This Convention shall enter into force on the sixtieth day following the date of deposit of the thirtieth instrument of ratification, acceptance, approval or accession with the Depositary between the States which have deposited such instrument. An instrument deposited by a Regional Economic Integration Organisation shall not be counted for the purpose of this paragraph.

7.   For other States and for other Regional Economic Integration Organisations, this Convention shall take effect sixty days following the date of deposit of the instrument of ratification, acceptance, approval or accession.

8.   The Depositary shall promptly notify all signatories and States Parties of:

(a)   each signature of this Convention and date thereof;

(b)   each deposit of an instrument of ratification, acceptance, approval or accession and date thereof;

(c)   the date of entry into force of this Convention;

(d)   the date of the coming into force of any revision of the limits of liability established under this Convention;

(e)   any denunciation under Article 54.

Article 54 - Denunciation

1.   Any State Party may denounce this Convention by written notification to the Depositary.

2.   Denunciation shall take effect one hundred and eighty days following the date on which notification is received by the Depositary.

Article 55 - Relationship with Other Warsaw Convention Instruments

This Convention shall prevail over any rules which apply to international carriage by air:

1.   between States Parties to this Convention by virtue of those States commonly being Party to

(a)   the Convention for the Unification of Certain Rules relating to International Carriage by Air signed at Warsaw on 12 October 1929 (hereinafter called the Warsaw Convention);

(b)   the Protocol to amend the Convention for the Unification of Certain Rules relating to International Carriage by Air signed at Warsaw on 12 October 1929, done at The Hague on 28 September 1955 (hereinafter called The Hague Protocol);

(c)   the Convention, Supplementary to the Warsaw Convention, for the Unification of Certain Rules relating to International Carriage by Air Performed by a Person other than the Contracting Carrier, signed at Guadalajara on 18 September 1961 (hereinafter called the Guadalajara Convention);

(d)   the Protocol to amend the Convention for the Unification of Certain Rules relating to International Carriage by Air signed at Warsaw on 12 October 1929 as amended by the Protocol done at The Hague on 28 September 1955, signed at Guatemala City on 8 March 1971 (hereinafter called the Guatemala City Protocol);

(e)   Additional Protocol Nos. 1 to 3 and Montreal Protocol No. 4 to amend the Warsaw Convention as amended by The Hague Protocol or the Warsaw Convention as amended by both

The Hague Protocol and the Guatemala City Protocol, signed at Montreal on 25 September 1975 (hereinafter called the Montreal Protocols); or

2.   within the territory of any single State Party to this Convention by virtue of that State being Party to one or more of the instruments referred to in sub-paragraphs (a) to (e) above.

Article 56 - States with More than One System of Law

1.   If a State has two or more territorial units in which different systems of law are applicable in relation to matters dealt with in this Convention, it may at the time of signature, ratification, acceptance, approval or accession declare that this Convention shall extend to all its territorial units or only to one or more of them and may modify this declaration by submitting another declaration at any time.

2.   Any such declaration shall be notified to the Depositary and shall state expressly the territorial units to which the Convention applies.

3.   In relation to a State Party which has made such a declaration:

(a)   references in Article 23 to "national currency" shall be construed as referring to the currency of the relevant territorial unit of that State; and

(b)   the reference in Article 28 to "national law" shall be construed as referring to the law of the relevant territorial unit of that State.

Article 57 - Reservations

No reservation may be made to this Convention except that a State Party may at any time declare by a notification addressed to the Depositary that this Convention shall not apply to:

(a)   international carriage by air performed and operated directly by that State Party for non-commercial purposes in respect to its functions and duties as a sovereign State; and/or

(b)   the carriage of persons, cargo and baggage for its military authorities on aircraft registered in or leased by that State Party, the whole capacity of which has been reserved by or on behalf of such authorities.

IN WITNESS WHEREOF the undersigned Plenipotentiaries, having been duly authorized, have signed this Convention.

DONE at Montreal on the 28th day of May of the year one thousand nine hundred and ninety-nine in the English, Arabic, Chinese, French, Russian and Spanish languages, all texts being equally authentic. This Convention shall remain deposited in the archives of the International Civil Aviation Organization, and certified copies thereof shall be transmitted by the Depositary to all States Parties to this Convention, as well as to all States Parties to the Warsaw Convention, The Hague Protocol, the Guadalajara Convention, the Guatemala City Protocol and the Montreal Protocols.

Entry into force: 4 November 2003
Ratification and binding effect: 102 Member States

UN CONVENTION ON THE CONTRACT FOR THE INTERNATIONAL CARRIAGE OF GOODS BY ROAD (CMR)[1]

(GENEVA, 19 MAY 1956)

PREAMBLE

THE CONTRACTING PARTIES,

HAVING RECOGNIZED the desirability of standardizing the conditions governing the contract for the international carriage of goods by road, particularly with respect to the documents used for such carriage and to the carrier's liability,

HAVE AGREED as follows:

CHAPTER 1 - SCOPE OF APPLICATION

Article 1

1.   This Convention shall apply to every contract for the carriage of goods by road in vehicles for reward, when the place of taking over of the goods and the place designated for delivery, as specified in the contract, are situated in two different countries, of which at least one is a contracting country, irrespective of the place of residence and the nationality of the parties.

2.   For the purpose of this Convention, "vehicles" means motor vehicles, articulated vehicles, trailers and semi-trailers as defined in Article 4 of the Convention on Road Traffic dated 19 September 1949.

3.   This Convention shall apply also where carriage coming within its scope is carried out by States or by governmental institutions or organizations.

4.   This Convention shall not apply:

(a)   To carriage performed under the terms of any international postal convention;

(b)   To funeral consignments;

(c)   To furniture removal.

5.   The Contracting Parties agree not to vary any of the provisions of this Convention by special agreements between two or more of them, except to make it inapplicable to their frontier traffic or to authorize the use in transport operations entirely confined to their territory of consignment notes representing a title to the goods.

Article 2

1.   Where the vehicle containing the goods is carried over part of the journey by sea, rail, inland waterways or air, and, except where the provisions of Article 14 are applicable, the goods are not unloaded from the vehicle, this Convention shall nevertheless apply to the whole of the carriage. Provided that to the extent it is proved that any loss, damage or delay in delivery of the goods which occurs during the carriage by the other means of transport was not caused by act or omission of the carrier by road, but by some event which could only occurred in the course of and by reason of the carriage by that other means of transport, the liability of the carrier by road shall be determined not by this convention but in the manner in which the liability of the carrier by the other means of transport would have been determined if a contract for the carriage the goods alone had been made by the sender with the carrier by the other means of transport in accordance with the conditions prescribed by law for the carriage of goods by that means of transport. If, however, there are no such prescribed conditions, the liability of the carrier by road shall be determined by this convention.

2.   If the carrier by road is also himself the carrier by the other means of transport, his liability shall also be determined in accordance with the provisions paragraph 1 of this article, but as if, in his capacities as carrier by road and carrier by the other means of transport, he were two separate persons.

---

1   © United Nations, 399 UNTS p. 189, all rights reserved.

CHAPTER II - PERSONS FOR WHOM THE CARRIER IS RESPONSIBLE
Article 3
For the purposes of this Convention the carrier shall be responsible for the acts of omissions of his agents and servants and of any other persons of whose services he makes use for the performance of the carriage, when such agents, servants or other persons are acting within the scope of their employment, as if such acts or omissions were his own.

CHAPTER III - CONCLUSION AND PERFORMANCE OF THE CONTRACT OF CARRIAGE
Article 4
The contract of carriage shall be confirmed by the making out of a consignment note. The absence, irregularity or loss of the consignment note shall not affect the existence or the validity of the contract of carriage which shall remain subject the provisions of this Convention.

Article 5
1.   The consignment note shall be made out in three original copies signed by the sender and by the carrier. These signatures may be printed or replaced by the stamps of the sender and the carrier if the law of the country in which the consignment note has been made out so permits. The first copy shall be handed to the sender, the second shall accompany the goods and the third shall be retained by the carrier.
2.   When the goods which are to be carried have to be loaded in different vehicles, or are of different kinds or are divided into different lots, the sender or the carrier shall have the right to require a separate consignment note to be made out for each vehicle used, or for each kind or lot of goods.

Article 6
1.   The consignment note shall contain the following particulars: (a) The date of the consignment note and the place at which it is made out;
(b)   The name and address of the sender;
(c)   The name and address of the carrier;
(d)   The place and the date of taking over of the goods and the place designated for delivery;
(e)   The name and address of the consignee;
(f)   The description in common use of the nature of the goods and the method of packing, and, in the case of dangerous goods, their generally recognized description;
(g)   The number of packages and their special marks and numbers;
(h)   The gross weight of the goods or their quantity otherwise expressed;
(i)   Charges relating to the carriage (carriage charges, supplementary charges, customs duties and other charges incurred from the making of the contract to the time of delivery);
(j)   The requisite instructions for Customs and other formalities;
(k)   A statement that the carriage is subject, notwithstanding any clause to the contrary, to the provisions of this Convention.
2.   Where applicable, the consignment note shall also contain the following particulars:
(a)   A statement that trans-shipment is not allowed;
(b)   Then charges which the sender undertakes to pay;
(c)   The amount of "cash on delivery" charges;
(d)   A declaration of the value of the goods and the amount representing special interest in delivery;
(e)   The sender's instructions to the carrier regarding insurance of the goods;
(f)   The agreed time limit within which the carriage is to be carried out;
(g)   A list of the documents handed to the carrier.
3.   The parties may enter in the consignment note any other particulars which they may deem useful.

Article 7
1.   The sender shall be responsible for all expenses, loss and damage sustained by the carrier by reason of the inaccuracy or inadequacy of:

(a) The particulars specified in Article 6, paragraph 1, (b), (d), (e), (f), (g), (h) and (j);
(b) The particular specified in Article 6, paragraph 2;
(c) Any other particulars or instructions given by him to enable the consignment note to be made out or for the purpose of their being entered therein.
2.   If, at the request of the sender, the carrier enters in the consignment note the particulars referred to in paragraph 1 of this article, he shall be deemed, unless the contrary is proved, to have done so on behalf of the sender.
3.   If the consignment note does not contain the statement specified in Article 6, paragraph 1 (k), the carrier shall be liable for all expenses, loss and damage sustained through such omission by the person entitled to dispose of the goods.

Article 8

1.   On taking over the goods, the carrier shall check:
(a) The accuracy of the statements in the consignment note as to the number of packages and their marks and numbers, and
(b) The apparent condition of the goods and their packaging.
2.   Where the carrier has no reasonable means of checking the accuracy of e statements referred to in paragraph 1 (a) of this article, he shall enter his reservations in the consignment note together with the grounds on which they are based. He shall likewise specify the grounds for any reservations which he makes with regard to the apparent condition of the goods and their packaging, such reservations shall not bind the sender unless he has expressly agreed to be bound by them in the consignment note.
3.   The sender shall be entitled to require the carrier to check the gross weight the goods or their quantity otherwise expressed. He may also require the contents of the packages to be checked.
        The carrier shall be entitled to claim the cost of such checking. The result of the checks shall be entered in the consignment note.

Article 9

1.   The consignment note shall be prima facie evidence of the making of the contract of carriage, the conditions of the contract and the receipt of the goods by the carrier.
2.   If the consignment note contains no specific reservations by the carrier, it shall be presumed, unless the contrary is proved, that the goods and their packaging appeared to be in good condition when the carrier took them over and that the number of packages, their marks and numbers corresponded with the statements in the consignment note.

Article 10

The sender shall be liable to the carrier for damage to persons, equipment or other goods, and for any expenses due to defective packing of the goods, unless the defect was apparent or known to the carrier at the time when he took over the goods and he made no reservations concerning it.

Article 11

1.   For the purposes of the Customs or other formalities which have to be completed before delivery of the goods, the sender shall attach the necessary documents to the consignment note or place them at the disposal of the carrier and shall furnish him with all the information which he requires.
2.   The carrier shall not be under any duty to enquire into either the accuracy or the adequacy of such documents and information. The sender shall be liable to the carrier for any damage caused by the absence, inadequacy or irregularity of such documents and information, except in the case of some wrongful act or neglect on the part of the carrier.
3.   The liability of the carrier for the consequences arising from the loss or incorrect use of the documents specified in and accompanying the consignment note or deposited with the carrier shall be that of an agent, provided that the compensation payable by the carrier shall not exceed that payable in the event of loss of the goods.

Article 12

1.   The sender has the right to dispose of the goods, in particular by asking the carrier to stop the goods in transit, to change the place at which delivery is to take place or to deliver the goods to a consignee other than the consignee indicated in the consignment note.

2.   This right shall cease to exist when the second copy of the consignment note is handed to the consignee or when the consignee exercises his right under Article 13, paragraph 1; from that time onwards the carrier shall obey the orders of the consignee.

3.   The consignee shall, however, have the right of disposal from the time when the consignment note is drawn up, if the sender makes an entry to that effect in the consignment note.

4.   If in exercising his right of disposal the consignee has ordered the delivery of the goods to another person, that other person shall not be entitled to name other consignees.

5.   The exercise of the right of disposal shall be subject to the following conditions:

(a)   That the sender or, in the case referred to in paragraph 3 of this article, the consignee who wishes to exercise the right produces the first copy of the consignment note on which the new instructions to the carrier have been entered and indemnifies the carrier against all expenses, loss and damage involved in carrying out such instructions;

(b)   That the carrying out of such instructions is possible at the time when the instructions reach the person who is to carry them out and does not either interfere with the normal working of the carriers' undertaking or prejudice the senders or consignees of other consignments;

(c)   That the instructions do not result in a division of the consignment.

6.   When, by reason of the provisions of paragraph 5 (b) of this article, the carrier cannot carry out the instructions which he receives, he shall immediately notify the person who gave him such instructions.

7.   A carrier who has not carried out the instructions given under the conditions provided for in this Article or who has carried them out without requiring the first copy of the consignment note to be produced, shall be liable to the person entitled to make a claim for any loss or damage caused thereby.

Article 13

1.   After arrival of the goods at the place designated for delivery, the consignee shall be entitled to require the carrier to deliver to him, against a receipt, the second copy of the consignment note and the goods. If the loss of the goods established or if the goods have not arrived after the expiry of the period provided for in Article 19, the consignee shall be entitled to enforce in his own name against the carrier any rights arising from the contract of carriage.

2.   The consignee who avails himself of the rights granted to him under paragraph 1 of this Article shall pay the charges shown to be due on the consignment note, but in the event of dispute on this matter the carrier shall not be required to deliver the goods unless security has been furnished by the consignee.

Article 14

1.   If for any reason it is or becomes impossible to carry out the contract in accordance with the terms laid down in the consignment note before the goods reach the place designated for delivery, the carrier shall ask for instructions from the person entitled to dispose of the goods in accordance with the provisions of Article 12.

2.   Nevertheless, if circumstances are such as to allow the carriage to be carried out under conditions differing from those laid down in the consignment note and if the carrier has been unable to obtain instructions in reasonable time the person entitled to dispose of the goods in accordance with the provisions of Article 12, he shall take such steps as seem to him to be in the best interests the person entitled to dispose of the goods.

Article 15

1.   Where circumstances prevent delivery of the goods after their arrival at the place designated for delivery, the carrier shall ask the sender for his instructions. If the consignee refuses the goods the sender shall be entitled to dispose of them without being obliged to produce the first copy of the consignment note.

2.   Even if he has refused the goods, the consignee may nevertheless require delivery so long as the carrier has not received instructions to the contrary from the sender.

3.   When circumstances preventing delivery of the goods arise after the consignee, in exercise of his rights under Article 12, paragraph 3, has given an order for the goods to be delivered to another person, paragraphs 1 and 2 of this Article shall apply as if the consignee were the sender and that other person were the consignee.

Article 16

1.   The carrier shall be entitled to recover the cost of his request for instructions and any expenses entailed in carrying out such instructions, unless such expenses were caused by the wrongful act or neglect of the carrier.

2.   In the cases referred to in Article 14, paragraph 1, and in Article 15, the carrier may immediately unload the goods for account of the person entitled to dispose of them and thereupon the carriage shall be deemed to be at an end. The carrier shall then hold the goods on behalf of the person so entitled. He may, however, entrust them to a third party, and in that case he shall not be under any liability except for the exercise of reasonable care in the choice of such third party. The charges due under the consignment note and all other expenses shall remain chargeable against the goods.

3.   The carrier may sell the goods, without awaiting instructions from the person entitled to dispose of them, if the goods are perishable or their condition warrants such a course, or when the storage expenses would be out of proportion to the value of the goods. He may also proceed to the sale of the goods in other cases if after the expiry of a reasonable period he has not received from the person entitled to dispose of the goods instructions to the contrary which he may reasonably be required to carry out.

4.   If the goods have been sold pursuant to this article, the proceeds of sale, after deduction of the expenses chargeable against the goods, shall be placed at the disposal of the person entitled to dispose of the goods. If these charges exceed the proceeds of sale, the carrier shall be entitled to the difference.

5.   The procedure in the case of sale shall be determined by the law or custom of the place where the goods are situated.

CHAPTER IV - LIABILITY OF THE CARRIER
Article 17

1.   The carrier shall be liable for the total or partial loss of the goods and for damage thereto occurring between the time when he takes over the goods and the time of delivery, as well as for any delay in delivery.

2.   The carrier shall, however, be relieved of liability if the loss, damage or delay was caused by the wrongful act or neglect of the claimant, by the instructions of the claimant given otherwise than as the result of a wrongful act or neglect on the part of the carrier, by inherent vice of the goods or through circumstances which the carrier could not avoid and the consequences of which he was unable to prevent.

3.   The carrier shall not be relieved of liability by reason of the defective condition of the vehicle used by him in order to perform the carriage, or by reason of the wrongful act or neglect of the person from whom he may have hired the vehicle or of the agents or servants of the latter.

4.   Subject to Article 18, paragraphs 2 to 5, the carrier shall be relieved of liability when the loss or damage arises from the special risks inherent in one more of the following circumstances:

(a) Use of open unsheeted vehicles, when their use has been expressly agreed and specified in the consignment note;

(b) The lack of, or defective condition of packing in the case of goods which, by their nature, are liable to wastage or to be damaged when not packed or when not properly packed;

(c) Handling, loading, stowage or unloading of the goods by the sender, the consignee or person acting on behalf of the sender or the consignee;

(d)   The nature of certain kinds of goods which particularly exposes them to total or partial loss or to damage, especially through breakage, rust, decay, desiccation, leakage, normal wastage, or the action of moth or vermin;
(f)   Insufficiency or inadequacy of marks or numbers on the packages;
(g)   The carriage of livestock.
5.   Where under this Article the carrier is not under any liability in respect some of the factors causing the loss, damage or delay, he shall only be liable the extent that those factors for which he is liable under this Article have contributed to the loss, damage or delay.

Article 18

1.   The burden of proving that loss, damage or delay was due to one of the specified in Article 17, paragraph 2, shall rest upon the carrier.
2.   When the carrier establishes that in the circumstances of the case, the loss damage could be attributed to one or more of the special risks referred to in Article 17, paragraph 4, it shall be resumed that it was so caused. The claimant shall, however, be entitled to prove that the loss or damage was not, in fact, attributable either wholly or partly to one of these risks.
3.   This presumption shall not apply in the circumstances set out in Article 17, paragraph 4 (a), if there has been an abnormal shortage, or a loss of any package.
4.   If the carriage is performed in vehicles specially equipped to protect the goods from the effects of heat, cold, variations in temperature or the humidity of the air, the carrier shall not be entitled to claim the benefit of Article 17, paragraph 4 (d), unless he proves that all steps incumbent on him in the circumstances with respect to the choice, maintenance and use of such equipment were taken and that he complied with any special instructions issued to him.
5.   The carrier shall not be entitled to claim the benefit of Article 17, paragraph 4 (f), unless he proves that all steps normally incumbent on him in the circumstances were taken and that he complied with any special instructions issued to him.

Article 19

Delay in delivery shall be said to occur when the goods have not been delivered within the agreed time-limit or when, failing an agreed time-limit, the actual duration of the carriage having regard to the circumstances of the case, and in particular, in the case of partial loads, the time required for making up a complete load in the normal way, exceeds the time it would be reasonable to allow a diligent carrier.

Article 20

1.   The fact that goods have not been delivered within thirty days following the expiry of the agreed time-limit, or, if there is no agreed time-limit, within sixty days from the time when the carrier took over the goods, shall be conclusive evidence of the loss of the goods, and the person entitled to make a claim may thereupon treat them as lost.
2.   The person so entitled may, on receipt of compensation for the missing goods, request in writing that he shall be notified immediately should the goods be recovered in the course of the year following the payment of compensation. He shall be given a written acknowledgement of such request.
3.   Within the thirty days following receipt of such notification, the person entitled as aforesaid may require the goods to be delivered to him against payment of the charges shown to be due on the consignment note and also against refund of the compensation he received less any charges included therein but without prejudice to any claims to compensation for delay in delivery under Article 23 and where applicable, Article 26.
4.   In the absence of the request mentioned in paragraph 2 or of any instructions given within the period of thirty days specified in paragraph 3, or if the goods are not recovered until more than one year after the payment of compensation, the carrier shall be entitled to deal with them in accordance with the law place where the goods are situated.

Article 21

Should the goods have been delivered to the consignee without collection of the "cash on delivery" charge which should have been collected by the carrier under terms of the contract of carriage, the carrier shall be liable to the sender for compensation not exceeding the amount of such charge without prejudice to his right of action against the consignee.

Article 22

1.   When the sender hands goods of a dangerous nature to the carrier, he shall inform the carrier of the exact nature of the danger and indicate if necessary, precautions to be taken. If this information has not been entered in the consignment note, the burden of proving, by some other means, that the carrier knew the exact nature of the danger constituted by the carriage of the said goods shall rest upon the sender or the consignee.
2.   Goods of a dangerous nature which, in the circumstance referred to in paragraph 1 of this article, the carrier did not know were dangerous, may, at any time or place, be unloaded, destroyed or rendered harmless by the carrier without compensation; further, the sender shall be liable for all expenses, loss or damage arising out of their handing over for carriage or of their carriage.

Article 23

1.   When, under the provisions of this Convention, a carrier is liable for compensation in respect of total or partial loss of goods, such compensation shall be calculated by reference to the value of the goods at the place and time at which they were accepted for carriage.
2.   The value of the goods shall be fixed according to the commodity exchange price or, if there is no such price, according to the current market price or, if there is no commodity exchange price or current market price, by reference to normal value of goods of the same kind and quality.
3.   Compensation shall not, however, exceed 25 francs per kilogram of gross weight short. "Franc" means the gold franc weighing 10/31 of a gramme and being of millesimal fineness 900.
4.   In addition, the carriage charges, Customs duties and other charges incurred in respect of the carriage of the goods shall be refunded in full in case of total loss and in proportion to the loss sustained in case of partial loss, but no further damage shall be payable.
5.   In the case of delay if the claimant proves that damage has resulted therefrom the carrier shall pay compensation for such damage not exceeding the carriage charges.
6.   Higher compensation may only be claimed where the value of the goods or a special interest in delivery has been declared in accordance with articles 24 and 26.

Article 24

The sender may, against payment of a surcharge to be agreed upon, declare in the consignment note a value for the goods exceeding the limit laid down in Article 23, paragraph 3, and in that case the amount of the declared value shall be substituted for that limit.

Article 25

1.   In case of damage, the carrier shall be liable for the amount by which the goods have diminished in value, calculated by reference to the value of the goods fixed in accordance with Article 23, paragraphs 1, 2 and 4.
2.   The compensation may not, however, exceed:
(a) If the whole consignment has been damaged, the amount payable in the case of total loss;
(b) If part only of the consignment has been damaged, the amount payable in the case of loss of the part affected.

Article 26

1.   The sender may, against payment of a surcharge to be agreed upon, fix the amount of a special interest in delivery in the case of loss or damage or of the agreed time-limit being exceeded, by entering such amount in the consignment note.
2.   If a declaration of a special interest in delivery has been made, compensation for the additional loss or damage proved may be claimed, up to the total amount of the interest declared, independently of the compensation provided for in articles 23, 24 and 25.

Article 27
1.   The claimant shall be entitled to claim interest on compensation payable. Such interest, calculated at five per centum per annum, shall accrue from the date on which the claim was sent
in writing to the carrier or, if no such claim has been made, from the date on which legal proceedings were instituted.
2.   When the amounts on which the calculation of the compensation is based are not expressed in the currency of the country in which payment is claimed, conversion shall be at the rate
of exchange applicable on the day and at the place of payment of compensation.

Article 28
1.   In cases where, under the law applicable, loss, damage or delay arising out of carriage under
this Convention gives rise to an extra-contractual claim, the carrier may avail himself of the provisions of this Convention which exclude his liability of which fix or limit the compensation due.
2.   In cases where the extra-contractual liability for loss, damage or delay of one of the persons
for whom the carrier is responsible under the terms of Article 3 is in issue, such person may also
avail himself of the provisions of this Convention which exclude the liability of the carrier or
which fix or limit the compensation due.

Article 29
1.   The carrier shall not be entitled to avail himself of the provisions of this chapter which exclude or limit his liability or which shift the burden of proof if the damage was caused by his wilful misconduct or by such default on his part as, in accordance with the law of the court or tribunal seised of the case, is considered as equivalent to wilful misconduct.
2.   The same provision shall apply if the wilful misconduct or default is committed by the
agents or servants of the carrier or by any other persons of whose services he makes use for the
performance of the carriage, when such agents, servants or other persons are acting within the
scope of their employment. Furthermore, in such a case such agents, servants or other persons
shall not be entitled to avail themselves, with regard to their personal liability, of the provisions
of this chapter referred to in paragraph 1.

CHAPTER V - CLAIMS AND ACTIONS
Article 30
1.   If the consignee takes delivery of the goods without duly checking their condition with the
carrier or without sending him reservations giving a general indication of the loss or damage,
not later than the time of delivery in the case of apparent loss or damage and within seven days
of delivery, Sundays and public holidays excepted, in the case of loss or damage which is not
apparent, the fact of this taking delivery shall be prima facie, evidence that he has received the
goods in the condition described in the consignment note. In the case of loss or damage which
is not apparent the reservations referred to shall be made in writing.
2.   When the condition of the goods has been duly checked by the consignee and the carrier,
evidence contradicting the result of this checking shall only be admissible in the case of loss or
damage which is not apparent and provided that the consignee has duly sent reservations in
writing to the carrier within seven days, Sundays and public holidays excepted, from the date of
checking.
3.   No compensation shall be payable for delay in delivery unless a reservation has been sent
in writing to the carrier, within twenty-one days from the time that the goods were placed at
the disposal of the consignee.
4.   In calculating the time-limits provided for in this Article the date of delivery, or the date of
checking, or the date when the goods were placed at the disposal of the consignee, as the case
may be, shall not be included.
5.   The carrier and the consignee shall give each other every reasonable facility for making the
requisite investigations and checks.

Article 31

1.   In legal proceedings arising out of carriage under this Convention, the plaintiff may bring an action in any court or tribunal of a contracting country designated by agreement between the parties and, in addition, in the courts or tribunals of a country within whose territory:
(a) The defendant is ordinarily resident, or has his principal place of business, or the branch or agency through which the contract of carriage was made, or
(b) The place where the goods were taken over by the carrier or the place designated for delivery is situated.

2.   Where in respect of a claim referred to in paragraph 1 of this Article an action is pending before a court or tribunal competent under that paragraph, or where in respect of such a claim a judgement has been entered by such a court or tribunal no new action shall be started between the same parties on the same grounds unless the judgement of the court or tribunal before which the first action was brought is not enforceable in the country in which the fresh proceedings are brought.

3.   When a judgement entered by a court or tribunal of a contracting country in any such action as is referred to in paragraph 1 of this Article has become enforceable in that country, it shall also become enforceable in each of the other contracting States, as soon as the formalities required in the country concerned have been complied with. These formalities shall not permit the merits of the case to be re-opened.

4.   The provisions of paragraph 3 of this Article shall apply to judgements after trial, judgements by default and settlements confirmed by an order of the court, but shall not apply to interim judgements or to awards of damages, in addition to costs against a plaintiff who wholly or partly fails in his action.

5.   Security for costs shall not be required in proceedings arising out of carriage under this Convention from nationals of contracting countries resident or having their place of business in one of those countries.

Article 32

1.   The period of limitation for an action arising out of carriage under this Convention shall be one year. Nevertheless, in the case of wilful misconduct, or such default as in accordance with the law of the court or tribunal seised of the case, is considered as equivalent to wilful misconduct, the period of limitation shall be three years. The period of limitation shall begin to run:
(a) In the case of partial loss, damage or delay in delivery, from the date of delivery;
(b) In the case of total loss, from the thirtieth day after the expiry of the agreed time-limit or where there is no agreed time-limit from the sixtieth day from the date on which the goods were taken over by the carrier;
(c) In all other cases, on the expiry of a period of three months after the making of the contract of carriage.
The day on which the period of limitation begins to run shall not be included in the period.

2.   A written claim shall suspend the period of limitation until such date as the carrier rejects the claim by notification in writing and returns the documents attached thereto. If a part of the claim is admitted the period of limitation shall start to run again only in respect of that part of the claim still in dispute. The burden of proof of the receipt of the claim, or of the reply and of the return of the documents, shall rest with the party relying upon these facts. The running of the period of limitation shall not be suspended by further claims having the same object.

3.   Subject to the provisions of paragraph 2 above, the extension of the period of limitation shall be governed by the law of the court or tribunal seized of the case. That law shall also govern the fresh accrual of rights of action.

4.   A right of action which has become barred by lapse of time may not be exercised by way of counterclaim or set-off.

Article 33

The contract of carriage may contain a clause conferring competence on an arbitration tribunal if the clause conferring competence on the tribunal provides that the tribunal shall apply this Convention.

CHAPTER VI - PROVISIONS RELATING TO CARRIAGE PERFORMED BY SUCCESSIVE CARRIERS

Article 34

If carriage governed by a single contract is performed by successive road carriers, each of them shall be responsible for the performance of the whole operation, the second carrier and each succeeding carrier becoming a party to the contract of carriage, under the terms of the consignment note, by reason of his acceptance of the goods and the consignment note.

Article 35

1.   A carrier accepting the goods from a previous carrier shall give the latter a dated and signed receipt. He shall enter his name and address on the second copy of the consignment note.

Where applicable, he shall enter on the second copy of the consignment note and on the receipt reservations of the kind provided for in Article 8, paragraph 2.

2.   The provisions of Article 9 shall apply to the relations between successive carriers.

Article 36

Except in the case of a counterclaim or a setoff raised in an action concerning a claim based on the same contract of carriage, legal proceedings in respect of liability for loss, damage or delay may only be brought against the first carrier, the last carrier or the carrier who was performing that portion of the carriage during which the event causing the loss, damage or delay occurred, an action may be brought at the same time against several of these carriers.

Article 37

A carrier who has paid compensation in compliance with the provisions of this Convention, shall be entitled to recover such compensation, together with interest thereon and all costs and expenses incurred by reason of the claim, from the other carriers who have taken part in the carriage, subject to the following provisions:

(a)   The carrier responsible for the loss or damage shall be solely liable for the compensation whether paid by himself or by another carrier;

(b)   When the loss or damage has been caused by the action of two or more carriers, each of them shall pay an amount proportionate to his share of liability; should it be impossible to apportion the liability, each carrier shall be liable in proportion to the share of the payment for the carriage which is due to him;

(c)   If it cannot be ascertained to which carriers liability is attributable for the loss or damage, the amount of the compensation shall be apportioned between all the carriers as laid down in (b) above.

Article 38

If one of the carriers is insolvent, the share of the compensation due from him and unpaid by him shall be divided among the other carriers in proportion to the share of the payment for the carriage due to them.

Article 39

1.   No carrier against whom a claim is made under articles 37 and 38 shall be entitled to dispute the validity of the payment made by the carrier making the claim if the amount of the compensation was determined by judicial authority after the first mentioned carrier had been given due notice of the proceedings and afforded an opportunity of entering an appearance.

2.   A carrier wishing to take proceedings to enforce his right of recovery may make his claim before the competent court or tribunal of the country in which one of the carriers concerned is ordinarily resident, or has his principal place of business or the branch or agency through which the contract of carriage was made. All the carriers concerned may be made defendants in the same action.

3.   The provisions of Article 31, paragraphs 3 and 4, shall apply to judgements entered in the proceedings referred to in articles 37 and 38.
4.   The provisions of Article 32 shall apply to claims between carriers. The period of limitation shall, however, begin to run either on the date of the final judicial decision fixing the amount of compensation payable under the provisions of this Convention, or, if there is no such judicial decision, from the actual date of payment.

Article 40
Carriers shall be free to agree among themselves on provisions other than those laid down in articles 37 and 38.

CHAPTER VII - NULLITY OF STIPULATION TO THE CONVENTION
Article 41
1.   Subject to the provisions of Article 40, any stipulation which would directly or indirectly derogate from the provisions of this Convention shall be null and void. The nullity of such a stipulation shall not involve the nullity of the other provisions of the contract.
2.   In particular, a benefit of insurance in favour of the carrier or any other similar clause, or any clause shifting the burden of proof shall be null and void.

CHAPTER VIII - FINAL PROVISIONS
Article 42
1.   This Convention is open for signature or accession by countries members of the Economic Commission for Europe and countries admitted to the Commission in a consultative capacity under paragraph 8 of the Commission's terms of reference.
2.   Such countries as may participate in certain activities of the Economic Commission for Europe in accordance with paragraph 11 of the Commission's terms of reference may become Contracting Parties to this Convention by acceding thereto after its entry into force.
3.   The Convention shall be open for signature until 31 August 1956 inclusive. Thereafter, it shall be open for accession.
4.   This Convention shall be ratified.
5.   Ratification or accession shall be effected by the deposit of an instrument with the Secretary-General of the United Nations.

Article 43
1.   This Convention shall come into force on the ninetieth day after five of the countries referred to in Article 42, paragraph 1, have deposited their instruments of ratification or accession.
2.   For any country ratifying or acceding to it after five countries have deposited their instruments of ratification of accession, this Convention shall enter into force on the ninetieth day after the said country has deposited its instrument of ratification or accession.

Article 44
1.   Any Contracting Party may denounce this Convention by so notifying the Secretary-General of the United Nations.
2.   Denunciation shall take effect twelve months after the date of receipt by the Secretary-General of the notification of denunciation.

Article 45
If, after the entry into force of this Convention, the number of Contracting Parties is reduced, as a result of denunciations, to less than five, the Convention shall cease to be in force from the date in which the last of such denunciations takes effect.

Article 46
1.   Any country may, at the time of depositing its instrument of ratification or accession or at any time thereafter, declare by notification addressed to the Secretary-General of the United Nations that this Convention shall extend to all or any of the territories for the international relations of which it is responsible. The Convention shall extend to the territory or territories named

in the notification as from the ninetieth day after its receipt by the Secretary-General or, if on that day the Convention has not yet entered into force, at the time of its entry into force.

2.   Any country which has made a declaration under the preceding paragraph extending this Convention to any territory for whose international relations it is responsible may denounce the Convention separately in respect of that territory in accordance with the provisions of Article 44.

Article 47

Any dispute between two or more Contracting Parties relating to the interpretation or application of this Convention, which the parties are unable to settle by negotiation or other means may, at the request of any one of the Contracting Parties concerned, be referred for settlement to the International Court of Justice

Article 48

1.   Each Contracting Party may, at the time of signing, ratifying, or acceding to, this Convention, declare that it does not consider itself as bound by Article 47 of the Convention. Other Contracting Parties shall not be bound by Article 47 in respect of any Contracting Party which has entered such a reservation.

2.   Any Contracting Party having entered a reservation as provided for in paragraph 1 may at any time withdraw such reservation by notifying the Secretary-General of the United Nations.

3.   No other reservation to this Convention shall be permitted.

Article 49

1.   After this Convention has been in force for three years, any Contracting Party may, by notification to the Secretary-General of the United Nations, request that a conference be convened for the purpose of reviewing the Convention. The Secretary-General shall notify all Contracting Parties of the request and a review conference shall be convened by the Secretary-General if, within a period of four months following the date of notification by the Secretary General, not less than one-fourth of the Contracting Parties notify him of their concurrence with the request.

2.   If a conference is convened in accordance with the preceding paragraph, the Secretary-General shall notify all the Contracting Parties and invite them to submit within a period of three months such proposals as they may wish the Conference to consider. The Secretary-General shall circulate to all Contracting Parties the provisional agenda for the conference together with the texts of such proposals at least three months before the date on which the conference is to meet.

3.   The Secretary-General shall invite to any conference convened in accordance with this Article all countries referred to in Article 42, paragraph 1, and countries which have become Contracting Parties under Article 42, paragraph 2.

Article 50

In addition to the notifications provided for in Article 49, the Secretary-General of the United Nations shall notify the countries referred to in Article 42, paragraph 1, and the countries which have become Contracting Parties under Article 42, paragraph 2, of:

(a)   Ratification and accessions under Article 42;
(b)   The dates of entry into force of this Convention in accordance with Article 43;
(c)   Denunciations under Article 44;
(d)   The termination of this Convention in accordance with Article 45;
(e)   Notifications received in accordance with Article 46;
(f)   Declarations and notifications received in accordance with Article 48, paragraphs 1 and 2.

Article 51

After 31 August 1956, the original of this Convention shall be deposited with the Secretary-General of the United Nations, who shall transmit certified true copies to each of the countries mentioned in Article 42, paragraphs 1 and 2.

Article 23 of the CMR, as amended by the 1978 Protocol

1.   When, under the provisions of this Convention, a carrier is liable for compensation in respect of total or partial loss of goods, such compensation shall be calculated by reference to the value of the goods at the place and time at which they were accepted for carriage.

2.   The value of the goods shall be fixed according to the commodity exchange price or, if there is no such price, according to the current market price or, if there is no commodity exchange price or current market price, by reference to normal value of goods of the same kind and quality.

3.   Compensation shall not, however, exceed 8.33 units of account per kilogram of gross weight short.

4.   In addition, the carriage charges, Customs duties and other charges incurred in respect of the carriage of the goods shall be refunded in full in case of total loss and in proportion to the loss sustained in case of partial loss, but no further damage shall be payable.

5.   In the case of delay if the claimant proves that damage has resulted therefrom the carrier shall pay compensation for such damage not exceeding the carriage charges.

6.   Higher compensation may only be claimed where the value of the goods or a special interest in delivery has been declared in accordance with articles 24 and 26.

7.   The unit of account mentioned in this Convention is the Special Drawing Right as defined by the International Monetary Fund. The amount mentioned in paragraph 3 of this Article shall be converted into the national currency of the State of the Court seized of the case on the basis of the value of that currency on the date of the judgment or the date agreed upon by the Parties. The value of the national currency, in terms of the Special Drawing Right, of a State which is a member of the International Monetary Fund, shall be calculated in accordance with the method of valuation applied by the International Monetary Fund in effect on the date in question for its operations and transactions. The value of the national currency, in terms of the Special Drawing Right, of a State which is not a member of the International Monetary Fund, shall be calculated in a manner determined by the State.

8.   Nevertheless, a State which is not a member of the International Monetary Fund and whose law does not permit the application of the provisions of paragraph 7 of this Article may, at the time of ratification of or accession to the Protocol to the CMR or at any time thereafter, declare that the limit of liability provided for in paragraph 3 of this Article to be applied in its territory shall be 25 monetary units. The monetary unit referred to in this paragraph corresponds to the 10/31 gram of gold of millesimal fineness nine hundred. The conversion shall be made according to the law of the State concerned.

9.   The calculation mentioned in the last sentence of paragraph 7 of this Article and the conversion mentioned in paragraph 8 of this Article shall be made in such a manner as to express in the national currency of the State as far as possible the same real value for the amount in paragraph 3 of this Article as is expressed there in units of account. States shall communicate to the Secretary-General of the United Nations the manner of calculation pursuant to paragraph 7 of this Article or the result of the conversion in paragraph 8 of this Article as the case may be, when depositing an instrument referred to in Article 3 of the Protocol to the CMR and whenever there is a change in either.

Entry into force: 2 July 1961
Ratification and binding effect: Albania (2006), Armenia (2006), Austria (1960), Azerbaijan (2006), Belarus (1993), Belgium (1962), Bosnia and Herzegovina (1993), Bulgaria (1977), Croatia (1992), Cyprus (2003), Czech Republic (1993), Denmark (1965), Estonia (1993), Finland (1973), France (1959), Georgia (1999), Germany (1961), Greece (1977), Hungary (1970), Iran (1998), Ireland (1991), Italy (1961), Jordan (2008), Kazakhstan (1996), Kyrgyzstan (1998), Latvia (1994), Lebanon (2006), Lithuania (1993), Luxembourg (1964), Macedonia (1997), Malta (2007), Moldova (1993), Mongolia (2003), Montenegro (2006), Morocco (1995), Netherlands (1960), Norway (1969), Poland (1962), Portugal (1969), Romania (1973), Russian Federation (1983), Serbia (2001), Slovakia (1993), Slovenia (1992), Spain (1974), Sweden (1969), Switzerland (1970), Syria (2008),

Tajikistan (1996), Tunisia (1994), Turkey (1995), Turkmenistan (1996), Ukraine (2007), United Kingdom (1967), Uzbekistan (1995)

US FEDERAL BILL OF LADING ACT
49 U.S.C §§80101 – 80116 *Der Hague Rules pg. 492*

§ 80101. Definitions

In this chapter –
(1)   "consignee" means the person named in a bill of lading as the person to whom the goods are to be delivered.
(2)   "consignor" means the person named in a bill of lading as the person from whom the goods have been received for shipment.
(3)   "goods" means merchandise or personal property that has been, is being, or will be transported.
(4)   "holder" means a person having possession of, and a property right in, a bill of lading.
(5)   "order" means an order by indorsement on a bill of lading.
(6)   "purchase" includes taking by mortgage or pledge.

§ 80102. Application

This chapter applies to a bill of lading when the bill is issued by a common carrier for the transportation of goods –
(1)   between a place in the District of Columbia and another place in the District of Columbia;
(2)   between a place in a territory or possession of the United States and another place in the same territory or possession;
(3)   between a place in a State and a place in another State;
(4)   between a place in a State and a place in the same State through another State or a foreign country; or
(5)   from a place in a State to a place in a foreign country.

§ 80103. Negotiable and Non-Negotiable Bills

(a)   Negotiable bills. –
(1)   A bill of lading is negotiable if the bill –
(A)   states that the goods are to be delivered to the order of a consignee; and
(B)   does not contain on its face an agreement with the shipper that the bill is not negotiable.
(2)   Inserting in a negotiable bill of lading the name of a person to be notified of the arrival of the goods –
(A)   does not limit its negotiability; and
(B)   is not notice to the purchaser of the goods of a right the named person has to the goods.
(b)   Non-negotiable bills. –
(1)   A bill of lading is non-negotiable if the bill states that the goods are to be delivered to a consignee. The indorsement of a non-negotiable bill does not –
(A)   make the bill negotiable; or
(B)   give the transferee any additional right.
(2)   A common carrier issuing a non-negotiable bill of lading must put "non-negotiable" or "not negotiable" on the bill. This paragraph does not apply to an informal memorandum or acknowledgment.

§ 80104. Form and Requirements for Negotiation

(a)   General rules. –

(1) A negotiable bill of lading may be negotiated by indorsement. An indorsement may be made in blank or to a specified person. If the goods are deliverable to the order of a specified person, then the bill must be indorsed by that person.

(2) A negotiable bill of lading may be negotiated by delivery when the common carrier, under the terms of the bill, undertakes to deliver the goods to the order of a specified person and that person or a subsequent indorsee has indorsed the bill in blank.

(3) A negotiable bill of lading may be negotiated by a person possessing the bill, regardless of the way in which the person got possession, if –

    (A) a common carrier, under the terms of the bill, undertakes to deliver the goods to that person; or

    (B) when the bill is negotiated, it is in a form that allows it to be negotiated by delivery.

(b) Validity not affected. – The validity of a negotiation of a bill of lading is not affected by the negotiation having been a breach of duty by the person making the negotiation, or by the owner of the bill having been deprived of possession by fraud, accident, mistake, duress, loss, theft, or conversion, if the person to whom the bill is negotiated, or a person to whom the bill is subsequently negotiated, gives value for the bill in good faith and without notice of the breach of duty, fraud, accident, mistake, duress, loss, theft, or conversion.

(c) Negotiation by seller, mortgagor, or pledgor to person without notice. – When goods for which a negotiable bill of lading has been issued are in a common carrier's possession, and the person to whom the bill has been issued retains possession of the bill after selling, mortgaging, or pledging the goods or bill, the subsequent negotiation of the bill by that person to another person receiving the bill for value, in good faith, and without notice of the prior sale, mortgage, or pledge has the same effect as if the first purchaser of the goods or bill had expressly authorized the subsequent negotiation.

§ 80105. Title and Rights Affected by Negotiation

(a) Title. – When a negotiable bill of lading is negotiated –

(1) the person to whom it is negotiated acquires the title to the goods that –

    (A) the person negotiating the bill had the ability to convey to a purchaser in good faith for value; and

    (B) the consignor and consignee had the ability to convey to such a purchaser; and

(2) the common carrier issuing the bill becomes obligated directly to the person to whom the bill is negotiated to hold possession of the goods under the terms of the bill the same as if the carrier had issued the bill to that person.

(b) Superiority of rights. – When a negotiable bill of lading is negotiated to a person for value in good faith, that person's right to the goods for which the bill was issued is superior to a seller's lien or to a right to stop the transportation of the goods. This subsection applies whether the negotiation is made before or after the common carrier issuing the bill receives notice of the seller's claim. The carrier may deliver the goods to an unpaid seller only if the bill first is surrendered for cancellation.

(c) Mortgagee and lien holder rights not affected. – Except as provided in subsection (b) of this section, this chapter does not limit a right of a mortgagee or lien holder having a mortgage or lien on goods against a person that purchased for value in good faith from the owner, and got possession of the goods immediately before delivery to the common carrier.

§ 80106. Transfer Without Negotiation

(a) Delivery and agreement. – The holder of a bill of lading may transfer the bill without negotiating it by delivery and agreement to transfer title to the bill or to the goods represented by it. Subject to the agreement, the person to whom the bill is transferred has title to the goods against the transferor.

(b) Compelling indorsement. – When a negotiable bill of lading is transferred for value by delivery without being negotiated and indorsement of the transferor is essential for negotiation, the transferee may compel the transferor to indorse the bill unless a contrary intention appears. The negotiation is effective when the indorsement is made.

(c)   Effect of notification. –
(1)   When a transferee notifies the common carrier that a nonnegotiable bill of lading has been transferred under subsection (a) of this section, the carrier is obligated directly to the transferee for any obligations the carrier owed to the transferor immediately before the notification. However, before the carrier is notified, the transferee's title to the goods and right to acquire the obligations of the carrier may be defeated by –
    (A)   garnishment, attachment, or execution on the goods by a creditor of the transferor; or
    (B)   notice to the carrier by the transferor or a purchaser from the transferor of a later purchase of the goods from the transferor.
(2)   A common carrier has been notified under this subsection only if –
    (A)   an officer or agent of the carrier, whose actual or apparent authority includes acting on the notification, has been notified; and
    (B)   the officer or agent has had time, exercising reasonable diligence, to communicate with the agent having possession or control of the goods.

§ 80107. Warranties and Liability

(a)   General rule. – Unless a contrary intention appears, a person negotiating or transferring a bill of lading for value warrants that –
(1)   the bill is genuine;
(2)   the person has the right to transfer the bill and the title to the goods described in the bill;
(3)   the person does not know of a fact that would affect the validity or worth of the bill; and
(4)   the goods are merchantable or fit for a particular purpose when merchantability or fitness would have been implied if the agreement of the parties had been to transfer the goods without a bill of lading.
(b)   Security for debt. – A person holding a bill of lading as security for a debt and in good faith demanding or receiving payment of the debt from another person does not warrant by the demand or receipt –
(1)   the genuineness of the bill; or
(2)   the quantity or quality of the goods described in the bill.
(c)   Duplicates. – A common carrier issuing a bill of lading, on the face of which is the word "duplicate" or another word indicating that the bill is not an original bill, is liable the same as a person that represents and warrants that the bill is an accurate copy of an original bill properly issued. The carrier is not otherwise liable under the bill.
(d)   Indorser liability.--Indorsement of a bill of lading does not make the indorser liable for failure of the common carrier or a previous indorser to fulfill its obligations.

§ 80108. Alterations and Additions

An alteration or addition to a bill of lading after its issuance by a common carrier, without authorization from the carrier in writing or noted on the bill, is void. However, the original terms of the bill are enforceable.

§ 80109. Liens Under Negotiable Bills

A common carrier issuing a negotiable bill of lading has a lien on the goods covered by the bill for –
(1)   charges for storage, transportation, and delivery (including demurrage and terminal charges), and expenses necessary to preserve the goods or incidental to transporting the goods after the date of the bill; and
(2)   other charges for which the bill expressly specifies a lien is claimed to the extent the charges are allowed by law and the agreement between the consignor and carrier.

§ 80110. Duty to Deliver Goods

(a)   General rules. – Except to the extent a common carrier establishes an excuse provided by law, the carrier must deliver goods covered by a bill of lading on demand of the consignee named in a nonnegotiable bill or the holder of a negotiable bill for the goods when the consignee or holder –

(1)   offers in good faith to satisfy the lien of the carrier on the goods;

(2)   has possession of the bill and, if a negotiable bill, offers to indorse and give the bill to the carrier; and

(3)   agrees to sign, on delivery of the goods, a receipt for delivery if requested by the carrier.

(b)   Persons to whom goods may be delivered. – Subject to section 80111 of this title, a common carrier may deliver the goods covered by a bill of lading to –

(1)   a person entitled to their possession;

(2)   the consignee named in a non-negotiable bill; or

(3)   a person in possession of a negotiable bill if –

  (A)   the goods are deliverable to the order of that person; or

  (B)   the bill has been indorsed to that person or in blank by the consignee or another indorsee.

(c)   Common carrier claims of title and possession. – A claim by a common carrier that the carrier has title to goods or right to their possession is an excuse for non-delivery of the goods only if the title or right is derived from –

(1)   a transfer made by the consignor or consignee after the shipment; or

(2)   the carrier's lien.

(d)   Adverse claims. – If a person other than the consignee or the person in possession of a bill of lading claims title to or possession of goods and the common carrier knows of the claim, the carrier is not required to deliver the goods to any claimant until the carrier has had a reasonable time to decide the validity of the adverse claim or to bring a civil action to require all claimants to interplead.

(e)   Interpleader. – If at least 2 persons claim title to or possession of the goods, the common carrier may –

(1)   bring a civil action to interplead all known claimants to the goods; or

(2)   require those claimants to interplead as a defense in an action brought against the carrier for non-delivery.

(f)   Third person claims not a defense. – Except as provided in subsections (b), (d), and (e) of this section, title or a right of a third person is not a defense to an action brought by the consignee of a nonnegotiable bill of lading or by the holder of a negotiable bill against the common carrier for failure to deliver the goods on demand unless enforced by legal process.

§ 80111. Liability for Delivery of Goods

(a)   General rules. – A common carrier is liable for damages to a person having title to, or right to possession of, goods when –

(1)   the carrier delivers the goods to a person not entitled to their possession unless the delivery is authorized under section 80110(b)(2) or (3) of this title;

(2)   the carrier makes a delivery under section 80110(b)(2) or (3) of this title after being requested by or for a person having title to, or right to possession of, the goods not to make the delivery; or

(3)   at the time of delivery under section 80110(b)(2) or (3) of this title, the carrier has information it is delivering the goods to a person not entitled to their possession.

(b)   Effectiveness of request or information. – A request or information is effective under subsection (a)(2) or (3) of this section only if –

(1)   an officer or agent of the carrier, whose actual or apparent authority includes acting on the request or information, has been given the request or information; and

(2)   the officer or agent has had time, exercising reasonable diligence, to stop delivery of the goods.

(c)   Failure to take and cancel bills. – Except as provided in subsection (d) of this section, if a common carrier delivers goods for which a negotiable bill of lading has been issued without taking and canceling the bill, the carrier is liable for damages for failure to deliver the goods to a person purchasing the bill for value in good faith whether the purchase was before or after delivery and even when delivery was made to the person entitled to the goods. The carrier also is liable under this paragraph if part of the goods are delivered without taking and canceling the bill or plainly noting on the bill that a partial delivery was made and generally describing the goods or the remaining goods kept by the carrier.

(d) Exceptions to liability. – A common carrier is not liable for failure to deliver goods to the consignee or owner of the goods or a holder of the bill if –

(1) a delivery described in subsection (c) of this section was compelled by legal process;

(2) the goods have been sold lawfully to satisfy the carrier's lien;

(3) the goods have not been claimed; or

(4) the goods are perishable or hazardous.

§ 80112. Liability Under Negotiable Bills Issued in Parts, Sets, or Duplicates

(a) Parts and sets. – A negotiable bill of lading issued in a State for the transportation of goods to a place in the 48 contiguous States or the District of Columbia may not be issued in parts or sets. A common carrier issuing a bill in violation of this subsection is liable for damages for failure to deliver the goods to a purchaser of one part for value in good faith even though the purchase occurred after the carrier delivered the goods to a holder of one of the other parts.

(b) Duplicates. – When at least 2 negotiable bills of lading are issued in a State for the same goods to be transported to a place in the 48 contiguous States or the District of Columbia, the word "duplicate" or another word indicating that the bill is not an original must be put plainly on the face of each bill except the original. A common carrier violating this subsection is liable for damages caused by the violation to a purchaser of the bill for value in good faith as an original bill even though the purchase occurred after the carrier delivered the goods to the holder of the original bill.

§ 80113. Liability for Nonreceipt, Misdescription, and Improper Loading

(a) Liability for non-receipt and misdescription. – Except as provided in this section, a common carrier issuing a bill of lading is liable for damages caused by non-receipt by the carrier of any part of the goods by the date shown in the bill or by failure of the goods to correspond with the description contained in the bill. The carrier is liable to the owner of goods transported under a nonnegotiable bill (subject to the right of stoppage in transit) or to the holder of a negotiable bill if the owner or holder gave value in good faith relying on the description of the goods in the bill or on the shipment being made on the date shown in the bill.

(b) Non-liability of carriers. – A common carrier issuing a bill of lading is not liable under subsection (a) of this section –

(1) when the goods are loaded by the shipper;

(2) when the bill –

(A) describes the goods in terms of marks or labels, or in a statement about kind, quantity, or condition; or

(B) is qualified by "contents or condition of contents of packages unknown", "said to contain", "shipper's weight, load, and count", or words of the same meaning; and

(3) to the extent the carrier does not know whether any part of the goods were received or conform to the description.

(c) Liability for improper loading. – A common carrier issuing a bill of lading is not liable for damages caused by improper loading if –

(1) the shipper loads the goods; and

(2) the bill contains the words "shipper's weight, load, and count", or words of the same meaning indicating the shipper loaded the goods.

(d) Carrier's duty to determine kind, quantity, and number. –

(1) When bulk freight is loaded by a shipper that makes available to the common carrier adequate facilities for weighing the freight, the carrier must determine the kind and quantity of the freight within a reasonable time after receiving the written request of the shipper

to make the determination. In that situation, inserting the words "shipper's weight" or words of the same meaning in the bill of lading has no effect.

(2) When goods are loaded by a common carrier, the carrier must count the packages of goods, if package freight, and determine the kind and quantity, if bulk freight. In that situation, inserting in the bill of lading or in a notice, receipt, contract, rule, or tariff, the words "shipper's weight, load, and count" or words indicating that the shipper described and loaded the goods, has no effect except for freight concealed by packages.

§ 80114. Lost, Stolen, and Destroyed Negotiable Bills

(a) Delivery on court order and surety bond. – If a negotiable bill of lading is lost, stolen, or destroyed, a court of competent jurisdiction may order the common carrier to deliver the goods if the person claiming the goods gives a surety bond, in an amount approved by the court, to indemnify the carrier or a person injured by delivery against liability under the outstanding original bill. The court also may order payment of reasonable costs and attorney's fees to the carrier. A voluntary surety bond, without court order, is binding on the parties to the bond.

(b) Liability to holder. – Delivery of goods under a court order under subsection (a) of this section does not relieve a common carrier from liability to a person to whom the negotiable bill has been or is negotiated for value without notice of the court proceeding or of the delivery of the goods.

§ 80115. Limitation on Use of Judicial Process to Obtain Possession of Goods from Common Carriers

(a) Attachment and levy. – Except when a negotiable bill of lading was issued originally on delivery of goods by a person that did not have the power to dispose of the goods, goods in the possession of a common carrier for which a negotiable bill has been issued may be attached through judicial process or levied on in execution of a judgment only if the bill is surrendered to the carrier or its negotiation is enjoined.

(b) Delivery. – A common carrier may be compelled by judicial process to deliver goods under subsection (a) of this section only when the bill is surrendered to the carrier or impounded by the court.

§ 80116. Criminal Penalty

A person shall be fined under title 18, imprisoned for not more than 5 years, or both, if the person –

(1) violates this chapter with intent to defraud; or
(2) knowingly or with intent to defraud –
    (A) falsely makes, alters, or copies a bill of lading subject to this chapter;
    (B) utters, publishes, or issues a falsely made, altered, or copied bill subject to this chapter; or
    (C) negotiates or transfers for value a bill containing a false statement.

Part IV - Insurance

YORK-ANTWERP RULES 2004[1]

Rule of Interpretation

In the adjustment of general average the following Rules shall apply to the exclusion of any Law and Practice inconsistent therewith.

Except as provided by the Rule Paramount and the numbered Rules, general average shall be adjusted according to the lettered Rules.

Rule Paramount

In no case shall there be any allowance for sacrifice or expenditure unless reasonably made or incurred.

Rule A

There is a general average act when, and only when, any extraordinary sacrifice or expenditure is intentionally and reasonably made or incurred for the common safety for the purpose of preserving from peril the property involved in a common maritime adventure.

General average sacrifices and expenditures shall be borne by the different contributing interests on the basis hereinafter provided.

Rule B

There is a common maritime adventure when one or more vessels are towing or pushing another vessel or vessels, provided that they are all involved in commercial activities and not in a salvage operation.

When measures are taken to preserve the vessels and their cargoes, if any, from a common peril, these Rules shall apply.

A vessel is not in common peril with another vessel or vessels if by simply disconnecting from the other vessel or vessels she is in safety; but if the disconnection is itself a general average act the common maritime adventure continues.

Rule C

Only such losses, damages or expenses which are the direct consequence of the general average act shall be allowed as general average.

In no case shall there be any allowance in general average for losses, damages or expenses incurred in respect of damage to the environment or in consequence of the escape or release of pollutant substances from the property involved in the common maritime adventure.

Demurrage, loss of market, and any loss or damage sustained or expense incurred by reason of delay, whether on the voyage or subsequently, and any indirect loss whatsoever, shall not be allowed as general average.

Rule D

Rights to contribution in general average shall not be affected, though the event which gave rise to the sacrifice or expenditure may have been due to the fault of one of the parties to the adventure, but this shall not prejudice any remedies or defences which may be open against or to that party in respect of such fault.

Rule E

The onus of proof is upon the party claiming in general average to show that the loss or expense claimed is properly allowable as general average.

All parties claiming in general average shall give notice in writing to the average adjuster of the loss or expense in respect of which they claim contribution within 12 months of the date of the termination of the common maritime adventure.

---

1   © Comité Maritime Internationale (CIM), 2004.

Failing such notification, or if within 12 months of a request for the same any of the parties shall fail to supply evidence in support of a notified claim, or particulars of value in respect of a contributory interest, the average adjuster shall be at liberty to estimate the extent of the allowance or the contributory value on the basis of the information available to him, which estimate may be challenged only on the ground that it is manifestly incorrect.

Rule F

Any additional expense incurred in place of another expense, which would have been allowable as general average shall be deemed to be general average and so allowed without regard to the saving, if any, to other interests, but only up to the amount of the general average expense avoided.

Rule G

General average shall be adjusted as regards both loss and contribution upon the basis of values at the time and place when and where the adventure ends.

This rule shall not affect the determination of the place at which the average statement is to be made up.

When a ship is at any port or place in circumstances which would give rise to an allowance in general average under the provisions of Rules X and XI, and the cargo or part thereof is forwarded to destination by other means, rights and liabilities in general average shall, subject to cargo interests being notified if practicable, remain as nearly as possible the same as they would have been in the absence of such forwarding, as if the adventure had continued in the original ship for so long as justifiable under the contract of affreightment and the applicable law.

The proportion attaching to cargo of the allowances made in general average by reason of applying the third paragraph of this Rule shall not exceed the cost which would have been borne by the owners of cargo if the cargo had been forwarded at their expense.

Rule I. Jettison of Cargo

No jettison of cargo shall be allowed as general average, unless such cargo is carried in accordance with the recognised custom of the trade.

Rule II. Loss or Damage by Sacrifices for the Common Safety

Loss of or damage to the property involved in the common maritime adventure by or in consequence of a sacrifice made for the common safety, and by water which goes down a ship's hatches opened or other opening made for the purpose of making a jettison for the common safety, shall be allowed as general average.

Rule III. Extinguishing Fire on Shipboard

Damage done to a ship and cargo, or either of them, by water or otherwise, including damage by beaching or scuttling a burning ship, in extinguishing a fire on board the ship, shall be allowed as general average; except that no allowance shall be made for damage by smoke however caused or by heat of the fire.

Rule IV. Cutting Away Wreck

Loss or damage sustained by cutting away wreck or parts of the ship which have been previously carried away or are effectively lost by accident shall not be allowed as general average.

Rule V. Voluntary Stranding

When a ship is intentionally run on shore for the common safety, whether or not she might have been driven on shore, the consequent loss or damage to the property involved in the common maritime adventure shall be allowed in general average.

Rule VI. Salvage Remuneration

a.   Salvage payments, including interest thereon and legal fees associated with such payments, shall lie where they fall and shall not be allowed in general average, save only that if one party to the salvage shall have paid all or any of the proportion of salvage (including interest and legal fees) due from another party (calculated on the basis of salved values and not general average contributory values), the unpaid contribution to salvage due from that other party shall be credited in the adjustment to the party that has paid it, and debited to the party on whose behalf the payment was made.

b.   Salvage payments referred to in paragraph (a) above shall include any salvage remuneration in which the skill and efforts of the salvors in preventing or minimising damage to the environment such as is referred to in Article 13 paragraph 1(b) of the International Convention on Salvage 1989 have been taken into account.

c.   Special compensation payable to a salvor by the shipowner under Article 14 of the said Convention to the extent specified in paragraph 4 of that Article or under any other provision similar in substance (such as SCOPIC) shall not be allowed in general average and shall not be considered a salvage payment as referred to in paragraph (a) of this Rule.

Rule VII. Damage to Machinery and Boilers

Damage caused to any machinery and boilers of a ship which is ashore and in a position of peril, in endeavouring to refloat, shall be allowed in general average when shown to have arisen from an actual intention to float the ship for the common safety at the risk of such damage; but where a ship is afloat no loss or damage caused by working the propelling machinery and boilers shall in any circumstances be allowed as general average.

Rule VIII. Expenses Lightening a Ship When Ashore and Consequent Damage

When a ship is ashore and cargo and ship's fuel and stores or any of them are discharged as a general average act, the extra cost of lightening, lighter hire and reshipping (if incurred), and any loss or damage to the property involved in the common maritime adventure in consequence thereof, shall be allowed as general average.

Rule IX. Cargo, Ship's Materials and Stores Used for Fuel

Cargo, ship's materials and stores, or any of them, necessarily used for fuel for the common safety at a time of peril shall be allowed as general average, but when such an allowance is made for the cost of ship's materials and stores the general average shall be credited with the estimated cost of the fuel which would otherwise have been consumed in prosecuting the intended voyage.

Rule X. Expenses at Port of Refuge, etc.

a. (i) When a ship shall have entered a port or place of refuge or shall have returned to her port or place of loading in consequence of accident, sacrifice or other extraordinary circumstances which render that necessary for the common safety, the expenses of entering such port or place shall be allowed as general average; and when she shall have sailed thence with her original cargo, or a part of it, the corresponding expenses of leaving such port or place consequent upon such entry or return shall likewise be allowed as general average.

(ii)   When a ship is at any port or place of refuge and is necessarily removed to another port or place of refuge because repairs cannot be carried out in the first port or place, the provisions of this Rule shall be applied to the second port or place of refuge as if it were a port or place of refuge and the cost of such removal including temporary repairs and towage shall be allowed as general average. The provisions of Rule XI shall be applied to the prolongation of the voyage occasioned by such removal.

b. (i) The cost of handling on board or discharging cargo, fuel or stores whether at a port or place of loading, call or refuge, shall be allowed as general average, when the handling or discharge was necessary for the common safety or to enable damage to the ship caused by sacrifice or accident to be repaired, if the repairs were necessary for the safe prosecution of the voyage, except in cases where the damage to the ship is discovered at a port or place of loading or call without any accident or other extraordinary circumstances connected with such damage having taken place during the voyage.

(ii)   The cost of handling on board or discharging cargo, fuel or stores shall not be allowable as general average when incurred solely for the purpose of restowage due to shifting during the voyage, unless such restowage is necessary for the common safety.

c.   Whenever the cost of handling or discharging cargo, fuel or stores is allowable as general average, the costs of storage, including insurance if reasonably incurred, reloading and stowing of such cargo, fuel or stores shall likewise be allowed as general average. The provisions of Rule XI shall be applied to the extra period of detention occasioned by such reloading or restowing. But when the ship is condemned or does not proceed on her original voyage, storage expenses shall be allowed as general average only up to the date of the ship's condemnation or of the abandonment of the voyage or up to the date of completion of discharge of cargo if the condemnation or abandonment takes place before that date.

Rule XI. Wages and Maintenance of Crew and Other Expenses Putting in to and at a Port of Refuge, etc.
a.   Wages and maintenance of master, officers and crew reasonably incurred and fuel and stores consumed during the prolongation of the voyage occasioned by a ship entering a port or place of refuge or returning to her port or place of loading shall be allowed as general average when the expenses of entering such port or place are allowable as general average in accordance with Rule X(a).
b.   For the purpose of this and the other Rules wages shall include all payments made to or for the benefit of the master, officers and crew, whether such payments be imposed by law upon the shipowners or be made under the terms of articles of employment.
c. (i) When a ship shall have entered or been detained in any port or place in consequence of accident, sacrifice or other extraordinary circumstances which render that necessary for the common safety, or to enable damage to the ship caused by sacrifice or accident to be repaired, if the repairs were necessary for the safe prosecution of the voyage, fuel and stores consumed during the extra period of detention in such port or place until the ship shall or should have been made ready to proceed upon her voyage, shall be allowed as general average, except such fuel and stores as are consumed in effecting repairs not allowable in general average.
(ii)   Port charges incurred during the extra period of detention shall likewise be allowed as general average except such charges as are incurred solely by reason of repairs not allowable in general average.
(iii) Provided that when damage to the ship is discovered at a port or place of loading or call without any accident or other extraordinary circumstance connected with such damage having taken place during the voyage, then fuel and stores consumed and port charges incurred during the extra detention for repairs to damages so discovered shall not be allowable as general average, even if the repairs are necessary for the safe prosecution of the voyage.
(iv)   When the ship is condemned or does not proceed on her original voyage, fuel and stores consumed and port charges shall be allowed as general average only up to the date of the ship's condemnation or of the abandonment of the voyage or up to the date of completion of discharge of cargo if the condemnation or abandonment takes place before that date.
d.   The cost of measures undertaken to prevent or minimise damage to the environment shall be allowed in general average when incurred in any or all of the following circumstances:
(i)   as part of an operation performed for the common safety which, had it been undertaken by a party outside the common maritime adventure, would have entitled such party to a salvage reward;
(ii)   as a condition of entry into or departure from any port or place in the circumstances prescribed in Rule X(a);
(iii) as a condition of remaining at any port or place in the circumstances prescribed in Rule XI(c), provided that when there is an actual escape or release of pollutant substances the cost of any additional measures required on that account to prevent or minimise pollution or environmental damage shall not be allowed as general average;
(iv)   necessarily in connection with the discharging, storing or reloading of cargo whenever the cost of those operations is allowable as general average.

Rule XII. Damage to Cargo in Discharging, etc.

Damage to or loss of cargo, fuel or stores sustained in consequence of their handling, discharging, storing, reloading and stowing shall be allowed as general average, when and only when the cost of those measures respectively is allowed as general average.

Rule XIII. Deductions from Cost of Repairs

a.   Repairs to be allowed in general average shall not be subject to deductions in respect of "new for old" where old material or parts are replaced by new unless the ship is over fifteen years old in which case there shall be a deduction of one third. The deductions shall be regulated by the age of the ship from the 31st December of the year of completion of construction to the date of the general average act, except for insulation, life and similar boats, communications and navigational apparatus and equipment, machinery and boilers for which the deductions shall be regulated by the age of the particular parts to which they apply.
b.   The deductions shall be made only from the cost of the new material or parts when finished and ready to be installed in the ship. No deduction shall be made in respect of provisions, stores, anchors and chain cables. Drydock and slipway dues and costs of shifting the ship shall be allowed in full.
c.   The costs of cleaning, painting or coating of bottom shall not be allowed in general average unless the bottom has been painted or coated within the twelve months preceding the date of the general average act in which case one half of such costs shall be allowed.

Rule XIV. Temporary Repairs

a.   Where temporary repairs are effected to a ship at a port of loading, call or refuge, for the common safety, or of damage caused by general average sacrifice, the cost of such repairs shall be allowed as general average.
b.   Where temporary repairs of accidental damage are effected in order to enable the adventure to be completed, the cost of such repairs shall be allowed as general average without regard to the saving, if any, to other interests, but only up to the saving in expense which would have been incurred and allowed in general average if such repairs had not been effected there. Provided that for the purposes of this paragraph only, the cost of temporary repairs falling for consideration shall be limited to the extent that the cost of temporary repairs effected at the port of loading, call or refuge, together with either the cost of permanent repairs eventually effected or, if unrepaired at the time of the adjustment, the reasonable depreciation in the value of the vessel at the completion of the voyage. exceeds the cost of permanent repairs had they been effected at the port of loading, call or refuge.
c.   No deductions "new for old" shall be made from the cost of temporary repairs allowable as general average.

Rule XV. Loss of Freight

Loss of freight arising from damage to or loss of cargo shall be allowed as general average, either when caused by a general average act, or when the damage to or loss of cargo is so allowed.

Deduction shall be made from the amount of gross freight lost, of the charges which the owner thereof would have incurred to earn such freight, but has, in consequence of the sacrifice, not incurred.

Rule XVI. Amount to Be Allowed for Cargo Lost or Damaged by Sacrifice

a.   The amount to be allowed as general average for damage to or loss of cargo sacrificed shall be the loss which has been sustained thereby based on the value at the time of discharge, ascertained from the commercial invoice rendered to the receiver or if there is no such invoice from the shipped value. The value at the time of discharge shall include the cost of insurance and freight except insofar as such freight is at the risk of interests other than the cargo.
b.   When cargo so damaged is sold and the amount of the damage has not been otherwise agreed, the loss to be allowed in general average shall be the difference between the net proceeds of sale and the net sound value as computed in the first paragraph of this Rule.

Rule XVII. Contributory Values

a. (i) The contribution to a general average shall be made upon the actual net values of the property at the termination of the adventure except that the value of cargo shall be the value at the time of discharge, ascertained from the commercial invoice rendered to the receiver or if there is no such invoice from the shipped value.

(ii) The value of the cargo shall include the cost of insurance and freight unless and insofar as such freight is at the risk of interests other than the cargo, deducting therefrom any loss or damage suffered by the cargo prior to or at the time of discharge.

(iii) The value of the ship shall be assessed without taking into account the beneficial or detrimental effect of any demise or time charterparty to which the ship may be committed.

b. To these values shall be added the amount allowed as general average for property sacrificed, if not already included, deduction being made from the freight and passage money at risk of such charges and crew's wages as would not have been incurred in earning the freight had the ship and cargo been totally lost at the date of the general average act and have not been allowed as general average; deduction being also made from the value of the property of all extra charges incurred in respect thereof subsequently to the general average act, except such charges as are allowed in general average or fall upon the ship by virtue of an award for special compensation under Art. 14 of the International Convention on Salvage, 1989 or under any other provision similar in substance.

c. In the circumstances envisaged in the third paragraph of Rule G, the cargo and other property shall contribute on the basis of its value upon delivery at original destination unless sold or otherwise disposed of short of that destination, and the ship shall contribute upon its actual net value at the time of completion of discharge of cargo.

d. Where cargo is sold short of destination, however, it shall contribute upon the actual net proceeds of sale, with the addition of any amount allowed as general average.

e. Mails, passengers' luggage, personal effects and accompanied private motor vehicles shall not contribute to general average.

Rule XVIII. Damage to Ship

The amount to be allowed as general average for damage or loss to the ship, her machinery and/or gear caused by a general average act shall be as follows:

a. When repaired or replaced,

The actual reasonable cost of repairing or replacing such damage or loss, subject to deductions in accordance with Rule XIII;

b. When not repaired or replaced,

The reasonable depreciation arising from such damage or loss, but not exceeding the estimated cost of repairs. But where the ship is an actual total loss or when the cost of repairs of the damage would exceed the value of the ship when repaired, the amount to be allowed as general average shall be the difference between the estimated sound value of the ship after deducting therefrom the estimated cost of repairing damage which is not general average and the value of the ship in her damaged state which may be measured by the net proceeds of sale, if any.

Rule XIX. Undeclared or Wrongfully Declared Cargo

a. Damage or loss caused to goods loaded without the knowledge of the shipowner or his agent or to goods wilfully misdescribed at time of shipment shall not be allowed as general average, but such goods shall remain liable to contribute, if saved.

b. Damage or loss caused to goods which have been wrongfully declared on shipment at a value which is lower than their real value shall be contributed for at the declared value, but such goods shall contribute upon their actual value.

Rule XX. Provision of Funds

a. The capital loss sustained by the owners of goods sold for the purpose of raising funds to defray general average disbursements shall be allowed in general average.

b. The cost of insuring average disbursements shall also be allowed in general average.

Rule XXI. Interest on Losses Allowed in General Average

a.   Interest shall be allowed on expenditure, sacrifices and allowances in general average until three months after the date of issue of the general average adjustment, due allowance being made for any payment on account by the contributory interests or from the general average deposit fund.

b.   Each year the Assembly of the Comité Maritime International shall decide the rate of interest which shall apply. This rate shall be used for calculating interest accruing during the following calendar year.

Rule XXII. Treatment of Cash Deposits

Where cash deposits have been collected in respect of cargo's liability for general average, salvage or special charges such deposits shall be paid without any delay into a special account in the joint names of a representative nominated on behalf of the shipowner and a representative nominated on behalf of the depositors in a bank to be approved by both. The sum so deposited together with accrued interest, if any, shall be held as security for payment to the parties entitled thereto of the general average, salvage or special charges payable by cargo in respect of which the deposits have been collected. Payments on account or refunds of deposits may be made if certified to in writing by the average adjuster. Such deposits and payments or refunds shall be without prejudice to the ultimate liability of the parties.

Rule XXIII. Time Bar for Contributions to General Average

a.   Subject always to any mandatory rule on time limitation contained in any applicable law:

(i)   Any rights to general average contribution, including any rights to claim under general average bonds and guarantees, shall be extinguished unless an action is brought by the party claiming such contribution within a period of one year after the date upon which the general average adjustment was issued. However, in no case shall such an action be brought after six years from the date of the termination of the common maritime adventure.

(ii) These periods may be extended if the parties so agree after the termination of the common maritime adventure.

b.   This Rule shall not apply as between the parties to the general average and their respective insurers.

UNCTAD MODEL CLAUSES ON MARINE HULL AND CARGO INSURANCE[1]

MARINE HULL INSURANCE [OMITTED]
VS.
CARGO INSURANCE   *doesn't really mean*
All Risks Cover   *all*
A. COVERAGE

1.   This insurance covers all risks of physical loss of or damage to the insured cargo, unless the insurer proves that one of the exclusions in Part B applies.

2.   This insurance also covers loss of or damage to the insured cargo caused by any act of any governmental authority to prevent or minimize pollution resulting from damage to the carrying vessel, provided such act of govern mental authority has not resulted from want of due diligence by the assured.

B. GENERAL EXCLUSIONS

3.   This insurance does not cover:

3.1   loss, damage, liability or expense caused by:

3.1.1   war, hostilities or warlike acts;

3.1.2   civil war, revolution, rebellion, insurrection, or civil strife arising therefrom;

---

1   © United Nations Conference on Trade and Development (UNCTAD), Geneva 1987; United Nations, New York 1989.

3.1.3   mines, torpedoes, bombs or other weapons of war;

3.1.4   capture, seizure other than by pirates, masters, officers or crew, arrest, restraint or detainment, and the consequences thereof or any attempt thereat;

3.1.5   sabotage or terrorism committed from a political motive;

3.1.6   detonation of an explosive caused by any person acting maliciously or from a political motive;

3.1.7   strikes, lock-outs or other similar labour disturbances;

3.1.8   civil commotions, riots or other similar events; or

3.1.9   confiscation, requisition, or other similar measures taken or attempted by any government or other similar organization assuming or wielding power;

3.2   loss, damage, liability or expense resulting from the personal act or omission of the assured done with the intent to cause such loss, damage, liability or expense, or recklessly and with knowledge that such loss, damage, liability or expense would probably result;

3.3   ordinary leakage, ordinary loss in weight or volume, or any other ordinary loss of or damage to the insured cargo;

3.4   loss, damage, liability or expense caused by insufficiency or unsuitability of packing or preparation of the insured cargo;

3.5   loss, damage, liability or expense caused by inadequacy or unsuitability of the stowage of the insured cargo in a container or liftvan where such stowage is carried out prior to attachment of this insurance;

3.6.1   loss, damage, liability or expense caused by

3.6.1.1   unseaworthiness of vessel or craft, or

3.6.1.2   unfitness of vessel, craft, conveyance, container or liftvan for the safe carriage of the insured cargo,

where the assured knew of or had recklessly refrained from obtaining knowledge of such unseaworthiness or unfitness by the time the insured cargo was loaded therein.

3.6.2   This exclusion 3.6 shall not be invoked against a party claiming under this insurance to whom the insurance has been assigned and who has bought the insured cargo in good faith without notice of such unseaworthiness or unfitness;

3.7   loss, damage, liability or expense caused by inherent vice or nature of the insured cargo;

3.8   loss, damage, liability or expense caused by delay, even though the delay is caused by a peril insured against, except liability or expense payable under clause S (the General Average and Salvage Clause);

3.9   Alternative A: loss, damage, liability or expense caused by insolvency or financial default of the owners, managers, charterers or operators of the vessel;

Alternative B

3.9.1   loss, damage, liability or expense caused by insolvency or financial default of the owners, managers, charterers or operators of the vessel, where the assured has failed to take all necessary and prudent measures to establish, or to ensure that his agents establish, the financial reliability of those parties.

3.9.2   This exclusion 3.9 shall not be invoked against a party claiming under this insurance to whom the insurance has been assigned and who has bought the insured cargo in good faith without notice of such insolvency or financial default and without notice that the original assured has failed to take such measures.

3.10   Additional exclusion clause (if expressly agreed by the parties): loss, damage, liability or expense caused by piracy.

3.11   Additional exclusion clause (if expressly agreed by the parties): loss, damage, liability or expense arising directly or indirectly from or in connection with nuclear, radioactive or similar material or from the use of or accidents in nuclear installations or reactors.

C. ADDITIONAL COVERAGE
4. Both to Blame Clause

Where the insured cargo is shipped under a contract of carriage or affreightment containing a "Both to Blame Collision" Clause, the insurer also agrees, as to all losses covered by this insurance, to indemnify the assured for the insured cargo's proportion of any amount up to the sum insured which the assured may be liable to pay to the shipowner or carrier under such clause. In the event of any claim by the shipowner or carrier under the said clause, the assured agrees to notify the insurer who shall have the right, at his own cost and expense, to defend the assured against such claim.

5. General Average and Salvage Clause

5.1   This insurance covers the insured cargo's proportion of general average, salvage and/or salvage charges, adjusted or determined according to the contract of carriage or affreightment and/or the governing law and practice. In case of general average sacrifice of the insured cargo, the assured has the right to recover in respect of the whole of such loss.

5.2   No claim under this clause shall in any case be allowed unless the general average act or salvage was undertaken to avoid, or in connection with the avoidance of, a peril insured against.

5.3   Where all the contributing interests are owned by the assured, the provisions of the York-Antwerp Rules, 1974, or similar provisions of other rules if expressly agreed, shall be applied as if the interests were owned by different persons, and the insurer shall pay the insured cargo's proportion as so calculated.

6. Sue and Labour and Forwarding Charges Clause

6.1   Where there has been loss of or damage to the cargo from a peril insured against, or where the cargo is in danger from such a peril, and as a result reasonable expenditure is incurred by the assured in order to avert or minimize a loss which would be recoverable under this insurance, the insurer shall pay to the assured the expenditure incurred.

6.2   Where, as a result of the operation of a peril insured against, the transit is terminated at a port or place other than the destination to which the cargo is insured hereunder, the insurer will reimburse the assured for any extra charges properly and reasonably incurred in unloading, storing and forwarding the cargo to that destination.

6.3   This clause shall not apply to general average, salvage or salvage charges.

6.4   The insurer's liability under this clause is in addition to his liability under the other provisions of this insurance, but shall not exceed an amount equal to the sum insured hereunder in respect of the cargo.

D. PERIOD OF COVERAGE
7. Commencement and Duration

The insurance commences from the time the insured cargo leaves the ware house or place of storage at the place named in this insurance for the commencement of the transit and shall continue during the ordinary course of transit.

8. Termination

This insurance shall terminate

8.1   on delivery of the insured cargo to the consignee's or other final warehouse or place of storage at the destination named in the insurance; or

8.2   Alternative A: on delivery of the insured cargo to any other warehouse or place of storage, whether prior to or at the destination named in the insurance, which the assured chooses to use either

8.2.1for storage other than in the ordinary course of transit, or

8.2.2for allocation or distribution; or

8.2   Alternative B: on any taking of delivery of the insured cargo by the assured, the shipper, the consignee or their representatives or other authorized persons before the time when the insurance would otherwise terminate as stipulated in 8.1 above; or

8.3 when ... days have elapsed after completion of discharge of the insured cargo from the oversea vessel at the final port or place of discharge;

8.4 when the insured cargo has been discharged from the oversea vessel at the final port or place of discharge, and transit commences to a destination other than that named in this insurance; whichever shall first occur.

9. Continuation

9.1 The insurance shall remain in force, subject to termination as provided by clauses 8 and 9.2, during delay beyond the control of the assured, any deviation, forced discharge, reshipment or transhipment, and during any variation of the adventure arising from the exercise of a liberty granted to shipowners or charterers under the contract of carriage or affreightment.

9.2 When, owing to circumstances beyond the control of the assured, the contract of carriage or affreightment is terminated at a port or place other than the destination named therein, or the transit is otherwise terminated before delivery of the insured cargo as provided for in clause 8 above, this insurance shall also terminate unless prompt notice is given to the insurer and continuation of cover is requested. In that case this insurance shall remain in force, subject to an additional premium if required by the insurer, either

9.2.1 until the insured cargo is sold and delivered at such port or place or, unless otherwise specially agreed, until the expiry of ... days after its arrival at such port or place, whichever shall first occur, or

9.2.2 if the insured cargo is forwarded within the above ... day period (or any agreed extension thereof) to the destination named in this insurance or to any other destination, until terminated in accordance with clause 8 above.

E. MEASURE OF INDEMNITY
10. General Rules

10.1 Agreed and insurable value

10.1.1 Where an agreed value is stated in this insurance this agreed value shall be conclusive between the assured and the insurer as to the value of the insured cargo in the absence of fraud.

10.1.2 Where there is no agreed value, the insurable value of the cargo is

Alternative A: the commercial invoice value or, if there is no such invoice, the market value of the cargo at the time and place of commencement of the cover, plus

10.1.2.1   if not already included, freight and other expenses incidental to the transport, customs duties, insurance costs, and

10.1.2.2   an expected profit of ... %

Alternative B: the market value at the place of destination at the time of the arrival of the cargo or, if the cargo does not arrive, at the time it should have arrived at the place of destination.

10.1.3 Where there is no agreed value and the term "agreed value" is used in other provisions of this insurance, this term shall be deemed also to cover the insurable value, as defined in 10.1.2 above.

10.2 Sum insured

The insurer's total liability under Part A and clauses 4 and 5 of Part C shall be limited to the sum insured. A separate limit shall apply to claims under clause 6 of Part C as provided therein.

10.3 Under- and over-insurance

10.3.1 Where the sum insured is less than the agreed value, the insurer is only liable to pay that proportion of any loss covered by this insurance that the sum insured bears to the agreed value.

10.3.2 Where the sum insured is higher than the agreed value, the assured may not recover more than the agreed value.

10.4 Under-valuation

Alternative A: Where the assured has a claim under Part C, clauses 5 and/or 6, the indemnity payable under this insurance shall not be reduced by reason of the agreed value being less than the actual or contributory value of the insured cargo.

Alternative B

10.4.1 Where the assured has a claim under Part C, clause 5, of this insurance other than for general average sacrifice of the cargo, and the agreed value is less than the full contributory value of the cargo, the insurer shall only pay such proportion of general average, salvage and salvage charges as the agreed value bears to the full contributory value.

10.4.2 Where the cargo has suffered damage covered by this insurance and such damage constitutes a deduction from the contributory value, the same amount must be deducted from the agreed value when determining whether the agreed value is less than the contributory value.

10.5 Co-insurance

Where two or more insurers are liable under this insurance,

10.5.1 each insurer is liable only for his proportion of the claim, which is the proportion that his subscription bears to the sum insured, and shall on no account be held jointly liable with his co-insurers.

10.5.2

Alternative A : each insurer agrees to be subject to the jurisdiction of the courts applicable to the leading insurer for all disputes under this insurance. The leading insurer is authorized by his co-insurers to accept and conduct legal proceedings on their behalf.

Alternative B: No provision.

11. Total Losses

11.1 A claim for loss by a peril insured against may be for a total loss, as herein defined, or otherwise for a partial loss.

11.2 Actual total loss occurs where the insured cargo is destroyed or so damaged as to cease to be a thing of the kind insured or where the assured is irretrievably deprived of the cargo.

11.3 Presumed total loss occurs where the carrying vessel is missing with the insured cargo and no news of the vessel or the cargo has been received within a reasonable time but not to exceed ... months.

11.4 Constructive total loss occurs:

11.4.1 where the assured has been deprived of the free use and disposal of the insured cargo, and

11.4.1.1 it is unlikely that he will be able to recover it within a reasonable time but not to exceed ... months, or

11.4.1.2 he could not recover it without incurring an expenditure which would exceed its value on recovery;

11.4.2 where the insured cargo has been damaged and it cannot be repaired or reconditioned and forwarded to its destination without:

11.4.2.1 becoming an actual total loss before arrival, or

11.4.2.2 incurring an expenditure which would exceed its value on arrival.

11.5 Where there is a valid claim for a total loss recoverable under this insurance, the amount payable by the insurer is the sum insured in respect of the cargo.

12. Abandonment

12.1 Where the assured elects to claim for a constructive total loss rather than for a partial loss, or where there is a presumed total loss, the assured shall with reasonable diligence notify the insurer that he wishes to abandon what remains of the cargo to the insurer.

12.2 Unless otherwise directed by applicable law, no notice of abandonment need be given if, at the time when the assured receives reliable information of the loss, there would be no possibility of benefit to the insurer if notice were given to him or where the insurer has expressly waived the need for such notice.

12.3 Notice of abandonment may be expressed in any terms which indicate the intention of the assured unconditionally to abandon his interest in the cargo to the insurer. The insurer shall advise the assured whether he accepts or rejects the notice of abandonment within a reasonable time from the date on which the notice is tendered.

12.4 Where notice of abandonment is given as provided herein, the rights of the assured shall not be prejudiced by the refusal of the insurer to accept the abandonment.

12.5 Where notice of abandonment is accepted, the abandonment is irrevocable and the acceptance of the notice of abandonment conclusively admits liability for the loss and the sufficiency of the notice. Upon acceptance of abandonment, the insurer may, if he so wishes, take over whatever may remain of the cargo, with all the rights and obligations attached thereto.

13. Partial Losses

13.1 Total loss of part: Where part of the cargo is totally lost, the assured is entitled to be indemnified for such proportion of the agreed value, if a value has been agreed, or of the insurable value, if no value has been agreed, as the insurable value of the part lost bears to the insurable value of the whole.

13.2 Damage

13.2.1 Where the whole or any part of the cargo has been delivered damaged at its destination, the assured is entitled to be indemnified for such proportion of the agreed value, if a value has been agreed, or of the insurable value, if no value has been agreed, as the difference between the gross sound and damaged values at the place of destination bears to the gross sound value.

13.2.2 If the assured chooses to recondition or to repair any part of the cargo which has been delivered damaged at its destination he may, alternatively, claim the reasonable cost of such reconditioning or repair at the time of arrival at its destination.

F. INSURABLE INTEREST

14.1 In order to recover under this insurance the assured must have an insurable interest in the insured cargo at the time of the loss.

14.2 Subject to 14.1 above, the assured shall be entitled to recover in respect of a loss occurring during the transit covered by this insurance, notwithstanding that the loss occurred before the contract of insurance was concluded, unless the assured was aware of the loss and the insurer was not.

CARGO INSURANCE - Intermediate Cover
A. COVERAGE

1. This insurance covers physical loss of or damage to the insured cargo caused by
1.1 vessel or craft being stranded, grounded, sunk or capsized;
1.2 collision or contact of vessel, craft or conveyance with any external object other than water;
1.3 derailment, overturning or falling of the transport conveyance;
1.4 explosion, fire or smoke emanating from that fire;
1.5 general average sacrifice;
1.6 jettison or washing overboard;
1.7 earthquake, volcanic eruption, lightning, or similar natural calamities;
1.8 entry of sea, lake or river water into the vessel, craft, hold, conveyance, container, liftvan or place of storage;
1.9 discharge of all or part of the cargo on the vessel or craft at a port of distress;
1.10 total loss of any package lost overboard or dropped whilst loading on to, or unloading from, vessel or craft.
2. This insurance also covers loss of or damage to the insured cargo caused by any act of any governmental authority to prevent or minimize pollution resulting from damage to the carrying vessel, provided that such act of governmental authority has not resulted from want of due diligence by the assured.

B. GENERAL EXCLUSIONS

3.   This insurance does not cover:

3.1   loss, damage, liability or expense caused by:

3.1.1war, hostilities or warlike acts;

3.1.2civil war, revolution, rebellion, insurrection, or civil strife arising therefrom;

3.1.3mines, torpedoes, bombs or other weapons of war;

3.1.4capture, seizure other than by pirates, masters, officers or crew, arrest, restraint or detainment, and the consequences thereof or any attempt thereat;

3.1.5sabotage or terrorism committed from a political motive;

3.1.6detonation of an explosive caused by any person acting maliciously or from a political motive;

3.1.7strikes, lock-outs or other similar labour disturbances;

3.1.8 civil commotions, riots or other similar events;

3.1.9 confiscation, requisition, or other similar measures taken or attempted by any government or other similar organization assuming or wielding power; or

3.1.10 deliberate damage to or deliberate destruction of the insured cargo or any part thereof by the wrongful act of any person or persons;

3.2   loss, damage, liability or expense resulting from the personal act or omission of the assured done with the intent to cause such loss, damage, liability or expense, or recklessly and with knowledge that such loss, damage, liability or expense would probably result;

3.3   ordinary leakage, ordinary loss in weight or volume, or any other ordinary loss of or damage to the insured cargo;

3.4   loss, damage, liability or expense caused by insufficiency or unsuitability of packing or preparation of the insured cargo;

3.5   loss, damage, liability or expense caused by inadequacy or unsuitability of the stowage of the insured cargo in a container or liftvan where such stowage is carried out prior to attachment of this insurance;

3.6.1loss, damage, liability or expense caused by

3.6.1.1   unseaworthiness of vessel or craft, or

3.6.1.2   unfitness of vessel, craft, conveyance, container or liftvan for the safe carriage of the insured cargo, where the assured knew of or had recklessly refrained from obtaining knowledge of such unseaworthiness of unfitness by the time the insured cargo was loaded therein.

3.6.2This exclusion 3.6 shall not be invoked against a party claiming under this insurance to whom the insurance has been assigned and who has bought the insured cargo in good faith without notice of such unseaworthiness or unfitness;

3.7   loss, damage, liability or expense caused by inherent vice or nature of the insured cargo;

3.8   loss, damage, liability or expense caused by delay, even though the delay is caused by a peril insured against, except liability or expense payable under clause 5 (the General Average and Salvage Clause);

3.9

Alternative A: loss, damage liability or expense caused by insolvency or financial default of the owners, managers, charterers or operators of the vessel;

Alternative B

3.9.1loss, damage, liability or expense caused by insolvency or financial default of the owners, managers, charterers or operators of the vessel, where the assured has failed to take all necessary and prudent measures to establish, or to ensure that his agents establish, the financial reliability of those parties.

3.9.2This exclusion 3.9 shall not be invoked against a party claiming under this insurance to whom the insurance has been assigned and who has bought the insured cargo in good faith without notice of such insolvency or financial default and without notice that the original assured has failed to take such measures.

3.10 Additional exclusion clause (if expressly agreed by the parties): loss, damage, liability or expense caused by piracy.

3.11 Additional exclusion clause (if expressly agreed by the parties): loss, damage, liability or expense arising directly or indirectly from or in connection with nuclear, radioactive or similar material or from the use of or accidents in nuclear installations or reactors.

C. ADDITIONAL COVERAGE
4. Both to Blame Clause

Where the insured cargo is shipped under a contract of carriage or affreightment containing a "Both to Blame Collision" Clause, the insurer also agrees, as to all losses covered by this insurance, to indemnify the assured for the insured cargo's proportion of any amount up to the sum insured which the assured may be liable to pay to the shipowner or carrier under such clause. In the event of any claim by the shipowner or carrier under the said clause the assured agrees to notify the insurer who shall have the right, at his own cost and expense, to defend the assured against such claim.

5. General Average and Salvage Clause

5.1 This insurance covers the insured cargo's proportion of general average, salvage and/or salvage charges, adjusted or determined according to the contract of carriage or affreightment and/or the governing law and practice. In case of general average sacrifice of the insured cargo, the assured has the right to recover in respect of the whole of such loss.

5.2 No claim under this clause shall in any case be allowed unless the general average act or salvage was undertaken to avoid or in connection with the avoidance of, a peril insured against.

5.3 Where all the contributing interests are owned by the assured the provisions of the York-Antwerp Rules, 1974, or similar provisions of other rules if expressly agreed, shall be applied as if the interests were owned by different persons, and the insurer shall pay the insured cargo's proportion as so calculated.

6. Sue and Labour and Forwarding Charges Clause

6.1 Where there has been loss of or damage to the cargo from a peril insured against, or where the cargo is in danger from such a peril, and as a result reasonable expenditure is incurred by the assured in order to avert or minimize a loss which would be recoverable under this insurance, the insurer shall pay to the assured the expenditure incurred.

6.2 Where, as a result of the operation of a peril insured against the transit is terminated at a port or place other than the destination to which the cargo is insured hereunder, the insurer will reimburse the assured for any extra charges properly and reasonably incurred in unloading, storing and forwarding the cargo to that destination.

6.3 This clause shall not apply to general average, salvage or salvage charges.

6.4 The insurer's liability under this clause is in addition to his liability under the other provisions of this insurance, but shall not exceed an amount equal to the sum insured hereunder in respect of the cargo.

D. PERIOD OF COVERAGE
7. Commencement and Duration

The insurance commences from the time the insured cargo leaves the warehouse or place of storage at the place named in this insurance for the commencement of the transit and shall continue during the ordinary course of transit.

8. Termination

This insurance shall terminate

8.1 on delivery of the insured cargo to the consignee's or other final warehouse or place of storage at the destination named in the insurance; or

8.2 Alternative A: on delivery of the insured cargo to any other warehouse or place of storage, whether prior to or at the destination named in the insurance, which the assured chooses to use either

8.2.1for storage other than in the ordinary course of transit, or

8.2.2for allocation or distribution; or

Alternative B: on any taking of delivery of the insured cargo by the assured, the shipper, the consignee or their representatives or other authorized persons before the time when the insurance would otherwise terminate as stipulated in 8.1 above; or

8.3 when ... days have elapsed after completion of discharge of the insured cargo from the oversea vessel at the final port or place of discharge;

8.4 when the insured cargo has been discharged from the oversea vessel at the final port or place of discharge, and transit commences to a destination other than that named in this insurance; whichever shall first occur.

9. Continuation

9.1 The insurance shall remain in force, subject to termination as provided by clauses 8 and 9.2, during delay beyond the control of the assured, any deviation, forced discharge, reshipment or transhipment, and during any variation of the adventure arising from the exercise of a liberty granted to shipowners or charterers under the contract of carriage or affreightment.

9.2 When, owing to circumstances beyond the control of the assured, the contract of carriage or affreightment is terminated at a port or place other than the destination named therein, or the transit is otherwise terminated before delivery of the insured cargo as provided for in clause 8 above, this insurance shall also terminate unless prompt notice is given to the insurer and continuation of cover is requested. In that case this insurance shall remain in force, subject to an additional premium if required by the insurer, either

9.2.1until the insured cargo is sold and delivered at such port or place or, unless otherwise specially agreed, until the expiry of ... days after its arrival at such port or place, whichever shall first occur, or

9.2.2if the insured cargo is forwarded within the above ... day period (or any agreed extension thereof) to the destination named in this insurance or to any other destination, until terminated in accordance with clause 8 above.

E. MEASURE OF INDEMNITY
10. General Rules

10.1 Agreed and insurable value

10.1.1 Where an agreed value is stated in this insurance this agreed value shall be conclusive between the assured and the insurer as to the value of the insured cargo in the absence of fraud.

10.1.2 Where there is no agreed value, the insurable value of the cargo is

Alternative A: the commercial invoice value or, if there is no such invoice, the market value of the cargo at the time and place of commencement of the cover, plus

10.1.2.1 if not already included, freight and other expenses incidental to the transport, customs duties, insurance costs, and

10.1.2.2 an expected profit of ... %.

Alternative B: the market value at the place of destination at the time of the arrival of the cargo or, if the cargo does not arrive, at the time it should have arrived at the place of destination.

10.1.3 Where there is no agreed value and the term "agreed value" is used in other provisions of this insurance, this term shall be deemed also to cover the insurable value, as defined in 10.1.2 above.

10.2 Sum insured

The insurer's total liability under Part A and clauses 4 and 5 of Part C shall be limited to the sum insured. A separate limit shall apply to claims under clause 6 of Part C as provided therein.

10.3 Under- and over-insurance

10.3.1 Where the sum insured is less than the agreed value, the insurer is only liable to pay that proportion of any loss covered by this insurance that the sum insured bears to the agreed value.

10.3.3 Where the sum insured is higher than the agreed value, the assured may not recover more than the agreed value.

10.4 Under-valuation

Alternative A: Where the assured has a claim under Part C, clauses 5 and/or 6, the indemnity payable under this insurance shall not be reduced by reason of the agreed value being less than the actual or contributory value of the insured cargo.

Alternative B

10.4.1 Where the assured has a claim under Part C, clause 5, of this insurance other than for general average sacrifice of the cargo, and the agreed value is less than the full contributory value of the cargo, the insurer shall only pay such proportion of general average, salvage and salvage charges as the agreed value bears to the full contributory value.

10.4.2 Where the cargo has suffered damage covered by this insurance and such damage constitutes a deduction from the contributory value, the same amount must be deducted from the agreed value when determining whether the agreed value is less than the contributory value.

10.5 Co-insurance: Where two or more insurers are liable under this insurance,

10.5.1 each insurer is liable only for his proportion of the claim, which is the proportion that his subscription bears to the sum insured, and shall on no account be held jointly liable with his co-insurers.

10.5.2 Alternative A: each insurer agrees to be subject to the jurisdiction of the courts applicable to the leading insurer for all disputes under this insurance. The leading insurer is authorized by his co-insurers to accept and conduct legal proceedings on their behalf.

Alternative B: No provision

11. Total Losses

11.1 A claim for loss by a peril insured against may be for a total loss, as herein defined, or otherwise for a partial loss.

11.2 Actual total loss occurs where the insured cargo is destroyed or so damaged as to cease to be a thing of the kind insured or where the assured is irretrievably deprived of the cargo.

11.3 Presumed total loss occurs where the carrying vessel is missing with the insured cargo and no news of the vessel or the cargo has been received within a reasonable time but not to exceed ... months.

11.4 Constructive total loss occurs:

11.4.1 where the assured has been deprived of the free use and disposal of the insured cargo, and

11.4.1.1 it is unlikely that he will be able to recover it within a reasonable time but not to exceed ... months, or

11.4.1.2 he could not recover it without incurring an expenditure which would exceed its value on recovery;

11.4.2 where the insured cargo has been damaged and it cannot be repaired or reconditioned and forwarded to its destination without:

11.4.2.1 becoming an actual total loss before arrival, or

11.4.2.2 incurring an expenditure which would exceed its value on arrival.

11.5 Where there is a valid claim for a total loss recoverable under this insurance, the amount payable by the insurer is the sum insured in respect of the cargo.

12. Abandonment

12.1 Where the assured elects to claim for a constructive total loss rather than for a partial loss, or where there is a presumed total loss, the assured shall with reasonable diligence notify the insurer that he wishes to abandon what remains of the cargo to the insurer.

12.2 Unless otherwise directed by applicable law, no notice of abandonment need be given if, at the time when the assured receives reliable information of the loss, there would be no possibility of benefit to the insurer if notice were given to him or where the insurer has expressly waived the need for such notice.

12.3 Notice of abandonment may be expressed in any terms which indicate the intention of the assured unconditionally to abandon his interest in the cargo to the insurer. The insurer shall advise the assured whether he accepts or rejects the notice of abandonment within a reasonable time from the date on which the notice is tendered.

12.4 Where notice of abandonment is given as provided herein, the rights of the assured shall not be prejudiced by the refusal of the insurer to accept the abandonment.

12.5 Where notice of abandonment is accepted, the abandonment is irrevocable and the acceptance of the notice of abandonment conclusively admits liability for the loss and the sufficiency of the notice. Upon acceptance of abandonment, the insurer may, if he so wishes, take over whatever may remain of the cargo, with all the rights and obligations attached thereto.

13. Partial Losses

13.1 Total loss of part: Where part of the cargo is totally lost, the assured is entitled to be indemnified for such proportion of the agreed value, if a value has been agreed, or of the insurable value, if no value has been agreed, as the insurable value of the part lost bears to the insurable value of the whole.

13.2 Damage

13.2.1 Where the whole or any part of the cargo has been delivered damaged at its destination, the assured is entitled to be indemnified for such proportion of the agreed value, if a value has been agreed, or of the insurable value, if no value has been agreed, as the difference between the gross sound and damaged values at the place of destination bears to the gross sound value.

13.2.2 If the assured chooses to recondition or to repair any part of the cargo which has been delivered damaged at its destination, he may, alternatively, claim the reasonable cost of such reconditioning or repair at the time of arrival at its destination.

F. INSURABLE INTEREST

14.1 In order to recover under this insurance the assured must have an insurable interest in the insured cargo at the time of the loss.

14.2 Subject to 14.1 above, the assured shall be entitled to recover in respect of a loss occurring during the transit covered by this insurance, notwithstanding that the loss occurred before the contract of insurance was concluded, unless the assured was aware of the loss and the insurer was not.

CARGO INSURANCE - Restricted Cover
A. COVERAGE

1. This insurance covers physical loss of or damage to the insured cargo caused by
1.1 vessel or craft being stranded, grounded, sunk or capsized;
1.2 collision or contact of vessel, craft or conveyance with any external object other than water;
1.3 derailment, overturning or falling of the transport conveyance;
1.4 explosion, fire or smoke emanating from that fire;
1.5 general average sacrifice;
1.6 jettison;
1.7 discharge of all or part of the cargo on the vessel or craft at a port of distress.

2. This insurance also covers loss of or damage to the insured cargo caused by any act of any governmental authority to prevent or minimize pollution resulting from damage to the carrying vessel, provided that such act of governmental authority has not resulted from want of due diligence by the assured.

B. GENERAL EXCLUSIONS

3. This insurance does not cover:
3.1 loss, damage, liability or expense caused by:
3.1.1 war, hostilities or warlike acts;
3.1.2 civil war, revolution, rebellion, insurrection, or civil strife arising therefrom;

3.1.3mines, torpedoes, bombs or other weapons of war;

3.1.4capture, seizure other than by pirates, masters, officers or crew, arrest, restraint or detainment, and the consequences thereof or any attempt thereat;

3.1.5sabotage or terrorism committed from a political motive;

3.1.6detonation of an explosive caused by any person acting maliciously or from a political motive;

3.1.7strikes, lock-outs or other similar labour disturbances;

3.1.8civil commotions, riots or other similar events;

3.1.9confiscation, requisition, or other similar measures taken or attempted by any government or other similar organization assuming or wielding power; or

3.1.10 deliberate damage to or deliberate destruction of the insured cargo or any part thereof by the wrongful act of any person or persons;

3.2 loss, damage, liability or expense resulting from the personal act or omission of the assured done with the intent to cause such loss, damage, liability or expense, or recklessly and with knowledge that such loss, damage, liability or expense would probably result;

3.3 ordinary leakage, ordinary loss in weight or volume, or any other ordinary loss of or damage to the insured cargo;

3.4 loss, damage, liability or expense caused by insufficiency or unsuitability of packing or preparation of the insured cargo;

3.5 loss, damage, liability or expense caused by inadequacy or unsuitability of the stowage of the insured cargo in a container or liftvan where such stowage is carried out prior to attachment of this insurance;

3.6.1loss damage, liability or expense caused by

3.6.1.1 unseaworthiness of vessel or craft, or

3.6.1.2 unfitness of vessel, craft, conveyance, container or liftvan for the safe carriage of the insured cargo, where the assured knew of or had recklessly refrained from obtaining knowledge of such unseaworthiness of unfitness by the time the insured cargo was loaded therein.

3.6.2This exclusion 3.6 shall not be invoked against a party claiming under this insurance to whom the insurance has been assigned and who has bought the insured cargo in good faith without notice of such unseaworthiness or unfitness;

3.7 loss, damage, liability or expense caused by inherent vice or nature of the insured cargo;

3.8 loss, damage, liability or expense caused by delay, even though the delay is caused by a peril insured against, except liability or expense payable under clause 5 (the General Average and Salvage Clause);

3.9 Alternative A: loss, damage, liability or expense caused by insolvency or financial default of the owners, managers, charterers or operators of the vessel;

Alternative B

3.9.1loss, damage, liability or expense caused by insolvency or financial default of the owners, managers, charterers or operators of the vessel, where the assured has failed to take all necessary and prudent measures to establish, or to ensure that his agents establish, the financial reliability of those parties.

3.9.2This exclusion 3.9 shall not be invoked against a party claiming under this insurance to whom the insurance has been assigned and who has bought the insured cargo in good faith without notice of such insolvency or financial default and without notice that the original assured has failed to take such measures.

3.10 Additional exclusion clause (if expressly agreed by the parties): loss, damage, liability or expense caused by piracy.

3.11 Additional exclusion clause (if expressly agreed by the parties): loss, damage, liability or expense arising directly or indirectly from or in connection with nuclear, radioactive or similar material or from the use of or accidents in nuclear installations or reactors.

C. ADDITIONAL COVERAGE
4. Both to Blame Clause

Where the insured cargo is shipped under a contract of carriage or affreightment containing a "Both to Blame Collision" Clause, the insurer also agrees, as to all losses covered by this insurance, to indemnify the assured for the insured cargo's proportion of any amount up to the sum insured which the assured may be liable to pay to the shipowner or carrier under such clause. In the event of any claim by the shipowner or carrier under the said clause, the assured agrees to notify the insurer who shall have the right, at his own cost and expense, to defend the assured against such claim.

5. General Average and Salvage Clause

5.1 This insurance covers the insured cargo's proportion of general average, salvage and/or salvage charges, adjusted or determined according to the contract of carriage or affreightment and/or the governing law and practice. In case of general average sacrifice of the insured cargo. the assured has the right to recover in respect of the whole of such loss.

5.2 No claim under this clause shall in any case be allowed unless the general average act or salvage was undertaken to avoid, or in connection with the avoidance of, a peril insured against.

5.3 Where all the contributing interests are owned by the assured, the provisions of the York-Antwerp Rules, 1974, or similar provisions of other rules if expressly agreed, shall be applied as if the interests were owned by different persons, and the insurer shall pay the insured cargo's proportion as so calculated.

6. Sue and Labour and Forwarding Charges Clause

6.1 Where there has been loss of or damage to the cargo from a peril insured against, or where the cargo is in danger from such a peril, and as a result reasonable expenditure is incurred by the assured in order to avert or minimize a loss which would be recoverable under this insurance, the insurer shall pay to the assured the expenditure incurred.

6.2 Where, as a result of the operation of a peril insured against, the transit is terminated at a port or place other than the destination to which the cargo is insured hereunder, the insurer will reimburse the assured for any extra charges properly and reasonably incurred in unloading, storing and forwarding the cargo to that destination.

6.3 This clause shall not apply to general average, salvage or salvage charges.

6.4 The insurer's liability under this clause is in addition to his liability under the other provisions of this insurance, but shall not exceed an amount equal to the sum insured hereunder in respect of the cargo.

D. PERIOD OF COVERAGE
7. Commencement and Duration

The insurance commences from the time the insured cargo leaves the ware house or place of storage at the place named in this insurance for the commencement of the transit and shall continue during the ordinary course of transit.

8. Termination

This insurance shall terminate

8.1 on delivery of the insured cargo to the consignee's or other final warehouse or place of storage at the destination named in the insurance; or

8.2 Alternative A: on delivery of the insured cargo to any other warehouse or place of storage, whether prior to or at the destination named in the insurance, which the assured chooses to use either

8.2.1for storage other than in the ordinary course of transit, or

8.2.2for allocation or distribution; or

8.2 Alternative B: on any taking of delivery of the insured cargo by the assured, the shipper, the consignee or their representatives or other authorized persons before the time when the insurance would otherwise terminate as stipulated in 8.1 above; or

8.3 when ... days have elapsed after completion of discharge of the insured cargo from the oversea vessel at the final port or place of discharge;

8.4 when the insured cargo has been discharged from the oversea vessel at the final port or place of discharge, and transit commences to a destination other than that named in this insurance; whichever shall first occur.

9. Continuation

9.1 The insurance shall remain in force, subject to termination as provided by clauses 8 and 9.2, during delay beyond the control of the assured, any deviation, forced discharge, reshipment or transhipment, and during any variation of the adventure arising from the exercise of a liberty granted to shipowners or charterers under the contract of carriage or affreightment.

9.2 When, owing to circumstances beyond the control of the assured, the contract of carriage or affreightment is terminated at a port or place other than the destination named therein, or the transit is otherwise terminated before delivery of the insured cargo as provided for in clause 8 above, this insurance shall also terminate unless prompt notice is given to the insurer and continuation of cover is requested. In that case this insurance shall remain in force, subject to an additional premium if required by the insurer, either

9.2.1 until the insured cargo is sold and delivered at such port or place or, unless otherwise specially agreed, until the expiry of ... days after its arrival at such port or place, whichever shall first occur, or

9.2.2 if the insured cargo is forwarded within the above ... day period (or any agreed extension thereof) to the destination named in this insurance or to any other destination, until terminated in accordance with clause 8 above.

E. MEASURE OF INDEMNITY
10. General Rules

10.1 Agreed and insurable value

10.1.1 Where an agreed value is stated in this insurance this agreed value shall be conclusive between the assured and the insurer as to the value of the insured cargo in the absence of fraud.

10.1.2 Where there is no agreed value, the insurable value of the cargo is

Alternative A: the commercial invoice value or, if there is no such invoice, the market value of the cargo at the time and place of commencement of the cover, plus

10.1.2.1 if not already included, freight and other expenses incidental to the transport, customs duties, insurance costs, and

10.1.2.2 an expected profit of ... %.

Alternative B: the market value at the place of destination at the time of the arrival of the cargo or, if the cargo does not arrive, at the time it should have arrived at the place of destination.

10.1.3 Where there is no agreed value and the term "agreed value" is used in other provisions of this insurance, this term shall be deemed also to cover the insurable value, as defined in 10.1.2 above.

10.2 Sum insured

The insurer's total liability under Part A and clauses 4 and 5 of Part C shall be limited to the sum insured. A separate limit shall apply to claims under clause 6 of Part C as provided therein.

10.3 Under- and over-insurance

10.3.1 Where the sum insured is less than the agreed value, the insurer is only liable to pay that proportion of any loss covered by this insurance that the sum insured bears to the agreed value.

10.3.2 Where the sum insured is higher than the agreed value, the assured may not recover more than the agreed value.

10.4 Under-valuation

Alternative A: Where the assured has a claim under Part C, clauses 5 and/or 6, the indemnity payable under this insurance shall not be reduced by reason of the agreed value being less than the actual or contributory value of the insured cargo.

Alternative B

10.4.1 Where the assured has a claim under Part C, clause 5, of this insurance other than for general average sacrifice of the cargo, and the agreed value is less than the full contributory value of the cargo, the insurer shall only pay such proportion of general average, salvage and salvage charges as the agreed value bears to the full contributory value.

10.4.2 Where the cargo has suffered damage covered by this insurance and such damage constitutes a deduction from the contributory value, the same amount must be deducted from the agreed value when determining whether the agreed value is less than the contributory value.

10.5 Co-insurance: Where two or more insurers are liable under this insurance,

10.5.1 each insurer is liable only for his proportion of the claim, which is the proportion that his subscription bears to the sum insured, and shall on no account be held jointly liable with his co-insurers.

10.5.2 Alternative A: each insurer agrees to be subject to the jurisdiction of the courts applicable to the leading insurer for all disputes under this insurance. The leading insurer is authorized by his co-insurers to accept and conduct legal proceedings on their behalf.

Alternative B: No provision

11. Total Losses

11.1 A claim for loss by a peril insured against may be for a total loss, as herein defined, or otherwise for a partial loss.

11.2 Actual total loss occurs where the insured cargo is destroyed or so damaged as to cease to be a thing of the kind insured or where the assured is irretrievably deprived of the cargo.

11.3 Presumed total loss occurs where the carrying vessel is missing with the insured cargo and no news of the vessel or the cargo has been received within a reasonable time but not to exceed ... months.

11.4 Constructive total loss occurs:

11.4.1 where the assured has been deprived of the free use and disposal of the insured cargo, and

11.4.1.1 it is unlikely that he will be able to recover it within a reasonable time but not to exceed ... months, or

11.4.1.2 he could not recover it without incurring an expenditure which would exceed its value on recovery;

11.4.2 where the insured cargo has been damaged and it cannot be repaired or reconditioned and forwarded to its destination without:

11.4.2.1 becoming an actual total loss before arrival, or

11.4.2.2 incurring an expenditure which would exceed its value on arrival.

11.5 Where there is a valid claim for a total loss recoverable under this insurance, the amount payable by the insurer is the sum insured in respect of the cargo.

12. Abandonment

12.1 Where the assured elects to claim for a constructive total loss rather than for a partial loss, or where there is a presumed total loss, the assured shall with reasonable diligence notify the insurer that he wishes to abandon what remains of the cargo to the insurer.

12.2 Unless otherwise directed by applicable law, no notice of abandonment need be given if, at the time when the assured receives reliable information of the loss, there would be no possibility of benefit to the insurer if notice were given to him or where the insurer has expressly waived the need for such notice.

12.3 Notice of abandonment may be expressed in any terms which indicate the intention of the assured unconditionally to abandon his interest in the cargo to the insurer. The insurer shall advise the assured whether he accepts or rejects the notice of abandonment within a reasonable time from the date on which the notice is tendered.

12.4 Where notice of abandonment is given as provided herein, the rights of the assured shall not be prejudiced by the refusal of the insurer to accept the abandonment.

12.5 Where notice of abandonment is accepted, the abandonment is irrevocable and the acceptance of the notice of abandonment conclusively admits liability for the loss and the sufficiency of the notice. Upon acceptance of abandonment, the insurer may, if he so wishes, take over whatever may remain of the cargo, with all the rights and obligations attached thereto.

13. Partial Losses

13.1 Total loss of part: Where part of the cargo is totally lost, the assured is entitled to be indemnified for such proportion of the agreed value, if a value has been agreed, or of the insurable value, if no value has been agreed, as the insurable value of the part lost bears to the insurable value of the whole.

13.2 Damage

13.2.1 Where the whole or any part of the cargo has been delivered damaged at its destination, the assured is entitled to be indemnified for such proportion of the agreed value, if a value has been agreed, or of the insurable value, if no value has been agreed, as the difference between the gross sound and damaged values at the place of destination bears to the gross sound value.

13.2.2 If the assured chooses to recondition or to repair any part of the cargo which has been delivered damaged at its destination, he may, alternatively, claim the reasonable cost of such reconditioning or repair at the time of arrival at its destination.

F. INSURABLE INTEREST

14.1 In order to recover under this insurance the assured must have an insurable interest in the insured cargo at the time of the loss.

14.2 Subject to 14.1 above, the assured shall be entitled to recover in respect of a loss occurring during the transit covered by this insurance, notwithstanding that the loss occurred before the contract of insurance was concluded, unless the assured was aware of the loss and the insurer was not.

INSTITUTE CARGO CLAUSES (A)[1]

RISKS COVERED

Risks

1. This insurance covers all risks of loss of or damage to the subject-matter insured except as excluded by the provisions of Clauses 4, 5, 6 and 7 below.

General Average

2. This insurance covers general average and salvage charges, adjusted or determined according to the contract of carriage and/or the governing law and practice, incurred to avoid or in connection with the avoidance of loss from any cause except those excluded in Clauses 4, 5, 6 and 7 below.

"Both to Blame Collision Clause"

3. This insurance indemnifies the Assured, in respect of any risk insured herein, against liability incurred under any Both to Blame Collision Clause in the contract of carriage. In the event of any claim by carriers under the said Clause, the Assured agree to notify the Insurers who shall have the right, at their own cost and expense, to defend the Assured against such claim.

EXCLUSIONS

4. In no case shall this insurance cover

4.1 loss damage or expense attributable to wilful misconduct of the Assured

4.2 ordinary leakage, ordinary loss in weight or volume, or ordinary wear and tear of the subject-matter insured

---

1   © International Underwriting Association, London, and Lloyd's Market Association, London.

4.3   loss damage or expense caused by insufficiency or unsuitability of packing or preparation of the subject-matter insured to withstand the ordinary incidents of the insured transit where such packing or preparation is carried out by the Assured or their employees or prior to the attachment of this insurance (for the purpose of these Clauses "packing" shall be deemed to include stowage in a container and "employees" shall not include independent contractors)

4.4   loss damage or expense caused by inherent vice or nature of the subject-matter insured

4.5   loss damage or expense caused by delay, even though the delay be caused by a risk insured against (except expenses payable under Clause 2 above)

4.6   loss damage or expense caused by insolvency or financial default of the owners managers charterers or operators of the vessel where, at the time of loading of the subject-matter insured on board the vessel, the Assured are aware, or in the ordinary course of business should be aware, that such insolvency or financial default could prevent the normal prosecution of the voyage This exclusion shall not apply where the contract of insurance has been assigned to the party claiming hereunder who has bought or agreed to buy the subject-matter insured in good faith under a binding contract

4.7   loss damage or expense directly or indirectly caused by or arising from the use of any weapon or device employing atomic or nuclear fission and/or fusion or other like reaction or radioactive force or matter.

5.1   In no case shall this insurance cover loss damage or expense arising from

5.1.1 unseaworthiness of vessel or craft or unfitness of vessel or craft for the safe carriage of the subject-matter insured, where the Assured are privy to such unseaworthiness or unfitness, at the time the subject-matter insured is loaded therein

5.1.2 unfitness of container or conveyance for the safe carriage of the subject-matter insured, where loading therein or thereon is carried out prior to attachment of this insurance or by the Assured or their employees and they are privy to such unfitness at the time of loading.

5.2   Exclusion 5.1.1 above shall not apply where the contract of insurance has been assigned to the party claiming hereunder who has bought or agreed to buy the subject-matter insured in good faith under a binding contract.

5.3   The Insurers waive any breach of the implied warranties of seaworthiness of the ship and fitness of the ship to carry the subject-matter insured to destination.

6.   In no case shall this insurance cover loss damage or expense caused by

6.1   war civil war revolution rebellion insurrection, or civil strife arising therefrom, or any hostile act by or against a belligerent power

6.2   capture seizure arrest restraint or detainment (piracy excepted), and the consequences thereof or any attempt thereat

6.3   derelict mines torpedoes bombs or other derelict weapons of war.

7.   In no case shall this insurance cover loss damage or expense

7.1   caused by strikers, locked-out workmen, or persons taking part in labour disturbances, riots or civil commotions

7.2   resulting from strikes, lock-outs, labour disturbances, riots or civil commotions

7.3   caused by any act of terrorism being an act of any person acting on behalf of, or in connection with, any organisation which carries out activities directed towards the overthrowing or influencing, by force or violence, of any government whether or not legally constituted

7.4   caused by any person acting from a political, ideological or religious motive.

DURATION
Transit Clause

8.1   Subject to Clause 11 below, this insurance attaches from the time the subject-matter insured is first moved in the warehouse or at the place of storage (at the place named in the contract of insurance) for the purpose of the immediate loading into or onto the carrying vehicle or other conveyance for the commencement of transit, continues during the ordinary course of transit and terminates either

8.1.1 on completion of unloading from the carrying vehicle or other conveyance in or at the final warehouse or place of storage at the destination named in the contract of insurance,

8.1.2 on completion of unloading from the carrying vehicle or other conveyance in or at any other warehouse or place of storage, whether prior to or at the destination named in the contract of insurance, which the Assured or their employees elect to use either for storage other than in the ordinary course of transit or for allocation or distribution, or

8.1.3 when the Assured or their employees elect to use any carrying vehicle or other conveyance or any container for storage other than in the ordinary course of transit or

8.1.4 on the expiry of 60 days after completion of discharge overside of the subject-matter insured from the oversea vessel at the final port of discharge, whichever shall first occur.

8.2 If, after discharge overside from the oversea vessel at the final port of discharge, but prior to termination of this insurance, the subject-matter insured is to be forwarded to a destination other than that to which it is insured, this insurance, whilst remaining subject to termination as provided in Clauses 8.1.1 to 8.1.4, shall not extend beyond the time the subject-matter insured is first moved for the purpose of the commencement of transit to such other destination.

8.3 This insurance shall remain in force (subject to termination as provided for in Clauses 8.1.1 to 8.1.4 above and to the provisions of Clause 9 below) during delay beyond the control of the Assured, any deviation, forced discharge, reshipment or transhipment and during any variation of the adventure arising from the exercise of a liberty granted to carriers under the contract of carriage.

Termination of Contract of Carriage

9. If owing to circumstances beyond the control of the Assured either the contract of carriage is terminated at a port or place other than the destination named therein or the transit is otherwise terminated before unloading of the subject-matter insured as provided for in Clause 8 above, then this insurance shall also terminate unless prompt notice is given to the Insurers and continuation of cover is requested when this insurance shall remain in force, subject to an additional premium if required by the Insurers, either

9.1 until the subject-matter insured is sold and delivered at such port or place, or, unless otherwise specially agreed, until the expiry of 60 days after arrival of the subject-matter insured at such port or place, whichever shall first occur, or

9.2 if the subject-matter insured is forwarded within the said period of 60 days (or any agreed extension thereof) to the destination named in the contract of insurance or to any other destination, until terminated in accordance with the provisions of Clause 8 above.

Change of Voyage

10.1 Where, after attachment of this insurance, the destination is changed by the Assured, this must be notified promptly to Insurers for rates and terms to be agreed. Should a loss occur prior to such agreement being obtained cover may be provided but only if cover would have been available at a reasonable commercial market rate on reasonable market terms.

10.2 Where the subject-matter insured commences the transit contemplated by this insurance (in accordance with Clause 8.1), but, without the knowledge of the Assured or their employees the ship sails for another destination, this insurance will nevertheless be deemed to have attached at commencement of such transit.

CLAIMS

Insurable Interest

11.1 In order to recover under this insurance the Assured must have an insurable interest in the subject-matter insured at the time of the loss.

11.2 Subject to Clause 11.1 above, the Assured shall be entitled to recover for insured loss occurring during the period covered by this insurance, notwithstanding that the loss occurred before the contract of insurance was concluded, unless the Assured were aware of the loss and the Insurers were not.

Forwarding Charges

12. Where, as a result of the operation of a risk covered by this insurance, the insured transit is terminated at a port or place other than that to which the subject-matter insured is covered under this insurance, the Insurers will reimburse the Assured for any extra charges properly and reasonably incurred in unloading storing and forwarding the subject-matter insured to the destination to which it is insured.

    This Clause 12, which does not apply to general average or salvage charges, shall be subject to the exclusions contained in Clauses 4, 5, 6 and 7 above, and shall not include charges arising from the fault negligence insolvency or financial default of the Assured or their employees.

Constructive Total Loss

13. No claim for Constructive Total Loss shall be recoverable hereunder unless the subject-matter insured is reasonably abandoned either on account of its actual total loss appearing to be unavoidable or because the cost of recovering, reconditioning and forwarding the subject-matter insured to the destination to which it is insured would exceed its value on arrival.

Increased Value

14.1 If any Increased Value insurance is effected by the Assured on the subject-matter insured under this insurance the agreed value of the subject-matter insured shall be deemed to be increased to the total amount insured under this insurance and all Increased Value insurances covering the loss, and liability under this insurance shall be in such proportion as the sum insured under this insurance bears to such total amount insured.

    In the event of claim the Assured shall provide the Insurers with evidence of the amounts insured under all other insurances.

14.2 Where this insurance is on Increased Value the following clause shall apply:

The agreed value of the subject-matter insured shall be deemed to be equal to the total amount insured under the primary insurance and all Increased Value insurances covering the loss and effected on the subject-matter insured by the Assured, and liability under this insurance shall be in such proportion as the sum insured under this insurance bears to such total amount insured.

    In the event of claim the Assured shall provide the Insurers with evidence of the amounts insured under all other insurances.

BENEFIT OF INSURANCE

15. This insurance

15.1 covers the Assured which includes the person claiming indemnity either as the person by or on whose behalf the contract of insurance was effected or as an assignee,

15.2 shall not extend to or otherwise benefit the carrier or other bailee.

MINIMISING LOSSES

Duty of Assured

16. It is the duty of the Assured and their employees and agents in respect of loss recoverable hereunder

16.1 to take such measures as may be reasonable for the purpose of averting or minimising such loss, and

16.2 to ensure that all rights against carriers, bailees or other third parties are properly preserved and exercised and the Insurers will, in addition to any loss recoverable hereunder, reimburse the Assured for any charges properly and reasonably incurred in pursuance of these duties.

Waiver

17. Measures taken by the Assured or the Insurers with the object of saving, protecting or recovering the subject-matter insured shall not be considered as a waiver or acceptance of abandonment or otherwise prejudice the rights of either party.

AVOIDANCE OF DELAY

18. It is a condition of this insurance that the Assured shall act with reasonable despatch in all circumstances within their control.

LAW AND PRACTICE

19. This insurance is subject to English law and practice.

NOTE:- Where a continuation of cover is requested under Clause 9, or a change of destination is notified under Clause 10, there is an obligation to give prompt notice to the Insurers and the right to such cover is dependent upon compliance with this obligation.

Part V - Enforcement of International Contracts and Agreements

2005 HAGUE CONVENTION ON CHOICE OF COURT AGREEMENTS[1]
(The Hague, 30 June 2005)

The States Parties to the present Convention,
Desiring to promote international trade and investment through enhanced judicial co-operation,
Believing that such co-operation can be enhanced by uniform rules on jurisdiction and on recognition and enforcement of foreign judgments in civil or commercial matters,
Believing that such enhanced co-operation requires in particular an international legal regime
that provides certainty and ensures the effectiveness of exclusive choice of court agreements
between parties to commercial transactions and that governs the recognition and enforcement
of judgments resulting from proceedings based on such agreements,
Have resolved to conclude this Convention and have agreed upon the following provisions -

Chapter I - Scope and Definitions
Article 1 Scope
(1)   This Convention shall apply in international cases to exclusive choice of court agreements
concluded in civil or commercial matters.
(2)   For the purposes of Chapter II, a case is international unless the parties are resident in the
same Contracting State and the relationship of the parties and all other elements relevant to the
dispute, regardless of the location of the chosen court, are connected only with that State.
(3)   For the purposes of Chapter III, a case is international where recognition or enforcement of
a foreign judgment is sought.
Article 2 Exclusions from Scope
(1)   This Convention shall not apply to exclusive choice of court agreements -
a)   to which a natural person acting primarily for personal, family or household purposes (a
     consumer) is a party;
b)   relating to contracts of employment, including collective agreements.
(2)   This Convention shall not apply to the following matters -
a)   the status and legal capacity of natural persons;
b)   maintenance obligations;
c)   other family law matters, including matrimonial property regimes and other rights or
     obligations arising out of marriage or similar relationships;
d)   wills and succession;
e)   insolvency, composition and analogous matters;
f)   the carriage of passengers and goods;
g)   marine pollution, limitation of liability for maritime claims, general average, and emergency
     towage and salvage;
h)   anti-trust (competition) matters;
i)   liability for nuclear damage;
j)   claims for personal injury brought by or on behalf of natural persons;
k)   tort or delict claims for damage to tangible property that do not arise from a contractual
     relationship;
l)   rights in rem in immovable property, and tenancies of immovable property;
m)   the validity, nullity, or dissolution of legal persons, and the validity of decisions of their
     organs;

---

1   © Hague Conference on Private International Law.

n)   the validity of intellectual property rights other than copyright and related rights;
o)   infringement of intellectual property rights other than copyright and related rights, except where infringement proceedings are brought for breach of a contract between the parties relating to such rights, or could have been brought for breach of that contract;
p)   the validity of entries in public registers.
(3)   Notwithstanding paragraph 2, proceedings are not excluded from the scope of this Convention where a matter excluded under that paragraph arises merely as a preliminary question and not as an object of the proceedings. In particular, the mere fact that a matter excluded under paragraph 2 arises by way of defence does not exclude proceedings from the Convention, if that matter is not an object of the proceedings.
(4)   This Convention shall not apply to arbitration and related proceedings.
(5)   Proceedings are not excluded from the scope of this Convention by the mere fact that a State, including a government, a governmental agency or any person acting for a State, is a party thereto.
(6)   Nothing in this Convention shall affect privileges and immunities of States or of international organisations, in respect of themselves and of their property.

Article 3 Exclusive Choice of Court Agreements

For the purposes of this Convention -
a)   "exclusive choice of court agreement" means an agreement concluded by two or more parties that meets the requirements of paragraph c) and designates, for the purpose of deciding disputes which have arisen or may arise in connection with a particular legal relationship, the courts of one Contracting State or one or more specific courts of one Contracting State to the exclusion of the jurisdiction of any other courts;
b)   a choice of court agreement which designates the courts of one Contracting State or one or more specific courts of one Contracting State shall be deemed to be exclusive unless the parties have expressly provided otherwise;
c)   an exclusive choice of court agreement must be concluded or documented -
i)   in writing; or
ii)   by any other means of communication which renders information accessible so as to be usable for subsequent reference;
d)   an exclusive choice of court agreement that forms part of a contract shall be treated as an agreement independent of the other terms of the contract. The validity of the exclusive choice of court agreement cannot be contested solely on the ground that the contract is not valid.

Article 4 Other Definitions

(1)   In this Convention, "judgment" means any decision on the merits given by a court, whatever it may be called, including a decree or order, and a determination of costs or expenses by the court (including an officer of the court), provided that the determination relates to a decision on the merits which may be recognised or enforced under this Convention. An interim measure of protection is not a judgment.
(2)   For the purposes of this Convention, an entity or person other than a natural person shall be considered to be resident in the State -
a)   where it has its statutory seat;
b)   under whose law it was incorporated or formed;
c)   where it has its central administration; or
d)   where it has its principal place of business.

Chapter II - Jurisdiction
Article 5 Jurisdiction of the Chosen Court

(1)   The court or courts of a Contracting State designated in an exclusive choice of court agreement shall have jurisdiction to decide a dispute to which the agreement applies, unless the agreement is null and void under the law of that State.

(2)   A court that has jurisdiction under paragraph 1 shall not decline to exercise jurisdiction on the ground that the dispute should be decided in a court of another State.
(3)   The preceding paragraphs shall not affect rules -
a)   on jurisdiction related to subject matter or to the value of the claim;
b)   on the internal allocation of jurisdiction among the courts of a Contracting State. However, where the chosen court has discretion as to whether to transfer a case, due consideration should be given to the choice of the parties.

Article 6 Obligations of a Court Not Chosen

A court of a Contracting State other than that of the chosen court shall suspend or dismiss proceedings to which an exclusive choice of court agreement applies unless -
a)   the agreement is null and void under the law of the State of the chosen court;
b)   a party lacked the capacity to conclude the agreement under the law of the State of the court seised;
c)   giving effect to the agreement would lead to a manifest injustice or would be manifestly contrary to the public policy of the State of the court seised;
d)   for exceptional reasons beyond the control of the parties, the agreement cannot reasonably be performed; or
e)   the chosen court has decided not to hear the case.

Article 7 Interim Measures of Protection

Interim measures of protection are not governed by this Convention. This Convention neither requires nor precludes the grant, refusal or termination of interim measures of protection by a court of a Contracting State and does not affect whether or not a party may request or a court should grant, refuse or terminate such measures.

Chapter III - Recognition and Enforcement
Article 8 Recognition and Enforcement

(1)   A judgment given by a court of a Contracting State designated in an exclusive choice of court agreement shall be recognised and enforced in other Contracting States in accordance with this Chapter. Recognition or enforcement may be refused only on the grounds specified in this Convention.
(2)   Without prejudice to such review as is necessary for the application of the provisions of this Chapter, there shall be no review of the merits of the judgment given by the court of origin. The court addressed shall be bound by the findings of fact on which the court of origin based its jurisdiction, unless the judgment was given by default.
(3)   A judgment shall be recognised only if it has effect in the State of origin, and shall be enforced only if it is enforceable in the State of origin.
(4)   Recognition or enforcement may be postponed or refused if the judgment is the subject of review in the State of origin or if the time limit for seeking ordinary review has not expired. A refusal does not prevent a subsequent application for recognition or enforcement of the judgment.
(5)   This Article shall also apply to a judgment given by a court of a Contracting State pursuant to a transfer of the case from the chosen court in that Contracting State as permitted by Article 5, paragraph 3. However, where the chosen court had discretion as to whether to transfer the case to another court, recognition or enforcement of the judgment may be refused against a party who objected to the transfer in a timely manner in the State of origin.

Article 9 Refusal of Recognition or Enforcement

Recognition or enforcement may be refused if -
a)   the agreement was null and void under the law of the State of the chosen court, unless the chosen court has determined that the agreement is valid;
b)   a party lacked the capacity to conclude the agreement under the law of the requested State;
c)   the document which instituted the proceedings or an equivalent document, including the essential elements of the claim,

i)   was not notified to the defendant in sufficient time and in such a way as to enable him to arrange for his defence, unless the defendant entered an appearance and presented his case without contesting notification in the court of origin, provided that the law of the State of origin permitted notification to be contested; or

ii)   was notified to the defendant in the requested State in a manner that is incompatible with fundamental principles of the requested State concerning service of documents;

d)   the judgment was obtained by fraud in connection with a matter of procedure;

e)   recognition or enforcement would be manifestly incompatible with the public policy of the requested State, including situations where the specific proceedings leading to the judgment were incompatible with fundamental principles of procedural fairness of that State;

f)   the judgment is inconsistent with a judgment given in the requested State in a dispute between the same parties; or

g)   the judgment is inconsistent with an earlier judgment given in another State between the same parties on the same cause of action, provided that the earlier judgment fulfils the conditions necessary for its recognition in the requested State.

Article 10 Preliminary Questions

(1)   Where a matter excluded under Article 2, paragraph 2, or under Article 21, arose as a preliminary question, the ruling on that question shall not be recognised or enforced under this Convention.

(2)   Recognition or enforcement of a judgment may be refused if, and to the extent that, the judgment was based on a ruling on a matter excluded under Article 2, paragraph 2.

(3)   However, in the case of a ruling on the validity of an intellectual property right other than copyright or a related right, recognition or enforcement of a judgment may be refused or postponed under the preceding paragraph only where -

a)   that ruling is inconsistent with a judgment or a decision of a competent authority on that matter given in the State under the law of which the intellectual property right arose; or

b)   proceedings concerning the validity of the intellectual property right are pending in that State.

(4)   Recognition or enforcement of a judgment may be refused if, and to the extent that, the judgment was based on a ruling on a matter excluded pursuant to a declaration made by the requested State under Article 21.

Article 11 Damages

(1)   Recognition or enforcement of a judgment may be refused if, and to the extent that, the judgment awards damages, including exemplary or punitive damages, that do not compensate a party for actual loss or harm suffered.

(2)   The court addressed shall take into account whether and to what extent the damages awarded by the court of origin serve to cover costs and expenses relating to the proceedings.

Article 12 Judicial Settlements (Transactions Judiciaires)

Judicial settlements (transactions judiciaires) which a court of a Contracting State designated in an exclusive choice of court agreement has approved, or which have been concluded before that court in the course of proceedings, and which are enforceable in the same manner as a judgment in the State of origin, shall be enforced under this Convention in the same manner as a judgment.

Article 13 Documents to Be Produced

(1)   The party seeking recognition or applying for enforcement shall produce -

a)   a complete and certified copy of the judgment;

b)   the exclusive choice of court agreement, a certified copy thereof, or other evidence of its existence;

c)   if the judgment was given by default, the original or a certified copy of a document establishing that the document which instituted the proceedings or an equivalent document was notified to the defaulting party;

d) any documents necessary to establish that the judgment has effect or, where applicable, is enforceable in the State of origin;
e) in the case referred to in Article 12, a certificate of a court of the State of origin that the judicial settlement or a part of it is enforceable in the same manner as a judgment in the State of origin.
(2) If the terms of the judgment do not permit the court addressed to verify whether the conditions of this Chapter have been complied with, that court may require any necessary documents.
(3) An application for recognition or enforcement may be accompanied by a document, issued by a court (including an officer of the court) of the State of origin, in the form recommended and published by the Hague Conference on Private International Law.
(4) If the documents referred to in this Article are not in an official language of the requested State, they shall be accompanied by a certified translation into an official language, unless the law of the requested State provides otherwise.

Article 14 Procedure

The procedure for recognition, declaration of enforceability or registration for enforcement, and the enforcement of the judgment, are governed by the law of the requested State unless this Convention provides otherwise. The court addressed shall act expeditiously.

Article 15 Severability

Recognition or enforcement of a severable part of a judgment shall be granted where recognition or enforcement of that part is applied for, or only part of the judgment is capable of being recognised or enforced under this Convention.

Chapter IV - General Clauses
Article 16 Transitional Provisions

(1) This Convention shall apply to exclusive choice of court agreements concluded after its entry into force for the State of the chosen court.
(2) This Convention shall not apply to proceedings instituted before its entry into force for the State of the court seised.

Article 17 Contracts of Insurance and Reinsurance

(1) Proceedings under a contract of insurance or reinsurance are not excluded from the scope of this Convention on the ground that the contract of insurance or reinsurance relates to a matter to which this Convention does not apply.
(2) Recognition and enforcement of a judgment in respect of liability under the terms of a contract of insurance or reinsurance may not be limited or refused on the ground that the liability under that contract includes liability to indemnify the insured or reinsured in respect of -
a) a matter to which this Convention does not apply; or
b) an award of damages to which Article 11 might apply.

Article 18 No Legalisation

All documents forwarded or delivered under this Convention shall be exempt from legalisation or any analogous formality, including an Apostille.

Article 19 Declarations Limiting Jurisdiction

A State may declare that its courts may refuse to determine disputes to which an exclusive choice of court agreement applies if, except for the location of the chosen court, there is no connection between that State and the parties or the dispute.

Article 20 Declarations Limiting Recognition and Enforcement

A State may declare that its courts may refuse to recognise or enforce a judgment given by a court of another Contracting State if the parties were resident in the requested State, and the relationship of the parties and all other elements relevant to the dispute, other than the location of the chosen court, were connected only with the requested State.

Article 21 Declarations with Respect to Specific Matters

(1)   Where a State has a strong interest in not applying this Convention to a specific matter, that State may declare that it will not apply the Convention to that matter. The State making such a declaration shall ensure that the declaration is no broader than necessary and that the specific matter excluded is clearly and precisely defined.

(2)   With regard to that matter, the Convention shall not apply -

a)   in the Contracting State that made the declaration;

b)   in other Contracting States, where an exclusive choice of court agreement designates the courts, or one or more specific courts, of the State that made the declaration.

Article 22 Reciprocal Declaratons on Non-Exclusive Choice of Court Agreements

(1)   A Contracting State may declare that its courts will recognise and enforce judgments given by courts of other Contracting States designated in a choice of court agreement concluded by two or more parties that meets the requirements of Article 3, paragraph c), and designates, for the purpose of deciding disputes which have arisen or may arise in connection with a particular legal relationship, a court or courts of one or more Contracting States (a non-exclusive choice of court agreement).

(2)   Where recognition or enforcement of a judgment given in a Contracting State that has made such a declaration is sought in another Contracting State that has made such a declaration, the judgment shall be recognised and enforced under this Convention, if -

a)   the court of origin was designated in a non-exclusive choice of court agreement;

b)   there exists neither a judgment given by any other court before which proceedings could be brought in accordance with the non-exclusive choice of court agreement, nor a proceeding pending between the same parties in any other such court on the same cause of action; and

c)   the court of origin was the court first seised.

Article 23 Uniform Interpretation

In the interpretation of this Convention, regard shall be had to its international character and to the need to promote uniformity in its application.

Article 24 Review of Operation of the Convention

The Secretary General of the Hague Conference on Private International Law shall at regular intervals make arrangements for -

a)   review of the operation of this Convention, including any declarations; and

b)   consideration of whether any amendments to this Convention are desirable.

Article 25 Non-Unified Legal Systems

(1)   In relation to a Contracting State in which two or more systems of law apply in different territorial units with regard to any matter dealt with in this Convention -

a)   any reference to the law or procedure of a State shall be construed as referring, where appropriate, to the law or procedure in force in the relevant territorial unit;

b)   any reference to residence in a State shall be construed as referring, where appropriate, to residence in the relevant territorial unit;

c)   any reference to the court or courts of a State shall be construed as referring, where appropriate, to the court or courts in the relevant territorial unit;

d)   any reference to a connection with a State shall be construed as referring, where appropriate, to a connection with the relevant territorial unit.

(2)   Notwithstanding the preceding paragraph, a Contracting State with two or more territorial units in which different systems of law apply shall not be bound to apply this Convention to situations which involve solely such different territorial units.

(3)   A court in a territorial unit of a Contracting State with two or more territorial units in which different systems of law apply shall not be bound to recognise or enforce a judgment from an-

other Contracting State solely because the judgment has been recognised or enforced in another territorial unit of the same Contracting State under this Convention.
(4)   This Article shall not apply to a Regional Economic Integration Organisation.

Article 26 Relationship with Other International Instruments
(1)   This Convention shall be interpreted so far as possible to be compatible with other treaties in force for Contracting States, whether concluded before or after this Convention.
(2)   This Convention shall not affect the application by a Contracting State of a treaty, whether concluded before or after this Convention, in cases where none of the parties is resident in a Contracting State that is not a Party to the treaty.
(3)   This Convention shall not affect the application by a Contracting State of a treaty that was concluded before this Convention entered into force for that Contracting State, if applying this Convention would be inconsistent with the obligations of that Contracting State to any non-Contracting State. This paragraph shall also apply to treaties that revise or replace a treaty concluded before this Convention entered into force for that Contracting State, except to the extent that the revision or replacement creates new inconsistencies with this Convention.
(4)   This Convention shall not affect the application by a Contracting State of a treaty, whether concluded before or after this Convention, for the purposes of obtaining recognition or enforcement of a judgment given by a court of a Contracting State that is also a Party to that treaty. However, the judgment shall not be recognised or enforced to a lesser extent than under this Convention.
(5)   This Convention shall not affect the application by a Contracting State of a treaty which, in relation to a specific matter, governs jurisdiction or the recognition or enforcement of judgments, even if concluded after this Convention and even if all States concerned are Parties to this Convention. This paragraph shall apply only if the Contracting State has made a declaration in respect of the treaty under this paragraph. In the case of such a declaration, other Contracting States shall not be obliged to apply this Convention to that specific matter to the extent of any inconsistency, where an exclusive choice of court agreement designates the courts, or one or more specific courts, of the Contracting State that made the declaration.
(6)   This Convention shall not affect the application of the rules of a Regional Economic Integration Organisation that is a Party to this Convention, whether adopted before or after this Convention -
a)   where none of the parties is resident in a Contracting State that is not a Member State of the Regional Economic Integration Organisation;
b)   as concerns the recognition or enforcement of judgments as between Member States of the Regional Economic Integration Organisation.

Chapter V - Final Clauses
Article 27 Signature, Ratification, Acceptance, Approval or Accession
(1)   This Convention is open for signature by all States.
(2)   This Convention is subject to ratification, acceptance or approval by the signatory States.
(3)   This Convention is open for accession by all States.
(4)   Instruments of ratification, acceptance, approval or accession shall be deposited with the Ministry of Foreign Affairs of the Kingdom of the Netherlands, depositary of the Convention.

Article 28 Declarations with Respect to Non-Unified Legal Systems
(1)   If a State has two or more territorial units in which different systems of law apply in relation to matters dealt with in this Convention, it may at the time of signature, ratification, acceptance, approval or accession declare that the Convention shall extend to all its territorial units or only to one or more of them and may modify this declaration by submitting another declaration at any time.
(2)   A declaration shall be notified to the depositary and shall state expressly the territorial units to which the Convention applies.

(3)   If a State makes no declaration under this Article, the Convention shall extend to all territorial units of that State.

(4)   This Article shall not apply to a Regional Economic Integration Organisation.

Article 29 Regional Economic Integration Organisations

(1)   A Regional Economic Integration Organisation which is constituted solely by sovereign States and has competence over some or all of the matters governed by this Convention may similarly sign, accept, approve or accede to this Convention. The Regional Economic Integration Organisation shall in that case have the rights and obligations of a Contracting State, to the extent that the Organisation has competence over matters governed by this Convention.

(2)   The Regional Economic Integration Organisation shall, at the time of signature, acceptance, approval or accession, notify the depositary in writing of the matters governed by this Convention in respect of which competence has been transferred to that Organisation by its Member States. The Organisation shall promptly notify the depositary in writing of any changes to its competence as specified in the most recent notice given under this paragraph.

(3)   For the purposes of the entry into force of this Convention, any instrument deposited by a Regional Economic Integration Organisation shall not be counted unless the Regional Economic Integration Organisation declares in accordance with Article 30 that its Member States will not be Parties to this Convention.

(4)   Any reference to a "Contracting State" or "State" in this Convention shall apply equally, where appropriate, to a Regional Economic Integration Organisation that is a Party to it.

Article 30 Accession by a Regional Economic Integration Organisation Without its Member States

(1)   At the time of signature, acceptance, approval or accession, a Regional Economic Integration Organisation may declare that it exercises competence over all the matters governed by this Convention and that its Member States will not be Parties to this Convention but shall be bound by virtue of the signature, acceptance, approval or accession of the Organisation.

(2)   In the event that a declaration is made by a Regional Economic Integration Organisation in accordance with paragraph 1, any reference to a "Contracting State" or "State" in this Convention shall apply equally, where appropriate, to the Member States of the Organisation.

Article 31 Entry into Force

(1)   This Convention shall enter into force on the first day of the month following the expiration of three months after the deposit of the second instrument of ratification, acceptance, approval or accession referred to in Article 27.

(2)   Thereafter this Convention shall enter into force -

a)   for each State or Regional Economic Integration Organisation subsequently ratifying, accepting, approving or acceding to it, on the first day of the month following the expiration of three months after the deposit of its instrument of ratification, acceptance, approval or accession;

b)   for a territorial unit to which this Convention has been extended in accordance with Article 28, paragraph 1, on the first day of the month following the expiration of three months after the notification of the declaration referred to in that Article.

Article 32 Declarations

(1)   Declarations referred to in Articles 19, 20, 21, 22 and 26 may be made upon signature, ratification, acceptance, approval or accession or at any time thereafter, and may be modified or withdrawn at any time.

(2)   Declarations, modifications and withdrawals shall be notified to the depositary.

(3)   A declaration made at the time of signature, ratification, acceptance, approval or accession shall take effect simultaneously with the entry into force of this Convention for the State concerned.

(4)   A declaration made at a subsequent time, and any modification or withdrawal of a declaration, shall take effect on the first day of the month following the expiration of three months after the date on which the notification is received by the depositary.
(5)   A declaration under Articles 19, 20, 21 and 26 shall not apply to exclusive choice of court agreements concluded before it takes effect.

Article 33 Denunciation

(1)   This Convention may be denounced by notification in writing to the depositary. The denunciation may be limited to certain territorial units of a non-unified legal system to which this Convention applies.
(2)   The denunciation shall take effect on the first day of the month following the expiration of twelve months after the date on which the notification is received by the depositary. Where a longer period for the denunciation to take effect is specified in the notification, the denunciation shall take effect upon the expiration of such longer period after the date on which the notification is received by the depositary.

Article 34 Notifications by the Depositary

The depositary shall notify the Members of the Hague Conference on Private International Law, and other States and Regional Economic Integration Organisations which have signed, ratified, accepted, approved or acceded in accordance with Articles 27, 29 and 30 of the following -
a)   the signatures, ratifications, acceptances, approvals and accessions referred to in Articles 27, 29 and 30;
b)   the date on which this Convention enters into force in accordance with Article 31;
c)   the notifications, declarations, modifications and withdrawals of declarations referred to in Articles 19, 20, 21, 22, 26, 28, 29 and 30;
d)   the denunciations referred to in Article 33.

In witness whereof the undersigned, being duly authorised thereto, have signed this Convention.

Done at The Hague, on 30 June 2005, in the English and French languages, both texts being equally authentic, in a single copy which shall be deposited in the archives of the Government of the Kingdom of the Netherlands, and of which a certified copy shall be sent, through diplomatic channels, to each of the Member States of the Hague Conference on Private International Law as of the date of its Twentieth Session and to each State which participated in that Session.

Entry into Force: not yet
Ratifications: Mexico
Signatures: European Union, USA

1965 CONVENTION ON THE SERVICE ABROAD OF JUDICIAL AND EXTRAJUDICIAL DOCUMENTS IN CIVIL OR COMMERCIAL MATTERS[1]
(The Hague, 15 November 1965)

The States signatory to the present Convention,
Desiring to create appropriate means to ensure that judicial and extrajudicial documents to be served abroad shall be brought to the notice of the addressee in sufficient time,
Desiring to improve the organisation of mutual judicial assistance for that purpose by simplifying and expediting the procedure,
Have resolved to conclude a Convention to this effect and have agreed upon the following provisions:

---

1   © Hague Conference on Private International Law.

Article 1

The present Convention shall apply in all cases, in civil or commercial matters, where there is occasion to transmit a judicial or extrajudicial document for service abroad.

This Convention shall not apply where the address of the person to be served with the document is not known.

Chapter I - Judicial Documents

Article 2

Each Contracting State shall designate a Central Authority which will undertake to receive requests for service coming from other Contracting States and to proceed in conformity with the provisions of Articles 3 to 6.

Each State shall organise the Central Authority in conformity with its own law.

Article 3

The authority or judicial officer competent under the law of the State in which the documents originate shall forward to the Central Authority of the State addressed a request conforming to the model annexed to the present Convention, without any requirement of legalisation or other equivalent formality.

The document to be served or a copy thereof shall be annexed to the request. The request and the document shall both be furnished in duplicate.

Article 4

If the Central Authority considers that the request does not comply with the provisions of the present Convention it shall promptly inform the applicant and specify its objections to the request.

Article 5

The Central Authority of the State addressed shall itself serve the document or shall arrange to have it served by an appropriate agency, either -

a) by a method prescribed by its internal law for the service of documents in domestic actions upon persons who are within its territory, or

b) by a particular method requested by the applicant, unless such a method is incompatible with the law of the State addressed.

Subject to sub-paragraph (b) of the first paragraph of this Article, the document may always be served by delivery to an addressee who accepts it voluntarily.

If the document is to be served under the first paragraph above, the Central Authority may require the document to be written in, or translated into, the official language or one of the official languages of the State addressed.

That part of the request, in the form attached to the present Convention, which contains a summary of the document to be served, shall be served with the document.

Article 6

The Central Authority of the State addressed or any authority which it may have designated for that purpose, shall complete a certificate in the form of the model annexed to the present Convention.

The certificate shall state that the document has been served and shall include the method, the place and the date of service and the person to whom the document was delivered. If the document has not been served, the certificate shall set out the reasons which have prevented service.

The applicant may require that a certificate not completed by a Central Authority or by a judicial authority shall be countersigned by one of these authorities.

The certificate shall be forwarded directly to the applicant.

Article 7

The standard terms in the model annexed to the present Convention shall in all cases be written either in French or in English. They may also be written in the official language, or in one of the official languages, of the State in which the documents originate.

The corresponding blanks shall be completed either in the language of the State addressed or in French or in English.

Article 8

Each Contracting State shall be free to effect service of judicial documents upon persons abroad, without application of any compulsion, directly through its diplomatic or consular agents.

Any State may declare that it is opposed to such service within its territory, unless the document is to be served upon a national of the State in which the documents originate.

Article 9

Each Contracting State shall be free, in addition, to use consular channels to forward documents, for the purpose of service, to those authorities of another Contracting State which are designated by the latter for this purpose.

Each Contracting State may, if exceptional circumstances so require, use diplomatic channels for the same purpose.

Article 10

Provided the State of destination does not object, the present Convention shall not interfere with -

a)   the freedom to send judicial documents, by postal channels, directly to persons abroad,

b)   the freedom of judicial officers, officials or other competent persons of the State of origin to effect service of judicial documents directly through the judicial officers, officials or other competent persons of the State of destination,

c)   the freedom of any person interested in a judicial proceeding to effect service of judicial documents directly through the judicial officers, officials or other competent persons of the State of destination.

Article 11

The present Convention shall not prevent two or more Contracting States from agreeing to permit, for the purpose of service of judicial documents, channels of transmission other than those provided for in the preceding Articles and, in particular, direct communication between their respective authorities.

Article 12

The service of judicial documents coming from a Contracting State shall not give rise to any payment or reimbursement of taxes or costs for the services rendered by the State addressed.

The applicant shall pay or reimburse the costs occasioned by --

a)   the employment of a judicial officer or of a person competent under the law of the State of destination,

b)   the use of a particular method of service.

Article 13

Where a request for service complies with the terms of the present Convention, the State addressed may refuse to comply therewith only if it deems that compliance would infringe its sovereignty or security.

It may not refuse to comply solely on the ground that, under its internal law, it claims exclusive jurisdiction over the subject-matter of the action or that its internal law would not permit the action upon which the application is based.

The Central Authority shall, in case of refusal, promptly inform the applicant and state the reasons for the refusal.

Article 14

Difficulties which may arise in connection with the transmission of judicial documents for service shall be settled through diplomatic channels.

Article 15

Where a writ of summons or an equivalent document had to be transmitted abroad for the purpose of service, under the provisions of the present Convention, and the defendant has not appeared, judgment shall not be given until it is established that -

a)   the document was served by a method prescribed by the internal law of the State addressed for the service of documents in domestic actions upon persons who are within its territory, or

b)   the document was actually delivered to the defendant or to his residence by another method provided for by this Convention,

and that in either of these cases the service or the delivery was effected in sufficient time to enable the defendant to defend.

Each Contracting State shall be free to declare that the judge, notwithstanding the provisions of the first paragraph of this Article, may give judgment even if no certificate of service or delivery has been received, if all the following conditions are fulfilled -

a)   the document was transmitted by one of the methods provided for in this Convention,

b)   a period of time of not less than six months, considered adequate by the judge in the particular case, has elapsed since the date of the transmission of the document,

c)   no certificate of any kind has been received, even though every reasonable effort has been made to obtain it through the competent authorities of the State addressed.

Notwithstanding the provisions of the preceding paragraphs the judge may order, in case of urgency, any provisional or protective measures.

Article 16

When a writ of summons or an equivalent document had to be transmitted abroad for the purpose of service, under the provisions of the present Convention, and a judgment has been entered against a defendant who has not appeared, the judge shall have the power to relieve the defendant from the effects of the expiration of the time for appeal from the judgment if the following conditions are fulfilled -

a)   the defendant, without any fault on his part, did not have knowledge of the document in sufficient time to defend, or knowledge of the judgment in sufficient time to appeal, and

b)   the defendant has disclosed a prima facie defence to the action on the merits.

An application for relief may be filed only within a reasonable time after the defendant has knowledge of the judgment.

Each Contracting State may declare that the application will not be entertained if it is filed after the expiration of a time to be stated in the declaration, but which shall in no case be less than one year following the date of the judgment.

This Article shall not apply to judgments concerning status or capacity of persons.

Chapter II - Extrajudicial Documents
Article 17

Extrajudicial documents emanating from authorities and judicial officers of a Contracting State may be transmitted for the purpose of service in another Contracting State by the methods and under the provisions of the present Convention.

Chapter III - General Clauses
Article 18

Each Contracting State may designate other authorities in addition to the Central Authority and shall determine the extent of their competence.

The applicant shall, however, in all cases, have the right to address a request directly to the Central Authority.

Federal States shall be free to designate more than one Central Authority.

Article 19

To the extent that the internal law of a Contracting State permits methods of transmission, other than those provided for in the preceding Articles, of documents coming from abroad, for service within its territory, the present Convention shall not affect such provisions.

Article 20

The present Convention shall not prevent an agreement between any two or more Contracting States to dispense with -
a)   the necessity for duplicate copies of transmitted documents as required by the second paragraph of Article 3,
b)   the language requirements of the third paragraph of Article 5 and Article 7,
c)   the provisions of the fourth paragraph of Article 5,
d)   the provisions of the second paragraph of Article 12.

Article 21

Each Contracting State shall, at the time of the deposit of its instrument of ratification or accession, or at a later date, inform the Ministry of Foreign Affairs of the Netherlands of the following -
a)   the designation of authorities, pursuant to Articles 2 and 18,
b)   the designation of the authority competent to complete the certificate pursuant to Article 6,
c)   the designation of the authority competent to receive documents transmitted by consular channels, pursuant to Article 9.
Each Contracting State shall similarly inform the Ministry, where appropriate, of -
a)   opposition to the use of methods of transmission pursuant to Articles 8 and 10,
b)   declarations pursuant to the second paragraph of Article 15 and the third paragraph of Article 16,
c)   all modifications of the above designations, oppositions and declarations.

Article 22

Where Parties to the present Convention are also Parties to one or both of the Conventions on civil procedure signed at The Hague on 17th July 1905, and on 1st March 1954, this Convention shall replace as between them Articles 1 to 7 of the earlier Conventions.

Article 23

The present Convention shall not affect the application of Article 23 of the Convention on civil procedure signed at The Hague on 17th July 1905, or of Article 24 of the Convention on civil procedure signed at The Hague on 1st March 1954.

These Articles shall, however, apply only if methods of communication, identical to those provided for in these Conventions, are used.

Article 24

Supplementary agreements between Parties to the Conventions of 1905 and 1954 shall be considered as equally applicable to the present Convention, unless the Parties have otherwise agreed.

Article 25

Without prejudice to the provisions of Articles 22 and 24, the present Convention shall not derogate from Conventions containing provisions on the matters governed by this Convention to which the Contracting States are, or shall become, Parties.

Article 26

The present Convention shall be open for signature by the States represented at the Tenth Session of the Hague Conference on Private International Law.

It shall be ratified, and the instruments of ratification shall be deposited with the Ministry of Foreign Affairs of the Netherlands.

Article 27

The present Convention shall enter into force on the sixtieth day after the deposit of the third instrument of ratification referred to in the second paragraph of Article 26.

The Convention shall enter into force for each signatory State which ratifies subsequently on the sixtieth day after the deposit of its instrument of ratification.

Article 28
Any State not represented at the Tenth Session of the Hague Conference on Private International Law may accede to the present Convention after it has entered into force in accordance with the first paragraph of Article 27. The instrument of accession shall be deposited with the Ministry of Foreign Affairs of the Netherlands.

The Convention shall enter into force for such a State in the absence of any objection from a State, which has ratified the Convention before such deposit, notified to the Ministry of Foreign Affairs of the Netherlands within a period of six months after the date on which the said Ministry has notified it of such accession.

In the absence of any such objection, the Convention shall enter into force for the acceding State on the first day of the month following the expiration of the last of the periods referred to in the preceding paragraph.

Article 29
Any State may, at the time of signature, ratification or accession, declare that the present Convention shall extend to all the territories for the international relations of which it is responsible, or to one or more of them. Such a declaration shall take effect on the date of entry into force of the Convention for the State concerned.

At any time thereafter, such extensions shall be notified to the Ministry of Foreign Affairs of the Netherlands.

The Convention shall enter into force for the territories mentioned in such an extension on the sixtieth day after the notification referred to in the preceding paragraph.

Article 30
The present Convention shall remain in force for five years from the date of its entry into force in accordance with the first paragraph of Article 27, even for States which have ratified it or acceded to it subsequently.

If there has been no denunciation, it shall be renewed tacitly every five years.

Any denunciation shall be notified to the Ministry of Foreign Affairs of the Netherlands at least six months before the end of the five year period.

It may be limited to certain of the territories to which the Convention applies.

The denunciation shall have effect only as regards the State which has notified it. The Convention shall remain in force for the other Contracting States.

Article 31
The Ministry of Foreign Affairs of the Netherlands shall give notice to the States referred to in Article 26, and to the States which have acceded in accordance with Article 28, of the following -
a)   the signatures and ratifications referred to in Article 26;
b)   the date on which the present Convention enters into force in accordance with the first paragraph of Article 27;
c)   the accessions referred to in Article 28 and the dates on which they take effect;
d)   the extensions referred to in Article 29 and the dates on which they take effect;
e)   the designations, oppositions and declarations referred to in Article 21;
f)   the denunciations referred to in the third paragraph of Article 30.

In witness whereof the undersigned, being duly authorised thereto, have signed the present Convention.

Done at The Hague, on the 15th day of November, 1965, in the English and French languages, both texts being equally authentic, in a single copy which shall be deposited in the archives of the Government of the Netherlands, and of which a certified copy shall be sent, through the diplomatic channel, to each of the States represented at the Tenth Session of the Hague Conference on Private International Law.

Entry into force: 10 February 1969
Ratifications and binding effect (as of July 2013):

No.	Country	Entry into Force	Reservations or Declarations
1	Albania	1 July 2007	
2	Antigua and Barbuda	1 Nov 1981	
3	Argentina	1 Dec 2001	D, R
4	Australia	1 Nov 2010	D
5	Bahamas	1 Feb 1998	
6	Barbados	1 Oct 1969	
7	Belarus	1 Feb 1998	
8	Belgium	18 Jan 1971	D
9	Belize	1 May 2010	
10	Bosnia and Herzegovina	1 Feb 2009	
11	Botswana	1 Sept 1969	D
12	Bulgaria	1 Aug 2000	D
13	Canada	1 May 1989	D
14	China	1 Jan 1992	D
15	Croatia	1 Nov 2006	D, R
16	Cyprus	1 June 1983	D
17	Czech Republic	1 Jan 1993	D, R
18	Denmark	1 Oct 1969	D
19	Egypt	10 Feb 1969	R
20	Estonia	1 Oct 1996	D
21	Finland	10 Nov 1969	D
22	France	1 Sept 1972	D
23	Germany	26 June 1979	D
24	Greece	18 Sept 1983	D
25	Hungary	1 April 2005	D
26	Iceland	1 July 2009	D, R
27	India	1 Aug 2007	D, R
28	Ireland	4 June 1994	D, R
29	Israel	13 Oct 1972	D, R
30	Italy	24 Jan 1982	D
31	Japan	27 July 1970	D
32	Korea, Republic of	1 Aug 2000	D, R
33	Kuwait	1 Dec 2002	D, R
34	Latvia	1 Nov 1995	D
35	Lithuania	1 June 2001	D, R
36	Luxembourg	7 Sept 1975	D, R
37	Macedonia	1 Sept 2009	D, R

38	Malawi	1 Dec 1972	
39	Malta	1 Oct 2011	D
40	Mexico	1 June 2000	D
41	Monaco	1 Nov 2007	D
42	Montenegro	1 Sept 2012	D
43	Morocco	1 Nov 2011	
44	Netherlands	2 Jan 1976	D
45	Norway	1 Oct 1969	D, R
46	Pakistan	1 Aug 1989	D
47	Poland	1 Sept 1996	R
48	Portugal	25 Feb 1974	D
49	Romania	1 April 2004	D
50	Russian Federation	1 Dec 2001	D, R
51	Saint Vincent and the Grenadines	27 Oct 1979	D
52	San Marino	1 Nov 2002	D
53	Serbia	1 Feb 2011	D
54	Seychelles	1 July 1981	D
55	Slovakia	1 Jan 1993	D
56	Slovenia	1 June 2001	
57	Spain	3 Aug 1987	D
58	Sri Lanka	1 June 2001	D
59	Sweden	1 Oct 1969	D
60	Switzerland	1 Jan 1995	D, R
61	Turkey	28 April 1972	D, R
62	Ukraine	1 Dec 2001	D, R
63	United Kingdom	10 Feb 1969	D
64	United States of America	10 Feb 1969	D
65	Venezuela	1 July 1994	D, R

1970 HAGUE CONVENTION ON THE TAKING OF EVIDENCE ABROAD IN CIVIL OR COMMERCIAL MATTERS[1]
(The Hague, 18 March 1970)

THE STATES SIGNATORY TO THE PRESENT CONVENTION,
DESIRING to facilitate the transmission and execution of Letters of Request and to further the accommodation of the different methods which they use for this purpose,
DESIRING to improve mutual judicial co-operation in civil or commercial matters,
HAVE RESOLVED to conclude a Convention to this effect and have agreed upon the following provisions -

---

1   © Hague Conference on Private International Law.

CHAPTER I - LETTERS OF REQUEST
Article 1 [Letters of Request]
In civil or commercial matters a judicial authority of a Contracting State may, in accordance with the provisions of the law of that State, request the competent authority of another Contracting State, by means of a Letter of Request, to obtain evidence, or to perform some other judicial act.

A Letter shall not be used to obtain evidence which is not intended for use in judicial proceedings, commenced or contemplated.

The expression "other judicial act" does not cover the service of judicial documents or the issuance of any process by which judgments or orders are executed or enforced, or orders for provisional or protective measures.

Article 2 [Central Authority]
A Contracting State shall designate a Central Authority which will undertake to receive Letters of Request coming from a judicial authority of another Contracting State and to transmit them to the authority competent to execute them. Each State shall organize the Central Authority in accordance with its own law.

Letters shall be sent to the Central Authority of the State of execution without being transmitted through any other authority of that State.

Article 3 [Contents of Letters of Request]
A Letter of Request shall specify -
(a)   the authority requesting its execution and the authority requested to execute it, if known to the requesting authority;
(b)   the names and addresses of the parties to the proceedings and their representatives, if any;
(c)   the nature of the proceedings for which the evidence is required, giving all necessary information in regard thereto;
(d)   the evidence to be obtained or other judicial act to be performed.
Where appropriate, the Letter shall specify, inter alia -
(e)   the names and addresses of the persons to be examined;
(f)   the questions to be put to the persons to be examined or a statement of the subject-matter about which they are to be examined;
(g)   the documents or other property, real or personal, to be inspected;
(h)   any requirement that the evidence is to be given on oath or affirmation, and any special form to be used;
(i)   any special method or procedure to be followed under Article 9.
A Letter may also mention any information necessary for the application of Article 11.

No legalization or other like formality may be required.

Article 4 [Language]
A Letter of Request shall be in the language of the authority requested to execute it or be accompanied by a translation into that language.

Nevertheless, a Contracting State shall accept a Letter in either English or French, or a translation into one of these languages, unless it has made the reservation authorized by Article 33.

A Contracting State which has more than one official language and cannot, for reasons of internal law, accept Letters in one of these languages for the whole of its territory, shall, by declaration, specify the language in which the Letter or translation thereof shall be expressed for execution in the specified parts of its territory. In case of failure to comply with this declaration, without justifiable excuse, the costs of translation into the required language shall be borne by the State of origin.

A Contracting State may, be declaration, specify the language or languages other than those referred to in the preceding paragraphs, in which a Letter may be sent to its Central Authority.

Any translation accompanying a Letter shall be certified as correct, either by a diplomatic officer or consular agent or by a sworn translator or by any other person so authorized in either State.

Article 5 [Objections to a Letter of Request]

If the Central Authority considers that the request does not comply with the provisions of the present Convention, it shall promptly inform the authority of the State of origin which transmitted the Letter of Request, specifying the objections to the Letter.

Article 6 [Automatic Forwarding to Competent Authority]

If the authority to whom a Letter of Request has been transmitted is not competent to execute it, the Letter shall be sent forthwith to the authority in the same State which is competent to execute it in accordance with the provisions of its own law.

Article 7 [Information on Time and Place of Proceedings]

The requesting authority shall, if it so desires, be informed of the time when, and the place where, the proceedings will take place, in order that the parties concerned, and their representatives, if any, may be present. This information shall be sent directly to the parties or their representatives when the authority of the State of origin so requests.

Article 8 [Participation in the Execution]

A Contracting State may declare that members of the judicial personnel of the requesting authority of another Contracting State may be present at the execution of a Letter of Request. Prior authorization by the competent authority designated by the declaring State may be required.

Article 9 [Applicable Procedural Laws]

The judicial authority which executes a Letter of Request shall apply its own law as to the methods and procedures to be followed.

However, it will follow a request of the requesting authority that a special method or procedure be followed, unless this is incompatible with the internal law of the State of execution or is impossible of performance by reason of its internal practice and procedure or by reason of practical difficulties.

A Letter of Request shall be executed expeditiously.

Article 10 [Use of Compulsion]

In executing a Letter of Request the requested authority shall apply the appropriate measures of compulsion in the instances and to the same extent as are provided by its internal law for the execution of orders issued by the authorities of its own country or of requests made by parties in internal proceedings.

Article 11 [Privilege Against Self-Incrimination]

In the execution of a Letter of Request the person concerned may refuse to give evidence in so far as he has a privilege or duty to refuse to give the evidence -
(a) under the law of the State of execution; or
(b) under the law of the State of origin, and the privilege or duty has been specified in the Letter, or, at the instance of the requested authority, has been otherwise confirmed to that authority by the requesting authority.

A Contracting State may declare that, in addition, it will respect privileges and duties existing under the law of States other than the State of origin and the State of execution, to the extent specified in that declaration.

Article 12 [Refusal of Execution]

The execution of a Letter of Request may be refused only to the extent that -
(a) in the State of execution the execution of the Letter does not fall within the functions of the judiciary; or
(b) the State addressed considers that its sovereignty or security would be prejudiced thereby. Execution may not be refused solely on the ground that under its internal law the State of execution claims exclusive jurisdiction over the subject-matter of the action or that its internal law would not admit a right of action on it.

Article 13 [Feedback to Requesting Authority After Execution]
The documents establishing the execution of the Letter of Request shall be sent by the requested authority to the requesting authority by the same channel which was used by the latter.

In every instance where the Letter is not executed in whole or in part, the requesting authority shall be informed immediately through the same channel and advised of the reasons.

Article 14 [Costs]
The execution of the Letter of Request shall not give rise to any reimbursement of taxes or costs of any nature.

Nevertheless, the State of execution has the right to require the State of origin to reimburse the fees paid to experts and interpreters and the costs occasioned by the use of a special procedure requested by the State of origin under Article 9, paragraph 2.

The requested authority whose law obliges the parties themselves to secure evidence, and which is not able itself to execute the Letter, may, after having obtained the consent of the requesting authority, appoint a suitable person to do so. When seeking this consent the requested authority shall indicate the approximate costs which would result from this procedure. If the requesting authority gives its consent it shall reimburse any costs incurred; without such consent the requesting authority shall not be liable for the costs.

CHAPTER II - TAKING OF EVIDENCE BY DIPLOMATIC OFFICERS, CONSULAR AGENTS AND COMMISSIONERS

Article 15
In a civil or commercial matter, a diplomatic officer or consular agent of a Contracting State may, in the territory of another Contracting State and within the area where he exercises his functions, take the evidence without compulsion of nationals of a State which he represents in aid of proceedings commenced in the courts of a State which he represents.

A Contracting State may declare that evidence may be taken by a diplomatic officer or consular agent only if permission to that effect is given upon application made by him or on his behalf to the appropriate authority designated by the declaring State.

Article 16
A diplomatic officer or consular agent of a Contracting State may, in the territory of another Contracting State and within the area where he exercises his functions, also take the evidence, without compulsion, of nationals of the State in which he exercises his functions or of a third State, in aid of proceedings commenced in the courts of a State which he represents, if -
(a)   a competent authority designated by the State in which he exercises his functions has given its permission either generally or in the particular case, and
(b)   he complies with the conditions which the competent authority has specified in the permission.

A Contracting State may declare that evidence may be taken under this Article without its prior permission.

Article 17
In a civil or commercial matter, a person duly appointed as a commissioner for the purpose may, without compulsion, take evidence in the territory of a Contracting State in aid of proceedings commenced in the courts of another Contracting State if -
(a)   a competent authority designated by the State where the evidence is to be taken has given its permission either generally or in the particular case; and
(b)   he complies with the conditions which the competent authority has specified in the permission.

A Contracting State may declare that evidence may be taken under this Article without its prior permission.

Article 18
A Contracting State may declare that a diplomatic officer, consular agent or commissioner authorized to take evidence under Articles 15, 16 or 17, may apply to the competent authority

designated by the declaring State for appropriate assistance to obtain the evidence by compulsion. The declaration may contain such conditions as the declaring State may see fit to impose.

If the authority grants the application it shall apply any measures of compulsion which are appropriate and are prescribed by its law for use in internal proceedings.

Article 19

The competent authority, in giving the permission referred to in Article 15, 16 or 17, or in granting the application referred to in Article 18, may lay down such conditions as it deems fit, inter alia, as to the time and place of the taking of the evidence. Similarly it may require that it be given reasonable advance notice of the time, date and place of the taking of the evidence; in such a case a representative of the authority shall be entitled to be present at the taking of the evidence.

Article 20

In the taking of evidence under any Article of this Chapter persons concerned may be legally represented.

Article 21

Where a diplomatic officer, consular agent or commissioner is authorized under Articles 15, 16 or 17 to take evidence -

(a) he may take all kinds of evidence which are not incompatible with the law of the State where the evidence is taken or contrary to any permission granted pursuant to the above Articles, and shall have power within such limits to administer an oath or take an affirmation;

(b) a request to a person to appear or to give evidence shall, unless the recipient is a national of the State where the action is pending, be drawn up in the language of the place where the evidence is taken or be accompanied by a translation into such language;

(c) the request shall inform the person that he may be legally represented and, in any State that has not filed a declaration under Article 18, shall also inform him that he is not compelled to appear or to give evidence;

(d) the evidence may be taken in the manner provided by the law applicable to the court in which the action is pending provided that such manner is not forbidden by the law of the State where the evidence is taken;

(e) a person requested to give evidence may invoke the privileges and duties to refuse to give the evidence contained in Article 11.

Article 22

The fact that an attempt to take evidence under the procedure laid down in this Chapter has failed, owing to the refusal of a person to give evidence, shall not prevent an application being subsequently made to take the evidence in accordance with Chapter I.

CHAPTER III - GENERAL CLAUSES

Article 23

A Contracting State may at the time of signature, ratification or accession, declare that it will not execute Letters of Request issued for the purpose of obtaining pre-trial discovery of documents as known in Common Law countries.

Article 24

A Contracting State may designate other authorities in addition to the Central Authority and shall determine the extent of their competence. However, Letters of Request may in all cases be sent to the Central Authority.

Federal States shall be free to designate more than one Central Authority.

Article 25

A Contracting State which has more than one legal system may designate the authorities of one of such systems, which shall have exclusive competence to execute Letters of Request pursuant to this Convention.

Article 26

A Contracting State, if required to do so because of constitutional limitations, may request the reimbursement by the State of origin of fees and costs, in connection with the execution of Letters of Request, for the service of process necessary to compel the appearance of a person to give evidence, the costs of attendance of such persons, and the cost of any transcript of the evidence.

Where a State has made a request pursuant to the above paragraph, any other Contracting State may request from that State the reimbursement of similar fees and costs.

Article 27

The provisions of the present Convention shall not prevent a Contracting State from -
(a)   declaring that Letters of Request may be transmitted to its judicial authorities through channels other than those provided for in Article 2;
(b)   permitting, by internal law or practice, any act provided for in this Convention to be performed upon less restrictive conditions;
(c)   permitting, by internal law or practice, methods of taking evidence other than those provided for in this Convention.

Article 28

The present Convention shall not prevent an agreement between any two or more Contracting States to derogate from -
(a)   the provisions of Article 2 with respect to methods of transmitting Letters of Request;
(b)   the provisions of Article 4 with respect to the languages which may be used;
(c)   the provisions of Article 8 with respect to the presence of judicial personnel at the execution of Letters;
(d)   the provisions of Article 11 with respect to the privileges and duties of witnesses to refuse to give evidence;
(e)   the provisions of Article 13 with respect to the methods of returning executed Letters to the requesting authority;
(f)   the provisions of Article 14 with respect to fees and costs;
(g)   the provisions of Chapter II.

Article 29

Between Parties to the present Convention who are also Parties to one or both of the Conventions on Civil Procedure signed at The Hague on the 17th of July 1905 and the 1st of March 1954, this Convention shall replace Articles 8-16 of the earlier Conventions.

Article 30

The present Convention shall not affect the application of Article 23 of the Convention of 1905, or of Article 24 of the Convention of 1954.

Article 31

Supplementary Agreements between Parties to the Conventions of 1905 and 1954 shall be considered as equally applicable to the present Convention unless the Parties have otherwise agreed.

Article 32

Without prejudice to the provisions of Articles 29 and 31, the present Convention shall not derogate from conventions containing provisions on the matters covered by this Convention to which the Contracting States are, or shall become Parties.

Article 33

A State may, at the time of signature, ratification or accession exclude, in whole or in part, the application of the provisions of paragraph 2 of Article 4 and of Chapter II. No other reservation shall be permitted.

Each Contracting State may at any time withdraw a reservation it has made; the reservation shall cease to have effect on the sixtieth day after notification of the withdrawal.

When a State has made a reservation, any other State affected thereby may apply the same rule against the reserving State.

Article 34

A State may at any time withdraw or modify a declaration.

Article 35

A Contracting State shall, at the time of the deposit of its instrument of ratification or accession, or at a later date, inform the Ministry of Foreign Affairs of the Netherlands of the designation of authorities, pursuant to Articles 2, 8, 24 and 25.

A Contracting State shall likewise inform the Ministry, where appropriate, of the following -
(a) the designation of the authorities to whom notice must be given, whose permission may be required, and whose assistance may be invoked in the taking of evidence by diplomatic officers and consular agents, pursuant to Articles 15, 16 and 18 respectively;
(b) the designation of the authorities whose permission may be required in the taking of evidence by commissioners pursuant to Article 17 and of those who may grant the assistance provided for in Article 18;
(c) declarations pursuant to Articles 4, 8, 11, 15, 16, 17, 18, 23 and 27;
(d) any withdrawal or modification of the above designations and declarations;
(e) the withdrawal of any reservation.

Article 36

Any difficulties which may arise between Contracting States in connection with the operation of this Convention shall be settled through diplomatic channels.

Article 37

The present Convention shall be open for signature by the States represented at the Eleventh Session of the Hague Conference on Private International Law.

It shall be ratified, and the instruments of ratification shall be deposited with the Ministry of Foreign Affairs of the Netherlands.

Article 38

The present Convention shall enter into force on the sixtieth day after the deposit of the third instrument of ratification referred to in the second paragraph of Article 37. The Convention shall enter into force for each signatory State which ratifies subsequently on the sixtieth day after the deposit of its instrument of ratification.

Article 39

Any State not represented at the Eleventh Session of the Hague Conference on Private International Law which is a Member of this Conference or of the United Nations or of a specialized agency of that Organization, or a Party to the Statute of the International Court of Justice may accede to the present Convention after it has entered into force in accordance with the first paragraph of Article 38.

The instrument of accession shall be deposited with the Ministry of Foreign Affairs of the Netherlands.

The Convention shall enter into force for a State acceding to it on the sixtieth day after the deposit of its instrument of accession. The accession will have effect only as regards the relations between the acceding State and such Contracting States as will have declared their acceptance of the accession. Such declaration shall be deposited at the Ministry of Foreign Affairs of the Netherlands; this Ministry shall forward, through diplomatic channels, a certified copy to each of the Contracting States.

The Convention will enter into force as between the acceding State and the State that has declared its acceptance of the accession on the sixtieth day after the deposit of the declaration of acceptance.

Article 40

Any State may, at the time of signature, ratification or accession, declare that the present Convention shall extend to all the territories for the international relations of which it is responsible, or to one or more of them. Such a declaration shall take effect on the date of entry into force of the Convention for the State concerned.

At any time thereafter, such extensions shall be notified to the Ministry of Foreign Affairs of the Netherlands.

The Convention shall enter into force for the territories mentioned in such an extension on the sixtieth day after the notification indicated in the preceding paragraph.

Article 41

The present Convention shall remain in force for five years from the date of its entry into force in accordance with the first paragraph of Article 38, even for States which have ratified it or acceded to it subsequently.

If there has been no denunciation, it shall be renewed tacitly every five years.

Any denunciation shall be notified to the Ministry of Foreign Affairs of the Netherlands at least six months before the end of the five year period.

It may be limited to certain of the territories to which the Convention applies.

The denunciation shall have effect only as regards the State which has notified it. The Convention shall remain in force for the other Contracting States.

Article 42

The Ministry of Foreign Affairs of the Netherlands shall give notice to the States referred to in Article 37, and to the States which have acceded in accordance with Article 39, of the following -
(a)   the signatures and ratifications referred to in Article 37;
(b)   the date on which the present Convention enters into force in accordance with the first paragraph of Article 38;
(c)   the accessions referred to in Article 39 and the dates on which they take effect;
(d)   the extensions referred to in Article 40 and the dates on which they take effect;
(e)   the designations, reservations and declarations referred to in Articles 33 and 35;
(f)   the denunciations referred to in the third paragraph of Article 41.

IN WITNESS WHEREOF the undersigned, being duly authorised thereto, have signed the present Convention.

DONE at The Hague, on the 18th day of March 1970, in the English and French languages, both texts being equally authentic, in a single copy which shall be deposited in the archives of the Government of the Netherlands, and of which a certified copy shall be sent, through the diplomatic channel, to each of the States represented at the Eleventh Session of the Hague Conference on Private International Law.

Entry into force: 7 October 1972
Ratification and binding effect (as of July 2013):

No.	Country	Entry into Force	Reservations or Declarations
1	Albania	14 Sept 2010	D
2	Argentina	7 July 1987	D, R
3	Armenia	27 June 2012	
4	Australia	22 Dec 1992	D, R
5	Barbados	4 May 1981	
6	Belarus	6 Oct 2001	D, R
7	Bosnia and Herzegovina	15 Aug 2008	
8	Bulgaria	22 Jan 2000	D, R
9	China	6 Feb 1998	D, R

10	Colombia	13 March 2012	
11	Croatia	30 Nov 2009	D, R
12	Cyprus	14 March 1983	D, R
13	Czech Republic	1 Jan 1993	D
14	Denmark	7 Oct 1972	D, R
15	Estonia	2 April 1996	D
16	Finland	6 June 1976	D, R
17	France	6 Oct 1974	D, R
18	Germany	26 June 1979	D, R
19	Greece	19 March 2005	D, R
20	Hungary	11 Sept 2004	D, R
21	Iceland	9 Jan 2009	D, R
22	India	8 April 2007	D
23	Israel	17 Sept 1979	D
24	Italy	21 Aug 1982	D
25	Korea, Republic of	12 Feb 2010	D, R
26	Kuwait	7 July 2002	
27	Latvia	27 May 1995	D
28	Liechtenstein	11 Jan 2009	D
29	Lithuania	1 Oct 2000	D, R
30	Luxembourg	24 Sept 1977	D, R
31	Macedonia	18 May 2009	D
32	Malta	24 April 2011	R
33	Mexico	25 Sept 1989	D, R
34	Monaco	18 March 1986	D, R
35	Montenegro	16 March 2012	D, R
36	Morocco	23 May 2011	
37	Netherlands	7 June 1981	D, R
38	Norway	7 Oct 1972	D, R
39	Poland	13 April 1996	R
40	Portugal	11 May 1975	D, R
41	Romania	20 Oct 2003	D, R
42	Russian Federation	30 June 2001	
43	Serbia	31 Aug 2010	D
44	Seychelles	7 March 2004	D
45	Singapore	26 Dec 1978	D, R
46	Slovakia	1 Jan 1993	D
47	Slovenia	18 Sept 2000	
48	South Africa	6 Sept 1997	D, R
49	Spain	21 July 1987	D, R
50	Sri Lanka	30 Oct 2000	D, R

51	Sweden	1 July 1975	D
52	Switzerland	1 Jan 1995	D, R
53	Turkey	12 Oct 2004	D, R
54	Ukraine	1 April 2001	D, R
55	United Kingdom	14 Sept 1976	D, R
56	United States of America	7 Oct 1972	D
57	Venezuela	31 Dec 1993	D, R

1971 CONVENTION ON THE RECOGNITION AND ENFORCEMENT OF FOREIGN JUDGMENTS IN CIVIL AND COMMERCIAL MATTERS[1]
(The Hague, 1 February 1971)

The States signatory to the present Convention,

Desiring to establish common provisions on mutual recognition and enforcement of judicial decisions rendered in their respective countries,

Have resolved to conclude a Convention to this effect and have agreed on the following provisions:

Chapter I - Scope of the Convention
Article 1

This Convention shall apply to decisions rendered in civil or commercial matters by the courts of Contracting States.

It shall not apply to decisions the main object of which is to determine -

(1) the status or capacity of persons or questions of family law, including personal or financial rights and obligations between parents and children or between spouses;
(2) the existence or constitution of legal persons or the powers of their officers;
(3) maintenance obligations, so far as not included in sub-paragraph (1) of this Article;
(4) questions of succession;
(5) questions of bankruptcy, compositions or analogous proceedings, including decisions which may result therefrom and which relate to the validity of the acts of the debtor;
(6) questions of social security;
(7) questions relating to damage or injury in nuclear matters.

This Convention does not apply to decisions for the payment of any customs duty, tax or penalty.

Article 2

This Convention shall apply to all decisions given by the courts of a Contracting State, irrespective of the name given by that State to the proceedings which gave rise to the decision or of the name given to the decision itself such as judgment, order or writ of execution.

However, it shall apply neither to decisions which order provisional or protective measures nor to decisions rendered by administrative tribunals.

Article 3

This Convention shall apply irrespective of the nationality of the parties.

Chapter II - Conditions of Recognition and Enforcement
Article 4

A decision rendered in one of the Contracting States shall be entitled to recognition and enforcement in another Contracting State under the terms of this Convention -

---

1   © Hague Conference on Private International Law.

(1)   if the decision was given by a court considered to have jurisdiction within the meaning of this Convention, and

(2)   if it is no longer subject to ordinary forms of review in the State of origin.

In addition, to be enforceable in the State addressed, a decision must be enforceable in the State of origin.

Article 5

Recognition or enforcement of a decision may nevertheless be refused in any of the following cases -

(1)   if recognition or enforcement of the decision is manifestly incompatible with the public policy of the State addressed or if the decision resulted from proceedings incompatible with the requirements of due process of law or if, in the circumstances, either party had no adequate opportunity fairly to present his case;

(2)   if the decision was obtained by fraud in the procedural sense;

(3)   if proceedings between the same parties, based on the same facts and having the same purpose -

a)   are pending before a court of the State addressed and those proceedings were the first to be instituted, or

b)   have resulted in a decision by a court of the State addressed, or

c)   have resulted in a decision by a court of another State which would be entitled to recognition and enforcement under the law of the State addressed.

Article 6

Without prejudice to the provisions of Article 5, a decision rendered by default shall neither be recognised nor enforced unless the defaulting party received notice of the institution of the proceedings in accordance with the law of the State of origin in sufficient time to enable him to defend the proceedings.

Article 7

Recognition or enforcement may not be refused for the sole reason that the court of the State of origin has applied a law other than that which would have been applicable according to the rules of private international law of the State addressed.

Nevertheless, recognition or enforcement may be refused if, to reach its decision, the court of the State of origin had to decide a question relating either to the status or the capacity of a party or to his rights in other matters excluded from this Convention by sub-paragraphs (1)-(4) of the second paragraph of Article 1, and has reached a result different from that which would have followed from the application to that question of the rules of private international law of the State addressed.

Article 8

Without prejudice to such review as is required by the terms of the preceding Articles, there shall be no review of the merits of the decision rendered by the court of origin.

Article 9

In questions relating to the jurisdiction of the court of the State of origin, the authority addressed shall be bound by the findings of fact on which that court based its jurisdiction, unless the decision was rendered by default.

Article 10

The court of the State of origin shall be considered to have jurisdiction for the purposes of this Convention -

(1)   if the defendant had, at the time when the proceedings were instituted, his habitual residence in the State of origin, or, if the defendant is not a natural person, its seat, its place of incorporation or its principal place of business in that State;

(2)   if the defendant had, in the State of origin, at the time when the proceedings were instituted, a commercial, industrial or other business establishment, or a branch office, and was cited there in proceedings arising from business transacted by such establishment or branch office;

(3)   if the action had as its object the determination of an issue relating to immovable property situated in the State of origin;

(4)   in the case of injuries to the person or damage to tangible property, if the facts which occasioned the damage occurred in the territory of the State of origin, and if the author of the injury or damage was present in that territory at the time when those facts occurred;

(5)   if, by a written agreement or by an oral agreement confirmed in writing within a reasonable time, the parties agreed to submit to the jurisdiction of the court of origin disputes which have arisen or which may arise in respect of a specific legal relationship, unless the law of the State addressed would not permit such an agreement because of the subject-matter of the dispute;

(6)   if the defendant has argued the merits without challenging the jurisdiction of the court or making reservations thereon; nevertheless such jurisdiction shall not be recognised if the defendant has argued the merits in order to resist the seisure of property or to obtain its release, or if the recognition of this jurisdiction would be contrary to the law of the State addressed because of the subject-matter of the dispute;

(7)   if the person against whom recognition or enforcement is sought was the plaintiff in the proceedings in the court of origin and was unsuccessful in those proceedings, unless the recognition of this jurisdiction would be contrary to the law of the State addressed because of the subject-matter of the dispute.

Article 11

The court of the State of origin shall be considered to have jurisdiction for the purposes of this Convention to try a counterclaim -

(1)   if that court would have had jurisdiction to try the action as a principal claim under sub-paragraphs (1)-(6) of Article 10, or

(2)   if that court had jurisdiction under Article 10 to try the principal claim and if the counterclaim arose out of the contract or out of the facts on which the principal claim was based.

Article 12

The jurisdiction of the court of the State of origin need not be recognised by the authority addressed in the following cases -

(1)   if the law of the State addressed confers upon its courts exclusive jurisdiction, either by reason of the subject-matter of the action or by virtue of an agreement between the parties as to the determination of the claim which gave rise to the foreign decision;

(2)   if the law of the State addressed recognises a different exclusive jurisdiction by reason of the subject-matter of the action, or if the authority addressed considers itself bound to recognise such an exclusive jurisdiction by reason of an agreement between the parties;

(3)   if the authority addressed considers itself bound to recognise an agreement by which exclusive jurisdiction is conferred upon arbitrators.

Chapter III - Recognition and Enforcement Procedures

Article 13

The party seeking recognition or applying for enforcement shall furnish -

(1)   a complete and authenticated copy of the decision;

(2)   if the decision was rendered by default, the originals or certified true copies of the documents required to establish that the summons was duly served on the defaulting party;

(3)   all documents required to establish that the decision fulfills the conditions of sub-paragraph (2) of the first paragraph of Article 4, and, where appropriate, of the second paragraph of Article 4;

(4)   unless the authority addressed otherwise requires, translations of the documents referred to above, certified as correct either by a diplomatic or consular agent or by a sworn translator or by any other person so authorised in either State.

   If the terms of the decision do not permit the authority addressed to verify whether the conditions of this Convention have been complied with, that authority may require the production of any other necessary documents.

   No legalisation or other like formality may be required.

Article 14
The procedure for the recognition or enforcement of foreign judgments is governed by the law of the State addressed so far as this Convention does not provide otherwise.

If the decision contains provisions which can be dissociated, any one or more of these may be separately recognised or enforced.

Article 15
Recognition or enforcement of an award of judicial costs or expenses may be accorded by virtue of this Convention only if this Convention is applicable to the decision on the merits.

This Convention shall apply to decisions relating to judicial costs or expenses even if such decisions do not proceed from a court, provided that they derive from a decision which may be recognised or enforced under this Convention and that the decision relating to costs or expenses could have been subject to judicial review.

Article 16
A judgment for costs or expenses given in connection with the granting or refusal of recognition or enforcement of a decision may be enforced under this Convention only if the applicant in the proceedings for recognition or enforcement relied on this Convention.

Article 17
No security, bond or deposit, however termed under the law of the State addressed, shall be required by reason of the nationality or domicile of the applicant to guarantee the payment of judicial costs or expenses if the applicant, being a natural person, has his habitual residence in or, not being a natural person, has a place of business in a State which has concluded with the State addressed a Supplementary Agreement in accordance with Article 21.

Article 18
A party granted legal aid in the State of origin shall be extended such aid in accordance with the law of the State addressed in any proceedings for the recognition or for the enforcement of a foreign decision.

Article 19
Settlements made in court in the course of a pending proceeding which may be enforced in the State of origin shall be enforceable in the State addressed under the same conditions as decisions falling within this Convention, so far as those conditions apply to settlements.

Chapter IV - Concurrent Actions
Article 20
If two States have concluded a Supplementary Agreement pursuant to Article 21, the judicial authorities of either State may dismiss an action brought before them or may stay such an action when other proceedings between the same parties, based on the same facts and having the same purpose, are pending in a court of another State and these proceedings may result in a decision which the authorities of the State in which the first mentioned action was brought would be bound to recognise under the terms of this Convention.

The authorities of these States may nevertheless order provisional or protective measures regardless of proceedings elsewhere.

Chapter V - Supplementary Agreements
Article 21
Decisions rendered in a Contracting State shall not be recognised or enforced in another Contracting State in accordance with the provisions of the preceding Articles unless the two States, being Parties to this Convention, have concluded a Supplementary Agreement to this effect.

Article 22
This Convention shall not apply to decisions rendered before the entry into force of the Supplementary Agreement provided for in Article 21 unless that Agreement otherwise provides.

The Supplementary Agreement shall continue to be applicable to decisions in respect of which recognition or enforcement proceedings have been instituted before any denunciation of that Agreement takes effect.

Article 23

In the Supplementary Agreements referred to in Article 21 the Contracting States may agree -

(1)   to clarify the meaning of the expression "civil and commercial matters", to determine the courts whose decisions shall be recognised and enforced under this Convention, to define the expression "social security" and to define the expression "habitual residence";

(2)   to clarify the meaning of the term "law" in States with more than one legal system;

(3)   to include within the scope of this Convention questions relating to damage or injury in nuclear matters;

(4)   to apply this Convention to decisions ordering provisional or protective measures;

(5)   not to apply this Convention to decisions rendered in the course of criminal proceedings;

(6)   to specify the cases under which a decision is no longer subject to ordinary forms of review;

(7)   to recognise and enforce decisions upon which enforcement could be obtained in the State of origin even if such decisions are still subject to ordinary forms of review and in such a case to define the conditions under which a stay of proceedings for recognition or enforcement is possible;

(8)   not to apply Article 6 if the decision rendered by default was notified to the defaulting party and the latter had the opportunity to lodge a timely appeal against such a decision;

(8bis) that the Authority addressed shall not be bound by the findings of fact on which the court of the State of origin based its jurisdiction;

(9)   to consider the courts of the State in which the defendant has his "domicile" as having juris- diction under Article 10:

(10) that the court of origin shall be considered as having jurisdiction under the terms of this Convention in cases where its jurisdiction is admitted by another Convention in force between the State of origin and the State addressed if that other Convention contains no special rules relating to the recognition or enforcement of foreign judgments;

(11) that the court of origin shall be considered as having jurisdiction under the terms of this Convention either when its jurisdiction is admitted by the law of the State addressed relating to the recognition or enforcement of foreign judgments, or on grounds additional to those in Article 10;

(12) to define, for the purposes of the application of Article 12, the bases of jurisdiction which are exclusive by reason of the subject-matter of the action;

(13) to exclude, in cases where jurisdiction is based on an agreement between the parties, the application of sub-paragraph (1) of Article 12 as well as to exclude that of sub-paragraph (3) of Article 12;

(14) to regulate the procedure for obtaining recognition or enforcement;

(15) to regulate the enforcement of judgments other than those which order the payment of a sum of money;

(16) that the enforcement of a foreign judgment may be refused when a specified period has elapsed from its date;

(17) to fix the rate of interest payable from the date of the judgment in the State of origin;

(18) to adapt to the requirements of their legal systems the list of documents required by Article 13, but with the sole object of enabling the authority addressed to verify whether the conditions of this Convention have been fulfilled;

(19) to subject the documents referred to in Article 13 to legalisation or to a similar formality;

(20) to depart from the provisions of Article 17 and to depart from the provisions of Article 18;

(21) to make the provisions of the first paragraph of Article 20 obligatory;

(22) to include within the scope of this Convention "actes authentiques", including documents upon which immediate enforcement can be obtained, and to specify those documents.

Chapter VI - Final Clauses
Article 24
This Convention shall not affect other Conventions relating to the recognition and enforcement of judgments to which the Contracting States are already Parties so long as those States have not concluded a Supplementary Agreement under the terms of Article 21.

Unless it is otherwise agreed, the provisions of a Supplementary Agreement concluded under Article 21 shall prevail over the terms of any prior Conventions in force between the Parties relating to the recognition and enforcement of judgments to the extent that their terms are mutually inconsistent.

Article 25
Whether or not they have concluded a Supplementary Agreement under Article 21, the Contracting States shall not conclude between themselves other Conventions relating to the recognition and enforcement of judgments within the scope of this Convention unless they consider it necessary, in particular, because of economic ties or of particular aspects of their legal systems.

Article 26
Notwithstanding the provisions of Articles 24 and 25, this Convention and the Supplementary Agreements made under Article 21 shall not prevail over Conventions to which the Contracting States are or may become Parties in special fields and which contain provisions for the recognition and enforcement of judgments.

Article 27
This Convention shall be open for signature by the States represented at the Tenth Session of the Hague Conference on Private International Law and Cyprus, Iceland and Malta.

It shall be ratified and the instruments of ratification shall be deposited with the Ministry of Foreign Affairs of the Netherlands.

Article 28
This Convention shall enter into force on the sixtieth day after the deposit of the second instrument of ratification.

This Convention shall enter into force for each State which ratifies it subsequently on the sixtieth day after the deposit of its instrument of ratification.

Article 29
Any State not falling within the provisions of the first paragraph of Article 27 may accede to this Convention after it has entered into force in accordance with the first paragraph of Article 28. The instrument of accession shall be deposited with the Ministry of Foreign Affairs of the Netherlands.

This Convention shall enter into force for such a State in the absence of any objection from a State which has ratified this Convention before such deposit, notified to the Ministry of Foreign Affairs of the Netherlands within a period of six months after the date on which the said Ministry has notified it of such accession.

In the absence of any such objection, this Convention shall enter into force for the acceding State on the first day of the month following the expiration of the last of the periods referred to in the preceding paragraph.

Article 30
Any State may, at the time of signature, ratification or accession, declare that this Convention shall extend to all the territories for the international relations of which it is responsible, or to one or more of them. Such a declaration shall take effect on the date of entry into force of this Convention for the State concerned.

At any time thereafter, such extensions shall be notified to the Ministry of Foreign Affairs of the Netherlands.

This Convention shall enter into force for the territories mentioned in such an extension on the sixtieth day after the notification referred to in the preceding paragraph.

The Parties to a Supplementary Agreement concluded under Article 21 shall determine its territorial application.

Article 31

This Convention shall have a duration of five years from the date on which it enters into force under the first paragraph of Article 28, even in its application to States which have subsequently ratified or acceded to it.

In the absence of any denunciation, this Convention shall be renewed tacitly every five years.

Any denunciation shall be notified to the Ministry of Foreign Affairs of the Netherlands at least six months before the end of the five year period.

Such denunciation may be limited to any one of the territories to which this Convention applies.

Such denunciation shall affect only the notifying State. This Convention shall remain in force for the other Contracting States.

Article 32

Each Supplementary Agreement concluded under Article 21 shall take effect from the date specified in such Agreement; a certified copy and, if necessary, a translation into French or English shall be communicated to the Ministry of Foreign Affairs of the Netherlands.

Any Contracting State may, without denouncing this Convention, denounce a Supplementary Agreement either under any provision for denunciation in such Agreement or, if such Agreement contains no such provision, by giving six months' notice to the other State. Any State denouncing a Supplementary Agreement shall so inform the Ministry of Foreign Affairs of the Netherlands.

Notwithstanding the denunciation of this Convention, it shall nevertheless continue to have effect between the denouncing State and any other State with which the former has concluded a Supplementary Agreement under Article 21, unless such Agreement provides otherwise.

Article 33

The Ministry of Foreign Affairs of the Netherlands shall give notice to the States referred to in Article 27, and to the States which have acceded in accordance with Article 29, of the following -
a)   the signatures and ratifications referred to in Article 27;
b)   the date on which the present Convention enters into force in accordance with the first paragraph of Article 28;
c)   the accessions referred to in Article 29 and the dates on which they take effect;
d)   the extensions referred to in Article 30 and the dates on which they take effect;
e)   a translation or a copy of the text in English or French of Supplementary Agreements concluded under Article 21;
f)   the denunciations referred to in the third paragraph of Article 31 and the second paragraph of Article 32.

In witness whereof the undersigned, being duly authorised thereto, have signed this Convention.

Done at The Hague, on the first day of February, 1971, in the English and French languages, both texts being equally authentic, in a single copy which shall be deposited in the archives of the Government of the Netherlands, and of which a certified copy shall be sent, through the diplomatic channel, to each of the States represented at the Tenth Session of the Hague Conference on Private International Law, and to Cyprus, Iceland and Malta.

Entry into force: 10 Nov 2010
Ratification and binding effect: Albania (2010), Cyprus (1979), Kuwait (2002), Netherlands (1979), Portugal (1983)

SUPPLEMENTARY PROTOCOL TO THE HAGUE CONVENTION ON THE RECOGNITION AND ENFORCEMENT OF FOREIGN JUDGMENTS IN CIVIL AND COMMERCIAL MATTERS[1]
(The Hague, 1 February 1971)

The States signatory to the present Protocol,

IN THE KNOWLEDGE that certain grounds of jurisdiction, which are not included in Articles 10 and 11 of the Hague Convention on the Recognition and Enforcement of Foreign Judgments in Civil and Commercial Matters, can only exceptionally justify the international recognition and enforcement of judgments,

CONVINCED that the principles upon which this Protocol is founded shall prevail both in Supplementary Agreements which will be concluded under Article 21 of the said Convention and in other Conventions to be concluded in the future,

HAVE RESOLVED to conclude a Protocol to this end, and agreed on the following provisions:

(1)   This Protocol shall apply to all foreign decisions, regardless of their State of origin, rendered in matters to which the Convention on the Recognition and Enforcement of Foreign Judgments in Civil and Commercial Matters extends, and directed against a person having his domicile or habitual residence in a Contracting State.

(2)   Recognition and enforcement of a decision to which Article 1 applies shall in a Contracting State be refused at the request of the person against whom recognition or enforcement is sought, where the decision was based, and in the circumstances could have been based, only on one or more of the grounds of jurisdiction specified in Article 4.

Recognition and enforcement need not, however, be refused where the jurisdiction of the court of the State of origin could in the circumstances also have been based upon another ground of jurisdiction which, as between the State of origin and the State of recognition, is sufficient to justify recognition and enforcement.

(3)   Contracting States for the purposes of Articles 1 and 2 are States which are Parties to the Convention, and are linked by a Supplementary Agreement in accordance with Article 21 thereof.

(4)   The grounds of jurisdiction referred to in the first paragraph of Article 2 are the following -

a)   the presence in the territory of the State of origin of property belonging to the defendant, or the seisure by the plaintiff of property situated there, unless -

-   the action is brought to assert proprietary or possessory rights in that property, or arises from another issue relating to such property,

-   the property constitutes the security for a debt which is the subject-matter of the action;

b)   the nationality of the plaintiff;

c)   the domicile, habitual residence or ordinary residence of the plaintiff within the territory of the State of origin unless the assumption of jurisdiction on such a ground is permitted by way of an exception made on account of the particular subject-matter of a class of contracts;

d)   the fact that the defendant carried on business within the territory of the State of origin, unless the action arises from that business;

e)   service of a writ upon the defendant within the territory of the State of origin during his temporary presence there;

f)   a unilateral specification of the forum by the plaintiff, particularly in an invoice.

(5)   A legal person shall be considered to have its domicile or habitual residence where it has its seat, its place of incorporation, or its principal place of business.

(6)   This Protocol shall not prevail over present or future Conventions which, in relation to special fields, provide for any of the grounds of jurisdiction specified in Article 4.

---

1   © Hague Conference on Private International Law.

(7) This Protocol applies subject to the provisions of existing Conventions relating to the recognition and enforcement of foreign judgments.

(8) In Supplementary Agreements concluded in accordance with Article 21 of the Convention on the Recognition and Enforcement of Foreign Judgments in Civil and Commercial Matters, States Parties to those Agreements will not regard a court as possessing jurisdiction when it has proceeded on one or more of the grounds of jurisdiction specified in Article 4, unless it is necessary to do so to prevent a denial of justice to a litigant.

(9) The present Protocol shall be open for signature by every State which has signed the Hague Convention on the Recognition and Enforcement of Foreign Judgments in Civil and Commercial Matters.

It may be signed and ratified by every State which is a Party to the Convention, and the instrument of ratification shall be deposited with the Ministry of Foreign Affairs of the Netherlands which shall give all necessary notifications.

It shall enter into force on the sixtieth day after the deposit of the second instrument of ratification.

For every State which ratifies it subsequently it shall enter into force on the sixtieth day after the deposit of the instrument of ratification.

A denunciation of the Convention entails the denunciation of the Protocol.

In witness whereof the undersigned, being duly authorised thereto, have signed this Protocol.

Done at The Hague, on the first day of February, 1971, in the English and French languages, both texts being equally authentic, in a single copy which shall be deposited in the archives of the Government of the Netherlands and of which a certified copy shall be sent, through the diplomatic channel, to each of the States represented at the Tenth Session of the Hague Conference on Private International Law, and to Cyprus, Iceland and Malta.

Entry into force: 20 Aug 1979
Ratifications and binding effect: Cyprus (1979), Kuwait (2002), Netherlands (1979), Portugal (1983)

COUNCIL REGULATION 44/2001 OF 22 DECEMBER 2000
ON JURISDICTION AND THE RECOGNITION AND ENFORCEMENT OF JUDGMENTS IN CIVIL AND COMMERCIAL MATTERS[1]

CHAPTER I - SCOPE
Article 1 [Scope of Application]

1. This Regulation shall apply in civil and commercial matters whatever the nature of the court or tribunal. It shall not extend, in particular, to revenue, customs or administrative matters.

2. The Regulation shall not apply to:

(a) the status or legal capacity of natural persons, rights in property arising out of a matrimonial relationship, wills and succession;

(b) bankruptcy, proceedings relating to the winding-up of insolvent companies or other legal persons, judicial arrangements, compositions and analogous proceedings;

(c) social security;

(d) arbitration.

3. In this Regulation, the term 'Member State' shall mean Member States with the exception of Denmark.

---

1 OJ 2001 L 12, pp. 1-23. The full text of this Regulation, as well as many other useful EU Law documents, can be found in Frank Emmert (ed.), European Union Law - Documents, The Hague 2011.

CHAPTER II - JURISDICTION
Section 1 – General Provisions
Article 2 [General Jurisdiction at Domicile of Defendant]
1. Subject to this Regulation, persons domiciled in a Member State shall, whatever their nationality, be sued in the courts of that Member State.
2. Persons who are not nationals of the Member State in which they are domiciled shall be governed by the rules of jurisdiction applicable to nationals of that State.

Article 3 [Alternative Jurisdictions Pursuant to Sections 2 to 7]
1. Persons domiciled in a Member State may be sued in the courts of another Member State only by virtue of the rules set out in Sections 2 to 7 of this Chapter.
2. In particular the rules of national jurisdiction set out in Annex I shall not be applicable as against them.

Article 4 [Jurisdiction Pursuant to Private Int'l Law in the Absence of Domicile]
1. If the defendant is not domiciled in a Member State, the jurisdiction of the courts of each Member State shall, subject to Articles 22 and 23, be determined by the law of that Member State.
2. As against such a defendant, any person domiciled in a Member State may, whatever his nationality, avail himself in that State of the rules of jurisdiction there in force, and in particular those specified in Annex I, in the same way as the nationals of that State.

Section 2 – Special Jurisdiction
Article 5 [Alternative Non-Exclusive Jurisdictions]
A person domiciled in a Member State may, in another Member State, be sued:

1.(a) in matters relating to a contract, in the courts for the place of performance of the obligation in question;

(b) for the purpose of this provision and unless otherwise agreed, the place of performance of the obligation in question shall be:

— in the case of the sale of goods, the place in a Member State where, under the contract, the goods were delivered or should have been delivered,

— in the case of the provision of services, the place in a Member State where, under the contract, the services were provided or should have been provided,

(c) if subparagraph (b) does not apply then subparagraph (a) applies;

2. in matters relating to maintenance, in the courts for the place where the maintenance creditor is domiciled or habitually resident or, if the matter is ancillary to proceedings concerning the status of a person, in the court which, according to its own law, has jurisdiction to entertain those proceedings, unless that jurisdiction is based solely on the nationality of one of the parties;

3. in matters relating to tort, *delict* or *quasi-delict*, in the courts for the place where the harmful event occurred or may occur;

4. as regards a civil claim for damages or restitution which is based on an act giving rise to criminal proceedings, in the court seised of those proceedings, to the extent that that court has jurisdiction under its own law to entertain civil proceedings;

5. as regards a dispute arising out of the operations of a branch, agency or other establishment, in the courts for the place in which the branch, agency or other establishment is situated;

6. as settlor, trustee or beneficiary of a trust created by the operation of a statute, or by a written instrument, or created orally and evidenced in writing, in the courts of the Member State in which the trust is domiciled;

7. as regards a dispute concerning the payment of remuneration claimed in respect of the salvage of a cargo or freight, in the court under the authority of which the cargo or freight in question:

(a) has been arrested to secure such payment, or

(b) could have been so arrested, but bail or other security has been given;

provided that this provision shall apply only if it is claimed that the defendant has an interest in the cargo or freight or had such an interest at the time of salvage.

Article 6 [Jurisdiction for Related Claims]
A person domiciled in a Member State may also be sued:
1.   where he is one of a number of defendants, in the courts for the place where any one of them is domiciled, provided the claims are so closely connected that it is expedient to hear and determine them together to avoid the risk of irreconcilable judgments resulting from separate proceedings;
2.   as a third party in an action on a warranty or guarantee or in any other third party proceedings, in the court seised of the original proceedings, unless these were instituted solely with the object of removing him from the jurisdiction of the court which would be competent in his case;
3.   on a counter-claim arising from the same contract or facts on which the original claim was based, in the court in which the original claim is pending;
4.   in matters relating to a contract, if the action may be combined with an action against the same defendant in matters relating to rights *in rem* in immovable property, in the court of the Member State in which the property is situated.

Article 7 [Liability of Ship Owners and Operators]
Where by virtue of this Regulation a court of a Member State has jurisdiction in actions relating to liability from the use or operation of a ship, that court, or any other court substituted for this purpose by the internal law of that Member State, shall also have jurisdiction over claims for limitation of such liability.

Section 3 – Jurisdiction in Matters Relating to Insurance
Article 8 [Insurers Domiciled in a Member State]
In matters relating to insurance, jurisdiction shall be determined by this Section, without prejudice to Article 4 and point 5 of Article 5.

Article 9 [Alternative Jurisdictions for Claims Against Insurers]
1.   An insurer domiciled in a Member State may be sued:
(a)   in the courts of the Member State where he is domiciled, or
(b)   in another Member State, in the case of actions brought by the policyholder, the insured or a beneficiary, in the courts for the place where the plaintiff is domiciled,
(c)   if he is a co-insurer, in the courts of a Member State in which proceedings are brought against the leading insurer.
2.   An insurer who is not domiciled in a Member State but has a branch, agency or other establishment in one of the Member States shall, in disputes arising out of the operations of the branch, agency or establishment, be deemed to be domiciled in that Member State.

Article 10 [Additional Jurisdictions in Tort and Property Liability Cases]
In respect of liability insurance or insurance of immovable property, the insurer may in addition be sued in the courts for the place where the harmful event occurred. The same applies if movable and immovable property are covered by the same insurance policy and both are adversely affected by the same contingency.

Article 11 [Jurisdiction for Claims of Injured Parties]
1.   In respect of liability insurance, the insurer may also, if the law of the court permits it, be joined in proceedings which the injured party has brought against the insured.
2.   Articles 8, 9 and 10 shall apply to actions brought by the injured party directly against the insurer, where such direct actions are permitted.
3.   If the law governing such direct actions provides that the policyholder or the insured may be joined as a party to the action, the same court shall have jurisdiction over them.

Article 12 [Jurisdiction for Claims Brought by Insurers]
1.   Without prejudice to Article 11(3), an insurer may bring proceedings only in the courts of the Member State in which the defendant is domiciled, irrespective of whether he is the policyholder, the insured or a beneficiary.

2.   The provisions of this Section shall not affect the right to bring a counter-claim in the court in which, in accordance with this Section, the original claim is pending.

Article 13 [Agreement on Jurisdiction]
The provisions of this Section may be departed from only by an agreement:
1.   which is entered into after the dispute has arisen, or
2.   which allows the policyholder, the insured or a beneficiary to bring proceedings in courts other than those indicated in this Section, or
3.   which is concluded between a policyholder and an insurer, both of whom are at the time of conclusion of the contract domiciled or habitually resident in the same Member State, and which has the effect of conferring jurisdiction on the courts of that State even if the harmful event were to occur abroad, provided that such an agreement is not contrary to the law of that State, or
4.   which is concluded with a policyholder who is not domiciled in a Member State, except in so far as the insurance is compulsory or relates to immovable property in a Member State, or
5.   which relates to a contract of insurance in so far as it covers one or more of the risks set out in Article 14.

Article 14 [Agreements Concerning Certain Risks]
The following are the risks referred to in Article 13(5):
1.   any loss of or damage to:
(a)   seagoing ships, installations situated offshore or on the high seas, or aircraft, arising from perils which relate to their use for commercial purposes;
(b)   goods in transit other than passengers' baggage where the transit consists of or includes carriage by such ships or aircraft;
2.   any liability, other than for bodily injury to passengers or loss of or damage to their baggage:
(a)   arising out of the use or operation of ships, installations or aircraft as referred to in point 1(a) in so far as, in respect of the latter, the law of the Member State in which such aircraft are registered does not prohibit agreements on jurisdiction regarding insurance of such risks;
(b)   for loss or damage caused by goods in transit as described in point 1(b);
3.   any financial loss connected with the use or operation of ships, installations or aircraft as referred to in point 1(a), in particular loss of freight or charter-hire;
4.   any risk or interest connected with any of those referred to in points 1 to 3;
5.   notwithstanding points 1 to 4, all "large risks" as defined in Council Directive 73/239[1] [...].

Section 4 – Jurisdiction over Consumer Contracts
Article 15 [Covered Consumer Contracts]
1.   In matters relating to a contract concluded by a person, the consumer, for a purpose which can be regarded as being outside his trade or profession, jurisdiction shall be determined by this Section, without prejudice to Article 4 and point 5 of Article 5, if:
(a)   it is a contract for the sale of goods on instalment credit terms; or
(b)   it is a contract for a loan repayable by instalments, or for any other form of credit, made to finance the sale of goods; or
(c)   in all other cases, the contract has been concluded with a person who pursues commercial or professional activities in the Member State of the consumer's domicile or, by any means, directs such activities to that Member State or to several States including that Member State, and the contract falls within the scope of such activities.
2.   Where a consumer enters into a contract with a party who is not domiciled in the Member State but has a branch, agency or other establishment in one of the Member States, that party

---

1   First Council Directive of 24 July 1973 on the Coordination of Laws, Regulations and Administrative Provisions Relating to the Taking-up and Pursuit of the Business of Direct Insurance Other than Life Assurance, OJ 1973 L 228, p. 3, as last amended by Directive 2000/26 of the European Parliament and of the Council, OJ 2000 L 181, p. 65.

shall, in disputes arising out of the operations of the branch, agency or establishment, be deemed to be domiciled in that State.
3.   This Section shall not apply to a contract of transport other than a contract which, for an
inclusive price, provides for a combination of travel and accommodation.

Article 16 [Jurisdiction]

1.   A consumer may bring proceedings against the other party to a contract either in the
courts of the Member State in which that party is domiciled or in the courts for the place where
the consumer is domiciled.
2.   Proceedings may be brought against a consumer by the other party to the contract only in
the courts of the Member State in which the consumer is domiciled.
3.   This Article shall not affect the right to bring a counter-claim in the court in which, in
accordance with this Section, the original claim is pending.

Article 17 [Agreements on Jurisdiction]

The provisions of this Section may be departed from only by an agreement:
1.   which is entered into after the dispute has arisen; or
2.   which allows the consumer to bring proceedings in courts other than those indicated in
this Section; or
3.   which is entered into by the consumer and the other party to the contract, both of whom
are at the time of conclusion of the contract domiciled or habitually resident in the same
Member State, and which confers jurisdiction on the courts of that Member State, provided that
such an agreement is not contrary to the law of that Member State.

Section 5 – Jurisdiction over Individual Contracts of Employment
Article 18 [Covered Contracts of Employment]

1.   In matters relating to individual contracts of employment, jurisdiction shall be determined
by this Section, without prejudice to Article 4 and point 5 of Article 5.
2.   Where an employee enters into an individual contract of employment with an employer
who is not domiciled in a Member State but has a branch, agency or other establishment in one
of the Member States, the employer shall, in disputes arising out of the operations of the
branch, agency or establishment, be deemed to be domiciled in that Member State.

Article 19 [Jurisdiction for Claims Against Employers]

An employer domiciled in a Member State may be sued:
1.   in the courts of the Member State where he is domiciled; or
2.   in another Member State:
(a)   in the courts for the place where the employee habitually carries out his work or in the
courts for the last place where he did so, or
(b)   if the employee does not or did not habitually carry out his work in any one country, in the
courts for the place where the business which engaged the employee is or was situated.

Article 20 [Jurisdiction for Claims by Employers]

1.   An employer may bring proceedings only in the courts of the Member State in which the
employee is domiciled.
2.   The provisions of this Section shall not affect the right to bring a counter-claim in the court
in which, in accordance with this Section, the original claim is pending.

Article 21 [Agreements on Jurisdiction]

The provisions of this Section may be departed from only by an agreement on jurisdiction:
1.   which is entered into after the dispute has arisen; or
2.   which allows the employee to bring proceedings in courts other than those indicated in
this Section.

Section 6 – Exclusive Jurisdiction
Article 22 [Jurisdictions Regardless of Domicile]

The following courts shall have exclusive jurisdiction, regardless of domicile:

1. in proceedings which have as their object rights *in rem* in immovable property or tenancies of immovable property, the courts of the Member State in which the property is situated.

However, in proceedings which have as their object tenancies of immovable property concluded for temporary private use for a maximum period of six consecutive months, the courts of the Member State in which the defendant is domiciled shall also have jurisdiction, provided that the tenant is a natural person and that the landlord and the tenant are domiciled in the same Member State;

2. in proceedings which have as their object the validity of the constitution, the nullity or the dissolution of companies or other legal persons or associations of natural or legal persons, or of the validity of the decisions of their organs, the courts of the Member State in which the company, legal person or association has its seat. In order to determine that seat, the court shall apply its rules of private international law;

3. in proceedings which have as their object the validity of entries in public registers, the courts of the Member State in which the register is kept;

4. in proceedings concerned with the registration or validity of patents, trade marks, designs, or other similar rights required to be deposited or registered, the courts of the Member State in which the deposit or registration has been applied for, has taken place or is under the terms of a Community instrument or an international convention deemed to have taken place.

Without prejudice to the jurisdiction of the European Patent Office under the Convention on the Grant of European Patents, signed at Munich on 5 October 1973, the courts of each Member State shall have exclusive jurisdiction, regardless of domicile, in proceedings concerned with the registration or validity of any European patent granted for that State;

5. in proceedings concerned with the enforcement of judgments, the courts of the Member State in which the judgment has been or is to be enforced.

Section 7 – Prorogation of Jurisdiction
Article 23 [Agreements Create Exclusive Jurisdiction]

1. If the parties, one or more of whom is domiciled in a Member State, have agreed that a court or the courts of a Member State are to have jurisdiction to settle any disputes which have arisen or which may arise in connection with a particular legal relationship, that court or those courts shall have jurisdiction. Such jurisdiction shall be exclusive unless the parties have agreed otherwise. Such an agreement conferring jurisdiction shall be either:

(a) in writing or evidenced in writing; or

(b) in a form which accords with practices which the parties have established between themselves; or

(c) in international trade or commerce, in a form which accords with a usage of which the parties are or ought to have been aware and which in such trade or commerce is widely known to, and regularly observed by, parties to contracts of the type involved in the particular trade or commerce concerned.

2. Any communication by electronic means which provides a durable record of the agreement shall be equivalent to 'writing'.

3. Where such an agreement is concluded by parties, none of whom is domiciled in a Member State, the courts of other Member States shall have no jurisdiction over their disputes unless the court or courts chosen have declined jurisdiction.

4. The court or courts of a Member State on which a trust instrument has conferred jurisdiction shall have exclusive jurisdiction in any proceedings brought against a settlor, trustee or beneficiary, if relations between these persons or their rights or obligations under the trust are involved.

5.   Agreements or provisions of a trust instrument conferring jurisdiction shall have no legal force if they are contrary to Articles 13, 17 or 21, or if the courts whose jurisdiction they purport to exclude have exclusive jurisdiction by virtue of Article 22.

Article 24 [Appearance Creates Jurisdiction]
Apart from jurisdiction derived from other provisions of this Regulation, a court of a Member State before which a defendant enters an appearance shall have jurisdiction. This rule shall not apply where appearance was entered to contest the jurisdiction, or where another court has exclusive jurisdiction by virtue of Article 22.

Section 8 – Examination as to Jurisdiction and Admissibility
Article 25 [Another Court Has Exclusive Jurisdiction]
Where a court of a Member State is seised of a claim which is principally concerned with a matter over which the courts of another Member State have exclusive jurisdiction by virtue of Article 22, it shall declare of its own motion that it has no jurisdiction.

Article 26 [Defendant Does Not Appear]
1.   Where a defendant domiciled in one Member State is sued in a court of another Member State and does not enter an appearance, the court shall declare of its own motion that it has no jurisdiction unless its jurisdiction is derived from the provisions of this Regulation.
2.   The court shall stay the proceedings so long as it is not shown that the defendant has been able to receive the document instituting the proceedings or an equivalent document in sufficient time to enable him to arrange for his defence, or that all necessary steps have been taken to this end.
3.   Article 19 of Council Regulation 1348/2000 of 29 May 2000 on the service in the Member States of judicial and extrajudicial documents in civil or commercial matters[1] shall apply instead of the provisions of paragraph 2 if the document instituting the proceedings or an equivalent document had to be transmitted from one Member State to another pursuant to this Regulation.
4.   Where the provisions of Regulation 1348/2000 are not applicable, Article 15 of the Hague Convention of 15 November 1965 on the Service Abroad of Judicial and Extrajudicial Documents in Civil or Commercial Matters shall apply if the document instituting the proceedings or an equivalent document had to be transmitted pursuant to that Convention.

Section 9 – Lis Pendens — Related Actions
Article 27 [Priority of the First Seised Court Over Alternative Jurisdictions]
1.   Where proceedings involving the same cause of action and between the same parties are brought in the courts of different Member States, any court other than the court first seised shall of its own motion stay its proceedings until such time as the jurisdiction of the court first seised is established.
2.   Where the jurisdiction of the court first seised is established, any court other than the court first seised shall decline jurisdiction in favour of that court.

Article 28 [Related Action Already Pending]
1.   Where related actions are pending in the courts of different Member States, any court other than the court first seised may stay its proceedings.
2.   Where these actions are pending at first instance, any court other than the court first seised may also, on the application of one of the parties, decline jurisdiction if the court first seised has jurisdiction over the actions in question and its law permits the consolidation thereof.
3.   For the purposes of this Article, actions are deemed to be related where they are so closely connected that it is expedient to hear and determine them together to avoid the risk of irreconcilable judgments resulting from separate proceedings.

---

1   OJ 2000 L 160, p. 37.

Article 29 [Several Seised Courts Have Exclusive Jurisdiction]
Where actions come within the exclusive jurisdiction of several courts, any court other than the court first seised shall decline jurisdiction in favour of that court.

Article 30 [Definition of "Seised Court"]
For the purposes of this Section, a court shall be deemed to be seised:
1.   at the time when the document instituting the proceedings or an equivalent document is lodged with the court, provided that the plaintiff has not subsequently failed to take the steps he was required to take to have service effected on the defendant, or
2.   if the document has to be served before being lodged with the court, at the time when it is received by the authority responsible for service, provided that the plaintiff has not subsequently failed to take the steps he was required to take to have the document lodged with the court.

Section 10 – Provisional, Including Protective, Measures
Article 31 [Jurisdiction for Provisional and Protective Measures]
Application may be made to the courts of a Member State for such provisional, including protective, measures as may be available under the law of that State, even if, under this Regulation, the courts of another Member State have jurisdiction as to the substance of the matter.

CHAPTER III - RECOGNITION AND ENFORCEMENT
Article 32 [Definition of "Judgment"]
For the purposes of this Regulation, 'judgment' means any judgment given by a court or tribunal of a Member State, whatever the judgment may be called, including a decree, order, decision or writ of execution, as well as the determination of costs or expenses by an officer of the court.

Section 1 – Recognition
Article 33 [General Principle of Recognition]
1.   A judgment given in a Member State shall be recognised in the other Member States without any special procedure being required.
2.   Any interested party who raises the recognition of a judgment as the principal issue in a dispute may, in accordance with the procedures provided for in Sections 2 and 3 of this Chapter, apply for a decision that the judgment be recognised.
3.   If the outcome of proceedings in a court of a Member State depends on the determination of an incidental question of recognition that court shall have jurisdiction over that question.

Article 34 [Exceptions]
A judgment shall not be recognised:
1.   if such recognition is manifestly contrary to public policy in the Member State in which recognition is sought;
2.   where it was given in default of appearance, if the defendant was not served with the document which instituted the proceedings or with an equivalent document in sufficient time and in such a way as to enable him to arrange for his defence, unless the defendant failed to commence proceedings to challenge the judgment when it was possible for him to do so;
3.   if it is irreconcilable with a judgment given in a dispute between the same parties in the Member State in which recognition is sought;
4.   if it is irreconcilable with an earlier judgment given in another Member State or in a third State involving the same cause of action and between the same parties, provided that the earlier judgment fulfils the conditions necessary for its recognition in the Member State addressed.

Article 35 [Non-Recognition for Lack of Jurisdiction]
1.   Moreover, a judgment shall not be recognised if it conflicts with Sections 3, 4 or 6 of Chapter II, or in a case provided for in Article 72.
2.   In its examination of the grounds of jurisdiction referred to in the foregoing paragraph, the court or authority applied to shall be bound by the findings of fact on which the court of the Member State of origin based its jurisdiction.

3.   Subject to the paragraph 1, the jurisdiction of the court of the Member State of origin may not be reviewed. The test of public policy referred to in point 1 of Article 34 may not be applied to the rules relating to jurisdiction.

Article 36 [No Substantive Review]
Under no circumstances may a foreign judgment be reviewed as to its substance.

Article 37 [Non-Recognition Pending Appeal]
1.   A court of a Member State in which recognition is sought of a judgment given in another Member State may stay the proceedings if an ordinary appeal against the judgment has been lodged.
2.   A court of a Member State in which recognition is sought of a judgment given in Ireland or the United Kingdom may stay the proceedings if enforcement is suspended in the State of origin, by reason of an appeal.

Section 2 – Enforcement
Article 38 [Enforcement by Application]
1.   A judgment given in a Member State and enforceable in that State shall be enforced in another Member State when, on the application of any interested party, it has been declared enforceable there.
2.   However, in the United Kingdom, such a judgment shall be enforced in England and Wales, in Scotland, or in Northern Ireland when, on the application of any interested party, it has been registered for enforcement in that part of the United Kingdom.

Article 39 [Competent Authorities]
1.   The application shall be submitted to the court or competent authority indicated in the list in Annex II.
2.   The local jurisdiction shall be determined by reference to the place of domicile of the party against whom enforcement is sought, or to the place of enforcement.

Article 40 [Procedural Rules]
1.   The procedure for making the application shall be governed by the law of the Member State in which enforcement is sought.
2.   The applicant must give an address for service of process within the area of jurisdiction of the court applied to. However, if the law of the Member State in which enforcement is sought does not provide for the furnishing of such an address, the applicant shall appoint a representative ad litem.
3.   The documents referred to in Article 53 shall be attached to the application.

Article 41 [Enforcement Without Review]
The judgment shall be declared enforceable immediately on completion of the formalities in Article 53 without any review under Articles 34 and 35. The party against whom enforcement is sought shall not at this stage of the proceedings be entitled to make any submissions on the application.

Article 42 [Decision on Enforceability]
1.   The decision on the application for a declaration of enforceability shall forthwith be brought to the notice of the applicant in accordance with the procedure laid down by the law of the Member State in which enforcement is sought.
2.   The declaration of enforceability shall be served on the party against whom enforcement is sought, accompanied by the judgment, if not already served on that party.

Article 43 [Appeals Against Decisions on Enforceability]
1.   The decision on the application for a declaration of enforceability may be appealed against by either party.
2.   The appeal is to be lodged with the court indicated in the list in Annex III.

3.   The appeal shall be dealt with in accordance with the rules governing procedure in contra-dictory matters.

4.   If the party against whom enforcement is sought fails to appear before the appellate court in proceedings concerning an appeal brought by the applicant, Article 26(2) to (4) shall apply even where the party against whom enforcement is sought is not domiciled in any of the Member States.

5.   An appeal against the declaration of enforceability is to be lodged within one month of service thereof. If the party against whom enforcement is sought is domiciled in a Member State other than that in which the declaration of enforceability was given, the time for appealing shall be two months and shall run from the date of service, either on him in person or at his residence. No extension of time may be granted on account of distance.

Article 44 [Second Appeal]

The judgment given on the appeal may be contested only by the appeal referred to in Annex IV.

Article 45 [Grounds for Revocation of a Decision on Enforceability]

1.   The court with which an appeal is lodged under Article 43 or Article 44 shall refuse or revoke a declaration of enforceability only on one of the grounds specified in Articles 34 and 35. It shall give its decision without delay.

2.   Under no circumstances may the foreign judgment be reviewed as to its substance.

Article 46 [Stay of Proceedings Pending Appeal in the Member State of Origin]

1.   The court with which an appeal is lodged under Article 43 or Article 44 may, on the applica-tion of the party against whom enforcement is sought, stay the proceedings if an ordinary appeal has been lodged against the judgment in the Member State of origin or if the time for such an appeal has not yet expired; in the latter case, the court may specify the time within which such an appeal is to be lodged.

2.   Where the judgment was given in Ireland or the United Kingdom, any form of appeal available in the Member State of origin shall be treated as an ordinary appeal for the purposes of paragraph 1.

3.   The court may also make enforcement conditional on the provision of such security as it shall determine.

Article 47 [Provisional and Protective Measures]

1.   When a judgment must be recognised in accordance with this Regulation, nothing shall prevent the applicant from availing himself of provisional, including protective, measures in accordance with the law of the Member State requested without a declaration of enforceability under Article 41 being required.

2.   The declaration of enforceability shall carry with it the power to proceed to any protective measures.

3.   During the time specified for an appeal pursuant to Article 43(5) against the declaration of enforceability and until any such appeal has been determined, no measures of enforcement may be taken other than protective measures against the property of the party against whom enforcement is sought.

Article 48 [Partial Enforceability]

1.   Where a foreign judgment has been given in respect of several matters and the declaration of enforceability cannot be given for all of them, the court or competent authority shall give it for one or more of them.

2.   An applicant may request a declaration of enforceability limited to parts of a judgment.

Article 49 [Enforcement of Periodic Payments]

A foreign judgment which orders a periodic payment by way of a penalty shall be enforceable in the Member State in which enforcement is sought only if the amount of the payment has been finally determined by the courts of the Member State of origin.

Article 50 [Legal Aid]

An applicant who, in the Member State of origin has benefited from complete or partial legal aid or exemption from costs or expenses, shall be entitled, in the procedure provided for in this Section, to benefit from the most favourable legal aid or the most extensive exemption from costs or expenses provided for by the law of the Member State addressed.

Article 51 [Non-Discrimination of Applicants from Other Member States]

No security, bond or deposit, however described, shall be required of a party who in one Member State applies for enforcement of a judgment given in another Member State on the ground that he is a foreign national or that he is not domiciled or resident in the State in which enforcement is sought.

Article 52 [Costs]

In proceedings for the issue of a declaration of enforceability, no charge, duty or fee calculated by reference to the value of the matter at issue may be levied in the Member State in which enforcement is sought.

Section 3 – Common Provisions

Article 53 [Submission of Original Documents for Recognition or Enforcement]

1.   A party seeking recognition or applying for a declaration of enforceability shall produce a copy of the judgment which satisfies the conditions necessary to establish its authenticity.
2.   A party applying for a declaration of enforceability shall also produce the certificate referred to in Article 54, without prejudice to Article 55.

Article 54 [Certificate]

The court or competent authority of a Member State where a judgment was given shall issue, at the request of any interested party, a certificate using the standard form in Annex V to this Regulation.

Article 55 [Alternatives to the Certificate]

1.   If the certificate referred to in Article 54 is not produced, the court or competent authority may specify a time for its production or accept an equivalent document or, if it considers that it has sufficient information before it, dispense with its production.
2.   If the court or competent authority so requires, a translation of the documents shall be produced. The translation shall be certified by a person qualified to do so in one of the Member States.

Article 56 [No Additional Requirements in National Law Allowed]

No legalisation or other similar formality shall be required in respect of the documents referred to in Article 53 or Article 55(2), or in respect of a document appointing a representative *ad litem*.

CHAPTER IV - AUTHENTIC INSTRUMENTS AND COURT SETTLEMENTS

Article 57 [Recognition and Enforcement of Other Documents and Decisions]

1.   A document which has been formally drawn up or registered as an authentic instrument and is enforceable in one Member State shall, in another Member State, be declared enforceable there, on application made in accordance with the procedures provided for in Articles 38, et seq. The court with which an appeal is lodged under Article 43 or Article 44 shall refuse or revoke a declaration of enforceability only if enforcement of the instrument is manifestly contrary to public policy in the Member State addressed.
2.   Arrangements relating to maintenance obligations concluded with administrative authorities or authenticated by them shall also be regarded as authentic instruments within the meaning of paragraph 1.
3.   The instrument produced must satisfy the conditions necessary to establish its authenticity in the Member State of origin.
4.   Section 3 of Chapter III shall apply as appropriate. The competent authority of a Member State where an authentic instrument was drawn up or registered shall issue, at the request of any interested party, a certificate using the standard form in Annex VI to this Regulation.

Article 58 [Enforcement of Settlements]

A settlement which has been approved by a court in the course of proceedings and is enforceable in the Member State in which it was concluded shall be enforceable in the State addressed under the same conditions as authentic instruments. The court or competent authority of a Member State where a court settlement was approved shall issue, at the request of any interested party, a certificate using the standard form in Annex V to this Regulation.

CHAPTER V - GENERAL PROVISIONS

Article 59 [Domicile of Natural Persons]

1.　In order to determine whether a party is domiciled in the Member State whose courts are seised of a matter, the court shall apply its internal law.

2.　If a party is not domiciled in the Member State whose courts are seised of the matter, then, in order to determine whether the party is domiciled in another Member State, the court shall apply the law of that Member State.

Article 60 [Domicile of Companies and Legal Persons]

1.　For the purposes of this Regulation, a company or other legal person or association of natural or legal persons is domiciled at the place where it has its:

(a)　statutory seat, or
(b)　central administration, or
(c)　principal place of business.

2.　For the purposes of the United Kingdom and Ireland 'statutory seat' means the registered office or, where there is no such office anywhere, the place of incorporation or, where there is no such place anywhere, the place under the law of which the formation took place.

3.　In order to determine whether a trust is domiciled in the Member State whose courts are seised of the matter, the court shall apply its rules of private international law.

PRELIMINARY DRAFT CONVENTION ON JURISDICTION AND FOREIGN JUDGMENTS IN CIVIL AND COMMERCIAL MATTERS[1]

adopted by the Special Commission on 30 October 1999
amended version (new numbering of articles)

CHAPTER I - SCOPE OF THE CONVENTION

Article 1 Substantive Scope

1.　The Convention applies to civil and commercial matters. It shall not extend in particular to revenue, customs or administrative matters.

2.　The Convention does not apply to -

a)　the status and legal capacity of natural persons;
b)　maintenance obligations;
c)　matrimonial property regimes and other rights and obligations arising out of marriage or similar relationships;
d)　wills and succession;
e)　insolvency, composition or analogous proceedings;
f)　social security;
g)　arbitration and proceedings related thereto;
h)　admiralty or maritime matters.

3.　A dispute is not excluded from the scope of the Convention by the mere fact that a government, a governmental agency or any other person acting for the State is a party thereto.

1　© The Hague Conference on Private International Law. All Rights Reserved.

4.   Nothing in this Convention affects the privileges and immunities of sovereign States or of entities of sovereign States, or of international organisations.

Article 2 Territorial Scope

1.   The provisions of Chapter II shall apply in the courts of a Contracting State unless all the parties are habitually resident in that State. However, even if all the parties are habitually resident in that State -
a)   Article 4 shall apply if they have agreed that a court or courts of another Contracting State have jurisdiction to determine the dispute;
b)   Article 12, regarding exclusive jurisdiction, shall apply;
c)   Articles 21 and 22 shall apply where the court is required to determine whether to decline jurisdiction or suspend its proceedings on the grounds that the dispute ought to be determined in the courts of another Contracting State.
2.   The provisions of Chapter III apply to the recognition and enforcement in a Contracting State of a judgment rendered in another Contracting State.

CHAPTER II - JURISDICTION

Article 3 Defendant's Forum

1.   Subject to the provisions of the Convention, a defendant may be sued in the courts of the State where that defendant is habitually resident.
2.   For the purposes of the Convention, an entity or person other than a natural person shall be considered to be habitually resident in the State -
a)   where it has its statutory seat,
b)   under whose law it was incorporated or formed,
c)   where it has its central administration, or
d)   where it has its principal place of business.

Article 4 Choice of Court

1.   If the parties have agreed that a court or courts of a Contracting State shall have jurisdiction to settle any dispute which has arisen or may arise in connection with a particular legal relationship, that court or those courts shall have jurisdiction, and that jurisdiction shall be exclusive unless the parties have agreed otherwise. Where an agreement having exclusive effect designates a court or courts of a non-Contracting State, courts in Contracting States shall decline jurisdiction or suspend proceedings unless the court or courts chosen have themselves declined jurisdiction.
2.   An agreement within the meaning of paragraph 1 shall be valid as to form, if it was entered into or confirmed -
a)   in writing;
b)   by any other means of communication which renders information accessible so as to be usable for subsequent reference;
c)   in accordance with a usage which is regularly observed by the parties;
d)   in accordance with a usage of which the parties were or ought to have been aware and which is regularly observed by parties to contracts of the same nature in the particular trade or commerce concerned.
3.   Agreements conferring jurisdiction and similar clauses in trust instruments shall be without effect if they conflict with the provisions of Article 7, 8 or 12.

Article 5 Appearance by the Defendant

1.   Subject to Article 12, a court has jurisdiction if the defendant proceeds on the merits without contesting jurisdiction.
2.   The defendant has the right to contest jurisdiction no later than at the time of the first defence on the merits.

Article 6 Contracts

A plaintiff may bring an action in contract in the courts of a State in which -

a)   in matters relating to the supply of goods, the goods were supplied in whole or in part;
b)   in matters relating to the provision of services, the services were provided in whole or in part;
c)   in matters relating both to the supply of goods and the provision of services, performance of the principal obligation took place in whole or in part.

Article 7 Contracts Concluded by Consumers

1.   A plaintiff who concluded a contract for a purpose which is outside its trade or profession, hereafter designated as the consumer, may bring a claim in the courts of the State in which it is habitually resident, if
a)   the conclusion of the contract on which the claim is based is related to trade or professional activities that the defendant has engaged in or directed to that State, in particular in soliciting business through means of publicity, and
b)   the consumer has taken the steps necessary for the conclusion of the contract in that State.
2.   A claim against the consumer may only be brought by a person who entered into the contract in the course of its trade or profession before the courts of the State of the habitual residence of the consumer.
3.   The parties to a contract within the meaning of paragraph 1 may, by an agreement which conforms with the requirements of Article 4, make a choice of court -
a)   if such agreement is entered into after the dispute has arisen, or
b)   to the extent only that it allows the consumer to bring proceedings in another court.

Article 8 Individual Contracts of Employment

1.   In matters relating to individual contracts of employment -
a)   an employee may bring an action against the employer,
    i)   in the courts of the State in which the employee habitually carries out his work or in the courts of the last State in which he did so, or
    ii) if the employee does not or did not habitually carry out his work in any one State, in the courts of the State in which the business that engaged the employee is or was situated;
b)   a claim against an employee may be brought by the employer only,
    i)   in the courts of the State where the employee is habitually resident, or
    ii) in the courts of the State in which the employee habitually carries out his work.
2.   The parties to a contract within the meaning of paragraph 1 may, by an agreement which conforms with the requirements of Article 4, make a choice of court -
a)   if such agreement is entered into after the dispute has arisen, or
b)   to the extent only that it allows the employee to bring proceedings in courts other than those indicated in this Article or in Article 3 of the Convention.

Article 9 Branches [and Regular Commercial Activity]

A plaintiff may bring an action in the courts of a State in which a branch, agency or any other establishment of the defendant is situated, [or where the defendant has carried on regular commercial activity by other means,] provided that the dispute relates directly to the activity of that branch, agency or establishment [or to that regular commercial activity].

Article 10 Torts or Delicts

1.   A plaintiff may bring an action in tort or delict in the courts of the State -
a)   in which the act or omission that caused injury occurred, or
b)   in which the injury arose, unless the defendant establishes that the person claimed to be responsible could not reasonably have foreseen that the act or omission could result in an injury of the same nature in that State.
2.   Paragraph 1 b) shall not apply to injury caused by anti-trust violations, in particular price-fixing or monopolisation, or conspiracy to inflict economic loss.
3.   A plaintiff may also bring an action in accordance with paragraph 1 when the act or omission, or the injury may occur.

4.   If an action is brought in the courts of a State only on the basis that the injury arose or may occur there, those courts shall have jurisdiction only in respect of the injury that occurred or may occur in that State, unless the injured person has his or her habitual residence in that State.

Article 11 Trusts
1.   In proceedings concerning the validity, construction, effects, administration or variation of a trust created voluntarily and evidenced in writing, the courts of a Contracting State designated in the trust instrument for this purpose shall have exclusive jurisdiction. Where the trust instrument designates a court or courts of a non-Contracting State, courts in Contracting States shall decline jurisdiction or suspend proceedings unless the court or courts chosen have themselves declined jurisdiction.
2.   In the absence of such designation, proceedings may be brought before the courts of a State
a)   in which is situated the principal place of administration of the trust;
b)   whose law is applicable to the trust;
c)   with which the trust has the closest connection for the purpose of the proceedings.

Article 12 Exclusive Jurisdiction
1.   In proceedings which have as their object rights in rem in immovable property or tenancies of immovable property, the courts of the Contracting State in which the property is situated have exclusive jurisdiction, unless in proceedings which have as their object tenancies of immovable property, the tenant is habitually resident in a different State.
2.   In proceedings which have as their object the validity, nullity, or dissolution of a legal person, or the validity or nullity of the decisions of its organs, the courts of a Contracting State whose law governs the legal person have exclusive jurisdiction.
3.   In proceedings which have as their object the validity or nullity of entries in public registers, the courts of the Contracting State in which the register is kept have exclusive jurisdiction.
4.   In proceedings which have as their object the registration, validity, [or] nullity[, or revocation or infringement,] of patents, trade marks, designs or other similar rights required to be deposited or registered, the courts of the Contracting State in which the deposit or registration has been applied for, has taken place or, under the terms of an international convention, is deemed to have taken place, have exclusive jurisdiction. This shall not apply to copyright or any neighbouring rights, even though registration or deposit of such rights is possible.
[5.   In relation to proceedings which have as their object the infringement of patents, the preceding paragraph does not exclude the jurisdiction of any other court under the Convention or under the national law of a Contracting State.]
[6.   The previous paragraphs shall not apply when the matters referred to therein arise as incidental questions.]

Article 13 Provisional and Protective Measures
1.   A court having jurisdiction under Articles 3 to 12 to determine the merits of the case has jurisdiction to order any provisional or protective measures.
2.   The courts of a State in which property is located have jurisdiction to order any provisional or protective measures in respect of that property.
3.   A court of a Contracting State not having jurisdiction under paragraphs 1 or 2 may order provisional or protective measures, provided that -
a)   their enforcement is limited to the territory of that State, and
b)   their purpose is to protect on an interim basis a claim on the merits which is pending or to be brought by the requesting party.

Article 14 Multiple Defendants
1.   A plaintiff bringing an action against a defendant in a court of the State in which that defendant is habitually resident may also proceed in that court against other defendants not habitually resident in that State if -

a)   the claims against the defendant habitually resident in that State and the other defendants are so closely connected that they should be adjudicated together to avoid a serious risk of inconsistent judgments, and

b)   as to each defendant not habitually resident in that State, there is a substantial connection between that State and the dispute involving that defendant.

2.   Paragraph 1 shall not apply to a co-defendant invoking an exclusive choice of court clause agreed with the plaintiff and conforming with Article 4.

Article 15 Counter-Claims

A court which has jurisdiction to determine a claim under the provisions of the Convention shall also have jurisdiction to determine a counter-claim arising out of the transaction or occurrence on which the original claim is based.

Article 16 Third Party Claims

1.   A court which has jurisdiction to determine a claim under the provisions of the Convention shall also have jurisdiction to determine a claim by a defendant against a third party for indemnity or contribution in respect of the claim against that defendant to the extent that such an action is permitted by national law, provided that there is a substantial connection between that State and the dispute involving that third party.

2.   Paragraph 1 shall not apply to a third party invoking an exclusive choice of court clause agreed with the defendant and conforming with Article 4.

Article 17 Jurisdiction Based on National Law

Subject to Articles 4, 5, 7, 8, 12 and 13, the Convention does not prevent the application by Contracting States of rules of jurisdiction under national law, provided that this is not prohibited under Article 18.

Article 18 Prohibited Grounds of Jurisdiction

1.   Where the defendant is habitually resident in a Contracting State, the application of a rule of jurisdiction provided for under the national law of a Contracting State is prohibited if there is no substantial connection between that State and the dispute.

2.   In particular, jurisdiction shall not be exercised by the courts of a Contracting State on the basis solely of one or more of the following -

a)   the presence or the seizure in that State of property belonging to the defendant, except where the dispute is directly related to that property;

b)   the nationality of the plaintiff;

c)   the nationality of the defendant;

d)   the domicile, habitual or temporary residence, or presence of the plaintiff in that State;

e)   the carrying on of commercial or other activities by the defendant in that State, except where the dispute is directly related to those activities;

f)   the service of a writ upon the defendant in that State;

g)   the unilateral designation of the forum by the plaintiff;

h)   proceedings in that State for declaration of enforceability or registration or for the enforcement of a judgment, except where the dispute is directly related to such proceedings;

i)   the temporary residence or presence of the defendant in that State;

j)   the signing in that State of the contract from which the dispute arises.

3.   Nothing in this Article shall prevent a court in a Contracting State from exercising jurisdiction under national law in an action [seeking relief] [claiming damages] in respect of conduct which constitutes -

[Variant One:

[a]   genocide, a crime against humanity or a war crime[, as defined in the Statute of the International Criminal Court]; or]

[b]   a serious crime against a natural person under international law; or]

[c]   a grave violation against a natural person of non-derogable fundamental rights established under international law, such as torture, slavery, forced labour and disappeared persons].

[Sub-paragraphs [b] and] c) above apply only if the party seeking relief is exposed to a risk of a denial of justice because proceedings in another State are not possible or cannot reasonably be required.]
Variant Two:
a serious crime under international law, provided that this State has established its criminal jurisdiction over that crime in accordance with an international treaty to which it is a party and that the claim is for civil compensatory damages for death or serious bodily injury arising from that crime.]

Article 19 Authority of the Court Seised

Where the defendant does not enter an appearance, the court shall verify whether Article 18 prohibits it from exercising jurisdiction if -
a)   national law so requires; or
b)   the plaintiff so requests; or
[c)   the defendant so requests, even after judgment is entered in accordance with procedures established under national law; or]
[d)   the document which instituted the proceedings or an equivalent document was served on the defendant in another Contracting State.] or
[d)   it appears from the documents filed by the plaintiff that the defendant's address is in another Contracting State.]

Article 20 [Verification of Service on Defendant]

1.   The court shall stay the proceedings so long as it is not established that the document which instituted the proceedings or an equivalent document, including the essential elements of the claim, was notified to the defendant in sufficient time and in such a way as to enable him to arrange for his defence, or that all necessary steps have been taken to that effect.
[2.   Paragraph 1 shall not affect the use of international instruments concerning the service abroad of judicial and extrajudicial documents in civil or commercial matters, in accordance with the law of the forum.]
[3.   Paragraph 1 shall not apply, in case of urgency, to any provisional or protective measures.]

Article 21 Lis Pendens

1.   When the same parties are engaged in proceedings in courts of different Contracting States and when such proceedings are based on the same causes of action, irrespective of the relief sought, the court second seised shall suspend the proceedings if the court first seised has jurisdiction and is expected to render a judgment capable of being recognised under the Convention in the State of the court second seised, unless the latter has exclusive jurisdiction under Article 4 or 12.
2.   The court second seised shall decline jurisdiction as soon as it is presented with a judgment rendered by the court first seised that complies with the requirements for recognition or enforcement under the Convention.
3.   Upon application of a party, the court second seised may proceed with the case if the plaintiff in the court first seised has failed to take the necessary steps to bring the proceedings to a decision on the merits or if that court has not rendered such a decision within a reasonable time.
4.   The provisions of the preceding paragraphs apply to the court second seised even in a case where the jurisdiction of that court is based on the national law of that State in accordance with Article 17.
5.   For the purpose of this Article, a court shall be deemed to be seised -
a)   when the document instituting the proceedings or an equivalent document is lodged with the court, or
b)   if such document has to be served before being lodged with the court, when it is received by the authority responsible for service or served on the defendant.
[As appropriate, universal time is applicable.]

6.   If in the action before the court first seised the plaintiff seeks a determination that it has no obligation to the defendant, and if an action seeking substantive relief is brought in the court second seised -

a)   the provisions of paragraphs 1 to 5 above shall not apply to the court second seised, and

b)   the court first seised shall suspend the proceedings at the request of a party if the court second seised is expected to render a decision capable of being recognised under the Convention.

7.   This Article shall not apply if the court first seised, on application by a party, determines that the court second seised is clearly more appropriate to resolve the dispute, under the conditions specified in Article 22.

Article 22 Exceptional Circumstances for Declining Jurisdiction

1.   In exceptional circumstances, when the jurisdiction of the court seised is not founded on an exclusive choice of court agreement valid under Article 4, or on Article 7, 8 or 12, the court may, on application by a party, suspend its proceedings if in that case it is clearly inappropriate for that court to exercise jurisdiction and if a court of another State has jurisdiction and is clearly more appropriate to resolve the dispute. Such application must be made no later than at the time of the first defence on the merits.

2.   The court shall take into account, in particular -

a)   any inconvenience to the parties in view of their habitual residence;

b)   the nature and location of the evidence, including documents and witnesses, and the procedures for obtaining such evidence;

c)   applicable limitation or prescription periods;

d)   the possibility of obtaining recognition and enforcement of any decision on the merits.

3.   In deciding whether to suspend the proceedings, a court shall not discriminate on the basis of the nationality or habitual residence of the parties.

4.   If the court decides to suspend its proceedings under paragraph 1, it may order the defendant to provide security sufficient to satisfy any decision of the other court on the merits. However, it shall make such an order if the other court has jurisdiction only under Article 17, unless the defendant establishes that sufficient assets exist in the State of that other court or in another State where the court's decision could be enforced.

5.   When the court has suspended its proceedings under paragraph 1,

a)   it shall decline to exercise jurisdiction if the court of the other State exercises jurisdiction, or if the plaintiff does not bring the proceedings in that State within the time specified by the court, or

b)   it shall proceed with the case if the court of the other State decides not to exercise jurisdiction.

CHAPTER III - RECOGNITION AND ENFORCEMENT

Article 23 Definition of "Judgment"

For the purposes of this Chapter, "judgment" means -

a)   any decision given by a court, whatever it may be called, including a decree or order, as well as the determination of costs or expenses by an officer of the court, provided that it relates to a decision which may be recognised or enforced under the Convention;

b)   decisions ordering provisional or protective measures in accordance with Article 13, paragraph 1.

Article 24 Judgments Excluded from Chapter III

This Chapter shall not apply to judgments based on a ground of jurisdiction provided for by national law in accordance with Article 17.

Article 25 Judgments to Be Recognised or Enforced

1.   A judgment based on a ground of jurisdiction provided for in Articles 3 to 13, or which is consistent with any such ground, shall be recognised or enforced under this Chapter.

2.   In order to be recognised, a judgment referred to in paragraph 1 must have the effect of res judicata in the State of origin.
3.   In order to be enforceable, a judgment referred to in paragraph 1 must be enforceable in the State of origin.
4.   However, recognition or enforcement may be postponed if the judgment is the subject of review in the State of origin or if the time limit for seeking a review has not expired.

Article 26 Judgments Not to Be Recognised or Enforced

A judgment based on a ground of jurisdiction which conflicts with Articles 4, 5, 7, 8 or 12, or whose application is prohibited by virtue of Article 18, shall not be recognised or enforced.

Article 27 Verification of Jurisdiction

1.   The court addressed shall verify the jurisdiction of the court of origin.
2.   In verifying the jurisdiction of the court of origin, the court addressed shall be bound by the findings of fact on which the court of origin based its jurisdiction, unless the judgment was given by default.
3.   Recognition or enforcement of a judgment may not be refused on the ground that the court addressed considers that the court of origin should have declined jurisdiction in accordance with Article 22.

Article 28 Grounds for Refusal of Recognition or Enforcement

1.   Recognition or enforcement of a judgment may be refused if -
a)   proceedings between the same parties and having the same subject matter are pending before a court of the State addressed, if first seised in accordance with Article 21;
b)   the judgment is inconsistent with a judgment rendered, either in the State addressed or in another State, provided that in the latter case the judgment is capable of being recognised or enforced in the State addressed;
c)   the judgment results from proceedings incompatible with fundamental principles of procedure of the State addressed, including the right of each party to be heard by an impartial and independent court;
d)   the document which instituted the proceedings or an equivalent document, including the essential elements of the claim, was not notified to the defendant in sufficient time and in such a way as to enable him to arrange for his defence;
e)   the judgment was obtained by fraud in connection with a matter of procedure;
f)   recognition or enforcement would be manifestly incompatible with the public policy of the State addressed.
2.   Without prejudice to such review as is necessary for the purpose of application of the provisions of this Chapter, there shall be no review of the merits of the judgment rendered by the court of origin.

Article 29 Documents to Be Produced

1.   The party seeking recognition or applying for enforcement shall produce -
a)   a complete and certified copy of the judgment;
b)   if the judgment was rendered by default, the original or a certified copy of a document establishing that the document which instituted the proceedings or an equivalent document was notified to the defaulting party;
c)   all documents required to establish that the judgment is res judicata in the State of origin or, as the case may be, is enforceable in that State;
d)   if the court addressed so requires, a translation of the documents referred to above, made by a person qualified to do so.
2.   No legalisation or similar formality may be required.
3.   If the terms of the judgment do not permit the court addressed to verify whether the conditions of this Chapter have been complied with, that court may require the production of any other necessary documents.

Article 30 Procedure
The procedure for recognition, declaration of enforceability or registration for enforcement, and the enforcement of the judgment, are governed by the law of the State addressed so far as the Convention does not provide otherwise. The court addressed shall act expeditiously.

Article 31 Costs of Proceedings
No security, bond or deposit, however described, to guarantee the payment of costs or expenses shall be required by reason only that the applicant is a national of, or has its habitual residence in, another Contracting State.

Article 32 Legal Aid
Natural persons habitually resident in a Contracting State shall be entitled, in proceedings for recognition or enforcement, to legal aid under the same conditions as apply to persons habitually resident in the requested State.

Article 33 Damages
1.   In so far as a judgment awards non-compensatory, including exemplary or punitive, damages, it shall be recognised at least to the extent that similar or comparable damages could have been awarded in the State addressed.
2. a) Where the debtor, after proceedings in which the creditor has the opportunity to be heard, satisfies the court addressed that in the circumstances, including those existing in the State of origin, grossly excessive damages have been awarded, recognition may be limited to a lesser amount.
   b)   In no event shall the court addressed recognise the judgment in an amount less than that which could have been awarded in the State addressed in the same circumstances, including those existing in the State of origin.
3.   In applying paragraph 1 or 2, the court addressed shall take into account whether and to what extent the damages awarded by the court of origin serve to cover costs and expenses relating to the proceedings.

Article 34 Severability
If the judgment contains elements which are severable, one or more of them may be separately recognised, declared enforceable, registered for enforcement, or enforced.

Article 35 Authentic Instruments
1.   Each Contracting State may declare that it will enforce, subject to reciprocity, authentic instruments formally drawn up or registered and enforceable in another Contracting State.
2.   The authentic instrument must have been authenticated by a public authority or a delegate of a public authority and the authentication must relate to both the signature and the content of the document.
[3.   The provisions concerning recognition and enforcement provided for in this Chapter shall apply as appropriate.]

Article 36 Settlements
Settlements to which a court has given its authority shall be recognised, declared enforceable or registered for enforcement in the State addressed under the same conditions as judgments falling within the Convention, so far as those conditions apply to settlements.

CHAPTER IV - GENERAL PROVISIONS
Article 37 Relationship with Other Conventions [See annex]

Article 38 Uniform Interpretation
1.   In the interpretation of the Convention, regard is to be had to its international character and to the need to promote uniformity in its application.
2.   The courts of each Contracting State shall, when applying and interpreting the Convention, take due account of the case law of other Contracting States.

[Article 39
1.   Each Contracting State shall, at the request of the Secretary General of the Hague Conference on Private International Law, send to the Permanent Bureau at regular intervals copies of
any significant decisions taken in applying the Convention and, as appropriate, other relevant
information.
2.   The Secretary General of the Hague Conference on Private International Law shall at
regular intervals convene a Special Commission to review the operation of the Convention.
3.   The Commission may make recommendations on the application or interpretation of the
Convention and may propose modifications or revisions of the Convention or the addition of
protocols.]

[Article 40
1.   Upon a joint request of the parties to a dispute in which the interpretation of the Convention is at issue, or of a court of a Contracting State, the Permanent Bureau of the Hague Conference on Private International Law shall assist in the establishment of a committee of experts to
make recommendations to such parties or such court.
[2.   The Secretary General of the Hague Conference on Private International Law shall, as soon
as possible, convene a Special Commission to draw up an optional protocol setting out rules
governing the composition and procedures of the committee of experts.]]

Article 41 Federal Clause

ANNEX
Article 37 Relationship with Other Conventions

Proposal 1
1.   The Convention does not affect any international instrument to which Contracting States
are or become Parties and which contains provisions on matters governed by the Convention,
unless a contrary declaration is made by the States Parties to such instrument.
2.   However, the Convention prevails over such instruments to the extent that they provide
for fora not authorized under the provisions of Article 18 of the Convention.
3.   The preceding paragraphs also apply to uniform laws based on special ties of a regional or
other nature between the States concerned and to instruments adopted by a community of
States.
Proposal 2
1.a) In this Article, the Brussels Convention [as amended], Regulation [...] of the European
      Union, and the Lugano Convention [as amended] shall be collectively referred to as "the
      European instruments".
b)   A State party to either of the above Conventions or a Member State of the European Union
      to which the above Regulation applies shall be collectively referred to as "European instru-
      ment States".
2.   Subject to the following provisions [of this Article], a European instrument State shall apply
the European instruments, and not the Convention, whenever the European instruments are
applicable according to their terms.
3.   Except where the provisions of the European instruments on -
a)   exclusive jurisdiction;
b)   prorogation of jurisdiction;
c)   lis pendens and related actions;
d)   protective jurisdiction for consumers or employees;
are applicable, a European instrument State shall apply Articles 3, 5 to 11, 14 to 16 and 18 of the
Convention whenever the defendant is not domiciled in a European instrument State.
4.   Even if the defendant is domiciled in a European instrument State, a court of such a State
shall apply -
a)   Article 4 of the Convention whenever the court chosen is not in a European instrument
      State;

b)   Article 12 of the Convention whenever the court with exclusive jurisdiction under that provision is not in a European instrument State; and

c)   Articles 21 and 22 of this Convention whenever the court in whose favour the proceedings are stayed or jurisdiction is declined is not a court of a European instrument State.

Note: Another provision will be needed for other conventions and instruments.

Proposal 3

5.   Judgments of courts of a Contracting State to this Convention based on jurisdiction granted under the terms of a different international convention ("other Convention") shall be recognised and enforced in courts of Contracting States to this Convention which are also Contracting States to the other Convention. This provision shall not apply if, by reservation under Article …., a Contracting State chooses -

a)   not to be governed by this provision, or

b)   not to be governed by this provision as to certain designated other conventions.

REVISED UNIFORM ENFORCEMENT OF FOREIGN JUDGMENTS ACT[1]

Section 1. Definitions

In this Act "foreign judgment" means any judgment, decree, or order of a court of the United States or of any other court which is entitled to full faith and credit in this state.

Section 2. Filing and Status of Foreign Judgments

A copy of any foreign judgment authenticated in accordance with the act of Congress or the statutes of this state may be filed in the office of the Clerk of any [District Court of any city or county] of this state. The Clerk shall treat the foreign judgment in the same manner as a judgment of the [District Court of any city or county] of this state. A judgment so filed has the same effect and is subject to the same procedures, defenses and proceedings for reopening, vacating, or staying as a judgment of a [District Court of any city or county] of this state and may be enforced or satisfied in like manner.

Section 3. Notice of Filing

(a)   At the time of the filing of the foreign judgment, the judgment creditor or his lawyer shall make and file with the Clerk of Court an affidavit setting forth the name and last known post office address of the judgment debtor, and the judgment creditor.

(b)   Promptly upon the filing of the foreign judgment and the affidavit, the Clerk shall mail notice of the filing of the foreign judgment to the judgment debtor at the address given and shall make a note of the mailing in the docket. The notice shall include the name and post office address of the judgment creditor and the judgment creditor's lawyer, if any, in this state. In addition, the judgment creditor may mail a notice of the filing of the judgment to the judgment debtor and may file proof of mailing with the Clerk. Lack of mailing notice of filing by the Clerk shall not affect the enforcement proceedings if proof of mailing by the judgment creditor has been filed.

[(c)   No execution or other process for enforcement of a foreign judgment filed hereunder shall issue until [_____] days after the date the judgment is filed.]

Section 4. Stay

(a)   If the judgment debtor shows the [District Court of any city or county] that an appeal from the foreign judgment is pending or will be taken, or that a stay of execution has been granted, the court shall stay enforcement of the foreign judgment until the appeal is concluded, the time for appeal expires, or the stay of execution expires or is vacated, upon proof that the judgment

---

1   As revised by the Uniform Law Commission, The National Conference of Commissioners on Uniform State Laws, 1964; enacted by all 50 States except California, Massachussets, and Vermont.

debtor has furnished the security for the satisfaction of the judgment required by the state in which it was rendered.

(b)   If the judgment debtor shows the [District Court of any city or county] any ground upon which enforcement of a judgment of any [District Court of any city or county] of this state would be stayed, the court shall stay enforcement of the foreign judgment for an appropriate period, upon requiring the same security for satisfaction of the judgment which is required in this state.

Section 5. Fees

Any person filing a foreign judgment shall pay to the clerk of Court _____ dollars. Fees for docketing, transcription or other enforcement proceedings shall be as provided for judgments of the [District Court of any city or county of this state].]

Section 6. Optional Procedure

The right of a judgment creditor to bring an action to enforce his judgment instead of procee-ding under this Act remains unimpaired.

Section 7. Uniformity of Interpretation

This Act shall be so interpreted and construed as to effectuate its general purpose to make uniform the law of those states which enact it.

Section 8. Short Title

This Act may be cited as the Uniform Enforcement of Foreign Judgments Act. [...]

CODE OF CIVIL PROCEDURE
SECTION 1713-1724

1713. [Official Title]

This chapter may be cited as the Uniform Foreign-Country Money Judgments Recognition Act.

1714. [Definitions]

As used in this chapter:

(a)   "Foreign country" means a government other than any of the following:

(1)   The United States.

(2)   A state, district, commonwealth, territory, or insular possession of the United States.

(3)   Any other government with regard to which the decision in this state as to whether to re-cognize a judgment of that government's courts is initially subject to determination under the Full Faith and Credit Clause of the United States Constitution.

(b)   "Foreign-country judgment" means a judgment of a court of a foreign country. "Foreign-country judgment" includes a judgment by any Indian tribe recognized by the government of the United States.

1715. [Scope of Application]

(a)   Except as otherwise provided in subdivision (b), this chapter applies to a foreign-country judgment to the extent that the judgment both:

(1)   Grants or denies recovery of a sum of money.

(2)   Under the law of the foreign country where rendered, is final, conclusive, and enforceable.

(b)   This chapter does not apply to a foreign-country judgment, even if the judgment grants or denies recovery of a sum of money, to the extent that the judgment is any of the following:

(1)   A judgment for taxes.

(2)   A fine or other penalty.

(3)   (A)   A judgment for divorce, support, or maintenance, or other judgment rendered in con-nection with domestic relations.

      (B)   A judgment for divorce, support, or maintenance, or other judgment rendered in con-nection with domestic relations may be recognized by a court of this state pursuant to Section 1723.

(c)   A party seeking recognition of a foreign-country judgment has the burden of establishing that the foreign-country judgment is entitled to recognition under this chapter.

1716. [The Duty to Recognize and Its Exceptions]

(a)   Except as otherwise provided in subdivisions (b) and (c), a court of this state shall recognize a foreign-country judgment to which this chapter applies.

(b)   A court of this state shall not recognize a foreign-country judgment if any of the following apply:

(1)   The judgment was rendered under a judicial system that does not provide impartial tribunals or procedures compatible with the requirements of due process of law.

(2)   The foreign court did not have personal jurisdiction over the defendant.

(3)   The foreign court did not have jurisdiction over the subject matter.

(c)   A court of this state is not required to recognize a foreign-country judgment if any of the following apply:

(1)   The defendant in the proceeding in the foreign court did not receive notice of the proceeding in sufficient time to enable the defendant to defend.

(2)   The judgment was obtained by fraud that deprived the losing party of an adequate opportunity to present its case.

(3)   The judgment or the cause of action or claim for relief on which the judgment is based is repugnant to the public policy of this state or of the United States.

(4)   The judgment conflicts with another final and conclusive judgment.

(5)   The proceeding in the foreign court was contrary to an agreement between the parties under which the dispute in question was to be determined otherwise than by proceedings in that foreign court.

(6)   In the case of jurisdiction based only on personal service, the foreign court was a seriously inconvenient forum for the trial of the action.

(7)   The judgment was rendered in circumstances that raise substantial doubt about the integrity of the rendering court with respect to the judgment.

(8)   The specific proceeding in the foreign court leading to the judgment was not compatible with the requirements of due process of law.

(9)   The judgment includes recovery for a claim of defamation unless the court determines that the defamation law applied by the foreign court provided at least as much protection for freedom of speech and the press as provided by both the United States and [applicable State] Constitutions.

(d)   If the party seeking recognition of a foreign-country judgment has met its burden of establishing recognition of the foreign-country judgment pursuant to subdivision (c) of Section 1715, a party resisting recognition of a foreign-country judgment has the burden of establishing that a ground for non-recognition stated in subdivision (b) or (c) exists.

1717. [Jurisdiction of the Foreign Court – Exception to Sec. 1716 (b)(2)]

(a)   A foreign-country judgment shall not be refused recognition for lack of personal jurisdiction if any of the following apply:

(1)   The defendant was served with process personally in the foreign country.

(2)   The defendant voluntarily appeared in the proceeding, other than for the purpose of protecting property seized or threatened with seizure in the proceeding or of contesting the jurisdiction of the court over the defendant.

(3)   The defendant, before the commencement of the proceeding, had agreed to submit to the jurisdiction of the foreign court with respect to the subject matter involved.

(4)   The defendant was domiciled in the foreign country when the proceeding was instituted or was a corporation or other form of business organization that had its principal place of business in, or was organized under the laws of, the foreign country.

(5)   The defendant had a business office in the foreign country and the proceeding in the foreign court involved a cause of action or claim for relief arising out of business done by the defendant through that office in the foreign country.

(6)   The defendant operated a motor vehicle or airplane in the foreign country and the proceeding involved a cause of action or claim for relief arising out of that operation.

(b)   The list of bases for personal jurisdiction in subdivision (a) is not exclusive. The courts of this state may recognize bases of personal jurisdiction other than those listed in subdivision (a) as sufficient to support a foreign-country judgment. [...]

1718. [Procedure of Recognition]

(a)   If recognition of a foreign-country judgment is sought as an original matter, the issue of recognition shall be raised by filing an action seeking recognition of the foreign-country judgment.

(b)   If recognition of a foreign-country judgment is sought in a pending action, the issue of recognition may be raised by counterclaim, cross-claim, or affirmative defense.

1719. [Effects of Recognition]

If the court in a proceeding under Section 1718 finds that the foreign-country judgment is entitled to recognition under this chapter then, to the extent that the foreign-country judgment grants or denies recovery of a sum of money, the foreign-country judgment is both of the following:

(a)   Conclusive between the parties to the same extent as the judgment of a sister state entitled to full faith and credit in this state would be conclusive.

(b)   Enforceable in the same manner and to the same extent as a judgment rendered in this state.

1720. [Appeal Pending in Foreign Court]

If a party establishes that an appeal from a foreign-country judgment is pending or will be taken in the foreign country, the court may stay any proceedings with regard to the foreign-country judgment until the appeal is concluded, the time for appeal expires, or the appellant has had sufficient time to prosecute the appeal and has failed to do so.

1721. [Deadline for Action to Recognize]

An action to recognize a foreign-country judgment shall be commenced within the earlier of the time during which the foreign-country judgment is effective in the foreign country or 10 years from the date that the foreign-country judgment became effective in the foreign country.

1722. [Interpretation]

In applying and construing this uniform act, consideration shall be given to the need to promote uniformity of the law with respect to its subject matter among states that enact it.

1723. [Recognition of Foreign Judgments Outside of this Act]

This chapter does not prevent the recognition under principles of comity or otherwise of a foreign-country judgment not within the scope of this chapter.

1724. [Transition]

(a)   This chapter applies to all actions commenced on or after the effective date of this chapter in which the issue of recognition of a foreign-country judgment is raised.

(b)   The former Uniform Foreign Money-Judgments Recognition Act (Chapter 2 (commencing with Section 1713) of Title 11 of Part 3) applies to all actions commenced before the effective date of this chapter in which the issue of recognition of a foreign-country judgment is raised.

1961 EUROPEAN CONVENTION ON INTERNATIONAL COMMERCIAL ARBITRATION[1]
(Geneva, 21 April 1961)

THE UNDERSIGNED, DULY AUTHORIZED,

CONVENED under the auspices of the Economic Commission for Europe of the United Nations.

Having noted that on 10th June 1958 at the United Nations Conference on International Commercial Arbitration has been signed in New York a Convention on the Recognition and Enforcement of Foreign Arbitral Awards,

DESIROUS of promoting the development of European trade by, as far as possible, removing certain difficulties that may impede the organization and operation of international commercial arbitration in relations between physical or legal persons of different European countries,

HAVE AGREED on the following provisions:

Article I - Scope of the Convention

1. This Convention shall apply:
(a) to arbitration agreements concluded for the purpose of settling disputes arising from international trade between physical or legal persons having, when concluding the agreement, their habitual place of residence or their seat in different Contracting States;
(b) to arbitral procedures and awards based on agreements referred to in paragraph 1(a) above.
2. For the purpose of this Convention,
(a) the term: "arbitration agreement" shall mean either an arbitral clause in a contract or an arbitration agreement, the contract or arbitration agreement being signed by the parties, or contained in an exchange of letters, telegrams, or in a communication by teleprinter and, in relations between States whose laws do not require that an arbitration agreement be made in writing, any arbitration agreement concluded in the form authorized by these laws;
(b) the term "arbitration" shall mean not only settlement by arbitrators appointed for each case (ad hoc arbitration) but also by permanent arbitral institutions;
(c) the term "seat" shall mean the place of the situation of the establishment that has made the arbitration agreement.

Article II - Right of Legal Persons of Public Law to Resort to Arbitration

1. In cases referred to in Article I, paragraph 1, of this Convention, legal persons considered by the law which is applicable to them as "legal persons of public law" have the right to conclude valid arbitration agreements.
2. On signing, ratifying or acceding to this Convention any State shall be entitled to declare that it limits the above faculty to such conditions as may be stated in its declaration.

Article III - Right of Foreign Nationals to Be Designated as Arbitrators

In arbitration covered by this Convention, foreign nationals may be designated as arbitrators.

Article IV - Organization of the Arbitration

1. The parties to an arbitration agreement shall be free to submit their disputes:
(a) to a permanent arbitral institution; in this case, the arbitration proceedings shall be held in conformity with the rules of the said institution;
(b) to an ad hoc arbitral procedure; in this case, they shall be free inter alia
  (i) to appoint arbitrators or to establish means for their appointment in the event of an actual dispute;
  (ii) to determine the place of arbitration; and
  (iii) to lay down the procedure to be followed by the arbitrators.

---

1   United Nations, Treaty Series , Vol. 484, p. 364 No. 7041 (1963-1964).

2.   Where the parties have agreed to submit any disputes to an ad hoc arbitration, and where within thirty days of the notification of the request for arbitration to the respondent one of the parties fails to appoint his arbitrator, the latter shall, unless otherwise provided, be appointed at the request of the other party by the President of the competent Chamber of Commerce of the country of the defaulting party's habitual place of residence or seat at the time of the introduction of the request for arbitration. This paragraph shall also apply to the replacement of the arbitrator(s) appointed by one of the parties or by the President of the Chamber of Commerce above referred to.

3.   Where the parties have agreed to submit any disputes to an ad hoc arbitration by one or more arbitrators and the arbitration agreement contains no indication regarding the organization of the arbitration, as mentioned in paragraph 1 of this Article, the necessary steps shall be taken by the arbitrator(s) already appointed, unless the parties are able to agree thereon and without prejudice to the case referred to in paragraph 2 above. Where the parties cannot agree on the appointment of the sole arbitrator or where the arbitrators appointed cannot agree on the measures to be taken, the claimant shall apply for the necessary action, where the place of arbitration has been agreed upon by the parties, at his option to the President of the Chamber of Commerce of the place of arbitration agreed upon or to the President of the competent Chamber of Commerce of the respondent's habitual place of residence or seat at the time of the introduction of the request for arbitration. Where such a place has not been agreed upon, the claimant shall be entitled at his option to apply for the necessary action either to the President of the competent Chamber of Commerce of the country of the respondent's habitual place of residence or seat at the time of the introduction of the request for arbitration, or to the Special Committee whose composition and procedure are specified in the Annex to this Convention. Where the claimant fails to exercise the rights given to him under this paragraph the respondent or the arbitrator(s) shall be entitled to do so.

4.   When seized of a request the President or the Special Committee shall be entitled as need be:

(a)   to appoint the sole arbitrator, presiding arbitrator, umpire, or referee;

(b)   to replace the arbitrator(s) appointed under any procedure other than that referred to in paragraph 2 above;

(c)   to determine the place of arbitration, provided that the arbitrator(s) may fix another place of arbitration;

(d)   to establish directly or by reference to the rules and statutes of a permanent arbitral institution the rules of procedure to be followed by the arbitrator(s), provided that the arbitrators have not established these rules themselves in the absence of any agreement thereon between the parties.

5.   Where the parties have agreed to submit their disputes to a permanent arbitral institution without determining the institution in question and cannot agree thereon, the claimant may request the determination of such institution in conformity with the procedure referred to in paragraph 3 above.

6.   Where the arbitration agreement does not specify the mode of arbitration (arbitration by a permanent arbitral institution or an ad hoc arbitration) to which the parties have agreed to submit their dispute, and where the parties cannot agree thereon, the claimant shall be entitled to have recourse in this case to the procedure referred to in paragraph 3 to determine the question. The President of the competent Chamber of Commerce or the Special Committee, shall be entitled either to refer the parties to a permanent arbitral institution or to request the parties to appoint their arbitrator within such time-limits as the President of the competent Chamber of Commerce or the Special Committee may have fixed and to agree within such time-limits on the necessary measures for the functioning of the arbitration. In the latter case, the provisions of paragraphs 2, 3 and 4 of this Article shall apply.

7.   Where within a period of sixty days from the moment when he was requested to fulfil one of the functions set out in paragraphs 2, 3, 4, 5 and 6 of this Article, the President of the

Chamber of Commerce designated by virtue of these paragraphs has not fulfilled one of these functions, the party requesting shall be entitled to ask the Special Committee to do so.

Article V - Plea as to Arbitral Jurisdiction

1.   The party which intends to raise a plea as to the arbitrator's jurisdiction based on the fact that the arbitration agreement was either non-existent or null and void or had lapsed shall do so during the arbitration proceedings, not later than the delivery of its statement of claim or defence relating to the substance of the dispute; those based on the fact that an arbitrator has exceeded his terms of reference shall be raised during the arbitration proceedings as soon as the question on which the arbitrator is alleged to have no jurisdiction is raised during the arbitral procedure. Where the delay in raising the plea is due to a cause which the arbitrator deems justified, the arbitrator shall declare the plea admissible.

2.   Pleas to the jurisdiction referred to in paragraph 1 above that have not been raised during the time-limits there referred to, may not be entered either during a subsequent stage of the arbitral proceedings where they are pleas left to the sole discretion of the parties under the law applicable by the arbitrator, or during subsequent court proceedings concerning the substance or the enforcement of the award where such pleas are left to the discretion of the parties under the rule of conflict of the court seized of the substance of the dispute or the enforcement of the award. The arbitrator's decision on the delay in raising the plea, will, however, be subject to judicial control.

3.   Subject to any subsequent judicial control provided for under the lex fori, the arbitrator whose jurisdiction is called in question shall be entitled to proceed with the arbitration, to rule on his own jurisdiction and to decide upon the existence or the validity of the arbitration agreement or of the contract of which the agreement forms part.

Article VI - Jurisdiction of Courts of Law

1.   A plea as to the jurisdiction of the court made before the court seized by either party to the arbitration agreement, on the basis of the fact that an arbitration agreement exists shall, under penalty of estoppel, be presented by the respondent before or at the same time as the presentation of his substantial defence, depending upon whether the law of the court seized regards this plea as one of procedure or of substance.

2.   In taking a decision concerning the existence or the validity of an arbitration agreement, courts of Contracting States shall examine the validity of such agreement with reference to the capacity of the parties, under the law applicable to them, and with reference to other questions.

(a)   under the law to which the parties have subjected their arbitration agreement;

(b)   failing any indication thereon, under the law of the country in which the award is to be made;

(c)   failing any indication as to the law to which the parties have subjected the agreement, and where at the time when the question is raised in court the country in which the award is to be made cannot be determined, under the competent law by virtue of the rules of conflict of the court seized of the dispute.

The courts may also refuse recognition of the arbitration agreement if under the law of their country the dispute is not capable of settlement by arbitration.

3.   Where either party to an arbitration agreement has initiated arbitration proceedings before any resort is had to a court, courts of Contracting States subsequently asked to deal with the same subject-matter between the same parties or with the question whether the arbitration agreement was non-existent or null and void or had lapsed, shall stay their ruling on the arbitrator's jurisdiction until the arbitral award is made, unless they have good and substantial reasons to the contrary.

4.   A request for interim measures or measures of conservation addressed to a judicial authority shall not be deemed incompatible with the arbitration agreement, or regarded as a submission of the substance of the case to the court.

Article VII - Applicable Law

1.   The parties shall be free to determine, by agreement, the law to be applied by the arbitrators to the substance of the dispute. Failing any indication by the parties as to the applicable law, the arbitrators shall apply the proper law under the rule of conflict that the arbitrators deem applicable. In both cases the arbitrators shall take account of the terms of the contract and trade usages.

2.   The arbitrators shall act as amiables compositeurs if the parties so decide and if they may do so under the law applicable to the arbitration.

Article VIII - Reasons for the Award

The parties shall be presumed to have agreed that reasons shall be given for the award unless they
(a)   either expressly declare that reasons shall not be given; or
(b)   have assented to an arbitral procedure under which it is not customary to give reasons for awards, provided that in this case neither party requests before the end of the hearing, or if there has not been a hearing then before the making of the award, that reasons be given.

Article IX - Setting Aside of the Arbitral Award

1.   The setting aside in a Contracting State of an arbitral award covered by this Convention shall only constitute a ground for the refusal of recognition or enforcement in another Contracting State where such setting aside took place in a State in which, or under the law of which, the award has been made and for one of the following reasons:
(a)   the parties to the arbitration agreement were under the law applicable to them, under some incapacity or the said agreement is not valid under the law to which the parties have subjected it or, failing any indication thereon, under the law of the country where the award was made, or
(b)   the party requesting the setting aside of the award was not given proper notice of the appointment of the arbitrator or of the arbitration proceedings or was otherwise unable to present his case; or
(c)   the award deals with a difference not contemplated by or not falling within the terms of the submission to arbitration, or it contains decisions on matters beyond the scope of the submission to arbitration, provided that, if the decisions on matters submitted to arbitration can be separated from those not so submitted, that part of the award which contains decisions on matters submitted to arbitration need not be set aside;
(d)   the composition of the arbitral authority or the arbitral procedure was not in accordance with the agreement of the parties, or failing such agreement, with the provisions of Article IV of this Convention.

2.   In relations between Contracting States that are also parties to the New York Convention on the Recognition and Enforcement of Foreign Arbitral Awards of 10th June 1958, paragraph 1 of this Article limits the application of Article V (1) (e) of the New York Convention solely to the cases of setting aside set out under paragraph 1 above.

Article X - Final Clauses

1.   This Convention is open for signature or accession by countries members of the Economic Commission for Europe and countries admitted to the Commission in a consultative capacity under paragraph 8 of the Commission's terms of reference.

2.   Such countries as may participate in certain activities of the Economic Commission for Europe in accordance with paragraph 11 of the Commission's terms of reference may become Contracting Parties to this Convention by acceding thereto after its entry into force.

3.   The Convention shall be open for signature until 31 December 1961 inclusive. Thereafter, it shall be open for accession.

4.   This Convention shall be ratified.

5.   Ratification or accession shall be effected by the deposit of an instrument with the Secretary-General of the United Nations.

6.   When signing, ratifying or acceding to this Convention, the Contracting Parties shall communicate to the Secretary-General of the United Nations a list of the Chambers of Commerce or other institutions in their country who will exercise the functions conferred by virtue of Article IV of this Convention on Presidents of the competent Chambers of Commerce.

7.   The provisions of the present Convention shall not affect the validity of multi-lateral or bilateral agreements concerning arbitration entered into by Contracting States.

8.   This Convention shall come into force on the ninetieth day after five of the countries referred to in paragraph 1 above have deposited their instruments of ratification or accession. For any country ratifying or acceding to it later this Convention shall enter into force on the ninetieth day after the said country has deposited its instrument of ratification or accession.

9.   Any Contracting Party may denounce this Convention by so notifying the Secretary-General of the United Nations. Denunciation shall take effect twelve months after the date of receipt by the Secretary-General of the notification of denunciation.

10.   If, after the entry into force of this Convention, the number of Contracting Parties is reduced, as a result of denunciations, to less than five, the Convention shall cease to be in force from the date on which the last of such denunciations takes effect.

11.   The Secretary-General of the United Nations shall notify the countries referred to in paragraph 1, and the countries which have become Contracting Parties under paragraph 2 above, of
(a)   declarations made under Article II, paragraph 2;
(b)   ratifications and accessions under paragraphs 1 and 2 above;
(c)   communications received in pursuance of paragraph 6 above;
(d)   the dates of entry into force of this Convention in accordance with paragraph 8 above;
(e)   denunciations under paragraph 9 above;
(f)   the termination of this Convention in accordance with paragraph 10 above.

12.   After 31 December 1961, the original of this Convention shall be deposited with the Secretary-General of the United Nations, who shall transmit certified true copies to each of the countries mentioned in paragraphs 1 and 2 above.

IN WITNESS THEREOF the undersigned, being duly authorized thereto, have signed this Convention.

DONE at Geneva, this twenty-first day of April, one thousand nine hundred and sixty-one, in a single copy in the English, French and Russian languages, each text being equally authentic.

Annex
COMPOSITION AND PROCEDURE OF THE SPECIAL COMMITTEE
REFERRED TO IN Article IV OF THE CONVENTION

1.   The Special Committee referred to in Article IV of the Convention shall consist of two regular members and a Chairman. One of the regular members shall be elected by the Chambers of Commerce or other institutions designated, under Article X, paragraph 6, of the Convention, by States in which at the time when the Convention is open to signature national Committees of the International Chamber of Commerce exist, and which at the time of the election are parties to the Convention. The other member shall be elected by the Chambers of Commerce or other institutions designated, under Article X, paragraph 6, of the Convention, by States in which at the time when the Convention is open to signature no National Committees of the International Chamber of Commerce exist and which at the time of the election are parties to the Convention.

2.   The persons who are to act as Chairman of the Special Committee pursuant to paragraph 7 of this Annex shall also be elected in like manner by the Chambers of Commerce or other institutions referred to in paragraph 1 of this Annex.

3.   The Chambers of Commerce or other institutions referred to in paragraph 1 of this Annex shall elect alternates at the same time and in the same manner as they elect the Chairman and other regular members, in case of the temporary inability of the Chairman or regular members to act. In the event of the permanent inability to act or of the resignation of a Chairman or of a

regular member, then the alternate elected to replace him shall become, as the case may be, the Chairman or regular member, and the group of Chambers of Commerce or other institutions which had elected the alternate who has become Chairman or regular member shall elect another alternate.

4.   The first elections to the Committee shall be held within ninety days from the date of the deposit of the fifth instrument of ratification or accession. Chambers of Commerce and other institutions designated by Signatory States who are not yet parties to the Convention shall also be entitled to take part in these elections. If however it should not be possible to hold elections within the prescribed period, the entry into force of paragraphs 3 to 7 of Article IV of the Convention shall be postponed until elections are held as provided for above.

5.   Subject to the provisions of paragraph 7 below, the members of the Special Committee shall be elected for a term of four years. New elections shall be held within the first six months of the fourth year following the previous elections. Nevertheless, if a new procedure for the election of the members of the Special Committee has not produced results, the members previously elected shall continue to exercise their functions until the election of new members.

6.   The results of the elections of the members of the Special Committee shall be communicated to the Secretary-General of the United Nations who shall notify the States referred to in Article X, paragraph 1, of the Convention and the States which have become Contracting Parties under Article X, paragraph 2. The Secretary-General shall likewise notify the said States of any postponement and of the entry into force of paragraphs 3 and 7 of Article IV of the Convention in pursuance of paragraph 4 of this Annex.

7.   The persons elected to the office of Chairman shall exercise their functions in rotation, each during a period of two years. The question which of these two persons shall act as chairman during the first two-year period after entry into force of the Convention shall be decided by the drawing of lots. The office of Chairman shall thereafter be vested, for each successive two year period, in the person elected Chairman by the group of countries other than that by which the Chairman exercising his functions during the immediately preceding two-year period was elected.

8.   The reference to the Special Committee of one of the requests referred to in paragraphs 3 to 7 of the aforesaid Article IV shall be addressed to the Executive Secretary of the Economic Commission for Europe. The Executive Secretary shall in the first instance lay the request before the member of the Special Committee elected by the group of countries other than that by which the Chairman holding office at the time of the introduction of the request was elected. The proposal of the member applied to in the first instance shall be communicated by the Executive Secretary to the other member of the Committee and, if that other member agrees to this proposal, it shall be deemed to be the Committee's ruling and shall be communicated as such by the Executive Secretary to the person who made the request.

9.   If the two members of the Special Committee applied to by the Executive Secretary are unable to agree on a ruling by correspondence, the Executive Secretary of the Economic Commission for Europe shall convene a meeting of the said Committee at Geneva in an attempt to secure a unanimous decision of unanimity, the Committee's decision shall be given by a majority vote and shall be communicated by the Executive Secretary to the person who made the request.

10.   The expenses connected with the Special Committee's action shall be advanced by the person requesting such action but shall be considered as costs in the cause.

Entry into force: 7 January 1964
Ratification and binding effect: Albania (2001), Austria (1964), Azerbaijan (2005), Belarus (1963), Belgium (1975), Bosnia and Herzegovina (1993), Bulgaria (1964), Burkina Faso (1965), Croatia (1993), Cuba (1965), Czech Republic (1993), Denmark (1972), France (1966), Germany (1964), Hungary (1963), Italy (1970), Kazakhstan (1995), Latvia (2003), Luxembourg (1982), Macedonia (1994), Moldova (1998), Montenegro (2006), Poland (1964), Romania (1963), Russian Federation (1962), Serbia (2001, Slovakia (1993), Slovenia (1992), Spain (1975), Turkey (1992), Ukraine (1963)

1975 INTER-AMERICAN CONVENTION ON INTERNATIONAL COMMERCIAL ARBITRATION [1]

The Governments of the Member States of the Organization of American States
DESIROUS of concluding a convention on international commercial arbitration,
HAVE AGREED as follows:

Article 1

An agreement in which the parties undertake to submit to arbitral decision any differences that may arise or have arisen between them with respect to a commercial transaction is valid. The agreement shall be set forth in an instrument signed by the parties, or in the form of an exchange of letters, telegrams, or telex communications.

Article 2

Arbitrators shall be appointed in the manner agreed upon by the parties. Their appointment may be delegated to a third party, whether a natural or juridical person. Arbitrators may be nationals or foreigners.

Article 3

In the absence of an express agreement between the parties, the arbitration shall be conducted in accordance with the rules of procedure of the Inter-American Commercial Arbitration Commission.

Article 4

An arbitral decision or award that is not appealable under the applicable law or procedural rules shall have the force of a final judicial judgment. Its execution or recognition may be ordered in the same manner as that of decisions handed down by national or foreign ordinary courts, in accordance with the procedural laws of the country where it is to be executed and the provisions of international treaties.

Article 5

1.   The recognition and execution of the decision may be refused, at the request of the party against which it is made, only if such party is able to prove to the competent authority of the State in which recognition and execution are requested:

a.   That the parties to the agreement were subject to some incapacity under the applicable law or that the agreement is not valid under the law to which the parties have submitted it, or, if such law is not specified, under the law of the State in which the decision was made; or

b.   That the party against which the arbitral decision has been made was not duly notified of the appointment of the arbitrator or of the arbitration procedure to be followed, or was unable, for any other reason, to present his defense; or

c.   That the decision concerns a dispute not envisaged in the agreement between the parties to submit to arbitration; nevertheless, if the provisions of the decision that refer to issues submitted to arbitration can be separated from those not submitted to arbitration, the former may be recognized and executed; or

d.   That the constitution of the arbitral tribunal or the arbitration procedure has not been carried out in accordance with the terms of the agreement signed by the parties or, in the absence of such agreement, that the constitution of the arbitral tribunal or the arbitration procedure has not been carried out in accordance with the law of the State where the arbitration took place; or

e.   That the decision is not yet binding on the parties or has been annulled or suspended by a competent authority of the State in which, or according to the law of which, the decision has been made.

2.   The recognition and execution of an arbitral decision may also be refused if the competent authority of the State in which the recognition and execution is requested finds:

---

1   © Organization of American States, Washington DC.

a.   That the subject of the dispute cannot be settled by arbitration under the law of that State; or
b.   That the recognition or execution of the decision would be contrary to the public policy ("ordre public") of that State.

Article 6

If the competent authority mentioned in Article 5. 1. e has been requested to annul or suspend the arbitral decision, the authority before which such decision is invoked may, if it deems it appropriate, postpone a decision on the execution of the arbitral decision and, at the request of the party requesting execution, may also instruct the other party to provide appropriate guaranties.

Article 7

This Convention shall be open for signature by the Member States of the Organization of American States.

Article 8

This Convention is subject to ratification. The instruments of ratification shall be deposited with the General Secretariat of the Organization of American States.

Article 9

This Convention shall remain open for accession by any other State. The instruments of accession shall be deposited with the General Secretariat of the Organization of American States.

Article 10

This Convention shall enter into force on the thirtieth day following the date of deposit of the second instrument of ratification.

For each State ratifying or acceding to the Convention after the deposit of the second instrument of ratification, the Convention shall enter into force on the thirtieth day after deposit by such State of its instrument of ratification or accession.

Article 11

If a State Party has two or more territorial units in which different systems of law apply in relation to the matters dealt with in this Convention, it may, at the time of signature, ratification or accession, declare that this Convention shall extend to all its territorial units or only to one or more of them.

Such declaration may be modified by subsequent declarations, which shall expressly indicate the territorial unit or units to which the Convention applies. Such subsequent declarations shall be transmitted to the General Secretariat of the Organization of American States, and shall become effective thirty days after the date of their receipt.

Article 12

This Convention shall remain in force indefinitely, but any of the States Parties may denounce it. The instrument of denunciation shall be deposited with the General Secretariat of the Organization of American States. After one year from the date of deposit of the instrument of denunciation, the Convention shall no longer be in effect for the denouncing State, but shall remain in effect for the other States Parties.

Article 13

The original instrument of this Convention, the English, French, Portuguese and Spanish texts of which are equally authentic, shall be deposited with the General Secretariat of the Organization of American States. The Secretariat shall notify the lumber States of the Organization of American States and the States that have acceded to the Convention of the signatures, deposits of instruments of ratification, accession, and denunciation as well as of reservations, if any. It shall also transmit the declarations referred to in Article 11 of this Convention.

IN WITNESS WHEREOF the undersigned Plenipotentiaries, being duly authorized thereto by their respective Governments, have signed this Convention.

DONE AT PANAMA CITY, Republic of Panama, this thirtieth day of January one thousand nine hundred and seventy-five.

Entry into force: 16 June 1976
Ratification and binding effect: Argentina (1995), Bolivia (1999), Brazil (1995), Chile (1976), Colombia (1986), Costa Rica (1978), Dominican Republic (2008), Ecuador (1991), El Salvador (1980), Guatemala (1986), Honduras (1979), Mexico (1978), Nicaragua (2003), Panama (1975), Paraguay (1976), Peru (1989), United States of America (1990), Uruguay (1977), Venezuela (1985)

UNCITRAL ARBITRATION RULES[1]
(as revised in 2010)
Section I. Introductory Rules
Article 1 Scope of Application
1.   Where parties have agreed that disputes between them in respect of a defined legal relationship, whether contractual or not, shall be referred to arbitration under the UNCITRAL Arbitration Rules, then such disputes shall be settled in accordance with these Rules subject to such modification as the parties may agree.
2.   The parties to an arbitration agreement concluded after 15 August 2010 shall be presumed to have referred to the Rules in effect on the date of commencement of the arbitration, unless the parties have agreed to apply a particular version of the Rules.

That presumption does not apply where the arbitration agreement has been concluded by accepting after 15 August 2010 an offer made before that date.
3.   These Rules shall govern the arbitration except that where any of these Rules is in conflict with a provision of the law applicable to the arbitration from which the parties cannot derogate, that provision shall prevail.

Article 2 Notice and Calculation of Periods of Time
1.   A notice, including a notification, communication or proposal, may be transmitted by any means of communication that provides or allows for a record of its transmission.
2.   If an address has been designated by a party specifically for this purpose or authorized by the arbitral tribunal, any notice shall be delivered to that party at that address, and if so delivered shall be deemed to have been received. Delivery by electronic means such as facsimile or e-mail may only be made to an address so designated or authorized.
3.   In the absence of such designation or authorization, a notice is:
(a)   Received if it is physically delivered to the addressee; or
(b)   Deemed to have been received if it is delivered at the place of business, habitual residence or mailing address of the addressee.
4.   If, after reasonable efforts, delivery cannot be effected in accordance with paragraphs 2 or 3, a notice is deemed to have been received if it is sent to the addressee's last-known place of business, habitual residence or mailing address by registered letter or any other means that provides a record of delivery or of attempted delivery.
5.   A notice shall be deemed to have been received on the day it is delivered in accordance with paragraphs 2, 3 or 4, or attempted to be delivered in accordance with paragraph 4. A notice transmitted by electronic means is deemed to have been received on the day it is sent, except that a notice of arbitration so transmitted is only deemed to have been received on the day when it reaches the addressee's electronic address.
6.   For the purpose of calculating a period of time under these Rules, such period shall begin to run on the day following the day when a notice is received. If the last day of such period is an official holiday or a non-business day at the residence or place of business of the addressee, the

---

1   © United Nations, GA Res. 65/22, New York 2011; and United Nations Commission on International Trade Law (UNCITRAL), Vienna 2010. All rights reserved.

period is extended until the first business day which follows. Official holidays or nonbusiness days occurring during the running of the period of time are included in calculating the period.

Article 3 Notice of Arbitration

1.   The party or parties initiating recourse to arbitration (hereinafter called the "claimant") shall communicate to the other party or parties (hereinafter called the "respondent") a notice of arbitration.
2.   Arbitral proceedings shall be deemed to commence on the date on which the notice of arbitration is received by the respondent.
3.   The notice of arbitration shall include the following:
(a)   A demand that the dispute be referred to arbitration;
(b)   The names and contact details of the parties;
(c)   Identification of the arbitration agreement that is invoked;
(d)   Identification of any contract or other legal instrument out of or in relation to which the dispute arises or, in the absence of such contract or instrument, a brief description of the relevant relationship;
(e)   A brief description of the claim and an indication of the amount involved, if any;
(f)   The relief or remedy sought;
(g)   A proposal as to the number of arbitrators, language and place of arbitration, if the parties have not previously agreed thereon.
4.   The notice of arbitration may also include:
(a)   A proposal for the designation of an appointing authority referred to in Article 6, paragraph 1;
(b)   A proposal for the appointment of a sole arbitrator referred to in Article 8, paragraph 1;
(c)   Notification of the appointment of an arbitrator referred to in Article 9 or 10.
5.   The constitution of the arbitral tribunal shall not be hindered by any controversy with respect to the sufficiency of the notice of arbitration, which shall be finally resolved by the arbitral tribunal.

Article 4 Response to the Notice of Arbitration

1.   Within 30 days of the receipt of the notice of arbitration, the respondent shall communicate to the claimant a response to the notice of arbitration, which shall include:
(a)   The name and contact details of each respondent;
(b)   A response to the information set forth in the notice of arbitration, pursuant to Article 3, paragraphs 3 (c) to (g).
2.   The response to the notice of arbitration may also include:
(a)   Any plea that an arbitral tribunal to be constituted under these Rules lacks jurisdiction;
(b)   A proposal for the designation of an appointing authority referred to in Article 6, paragraph 1;
(c)   A proposal for the appointment of a sole arbitrator referred to in Article 8, paragraph 1;
(d)   Notification of the appointment of an arbitrator referred to in Article 9 or 10;
(e)   A brief description of counterclaims or claims for the purpose of a set-off, if any, including where relevant, an indication of the amounts involved, and the relief or remedy sought;
(f)   A notice of arbitration in accordance with Article 3 in case the respondent formulates a claim against a party to the arbitration agreement other than the claimant.
3.   The constitution of the arbitral tribunal shall not be hindered by any controversy with respect to the respondent's failure to communicate a response to the notice of arbitration, or an incomplete or late response to the notice of arbitration, which shall be finally resolved by the arbitral tribunal.

Article 5 Representation and Assistance

Each party may be represented or assisted by persons chosen by it.
         The names and addresses of such persons must be communicated to all parties and to the arbitral tribunal. Such communication must specify whether the appointment is being made for purposes of representation or assistance. Where a person is to act as a representative of a party, the arbitral tribunal, on its own initiative or at the request of any party, may at any time require

proof of authority granted to the representative in such a form as the arbitral tribunal may determine.

Article 6 Designating and Appointing Authorities

1.   Unless the parties have already agreed on the choice of an appointing authority, a party may at any time propose the name or names of one or more institutions or persons, including the Secretary-General of the Permanent Court of Arbitration at The Hague (hereinafter called the "PCA"), one of whom would serve as appointing authority.

2.   If all parties have not agreed on the choice of an appointing authority within 30 days after a proposal made in accordance with paragraph 1 has been received by all other parties, any party may request the Secretary-General of the PCA to designate the appointing authority.

3.   Where these Rules provide for a period of time within which a party must refer a matter to an appointing authority and no appointing authority has been agreed on or designated, the period is suspended from the date on which a party initiates the procedure for agreeing on or designating an appointing authority until the date of such agreement or designation.

4.   Except as referred to in Article 41, paragraph 4, if the appointing authority refuses to act, or if it fails to appoint an arbitrator within 30 days after it receives a party's request to do so, fails to act within any other period provided by these Rules, or fails to decide on a challenge to an arbitrator within a reasonable time after receiving a party's request to do so, any party may request the Secretary-General of the PCA to designate a substitute appointing authority.

5.   In exercising their functions under these Rules, the appointing authority and the Secretary-General of the PCA may require from any party and the arbitrators the information they deem necessary and they shall give the parties and, where appropriate, the arbitrators, an opportunity to present their views in any manner they consider appropriate. All such communications to and from the appointing authority and the Secretary-General of the PCA shall also be provided by the sender to all other parties.

6.   When the appointing authority is requested to appoint an arbitrator pursuant to articles 8, 9, 10 or 14, the party making the request shall send to the appointing authority copies of the notice of arbitration and, if it exists, any response to the notice of arbitration.

7.   The appointing authority shall have regard to such considerations as are likely to secure the appointment of an independent and impartial arbitrator and shall take into account the advisability of appointing an arbitrator of a nationality other than the nationalities of the parties.

Section II. Composition of the Arbitral Tribunal

Article 7 Number of Arbitrators

1.   If the parties have not previously agreed on the number of arbitrators, and if within 30 days after the receipt by the respondent of the notice of arbitration the parties have not agreed that there shall be only one arbitrator, three arbitrators shall be appointed.

2.   Notwithstanding paragraph 1, if no other parties have responded to a party's proposal to appoint a sole arbitrator within the time limit provided for in paragraph 1 and the party or parties concerned have failed to appoint a second arbitrator in accordance with Article 9 or 10, the appointing authority may, at the request of a party, appoint a sole arbitrator pursuant to the procedure provided for in Article 8, paragraph 2, if it determines that, in view of the circumstances of the case, this is more appropriate.

Article 8 Appointment of Arbitrators (Articles 8 to 10)

1.   If the parties have agreed that a sole arbitrator is to be appointed and if within 30 days after receipt by all other parties of a proposal for the appointment of a sole arbitrator the parties have not reached agreement thereon, a sole arbitrator shall, at the request of a party, be appointed by the appointing authority.

2.   The appointing authority shall appoint the sole arbitrator as promptly as possible. In making the appointment, the appointing authority shall use the following list-procedure, unless the parties agree that the list-procedure should not be used or unless the appointing authority determines in its discretion that the use of the list-procedure is not appropriate for the case:

(a) The appointing authority shall communicate to each of the parties an identical list containing at least three names;
(b) Within 15 days after the receipt of this list, each party may return the list to the appointing authority after having deleted the name or names to which it objects and numbered the remaining names on the list in the order of its preference;
(c) After the expiration of the above period of time the appointing authority shall appoint the sole arbitrator from among the names approved on the lists returned to it and in accordance with the order of preference indicated by the parties;
(d) If for any reason the appointment cannot be made according to this procedure, the appointing authority may exercise its discretion in appointing the sole arbitrator.

Article 9

1. If three arbitrators are to be appointed, each party shall appoint one arbitrator. The two arbitrators thus appointed shall choose the third arbitrator who will act as the presiding arbitrator of the arbitral tribunal.
2. If within 30 days after the receipt of a party's notification of the appointment of an arbitrator the other party has not notified the first party of the arbitrator it has appointed, the first party may request the appointing authority to appoint the second arbitrator.
3. If within 30 days after the appointment of the second arbitrator the two arbitrators have not agreed on the choice of the presiding arbitrator, the presiding arbitrator shall be appointed by the appointing authority in the same way as a sole arbitrator would be appointed under Article 8.

Article 10

1. For the purposes of Article 9, paragraph 1, where three arbitrators are to be appointed and there are multiple parties as claimant or as respondent, unless the parties have agreed to another method of appointment of arbitrators, the multiple parties jointly, whether as claimant or as respondent, shall appoint an arbitrator.
2. If the parties have agreed that the arbitral tribunal is to be composed of a number of arbitrators other than one or three, the arbitrators shall be appointed according to the method agreed upon by the parties.
3. In the event of any failure to constitute the arbitral tribunal under these Rules, the appointing authority shall, at the request of any party, constitute the arbitral tribunal and, in doing so, may revoke any appointment already made and appoint or reappoint each of the arbitrators and designate one of them as the presiding arbitrator.

Article 11 Disclosures by and Challenge of Arbitrators (Articles 11 to 13)

When a person is approached in connection with his or her possible appointment as an arbitrator, he or she shall disclose any circumstances likely to give rise to justifiable doubts as to his or her impartiality or independence. An arbitrator, from the time of his or her appointment and throughout the arbitral proceedings, shall without delay disclose any such circumstances to the parties and the other arbitrators unless they have already been informed by him or her of these circumstances.

Article 12

1. Any arbitrator may be challenged if circumstances exist that give rise to justifiable doubts as to the arbitrator's impartiality or independence.
2. A party may challenge the arbitrator appointed by it only for reasons of which it becomes aware after the appointment has been made.
3. In the event that an arbitrator fails to act or in the event of the de jure or de facto impossibility of his or her performing his or her functions, the procedure in respect of the challenge of an arbitrator as provided in Article 13 shall apply.

Article 13

1. A party that intends to challenge an arbitrator shall send notice of its challenge within 15 days after it has been notified of the appointment of the challenged arbitrator, or within 15 days

after the circumstances mentioned in articles 11 and 12 became known to that party.

2.   The notice of challenge shall be communicated to all other parties, to the arbitrator who is challenged and to the other arbitrators. The notice of challenge shall state the reasons for the challenge.

3.   When an arbitrator has been challenged by a party, all parties may agree to the challenge. The arbitrator may also, after the challenge, withdraw from his or her office. In neither case does this imply acceptance of the validity of the grounds for the challenge.

4.   If, within 15 days from the date of the notice of challenge, all parties do not agree to the challenge or the challenged arbitrator does not withdraw, the party making the challenge may elect to pursue it. In that case, within 30 days from the date of the notice of challenge, it shall seek a decision on the challenge by the appointing authority.

Article 14 Replacement of an Arbitrator

1.   Subject to paragraph 2, in any event where an arbitrator has to be replaced during the course of the arbitral proceedings, a substitute arbitrator shall be appointed or chosen pursuant to the procedure provided for in articles 8 to 11 that was applicable to the appointment or choice of the arbitrator being replaced. This procedure shall apply even if during the process of appointing the arbitrator to be replaced, a party had failed to exercise its right to appoint or to participate in the appointment.

2.   If, at the request of a party, the appointing authority determines that, in view of the exceptional circumstances of the case, it would be justified for a party to be deprived of its right to appoint a substitute arbitrator, the appointing authority may, after giving an opportunity to the parties and the remaining arbitrators to express their views: (a) appoint the substitute arbitrator; or (b) after the closure of the hearings, authorize the other arbitrators to proceed with the arbitration and make any decision or award.

Article 15 Repetition of Hearings in the Event of the Replacement of an Arbitrator

If an arbitrator is replaced, the proceedings shall resume at the stage where the arbitrator who was replaced ceased to perform his or her functions, unless the arbitral tribunal decides otherwise.

Article 16 Exclusion of Liability

Save for intentional wrongdoing, the parties waive, to the fullest extent permitted under the applicable law, any claim against the arbitrators, the appointing authority and any person appointed by the arbitral tribunal based on any act or omission in connection with the arbitration.

Section III. Arbitral Proceedings

Article 17 General Provisions

1.   Subject to these Rules, the arbitral tribunal may conduct the arbitration in such manner as it considers appropriate, provided that the parties are treated with equality and that at an appropriate stage of the proceedings each party is given a reasonable opportunity of presenting its case. The arbitral tribunal, in exercising its discretion, shall conduct the proceedings so as to avoid unnecessary delay and expense and to provide a fair and efficient process for resolving the parties' dispute.

2.   As soon as practicable after its constitution and after inviting the parties to express their views, the arbitral tribunal shall establish the provisional timetable of the arbitration. The arbitral tribunal may, at any time, after inviting the parties to express their views, extend or abridge any period of time prescribed under these Rules or agreed by the parties.

3.   If at an appropriate stage of the proceedings any party so requests, the arbitral tribunal shall hold hearings for the presentation of evidence by witnesses, including expert witnesses, or for oral argument. In the absence of such a request, the arbitral tribunal shall decide whether to hold such hearings or whether the proceedings shall be conducted on the basis of documents and other materials.

4.   All communications to the arbitral tribunal by one party shall be communicated by that party to all other parties. Such communications shall be made at the same time, except as otherwise permitted by the arbitral tribunal if it may do so under applicable law.

5.   The arbitral tribunal may, at the request of any party, allow one or more third persons to be joined in the arbitration as a party provided such person is a party to the arbitration agreement, unless the arbitral tribunal finds, after giving all parties, including the person or persons to be joined, the opportunity to be heard, that joinder should not be permitted because of prejudice to any of those parties. The arbitral tribunal may make a single award or several awards in respect of all parties so involved in the arbitration.

Article 18 Place of Arbitration

1.   If the parties have not previously agreed on the place of arbitration, the place of arbitration shall be determined by the arbitral tribunal having regard to the circumstances of the case. The award shall be deemed to have been made at the place of arbitration.

2.   The arbitral tribunal may meet at any location it considers appropriate for deliberations. Unless otherwise agreed by the parties, the arbitral tribunal may also meet at any location it considers appropriate for any other purpose, including hearings.

Article 19 Language

1.   Subject to an agreement by the parties, the arbitral tribunal shall, promptly after its appointment, determine the language or languages to be used in the proceedings. This determination shall apply to the statement of claim, the statement of defence, and any further written statements and, if oral hearings take place, to the language or languages to be used in such hearings.

2.   The arbitral tribunal may order that any documents annexed to the statement of claim or statement of defence, and any supplementary documents or exhibits submitted in the course of the proceedings, delivered in their original language, shall be accompanied by a translation into the language or languages agreed upon by the parties or determined by the arbitral tribunal.

Article 20 Statement of Claim

1.   The claimant shall communicate its statement of claim in writing to the respondent and to each of the arbitrators within a period of time to be determined by the arbitral tribunal. The claimant may elect to treat its notice of arbitration referred to in Article 3 as a statement of claim, provided that the notice of arbitration also complies with the requirements of paragraphs 2 to 4 of this article.

2.   The statement of claim shall include the following particulars:
(a)   The names and contact details of the parties;
(b)   A statement of the facts supporting the claim;
(c)   The points at issue;
(d)   The relief or remedy sought;
(e)   The legal grounds or arguments supporting the claim.

3.   A copy of any contract or other legal instrument out of or in relation to which the dispute arises and of the arbitration agreement shall be annexed to the statement of claim.

4.   The statement of claim should, as far as possible, be accompanied by all documents and other evidence relied upon by the claimant, or contain references to them.

Article 21 Statement of Defence

1.   The respondent shall communicate its statement of defence in writing to the claimant and to each of the arbitrators within a period of time to be determined by the arbitral tribunal. The respondent may elect to treat its response to the notice of arbitration referred to in Article 4 as a statement of defence, provided that the response to the notice of arbitration also complies with the requirements of paragraph 2 of this article.

2.   The statement of defence shall reply to the particulars (b) to (e) of the statement of claim (art. 20, para. 2). The statement of defence should, as far as possible, be accompanied by all documents and other evidence relied upon by the respondent, or contain references to them.
3.   In its statement of defence, or at a later stage in the arbitral proceedings if the arbitral tribu-nal decides that the delay was justified under the circumstances, the respondent may make a counterclaim or rely on a claim for the purpose of a set-off provided that the arbitral tribunal has jurisdiction over it.
4.   The provisions of Article 20, paragraphs 2 to 4, shall apply to a counterclaim, a claim under Article 4, paragraph 2 (f), and a claim relied on for the purpose of a set-off.

Article 22 Amendments to the Claim or Defence

During the course of the arbitral proceedings, a party may amend or supplement its claim or defence, including a counterclaim or a claim for the purpose of a set-off, unless the arbitral tri-bunal considers it inappropriate to allow such amendment or supplement having regard to the delay in making it or prejudice to other parties or any other circumstances. However, a claim or defence, including a counterclaim or a claim for the purpose of a set-off, may not be amended or supplemented in such a manner that the amended or supplemented claim or defence falls outside the jurisdiction of the arbitral tribunal.

Article 23 Pleas as to the Jurisdiction of the Arbitral Tribunal

1.   The arbitral tribunal shall have the power to rule on its own jurisdiction, including any objections with respect to the existence or validity of the arbitration agreement. For that pur-pose, an arbitration clause that forms part of a contract shall be treated as an agreement inde-pendent of the other terms of the contract. A decision by the arbitral tribunal that the contract is null shall not entail automatically the invalidity of the arbitration clause.
2.   A plea that the arbitral tribunal does not have jurisdiction shall be raised no later than in the statement of defence or, with respect to a counterclaim or a claim for the purpose of a set-off, in the reply to the counterclaim or to the claim for the purpose of a set-off. A party is not precluded from raising such a plea by the fact that it has appointed, or participated in the appointment of, an arbitrator. A plea that the arbitral tribunal is exceeding the scope of its authority shall be raised as soon as the matter alleged to be beyond the scope of its authority is raised during the arbitral proceedings. The arbitral tribunal may, in either case, admit a later plea if it considers the delay justified.
3.   The arbitral tribunal may rule on a plea referred to in paragraph 2 either as a preliminary question or in an award on the merits. The arbitral tribunal may continue the arbitral procee-dings and make an award, notwithstanding any pending challenge to its jurisdiction before a court.

Article 24 Further Written Statements

The arbitral tribunal shall decide which further written statements, in addition to the statement of claim and the statement of defence, shall be required from the parties or may be presented by them and shall fix the periods of time for communicating such statements.

Article 25 Periods of Time

The periods of time fixed by the arbitral tribunal for the communication of written statements (including the statement of claim and statement of defence) should not exceed 45 days. How-ever, the arbitral tribunal may extend the time limits if it concludes that an extension is justified.

Article 26 Interim Measures

1.   The arbitral tribunal may, at the request of a party, grant interim measures.
2.   An interim measure is any temporary measure by which, at any time prior to the issuance of the award by which the dispute is finally decided, the arbitral tribunal orders a party, for example and without limitation, to:
(a)   Maintain or restore the status quo pending determination of the dispute;

(b)   Take action that would prevent, or refrain from taking action that is likely to cause, (i) current or imminent harm or (ii) prejudice to the arbitral process itself;
(c)   Provide a means of preserving assets out of which a subsequent award may be satisfied; or
(d)   Preserve evidence that may be relevant and material to the resolution of the dispute.
3.   The party requesting an interim measure under paragraphs 2 (a) to (c) shall satisfy the arbitral tribunal that:
(a)   Harm not adequately reparable by an award of damages is likely to result if the measure is not ordered, and such harm substantially outweighs the harm that is likely to result to the party against whom the measure is directed if the measure is granted; and
(b)   There is a reasonable possibility that the requesting party will succeed on the merits of the claim. The determination on this possibility shall not affect the discretion of the arbitral tribunal in making any subsequent determination.
4.   With regard to a request for an interim measure under paragraph 2 (d), the requirements in paragraphs 3 (a) and (b) shall apply only to the extent the arbitral tribunal considers appropriate.
5.   The arbitral tribunal may modify, suspend or terminate an interim measure it has granted, upon application of any party or, in exceptional circumstances and upon prior notice to the parties, on the arbitral tribunal's own initiative.
6.   The arbitral tribunal may require the party requesting an interim measure to provide appropriate security in connection with the measure.
7.   The arbitral tribunal may require any party promptly to disclose any material change in the circumstances on the basis of which the interim measure was requested or granted.
8.   The party requesting an interim measure may be liable for any costs and damages caused by the measure to any party if the arbitral tribunal later determines that, in the circumstances then prevailing, the measure should not have been granted. The arbitral tribunal may award such costs and damages at any point during the proceedings.
9.   A request for interim measures addressed by any party to a judicial authority shall not be deemed incompatible with the agreement to arbitrate, or as a waiver of that agreement.

Article 27 Evidence
1.   Each party shall have the burden of proving the facts relied on to support its claim or defence.
2.   Witnesses, including expert witnesses, who are presented by the parties to testify to the arbitral tribunal on any issue of fact or expertise may be any individual, notwithstanding that the individual is a party to the arbitration or in any way related to a party. Unless otherwise directed by the arbitral tribunal, statements by witnesses, including expert witnesses, may be presented in writing and signed by them.
3.   At any time during the arbitral proceedings the arbitral tribunal may require the parties to produce documents, exhibits or other evidence within such a period of time as the arbitral tribunal shall determine.
4.   The arbitral tribunal shall determine the admissibility, relevance, materiality and weight of the evidence offered.

Article 28 Hearings
1.   In the event of an oral hearing, the arbitral tribunal shall give the parties adequate advance notice of the date, time and place thereof.
2.   Witnesses, including expert witnesses, may be heard under the conditions and examined in the manner set by the arbitral tribunal.
3.   Hearings shall be held in camera unless the parties agree otherwise. The arbitral tribunal may require the retirement of any witness or witnesses, including expert witnesses, during the testimony of such other witnesses, except that a witness, including an expert witness, who is a party to the arbitration shall not, in principle, be asked to retire.
4.   The arbitral tribunal may direct that witnesses, including expert witnesses, be examined through means of telecommunication that do not require their physical presence at the hearing (such as videoconference).

Article 29 Experts Appointed by the Arbitral Tribunal

1.   After consultation with the parties, the arbitral tribunal may appoint one or more independent experts to report to it, in writing, on specific issues to be determined by the arbitral tribunal. A copy of the expert's terms of reference, established by the arbitral tribunal, shall be communicated to the parties.

2.   The expert shall, in principle before accepting appointment, submit to the arbitral tribunal and to the parties a description of his or her qualifications and a statement of his or her impartiality and independence. Within the time ordered by the arbitral tribunal, the parties shall inform the arbitral tribunal whether they have any objections as to the expert's qualifications, impartiality or independence. The arbitral tribunal shall decide promptly whether to accept any such objections. After an expert's appointment, a party may object to the expert's qualifications, impartiality or independence only if the objection is for reasons of which the party becomes aware after the appointment has been made. The arbitral tribunal shall decide promptly what, if any, action to take.

3.   The parties shall give the expert any relevant information or produce for his or her inspection any relevant documents or goods that he or she may require of them. Any dispute between a party and such expert as to the relevance of the required information or production shall be referred to the arbitral tribunal for decision.

4.   Upon receipt of the expert's report, the arbitral tribunal shall communicate a copy of the report to the parties, which shall be given the opportunity to express, in writing, their opinion on the report. A party shall be entitled to examine any document on which the expert has relied in his or her report.

5.   At the request of any party, the expert, after delivery of the report, may be heard at a hearing where the parties shall have the opportunity to be present and to interrogate the expert. At this hearing, any party may present expert witnesses in order to testify on the points at issue. The provisions of Article 28 shall be applicable to such proceedings.

Article 30 Default

1.   If, within the period of time fixed by these Rules or the arbitral tribunal, without showing sufficient cause:

(a)   The claimant has failed to communicate its statement of claim, the arbitral tribunal shall issue an order for the termination of the arbitral proceedings, unless there are remaining matters that may need to be decided and the arbitral tribunal considers it appropriate to do so;

(b)   The respondent has failed to communicate its response to the notice of arbitration or its statement of defence, the arbitral tribunal shall order that the proceedings continue, without treating such failure in itself as an admission of the claimant's allegations; the provisions of this subparagraph also apply to a claimant's failure to submit a defence to a counterclaim or to a claim for the purpose of a set-off.

2.   If a party, duly notified under these Rules, fails to appear at a hearing, without showing sufficient cause for such failure, the arbitral tribunal may proceed with the arbitration.

3.   If a party, duly invited by the arbitral tribunal to produce documents, exhibits or other evidence, fails to do so within the established period of time, without showing sufficient cause for such failure, the arbitral tribunal may make the award on the evidence before it.

Article 31 Closure of Hearings

1.   The arbitral tribunal may inquire of the parties if they have any further proof to offer or witnesses to be heard or submissions to make and, if there are none, it may declare the hearings closed.

2.   The arbitral tribunal may, if it considers it necessary owing to exceptional circumstances, decide, on its own initiative or upon application of a party, to reopen the hearings at any time before the award is made.

Article 32 Waiver of Right to Object

A failure by any party to object promptly to any non-compliance with these Rules or with any requirement of the arbitration agreement shall be deemed to be a waiver of the right of such party to make such an objection, unless such party can show that, under the circumstances, its failure to object was justified.

Section IV. The Award
Article 33 Decisions

1.   When there is more than one arbitrator, any award or other decision of the arbitral tribunal shall be made by a majority of the arbitrators.
2.   In the case of questions of procedure, when there is no majority or when the arbitral tribunal so authorizes, the presiding arbitrator may decide alone, subject to revision, if any, by the arbitral tribunal.

Article 34 Form and Effect of the Award

1.   The arbitral tribunal may make separate awards on different issues at different times.
2.   All awards shall be made in writing and shall be final and binding on the parties. The parties shall carry out all awards without delay.
3.   The arbitral tribunal shall state the reasons upon which the award is based, unless the parties have agreed that no reasons are to be given.
4.   An award shall be signed by the arbitrators and it shall contain the date on which the award was made and indicate the place of arbitration. Where there is more than one arbitrator and any of them fails to sign, the award shall state the reason for the absence of the signature.
5.   An award may be made public with the consent of all parties or where and to the extent disclosure is required of a party by legal duty, to protect or pursue a legal right or in relation to legal proceedings before a court or other competent authority.
6.   Copies of the award signed by the arbitrators shall be communicated to the parties by the arbitral tribunal.

Article 35 Applicable Law, amiable compositeur

1.   The arbitral tribunal shall apply the rules of law designated by the parties as applicable to the substance of the dispute. Failing such designation by the parties, the arbitral tribunal shall apply the law which it determines to be appropriate.
2.   The arbitral tribunal shall decide as *amiable compositeur* or *ex aequo et bono* only if the parties have expressly authorized the arbitral tribunal to do so.
3.   In all cases, the arbitral tribunal shall decide in accordance with the terms of the contract, if any, and shall take into account any usage of trade applicable to the transaction.

Article 36 Settlement or Other Grounds for Termination

1.   If, before the award is made, the parties agree on a settlement of the dispute, the arbitral tribunal shall either issue an order for the termination of the arbitral proceedings or, if requested by the parties and accepted by the arbitral tribunal, record the settlement in the form of an arbitral award on agreed terms. The arbitral tribunal is not obliged to give reasons for such an award.
2.   If, before the award is made, the continuation of the arbitral proceedings becomes unnecessary or impossible for any reason not mentioned in paragraph 1, the arbitral tribunal shall inform the parties of its intention to issue an order for the termination of the proceedings. The arbitral tribunal shall have the power to issue such an order unless there are remaining matters that may need to be decided and the arbitral tribunal considers it appropriate to do so.
3.   Copies of the order for termination of the arbitral proceedings or of the arbitral award on agreed terms, signed by the arbitrators, shall be communicated by the arbitral tribunal to the parties. Where an arbitral award on agreed terms is made, the provisions of Article 34, paragraphs 2, 4 and 5, shall apply.

Article 37 Interpretation of the Award

1.   Within 30 days after the receipt of the award, a party, with notice to the other parties, may request that the arbitral tribunal give an interpretation of the award.

2.   The interpretation shall be given in writing within 45 days after the receipt of the request. The interpretation shall form part of the award and the provisions of Article 34, paragraphs 2 to 6, shall apply.

Article 38 Correction of the Award

1.   Within 30 days after the receipt of the award, a party, with notice to the other parties, may request the arbitral tribunal to correct in the award any error in computation, any clerical or typographical error, or any error or omission of a similar nature. If the arbitral tribunal considers that the request is justified, it shall make the correction within 45 days of receipt of the request.

2.   The arbitral tribunal may within 30 days after the communication of the award make such corrections on its own initiative.

3.   Such corrections shall be in writing and shall form part of the award. The provisions of Article 34, paragraphs 2 to 6, shall apply.

Article 39 Additional Award

1.   Within 30 days after the receipt of the termination order or the award, a party, with notice to the other parties, may request the arbitral tribunal to make an award or an additional award as to claims presented in the arbitral proceedings but not decided by the arbitral tribunal.

2.   If the arbitral tribunal considers the request for an award or additional award to be justified, it shall render or complete its award within 60 days after the receipt of the request. The arbitral tribunal may extend, if necessary, the period of time within which it shall make the award.

3.   When such an award or additional award is made, the provisions of Article 34, paragraphs 2 to 6, shall apply.

Article 40 Definition of Costs

1.   The arbitral tribunal shall fix the costs of arbitration in the final award and, if it deems appropriate, in another decision.

2.   The term "costs" includes only:

(a)   The fees of the arbitral tribunal to be stated separately as to each arbitrator and to be fixed by the tribunal itself in accordance with Article 41;

(b)   The reasonable travel and other expenses incurred by the arbitrators;

(c)   The reasonable costs of expert advice and of other assistance required by the arbitral tribunal;

(d)   The reasonable travel and other expenses of witnesses to the extent such expenses are approved by the arbitral tribunal;

(e)   The legal and other costs incurred by the parties in relation to the arbitration to the extent that the arbitral tribunal determines that the amount of such costs is reasonable;

(f)   Any fees and expenses of the appointing authority as well as the fees and expenses of the Secretary-General of the PCA.

3.   In relation to interpretation, correction or completion of any award under Articles 37 to 39, the arbitral tribunal may charge the costs referred to in paragraphs 2 (b) to (f), but no additional fees.

Article 41 Fees and Expenses of Arbitrators

1.   The fees and expenses of the arbitrators shall be reasonable in amount, taking into account the amount in dispute, the complexity of the subject matter, the time spent by the arbitrators and any other relevant circumstances of the case.

2.   If there is an appointing authority and it applies or has stated that it will apply a schedule or particular method for determining the fees for arbitrators in international cases, the arbitral tribunal in fixing its fees shall take that schedule or method into account to the extent that it considers appropriate in the circumstances of the case.

3.   Promptly after its constitution, the arbitral tribunal shall inform the parties as to how it proposes to determine its fees and expenses, including any rates it intends to apply. Within 15 days of receiving that proposal, any party may refer the proposal to the appointing authority for review. If, within 45 days of receipt of such a referral, the appointing authority finds that the proposal of the arbitral tribunal is inconsistent with paragraph 1, it shall make any necessary adjustments thereto, which shall be binding upon the arbitral tribunal.

4.(a) When informing the parties of the arbitrators' fees and expenses that have been fixed pursuant to Article 40, paragraphs 2 (a) and (b), the arbitral tribunal shall also explain the manner in which the corresponding amounts have been calculated;

(b)   Within 15 days of receiving the arbitral tribunal's determination of fees and expenses, any party may refer for review such determination to the appointing authority. If no appointing authority has been agreed upon or designated, or if the appointing authority fails to act within the time specified in these Rules, then the review shall be made by the Secretary-General of the PCA;

(c)   If the appointing authority or the Secretary-General of the PCA finds that the arbitral tribunal's determination is inconsistent with the arbitral tribunal's proposal (and any adjustment thereto) under paragraph 3 or is otherwise manifestly excessive, it shall, within 45 days of receiving such a referral, make any adjustments to the arbitral tribunal's determination that are necessary to satisfy the criteria in paragraph 1. Any such adjustments shall be binding upon the arbitral tribunal;

(d)   Any such adjustments shall either be included by the arbitral tribunal in its award or, if the award has already been issued, be implemented in a correction to the award, to which the procedure of Article 38, paragraph 3, shall apply.

5.   Throughout the procedure under paragraphs 3 and 4, the arbitral tribunal shall proceed with the arbitration, in accordance with Article 17, paragraph 1.

6.   A referral under paragraph 4 shall not affect any determination in the award other than the arbitral tribunal's fees and expenses; nor shall it delay the recognition and enforcement of all parts of the award other than those relating to the determination of the arbitral tribunal's fees and expenses.

Article 42 Allocation of Costs

1.   The costs of the arbitration shall in principle be borne by the unsuccessful party or parties. However, the arbitral tribunal may apportion each of such costs between the parties if it determines that apportionment is reasonable, taking into account the circumstances of the case.

2.   The arbitral tribunal shall in the final award or, if it deems appropriate, in any other award, determine any amount that a party may have to pay to another party as a result of the decision on allocation of costs.

Article 43 Deposit of Costs

1.   The arbitral tribunal, on its establishment, may request the parties to deposit an equal amount as an advance for the costs referred to in Article 40, paragraphs 2 *(a)* to *(c)*.

2.   During the course of the arbitral proceedings the arbitral tribunal may request supplementary deposits from the parties.

3.   If an appointing authority has been agreed upon or designated, and when a party so requests and the appointing authority consents to perform the function, the arbitral tribunal shall fix the amounts of any deposits or supplementary deposits only after consultation with the appointing authority, which may make any comments to the arbitral tribunal that it deems appropriate concerning the amount of such deposits and supplementary deposits.

4.   If the required deposits are not paid in full within 30 days after the receipt of the request, the arbitral tribunal shall so inform the parties in order that one or more of them may make the required payment. If such payment is not made, the arbitral tribunal may order the suspension or termination of the arbitral proceedings.

5.   After a termination order or final award has been made, the arbitral tribunal shall render an accounting to the parties of the deposits received and return any unexpended balance to the parties.

Annex: Model Arbitration Clause for Contracts

Any dispute, controversy or claim arising out of or relating to this contract, or the breach, termination or invalidity thereof, shall be settled by arbitration in accordance with the UNCITRAL
Arbitration Rules.

Note. Parties should consider adding:
(a)   The appointing authority shall be ... [name of institution or person];
(b)   The number of arbitrators shall be ... [one or three];
(c)   The place of arbitration shall be ... [town and country];
(d)   The language to be used in the arbitral proceedings shall be ... .

Possible Waiver Statement

Note. If the parties wish to exclude recourse against the arbitral award that may be available under the applicable law, they may consider adding a provision to that effect as suggested below, considering, however, that the effectiveness and conditions of such an exclusion depend on the applicable law.

Waiver: The parties hereby waive their right to any form of recourse against an award to any court or other competent authority, insofar as such waiver can validly be made under the applicable law.

Model Statements of Independence Pursuant to Article 11 of the Rules

No circumstances to disclose
I am impartial and independent of each of the parties and intend to remain so. To the best of my knowledge, there are no circumstances, past or present, likely to give rise to justifiable doubts as to my impartiality or independence. I shall promptly notify the parties and the other arbitrators of any such circumstances that may subsequently come to my attention during this arbitration.

Circumstances to disclose
I am impartial and independent of each of the parties and intend to remain so. Attached is a statement made pursuant to Article 11 of the UNCITRAL Arbitration Rules of (a) my past and present professional, business and other relationships with the parties and (b) any other relevant circumstances.

[Include statement.] I confirm that those circumstances do not affect my independence and impartiality. I shall promptly notify the parties and the other arbitrators of any such further relationships or circumstances that may subsequently come to my attention during this arbitration.

Note. Any party may consider requesting from the arbitrator the following addition to the statement of independence:

I confirm, on the basis of the information presently available to me, that I can devote the time necessary to conduct this arbitration diligently, efficiently and in accordance with the time limits in the Rules.

1985 UNCITRAL MODEL LAW ON INTERNATIONAL COMMERCIAL ARBITRATION[1]
(with amendments as adopted in 2006)

CHAPTER I. GENERAL PROVISIONS
Article 1. Scope of Application[2]

(1)   This Law applies to international commercial[3] arbitration, subject to any agreement in force between this State and any other State or States.

(2)   The provisions of this Law, except articles 8, 9, 17 H, 17 I, 17 J, 35 and 36, apply only if the place of arbitration is in the territory of this State.

(Article 1(2) has been amended by the Commission at its thirty-ninth session, in 2006)

(3)   An arbitration is international if:

(a)   the parties to an arbitration agreement have, at the time of the conclusion of that agreement, their places of business in different States; or

(b)   one of the following places is situated outside the State in which the parties have their places of business:

   (i)   the place of arbitration if determined in, or pursuant to, the arbitration agreement;

   (ii)   any place where a substantial part of the obligations of the commercial relationship is to be performed or the place with which the subject-matter of the dispute is most closely connected; or

(c)   the parties have expressly agreed that the subject matter of the arbitration agreement relates to more than one country.

(4)   For the purposes of paragraph (3) of this article:

(a)   if a party has more than one place of business, the place of business is that which has the closest relationship to the arbitration agreement;

(b)   if a party does not have a place of business, reference is to be made to his habitual residence.

(5)   This Law shall not affect any other law of this State by virtue of which certain disputes may not be submitted to arbitration or may be submitted to arbitration only according to provisions other than those of this Law.

Article 2. Definitions and Rules of Interpretation

For the purposes of this Law:

(a)   "arbitration" means any arbitration whether or not administered by a permanent arbitral institution;

(b)   "arbitral tribunal" means a sole arbitrator or a panel of arbitrators;

(c)   "court" means a body or organ of the judicial system of a State;

(d)   where a provision of this Law, except Article 28, leaves the parties free to determine a certain issue, such freedom includes the right of the parties to authorize a third party, including an institution, to make that determination;

---

1   © United Nations, GA Res. 61/22, New York 2006; and United Nations Commission on International Trade Law (UNCITRAL), Vienna 2006. All rights reserved. The UNCITRAL website provides a list of some 66 countries that have adopted legislation based on the Model Law, see http://www.uncitral.org/uncitral/en/uncitral_texts/arbitration/1985Model_arbitration_status.html.

2   Article headings are for reference purposes only and are not to be used for purposes of interpretation.

3   The term "commercial" should be given a wide interpretation so as to cover matters arising from all relationships of a commercial nature, whether contractual or not. Relationships of a commercial nature include, but are not limited to, the following transactions: any trade transaction for the supply or exchange of goods or services; distribution agreement; commercial representation or agency; factoring; leasing; construction of works; consulting; engineering; licensing; investment; financing; banking; insurance; exploitation agreement or concession; joint venture and other forms of industrial or business cooperation; carriage of goods or passengers by air, sea, rail or road.

(e)   where a provision of this Law refers to the fact that the parties have agreed or that they may agree or in any other way refers to an agreement of the parties, such agreement includes any arbitration rules referred to in that agreement;

(f)   where a provision of this Law, other than in articles 25(a) and 32(2) (a), refers to a claim, it also applies to a counter-claim, and where it refers to a defence, it also applies to a defence to such counter-claim.

Article 2 A. International Origin and General Principles
(As adopted by the Commission at its thirty-ninth session, in 2006)

(1)   In the interpretation of this Law, regard is to be had to its international origin and to the need to promote uniformity in its application and the observance of good faith.

(2)   Questions concerning matters governed by this Law which are not expressly settled in it are to be settled in conformity with the general principles on which this Law is based.

Article 3. Receipt of Written Communications

(1)   Unless otherwise agreed by the parties:

(a)   any written communication is deemed to have been received if it is delivered to the addressee personally or if it is delivered at his place of business, habitual residence or mailing address; if none of these can be found after making a reasonable inquiry, a written communication is deemed to have been received if it is sent to the addressee's last-known place of business, habitual residence or mailing address by registered letter or any other means which provides a record of the attempt to deliver it;

(b)   the communication is deemed to have been received on the day it is so delivered.

(2)   The provisions of this Article do not apply to communications in court proceedings.

Article 4. Waiver of Right to Object

A party who knows that any provision of this Law from which the parties may derogate or any requirement under the arbitration agreement has not been complied with and yet proceeds with the arbitration without stating his objection to such non-compliance without undue delay or, if a time-limit is provided therefor, within such period of time, shall be deemed to have waived his right to object.

Article 5. Extent of Court Intervention

In matters governed by this Law, no court shall intervene except where so provided in this Law.

Article 6. Court or Other Authority for Certain Functions of Arbitration Assistance and Supervision

The functions referred to in Articles 11(3), 11(4), 13(3), 14, 16(3) and 34(2) shall be performed by ... [Each State enacting this model law specifies the court, courts or, where referred to therein, other authority competent to perform these functions.]

CHAPTER II. ARBITRATION AGREEMENT

Option I
Article 7. Definition and Form of Arbitration Agreement
(As adopted by the Commission at its thirty-ninth session, in 2006)

(1)   "Arbitration agreement" is an agreement by the parties to submit to arbitration all or certain disputes which have arisen or which may arise between them in respect of a defined legal relationship, whether contractual or not. An arbitration agreement may be in the form of an arbitration clause in a contract or in the form of a separate agreement.

(2)   The arbitration agreement shall be in writing.

(3)   An arbitration agreement is in writing if its content is recorded in any form, whether or not the arbitration agreement or contract has been concluded orally, by conduct, or by other means.

(4)   The requirement that an arbitration agreement be in writing is met by an electronic communication if the information contained therein is accessible so as to be useable for subsequent reference; "electronic communication" means any communication that the parties make by means of data messages; "data message" means information generated, sent, received or sto-

red by electronic, magnetic, optical or similar means, including, but not limited to, electronic data interchange (EDI), electronic mail, telegram, telex or telecopy.

(5)   Furthermore, an arbitration agreement is in writing if it is contained in an exchange of statements of claim and defence in which the existence of an agreement is alleged by one party and not denied by the other.

(6)   The reference in a contract to any document containing an arbitration clause constitutes an arbitration agreement in writing, provided that the reference is such as to make that clause part of the contract.

Option II
Article 7. Definition of Arbitration Agreement
(As adopted by the Commission at its thirty-ninth session, in 2006)
"Arbitration agreement" is an agreement by the parties to submit to arbitration all or certain disputes which have arisen or which may arise between them in respect of a defined legal relationship, whether contractual or not.

Article 8. Arbitration Agreement and Substantive Claim Before Court
(1)   A court before which an action is brought in a matter which is the subject of an arbitration agreement shall, if a party so requests not later than when submitting his first statement on the substance of the dispute, refer the parties to arbitration unless it finds that the agreement is null and void, inoperative or incapable of being performed.

(2)   Where an action referred to in paragraph (1) of this Article has been brought, arbitral proceedings may nevertheless be commenced or continued, and an award may be made, while the issue is pending before the court.

Article 9. Arbitration Agreement and Interim Measures by Court
It is not incompatible with an arbitration agreement for a party to request, before or during arbitral proceedings, from a court an interim measure of protection and for a court to grant such measure.

CHAPTER III. COMPOSITION OF ARBITRAL TRIBUNAL
Article 10. Number of Arbitrators
(1)   The parties are free to determine the number of arbitrators.

(2)   Failing such determination, the number of arbitrators shall be three.

Article 11. Appointment of Arbitrators
(1)   No person shall be precluded by reason of his nationality from acting as an arbitrator, unless otherwise agreed by the parties.

(2)   The parties are free to agree on a procedure of appointing the arbitrator or arbitrators, subject to the provisions of paragraphs (4) and (5) of this article.

(3)   Failing such agreement,

(a)   in an arbitration with three arbitrators, each party shall appoint one arbitrator, and the two arbitrators thus appointed shall appoint the third arbitrator; if a party fails to appoint the arbitrator within thirty days of receipt of a request to do so from the other party, or if the two arbitrators fail to agree on the third arbitrator within thirty days of their appointment, the appointment shall be made, upon request of a party, by the court or other authority specified in Article 6;

(b)   in an arbitration with a sole arbitrator, if the parties are unable to agree on the arbitrator, he shall be appointed, upon request of a party, by the court or other authority specified in Article 6.

(4)   Where, under an appointment procedure agreed upon by the parties,

(a)   a party fails to act as required under such procedure, or

(b)   the parties, or two arbitrators, are unable to reach an agreement expected of them under such procedure, or

(c)   a third party, including an institution, fails to perform any function entrusted to it under such procedure, any party may request the court or other authority specified in Article 6 to take the necessary measure, unless the agreement on the appointment procedure provides other means for securing the appointment.

(5)   A decision on a matter entrusted by paragraph (3) or (4) of this Article to the court or other authority specified in Article 6 shall be subject to no appeal. The court or other authority, in appointing an arbitrator, shall have due regard to any qualifications required of the arbitrator by the agreement of the parties and to such considerations as are likely to secure the appointment of an independent and impartial arbitrator and, in the case of a sole or third arbitrator, shall take into account as well the advisability of appointing an arbitrator of a nationality other than those of the parties.

Article 12. Grounds for Challenge

(1)   When a person is approached in connection with his possible appointment as an arbitrator, he shall disclose any circumstances likely to give rise to justifiable doubts as to his impartiality or independence. An arbitrator, from the time of his appointment and throughout the arbitral proceedings, shall without delay disclose any such circumstances to the parties unless they have already been informed of them by him.

(2)   An arbitrator may be challenged only if circumstances exist that give rise to justifiable doubts as to his impartiality or independence, or if he does not possess qualifications agreed to by the parties. A party may challenge an arbitrator appointed by him, or in whose appointment he has participated, only for reasons of which he becomes aware after the appointment has been made.

Article 13. Challenge Procedure

(1)   The parties are free to agree on a procedure for challenging an arbitrator, subject to the provisions of paragraph (3) of this article.

(2)   Failing such agreement, a party who intends to challenge an arbitrator shall, within fifteen days after becoming aware of the constitution of the arbitral tribunal or after becoming aware of any circumstance referred to in Article 12(2), send a written statement of the reasons for the challenge to the arbitral tribunal. Unless the challenged arbitrator withdraws from his office or the other party agrees to the challenge, the arbitral tribunal shall decide on the challenge.

(3)   If a challenge under any procedure agreed upon by the parties or under the procedure of paragraph (2) of this Article is not successful, the challenging party may request, within thirty days after having received notice of the decision rejecting the challenge, the court or other authority specified in Article 6 to decide on the challenge, which decision shall be subject to no appeal; while such a request is pending, the arbitral tribunal, including the challenged arbitrator, may continue the arbitral proceedings and make an award.

Article 14. Failure or Impossibility to Act

(1)   If an arbitrator becomes *de jure* or *de facto* unable to perform his functions or for other reasons fails to act without undue delay, his mandate terminates if he withdraws from his office or if the parties agree on the termination. Otherwise, if a controversy remains concerning any of these grounds, any party may request the court or other authority specified in Article 6 to decide on the termination of the mandate, which decision shall be subject to no appeal.

(2)   If, under this Article or Article 13(2), an arbitrator withdraws from his office or a party agrees to the termination of the mandate of an arbitrator, this does not imply acceptance of the validity of any ground referred to in this Article or Article 12(2).

Article 15. Appointment of Substitute Arbitrator

Where the mandate of an arbitrator terminates under Article 13 or 14 or because of his withdrawal from office for any other reason or because of the revocation of his mandate by agreement of the parties or in any other case of termination of his mandate, a substitute arbitrator shall be appointed according to the rules that were applicable to the appointment of the arbitrator being replaced.

CHAPTER IV. JURISDICTION OF ARBITRAL TRIBUNAL
Article 16. Competence of Arbitral Tribunal to Rule on its Jurisdiction
(1)   The arbitral tribunal may rule on its own jurisdiction, including any objections with respect to the existence or validity of the arbitration agreement. For that purpose, an arbitration clause which forms part of a contract shall be treated as an agreement independent of the other terms of the contract. A decision by the arbitral tribunal that the contract is null and void shall not entail *ipso jure* the invalidity of the arbitration clause.
(2)   A plea that the arbitral tribunal does not have jurisdiction shall be raised not later than the submission of the statement of defence. A party is not precluded from raising such a plea by the fact that he has appointed, or participated in the appointment of, an arbitrator. A plea that the arbitral tribunal is exceeding the scope of its authority shall be raised as soon as the matter alleged to be beyond the scope of its authority is raised during the arbitral proceedings. The arbitral tribunal may, in either case, admit a later plea if it considers the delay justified.
(3)   The arbitral tribunal may rule on a plea referred to in paragraph (2) of this Article either as a preliminary question or in an award on the merits. If the arbitral tribunal rules as a preliminary question that it has jurisdiction, any party may request, within thirty days after having received notice of that ruling, the court specified in Article 6 to decide the matter, which decision shall be subject to no appeal; while such a request is pending, the arbitral tribunal may continue the arbitral proceedings and make an award.

CHAPTER IV A. INTERIM MEASURES AND PRELIMINARY ORDERS
(As adopted by the Commission at its thirty-ninth session, in 2006)
Section 1. Interim Measures
Article 17. Power of Arbitral Tribunal to Order Interim Measures
(1)   Unless otherwise agreed by the parties, the arbitral tribunal may, at the request of a party, grant interim measures.
(2)   An interim measure is any temporary measure, whether in the form of an award or in another form, by which, at any time prior to the issuance of the award by which the dispute is finally decided, the arbitral tribunal orders a party to:
(a)   Maintain or restore the status quo pending determination of the dispute;
(b)   Take action that would prevent, or refrain from taking action that is likely to cause, current or imminent harm or prejudice to the arbitral process itself;
(c)   Provide a means of preserving assets out of which a subsequent award may be satisfied; or
(d)   Preserve evidence that may be relevant and material to the resolution of the dispute.

Article 17 A. Conditions for Granting Interim Measures
(1)   The party requesting an interim measure under Article 17(2)(a), (b) and (c) shall satisfy the arbitral tribunal that:
(a)   Harm not adequately reparable by an award of damages is likely to result if the measure is not ordered, and such harm substantially outweighs the harm that is likely to result to the party against whom the measure is directed if the measure is granted; and
(b)   There is a reasonable possibility that the requesting party will succeed on the merits of the claim. The determination on this possibility shall not affect the discretion of the arbitral tribunal in making any subsequent determination.
(2)   With regard to a request for an interim measure under Article 17(2)(d), the requirements in paragraphs (1)(a) and (b) of this Article shall apply only to the extent the arbitral tribunal considers appropriate.
Section 2. Preliminary Orders
Article 17 B. Applications for Preliminary Orders and Conditions for Granting Preliminary Orders
(1)   Unless otherwise agreed by the parties, a party may, without notice to any other party, make a request for an interim measure together with an application for a preliminary order directing a party not to frustrate the purpose of the interim measure requested.

(2)   The arbitral tribunal may grant a preliminary order provided it considers that prior disclosure of the request for the interim measure to the party against whom it is directed risks frustrating the purpose of the measure.

(3)   The conditions defined under Article 17A apply to any preliminary order, provided that the harm to be assessed under Article 17A(1)*(a)*, is the harm likely to result from the order being granted or not.

Article 17 C. Specific Regime for Preliminary Orders

(1)   Immediately after the arbitral tribunal has made a determination in respect of an application for a preliminary order, the arbitral tribunal shall give notice to all parties of the request for the interim measure, the application for the preliminary order, the preliminary order, if any, and all other communications, including by indicating the content of any oral communication, between any party and the arbitral tribunal in relation thereto.

(2)   At the same time, the arbitral tribunal shall give an opportunity to any party against whom a preliminary order is directed to present its case at the earliest practicable time.

(3)   The arbitral tribunal shall decide promptly on any objection to the preliminary order.

(4)   A preliminary order shall expire after twenty days from the date on which it was issued by the arbitral tribunal. However, the arbitral tribunal may issue an interim measure adopting or modifying the preliminary order, after the party against whom the preliminary order is directed has been given notice and an opportunity to present its case.

(5)   A preliminary order shall be binding on the parties but shall not be subject to enforcement by a court. Such a preliminary order does not constitute an award.

Section 3. Provisions Applicable to Interim Measures and Preliminary Orders
Article 17 D. Modification, Suspension, Termination

The arbitral tribunal may modify, suspend or terminate an interim measure or a preliminary order it has granted, upon application of any party or, in exceptional circumstances and upon prior notice to the parties, on the arbitral tribunal's own initiative.

Article 17 E. Provision of Security

(1)   The arbitral tribunal may require the party requesting an interim measure to provide appropriate security in connection with the measure.

(2)   The arbitral tribunal shall require the party applying for a preliminary order to provide security in connection with the order unless the arbitral tribunal considers it inappropriate or unnecessary to do so.

Article 17 F. Disclosure

(1)   The arbitral tribunal may require any party promptly to disclose any material change in the circumstances on the basis of which the measure was requested or granted.

(2)   The party applying for a preliminary order shall disclose to the arbitral tribunal all circumstances that are likely to be relevant to the arbitral tribunal's determination whether to grant or maintain the order, and such obligation shall continue until the party against whom the order has been requested has had an opportunity to present its case. Thereafter, paragraph (1) of this Article shall apply.

Article 17 G. Costs and Damages

The party requesting an interim measure or applying for a preliminary order shall be liable for any costs and damages caused by the measure or the order to any party if the arbitral tribunal later determines that, in the circumstances, the measure or the order should not have been granted. The arbitral tribunal may award such costs and damages at any point during the proceedings.

Section 4. Recognition and Enforcement of Interim Measures
Article 17 H. Recognition and Enforcement

(1)   An interim measure issued by an arbitral tribunal shall be recognized as binding and, unless otherwise provided by the arbitral tribunal, enforced upon application to the competent court, irrespective of the country in which it was issued, subject to the provisions of Article 17 I.

(2)   The party who is seeking or has obtained recognition or enforcement of an interim measure shall promptly inform the court of any termination, suspension or modification of that interim measure.

(3)   The court of the State where recognition or enforcement is sought may, if it considers it proper, order the requesting party to provide appropriate security if the arbitral tribunal has not already made a determination with respect to security or where such a decision is necessary to protect the rights of third parties.

Article 17 I. Grounds for Refusing Recognition or Enforcement[1]

(1)   Recognition or enforcement of an interim measure may be refused only:

(a)   At the request of the party against whom it is invoked if the court is satisfied that:

   (i)   Such refusal is warranted on the grounds set forth in Article 36(1)(a)(i), (ii), (iii) or (iv); or

   (ii) The arbitral tribunal's decision with respect to the provision of security in connection with the interim measure issued by the arbitral tribunal has not been complied with; or

   (iii) The interim measure has been terminated or suspended by the arbitral tribunal or, where so empowered, by the court of the State in which the arbitration takes place or under the law of which that interim measure was granted; or

(b)   If the court finds that:

   (i)   The interim measure is incompatible with the powers conferred upon the court unless the court decides to reformulate the interim measure to the extent necessary to adapt it to its own powers and procedures for the purposes of enforcing that interim measure and without modifying its substance; or

   (ii) Any of the grounds set forth in Article 36(1)(b)(i) or (ii), apply to the recognition and enforcement of the interim measure.

(2)   Any determination made by the court on any ground in paragraph (1) of this Article shall be effective only for the purposes of the application to recognize and enforce the interim measure. The court where recognition or enforcement is sought shall not, in making that determination, undertake a review of the substance of the interim measure.

Section 5. Court-Ordered Interim Measures
Article 17 J. Court-Ordered Interim Measures

A court shall have the same power of issuing an interim measure in relation to arbitration proceedings, irrespective of whether their place is in the territory of this State, as it has in relation to proceedings in courts. The court shall exercise such power in accordance with its own procedures in consideration of the specific features of international arbitration.

CHAPTER V. CONDUCT OF ARBITRAL PROCEEDINGS
Article 18. Equal Treatment of Parties

The parties shall be treated with equality and each party shall be given a full opportunity of presenting his case.

Article 19. Determination of Rules of Procedure

(1)   Subject to the provisions of this Law, the parties are free to agree on the procedure to be followed by the arbitral tribunal in conducting the proceedings.

(2)   Failing such agreement, the arbitral tribunal may, subject to the provisions of this Law, conduct the arbitration in such manner as it considers appropriate. The power conferred upon the arbitral tribunal includes the power to determine the admissibility, relevance, materiality and weight of any evidence.

---

1   The conditions set forth in Article 17 I are intended to limit the number of circumstances in which the court may refuse to enforce an interim measure. It would not be contrary to the level of harmonization sought to be achieved by these model provisions if a State were to adopt fewer circumstances in which enforcement may be refused.

Article 20. Place of Arbitration

(1)   The parties are free to agree on the place of arbitration. Failing such agreement, the place of arbitration shall be determined by the arbitral tribunal having regard to the circumstances of the case, including the convenience of the parties.

(2)   Notwithstanding the provisions of paragraph (1) of this Article, the arbitral tribunal may, unless otherwise agreed by the parties, meet at any place it considers appropriate for consultation among its members, for hearing witnesses, experts or the parties, or for inspection of goods, other property or documents.

Article 21. Commencement of Arbitral Proceedings

Unless otherwise agreed by the parties, the arbitral proceedings in respect of a particular dispute commence on the date on which a request for that dispute to be referred to arbitration is received by the respondent.

Article 22. Language

(1)   The parties are free to agree on the language or languages to be used in the arbitral proceedings. Failing such agreement, the arbitral tribunal shall determine the language or languages to be used in the proceedings. This agreement or determination, unless otherwise specified therein, shall apply to any written statement by a party, any hearing and any award, decision or other communication by the arbitral tribunal.

(2)   The arbitral tribunal may order that any documentary evidence shall be accompanied by a translation into the language or languages agreed upon by the parties or determined by the arbitral tribunal.

Article 23. Statements of Claim and Defence

(1)   Within the period of time agreed by the parties or determined by the arbitral tribunal, the claimant shall state the facts supporting his claim, the points at issue and the relief or remedy sought, and the respondent shall state his defence in respect of these particulars, unless the parties have otherwise agreed as to the required elements of such statements. The parties may submit with their statements all documents they consider to be relevant or may add a reference to the documents or other evidence they will submit.

(2) Unless otherwise agreed by the parties, either party may amend or supplement his claim or defence during the course of the arbitral proceedings, unless the arbitral tribunal considers it inappropriate to allow such amendment having regard to the delay in making it.

Article 24. Hearings and Written Proceedings

(1)   Subject to any contrary agreement by the parties, the arbitral tribunal shall decide whether to hold oral hearings for the presentation of evidence or for oral argument, or whether the proceedings shall be conducted on the basis of documents and other materials. However, unless the parties have agreed that no hearings shall be held, the arbitral tribunal shall hold such hearings at an appropriate stage of the proceedings, if so requested by a party.

(2)   The parties shall be given sufficient advance notice of any hearing and of any meeting of the arbitral tribunal for the purposes of inspection of goods, other property or documents.

(3)   All statements, documents or other information supplied to the arbitral tribunal by one party shall be communicated to the other party. Also any expert report or evidentiary document on which the arbitral tribunal may rely in making its decision shall be communicated to the parties.

Article 25. Default of a Party

Unless otherwise agreed by the parties, if, without showing sufficient cause,

(a)   the claimant fails to communicate his statement of claim in accordance with Article 23(1), the arbitral tribunal shall terminate the proceedings;

(b)   the respondent fails to communicate his statement of defence in accordance with Article 23(1), the arbitral tribunal shall continue the proceedings without treating such failure in itself as an admission of the claimant's allegations;

(c) any party fails to appear at a hearing or to produce documentary evidence, the arbitral tribunal may continue the proceedings and make the award on the evidence before it.

Article 26. Expert Appointed by Arbitral Tribunal

(1) Unless otherwise agreed by the parties, the arbitral tribunal

(a) may appoint one or more experts to report to it on specific issues to be determined by the arbitral tribunal;

(b) may require a party to give the expert any relevant information or to produce, or to provide access to, any relevant documents, goods or other property for his inspection.

(2) Unless otherwise agreed by the parties, if a party so requests or if the arbitral tribunal considers it necessary, the expert shall, after delivery of his written or oral report, participate in a hearing where the parties have the opportunity to put questions to him and to present expert witnesses in order to testify on the points at issue.

Article 27. Court Assistance in Taking Evidence

The arbitral tribunal or a party with the approval of the arbitral tribunal may request from a competent court of this State assistance in taking evidence. The court may execute the request within its competence and according to its rules on taking evidence.

CHAPTER VI. MAKING OF AWARD AND TERMINATION OF PROCEEDINGS

Article 28. Rules Applicable to Substance of Dispute

(1) The arbitral tribunal shall decide the dispute in accordance with such rules of law as are chosen by the parties as applicable to the substance of the dispute. Any designation of the law or legal system of a given State shall be construed, unless otherwise expressed, as directly referring to the substantive law of that State and not to its conflict of laws rules.

(2) Failing any designation by the parties, the arbitral tribunal shall apply the law determined by the conflict of laws rules which it considers applicable.

(3) The arbitral tribunal shall decide *ex aequo et bono* or as *amiable compositeur* only if the parties have expressly authorized it to do so.

(4) In all cases, the arbitral tribunal shall decide in accordance with the terms of the contract and shall take into account the usages of the trade applicable to the transaction.

Article 29. Decision-Making by Panel of Arbitrators

In arbitral proceedings with more than one arbitrator, any decision of the arbitral tribunal shall be made, unless otherwise agreed by the parties, by a majority of all its members. However, questions of procedure may be decided by a presiding arbitrator, if so authorized by the parties or all members of the arbitral tribunal.

Article 30. Settlement

(1) If, during arbitral proceedings, the parties settle the dispute, the arbitral tribunal shall terminate the proceedings and, if requested by the parties and not objected to by the arbitral tribunal, record the settlement in the form of an arbitral award on agreed terms.

(2) An award on agreed terms shall be made in accordance with the provisions of Article 31 and shall state that it is an award. Such an award has the same status and effect as any other award on the merits of the case.

Article 31. Form and Contents of Award

(1) The award shall be made in writing and shall be signed by the arbitrator or arbitrators. In arbitral proceedings with more than one arbitrator, the signatures of the majority of all members of the arbitral tribunal shall suffice, provided that the reason for any omitted signature is stated.

(2) The award shall state the reasons upon which it is based, unless the parties have agreed that no reasons are to be given or the award is an award on agreed terms under Article 30.

(3) The award shall state its date and the place of arbitration as determined in accordance with Article 20(1). The award shall be deemed to have been made at that place.

(4)   After the award is made, a copy signed by the arbitrators in accordance with paragraph (1) of this Article shall be delivered to each party.

Article 32. Termination of Proceedings

(1)   The arbitral proceedings are terminated by the final award or by an order of the arbitral tribunal in accordance with paragraph (2) of this article.

(2)   The arbitral tribunal shall issue an order for the termination of the arbitral proceedings when:

(a)   the claimant withdraws his claim, unless the respondent objects thereto and the arbitral tribunal recognizes a legitimate interest on his part in obtaining a final settlement of the dispute;

(b)   the parties agree on the termination of the proceedings;

(c)   the arbitral tribunal finds that the continuation of the proceedings has for any other reason become unnecessary or impossible.

(3)   The mandate of the arbitral tribunal terminates with the termination of the arbitral proceedings, subject to the provisions of articles 33 and 34(4).

Article 33. Correction and Interpretation of Award; Additional Award

(1)   Within thirty days of receipt of the award, unless another period of time has been agreed upon by the parties:

(a)   a party, with notice to the other party, may request the arbitral tribunal to correct in the award any errors in computation, any clerical or typographical errors or any errors of similar nature;

(b)   if so agreed by the parties, a party, with notice to the other party, may request the arbitral tribunal to give an interpretation of a specific point or part of the award.

If the arbitral tribunal considers the request to be justified, it shall make the correction or give the interpretation within thirty days of receipt of the request. The interpretation shall form part of the award.

(2)   The arbitral tribunal may correct any error of the type referred to in paragraph (1)(a) of this Article on its own initiative within thirty days of the date of the award.

(3)   Unless otherwise agreed by the parties, a party, with notice to the other party, may request, within thirty days of receipt of the award, the arbitral tribunal to make an additional award as to claims presented in the arbitral proceedings but omitted from the award. If the arbitral tribunal considers the request to be justified, it shall make the additional award within sixty days.

(4)   The arbitral tribunal may extend, if necessary, the period of time within which it shall make a correction, interpretation or an additional award under paragraph (1) or (3) of this article.

(5)   The provisions of Article 31 shall apply to a correction or interpretation of the award or to an additional award.

CHAPTER VII. RECOURSE AGAINST AWARD

Article 34. Application for Setting Aside as Exclusive Recourse Against Arbitral Award

(1)   Recourse to a court against an arbitral award may be made only by an application for setting aside in accordance with paragraphs (2) and (3) of this article.

(2)   An arbitral award may be set aside by the court specified in Article 6 only if:

(a)   the party making the application furnishes proof that:

    (i)   a party to the arbitration agreement referred to in Article 7 was under some incapacity; or the said agreement is not valid under the law to which the parties have subjected it or, failing any indication thereon, under the law of this State; or

    (ii)   the party making the application was not given proper notice of the appointment of an arbitrator or of the arbitral proceedings or was otherwise unable to present his case; or

    (iii) the award deals with a dispute not contemplated by or not falling within the terms of the submission to arbitration, or contains decisions on matters beyond the scope of the submission to arbitration, provided that, if the decisions on matters submitted to arbitration can be separated from those not so submitted, only that part of the award which contains decisions on matters not submitted to arbitration may be set aside; or

(iv) the composition of the arbitral tribunal or the arbitral procedure was not in accordance with the agreement of the parties, unless such agreement was in conflict with a provision of this Law from which the parties cannot derogate, or, failing such agreement, was not in accordance with this Law; or

(b) the court finds that:

(i) the subject-matter of the dispute is not capable of settlement by arbitration under the law of this State; or

(ii) the award is in conflict with the public policy of this State.

(3) An application for setting aside may not be made after three months have elapsed from the date on which the party making that application had received the award or, if a request had been made under Article 33, from the date on which that request had been disposed of by the arbitral tribunal.

(4) The court, when asked to set aside an award, may, where appropriate and so requested by a party, suspend the setting aside proceedings for a period of time determined by it in order to give the arbitral tribunal an opportunity to resume the arbitral proceedings or to take such other action as in the arbitral tribunal's opinion will eliminate the grounds for setting aside.

CHAPTER VIII. RECOGNITION AND ENFORCEMENT OF AWARDS

Article 35. Recognition and Enforcement

(1) An arbitral award, irrespective of the country in which it was made, shall be recognized as binding and, upon application in writing to the competent court, shall be enforced subject to the provisions of this article and of Article 36.

(2) The party relying on an award or applying for its enforcement shall supply the original award or a copy thereof. If the award is not made in an official language of this State, the court may request the party to supply a translation thereof into such language.[1]

(Article 35(2) has been amended by the Commission at its thirty-ninth session, in 2006)

Article 36. Grounds for Refusing Recognition or Enforcement

(1) Recognition or enforcement of an arbitral award, irrespective of the country in which it was made, may be refused only:

(a) at the request of the party against whom it is invoked, if that party furnishes to the competent court where recognition or enforcement is sought proof that:

(i) a party to the arbitration agreement referred to in Article 7 was under some incapacity; or the said agreement is not valid under the law to which the parties have subjected it or, failing any indication thereon, under the law of the country where the award was made; or

(ii) the party against whom the award is invoked was not given proper notice of the appointment of an arbitrator or of the arbitral proceedings or was otherwise unable to present his case; or

(iii) the award deals with a dispute not contemplated by or not falling within the terms of the submission to arbitration, or it contains decisions on matters beyond the scope of the submission to arbitration, provided that, if the decisions on matters submitted to arbitration can be separated from those not so submitted, that part of the award which contains decisions on matters submitted to arbitration may be recognized and enforced; or

---

1   The conditions set forth in this paragraph are intended to set maximum standards. It would, thus, not be contrary to the harmonization to be achieved by the model law if a State retained even less onerous conditions.

(iv) the composition of the arbitral tribunal or the arbitral procedure was not in accordance with the agreement of the parties or, failing such agreement, was not in accordance with the law of the country where the arbitration took place; or

(v) the award has not yet become binding on the parties or has been set aside or suspended by a court of the country in which, or under the law of which, that award was made; or

(b) if the court finds that:

(i) the subject-matter of the dispute is not capable of settlement by arbitration under the law of this State; or

(ii) the recognition or enforcement of the award would be contrary to the public policy of this State.

(2) If an application for setting aside or suspension of an award has been made to a court referred to in paragraph (1)*(a)*(v) of this article, the court where recognition or enforcement is sought may, if it considers it proper, adjourn its decision and may also, on the application of the party claiming recognition or enforcement of the award, order the other party to provide appropriate security.

1996 UNCITRAL NOTES ON ORGANIZING ARBITRAL PROCEEDINGS[1]

INTRODUCTION

Purpose of the Notes

1.   The purpose of the Notes is to assist arbitration practitioners by listing and briefly describing questions on which appropriately timed decisions on organizing arbitral proceedings may be useful. The text, prepared with a particular view to international arbitrations, may be used whether or not the arbitration is administered by an arbitral institution.

Non-Binding Character of the Notes

2.   No legal requirement binding on the arbitrators or the parties is imposed by the Notes. The arbitral tribunal remains free to use the Notes as it sees fit and is not required to give reasons for disregarding them.

3.   The Notes are not suitable to be used as arbitration rules, since they do not establish any obligation of the arbitral tribunal or the parties to act in a particular way. Accordingly, the use of the Notes cannot imply any modification of the arbitration rules that the parties may have agreed upon.

Discretion in Conduct of Proceedings and Usefulness of Timely Decisions on Organizing Proceedings

4.   Laws governing the arbitral procedure and arbitration rules that parties may agree upon typically allow the arbitral tribunal broad discretion and flexibility in the conduct of arbitral proceedings. This is useful in that it enables the arbitral tribunal to take decisions on the organization of proceedings that take into account the circumstances of the case, the expectations of the parties and of the members of the arbitral tribunal, and the need for a just and cost-efficient resolution of the dispute.

5.   Such discretion may make it desirable for the arbitral tribunal to give the parties a timely indication as to the organization of the proceedings and the manner in which the tribunal intends to proceed. This is particularly desirable in international arbitrations, where the participants may be accustomed to differing styles of conducting arbitrations. Without such guidance, a party may find aspects of the proceedings unpredictable and difficult to prepare for. That may lead to misunderstandings, delays and increased costs.

1   © United Nations: United Nations Commission on International Trade Law (UNCITRAL). All rights reserved.

Multi-Party Arbitration

6.   These Notes are intended for use not only in arbitrations with two parties but also in arbitrations with three or more parties. Use of the Notes in multi-party arbitration is referred to below in paragraphs 86-88 (item 18).

Process of Making Decisions on Organizing Arbitral Proceedings

7.   Decisions by the arbitral tribunal on organizing arbitral proceedings may be taken with or without previous consultations with the parties. The method chosen depends on whether, in view of the type of the question to be decided, the arbitral tribunal considers that consultations are not necessary or that hearing the views of the parties would be beneficial for increasing the predictability of the proceedings or improving the procedural atmosphere.

8.   The consultations, whether they involve only the arbitrators or also the parties, can be held in one or more meetings, or can be carried out by correspondence or telecommunications such as telefax or conference telephone calls or other electronic means. Meetings may be held at the venue of arbitration or at some other appropriate location.

9.   In some arbitrations a special meeting may be devoted exclusively to such procedural consultations; alternatively, the consultations may be held in conjunction with a hearing on the substance of the dispute. Practices differ as to whether such special meetings should be held and how they should be organized. Special procedural meetings of the arbitrators and the parties separate from hearings are in practice referred to by expressions such as "preliminary meeting", "pre-hearing conference", "preparatory conference", "pre-hearing review", or terms of similar meaning. The terms used partly depend on the stage of the proceedings at which the meeting is taking place.

List of Matters for Possible Consideration in Organizing Arbitral Proceedings

10.   The Notes provide a list, followed by annotations, of matters on which the arbitral tribunal may wish to formulate decisions on organizing arbitral proceedings.

11.   Given that procedural styles and practices in arbitration vary widely, that the purpose of the Notes is not to promote any practice as best practice, and that the Notes are designed for universal use, it is not attempted in the Notes to describe in detail different arbitral practices or express a preference for any of them.

12.   The list, while not exhaustive, covers a broad range of situations that may arise in an arbitration. In many arbitrations, however, only a limited number of the matters mentioned in the list need to be considered. It also depends on the circumstances of the case at which stage or stages of the proceedings it would be useful to consider matters concerning the organization of the proceedings. Generally, in order not to create opportunities for unnecessary discussions and delay, it is advisable not to raise a matter prematurely, i.e. before it is clear that a decision is needed.

13.   When the Notes are used, it should be borne in mind that the discretion of the arbitral tribunal in organizing the proceedings may be limited by arbitration rules, by other provisions agreed to by the parties and by the law applicable to the arbitral procedure. When an arbitration is administered by an arbitral institution, various matters discussed in the Notes may be covered by the rules and practices of that institution.

ANNOTATIONS
1. Set of Arbitration Rules
If the parties have not agreed on a set of arbitration rules, would they wish to do so?

14.   Sometimes parties who have not included in their arbitration agreement a stipulation that a set of arbitration rules will govern their arbitral proceedings might wish to do so after the arbitration has begun. If that occurs, the UNCITRAL Arbitration Rules may be used either without modification or with such modifications as the parties might wish to agree upon. In the alternative, the parties might wish to adopt the rules of an arbitral institution; in that case, it may be necessary to secure the agreement of that institution and to stipulate the terms under which the arbitration could be carried out in accordance with the rules of that institution.

15. However, caution is advised as consideration of a set of arbitration rules might delay the proceedings or give rise to unnecessary controversy.

16. It should be noted that agreement on arbitration rules is not a necessity and that, if the parties do not agree on a set of arbitration rules, the arbitral tribunal has the power to continue the proceedings and determine how the case will be conducted.

2. Language of Proceedings

17. Many rules and laws on arbitral procedure empower the arbitral tribunal to determine the language or languages to be used in the proceedings, if the parties have not reached an agreement thereon.

(a) Possible need for translation of documents, in full or in part

18. Some documents annexed to the statements of claim and defence or submitted later may not be in the language of the proceedings. Bearing in mind the needs of the proceedings and economy, it may be considered whether the arbitral tribunal should order that any of those documents or parts thereof should be accompanied by a translation into the language of the proceedings.

(b) Possible need for interpretation of oral presentations

19. If interpretation will be necessary during oral hearings, it is advisable to consider whether the interpretation will be simultaneous or consecutive and whether the arrangements should be the responsibility of a party or the arbitral tribunal. In an arbitration administered by an institution, interpretation as well as translation services are often arranged by the arbitral institution.

(c) Cost of translation and interpretation

20. In taking decisions about translation or interpretation, it is advisable to decide whether any or all of the costs are to be paid directly by a party or whether they will be paid out of the deposits and apportioned between the parties along with the other arbitration costs.

3. Place of Arbitration

(a) Determination of the place of arbitration, if not already agreed upon by the parties

21. Arbitration rules usually allow the parties to agree on the place of arbitration, subject to the requirement of some arbitral institutions that arbitrations under their rules be conducted at a particular place, usually the location of the institution. If the place has not been so agreed upon, the rules governing the arbitration typically provide that it is in the power of the arbitral tribunal or the institution administering the arbitration to determine the place. If the arbitral tribunal is to make that determination, it may wish to hear the views of the parties before doing so.

22. Various factual and legal factors influence the choice of the place of arbitration, and their relative importance varies from case to case. Among the more prominent factors are: (a) suitability of the law on arbitral procedure of the place of arbitration; (b) whether there is a multilateral or bilateral treaty on enforcement of arbitral awards between the State where the arbitration takes place and the State or States where the award may have to be enforced; (c) convenience of the parties and the arbitrators, including the travel distances; (d) availability and cost of support services needed; and (e) location of the subject-matter in dispute and proximity of evidence.

(b) Possibility of meetings outside the place of arbitration

23. Many sets of arbitration rules and laws on arbitral procedure expressly allow the arbitral tribunal to hold meetings elsewhere than at the place of arbitration. For example, under the UNCITRAL Model Law on International Commercial Arbitration "the arbitral tribunal may, unless otherwise agreed by the parties, meet at any place it considers appropriate for consultation among its members, for hearing witnesses, experts or the parties, or for inspection of goods, other property or documents" (article 20(2)). The purpose of this discretion is to permit arbitral proceedings to be carried out in a manner that is most efficient and economical.

4. Administrative Services That May Be Needed for the Arbitral Tribunal to Carry out its Functions
24.   Various administrative services (e.g. hearing rooms or secretarial services) may need to be procured for the arbitral tribunal to be able to carry out its functions. When the arbitration is administered by an arbitral institution, the institution will usually provide all or a good part of the required administrative support to the arbitral tribunal. When an arbitration administered by an arbitral institution takes place away from the seat of the institution, the institution may be able to arrange for administrative services to be obtained from another source, often an arbitral institution; some arbitral institutions have entered into cooperation agreements with a view to providing mutual assistance in servicing arbitral proceedings.
25.   When the case is not administered by an institution, or the involvement of the institution does not include providing administrative support, usually the administrative arrangements for the proceedings will be made by the arbitral tribunal or the presiding arbitrator; it may also be acceptable to leave some of the arrangements to the parties, or to one of the parties subject to agreement of the other party or parties. Even in such cases, a convenient source of administrative support might be found in arbitral institutions, which often offer their facilities to arbitrations not governed by the rules of the institution. Otherwise, some services could be procured from entities such as chambers of commerce, hotels or specialized firms providing secretarial or other support services.
26.   Administrative services might be secured by engaging a secretary of the arbitral tribunal (also referred to as registrar, clerk, administrator or rapporteur), who carries out the tasks under the direction of the arbitral tribunal. Some arbitral institutions routinely assign such persons to the cases administered by them. In arbitrations not administered by an institution or where the arbitral institution does not appoint a secretary, some arbitrators frequently engage such persons, at least in certain types of cases, whereas many others normally conduct the proceedings without them.
27.   To the extent the tasks of the secretary are purely organizational (e.g. obtaining meeting rooms and providing or coordinating secretarial services), this is usually not controversial. Differences in views, however, may arise if the tasks include legal research and other professional assistance to the arbitral tribunal (e.g. collecting case law or published commentaries on legal issues defined by the arbitral tribunal, preparing summaries from case law and publications, and sometimes also preparing drafts of procedural decisions or drafts of certain parts of the award, in particular those concerning the facts of the case). Views or expectations may differ especially where a task of the secretary is similar to professional functions of the arbitrators. Such a role of the secretary is in the view of some commentators inappropriate or is appropriate only under certain conditions, such as that the parties agree thereto. However, it is typically recognized that it is important to ensure that the secretary does not perform any decision-making function of the arbitral tribunal.

5. Deposits in Respect of Costs
(a) Amount to be deposited
28.   In an arbitration administered by an institution, the institution often sets, on the basis of an estimate of the costs of the proceedings, the amount to be deposited as an advance for the costs of the arbitration. In other cases it is customary for the arbitral tribunal to make such an estimate and request a deposit. The estimate typically includes travel and other expenses by the arbitrators, expenditures for administrative assistance required by the arbitral tribunal, costs of any expert advice required by the arbitral tribunal, and the fees for the arbitrators. Many arbitration rules have provisions on this matter, including on whether the deposit should be made by the two parties (or all parties in a multi-party case) or only by the claimant.

(b) Management of deposits
29.   When the arbitration is administered by an institution, the institution's services may include managing and accounting for the deposited money. Where that is not the case, it might be

useful to clarify matters such as the type and location of the account in which the money will be kept and how the deposits will be managed.

(c) Supplementary deposits

30. If during the course of proceedings it emerges that the costs will be higher than anticipated, supplementary deposits may be required (e.g. because the arbitral tribunal decides pursuant to the arbitration rules to appoint an expert).

6. Confidentiality of Information Relating to the Arbitration; Possible Agreement Thereon

31. It is widely viewed that confidentiality is one of the advantageous and helpful features of arbitration. Nevertheless, there is no uniform answer in national laws as to the extent to which the participants in an arbitration are under the duty to observe the confidentiality of information relating to the case. Moreover, parties that have agreed on arbitration rules or other provisions that do not expressly address the issue of confidentiality cannot assume that all jurisdictions would recognize an implied commitment to confidentiality. Furthermore, the participants in an arbitration might not have the same understanding as regards the extent of confidentiality that is expected. Therefore, the arbitral tribunal might wish to discuss that with the parties and, if considered appropriate, record any agreed principles on the duty of confidentiality.

32. An agreement on confidentiality might cover, for example, one or more of the following matters: the material or information that is to be kept confidential (e.g. pieces of evidence, written and oral arguments, the fact that the arbitration is taking place, identity of the arbitrators, content of the award); measures for maintaining confidentiality of such information and hearings; whether any special procedures should be employed for maintaining the confidentiality of information transmitted by electronic means (e.g. because communication equipment is shared by several users, or because electronic mail over public networks is considered not sufficiently protected against unauthorized access); circumstances in which confidential information may be disclosed in part or in whole (e.g. in the context of disclosures of information in the public domain, or if required by law or a regulatory body).

7. Routing of Written Communications among the Parties and the Arbitrators

33. To the extent the question how documents and other written communications should be routed among the parties and the arbitrators is not settled by the agreed rules, or, if an institution administers the case, by the practices of the institution, it is useful for the arbitral tribunal to clarify the question suitably early so as to avoid misunderstandings and delays.

34. Among various possible patterns of routing, one example is that a party transmits the appropriate number of copies to the arbitral tribunal, or to the arbitral institution, if one is involved, which then forwards them as appropriate. Another example is that a party is to send copies simultaneously to the arbitrators and the other party or parties. Documents and other written communications directed by the arbitral tribunal or the presiding arbitrator to one or more parties may also follow a determined pattern, such as through the arbitral institution or by direct transmission. For some communications, in particular those on organizational matters (e.g. dates for hearings), more direct routes of communication may be agreed, even if, for example, the arbitral institution acts as an intermediary for documents such as the statements of claim and defence, evidence or written arguments.

8. Telefax and Other Electronic Means of Sending Documents
(a) Telefax

35. Telefax, which offers many advantages over traditional means of communication, is widely used in arbitral proceedings. Nevertheless, should it be thought that, because of the characteristics of the equipment used, it would be preferable not to rely only on a telefacsimile of a document, special arrangements may be considered, such as that a particular piece of written evidence should be mailed or otherwise physically delivered, or that certain telefax messages should be confirmed by mailing or otherwise delivering documents whose facsimile were transmitted by electronic means. When a document should not be sent by telefax, it may, however,

be appropriate, in order to avoid an unnecessarily rigid procedure, for the arbitral tribunal to retain discretion to accept an advance copy of a document by telefax for the purposes of meeting a deadline, provided that the document itself is received within a reasonable time thereafter.

(b) Other electronic means (e.g. electronic mail and magnetic or optical disk)

36. It might be agreed that documents, or some of them, will be exchanged not only in paper-based form, but in addition also in an electronic form other than telefax (e.g. as electronic mail, or on a magnetic or optical disk), or only in electronic form. Since the use of electronic means depends on the aptitude of the persons involved and the availability of equipment and computer programs, agreement is necessary for such means to be used. If both paper-based and electronic means are to be used, it is advisable to decide which one is controlling and, if there is a time-limit for submitting a document, which act constitutes submission.

37. When the exchange of documents in electronic form is planned, it is useful, in order to avoid technical difficulties, to agree on matters such as: data carriers (e.g. electronic mail or computer disks) and their technical characteristics; computer programs to be used in preparing the electronic records; instructions for transforming the electronic records into human-readable form; keeping of logs and back.up records of communications sent and received; information in human-readable form that should accompany the disks (e.g. the names of the originator and recipient, computer program, titles of the electronic files and the back-up methods used); procedures when a message is lost or the communication system otherwise fails; and identification of persons who can be contacted if a problem occurs.

9. Arrangements for the Exchange of Written Submissions

38. After the parties have initially stated their claims and defences, they may wish, or the arbitral tribunal might request them, to present further written submissions so as to prepare for the hearings or to provide the basis for a decision without hearings. In such submissions, the parties, for example, present or comment on allegations and evidence, cite or explain law, or make or react to proposals. In practice such submissions are referred to variously as, for example, statement, memorial, counter-memorial, brief, counter-brief, reply, réplique, duplique, rebuttal or rejoinder; the terminology is a matter of linguistic usage and the scope or sequence of the submission.

(a) Scheduling of written submissions

39. It is advisable that the arbitral tribunal set time.limits for written submissions. In enforcing the time-limits, the arbitral tribunal may wish, on the one hand, to make sure that the case is not unduly protracted and, on the other hand, to reserve a degree of discretion and allow late submissions if appropriate under the circumstances. In some cases the arbitral tribunal might prefer not to plan the written submissions in advance, thus leaving such matters, including time-limits, to be decided in light of the developments in the proceedings. In other cases, the arbitral tribunal may wish to determine, when scheduling the first written submissions, the number of subsequent submissions.

40. Practices differ as to whether, after the hearings have been held, written submissions are still acceptable. While some arbitral tribunals consider post-hearing submissions unacceptable, others might request or allow them on a particular issue. Some arbitral tribunals follow the procedure according to which the parties are not requested to present written evidence and legal arguments to the arbitral tribunal before the hearings; in such a case, the arbitral tribunal may regard it as appropriate that written submissions be made after the hearings.

(b) Consecutive or simultaneous submissions

41. Written submissions on an issue may be made consecutively, i.e. the party who receives a submission is given a period of time to react with its counter submission. Another possibility is to request each party to make the submission within the same time period to the arbitral tribunal or the institution administering the case; the received submissions are then forwarded simultaneously to the respective other party or parties. The approach used may depend on the type of issues to be commented upon and the time in which the views should be clarified. With

consecutive submissions, it may take longer than with simultaneous ones to obtain views of the parties on a given issue. Consecutive submissions, however, allow the reacting party to comment on all points raised by the other party or parties, which simultaneous submissions do not; thus, simultaneous submissions might possibly necessitate further submissions.

10. Practical Details Concerning Written Submissions and Evidence
(e.g. Method of Submission, Copies, Numbering, References)

42.   Depending on the volume and kind of documents to be handled, it might be considered whether practical arrangements on details such as the following would be helpful:

-   Whether the submissions will be made as paper documents or by electronic means, or both (see paragraphs 35.37);
-   The number of copies in which each document is to be submitted;
-   A system for numbering documents and items of evidence, and a method for marking them, including by tabs;
-   The form of references to documents (e.g. by the heading and the number assigned to the document or its date);
-   Paragraph numbering in written submissions, in order to facilitate precise references to parts of a text;
-   When translations are to be submitted as paper documents, whether the translations are to be contained in the same volume as the original texts or included in separate volumes.

11. Defining Points at Issue; Order of Deciding Issues; Defining Relief or Remedy Sought
(a) Should a list of points at issue be prepared?

43.   In considering the parties' allegations and arguments, the arbitral tribunal may come to the conclusion that it would be useful for it or for the parties to prepare, for analytical purposes and for ease of discussion, a list of the points at issue, as opposed to those that are undisputed. If the arbitral tribunal determines that the advantages of working on the basis of such a list outweigh the disadvantages, it chooses the appropriate stage of the proceedings for preparing a list, bearing in mind also that subsequent developments in the proceedings may require a revision of the points at issue. Such an identification of points at issue might help to concentrate on the essential matters, to reduce the number of points at issue by agreement of the parties, and to select the best and most economical process for resolving the dispute. However, possible disadvantages of preparing such a list include delay, adverse effect on the flexibility of the proceedings, or unnecessary disagreements about whether the arbitral tribunal has decided all issues submitted to it or whether the award contains decisions on matters beyond the scope of the submission to arbitration. The terms of reference required under some arbitration rules, or in agreements of parties, may serve the same purpose as the above.described list of points at issue.

(b) In which order should the points at issue be decided?

44.   While it is often appropriate to deal with all the points at issue collectively, the arbitral tribunal might decide to take them up during the proceedings in a particular order. The order may be due to a point being preliminary relative to another (e.g. a decision on the jurisdiction of the arbitral tribunal is preliminary to consideration of substantive issues, or the issue of responsibility for a breach of contract is preliminary to the issue of the resulting damages). A particular order may be decided also when the breach of various contracts is in dispute or when damages arising from various events are claimed.

45.   If the arbitral tribunal has adopted a particular order of deciding points at issue, it might consider it appropriate to issue a decision on one of the points earlier than on the other ones. This might be done, for example, when a discrete part of a claim is ready for decision while the other parts still require extensive consideration, or when it is expected that after deciding certain issues the parties might be more inclined to settle the remaining ones. Such earlier decisions are referred to by expressions such as "partial", "interlocutory" or "interim" awards or decisions, depending on the type of issue dealt with and on whether the decision is final with respect to the

issue it resolves. Questions that might be the subject of such decisions are, for example, jurisdiction of the arbitral tribunal, interim measures of protection, or the liability of a party.

(c) Is there a need to define more precisely the relief or remedy sought?
46.   If the arbitral tribunal considers that the relief or remedy sought is insufficiently definite, it may wish to explain to the parties the degree of definiteness with which their claims should be formulated. Such an explanation may be useful since criteria are not uniform as to how specific the claimant must be in formulating a relief or remedy.

12. Possible Settlement Negotiations and Their Effect on Scheduling Proceedings
47.   Attitudes differ as to whether it is appropriate for the arbitral tribunal to bring up the possibility of settlement. Given the divergence of practices in this regard, the arbitral tribunal should only suggest settlement negotiations with caution. However, it may be opportune for the arbitral tribunal to schedule the proceedings in a way that might facilitate the continuation or initiation of settlement negotiations.

13. Documentary Evidence
(a) Time-limits for submission of documentary evidence intended to be submitted by the parties; consequences of late submission
48.   Often the written submissions of the parties contain sufficient information for the arbitral tribunal to fix the time-limit for submitting evidence. Otherwise, in order to set realistic time periods, the arbitral tribunal may wish to consult with the parties about the time that they would reasonably need.
49.   The arbitral tribunal may wish to clarify that evidence submitted late will as a rule not be accepted. It may wish not to preclude itself from accepting a late submission of evidence if the party shows sufficient cause for the delay.

(b) Whether the arbitral tribunal intends to require a party to produce documentary evidence
50.   Procedures and practices differ widely as to the conditions under which the arbitral tribunal may require a party to produce documents. Therefore, the arbitral tribunal might consider it useful, when the agreed arbitration rules do not provide specific conditions, to clarify to the parties the manner in which it intends to proceed.
51.   The arbitral tribunal may wish to establish time-limits for the production of documents. The parties might be reminded that, if the requested party duly invited to produce documentary evidence fails to do so within the established period of time, without showing sufficient cause for such failure, the arbitral tribunal is free to draw its conclusions from the failure and may make the award on the evidence before it.

(c) Should assertions about the origin and receipt of documents and about the correctness of photocopies be assumed as accurate?
52.   It may be helpful for the arbitral tribunal to inform the parties that it intends to conduct the proceedings on the basis that, unless a party raises an objection to any of the following conclusions within a specified period of time: *(a)* a document is accepted as having originated from the source indicated in the document; *(b)* a copy of a dispatched communication (e.g. letter, telex, telefax or other electronic message) is accepted without further proof as having been received by the addressee; and *(c)* a copy is accepted as correct. A statement by the arbitral tribunal to that effect can simplify the introduction of documentary evidence and discourage unfounded and dilatory objections, at a late stage of the proceedings, to the probative value of documents. It is advisable to provide that the time-limit for objections will not be enforced if the arbitral tribunal considers the delay justified.

(d) Are the parties willing to submit jointly a single set of documentary evidence?
53.   The parties may consider submitting jointly a single set of documentary evidence whose authenticity is not disputed. The purpose would be to avoid duplicate submissions and unnecessary discussions concerning the authenticity of documents, without prejudicing the position of the parties concerning the content of the documents. Additional documents may be inserted

later if the parties agree. When a single set of documents would be too voluminous to be easily manageable, it might be practical to select a number of frequently used documents and establish a set of "working" documents. A convenient arrangement of documents in the set may be according to chronological order or subject-matter. It is useful to keep a table of contents of the documents, for example, by their short headings and dates, and to provide that the parties will refer to documents by those headings and dates.

(e) Should voluminous and complicated documentary evidence be presented through summaries, tabulations, charts, extracts or samples?

54.   When documentary evidence is voluminous and complicated, it may save time and costs if such evidence is presented by a report of a person competent in the relevant field (e.g. public accountant or consulting engineer). The report may present the information in the form of summaries, tabulations, charts, extracts or samples. Such presentation of evidence should be combined with arrangements that give the interested party the opportunity to review the underlying data and the methodology of preparing the report.

14. Physical Evidence Other than Documents

55.   In some arbitrations the arbitral tribunal is called upon to assess physical evidence other than documents, for example, by inspecting samples of goods, viewing a video recording or observing the functioning of a machine.

(a) What arrangements should be made if physical evidence will be submitted?

56.   If physical evidence will be submitted, the arbitral tribunal may wish to fix the time schedule for presenting the evidence, make arrangements for the other party or parties to have a suitable opportunity to prepare itself for the presentation of the evidence, and possibly take measures for safekeeping the items of evidence.

(b) What arrangements should be made if an on-site inspection is necessary?

57.   If an on-site inspection of property or goods will take place, the arbitral tribunal may consider matters such as timing, meeting places, other arrangements to provide the opportunity for all parties to be present, and the need to avoid communications between arbitrators and a party about points at issue without the presence of the other party or parties.

58.   The site to be inspected is often under the control of one of the parties, which typically means that employees or representatives of that party will be present to give guidance and explanations. It should be borne in mind that statements of those representatives or employees made during an on-site inspection, as contrasted with statements those persons might make as witnesses in a hearing, should not be treated as evidence in the proceedings.

15. Witnesses

59.   While laws and rules on arbitral procedure typically leave broad freedom concerning the manner of taking evidence of witnesses, practices on procedural points are varied. In order to facilitate the preparations of the parties for the hearings, the arbitral tribunal may consider it appropriate to clarify, in advance of the hearings, some or all of the following issues.

(a) Advance notice about a witness whom a party intends to present; written witnesses' statements

60.   To the extent the applicable arbitration rules do not deal with the matter, the arbitral tribunal may wish to require that each party give advance notice to the arbitral tribunal and the other party or parties of any witness it intends to present. As to the content of the notice, the following is an example of what might be required, in addition to the names and addresses of the witnesses:

(a)   the subject upon which the witnesses will testify;
(b)   the language in which the witnesses will testify; and
(c)   the nature of the relationship with any of the parties, qualifications and experience of the witnesses if and to the extent these are relevant to the dispute or the testimony, and how the witnesses learned about the facts on which they will testify. However, it may not be ne-

cessary to require such a notice, in particular if the thrust of the testimony can be clearly ascertained from the party's allegations.

61.   Some practitioners favour the procedure according to which the party presenting witness evidence submits a signed witness's statement containing testimony itself. It should be noted, however, that such practice, which implies interviewing the witness by the party presenting the testimony, is not known in all parts of the world and, moreover, that some practitioners disapprove of it on the ground that such contacts between the party and the witness may compromise the credibility of the testimony and are therefore improper (see paragraph 67). Notwithstanding these reservations, signed witness's testimony has advantages in that it may expedite the proceedings by making it easier for the other party or parties to prepare for the hearings or for the parties to identify uncontested matters. However, those advantages might be outweighed by the time and expense involved in obtaining the written testimony.

62.   If a signed witness's statement should be made under oath or similar affirmation of truth-fulness, it may be necessary to clarify by whom the oath or affirmation should be administered and whether any formal authentication will be required by the arbitral tribunal.

(b) Manner of taking oral evidence of witnesses
(i) Order in which questions will be asked and the manner in which the hearing of witnesses will be conducted

63.   To the extent that the applicable rules do not provide an answer, it may be useful for the arbitral tribunal to clarify how witnesses will be heard. One of the various possibilities is that a witness is first questioned by the arbitral tribunal, whereupon questions are asked by the par-ties, first by the party who called the witness. Another possibility is for the witness to be questio-ned by the party presenting the witness and then by the other party or parties, while the arbitral tribunal might pose questions during the questioning or after the parties on points that in the tribunal's view have not been sufficiently clarified. Differences exist also as to the degree of con-trol the arbitral tribunal exercises over the hearing of witnesses. For example, some arbitrators prefer to permit the parties to pose questions freely and directly to the witness, but may dis-allow a question if a party objects; other arbitrators tend to exercise more control and may dis-allow a question on their initiative or even require that questions from the parties be asked through the arbitral tribunal.

(ii) Whether oral testimony will be given under oath or affirmation and, if so, in what form an oath or affirmation should be made

64.   Practices and laws differ as to whether or not oral testimony is to be given under oath or affirmation. In some legal systems, the arbitrators are empowered to put witnesses on oath, but it is usually in their discretion whether they want to do so. In other systems, oral testimony under oath is either unknown or may even be considered improper as only an official such as a judge or notary may have the authority to administer oaths.

(iii) May witnesses be in the hearing room when they are not testifying?

65.   Some arbitrators favour the procedure that, except if the circumstances suggest otherwise, the presence of a witness in the hearing room is limited to the time the witness is testifying; the purpose is to prevent the witness from being influenced by what is said in the hearing room, or to prevent that the presence of the witness would influence another witness. Other arbitrators consider that the presence of a witness during the testimony of other witnesses may be beneficial in that possible contradictions may be readily clarified or that their presence may act as a deterrent against untrue statements. Other possible approaches may be that witnesses are not present in the hearing room before their testimony, but stay in the room after they have tes-tified, or that the arbitral tribunal decides the question for each witness individually depending on what the arbitral tribunal considers most appropriate. The arbitral tribunal may leave the procedure to be decided during the hearings, or may give guidance on the question in advance of the hearings.

(c) The order in which the witnesses will be called

66. When several witnesses are to be heard and longer testimony is expected, it is likely to reduce costs if the order in which they will be called is known in advance and their presence can be scheduled accordingly. Each party might be invited to suggest the order in which it intends to present the witnesses, while it would be up to the arbitral tribunal to approve the scheduling and to make departures from it.

(d) Interviewing witnesses prior to their appearance at a hearing

67. In some legal systems, parties or their representatives are permitted to interview witnesses, prior to their appearance at the hearing, as to such matters as their recollection of the relevant events, their experience, qualifications or relation with a participant in the proceedings. In those legal systems such contacts are usually not permitted once the witness's oral testimony has begun. In other systems such contacts with witnesses are considered improper. In order to avoid misunderstandings, the arbitral tribunal may consider it useful to clarify what kind of contacts a party is permitted to have with a witness in the preparations for the hearings.

(e) Hearing representatives of a party

68. According to some legal systems, certain persons affiliated with a party may only be heard as representatives of the party but not as witnesses. In such a case, it may be necessary to consider ground rules for determining which persons may not testify as witnesses (e.g. certain executives, employees or agents) and for hearing statements of those persons and for questioning them.

16. Experts and Expert Witnesses

69. Many arbitration rules and laws on arbitral procedure address the participation of experts in arbitral proceedings. A frequent solution is that the arbitral tribunal has the power to appoint an expert to report on issues determined by the tribunal; in addition, the parties may be permitted to present expert witnesses on points at issue. In other cases, it is for the parties to present expert testimony, and it is not expected that the arbitral tribunal will appoint an expert.

(a) Expert appointed by the arbitral tribunal

70. If the arbitral tribunal is empowered to appoint an expert, one possible approach is for the tribunal to proceed directly to selecting the expert. Another possibility is to consult the parties as to who should be the expert; this may be done, for example, without mentioning a candidate, by presenting to the parties a list of candidates, soliciting proposals from the parties, or by discussing with the parties the "profile" of the expert the arbitral tribunal intends to appoint, i.e. the qualifications, experience and abilities of the expert.

(i) The expert's terms of reference

71. The purpose of the expert's terms of reference is to indicate the questions on which the expert is to provide clarification, to avoid opinions on points that are not for the expert to assess and to commit the expert to a time schedule. While the discretion to appoint an expert normally includes the determination of the expert's terms of reference, the arbitral tribunal may decide to consult the parties before finalizing the terms. It might also be useful to determine details about how the expert will receive from the parties any relevant information or have access to any relevant documents, goods or other property, so as to enable the expert to prepare the report. In order to facilitate the evaluation of the expert's report, it is advisable to require the expert to include in the report information on the method used in arriving at the conclusions and the evidence and information used in preparing the report.

(ii) The opportunity of the parties to comment on the expert's report, including by presenting expert testimony

72. Arbitration rules that contain provisions on experts usually also have provisions on the right of a party to comment on the report of the expert appointed by the arbitral tribunal. If no such provisions apply or more specific procedures than those prescribed are deemed necessary, the arbitral tribunal may, in light of those provisions, consider it opportune to determine,

for example, the time period for presenting written comments of the parties, or, if hearings are to be held for the purpose of hearing the expert, the procedures for interrogating the expert by the parties or for the participation of any expert witnesses presented by the parties.

(b) Expert opinion presented by a party (expert witness)

73. If a party presents an expert opinion, the arbitral tribunal might consider requiring, for example, that the opinion be in writing, that the expert should be available to answer questions at hearings, and that, if a party will present an expert witness at a hearing, advance notice must be given or that the written opinion must be presented in advance, as in the case of other witnesses (see paragraphs 60-62).

17. Hearings

(a) Decision whether to hold hearings

74. Laws on arbitral procedure and arbitration rules often have provisions as to the cases in which oral hearings must be held and as to when the arbitral tribunal has discretion to decide whether to hold hearings.

75. If it is up to the arbitral tribunal to decide whether to hold hearings, the decision is likely to be influenced by factors such as, on the one hand, that it is usually quicker and easier to clarify points at issue pursuant to a direct confrontation of arguments than on the basis of correspondence and, on the other hand, the travel and other cost of holding hearings, and that the need of finding acceptable dates for the hearings might delay the proceedings. The arbitral tribunal may wish to consult the parties on this matter.

(b) Whether one period of hearings should be held or separate periods of hearings

76. Attitudes vary as to whether hearings should be held in a single period of hearings or in separate periods, especially when more than a few days are needed to complete the hearings. According to some arbitrators, the entire hearings should normally be held in a single period, even if the hearings are to last for more than a week. Other arbitrators in such cases tend to schedule separate periods of hearings. In some cases issues to be decided are separated, and separate hearings set for those issues, with the aim that oral presentation on those issues will be completed within the allotted time. Among the advantages of one period of hearings are that it involves less travel costs, memory will not fade, and it is unlikely that people representing a party will change. On the other hand, the longer the hearings, the more difficult it may be to find early dates acceptable to all participants. Furthermore, separate periods of hearings may be easier to schedule, the subsequent hearings may be tailored to the development of the case, and the period between the hearings leaves time for analysing the records and negotiations between the parties aimed at narrowing the points at issue by agreement.

(c) Setting dates for hearings

77. Typically, firm dates will be fixed for hearings. Exceptionally, the arbitral tribunal may initially wish to set only "target dates" as opposed to definitive dates. This may be done at a stage of the proceedings when not all information necessary to schedule hearings is yet available, with the understanding that the target dates will either be confirmed or rescheduled within a reasonably short period. Such provisional planning can be useful to participants who are generally not available on short notice.

(d) Whether there should be a limit on the aggregate amount of time each party will have for oral arguments and questioning witnesses

78. Some arbitrators consider it useful to limit the aggregate amount of time each party has for any of the following: (a) making oral statements; (b) questioning its witnesses; and (c) questioning the witnesses of the other party or parties. In general, the same aggregate amount of time is considered appropriate for each party, unless the arbitral tribunal considers that a different allocation is justified. Before deciding, the arbitral tribunal may wish to consult the parties as to how much time they think they will need.

79. Such planning of time, provided it is realistic, fair and subject to judiciously firm control by the arbitral tribunal, will make it easier for the parties to plan the presentation of the various items of evidence and arguments, reduce the likelihood of running out of time towards the end of the hearings and avoid that one party would unfairly use up a disproportionate amount of time.

(e) The order in which the parties will present their arguments and evidence

80. Arbitration rules typically give broad latitude to the arbitral tribunal to determine the order of presentations at the hearings. Within that latitude, practices differ, for example, as to whether opening or closing statements are heard and their level of detail; the sequence in which the claimant and the respondent present their opening statements, arguments, witnesses and other evidence; and whether the respondent or the claimant has the last word. In view of such differences, or when no arbitration rules apply, it may foster efficiency of the proceedings if the arbitral tribunal clarifies to the parties, in advance of the hearings, the manner in which it will conduct the hearings, at least in broad lines.

(f) Length of hearings

81. The length of a hearing primarily depends on the complexity of the issues to be argued and the amount of witness evidence to be presented. The length also depends on the procedural style used in the arbitration. Some practitioners prefer to have written evidence and written arguments presented before the hearings, which thus can focus on the issues that have not been sufficiently clarified. Those practitioners generally tend to plan shorter hearings than those practitioners who prefer that most if not all evidence and arguments are presented to the arbitral tribunal orally and in full detail. In order to facilitate the parties' preparations and avoid misunderstandings, the arbitral tribunal may wish to clarify to the parties, in advance of the hearings, the intended use of time and style of work at the hearings.

(g) Arrangements for a record of the hearings

82. The arbitral tribunal should decide, possibly after consulting with the parties, on the method of preparing a record of oral statements and testimony during hearings. Among different possibilities, one method is that the members of the arbitral tribunal take personal notes. Another is that the presiding arbitrator during the hearing dictates to a typist a summary of oral statements and testimony. A further method, possible when a secretary of the arbitral tribunal has been appointed, may be to leave to that person the preparation of a summary record. A useful, though costly, method is for professional stenographers to prepare verbatim transcripts, often within the next day or a similarly short time period. A written record may be combined with tape-recording, so as to enable reference to the tape in case of a disagreement over the written record.

83. If transcripts are to be produced, it may be considered how the persons who made the statements will be given an opportunity to check the transcripts. For example, it may be determined that the changes to the record would be approved by the parties or, failing their agreement, would be referred for decision to the arbitral tribunal.

(h) Whether and when the parties are permitted to submit notes summarizing their oral arguments

84. Some legal counsel are accustomed to giving notes summarizing their oral arguments to the arbitral tribunal and to the other party or parties. If such notes are presented, this is usually done during the hearings or shortly thereafter; in some cases, the notes are sent before the hearing. In order to avoid surprise, foster equal treatment of the parties and facilitate preparations for the hearings, advance clarification is advisable as to whether submitting such notes is acceptable and the time for doing so.

85. In closing the hearings, the arbitral tribunal will normally assume that no further proof is to be offered or submission to be made. Therefore, if notes are to be presented to be read after the closure of the hearings, the arbitral tribunal may find it worthwhile to stress that the notes should be limited to summarizing what was said orally and in particular should not refer to new evidence or new argument.

18. Multi-Party Arbitration

86.   When a single arbitration involves more than two parties (multi-party arbitration), considerations regarding the need to organize arbitral proceedings, and matters that may be considered in that connection, are generally not different from two-party arbitrations. A possible difference may be that, because of the need to deal with more than two parties, multi-party proceedings can be more complicated to manage than bilateral proceedings. The Notes, notwithstanding a possible greater complexity of multi-party arbitration, can be used in multi-party as well as in two-party proceedings.

87.   The areas of possibly increased complexity in multi-party arbitration are, for example, the flow of communications among the parties and the arbitral tribunal (see paragraphs 33, 34 and 38-41); if points at issue are to be decided at different points in time, the order of deciding them (paragraphs 44-45); the manner in which the parties will participate in hearing witnesses (paragraph 63); the appointment of experts and the participation of the parties in considering their reports (paragraphs 70-72); the scheduling of hearings (paragraph 76); the order in which the parties will present their arguments and evidence at hearings (paragraph 80).

88.   The Notes, which are limited to pointing out matters that may be considered in organizing arbitral proceedings in general, do not cover the drafting of the arbitration agreement or the constitution of the arbitral tribunal, both issues that give rise to special questions in multi-party arbitration as compared to two-party arbitration.

19. Possible Requirements Concerning Filing or Delivering the Award

89.   Some national laws require that arbitral awards be filed or registered with a court or similar authority, or that they be delivered in a particular manner or through a particular authority. Those laws differ with respect to, for example, the type of award to which the requirement applies (e.g. to all awards or only to awards not rendered under the auspices of an arbitral institution); time periods for filing, registering or delivering the award (in some cases those time periods may be rather short); or consequences for failing to comply with the requirement (which might be, for example, invalidity of the award or inability to enforce it in a particular manner).

Who should take steps to fulfil any requirement?

90.   If such a requirement exists, it is useful, some time before the award is to be issued, to plan who should take the necessary steps to meet the requirement and how the costs are to be borne.

2012 RULES OF ARBITRATION
ICC Publication No. 850[1]

Introductory Provisons
Article 1 International Court of Arbitration

1   The International Court of Arbitration (the "Court") of the International Chamber of Commerce (the "ICC") is the independent arbitration body of the ICC. The statutes of the Court are set forth in Appendix I.

2   The Court does not itself resolve disputes. It administers the resolution of disputes by arbitral tribunals, in accordance with the Rules of Arbitration of the ICC (the "Rules"). The Court is the only body authorized to administer arbitrations under the Rules, including the scrutiny and

---

1   © ICC. The text reproduced here is valid at the time of reproduction in June 2012. As amendments may from time to time be made to the text, please refer to the website <www.iccarbitration.org> for the latest version and for more information on this ICC dispute resolution service. The text is also available in the ICC Dispute Resolution Library at <www.iccdrl.com>.

approval of awards rendered in accordance with the Rules. It draws up its own internal rules, which are set forth in Appendix II (the "Internal Rules").

3   The President of the Court (the "President") or, in the President's absence or otherwise at the President's request, one of its Vice-Presidents shall have the power to take urgent decisions on behalf of the Court, provided that any such decision is reported to the Court at its next session.

4   As provided for in the Internal Rules, the Court may delegate to one or more committees composed of its members the power to take certain decisions, provided that any such decision is reported to the Court at its next session.

5   The Court is assisted in its work by the Secretariat of the Court (the "Secretariat") under the direction of its Secretary General (the "Secretary General").

Article 2 Definitions

In the Rules:

(i)   "arbitral tribunal" includes one or more arbitrators;

(ii)   "claimant" includes one or more claimants, "respondent" includes one or more respondents, and "additional party" includes one or more additional parties;

(iii)   "party" or "parties" include claimants, respondents or additional parties;

(iv)   "claim" or "claims" include any claim by any party against any other party;

(v)   "award" includes, *inter alia*, an interim, partial or final award.

Article 3 Written Notifications or Communications; Time Limits

1   All pleadings and other written communications submitted by any party, as well as all documents annexed thereto, shall be supplied in a number of copies sufficient to provide one copy for each party, plus one for each arbitrator, and one for the Secretariat. A copy of any notification or communication from the arbitral tribunal to the parties shall be sent to the Secretariat.

2   All notifications or communications from the Secretariat and the arbitral tribunal shall be made to the last address of the party or its representative for whom the same are intended, as notified either by the party in question or by the other party. Such notification or communication may be made by delivery against receipt, registered post, courier, email, or any other means of telecommunication that provides a record of the sending thereof.

3   A notification or communication shall be deemed to have been made on the day it was received by the party itself or by its representative, or would have been received if made in accordance with Article 3(2).

4   Periods of time specified in or fixed under the Rules shall start to run on the day following the date a notification or communication is deemed to have been made in accordance with Article 3(3). When the day next following such date is an official holiday, or a non-business day in the country where the notification or communication is deemed to have been made, the period of time shall commence on the first following business day. Official holidays and non-business days are included in the calculation of the period of time. If the last day of the relevant period of time granted is an official holiday or a nonbusiness day in the country where the notification or communication is deemed to have been made, the period of time shall expire at the end of the first following business day.

Commencing the Arbitration
Article 4 Request for Arbitration

1   A party wishing to have recourse to arbitration under the Rules shall submit its Request for Arbitration (the "Request") to the Secretariat at any of the offices specified in the Internal Rules. The Secretariat shall notify the claimant and respondent of the receipt of the Request and the date of such receipt.

2   The date on which the Request is received by the Secretariat shall, for all purposes, be deemed to be the date of the commencement of the arbitration.

3   The Request shall contain the following information:

a)   the name in full, description, address and other contact details of each of the parties;

b)   the name in full, address and other contact details of any person(s) representing the clai-
     mant in the arbitration;
c)   a description of the nature and circumstances of the dispute giving rise to the claims and of
     the basis upon which the claims are made;
d)   a statement of the relief sought, together with the amounts of any quantified claims and,
     to the extent possible, an estimate of the monetary value of any other claims;
e)   any relevant agreements and, in particular, the arbitration agreement(s);
f)   where claims are made under more than one arbitration agreement, an indication of the
     arbitration agreement under which each claim is made;
g)   all relevant particulars and any observations or proposals concerning the number of arbi-
     trators and their choice in accordance with the provisions of Articles 12 and 13, and any no-
     mination of an arbitrator required thereby; and
h)   all relevant particulars and any observations or proposals as to the place of the arbitration,
     the applicable rules of law and the language of the arbitration.
The claimant may submit such other documents or information with the Request as it
considers appropriate or as may contribute to the efficient resolution of the dispute.
4   Together with the Request, the claimant shall:
a)   submit the number of copies thereof required by Article 3(1); and
b)   make payment of the filing fee required by Appendix III ("Arbitration Costs and Fees") in
     force on the date the Request is submitted.
In the event that the claimant fails to comply with either of these requirements, the Secretariat
may fix a time limit within which the claimant must comply, failing which the file shall be closed
without prejudice to the claimant's right to submit the same claims at a later date in another
Request.
5   The Secretariat shall transmit a copy of the Request and the documents annexed thereto
to the respondent for its Answer to the Request once the Secretariat has sufficient copies of the
Request and the required filing fee.

Article 5 Answer to the Request; Counterclaims
1   Within 30 days from the receipt of the Request from the Secretariat, the respondent shall
submit an Answer (the "Answer") which shall contain the following information:
a)   its name in full, description, address and other contact details;
b)   the name in full, address and other contact details of any person(s) representing the
     respondent in the arbitration;
c)   its comments as to the nature and circumstances of the dispute giving rise to the claims
     and the basis upon which the claims are made;
d)   its response to the relief sought;
e)   any observations or proposals concerning the number of arbitrators and their choice in
     light of the claimant's proposals and in accordance with the provisions of Articles 12 and
     13, and any nomination of an arbitrator required thereby; and
f)   any observations or proposals as to the place of the arbitration, the applicable rules of law
     and the language of the arbitration.
The respondent may submit such other documents or information with the Answer as it considers appropriate or as may contribute to the efficient resolution of the dispute.
2   The Secretariat may grant the respondent an extension of the time for submitting the
Answer, provided the application for such an extension contains the respondent's observations
or proposals concerning the number of arbitrators and their choice and, where required by
Articles 12 and 13, the nomination of an arbitrator. If the respondent fails to do so, the Court
shall proceed in accordance with the Rules.
3   The Answer shall be submitted to the Secretariat in the number of copies specified by
Article 3(1).
4   The Secretariat shall communicate the Answer and the documents annexed thereto to all
other parties.

5   Any counterclaims made by the respondent shall be submitted with the Answer and shall provide:

a)   a description of the nature and circumstances of the dispute giving rise to the counter-claims and of the basis upon which the counterclaims are made;

b)   a statement of the relief sought together with the amounts of any quantified counter-claims and, to the extent possible, an estimate of the monetary value of any other counter-claims;

c)   any relevant agreements and, in particular, the arbitration agreement(s); and

d)   where counterclaims are made under more than one arbitration agreement, an indication of the arbitration agreement under which each counterclaim is made.

The respondent may submit such other documents or information with the counterclaims as it considers appropriate or as may contribute to the efficient resolution of the dispute.

6   The claimant shall submit a reply to any counterclaim within 30 days from the date of receipt of the counterclaims communicated by the Secretariat. Prior to the transmission of the file to the arbitral tribunal, the Secretariat may grant the claimant an extension of time for submitting the reply.

Article 6 Effect of the Arbitration Agreement

1   Where the parties have agreed to submit to arbitration under the Rules, they shall be deemed to have submitted *ipso facto* to the Rules in effect on the date of commencement of the arbitration, unless they have agreed to submit to the Rules in effect on the date of their arbitration agreement.

2   By agreeing to arbitration under the Rules, the parties have accepted that the arbitration shall be administered by the Court.

3   If any party against which a claim has been made does not submit an answer, or raises one or more pleas concerning the existence, validity or scope of the arbitration agreement or concerning whether all of the claims made in the arbitration may be determined together in a single arbitration, the arbitration shall proceed and any question of jurisdiction or of whether the claims may be determined together in that arbitration shall be decided directly by the arbitral tribunal, unless the Secretary General refers the matter to the Court for its decision pursuant to Article 6(4).

4   In all cases referred to the Court under Article 6(3), the Court shall decide whether and to what extent the arbitration shall proceed. The arbitration shall proceed if and to the extent that the Court is *prima facie* satisfied that an arbitration agreement under the Rules may exist. In particular:

(i)   where there are more than two parties to the arbitration, the arbitration shall proceed between those of the parties, including any additional parties joined pursuant to Article 7, with respect to which the Court is *prima facie* satisfied that an arbitration agreement under the Rules that binds them all may exist; and

(ii)   where claims pursuant to Article 9 are made under more than one arbitration agreement, the arbitration shall proceed as to those claims with respect to which the Court is *prima facie* satisfied (a) that the arbitration agreements under which those claims are made may be compatible, and (b) that all parties to the arbitration may have agreed that those claims can be determined together in a single arbitration.

The Court's decision pursuant to Article 6(4) is without prejudice to the admissibility or merits of any party's plea or pleas.

5   In all matters decided by the Court under Article 6(4), any decision as to the jurisdiction of the arbitral tribunal, except as to parties or claims with respect to which the Court decides that the arbitration cannot proceed, shall then be taken by the arbitral tribunal itself.

6   Where the parties are notified of the Court's decision pursuant to Article 6(4) that the arbitration cannot proceed in respect of some or all of them, any party retains the right to ask any court having jurisdiction whether or not, and in respect of which of them, there is a binding arbitration agreement.

7   Where the Court has decided pursuant to Article 6(4) that the arbitration cannot proceed in respect of any of the claims, such decision shall not prevent a party from reintroducing the same claim at a later date in other proceedings.

8   If any of the parties refuses or fails to take part in the arbitration or any stage thereof, the arbitration shall proceed notwithstanding such refusal or failure.

9   Unless otherwise agreed, the arbitral tribunal shall not cease to have jurisdiction by reason of any allegation that the contract is non-existent or null and void, provided that the arbitral tribunal upholds the validity of the arbitration agreement. The arbitral tribunal shall continue to have jurisdiction to determine the parties' respective rights and to decide their claims and pleas even though the contract itself may be non-existent or null and void.

Multiple Parties, Multiple Contracts, and Consolidation
Article 7 Joinder of Additional Parties

1   A party wishing to join an additional party to the arbitration shall submit its request for arbitration against the additional party (the "Request for Joinder") to the Secretariat. The date on which the Request for Joinder is received by the Secretariat shall, for all purposes, be deemed to be the date of the commencement of arbitration against the additional party. Any such joinder shall be subject to the provisions of Articles 6(3)–6(7) and 9. No additional party may be joined after the confirmation or appointment of any arbitrator, unless all parties, including the additional party, otherwise agree. The Secretariat may fix a time limit for the submission of a Request for Joinder.

2   The Request for Joinder shall contain the following information:
a)   the case reference of the existing arbitration;
b)   the name in full, description, address and other contact details of each of the parties, including the additional party; and
c)   the information specified in Article 4(3) subparagraphs c), d), e) and f).

The party filing the Request for Joinder may submit therewith such other documents or information as it considers appropriate or as may contribute to the efficient resolution of the dispute.

3   The provisions of Articles 4(4) and 4(5) shall apply, *mutatis mutandis*, to the Request for Joinder.

4   The additional party shall submit an Answer in accordance, *mutatis mutandis*, with the provisions of Articles 5(1)–5(4). The additional party may make claims against any other party in accordance with the provisions of Article 8.

Article 8 Claims Between Multiple Parties

1   In an arbitration with multiple parties, claims may be made by any party against any other party, subject to the provisions of Articles 6(3)–6(7) and 9 and provided that no new claims may be made after the Terms of Reference are signed or approved by the Court without the authorization of the arbitral tribunal pursuant to Article 23(4).

2   Any party making a claim pursuant to Article 8(1) shall provide the information specified in Article 4(3) subparagraphs c), d), e) and f).

3   Before the Secretariat transmits the file to the arbitral tribunal in accordance with Article 16, the following provisions shall apply, *mutatis mutandis*, to any claim made: Article 4(4) subparagraph a); Article 4(5); Article 5(1) except for subparagraphs a), b), e) and f); Article 5(2); Article 5(3) and Article 5(4). Thereafter, the arbitral tribunal shall determine the procedure for making a claim.

Article 9 Multiple Contracts

Subject to the provisions of Articles 6(3)–6(7) and 23(4), claims arising out of or in connection with more than one contract may be made in a single arbitration, irrespective of whether such claims are made under one or more than one arbitration agreement under the Rules.

Article 10 Consolidation of Arbitrations

The Court may, at the request of a party, consolidate two or more arbitrations pending under the Rules into a single arbitration, where:

a)   the parties have agreed to consolidation; or
b)   all of the claims in the arbitrations are made under the same arbitration agreement; or
c)   where the claims in the arbitrations are made under more than one arbitration agreement, the arbitrations are between the same parties, the disputes in the arbitrations arise in connection with the same legal relationship, and the Court finds the arbitration agreements to be compatible.

In deciding whether to consolidate, the Court may take into account any circumstances it considers to be relevant, including whether one or more arbitrators have been confirmed or appointed in more than one of the arbitrations and, if so, whether the same or different persons have been confirmed or appointed.

When arbitrations are consolidated, they shall be consolidated into the arbitration that commenced first, unless otherwise agreed by all parties.

The Arbitral Tribunal
Article 11 General Provisions

1   Every arbitrator must be and remain impartial and independent of the parties involved in the arbitration.

2   Before appointment or confirmation, a prospective arbitrator shall sign a statement of acceptance, availability, impartiality and independence. The prospective arbitrator shall disclose in writing to the Secretariat any facts or circumstances which might be of such a nature as to call into question the arbitrator's independence in the eyes of the parties, as well as any circumstances that could give rise to reasonable doubts as to the arbitrator's impartiality. The Secretariat shall provide such information to the parties in writing and fix a time limit for any comments from them.

3   An arbitrator shall immediately disclose in writing to the Secretariat and to the parties any facts or circumstances of a similar nature to those referred to in Article 11(2) concerning the arbitrator's impartiality or independence which may arise during the arbitration.

4   The decisions of the Court as to the appointment, confirmation, challenge or replacement of an arbitrator shall be final, and the reasons for such decisions shall not be communicated.

5   By accepting to serve, arbitrators undertake to carry out their responsibilities in accordance with the Rules.

6   Insofar as the parties have not provided otherwise, the arbitral tribunal shall be constituted in accordance with the provisions of Articles 12 and 13.

Article 12 Constitution of the Arbitral Tribunal
Number of Arbitrators

1   The disputes shall be decided by a sole arbitrator or by three arbitrators.

2   Where the parties have not agreed upon the number of arbitrators, the Court shall appoint a sole arbitrator, save where it appears to the Court that the dispute is such as to warrant the appointment of three arbitrators. In such case, the claimant shall nominate an arbitrator within a period of 15 days from the receipt of the notification of the decision of the Court, and the respondent shall nominate an arbitrator within a period of 15 days from the receipt of the notification of the nomination made by the claimant. If a party fails to nominate an arbitrator, the appointment shall be made by the Court.

Sole Arbitrator

3   Where the parties have agreed that the dispute shall be resolved by a sole arbitrator, they may, by agreement, nominate the sole arbitrator for confirmation. If the parties fail to nominate a sole arbitrator within 30 days from the date when the claimant's Request for Arbitration has been received by the other party, or within such additional time as may be allowed by the Secretariat, the sole arbitrator shall be appointed by the Court.

Three Arbitrators

4   Where the parties have agreed that the dispute shall be resolved by three arbitrators, each party shall nominate in the Request and the Answer, respectively, one arbitrator for confirmation. If a party fails to nominate an arbitrator, the appointment shall be made by the Court.
5   Where the dispute is to be referred to three arbitrators, the third arbitrator, who will act as president of the arbitral tribunal, shall be appointed by the Court, unless the parties have agreed upon another procedure for such appointment, in which case the nomination will be subject to confirmation pursuant to Article 13. Should such procedure not result in a nomination within 30 days from the confirmation or appointment of the co-arbitrators or any other time limit agreed by the parties or fixed by the Court, the third arbitrator shall be appointed by the Court.
6   Where there are multiple claimants or multiple respondents, and where the dispute is to be referred to three arbitrators, the multiple claimants, jointly, and the multiple respondents, jointly, shall nominate an arbitrator for confirmation pursuant to Article 13.
7   Where an additional party has been joined, and where the dispute is to be referred to three arbitrators, the additional party may, jointly with the claimant(s) or with the respondent(s), nominate an arbitrator for confirmation pursuant to Article 13.
8   In the absence of a joint nomination pursuant to Articles 12(6) or 12(7) and where all parties are unable to agree to a method for the constitution of the arbitral tribunal, the Court may appoint each member of the arbitral tribunal and shall designate one of them to act as president. In such case, the Court shall be at liberty to choose any person it regards as suitable to act as arbitrator, applying Article 13 when it considers this appropriate.

Article 13 Appointment and Confirmation of the Arbitrators

1   In confirming or appointing arbitrators, the Court shall consider the prospective arbitrator's nationality, residence and other relationships with the countries of which the parties or the other arbitrators are nationals and the prospective arbitrator's availability and ability to conduct the arbitration in accordance with the Rules. The same shall apply where the Secretary General confirms arbitrators pursuant to Article 13(2).
2   The Secretary General may confirm as co-arbitrators, sole arbitrators and presidents of arbitral tribunals persons nominated by the parties or pursuant to their particular agreements, provided that the statement they have submitted contains no qualification regarding impartiality or independence or that a qualified statement regarding impartiality or independence has not given rise to objections. Such confirmation shall be reported to the Court at its next session. If the Secretary General considers that a co-arbitrator, sole arbitrator or president of an arbitral tribunal should not be confirmed, the matter shall be submitted to the Court.
3   Where the Court is to appoint an arbitrator, it shall make the appointment upon proposal of a National Committee or Group of the ICC that it considers to be appropriate. If the Court does not accept the proposal made, or if the National Committee or Group fails to make the proposal requested within the time limit fixed by the Court, the Court may repeat its request, request a proposal from another National Committee or Group that it considers to be appropriate, or appoint directly any person whom it regards as suitable.
4   The Court may also appoint directly to act as arbitrator any person whom it regards as suitable where:
a)   one or more of the parties is a state or claims to be a state entity; or
b)   the Court considers that it would be appropriate to appoint an arbitrator from a country or territory where there is no National Committee or Group; or
c)   the President certifies to the Court that circumstances exist which, in the President's opinion, make a direct appointment necessary and appropriate.
5   The sole arbitrator or the president of the arbitral tribunal shall be of a nationality other than those of the parties. However, in suitable circumstances and provided that none of the parties objects within the time limit fixed by the Court, the sole arbitrator or the president of the arbitral tribunal may be chosen from a country of which any of the parties is a national.

Article 14 Challenge of Arbitrators

1   A challenge of an arbitrator, whether for an alleged lack of impartiality or independence, or otherwise, shall be made by the submission to the Secretariat of a written statement specifying the facts and circumstances on which the challenge is based.

2   For a challenge to be admissible, it must be submitted by a party either within 30 days from receipt by that party of the notification of the appointment or confirmation of the arbitrator, or within 30 days from the date when the party making the challenge was informed of the facts and circumstances on which the challenge is based if such date is subsequent to the receipt of such notification.

3   The Court shall decide on the admissibility and, at the same time, if necessary, on the merits of a challenge after the Secretariat has afforded an opportunity for the arbitrator concerned, the other party or parties and any other members of the arbitral tribunal to comment in writing within a suitable period of time. Such comments shall be communicated to the parties and to the arbitrators.

Article 15 Replacement of Arbitrators

1   An arbitrator shall be replaced upon death, upon acceptance by the Court of the arbitrator's resignation, upon acceptance by the Court of a challenge, or upon acceptance by the Court of a request of all the parties.

2   An arbitrator shall also be replaced on the Court's own initiative when it decides that the arbitrator is prevented *de jure* or *de facto* from fulfilling the arbitrator's functions, or that the arbitrator is not fulfilling those functions in accordance with the Rules or within the prescribed time limits.

3   When, on the basis of information that has come to its attention, the Court considers applying Article 15(2), it shall decide on the matter after the arbitrator concerned, the parties and any other members of the arbitral tribunal have had an opportunity to comment in writing within a suitable period of time. Such comments shall be communicated to the parties and to the arbitrators.

4   When an arbitrator is to be replaced, the Court has discretion to decide whether or not to follow the original nominating process. Once reconstituted, and after having invited the parties to comment, the arbitral tribunal shall determine if and to what extent prior proceedings shall be repeated before the reconstituted arbitral tribunal.

5   Subsequent to the closing of the proceedings, instead of replacing an arbitrator who has died or been removed by the Court pursuant to Articles 15(1) or 15(2), the Court may decide, when it considers it appropriate, that the remaining arbitrators shall continue the arbitration. In making such determination, the Court shall take into account the views of the remaining arbitrators and of the parties and such other matters that it considers appropriate in the circumstances.

The Arbitral Proceedings

Article 16 Transmission of the File to the Arbitral Tribunal

The Secretariat shall transmit the file to the arbitral tribunal as soon as it has been constituted, provided the advance on costs requested by the Secretariat at this stage has been paid.

Article 17 Proof of Authority

At any time after the commencement of the arbitration, the arbitral tribunal or the Secretariat may require proof of the authority of any party representatives.

Article 18 Place of the Arbitration

1   The place of the arbitration shall be fixed by the Court, unless agreed upon by the parties.

2   The arbitral tribunal may, after consultation with the parties, conduct hearings and meetings at any location it considers appropriate, unless otherwise agreed by the parties.

3   The arbitral tribunal may deliberate at any location it considers appropriate.

Article 19 Rules Governing the Proceedings

The proceedings before the arbitral tribunal shall be governed by the Rules and, where the Rules are silent, by any rules which the parties or, failing them, the arbitral tribunal may settle on, whether or not reference is thereby made to the rules of procedure of a national law to be applied to the arbitration.

Article 20 Language of the Arbitration

In the absence of an agreement by the parties, the arbitral tribunal shall determine the language or languages of the arbitration, due regard being given to all relevant circumstances, including the language of the contract.

Article 21 Applicable Rules of Law

1   The parties shall be free to agree upon the rules of law to be applied by the arbitral tribunal to the merits of the dispute. In the absence of any such agreement, the arbitral tribunal shall apply the rules of law which it determines to be appropriate.
2   The arbitral tribunal shall take account of the provisions of the contract, if any, between the parties and of any relevant trade usages.
3   The arbitral tribunal shall assume the powers of an *amiable compositeur* or decide *ex aequo et bono* only if the parties have agreed to give it such powers.

Article 22 Conduct of the Arbitration

1   The arbitral tribunal and the parties shall make every effort to conduct the arbitration in an expeditious and cost-effective manner, having regard to the complexity and value of the dispute.
2   In order to ensure effective case management, the arbitral tribunal, after consulting the parties, may adopt such procedural measures as it considers appropriate, provided that they are not contrary to any agreement of the parties.
3   Upon the request of any party, the arbitral tribunal may make orders concerning the confidentiality of the arbitration proceedings or of any other matters in connection with the arbitration and may take measures for protecting trade secrets and confidential information.
4   In all cases, the arbitral tribunal shall act fairly and impartially and ensure that each party has a reasonable opportunity to present its case.
5   The parties undertake to comply with any order made by the arbitral tribunal.

Article 23 Terms of Reference

1   As soon as it has received the file from the Secretariat, the arbitral tribunal shall draw up, on the basis of documents or in the presence of the parties and in the light of their most recent submissions, a document defining its Terms of Reference. This document shall include the following particulars:
a)   the names in full, description, address and other contact details of each of the parties and of any person(s) representing a party in the arbitration;
b)   the addresses to which notifications and communications arising in the course of the arbitration may be made;
c)   a summary of the parties' respective claims and of the relief sought by each party, together with the amounts of any quantified claims and, to the extent possible, an estimate of the monetary value of any other claims;
d)   unless the arbitral tribunal considers it inappropriate, a list of issues to be determined;
e)   the names in full, address and other contact details of each of the arbitrators;
f)   the place of the arbitration; and
g)   particulars of the applicable procedural rules and, if such is the case, reference to the power conferred upon the arbitral tribunal to act as *amiable compositeur* or to decide *ex aequo et bono*.
2   The Terms of Reference shall be signed by the parties and the arbitral tribunal. Within two months of the date on which the file has been transmitted to it, the arbitral tribunal shall transmit to the Court the Terms of Reference signed by it and by the parties. The Court may extend this time limit pursuant to a reasoned request from the arbitral tribunal or on its own initiative if it decides it is necessary to do so.

3   If any of the parties refuses to take part in the drawing up of the Terms of Reference or to sign the same, they shall be submitted to the Court for approval. When the Terms of Reference have been signed in accordance with Article 23(2) or approved by the Court, the arbitration shall proceed.

4   After the Terms of Reference have been signed or approved by the Court, no party shall make new claims which fall outside the limits of the Terms of Reference unless it has been authorized to do so by the arbitral tribunal, which shall consider the nature of such new claims, the stage of the arbitration and other relevant circumstances.

Article 24 Case Management Conference and Procedural Timetable

1   When drawing up the Terms of Reference or as soon as possible thereafter, the arbitral tribunal shall convene a case management conference to consult the parties on procedural measures that may be adopted pursuant to Article 22(2). Such measures may include one or more of the case management techniques described in Appendix IV.

2   During or following such conference, the arbitral tribunal shall establish the procedural timetable that it intends to follow for the conduct of the arbitration. The procedural timetable and any modifications thereto shall be communicated to the Court and the parties.

3   To ensure continued effective case management, the arbitral tribunal, after consulting the parties by means of a further case management conference or otherwise, may adopt further procedural measures or modify the procedural timetable.

4   Case management conferences may be conducted through a meeting in person, by video conference, telephone or similar means of communication. In the absence of an agreement of the parties, the arbitral tribunal shall determine the means by which the conference will be conducted. The arbitral tribunal may request the parties to submit case management proposals in advance of a case management conference and may request the attendance at any case management conference of the parties in person or through an internal representative.

Article 25 Establishing the Facts of the Case

1   The arbitral tribunal shall proceed within as short a time as possible to establish the facts of the case by all appropriate means.

2   After studying the written submissions of the parties and all documents relied upon, the arbitral tribunal shall hear the parties together in person if any of them so requests or, failing such a request, it may of its own motion decide to hear them.

3   The arbitral tribunal may decide to hear witnesses, experts appointed by the parties or any other person, in the presence of the parties, or in their absence provided they have been duly summoned.

4   The arbitral tribunal, after having consulted the parties, may appoint one or more experts, define their terms of reference and receive their reports. At the request of a party, the parties shall be given the opportunity to question at a hearing any such expert.

5   At any time during the proceedings, the arbitral tribunal may summon any party to provide additional evidence.

6   The arbitral tribunal may decide the case solely on the documents submitted by the parties unless any of the parties requests a hearing.

Article 26 Hearings

1   When a hearing is to be held, the arbitral tribunal, giving reasonable notice, shall summon the parties to appear before it on the day and at the place fixed by it.

2   If any of the parties, although duly summoned, fails to appear without valid excuse, the arbitral tribunal shall have the power to proceed with the hearing.

3   The arbitral tribunal shall be in full charge of the hearings, at which all the parties shall be entitled to be present. Save with the approval of the arbitral tribunal and the parties, persons not involved in the proceedings shall not be admitted.

4   The parties may appear in person or through duly authorized representatives. In addition, they may be assisted by advisers.

Article 27 Closing of the Proceedings and Date for Submission of Draft Awards
As soon as possible after the last hearing concerning matters to be decided in an award or the filing of the last authorized submissions concerning such matters, whichever is later, the arbitral tribunal shall:
a)   declare the proceedings closed with respect to the matters to be decided in the award; and
b)   inform the Secretariat and the parties of the date by which it expects to submit its draft award to the Court for approval pursuant to Article 33.
After the proceedings are closed, no further submission or argument may be made, or evidence produced, with respect to the matters to be decided in the award, unless requested or authorized by the arbitral tribunal.

Article 28 Conservatory and Interim Measures
1   Unless the parties have otherwise agreed, as soon as the file has been transmitted to it, the arbitral tribunal may, at the request of a party, order any interim or conservatory measure it deems appropriate. The arbitral tribunal may make the granting of any such measure subject to appropriate security being furnished by the requesting party. Any such measure shall take the form of an order, giving reasons, or of an award, as the arbitral tribunal considers appropriate.
2   Before the file is transmitted to the arbitral tribunal, and in appropriate circumstances even thereafter, the parties may apply to any competent judicial authority for interim or conservatory measures. The application of a party to a judicial authority for such measures or for the implementation of any such measures ordered by an arbitral tribunal shall not be deemed to be an infringement or a waiver of the arbitration agreement and shall not affect the relevant powers reserved to the arbitral tribunal.
    Any such application and any measures taken by the judicial authority must be notified without delay to the Secretariat. The Secretariat shall inform the arbitral tribunal thereof.

Article 29 Emergency Arbitrator
1   A party that needs urgent interim or conservatory measures that cannot await the constitution of an arbitral tribunal ("Emergency Measures") may make an application for such measures pursuant to the Emergency Arbitrator Rules in Appendix V. Any such application shall be accepted only if it is received by the Secretariat prior to the transmission of the file to the arbitral tribunal pursuant to Article 16 and irrespective of whether the party making the application has already submitted its Request for Arbitration.
2   The emergency arbitrator's decision shall take the form of an order. The parties undertake to comply with any order made by the emergency arbitrator.
3   The emergency arbitrator's order shall not bind the arbitral tribunal with respect to any question, issue or dispute determined in the order. The arbitral tribunal may modify, terminate or annul the order or any modification thereto made by the emergency arbitrator.
4   The arbitral tribunal shall decide upon any party's requests or claims related to the emergency arbitrator proceedings, including the reallocation of the costs of such proceedings and any claims arising out of or in connection with the compliance or non-compliance with the order.
5   Articles 29(1)–29(4) and the Emergency Arbitrator Rules set forth in Appendix V (collectively the "Emergency Arbitrator Provisions") shall apply only to parties that are either signatories of the arbitration agreement under the Rules that is relied upon for the application or successors to such signatories.
6   The Emergency Arbitrator Provisions shall not apply if:
a)   the arbitration agreement under the Rules was concluded before the date on which the Rules came into force;
b)   the parties have agreed to opt out of the Emergency Arbitrator Provisions; or
c)   the parties have agreed to another pre-arbitral procedure that provides for the granting of conservatory, interim or similar measures.

7   The Emergency Arbitrator Provisions are not intended to prevent any party from seeking urgent interim or conservatory measures from a competent judicial authority at any time prior to making an application for such measures, and in appropriate circumstances even thereafter, pursuant to the Rules. Any application for such measures from a competent judicial authority shall not be deemed to be an infringement or a waiver of the arbitration agreement. Any such application and any measures taken by the judicial authority must be notified without delay to the Secretariat.

Awards
Article 30 Time Limit for the Final Award

1   The time limit within which the arbitral tribunal must render its final award is six months. Such time limit shall start to run from the date of the last signature by the arbitral tribunal or by the parties of the Terms of Reference or, in the case of application of Article 23(3), the date of the notification to the arbitral tribunal by the Secretariat of the approval of the Terms of Reference by the Court. The Court may fix a different time limit based upon the procedural timetable established pursuant to Article 24(2).

2   The Court may extend the time limit pursuant to a reasoned request from the arbitral tribunal or on its own initiative if it decides it is necessary to do so.

Article 31 Making of the Award

1   When the arbitral tribunal is composed of more than one arbitrator, an award is made by a majority decision. If there is no majority, the award shall be made by the president of the arbitral tribunal alone.

2   The award shall state the reasons upon which it is based.

3   The award shall be deemed to be made at the place of the arbitration and on the date stated therein.

Article 32 Award by Consent

If the parties reach a settlement after the file has been transmitted to the arbitral tribunal in accordance with Article 16, the settlement shall be recorded in the form of an award made by consent of the parties, if so requested by the parties and if the arbitral tribunal agrees to do so.

Article 33 Scrutiny of the Award by the Court

Before signing any award, the arbitral tribunal shall submit it in draft form to the Court. The Court may lay down modifications as to the form of the award and, without affecting the arbitral tribunal's liberty of decision, may also draw its attention to points of substance. No award shall be rendered by the arbitral tribunal until it has been approved by the Court as to its form.

Article 34 Notification, Deposit and Enforceability of the Award

1   Once an award has been made, the Secretariat shall notify to the parties the text signed by the arbitral tribunal, provided always that the costs of the arbitration have been fully paid to the ICC by the parties or by one of them.

2   Additional copies certified true by the Secretary General shall be made available on request and at any time to the parties, but to no one else.

3   By virtue of the notification made in accordance with Article 34(1), the parties waive any other form of notification or deposit on the part of the arbitral tribunal.

4   An original of each award made in accordance with the Rules shall be deposited with the Secretariat.

5   The arbitral tribunal and the Secretariat shall assist the parties in complying with whatever further formalities may be necessary.

6   Every award shall be binding on the parties. By submitting the dispute to arbitration under the Rules, the parties undertake to carry out any award without delay and shall be deemed to have waived their right to any form of recourse insofar as such waiver can validly be made.

Article 35 Correction and Interpretation of the Award; Remission of Awards
1   On its own initiative, the arbitral tribunal may correct a clerical, computational or typographical error, or any errors of similar nature contained in an award, provided such correction is submitted for approval to the Court within 30 days of the date of such award.
2   Any application of a party for the correction of an error of the kind referred to in Article 35(1), or for the interpretation of an award, must be made to the Secretariat within 30 days of the receipt of the award by such party, in a number of copies as stated in Article 3(1). After transmittal of the application to the arbitral tribunal, the latter shall grant the other party a short time limit, normally not exceeding 30 days, from the receipt of the application by that party, to submit any comments thereon. The arbitral tribunal shall submit its decision on the application in draft form to the Court not later than 30 days following the expiration of the time limit for the receipt of any comments from the other party or within such other period as the Court may decide.
3   A decision to correct or to interpret the award shall take the form of an addendum and shall constitute part of the award. The provisions of Articles 31, 33 and 34 shall apply *mutatis mutandis*.
4   Where a court remits an award to the arbitral tribunal, the provisions of Articles 31, 33, 34 and this Article 35 shall apply *mutatis mutandis* to any addendum or award made pursuant to the terms of such remission. The Court may take any steps as may be necessary to enable the arbitral tribunal to comply with the terms of such remission and may fix an advance to cover any additional fees and expenses of the arbitral tribunal and any additional ICC administrative expenses.

Costs
Article 36 Advance to Cover the Costs of the Arbitration
1   After receipt of the Request, the Secretary General may request the claimant to pay a provisional advance in an amount intended to cover the costs of the arbitration until the Terms of Reference have been drawn up. Any provisional advance paid will be considered as a partial payment by the claimant of any advance on costs fixed by the Court pursuant to this Article 36.
2   As soon as practicable, the Court shall fix the advance on costs in an amount likely to cover the fees and expenses of the arbitrators and the ICC administrative expenses for the claims which have been referred to it by the parties, unless any claims are made under Article 7 or 8 in which case Article 36(4) shall apply. The advance on costs fixed by the Court pursuant to this Article 36(2) shall be payable in equal shares by the claimant and the respondent.
3   Where counterclaims are submitted by the respondent under Article 5 or otherwise, the Court may fix separate advances on costs for the claims and the counterclaims. When the Court has fixed separate advances on costs, each of the parties shall pay the advance on costs corresponding to its claims.
4   Where claims are made under Article 7 or 8, the Court shall fix one or more advances on costs that shall be payable by the parties as decided by the Court. Where the Court has previously fixed any advance on costs pursuant to this Article 36, any such advance shall be replaced by the advance(s) fixed pursuant to this Article 36(4), and the amount of any advance previously paid by any party will be considered as a partial payment by such party of its share of the advance(s) on costs as fixed by the Court pursuant to this Article 36(4).
5   The amount of any advance on costs fixed by the Court pursuant to this Article 36 may be subject to readjustment at any time during the arbitration. In all cases, any party shall be free to pay any other party's share of any advance on costs should such other party fail to pay its share.
6   When a request for an advance on costs has not been complied with, and after consultation with the arbitral tribunal, the Secretary General may direct the arbitral tribunal to suspend its work and set a time limit, which must be not less than 15 days, on the expiry of which the relevant claims shall be considered as withdrawn. Should the party in question wish to object to this measure, it must make a request within the aforementioned period for the matter to be decided by the Court. Such party shall not be prevented, on the ground of such withdrawal, from reintroducing the same claims at a later date in another proceeding.

7   If one of the parties claims a right to a set-off with regard to any claim, such set-off shall be taken into account in determining the advance to cover the costs of the arbitration in the same way as a separate claim insofar as it may require the arbitral tribunal to consider additional matters.

Article 37 Decision as to the Costs of the Arbitration

1   The costs of the arbitration shall include the fees and expenses of the arbitrators and the ICC administrative expenses fixed by the Court, in accordance with the scale in force at the time of the commencement of the arbitration, as well as the fees and expenses of any experts appointed by the arbitral tribunal and the reasonable legal and other costs incurred by the parties for the arbitration.

2   The Court may fix the fees of the arbitrators at a figure higher or lower than that which would result from the application of the relevant scale should this be deemed necessary due to the exceptional circumstances of the case.

3   At any time during the arbitral proceedings, the arbitral tribunal may make decisions on costs, other than those to be fixed by the Court, and order payment.

4   The final award shall fix the costs of the arbitration and decide which of the parties shall bear them or in what proportion they shall be borne by the parties.

5   In making decisions as to costs, the arbitral tribunal may take into account such circumstances as it considers relevant, including the extent to which each party has conducted the arbitration in an expeditious and cost-effective manner.

6   In the event of the withdrawal of all claims or the termination of the arbitration before the rendering of a final award, the Court shall fix the fees and expenses of the arbitrators and the ICC administrative expenses. If the parties have not agreed upon the allocation of the costs of the arbitration or other relevant issues with respect to costs, such matters shall be decided by the arbitral tribunal. If the arbitral tribunal has not been constituted at the time of such withdrawal or termination, any party may request the Court to proceed with the constitution of the arbitral tribunal in accordance with the Rules so that the arbitral tribunal may make decisions as to costs.

Miscellaneous

Article 38 Modified Time Limits

1   The parties may agree to shorten the various time limits set out in the Rules. Any such agreement entered into subsequent to the constitution of an arbitral tribunal shall become effective only upon the approval of the arbitral tribunal.

2   The Court, on its own initiative, may extend any time limit which has been modified pursuant to Article 38(1) if it decides that it is necessary to do so in order that the arbitral tribunal and the Court may fulfil their responsibilities in accordance with the Rules.

Article 39 Waiver

A party which proceeds with the arbitration without raising its objection to a failure to comply with any provision of the Rules, or of any other rules applicable to the proceedings, any direction given by the arbitral tribunal, or any requirement under the arbitration agreement relating to the constitution of the arbitral tribunal or the conduct of the proceedings, shall be deemed to have waived its right to object.

Article 40 Limitation of Liability

The arbitrators, any person appointed by the arbitral tribunal, the emergency arbitrator, the Court and its members, the ICC and its employees, and the ICC National Committees and Groups and their employees and representatives shall not be liable to any person for any act or omission in connection with the arbitration, except to the extent such limitation of liability is prohibited by applicable law.

Article 41 General Rule

In all matters not expressly provided for in the Rules, the Court and the arbitral tribunal shall act in the spirit of the Rules and shall make every effort to make sure that the award is enforceable at law.

Appendix I - Statutes of the International Court of Arbitration
Article 1 Function

1   The function of the International Court of Arbitration of the International Chamber of Commerce (the "Court") is to ensure the application of the Rules of Arbitration of the International Chamber of Commerce, and it has all the necessary powers for that purpose.

2   As an autonomous body, it carries out these functions in complete independence from the ICC and its organs.

3   Its members are independent from the ICC National Committees and Groups.

Article 2 Composition of the Court

The Court shall consist of a President,[1] Vice-Presidents,[2] and members and alternate members (collectively designated as members). In its work it is assisted by its Secretariat (Secretariat of the Court).

Article 3 Appointment

1   The President is elected by the ICC World Council upon the recommendation of the Executive Board of the ICC.

2   The ICC World Council appoints the Vice-Presidents of the Court from among the members of the Court or otherwise.

3   Its members are appointed by the ICC World Council on the proposal of National Committees or Groups, one member for each National Committee or Group.

4   On the proposal of the President of the Court, the World Council may appoint alternate members.

5   The term of office of all members, including, for the purposes of this paragraph, the President and Vice-Presidents, is three years. If a member is no longer in a position to exercise the member's functions, a successor is appointed by the World Council for the remainder of the term. Upon the recommendation of the Executive Board, the duration of the term of office of any member may be extended beyond three years if the World Council so decides.

Article 4 Plenary Session of the Court

The Plenary Sessions of the Court are presided over by the President or, in the President's absence, by one of the Vice-Presidents designated by the President. The deliberations shall be valid when at least six members are present. Decisions are taken by a majority vote, the President or Vice-President, as the case may be, having a casting vote in the event of a tie.

Article 5 Committees

The Court may set up one or more Committees and establish the functions and organization of such Committees.

Article 6 Confidentiality

The work of the Court is of a confidential nature which must be respected by everyone who participates in that work in whatever capacity. The Court lays down the rules regarding the persons who can attend the meetings of the Court and its Committees and who are entitled to have access to materials related to the work of the Court and its Secretariat.

Article 7 Modification of the Rules of Arbitration

Any proposal of the Court for a modification of the Rules is laid before the Commission on Arbitration before submission to the Executive Board of the ICC for approval, provided, however, that the Court, in order to take account of developments in information technology, may

---

1   Referred to as "Chairman of the International Court of Arbitration" in the Constitution of the International Chamber of Commerce.

2   Referred to as "Vice-Chairmen of the International Court of Arbitration" in the Constitution of the International Chamber of Commerce.

propose to modify or supplement the provisions of Article 3 of the Rules or any related provisions in the Rules without laying any such proposal before the Commission.

Appendix II - Internal Rules of the International Court of Arbitration

Article 1 Confidential Character of the Work of the International Court of Arbitration

1   For the purposes of this Appendix, members of the Court include the President and Vice-Presidents of the Court.

2   The sessions of the Court, whether plenary or those of a Committee of the Court, are open only to its members and to the Secretariat.

3   However, in exceptional circumstances, the President of the Court may invite other persons to attend. Such persons must respect the confidential nature of the work of the Court.

4   The documents submitted to the Court, or drawn up by it or the Secretariat in the course of the Court's proceedings, are communicated only to the members of the Court and to the Secretariat and to persons authorized by the President to attend Court sessions.

5   The President or the Secretary General of the Court may authorize researchers undertaking work of an academic nature to acquaint themselves with awards and other documents of general interest, with the exception of memoranda, notes, statements and documents remitted by the parties within the framework of arbitration proceedings.

6   Such authorization shall not be given unless the beneficiary has undertaken to respect the confidential character of the documents made available and to refrain from publishing anything based upon information contained therein without having previously submitted the text for approval to the Secretary General of the Court.

7   The Secretariat will in each case submitted to arbitration under the Rules retain in the archives of the Court all awards, Terms of Reference and decisions of the Court, as well as copies of the pertinent correspondence of the Secretariat.

8   Any documents, communications or correspondence submitted by the parties or the arbitrators may be destroyed unless a party or an arbitrator requests in writing within a period fixed by the Secretariat the return of such documents, communications or correspondence. All related costs and expenses for the return of those documents shall be paid by such party or arbitrator.

Article 2 Participation of Members of the International Court of Arbitration in ICC Arbitration

1   The President and the members of the Secretariat of the Court may not act as arbitrators or as counsel in cases submitted to ICC arbitration.

2   The Court shall not appoint Vice-Presidents or members of the Court as arbitrators. They may, however, be proposed for such duties by one or more of the parties, or pursuant to any other procedure agreed upon by the parties, subject to confirmation.

3   When the President, a Vice-President or a member of the Court or of the Secretariat is involved in any capacity whatsoever in proceedings pending before the Court, such person must inform the Secretary General of the Court upon becoming aware of such involvement.

4   Such person must be absent from the Court session whenever the matter is considered by the Court and shall not participate in the discussions or in the decisions of the Court.

5   Such person will not receive any material documentation or information pertaining to such proceedings.

Article 3 Relations between the Members of the Court and the ICC National Committees and Groups

1   By virtue of their capacity, the members of the Court are independent of the ICC National Committees and Groups which proposed them for appointment by the ICC World Council.

2   Furthermore, they must regard as confidential, vis-a-vis the said National Committees and Groups, any information concerning individual cases with which they have become acquainted in their capacity as members of the Court, except when they have been requested by the President of the Court, by a Vice-President of the Court authorized by the President of the Court, or by the Court's Secretary General to communicate specific information to their respective National Committees or Groups.

Article 4 Committee of the Court

1   In accordance with the provisions of Article 1(4) of the Rules and Article 5 of its statutes (Appendix I), the Court hereby establishes a Committee of the Court.

2   The members of the Committee consist of a president and at least two other members. The President of the Court acts as the president of the Committee. In the President's absence or otherwise at the President's request, a Vice-President of the Court or, in exceptional circumstances, another member of the Court may act as president of the Committee.

3   The other two members of the Committee are appointed by the Court from among the Vice-Presidents or the other members of the Court. At each Plenary Session the Court appoints the members who are to attend the meetings of the Committee to be held before the next Plenary Session.

4   The Committee meets when convened by its president. Two members constitute a quorum. 5 (a)The Court shall determine the decisions that may be taken by the Committee.

(b)   The decisions of the Committee are taken unanimously.

(c)   When the Committee cannot reach a decision or deems it preferable to abstain, it transfers the case to the next Plenary Session, making any suggestions it deems appropriate.

(d)   The Committee's decisions are brought to the notice of the Court at its next Plenary Session.

Article 5 Court Secretariat

1   In the Secretary General's absence or otherwise at the Secretary General's request, the Deputy Secretary General and/or the General Counsel shall have the authority to refer matters to the Court, confirm arbitrators, certify true copies of awards and request the payment of a provisional advance, respectively provided for in Articles 6(3), 13(2), 34(2) and 36(1) of the Rules.

2   The Secretariat may, with the approval of the Court, issue notes and other documents for the information of the parties and the arbitrators, or as necessary for the proper conduct of the arbitral proceedings.

3   Offices of the Secretariat may be established outside the headquarters of the ICC. The Secretariat shall keep a list of offices designated by the Secretary General. Requests for Arbitration may be submitted to the Secretariat at any of its offices, and the Secretariat's functions under the Rules may be carried out from any of its offices, as instructed by the Secretary General, Deputy Secretary General or General Counsel.

Article 6 Scrutiny of Arbitral Awards

When the Court scrutinizes draft awards in accordance with Article 33 of the Rules, it considers, to the extent practicable, the requirements of mandatory law at the place of the arbitration.

Appendix III - Arbitration Costs and Fees

Article 1 Advance on Costs

1   Each request to commence an arbitration pursuant to the Rules must be accompanied by a filing fee of US$ 3,000. Such payment is non-refundable and shall be credited to the claimant's portion of the advance on costs.

2   The provisional advance fixed by the Secretary General according to Article 36(1) of the Rules shall normally not exceed the amount obtained by adding together the ICC administrative expenses, the minimum of the fees (as set out in the scale hereinafter) based upon the amount of the claim and the expected reimbursable expenses of the arbitral tribunal incurred with respect to the drafting of the Terms of Reference. If such amount is not quantified, the provisional advance shall be fixed at the discretion of the Secretary General. Payment by the claimant shall be credited to its share of the advance on costs fixed by the Court.

3   In general, after the Terms of Reference have been signed or approved by the Court and the procedural timetable has been established, the arbitral tribunal shall, in accordance with Article 36(6) of the Rules, proceed only with respect to those claims or counterclaims in regard to which the whole of the advance on costs has been paid.

4   The advance on costs fixed by the Court according to Articles 36(2) or 36(4) of the Rules comprises the fees of the arbitrator or arbitrators (hereinafter referred to as "arbitrator"), any arbitration-related expenses of the arbitrator and the ICC administrative expenses.
5   Each party shall pay its share of the total advance on costs in cash. However, if a party's share of the advance on costs is greater than US$ 500,000 (the "Threshold Amount"), such party may post a bank guarantee for any amount above the Threshold Amount. The Court may modify the Threshold Amount at any time at its discretion.
6   The Court may authorize the payment of advances on costs, or any party's share thereof, in instalments, subject to such conditions as the Court thinks fit, including the payment of additional ICC administrative expenses.
7   A party that has already paid in full its share of the advance on costs fixed by the Court may, in accordance with Article 36(5) of the Rules, pay the unpaid portion of the advance owed by the defaulting party by posting a bank guarantee.
8   When the Court has fixed separate advances on costs pursuant to Article 36(3) of the Rules, the Secretariat shall invite each party to pay the amount of the advance corresponding to its respective claim(s).
9   When, as a result of the fixing of separate advances on costs, the separate advance fixed for the claim of either party exceeds one half of such global advance as was previously fixed (in respect of the same claims and counterclaims that are the subject of separate advances), a bank guarantee may be posted to cover any such excess amount. In the event that the amount of the separate advance is subsequently increased, at least one half of the increase shall be paid in cash.
10   The Secretariat shall establish the terms governing all bank guarantees which the parties may post pursuant to the above provisions.
11   As provided in Article 36(5) of the Rules, the advance on costs may be subject to readjustment at any time during the arbitration, in particular to take into account fluctuations in the amount in dispute, changes in the amount of the estimated expenses of the arbitrator, or the evolving difficulty or complexity of arbitration proceedings.
12   Before any expertise ordered by the arbitral tribunal can be commenced, the parties, or one of them, shall pay an advance on costs fixed by the arbitral tribunal sufficient to cover the expected fees and expenses of the expert as determined by the arbitral tribunal. The arbitral tribunal shall be responsible for ensuring the payment by the parties of such fees and expenses.
13   The amounts paid as advances on costs do not yield interest for the parties or the arbitrator.

Article 2 Costs and Fees

1   Subject to Article 37(2) of the Rules, the Court shall fix the fees of the arbitrator in accordance with the scale hereinafter set out or, where the amount in dispute is not stated, at its discretion.
2   In setting the arbitrator's fees, the Court shall take into consideration the diligence and efficiency of the arbitrator, the time spent, the rapidity of the proceedings, the complexity of the dispute and the timeliness of the submission of the draft award, so as to arrive at a figure within the limits specified or, in exceptional circumstances (Article 37(2) of the Rules), at a figure higher or lower than those limits.
3   When a case is submitted to more than one arbitrator, the Court, at its discretion, shall have the right to increase the total fees up to a maximum which shall normally not exceed three times the fees of one arbitrator.
4   The arbitrator's fees and expenses shall be fixed exclusively by the Court as required by the Rules. Separate fee arrangements between the parties and the arbitrator are contrary to the Rules.
5   The Court shall fix the ICC administrative expenses of each arbitration in accordance with the scale hereinafter set out or, where the amount in dispute is not stated, at its discretion. In exceptional circumstances, the Court may fix the ICC administrative expenses at a lower or higher figure than that which would result from the application of such scale, provided that such expenses shall normally not exceed the maximum amount of the scale.

6   At any time during the arbitration, the Court may fix as payable a portion of the ICC administrative expenses corresponding to services that have already been performed by the Court and the Secretariat.

7   The Court may require the payment of administrative expenses in addition to those provided in the scale of administrative expenses as a condition for holding an arbitration in abeyance at the request of the parties or of one of them with the acquiescence of the other.

8   If an arbitration terminates before the rendering of a final award, the Court shall fix the fees and expenses of the arbitrators and the ICC administrative expenses at its discretion, taking into account the stage attained by the arbitral proceedings and any other relevant circumstances.

9   Any amount paid by the parties as an advance on costs exceeding the costs of the arbitration fixed by the Court shall be reimbursed to the parties having regard to the amounts paid.

10   In the case of an application under Article 35(2) of the Rules or of a remission pursuant to Article 35(4) of the Rules, the Court may fix an advance to cover additional fees and expenses of the arbitral tribunal and additional ICC administrative expenses and may make the transmission of such application to the arbitral tribunal subject to the prior cash payment in full to the ICC of such advance. The Court shall fix at its discretion the costs of the procedure following an application or a remission, which shall include any possible fees of the arbitrator and ICC administrative expenses, when approving the decision of the arbitral tribunal.

11   The Secretariat may require the payment of administrative expenses in addition to those provided in the scale of administrative expenses for any expenses arising in relation to a request pursuant to Article 34(5) of the Rules.

12   When an arbitration is preceded by an attempt at amicable resolution pursuant to the ICC ADR Rules, one half of the ICC administrative expenses paid for such ADR proceedings shall be credited to the ICC administrative expenses of the arbitration.

13   Amounts paid to the arbitrator do not include any possible value added tax (VAT) or other taxes or charges and imposts applicable to the arbitrator's fees. Parties have a duty to pay any such taxes or charges; however, the recovery of any such charges or taxes is a matter solely between the arbitrator and the parties.

14   Any ICC administrative expenses may be subject to value added tax (VAT) or charges of a similar nature at the prevailing rate.

Article 3 ICC as Appointing Authority

Any request received for an authority of the ICC to act as appointing authority will be treated in accordance with the Rules of ICC as Appointing Authority in UNCITRAL or Other *Ad Hoc* Arbitration Proceedings and shall be accompanied by a non-refundable filing fee of US$ 3,000. No request shall be processed unless accompanied by the said filing fee. For additional services, ICC may at its discretion fix ICC administrative expenses, which shall be commensurate with the services provided and shall normally not exceed the maximum amount of US$ 10,000.

Article 4 Scales of Administrative Expenses and Arbitrator's Fees

1   The Scales of Administrative Expenses and Arbitrator's Fees set forth below shall be effective as of 1 January 2012 in respect of all arbitrations commenced on or after such date, irrespective of the version of the Rules applying to such arbitrations.

2   To calculate the ICC administrative expenses and the arbitrator's fees, the amounts calculated for each successive tranche of the amount in dispute must be added together, except that where the amount in dispute is over US$ 500 million, a flat amount of US$ 113,215 shall constitute the entirety of the ICC administrative expenses.

3   All amounts fixed by the Court or pursuant to any of the appendices to the Rules are payable in US$ except where prohibited by law, in which case the ICC may apply a different scale and fee arrangement in another currency.

Table I

Amount in Dispute	Administrative Expenses
up to 50,000$	3,000$
from 50,001 - 100,000$	3,000$ + 4.73% of amt. over 50,000$
from 100,001 - 200,000$	5,365$ + 2.53% of amt. over 100,000$
from 200,001 - 500,000$	7,895$ + 2.09% of amt. over 200,000$
from 500,001 - 1,000,000$	14,165$ + 1.51% of amt. over 500,000$
from 1,000,001 - 2,000,000$	21,715$ + 0.95% of amt. over 1,000,000$
from 2,000,001 - 5,000,000$	31,215$ + 0.46% of amt. over 2,000,000$
from 5,000,001 - 10,000,000$	45,015$ + 0.25% of amt. over 5,000,000$
from 10,000,001 - 30,000,000$	57,515$ + 0.10% of amt. over 10,000,000$
from 30,000,001 - 50,000,000$	77,515$ + 0.09% of amt. over 30,000,000$
from 50,000,001 - 80,000,000$	95,515$ + 0.01% of amt. over 50,000,000$
from 80,000,001 - 100,000,000$	98,515$ + 0.0035% of amt. over 80,000,000$
from 100,000,001 - 500,000,000$	99,215$ + 0.0035% of amt. over 100,000,000$
over 500,000,000$	113,215$

Table II

Amount in Dispute	Arbitrator's Fees[1] min	max
up to 50,000$	3,000$	18.020%
from 50,001 - 100,000$	2.650%	13.568%
from 100,001 - 200,000$	1.431%	7.685%
from 200,001 - 500,000$	1.367%	6.837%
from 500,001 - 1,000,000$	0.954%	4.028%
from 1,000,001 - 2,000,000$	0.689%	3.604%
from 2,000,001 - 5,000,000$	0.375%	1.391%
from 5,000,001 - 10,000,000$	0.128%	0.910%
from 10,000,001 - 30,000,000$	0.064%	0.241%
from 30,000,001 - 50,000,000$	0.059%	0.228%
from 50,000,001 - 80,000,000$	0.033%	0.157%
from 80,000,001 - 100,000,000$	0.021%	0.115%
from 100,000,001 - 500,000,000$	0.011%	0.058%
over 500,000,000$	0.010%	0.040%

Appendix IV - Case Management Techniques

The following are examples of case management techniques that can be used by the arbitral tribunal and the parties for controlling time and cost. Appropriate control of time and cost is important in all cases. In cases of low complexity and low value, it is particularly important to ensure that time and costs are proportionate to what is at stake in the dispute.

---

1   The amounts are cumulative. For example, for a dispute of 15 mio US$, the arbitrator's fees are min. 3,000$ + (2.650% of the amount between 50,001 and 100,000$) + (1.431% of the amount between 100,001 and 200,000$) + (1.367% of the amount between 200,001 and 500,000$) + (0.954% of the amount between 500,001 and 1,000,000$) + (0.689% of the amount between 1,000,001 and 2,000,000$) + (0.375% of the amount between 2,000,001 and 5,000,000$) + (0.128% of the amount between 5,000,001 and 10,000,000$) + (0.064% of the amount over 10,000,000$) = 42,367$. The fees are per arbitrator.

a) Bifurcating the proceedings or rendering one or more partial awards on key issues, when doing so may genuinely be expected to result in a more efficient resolution of the case.

b) Identifying issues that can be resolved by agreement between the parties or their experts.

c) Identifying issues to be decided solely on the basis of documents rather than through oral evidence or legal argument at a hearing.

d) Production of documentary evidence:

(i) requiring the parties to produce with their submissions the documents on which they rely;

(ii) avoiding requests for document production when appropriate in order to control time and cost;

(iii) in those cases where requests for document production are considered appropriate, limiting such requests to documents or categories of documents that are relevant and material to the outcome of the case;

(iv) establishing reasonable time limits for the production of documents;

(v) using a schedule of document production to facilitate the resolution of issues in relation to the production of documents.

e) Limiting the length and scope of written submissions and written and oral witness evidence (both fact witnesses and experts) so as to avoid repetition and maintain a focus on key issues.

f) Using telephone or video conferencing for procedural and other hearings where attendance in person is not essential and use of IT that enables online communication among the parties, the arbitral tribunal and the Secretariat of the Court.

g) Organizing a pre-hearing conference with the arbitral tribunal at which arrangements for a hearing can be discussed and agreed and the arbitral tribunal can indicate to the parties issues on which it would like the parties to focus at the hearing.

h) Settlement of disputes:

(i) informing the parties that they are free to settle all or part of the dispute either by negotiation or through any form of amicable dispute resolution methods such as, for example, mediation under the ICC ADR Rules;

(ii) where agreed between the parties and the arbitral tribunal, the arbitral tribunal may take steps to facilitate settlement of the dispute, provided that every effort is made to ensure that any subsequent award is enforceable at law.

Additional techniques are described in the ICC publication entitled "Techniques for Controlling Time and Costs in Arbitration".

Appendix V - Emergency Arbitrator Rules

Article 1 Application for Emergency Measures

1 A party wishing to have recourse to an emergency arbitrator pursuant to Article 29 of the Rules of Arbitration of the ICC (the "Rules") shall submit its Application for Emergency Measures (the "Application") to the Secretariat at any of the offices specified in the Internal Rules of the Court in Appendix II to the Rules.

2 The Application shall be supplied in a number of copies sufficient to provide one copy for each party, plus one for the emergency arbitrator, and one for the Secretariat.

3 The Application shall contain the following information:

a) the name in full, description, address and other contact details of each of the parties;

b) the name in full, address and other contact details of any person(s) representing the applicant;

c) a description of the circumstances giving rise to the Application and of the underlying dispute referred or to be referred to arbitration;

d) a statement of the Emergency Measures sought;

e) the reasons why the applicant needs urgent interim or conservatory measures that cannot await the constitution of an arbitral tribunal;

f) any relevant agreements and, in particular, the arbitration agreement;

g) any agreement as to the place of the arbitration, the applicable rules of law or the language of the arbitration;

h)   proof of payment of the amount referred to in Article 7(1) of this Appendix; and
i)   any Request for Arbitration and any other submissions in connection with the underlying dispute, which have been filed with the Secretariat by any of the parties to the emergency arbitrator proceedings prior to the making of the Application.

The Application may contain such other documents or information as the applicant considers appropriate or as may contribute to the efficient examination of the Application.

4   The Application shall be drawn up in the language of the arbitration if agreed upon by the parties or, in the absence of any such agreement, in the language of the arbitration agreement.

5   If and to the extent that the President of the Court (the "President") considers, on the basis of the information contained in the Application, that the Emergency Arbitrator Provisions apply with reference to Article 29(5) and Article 29(6) of the Rules, the Secretariat shall transmit a copy of the Application and the documents annexed thereto to the responding party. If and to the extent that the President considers otherwise, the Secretariat shall inform the parties that the emergency arbitrator proceedings shall not take place with respect to some or all of the parties and shall transmit a copy of the Application to them for information.

6   The President shall terminate the emergency arbitrator proceedings if a Request for Arbitration has not been received by the Secretariat from the applicant within 10 days of the Secretariat's receipt of the Application, unless the emergency arbitrator determines that a longer period of time is necessary.

Article 2 Appointment of the Emergency Arbitrator; Transmission of the File

1   The President shall appoint an emergency arbitrator within as short a time as possible, normally within two days from the Secretariat's receipt of the Application.

2   No emergency arbitrator shall be appointed after the file has been transmitted to the arbitral tribunal pursuant to Article 16 of the Rules. An emergency arbitrator appointed prior thereto shall retain the power to make an order within the time limit permitted by Article 6(4) of this Appendix.

3   Once the emergency arbitrator has been appointed, the Secretariat shall so notify the parties and shall transmit the file to the emergency arbitrator. Thereafter, all written communications from the parties shall be submitted directly to the emergency arbitrator with a copy to the other party and the Secretariat. A copy of any written communications from the emergency arbitrator to the parties shall be submitted to the Secretariat.

4   Every emergency arbitrator shall be and remain impartial and independent of the parties involved in the dispute.

5   Before being appointed, a prospective emergency arbitrator shall sign a statement of acceptance, availability, impartiality and independence. The Secretariat shall provide a copy of such statement to the parties.

6   An emergency arbitrator shall not act as an arbitrator in any arbitration relating to the dispute that gave rise to the Application.

Article 3 Challenge of an Emergency Arbitrator

1   A challenge against the emergency arbitrator must be made within three days from receipt by the party making the challenge of the notification of the appointment or from the date when that party was informed of the facts and circumstances on which the challenge is based if such date is subsequent to the receipt of such notification.

2   The challenge shall be decided by the Court after the Secretariat has afforded an opportunity for the emergency arbitrator and the other party or parties to provide comments in writing within a suitable period of time.

Article 4 Place of the Emergency Arbitrator Proceedings

1   If the parties have agreed upon the place of the arbitration, such place shall be the place of the emergency arbitrator proceedings. In the absence of such agreement, the President shall fix the place of the emergency arbitrator proceedings, without prejudice to the determination of the place of the arbitration pursuant to Article 18(1) of the Rules.

2   Any meetings with the emergency arbitrator may be conducted through a meeting in person at any location the emergency arbitrator considers appropriate or by video conference, telephone or similar means of communication.

Article 5 Proceedings

1   The emergency arbitrator shall establish a procedural timetable for the emergency arbitrator proceedings within as short a time as possible, normally within two days from the transmission of the file to the emergency arbitrator pursuant to Article 2(3) of this Appendix.

2   The emergency arbitrator shall conduct the proceedings in the manner which the emergency arbitrator considers to be appropriate, taking into account the nature and the urgency of the Application. In all cases, the emergency arbitrator shall act fairly and impartially and ensure that each party has a reasonable opportunity to present its case.

Article 6 Order

1   Pursuant to Article 29(2) of the Rules, the emergency arbitrator's decision shall take the form of an order (the "Order").

2   In the Order, the emergency arbitrator shall determine whether the Application is admissible pursuant to Article 29(1) of the Rules and whether the emergency arbitrator has jurisdiction to order Emergency Measures.

3   The Order shall be made in writing and shall state the reasons upon which it is based. It shall be dated and signed by the emergency arbitrator.

4   The Order shall be made no later than 15 days from the date on which the file was transmitted to the emergency arbitrator pursuant to Article 2(3) of this Appendix. The President may extend the time limit pursuant to a reasoned request from the emergency arbitrator or on the President's own initiative if the President decides it is necessary to do so.

5   Within the time limit established pursuant to Article 6(4) of this Appendix, the emergency arbitrator shall send the Order to the parties, with a copy to the Secretariat, by any of the means of communication permitted by Article 3(2) of the Rules that the emergency arbitrator considers will ensure prompt receipt.

6   The Order shall cease to be binding on the parties upon:
a)   the President's termination of the emergency arbitrator proceedings pursuant to Article 1(6) of this Appendix;
b)   the acceptance by the Court of a challenge against the emergency arbitrator pursuant to Article 3 of this Appendix;
c)   the arbitral tribunal's final award, unless the arbitral tribunal expressly decides otherwise; or
d)   the withdrawal of all claims or the termination of the arbitration before the rendering of a final award.

7   The emergency arbitrator may make the Order subject to such conditions as the emergency arbitrator thinks fit, including requiring the provision of appropriate security.

8   Upon a reasoned request by a party made prior to the transmission of the file to the arbitral tribunal pursuant to Article 16 of the Rules, the emergency arbitrator may modify, terminate or annul the Order.

Article 7 Costs of the Emergency Arbitrator Proceedings

1   The applicant must pay an amount of US$ 40,000, consisting of US$ 10,000 for ICC administrative expenses and US$ 30,000 for the emergency arbitrator's fees and expenses. Notwithstanding Article 1(5) of this Appendix, the Application shall not be notified until the payment of US$ 40,000 is received by the Secretariat.

2   The President may, at any time during the emergency arbitrator proceedings, decide to increase the emergency arbitrator's fees or the ICC administrative expenses taking into account, *inter alia*, the nature of the case and the nature and amount of work performed by the emergency arbitrator, the Court, the President and the Secretariat. If the party which submitted the Application fails to pay the increased costs within the time limit fixed by the Secretariat, the Application shall be considered as withdrawn.

3   The emergency arbitrator's Order shall fix the costs of the emergency arbitrator proceedings and decide which of the parties shall bear them or in what proportion they shall be borne by the parties.

4   The costs of the emergency arbitrator proceedings include the ICC administrative expenses, the emergency arbitrator's fees and expenses and the reasonable legal and other costs incurred by the parties for the emergency arbitrator proceedings.

5   In the event that the emergency arbitrator proceedings do not take place pursuant to Article 1(5) of this Appendix or are otherwise terminated prior to the making of an Order, the President shall determine the amount to be reimbursed to the applicant, if any. An amount of US$ 5,000 for ICC administrative expenses is non-refundable in all cases.

Article 8 General Rule

1   The President shall have the power to decide, at the President's discretion, all matters relating to the administration of the emergency arbitrator proceedings not expressly provided for in this Appendix.

2   In the President's absence or otherwise at the President's request, any of the Vice-Presidents of the Court shall have the power to take decisions on behalf of the President.

3   In all matters concerning emergency arbitrator proceedings not expressly provided for in this Appendix, the Court, the President and the emergency arbitrator shall act in the spirit of the Rules and this Appendix.

ADR RULES OF THE INTERNATIONAL CHAMBER OF COMMERCE[1]
(1 July 2001)

Preamble

Amicable settlement is a desirable solution for business disputes and differences. It can occur before or during the litigation or arbitration of a dispute and can often be facilitated through the aid of a third party (the "Neutral") acting in accordance with simple rules. The parties can agree to submit to such rules in their underlying contract or at any other time.

The International Chamber of Commerce (the "ICC") sets out these amicable dispute resolution rules, entitled the ICC ADR Rules (the "Rules"), which permit the parties to agree upon whatever settlement technique they believe to be appropriate to help them settle their dispute. In the absence of an agreement of the parties on a settlement technique, mediation shall be the settlement technique used under the Rules. The Guide to ICC ADR [available at <www.icc-adr.org>], which does not form part of the Rules, provides an explanation of the Rules and of various settlement techniques which can be used pursuant to the Rules.

Article 1 Scope of the ICC ADR Rules

All business disputes, whether or not of an international character, may be referred to ADR proceedings pursuant to these Rules. The provisions of these Rules may be modified by agreement of all of the parties, subject to the approval of the ICC.

---

1   © International Chamber of Commerce, Paris.

Article 2 Commencement of the ADR Proceedings

A   Where there is an agreement to refer to the Rules

1   Where there is an agreement between the parties to refer their dispute to the ICC ADR Rules, any party or parties wishing to commence ADR proceedings pursuant to the Rules shall send to the ICC a written Request for ADR, which shall include:

a)   the names, addresses, telephone and facsimile numbers and email addresses of the parties to the dispute and their authorized representatives, if any;

b)   a description of the dispute including, if possible, an assessment of its value;

c)   any joint designation by all of the parties of a Neutral or any agreement of all of the parties upon the qualifications of a Neutral to be appointed by the ICC where no joint designation has been made;

d)   a copy of any written agreement under which the Request for ADR is made; and

e)   the registration fee of the ADR proceedings, as set out in the Appendix hereto.

2   Where the Request for ADR is not filed jointly by all of the parties, the party or parties filing the Request shall simultaneously send the Request to the other party or parties. Such Request may include any proposal regarding the qualifications of a Neutral or any proposal of one or more Neutrals to be designated by all of the parties. Thereafter, all of the parties may jointly designate a Neutral or may agree upon the qualifications of a Neutral to be appointed by the ICC. In either case, the parties shall promptly notify the ICC thereof.

3   The ICC shall promptly acknowledge receipt of the Request for ADR in writing to the parties.

B   Where there is no agreement to refer to the Rules

1   Where there is no agreement between the parties to refer their dispute to the ICC ADR Rules, any party or parties wishing to commence ADR proceedings pursuant to the Rules shall send to the ICC a written Request for ADR, which shall include:

a)   the names, addresses, telephone and facsimile numbers and email addresses of the parties to the dispute and their authorized representatives, if any;

b)   a description of the dispute including, if possible, an assessment of its value; and

c)   the registration fee of the ADR proceedings, as set out in the Appendix hereto.

The Request for ADR may also include any proposal regarding the qualifications of a Neutral or any proposal of one or more Neutrals to be designated by all of the parties.

2   The ICC shall promptly inform the other party or parties in writing of the Request for ADR. Such party or parties shall be asked to inform the ICC in writing, within 15 days of receipt of the Request for ADR, as to whether they agree or decline to participate in the ADR proceedings. In the former case, they may provide any proposal regarding the qualifications of a Neutral and may propose one or more Neutrals to be designated by the parties. Thereafter, all of the parties may jointly designate a Neutral or may agree upon the qualifications of a Neutral to be appointed by the ICC. In either case, the parties shall promptly notify the ICC thereof.

In the absence of any reply within such 15-day period, or in the case of a negative reply, the Request for ADR shall be deemed to have been declined and ADR proceedings shall not be commenced. The ICC shall promptly so inform in writing the party or parties which filed the Request for ADR.

Article 3 Selection of the Neutral

1   Where all of the parties have jointly designated a Neutral, the ICC shall take note of that designation, and such person, upon notifying the ICC of his or her agreement to serve, shall act as the Neutral in the ADR proceedings. Where a Neutral has not been designated by all of the parties, or where the designated Neutral does not agree to serve, the ICC shall promptly appoint a Neutral, either through an ICC National Committee or otherwise, and notify the parties thereof. The ICC shall make all reasonable efforts to appoint a Neutral having the qualifications, if any, which have been agreed upon by all of the parties.

2   Every prospective Neutral shall promptly provide the ICC with a *curriculum vitae* and a statement of independence, both duly signed and dated. The prospective Neutral shall disclose to the ICC in the statement of independence any facts or circumstances which might be of such

a nature as to call into question his or her independence in the eyes of the parties. The ICC shall provide such information to the parties in writing.

3   If any party objects to the Neutral appointed by the ICC and notifies the ICC and the other party or parties thereof in writing, stating the reasons for such objection, within 15 days of receipt of notification of the appointment, the ICC shall promptly appoint another Neutral.

4   Upon agreement of all of the parties, the parties may designate more than one Neutral or request the ICC to appoint more than one Neutral, in accordance with the provisions of these Rules. In appropriate circumstances, the ICC may propose the appointment of more than one Neutral to the parties.

Article 4 Fees and Costs

1   The party or parties filing a Request for ADR shall include with the Request a non-refundable registration fee, as set out in the Appendix hereto. No Request for ADR shall be processed unless accompanied by the requisite payment.

2   Following the receipt of a Request for ADR, the ICC shall request the parties to pay a deposit in an amount likely to cover the administrative expenses of the ICC and the fees and expenses of the Neutral for the ADR proceedings, as set out in the Appendix hereto. The ADR proceedings shall not go forward until payment of such deposit has been received by the ICC.

3   In any case where the ICC considers that the deposit is not likely to cover the total costs of the ADR proceedings, the amount of such deposit may be subject to readjustment. The ICC may stay the ADR proceedings until the corresponding payments are made by the parties.

4   Upon termination of the ADR proceedings, the ICC shall settle the total costs of the proceedings and shall, as the case may be, reimburse the parties for any excess payment or bill the parties for any balance required pursuant to these Rules.

5   All above deposits and costs shall be borne in equal shares by the parties, unless they agree otherwise in writing. However, any party shall be free to pay the unpaid balance of such deposits and costs should another party fail to pay its share.

6   A party's other expenditure shall remain the responsibility of that party.

Article 5 Conduct of the ADR Procedure

1   The Neutral and the parties shall promptly discuss, and seek to reach agreement upon, the settlement technique to be used, and shall discuss the specific ADR procedure to be followed.

2   In the absence of an agreement of the parties on the settlement technique to be used, mediation shall be used.

3   The Neutral shall conduct the procedure in such manner as the Neutral sees fit. In all cases the Neutral shall be guided by the principles of fairness and impartiality and by the wishes of the parties.

4   In the absence of an agreement of the parties, the Neutral shall determine the language or languages of the proceedings and the place of any meetings to be held.

5   Each party shall cooperate in good faith with the Neutral.

Article 6 Termination of the ADR Proceedings

1   ADR proceedings which have been commenced pursuant to these Rules shall terminate upon the earlier of:

a)   the signing by the parties of a settlement agreement;

b)   the notification in writing to the Neutral by one or more parties, at any time after the discussion referred to in Article 5(1) has occurred, of a decision no longer to pursue the ADR proceedings;

c)   the completion of the procedure established pursuant to Article 5 and the notification in writing thereof by the Neutral to the parties;

d)   the notification in writing by the Neutral to the parties that the ADR proceedings will not, in the Neutral's opinion, resolve the dispute between the parties;

e)   the expiration of any time limit set for the ADR proceedings, if not extended by all of the parties, such expiration to be notified in writing by the Neutral to the parties;

f)   the notification in writing by the ICC to the parties and the Neutral, not less than 15 days after the due date for any payment by one or more parties pursuant to these Rules, stating that such payment has not been made; or

g)   the notification in writing by the ICC to the parties stating, in the judgment of the ICC, that there has been a failure to designate a Neutral or that it has not been reasonably possible to appoint a Neutral.

2   The Neutral, upon any termination of the ADR proceedings pursuant to Article 6(1), (a)–(e), shall promptly notify the ICC of the termination of the ADR proceedings and shall provide the ICC with a copy of any notification referred to in Article 6(1), (b)–(e). In all cases the ICC shall confirm in writing the termination of the ADR proceedings to the parties and the Neutral, if a Neutral has already been designated or appointed.

Article 7 General Provisions

1   In the absence of any agreement of the parties to the contrary and unless prohibited by applicable law, the ADR proceedings, including their outcome, are private and confidential. Any settlement agreement between the parties shall similarly be kept confidential except that a party shall have the right to disclose it to the extent that such disclosure is required by applicable law or necessary for purposes of its implementation or enforcement.

2   Unless required to do so by applicable law and in the absence of any agreement of the parties to the contrary, a party shall not in any manner produce as evidence in any judicial, arbitration or similar proceedings:

a)   any documents, statements or communications which are submitted by another party or by the Neutral in the ADR proceedings, unless they can be obtained independently by the party seeking to produce them in the judicial, arbitration or similar proceedings;

b)   any views expressed or suggestions made by any party within the ADR proceedings with regard to the possible settlement of the dispute;

c)   any admissions made by another party within the ADR proceedings;

d)   any views or proposals put forward by the Neutral; or

e)   the fact that any party had indicated within the ADR proceedings that it was ready to accept a proposal for a settlement.

3   Unless all of the parties agree otherwise in writing, a Neutral shall not act nor shall have acted in any judicial, arbitration or similar proceedings relating to the dispute which is or was the subject of the ADR proceedings, whether as a judge, as an arbitrator, as an expert or as a representative or advisor of a party.

4   The Neutral, unless required by applicable law or unless all of the parties agree otherwise in writing, shall not give testimony in any judicial, arbitration or similar proceedings concerning any aspect of the ADR proceedings.

5   Neither the Neutral, nor the ICC and its employees, nor the ICC National Committees shall be liable to any person for any act or omission in connection with the ADR proceedings.

Appendix - Schedule of ADR Costs

A   The party or parties filing a Request for ADR shall include with the Request a non-refundable registration fee of US$ 1,500 to cover the costs of processing the Request for ADR. No Request for ADR shall be processed unless accompanied by the requisite payment.

B   The administrative expenses of the ICC for the ADR proceedings shall be fixed at the ICC's discretion depending on the tasks carried out by the ICC. Such administrative expenses shall not exceed the maximum sum of US$ 10,000.

C   The fees of the Neutral shall be calculated on the basis of the time reasonably spent by the Neutral in the ADR proceedings, at an hourly rate fixed for such proceedings by the ICC in consultation with the Neutral and the parties. Such hourly rate shall be reasonable in amount and shall be determined in light of the complexity of the dispute and any other relevant circumstances. The amount of reasonable expenses of the Neutral shall be fixed by the ICC.

D   Amounts paid to the Neutral do not include any possible value added taxes (VAT) or other taxes or charges and imposts applicable to the Neutral's fees. Parties have a duty to pay any such taxes or charges; however, the recovery of any such taxes or charges is a matter solely between the Neutral and the parties.

Standard and Suggested Clauses

Below are standard and suggested clauses for use by parties who wish to have recourse to ICC arbitration and/or ICC ADR under the foregoing Rules.

Arbitration

"All disputes arising out of or in connection with the present contract shall be finally settled under the Rules of Arbitration of the International Chamber of Commerce by one or more arbitrators appointed in accordance with the said Rules."

Arbitration Without Emergency Arbitrator

"All disputes arising out of or in connection with the present contract shall be finally settled under the Rules of Arbitration of the International Chamber of Commerce by one or more arbitrators appointed in accordance with the said Rules. The Emergency Arbitrator Provisions shall not apply."

Optional ADR

"The parties may at any time, without prejudice to any other proceedings, seek to settle any dispute arising out of or in connection with the present contract in accordance with the ICC ADR Rules."

Obligation to Consider ADR

"In the event of any dispute arising out of or in connection with the present contract, the parties agree in the first instance to discuss and consider submitting the matter to settlement proceedings under the ICC ADR Rules."

Obligation to Submit Dispute to ADR with an Automatic Expiration Mechanism

"In the event of any dispute arising out of or in connection with the present contract, the parties agree to submit the matter to settlement proceedings under the ICC ADR Rules. If the dispute has not been settled pursuant to the said Rules within 45 days following the filing of a Request for ADR or within such other period as the parties may agree in writing, the parties shall have no further obligations under this paragraph."

Obligation to Submit Dispute to ADR , Followed by Arbitration If Required

"In the event of any dispute arising out of or in connection with the present contract, the parties agree to submit the matter to settlement proceedings under the ICC ADR Rules. If the dispute has not been settled pursuant to the said Rules within 45 days following the filing of a Request for ADR or within such other period as the parties may agree in writing, such dispute shall be finally settled under the Rules of Arbitration of the International Chamber of Commerce by one or more arbitrators appointed in accordance with the said Rules of Arbitration."

How to Use These Clauses

Parties wishing to use ICC arbitration and/or ICC ADR should choose one of the above clauses, which cover different situations and needs.

If the parties do not want the Emergency Arbitrator Provisions to apply, they must expressly opt out by using the second of the two arbitration clauses.

Parties are free to adapt the chosen clause to their particular circumstances. For instance, when providing for arbitration, they may wish to stipulate the number of arbitrators, given that the Rules of Arbitration contain a presumption in favour of a sole arbitrator. They may also wish to stipulate the language and place of the arbitration and the law applicable to the merits. When providing for ADR, they may wish to specify the settlement technique to be applied, failing which mediation, the default mechanism, will be used.

The last clause above is a two-tiered clause providing for ADR followed by arbitration. Other combinations of services are also possible. Combined and multi-tiered dispute resolution clauses may help to facilitate dispute management. However, it is also possible for parties to file requests under the ICC ADR Rules or the ICC Rules for Expertise at any time, even after a dispute has arisen or in the course of other dispute resolution proceedings.

At all times, care must be taken to avoid any risk of ambiguity in the drafting of the clause. Unclear wording causes uncertainty and delay and can hinder or even compromise the dispute resolution process.

When incorporating any of the above clauses in their contracts, parties are advised to take account of any factors that may affect their enforceability under applicable law. For instance, they should have regard to any mandatory requirements at the place of arbitration and the place of enforcement.

Translations of the above clauses and clauses providing for other procedures and combinations of procedures can be found at <www.iccarbitration.org>.

IBA RULES ON THE TAKING OF EVIDENCE IN INTERNATIONAL ARBITRATION
Adopted by a Resolution of the IBA Council on 29 May 2010[1]

Preamble

1.   These IBA Rules on the Taking of Evidence in International Arbitration are intended to provide an efficient, economical and fair process for the taking of evidence in international arbitrations, particularly those between Parties from different legal traditions. They are designed to supplement the legal provisions and the institutional, ad hoc or other rules that apply to the conduct of the arbitration.

2.   Parties and Arbitral Tribunals may adopt the IBA Rules of Evidence, in whole or in part, to govern arbitration proceedings, or they may vary them or use them as guidelines in developing their own procedures. The Rules are not intended to limit the flexibility that is inherent in, and an advantage of, international arbitration, and Parties and Arbitral Tribunals are free to adapt them to the particular circumstances of each arbitration.

3.   The taking of evidence shall be conducted on the principles that each Party shall act in good faith and be entitled to know, reasonably in advance of any Evidentiary Hearing or any fact or merits determination, the evidence on which the other Parties rely.

Definitions

In the IBA Rules of Evidence:

Arbitral Tribunal means a sole arbitrator or a panel of arbitrators;

Claimant means the Party or Parties who commenced the arbitration and any Party who, through joinder or otherwise, becomes aligned with such Party or Parties;

Document means a writing, communication, picture, drawing, program or data of any kind, whether recorded or maintained on paper or by electronic, audio, visual or any other means;

Evidentiary Hearing means any hearing, whether or not held on consecutive days, at which the Arbitral Tribunal, whether in person, by teleconference, video-conference or other method, receives oral or other evidence;

Expert Report means a written statement by a Tribunal-Appointed Expert or a Party-Appointed Expert;

General Rules mean the institutional, ad hoc or other rules that apply to the conduct of the arbitration;

IBA Rules of Evidence or **Rules** means these IBA Rules on the Taking of Evidence in International Arbitration, as they may be revised or amended from time to time;

---

1   © International Bar Association, London.

Party means a party to the arbitration;

Party-Appointed Expert means a person or organisation appointed by a Party in order to report on specific issues determined by the Party;

Request to Produce means a written request by a Party that another Party produce Documents;

Respondent means the Party or Parties against whom the Claimant made its claim, and any Party who, through joinder or otherwise, becomes aligned with such Party or Parties, and includes a Respondent making a counterclaim;

Tribunal-Appointed Expert means a person or organisation appointed by the Arbitral Tribunal in order to report to it on specific issues determined by the Arbitral Tribunal; and

Witness Statement means a written statement of testimony by a witness of fact.

Article 1 Scope of Application

1.   Whenever the Parties have agreed or the Arbitral Tribunal has determined to apply the IBA Rules of Evidence, the Rules shall govern the taking of evidence, except to the extent that any specific provision of them may be found to be in conflict with any mandatory provision of law determined to be applicable to the case by the Parties or by the Arbitral Tribunal.

2.   Where the Parties have agreed to apply the IBA Rules of Evidence, they shall be deemed to have agreed, in the absence of a contrary indication, to the version as current on the date of such agreement.

3.   In case of conflict between any provisions of the IBA Rules of Evidence and the General Rules, the Arbitral Tribunal shall apply the IBA Rules of Evidence in the manner that it determines best in order to accomplish the purposes of both the General Rules and the IBA Rules of Evidence, unless the Parties agree to the contrary.

4.   In the event of any dispute regarding the meaning of the IBA Rules of Evidence, the Arbitral Tribunal shall interpret them according to their purpose and in the manner most appropriate for the particular arbitration.

5.   Insofar as the IBA Rules of Evidence and the General Rules are silent on any matter concerning the taking of evidence and the Parties have not agreed otherwise, the Arbitral Tribunal shall conduct the taking of evidence as it deems appropriate, in accordance with the general principles of the IBA Rules of Evidence.

Article 2 Consultation on Evidentiary Issues

1.   The Arbitral Tribunal shall consult the Parties at the earliest appropriate time in the proceedings and invite them to consult each other with a view to agreeing on an efficient, economical and fair process for the taking of evidence.

2.   The consultation on evidentiary issues may address the scope, timing and manner of the taking of evidence, including:

(a)   the preparation and submission of Witness Statements and Expert Reports;

(b)   the taking of oral testimony at any Evidentiary Hearing;

(c)   the requirements, procedure and format applicable to the production of Documents;

(d)   the level of confidentiality protection to be afforded to evidence in the arbitration; and

(e)   the promotion of efficiency, economy and conservation of resources in connection with the taking of evidence.

3.   The Arbitral Tribunal is encouraged to identify to the Parties, as soon as it considers it to be appropriate, any issues:

(a)   that the Arbitral Tribunal may regard as relevant to the case and material to its outcome; and/or

(b)   for which a preliminary determination may be appropriate.

Article 3 Documents

1.   Within the time ordered by the Arbitral Tribunal, each Party shall submit to the Arbitral Tribunal and to the other Parties all Documents available to it on which it relies, including public

Documents and those in the public domain, except for any Documents that have already been submitted by another Party.

2.   Within the time ordered by the Arbitral Tribunal, any Party may submit to the Arbitral Tribunal and to the other Parties a Request to Produce.

3.   A Request to Produce shall contain:

(a)   (i)   a description of each requested Document sufficient to identify it, or

      (ii)   a description in sufficient detail (including subject matter) of a narrow and specific re-quested category of Documents that are reasonably believed to exist; in the case of Documents maintained in electronic form, the requesting Party may, or the Arbitral Tribunal may order that it shall be required to, identify specific files, search terms, indi-viduals or other means of searching for such Documents in an efficient and economi-cal manner;

(b)   a statement as to how the Documents requested are relevant to the case and material to its outcome; and

(c)   (i)   a statement that the Documents requested are not in the possession, custody or con-trol of the requesting Party or a statement of the reasons why it would be unreason-ably burdensome for the requesting Party to produce such Documents, and

      (ii)   a statement of the reasons why the requesting Party assumes the Documents reques-ted are in the possession, custody or control of another Party.

4.   Within the time ordered by the Arbitral Tribunal, the Party to whom the Request to Produce is addressed shall produce to the other Parties and, if the Arbitral Tribunal so orders, to it, all the Documents requested in its possession, custody or control as to which it makes no objection.

5.   If the Party to whom the Request to Produce is addressed has an objection to some or all of the Documents requested, it shall state the objection in writing to the Arbitral Tribunal and the other Parties within the time ordered by the Arbitral Tribunal. The reasons for such objection shall be any of those set forth in Article 9.2 or a failure to satisfy any of the requirements of Article 3.3.

6.   Upon receipt of any such objection, the Arbitral Tribunal may invite the relevant Parties to consult with each other with a view to resolving the objection.

7.   Either Party may, within the time ordered by the Arbitral Tribunal, request the Arbitral Tri-bunal to rule on the objection. The Arbitral Tribunal shall then, in consultation with the Parties and in timely fashion, consider the Request to Produce and the objection. The Arbitral Tribunal may order the Party to whom such Request is addressed to produce any requested Document in its possession, custody or control as to which the Arbitral Tribunal determines that (i) the issues that the requesting Party wishes to prove are relevant to the case and material to its outcome; (ii) none of the reasons for objection set forth in Article 9.2 applies; and (iii) the requirements of Article 3.3 have been satisfied. Any such Document shall be produced to the other Parties and, if the Arbitral Tribunal so orders, to it.

8.   In exceptional circumstances, if the propriety of an objection can be determined only by review of the Document, the Arbitral Tribunal may determine that it should not review the Document. In that event, the Arbitral Tribunal may, after consultation with the Parties, appoint an independent and impartial expert, bound to confidentiality, to review any such Document and to report on the objection. To the extent that the objection is upheld by the Arbitral Tribu-nal, the expert shall not disclose to the Arbitral Tribunal and to the other Parties the contents of the Document reviewed.

9.   If a Party wishes to obtain the production of Documents from a person or organisation who is not a Party to the arbitration and from whom the Party cannot obtain the Documents on its own, the Party may, within the time ordered by the Arbitral Tribunal, ask it to take whatever steps are legally available to obtain the requested Documents, or seek leave from the Arbitral Tribunal to take such steps itself. The Party shall submit such request to the Arbitral Tribunal and to the other Parties in writing, and the request shall contain the particulars set forth in Article 3.3, as applicable. The Arbitral Tribunal shall decide on this request and shall take, authorize the re-

questing Party to take, or order any other Party to take, such steps as the Arbitral Tribunal considers appropriate if, in its discretion, it determines that (i) the Documents would be relevant to the case and material to its outcome, (ii) the requirements of Article 3.3, as applicable, have been satisfied and (iii) none of the reasons for objection set forth in Article 9.2 applies.

10.   At any time before the arbitration is concluded, the Arbitral Tribunal may (i) request any Party to produce Documents, (ii) request any Party to use its best efforts to take or (iii) itself take, any step that it considers appropriate to obtain Documents from any person or organisation. A Party to whom such a request for Documents is addressed may object to the request for any of the reasons set forth in Article 9.2. In such cases, Article 3.4 to Article 3.8 shall apply correspondingly.

11.   Within the time ordered by the Arbitral Tribunal, the Parties may submit to the Arbitral Tribunal and to the other Parties any additional Documents on which they intend to rely or which they believe have become relevant to the case and material to its outcome as a consequence of the issues raised in Documents, Witness Statements or Expert Reports submitted or produced, or in other submissions of the Parties.

12.   With respect to the form of submission or production of Documents:

(a)   copies of Documents shall conform to the originals and, at the request of the Arbitral Tribunal, any original shall be presented for inspection;

(b)   Documents that a Party maintains in electronic form shall be submitted or produced in the form most convenient or economical to it that is reasonably usable by the recipients, unless the Parties agree otherwise or, in the absence of such agreement, the Arbitral Tribunal decides otherwise;

(c)   a Party is not obligated to produce multiple copies of Documents which are essentially identical unless the Arbitral Tribunal decides otherwise; and

(d)   translations of Documents shall be submitted together with the originals and marked as translations with the original language identified.

13.   Any Document submitted or produced by a Party or non-Party in the arbitration and not otherwise in the public domain shall be kept confidential by the Arbitral Tribunal and the other Parties, and shall be used only in connection with the arbitration. This requirement shall apply except and to the extent that disclosure may be required of a Party to fulfil a legal duty, protect or pursue a legal right, or enforce or challenge an award in bona fide legal proceedings before a state court or other judicial authority. The Arbitral Tribunal may issue orders to set forth the terms of this confidentiality. This requirement shall be without prejudice to all other obligations of confidentiality in the arbitration.

14.   If the arbitration is organised into separate issues or phases (such as jurisdiction, preliminary determinations, liability or damages), the Arbitral Tribunal may, after consultation with the Parties, schedule the submission of Documents and Requests to Produce separately for each issue or phase.

Article 4 Witnesses of Fact

1.   Within the time ordered by the Arbitral Tribunal, each Party shall identify the witnesses on whose testimony it intends to rely and the subject matter of that testimony.

2.   Any person may present evidence as a witness, including a Party or a Party's officer, employee or other representative.

3.   It shall not be improper for a Party, its officers, employees, legal advisors or other representatives to interview its witnesses or potential witnesses and to discuss their prospective testimony with them.

4.   The Arbitral Tribunal may order each Party to submit within a specified time to the Arbitral Tribunal and to the other Parties Witness Statements by each witness on whose testimony it intends to rely, except for those witnesses whose testimony is sought pursuant to Articles 4.9 or 4.10. If Evidentiary Hearings are organised into separate issues or phases (such as jurisdiction, preliminary determinations, liability or damages), the Arbitral Tribunal or the Parties by agreement may schedule the submission of Witness Statements separately for each issue or phase.

5.   Each Witness Statement shall contain:

(a) the full name and address of the witness, a statement regarding his or her present and past relationship (if any) with any of the Parties, and a description of his or her background, qualifications, training and experience, if such a description may be relevant to the dispute or to the contents of the statement;

(b) a full and detailed description of the facts, and the source of the witness's information as to those facts, sufficient to serve as that witness's evidence in the matter in dispute. Documents on which the witness relies that have not already been submitted shall be provided;

(c) a statement as to the language in which the Witness Statement was originally prepared and the language in which the witness anticipates giving testimony at the Evidentiary Hearing;

(d) an affirmation of the truth of the Witness Statement; and

(e) the signature of the witness and its date and place.

6. If Witness Statements are submitted, any Party may, within the time ordered by the Arbitral Tribunal, submit to the Arbitral Tribunal and to the other Parties revised or additional Witness Statements, including statements from persons not previously named as witnesses, so long as any such revisions or additions respond only to matters contained in another Party's Witness Statements, Expert Reports or other submissions that have not been previously presented in the arbitration.

7. If a witness whose appearance has been requested pursuant to Article 8.1 fails without a valid reason to appear for testimony at an Evidentiary Hearing, the Arbitral Tribunal shall disregard any Witness Statement related to that Evidentiary Hearing by that witness unless, in exceptional circumstances, the Arbitral Tribunal decides otherwise.

8. If the appearance of a witness has not been requested pursuant to Article 8.1, none of the other Parties shall be deemed to have agreed to the correctness of the content of the Witness Statement.

9. If a Party wishes to present evidence from a person who will not appear voluntarily at its request, the Party may, within the time ordered by the Arbitral Tribunal, ask it to take whatever steps are legally available to obtain the testimony of that person, or seek leave from the Arbitral Tribunal to take such steps itself. In the case of a request to the Arbitral Tribunal, the Party shall identify the intended witness, shall describe the subjects on which the witness's testimony is sought and shall state why such subjects are relevant to the case and material to its outcome. The Arbitral Tribunal shall decide on this request and shall take, authorize the requesting Party to take or order any other Party to take, such steps as the Arbitral Tribunal considers appropriate if, in its discretion, it determines that the testimony of that witness would be relevant to the case and material to its outcome.

10. At any time before the arbitration is concluded, the Arbitral Tribunal may order any Party to provide for, or to use its best efforts to provide for, the appearance for testimony at an Evidentiary Hearing of any person, including one whose testimony has not yet been offered. A Party to whom such a request is addressed may object for any of the reasons set forth in Article 9.2.

Article 5 Party-Appointed Experts

1. A Party may rely on a Party-Appointed Expert as a means of evidence on specific issues. Within the time ordered by the Arbitral Tribunal, (i) each Party shall identify any Party-Appointed Expert on whose testimony it intends to rely and the subject-matter of such testimony; and (ii) the Party-Appointed Expert shall submit an Expert Report.

2. The Expert Report shall contain:

(a) the full name and address of the Party-Appointed Expert, a statement regarding his or her present and past relationship (if any) with any of the Parties, their legal advisors and the Arbitral Tribunal, and a description of his or her background, qualifications, training and experience;

(b) a description of the instructions pursuant to which he or she is providing his or her opinions and conclusions;

(c)   a statement of his or her independence from the Parties, their legal advisors and the Arbitral Tribunal;

(d)   a statement of the facts on which he or she is basing his or her expert opinions and conclusions;

(e)   his or her expert opinions and conclusions, including a description of the methods, evidence and information used in arriving at the conclusions. Documents on which the Party-Appointed Expert relies that have not already been submitted shall be provided;

(f)   if the Expert Report has been translated, a statement as to the language in which it was originally prepared, and the language in which the Party-Appointed Expert anticipates giving testimony at the Evidentiary Hearing;

(g)   an affirmation of his or her genuine belief in the opinions expressed in the Expert Report;

(h)   the signature of the Party-Appointed Expert and its date and place; and

(i)   if the Expert Report has been signed by more than one person, an attribution of the entirety or specific parts of the Expert Report to each author.

3.   If Expert Reports are submitted, any Party may, within the time ordered by the Arbitral Tribunal, submit to the Arbitral Tribunal and to the other Parties revised or additional Expert Reports, including reports or statements from persons not previously identified as Party-Appointed Experts, so long as any such revisions or additions respond only to matters contained in another Party's Witness Statements, Expert Reports or other submissions that have not been previously presented in the arbitration.

4.   The Arbitral Tribunal in its discretion may order that any Party-Appointed Experts who will submit or who have submitted Expert Reports on the same or related issues meet and confer on such issues. At such meeting, the Party-Appointed Experts shall attempt to reach agreement on the issues within the scope of their Expert Reports, and they shall record in writing any such issues on which they reach agreement, any remaining areas of disagreement and the reasons therefore.

5.   If a Party-Appointed Expert whose appearance has been requested pursuant to Article 8.1 fails without a valid reason to appear for testimony at an Evidentiary Hearing, the Arbitral Tribunal shall disregard any Expert Report by that Party-Appointed Expert related to that Evidentiary Hearing unless, in exceptional circumstances, the Arbitral Tribunal decides otherwise.

6.   If the appearance of a Party-Appointed Expert has not been requested pursuant to Article 8.1, none of the other Parties shall be deemed to have agreed to the correctness of the content of the Expert Report.

Article 6 Tribunal-Appointed Experts

1.   The Arbitral Tribunal, after consulting with the Parties, may appoint one or more independent Tribunal-Appointed Experts to report to it on specific issues designated by the Arbitral Tribunal. The Arbitral Tribunal shall establish the terms of reference for any Tribunal-Appointed Expert Report after consulting with the Parties. A copy of the final terms of reference shall be sent by the Arbitral Tribunal to the Parties.

2.   The Tribunal-Appointed Expert shall, before accepting appointment, submit to the Arbitral Tribunal and to the Parties a description of his or her qualifications and a statement of his or her independence from the Parties, their legal advisors and the Arbitral Tribunal. Within the time ordered by the Arbitral Tribunal, the Parties shall inform the Arbitral Tribunal whether they have any objections as to the Tribunal-Appointed Expert's qualifications and independence. The Arbitral Tribunal shall decide promptly whether to accept any such objection. After the appointment of a Tribunal-Appointed Expert, a Party may object to the expert's qualifications or independence only if the objection is for reasons of which the Party becomes aware after the appointment has been made. The Arbitral Tribunal shall decide promptly what, if any, action to take.

3.   Subject to the provisions of Article 9.2, the Tribunal-Appointed Expert may request a Party to provide any information or to provide access to any Documents, goods, samples, property, machinery, systems, processes or site for inspection, to the extent relevant to the case and material to its outcome. The authority of a Tribunal-Appointed Expert to request such informa-

tion or access shall be the same as the authority of the Arbitral Tribunal. The Parties and their representatives shall have the right to receive any such information and to attend any such inspection. Any disagreement between a Tribunal-Appointed Expert and a Party as to the relevance, materiality or appropriateness of such a request shall be decided by the Arbitral Tribunal, in the manner provided in Articles 3.5 through 3.8. The Tribunal-Appointed Expert shall record in the Expert Report any non-compliance by a Party with an appropriate request or decision by the Arbitral Tribunal and shall describe its effects on the determination of the specific issue.

4.   The Tribunal-Appointed Expert shall report in writing to the Arbitral Tribunal in an Expert Report. The Expert Report shall contain:

(a)   the full name and address of the Tribunal-Appointed Expert, and a description of his or her background, qualifications, training and experience;

(b)   a statement of the facts on which he or she is basing his or her expert opinions and conclusions;

(c)   his or her expert opinions and conclusions, including a description of the methods, evidence and information used in arriving at the conclusions. Documents on which the Tribunal-Appointed Expert relies that have not already been submitted shall be provided;

(d)   if the Expert Report has been translated, a statement as to the language in which it was originally prepared, and the language in which the Tribunal-Appointed Expert anticipates giving testimony at the Evidentiary Hearing;

(e)   an affirmation of his or her genuine belief in the opinions expressed in the Expert Report;

(f)   the signature of the Tribunal-Appointed Expert and its date and place; and

(g)   if the Expert Report has been signed by more than one person, an attribution of the entirety or specific parts of the Expert Report to each author.

5.   The Arbitral Tribunal shall send a copy of such Expert Report to the Parties. The Parties may examine any information, Documents, goods, samples, property, machinery, systems, processes or site for inspection that the Tribunal-Appointed Expert has examined and any correspondence between the Arbitral Tribunal and the Tribunal-Appointed Expert. Within the time ordered by the Arbitral Tribunal, any Party shall have the opportunity to respond to the Expert Report in a submission by the Party or through a Witness Statement or an Expert Report by a Party-Appointed Expert. The Arbitral Tribunal shall send the submission, Witness Statement or Expert Report to the Tribunal-Appointed Expert and to the other Parties.

6.   At the request of a Party or of the Arbitral Tribunal, the Tribunal-Appointed Expert shall be present at an Evidentiary Hearing. The Arbitral Tribunal may question the Tribunal-Appointed Expert, and he or she may be questioned by the Parties or by any Party-Appointed Expert on issues raised in his or her Expert Report, the Parties' submissions or Witness Statement or the Expert Reports made by the Party-Appointed Experts pursuant to Article 6.5.

7.   Any Expert Report made by a Tribunal-Appointed Expert and its conclusions shall be assessed by the Arbitral Tribunal with due regard to all circumstances of the case.

8.   The fees and expenses of a Tribunal-Appointed Expert, to be funded in a manner determined by the Arbitral Tribunal, shall form part of the costs of the arbitration.

Article 7 Inspection

Subject to the provisions of Article 9.2, the Arbitral Tribunal may, at the request of a Party or on its own motion, inspect or require the inspection by a Tribunal-Appointed Expert or a Party-Appointed Expert of any site, property, machinery or any other goods, samples, systems, processes or Documents, as it deems appropriate. The Arbitral Tribunal shall, in consultation with the Parties, determine the timing and arrangement for the inspection. The Parties and their representatives shall have the right to attend any such inspection.

Article 8 Evidentiary Hearing

1.   Within the time ordered by the Arbitral Tribunal, each Party shall inform the Arbitral Tribunal and the other Parties of the witnesses whose appearance it requests. Each witness (which

term includes, for the purposes of this Article, witnesses of fact and any experts) shall, subject to Article 8.2, appear for testimony at the Evidentiary Hearing if such person's appearance has been requested by any Party or by the Arbitral Tribunal. Each witness shall appear in person unless the Arbitral Tribunal allows the use of video-conference or similar technology with respect to a particular witness.

2.   The Arbitral Tribunal shall at all times have complete control over the Evidentiary Hearing. The Arbitral Tribunal may limit or exclude any question to, answer by or appearance of a witness, if it considers such question, answer or appearance to be irrelevant, immaterial, unreasonably burdensome, duplicative or otherwise covered by a reason for objection set forth in Article 9.2. Questions to a witness during direct and re-direct testimony may not be unreasonably leading.

3.   With respect to oral testimony at an Evidentiary Hearing:

(a)   the Claimant shall ordinarily first present the testimony of its witnesses, followed by the Respondent presenting the testimony of its witnesses;

(b)   following direct testimony, any other Party may question such witness, in an order to be determined by the Arbitral Tribunal. The Party who initially presented the witness shall subsequently have the opportunity to ask additional questions on the matters raised in the other Parties' questioning;

(c)   thereafter, the Claimant shall ordinarily first present the testimony of its Party-Appointed Experts, followed by the Respondent presenting the testimony of its Party-Appointed Experts. The Party who initially presented the Party-Appointed Expert shall subsequently have the opportunity to ask additional questions on the matters raised in the other Parties' questioning;

(d)   the Arbitral Tribunal may question a Tribunal-Appointed Expert, and he or she may be questioned by the Parties or by any Party-Appointed Expert, on issues raised in the Tribunal-Appointed Expert Report, in the Parties' submissions or in the Expert Reports made by the Party-Appointed Experts;

(e)   if the arbitration is organised into separate issues or phases (such as jurisdiction, preliminary determinations, liability and damages), the Parties may agree or the Arbitral Tribunal may order the scheduling of testimony separately for each issue or phase;

(f)   the Arbitral Tribunal, upon request of a Party or on its own motion, may vary this order of proceeding, including the arrangement of testimony by particular issues or in such a manner that witnesses be questioned at the same time and in confrontation with each other (witness conferencing);

(g)   the Arbitral Tribunal may ask questions to a witness at any time.

4.   A witness of fact providing testimony shall first affirm, in a manner determined appropriate by the Arbitral Tribunal, that he or she commits to tell the truth or, in the case of an expert witness, his or her genuine belief in the opinions to be expressed at the Evidentiary Hearing. If the witness has submitted a Witness Statement or an Expert Report, the witness shall confirm it. The Parties may agree or the Arbitral Tribunal may order that the Witness Statement or Expert Report shall serve as that witness's direct testimony.

5.   Subject to the provisions of Article 9.2, the Arbitral Tribunal may request any person to give oral or written evidence on any issue that the Arbitral Tribunal considers to be relevant to the case and material to its outcome. Any witness called and questioned by the Arbitral Tribunal may also be questioned by the Parties.

Article 9 Admissibility and Assessment of Evidence

1.   The Arbitral Tribunal shall determine the admissibility, relevance, materiality and weight of evidence.

2.   The Arbitral Tribunal shall, at the request of a Party or on its own motion, exclude from evidence or production any Document, statement, oral testimony or inspection for any of the following reasons:

(a)   lack of sufficient relevance to the case or materiality to its outcome;

(b)   legal impediment or privilege under the legal or ethical rules determined by the Arbitral Tribunal to be applicable;

(c)   unreasonable burden to produce the requested evidence;

(d)   loss or destruction of the Document that has been shown with reasonable likelihood to have occurred;

(e)   grounds of commercial or technical confidentiality that the Arbitral Tribunal determines to be compelling;

(f)   grounds of special political or institutional sensitivity (including evidence that has been classified as secret by a government or a public international institution) that the Arbitral Tribunal determines to be compelling; or

(g)   considerations of procedural economy, proportionality, fairness or equality of the Parties that the Arbitral Tribunal determines to be compelling.

3.   In considering issues of legal impediment or privilege under Article 9.2(b), and insofar as permitted by any mandatory legal or ethical rules that are determined by it to be applicable, the Arbitral Tribunal may take into account:

(a)   any need to protect the confidentiality of a Document created or statement or oral communication made in connection with and for the purpose of providing or obtaining legal advice;

(b)   any need to protect the confidentiality of a Document created or statement or oral communication made in connection with and for the purpose of settlement negotiations;

(c)   the expectations of the Parties and their advisors at the time the legal impediment or privilege is said to have arisen;

(d)   any possible waiver of any applicable legal impediment or privilege by virtue of consent, earlier disclosure, affirmative use of the Document, statement, oral communication or advice contained therein, or otherwise; and

(e)   the need to maintain fairness and equality as between the Parties, particularly if they are subject to different legal or ethical rules.

4.   The Arbitral Tribunal may, where appropriate, make necessary arrangements to permit evidence to be presented or considered subject to suitable confidentiality protection.

5.   If a Party fails without satisfactory explanation to produce any Document requested in a Request to Produce to which it has not objected in due time or fails to produce any Document ordered to be produced by the Arbitral Tribunal, the Arbitral Tribunal may infer that such document would be adverse to the interests of that Party.

6.   If a Party fails without satisfactory explanation to make available any other relevant evidence, including testimony, sought by one Party to which the Party to whom the request was addressed has not objected in due time or fails to make available any evidence, including testimony, ordered by the Arbitral Tribunal to be produced, the Arbitral Tribunal may infer that such evidence would be adverse to the interests of that Party.

7.   If the Arbitral Tribunal determines that a Party has failed to conduct itself in good faith in the taking of evidence, the Arbitral Tribunal may, in addition to any other measures available under these Rules, take such failure into account in its assignment of the costs of the arbitration, including costs arising out of or in connection with the taking of evidence.

LONDON COURT OF INTERNATIONAL ARBITRATION
1998 ARBITRATION RULES[1]

Article 1 The Request for Arbitration

1.1   Any party wishing to commence an arbitration under these Rules ("the Claimant") shall send to the Registrar of the LCIA Court ("the Registrar") a written request for arbitration ("the Request"), containing or accompanied by:

(a)   the names, addresses, telephone, facsimile, telex and e-mail numbers (if known) of the parties to the arbitration and of their legal representatives;

(b)   a copy of the written arbitration clause or separate written arbitration agreement invoked by the Claimant ("the Arbitration Agreement"), together with a copy of the contractual documentation in which the arbitration clause is contained or in respect of which the arbitration arises;

(c)   a brief statement describing the nature and circumstances of the dispute, and specifying the claims advanced by the Claimant against another party to the arbitration ("the Respondent");

(d)   a statement of any matters (such as the seat or language(s) of the arbitration, or the number of arbitrators, or their qualifications or identities) on which the parties have already agreed in writing for the arbitration or in respect of which the Claimant wishes to make a proposal;

(e)   if the Arbitration Agreement calls for party nomination of arbitrators, the name, address, telephone, facsimile, telex and e-mail numbers (if known) of the Claimant's nominee;

(f)   the fee prescribed in the Schedule of Costs (without which the Request shall be treated as not having been received by the Registrar and the arbitration as not having been commenced);

(g)   confirmation to the Registrar that copies of the Request (including all accompanying documents) have been or are being served simultaneously on all other parties to the arbitration by one or more means of service to be identified in such confirmation.

1.2   The date of receipt by the Registrar of the Request shall be treated as the date on which the arbitration has commenced for all purposes. The Request (including all accompanying documents) should be submitted to the Registrar in two copies where a sole arbitrator should be appointed, or, if the parties have agreed or the Claimant considers that three arbitrators should be appointed, in four copies.

Article 2 The Response

2.1   Within 30 days of service of the Request on the Respondent, (or such lesser period fixed by the LCIA Court), the Respondent shall send to the Registrar a written response to the Request ("the Response"), containing or accompanied by:

(a)   confirmation or denial of all or part of the claims advanced by the Claimant in the Request;

(b)   a brief statement describing the nature and circumstances of any counterclaims advanced by the Respondent against the Claimant;

(c)   comment in response to any statements contained in the Request, as called for under Article 1.1(d), on matters relating to the conduct of the arbitration;

(d)   if the Arbitration Agreement calls for party nomination of arbitrators, the name, address, telephone, facsimile, telex and e-mail numbers (if known) of the Respondent's nominee; and

(e)   confirmation to the Registrar that copies of the Response (including all accompanying documents) have been or are being served simultaneously on all other parties to the arbitration by one or more means of service to be identified in such confirmation.

2.2   The Response (including all accompanying documents) should be submitted to the Registrar in two copies, or if the parties have agreed or the Respondent considers that three arbitrators should be appointed, in four copies.

2.3   Failure to send a Response shall not preclude the Respondent from denying any claim or from advancing a counterclaim in the arbitration. However, if the Arbitration Agreement calls

1   © London Court of International Arbitration, Document no. 80, www.lcia.org. All rights reserved.

for party nomination of arbitrators, failure to send a Response or to nominate an arbitrator within time or at all shall constitute an irrevocable waiver of that party's opportunity to nominate an arbitrator.

Article 3 The LCIA Court and Registrar

3.1   The functions of the LCIA Court under these Rules shall be performed in its name by the President or a Vice-President of the LCIA Court or by a division of three or five members of the LCIA Court appointed by the President or a Vice-President of the LCIA Court, as determined by the President.

3.2   The functions of the Registrar under these Rules shall be performed by the Registrar or any deputy Registrar of the LCIA Court under the supervision of the LCIA Court.

3.3   All communications from any party or arbitrator to the LCIA Court shall be addressed to the Registrar.

Article 4 Notices and Periods of Time

4.1   Any notice or other communication that may be or is required to be given by a party under these Rules shall be in writing and shall be delivered by registered postal or courier service or transmitted by facsimile, telex, e-mail or any other means of telecommunication that provide a record of its transmission.

4.2   A party's last-known residence or place of business during the arbitration shall be a valid address for the purpose of any notice or other communication in the absence of any notification of a change to such address by that party to the other parties, the Arbitral Tribunal and the Registrar.

4.3   For the purpose of determining the date of commencement of a time limit, a notice or other communication shall be treated as having been received on the day it is delivered or, in the case of telecommunications, transmitted in accordance with Articles 4.1 and 4.2.

4.4   For the purpose of determining compliance with a time limit, a notice or other communication shall be treated as having been sent, made or transmitted if it is dispatched in accordance with Articles 4.1 and 4.2 prior to or on the date of the expiration of the time-limit.

4.5   Notwithstanding the above, any notice or communication by one party may be addressed to another party in the manner agreed in writing between them or, failing such agreement, according to the practice followed in the course of their previous dealings or in whatever manner ordered by the Arbitral Tribunal.

4.6   For the purpose of calculating a period of time under these Rules, such period shall begin to run on the day following the day when a notice or other communication is received. If the last day of such period is an official holiday or a non-business day at the residence or place of business of the addressee, the period is extended until the first business day which follows. Official holidays or non-business days occurring during the running of the period of time are included in calculating that period.

4.7   The Arbitral Tribunal may at any time extend (even where the period of time has expired) or abridge any period of time prescribed under these Rules or under the Arbitration Agreement for the conduct of the arbitration, including any notice or communication to be served by one party on any other party.

Article 5 Formation of the Arbitral Tribunal

5.1   The expression "the Arbitral Tribunal" in these Rules includes a sole arbitrator or all the arbitrators where more than one. All references to an arbitrator shall include the masculine and feminine. (References to the President, Vice-President and members of the LCIA Court, the Registrar or deputy Registrar, expert, witness, party and legal representative shall be similarly understood).

5.2   All arbitrators conducting an arbitration under these Rules shall be and remain at all times impartial and independent of the parties; and none shall act in the arbitration as advocates for any party. No arbitrator, whether before or after appointment, shall advise any party on the merits or outcome of the dispute.

5.3   Before appointment by the LCIA Court, each arbitrator shall furnish to the Registrar a written resume of his past and present professional positions; he shall agree in writing upon fee rates conforming to the Schedule of Costs; and he shall sign a declaration to the effect that there are no circumstances known to him likely to give rise to any justified doubts as to his impartiality or independence, other than any circumstances disclosed by him in the declaration. Each arbitrator shall thereby also assume a continuing duty forthwith to disclose any such circumstances to the LCIA Court, to any other members of the Arbitral Tribunal and to all the parties if such circumstances should arise after the date of such declaration and before the arbitration is concluded.

5.4   The LCIA Court shall appoint the Arbitral Tribunal as soon as practicable after receipt by the Registrar of the Response or after the expiry of 30 days following service of the Request upon the Respondent if no Response is received by the Registrar (or such lesser period fixed by the LCIA Court). The LCIA Court may proceed with the formation of the Arbitral Tribunal notwithstanding that the Request is incomplete or the Response is missing, late or incomplete. A sole arbitrator shall be appointed unless the parties have agreed in writing otherwise, or unless the LCIA Court determines that in view of all the circumstances of the case a three-member tribunal is appropriate.

5.5   The LCIA Court alone is empowered to appoint arbitrators. The LCIA Court will appoint arbitrators with due regard for any particular method or criteria of selection agreed in writing by the parties. In selecting arbitrators consideration will be given to the nature of the transaction, the nature and circumstances of the dispute, the nationality, location and languages of the parties and (if more than two) the number of parties.

5.6   In the case of a three-member Arbitral Tribunal, the chairman (who will not be a party-nominated arbitrator) shall be appointed by the LCIA Court.

Article 6 Nationality of Arbitrators

6.1   Where the parties are of different nationalities, a sole arbitrator or chairman of the Arbitral Tribunal shall not have the same nationality as any party unless the parties who are not of the same nationality as the proposed appointee all agree in writing otherwise.

6.2   The nationality of parties shall be understood to include that of controlling shareholders or interests.

6.3   For the purpose of this Article, a person who is a citizen of two or more states shall be treated as a national of each state; and citizens of the European Union shall be treated as nationals of its different Member States and shall not be treated as having the same nationality.

Article 7 Party and Other Nominations

7.1   If the parties have agreed that any arbitrator is to be appointed by one or more of them or by any third person, that agreement shall be treated as an agreement to nominate an arbitrator for all purposes. Such nominee may only be appointed by the LCIA Court as arbitrator subject to his prior compliance with Article 5.3. The LCIA Court may refuse to appoint any such nominee if it determines that he is not suitable or independent or impartial.

7.2   Where the parties have howsoever agreed that the Respondent or any third person is to nominate an arbitrator and such nomination is not made within time or at all, the LCIA Court may appoint an arbitrator notwithstanding the absence of the nomination and without regard to any late nomination. Likewise, if the Request for Arbitration does not contain a nomination by the Claimant where the parties have howsoever agreed that the Claimant or a third person is to nominate an arbitrator, the LCIA Court may appoint an arbitrator notwithstanding the absence of the nomination and without regard to any late nomination.

Article 8 Three or More Parties

8.1   Where the Arbitration Agreement entitles each party howsoever to nominate an arbitrator, the parties to the dispute number more than two and such parties have not all agreed in writing that the disputant parties represent two separate sides for the formation of the Arbitral Tribunal as Claimant and Respondent respectively, the LCIA Court shall appoint the Arbitral Tribunal without regard to any party's nomination.

8.2   In such circumstances, the Arbitration Agreement shall be treated for all purposes as a written agreement by the parties for the appointment of the Arbitral Tribunal by the LCIA Court.

Article 9 Expedited Formation

9.1   In exceptional urgency, on or after the commencement of the arbitration, any party may apply to the LCIA Court for the expedited formation of the Arbitral Tribunal, including the appointment of any replacement arbitrator under Articles 10 and 11 of these Rules.

9.2   Such an application shall be made in writing to the LCIA Court, copied to all other parties to the arbitration; and it shall set out the specific grounds for exceptional urgency in the formation of the Arbitral Tribunal.

9.3   The LCIA Court may, in its complete discretion, abridge or curtail any time-limit under these Rules for the formation of the Arbitral Tribunal, including service of the Response and of any matters or documents adjudged to be missing from the Request. The LCIA Court shall not be entitled to abridge or curtail any other time-limit.

Article 10 Revocation of Arbitrator's Appointment

10.1 If either (a) any arbitrator gives written notice of his desire to resign as arbitrator to the LCIA Court, to be copied to the parties and the other arbitrators (if any) or (b) any arbitrator dies, falls seriously ill, refuses, or becomes unable or unfit to act, either upon challenge by a party or at the request of the remaining arbitrators, the LCIA Court may revoke that arbitrator's appointment and appoint another arbitrator. The LCIA Court shall decide upon the amount of fees and expenses to be paid for the former arbitrator's services (if any) as it may consider appropriate in all the circumstances.

10.2 If any arbitrator acts in deliberate violation of the Arbitration Agreement (including these Rules) or does not act fairly and impartially as between the parties or does not conduct or participate in the arbitration proceedings with reasonable diligence, avoiding unnecessary delay or expense, that arbitrator may be considered unfit in the opinion of the LCIA Court.

10.3 An arbitrator may also be challenged by any party if circumstances exist that give rise to justifiable doubts as to his impartiality or independence. A party may challenge an arbitrator it has nominated, or in whose appointment it has participated, only for reasons of which it becomes aware after the appointment has been made.

10.4 A party who intends to challenge an arbitrator shall, within 15 days of the formation of the Arbitral Tribunal or (if later) after becoming aware of any circumstances referred to in Article 10.1, 10.2 or 10.3, send a written statement of the reasons for its challenge to the LCIA Court, the Arbitral Tribunal and all other parties. Unless the challenged arbitrator withdraws or all other parties agree to the challenge within 15 days of receipt of the written statement, the LCIA Court shall decide on the challenge.

Article 11 Nomination and Replacement of Arbitrators

11.1 In the event that the LCIA Court determines that any nominee is not suitable or independent or impartial or if an appointed arbitrator is to be replaced for any reason, the LCIA Court shall have a complete discretion to decide whether or not to follow the original nominating process.

11.2 If the LCIA Court should so decide, any opportunity given to a party to make a renomination shall be waived if not exercised within 15 days (or such lesser time as the LCIA Court may fix), after which the LCIA Court shall appoint the replacement arbitrator.

Article 12 Majority Power to Continue Proceedings

12.1 If any arbitrator on a three-member Arbitral Tribunal refuses or persistently fails to participate in its deliberations, the two other arbitrators shall have the power, upon their written notice of such refusal or failure to the LCIA Court, the parties and the third arbitrator, to continue the arbitration (including the making of any decision, ruling or award), notwithstanding the absence of the third arbitrator.

12.2 In determining whether to continue the arbitration, the two other arbitrators shall take into account the stage of the arbitration, any explanation made by the third arbitrator for his non-participation and such other matters as they consider appropriate in the circumstances of the case. The reasons for such determination shall be stated in any award, order or other decision made by the two arbitrators without the participation of the third arbitrator.

12.3 In the event that the two other arbitrators determine at any time not to continue the arbitration without the participation of the third arbitrator missing from their deliberations, the two arbitrators shall notify in writing the parties and the LCIA Court of such determination; and in that event, the two arbitrators or any party may refer the matter to the LCIA Court for the revocation of that third arbitrator's appointment and his replacement under Article 10.

Article 13 Communications Between Parties and the Arbitral Tribunal

13.1 Until the Arbitral Tribunal is formed, all communications between parties and arbitrators shall be made through the Registrar.

13.2 Thereafter, unless and until the Arbitral Tribunal directs that communications shall take place directly between the Arbitral Tribunal and the parties (with simultaneous copies to the Registrar), all written communications between the parties and the Arbitral Tribunal shall continue to be made through the Registrar.

13.3 Where the Registrar sends any written communication to one party on behalf of the Arbitral Tribunal, he shall send a copy to each of the other parties. Where any party sends to the Registrar any communication (including Written Statements and Documents under Article 15), it shall include a copy for each arbitrator; and it shall also send copies direct to all other parties and confirm to the Registrar in writing that it has done or is doing so.

Article 14 Conduct of the Proceedings

14.1 The parties may agree on the conduct of their arbitral proceedings and they are encouraged to do so, consistent with the Arbitral Tribunal's general duties at all times:
(i)   to act fairly and impartially as between all parties, giving each a reasonable opportunity of putting its case and dealing with that of its opponent; and
(ii)   to adopt procedures suitable to the circumstances of the arbitration, avoiding unnecessary delay or expense, so as to provide a fair and efficient means for the final resolution of the parties' dispute.

Such agreements shall be made by the parties in writing or recorded in writing by the Arbitral Tribunal at the request of and with the authority of the parties.

14.2 Unless otherwise agreed by the parties under Article 14.1, the Arbitral Tribunal shall have the widest discretion to discharge its duties allowed under such law(s) or rules of law as the Arbitral Tribunal may determine to be applicable; and at all times the parties shall do everything necessary for the fair, efficient and expeditious conduct of the arbitration.

14.3 In the case of a three-member Arbitral Tribunal the chairman may, with the prior consent of the other two arbitrators, make procedural rulings alone.

Article 15 Submission of Written Statements and Documents

15.1 Unless the parties have agreed otherwise under Article 14.1 or the Arbitral Tribunal should determine differently, the written stage of the proceedings shall be as set out below.

15.2 Within 30 days of receipt of written notification from the Registrar of the formation of the Arbitral Tribunal, the Claimant shall send to the Registrar a Statement of Case setting out in sufficient detail the facts and any contentions of law on which it relies, together with the relief claimed against all other parties, save and insofar as such matters have not been set out in its Request.

15.3 Within 30 days of receipt of the Statement of Case or written notice from the Claimant that it elects to treat the Request as its Statement of Case, the Respondent shall send to the Registrar a Statement of Defence setting out in sufficient detail which of the facts and contentions of law in the Statement of Case or Request (as the case may be) it admits or denies, on what grounds and on what other facts and contentions of law it relies. Any counterclaims shall be submitted with the Statement of Defence in the same manner as claims are to be set out in the Statement of Case.

15.4 Within 30 days of receipt of the Statement of Defence, the Claimant shall send to the Registrar a Statement of Reply which, where there are any counterclaims, shall include a Defence to Counterclaim in the same manner as a defence is to be set out in the Statement of Defence.

15.5 If the Statement of Reply contains a Defence to Counterclaim, within 30 days of its receipt the Respondent shall send to the Registrar a Statement of Reply to Counterclaim.

15.6 All Statements referred to in this Article shall be accompanied by copies (or, if they are especially voluminous, lists) of all essential documents on which the party concerned relies and which have not previously been submitted by any party, and (where appropriate) by any relevant samples and exhibits.

15.7 As soon as practicable following receipt of the Statements specified in this Article, the Arbitral Tribunal shall proceed in such manner as has been agreed in writing by the parties or pursuant to its authority under these Rules.

15.8 If the Respondent fails to submit a Statement of Defence or the Claimant a Statement of Defence to Counterclaim, or if at any point any party fails to avail itself of the opportunity to present its case in the manner determined by Article 15.2 to 15.6 or directed by the Arbitral Tribunal, the Arbitral Tribunal may nevertheless proceed with the arbitration and make an award.

Article 16 Seat of Arbitration and Place of Hearings

16.1 The parties may agree in writing the seat (or legal place) of their arbitration. Failing such a choice, the seat of arbitration shall be London, unless and until the LCIA Court determines in view of all the circumstances, and after having given the parties an opportunity to make written comment, that another seat is more appropriate.

16.2 The Arbitral Tribunal may hold hearings, meetings and deliberations at any convenient geographical place in its discretion; and if elsewhere than the seat of the arbitration, the arbitration shall be treated as an arbitration conducted at the seat of the arbitration and any award as an award made at the seat of the arbitration for all purposes.

16.3 The law applicable to the arbitration (if any) shall be the arbitration law of the seat of arbitration, unless and to the extent that the parties have expressly agreed in writing on the application of another arbitration law and such agreement is not prohibited by the law of the arbitral seat.

Article 17 Language of Arbitration

17.1 The initial language of the arbitration shall be the language of the Arbitration Agreement, unless the parties have agreed in writing otherwise and providing always that a non-participating or defaulting party shall have no cause for complaint if communications to and from the Registrar and the arbitration proceedings are conducted in English.

17.2 In the event that the Arbitration Agreement is written in more than one language, the LCIA Court may, unless the Arbitration Agreement provides that the arbitration proceedings shall be conducted in more than one language, decide which of those languages shall be the initial language of the arbitration.

17.3 Upon the formation of the Arbitral Tribunal and unless the parties have agreed upon the language or languages of the arbitration, the Arbitration Tribunal shall decide upon the language(s) of the arbitration, after giving the parties an opportunity to make written comment and taking into account the initial language of the arbitration and any other matter it may consider appropriate in all the circumstances of the case.

17.4 If any document is expressed in a language other than the language(s) of the arbitration and no translation of such document is submitted by the party relying upon the document, the Arbitral Tribunal or (if the Arbitral Tribunal has not been formed) the LCIA Court may order that party to submit a translation in a form to be determined by the Arbitral Tribunal or the LCIA Court, as the case may be.

Article 18 Party Representation

18.1 Any party may be represented by legal practitioners or any other representatives.

18.2 At any time the Arbitral Tribunal may require from any party proof of authority granted to its representative(s) in such form as the Arbitral Tribunal may determine.

Article 19 Hearings

19.1 Any party which expresses a desire to that effect has the right to be heard orally before the Arbitral Tribunal on the merits of the dispute, unless the parties have agreed in writing on documents-only arbitration.

19.2 The Arbitral Tribunal shall fix the date, time and physical place of any meetings and hearings in the arbitration, and shall give the parties reasonable notice thereof.

19.3 The Arbitral Tribunal may in advance of any hearing submit to the parties a list of questions which it wishes them to answer with special attention.

19.4 All meetings and hearings shall be in private unless the parties agree otherwise in writing or the Arbitral Tribunal directs otherwise.

19.5 The Arbitral Tribunal shall have the fullest authority to establish time-limits for meetings and hearings, or for any parts thereof.

Article 20 Witnesses

20.1 Before any hearing, the Arbitral Tribunal may require any party to give notice of the identity of each witness that party wishes to call (including rebuttal witnesses), as well as the subject matter of that witness's testimony, its content and its relevance to the issues in the arbitration.

20.2 The Arbitral Tribunal may also determine the time, manner and form in which such materials should be exchanged between the parties and presented to the Arbitral Tribunal; and it has a discretion to allow, refuse, or limit the appearance of witnesses (whether witness of fact or expert witness).

20.3 Subject to any order otherwise by the Arbitral Tribunal, the testimony of a witness may be presented by a party in written form, either as a signed statement or as a sworn affidavit.

20.4 Subject to Article 14.1 and 14.2, any party may request that a witness, on whose testimony another party seeks to rely, should attend for oral questioning at a hearing before the Arbitral Tribunal. If the Arbitral Tribunal orders that other party to produce the witness and the witness fails to attend the oral hearing without good cause, the Arbitral Tribunal may place such weight on the written testimony (or exclude the same altogether) as it considers appropriate in the circumstances of the case.

20.5 Any witness who gives oral evidence at a hearing before the Arbitral Tribunal may be questioned by each of the parties under the control of the Arbitral Tribunal. The Arbitral Tribunal may put questions at any stage of his evidence.

20.6 Subject to the mandatory provisions of any applicable law, it shall not be improper for any party or its legal representatives to interview any witness or potential witness for the purpose of presenting his testimony in written form or producing him as an oral witness.

20.7 Any individual intending to testify to the Arbitral Tribunal on any issue of fact or expertise shall be treated as a witness under these Rules notwithstanding that the individual is a party to the arbitration or was or is an officer, employee or shareholder of any party.

Article 21 Experts to the Arbitral Tribunal

21.1 Unless otherwise agreed by the parties in writing, the Arbitral Tribunal:

(a)   may appoint one or more experts to report to the Arbitral Tribunal on specific issues, who shall be and remain impartial and independent of the parties throughout the arbitration proceedings; and

(b)   may require a party to give any such expert any relevant information or to provide access to any relevant documents, goods, samples, property or site for inspection by the expert.

21.2 Unless otherwise agreed by the parties in writing, if a party so requests or if the Arbitral Tribunal considers it necessary, the expert shall, after delivery of his written or oral report to the Arbitral Tribunal and the parties, participate in one or more hearings at which the parties shall have the opportunity to question the expert on his report and to present expert witnesses in order to testify on the points at issue.

21.3 The fees and expenses of any expert appointed by the Arbitral Tribunal under this Article shall be paid out of the deposits payable by the parties under Article 24 and shall form part of the costs of the arbitration.

Article 22 Additional Powers of the Arbitral Tribunal

22.1 Unless the parties at any time agree otherwise in writing, the Arbitral Tribunal shall have the power, on the application of any party or of its own motion, but in either case only after giving the parties a reasonable opportunity to state their views:

(a)   to allow any party, upon such terms (as to costs and otherwise) as it shall determine, to amend any claim, counterclaim, defence and reply;

(b)   to extend or abbreviate any time-limit provided by the Arbitration Agreement or these Rules for the conduct of the arbitration or by the Arbitral Tribunal's own orders;

(c)   to conduct such enquiries as may appear to the Arbitral Tribunal to be necessary or expedient, including whether and to what extent the Arbitral Tribunal should itself take the initiative in identifying the issues and ascertaining the relevant facts and the law(s) or rules of law applicable to the arbitration, the merits of the parties' dispute and the Arbitration Agreement;

(d)   to order any party to make any property, site or thing under its control and relating to the subject matter of the arbitration available for inspection by the Arbitral Tribunal, any other party, its expert or any expert to the Arbitral Tribunal;

(e)   to order any party to produce to the Arbitral Tribunal, and to the other parties for inspection, and to supply copies of, any documents or classes of documents in their possession, custody or power which the Arbitral Tribunal determines to be relevant;

(f)   to decide whether or not to apply any strict rules of evidence (or any other rules) as to the admissibility, relevance or weight of any material tendered by a party on any matter of fact or expert opinion; and to determine the time, manner and form in which such material should be exchanged between the parties and presented to the Arbitral Tribunal;

(g)   to order the correction of any contract between the parties or the Arbitration Agreement, but only to the extent required to rectify any mistake which the Arbitral Tribunal determines to be common to the parties and then only if and to the extent to which the law(s) or rules of law applicable to the contract or Arbitration Agreement permit such correction; and

(h)   to allow, only upon the application of a party, one or more third persons to be joined in the arbitration as a party provided any such third person and the applicant party have consented thereto in writing, and thereafter to make a single final award, or separate awards, in respect of all parties so implicated in the arbitration;

22.2 By agreeing to arbitration under these Rules, the parties shall be treated as having agreed not to apply to any state court or other judicial authority for any order available from the Arbitral Tribunal under Article 22.1, except with the agreement in writing of all parties.

22.3 The Arbitral Tribunal shall decide the parties' dispute in accordance with the law(s) or rules of law chosen by the parties as applicable to the merits of their dispute. If and to the extent that the Arbitral Tribunal determines that the parties have made no such choice, the Arbitral Tribunal shall apply the law(s) or rules of law which it considers appropriate.

22.4 The Arbitral Tribunal shall only apply to the merits of the dispute principles deriving from "ex aequo et bono", "amiable composition" or "honourable engagement" where the parties have so agreed expressly in writing.

Article 23 Jurisdiction of the Arbitral Tribunal

23.1 The Arbitral Tribunal shall have the power to rule on its own jurisdiction, including any objection to the initial or continuing existence, validity or effectiveness of the Arbitration Agreement. For that purpose, an arbitration clause which forms or was intended to form part of another agreement shall be treated as an arbitration agreement independent of that other agreement. A decision by the Arbitral Tribunal that such other agreement is non-existent, invalid or ineffective shall not entail ipso jure the non-existence, invalidity or ineffectiveness of the arbitration clause.

23.2 A plea by a Respondent that the Arbitral Tribunal does not have jurisdiction shall be treated as having been irrevocably waived unless it is raised not later than the Statement of Defence; and a like plea by a Respondent to Counterclaim shall be similarly treated unless it is raised no later than the Statement of Defence to Counterclaim. A plea that the Arbitral Tribunal is exceeding the scope of its authority shall be raised promptly after the Arbitral Tribunal has indicated its intention to decide on the matter alleged by any party to be beyond the scope of its authority, failing which such plea shall also be treated as having been waived irrevocably. In any case, the Arbitral Tribunal may nevertheless admit an untimely plea if it considers the delay justified in the particular circumstances.

23.3 The Arbitral Tribunal may determine the plea to its jurisdiction or authority in an award as to jurisdiction or later in an award on the merits, as it considers appropriate in the circumstances.

23.4 By agreeing to arbitration under these Rules, the parties shall be treated as having agreed not to apply to any state court or other judicial authority for any relief regarding the Arbitral Tribunal's jurisdiction or authority, except with the agreement in writing of all parties to the arbitration or the prior authorisation of the Arbitral Tribunal or following the latter's award ruling on the objection to its jurisdiction or authority.

Article 24 Deposits

24.1 The LCIA Court may direct the parties, in such proportions as it thinks appropriate, to make one or several interim or final payments on account of the costs of the arbitration. Such deposits shall be made to and held by the LCIA and from time to time may be released by the LCIA Court to the arbitrator(s), any expert appointed by the Arbitral Tribunal and the LCIA itself as the arbitration progresses.

24.2 The Arbitral Tribunal shall not proceed with the arbitration without ascertaining at all times from the Registrar or any deputy Registrar that the LCIA is in requisite funds.

24.3 In the event that a party fails or refuses to provide any deposit as directed by the LCIA Court, the LCIA Court may direct the other party or parties to effect a substitute payment to allow the arbitration to proceed (subject to any award on costs). In such circumstances, the party paying the substitute payment shall be entitled to recover that amount as a debt immediately due from the defaulting party.

24.4 Failure by a claimant or counterclaiming party to provide promptly and in full the required deposit may be treated by the LCIA Court and the Arbitral Tribunal as a withdrawal of the claim or counterclaim respectively.

Article 25 Interim and Conservatory Measures

25.1 The Arbitral Tribunal shall have the power, unless otherwise agreed by the parties in writing, on the application of any party:

(a) to order any respondent party to a claim or counterclaim to provide security for all or part of the amount in dispute, by way of deposit or bank guarantee or in any other manner and upon such terms as the Arbitral Tribunal considers appropriate. Such terms may include the provision by the claiming or counterclaiming party of a cross-indemnity, itself secured in such manner as the Arbitral Tribunal considers appropriate, for any costs or losses incurred by such respondent in providing security. The amount of any costs and losses payable under such cross-indemnity may be determined by the Arbitral Tribunal in one or more awards;

(b) to order the preservation, storage, sale or other disposal of any property or thing under the control of any party and relating to the subject matter of the arbitration; and

(c) to order on a provisional basis, subject to final determination in an award, any relief which the Arbitral Tribunal would have power to grant in an award, including a provisional order for the payment of money or the disposition of property as between any parties.

25.2 The Arbitral Tribunal shall have the power, upon the application of a party, to order any claiming or counterclaiming party to provide security for the legal or other costs of any other party by way of deposit or bank guarantee or in any other manner and upon such terms as the Arbitral Tribunal considers appropriate. Such terms may include the provision by that other party of a cross-indemnity, itself secured in such manner as the Arbitral Tribunal considers appropriate, for any costs and losses incurred by such claimant or counterclaimant in providing security. The amount of any costs and losses payable under such cross-indemnity may be determined by the Arbitral Tribunal in one or more awards. In the event that a claiming or counterclaiming party does not comply with any order to provide security, the Arbitral Tribunal may stay that party's claims or counterclaims or dismiss them in an award.

25.3 The power of the Arbitral Tribunal under Article 25.1 shall not prejudice howsoever any party's right to apply to any state court or other judicial authority for interim or conservatory measures before the formation of the Arbitral Tribunal and, in exceptional cases, thereafter. Any application and any order for such measures after the formation of the Arbitral Tribunal shall be promptly communicated by the applicant to the Arbitral Tribunal and all other parties. However, by agreeing to arbitration under these Rules, the parties shall be taken to have agreed not to apply to any state court or other judicial authority for any order for security for its legal or other costs available from the Arbitral Tribunal under Article 25.2.

Article 26 The Award

26.1 The Arbitral Tribunal shall make its award in writing and, unless all parties agree in writing otherwise, shall state the reasons upon which its award is based. The award shall also state the date when the award is made and the seat of the arbitration; and it shall be signed by the Arbitral Tribunal or those of its members assenting to it.

26.2 If any arbitrator fails to comply with the mandatory provisions of any applicable law relating to the making of the award, having been given a reasonable opportunity to do so, the remaining arbitrators may proceed in his absence and state in their award the circumstances of the other arbitrator's failure to participate in the making of the award.

26.3 Where there are three arbitrators and the Arbitral Tribunal fails to agree on any issue, the arbitrators shall decide that issue by a majority. Failing a majority decision on any issue, the chairman of the Arbitral Tribunal shall decide that issue.

26.4 If any arbitrator refuses or fails to sign the award, the signatures of the majority or (failing a majority) of the chairman shall be sufficient, provided that the reason for the omitted signature is stated in the award by the majority or chairman.

26.5 The sole arbitrator or chairman shall be responsible for delivering the award to the LCIA Court, which shall transmit certified copies to the parties provided that the costs of arbitration have been paid to the LCIA in accordance with Article 28.

26.6 An award may be expressed in any currency. The Arbitral Tribunal may order that simple or compound interest shall be paid by any party on any sum awarded at such rates as the Arbitral Tribunal determines to be appropriate, without being bound by legal rates of interest imposed by any state court, in respect of any period which the Arbitral Tribunal determines to be appropriate ending not later than the date upon which the award is complied with.

26.7 The Arbitral Tribunal may make separate awards on different issues at different times. Such awards shall have the same status and effect as any other award made by the Arbitral Tribunal.

26.8 In the event of a settlement of the parties' dispute, the Arbitral Tribunal may render an award recording the settlement if the parties so request in writing (a "Consent Award"), provided always that such award contains an express statement that it is an award made by the parties' consent. A Consent Award need not contain reasons. If the parties do not require a consent award, then on written confirmation by the parties to the LCIA Court that a settlement has been reached, the Arbitral Tribunal shall be discharged and the arbitration proceedings concluded, subject to payment by the parties of any outstanding costs of the arbitration under Article 28.

26.9 All awards shall be final and binding on the parties. By agreeing to arbitration under these Rules, the parties undertake to carry out any award immediately and without any delay (subject only to Article 27); and the parties also waive irrevocably their right to any form of appeal, review or recourse to any state court or other judicial authority, insofar as such waiver may be validly made.

Article 27 Correction of Awards and Additional Awards

27.1 Within 30 days of receipt of any award, or such lesser period as may be agreed in writing by the parties, a party may by written notice to the Registrar (copied to all other parties) request the Arbitral Tribunal to correct in the award any errors in computation, clerical or typographical errors or any errors of a similar nature. If the Arbitral Tribunal considers the request to be justified, it shall make the corrections within 30 days of receipt of the request. Any correction shall take the form of separate memorandum dated and signed by the Arbitral Tribunal or (if three arbitrators) those of its members assenting to it; and such memorandum shall become part of the award for all purposes.

27.2 The Arbitral Tribunal may likewise correct any error of the nature described in Article 27.1 on its own initiative within 30 days of the date of the award, to the same effect.

27.3 Within 30 days of receipt of the final award, a party may by written notice to the Registrar (copied to all other parties), request the Arbitral Tribunal to make an additional award as to claims or counterclaims presented in the arbitration but not determined in any award. If the Arbitral Tribunal considers the request to be justified, it shall make the additional award within 60 days of receipt of the request. The provisions of Article 26 shall apply to any additional award.

Article 28 Arbitration and Legal Costs

28.1 The costs of the arbitration (other than the legal or other costs incurred by the parties themselves) shall be determined by the LCIA Court in accordance with the Schedule of Costs. The parties shall be jointly and severally liable to the Arbitral Tribunal and the LCIA for such arbitration costs.

28.2 The Arbitral Tribunal shall specify in the award the total amount of the costs of the arbitration as determined by the LCIA Court. Unless the parties agree otherwise in writing, the Arbitral Tribunal shall determine the proportions in which the parties shall bear all or part of such arbitration costs. If the Arbitral Tribunal has determined that all or any part of the arbitration costs shall be borne by a party other than a party which has already paid them to the LCIA, the latter party shall have the right to recover the appropriate amount from the former party.

28.3 The Arbitral Tribunal shall also have the power to order in its award that all or part of the legal or other costs incurred by a party be paid by another party, unless the parties agree otherwise in writing. The Arbitral Tribunal shall determine and fix the amount of each item comprising such costs on such reasonable basis as it thinks fit.

28.4 Unless the parties otherwise agree in writing, the Arbitral Tribunal shall make its orders on both arbitration and legal costs on the general principle that costs should reflect the parties' relative success and failure in the award or arbitration, except where it appears to the Arbitral Tribunal that in the particular circumstances this general approach is inappropriate. Any order for costs shall be made with reasons in the award containing such order.

28.5 If the arbitration is abandoned, suspended or concluded, by agreement or otherwise, before the final award is made, the parties shall remain jointly and severally liable to pay to the LCIA and the Arbitral Tribunal the costs of the arbitration as determined by the LCIA Court in accordance with the Schedule of Costs. In the event that such arbitration costs are less than the deposits made by the parties, there shall be a refund by the LCIA in such proportion as the parties may agree in writing, or failing such agreement, in the same proportions as the deposits were made by the parties to the LCIA.

Article 29 Decisions by the LCIA Court

29.1 The decisions of the LCIA Court with respect to all matters relating to the arbitration shall be conclusive and binding upon the parties and the Arbitral Tribunal. Such decisions are to be treated as administrative in nature and the LCIA Court shall not be required to give any reasons.

29.2 To the extent permitted by the law of the seat of the arbitration, the parties shall be taken to have waived any right of appeal or review in respect of any such decisions of the LCIA Court to any state court or other judicial authority. If such appeals or review remain possible due to mandatory provisions of any applicable law, the LCIA Court shall, subject to the provisions of that applicable law, decide whether the arbitral proceedings are to continue, notwithstanding an appeal or review.

Article 30 Confidentiality

30.1 Unless the parties expressly agree in writing to the contrary, the parties undertake as a general principle to keep confidential all awards in their arbitration, together with all materials in the proceedings created for the purpose of the arbitration and all other documents produced by another party in the proceedings not otherwise in the public domain - save and to the extent that disclosure may be required of a party by legal duty, to protect or pursue a legal right or to enforce or challenge an award in bona fide legal proceedings before a state court or other judicial authority.

30.2 The deliberations of the Arbitral Tribunal are likewise confidential to its members, save and to the extent that disclosure of an arbitrator's refusal to participate in the arbitration is required of the other members of the Arbitral Tribunal under Articles 10, 12 and 26.

30.3 The LCIA Court does not publish any award or any part of an award without the prior written consent of all parties and the Arbitral Tribunal.

Article 31 Exclusion of Liability

31.1 None of the LCIA, the LCIA Court (including its President, Vice-Presidents and individual members), the Registrar, any deputy Registrar, any arbitrator and any expert to the Arbitral Tribunal shall be liable to any party howsoever for any act or omission in connection with any arbitration conducted by reference to these Rules, save where the act or omission is shown by that party to constitute conscious and deliberate wrongdoing committed by the body or person alleged to be liable to that party.

31.2 After the award has been made and the possibilities of correction and additional awards referred to in Article 27 have lapsed or been exhausted, neither the LCIA, the LCIA Court (including its President, Vice-Presidents and individual members), the Registrar, any deputy Registrar, any arbitrator or expert to the Arbitral Tribunal shall be under any legal obligation to make any statement to any person about any matter concerning the arbitration, nor shall any party seek to make any of these persons a witness in any legal or other proceedings arising out of the arbitration.

Article 32 General Rules

32.1 A party who knows that any provision of the Arbitration Agreement (including these Rules) has not been complied with and yet proceeds with the arbitration without promptly stating its objection to such non-compliance, shall be treated as having irrevocably waived its right to object.

32.2 In all matters not expressly provided for in these Rules, the LCIA Court, the Arbitral Tribunal and the parties shall act in the spirit of these Rules and shall make every reasonable effort to ensure that an award is legally enforceable.

AMERICAN ARBITRATION ASSOCIATION
International Centre for Dispute Resolution
International Dispute Resolution Procedures, Mediation and Arbitration Rules[1]
Rules Amended and Effective 1 June 2009
Fee Schedule Amended and Effective 1 June 2010

INTRODUCTION

The international business community uses arbitration to resolve commercial disputes arising in the global marketplace. Supportive laws are in place. The New York Convention of 1958 has been widely adopted, providing a favorable legislative climate that enables the enforcement of arbitration clauses. International commercial arbitration awards are recognized by national courts in most parts of the world, even more than foreign court judgments. A key component to the successful resolution of an international commercial dispute is the role played by the administrative institution. The International Centre for Dispute Resolution® (ICDR) is the international division of the American Arbitration Association (AAA) charged with the exclusive administration of all of the AAA's international matters. The ICDR's experience, international expertise and multilingual staff forms an integral part of the dispute resolution process. The ICDR's international system is premised on its ability to move the matter forward, facilitate communications, ensure that qualified arbitrators and mediators are appointed, control costs, understand cultural sensitivities, resolve procedural impasses and properly interpret and apply its International Mediation and Arbitration Rules. Additionally, the ICDR has many cooperative agreements with arbitral institutions around the world for facilitating the administration of its international cases.

International Mediation

The parties might wish to submit their dispute to an international mediation prior to arbitration. In mediation, an impartial and independent mediator assists the parties in reaching a settlement but does not have the authority to make a binding decision or award. International Mediation is administered by the ICDR in accordance with its International Mediation Rules. There is no additional administrative fee where parties to a pending arbitration attempt to mediate their dispute under the ICDR's auspices.

If the parties want to adopt mediation as a part of their contractual dispute settlement procedure, they can insert the following mediation clause into their contract in conjunction with a standard arbitration provision: *"If a dispute arises out of or relates to this contract, or the breach thereof, and if the dispute cannot be settled through negotiation, the parties agree first to try in good faith to settle the dispute by mediation in accordance with the International Mediation Rules of the International Centre for Dispute Resolution before resorting to arbitration, litigation or some other dispute resolution procedure."*

If the parties want to use a mediator to resolve an existing dispute, they can enter into the following submission: *"The parties hereby submit the following dispute to mediation administered by the International Centre for Dispute Resolution in accordance with its International Mediation Rules. (The clause may also provide for the qualifications of the mediator(s), method of payment, locale of meetings and any other item of concern to the parties.)"*

The ICDR can schedule the mediation anywhere in the world and will propose a list of specialized international mediators.

International Arbitration

As the ICDR is a division of the AAA, parties can arbitrate future disputes under these Rules by inserting either of the following clauses into their contracts:

---

1   © 2011 International Centre for Dispute Resolution and American Arbitration Association, Inc. All rights reserved.

"Any controversy or claim arising out of or relating to this contract, or the breach thereof, shall be determined by arbitration administered by the International Centre for Dispute Resolution in accordance with its International Arbitration Rules." or

"Any controversy or claim arising out of or relating to this contract, or the breach thereof, shall be determined by arbitration administered by the American Arbitration Association in accordance with its International Arbitration Rules."

The parties may wish to consider adding:

(a) "The number of arbitrators shall be (one or three)";
(b) "The place of arbitration shall be (city and/or country)"; or
(c) "The language(s) of the arbitration shall be _____."

Parties are encouraged, when writing their contracts or when a dispute arises, to request a conference, in person or by telephone, with the ICDR, to discuss an appropriate method for selection of arbitrators or any other matter that might facilitate efficient arbitration of the dispute.

Under these Rules, the parties are free to adopt any mutually agreeable procedure for appointing arbitrators, or may designate arbitrators upon whom they agree. Parties can reach agreements concerning appointing arbitrators either when writing their contracts or after a dispute has arisen. This flexible procedure permits parties to utilize whatever method they consider best suits their needs. For example, parties may choose to have a sole arbitrator or a tribunal of three or more. They may agree that arbitrators shall be appointed by the ICDR, or that each side shall designate one arbitrator and those two shall name a third, with the ICDR making appointments if the tribunal is not promptly formed by that procedure. Parties may mutually request the ICDR to submit to them a list of arbitrators from which each can delete names not acceptable to it, or the parties may instruct the ICDR to appoint arbitrators without the submission of lists, or may leave that matter to the sole discretion of the ICDR. Parties also may agree on a variety of other methods for establishing the tribunal. In any event, if parties are unable to agree on a procedure for appointing arbitrators or on the designation of arbitrators, the ICDR, after inviting consultation by the parties, will appoint the arbitrators. The Rules thus provide for the fullest exercise of party autonomy, while assuring that the ICDR is available to act if the parties cannot reach mutual agreement. By providing for arbitration under these Rules, parties can avoid the uncertainty of having to petition a local court to resolve procedural impasses. These Rules, as administered by the IDCR, are intended to provide prompt, effective and economical arbitration services to the global business community.

Whenever a singular term is used in the Rules, such as "party," "claimant" or "arbitrator," that term shall include the plural if there is more than one such entity.

Parties filing an international case with the International Centre for Dispute Resolution, or the American Arbitration Association, may file online via AAAWebFile® at www.adr.org. For filing assistance, parties may directly contact the ICDR in New York, Bahrain, Singapore or any one of the AAA's regional offices.

If you would like to file a case by mail or fax, please complete the appropriate form(s) and forward to AAA/ICDR Case Filing Services.

International Centre for Dispute Resolution
A Division of the American Arbitration Association
Case Filing Services
1101 Laurel Oak Road, Suite 100
Voorhees, NJ 08043
Phone: 856-435-6401
Toll free number in the US 877-495-4185
Fax number 877-304-8457
Fax number outside the US: 212-484-4178
Email box: casefiling@adr.org

Further information about these Rules can be secured by contacting the International Centre for Dispute Resolution at 212.484.4181 or by visiting the ICDR's Web site at www.icdr.org.

The English language version of the Rules is the official text for questions of interpretation.

INTERNATIONAL MEDIATION RULES

1. Agreement of Parties

Whenever parties have agreed in writing to mediate disputes under these International Mediation Rules, or have provided for mediation or conciliation of existing or future international disputes under the auspices of the International Centre for Dispute Resolution, the international division of the American Arbitration Association, or the American Arbitration Association without designating particular Rules, they shall be deemed to have made these Rules, as amended and in effect as of the date of the submission of the dispute, a part of their agreement.

The parties by mutual agreement may vary any part of these Rules including, but not limited to, agreeing to conduct the mediation via telephone or other electronic or technical means.

2. Initiation of Mediation

Any party or parties to a dispute may initiate mediation under the ICDR's auspices by making a request for mediation to any of the ICDR's regional offices or case management centers via telephone, email, regular mail or fax. Requests for mediation may also be filed online via AAA WebFile at www.adr.org.

The party initiating the mediation shall simultaneously notify the other party or parties of the request. The initiating party shall provide the following information to the ICDR and the other party or parties as applicable:
a) A copy of the mediation provision of the parties' contract or the parties' stipulation to mediate.
b) The names, regular mail addresses, email addresses, and telephone numbers of all parties to the dispute and representatives, if any, in the mediation.
c) A brief statement of the nature of the dispute and the relief requested.
d) Any specific qualifications the mediator should possess.

Where there is no preexisting stipulation or contract by which the parties have provided for mediation of existing or future disputes under the auspices of the ICDR, a party may request the ICDR to invite another party to participate in "mediation by voluntary submission". Upon receipt of such a request, the ICDR will contact the other party or parties involved in the dispute and attempt to obtain a submission to mediation.

3. Representation

Subject to any applicable law, any party may be represented by persons of the party's choice. The names and addresses of such persons shall be communicated in writing to all parties and to the ICDR.

4. Appointment of the Mediator

Parties may search the online profiles of the ICDR's Panel of Mediators at www.aaamediation.com in an effort to agree on a mediator. If the parties have not agreed to the appointment of a mediator and have not provided any other method of appointment, the mediator shall be appointed in the following manner:
a.   Upon receipt of a request for mediation, the ICDR will send to each party a list of mediators from the ICDR's Panel of Mediators. The parties are encouraged to agree to a mediator from the submitted list and to advise the ICDR of their agreement.
b.   If the parties are unable to agree upon a mediator, each party shall strike unacceptable names from the list, number the remaining names in order of preference, and return the list to the ICDR. If a party does not return the list within the time specified, all mediators on the list shall be deemed acceptable. From among the mediators who have been mutually approved by the parties, and in accordance with the designated order of mutual preference, the ICDR shall invite a mediator to serve.
c.   If the parties fail to agree on any of the mediators listed, or if acceptable mediators are unable to serve, or if for any other reason the appointment cannot be made from the submitted list, the ICDR shall have the authority to make the appointment from among other members of the Panel of Mediators without the submission of additional lists.

5. Mediator's Impartiality and Duty to Disclose

ICDR mediators are required to abide by the Model Standards of Conduct for Mediators in effect at the time a mediator is appointed to a case. Where there is a conflict between the Model Standards and any provision of these Mediation Rules, these Mediation Rules shall govern. The Standards require mediators to (i) decline a mediation if the mediator cannot conduct it in an impartial manner, and (ii) disclose, as soon as practicable, all actual and potential conflicts of interest that are reasonably known to the mediator and could reasonably be seen as raising a question about the mediator's impartiality.

Prior to accepting an appointment, ICDR mediators are required to make a reasonable inquiry to determine whether there are any facts that a reasonable individual would consider likely to create a potential or actual conflict of interest for the mediator. ICDR mediators are required to disclose any circumstance likely to create a presumption of bias or prevent a resolution of the parties' dispute within the time frame desired by the parties. Upon receipt of such disclosures, the ICDR shall immediately communicate the disclosures to the parties for their comments.

The parties may, upon receiving disclosure of actual or potential conflicts of interest of the mediator, waive such conflicts and proceed with the mediation. In the event that a party disagrees as to whether the mediator shall serve, or in the event that the mediator's conflict of interest might reasonably be viewed as undermining the integrity of the mediation, the mediator shall be replaced.

6. Vacancies

If any mediator shall become unwilling or unable to serve, the ICDR will appoint another mediator, unless the parties agree otherwise, in accordance with section 4.

7. Duties and Responsibilities of the Mediator

a. The mediator shall conduct the mediation based on the principle of party self-determination. Self-determination is the act of coming to a voluntary, uncoerced decision in which each party makes free and informed choices as to process and outcome.

b. The mediator is authorized to conduct separate or ex parte meetings and other communications with the parties and/or their representatives, before, during, and after any scheduled mediation conference. Such communications may be conducted via telephone, in writing, via email, online, in person or otherwise.

c. The parties are encouraged to exchange all documents pertinent to the relief requested. The mediator may request the exchange of memoranda on issues, including the underlying interests and the history of the parties' negotiations. Information that a party wishes to keep confidential may be sent to the mediator, as necessary, in a separate communication with the mediator.

d. The mediator does not have the authority to impose a settlement on the parties but will attempt to help them reach a satisfactory resolution of their dispute. Subject to the discretion of the mediator, the mediator may make oral or written recommendations for settlement to a party privately or, if the parties agree, to all parties jointly.

e. In the event that a complete settlement of all or some issues in dispute is not achieved within the scheduled mediation conference(s), the mediator may continue to communicate with the parties, for a period of time, in an ongoing effort to facilitate a complete settlement.

f. The mediator is not a legal representative of any party and has no fiduciary duty to any party.

8. Responsibilities of the Parties

The parties shall ensure that appropriate representatives of each party, having authority to consummate a settlement, attend the mediation conference.

Prior to and during the scheduled mediation conference(s) the parties and their representatives shall, as appropriate to each party's circumstances, exercise their best efforts to prepare for and engage in a meaningful and productive mediation.

9. Privacy

Mediation conferences and related mediation communications are private proceedings. The parties and their representatives may attend mediation conferences. Other persons may attend only with the permission of the parties and with the consent of the mediator.

10. Confidentiality

Subject to applicable law or the parties' agreement, confidential information disclosed to a mediator by the parties or by other participants (witnesses) in the course of the mediation shall not be divulged by the mediator. The mediator shall maintain the confidentiality of all information obtained in the mediation, and all records, reports, or other documents received by a mediator while serving in that capacity shall be confidential.

The mediator shall not be compelled to divulge such records or to testify in regard to the mediation in any adversary proceeding or judicial forum.

The parties shall maintain the confidentiality of the mediation and shall not rely on, or introduce as evidence in any arbitral, judicial, or other proceeding the following, unless agreed to by the parties or required by applicable law:

a.   Views expressed or suggestions made by a party or other participant with respect to a possible settlement of the dispute;
b.   Admissions made by a party or other participant in the course of the mediation proceedings;
c.   Proposals made or views expressed by the mediator; or
d.   The fact that a party had or had not indicated willingness to accept a proposal for settlement made by the mediator.

11. No Stenographic Record

There shall be no stenographic record of the mediation process.

12. Termination of Mediation

The mediation shall be terminated:

a.   By the execution of a settlement agreement by the parties; or
b.   By a written or verbal declaration of the mediator to the effect that further efforts at mediation would not contribute to a resolution of the parties' dispute; or
c.   By a written or verbal declaration of all parties to the effect that the mediation proceedings are terminated; or
d.   When there has been no communication between the mediator and any party or party's representative for 21 days following the conclusion of the mediation conference.

13. Exclusion of Liability

Neither the ICDR nor any mediator is a necessary party in judicial proceedings relating to the mediation. Neither the ICDR nor any mediator shall be liable to any party for any error, act or omission in connection with any mediation conducted under these Rules.

14. Interpretation and Application of Rules

The mediator shall interpret and apply these Rules insofar as they relate to the mediator's duties and responsibilities. All other Rules shall be interpreted and applied by the ICDR.

15. Deposits

Unless otherwise directed by the mediator, the ICDR will require the parties to deposit in advance of the mediation conference such sums of money as it, in consultation with the mediator, deems necessary to cover the costs and expenses of the mediation and shall render an accounting to the parties and return any unexpended balance at the conclusion of the mediation.

16. Expenses

All expenses of the mediation, including required traveling and other expenses or charges of the mediator, shall be borne equally by the parties unless they agree otherwise. The expenses of participants for either side shall be paid by the party requesting the attendance of such participants.

17. Cost of the Mediation

There is no filing fee to initiate a mediation or a fee to request the ICDR to invite parties to mediate.

The cost of mediation is based on the hourly mediation rate published on the mediator's ICDR profile. This rate covers both mediator compensation and an allocated portion for the ICDR's services. There is a four-hour minimum charge for a mediation conference. Expenses referenced in Section M-16 may also apply.

If a matter submitted for mediation is withdrawn or cancelled or results in a settlement after the agreement to mediate is filed but prior to the mediation conference the cost is $250 plus any mediator time and charges incurred.

The parties will be billed equally for all costs unless they agree otherwise.

If you have questions about mediation costs or services visit our website at www.icdr.org or contact us at + 1 212.484.4181.

18. Language

If the parties have not agreed otherwise, the language(s) of the mediation shall be that of the documents containing the mediation agreement.

Conference Room Rental

The costs described above do not include the use of ICDR conference rooms. Conference rooms are available on a rental basis. Please contact your local ICDR office for availability and rates.

INTERNATIONAL ARBITRATION RULES
Article 1 [Scope of Application]

a.   Where parties have agreed in writing to arbitrate disputes under these International Arbitration Rules or have provided for arbitration of an international dispute by the International Centre for Dispute Resolution or the American Arbitration Association without designating particular Rules, the arbitration shall take place in accordance with these Rules, as in effect at the date of commencement of the arbitration, subject to whatever modifications the parties may adopt in writing.

b.   These Rules govern the arbitration, except that, where any such rule is in conflict with any provision of the law applicable to the arbitration from which the parties cannot derogate, that provision shall prevail.

c.   These Rules specify the duties and responsibilities of the administrator, the International Centre for Dispute Resolution, a division of the American Arbitration Association. The administrator may provide services through its Centre, located in New York, or through the facilities of arbitral institutions with which it has agreements of cooperation.

Commencing the Arbitration
Article 2 Notice of Arbitration and Statement of Claim

1.   The party initiating arbitration ("claimant") shall give written notice of arbitration to the administrator and at the same time to the party against whom a claim is being made ("respondent").

2.   Arbitral proceedings shall be deemed to commence on the date on which the administrator receives the notice of arbitration.

3.   The notice of arbitration shall contain a statement of claim including the following:

(a)   a demand that the dispute be referred to arbitration;

(b)   the names, addresses and telephone numbers of the parties;

(c)   a reference to the arbitration clause or agreement that is invoked;

(d)   a reference to any contract out of or in relation to which the dispute arises;

(e)   a description of the claim and an indication of the facts supporting it;

(f)   the relief or remedy sought and the amount claimed; and

(g)   may include proposals as to the means of designating and the number of arbitrators, the place of arbitration and the language(s) of the arbitration.

4.   Upon receipt of the notice of arbitration, the administrator shall communicate with all parties with respect to the arbitration and shall acknowledge the commencement of the arbitration.

Article 3 Statement of Defense and Counterclaim

1.   Within 30 days after the commencement of the arbitration, a respondent shall submit a written statement of defense, responding to the issues raised in the notice of arbitration, to the claimant and any other parties, and to the administrator.
2.   At the time a respondent submits its statement of defense, a respondent may make counterclaims or assert setoffs as to any claim covered by the agreement to arbitrate, as to which the claimant shall within 30 days submit a written statement of defense to the respondent and any other parties and to the administrator.
3.   A respondent shall respond to the administrator, the claimant and other parties within 30 days after the commencement of the arbitration as to any proposals the claimant may have made as to the number of arbitrators, the place of the arbitration or the language(s) of the arbitration, except to the extent that the parties have previously agreed as to these matters.
4.   The arbitral tribunal, or the administrator if the arbitral tribunal has not yet been formed, may extend any of the time limits established in this article if it considers such an extension justified.

Article 4 Amendments to Claims

During the arbitral proceedings, any party may amend or supplement its claim, counterclaim or defense, unless the tribunal considers it inappropriate to allow such amendment or supplement because of the party's delay in making it, prejudice to the other parties or any other circumstances. A party may not amend or supplement a claim or counterclaim if the amendment or supplement would fall outside the scope of the agreement to arbitrate.

The Tribunal

Article 5 Number of Arbitrators

If the parties have not agreed on the number of arbitrators, one arbitrator shall be appointed unless the administrator determines in its discretion that three arbitrators are appropriate because of the large size, complexity or other circumstances of the case.

Article 6 Appointment of Arbitrators

1.   The parties may mutually agree upon any procedure for appointing arbitrators and shall inform the administrator as to such procedure.
2.   The parties may mutually designate arbitrators, with or without the assistance of the administrator. When such designations are made, the parties shall notify the administrator so that notice of the appointment can be communicated to the arbitrators, together with a copy of these Rules.
3.   If within 45 days after the commencement of the arbitration, all of the parties have not mutually agreed on a procedure for appointing the arbitrator(s) or have not mutually agreed on the designation of the arbitrator(s), the administrator shall, at the written request of any party, appoint the arbitrator(s) and designate the presiding arbitrator. If all of the parties have mutually agreed upon a procedure for appointing the arbitrator(s), but all appointments have not been made within the time limits provided in that procedure, the administrator shall, at the written request of any party, perform all functions provided for in that procedure that remain to be performed.
4.   In making such appointments, the administrator, after inviting consultation with the parties, shall endeavor to select suitable arbitrators. At the request of any party or on its own initiative, the administrator may appoint nationals of a country other than that of any of the parties.
5.   Unless the parties have agreed otherwise no later than 45 days after the commencement of the arbitration, if the notice of arbitration names two or more claimants or two or more respondents, the administrator shall appoint all the arbitrators.

Article 7 Impartiality and Independence of Arbitrators

1.   Arbitrators acting under these Rules shall be impartial and independent. Prior to accepting appointment, a prospective arbitrator shall disclose to the administrator any circumstance likely to give rise to justifiable doubts as to the arbitrator's impartiality or independence. If, at any stage during the arbitration, new circumstances arise that may give rise to such doubts, an arbitrator shall promptly disclose such circumstances to the parties and to the administrator. Upon receipt of such information from an arbitrator or a party, the administrator shall communicate it to the other parties and to the tribunal.

2.   No party or anyone acting on its behalf shall have any ex parte communication relating to the case with any arbitrator, or with any candidate for appointment as party-appointed arbitrator except to advise the candidate of the general nature of the controversy and of the anticipated proceedings and to discuss the candidate's qualifications, availability or independence in relation to the parties, or to discuss the suitability of candidates for selection as a third arbitrator where the parties or party designated arbitrators are to participate in that selection. No party or anyone acting on its behalf shall have any ex parte communication relating to the case with any candidate for presiding arbitrator.

Article 8 Challenge of Arbitrators

1.   A party may challenge any arbitrator whenever circumstances exist that give rise to justifiable doubts as to the arbitrator's impartiality or independence. A party wishing to challenge an arbitrator shall send notice of the challenge to the administrator within 15 days after being notified of the appointment of the arbitrator or within 15 days after the circumstances giving rise to the challenge become known to that party.

2.   The challenge shall state in writing the reasons for the challenge.

3.   Upon receipt of such a challenge, the administrator shall notify the other parties of the challenge. When an arbitrator has been challenged by one party, the other party or parties may agree to the acceptance of the challenge and, if there is agreement, the arbitrator shall withdraw. The challenged arbitrator may also withdraw from office in the absence of such agreement. In neither case does withdrawal imply acceptance of the validity of the grounds for the challenge.

Article 9 [Decision in the Absence of Agreement]

If the other party or parties do not agree to the challenge or the challenged arbitrator does not withdraw, the administrator in its sole discretion shall make the decision on the challenge.

Article 10 Replacement of an Arbitrator

If an arbitrator withdraws after a challenge, or the administrator sustains the challenge, or the administrator determines that there are sufficient reasons to accept the resignation of an arbitrator, or an arbitrator dies, a substitute arbitrator shall be appointed pursuant to the provisions of Article 6, unless the parties otherwise agree.

Article 11 [Failure of an Arbitrator to Participate]

1.   If an arbitrator on a three-person tribunal fails to participate in the arbitration for reasons other than those identified in Article 10, the two other arbitrators shall have the power in their sole discretion to continue the arbitration and to make any decision, ruling or award, notwithstanding the failure of the third arbitrator to participate. In determining whether to continue the arbitration or to render any decision, ruling or award without the participation of an arbitrator, the two other arbitrators shall take into account the stage of the arbitration, the reason, if any, expressed by the third arbitrator for such nonparticipation and such other matters as they consider appropriate in the circumstances of the case. In the event that the two other arbitrators determine not to continue the arbitration without the participation of the third arbitrator, the administrator on proof satisfactory to it shall declare the office vacant, and a substitute arbitrator shall be appointed pursuant to the provisions of Article 6, unless the parties otherwise agree.

2.   If a substitute arbitrator is appointed under either Article 10 or Article 11, the tribunal shall determine at its sole discretion whether all or part of any prior hearings shall be repeated.

General Conditions
Article 12 Representation

Any party may be represented in the arbitration. The names, addresses and telephone numbers of representatives shall be communicated in writing to the other parties and to the administrator. Once the tribunal has been established, the parties or their representatives may communicate in writing directly with the tribunal.

Article 13 Place of Arbitration

1.   If the parties disagree as to the place of arbitration, the administrator may initially determine the place of arbitration, subject to the power of the tribunal to determine finally the place of arbitration within 60 days after its constitution. All such determinations shall be made having regard for the contentions of the parties and the circumstances of the arbitration.
2.   The tribunal may hold conferences or hear witnesses or inspect property or documents at any place it deems appropriate. The parties shall be given sufficient written notice to enable them to be present at any such proceedings.

Article 14 Language

If the parties have not agreed otherwise, the language(s) of the arbitration shall be that of the documents containing the arbitration agreement, subject to the power of the tribunal to determine otherwise based upon the contentions of the parties and the circumstances of the arbitration. The tribunal may order that any documents delivered in another language shall be accompanied by a translation into the language(s) of the arbitration.

Article 15 Pleas as to Jurisdiction

1.   The tribunal shall have the power to rule on its own jurisdiction, including any objections with respect to the existence, scope or validity of the arbitration agreement.
2.   The tribunal shall have the power to determine the existence or validity of a contract of which an arbitration clause forms a part. Such an arbitration clause shall be treated as an agreement independent of the other terms of the contract. A decision by the tribunal that the contract is null and void shall not for that reason alone render invalid the arbitration clause.
3.   A party must object to the jurisdiction of the tribunal or to the arbitrability of a claim or counterclaim no later than the filing of the statement of defense, as provided in Article 3, to the claim or counterclaim that gives rise to the objection. The tribunal may rule on such objections as a preliminary matter or as part of the final award.

Article 16 Conduct of the Arbitration

1.   Subject to these Rules, the tribunal may conduct the arbitration in whatever manner it considers appropriate, provided that the parties are treated with equality and that each party has the right to be heard and is given a fair opportunity to present its case.
2.   The tribunal, exercising its discretion, shall conduct the proceedings with a view to expediting the resolution of the dispute. It may conduct a preparatory conference with the parties for the purpose of organizing, scheduling and agreeing to procedures to expedite the subsequent proceedings.
3.   The tribunal may in its discretion direct the order of proof, bifurcate proceedings, exclude cumulative or irrelevant testimony or other evidence and direct the parties to focus their presentations on issues the decision of which could dispose of all or part of the case.
4.   Documents or information supplied to the tribunal by one party shall at the same time be communicated by that party to the other party or parties.

Article 17 Further Written Statements

1.   The tribunal may decide whether the parties shall present any written statements in addition to statements of claims and counterclaims and statements of defense, and it shall fix the periods of time for submitting any such statements.

2.   The periods of time fixed by the tribunal for the communication of such written statements should not exceed 45 days. However, the tribunal may extend such time limits if it considers such an extension justified.

Article 18 Notices

1.   Unless otherwise agreed by the parties or ordered by the tribunal, all notices, statements and written communications may be served on a party by air mail, air courier, facsimile transmission, telex, telegram or other written forms of electronic communication addressed to the party or its representative at its last known address or by personal service.
2.   For the purpose of calculating a period of time under these Rules, such period shall begin to run on the day following the day when a notice, statement or written communication is received. If the last day of such period is an official holiday at the place received, the period is extended until the first business day which follows. Official holidays occurring during the running of the period of time are included in calculating the period.

Article 19 Evidence

1.   Each party shall have the burden of proving the facts relied on to support its claim or defense.
2.   The tribunal may order a party to deliver to the tribunal and to the other parties a summary of the documents and other evidence which that party intends to present in support of its claim, counterclaim or defense.
3.   At any time during the proceedings, the tribunal may order parties to produce other documents, exhibits or other evidence it deems necessary or appropriate.

Article 20 Hearings

1.   The tribunal shall give the parties at least 30 days advance notice of the date, time and place of the initial oral hearing. The tribunal shall give reasonable notice of subsequent hearings.
2.   At least 15 days before the hearings, each party shall give the tribunal and the other parties the names and addresses of any witnesses it intends to present, the subject of their testimony and the languages in which such witnesses will give their testimony.
3.   At the request of the tribunal or pursuant to mutual agreement of the parties, the administrator shall make arrangements for the interpretation of oral testimony or for a record of the hearing.
4.   Hearings are private unless the parties agree otherwise or the law provides to the contrary. The tribunal may require any witness or witnesses to retire during the testimony of other witnesses. The tribunal may determine the manner in which witnesses are examined.
5.   Evidence of witnesses may also be presented in the form of written statements signed by them.
6.   The tribunal shall determine the admissibility, relevance, materiality and weight of the evidence offered by any party. The tribunal shall take into account applicable principles of legal privilege, such as those involving the confidentiality of communications between a lawyer and client.

Article 21 Interim Measures of Protection

1.   At the request of any party, the tribunal may take whatever interim measures it deems necessary, including injunctive relief and measures for the protection or conservation of property.
2.   Such interim measures may take the form of an interim award, and the tribunal may require security for the costs of such measures.
3.   A request for interim measures addressed by a party to a judicial authority shall not be deemed incompatible with the agreement to arbitrate or a waiver of the right to arbitrate.
4.   The tribunal may in its discretion apportion costs associated with applications for interim relief in any interim award or in the final award.

Article 22 Experts

1.   The tribunal may appoint one or more independent experts to report to it, in writing, on specific issues designated by the tribunal and communicated to the parties.

2.   The parties shall provide such an expert with any relevant information or produce for inspection any relevant documents or goods that the expert may require. Any dispute between a party and the expert as to the relevance of the requested information or goods shall be referred to the tribunal for decision.

3.   Upon receipt of an expert's report, the tribunal shall send a copy of the report to all parties and shall give the parties an opportunity to express, in writing, their opinion on the report. A party may examine any document on which the expert has relied in such a report.

4.   At the request of any party, the tribunal shall give the parties an opportunity to question the expert at a hearing. At this hearing, parties may present expert witnesses to testify on the points at issue.

Article 23 Default

1.   If a party fails to file a statement of defense within the time established by the tribunal without showing sufficient cause for such failure, as determined by the tribunal, the tribunal may proceed with the arbitration.

2.   If a party, duly notified under these Rules, fails to appear at a hearing without showing sufficient cause for such failure, as determined by the tribunal, the tribunal may proceed with the arbitration.

3.   If a party, duly invited to produce evidence or take any other steps in the proceedings, fails to do so within the time established by the tribunal without showing sufficient cause for such failure, as determined by the tribunal, the tribunal may make the award on the evidence before it.

Article 24 Closure of Hearing

1.   After asking the parties if they have any further testimony or evidentiary submissions and upon receiving negative replies or if satisfied that the record is complete, the tribunal may declare the hearings closed.

2.   The tribunal in its discretion, on its own motion or upon application of a party, may reopen the hearings at any time before the award is made.

Article 25 Waiver of Rules

A party who knows that any provision of the Rules or requirement under the Rules has not been complied with, but proceeds with the arbitration without promptly stating an objection in writing thereto, shall be deemed to have waived the right to object.

Article 26 Awards, Decisions and Rulings

1.   When there is more than one arbitrator, any award, decision or ruling of the arbitral tribunal shall be made by a majority of the arbitrators. If any arbitrator fails to sign the award, it shall be accompanied by a statement of the reason for the absence of such signature.

2.   When the parties or the tribunal so authorize, the presiding arbitrator may make decisions or rulings on questions of procedure, subject to revision by the tribunal.

Article 27 Form and Effect of the Award

1.   Awards shall be made in writing, promptly by the tribunal, and shall be final and binding on the parties. The parties undertake to carry out any such award without delay.

2.   The tribunal shall state the reasons upon which the award is based, unless the parties have agreed that no reasons need be given.

3.   The award shall contain the date and the place where the award was made, which shall be the place designated pursuant to Article 13.

4.   An award may be made public only with the consent of all parties or as required by law.

5.   Copies of the award shall be communicated to the parties by the administrator.

6.   If the arbitration law of the country where the award is made requires the award to be filed or registered, the tribunal shall comply with such requirement.

7.   In addition to making a final award, the tribunal may make interim, interlocutory or partial orders and awards.

8.   Unless otherwise agreed by the parties, the administrator may publish or otherwise make publicly available selected awards, decisions and rulings that have been edited to conceal the names of the parties and other identifying details or that have been made publicly available in the course of enforcement or otherwise.

Article 28 Applicable Laws and Remedies

1.   The tribunal shall apply the substantive law(s) or rules of law designated by the parties as applicable to the dispute. Failing such a designation by the parties, the tribunal shall apply such law(s) or rules of law as it determines to be appropriate.

2.   In arbitrations involving the application of contracts, the tribunal shall decide in accordance with the terms of the contract and shall take into account usages of the trade applicable to the contract.

3.   The tribunal shall not decide as amiable *compositeur* or *ex aequo et bono* unless the parties have expressly authorized it to do so.

4.   A monetary award shall be in the currency or currencies of the contract unless the tribunal considers another currency more appropriate, and the tribunal may award such pre-award and post-award interest, simple or compound, as it considers appropriate, taking into consideration the contract and applicable law.

5.   Unless the parties agree otherwise, the parties expressly waive and forego any right to punitive, exemplary or similar damages unless a statute requires that compensatory damages be increased in a specified manner. This provision shall not apply to any award of arbitration costs to a party to compensate for dilatory or bad faith conduct in the arbitration.

Article 29 Settlement or Other Reasons for Termination

1.   If the parties settle the dispute before an award is made, the tribunal shall terminate the arbitration and, if requested by all parties, may record the settlement in the form of an award on agreed terms. The tribunal is not obliged to give reasons for such an award.

2.   If the continuation of the proceedings becomes unnecessary or impossible for any other reason, the tribunal shall inform the parties of its intention to terminate the proceedings. The tribunal shall thereafter issue an order terminating the arbitration, unless a party raises justifiable grounds for objection.

Article 30 Interpretation or Correction of the Award

1.   Within 30 days after the receipt of an award, any party, with notice to the other parties, may request the tribunal to interpret the award or correct any clerical, typographical or computation errors or make an additional award as to claims presented but omitted from the award.

2.   If the tribunal considers such a request justified, after considering the contentions of the parties, it shall comply with such a request within 30 days after the request.

Article 31 Costs

The tribunal shall fix the costs of arbitration in its award. The tribunal may apportion such costs among the parties if it determines that such apportionment is reasonable, taking into account the circumstances of the case.

Such costs may include:

(a)   the fees and expenses of the arbitrators;

(b)   the costs of assistance required by the tribunal, including its experts;

(c)   the fees and expenses of the administrator;

(d)   the reasonable costs for legal representation of a successful party; and

(e)   any such costs incurred in connection with an application for interim or emergency relief pursuant to Article 21.

Article 32 Compensation of Arbitrators

Arbitrators shall be compensated based upon their amount of service, taking into account their stated rate of compensation and the size and complexity of the case. The administrator shall arrange an appropriate daily or hourly rate, based on such considerations, with the parties and with each of the arbitrators as soon as practicable after the commencement of the arbitration. If the parties fail to agree on the terms of compensation, the administrator shall establish an appropriate rate and communicate it in writing to the parties.

Article 33 Deposit of Costs
1.   When a party files claims, the administrator may request the filing party to deposit appropriate amounts as an advance for the costs referred to in Article 31, paragraphs (a.), (b.) and (c.).
2.   During the course of the arbitral proceedings, the tribunal may request supplementary deposits from the parties.
3.   If the deposits requested are not paid in full within 30 days after the receipt of the request, the administrator shall so inform the parties, in order that one or the other of them may make the required payment. If such payments are not made, the tribunal may order the suspension or termination of the proceedings.
4.   After the award has been made, the administrator shall render an accounting to the parties of the deposits received and return any unexpended balance to the parties.

Article 34 Confidentiality
Confidential information disclosed during the proceedings by the parties or by witnesses shall not be divulged by an arbitrator or by the administrator. Except as provided in Article 27, unless otherwise agreed by the parties, or required by applicable law, the members of the tribunal and the administrator shall keep confidential all matters relating to the arbitration or the award.

Article 35 Exclusion of Liability
The members of the tribunal and the administrator shall not be liable to any party for any act or omission in connection with any arbitration conducted under these Rules, except that they may be liable for the consequences of conscious and deliberate wrongdoing.

Article 36 Interpretation of Rules
The tribunal shall interpret and apply these Rules insofar as they relate to its powers and duties. The administrator shall interpret and apply all other Rules.

Article 37 Emergency Measures of Protection
1.   Unless the parties agree otherwise, the provisions of this Article 37 shall apply to arbitrations conducted under arbitration clauses or agreements entered on or after May 1, 2006.
2.   A party in need of emergency relief prior to the constitution of the tribunal shall notify the administrator and all other parties in writing of the nature of the relief sought and the reasons why such relief is required on an emergency basis. The application shall also set forth the reasons why the party is entitled to such relief. Such notice may be given by e-mail, facsimile transmission or other reliable means, but must include a statement certifying that all other parties have been notified or an explanation of the steps taken in good faith to notify other parties.
3.   Within one business day of receipt of notice as provided in paragraph 2, the administrator shall appoint a single emergency arbitrator from a special panel of emergency arbitrators designated to rule on emergency applications. Prior to accepting appointment, a prospective emergency arbitrator shall disclose to the administrator any circumstance likely to give rise to justifiable doubts to the arbitrator's impartiality or independence. Any challenge to the appointment of the emergency arbitrator must be made within one business day of the communication by the administrator to the parties of the appointment of the emergency arbitrator and the circumstances disclosed.
4.   The emergency arbitrator shall as soon as possible, but in any event within two business days of appointment, establish a schedule for consideration of the application for emergency relief. Such schedule shall provide a reasonable opportunity to all parties to be heard, but may provide for proceedings by telephone conference or on written submissions as alternatives to a formal hearing. The emergency arbitrator shall have the authority vested in the tribunal under

Article 15, including the authority to rule on her/his own jurisdiction, and shall resolve any disputes over the applicability of this Article 37.

5.   The emergency arbitrator shall have the power to order or award any interim or conservancy measure the emergency arbitrator deems necessary, including injunctive relief and measures for the protection or conservation of property. Any such measure may take the form of an interim award or of an order. The emergency arbitrator shall give reasons in either case. The emergency arbitrator may modify or vacate the interim award or order for good cause shown.

6.   The emergency arbitrator shall have no further power to act after the tribunal is constituted. Once the tribunal has been constituted, the tribunal may reconsider, modify or vacate the interim award or order of emergency relief issued by the emergency arbitrator. The emergency arbitrator may not serve as a member of the tribunal unless the parties agree otherwise.

7.   Any interim award or order of emergency relief may be conditioned on provision by the party seeking such relief of appropriate security.

8.   A request for interim measures addressed by a party to a judicial authority shall not be deemed incompatible with this Article 37 or with the agreement to arbitrate or a waiver of the right to arbitrate. If the administrator is directed by a judicial authority to nominate a special master to consider and report on an application for emergency relief, the administrator shall proceed as in Paragraph 2 of this article and the references to the emergency arbitrator shall be read to mean the special master, except that the special master shall issue a report rather than an interim award.

9.   The costs associated with applications for emergency relief shall initially be apportioned by the emergency arbitrator or special master, subject to the power of the tribunal to determine finally the apportionment of such costs.

Administrative Fees
Administrative Fee Schedules (Standard and Flexible Fee)

The ICDR has two administrative fee options for parties filing claims or counterclaims, the Standard Fee Schedule and Flexible Fee Schedule. The Standard Fee Schedule has a two payment schedule, and the Flexible Fee Schedule has a three payment schedule which offers lower initial filing fees, but potentially higher total administrative fees of approximately 12% to 19% for cases that proceed to a hearing. The administrative fees of the ICDR are based on the amount of the claim or counterclaim. Arbitrator compensation is not included in this schedule. Unless the parties agree otherwise, arbitrator compensation and administrative fees are subject to allocation by the arbitrator in the award.

Fees for Incomplete or Deficient Filings

Where the applicable arbitration agreement does not reference the ICDR or the AAA, the ICDR will attempt to obtain the agreement of the other parties to the dispute to have the arbitration administered by the ICDR. However, where the ICDR is unable to obtain the agreement of the parties to have the ICDR administer the arbitration, the ICDR will administratively close the case and will not proceed with the administration of the arbitration. In these cases, the ICDR will return the filing fees to the filing party, less the amount specified in the fee schedule below for deficient filings.

Parties that file demands for arbitration that are incomplete or otherwise do not meet the filing requirements contained in these Rules shall also be charged the amount specified below for deficient filings if they fail or are unable to respond to the ICDR's request to correct the deficiency.

Fees for Additional Services

The ICDR reserves the right to assess additional administrative fees for services performed by the ICDR beyond those provided for in these Rules which may be required by the parties' agreement or stipulation.

Suspension for Nonpayment

If arbitrator compensation or administrative charges have not been paid in full, the administrator may so inform the parties in order that one of them may advance the required payment.

If such payments are not made, the tribunal may order the suspension or termination of the proceedings. If no arbitrator has yet been appointed, the ICDR may suspend the proceedings.

Standard Fee Schedule

An Initial Filing Fee is payable in full by a filing party when a claim, counterclaim, or additional claim is filed. A Final Fee will be incurred for all cases that proceed to their first hearing. This fee will be payable in advance at the time that the first hearing is scheduled. This fee will be refunded at the conclusion of the case if no hearings have occurred. However, if the administrator is not notified at least 24 hours before the time of the scheduled hearing, the Final Fee will remain due and will not be refunded.

These fees will be billed in accordance with the following schedule:

Amount of Claim	Initial Filing Fee	Final Fee
Up to $10,000	$775	$200
From $10,000 - $75,000	$975	$300
From $75,000 to $150,000	$1,850	$750
From $150,000 to $300,000	$2,800	$1,250
From $300,000 to $500,000	$4,350	$1,750
From $500,000 to $1,000,000	$6,200	$2,500
From $1,000,000 to $5,000,000	$8,200	$3,250
From $5,000,000 to $10,000,000	$10,200	$4,000
Above $10,000,000	Base fee of $12,800 plus 0.01% of the amount of claim above $10,000,000 Fee Capped at $65,000	$6,000
Non-Monetary Claims[1]	$3,350	$1,250
Deficient Claim Filing[2]	$350	
Additional Services[3]		

Fees are subject to increase if the amount of a claim or counterclaim is modified after the initial filing date. Fees are subject to decrease if the amount of a claim or counterclaim is modified before the first hearing.

The minimum fees for any case having three or more arbitrators are $2,800 for the filing fee, plus a $1,250 Case Service Fee.

Parties on cases filed under either the Flexible Fee Schedule or the Standard Fee Schedule that are held in abeyance for one year will be assessed an annual abeyance fee of $300. If a party refuses to pay the assessed fee, the other party or parties may pay the entire fee on behalf of all parties, otherwise the matter will be administratively closed.

For more information, please contact the ICDR at +212.484.4181.

---

1   This fee is applicable when a claim or counterclaim is not for a monetary amount. Where a monetary claim amount is not known, parties will be required to state a range of claims or be subject to a filing fee of $10,200.

2   The Deficient Claim Filing Fee shall not be charged in cases filed by a consumer in an arbitration governed by the Supplementary Procedures for the Resolution of Consumer-Related Disputes, or in cases filed by an Employee who is submitting their dispute to arbitration pursuant to an employer promulgated plan.

3   The ICDR may assess additional fees where procedures or services outside the Rules sections are required under the parties' agreement or by stipulation.

Refund Schedule for Standard Fee Schedule

The ICDR offers a refund schedule on filing fees connected with the Standard Fee Schedule. For cases with claims up to $75,000, a minimum filing fee of $350 will not be refunded. For all other cases, a minimum fee of $600 will not be refunded. Subject to the minimum fee requirements, refunds will be calculated as follows:

- 100% of the filing fee, above the minimum fee, will be refunded if the case is settled or withdrawn within five calendar days of filing.
- 50% of the filing fee will be refunded if the case is settled or withdrawn between six and 30 calendar days of filing.
- 25% of the filing fee will be refunded if the case is settled or withdrawn between 31 and 60 calendar days of filing.

No refund will be made once an arbitrator has been appointed (this includes one arbitrator on a three-arbitrator panel). No refunds will be granted on awarded cases.

Note: The date of receipt of the demand for arbitration with the ICDR will be used to calculate refunds of filing fees for both claims and counterclaims.

Flexible Fee Schedule

A non-refundable Initial Filing Fee is payable in full by a filing party when a claim, counterclaim, or additional claim is filed. Upon receipt of the Demand for Arbitration, the ICDR will promptly initiate the case and notify all parties as well as establish the due date for filing of an Answer, which may include a Counterclaim. In order to proceed with the further administration of the arbitration and appointment of the arbitrator(s), the appropriate, non-refundable Proceed Fee outlined below must be paid.

If a Proceed Fee is not submitted within ninety (90) days of the filing of the Claimant's Demand for Arbitration, the ICDR will administratively close the file and notify all parties.

No refunds or refund schedule will apply to the Filing or Proceed Fees once received.

The Flexible Fee Schedule below also may be utilized for the filing of counterclaims. However, as with the Claimant's claim, the counterclaim will not be presented to the arbitrator until the Proceed Fee is paid.

A Final Fee will be incurred for all claims and/or counterclaims that proceed to their first hearing. This fee will be payable in advance when the first hearing is scheduled, but will be refunded at the conclusion of the case if no hearings have occurred. However, if the administrator is not notified of a cancellation at least 24 hours before the time of the scheduled hearing, the Final Fee will remain due and will not be refunded.

All fees will be billed in accordance with the following schedule:

Amount of Claim	Initial Filing Fee	Proceed Fee	Final Fee
Up to $10,000	$400	$475	$200
From $10,000 - $75,000	$625	$500	$300
From $75,000 to $150,000	$850	$1,250	$750
From $150,000 to $300,000	$1,000	$2,125	$1,250
From $300,000 to $500,000	$1,500	$3,400	$1,750
From $500,000 to $1,000,000	$2,500	$4,500	$2,500
From $1,000,000 to $5,000,000	$2,500	$6,700	$3,250
From $5,000,000 to $10,000,000	$3,500	$8,200	$4,000
Above $10,000,000	$4,500	$10,300 plus 0.01% of claim amount over $10,000,000 up to $65,000	$6,000

Non-Monetary Claims[1]	$2,000	$2,000	$1,250
Deficient Claim Filing	$350		
Additional Services[2]			

All fees are subject to increase if the amount of a claim or counterclaim is modified after the initial filing date. Fees are subject to decrease if the amount of a claim or counterclaim is modified before the first hearing.

The minimum fees for any case having three or more arbitrators are $1,000 for the Initial Filing Fee; $2,125 for the Proceed Fee; and $1,250 for the Final Fee.

Under the Flexible Fee Schedule, a party's obligation to pay the Proceed Fee shall remain in effect regardless of any agreement of the parties to stay, postpone or otherwise modify the arbitration proceedings. Parties that, through mutual agreement, have held their case in abeyance for one year will be assessed an annual abeyance fee of $300. If a party refuses to pay the assessed fee, the other party or parties may pay the entire fee on behalf of all parties, otherwise the matter will be closed.

Note: The date of receipt by the ICDR of the demand/notice for arbitration will be used to calculate the ninety(90)-day time limit for payment of the Proceed Fee.

For more information, please contact the ICDR at +212.484.4181.

There is no Refund Schedule in the Flexible Fee Schedule.

Hearing Room Rental

The fees described above do not cover the cost of hearing rooms, which are available on a rental basis. Check with the ICDR for availability and rates.

1987 IBA RULES OF ETHICS FOR INTERNATIONAL ARBITRATORS[3]

Introductory Note

International arbitrators should be impartial, independent, competent, diligent and discreet. These rules seek to establish the manner in which these abstract qualities may be assessed in practice. Rather than rigid rules, they reflect internationally acceptable guidelines developed by practising lawyers from all continents. They will attain their objectives only if they are applied in good faith.

The rules cannot be directly binding either on arbitrators, or on the parties themselves, unless they are adopted by agreement. Whilst the International Bar Association hopes that they will be taken into account in the context of challenges to arbitrators, it is emphasised that these guidelines are not intended to create grounds for the setting aside of awards by national courts. If parties wish to adopt the rules they may add the following to their arbitration clause or arbitration agreement:

"The parties agree that the Rules of Ethics for International Arbitrators established by the International Bar Association, in force at the date of the commencement of any arbitration under this clause, shall be applicable to the arbitrators appointed in respect of such arbitration."

The International Bar Association takes the position that (whatever may be the case in domestic arbitration) international arbitrators should in principle be granted immunity from suit under national laws, except in extreme cases of wilful or reckless disregard of their legal obliga-

---

1   This fee is applicable when a claim or counterclaim is not for a monetary amount. Where a monetary claim amount is not known, parties will be required to state a range of claims or be subject to a filing fee of $3,500 and a proceed fee of $8,200.

2   The ICDR reserves the right to assess additional administrative fees for services performed by the ICDR beyond those provided for in these Rules and which may be required by the parties' agreement or stipulation.

3   © International Bar Association, London.

tions. Accordingly, the International Bar Association wishes to make it clear that it is not the intention of these rules to create opportunities for aggrieved parties to sue international arbitrators in national courts. The normal sanction for breach of an ethical duty is removal from office, with consequent loss of entitlement to remuneration. The International Bar Association also emphasises that these rules do not affect, and are intended to be consistent with, the International Code of Ethics for Lawyers, adopted at Oslo on 25 July 1956, and amended by the General Meeting of the International Bar Association at Mexico City on 24 July 1964.

1. Fundamental Rule

Arbitrators shall proceed diligently and efficiently to provide the parties with a just and effective resolution of their disputes, and shall be and shall remain free from bias.

2. Acceptance of Appointment

2.1   A prospective arbitrator shall accept an appointment only if he is fully satisfied that he is able to discharge his duties without bias.

2.2   A prospective arbitrator shall accept an appointment only if he is fully satisfied that he is competent to determine the issues in dispute, and has an adequate knowledge of the language of the arbitration.

2.3   A prospective arbitrator should accept an appointment only if he is able to give to the arbitration the time and attention which the parties are reasonably entitled to expect.

2.4   It is inappropriate to contact parties in order to solicit appointment as arbitrator.

3. Elements of Bias

3.1   The criteria for assessing questions relating to bias are impartiality and independence. Partiality arises when an arbitrator favours one of the parties, or where he is prejudiced in relation to the subject-matter of the dispute. Dependence arises from relationships between an arbitrator and one of the parties, or with someone closely connected with one of the parties.

3.2   Facts which might lead a reasonable person, not knowing the arbitrator's true state of mind, to consider that he is dependent on a party create an appearance of bias. The same is true if an arbitrator has a material interest in the outcome of the dispute, or if he has already taken a position in relation to it. The appearance of bias is best overcome by full disclosure as described in Article 4 below.

3.3   Any current direct or indirect business relationship between an arbitrator and a party, or with a person who is known to be a potentially important witness, will normally give rise to justifiable doubts as to a prospective arbitrator's impartiality or independence. He should decline to accept an appointment in such circumstances unless the parties agree in writing that he may proceed. Examples of indirect relationships are where a member of the prospective arbitrator's family, his firm, or any business partner has a business relationship with one of the parties.

3.4   Past business relationships will not operate as an absolute bar to acceptance of appointment, unless they are of such magnitude or nature as to be likely to affect a prospective arbitrator's judgment.

3.5   Continuous and substantial social or professional relationships between a prospective arbitrator and a party, or with a person who is known to be a potentially important witness in the arbitration, will normally give rise to justifiable doubts as to the impartiality or independence of a prospective arbitrator.

4. Duty of Disclosure

4.1   A prospective arbitrator should disclose all facts or circumstances that may give rise to justifiable doubts as to his impartiality or independence. Failure to make such disclosure creates an appearance of bias, and may of itself be a ground for disqualification even though he nondisclosed facts or circumstances would not of themselves justify disqualification.

4.2   A prospective arbitrator should disclose:

(a)   any past or present business relationship, whether direct or indirect as illustrated in Article 3.3, including prior appointment as arbitrator, with any party to the dispute, or any representative of a party, or any person known to be a potentially important witness in the arbitration. With regard to present relationships, the duty of disclosure applies irrespective of their magnitude, but with regard to past relationships only if they were of more than a trivial nature in relation to the arbitrator's professional or business affairs. Nondisclosure of an indirect relationship unknown to a prospective arbitrator will not be a ground for disqualification unless it could have been ascertained by making reasonable enquiries;

(b)   the nature and duration of any substantial social relationships with any party or any person known to be likely to be an important witness in the arbitration;

(c)   the nature of any previous relationship with any fellow arbitrator (including prior joint service as an arbitrator);

(d)   the extent of any prior knowledge he may have of the dispute;

(e)   the extent of any commitments which may affect his availability to perform his duties as arbitrator as may be reasonably anticipated.

4.3   The duty of disclosure continues throughout the arbitral proceedings as regards new facts or circumstances.

4.4   Disclosure should be made in writing and communicated to all parties and arbitrators. When an arbitrator has been appointed, any previous disclosure made to the parties should be communicated to the other arbitrators.

5. Communications with Parties

5.1   When approached with a view to appointment, a prospective arbitrator should make sufficient enquiries in order to inform himself whether there may be any justifiable doubts regarding his impartiality or independence; whether he is competent to determine the issues in dispute; and whether he is able to give the arbitration the time and attention required. He may also respond to enquiries from those approaching him, provided that such enquiries are designed to determine his suitability and availability for the appointment and provided that the merits of the case are not discussed. In the event that a prospective sole arbitrator or presiding arbitrator is approached by one party alone, or by one arbitrator chosen unilaterally by a party (a 'party-nominated' arbitrator), he should ascertain that the other party or parties, or the other arbitrator, has consented to the manner in which he has been approached. In such circumstances he should, in writing or orally, inform the other party or parties, or the other arbitrator, of the substance of the initial conversation.

5.2   If a party-nominated arbitrator is required to participate in the selection of a third or presiding arbitrator, it is acceptable for him (although he is not so required) to obtain the views of the party who nominated him as to the acceptability of candidates being considered.

5.3   Throughout the arbitral proceedings, an arbitrator should avoid any unilateral communications regarding the case with any party, or its representatives. If such communication should occur, the arbitrator should inform the other party or parties and arbitrators of its substance.

5.4   If an arbitrator becomes aware that a fellow arbitrator has been in improper communication with a party, he may inform the remaining arbitrators and they should together determine what action should be taken. Normally, the appropriate initial course of action is for the offending arbitrator to be requested to refrain from making any further improper communications with the party. Where the offending arbitrator fails or refuses to refrain from improper communications, the remaining arbitrators may inform the innocent party in order that he may consider what action he should take. An arbitrator may act unilaterally to inform a party of the conduct of another arbitrator in order to allow the said party to consider a challenge of the offending arbitrator only in extreme circumstances, and after communicating his intention to his fellow arbitrators in writing.

5.5   No arbitrator should accept any gift or substantial, hospitality, directly or indirectly, from any party to the arbitration. Sole arbitrators and presiding arbitrators should be particularly meticulous in avoiding significant social or professional contacts with any party to the arbitration other than in the presence of the other parties.

6. Fees

Unless the parties agree otherwise or a party defaults, an arbitrator shall make no unilateral arrangements for fees or expenses.

7. Duty of Diligence

All arbitrators should devote such time and attention as the parties may reasonably require having regard to all the circumstances of the case, and shall do their best to conduct the arbitration in such a manner that costs do not rise to an unreasonable proportion of the interests at stake.

8. Involvement in Settlement Proposals

Where the parties have so requested, or consented to a suggestion to this effect by the arbitral tribunal, the tribunal as a whole (or the presiding arbitrator where appropriate), may make proposals for settlement to both parties simultaneously, and preferably in the presence of each other. Although any procedure is possible with the agreement of the parties, the arbitral tribunal should point out to the parties that it is undesirable that any arbitrator should discuss settlement terms with a party in the absence of the other parties since this will normally have the result that any arbitrator involved in such discussions will become disqualified from any future participation in the arbitration.

9. Confidentiality of the Deliberations

The deliberations of the arbitral tribunal, and the contents of the award itself, remain confidential in perpetuity unless the parties release the arbitrators from this obligation. An arbitrator should not participate in, or give any information for the purpose of assistance in, any proceedings to consider the award unless, exceptionally, he considers it his duty to disclose any material misconduct or fraud on the part of his fellow arbitrators.

2004 IBA GUIDELINES ON CONFLICTS OF INTEREST
IN INTERNATIONAL ARBITRATION[1]

Approved on 22 May 2004 by the Council of the International Bar Association

Introduction

1.   Problems of conflicts of interest increasingly challenge international arbitration. Arbitrators are often unsure about what facts need to be disclosed, and they may make different choices about disclosures than other arbitrators in the same situation. The growth of international business and the manner in which it is conducted, including interlocking corporate relationships and larger international law firms, have caused more disclosures and have created more difficult conflict of interest issues to determine. Reluctant parties have more opportunities to use challenges of arbitrators to delay arbitrations or to deny the opposing party the arbitrator of its choice. Disclosure of any relationship, no matter how minor or serious, has too often led to objections, challenge and withdrawal or removal of the arbitrator.

2.   Thus, parties, arbitrators, institutions and courts face complex decisions about what to disclose and what standards to apply. In addition, institutions and courts face difficult decisions if an objection or a challenge is made after a disclosure. There is a tension between, on the one hand, the parties' right to disclosure of situations that may reasonably call into question an arbitrator's impartiality or independence and their right to a fair hearing and, on the other hand, the parties' right to select arbitrators of their choosing. Even though laws and arbitration rules provide some standards, there is a lack of detail in their guidance and of uniformity in their application. As a result, quite often members of the international arbitration community apply different standards in making decisions concerning disclosure, objections and challenges.

---

1   © International Bar Association, London.

3.   It is in the interest of everyone in the international arbitration community that international arbitration proceedings not be hindered by these growing conflicts of interest issues. The Committee on Arbitration and ADR of the International Bar Association appointed a Working Group of 19 experts in international arbitration from 14 countries to study, with the intent of helping this decision-making process, national laws, judicial decisions, arbitration rules and practical considerations and applications regarding impartiality and independence and disclosure in international arbitration. The Working Group has determined that existing standards lack sufficient clarity and uniformity in their application. It has therefore prepared these Guidelines, which set forth some General Standards and Explanatory Notes on the Standards. Moreover, the Working Group believes that greater consistency and fewer unnecessary challenges and arbitrator withdrawals and removals could be achieved by providing lists of specific situations that, in the view of the Working Group, do or do not warrant disclosure or disqualification of an arbitrator. Such lists – designated Red, Orange and Green (the "Application Lists") – appear at the end of these Guidelines.[1]

4.   The Guidelines reflect the Working Group's understanding of the best current international practice firmly rooted in the principles expressed in the General Standards. The Working Group has based the General Standards and the Application Lists upon statutes and case law in jurisdictions and upon the judgment and experience of members of the Working Group and others involved in international commercial arbitration. The Working Group has attempted to balance the various interests of parties, representatives, arbitrators and arbitration institutions, all of whom have a responsibility for ensuring the integrity, reputation and efficiency of international commercial arbitration. In particular, the Working Group has sought and considered the views of many leading arbitration institutions, as well as corporate counsel and other persons involved in international arbitration. The Working Group also published drafts of the Guidelines and sought comments at two annual meetings of the International Bar Association and other meetings of arbitrators. While the comments received by the Working Group varied, and included some points of criticisms, the arbitration community generally supported and encouraged these efforts to help reduce the growing problems of conflicts of interests. The Working Group has studied all the comments received and has adopted many of the proposals that it has received. The Working Group is very grateful indeed for the serious considerations given to its proposals by so many institutions and individuals all over the globe and for the comments and proposals received.

5.   Originally, the Working Group developed the Guidelines for international commercial arbitration. However, in the light of comments received, it realized that the Guidelines should equally apply to other types of arbitration, such as investment arbitrations (insofar as these may not be considered as commercial arbitrations).[2]

6.   These Guidelines are not legal provisions and do not override any applicable national law or arbitral rules chosen by the parties. However, the Working Group hopes that these Guidelines will find general acceptance within the international arbitration community (as was the case with the IBA Rules on the Taking of Evidence in International Commercial Arbitration) and that they thus will help parties, practitioners, arbitrators, institutions and the courts in their decision-making process on these very important questions of impartiality, independence, disclosure, objections and challenges made in that connection. The Working Group trusts that the Guidelines will be applied with robust common sense and without pedantic and unduly formalistic interpretation. The Working Group is also publishing a Background and History, which describes the studies made by the Working Group and may be helpful in interpreting the Guidelines.

---

1   Detailed Background Information to the Guidelines has been published in *Business Law International* at BLI Vol 5, No 3, September 2004, pp 433-458 and is available at the IBA website www.ibanet.org.

2   Similarly, the Working Group is of the opinion that these Guidelines should apply by analogy to civil servants and government officers who are appointed as arbitrators by States or State entities that are parties to arbitration proceedings.

7.   The IBA and the Working Group view these Guidelines as a beginning, rather than an end, of the process. The Application Lists cover many of the varied situations that commonly arise in practice, but they do not purport to be comprehensive, nor could they be. Nevertheless, the Working Group is confident that the Application Lists provide better concrete guidance than the General Standards (and certainly more than existing standards). The IBA and the Working Group seek comments on the actual use of the Guidelines, and they plan to supplement, revise and refine the Guidelines based on that practical experience.

8.   In 1987, the IBA published Rules of Ethics for International Arbitrators.[1] Those Rules cover more topics than these Guidelines, and they remain in effect as to subjects that are not discussed in the Guidelines. The Guidelines supersede the Rules of Ethics as to the matters treated here.

PART I: GENERAL STANDARDS REGARDING IMPARTIALITY, INDEPENDENCE AND DISCLOSURE

(1) General Principle

Every arbitrator shall be impartial and independent of the parties at the time of accepting an appointment to serve and shall remain so during the entire arbitration proceeding until the final award has been rendered or the proceeding has otherwise finally terminated.

Explanation to General Standard 1:

The Working Group is guided by the fundamental principle in international arbitration that each arbitrator must be impartial and independent of the parties at the time he or she accepts an appointment to act as arbitrator and must remain so during the entire course of the arbitration proceedings. The Working Group considered whether this obligation should extend even during the period that the award may be challenged but has decided against this. The Working Group takes the view that the arbitrator's duty ends when the Arbitral Tribunal has rendered the final award or the proceedings have otherwise been finally terminated (e.g., because of a settlement). If, after setting aside or other proceedings, the dispute is referred back to the same arbitrator, a fresh round of disclosure may be necessary.

(2) Conflicts of Interest

(a)   An arbitrator shall decline to accept an appointment or, if the arbitration has already been commenced, refuse to continue to act as an arbitrator if he or she has any doubts as to his or her ability to be impartial or independent.

(b)   The same principle applies if facts or circumstances exist, or have arisen since the appointment, that, from a reasonable third person's point of view having knowledge of the relevant facts, give rise to justifiable doubts as to the arbitrator's impartiality or independence, unless the parties have accepted the arbitrator in accordance with the requirements set out in General Standard (4).

(c)   Doubts are justifiable if a reasonable and informed third party would reach the conclusion that there was a likelihood that the arbitrator may be influenced by factors other than the merits of the case as presented by the parties in reaching his or her decision.

(d)   Justifiable doubts necessarily exist as to the arbitrator's impartiality or independence if there is an identity between a party and the arbitrator, if the arbitrator is a legal representative of a legal entity that is a party in the arbitration, or if the arbitrator has a significant financial or personal interest in the matter at stake.

Explanation to General Standard 2:

(a)   It is the main ethical guiding principle of every arbitrator that actual bias from the arbitrator's own point of view must lead to that arbitrator declining his or her appointment. This standard should apply regardless of the stage of the proceedings. This principle is so self-evident

---

1   See above, p. 781.

that many national laws do not explicitly say so, see e.g. Article 12, UNCITRAL Model Law. The Working Group, however, has included it in the General Standards because explicit expression in these Guidelines helps to avoid confusion and to create confidence in procedures before arbitral tribunals. In addition, the Working Group believes that the broad standard of 'any doubts as to an ability to be impartial and independent' should lead to the arbitrator declining the appointment.

(b)   In order for standards to be applied as consistently as possible, the Working Group believes that the test for disqualification should be an objective one. The Working Group uses the wording 'impartiality or independence' derived from the broadly adopted Article 12 of the UNCITRAL Model Law, and the use of an appearance test, based on justifiable doubts as to the impartiality or independence of the arbitrator, as provided in Article 12(2) of the UNCITRAL Model Law, to be applied objectively (a 'reasonable third person test'). As described in the Explanation to General Standard 3(d), this standard should apply regardless of the stage of the proceedings.

(c)   Most laws and rules that apply the standard of justifiable doubts do not further define that standard. The Working Group believes that this General Standard provides some context for making this determination.

(d)   The Working Group supports the view that no one is allowed to be his or her own judge; i.e., there cannot be identity between an arbitrator and a party. The Working Group believes that this situation cannot be waived by the parties. The same principle should apply to persons who are legal representatives of a legal entity that is a party in the arbitration, like board members, or who have a significant economic interest in the matter at stake. Because of the importance of this principle, this non-waivable situation is made a General Standard, and examples are provided in the non-waivable Red List. The General Standard purposely uses the terms 'identity' and 'legal representatives.' In the light of comments received, the Working Group considered whether these terms should be extended or further defined, but decided against doing so. It realizes that there are situations in which an employee of a party or a civil servant can be in a position similar, if not identical, to the position of an official legal representative. The Working Group decided that it should suffice to state the principle.

(3) Disclosure by the Arbitrator

(a)   If facts or circumstances exist that may, in the eyes of the parties, give rise to doubts as to the arbitrator's impartiality or independence, the arbitrator shall disclose such facts or circumstances to the parties, the arbitration institution or other appointing authority (if any, and if so required by the applicable institutional rules) and to the co-arbitrators, if any, prior to accepting his or her appointment or, if thereafter, as soon as he or she learns about them.

(b)   It follows from General Standards 1 and 2(a) that an arbitrator who has made a disclosure considers himself or herself to be impartial and independent of the parties despite the disclosed facts and therefore capable of performing his or her duties as arbitrator. Otherwise, he or she would have declined the nomination or appointment at the outset or resigned.

(c)   Any doubt as to whether an arbitrator should disclose certain facts or circumstances should be resolved in favour of disclosure.

(d)   When considering whether or not facts or circumstances exist that should be disclosed, the arbitrator shall not take into account whether the arbitration proceeding is at the beginning or at a later stage.

Explanation to General Standard 3:

(a)   General Standard 2(b) above sets out an objective test for disqualification of an arbitrator. However, because of varying considerations with respect to disclosure, the proper standard for disclosure may be different. A purely objective test for disclosure exists in the majority of the jurisdictions analyzed and in the UNCITRAL Model Law. Nevertheless, the Working Group recognizes that the parties have an interest in being fully informed about any circumstances that may be relevant in their view.

Because of the strongly held views of many arbitration institutions (as reflected in their rules and as stated to the Working Group) that the disclosure test should reflect the perspectives of the parties, the Working Group in principle accepted, after much debate, a subjective approach for disclosure. The Working Group has adapted the language of Article 7(2) of the ICC Rules for this standard. However, the Working Group believes that this principle should not be applied without limitations. Because some situations should never lead to disqualification under the objective test, such situations need not be disclosed, regardless of the parties' perspective. These limitations to the subjective test are reflected in the Green List, which lists some situations in which disclosure is not required.

Similarly, the Working Group emphasizes that the two tests (objective test for disqualification and subjective test for disclosure) are clearly distinct from each other, and that a disclosure shall not automatically lead to disqualification, as reflected in General Standard 3(b).

In determining what facts should be disclosed, an arbitrator should take into account all circumstances known to him or her, including to the extent known the culture and the customs of the country of which the parties are domiciled or nationals.

(b) Disclosure is not an admission of a conflict of interest. An arbitrator who has made a disclosure to the parties considers himself or herself to be impartial and independent of the parties, despite the disclosed facts, or else he or she would have declined the nomination or resigned. An arbitrator making disclosure thus feels capable of performing his or her duties. It is the purpose of disclosure to allow the parties to judge whether or not they agree with the evaluation of the arbitrator and, if they so wish, to explore the situation further. The Working Group hopes that the promulgation of this General Standard will eliminate the misunderstanding that disclosure demonstrates doubts sufficient to disqualify the arbitrator. Instead, any challenge should be successful only if an objective test, as set forth above, is met.

(c) Unnecessary disclosure sometimes raises an incorrect implication in the minds of the parties that the disclosed circumstances would affect his or her impartiality or independence. Excessive disclosures thus unnecessarily undermine the parties' confidence in the process. Nevertheless, after some debate, the Working Group believes it important to provide expressly in the General Standards that in case of doubt the arbitrator should disclose. If the arbitrator feels that he or she should disclose but that professional secrecy rules or other rules of practice prevent such disclosure, he or she should not accept the appointment or should resign.

(d) The Working Group has concluded that disclosure or disqualification (as set out in General Standard 2) should not depend on the particular stage of the arbitration. In order to determine whether the arbitrator should disclose, decline the appointment or refuse to continue to act or whether a challenge by a party should be successful, the facts and circumstances alone are relevant and not the current stage of the procedure or the consequences of the withdrawal.

As a practical matter, institutions make a distinction between the commencement of an arbitration proceeding and a later stage. Also, courts tend to apply different standards. Nevertheless, the Working Group believes it important to clarify that no distinction should be made regarding the stage of the arbitral procedure. While there are practical concerns if an arbitrator must withdraw after an arbitration has commenced, a distinction based on the stage of arbitration would be inconsistent with the General Standards.

(4) Waiver by the Parties

(a) If, within 30 days after the receipt of any disclosure by the arbitrator or after a party learns of facts or circumstances that could constitute a potential conflict of interest for an arbitrator, a party does not raise an express objection with regard to that arbitrator, subject to paragraphs (b) and (c) of this General Standard, the party is deemed to have waived any potential conflict of interest by the arbitrator based on such facts or circumstances and may not raise any objection to such facts or circumstances at a later stage.

(b) However, if facts or circumstances exist as described in General Standard 2(d), any waiver by a party or any agreement by the parties to have such a person serve as arbitrator shall be regarded as invalid.

(c)   A person should not serve as an arbitrator when a conflict of interest, such as those exemplified in the waivable Red List, exists. Nevertheless, such a person may accept appointment as arbitrator or continue to act as an arbitrator, if the following conditions are met:

(i)   All parties, all arbitrators and the arbitration institution or other appointing authority (if any) must have full knowledge of the conflict of interest; and

(ii)   All parties must expressly agree that such person may serve as arbitrator despite the conflict of interest.

(d)   An arbitrator may assist the parties in reaching a settlement of the dispute at any stage of the proceedings. However, before doing so, the arbitrator should receive an express agreement by the parties that acting in such a manner shall not disqualify the arbitrator from continuing to serve as arbitrator. Such express agreement shall be considered to be an effective waiver of any potential conflict of interest that may arise from the arbitrator's participation in such process or from information that the arbitrator may learn in the process. If the assistance by the arbitrator does not lead to final settlement of the case, the parties remain bound by their waiver. However, consistent with General Standard 2(a) and notwithstanding such agreement, the arbitrator shall resign if, as a consequence of his or her involvement in the settlement process, the arbitrator develops doubts as to his or her ability to remain impartial or independent in the future course of the arbitration proceedings.

Explanation to General Standard 4:

(a)   The Working Group suggests a requirement of an explicit objection by the parties within a certain time limit. In the view of the Working Group, this time limit should also apply to a party who refuses to be involved.

(b)   This General Standard is included to make General Standard 4(a) consistent with the non-waivable provisions of General Standard 2(d). Examples of such circumstances are described in the non-waivable Red List.

(c)   In a serious conflict of interest, such as those that are described by way of example in the waivable Red List, the parties may nevertheless wish to use such a person as an arbitrator. Here, party autonomy and the desire to have only impartial and independent arbitrators must be balanced. The Working Group believes persons with such a serious conflict of interests may serve as arbitrators only if the parties make fully informed, explicit waivers.

(d)   The concept of the Arbitral Tribunal assisting the parties in reaching a settlement of their dispute in the course of the arbitration proceedings is well established in some jurisdictions but not in others. Informed consent by the parties to such a process prior to its beginning should be regarded as effective waiver of a potential conflict of interest. Express consent is generally sufficient, as opposed to a consent made in writing which in certain jurisdictions requires signature. In practice, the requirement of an express waiver allows such consent to be made in the minutes or transcript of a hearing. In addition, in order to avoid parties using an arbitrator as mediator as a means of disqualifying the arbitrator, the General Standard makes clear that the waiver should remain effective if the mediation is unsuccessful. Thus, parties assume the risk of what the arbitrator may learn in the settlement process. In giving their express consent, the parties should realize the consequences of the arbitrator assisting the parties in a settlement process and agree on regulating this special position further where appropriate.

(5) Scope

These Guidelines apply equally to tribunal chairs, sole arbitrators and party-appointed arbitrators. These Guidelines do not apply to non-neutral arbitrators, who do not have an obligation to be independent and impartial, as may be permitted by some arbitration rules or national laws.

Explanation to General Standard 5:

Because each member of an Arbitral Tribunal has an obligation to be impartial and independent, the General Standards should not distinguish among sole arbitrators, party-appointed arbitrators and tribunal chairs. With regard to secretaries of Arbitral Tribunals, the Working

Group takes the view that it is the responsibility of the arbitrator to ensure that the secretary is and remains impartial and independent.

Some arbitration rules and domestic laws permit party-appointed arbitrators to be non-neutral. When an arbitrator is serving in such a role, these Guidelines should not apply to him or her, since their purpose is to protect impartiality and independence.

(6) Relationships

(a)   When considering the relevance of facts or circumstances to determine whether a potential conflict of interest exists or whether disclosure should be made, the activities of an arbitrator's law firm, if any, should be reasonably considered in each individual case. Therefore, the fact that the activities of the arbitrator's firm involve one of the parties shall not automatically constitute a source of such conflict or a reason for disclosure.

(b)   Similarly, if one of the parties is a legal entity which is a member of a group with which the arbitrator's firm has an involvement, such facts or circumstances should be reasonably considered in each individual case. Therefore, this fact alone shall not automatically constitute a source of a conflict of interest or a reason for disclosure.

(c)   If one of the parties is a legal entity, the managers, directors and members of a supervisory board of such legal entity and any person having a similar controlling influence on the legal entity shall be considered to be the equivalent of the legal entity.

Explanation to General Standard 6:

(a)   The growing size of law firms should be taken into account as part of today's reality in international arbitration. There is a need to balance the interests of a party to use the arbitrator of its choice and the importance of maintaining confidence in the impartiality and independence of international arbitration. In the opinion of the Working Group, the arbitrator must in principle be considered as identical to his or her law firm, but nevertheless the activities of the arbitrator's firm should not automatically constitute a conflict of interest.

The relevance of such activities, such as the nature, timing and scope of the work by the law firm, should be reasonably considered in each individual case. The Working Group uses the term 'involvement' rather than 'acting for' because a law firm's relevant connections with a party may include activities other than representation on a legal matter.

(b)   When a party to an arbitration is a member of a group of companies, special questions regarding conflict of interest arise. As in the prior paragraph, the Working Group believes that because individual corporate structure arrangements vary so widely an automatic rule is not appropriate. Instead, the particular circumstances of an affiliation with another entity within the same group of companies should be reasonably considered in each individual case.

(c)   The party in international arbitration is usually a legal entity. Therefore, this General Standard clarifies which individuals should be considered effectively to be that party.

(7) Duty of Arbitrator and Parties

(a)   A party shall inform an arbitrator, the Arbitral Tribunal, the other parties and the arbitration institution or other appointing authority (if any) about any direct or indirect relationship between it (or another company of the same group of companies) and the arbitrator. The party shall do so on its own initiative before the beginning of the proceeding or as soon as it becomes aware of such relationship.

(b)   In order to comply with General Standard 7(a), a party shall provide any information already available to it and shall perform a reasonable search of publicly available information.

(c)   An arbitrator is under a duty to make reasonable enquiries to investigate any potential conflict of interest, as well as any facts or circumstances that may cause his or her impartiality or independence to be questioned. Failure to disclose a potential conflict is not excused by lack of knowledge if the arbitrator makes no reasonable attempt to investigate.

Explanation to General Standard 7:

To reduce the risk of abuse by unmeritorious challenge of an arbitrator's impartiality or independence, it is necessary that the parties disclose any relevant relationship with the arbitrator. In addition, any party or potential party to an arbitration is, at the outset, required to make a reasonable effort to ascertain and to disclose publicly available information that, applying the general standard, might affect the arbitrator's impartiality and independence. It is the arbitrator or putative arbitrator's obligation to make similar enquiries and to disclose any information that may cause his or her impartiality or independence to be called into question.

PART II: PRACTICAL APPLICATION OF THE GENERAL STANDARDS

1.   The Working Group believes that if the Guidelines are to have an important practical influence, they should reflect situations that are likely to occur in today's arbitration practice. The Guidelines should provide specific guidance to arbitrators, parties, institutions and courts as to what situations do or do not constitute conflicts of interest or should be disclosed.

For this purpose, the members of the Working Group analyzed their respective case law and categorized situations that can occur in the following Application Lists. These lists obviously cannot contain every situation, but they provide guidance in many circumstances, and the Working Group has sought to make them as comprehensive as possible. In all cases, the General Standards should control.

2.   The Red List consists of two parts: 'a non-waivable Red List' (see General Standards 2(c) and 4(b)) and 'a waivable Red List' (see General Standard 4(c)). These lists are a non-exhaustive enumeration of specific situations which, depending on the facts of a given case, give rise to justifiable doubts as to the arbitrator's impartiality and independence; i.e., in these circumstances an objective conflict of interest exists from the point of view of a reasonable third person having knowledge of the relevant facts (see General Standard 2(b)). The non-waivable Red List includes situations deriving from the overriding principle that no person can be his or her own judge. Therefore, disclosure of such a situation cannot cure the conflict. The waivable Red List encompasses situations that are serious but not as severe. Because of their seriousness, unlike circumstances described in the Orange List, these situations should be considered waivable only if and when the parties, being aware of the conflict of interest situation, nevertheless expressly state their willingness to have such a person act as arbitrator, as set forth in General Standard 4(c).

3.   The Orange List is a non-exhaustive enumeration of specific situations which (depending on the facts of a given case) in the eyes of the parties may give rise to justifiable doubts as to the arbitrator's impartiality or independence. The Orange List thus reflects situations that would fall under General Standard 3(a), so that the arbitrator has a duty to disclose such situations. In all these situations, the parties are deemed to have accepted the arbitrator if, after disclosure, no timely objection is made. (General Standard 4(a)).

4.   It should be stressed that, as stated above, such disclosure should not automatically result in a disqualification of the arbitrator; no presumption regarding disqualification should arise from a disclosure. The purpose of the disclosure is to inform the parties of a situation that they may wish to explore further in order to determine whether objectively - i.e., from a reasonable third person's point of view having knowledge of the relevant facts - there is a justifiable doubt as to the arbitrator's impartiality or independence. If the conclusion is that there is no justifiable doubt, the arbitrator can act. He or she can also act if there is no timely objection by the parties or, in situations covered by the waivable Red List, a specific acceptance by the parties in accordance with General Standard 4(c). Of course, if a party challenges the appointment of the arbitrator, he or she can nevertheless act if the authority that has to rule on the challenge decides that the challenge does not meet the objective test for disqualification.

5.   In addition, a later challenge based on the fact that an arbitrator did not disclose such facts or circumstances should not result automatically in either non-appointment, later disqualification or a successful challenge to any award. In the view of the Working Group, non-disclosure cannot make an arbitrator partial or lacking independence; only the facts or circumstances that he or she did not disclose can do so.

6.   The Green List contains a non-exhaustive enumeration of specific situations where no appearance of, and no actual, conflict of interest exists from the relevant objective point of view. Thus, the arbitrator has no duty to disclose situations falling within the Green List. In the opinion of the Working Group, as already expressed in the Explanation to General Standard 3(a), there should be a limit to disclosure, based on reasonableness; in some situations, an objective test should prevail over the purely subjective test of 'the eyes of the parties.'

7.   Situations falling outside the time limit used in some of the Orange List situations should generally be considered as falling in the Green List, even though they are not specifically stated. An arbitrator may nevertheless wish to make disclosure if, under the General Standards, he or she believes it to be appropriate. While there has been much debate with respect to the time limits used in the Lists, the Working Group has concluded that the limits indicated are appropriate and provide guidance where none exists now. For example, the three-year period in Orange List 3.1 may be too long in certain circumstances and too short in others, but the Working Group believes that the period is an appropriate general criterion, subject to the special circumstances of any case.

8.   The borderline between the situations indicated is often thin. It can be debated whether a certain situation should be on one List of instead of another. Also, the Lists contain, for various situations, open norms like 'significant'. The Working Group has extensively and repeatedly discussed both of these issues, in the light of comments received. It believes that the decisions reflected in the Lists reflect international principles to the best extent possible and that further definition of the norms, which should be interpreted reasonably in light of the facts and circumstances in each case, would be counter-productive.

9.   There has been much debate as to whether there should be a Green List at all and also, with respect to the Red List, whether the situations on the non-waivable Red List should be waivable in light of party autonomy. With respect to the first question, the Working Group has maintained its decision that the subjective test for disclosure should not be the absolute criterion but that some objective thresholds should be added. With respect to the second question, the conclusion of the Working Group was that party autonomy, in this respect, has its limits.

1. Non-Waivable Red List

1.1. There is an identity between a party and the arbitrator, or the arbitrator is a legal representative of an entity that is a party in the arbitration.

1.2. The arbitrator is a manager, director or member of the supervisory board, or has a similar controlling influence in one of the parties.

1.3. The arbitrator has a significant financial interest in one of the parties or the outcome of the case.

1.4. The arbitrator regularly advises the appointing party or an affiliate of the appointing party, and the arbitrator or his or her firm derives a significant financial income therefrom.

2. Waivable Red List

2.1. Relationship of the arbitrator to the dispute

2.1.1 The arbitrator has given legal advice or provided an expert opinion on the dispute to a party or an affiliate of one of the parties.

2.1.2 The arbitrator has previous involvement in the case.

2.2. Arbitrator's direct or indirect interest in the dispute

2.2.1 The arbitrator holds shares, either directly or indirectly, in one of the parties or an affiliate of one of the parties that is privately held.

2.2.2 A close family member[1] of the arbitrator has a significant financial interest in the outcome of the dispute.

---

1   Throughout the Application Lists, the term 'close family member' refers to a spouse, sibling, child, parent or life partner.

2.2.3 The arbitrator or a close family member of the arbitrator has a close relationship with a third party who may be liable to recourse on the part of the unsuccessful party in the dispute.

2.3. Arbitrator's relationship with the parties or counsel

2.3.1 The arbitrator currently represents or advises one of the parties or an affiliate of one of the parties.

2.3.2 The arbitrator currently represents the lawyer or law firm acting as counsel for one of the parties.

2.3.3 The arbitrator is a lawyer in the same law firm as the counsel to one of the parties.

2.3.4 The arbitrator is a manager, director or member of the supervisory board, or has a similar controlling influence, in an affiliate[1] of one of the parties if the affiliate is directly involved in the matters in dispute in the arbitration.

2.3.5 The arbitrator's law firm had a previous but terminated involvement in the case without the arbitrator being involved himself or herself.

2.3.6 The arbitrator's law firm currently has a significant commercial relationship with one of the parties or an affiliate of one of the parties.

2.3.7 The arbitrator regularly advises the appointing party or an affiliate of the appointing party, but neither the arbitrator nor his or her firm derives a significant financial income therefrom.

2.3.8 The arbitrator has a close family relationship with one of the parties or with a manager, director or member of the supervisory board or any person having a similar controlling influence in one of the parties or an affiliate of one of the parties or with a counsel representing a party.

2.3.9 A close family member of the arbitrator has a significant financial interest in one of the parties or an affiliate of one of the parties.

3. Orange List

3.1. Previous services for one of the parties or other involvement in the case

3.1.1 The arbitrator has within the past three years served as counsel for one of the parties or an affiliate of one of the parties or has previously advised or been consulted by the party or an affiliate of the party making the appointment in an unrelated matter, but the arbitrator and the party or the affiliate of the party have no ongoing relationship.

3.1.2 The arbitrator has within the past three years served as counsel against one of the parties or an affiliate of one of the parties in an unrelated matter.

3.1.3 The arbitrator has within the past three years been appointed as arbitrator on two or more occasions by one of the parties or an affiliate of one of the parties.[2]

3.1.4 The arbitrator's law firm has within the past three years acted for one of the parties or an affiliate of one of the parties in an unrelated matter without the involvement of the arbitrator.

3.1.5 The arbitrator currently serves, or has served within the past three years, as arbitrator in another arbitration on a related issue involving one of the parties or an affiliate of one of the parties.

---

1 Throughout the Application Lists, the term 'affiliate' encompasses all companies in one group of companies including the parent company.

2 It may be the practice in certain specific kinds of arbitration, such as maritime or commodities arbitration, to draw arbitrators from a small, specialized pool. If in such fields it is the custom and practice for parties frequently to appoint the same arbitrator in different cases, no disclosure of this fact is required where all parties in the arbitration should be familiar with such custom and practice.

3.2. Current services for one of the parties

3.2.1 The arbitrator's law firm is currently rendering services to one of the parties or to an affiliate of one of the parties without creating a significant commercial relationship and without the involvement of the arbitrator.

3.2.2 A law firm that shares revenues or fees with the arbitrator's law firm renders services to one of the parties or an affiliate of one of the parties before the arbitral tribunal.

3.2.3 The arbitrator or his or her firm represents a party or an affiliate to the arbitration on a regular basis but is not involved in the current dispute.

3.3. Relationship between an arbitrator and another arbitrator or counsel.

3.3.1 The arbitrator and another arbitrator are lawyers in the same law firm.

3.3.2 The arbitrator and another arbitrator or the counsel for one of the parties are members of the same barristers' chambers.

3.3.3 The arbitrator was within the past three years a partner of, or otherwise affiliated with, another arbitrator or any of the counsel in the same arbitration.

3.3.4 A lawyer in the arbitrator's law firm is an arbitrator in another dispute involving the same party or parties or an affiliate of one of the parties.

3.3.5 A close family member of the arbitrator is a partner or employee of the law firm representing one of the parties, but is not assisting with the dispute.

3.3.6 A close personal friendship exists between an arbitrator and a counsel of one party, as demonstrated by the fact that the arbitrator and the counsel regularly spend considerable time together unrelated to professional work commitments or the activities of professional associations or social organizations.

3.3.7 The arbitrator has within the past three years received more than three appointments by the same counsel or the same law firm.

3.4. Relationship between arbitrator and party and others involved in the arbitration

3.4.1 The arbitrator's law firm is currently acting adverse to one of the parties or an affiliate of one of the parties.

3.4.2 The arbitrator had been associated within the past three years with a party or an affiliate of one of the parties in a professional capacity, such as a former employee or partner.

3.4.3 A close personal friendship exists between an arbitrator and a manager or director or a member of the supervisory board or any person having a similar controlling influence in one of the parties or an affiliate of one of the parties or a witness or expert, as demonstrated by the fact that the arbitrator and such director, manager, other person, witness or expert regularly spend considerable time together unrelated to professional work commitments or the activities of professional associations or social organizations.

3.4.4 If the arbitrator is a former judge, he or she has within the past three years heard a significant case involving one of the parties.

3.5. Other circumstances

3.5.1 The arbitrator holds shares, either directly or indirectly, which by reason of number or denomination constitute a material holding in one of the parties or an affiliate of one of the parties that is publicly listed.

3.5.2 The arbitrator has publicly advocated a specific position regarding the case that is being arbitrated, whether in a published paper or speech or otherwise.

3.5.3 The arbitrator holds one position in an arbitration institution with appointing authority over the dispute.

3.5.4 The arbitrator is a manager, director or member of the supervisory board, or has a similar controlling influence, in an affiliate of one of the parties, where the affiliate is not directly involved in the matters in dispute in the arbitration.

4. Green List

4.1. Previously expressed legal opinions

4.1.1 The arbitrator has previously published a general opinion (such as in a law review article or public lecture) concerning an issue which also arises in the arbitration (but this opinion is not focused on the case that is being arbitrated).

4.2. Previous services against one party

4.2.1 The arbitrator's law firm has acted against one of the parties or an affiliate of one of the parties in an unrelated matter without the involvement of the arbitrator.

4.3. Current services for one of the parties

4.3.1 A firm in association or in alliance with the arbitrator's law firm, but which does not share fees or other revenues with the arbitrator's law firm, renders services to one of the parties or an affiliate of one of the parties in an unrelated matter.

4.4. Contacts with another arbitrator or with counsel for one of the parties

4.4.1 The arbitrator has a relationship with another arbitrator or with the counsel for one of the parties through membership in the same professional association or social organization.

4.4.2 The arbitrator and counsel for one of the parties or another arbitrator have previously served together as arbitrators or as co-counsel.

4.5. Contacts between the arbitrator and one of the parties

4.5.1 The arbitrator has had an initial contact with the appointing party or an affiliate of the appointing party (or the respective counsels) prior to appointment, if this contact is limited to the arbitrator's availability and qualifications to serve or to the names of possible candidates for a chairperson and did not address the merits or procedural aspects of the dispute.

4.5.2 The arbitrator holds an insignificant amount of shares in one of the parties or an affiliate of one of the parties, which is publicly listed.

4.5.3 The arbitrator and a manager, director or member of the supervisory board, or any person having a similar controlling influence, in one of the parties or an affiliate of one of the parties, have worked together as joint experts or in another professional capacity, including as arbitrators in the same case.

A flow chart is attached to these Guidelines for easy reference to the application of the Lists. However, it should be stressed that this is only a schematic reflection of the very complex reality. Always, the specific circumstances of the case prevail.

Flow Chart IBA Guidelines on Conflicts of Interest in International Arbitration

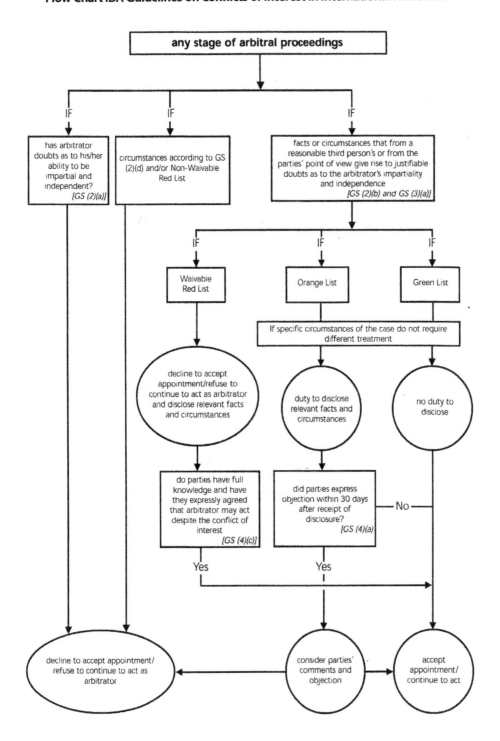

UNITED NATIONS CONVENTION ON THE RECOGNITION AND ENFORCEMENT OF FOREIGN ARBITRAL AWARDS[1]
(New York, 10 June 1958)

Article I

1.   This Convention shall apply to the recognition and enforcement of arbitral awards made in the territory of a State other than the State where the recognition and enforcement of such awards are sought, and arising out of differences between persons, whether physical or legal. It shall also apply to arbitral awards not considered as domestic awards in the State where their recognition and enforcement are sought.

2.   The term "arbitral awards" shall include not only awards made by arbitrators appointed for each case but also those made by permanent arbitral bodies to which the parties have submitted.

3.   When signing, ratifying or acceding to this Convention, or notifying extension under Article X hereof, any State may on the basis of reciprocity declare that it will apply the Convention to the recognition and enforcement of awards made only in the territory of another Contracting State. It may also declare that it will apply the Convention only to differences arising out of legal relationships, whether contractual or not, which are considered as commercial under the national law of the State making such declaration.

Article II

1.   Each Contracting State shall recognize an agreement in writing under which the parties undertake to submit to arbitration all or any differences which have arisen or which may arise between them in respect of a defined legal relationship, whether contractual or not, concerning a subject matter capable of settlement by arbitration.

2.   The term "agreement in writing" shall include an arbitral clause in a contract or an arbitration agreement, signed by the parties or contained in an exchange of letters or telegrams.

3.   The court of a Contracting State, when seized of an action in a matter in respect of which the parties have made an agreement within the meaning of this article, at the request of one of the parties, refer the parties to arbitration, unless it finds that the said agreement is null and void, inoperative or incapable of being performed.

Article III

Each Contracting State shall recognize arbitral awards as binding and enforce them in accordance with the rules of procedure of the territory where the award is relied upon, under the conditions laid down in the following articles. There shall not be imposed substantially more onerous conditions or higher fees or charges on the recognition or enforcement of arbitral awards to which this Convention applies than are imposed on the recognition or enforcement of domestic arbitral awards.

Article IV

1.   To obtain the recognition and enforcement mentioned in the preceding article, the party applying for recognition and enforcement shall, at the time of the application, supply:

(a)   The duly authenticated original award or a duly certified copy thereof;

(b)   The original agreement referred to in Article II or a duly certified copy thereof.

2.   If the said award or agreement is not made in an official language of the country in which the award is relied upon, the party applying for recognition and enforcement of the award shall produce a translation of these documents into such language. The translation shall be certified by an official or sworn translator or by a diplomatic or consular agent.

---

1   © United Nations, 330 UNTS p. 3, all rights reserved.

Article V

1.   Recognition and enforcement of the award may be refused, at the request of the party against whom it is invoked, only if that party furnishes to the competent authority where the recognition and enforcement is sought, proof that:
(a)   The parties to the agreement referred to in Article II were, under the law applicable to them, under some incapacity, or the said agreement is not valid under the law to which the parties have subjected it or, failing any indication thereon, under the law of the country where the award was made; or
(b)   The party against whom the award is invoked was not given proper notice of the appointment of the arbitrator or of the arbitration proceedings or was otherwise unable to present his case; or
(c)   The award deals with a difference not contemplated by or not falling within the terms of the submission to arbitration, or it contains decisions on matters beyond the scope of the submission to arbitration, provided that, if the decisions on matters submitted to arbitration can be separated from those not so submitted, that part of the award which contains decisions on matters submitted to arbitration may be recognized and enforced; or
(d)   The composition of the arbitral authority or the arbitral procedure was not in accordance with the agreement of the parties, or, failing such agreement, was not in accordance with the law of the country where the arbitration took place; or
(e)   The award has not yet become binding on the parties, or has been set aside or suspended by a competent authority of the country in which, or under the law of which, that award was made.
2.   Recognition and enforcement of an arbitral award may also be refused if the competent authority in the country where recognition and enforcement is sought finds that:
(a)   The subject matter of the difference is not capable of settlement by arbitration under the law of that country; or
(b)   The recognition or enforcement of the award would be contrary to the public policy of that country.

Article VI

If an application for the setting aside or suspension of the award has been made to a competent authority referred to in Article V (1) (e), the authority before which the award is sought to be relied upon may, if it considers it proper, adjourn the decision on the enforcement of the award and may also, on the application of the party claiming enforcement of the award, order the other party to give suitable security.

Article VII

1.   The provisions of the present Convention shall not affect the validity of multilateral or bilateral agreements concerning the recognition and enforcement of arbitral awards entered into by the Contracting States nor deprive any interested party of any right he may have to avail himself of an arbitral award in the manner and to the extent allowed by the law or the treaties of the country where such award is sought to be relied upon.
2.   The Geneva Protocol on Arbitration Clauses of 1923 and the Geneva Convention on the Execution of Foreign Arbitral Awards of 1927 shall cease to have effect between Contracting States on their becoming bound and to the extent that they become bound, by this Convention.

Article VIII

1.   This Convention shall be open until 31 December 1958 for signature on behalf of any Member of the United Nations and also on behalf of any other State which is or hereafter becomes a member of any specialized agency of the United Nations, or which is or hereafter becomes a party to the Statute of the International Court of Justice, or any other State to which an invitation has been addressed by the General Assembly of the United Nations.
2.   This Convention shall be ratified and the instrument of ratification shall be deposited with the Secretary-General of the United Nations.

Article IX

1.   This Convention shall be open for accession to all States referred to in Article VIII.
2.   Accession shall be effected by the deposit of an instrument of accession with the Secretary-General of the United Nations.

Article X

1.   Any State may, at the time of signature, ratification or accession, declare that this Convention shall extend to all or any of the territories for the international relations of which it is responsible. Such a declaration shall take effect when the Convention enters into force for the State concerned.
2.   At any time thereafter any such extension shall be made by notification addressed to the Secretary-General of the United Nations and shall take effect as from the ninetieth day after the day of receipt by the Secretary-General of the United Nations of this notification, or as from the date of entry into force of the Convention for the State concerned, whichever is the later.
3.   With respect to those territories to which this Convention is not extended at the time of signature, ratification or accession, each State concerned shall consider the possibility of taking the necessary steps in order to extend the application of this Convention to such territories, subject, where necessary for constitutional reasons, to the consent of the Governments of such territories.

Article XI

In the case of a federal or non-unitary State, the following provisions shall apply:
(a)   With respect to those articles of this Convention that come within the legislative jurisdiction of the federal authority, the obligations of the federal Government shall to this extent be the same as those of Contracting States which are not federal States;
(b)   With respect to those articles of this Convention that come within the legislative jurisdiction of constituent states or provinces which are not, under the constitutional system of the federation, bound to take legislative action, the federal Government shall bring such articles with a favourable recommendation to the notice of the appropriate authorities of constituent states or provinces at the earliest possible moment;
(c)   A federal State Party to this Convention shall, at the request of any other Contracting State transmitted through the Secretary-General of the United Nations, supply a statement of the law and practice of the federation and its constituent units in regard to any particular provision of this Convention, showing the extent to which effect has been given to that provision by legislative or other action.

Article XII

1.   This Convention shall come into force on the ninetieth day following the date of deposit of the third instrument of ratification or accession.
2.   For each State ratifying or acceding to this Convention after the deposit of the third instrument of ratification or accession, this Convention shall enter into force on the ninetieth day after deposit by such State of its instrument of ratification or accession.

Article XIII

1.   Any Contracting State may denounce this Convention by a written notification to the Secretary-General of the United Nations. Denunciation shall take effect one year after the date of receipt of the notification by the Secretary-General.
2.   Any State which has made a declaration or notification under Article X may, at any time thereafter, by notification to the Secretary-General of the United Nations, declare that this Convention shall cease to extend to the territory concerned one year after the date of the receipt of the notification by the Secretary-General.
3.   This Convention shall continue to be applicable to arbitral awards in respect of which recognition and enforcement proceedings have been instituted before the denunciation takes effect.

Article XIV

A Contracting State shall not be entitled to avail itself of the present Convention against other Contracting States except to the extent that it is itself bound to apply the Convention.

Article XV

The Secretary-General of the United Nations shall notify the States contemplated in Article VIII of the following:
(a)   Signatures and ratifications in accordance with Article VIII;
(b)   Accessions in accordance with Article IX;
(c)   Declarations and notifications under articles I, X and XI;
(d)   The date upon which this Convention enters into force in accordance with Article XII;
(e)   Denunciations and notifications in accordance with Article XIII.

Article XVI

1.   This Convention, of which the Chinese, English, French, Russian and Spanish texts shall be equally authentic, shall be deposited in the archives of the United Nations.
2.   The Secretary-General of the United Nations shall transmit a certified copy of this Convention to the States contemplated in Article VIII.

Entry into force: 7 June 1959
Ratification and binding effect: 149 countries

1925 UNITED STATES FEDERAL ARBITRATION ACT
United States Code Title 9. Arbitration (as last amended in 1990)

Chapter 1. General Provisions

§ 1 - "Maritime Transactions" and "Commerce" Defined; Exceptions to Operation of Title

"Maritime transactions", as herein defined, means charter parties, bills of lading of water carriers, agreements relating to wharfage, supplies furnished vessels or repairs to vessels, collisions, or any other matters in foreign commerce which, if the subject of controversy, would be embraced within admiralty jurisdiction; "commerce", as herein defined, means commerce among the several States or with foreign nations, or in any Territory of the United States or in the District of Columbia, or between any such Territory and another, or between any such Territory and any State or foreign nation, or between the District of Columbia and any State or Territory or foreign nation, but nothing herein contained shall apply to contracts of employment of seamen, railroad employees, or any other class of workers engaged in foreign or interstate commerce.

§ 2 - Validity, Irrevocability, and Enforcement of Agreements to Arbitrate

A written provision in any maritime transaction or a contract evidencing a transaction involving commerce to settle by arbitration a controversy thereafter arising out of such contract or transaction, or the refusal to perform the whole or any part thereof, or an agreement in writing to submit to arbitration an existing controversy arising out of such a contract, transaction, or refusal, shall be valid, irrevocable, and enforceable, save upon such grounds as exist at law or in equity for the revocation of any contract.

§ 3 - Stay of Proceedings Where Issue Therein Referable to Arbitration

If any suit or proceeding be brought in any of the courts of the United States upon any issue referable to arbitration under an agreement in writing for such arbitration, the court in which such suit is pending, upon being satisfied that the issue involved in such suit or proceeding is referable to arbitration under such an agreement, shall on application of one of the parties stay the trial of the action until such arbitration has been had in accordance with the terms of the agreement, providing the applicant for the stay is not in default in proceeding with such arbitration.

§ 4 - Failure to Arbitrate under Agreement; Petition to United States Court Having Jurisdiction for Order to Compel Arbitration; Notice and Service Thereof; Hearing and Determination

A party aggrieved by the alleged failure, neglect, or refusal of another to arbitrate under a written agreement for arbitration may petition any United States district court which, save for such agreement, would have jurisdiction under title 28, in a civil action or in admiralty of the subject matter of a suit arising out of the controversy between the parties, for an order directing that such arbitration proceed in the manner provided for in such agreement. Five days' notice in writing of such application shall be served upon the party in default. Service thereof shall be made in the manner provided by the Federal Rules of Civil Procedure. The court shall hear the parties, and upon being satisfied that the making of the agreement for arbitration or the failure to comply therewith is not in issue, the court shall make an order directing the parties to proceed to arbitration in accordance with the terms of the agreement. The hearing and proceedings, under such agreement, shall be within the district in which the petition for an order directing such arbitration is filed. If the making of the arbitration agreement or the failure, neglect, or refusal to perform the same be in issue, the court shall proceed summarily to the trial thereof. If no jury trial be demanded by the party alleged to be in default, or if the matter in dispute is within admiralty jurisdiction, the court shall hear and determine such issue. Where such an issue is raised, the party alleged to be in default may, except in cases of admiralty, on or before the return day of the notice of application, demand a jury trial of such issue, and upon such demand the court shall make an order referring the issue or issues to a jury in the manner provided by the Federal Rules of Civil Procedure, or may specially call a jury for that purpose. If the jury find that no agreement in writing for arbitration was made or that there is no default in proceeding thereunder, the proceeding shall be dismissed. If the jury find that an agreement for arbitration was made in writing and that there is a default in proceeding thereunder, the court shall make an order summarily directing the parties to proceed with the arbitration in accordance with the terms thereof.

§ 5 - Appointment of Arbitrators or Umpire

If in the agreement provision be made for a method of naming or appointing an arbitrator or arbitrators or an umpire, such method shall be followed; but if no method be provided therein, or if a method be provided and any party thereto shall fail to avail himself of such method, or if for any other reason there shall be a lapse in the naming of an arbitrator or arbitrators or umpire, or in filling a vacancy, then upon the application of either party to the controversy the court shall designate and appoint an arbitrator or arbitrators or umpire, as the case may require, who shall act under the said agreement with the same force and effect as if he or they had been specifically named therein; and unless otherwise provided in the agreement the arbitration shall be by a single arbitrator.

§ 6 - Application Heard as Motion

Any application to the court hereunder shall be made and heard in the manner provided by law for the making and hearing of motions, except as otherwise herein expressly provided.

§ 7 - Witnesses Before Arbitrators; Fees; Compelling Attendance

The arbitrators selected either as prescribed in this title or otherwise, or a majority of them, may summon in writing any person to attend before them or any of them as a witness and in a proper case to bring with him or them any book, record, document, or paper which may be deemed material as evidence in the case. The fees for such attendance shall be the same as the fees of witnesses before masters of the United States courts. Said summons shall issue in the name of the arbitrator or arbitrators, or a majority of them, and shall be signed by the arbitrators, or a majority of them, and shall be directed to the said person and shall be served in the same manner as subpoenas to appear and testify before the court; if any person or persons so summoned to testify shall refuse or neglect to obey said summons, upon petition the United States district court for the district in which such arbitrators, or a majority of them, are sitting may compel the attendance of such person or persons before said arbitrator or arbitrators, or punish said person or persons for contempt in the same manner provided by law for securing the attendance of witnesses or their punishment for neglect or refusal to attend in the courts of the United States.

§ 8 - Proceedings Begun by Libel in Admiralty and Seizure of Vessel or Property

If the basis of jurisdiction be a cause of action otherwise justiciable in admiralty, then, notwithstanding anything herein to the contrary, the party claiming to be aggrieved may begin his proceeding hereunder by libel and seizure of the vessel or other property of the other party according to the usual course of admiralty proceedings, and the court shall then have jurisdiction to direct the parties to proceed with the arbitration and shall retain jurisdiction to enter its decree upon the award.

§ 9 - Award of Arbitrators; Confirmation; Jurisdiction; Procedure

If the parties in their agreement have agreed that a judgment of the court shall be entered upon the award made pursuant to the arbitration, and shall specify the court, then at any time within one year after the award is made any party to the arbitration may apply to the court so specified for an order confirming the award, and thereupon the court must grant such an order unless the award is vacated, modified, or corrected as prescribed in sections 10 and 11 of this title. If no court is specified in the agreement of the parties, then such application may be made to the United States court in and for the district within which such award was made. Notice of the application shall be served upon the adverse party, and thereupon the court shall have jurisdiction of such party as though he had appeared generally in the proceeding. If the adverse party is a resident of the district within which the award was made, such service shall be made upon the adverse party or his attorney as prescribed by law for service of notice of motion in an action in the same court. If the adverse party shall be a nonresident, then the notice of the application shall be served by the marshal of any district within which the adverse party may be found in like manner as other process of the court.

§ 10 - Same; Vacation; Grounds; Rehearing

(a)   In any of the following cases the United States court in and for the district wherein the award was made may make an order vacating the award upon the application of any party to the arbitration –

(1)   where the award was procured by corruption, fraud, or undue means;

(2)   where there was evident partiality or corruption in the arbitrators, or either of them;

(3)   where the arbitrators were guilty of misconduct in refusing to postpone the hearing, upon sufficient cause shown, or in refusing to hear evidence pertinent and material to the controversy; or of any other misbehavior by which the rights of any party have been prejudiced; or

(4)   where the arbitrators exceeded their powers, or so imperfectly executed them that a mutual, final, and definite award upon the subject matter submitted was not made.

(b)   If an award is vacated and the time within which the agreement required the award to be made has not expired, the court may, in its discretion, direct a rehearing by the arbitrators.

(c)   The United States district court for the district wherein an award was made that was issued pursuant to section 580 of title 5 may make an order vacating the award upon the application of a person, other than a party to the arbitration, who is adversely affected or aggrieved by the award, if the use of arbitration or the award is clearly inconsistent with the factors set forth in section 572 of title 5.

§ 11 - Same; Modification or Correction; Grounds; Order

In either of the following cases the United States court in and for the district wherein the award was made may make an order modifying or correcting the award upon the application of any party to the arbitration –

(a)   Where there was an evident material miscalculation of figures or an evident material mistake in the description of any person, thing, or property referred to in the award.

(b)   Where the arbitrators have awarded upon a matter not submitted to them, unless it is a matter not affecting the merits of the decision upon the matter submitted.

(c)   Where the award is imperfect in matter of form not affecting the merits of the controversy. The order may modify and correct the award, so as to effect the intent thereof and promote justice between the parties.

§ 12 - Notice of Motions to Vacate or Modify; Service; Stay of Proceedings
Notice of a motion to vacate, modify, or correct an award must be served upon the adverse party or his attorney within three months after the award is filed or delivered. If the adverse party is a resident of the district within which the award was made, such service shall be made upon the adverse party or his attorney as prescribed by law for service of notice of motion in an action in the same court. If the adverse party shall be a nonresident then the notice of the application shall be served by the marshal of any district within which the adverse party may be found in like manner as other process of the court. For the purposes of the motion any judge who might make an order to stay the proceedings in an action brought in the same court may make an order, to be served with the notice of motion, staying the proceedings of the adverse party to enforce the award.

§ 13 - Papers Filed with Order on Motions; Judgment; Docketing; Force and Effect; Enforcement
The party moving for an order confirming, modifying, or correcting an award shall, at the time such order is filed with the clerk for the entry of judgment thereon, also file the following papers with the clerk:
(a)   The agreement; the selection or appointment, if any, of an additional arbitrator or umpire; and each written extension of the time, if any, within which to make the award.
(b)   The award.
(c)   Each notice, affidavit, or other paper used upon an application to confirm, modify, or correct the award, and a copy of each order of the court upon such an application.
The judgment shall be docketed as if it was rendered in an action.
The judgment so entered shall have the same force and effect, in all respects, as, and be subject to all the provisions of law relating to, a judgment in an action; and it may be enforced as if it had been rendered in an action in the court in which it is entered.

§ 14 - Contracts Not Affected
This title shall not apply to contracts made prior to January 1, 1926.

§ 15 - Inapplicability of the Act of State Doctrine
Enforcement of arbitral agreements, confirmation of arbitral awards, and execution upon judgments based on orders confirming such awards shall not be refused on the basis of the Act of State doctrine.

§ 16 - Appeals
(a)   An appeal may be taken from –
(1)   an order –
   (A)   refusing a stay of any action under section 3 of this title,
   (B)   denying a petition under section 4 of this title to order arbitration to proceed,
   (C)   denying an application under section 206 of this title to compel arbitration,
   (D)   confirming or denying confirmation of an award or partial award, or
   (E)   modifying, correcting, or vacating an award;
(2)   an interlocutory order granting, continuing, or modifying an injunction against an arbitration that is subject to this title; or
(3)   a final decision with respect to an arbitration that is subject to this title.
(b)   Except as otherwise provided in section 1292(b) of title 28, an appeal may not be taken from an interlocutory order –
(1)   granting a stay of any action under section 3 of this title;
(2)   directing arbitration to proceed under section 4 of this title;
(3)   compelling arbitration under section 206 of this title; or
(4)   refusing to enjoin an arbitration that is subject to this title.

Chapter 2 - Convention on the Recognition and Enforcement of Foreign Arbitral Awards

§ 201 - Enforcement of Convention

The Convention on the Recognition and Enforcement of Foreign Arbitral Awards of June 10, 1958, shall be enforced in United States courts in accordance with this chapter.

§ 202 - Agreement or Award Falling under the Convention

An arbitration agreement or arbitral award arising out of a legal relationship, whether contractual or not, which is considered as commercial, including a transaction, contract, or agreement described in section 2 of this title, falls under the Convention. An agreement or award arising out of such a relationship which is entirely between citizens of the United States shall be deemed not to fall under the Convention unless that relationship involves property located abroad, envisages performance or enforcement abroad, or has some other reasonable relation with one or more foreign states. For the purpose of this section a corporation is a citizen of the United States if it is incorporated or has its principal place of business in the United States.

§ 203 - Jurisdiction; Amount in Controversy

An action or proceeding falling under the Convention shall be deemed to arise under the laws and treaties of the United States. The district courts of the United States (including the courts enumerated in section 460 of title 28) shall have original jurisdiction over such an action or proceeding, regardless of the amount in controversy.

§ 204 - Venue

An action or proceeding over which the district courts have jurisdiction pursuant to section 203 of this title may be brought in any such court in which save for the arbitration agreement an action or proceeding with respect to the controversy between the parties could be brought, or in such court for the district and division which embraces the place designated in the agreement as the place of arbitration if such place is within the United States.

§ 205 - Removal of Cases from State Courts

Where the subject matter of an action or proceeding pending in a State court relates to an arbitration agreement or award falling under the Convention, the defendant or the defendants may, at any time before the trial thereof, remove such action or proceeding to the district court of the United States for the district and division embracing the place where the action or proceeding is pending. The procedure for removal of causes otherwise provided by law shall apply, except that the ground for removal provided in this section need not appear on the face of the complaint but may be shown in the petition for removal. For the purposes of Chapter 1 of this title any action or proceeding removed under this section shall be deemed to have been brought in the district court to which it is removed.

§ 206 - Order to Compel Arbitration; Appointment of Arbitrators

A court having jurisdiction under this chapter may direct that arbitration be held in accordance with the agreement at any place therein provided for, whether that place is within or without the United States. Such court may also appoint arbitrators in accordance with the provisions of the agreement.

§ 207 - Award of Arbitrators; Confirmation; Jurisdiction; Proceeding

Within three years after an arbitral award falling under the Convention is made, any party to the arbitration may apply to any court having jurisdiction under this chapter for an order confirming the award as against any other party to the arbitration. The court shall confirm the award unless it finds one of the grounds for refusal or deferral of recognition or enforcement of the award specified in the said Convention.

§ 208 - Chapter 1; Residual Application

Chapter 1 applies to actions and proceedings brought under this chapter to the extent that chapter is not in conflict with this chapter or the Convention as ratified by the United States.

Chapter 3 - Inter-American Convention on International Commercial Arbitration

§ 301 - Enforcement of Convention

The Inter-American Convention on International Commercial Arbitration of January 30, 1975, shall be enforced in United States courts in accordance with this chapter.

§ 302 - Incorporation by Reference

Sections 202, 203, 204, 205, and 207 of this title shall apply to this chapter as if specifically set forth herein, except that for the purposes of this chapter "the Convention" shall mean the Inter-American Convention.

§ 303 - Order to Compel Arbitration; Appointment of Arbitrators; Locale

(a)   A court having jurisdiction under this chapter may direct that arbitration be held in accordance with the agreement at any place therein provided for, whether that place is within or without the United States. The court may also appoint arbitrators in accordance with the provisions of the agreement.

(b)   In the event the agreement does not make provision for the place of arbitration or the appointment of arbitrators, the court shall direct that the arbitration shall be held and the arbitrators be appointed in accordance with Article 3 of the Inter-American Convention.

§ 304 - Recognition and Enforcement of Foreign Arbitral Decisions and Awards; Reciprocity

Arbitral decisions or awards made in the territory of a foreign State shall, on the basis of reciprocity, be recognized and enforced under this chapter only if that State has ratified or acceded to the Inter-American Convention.

§ 305 - Relationship Between the Inter-American Convention and the Convention on the Recognition and Enforcement of Foreign Arbitral Awards of June 10, 1958

When the requirements for application of both the Inter-American Convention and the Convention on the Recognition and Enforcement of Foreign Arbitral Awards of June 10, 1958, are met, determination as to which Convention applies shall, unless otherwise expressly agreed, be made as follows:

(1)   If a majority of the parties to the arbitration agreement are citizens of a State or States that have ratified or acceded to the Inter-American Convention and are member States of the Organization of American States, the Inter-American Convention shall apply.

(2)   In all other cases the Convention on the Recognition and Enforcement of Foreign Arbitral Awards of June 10, 1958, shall apply.

§ 306 - Applicable Rules of Inter-American Commercial Arbitration Commission

(a)   For the purposes of this chapter the rules of procedure of the Inter-American Commercial Arbitration Commission referred to in Article 3 of the Inter-American Convention shall, subject to subsection (b) of this section, be those rules as promulgated by the Commission on July 1, 1988.

(b)   In the event the rules of procedure of the Inter-American Commercial Arbitration Commission are modified or amended in accordance with the procedures for amendment of the rules of that Commission, the Secretary of State, by regulation in accordance with section 553 of title 5, consistent with the aims and purposes of this Convention, may prescribe that such modifications or amendments shall be effective for purposes of this chapter.

§ 307 - Chapter 1; Residual Application

Chapter 1 applies to actions and proceedings brought under this chapter to the extent chapter 1 is not in conflict with this chapter or the Inter-American Convention as ratified by the United States.

Index